CCNP SPCOR 350-501 Official Cert Guide

Companion Website and Pearson Test Prep Access Code

Access interactive study tools on this book's companion website, including practice test software, review exercises, Key Term flash card application, a study planner, and more!

To access the companion website, simply follow these steps:

1. Go to www.ciscopress.com/register by December 31, 2027.

2. Enter the **print book ISBN**: 9780135324806.

3. Answer the security question to validate your purchase.

4. Go to your account page.

5. Click on the **Registered Products** tab.

6. Under the book listing, click on the **Access Bonus Content** link.

When you register your book, your Pearson Test Prep practice test access code will automatically be populated with the book listing under the Registered Products tab. You will need this code to access the practice test that comes with this book. You can redeem the code at **PearsonTestPrep.com**. Simply choose Pearson IT Certification as your product group and log into the site with the same credentials you used to register your book. Click the **Activate New Product** button and enter the access code. More detailed instructions on how to redeem your access code for both the online and desktop versions can be found on the companion website.

If you have any issues accessing the companion website or obtaining your Pearson Test Prep practice test access code, you can contact our support team by going to **pearsonitp.echelp.org**.

CCNP SPCOR 350-501

Official Cert Guide

BRADLEY RIAPOLOV, CCIE No. 18921

MOHAMMAD KHALIL, CCDE No. 2023::57, CCIE No. 35484

Cisco Press

CCNP SPCOR 350-501 Official Cert Guide

Bradley Riapolov

Mohammad Khalil

Published by:
Cisco Press
Hoboken, New Jersey

$PrintCode

Library of Congress Control Number: 2024947468

ISBN-13: 978-0-13-532480-6

ISBN-10: 0-13-532480-7

Warning and Disclaimer

This book is designed to provide information about the Implementing and Operating Cisco Service Provider Network Core Technologies (SPCOR 350-501) exam. Every effort has been made to make this book as complete and as accurate as possible, but no warranty or fitness is implied.

The information is provided on an "as is" basis. The authors, Cisco Press, and Cisco Systems, Inc. shall have neither liability nor responsibility to any person or entity with respect to any loss or damages arising from the information contained in this book or from the use of the discs or programs that may accompany it.

The opinions expressed in this book belong to the author and are not necessarily those of Cisco Systems, Inc.

Please contact us with concerns about any potential bias at https://www.pearson.com/report-bias.html.

Trademark Acknowledgments

All terms mentioned in this book that are known to be trademarks or service marks have been appropriately capitalized. Cisco Press or Cisco Systems, Inc., cannot attest to the accuracy of this information. Use of a term in this book should not be regarded as affecting the validity of any trademark or service mark.

Feedback Information

At Cisco Press, our goal is to create in-depth technical books of the highest quality and value. Each book is crafted with care and precision, undergoing rigorous development that involves the unique expertise of members from the professional technical community.

Readers' feedback is a natural continuation of this process. If you have any comments regarding how we could improve the quality of this book, or otherwise alter it to better suit your needs, you can contact us through email at feedback@ciscopress.com. Please make sure to include the book title and ISBN in your message.

We greatly appreciate your assistance.

GM K12, Early Career and Professional Learning: Soo Kang

Alliances Manager, Cisco Press: Caroline Antonio

Director, ITP Product Management: Brett Bartow

Executive Editor: James Manly

Managing Editor: Sandra Schroeder

Development Editor: Christopher A. Cleveland

Senior Project Editor: Tonya Simpson

Copy Editor: CAH Editorial

Technical Editor: Brad Edgeworth

Editorial Assistant: Cindy Teeters

Cover Designer: Chuti Prasertsith

Composition: codeMantra

Indexer: Timothy Wright

Proofreader: Jennifer Hinchliffe

About the Authors

Bradley Riapolov is a seasoned technical solutions architect at Cisco Systems, currently serving in the MassScale Infrastructure Group. Since joining Cisco in 2008, he has been at the forefront of designing and deploying cutting-edge networking solutions, leveraging his extensive expertise to meet the complex demands of today's technology landscape.

Before his tenure at Cisco, Bradley gained invaluable experience working with various Fortune 500 companies, where he was instrumental in designing and operating small, medium, and large networks. His 20-year career is marked by a diverse background in successfully implementing technical campaigns across multiple industries, including transport, service provider, enterprise, industrial, and mobility networking.

In addition to his role at Cisco, Bradley is a recognized thought leader and educator. As a Cisco Press author and a distinguished speaker at Cisco Live, he has contributed to the body of knowledge in networking, sharing his insights and expertise through various publications. Moreover, his dedication to education is widely demonstrated, not only within Cisco but also through his role as a NetAcad instructor, where he has mentored and guided aspiring network professionals.

Bradley's dedication to excellence and his ability to simplify complex concepts have made him a respected figure in the networking community. His contributions continue to shape the future of networking, driving innovation and excellence in the industry. Bradley's refreshing no-nonsense approach to problem-solving has earned him a credible reputation among customers and peers alike.

Mohammad Khalil is an experienced service provider and enterprise expert, having worked in several service provider networks within the MENA region. Currently, he is a leader with the Cisco Competitive Win Center team covering enterprise architecture and working closely with Cisco sales/technical teams on designing their solutions.

Mohammad is a passionate networking expert, following technology trends and certifications development by writing several work labs and design scenarios. He was honored to be one of the SMEs for the CCIE Service Provider blueprint, SME for updated content of the CCIE Enterprise, and president of the Jordan IPv6 Council (part of the IPv6FORUM).

About the Technical Reviewer

Brad Edgeworth, CCIE No. 31574 (R&S and SP), is an SD-WAN technical solutions architect at Cisco Systems. Brad is a distinguished speaker at Cisco Live, where he has presented on various topics. Before joining Cisco, Brad worked as a network architect and consultant for various Fortune 500 companies. Brad's expertise is based on enterprise and service provider environments, with an emphasis on architectural and operational simplicity. Brad holds a bachelor of arts degree in computer systems management from St. Edward's University in Austin, Texas. Brad can be found on X (formerly Twitter) as @BradEdgeworth.

Dedications

To my beautiful wife, Evelina, who has supported me throughout the development of this book. You have challenged my assumptions, sharpened my ideas, and made some parts truly exceptional.

—*Bradley Riapolov*

I want to dedicate this book with affection to my wife, Qamar, and my precious children, Sireen and Saeed, who have supported me and motivated me to accomplish this effort. To my wise father, who believed in me and encouraged me all the way. Lastly, to my second home Estarta, which provided me with the support and environment to walk through.

—*Mohammad Khalil*

Acknowledgments

I would like to thank the Cisco Press team, especially James Manly and Christopher Cleveland, for their patience, guidance, and consideration.

I would like to thank the technical editor, colleague, and friend, Brad Edgeworth, for his time, technical expertise, and readiness to generously share knowledge without expecting anything in return.

I would like to thank Bikram Gandhok, Cisco Certification Program Manager, for driving Cisco Certifications to stay relevant and impactful.

I would like to thank Kent Dailey, my steadfast accomplice, who has navigated both challenges and victories with equal zeal.

I would like to thank my mentors, Marty Fierbaugh and Emerson Moura, for helping me gain insights that extend beyond my own perceptions.

Finally, I would like to thank my co-author, Mohammad, for sharing the burden of this challenging endeavor.

—Bradley Riapolov

I would like to massively thank our development editor, Chris Cleveland, for his guidance and the contribution he provided. James Manly's support was remarkable; a big thanks for his kindness.

I want to thank our technical editor, Brad, for his great insights, patience, and kindness for sharing his amazing practical experience and guiding us throughout the content development.

And I don't want to forget to thank my friend, Adeeb Al-Husseini, for his time sharing his practical experience and insights.

Finally, I would like to thank my partner, Bradley, for his seamless cooperation, contribution, and kindness to share his ideas and thoughts with me.

—Mohammad Khalil

Contents at a Glance

Introduction   xxx

Contents

Chapter 7   **BGP Fundamentals   228**

Command Syntax Conventions

The conventions used to present command syntax in this book are the same conventions used in the IOS Command Reference. The Command Reference describes these conventions as follows:

- **Boldface** indicates commands and keywords that are entered literally as shown. In actual configuration examples and output (not general command syntax), boldface indicates commands that are manually input by the user (such as a **show** command).

- *Italic* indicates arguments for which you supply actual values.

- Vertical bars (|) separate alternative, mutually exclusive elements.

- Square brackets ([ ]) indicate an optional element.

- Braces ({ }) indicate a required choice.

- Braces within brackets ([{ }]) indicate a required choice within an optional element.

Preface

I'm not an academic or engineer with a PhD, just an ordinary person like many of you. Back in 2000, when I lost my job, my college roommate's brother-in-law handed me a book on networking (*The CCNA Certification Guide*). I started my career at the very bottom, shlepping printers. I worked with various customers for eight years, thinking I was a pretty smart engineer until I joined Cisco, where smart engineers were as common as raindrops in a storm. Throughout my career, I've been fortunate to work with many networks, from small to massive, for over a quarter of a century. The insights in this book come from someone who's built real networks and learned from clever mentors, mistakes, and experiences.

While my writing style might not adhere to academic conventions, it remains practical, mirroring my approach to problem-solving. It offers an opportunity to assess your problem-solving approach and perhaps discover new perspectives. I aim to help you pass a particularly challenging exam and impart valuable skills to those who build networks, not just academics, whom I deeply respect. So, expect my approach to differ from what you're used to, with a focus on hands-on, real-world scenarios.

What makes this exam so tough? Having worked across various networking domains, I find that service provider networks are especially complex compared to their enterprise, data center, or mobility counterparts. Cisco acknowledges this complexity in its exam structure. Expect tough questions, and be pleasantly surprised when you encounter the ones easier than that.

As you prepare, pay close attention to the exam blueprint and how its sections are worded. Questions deliberately fall into four categories: Describe, Compare, Configure, and Troubleshoot. "Describe" sections assume a solid grasp of general knowledge and concepts. "Compare" sections probe deeper, expecting candidates to differentiate between similar topics. "Configure" sections require advanced familiarity to configure or spot errors accurately. "Troubleshoot" sections demand the highest skill level, testing your ability to solve complex problems with twists.

What's my top tip for acing the exam on your first attempt? Practice. I have structured my portions of the content for you to follow in the book and the command line. In theory, there is no difference between theory and practice. I can tell you that in practice, there is. There's no substitute for hands-on keyboard time in mastering service provider networks.

Once, at a networking convention, I spotted someone wearing a humorous T-shirt defining "engineer" as "someone who does precision guesswork based on unreliable data provided by those of questionable knowledge." During the exam and throughout your career, you might feel like that. But remember, you're not alone. This book is dedicated to those who've tackled the seemingly impossible in the past, those fixing networks alongside me today, and those learning to do the same in the near future. May some of us meet and recognize each other.

—Bradley Riapolov

To add to what Bradley mentioned, we tried our best to add new terms within the book from brainstorming and use cases to make it more realistic from practical experience and to assist with some design guidelines for the service provider technologies.

—Mohammad Khalil

Introduction

The Implementing and Operating Cisco Service Provider Network Core Technologies (SPCOR 350-501) exam is the required "core" exam for the CCNP Service Provider certifications. This exam tests your knowledge of implementing core service provider network technologies including architecture, services, networking, automation, quality of service, security, and network assurance.

Implementing and Operating Cisco Service Provider Network Core Technologies (SPCOR 350-501) is a 120-minute exam.

TIP   You can review the exam blueprint from Cisco's website at https://learningnetwork.cisco.com/s/spcor-exam-topics.

This book gives you the foundation and covers the topics necessary to start your CCNP Service Provider or CCIE Service Provider journey.

The CCNP Service Provider Certification

The CCNP Service Provider certification is one of the industry's most respected certifications. In order for you to earn the CCNP Service Provider certification, you must pass two exams: the SPCOR exam covered in this book (which covers core security technologies) and one of four available service provider concentration exams of your choice, so you can customize your certification to your technical area of focus.

TIP   The SPCOR core exam is also the qualifying exam for the CCIE Service Provider certification. Passing this exam is the first step toward earning both of these certifications.

The following are the CCNP Service Provider concentration exams:

- Implementing Cisco Service Provider Advanced Routing Solutions (300-510 SPRI)

- Implementing Cisco Service Provider VPN Services (300-515 SPVI)

- Automating Cisco Service Provider Solutions (300-535 SPAUTO)

- Designing and Implementing Cisco Service Provider Cloud Network Infrastructure (300-540 SPCNI)

The CCIE Service Provider Certification

The CCIE Service Provider certification is one of the most admired, elite, and challenging certifications in the industry. The CCIE Service Provider program prepares you to be a recognized technical leader. In order to earn the CCIE Service Provider certification, you must pass the SPCOR 350-501 exam and an eight-hour, hands-on lab exam. The lab exam covers very complex network service provider network scenarios. These scenarios range from designing through implementing, operating, and optimizing dual-stack solutions (IPv4 and IPv6) of complex service provider networks.

Cisco considers ideal candidates to be those who possess the following:

- Extensive hands-on experience with Cisco's Service Provider portfolio

- Experience deploying Cisco's wide assortment of legacy and modern service provider technologies

- Deep understanding of multiple transport protocols and multitenant segmentation solutions

- Hands-on experience with MPLS networks and VPN solutions

- Configuring and troubleshooting QoS, mobility networking, device hardening, and general and access control

- Deep understanding of network automation and orchestration constructs

The Exam Objectives (Domains)

The Implementing and Operating Cisco Service Provider Network Core Technologies (SPCOR 350-501) exam is broken down into five major domains. The contents of this book cover each of the domains and the subtopics included in them, as illustrated in the following descriptions.

The following table breaks down each of the domains represented in the exam.

Domain	Percentage of Representation in Exam
1: Architecture	15%
2: Networking	30%
3: MPLS and Segment Routing	20%
4: Services	20%
5: Automation and Assurance	15%
	Total 100%

Here are the details of each domain:

Domain 1: Architecture: This domain is covered in Chapters 1–3, 14, 16–18, and 21.

    1.1 Describe service provider architectures

        1.1.a Core architectures (Metro Ethernet, MPLS, unified MPLS, SR, SRTE, SRv6)

        1.1.b Transport technologies (xDSL, DWDM, DOCSIS, TDM, and xPON)

        1.1.c Mobility (packet core, RAN xhaul transport for 5G vRAN and ORAN transport)

        1.1.d Routed optical network

    1.2 Describe Cisco network software architecture

        1.2.a IOS

        1.2.b IOS XE

        1.2.c IOS XR

3.3.d TI-LFa

3.3.e PCE-PCC architectures

3.3.f Flexible algorithm

3.3.g SRv6 (locator, micro-segment, encapsulation, interworking gateway)

Domain 4: Services: This domain is covered in Chapters 9, 11–13, and 21.

4.1 Describe VPN services

4.1.a EVPN

4.1.b Inter-AS VPN

4.1.c CSC

4.1.d mVPN

4.2 Configure L2VPN and Carrier Ethernet

4.2.a Ethernet services (E-Line, E-Tree, E-Access, E-LAN)

4.2.b IEEE 802.1ad, IEEE 802.1ah, and ITU G.8032

4.2.c Ethernet OAM

4.2.d VLAN tag manipulation

4.3 Configure L3VPN

4.3.a Intra-AS VPN

4.3.b Shared services (extranet and Internet)

4.4 Implement multicast services

4.4.a PIM (PIM-SM, PIM-SSM, and PIM-BIDIR, PIMv6)

4.4.b IGMP v1/v2/v3 and MLD

4.5 Implement QoS services

4.5.a Classification and marking

4.5.b Congestion avoidance, traffic policing, and shaping

Domain 5: Automation and Assurance: This domain is covered in Chapter 22.

5.1 Describe the programmable APIs used to include Cisco devices in network automation

5.2 Interpret an external script to configure a Cisco device using a REST API

5.3 Describe the role of Network Services Orchestration (NSO)

5.4 Describe the high-level principles and benefits of a data modeling language, such as YANG

5.5 Describe configuration management tools, such as Ansible and Terraform

5.6 Describe Secure ZTP

5.7 Configure dial-in/out, TCP, TLS, and mTLS certificates using gRPC and gNMI

5.8 Configure and verify NetFlow/IPFIX

5.9 Configure and verify NETCONF and RESTCONF

5.10 Configure and verify SNMP (v2c/v3)

Steps to Pass the SPCOR Exam

There are no prerequisites for the SPCOR exam. However, students must have an understanding of networking and cybersecurity concepts.

Signing Up for the Exam

The steps required to sign up for the Implementing and Operating Cisco Service Provider Network Core Technologies (SPCOR 350-501) exam:

1. Create a Certiport account at https://www.certiport.com/portal/SSL/Login.aspx.

2. Once you have logged in, make sure that "Test Candidate" from the drop-down menu is selected.

3. Click the **Shop Available Exams** button.

4. Select the **Schedule exam** button under the exam you wish to take.

5. Verify your information and continue throughout the next few screens.

6. On the **Enter payment and billing** page, click the **Add Voucher or Promo Code** button if applicable. Enter the voucher number or promo/discount code in the field below and click the **Apply** button.

7. Continue through the next two screens to finish scheduling your exam.

Facts About the Exam

The exam is a computer-based test. The exam consists of multiple-choice questions only. You must bring a government-issued identification card. No other forms of ID will be accepted. You can take the exam at a Pearson Vue center or online via the OnVUE platform. Visit the OnVUE page for your exam program: https://home.pearsonvue.com/Test-takers/OnVUE-online-proctoring/View-all.aspx

Once there, navigate to the FAQs section of the page, where you'll find helpful information on everything from scheduling your exam to system requirements, testing policies, and more.

> **NOTE**   Refer to the Cisco Certification site at https://cisco.com/go/certifications for more information regarding this, and other, Cisco certifications.

About the *CCNP SPCOR 350-501 Official Cert Guide*

This book maps directly to the topic areas of the SPCOR exam and uses a number of features to help you understand the topics and prepare for the exam.

Objectives and Methods

This book uses several key methodologies to help you discover the exam topics that need more review, to help you fully understand and remember those details, and to help you prove to yourself that you have retained your knowledge of those topics. The book does not try to help you pass the exam only by memorization; it seeks to help you to truly learn and understand the topics. This book is designed to help you pass the Implementing and Operating Cisco Service Provider Network Core Technologies (SPCOR 350-501) exam by using the following methods:

- Helping you discover which exam topics you have not mastered

- Providing explanations and information to fill in your knowledge gaps

- Supplying exercises that enhance your ability to recall and deduce the answers to test questions

- Providing practice exercises on the topics and the testing process via test questions on the companion website

How to Use This Book

To help you customize your study time using this book, the core chapters have several features that help you make the best use of your time:

- **Foundation Topics:** These are the core sections of each chapter. They explain the concepts for the topics in that chapter.

- **Brainstorming:** These encourage you to actively apply their knowledge. You are invited to take a step beyond mere fact retrieval and engage deeply with the material you've covered. This is your opportunity to think critically about what you've learned and attempt to apply it on your own. Most of the time, we guide you through the process, but these exercises are designed to help you assess an exam question and provide an educated, well-reasoned answer. By participating in these sessions, you'll develop the skills to approach challenges with confidence and creativity, ensuring you're prepared to succeed independently.

- **Exam Preparation Tasks:** After the "Foundation Topics" section of each chapter, the "Exam Preparation Tasks" section lists a series of study activities that you should do at the end of the chapter:

  - **Review All Key Topics:** The Key Topic icon appears next to the most important items in the "Foundation Topics" section of the chapter. The Review All Key Topics activity lists the key topics from the chapter, along with their page numbers. Although the contents of the entire chapter could be on the exam, you should definitely know the information listed in each key topic, so you should review these.

  - **Define Key Terms:** Although the Implementing and Operating Cisco Service Provider Network Core Technologies (SPCOR 350-501) exam may be unlikely to ask a question such as "Define this term," the exam does require that you learn and know a lot of cybersecurity terminology. This section lists the most important terms from the chapter, asking you to write a short definition and compare your answer to the glossary at the end of the book.

- **Review Questions:** Confirm that you understand the content you just covered by answering these questions and reading the answer explanations in Appendix A.

- **Web-based practice exam:** The companion website includes the Pearson Cert Practice Test engine, which allows you to take practice exam questions. Use it to prepare with a sample exam and to pinpoint topics where you need more study.

How This Book Is Organized

This book contains 22 core chapters—Chapters 1 through 22. Chapter 23 includes preparation tips and suggestions for how to approach the exam. Each core chapter covers a subset of the topics on the Implementing and Operating Cisco Service Provider Network Core Technologies (SPCOR 350-501) exam. The core chapters map to the SPCOR topic areas and cover the concepts and technologies you will encounter on the exam.

The Companion Website for Online Content Review

All the electronic review elements, as well as other electronic components of the book, exist on this book's companion website.

To access the companion website, which gives you access to the electronic content that accompanies this book, start by establishing a login at www.ciscopress.com and registering your book by December 31, 2027. To do so, simply go to www.ciscopress.com/register and enter the ISBN of the print book: 9780135324806. After you have registered your book, go to your account page and click the **Registered Products** tab. From there, click the **Access Bonus Content** link to get access to the book's companion website.

Note that if you buy the Premium Edition eBook and Practice Test version of this book from Cisco Press, your book will automatically be registered on your account page. Simply go to your account page, click the **Registered Products** tab, and select **Access Bonus Content** to access the book's companion website.

Please note that many of our companion content files can be very large, especially image and video files.

If you are unable to locate the files for this title by following these steps, please visit www.pearsonITcertification.com/contact and select the **Site Problems/Comments** option. Our customer service representatives will assist you.

How to Access the Pearson Test Prep (PTP) App

You have two options for installing and using the Pearson Test Prep application: a web app and a desktop app. To use the Pearson Test Prep application, start by accessing the registration code that comes with the book. You can access the code in these ways:

- You can get your access code by registering the print ISBN 9780135324806 on https://www.ciscopress.com/register. Make sure to use the print book ISBN, regardless of whether you purchased an eBook or the print book. After you register the book, your access code will be populated on your account page under the Registered Products tab. Instructions for how to redeem the code are available on the book's companion website by clicking the **Access Bonus Content** link.

■ If you purchase the Premium Edition eBook and Practice Test directly from the Pearson IT Certification website, the code will be populated on your account page after purchase. Just log in at https://www.ciscopress.com, click **Account** to see details of your account, and click the **Digital Purchases** tab.

NOTE   After you register your book, your code can always be found in your account under the Registered Products tab.

Once you have the access code, to find instructions about both the PTP web app and the desktop app, follow these steps:

Step 1.   Open this book's companion website, as was shown earlier in this Introduction under the heading "The Companion Website for Online Content Review."

Step 2.   Click the **Practice Exams** button.

Step 3.   Follow the instructions listed there both for installing the desktop app and for using the web app.

Note that if you want to use the web app only at this point, just navigate to www.pearsontestprep.com, establish a free login if you do not already have one, and register this book's practice tests using the registration code you just found. The process should take only a couple of minutes.

Customizing Your Exams

Once you are in the exam settings screen, you can choose to take exams in one of three modes:

■ **Study mode:** Allows you to fully customize your exams and review answers as you are taking the exam. This is typically the mode you would use first to assess your knowledge and identify information gaps.

■ **Practice Exam mode:** Locks certain customization options, as it is presenting a realistic exam experience. Use this mode when you are preparing to test your exam readiness.

■ **Flash Card mode:** Strips out the answers and presents you with only the question stem. This mode is great for late-stage preparation when you really want to challenge yourself to provide answers without the benefit of seeing multiple-choice options. This mode does not provide the detailed score reports that the other two modes do, so you should not use it if you are trying to identify knowledge gaps.

In addition to these three modes, you will be able to select the source of your questions. You can choose to take exams that cover all of the chapters or you can narrow your selection to just a single chapter or the chapters that make up specific parts in the book. All chapters are selected by default. If you want to narrow your focus to individual chapters, simply deselect all the chapters and then select only those on which you wish to focus in the Objectives area.

You can also select the exam banks on which to focus. Each exam bank comes complete with a full exam of questions that cover topics in every chapter. The two exams printed in the book are available to you as well as two additional exams of unique questions. You can have the test engine serve up exams from all four banks or just from one individual bank by selecting the desired banks in the exam bank area.

There are several other customizations you can make to your exam from the exam settings screen, such as the time of the exam, the number of questions served up, whether to randomize questions and answers, whether to show the number of correct answers for multiple-answer questions, and whether to serve up only specific types of questions. You can also create custom test banks by selecting only questions that you have marked or questions on which you have added notes.

Updating Your Exams

If you are using the online version of the Pearson Test Prep software, you should always have access to the latest version of the software as well as the exam data. If you are using the Windows desktop version, every time you launch the software while connected to the Internet, it checks if there are any updates to your exam data and automatically downloads any changes that were made since the last time you used the software.

Sometimes, due to many factors, the exam data may not fully download when you activate your exam. If you find that figures or exhibits are missing, you may need to manually update your exams. To update a particular exam you have already activated and downloaded, simply click the **Tools** tab and click the **Update Products** button. Again, this is only an issue with the desktop Windows application.

If you wish to check for updates to the Pearson Test Prep exam engine software, Windows desktop version, simply click the **Tools** tab and click the **Update Application** button. This ensures that you are running the latest version of the software engine.

Figure Credits

Figure 1-15 © ITU 2024

Figure 7-2, baranoski.ca

Figures 17-1 and 17-2 © 2024 Postman, Inc.

Cover, insta_photos/shutterstock

Service Provider Architectures

This chapter covers the following exam topics:

1.1 Describe service provider architectures

- 1.1a Core architectures (Metro Ethernet, MPLS, unified MPLS, SR, SRTE, SRv6)
- 1.1b Transport technologies (xDSL, DWDM, DOCSIS, TDM, and xPON)
- 1.1c Mobility (packet core, RAN xhaul transport for 5G vRAN and O-RAN transport)
- 1.1d Routed optical network

Service provider networks are complex and sophisticated infrastructures that enable the delivery of various communication services to end users. These networks are typically operated by telecommunications companies (or service providers) and play a crucial role in connecting people, devices, and organizations. They consist of a vast physical infrastructure, including a combination of fiber-optic cables, coaxial cables, microwave links, radio, and other transmission mediums. Some of these infrastructures are limited to relatively small areas, whereas others span across various geographical regions to provide wide coverage.

Over the span of decades, service provider networks have witnessed the rise and fall of numerous technologies, protocols, and architectures, each claiming its place as the most efficient conduit for transferring data across networks. This dynamic evolution continually gives birth to new innovations while sometimes reviving age-old methods. In this chapter, we explore the vibrant landscape of network technologies that you're likely to encounter in your exam journey.

"Do I Know This Already?" Quiz

The "Do I Know This Already?" quiz allows you to assess whether you should read this entire chapter thoroughly or jump to the "Exam Preparation Tasks" section. If you are in doubt about your answers to these questions or your own assessment of your knowledge of the topics, read the entire chapter. Table 1-1 lists the major headings in this chapter and their corresponding "Do I Know This Already?" quiz questions. You can find the answers in Appendix A, "Answers to the 'Do I Know This Already?' Quizzes and Review Questions."

Table 1-1 "Do I Know This Already?" Section-to-Question Mapping

Foundation Topics Section	Questions
Network Core Architectures	1–2
Transport Technologies	3–4
Mobility (Packet Core, RAN xhaul Transport for 5G vRAN and ORAN Transport)	5–6

1. Unified MPLS makes use of
   a. SR labels
   b. BGP
   c. Inter-AS options
   d. IS-IS extensions
2. Valid Metro Services include these two offerings:
   a. E-Lane
   b. E-Tree
   c. E-LAN
   d. E-Mesh
3. What is the center wavelength for 100 GHz spacing?
   a. 1550.12 nm
   b. 1550.92 nm
   c. 1551.72 nm
   d. 1552.52 nm
4. Wavelength separation is provided by
   a. Amplifier
   b. Router
   c. Transponder
   d. ROADM
5. Processed data between the BBU and RRH is a function of
   a. Pre-aggregation
   b. Midhaul
   c. Fronthaul
   d. Backhaul
6. A low-level split should allow for the following two considerations:
   a. Careful coordination
   b. Accommodation of diverse use cases
   c. Efficient resource utilization
   d. Management of distributed network elements

Foundation Topics

Network Core Architectures

Service provider core architecture refers to the network design and infrastructure that telecommunication service providers use to deliver a variety of services to their customers. Service provider networks tend to be much larger than their enterprise or data center counterparts. They offer a diverse range of services such as Internet access, voice communication, video streaming, private circuits, virtual private networks (VPNs, which are introduced in later chapters), mobility, and many more. The core architecture is critical for ensuring high performance, scalability, and reliability.

In the past, telephone companies (telcos) and Internet service providers (ISPs) varied in their approaches to offering network services. Telcos offered a wide assortment of services to their customers:

- Time-division multiplexing (TDM) provided telephony or data circuits.

- ATM or Frame Relay provided VPNs.

- SONET/Synchronous Digital Hierarchy (SDH) carried TDM and ATM across optical networks.

- Quality of service (QoS) gave priority to customers who were willing to pay for it.

- IP provided Internet access.

Such networks offered a variety of services but also carried significant costs (both customer and internal). At the same time, ISPs narrowly focused on a single cost-effective technology, IP. This allowed them to offer competitive pricing at the expense of limiting their service to only Internet access. As technology has evolved, so has the role of a service provider. To stay in business, modern service providers have had to change their approach to meet the ever-increasing customer demands. Today's service provider offers

- High-speed broadband and fiber-optic Internet access.

- 4G and 5G ultra-fast and low-latency cellular broadband.

- Voice over IP (VoIP) services in a Unified Communications platform.

- Cloud services, including Infrastructure as a Service (IaaS), Platform as a Service (PaaS), and Software as a Service (SaaS), allowing businesses to leverage scalable and flexible computing resources.

- Managed Security Services to protect networks, data, and systems from cyber threats through solutions like firewalls, intrusion detection/prevention, and threat intelligence.

- Software-defined networking (SDN) and network function virtualization (NFV) for virtualization and automation of network functions.

- Internet of Things (IoT) connectivity for a growing number of IoT devices, enabling communication and data exchange between devices for applications such as smart cities, industrial IoT, and healthcare.

- Content Delivery Networks (CDNs) for optimized delivery of content by distributing it across strategic geographies, reducing latency, and improving the performance of websites.

- Dense wavelength-division multiplexing (DWDM) services to maximize the amount of throughput that is available via a single strand of optical fiber.

- Collaboration tools for remote teamwork, video conferencing, and document sharing, supporting the evolving nature of work and communication.

- Managed Wi-Fi Services for businesses and homes with features like guest access, network monitoring, and performance optimization.

- Data Center Services such as co-location, hosting, and cloud infrastructure to meet the growing demands for storage, processing, and application deployment.

- Integrated solutions for smart homes, including connected devices, home automation, and entertainment services.

These services reflect the industry's response to technological advancements and the changing requirements of businesses and consumers. As technology continues to evolve, service providers are likely to introduce new services and enhancements to stay at the forefront of the telecommunications landscape. Our goal is to introduce you to several aspects of the service provider core architectures you are likely to see on the exam.

Metro Ethernet

Metro Ethernet refers to the use of Ethernet technology in metropolitan area networks (MANs) to create high-speed, scalable, and cost-effective network infrastructures. It extends the principles of Ethernet, commonly used in local area networks (LANs), to cover larger geographic areas within a city or metropolitan region. Metro Ethernet allows for the creation of scalable networks that can cover larger geographical areas than traditional LANs. It is well suited for connecting multiple sites within a city or metropolitan region. Metro Ethernet provides high-speed connectivity, offering bandwidth options that can meet the demands of businesses, service providers, and institutions requiring fast and reliable data transmission. Leveraging Ethernet technology powers up cost-effective network solutions, and the use of standardized Ethernet equipment and protocols contributes to affordability and ease of deployment. Metro Ethernet is based on industry-standard Ethernet technologies, including IEEE 802.1Q (VLAN tagging) and IEEE 802.1ad (provider bridging or Q-in-Q). This adherence to standards promotes interoperability and compatibility among different vendors' equipment. You should be familiar with the following three aspects of Metro Ethernet services and topologies, which are covered in the following pages.

- E-Line

- E-LAN

- E-Tree

E-Line (Ethernet Line Service)

E-Line service, often referred to as Ethernet Line or Ethernet Virtual Private Line (EVPL), is a type of Ethernet service that establishes a point-to-point or point-to-multipoint

Ethernet connection between two or more locations, as illustrated in Figure 1-1. This service is commonly used to provide a dedicated and transparent communication channel between different sites. It uses Ethernet, thus providing a familiar and widely used networking protocol and making it compatible with various types of Ethernet-enabled devices. Its transparent nature allows customers to run any networking protocol over established Ethernet connections. Supporting high-bandwidth speeds makes it suitable for applications that require significant data transfer rates.

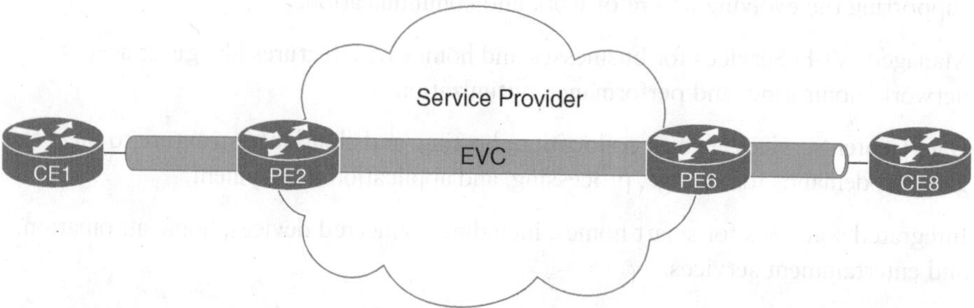

Figure 1-1 *E-Line Metro Ethernet Point-to-Point Service*

Note how, in Figure 1-1, a service provider delivers an E-Line service to the customer's two locations on opposite sides of an imaginary town. This Ethernet Virtual Circuit (EVC) is the simplest possible point-to-point Layer 2 link between two sites. In fact, routers CE1 (Customer Edge 1) and CE8 (Customer Edge 8) are clueless that this circuit, or the service provider network, for that matter, even exist! Routers CE1 and CE8 are on the same Layer 2 LAN (same Layer 3 subnet) and from their perspective are connected via a crossover cable because they do not detect any infrastructure in between (unless the service provider allows this behavior).

Another variation of the E-Line service is found in Figure 1-2, where an additional Metro location CE9 is connected via a separate E-Line service to the CE1 location. Two separate EVCs are used, and most likely CE1 is trunked to PE2, carrying discreet VLANs for each of the EVCs.

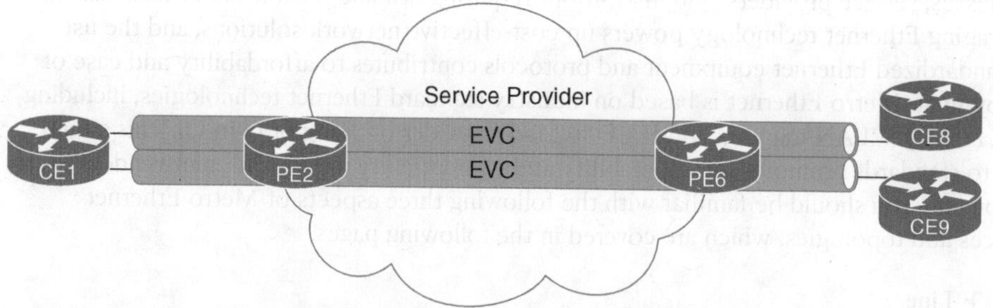

Figure 1-2 *E-Line Metro Ethernet Multiple Point-to-Point Services*

In Figure 1-2, it is assumed that the service provider used Ethernet inside their network. If the service provider uses MPLS in their network, this service will be referred to as Virtual Private Wire Service (VPWS). These are constructed with "pseudowires" (equivalents of EVCs in the MPLS domain), which are virtual connections between any two routers. If a service provider builds these connections locally on a single router (connecting different ports together), Cisco's documentation refers to these as *xconnects* (cross-connects).

E-LAN (Ethernet LAN Service)

E-LAN (Ethernet LAN) is a type of Ethernet service that provides multipoint-to-multipoint connectivity, allowing multiple sites to communicate with each other over a shared network as if they were on the same local area network (LAN). In Figure 1-3, we expand our network and introduce a couple more routers in the service provider network. We also add another site, CE10. In this offering, the EVC connects all sites with a full-mesh interconnect because they are sharing the same LAN. Distance wise, these sites have long ago exhausted the limits of LAN Ethernet reach, but this service removes this physical limitation. Sometimes, it helps to think of the service provider's network as one giant switch that provides multipoint-to-multipoint services. If a service provider is running MPLS, this EVC would be referred to as a Virtual Private LAN Service (VPLS), which is created on Cisco routers with bridge domains.

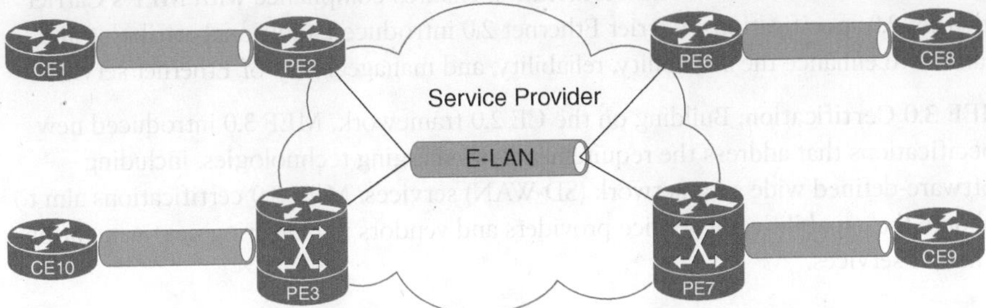

Figure 1-3 *E-LAN Metro Multipoint-to-Multipoint Ethernet Services*

Note that one of the advantages of VPLS is that it eliminates the need for Spanning Tree Protocol (STP) in the core of the service provider network. By encapsulating Layer 2 frames within MPLS tunnels, VPLS allows traffic to be forwarded based on MPLS labels rather than MAC addresses. This configuration eliminates the risk of loops in the core network and allows for more efficient use of network resources. As a result, service providers can deploy VPLS without relying on STP in the core, leading to simpler network designs and improved scalability.

E-Tree (Ethernet Tree Service)

E-Tree services are likely to connect multiple sites to the central CE1 site to access shared resources at that site, as illustrated in Figure 1-4. Think of this topology as similar to hub-and-spoke, where the spokes can still communicate with each other, but not directly, only going through the central CE1 site. Think of this as a point-to-multipoint service.

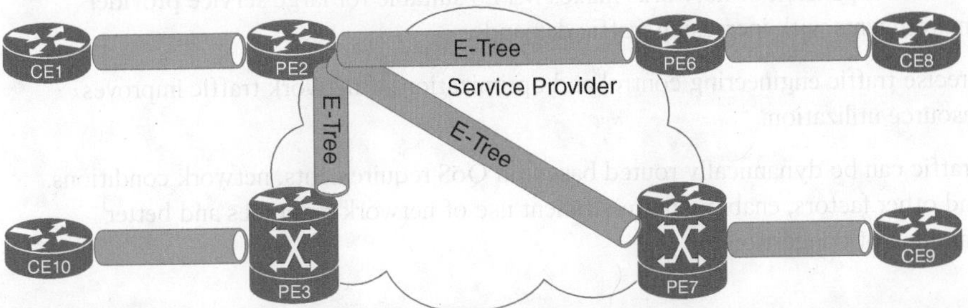

Figure 1-4 *E-Tree Metro Point-to-Multipoint Ethernet Services*

Metro Ethernet Forum (MEF)

Metro Ethernet Forum (MEF) Ethernet certification refers to a set of standardized certifications provided by the MEF organization to ensure compliance with industry-defined specifications for Ethernet services. MEF is a global alliance of telecommunication service providers, vendors, and other stakeholders focused on developing and standardizing Carrier Ethernet services.

The MEF Ethernet certification program is designed to validate that service providers and vendors adhere to MEF-defined standards, ensuring interoperability, reliability, and consistency in the deployment of Ethernet services. This program includes various certifications, each focusing on specific aspects of Carrier Ethernet services to ensure that vendors' products meet these criteria. Some key MEF Ethernet certifications include

- **MEF CE 2.0 Certification:** This certification ensures compliance with MEF's Carrier Ethernet 2.0 specifications. Carrier Ethernet 2.0 introduced additional attributes and features to enhance the scalability, reliability, and manageability of Ethernet services.

- **MEF 3.0 Certification:** Building on the CE 2.0 framework, MEF 3.0 introduced new specifications that address the requirements of emerging technologies, including software-defined wide area network (SD-WAN) services. MEF 3.0 certifications aim to validate the capabilities of service providers and vendors in delivering next-generation Ethernet services.

In summary, Metro Ethernet plays a crucial role in enabling efficient and high-performance connectivity for businesses, institutions, and service providers operating within a metropolitan area. It provides a cost-effective solution for extending Ethernet networks beyond the local office or campus, supporting the growing demand for high-speed and reliable communication in urban environments.

MPLS

Without question, MPLS is a dominantly popular technology in the core architecture of today's service providers. Why? Because it enhances the efficiency of routing data traffic while keeping down costs. It enables the creation of virtual private networks (VPNs), traffic engineering (TE), and quality of service (QoS) capabilities at immense scale. MPLS allows service providers to offer services with varying levels of performance and reliability.

Briefly, MPLS works by assigning labels to data packets, allowing routers to make faster and more predictable forwarding decisions. Consider the following MPLS benefits:

- Scalable expansion of networks makes MPLS suitable for large service provider environments with increasing traffic demands.

- Precise traffic engineering control and optimization of network traffic improves resource utilization.

- Traffic can be dynamically routed based on QoS requirements, network conditions, and other factors, enabling more efficient use of network resources and better handling of congestion.

- Creation of discreet and scalable VPNs supports traffic isolation for different customers or business entities.

- Unmatched network reliability is accomplished via fast rerouting capabilities, reducing downtime in the event of link or node failures.

- Segmentation of any network traffic isolates and manages various services or applications more effectively.

- Simplified network management abstracts the complexities of underlying protocols, making it easier to configure and maintain large networks.

- The protocol-agnostic nature of MPLS allows it to carry several types of network protocols, making it versatile for diverse applications.

- Most importantly, MPLS is a cost-efficient construct that can lead to cost savings by improving network utilization, reducing the need for additional bandwidth, and streamlining network management processes.

MPLS improved traditional IP routing because it introduced an additional packet header known as the MPLS label. MPLS is an encapsulation between the OSI Layer 3 IP header and any chosen OSI Layer 2 header. Observe Figure 1-5, which shows the packet header structure; Chapter 10, "MPLS Fundamentals," explains this topic in further detail.

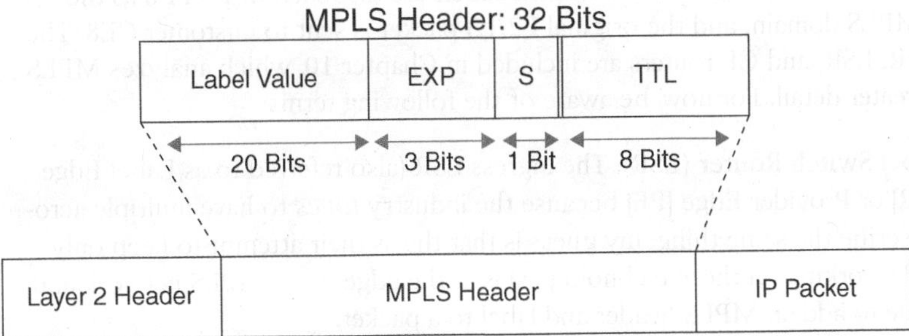

Figure 1-5 *IP Packet Header Structure with MPLS Encapsulation*

The MPLS label value in Figure 1-5 is used to switch packets based on label lookup rather than IP address lookup. Such labels align with destination IP networks, with each router within an MPLS-enabled network associating specific labels with a corresponding destination IP prefix. In service provider networks, the adoption of MPLS allows for service providers to provide connectivity and services with only Edge routers in an MPLS domain performing route lookup. All other routers forward packets based on the assigned labels, simplifying the overall packet forwarding process.

Figure 1-6 shows the basics of how labels are used in MPLS networks (this figure appears again in subsequent chapters).

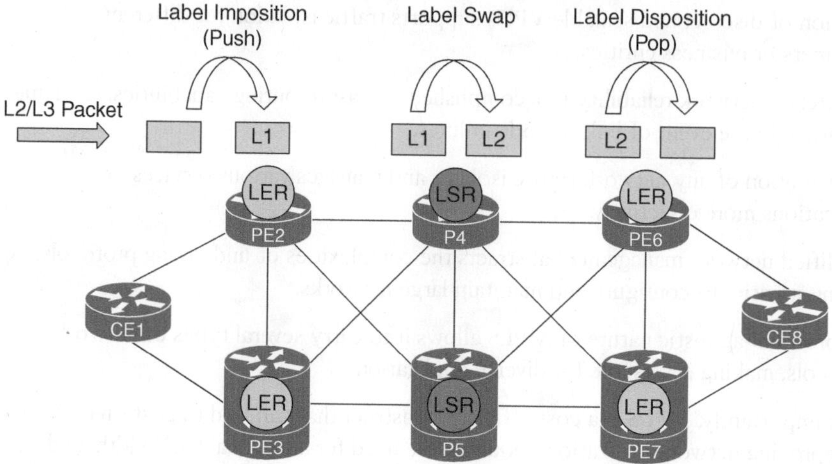

Figure 1-6 *MPLS Basics*

As a packet from Customer Edge 1 (CE1) enters this service provider's domain, the packet's Layer 3 header is examined by Provider Edge x (PE) only once at this point of entry into the MPLS domain. At the service provider's entry point, Router Provider Edge 2 (PE2) adds labels to the packet and forwards it through the MPLS domain. The packet continues through the domain until it reaches PE6, where the labels are disposed of by PE6 as the packet exits the MPLS domain, and the original L2/L3 packet is sent to customer CE8. The definitions for LER, LSR, and CE routers are included in Chapter 10, which analyzes MPLS networks in far greater detail. For now, be aware of the following terms:

- **Ingress Label Switch Router (LSR):** The ingress LSR (also referred to as Label Edge Router [LER] or Provider Edge [PE] because the industry *loves* to have multiple acronyms to describe the same thing; my guess is that this is their attempt to keep only smart people working on these technologies) is at the edge of an MPLS network and the first node to add an MPLS header and label to a packet.

- **Intermediate LSR:** LSRs (or Provider Core [P]) exist within the network and are responsible for manipulating (pushing, popping, and swapping labels based on the routing with the MPLS network).

- **Egress LSR:** The egress LSR (also referred to as Label Edge Router [LER] or Provider Edge [PE]) is at the edge of the network. It is the last checkpoint before leaving the network. It removes all the MPLS labels and header.

- **LSP (Label Switched Path):** This is a series of labels used to reach a destination. LSPs operate in a one-way manner: the path for return traffic employs a separate LSP.

Here's MPLS in a nutshell: it's the VIP pass for your data packets, making them travel through the network in style!

Unified MPLS

Unified MPLS is not an industry term. It is Cisco's technology framework to describe seamless or hierarchical MPLS—a method to efficiently scale expansive service provider networks featuring multiple Interior Gateway Protocols (IGPs, such as IS-IS and OSPF) domains. Unified MPLS uses existing MPLS forwarding architecture but introduces a capability to identify traffic using a single label that spans multiple segments within a service provider network. To achieve this, BGP is deployed to carry the label, identifying the destination router, and advertising a specific service end to end. The goal is to keep the MPLS services (MPLS L3VPN, MPLS L2VPN) as they are but to introduce greater scalability of service provider networks beyond what was achievable with earlier technologies. It combines the advantages of a hierarchical structure, improves scalability, and simplifies network designs. Figure 1-7 shows Cisco's visualization of this framework.

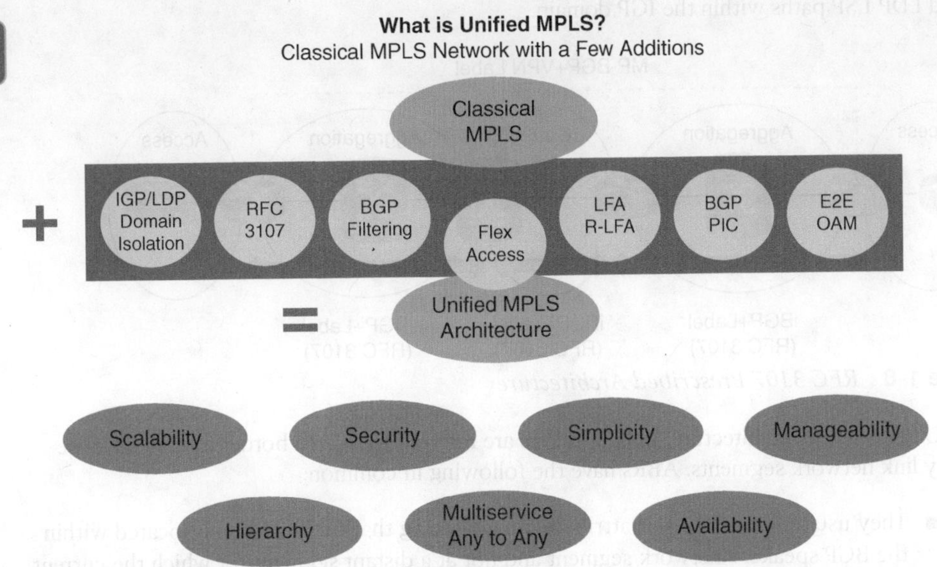

Figure 1-7 *Unified MPLS*

Scalability demands efficient prefix exchange between network segments. While merging several IGPs (Open Shortest Path First [OSPF] or Intermediate System-to-Intermediate System [IS-IS]) into a single domain is a possible approach, this approach falls short when dealing with a large number of prefixes, because IGPs are not designed to handle such extensive loads. No IGP is able to carry hundreds of thousands of prefixes. The optimal solution would be BGP, a well-established protocol supporting today's Internet route table with over 900,000 prefixes and additional MPLS-VPN environments with millions of entries. Cisco Unified MPLS utilizes BGP-4 for label information exchange, following the RFC 3107 standard.

In the Unified MPLS framework, BGP uses label mapping to associate MPLS labels with routes during route distribution. The MPLS label information is distributed in the BGP update message containing details about the route. The label is preserved if the next hop remains unchanged, and it changes if the next hop changes. This typically occurs at area border routers (ABRs). Enabling RFC 3107 on both BGP routers signals their ability to exchange MPLS labels. Successful negotiation results in the addition of MPLS labels to all outgoing BGP updates.

The label exchange is essential for maintaining end-to-end path information between segments. This ensures that each segment remains manageable for operators, and circuit information is distributed for path awareness between different IP speakers.

In Figure 1-8, core and aggregation segments use Label Distribution Protocol (LDP) labeled switched paths (LSPs), while the access network does not run LDP. The goal is to connect these segments into a Unified MPLS path (Internal BGP [iBGP] hierarchical LSP) between aggregation routers. This way, the network will operate as a single BGP autonomous system (AS), and all sessions will be iBGP sessions. Each segment operates its own IGP (OSPF, IS-IS) and LDP LSP paths within the IGP domain.

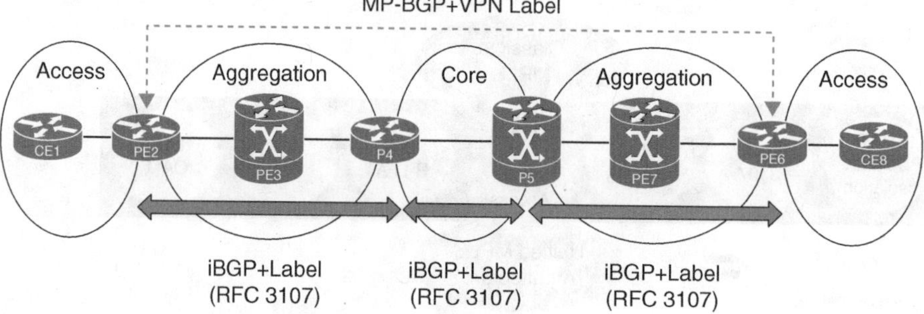

Figure 1-8 *RFC 3107 Prescribed Architecture*

In Unified MPLS architecture, BGP speakers are referred to as area border routers because they link network segments. ABRs have the following in common:

■ They use the next-hop-self attribute, guaranteeing that the next-hop is located within the BGP speaker's network segment and not at a distant segment for which the current speaker lacks the IGP route.

■ They use RFC 3107 methodology to carry an IPv4 with label configurations; this enables Unified MPLS.

■ They function as BGP inline route reflectors. Wait a minute. Why route reflectors? In Unified MPLS, all connections are iBGP peerings and require full-mesh connectivity for all iBGP speakers across the entire network (if iBGP, eBGP, or route-reflector terms are new to you, they are covered in detail in Chapter 7, "BGP Fundamentals"). Without this function, the setup would quickly become terribly impractical with a large number of BGP speakers that can potentially number in the thousands. By making the ABRs route reflectors, the number of iBGP peerings is reduced to the count of BGP speakers within each segment, rather than requiring connections among every BGP speaker across the entire autonomous system.

Figure 1-8 shows three independent IGP domains, each using a discreet LDP domain to build *intradomain* LSPs. This approach reduces the size of routing and forwarding tables on routers while enhancing stability and accelerating convergence. RFC 3107 uses BGP labels to construct hierarchical *interdomain* LSPs. Figure 1-9 shows the additional label in the forwarding stack to enable Unified MPLS.

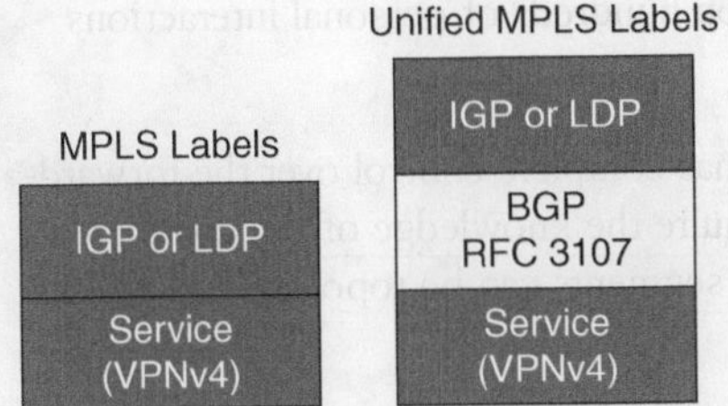

Figure 1-9 *Additional Unified MPLS BGP Label*

You should be aware of a couple of additional features that improve Unified MPLS operations:

- **BGP Prefix-Independent Convergence (BGP PIC):** This feature enhances BGP convergence following a network failure. This applies to both core and edge failures and is applicable in both IP and MPLS networks. The feature calculates and stores a backup (or alternate) path in the routing information base (RIB) and forwarding information base (FIB) tables. Upon detecting a failure, this backup path can swiftly take over, ensuring rapid failover. You can think of this feature as *fast-reroute* (FRR, which is described in Chapter 10) for BGP. Note that BGP PIC Core and BGP PIC Edge work distinctly differently.

- **BGP Add-Path:** When a BGP speaker has multiple entries for a specific destination, it typically transmits only its best path to neighbors, restricting the advertisement of multiple paths for the same destination. This feature addresses the "best path" limitation, allowing multiple paths for the same destination without automatically replacing any existing ones—thus assisting BGP PIC.

In Chapter 14, "MPLS Traffic Engineering," we investigate the technicalities behind Unified MPLS.

Segment Routing

Traffic engineering is a must-have tool on today's networks for technical and economic reasons. It addresses the most glaring limitation of using IGP metrics to manipulate traffic—the "all-or-nothing" approach. When relying on IGP metrics alone, even the simplest networks will overutilize and congest some of the links while underutilizing others, even though those may be high bandwidth or low latency. IGP metrics lack optimization capabilities because they do not allow network operators to map different services to different paths between same source and destination nodes.

In fact, a distinct variety of problems cannot be solved with IGP manipulations and destination-based routing. **Segment Routing** (also referred to as *Source Routing* by the wider industry) is a modern approach to traffic engineering in service provider networks. Instead of many routers reserving hundreds or possibly thousands of stateful tunnels along with backup paths (burning compute, memory, and storage resources), only the source (ingress router) specifies the entire path in advance and can force the traffic anywhere on the network. The source router accomplishes this through a list of instructions called *segments* in the data packet. This makes networks more flexible, scalable, and easier to manage. Segment Routing is used for efficient traffic control and works well in various network environments, offering a simpler and more adaptable way of handling data paths.

Among the chief benefits of Segment Routing, based on hundreds of personal interactions with customers, are

- **Optimized Traffic Delivery:** The ingress router has complete control over the forwarding path of the packet. Transit routers do not require the knowledge of the complete path, only how to get to the next segment. Such segments can be topology or services based.

- **Network Simplification:** There is significant reduction of involved protocols. LDP and RSVP-TE are removed, along with their problematic synchronization issues, because IGP takes over the entire management of both routing and label distribution. The notion of MPLS tunnels is drastically simplified as IGP becomes the client of the control plane.

- **Network Resiliency:** Fast-reroute (FRR) now works under any conceivable topology with the improved topology-independent loop-free alternate (TI-LFA), thereby finally addressing loop-free alternate/remote loop-free alternate (LFA/RLFA) limitations.

- **Software-Defined Application-Engineered Routing:** This becomes a reality as SDN controllers are integrated into the networking domain to enable optimal path selection. Balance between distributed intelligence and centralized optimization is finally realized.

- **Cost Savings:** Segment Routing promotes better network utilization because most of today's networks are 50 percent overengineered to support suboptimal routing. It lowers resource consumption and promotes resource conservation, minimizing network control plane pressure because it avoids thousands of LDP labels in the core of the network.

Segment Routing Traffic Engineering (SRTE)

Traffic engineering has evolved significantly over the years, adapting to the changing landscape of network technologies and requirements. Initially, traffic engineering focused on optimizing network resources to ensure efficient data transmission, primarily through the use of static routing protocols and manual configurations. As networks grew in size and complexity, the need for more dynamic and automated traffic management solutions became apparent. This led to the development of technologies such as Multiprotocol Label Switching (MPLS) and Resource Reservation Protocol (RSVP), which introduced the concept of traffic engineering in the context of label-switched paths and explicit route setup.

More recently, advancements in software-defined networking (SDN) and Segment Routing have further revolutionized traffic engineering, offering more flexible and scalable approaches to traffic optimization and path selection. Prior to the introduction of Segment Routing Traffic Engineering (SRTE), IP networks relied on connection-oriented circuits such as frame relay and ATM, as well as RSVP MPLS LSPs. However, these traditional methods lacked ECMP-based capabilities, which proved to be a substantial drawback because the network was not trained to automatically find and consume all available resources. The transition to Segment Routing presents an opportunity for IP networks to leverage their inherent ECMP properties, allowing for the efficient utilization of multiple available paths throughout the network. In an SR-MPLS-enabled network, an MPLS label represents an instruction. The source nodes program the path to a destination in the packet header as a stack of labels. Segment Routing policies articulate these paths as the shortest ECMP-aware routes to specified reference points, offering a significant advantage over older methods. This advantage extends directly to both SR-MPLS (MPLS data plane) and SRv6 (IPv6 data plane), enhancing network efficiency and flexibility.

Over the years, SRTE has undergone significant evolution and refinement, reaching a level of maturity that rivals traditional Resource Reservation Protocol Traffic Engineering (RSVP-TE) functionalities. SRTE has emerged as a robust and scalable solution that addresses many of the limitations and challenges that RSVP-TE encountered. Unlike RSVP-TE, which relies on complex signaling protocols and explicit path setup, SRTE offers a simpler, more efficient approach to traffic engineering. Network operators can define explicit paths through the network using segments with greater flexibility and control over traffic flows. With its maturation, SRTE has proven to be a viable alternative to RSVP-TE, offering improved scalability, operational simplicity, and compatibility with emerging network architectures.

One of the significant advantages of SRTE is its integration with the Path Computation Element Protocol (PCEP) controller for traffic policy optimization. Network operators can dynamically optimize traffic flows based on real-time network conditions and policy requirements. By leveraging a two-way feedback mechanism facilitated by Border Gateway Protocol Link State (BGP-LS), SRTE can gather comprehensive network topology and traffic information in real time. The PCEP controller uses this data to compute optimal paths and traffic policies, considering factors such as link utilization, delay, network congestion, and quality of service constraints. This dynamic optimization capability allows for efficient resource utilization, improved network performance, and enhanced service delivery. Additionally, the integration of PCEP controller-based optimization with SRTE provides a centralized and automated approach to traffic engineering, simplifying network operations and reducing manual configuration overhead. Overall, this synergy between SRTE and PCEP controller-based optimization represents a significant advancement in traffic engineering methodologies, enabling networks to adapt dynamically to changing traffic patterns and operational requirements.

SRv6 (Segment Routing IPv6)

Segment Routing over IPv6 (SRv6) extends Segment Routing support with the IPv6 data plane and offers a multitude of advantages that make it a compelling choice for modern networking environments. One of the primary benefits of SRv6 is its inherent simplicity and flexibility. By leveraging IPv6 data plane capabilities, SRv6 eliminates the need for additional encapsulation or tunneling mechanisms, resulting in a streamlined architecture and reduced overhead. SRv6 brings in a network programming framework, allowing network operators or applications to define how packets are processed. This is done by encoding instructions in the IPv6 packet header. These instructions, identified by SRv6 Segment Identifiers (SIDs), dictate actions taken at various network nodes.

Furthermore, SRv6 provides granular control over traffic engineering and service chaining, allowing operators to define explicit paths and service functions using IPv6 segment identifiers. This level of programmability enables dynamic and efficient network resource utilization, optimized traffic distribution, and simplified service deployment. SRv6 works seamlessly with existing IPv6 infrastructure, enabling gradual deployment and coexistence with legacy IPv4 networks. It also inherently supports network slicing, enabling the creation of isolated and customized network segments for diverse use cases such as 5G, edge computing, and IoT. Overall, SRv6 represents a revolutionary paradigm shift in networking, offering unprecedented levels of flexibility, scalability, and innovation to meet the evolving demands of modern applications and services.

We deal with Segment Routing in great detail in Chapter 15, "Segment Routing." Until then, let's look at the transport technologies that service providers use to construct networks.

Transport Technologies

Transport technologies refer to the various methods and systems used to move data, voice, and video signals from one point to another within a network. These technologies are essential for communication between devices and systems. They collectively form the backbone of modern communication networks, facilitating the exchange of information across local and global scales. Advances in technology continue to shape and improve these transport methods for greater efficiency, speed, and reliability. They create the physical underlay for the network that sits on top it. In the following sections, we describe some of the common transport technologies you may see on the exam.

DOCSIS

Data Over Cable Service Interface Specification (DOCSIS) is an international standard developed by CableLabs for the transmission of data over cable television (CATV) systems. CableLabs' influence on major cable TV companies can be compared to Bell Labs' contributions to major telephone companies. DOCSIS has played a significant role in the widespread adoption of broadband Internet services over cable television infrastructure, offering consumers high-speed connectivity for various online activities.

DOCSIS architecture was introduced as a standard in the late 1990s and laid the foundation for cable modems. It included two primary components to connect to a cable TV line for high-speed Internet access, as seen in Figure 1-10:

- A cable modem located at the customer premises with (typically) two connections: one to the cable TV line and another to a computer or a home network.

- A Cable Modem Termination System (CMTS) located at the CATV headend.

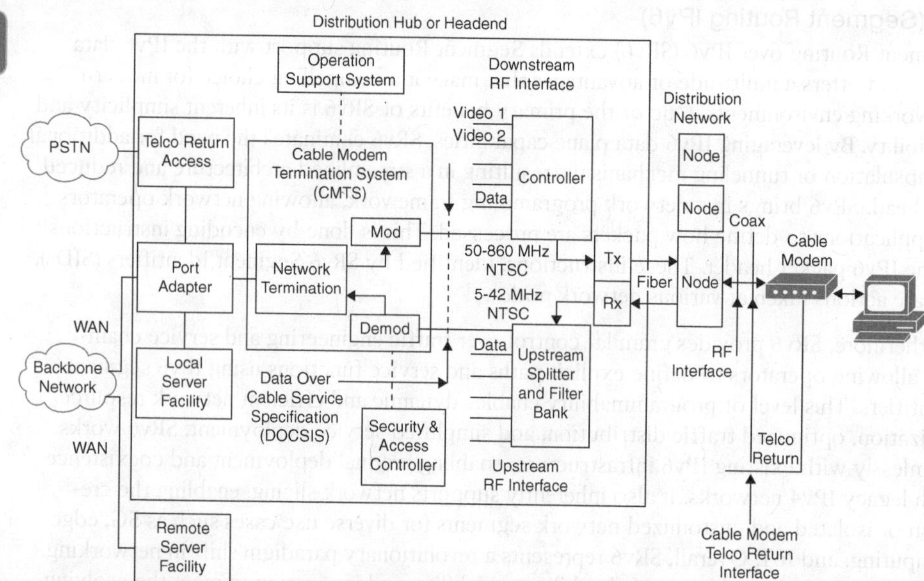

Figure 1-10 *DOCSIS Architecture*

As you can see, the standard called for both downstream (from the Internet to the user) and upstream (from the user to the Internet) communication channels that operated on different frequency ranges, allowing for bidirectional data transmission over the same cable. A customer PC and associated peripherals were referred to as customer-premises equipment (CPE). The CPE connected to the cable modem, which, in turn, connected through the hybrid fiber coaxial (HFC) network to the CMTS. The CMTS then routed traffic between HFC and the Internet. Using provisioning systems and CMTS, the cable operator exercised control over the cable modem's configuration. HFC networks are shared access mediums, meaning all homes in the neighborhood share the bandwidth. Years ago, I moved into a new neighborhood that had few homes, and Internet connectivity was great. A couple of years later, as houses filled the neighborhood, the connection became far worse because many households were sharing the same service. This is the nature of shared infrastructures.

Table 1-2 briefly shows the evolution of DOCSIS technology.

Table 1-2 DOCSIS Standards

DOCSIS Standard	Issue Date	Downstream Bandwidth	Upstream Bandwidth	Distinct Contributions
1.0	1997	~40 Mbps	~10 Mbps	The initial Internet access specification was made over cable infrastructure, DES 56 encryption.
1.1	1999	~40 Mbps	~10 Mbps	Quality of service (QoS) empowered cable systems to carry and prioritize voice calls.
2.0	2001	~40 Mbps	~30 Mbps	Transmission speeds were upgraded.
3.0	2006	~1 Gbps	~300 Mbps	Channel bonding was introduced to allow higher transmission rates, cross-version compatibility, IP multicast, IPv6, and AES encryption.
3.1	2013	~10 Gbps	~2 Gbps	A staggering capacity increase occurred with Orthogonal Frequency Division Multiplexing (OFDM) sub-carriers and Forward Error Correction (FEC) mechanisms.
4.0	2023	~10 Gbps	~6 Gbps	Multi-gigabit symmetric services were introduced in limited markets.

As high-speed fiber-optic Internet gained popularity, cable networks faced a gradual decline. Despite formidable competition, the well-established but older coaxial cable technology has not faded away. The DOCSIS standard emerged as a key element that allowed coaxial cable technology to remain competitive. It has played a major role in facilitating increasingly faster Internet access without the daunting and costly task of replacing the entire physical network infrastructure. In my mind, DOCSIS has breathed new life into hybrid fiber coaxial (HFC) networks, as the industry prepared to wage another war fighting fiber with…fiber.

xDSL

Digital Subscriber Line (DSL) refers to technologies that digitally transmit information over a single telephone line using the voice frequency to send and receive Internet data and traffic. This type of connection enabled high-speed downloads and can be categorized into two main groups based on how they send data:

- **Symmetric DSL (SDSL):** Characterized by symmetric transmission, where upload and download speeds are the same. It has been traditionally used to back up large amounts of information to cloud storage or VPN users due to required capacity.

- **Asymmetric DSL (ADSL):** Characterized by asymmetric transmission, where download speeds are faster than upload speeds. This is a less expensive service and more widely deployed because of its quicker download speed as opposed to upload speed.

The term *xDSL* covers various types of DSL. In general, xDSL services offer dedicated, point-to-point, and public network access through twisted-pair copper wires in the local loop, commonly known as the "last mile." DSL initially worked over OSI model physical Layer 1. The DSL Layer 1 connection consists of a pair of DSL modems on either end of a copper wire pair—at the subscriber end and at a central office (CO; metal cages often seen at the front of a neighborhood or around town) or other points of presence (POPs).

Many households use four wires (two pairs) of copper unshielded twisted-pair (UTP) cables. This setup can accommodate two phone lines, with one dedicated to specific data services like DSL, ISDN, or a dial-up modem connection. For plain old telephone service (POTS) line voice services, frequencies up to 4 kHz were used. The upstream data occupied the 20–240 kHz range and downstream data in the 250–1 kHz range. DSL subscribers' CPE equipment linked directly to DSLAM equipment (specifically the DSL modem cards within the Digital Subscriber Line Access Multiplexer, or DSLAM). These cards came with different port capacities, with each port connecting to an individual subscriber. Later DSLAM generations added Layer 3 intelligence for IP switching alongside Layer 1 multiplexing capabilities. Figure 1-11 helps to visualize DSL technology.

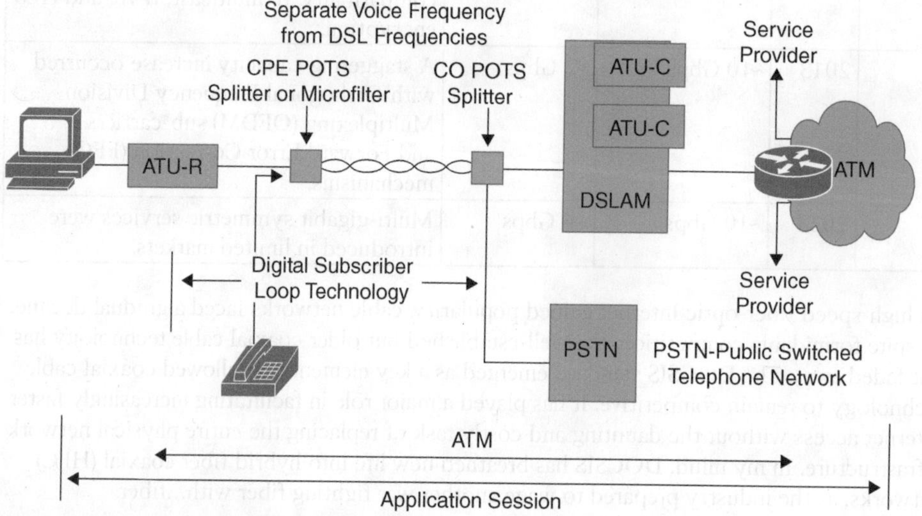

Figure 1-11 *Basic DSL Architecture*

DLS technology was not without problems. Wire crosstalk, frequency interference, copper impedance mismatches, and other issues brought distinct impairments to the technology, but most were addressed in one way or another. Yet the most notable drawback remained—distance, specifically the 12,000-foot limit (~2 miles). Some providers quoted better distances, but no one has been able to beat physics. The greater the distance away from the central office, the slower the connection speed. As you moved away from the central office, the signal quality diminished due to increased line distortion. To address this issue, the phone company would reduce transmission rates, for instance, from 1.5 Mbps to 384 Kbps, but slowing down the speed was effective only to a certain extent. As you moved past this 2-mile limit, quality problems showed up in droves until finally the DSL service became unusable and unavailable. To address these limitations, some companies started offering DSL repeaters, extending the reach past that limit. Familiarize yourself with Table 1-3, which shows the more notable xDSL highlights.

Table 1-3   xDSL Service Provider Offerings

xDSL	Full Name	Description
Asymmetric		
ADSL	Asymmetric DSL	8 Mbps download, 756 Kpbs upload
ADSL2	Asymmetric DSL2	ADSL speed increase to 12 Mbps download, up to 3.5 Mbps upload
ADSL2+	Asymmetric DSL2+	ADSL2 2X speed increase due to higher frequencies
Symmetric		
HDSL	High bitrate DSL	Constant symmetric 1.5–2 Mbps, divided digital trunk into two or three wire pairs
HDSL2	High bitrate DSL2	Distance reach enhancement over HDSL
SDSL	Symmetrical DSL	Deployed over a single pair of copper wire, featured variable rates from 192 Kbps to 2.3 Mbps
SHDSL	Symmetrical Highspeed DSL	2X speed OR distance with the second wire pair
Symmetric and Asymmetric		
VDSL	Very high bitrate DSL	A single flat untwisted or twisted pair of copper wires, up to 52 Mbps downstream and 16 Mpbs upstream
VDSL2	Very high bitrate DSL 2	Version 2; exceeds 100 Mbps simultaneously for upstream and downstream

TDM

Time-division multiplexing (TDM) is a method of transmitting multiple signals or data streams over a common communication channel by dividing the channel into time slots. Each input signal or data stream is allocated a specific time slot, and the signals take turns using the channel during their designated time periods. Just as passengers board a bus one at a time, TDM allows various signals to share the same channel by taking turns during their designated time intervals. This enables multiple signals to share the same communication medium without interfering with each other: all passengers can get on or get off the bus if they wait for their turn because they cannot all do it at once.

TDM is widely used in telecommunications for various applications, including voice and data transmission. It allows efficient utilization of bandwidth by time-slicing the available resources and guarantees that each participant gets dedicated time intervals for communication. TDM is employed in technologies like T1 and E1 lines for digital voice and data communication, as well as in older telephony systems. It has proven to be a versatile and effective method for optimizing the use of communication channels in various applications.

Synchronous Optical Networking (SONET) and Synchronous Digital Hierarchy (SDH) are two related but different standards that use TDM to send multiple data streams simultaneously on fiber-optic networks. They both have been around longer than I have been in my networking career. When I started my first networking job in 2000, the industry was discussing ways to get off these technologies, and here we are twenty-five years later discussing the same in my current job role. At times, it feels like a never-ending Netflix series—just when you think it's over, a new season begins.

Originally, SONET and SDH were created to transport 64 KB pulse-code modulation (PCM) voice channels, a common standard in telecommunications. There are notable differences and similarities between SONET and SDH, summarized in Table 1-4.

Table 1-4 SONET and SDH Differences

Differences	SONET	SDH
Regional	Primarily used in North America; sets the standard for optical telecommunications	Commonly used in international contexts; the dominant standard in Europe and many other parts of the world
Terminology	Uses Optical Carrier (OC) levels to specify data rates (e.g., OC-3, OC-12)	Uses Synchronous Transport Module (STM) levels (e.g., STM-1, STM-4) to specify data rates
Frame Structures	Uses synchronous frames; the basic unit is the Synchronous Transport Signal 1 (STS-1) frame	Uses synchronous frames as well; the basic unit is the Synchronous Transport Module (STM-1) frame
Frame Overhead	Uses Transport Overhead, Section Overhead, Line Overhead, and Path Overhead.	Uses Administrative Unit (AU) Overhead, Multiplex Section Overhead (MSOH), and Path Overhead (POH)
Error Detection	Uses Bit Interleaved Parity 8 (BIP-8)	Has its own version of BIP-8
Network Synchronization	Uses a synchronization network called the Synchronous Status Message (SSM)	

Despite these differences, SONET and SDH are functionally similar and serve the same purpose of providing a standardized framework for synchronous optical communication. Keep Table 1-5 handy for conversion purposes.

Table 1-5   SONET and SDH Conversion Chart

SONET				SDH			
Bit Rate	Signal	Channels		Signal	Channels		Speed
Mbps		DS1	DS3		E1	E4	Gbps
51.84	STS-1	28	1	STM-0	21	0	
155.52	STS-3	84	3	STM-1	63	1	
622.08	STS-12	336	12	STM-4	252	4	
2488.32	STS-48	1344	48	STM-16	1008	16	2.5
9953.28	STS-192	5376	192	STM-64	4032	64	10
39813.1	STS-786	21504	786	STM-256	16128	256	40

NOTE   A DS1 (T1) line has a transmission rate of 1.544 Mbps and consists of 24 channels, each capable of carrying 64 Kbps of data. A DS1 line can be considered as a single unit that can be divided, or "fractaled," into smaller channels or circuits, each capable of carrying individual voice or data streams.

A DS3 (T3) line has a transmission rate of 44.736 Mbps and consists of 28 DS1 channels multiplexed together. A DS3 line can be considered as a higher-level unit that contains multiple DS1 channels. Each DS1 channel within the DS3 line retains its capacity of 1.544 Mbps.

In the recent past, Time-Division Multiplexing over Internet Protocol (TDMoIP) and Private Line Emulation (PLE) are the two technologies that have emerged as modern alternatives to the older SONET/SDH technology. TDMoIP enables the transport of TDM voice or data streams over IP networks. It allows the emulation of TDM circuit-switched connections over packet-switched networks like the Internet.

PLE also enables the transmission of private line services over a unified IP network, extending its applicability beyond Ethernet-type services to encompass technologies like SONET/SDH and Fibre Channel. Through PLE, consistent service-level agreements and characteristics, such as assured bandwidth and enduring bidirectional paths, are retained. This is achieved through advancements in Circuit-Style Segment Routing (CS-SR). PLE incorporates extensions for Ethernet virtual private network (EVPN) for configuration and control, along with circuit emulation to ensure bit transparency. Both TDMoIP and PLE are effective substitutes addressing the aging SONET/SDH product lines and the noticeable absence of SONET/SDH standards evolution.

Dense Wavelength-Division Multiplexing (DWDM)

Wavelength-division multiplexing (WDM) adopts a distinct strategy for maximizing the capacity of the physical medium (fiber) by using multiple wavelengths. In WDM, incoming optical signals are assigned to specific light frequencies, known as *wavelengths* or *lambdas* or *channels*, within a designated frequency band. Do you remember the passengers getting on or off a bus? WDM operates akin to radio stations broadcasting on varied wavelengths simultaneously, ensuring no interference occurs between them. Because each channel transmits at a distinct frequency, a tuner selects from these channels. An even better analogy for WDM is to envision each channel as a different color of light and, when combined, they form a rainbow.

Over the years, there have been several implementations of WDM; among more notable ones are coarse wavelength-division multiplexing (CWDM), which used wider channel spacing, and **dense wavelength-division multiplexing (DWDM)**, which used tighter spacing, hence allowing for more channels (wavelengths or lambdas). DWDM refers to optical signals that are multiplexed within the 1550-nm band. In Figure 1-12, three discreet wavelengths are multiplexed (through the use of a filter, or a mux/demux, which is a passive mechanical device) into a single composite signal. The image here is in gray and white, but the original picture is in color and the individual colors of blue, green, and red coming into the filter are multiplexed into a rainbow-like single composite signal. The 1550 nm composite signal is then amplified by an Erbium-doped fiber amplifier (EDFA) or Raman amplifier. An EDFA amplifier works through interaction with the doping Erbium (look up symbol Er and atomic number 68 in the Periodic Table of Elements) ions, which are excited to provide higher power to the weak signal to propel it over longer distances. Raman amplifiers are named after a talented Indian physicist who won the Nobel Prize in physics in 1930 for his discovery of a light-scattering phenomenon.

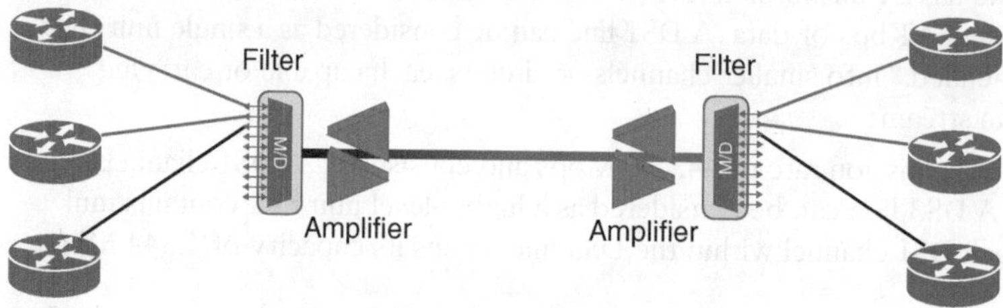

Figure 1-12 *Wavelength Division Multiplexing*

The composite signal then travels to the other side of this point-to-point link, where it is demultiplexed and groomed onto discreetly colored wavelengths. The ITU draft standard G.694.1 "Spectral grids for WDM applications: DWDM frequency grid" defines a laser grid for point-to-point WDM systems. Figure 1-13 shows Cisco's implementation of ONS 15216 exposed faceplate Mux/Demux 40-Channel Patch Panels, which support 100 GHz spacing with the ODD filter and 50 GHz spacing with the EVEN filter. Notice that the center wavelength is located at 1552.52 nm.

Additionally, back in Figure 1-12, look at the "rainbow" section between the multiplexing and demultiplexing points (between the filters) where multiple wavelengths coexist in a form of a composite signal. If you ever need to selectively add or remove specific wavelengths from the composite signal, you can accomplish this with an optical add/drop multiplexer (OADM). Unlike the complete combination or separation of all wavelengths, an OADM can selectively (but *manually*) remove certain wavelengths while allowing others to pass through. A **reconfigurable optical add-drop multiplexer (ROADM)** is an improvement to OADM. This device is used in optical fiber networks to manage and *dynamically* control the flow of data carried by different wavelengths of light, and you are likely to see references to it on the exam. The primary function of a ROADM is to add (insert), drop (remove), or pass through specific wavelengths of light in an optical signal without affecting the others. This enables flexible and efficient wavelength routing and allows for dynamic reconfiguration of the network—something that OADM devices could not do, because manual onsite intervention was required. Wavelengths that are neither added nor dropped at a site are referred to as *express* because they pass through a site without stopping, much like express trains that skip certain stops. Figure 1-14 shows a Cisco 20-port single module ROADM card for the NCS 2000 platform.

15216-MD-40-ODD			15216-MD-40-EVEN		
Channel ID	Frequency (THz)	Wavelength (nm)	Channel ID	Frequency (THz)	Wavelength (nm)
1	195.9	1530.33	1	195.85	1530.72
2	195.8	1531.12	2	195.75	1531.51
3	195.7	1531.90	3	195.65	1532.29
4	195.6	1532.68	4	195.55	1533.07
5	195.5	1533.47	5	195.45	1533.86
6	195.4	1534.25	6	195.35	1534.64
7	195.3	1535.04	7	195.25	1535.43
8	195.2	1535.82	8	195.15	1536.22
9	195.1	1536.61	9	195.05	1537.00
10	195.0	1537.40	10	194.95	1537.79
11	194.9	1538.19	11	194.85	1538.58
12	194.8	1538.98	12	194.75	1539.37
13	194.7	1539.77	13	194.65	1540.16
14	194.6	1540.56	14	194.55	1540.95
15	194.5	1541.35	15	194.45	1541.75
16	194.4	1542.14	16	194.35	1542.54
17	194.3	1542.94	17	194.25	1543.33
18	194.2	1543.73	18	194.15	1544.13
19	194.1	1544.53	19	194.05	1544.92
20	194.0	1545.32	20	193.95	1545.72
21	193.9	1546.12	21	193.85	1546.52
22	193.8	1546.92	22	193.75	1547.32
23	193.7	1547.72	23	193.65	1548.11
24	193.6	1548.51	24	193.55	1548.91
25	193.5	1549.32	25	193.45	1549.72
26	193.4	1550.12	26	193.35	1550.52
27	193.3	1550.92	27	193.25	1551.32
28	193.2	1551.72	28	193.15	1552.12
29	193.1	1552.52	29	193.05	1552.93
30	193.0	1553.33	30	192.95	1553.73
31	192.9	1554.13	31	192.85	1554.54
32	192.8	1554.94	32	192.75	1555.34
33	192.7	1555.75	33	192.65	1556.15
34	192.6	1556.55	34	192.55	1556.96
35	192.5	1557.36	35	192.45	1557.77
36	192.4	1558.17	36	192.35	1558.58
37	192.3	1558.98	37	192.25	1559.39
38	192.2	1559.79	38	192.15	1560.20
39	192.1	1560.61	39	192.05	1561.01
40	192.0	1561.42	40	191.95	1561.83

Figure 1-13   *Cisco ONS 15216 Exposed Faceplate Mux/Demux 40-Channel Patch Panel Channel Plan*

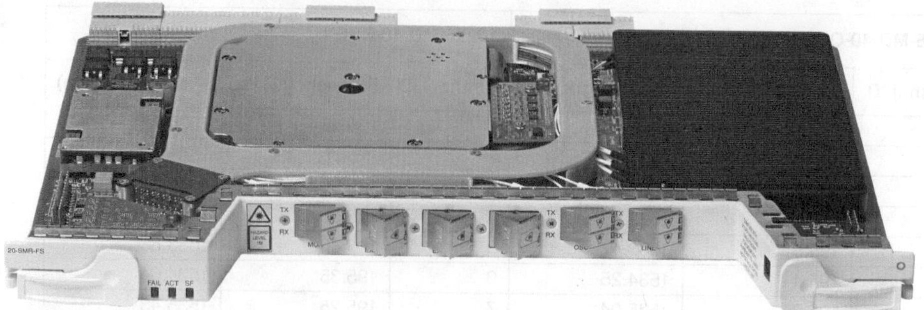

Figure 1-14   *Cisco 20-Port Single Module ROADM*

xPON

xPON (Passive Optical Network) technology is a type of fiber-optic network architecture that is commonly used for delivering broadband services, including high-speed Internet access, voice, and video. The *x* in xPON refers to various PON standards, with the most notable ones being Ethernet Passive Optical Network (EPON), Gigabit Passive Optical Network (GPON), and 10G Symmetrical PON (XGS-PON). These standards determine the specific protocols and technologies used within the XPON network. Refer to Table 1-6 for different xPON standards.

Table 1-6   Passive Optical Network Standards

	GE-PON	GPON	10G-EPON	XGS-PON	NG-PON2	100G-EPON
Standard	IEEE 802.3ah (2004)	ITU-T G.984 (2003)	IEEE 802.3av (2009)	ITU-T G.9807.1 (2016)	ITU-T G.989 (2015)	IEEE 802.3ca (2019 TBD)
Downstream Rate	1.25 Gbps	2.4 Gbps	10 Gbps	10 Gbps	40 Gbps	100 Gbps
Upstream Rate	1.25 Gbps	1.2 Gbps	10 Gbps	10 Gbps	10 Gbps	100 Gbps
Splitting Ratio	Up to 1:64	Up to 1:64 (128)	Up to 1:128	Up to 1:128 (256)	Up to 1:128 (256)	TBD
Coexistence	No	No	GE-PON	GPON	GPON	GE-PON

- **Ethernet Passive Optical Network (EPON)** is a type of passive optical network technology that uses the IEEE 802.3 Ethernet standard to provide efficient and cost-effective solutions for delivering Internet access and other broadband services and supports speed up to 1 Gbps.

- **Gigabit Passive Optical Network (GPON)** is a type of passive asymmetric optical network technology that uses the ITU-T G.984 standard and is widely deployed for Fiber-to-the-Home (FTTH) and Fiber-to-the-Premises (FTTP) deployments and supports speeds of up to 2.5 Gpbs downstream and 1.25 Gbps upstream.

- **10 Gigabit Symmetric Passive Optical Network (XGS-PON)** is an advanced passive optical network technology that is standardized by the ITU-T G.9807 series and supports symmetrical data rates of up to 10 Gbps in both the downstream and upstream directions.

Recommendation ITU-T G.984.1 illustrates different components of an xPON network in Figure 1-15.

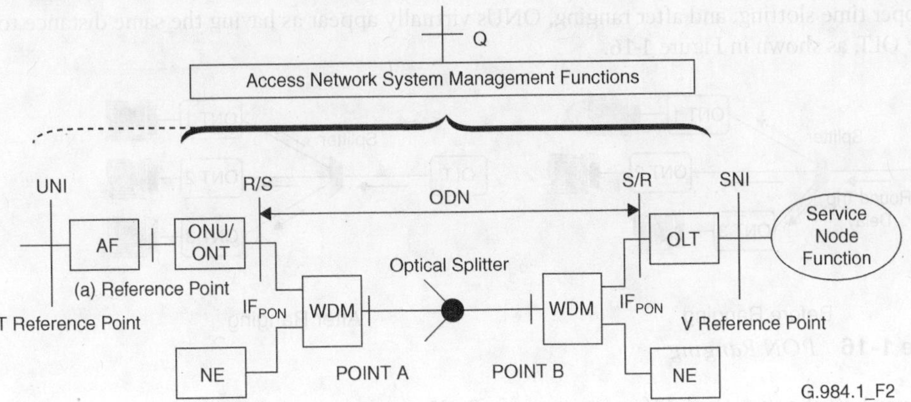

Figure 1-15 *GPON Reference Diagram*

Be familiar with the following terms starting from the left side of Figure 1-15:

- **UNI:** User Network Interface (a reference point between CPE and ONT).

- **ONU/ONT:** Optical Network Unit and Optical Network Terminal. These terms refer to the consumer-side equipment in an optical Fiber-to-the-Home (FTTH) communication link. ONU and ONT are the same thing; the only difference is that ONT is an ITU-T term, whereas ONU is an IEEE term.

- **NE:** A network element using a different wavelength that ONT/OLT uses.

- **WDM:** Wavelength-division multiplexing, which transmits data of different upstream/downstream wavelengths over the same ODN.

- **ODN:** Optical Distribution Network (the entire xPON fiber infrastructure).

- **Optical Splitter:** A passive mechanical device that splits a physical fiber into a point-to-multipoint physical topology. A clever way to think of it is to visualize a colander that creates multiple water streams when water is poured into it.

- **OLT:** Optical Line Termination, a service provider–side device or shelf aggregating connections from hundreds to thousands of ONTs.

Just like other technologies, xPON variants have their own limits. Maximum fiber distance between send/receive (S/R) and receive/send (R/S) points is 20 km. The split ratio is restricted by the number of splits (16, 32, or 64) supported by the specific standard or implementation. Just like in other optical networks, loss of optical power must be accounted for. This loss of power can be introduced in a variety of ways—loss within splitters, path loss per kilometer of fiber (0.25 dB or 0.35 dB per km depending on what fiber is being used), loss in splices (> 0.2 dB), connector loss (0.6 dB), and fiber bends.

Another important concept is *ranging*. To avoid data conflicts (collisions), the OLT needs accurate distance measurements to each ONU. This enables the allocation of precise time slots for upstream data transmission by the ONUs. This timing coordination, essential for preventing upstream issues, is accomplished using a method known as *ranging*. During the first registration, OLT obtains the roundtrip delay value from each ONU; they are located at varying distances (think of a neighborhood where homes toward the back are further away from the central office than the homes at the front). The distances are normalized through proper time slotting, and after ranging, ONUs virtually appear as having the same distance to the OLT, as shown in Figure 1-16.

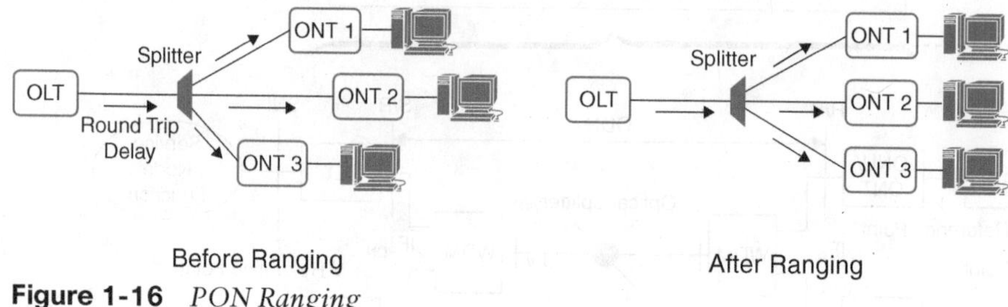

Figure 1-16 *PON Ranging*

Figure 1-17 shows several different types of xPON network protection modes.

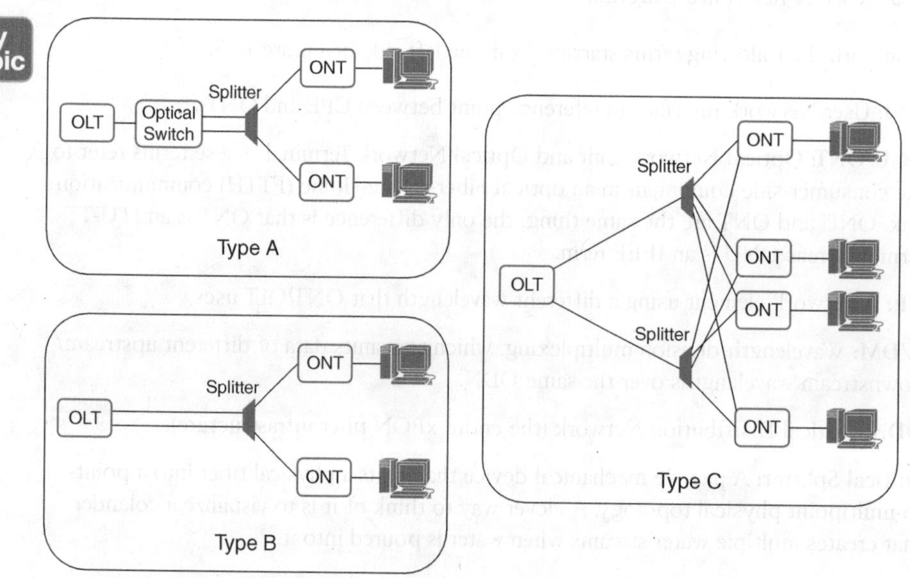

Figure 1-17 *Network Protection Modes*

In Figure 1-17, Type A uses a single OLT port, and when the primary fiber to the splitter fails, services are transferred to the secondary fiber. The outage lasts as long as it is necessary to recover the line. Should the failure occur on the line between the splitter and ONT, there is no backup.

Type B offers redundancy to OLT ports, and protection is restricted to the line between the OLT and splitter. There is no redundancy between splitter and ONT.

Type C offers full redundancy for the OLT, ODN, and ONTs. In 1+1 protection mode, normal traffic is copied and sent on both paths to the ONT simultaneously, with the backup path discarded at the ONT. The 1:1 protection mode uses only a single path but provides automatic protection in case of failure. For obvious reasons, Type C provides maximum availability but is far more costly.

Note that in PON networks data is *broadcast in the downstream* direction (network Ð home) on wavelengths ranging from 1480 nm to 1603 nm in a *downstream continuous mode of operation*, meaning that there is always a signal even when there is no user data (unless the operator has turned off the laser).

Data is transmitted in the *TDMA mode (based on timeslots) in the upstream direction* (home Ð network) on wavelengths ranging from 1270 nm to 1390 nm for GPON and from 1532 nm to 1539 nm for NGPON2. ONTs send a signal only when needed and only during their exclusive timeslots, which are allocated by the OLT based on the distance from the OLT (this way, the ONT that is physically closest to the OLT does not have to wait the same time as the ONT that is at the end of the neighborhood), maximizing the available timeslots for all available ONTs.

The most recent addition to Cisco's product portfolio is Cisco 10G Routed XGS-PON OLT. It simplifies the network with pluggable form factor optical line terminals (OLTs), seen in Figure 1-18.

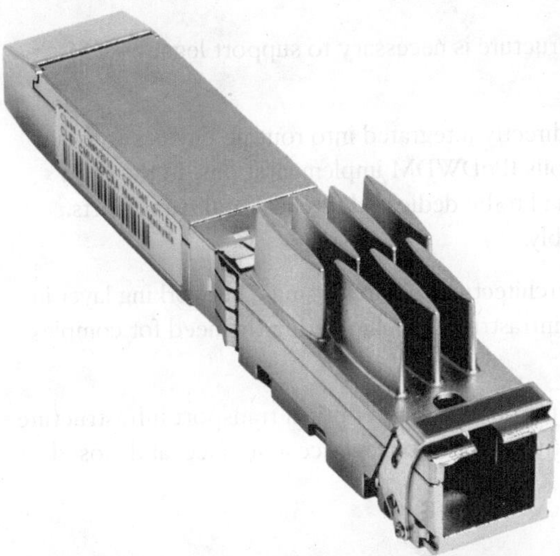

Figure 1-18   *XGS-PON OLT Pluggable*

The Cisco Routed PON Solution replaces dedicated PON chassis with a multiservice router, increasing flexibility and reducing network footprint and power consumption. This solution is available on Cisco NCS 540, NCS 5500, and NCS 5700, and with the help of a software controller converges Ethernet and PON services.

Routed Optical Networking

Cisco *Routed Optical Networking* refers to a network architecture that integrates IP and optical transport technologies to create a scalable and efficient communication infrastructure. In this architecture, introduced in 2020, IP routers are interconnected using dense wavelength-division multiplexing (DWDM) optical links, enabling high-capacity and low-latency data transmission over long distances. I was lucky enough to be a part of the team that championed this cause internally within Cisco and externally with Cisco's customers. Routed Optical Networking (or RON for short) was at first met with skepticism by the traditional DWDM providers but soon gained massive adoption due to tangible technological and financial advantages. Each vendor has its own name for this architecture.

Briefly, RON combines (where economically possible and technically beneficial) IP packet and optical DWDM technologies in a single device with the use of intelligent pluggables (pluggable transceivers).

Traditional network architectures consist of multiple layers, each with its own set of equipment and management systems. This setup is inefficient and costly because it requires a lot of equipment and manual effort to connect services between the layers. Additionally, managing each layer separately creates complications for ensuring services work smoothly, fixing problems, and planning for future needs. As a result, the overall cost of maintaining this kind of network is high, making it difficult for service providers to expand their networks affordably to meet growing demands for Internet services.

This new approach, shown in Figure 1-19, transitions networks from the siloed infrastructure to a new architecture that relies on a single IP/MPLS control plane in a converged router-to-router IP and optical network. This drives significant simplification and cost savings. It addresses the complexities and redundant networking layers that present bottlenecks to scalability. The key aspects of RON include the following:

- Integration of OTN switching infrastructure is necessary to support legacy TDM services.

- High-capacity optical interfaces are directly integrated into routing devices without compromising IP fabric seen in previous IPoDWDM implementations. In the older IPoDWDM approach, certain ports had to be dedicated to client and trunk ports. RON ports can be used interchangeably.

- The core router-to-router IP routing architecture features a single networking layer in the IP domain and simplified optical infrastructure, eliminating the need for complex ROADM technologies.

- A unified transport SDN is implemented across IP and optical transport infrastructure for streamlined capacity planning, path optimization, service assurance, and closed-loop automation.

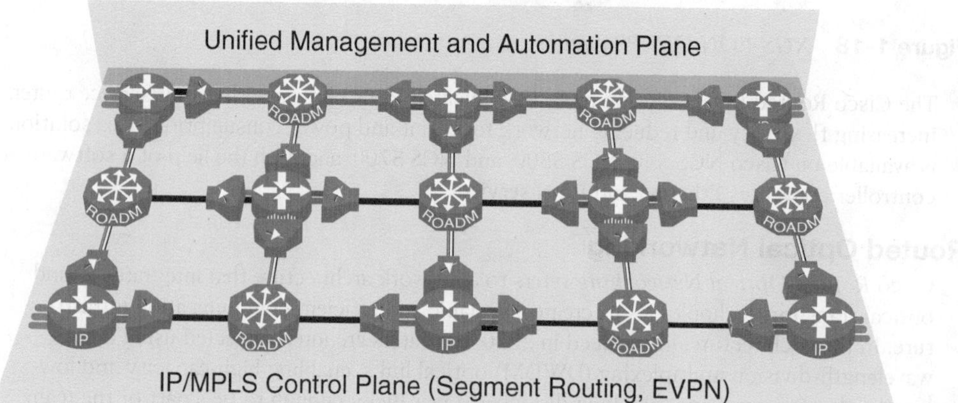

Figure 1-19 *Routed Optical Network Architecture*

Figure 1-20 shows an example of RON consolidating DWDM and packet technologies. The line card is a 400G-capable 2-RU (two rack units) muxponder that requires 330W of power and must be housed in a 6-RU NCS 2006 chassis. Shown below is a 400G ZR+ optic capable of the same bandwidth that fits into the palm of your hand and consumes only 23W. You can put 32 of these into a 1RU router today. That is a massive improvement in bandwidth and significant reduction in power consumption.

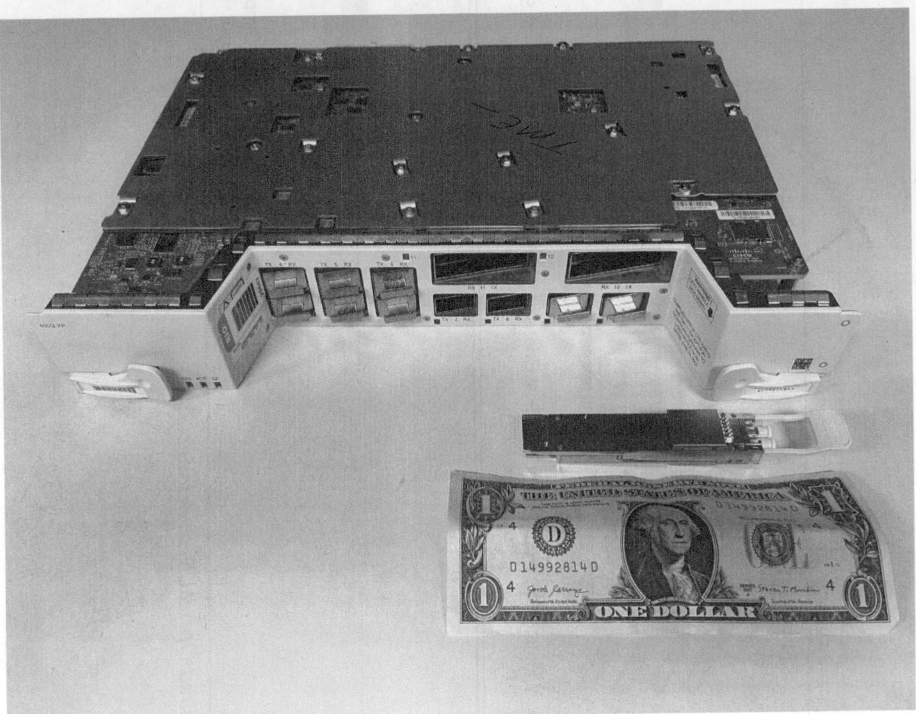

Figure 1-20 *Intelligent DWDM Pluggables Used in Routers*

Figure 1-21 shows further components that RON can consolidate—gray pluggables (1310 nm and 850 nm), jumpers, muxponders, and optical chassis. Again, customers can take advantage of this consolidation where operationally possible and economically advantageous. Support, operations, power consumption, and complexity are optimized.

Modern router chipsets can match the bandwidth traditionally available only in the optical products. Technical advantages of Routed Optical Networking come from IP, which is a far simpler alternative to Layer 2 Ethernet rings that have underpinned optical networks for decades. Constructs such as Segment Routing, EVPN, and L3VPNs can protect, restore, reroute, traffic engineer, and provide discrete segmentation better, faster, and cheaper. Packet networks are no longer "slow" thanks to hardware-based packet forwarding. Transfer delay of a packet node is <10 μs per hop (equal to roughly 2 km of fiber), so the latency nowadays comes from path propagation delay, not from the packet elements.

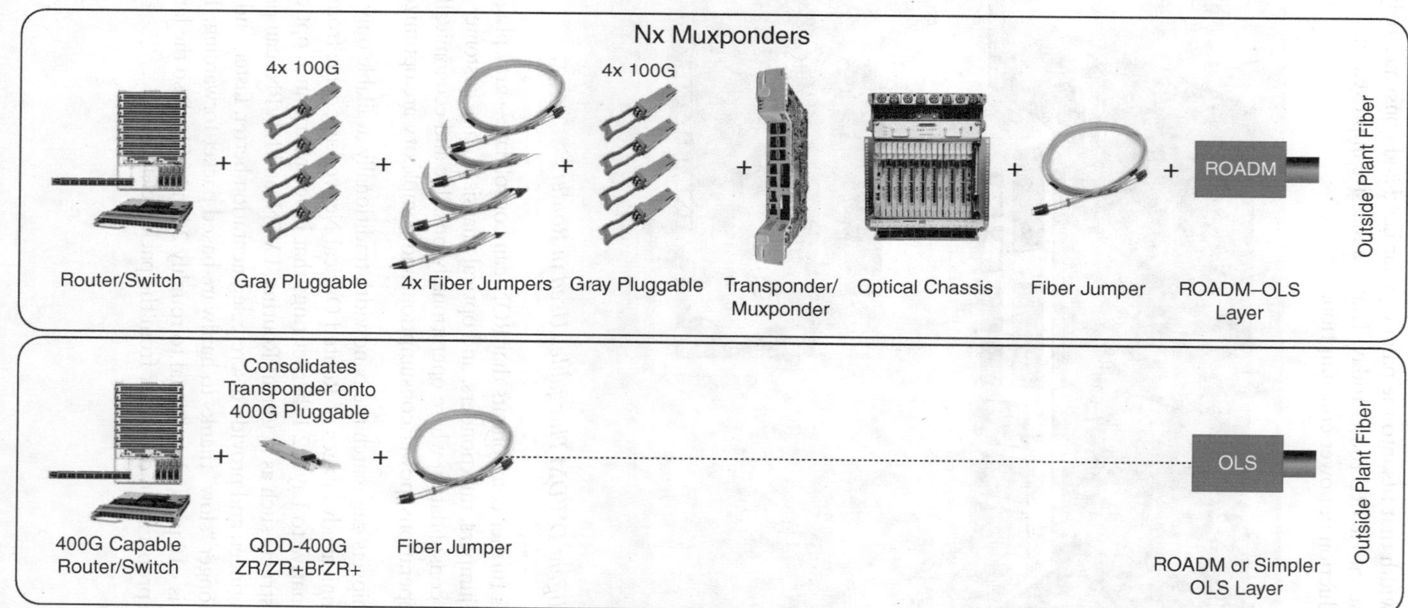

Figure 1-21   *Infrastructure Simplification with Routed Optical Networking*

The automation and orchestration components are also strengths of Routed Optical Networking. Figure 1-22 shows a visualization approach provided by Cisco's Hierarchical Controller (HCO), which stitches together a single pane view for fiber infrastructure, optical, IP, and service elements.

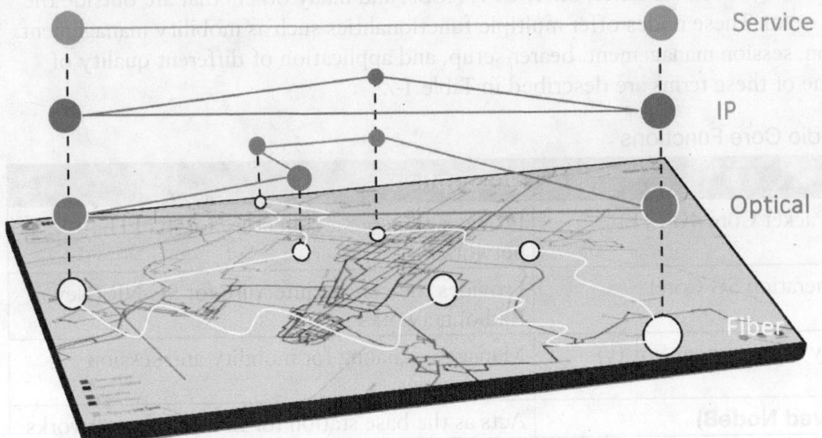

Figure 1-22 *Managing Routed Optical Automation Network Stack*

Will RON architecture completely replace optical networking? I do not believe so. Optical networks are here to stay; it is just that some DWDM elements will naturally find their home in high-capacity routers equipped with intelligent pluggables. So will the optical engineers whose skillset is not disappearing but is relocating when it makes sense to companies and operators.

Mobility (Packet Core, RAN xhaul Transport for 5G vRAN and ORAN Transport)

Mobility radio technology refers to the set of technologies that enable wireless communication and seamless movement of devices or users within a network. This technology is crucial for mobile communication systems, such as cellular networks and wireless LANs, where devices need to maintain connectivity while in motion. Fourth Generation (4G) and Fifth Generation (5G) radio networks represent successive leaps in mobile communication technology, each introducing transformative capabilities to meet the evolving demands of our connected world. Primarily based on Long-Term Evolution (LTE), 4G delivered faster data speeds, lower latency, and enhanced spectral efficiency compared to its predecessor, 3G. It facilitated seamless multimedia experiences, paving the way for high-quality video streaming and online gaming. In contrast, 5G stands as a quantum leap forward, promising unprecedented data speeds reaching up to 20 Gbps, almost negligible latency, and the ability to support a massive number of devices through concepts like network slicing. The introduction of 5G New Radio (NR) and utilization of a broader spectrum, including mmWave bands, enable revolutionary applications such as augmented reality, virtual reality, and diverse IoT scenarios. With 5G, we witness not just an evolution in speed but a fundamental shift in the capabilities and possibilities of wireless communication, opening doors to innovation across industries and transforming the way we connect and communicate.

Packet Core

While the exam focuses on 5G networks, its components are better understood with a perspective of the past. In radio cellular networks, the core is formed by multiple nodes. In EPC 4G LTE, the main ones are MME, SGW, PGW, and HSS. In 5GC, new elements have been added, among which are AMF, SMF, UPF, AUSF, and many others that are outside the scope of the exam. These nodes offer multiple functionalities such as mobility management, authentication, session management, bearer setup, and application of different quality of services. Some of these terms are described in Table 1-7.

Table 1-7   Radio Core Functions

Function	Description
EPC (Evolved Packet Core 4G LTE)	Provides the core architecture for 4G LTE networks
5GC (Next Generation 5G Core)	Provides the core architecture for 5G NR (New Radio) networks
MME (Mobility Management Entity)	Manages signaling for mobility and session management
eNodeB (Evolved NodeB)	Acts as the base station for LTE cellular networks
SGW (Service Gateway)	Manages user plane functionality (data traffic) between the mobile device and the eNodeB
PGW (Packet Data Network Gateway)	Connects the LTE network to external packet data networks, such as the Internet
HSS (Home Subscriber Server)	Provides a database to manage subscribers in real time
AMF (Access and Mobility Management Function)	Manages access and mobility for devices
SMF (Session Management Function)	Manages session-related functions, such as establishment, modification, and termination
UPF (User Plane Function)	Manages the user plane and data forwarding
AUSF (Authentication Server Function)	Is responsible for authentication and key management

Table 1-8 shows some of the notable differences between the 4G LTE and 5G NR architectures.

Table 1-8   Key Differences Between 4G and 5G Architectures

Feature	4G LTE	5G NR
Network Core	**Evolved Packet Core (EPC)**	5GC Core
Services-Based Architecture (SBA)	No	Network functions access services from other functions
Base Station	Evolved NodeB (eNodeB)	**Next-Generation NodeB (gNodeB)**
Bandwidth	< 1 Gb	< 20 Gb
Latency	~30–50 ms	~1 ms

Feature	4G LTE	5G NR
Slicing	Not native	Native (multiple networks with varied characteristics)
State	Stateful (rigid)	Stateless (improves reliability and fault tolerance)
Control and User Plane Separation	Present	Further decoupled for flexible deployments and scale
Common interface	Proprietary CPRI (Common Public Radio Interface)	Open standards-based O-RAN (Open Radio Access Network)

xHaul

In the context of cellular networks like 4G LTE and 5G, the terms *fronthaul*, *midhaul*, and *backhaul* refer to different segments of the network architecture responsible for carrying data between various network elements. These segments play crucial roles in ensuring efficient communication and data transfer within the network. Figure 1-23 helps to visualize xHaul segments and how they relate to both 4G LTE and 5G NR architectures.

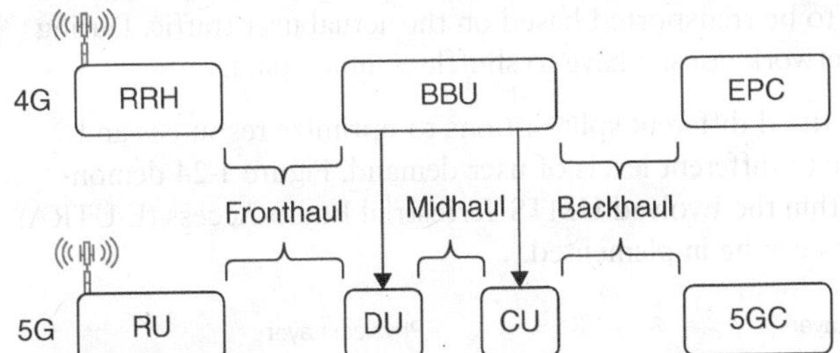

Figure 1-23 *xHaul Segments*

In 4G LTE networks, the baseband unit (BBU) is a fundamental element of the base station. It handles radio communications and control processing, turning data into a digital signal. This signal is then sent to the remote radio head (RRH), which converts it into an analog signal for wireless transmission.

In Distributed Radio Access Networks (D-RANs), BBUs are placed alongside RRH radio frequency components at the base of macro cell towers. In Cloud Radio Access Network (C-RAN) setups, RRH remains at the cell tower, while BBU is moved to a distant geographical location for central management.

In 5G RANs, things have evolved. The traditional BBU and RRH have transformed into the distributed unit (DU), centralized unit (CU), and radio unit (RU). These components work together, and Figure 1-23 shows how they connect.

- **Fronthaul** links remote radio heads (RRHs) with BBUs, sometimes spanning considerable distances (in kilometers). Fronthaul does the job of sending processed data between the BBU (which manages baseband tasks) and the RRH (which holds the radio components for wireless signals). This segment requires low latency and high bandwidth to ensure that the radio signals are processed and transmitted/received without significant delay. Common fronthaul interfaces include **Common Public Radio Interface (CPRI)** and **enhanced Common Public Radio Interface (eCPRI)**.

- **Midhaul** denotes the connection between the DU and CU. It aggregates and transports data from multiple cell sites or base stations to the core network. It serves as an intermediate link between the fronthaul and backhaul segments and needs sufficient capacity to handle the aggregated traffic from multiple fronthaul connections. It may use high-capacity optical fiber links and technologies like Ethernet for efficient data transport.

- **Backhaul** signifies the link between the CU and the core network. Backhaul requires high capacity to handle the aggregated traffic from multiple midhaul connections and transports aggregated data to the core network.

Functional Splits Options

In traditional fronthaul, CPRI constantly transmits data regardless of whether users are actively using the network. Data flows continuously, even during idle times. The architecture of 5G seeks to adjust resources smartly to make the network more flexible to changing user needs. It aims to deliver a service-oriented, adaptable, and highly efficient architecture that pushes the boundaries of performance. To accomplish this, functions have to be disaggregated to scale the amount of data to be transported based on the actual user traffic. During periods of low user activity, the network doesn't have to shuffle as much data.

Several standards bodies have identified different split options to optimize resources and make the network more responsive to different levels of user demand. Figure 1-24 demonstrates every potential location within the Evolved UMTS Terrestrial Radio Access (E-UTRA) protocol stack where enhancements can be implemented.

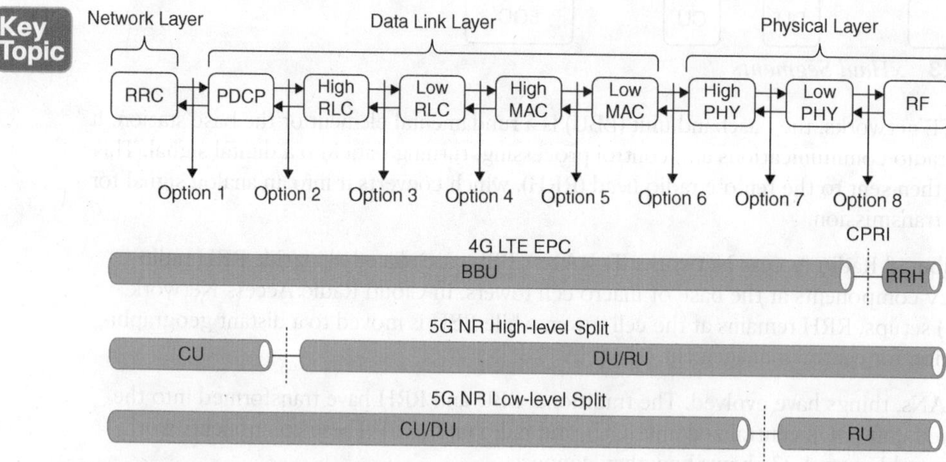

Figure 1-24 *Functional Split Options*

As data travels between the Radio Resource Control (RRC) control plane of the IP network layer and the radio frequency (RF; i.e., the actual radio signals), specific points in the protocol stack mark transitions where improvements can be explored. Each of these split points involves its own set of trade-offs, and detailed explanations of these terms and definitions are complex and outside of the scope of this book and exam. We encourage you to explore these on your own.

Notice how in traditional 4G LTE, the CPRI protocol provided the fronthaul connection between the RF and the remaining L1/L2/L3 functions at the Option 8 split point. This particular split point option enabled the centralization of all high-layer processing functions but came at the cost of imposing the most demanding fronthaul latency and bandwidth requirements.

Among several possible Radio Access Network (RAN) split points, two specific splits provide better locations to optimize network performance, efficiency, and resource utilization. High-level and low-level splits refer to the distribution of functions between different network elements.

- **High-level split (Centralized Architecture)** is a high-layer split (because it occurs higher in the protocol stack). It is known as Option 2 (PDCP-High RLC split point, Packet Data Convergence Protocol–High Radio Link Control). Recall that it is accomplished by splitting the BBU functions in Figure 1-23 into CU/DU components where more functions are centralized in a centralized unit (CU). Since CU can compute complex processing tasks, such as baseband processing and coordination, this allows for efficient resource utilization and easier management of network functions. It can lead to better optimization and coordination across the network.

- **Low-Level Split (Distributed Architecture)** is a low-layer split (since it occurs lower in the protocol stack). It is also known as an Option 7 split and focuses on the intra-PHY connections (High PHY and Low PHY in Figure 1-24). In this low-level split architecture, functions are distributed across different units, with some processing taking place closer to the cell site. This includes distributing baseband processing functions to distributed units (DUs) located closer to the radio heads. Such distribution reduces latency by processing certain functions closer to the edge of the network. It allows for more flexibility in deploying network elements and adapting to specific use cases.

High-level splits can deliver improved throughput and reduced latency because centralizing certain functions can optimize their processing. Low-level splits can reduce latency by distributing processing functions closer to the edge. Nevertheless, the trade-offs remain. While offering centralized optimization, high-level splits may face challenges in accommodating diverse use cases with varying latency requirements.

Conversely, while reducing latency, low-level splits may require more careful coordination and management of distributed network elements.

In summary, high-level and low-level splits in RAN networks aim to strike a balance between centralized and distributed processing to achieve optimal network performance, considering factors such as throughput, latency, and resource utilization. The choice between these splits depends on the specific requirements and goals of the network deployment. If you are less than clear about this topic, keep rereading this section until it makes sense. It is carefully worded to provide good and succinct explanation of this complex topic.

O-RAN

Open Radio Access Network (O-RAN) is a groundbreaking initiative in the telecommunications industry that champions openness and collaboration. Traditionally, mobile networks have been built on closed, proprietary systems, but this approach challenges this status quo by advocating for open standards and interfaces. By embracing O-RAN, operators can break free from vendor lock-in and customize their networks with components from different suppliers. This not only fosters innovation but also drives down costs and accelerates the deployment of new technologies. It represents a paradigm shift toward a more dynamic and inclusive approach to network architecture, promising a future where mobile connectivity is more accessible, efficient, and resilient.

O-RAN represents the collaborative efforts of the O-RAN Alliance, a consortium comprising approximately 200 entities, including mobile operators, vendors, and research institutions. This group is dedicated to crafting cutting-edge specifications for future RAN infrastructures, driven by the principles of intelligence and openness. With a global reach, the O-RAN Alliance endeavors to revolutionize the RAN industry by advocating for more intelligent, virtualized network components, embracing white-box hardware, and championing standardized and open interfaces. The term *O-RAN* can refer to the interfaces and architectural components delineated by the O-RAN Alliance's specifications.

Cisco plays a pivotal role in the O-RAN ecosystem as a leading provider of networking solutions and expertise. As O-RAN gains momentum, Cisco is actively engaged in developing open and interoperable technologies that align with O-RAN principles. This includes contributing to industry forums, standards bodies, and open-source initiatives focused on defining O-RAN specifications and interfaces. Additionally, Cisco leverages its extensive portfolio of networking products and services to support operators in deploying O-RAN–compliant solutions. By collaborating with industry partners and customers, Cisco aims to drive innovation and accelerate the adoption of O-RAN, empowering operators to build more flexible, scalable, and efficient mobile networks.

To this end, an O-RAN solution may have multiple vendors. The radio unit (RU) software comes from the same company that manufactures the antennae, while the distribution unit (DU) and centralized unit (CU) could originate from another company.

O-RAN operates on the premise of interoperable lower-layer splits, posing a multifaceted challenge of determining the optimal split location. This decision hinges on balancing factors like RU simplification, support for advanced multipoint radio frequency capabilities, and fronthaul transport requirements.

As discussed earlier, assigning numerical values to splits aids in comparing the plethora of available options. Higher numbers denote splits residing deeper within the protocol stack, featuring reduced functionality beneath the RU split.

Lower-layer splits primarily reside beneath the Medium Access Control (MAC) layer in the protocol stack. Placement options include between the MAC and Physical (PHY) layers (Split 6), within the PHY layer (Split 7), and between the PHY layer and RF functionality (Split 8).

Cisco has been at the forefront of integrating open networking principles into the RAN domain for over six years through active participation in the O-RAN Alliance. The company's pivotal role began in 2018 with the initiation of a multivendor Open vRAN ecosystem showcased at the Mobile World Congress trade show. Subsequently, in 2019, Cisco led the architectural design and network deployment for the inaugural fully software-defined network worldwide. Building on this momentum, in 2020, Cisco achieved another milestone by collaborating with a communication service provider to successfully conduct a fully packetized phone call over a fronthaul network.

In February 2020, Cisco expanded its NCS 540 portfolio with the introduction of the cutting-edge NCS 540 Fronthaul router (see Figure 1-25), specifically engineered for packet-based fronthaul applications. This advancement significantly enhanced various aspects of the NCS 540, particularly in relation to 5G, encompassing improvements in timing, latency, bandwidth, programmability, and security. Today, the NCS 540 Fronthaul features support for open fronthaul gateways, further augmenting its capabilities.

Figure 1-25 *Cisco NCS 540 FrontHaul Routers*

Designed to facilitate the transport of O-RAN 7.2x eCPRI and legacy CPRI traffic over a unified packet network, the NCS 540 Fronthaul router offers robust transport functionalities—Segment Routing, hierarchical quality of service (QoS), and Ethernet virtual private network pseudowire emulation, all tailored to meet the stringent latency and jitter requirements of packet-based fronthaul. Additionally, the platform complies with IEEE 802.1CM standards profiles A and B, ensuring adherence to fronthaul specifications for latency, QoS, and timing.

Supporting various CPRI bit rates, spanning CPRI options 3 to 8, the platform offers versatile connectivity options. Many leading operators worldwide have already leveraged Cisco's CPRI to Radio over Ethernet (RoE) mapper-based packet fronthaul solution to convert CPRI streams to packets in line with IEEE 1914.1 and 1914.3 standards. Cisco's extensive portfolio of patented innovations in this domain plays a pivotal role in advancing industry standards, facilitating the widespread adoption of CPRI and RoE technologies.

In June 2023, Cisco and Intel validated interoperability between Cisco Nexus 93180YC-FX3 Switch and Intel Ethernet 800 Series network adapters that feature enhanced timing capabilities for faster and lower-cost Open Radio Access Network deployments. I suspect Cisco's contribution to the Open RAN initiative will only continue to increase.

Exam Preparation Tasks

As mentioned in the section "How to Use This Book" in the Introduction, you have a few choices for exam preparation: the exercises here, Chapter 23, "Final Preparation," and the exam simulation questions in the Pearson Test Prep Software Online.

Review All Key Topics

Review the most important topics in this chapter, noted with the Key Topic icon in the margin of the page. Table 1-9 lists a reference of these key topics and the page numbers on which each is found.

Table 1-9   Key Topics for Chapter 1

Key Topic Element	Description	Page Number
Figure 1-7	Unified MPLS	11
Figure 1-9	Additional Unified MPLS BGP Label	13
Figure 1-10	DOCSIS Architecture	16
Table 1-2	DOCSIS Standards	17
Table 1-3	xDSL Service Provider Offerings	19
Table 1-4	SONET and SDH Differences	20
Table 1-5	SONET and SDH Conversion Chart	21
Figure 1-13	Cisco ONS 15216 Exposed Faceplate Mux/Demux 40-Channel Patch Panel Channel Plan	23
Table 1-6	Passive Optical Network Standards	24
Figure 1-17	Network Protection Modes	26
Table 1-7	Radio Core Functions	32
Figure 1-23	xHaul Segments	33
Figure 1-24	Functional Split Options	34

Define Key Terms

Define the following key terms from this chapter and check the answers in the glossary:

CPRI (Common Public Radio Interface), DOCSIS (Data Over Cable Service Interface Specification), DSL (Digital Subscriber Line), DWDM (Dense Wavelength-Division Multiplexing), eCPRI (Enhanced Common Public Radio Interface), E-LAN, E-Line, eNodeB (Evolved NodeB), EPC (Evolved Packet Core), E-Tree, gNodeB (Next-Generation NodeB), Metro Ethernet, Metro Ethernet Forum (MEF), O-RAN (Open Radio Access Network), ROADM (Reconfigurable Optical Add-Drop Multiplexer), TDM (Time-Division Multiplexing), Unified MPLS, Segment Routing

Review Questions

As a part of the review, we encourage you to provide *a single-sentence answer* (keep your answers as short as possible) to the following questions. If you struggle to complete this answer in a single sentence, this may indicate a lack of clarity or reveal gaps in your understanding. We have constructed these questions to help you consolidate this chapter's information and extract the essence of the covered content.

The answers to these questions appear in Appendix A. For more practice with exam format questions, use the Pearson Test Prep Software Online.

1. Can you explain what you think we mean by the combination of distributed intelligence alongside of centralized optimization when describing Segment Routing?

2. How does the role of ROADM contribute to the flexibility and efficiency of wavelength management in a DWDM system?

3. What is the role of MIMO in 5G RAN networks?

4. Which Metro technology is cheaper to deploy—E-LAN or E-Tree—and why?

Bibliography

3GPP Documents:

> https://www.3gpp.org/specifications-technologies/releases

> https://www.3gpp.org/specifications-technologies/releases/release-14

Cisco Live DWDM Content: https://www.ciscolive.com/on-demand/on-demand-library.html?search=riapolov#/

Cisco ONS 15216 Exposed Faceplate Mux/Demux 40-Channel Patch Panel: https://www.cisco.com/c/en/us/products/collateral/optical-networking/ons-15200-series-dwdm-systems/data_sheet_c78-720170.html

DOCSIS and CMTS Architectural Overview: https://www.cisco.com/c/en/us/td/docs/ios/cable/configuration/guide/u10k_cmts_dsis_ov.html

The International Telecommunications Union Telecommunications Standardization Sector (ITU-T) has approved the various versions of DOCSIS as international standards.

> DOCSIS 1.0 ITU-T Recommendation J.112 Annex B

> DOCSIS 1.1 ITU-T Recommendation J.112 Annex B

> DOCSIS 2.0 ITU-T Recommendation J.122

> DOCSIS 3.0 ITU-T Recommendation J.222 (J.222.1, J.222.2, J.222.3).

Introduction to DWDM Technology: https://www.cisco.com/c/dam/global/de_at/assets/docs/dwdm.pdf

MEF Educational Materials: https://www.mef.net/certify/certifications-for-services/carrier-ethernet-certifications-for-services/

Spectral grids for WDM applications: DWDM frequency grid (ITU-T Recommendation G.694.1 (10/20))

Unified MPLS Functionality, Features, and Configuration Example: https://www.cisco.com/c/en/us/support/docs/multiprotocol-label-switching-mpls/mpls/118846-config-mpls-00.html

W. Vermillion. *End-to-End DSL Architectures*. Cisco Press. Apr 2, 2003. ISBN-13: 978-1-58705-087-9: https://www.ciscopress.com/store/end-to-end-dsl-architectures-9781587050879

Y. Rekhter and E. Rosen. RFC 3107, *Carrying Label Information in BGP-4*, IETF, https://tools.ietf.org/html/rfc3107, May 2001.

CHAPTER 2

Software Architectures

This chapter covers the following exam topics:

1.2 Describe Cisco network architecture

- 1.2.a IOS
- 1.2.b IOS XE
- 1.2.c IOS XR

Network operating systems (NOS) are crucial for managing diverse networks and devices efficiently. The Cisco network operating systems have been instrumental in shaping the landscape of service provider networks. With offerings like Cisco IOS XR and Cisco IOS XE, Cisco has provided robust and scalable solutions tailored to the needs of service providers. These solutions offer advanced features such as high availability, seamless scalability, and extensive programmability, enabling service providers to build and manage complex networks with ease. Through innovations like Segment Routing, network function virtualization (NFV), and software-defined networking (SDN) capabilities, the Cisco NOS platforms keep evolving to meet ever-changing customer demands for businesses to remain competitive and relevant in today's dynamic marketplace. In this chapter, we explore these network operating systems that have played a significant role over the past decades.

"Do I Know This Already?" Quiz

The "Do I Know This Already?" quiz allows you to assess whether you should read this entire chapter thoroughly or jump to the "Exam Preparation Tasks" section. If you are in doubt about your answers to these questions or your own assessment of your knowledge of the topics, read the entire chapter. Table 2-1 lists the major heading in this chapter and its corresponding "Do I Know This Already?" quiz questions. You can find the answers in Appendix A, "Answers to the 'Do I Know This Already?' Quizzes and Review Questions."

Table 2-1 "Do I Know This Already?" Section-to-Question Mapping

Foundation Topics Section	Questions
Software Architectures	1–4

CAUTION The goal of self-assessment is to gauge your mastery of the topics in this chapter. If you do not know the answer to a question or are only partially sure of the answer, you should mark that question as wrong for purposes of the self-assessment. Giving yourself credit for an answer you correctly guess skews your self-assessment results and might provide you with a false sense of security.

1. IOS XR is best characterized by which of the following attributes? (Choose two.)

   a. A uniform full-featured image

   b. Preemptive multitasking

   c. Licenses to activate feature access

   d. Two-stage commit

2. Cisco IOS XR software packages can be which of the following? (Choose three.)

   a. Committed

   b. Extracted

   c. Activated

   d. Added

3. Which of the following best defines a *run-to-completion scheduler* in the context of operating systems?

   a. This term refers to a scheduling algorithm that allows tasks to run indefinitely, ignoring any predefined time limits or constraints.

   b. This scheduler prioritizes tasks based on their completion time, favoring those that have been running for the longest duration.

   c. This scheduling mechanism enables tasks to be assigned fixed time slices to execute, regardless of whether they have completed their operations.

   d. This type of scheduling algorithm is employed by operating systems to manage the execution of tasks or processes.

4. Which is the proper command to restore router configuration prior to two last commit changes?

   a. RP/0/RP0/CPU0:Router# **rollback 2**

   b. RP/0/RP0/CPU0:Router(config)# **rollback configuration last 2**

   c. RP/0/RP0/CPU0:Router# **rollback configuration commit changes last 2**

   d. RP/0/RP0/CPU0:Router# **rollback configuration last 2**

Foundation Topics

Software Architectures

Since its establishment in 1984, Cisco Systems has played a key role in powering global networks. Cisco Internetworking Operating System (IOS) stands as the driving force behind countless families of routers used worldwide. Over the years, IOS has demonstrated a rich legacy of adeptly addressing the ever-shifting landscape of multiprotocol routing challenges. The evolution continues with the latest iterations, IOS XE and IOS XR, marking advancements in the software to keep pace with the dynamic changes and technological improvements that have unfolded over the span of 40 years.

The book *IP Routing on Cisco IOS, IOS XE, and IOS XR: An Essential Guide to Understanding and Implementing IP Routing Protocols* (ISBN-13: 978-1-58714-423-3) provides a detailed overview of the differences in these flavors of Cisco IOS. For the purposes of the 350-501 exam, we have chosen to focus on the material you are likely to see during the test.

IOS

IOS, originally developed in the 1980s, was designed during an era when routers faced constraints of limited memory (256 KB) and relatively low CPU processing power. As hardware capabilities evolved and customer demands increased, IOS seamlessly adapted to incorporate advanced routing features requested by Cisco customers. Remarkably, IOS remains as robust and powerful today as it was at its inception, showcasing its adaptability to the dynamic landscape of networking technologies.

This original Cisco IOS featured a monolithic kernel architecture, meaning that the entire operating system ran a single software image. In this approach, all software components and processes directly accessed hardware to conserve processing time. This was an efficient approach in smaller routers and networks and featured a *run-to-completion scheduler* to plan router tasks. Many processes ran until they finished or the scheduler forcefully reclaimed the resources. The CPU did not have to multitask between multiple processes (a CPU-intensive task due to context switch), which is a benefit of the run-to-completion schedulers. A downside of the run-to-completion schedulers is runaway processes, which can disrupt system stability. Additionally, to improve performance and minimize operational overhead, IOS did not implement memory protection between processes or memory pools because the entire physical memory was used as one flat address space. The trade-off was the possibility that corrupted data in one of the processes could destabilize the entire system and even crash software on the router—something only a complete router reload could fix. As routers advanced to handle a more extensive array of functions and networks expanded in scale, Cisco evolved the operating system to meet the growing needs of increasingly complex and expansive networking environments.

IOS XE

In 2004, Cisco engineers improved the weaker points of the IOS kernel and created IOS XE specifically for the Cisco 1000 Series Aggregation Services Router (ASR 1000) router family. IOS XE maintained a command-line interface and configuration approach that closely resembled the original IOS. The similarity was so striking that many engineers well versed in IOS could not discern any difference when working with the IOS XE operating system.

Under the covers, however, the differences were notable. IOS XE innovatively integrated a Linux kernel and autonomous processes to realize the segregation of the control plane and the data plane—a distinct attribute of a stable platform. The Linux kernel and drivers were now the only components with direct access to hardware, which provided additional platform stability. The Linux kernel could now execute processes across multiple CPUs. Most importantly, the operating system was divided into separate functional modules. All the routing protocols were confined to a process called IOSd. Hardware programming ran in another process. Platform management had its own process.

With the integration of the Linux kernel, IOS XE introduced support for virtual memory and a 64-bit architecture, effectively surpassing the recognized 4 GB limit of the 32-bit architecture. The inclusion of memory protection served to prevent corruption between processes. While IOS XE still ran a universal image, certain features could be enabled by activating software licenses associated with these "feature sets."

Equipped with these advancements, IOS XE routers were ready to deliver stability and the growing demands of the new century. In this book, we use IOS XE for configurations associated with both IOS and IOS XE, since there are no functional differences between the two operating systems. We refer to IOS XE as *IOS* for the remainder of the book as much as possible.

IOS uses three CLI modes. Please note that throughout the rest of the book, every typed or entered command appears in **bold**.

- **User EXEC Mode:** Where the CLI prompt ends with the greater-than sign (>). This mode gives limited access to basic monitoring and operational commands, such as checking system status and running show commands. Limited configuration changes are permitted. Example 2-1 shows an interrupted (not full) output of possible commands. Generally, I plan to provide full command output and note where content is omitted for brevity.

Example 2-1   *User EXEC Mode*

```
CE1> ?
Exec commands:
  access-enable    Create a temporary Access-List entry
  access-profile   Apply user-profile to interface
  clear            Reset functions
  connect          Open a terminal connection
  crypto           Encryption related commands.
  disable          Turn off privileged commands
  disconnect       Disconnect an existing network connection
  do-exec          Mode-independent "do-exec" prefix support
  enable           Turn on privileged commands
  ethernet         Ethernet parameters
  exit             Exit from the EXEC
  help             Description of the interactive help system
  ip               IP SLA Exec Command
  ips              Intrusion Prevention System
  lat              Open a lat connection
  lig              LISP Internet Groper
  lock             Lock the terminal
  login            Log in as a particular user
  logout           Exit from the EXEC
  modemui          Start a modem-like user interface
  mrinfo           Request neighbor and version information from a multicast

CE1>
```

- **Privileged EXEC Mode:** Where the CLI prompt ends with the hash symbol (#). This mode provides elevated access with privileges for configuration and more advanced monitoring; plus, it offers a broader range of commands, including configuration commands for modifying the device's settings. In Example 2-2, notice how several new commands appear.

Example 2-2 *Privileged EXEC Mode*

```
CE1> enable
CE1#?
Exec commands:
 access-enable   Create a temporary Access-List entry
 access-profile  Apply user-profile to interface
 access-template Create a temporary Access-List entry
 alps            ALPS exec commands
 archive         manage archive files
 auto            Exec level Automation
 beep            Blocks Extensible Exchange Protocol commands
 bfe             For manual emergency modes setting
 bulkstat        Bulkstat exec commands
 calendar        Manage the hardware calendar
 cd              Change current directory
 clear           Reset functions
 clock           Manage the system clock
 cns             CNS agents
 configure       Enter configuration mode
 connect         Open a terminal connection
 copy            Copy from one file to another
 crypto          Encryption related commands.
 cts             Cisco Trusted Security Exec Commands
 debug           Debugging functions (see also 'undebug')
 delete          Delete a file
! Output omitted for brevity
CE1#
```

- **Global Configuration Mode:** Where the CLI prompt appears as (config)#. This mode allows users to make changes to the device's configuration, including interface settings, routing parameters, and other global configurations. Commands entered in this mode affect the overall behavior of the device. Example 2-3 shows the operator changing the configuration of the router's name.

Example 2-3 *Global Configuration Mode*

```
CE1# configure terminal
Enter configuration commands, one per line. End with CNTL/Z.
CE1(config)# hostname ?
 WORD This system's network name
CE1(config)# hostname 305-501
305-501(config)# exit
305-501#
*Jan 9 11:50:42.572: %SYS-5-CONFIG_I: Configured from console by console
305-501#
```

This is an important distinction about IOS XE. Notice that as soon as we pressed the Enter key, the change of hostname was immediate. There were no semantic checks or warnings whether the configuration we just made would not work with the rest of the working configuration. If you have worked on larger networks, you likely know the feeling of your soul momentarily leaving your body when the command prompt freezes for a couple of seconds after you hit the Enter key…. As you imagine that the SSH connection has dropped, you can feel the weight of potential network chaos bearing down on you. Panic quickly sets in, and the horror of having broken the entire system invades your body. Then, out of nowhere, connectivity is restored, the prompt is back, and your sigh of relief could blow the server room door off its hinges. You still have your job. Time to get some coffee.

Additionally, observe that no quick and easy way to overwrite the current configuration with the previous one(s) is available in IOS XE by default. Here's a pop quiz for experienced CLI jockeys…who are sipping coffee with adrenalin and thinking that this can be *the* legal mixture you need to conquer the day, one jittery keystroke at a time: Can you actually undo this configuration? Well, this is not a big deal if you only changed a hostname, but if you have just copied and pasted a multipage text file that has generated undesired network behaviors, oh yes, you are in for a wild ride! There isn't a simple Ctrl+Z situation (note to self: this can be the software enhancement I have been looking for to get the next promotion). No problem. Copying and pasting the original file—which we smart engineers have saved—should do the job. So far, so good. But halfway through the paste: "Paste denied!" Noooo!! Now you have a real mess on your hands, and this is why your employer pays you the big dollars. You have to be methodical and careful not to destabilize the network.

By the way, have you thought about how to revert the configuration? If you answered **copy startup-config running-config**, you just failed the pop quiz. What?! Because your copy action acts as a merge, now you have to remove some of the settings. A better answer would be to **archive** the config and **replace** it as shown in Example 2-4, where we take router PE2 (you will get to know this topology soon enough) for a spin.

Example 2-4 *Archiving and Replacing IOS XE Configurations*

```
PE2# show archive
 Archive feature not enabled
PE2# configure terminal
Enter configuration commands, one per line. End with CNTL/Z.
PE2(config)# archive
PE2(config-archive)# path flash:
PE2(config-archive)# time-period 1440
PE2(config-archive)# end
PE2# write memory
Building configuration...
[OK]
PE2# show archive
The maximum archive configurations allowed is 10.
There are currently 1 archive configurations saved.
The next archive file will be named bootflash:-<timestamp>-1
```

```
 Archive # Name
    1     bootflash:-Jan--9-13-56-11.092-0 <- Most Recent
    2
    3
    4
    5
    6
    7
    8
    9
   10
PE2# configure terminal
Enter configuration commands, one per line. End with CNTL/Z.
PE2(config)# hostname 350-501
350-501(config)# exit
350-501#
350-501# show archive config differences bootflash:-Jan--9-13-56-11.092-0
!Contextual Config Diffs:
+hostname PE2
-hostname 350-501
line con 0
 -length 0

350-501# configure replace bootflash:-Jan--9-13-56-11.092-0
This will apply all necessary additions and deletions
to replace the current running configuration with the
contents of the specified configuration file, which is
assumed to be a complete configuration, not a partial
configuration. Enter Y if you are sure you want to proceed. ? [no]: y

*Jan 9 13:59:30.223: Rollback:Acquired Configuration lock.
*Jan 9 13:59:30.223: %SYS-5-CONFIG_R: Config Replace is Done
*Jan 9 13:59:31.045: %SYS-5-CONFIG_P: Configured programmatically by process Exec
from console as console
Total number of passes: 1
Rollback Done

PE2#
```

Now you are back to the original configuration with the hostname PE2. After you master this little technique, it is important to note that sufficient memory is essential to accommodate both the running and source configurations. Some commands may not be removed, and a device reload might be necessary. Always, always triple-check everything (a hint for when you take your 350-501 test) in production.

Additionally, after you set up the archiving feature, IOS enables you to apply a revert timer to your configuration, as shown in Example 2-5. Notice how the router replaces all the changes after you deliberately choose not to enter **configure confirm**. This way, you can prepare the router to load the last known good configuration.

Example 2-5 *Reverting Configurations with a Revert Timer*

```
PE2# configure terminal revert timer 1
Rollback Confirmed Change: Backing up current running config to
bootflash:0-Jul--1-13-27-56.595-0
Enter configuration commands, one per line.  End with CNTL/Z.
PE2(config)#Rollback Confirmed Change: Rollback will begin in one minute.
Enter "configure confirm" if you wish to keep what you've configured
*Jul  1 13:27:56.815: %ARCHIVE_DIFF-5-ROLLBK_CNFMD_CHG_BACKUP: Backing up current
running config to bootflash:0-Jul--1-13-27-56.595-0
*Jul  1 13:27:56.815: %ARCHIVE_DIFF-5-ROLLBK_CNFMD_CHG_START_ABSTIMER:
User: console(Priv: 15, View: 0): Scheduled to rollback to config bootflash:
0-Jul--1-13-27-56.595-0 in 1 minutes
*Jul  1 13:27:56.818: %ARCHIVE_DIFF-5-ROLLBK_CNFMD_CHG_WARNING_ABSTIMER: System will
rollback to config bootflash:0-Jul--1-13-27-56.595-0 in one minute. Enter "configure
confirm" if you wish to keep what you've configured
PE2(config)# hostname R999
R999(config)#
R999(config)#Rollback Confirmed Change: rolling to:bootflash:0-Jul--1-13-27-56.595-0
*Jul  1 13:28:56.815: %ARCHIVE_DIFF-5-ROLLBK_CNFMD_CHG_ROLLBACK_START: Start rolling
to: bootflash:0-Jul--1-13-27-56.595-0
*Jul  1 13:28:56.932: Rollback:Acquired Configuration lock.
Total number of passes: 1
Rollback Done
*Jul  1 13:28:56.932: %SYS-5-CONFIG_R: Config Replace is Done
*Jul  1 13:28:57.052: %SYS-5-CONFIG_P: Configured programmatically by process Policy
Manager from console as console
PE2(config)#
```

IOS XR

With the explosion of service provider networks, a far greater scrutiny was given to organizations offering various communication services to their customers. The "five nines" (99.999%) availability represented a very low level of downtime, allowing for only a few minutes of service interruption per year. This level of reliability is crucial for mission-critical applications and services where continuous availability is paramount. To meet this challenge, Cisco launched yet another flavor of IOS, the IOS XR operating system in May of 2004 with the CSR-1 router.

IOS XR is designed for high-end routers and carrier-grade systems, featuring a distributed architecture that separates control plane and data plane functions and employs a modular design with additional safety mechanisms. This modular approach enhances scalability, ease of maintenance, and the ability to introduce new features without disrupting the entire system. The microkernel architecture of IOS XR operates by running nearly all system services and processes outside the kernel. Consequently, processes function as user programs without the need for a complete system reload. IOS XR also introduced preemptive multitasking, enabling lower-priority processes to be temporarily suspended through a context switch.

This approach allowed higher-priority processes to take precedence, resulting in a "fairer" scheduler and reducing the likelihood of overwhelming the CPU. Additionally, IOS XR introduced a dedicated memory management unit (MMU) controller to manage physical to virtual address space mapping to deal with memory corruption issues.

IOS XR also introduced software packages instead of the feature sets you have learned about in IOS XE. Operators could now install, remove, and modify packages without having to reload the entire system. These packages fell into two categories:

- Package Installation Envelopes (PIEs)

- Software Maintenance Upgrades (SMUs)

PIEs are files containing code for software features. Mandatory PIEs were a part of a core "mini" image loaded on XR routers. Table 2-2 lists the mandatory and optional PIEs.

Table 2-2 Package Installation Envelopes

Mandatory (Core Mini Image) PIEs	Optional PIEs
OS (kernel, file system, memory management)	MPLS
Base (interface manager, SysDB, configuration manager, checkpoint services)	Multicast
Admin (line cards, fabric)	BNG
Forwarding (FIB, ACL, QoS, ARP, others)	Satellite
Line Card drivers	Carrier Grade NAT
Routing (RIB, OSPF, IS-IS, BGP, RPL)	Security
	Lawful Intercept
	Virtual Services Module

Example 2-6 shows the output of the **show install active summary** command where you can see some of these packages. Note that different hardware platforms produce different output, but the concept remains, and you will be able to recognize it on the exam regardless of what output you see. Can you guess what some of these packages do?

Example 2-6 *Identifying Package Installation Envelopes*

```
RP/0/RSP0/CPU0:ASR9K# show install active summary
Active Packages:
 disk0:asr9k-mgbl-px-6.3.2
 disk0:asr9k-mini-px-6.3.2
 disk0:asr9k-li-px-6.3.2
 disk0:asr9k-k9sec-px-6.3.2
 disk0:asr9k-doc-px-6.3.2
 disk0:asr9k-mcast-px-6.3.2
 disk0:asr9k-optic-px-6.3.2
 disk0:asr9k-fpd-px-6.3.2
 disk0:asr9k-mpls-px-6.3.2
```

SMUs are PIEs that provide software patches for defects while allowing the router to stay on the same software version. They serve as emergency point fixes. This expedited solution is specifically tailored to address critical issues causing network downtime or impacting revenue. In the event of a software deficiency or bug, Cisco can promptly deliver a targeted fix within the existing Cisco IOS XR release.

These packages have to be added (copied to the router), activated (processes have to be restarted with the new code), and committed (locked in the configuration to survive router reloads). The last one catches newcomers to XR by surprise...and lost time when they forget to **commit** because the system does not retain the changes after a reboot. Old packages have to be removed from the system by deactivating them (removing them from runtime), committing them (locking to service reloads), and deleting them (removing them from local storage). It is best to follow the exact steps provided in the specific documentation for the particular hardware and software version for successful addition or removal of these elements.

As soon as you log in to an IOS XR router, you notice right away that the concept of a user mode (>) does not exist. The familiar # indicates that the user is in EXEC mode and privileges are determined during login, as you will see in the upcoming example. I highly doubt that you will see this question on the exam, but at this level of your career, you have to know that there have been several flavors of IOS XR. You have far more important things to remember for this exam, but be aware that differences in IOS XR flavors do exist, so you should not be surprised that some commands work differently. You will have to poke around and learn this through your own research; this book would turn into a multivolume encyclopedia if we were to address this level of detail. Now that we've said this, be aware of the following, and you will know where to start.

1. Classic IOS XR a.k.a. **Classic XR** (or cXR): It ran distributed multichassis systems with a 32-bit operating system on a QNX microkernel.

2. Linux-based **Virtualized XR**: This 64-bit OS ran in a virtual machine and brought hardware-enabled true zero-packet loss, zero-topology loss (ZPL/ZTL) with In-Service-Software-Upgrades (**ISSU**) and a separate admin context for multitenancy (called SDR for Secure Domain Router), as shown in Example 2-7, which is missing in the newer versions of IOS XR. The admin context provides access to control software versions, PIEs, SMUs, and others device states.

Example 2-7 *EXEC and Admin Mode Prompts*

```
RP/0/0/CPU0:PE4# admin
Tue Jan 9 14:33:15.374 UTC
RP/0/0/CPU0:PE4(admin)#
```

Cisco has since evicted the SDR feature due to complexity and lack of demand. Some other vendors have kept it, but I rarely run into this.

3. **Evolved XR (eXR)**: This LXC-based (Linux Containers) lighter-weight version has several manageability, telemetry, and application hosting enhancements. It still retained the admin control plane, which also ran in a separate Linux container.

4. **XR LNT** (pronounced "lint"): You will see this on the newer Cisco routers (see Example 2-8). It is an attempt to arrive at a minimal set of XR binaries, with minimal "XR-isms" (i.e., infra-structure, middleware, XR libraries) for simplified operations. LNT achieved faster boot times, removed the admin context along with the SDR functionality mentioned previously, disaggregated the software, and featured superior security. ISSUs are gone as well. I have never been a big fan of these due to what I have seen in real production networks with multiple vendors implementing this feature, but that is for another book. Some people love ISSUs and keep asking when Cisco will bring them back. Time will tell. It looks as though they have had their day.

Example 2-8   *IOS XR LNT*

```
RP/0/RP0/CPU0:8201# show version
Tue Jan 9 11:34:04.147 UTC
Cisco IOS XR Software, Version 7.7.2 LNT
Copyright (c) 2013-2022 by Cisco Systems, Inc.

Build Information:
 Built By     : ingunawa
 Built On     : Wed Oct 26 17:22:02 UTC 2022
 Build Host   : iox-ucs-060
 Workspace    : /auto/srcarchive14/prod/7.7.2/8000/ws
 Version      : 7.7.2
 Label        : 7.7.2

cisco 8000 (Intel(R) Xeon(R) CPU D-1530 @ 2.40GHz)
cisco 8201-32FH (Intel(R) Xeon(R) CPU D-1530 @ 2.40GHz) processor with 32GB of
memory
8201 uptime is 1 day, 2 hours, 28 minutes
Cisco 8000 Series 32x400G QSFPDD 1RU Fixed System w/HBM

RP/0/RP0/CPU0:8201#
```

Software packaging has changed over time as well. Depending on which flavor of XR you work with, you should be able to recognize that there is a base package, and optional package operators can load based on their preferences, as shown in Example 2-9.

Example 2-9   *Viewing Software Packages on XR LNT*

```
RP/0/RP0/CPU0:8201# show install active summary
Tue Jan 9 11:42:00.420 UTC
Active Packages:  XR: 197  All: 1482
Label:            7.7.2
Software Hash:    ce2b19e5dc0506706b9c3fb48e0a8b21042b10eb0e02ccf773cb2f18eb645cca

Optional Packages                                    Version
---------------------------------------------------  --------------------------
```

```
xr-8000-l2mcast                            7.7.2v1.0.0-1
xr-8000-mcast                              7.7.2v1.0.0-1
xr-8000-netflow                            7.7.2v1.0.0-1
xr-bgp                                     7.7.2v1.0.0-1
xr-ipsla                                   7.7.2v1.0.0-1
xr-is-is                                   7.7.2v1.0.0-1
xr-lldp                                    7.7.2v1.0.0-1
xr-mcast                                   7.7.2v1.0.0-1
xr-mpls-oam                                7.7.2v1.0.0-1
xr-netflow                                 7.7.2v1.0.0-1
xr-ospf                                    7.7.2v1.0.0-1
xr-perf-meas                               7.7.2v1.0.0-1
xr-perfmgmt                                7.7.2v1.0.0-1
xr-track                                   7.7.2v1.0.0-1
RP/0/RP0/CPU0:8201#
```

Unlike IOS (IOS XE), where pressing the Enter key applies the configuration, IOS XR uses a
two-stage commit to process configuration changes. During the first stage, a user creates
a target configuration that contains only the intended changes. It does not contain a copy of
the running configuration. During the second stage, when a user types in **commit**, IOS XR
parses the configuration for syntax and transport errors, and if they pass the checks, these
commands are added to the running configuration, as shown in Figure 2-1.

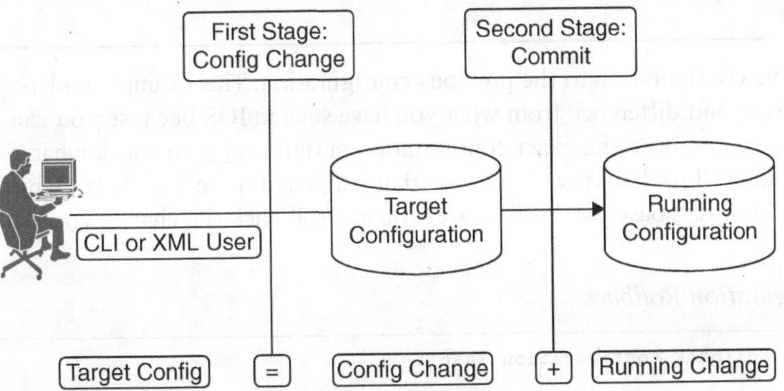

Figure 2-1   *Two-Stage Commit in IOS XR*

Knowing how to make IOS XR configuration changes is fundamental to the job. Be sure to
spend time doing this in a lab. I will take you through some of the basics to get you started.
In Example 2-10, let's change the hostname again and observe differences with IOS (XE).

Example 2-10   *Two-Stage Commit Example from IOS XR*

```
RP/0/RP0/CPU0:8201# configure
RP/0/RP0/CPU0:8201(config)# hostname 350-501
RP/0/RP0/CPU0:8201(config)# commit
RP/0/RP0/CPU0:Jan 9 18:01:337.317 UTC: config[77183]: <commit confirmation message>
RP/0/RP0/CPU0:350-501(config)# end
RP/0/RP0/CPU0:350-501#
```

This behavior is different from IOS because the prompt does not change until you enter the **commit** command. You can find your change-id as a database entry by using **show configuration commit list command**. The latest commit change appears at the top of the list, and your change-id will vary from what is shown in Example 2-11. Example 2-11 shows 1000000003.

Example 2-11 *Display Configuration Database*

```
RP/0/RP0/CPU0:350-501# show configuration commit list
SNo.   Label/ID    User    Line     Client      Time Stamp
~~~~   ~~~~~~~~    ~~~~    ~~~~     ~~~~~~      ~~~~~~~~~~
1      1000000003  cisco   con0_RP0_CPU0 CLI   Mon Jan 9 18:03:36 2024
! Output omitted for brevity
RP/0/RP0/CPU0:350-501#
```

Enter the following **show configuration commit changes last 1** command on the router to look at the last configuration change, as demonstrated in Example 2-12.

Example 2-12 *Viewing the Contents of the Last Configuration*

```
RP/0/RP0/CPU0:350-501# show configuration commit changes last 1
Building configuration...
!! IOS XR Configuration 7.7.2
hostname 350-501
end
RP/0/RP0/CPU0:350-501#
```

Example 2-13 returns the configuration to the previous configuration. This example underscores the operational ease and difference from what you have seen in IOS because you can go back several changes and point to the exact configuration in time and even check what was committed. You could roll back to a configuration that happened quite a while back by specifying a number in your database list. In this case, you just roll back the change you just made.

Example 2-13 *Configuration Rollback*

```
RP/0/RP0/CPU0:350-501# rollback configuration last 1

Loading Rollback Changes.
Loaded Rollback Changes in 1 sec
Committing.
1 items committed in 1 sec (1)items/sec
Updating.
Updated Commit database in 1 sec
Configuration successfully rolled back 1 commits.
RP/0/RP0/CPU0:8201#
```

Working with configuration IDs can be inconvenient. Labels are friendlier names you can use to identify what has been done, as demonstrated in Example 2-14.

Example 2-14 *Working with Commit Labels*

```
RP/0/RP0/CPU0:8201(config)# hostname 350-501
RP/0/RP0/CPU0:8201(config)# commit label new_hostname
Tue Jan 9 19:00:03.336 UTC
RP/0/RP0/CPU0:350-501(config)# end
RP/0/RP0/CPU0:350-501# show configuration commit list
Tue Jan 9 19:01:07.968 UTC
SNo. Label/ID    User  Line        Client  Time Stamp
~~~~ ~~~~~~~~~   ~~~~  ~~~~        ~~~~~~  ~~~~~~~~~~~
1  new_hostname  cisco  con0_RP0_CPU0 CLI    Tue Jan 9 19:00:05 2024
! Output omitted for brevity
RP/0/RP0/CPU0:350-501# rollback configuration new_hostname

Loading Rollback Changes.
Loaded Rollback Changes in 1 sec
Committing.
1 items committed in 1 sec (0)items/sec
Updating.
Updated Commit database in 1 sec
Configuration successfully rolled back commit 'new_hostname'.
RP/0/RP0/CPU0:8201#
```

I strongly encourage you to explore working with IOS XR on your own to feel comfortable
with it because it is not possible for us to cover all options in this volume. Example 2-15
encourages you to explore the following options on your own.

Example 2-15 *Exploring IOS XR Command Options*

```
RP/0/RP0/CPU0:8201# configure
Tue Jan 9 19:20:29.987 UTC
RP/0/RP0/CPU0:8201(config)# commit ?
 best-effort  Commit the configuration changes via best-effort operation
 comment      Assign a comment to this commit
 confirmed    Rollback this commit unless there is a confirming commit
 force        Override the memory checks
 label        Assign a label to this commit
 replace      Replace the contents of running configuration
 save-running Save running configuration to a file
 show-error   Displays commit failures immediately
 <cr>      Commit the configuration changes via pseudo-atomic operation
RP/0/RP0/CPU0:8201(config)# commit confirmed minutes ?
  <1-1024>  Minutes until rollback unless there is a confirming commit
RP/0/RP0/CPU0:8201(config)# commit confirmed minutes 10 ?
  comment      Assign a comment to this commit
  force        Override the memory checks
```

```
 label           Assign a label to this commit
 save-running    Save running configuration to a file
 show-error      Displays commit failures immediately
 <cr>            Commit the configuration changes via pseudo-atomic operation
RP/0/RP0/CPU0:8201(config)# commit replace ?
 best-effort     Commit the configuration changes via best-effort operation
 comment         Assign a comment to this commit
 confirmed       Rollback this commit unless there is a confirming commit
 force           Override the memory checks
 label           Assign a label to this commit
 save-running    Save running configuration to a file
 show-error      Displays commit failures immediately
 <cr>            Commit the configuration changes via pseudo-atomic operation
RP/0/RP0/CPU0:8201(config)#
```

Example 2-15 explores the options associated with the **commit** command. Initially, it presents a convenient feature allowing a return to the current configuration within 10 minutes unless human confirmation affirms the intended changes as permanent. In scenarios where changes lead to unintended consequences and router access is lost, this feature becomes invaluable. Within 10 minutes, configurations automatically revert to their prior state. Following this, you can explore the **commit replace** command, akin to the IOS **write erase** command, which wipes all router configurations.

On IOS devices, many configurations may appear in several different parts of the configuration file. For example, routing protocol configurations may be found under the routing process, global configuration, and the interface configuration submode. If you are not familiar with all possible occurring sections, you can easily get confused about why the router is behaving differently than expected. In contrast, IOS XR has a hierarchical command-line interface structure. All commands logically cascade to their own respective decision trees. You might be in one configuration submode (for example, IS-IS) and must change to another configuration submode (for example, configuring an IP address). This will result in an error because you do not leave the original subconfiguration, and commands are entered under the wrong subconfiguration, as demonstrated in Example 2-16. The advantage of this approach is that when you get used to it, you can more easily navigate it and understand where to make all the necessary changes.

Example 2-16 *IOS XR Hierarchy Demonstrated*

```
RP/0/0/CPU0:PE4# configure
RP/0/0/CPU0:PE4(config)# router isis CCNP
RP/0/0/CPU0:PE4(config-isis)# net 49.0001.0000.0000.0004.00
RP/0/0/CPU0:PE4(config-isis)# interface Loopback0
RP/0/0/CPU0:PE4(config-isis-if)# interface FourHundredGigE0/0/0/1
RP/0/0/CPU0:PE4(config-isis-if)# ipv4 address 1.1.1.1 255.255.255.255
                                  ^
% Invalid input detected at '^' marker.
RP/0/0/CPU0:PE4 (config-isis-if)# pwd
```

```
router isis lab
 interface FourHundredGigE0/0/0/1
RP/0/0/CPU0:PE4(config-isis-if)# root
RP/0/0/CPU0:PE4(config)# interface FourHundredGigE0/0/0/1
RP/0/0/CPU0:PE4(config-if)# ipv4 address 1.1.1.1 255.255.255.255
RP/0/0/CPU0:PE4 (config-if)#
```

In Example 2-16, notice how the interface Loopback0 is added to the IS-IS routing process. The operator wants to exit the IS-IS process to configure an IP address to interface FourHundredGigE0/0/0/1 as customary in IOS but does not realize that they are still within the tree branch of the IS-IS hierarchy. When the configuration is not accepted, you can check the hierarchy position with the **pwd** command. After realizing the mistake, you can use the **root** command to return to the top of the hierarchy, where you can successfully navigate to the appropriate tree branch to make the changes. Although the **root** command is quicker, using the **exit** command multiple times accomplishes the same thing, as shown in Example 2-17.

Example 2-17 *IOS XR Hierarchy Demonstrated with* **exit** *Command*

```
RP/0/0/CPU0:PE4(config-if)# router isis lab
RP/0/0/CPU0:PE4(config-isis)# net 49.0001.0000.0000.0004.00
RP/0/0/CPU0:PE4(config-isis)# interface Loopback0
RP/0/0/CPU0:PE4(config-isis-if)# interface FourHundredGigE0/0/0/1
RP/0/0/CPU0:PE4(config-isis-if)# ipv4 address 1.1.1.1 255.255.255.255
                                                 ^
% Invalid input detected at '^' marker.
RP/0/0/CPU0:PE4(config-isis-if)# exit
RP/0/0/CPU0:PE4(config-isis)# exit
RP/0/0/CPU0:PE4(config)# interface FourHundredGigE0/0/0/1
RP/0/0/CPU0:PE4(config-if)# ipv4 address 1.1.1.1 255.255.255.255
RP/0/0/CPU0:PE4(config-if)#
```

As previously stated, IOS XR includes an intrinsic check to prevent you from making syntax and transport errors that are nonsensical to the configuration check parser. The **show configuration failed** command can offer insights into why the router rejects incorrect configurations, aiding you in troubleshooting, as shown in Example 2-18.

Example 2-18 *IOS XR Configuration Parser Dislikes Incomplete Instructions*

```
RP/0/RP0/CPU0:8201(config)# taskgroup ?
  WORD  Taskgroup name
RP/0/RP0/CPU0:8201(config)# taskgroup ospf
RP/0/RP0/CPU0:8201(config-tg)# commit
Sun May  5 06:14:35.662 CDT

% Failed to commit one or more configuration items during a pseudo-atomic operation.
All changes made have been reverted. Please issue 'show configuration failed
[inheritance]' from this session to view the errors
```

```
RP/0/RP0/CPU0:8201(config-tg)# show configuration failed
Sun May  5 06:15:01.193 CDT
!! SEMANTIC ERRORS: This configuration was rejected by
!! the system due to semantic errors. The individual
!! errors with each failed configuration command can be
!! found below.

taskgroup ospf
!!% 'LOCALD' detected the 'fatal' condition 'Usergroup/Taskgroup names cannot be
taskid names'
!
end
RP/0/RP0/CPU0:8201(config-tg)# task ?
  debug     Specify a debug-type task ID
  execute   Specify a execute-type task ID
  notify    Config deprecated. Will be removed in 7.7.1. Specify 'read' instead.
  read      Specify a read-type task ID
  write     Specify a read-write-type task ID
RP/0/RP0/CPU0:8201(config-tg)# task read o
ospf  otn  ouni
RP/0/RP0/CPU0:8201(config-tg)#
```

Example 2-18 illustrates what occurs when the parser rejects the input intended for committing. IOS XR boasts a strong embedded mechanism for user authentication and authorization. Unlike IOS, which employs privilege levels, XR doesn't utilize this concept. However, its embedded user task group management is exceptionally robust, enabling the creation of various task groups with precision. When attempting to define a task group aimed at granting permissions to view OSPF process tasks, the parser rejects this attempt due to conflicts with the task names, such as "ospf," as you confirm the existence of this task. Choosing a task group name that doesn't conflict with existing tasks will enable you to successfully commit the configuration.

Example 2-19 shows what happens when you attempt to exit the Configuration mode. You are asked to commit the changes or abort them or cancel the exit itself with **cancel** as the default option, which is chosen here. Notice also the two helpful commands that are highlighted. The **abort** command enables you to discard all uncommitted changes and exit the Configuration mode. The **clear** command conveniently cancels all uncommitted changes without exiting the Configuration mode. This feature proves helpful when you are troubleshooting or experimenting with configurations, eliminating the need to manually undo each command entered.

Example 2-19 *Exiting the Configuration Mode*

```
RP/0/RP0/CPU0:8201(config-tg)# end
Uncommitted changes found, commit them before exiting(yes/no/cancel)? [cancel]:
RP/0/RP0/CPU0:8201(config-tg)# exit
RP/0/RP0/CPU0:8201(config)# ?
```

```
aaa                    Authentication, Authorization and Accounting
abort                  Abort this configuration session
accounting             Enable accounting
address-family         AFI/SAFI configuration
adt                    ADT configuration commands
alias                  Create an alias for entity
apply-group            Apply configuration from a group
apply-group-append     Append apply-group configuration from a group
apply-group-remove     Remove a group from apply-group configuration
apply-template         Apply configuration from a template
appmgr                 appmgr configuration
arp                    Global ARP configuration
as-format              Autonomous system number format
as-path-set            Define an AS-path set
as-set                 Configuration for a as set
attestation            Attestation Agent configuration
auto-ip-ring           Enable auto-ip-ring
banner                 Define a login banner
bfd                    Global BFD configuration commands
bmp                    BGP Monitoring Protocol commands
bundle                 Bundle global command
call-home              Enter call-home configuration mode
cef                    CEF configuration
cinetd                 Global Cisco inetd configuration commands
class-map              Configure a class-map
clear                  Clear the uncommitted configuration
clock                  Configure time-of-day clock
clock-interface        Clock interface configuration commands
```

Something else applies to both the IOS and IOS XR routers. This point might seem trivial to experienced users but can be an indispensable time-saver for newcomers to Cisco. It is the use of the **do** command in the Configuration mode, as demonstrated in Example 2-20. Note how you are restricted to issuing EXEC mode commands in the Configuration mode, which this command keyword helps you overcome. We use it extensively in the following chapters.

Example 2-20   *Use of the* **do** *Keyword in the Configuration Mode*

```
RP/0/RP0/CPU0:R4(config)# show clock
                            ^
% Invalid input detected at '^' marker.
RP/0/RP0/CPU0:R4(config)# do show clock
Wed Jan 9 23:54:54.488 UTC
23:54:54.531 UTC Wed Jan 9 2024
RP/0/RP0/CPU0:R4(config)#
```

The output from XR routers differs from that of IOS-based platforms in that it includes timestamps for many configuration, **show**, and **commit** commands. This chapter shows several XR output examples, which illustrate how the timestamps make it easier to track when specific actions occurred. This is a distinct difference between the operating systems, and in this book, I've aimed to preserve the look and feel of XR. However, to maintain brevity and focus on relevant content, I omit timestamps from the output unless they are essential for understanding certain behaviors. Please keep this in mind as you go through the book.

After reading this section, you should possess a foundational comprehension of the IOS, IOS XE, and IOS XR network operating systems, along with an awareness of their respective advantages and disadvantages that impact their operational characteristics. We have provided guidance on accessing a router and showed the initial steps to facilitate your understanding. We encourage you to invest the time needed to familiarize yourself more thoroughly with these operating systems.

Exam Preparation Tasks

As mentioned in the section "How to Use This Book" in the Introduction, you have a few choices for exam preparation: the exercises here, Chapter 23, "Final Preparation," and the exam simulation questions in the Pearson Test Prep Software Online.

Review All Key Topics

Review the most important topics in this chapter, noted with the Key Topic icon in the margin of the page. Table 2-3 lists a reference of these key topics and the page numbers on which each is found.

Table 2-3   Key Topics for Chapter 2

Key Topic Element	Description	Page Number
Table 2-2	Package Installation Envelopes	48
Figure 2-1	Two-stage Commit in IOS XR	51

Define Key Terms

Define the following key terms from this chapter and check the answers in the glossary:

Classic XR, Evolved XR (eXR), Global Configuration Mode, ISSU, Privileged EXEC Mode, two-stage commit, User EXEC Mode, Virtualized XR, XR LNT

Command Reference to Check Your Memory

This section includes the most important configuration and EXEC commands covered in this chapter. It might not be necessary to memorize the complete syntax of every command, but you should be able to remember the basic keywords that are needed.

To test your memory of the commands, cover the right side of Table 2-4 with a piece of paper, read the description on the left side, and then see how much of the command you can remember.

The 350-501 exam focuses on practical, hands-on skills that are used by networking professionals. Therefore, you should be able to identify the commands needed to configure and test. Note that not all commands are fully covered in the chapter, but their presence in the following table should lead you to investigate them further to understand this technology.

Table 2-4   CLI Commands to Know

Task	Command Syntax
Display configuration database	RP/0/RP0/CPU0:Router# **show configuration commit list**
Display changes during the last configuration	RP/0/RP0/CPU0:Router# **show configuration commit changes last 1**
Load the previous configuration	RP/0/RP0/CPU0:Router# **rollback configuration last 1**
Commit a configuration with humanly identifiable label	RP/0/RP0/CPU0:Router(config)# **commit label new_hostname**
Display the hierarchical CLI path	RP/0/0/CPU0:Router(config-isis-if)# **pwd**
Return to the top of the CLI tree	RP/0/0/CPU0:Router(config-isis-if)# **root**
Display candidate configuration at the top of the tree	RP/0/0/CPU0: Router(config)# **show**
Replace the contents of the running-configuration	RP/0/RP0/CPU0:Router(config)# **commit replace**
Get clues as to why the candidate configuration is not committing	RP/0/RP0/CPU0:Router(config)# **show configuration failed**
Discard uncommitted changes and exit Configuration Mode	RP/0/0/CPU0: Router(config)# **abort**
Discard uncommitted changes	RP/0/0/CPU0: Router(config)# **clear**

Review Questions

As a part of the review, we encourage you to provide *a single-sentence answer* (keep your answers as short as possible) to the questions that follow. If you struggle to complete this answer in a single sentence, this might indicate a lack of clarity or reveal gaps in your understanding. We have constructed these questions to help you consolidate this chapter's information and extract the essence of the covered content.

The answers to these questions appear in Appendix A. For more practice with exam format questions, use the Pearson Test Prep Software Online.

1. Can you describe the IOS XR mechanisms for implementing configuration changes?

2. How does Cisco IOS XR facilitate modularity in configuration management?

3. What is the IOS-XR command syntax to deploy a new software package? (You will have to look this up.)

## CHAPTER 3

Service Provider Virtualization

This chapter covers the following exam topics:

1.3 Describe service provider virtualization

- 1.3.a NFV infrastructure
- 1.3.b VNF workloads
- 1.3.c Containers
- 1.3.d Application hosting

A key trend—and necessity—in modern deployments has been network virtualization. This approach has revolutionized the traditional networking paradigm by decoupling network functions from underlying hardware, enabling the creation of virtualized network environments. Leveraging software-defined networking (SDN) principles to abstract network resources and services allows for greater flexibility, scalability, and agility in network operations. By virtualizing network components such as switches, routers, firewalls, and load balancers, organizations can dynamically provision, configure, and manage network infrastructure to meet evolving business needs. Chapter 3 sets the stage for exploring various network virtualization technologies and their transformative impact on modern networking architectures.

"Do I Know This Already?" Quiz

The "Do I Know This Already?" quiz allows you to assess whether you should read this entire chapter thoroughly or jump to the "Exam Preparation Tasks" section. If you are in doubt about your answers to these questions or your own assessment of your knowledge of the topics, read the entire chapter. Table 3-1 lists the major heading in this chapter and its corresponding "Do I Know This Already?" quiz questions. You can find the answers in Appendix A, "Answers to the 'Do I Know This Already?' Quizzes and Review Questions."

Table 3-1 "Do I Know This Already?" Section-to-Question Mapping

Foundation Topics Section	Questions
Virtualization Technologies	1–4

CAUTION The goal of self-assessment is to gauge your mastery of the topics in this chapter. If you do not know the answer to a question or are only partially sure of the answer, you should mark that question as wrong for purposes of the self-assessment. Giving yourself credit for an answer you correctly guess skews your self-assessment results and might provide you with a false sense of security.

1. Cisco NFV physical infrastructure includes which of the following? (Select all that apply.)

   a. Networking

   b. Storage

   c. Fully integrated KVM stack

   d. Compute

2. Which of the following best describes Cisco VIM?

   a. Cisco UCS rack-and-blade server manager

   b. A full lifecycle management tool for software and hardware

   c. Nexus switches fabric manager

   d. WAN Orchestration platform

3. Which of the following containers runs on XR routers?

   a. containerd

   b. Podman

   c. Kubernetes

   d. Docker

4. Which of the following is not a valid Docker command?

   a. attach

   b. abort

   c. build

   d. commit

Foundation Topics

Virtualization Technologies

Virtualization technologies play a major role in modern computing environments, revolutionizing the way resources are used and managed. Virtualization enables creation of virtual instances of operating systems, servers, storage, or networks on a single physical hardware platform. This technology optimizes resource utilization, enhances scalability, and simplifies management to allow multiple virtual environments to coexist independently. Hypervisors, the core components of virtualization, facilitate the allocation of resources and isolation between virtual instances. Moreover, virtualization contributes significantly to cost reduction because it minimizes the need for dedicated hardware and provides a flexible infrastructure that adapts to varying workloads. Cloud computing heavily relies on virtualization to deliver on-demand services, and its applications extend to areas such as server virtualization, desktop virtualization, and network virtualization, fostering efficiency and agility in diverse computing landscapes.

NFV Infrastructure

Network Functions Virtualization Infrastructure (**NFVI**) is a solution provided by Cisco to enable service providers to deploy and manage network functions more efficiently. It integrates open-source hardware and software components with a certified design for superior throughput and performance. It ensures carrier-grade high availability and offers automated deployment on day zero, along with intelligent operation tools for day one to two activities. Notable attributes and benefits of the Cisco NFVI solution include

- **Optimized architecture:**

    - Specialized for virtualized service delivery

    - Designed to support NFV evolution, optimized investment

    - Integrated solution that avoids risks and cost

    - Scale to support edge architecture with centralized storage and management

    - Network data center SDN that supports bare-metal, OpenStack, and Kubernetes

- **Simplified operations:**

    - Fully instrumental for carrier class operations

    - Simple, automated installation inclusive of hardware and OpenStack services

    - Designed for reliable upgrade with telemetry and visibility to identify hot spots

    - Simplified E2E operation and complexity of virtualization

- **Faster service delivery and time-to-market:**

    - Modular design for rapid and efficient deployment

    - Integrated, validated, and certified design reduces deployment from month to weeks

    - Hardware and software upgrades made modular and simpler

    - General multivendor and open-source NFV

Figure 3-1 illustrates the scope of Cisco's NFVI solution.

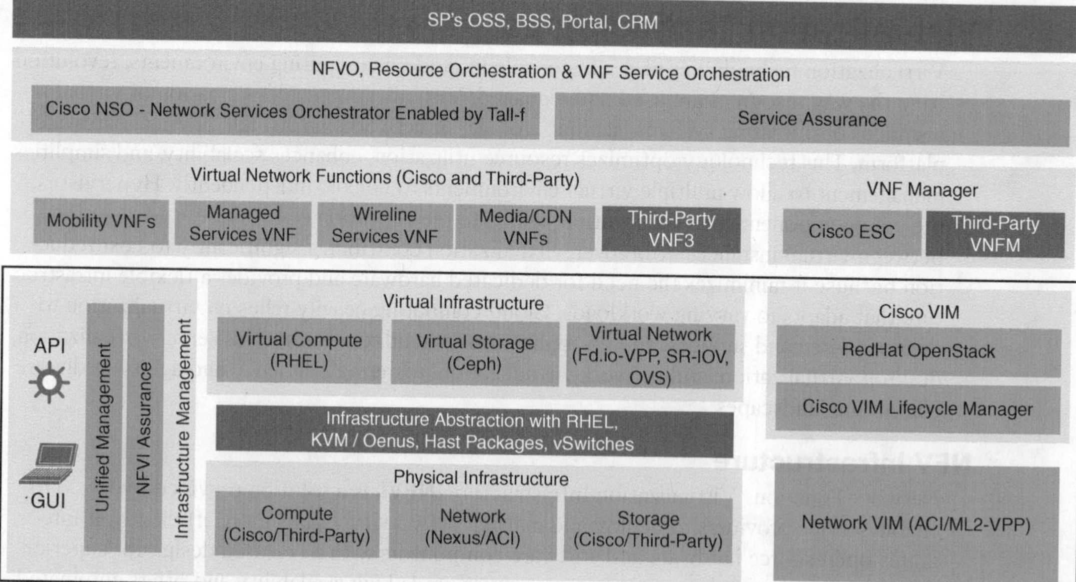

Figure 3-1   *Scope of Cisco NFVI Solution*

The components of the NFVI Solutions are

- **Cisco Virtualized Infrastructure Manager (VIM):** This full lifecycle management tool for software and hardware is used to control and manage your NFVI compute, storage, and network resources.

- **Cisco UCS Servers:** NFVI servers are the best-in-class Cisco UCS rack and blade servers that provide high levels of scalability and availability.

- **Cisco Nexus Switches:** These data center switches are built for scale, industry-leading automation, programmability, and real-time visibility.

- **Cisco Mass Scale Routers:** These routers provide an advanced routing portfolio with multidimensional programmability.

VNF Workloads

A virtual network function (**VNF**) is the software-based counterpart of a hardware device's network function. These are accessible in the form of virtual machines (VMs) or containers, offering flexibility and scalability in network deployment and management. Instead of being tied to a specific element of hardware, they have been turned into software applications that run on a virtual machine, container, or cloud infrastructure.

The term **VNF workloads** refers to the amount of processing the computer has been tasked with. Some examples of Cisco's implementations are as follows:

- Cloud Services Platform (CSP) 2100 (reached end-of-sale status)

- vEdge Cloud (reached end-of-sale status)

- CSR1000v (reached end-of-sale status)

- ASAv

- XRv 9000

- Nexus 9000v

- Cisco 8000v

- Cisco c8000v

- Firepower FTDv

- Web Security Virtual Appliance (WSAv)

- Email Security Virtual Appliance

- Advanced Malware Protection Virtual (AMPv)

Containers

A container is a unit of lightweight, executable software that packages application code and its dependencies in a standardized way. This packaging allows an application to be mobile and executed across different locations. The container image contains all the information for the container to run, such as application code, operating system, and other dependencies (e.g., libraries).

There are a number of container engines such as Docker, RKT (pronounced "rocket," from Red Hat), LXD (Linux containers), among others. Container engines can run on any container host, such as on a laptop, on a data center physical server, or in the public cloud. **Kubernetes** is an open-source orchestration platform designed to automate deploying, scaling, and managing containerized applications.

Containers and virtual machines are often compared due to their similarities, but they serve different purposes. While VMs abstract an entire operating system from the physical server, containers provide an environment for executing application code. Just as VM hypervisors virtualize hardware to host multiple isolated operating systems, container engines virtualize the operating system to host multiple isolated applications. Containers are typically smaller in size than VMs because they are tailored for running applications and package only essential data and executables. One notable concept introduced by containers is immutability. Unlike VMs, containers do not require regular updates or patches. Instead, any updates necessitate replacing the existing container with a new one.

Containers offer significant advantages to both developers and IT operations teams, primarily through consistency and reduced overhead. Containerized applications operate independently from both virtualized and physical infrastructure, enabling developers to modify their code and incorporate new dependencies seamlessly into updated containers. To put this concept into perspective, one of the engineers on my team (Brad's team) used containerlab (https:// containerlab.dev/) to stand up 10 of the latest virtual Cisco 8202 routers (32×400G each). How long would it take us to cable, load, and pay for this massive amount of expensive hardware? It took him only 20 minutes and 130 GB of memory on a Cisco UCS chassis (see Figure 3-2).

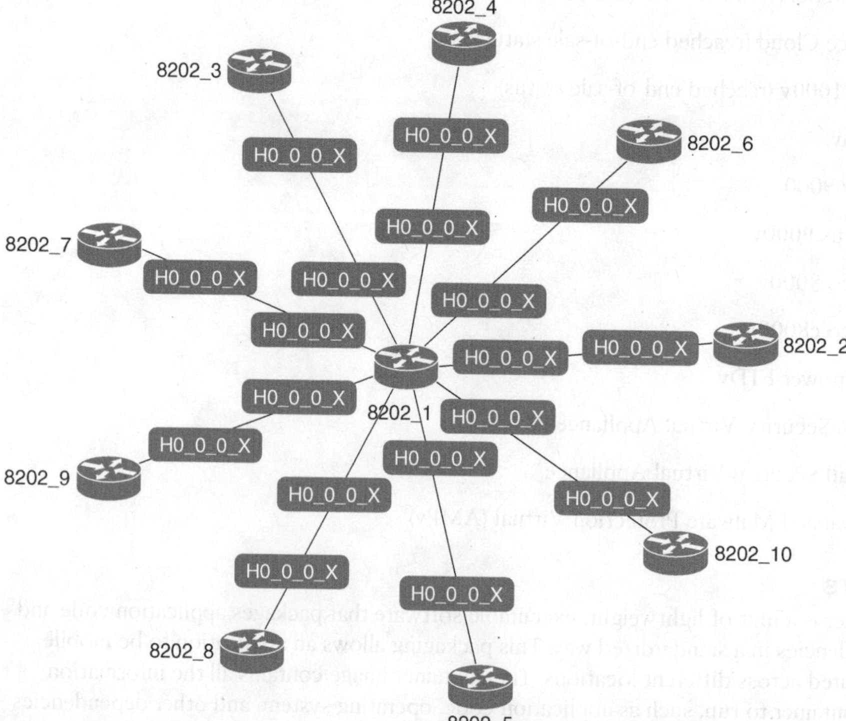

Figure 3-2 *Containerlab 10 Routers in 20 Minutes*

Docker is an open-source platform licensed under Apache, designed for developing, packaging, and deploying applications within containers. It distinguishes applications from infrastructure by furnishing a comprehensive suite of tools for orchestrating and overseeing containers that support various services. In addition to furnishing a container runtime, Docker offers tooling and a platform for overseeing the complete lifecycle of containerized applications. Understanding container technologies is valuable because they are widely deployed across various industries and applications.

As an example, the PON Controller software that I mentioned in the "xPON" section in Chapter 1, runs in a Docker container on NCS routers. It's essential to familiarize yourself with Docker commands because they are frequently tested in the exams. Example 3-1 includes some fundamental Docker commands that you should know.

Example 3-1   *Using Docker to View PON Controller on Cisco NCS-55A2*

```
RP/0/RP0/CPU0:PON-OLT1# run
Thu Apr 25 09:06:59.685 CDT
[xr-vm_node0_RP0_CPU0:~]$ docker ps
CONTAINER ID    IMAGE              COMM          CREATED      STATUS        PORTS       NAMES
8fe6b60b494c    tibit-poncntl.xr:R4.0.0   "/usr/bin/supervisor…"   4 weeks ago    Up 2
weeks           pon_ctlr
[xr-vm_node0_RP0_CPU0:~]$ docker --help
Usage:  docker [OPTIONS] COMMAND
A self-sufficient runtime for containers
Options:
      --config string       Location of client config files (default "/disk0:/.docker")
  -c, --context string      Name of the context to use to connect to the daemon
(overrides DOCKER_HOST env var and
                            default context set with "docker context use")
  -D, --debug               Enable debug mode
  -H, --host list           Daemon socket(s) to connect to
  -l, --log-level string    Set the logging level ("debug"|"info"|"warn"|"error"|
"fatal") (default "info")
      --tls                 Use TLS; implied by --tlsverify
      --tlscacert string    Trust certs signed only by this CA (default "/disk0:/.
docker/ca.pem")
      --tlscert string      Path to TLS certificate file (default "/disk0:/.docker/
cert.pem")
      --tlskey string       Path to TLS key file (default "/disk0:/.docker/key.pem")
      --tlsverify           Use TLS and verify the remote
  -v, --version             Print version information and quit


Management Commands:
  builder     Manage builds
  config      Manage Docker configs
  container   Manage containers
  context     Manage contexts
  image       Manage images
```

```
  manifest    Manage Docker image manifests and manifest lists
  network     Manage networks
  node        Manage Swarm nodes
  plugin      Manage plugins
  secret      Manage Docker secrets
  service     Manage services
  stack       Manage Docker stacks
  swarm       Manage Swarm
  system      Manage Docker
  trust       Manage trust on Docker images
  volume      Manage volumes

Commands:
  attach      Attach local standard input, output, and error streams to a running
container
  build       Build an image from a Dockerfile
  commit      Create a new image from a container's changes
  cp          Copy files/folders between a container and the local filesystem
  create      Create a new container
  diff        Inspect changes to files or directories on a container's filesystem
  events      Get real time events from the server
  exec        Run a command in a running container
  export      Export a container's filesystem as a tar archive
  history     Show the history of an image
  images      List images
  import      Import the contents from a tarball to create a filesystem image
  info        Display system-wide information
  inspect     Return low-level information on Docker objects
  kill        Kill one or more running containers
  load        Load an image from a tar archive or STDIN
  login       Log in to a Docker registry
  logout      Log out from a Docker registry
  logs        Fetch the logs of a container
  pause       Pause all processes within one or more containers
  port        List port mappings or a specific mapping for the container
  ps          List containers
  pull        Pull an image or a repository from a registry
  push        Push an image or a repository to a registry
  rename      Rename a container
  restart     Restart one or more containers
  rm          Remove one or more containers
  rmi         Remove one or more images
  run         Run a command in a new container
  save        Save one or more images to a tar archive (streamed to STDOUT by default)
  search      Search the Docker Hub for images
```

```
start           Start one or more stopped containers
stats           Display a live stream of container(s) resource usage statistics
stop            Stop one or more running containers
tag             Create a tag TARGET_IMAGE that refers to SOURCE_IMAGE
top             Display the running processes of a container
unpause         Unpause all processes within one or more containers
update          Update configuration of one or more containers
version         Show the Docker version information
wait            Block until one or more containers stop, then print their exit codes

Run 'docker COMMAND --help' for more information on a command.
To get more help with docker, check out our guides at https://docs.docker.com/go/guides/
[xr-vm_node0_RP0_CPU0:~]$ docker logs pon_ctlr --tail 50
        "ONUs": {
            "CIGG21b00cb2": "Registered"

        }

    }

}
2024-04-25 13:15:40.244         PonCntl         System Status
{

    "ac:89:d2:c4:d2:36": {

        "OLT State": "Unspecified",

        "ONU Active Count": 1,

        "ONUs": {

            "CIGG21b00cb2": "Registered"

        }

    }

}
2024-04-25 13:22:00.579 NOTICE   PonCntl         OLT ac:89:d2:c4:d2:36
ONU CIGG21b00cb2  MIB Upload Needed - Refresh Interval expired
2024-04-25 13:22:00.595 INFO     TAPI            ONU CIGG21b00cb2
Uploading MIB: 242 commands
2024-04-25 13:22:03.531 INFO     TAPI            ONU CIGG21b00cb2    MIB Upload complete
2024-04-25 13:22:03.656 ERROR    TAPI            ONU CIGG21b00cb2
Unknown Entity error getting OMCI ME Class: Omci ID: 0
2024-04-25 13:22:03.664 ERROR    TAPI            ONU CIGG21b00cb2
Unknown Entity error getting OMCI ME Class: Omci ID: 0
2024-04-25 13:30:44.070         PonCntl         System Status
{

    "ac:89:d2:c4:d2:36": {

        "OLT State": "Unspecified",

        "ONU Active Count": 1,

        "ONUs": {

            "CIGG21b00cb2": "Registered"

        }

    }

}
```

```
2024-04-25 13:45:50.899              PonCntl        System Status
{
    "ac:89:d2:c4:d2:36": {
        "OLT State": "Unspecified",
        "ONU Active Count": 1,
        "ONUs": {
            "CIGG21b00cb2": "Registered"
        }
    }
}
2024-04-25 14:00:51.012              PonCntl        System Status
{
    "ac:89:d2:c4:d2:36": {
        "OLT State": "Unspecified",
        "ONU Active Count": 1,
        "ONUs": {
            "CIGG21b00cb2": "Registered"
        }
    }
}
[xr-vm_node0_RP0_CPU0:~]$
```

In this example, first, you enter the **run** command to launch the IOS XR Linux bash shell and highlight the most useful Docker commands at the top of the root of the command hierarchy. Then you look at the last 50 lines of the log file to retrieve ONU registrations.

Application Hosting

Container application hosting makes it possible for applications to be hosted in their own environment and process space (namespace) containers on both IOS and Cisco IOS XR. Over time, I've encountered a diverse array of instances involving the deployment of applications on Cisco routers and switches—from running iperf test performance tools to Wireshark packet captures to more sophisticated IoT room temperature sensors, the PON controller in the previous example, and Radware containers that now run DDoS protection directly on Cisco IOS XR routers. In the virtualization realm, Cisco routers boast significant potential, with uncharted territories awaiting exploration—though, of course, fueled by RAM, disk space, and a hearty dose of imagination and determination to reach your networking goals. Example 3-2 demonstrates running the Wireshark application on an IOS router.

Example 3-2 *Running Wireshark on an IOS Router*

```
PE2# show app-hosting detail


State                       : Running
Author                      : Cisco Systems, Inc
Application
  Type                      : vm
  App id                    : Wireshark
  Name                      : Wireshark
```

```
 Version                    : 3.4
 Activated Profile Name     : custom
 Description                : Ubuntu based Wireshark
Resource Reservation
 Memory                     : 1900 MB
 Disk                       : 10 MB
 CPU                        : 4000 units
 VCPU                       : 2
Attached devices
 Type          Name          Alias
-----------------------------------------------------------------
Serial/shell
Serial/aux
Serial/Syslog               serial2
Serial/Trace                serial3
Network Interfaces
-----------------------------------------------------------------
eth0:
 MAC address                : 52:54:dd:80:bd:59
 IPv4 address
eth1:
 MAC address                : 52:54:dd:c7:7c:aa
 IPv4 address
```

Example 3-3 demonstrates running **iperf** on an IOS XR router. Again, observe the use of the **run** command to access the Linux bash shell to access the container and finally launch the application itself.

Example 3-3 *Running* **iperf** *in a Docker Container on ASR9K*

```
RP/0/RP0/CPU0:PE3# run
[xr-vm_node0_RP0_CPU0:~]$ virsh -c lxc+tcp://10.1.99.50:16509/ -e ^Q console spcor
Connected to domain spcor
Escape character is ^Q
Kernel 3.14.23-WR7.0.0.2_standard on an x86_64

host login: Password:

[root@host ~]# iperf -v
iperf version 2.0.13 (01 Jul 2018) pthreads
[root@host ~]# iperf -s -B 10.100.100.3 -p 5001

Server listening on TCP port 5001
TCP window size: 85.3 KByte (default)
-----------------------------------------------------------------
[  4] local 10.100.100.3 port 5001 connected with 10.1.23.100 port 53710
[ ID] Interval       Transfer     Bandwidth
[  4]  0.0-10.0 sec  1.09 GBytes   939 Mbits/sec
```

A comprehensive understanding of containers can prove invaluable for success in this exam. Given their widespread adoption and pivotal role in modern software development and deployment practices, having a nuanced grasp of container technologies offers a significant advantage. Familiarity with container concepts, orchestration platforms, and associated tools not only enhances your proficiency in managing complex IT environments but also demonstrates your adaptability and readiness to tackle contemporary challenges.

Exam Preparation Tasks

As mentioned in the section "How to Use This Book" in the Introduction, you have a few choices for exam preparation: the exercises here, Chapter 23, "Final Preparation," and the exam simulation questions in the Pearson Test Prep Software Online.

Review All Key Topics

Review the most important topics in this chapter, noted with the Key Topic icon in the margin of the page. Table 3-2 lists a reference of these key topics and the page numbers on which each is found.

Table 3-2   Key Topics for Chapter 3

Key Topic Element	Description	Page Number
Figure 3-1	Scope of Cisco NFVI Solution	62
List	Components of VNF workloads	63

Define Key Terms

Define the following key terms from this chapter and check the answers in the glossary:

Containers, Docker, Kubernetes, NFVI, VIM, VNF, VNF workload

Command Reference to Check Your Memory

This section includes the most important configuration and EXEC commands covered in this chapter. It might not be necessary to memorize the complete syntax of every command, but you should be able to remember the basic keywords that are needed.

To test your memory of the commands, cover the right side of Table 3-3 with a piece of paper, read the description on the left side, and then see how much of the command you can remember.

The 350-501 exam focuses on practical, hands-on skills that are used by networking professionals. Therefore, you should be able to identify the commands needed to configure and test. Note that not all commands are fully covered in the chapter, but their presence in the following table should lead you to investigate them further to understand this technology.

Table 3-3   CLI Commands to Know

Task	Command Syntax
Launch the IOS XR Linux bash shell	RP/0/RP0/CPU0:Router# **run**
List the currently running Docker containers on your system	[xr-vm_node0_RP0_CPU0:~]$ **docker ps**
Display a summary of available Docker commands and their options	[xr-vm_node0_RP0_CPU0:~]$ **docker --help**
Display detailed information about the currently hosted applications on IOS routers	Router# PE2# **show app-hosting detail**
Start one or more stopped containers	[xr-vm_node0_RP0_CPU0:~]$ **docker start**
Stop one or more running containers	[xr-vm_node0_RP0_CPU0:~]$ **docker stop**

Review Questions

As a part of the review, we encourage you to provide *a single-sentence answer* (keep your answers as short as possible) to the following questions. If you struggle to complete this answer in a single sentence, this may indicate a lack of clarity or reveal gaps in your understanding. We have constructed these questions to help you consolidate this chapter's information and extract the essence of the covered content.

The answers to these questions appear in Appendix A. For more practice with exam format questions, use the Pearson Test Prep Software Online.

1. Can you explain the architectural components and deployment considerations of Virtualized Network Function Infrastructure (VNFI) in the context of software-defined networking (SDN) and network function virtualization (NFV) environments?

2. What is the difference between **docker create** and **docker start** commands?

3. What are the key challenges and strategies for hosting and managing containerized applications on Cisco IOS XR-based devices in service provider networks?

4. Do Cisco routers run Kubernetes by default?

## CHAPTER 4

Routing Fundamentals

This chapter covers the following exam topic:

2.5 Implement routing policy language and route maps (BGP, OSPF, IS-IS)

IP routing refers to the process of forwarding data packets from one network device to another. This process involves routers or Layer 3 switches making decisions about the best path for packet delivery by consulting routing tables, which contain information about network destinations and the next hops to reach them. IP routing enables communication between devices on different networks and forms the foundation of inter-network communication on the Internet and other TCP/IP-based networks.

"Do I Know This Already?" Quiz

The "Do I Know This Already?" quiz allows you to assess whether you should read this entire chapter thoroughly or jump to the "Exam Preparation Tasks" section. If you are in doubt about your answers to these questions or your own assessment of your knowledge of the topics, read the entire chapter. Table 4-1 lists the major headings in this chapter and their corresponding "Do I Know This Already?" quiz questions. You can find the answers in Appendix A, "Answers to the 'Do I Know This Already?' Quizzes and Review Questions."

Table 4-1 "Do I Know This Already?" Section-to-Question Mapping

Foundation Topics Section	Questions
IP Routing	1–3
Route Maps	3–6
Route Policy Language (RPL)	6–9
Prefix Lists	10

CAUTION The goal of self-assessment is to gauge your mastery of the topics in this chapter. If you do not know the answer to a question or are only partially sure of the answer, you should mark that question as wrong for purposes of the self-assessment. Giving yourself credit for an answer you correctly guess skews your self-assessment results and might provide you with a false sense of security.

1. In OSPF, what specific advantage does the link-state routing algorithm offer over traditional distance-vector routing protocols?

  a. Provides better compatibility with legacy routing equipment

  b. Requires less CPU and memory resources compared to distance-vector protocols

    c. Offers faster convergence, loop-free topology, and efficient resource utilization

    d. Offers simpler configuration and management compared to other routing protocols

2. What specific advantage does IS-IS offer over OSPF in terms of scalability and hierarchical design?

    a. Provides faster convergence due to its optimized routing algorithm

    b. Offers superior scalability and hierarchical design because of its efficient use of TLVs (Type-Length-Value) and support for multiple network topologies

    c. Offers better support for MPLS traffic engineering

    d. Requires less administrative overhead and is easier to configure

3. What specific advantage does BGP offer over interior routing protocols like OSPF and IS-IS in terms of its ability to scale and support diverse network topologies?

    a. It provides faster convergence due to its advanced routing algorithms.

    b. The advantage is in the inter-domain routing, policy-based routing approach and support for multiple path attributes.

    c. It provides better support for MPLS traffic engineering.

    d. It requires less administrative overhead and is easier to configure.

4. The global route map feature is supported in which of the following Cisco OS versions? (Select all that apply.)

    a. IOS

    b. IOS XE

    c. NX-OS

    d. IOS XR

5. In Boolean logic, what is the result of an OR operation when one operand is *true* and the other is *false*?

    a. Undefined

    b. Null

    c. True

    d. False

6. What is true regarding sequence numbers in a route map and how they affect the processing order of route map entries in a routing configuration?

    a. They are randomly assigned and do not impact the processing order.

    b. They are processed alphabetically, based on their names rather than their sequence numbers.

    c. Higher sequence numbers indicate a higher priority, causing those entries to be evaluated first in the route map processing order.

    d. They determine the order in which route map entries are processed with lower sequence numbers evaluated first.

7. In Boolean logic, what is the result of an AND operation when one operand is *true* and the other is *false*?

   a. False

   b. True

   c. Undefined

   d. Null

8. Which of the following are valid actions in an RPL policy? (Select all that apply.)

   a. Pass

   b. Redirect

   c. Done

   d. Modify

9. RPL is based on which programming logic?

   a. while loops

   b. do-while loops

   c. for loops

   d. if-then statements

10. In the prefix list entry 10.0.0.0/16 ge 24, "ge 24" specifies that the correct prefix length must be which of the following?

   a. Exactly 24 bits, so routes with a prefix length longer than 24 bits will not be permitted.

   b. Less than 24 bits will be permitted because they are greater than or equal to 24.

   c. Greater than or equal to 24 bits will be permitted.

   d. There must be greater than or equal to 24 bits, so routes with a prefix length of exactly 24 bits will be permitted.

Foundation Topics

IP Routing

The fundamental job of a network router is to forward data packets between different networks, ensuring that packets reach their intended destinations efficiently and accurately. Routers make decisions based on the destination IP address of each packet, consulting their routing tables to determine the best path for packet delivery. They are responsible for directing traffic, managing network congestion, and maintaining communication between devices on separate networks, enabling inter-network connectivity and facilitating data exchange across the Internet and other network infrastructures.

The service provider routing environment is rigorous and demanding, requiring the highest level of networking expertise. It is a less forgiving landscape, where the slightest misconfiguration or oversight can have significant consequences. Service providers operate at large scales, handling vast amounts of traffic and supporting critical services. Network engineers must navigate complex infrastructures, optimize routing protocols, and troubleshoot issues swiftly and effectively. The reliability and performance of the network are paramount, with downtime or disruptions posing substantial risks to both the provider's reputation and customers' experience. In this challenging environment, mastery of networking fundamentals, meticulous attention to detail, and the ability to adapt quickly to evolving technologies are essential for success.

A fundamental block of router instructions is static routing, which involves manually configuring routes on network devices. Administrators specify the routes directly by entering static route commands into the device's configuration. Once configured, static routes do not change unless explicitly modified by the administrator. This method is suitable for smaller networks or those with simple, stable topologies where network changes are infrequent. Static routing imposes less overhead on network devices and is simpler to configure compared to dynamic routing protocols and is predictable.

In contrast, dynamic routing protocols automatically discover and update routing information based on network changes. Routers exchange routing updates with neighboring routers to learn about reachable networks and determine the best paths to reach them. Routes are dynamically learned and adjusted, providing flexibility and scalability. Dynamic routing is well suited for larger networks or those with complex, dynamic topologies where network changes occur frequently. While dynamic routing offers benefits such as faster convergence and better fault tolerance, it requires more overhead on network devices and more complex configuration compared to static routing.

Distance-vector routing algorithms (which are older), such as the Routing Information Protocol (RIP), lost their luster and appeal due to growing networking demands, operated by routers exchanging routing information with their neighboring routers. Each router maintained a table containing distance estimates (typically hop counts) to all known destinations. Periodically, routers sent updates containing their routing table to neighboring routers. Upon receiving an update, a router updated its own routing table based on the information received. The router then advertised its updated table to its neighbors, and this process continued until convergence was reached. Distance-vector algorithms relied on the principle of each router sharing its routing table with its neighbors, allowing them to collectively build a view of the network topology. However, they had limitations such as slow convergence and the potential for routing loops. To mitigate these issues, techniques like split horizon and poison reverse were employed. Despite their limitations, distance-vector algorithms were relatively simple to implement and were suitable for small to medium-sized networks with low to moderate traffic.

Enhanced distance-vector routing algorithms, such as the Enhanced Interior Gateway Routing Protocol (EIGRP), improved the shortcomings of traditional distance-vector algorithms while retaining their simplicity. EIGRP introduces several enhancements, including faster convergence, loop prevention mechanisms, and support for variable-length subnet masks (VLSMs) and classless inter-domain routing (CIDR). One key enhancement of EIGRP is the use of the diffusing update algorithm (DUAL) to achieve rapid convergence by minimizing the propagation of routing updates when network topology changes occur. DUAL allows routers to quickly update their routing tables without waiting for periodic updates or full routing table exchanges. EIGRP provided the benefits of traditional distance-vector protocols with added features for faster convergence, loop prevention, and support for modern networking practices.

In service provider networks, link-state routing algorithms, such as the Open Shortest Path First (OSPF) and Intermediate System to Intermediate System (IS-IS) protocols, dominate routing preferences. These two protocols are used for building the service provider underlay networks and play a crucial role in efficiently routing traffic across complex network infrastructures. Link-state algorithms operate by routers exchanging information about the state of their directly connected links with neighboring routers. Each router constructs a detailed view of the entire network topology based on the received link-state advertisements (LSAs) or link-state packets (LSPs). This view includes information about neighboring routers, link costs, and network topology changes. Where scalability, fast convergence, reliability, loop-free routing, traffic engineering, and efficient resource utilization are paramount, link-state routing algorithms offer several advantages—making them a cornerstone of modern Internet routing infrastructure. IS-IS has been around in service provider networks for a long time primarily due to its efficient use of **TLVs** (Type-Length-Value) and support for multiple network topologies.

The path vector routing algorithm, the Border Gateway Protocol (BGP), is instrumental in facilitating inter-domain routing and connecting disparate networks across the Internet.

Path vector algorithms differ from distance-vector and link-state algorithms in that they track the path, or sequence of autonomous systems (ASes), through which routing updates traverse to reach a destination network. Instead of solely relying on metrics like hop count or link costs, path vector protocols consider policies and attributes associated with each route, making them well suited for routing between autonomous systems with diverse policies and preferences. In service provider networks, BGP is the primary path vector protocol. Key characteristics of BGP in service provider environments are inter-domain routing, enforcing policy controls, and maintaining the stability and security of the global Internet routing infrastructure.

Changing Natural Routing Protocol Behaviors

On the exam, significant focus is placed on Intermediate System to Intermediate System (IS-IS), Open Shortest Path First (OSPF), and Border Gateway Protocol (BGP). While we dedicate extensive coverage to understanding their functionalities in the following chapters, an essential aspect of assessment will be your proficiency in manipulating these protocols using route maps and Route Policy Language (RPL). A good network engineer is skilled in these techniques, so we start with it first before diving into the intricacies of the protocols themselves.

Route maps and RPL play a critical role in configuring and controlling the behavior of routing protocols in network environments. They both provide a flexible framework for defining policies that influence how routing updates are processed, filtered, redistributed, and manipulated within a network. They are commonly used in conjunction with routing protocols such as OSPF, BGP, and IS-IS. Here's how they relate to these protocols:

In **BGP**, they are extensively used to manipulate BGP routing information, apply inbound and outbound filtering, modify BGP attributes, and control route redistribution between BGP and other routing protocols. They allow network administrators to define complex policies based on BGP attributes (such as as-path, next-hop, and community values) and route attributes to influence BGP route selection and propagation decisions.

In **OSPF**, they are used to filter and manipulate OSPF routing updates, control redistribution of routes between OSPF and other routing protocols, and adjust OSPF metric values. They enable administrators to implement fine-grained filtering based on IP prefix, route type, or other criteria, as well as to modify OSPF attributes like administrative distance and cost.

In **IS-IS**, they are used to filter, manipulate, and redistribute IS-IS routing information, control route redistribution with other routing protocols, adjust metrics, and implement route summarization. They are typically applied at the boundary between different routing domains or at the edge of the network where routing information is exchanged with other protocols such as OSPF or BGP. These policies allow network administrators to enforce routing policies, optimize routing behavior, and ensure proper routing convergence and stability in IS-IS networks.

Route Maps

A *route map* (or *route-map* in the configuration files) in Cisco IOS (not IOS XR) network devices is a configuration tool that enables you to define a set of sequential rules or statements (each with a permit or deny condition) which select components and prescribe enhanced intended behavior.

Example 4-1 demonstrates a basic route map.

Example 4-1   *Basic Route Map Template*

```
P4# show running-config | begin route-map
route-map RULES permit 10
 match ip address 110
!
route-map RULES deny 20
 match ip address 120
!
route-map RULES permit 30
 match ip address 130
 continue 50
!
route-map RULES permit 40
 match ip address 140
 set local-preference 200
!
route-map RULES permit 50
```

Carefully study Example 4-1, which shows a basic route map configured on one the routers you will see later. Follow this route map's structure and logic with the following top-10 list.

Sequence matters because route maps are read from top to bottom.

1. If you fail to provide a sequence number, sequence number 10 will be used and will not increment if you repeat the entry (you will end up overwriting the previous entry).

2. If there is a match, the route map will stop processing the entries below. If sequence 10 matches access-list 110, the route map will not examine sequences 20, 30, 40, and 50.

3. In sequence 10, access-list 110 matching entries will be permitted (and route map processing stops).

4. In sequence 20, access-list 120 matching entries will be denied (and route map processing stops).

5. In sequence 30, access-list 130 matching entries will be permitted, and the continue clause will jump to sequence 50, skipping sequence 40.

6. In sequence 40 (if sequence 30 had no match, that is), access-list 140 matching entries will be permitted, and the local-preference attribute (for BGP) will be modified (and route map processing stops).

7. In sequence 50, because the match statement is absent, it will match all prefixes.

8. If sequence 50 were not present, all prefixes after sequence 40 would be implicitly denied.

9. If you delete a specific route map statement and do not include its sequence number, you will delete the entire route map.

10. If you do not specify a match (as in sequence 50), an all-match will be presumed. In all previous sequences, a single example of conditional matching was used because of the conditional selection.

Example 4-2 shows a full list of possible route map conditional matches. Study them to understand what is available, but you don't need to memorize them. I have highlighted the ones I have seen used more frequently than others.

Example 4-2 *Route Map Conditional Matching Options*

```
P4(config-route-map)# match ?
  additional-paths  BGP Add-Path match policies
  address           Match address of route or match packet
  as-path           Match BGP AS path list
  clns              CLNS information
  community         Match BGP community list
  extcommunity      Match BGP/VPN extended community list
  interface         Match first hop interface of route
  ip                IP specific information
  ipv6              IPv6 specific information
  length            Packet length
  local-preference  Local preference for route
  mdt-group         Match routes corresponding to MDT group
  metric            Match metric of route
  mpls-label        Match routes which have MPLS labels
  next-hop          Match next-hop address of route
  nlri              BGP NLRI type
  omp-tag           Match OMP tag of route
  policy-list       Match IP policy list
  route-source      Match advertising source address of route
  route-type        Match route-type of route
  rpki              Match RPKI state of route
  security-group    Security Group
  source-protocol   Match source-protocol of route
  tag               Match tag of route
  track             tracking object
```

Example 4-3 shows complex matching you can accomplish with route maps. What do you suppose they do? Be aware that in both IOS and IOS XR, you can issue EXEC level commands from the Global Configuration mode by prepending **do** in front of the command. This approach can certainly save you time, but you must be careful, particularly in IOS when every command followed by the Enter key will go into immediate effect. For this reason, I advise you to be extremely careful with what you type from the Global Configuration mode. On production networks, I strongly advise against this approach because the risk of making a mistake is high, even among the most seasoned engineers.

Example 4-3 *Route Map Conditional Matching with Multiple Entries*

```
P4(config-route-map)# do show running-config | begin route-map
route-map COMPLEX-RULES permit 10
 match ip address 110 120
!
route-map COMPLEX-RULES permit 20
 match ip next-hop 10
 match mpls-label
```

In Example 4-3, sequence 10 shows two access lists specified in a single line. Multiple variables of the same type are permitted, and a **Boolean or** operator is used, meaning that matches can come from entries in access-list 110 or access-list 120. Sequence 20 has two separate lines with two different match types, and a Boolean **and** operator is used, meaning that a match of the next hop specified in access-list 10 and presence of an MPLS label are *both* required for the match to occur.

Example 4-4 shows a wide variety of actions you can take on matched components. I highlighted the options I have most frequently encountered in customer networks.

Example 4-4 *Taking an Action on Matched Components*

```
P4(config-route-map)# set ?
  aigp-metric      accumulated metric value
  as-path          Modify BGP AS-path attribute
  attribute-set    Set attribute
  automatic-tag    Automatically compute TAG value
  clns             OSI summary address
  comm-list        set BGP community list (for deletion)
  community        BGP community attribute
  dampening        Set BGP route flap dampening parameters
  default          Set default information
  extcomm-list     Set BGP/VPN extended community list (for deletion)
  extcommunity     BGP extended community attribute
  global           Set to global routing table
  interface        Output interface
  ip               IP specific information
  ipv6             IPv6 specific information
  level            Where to import route
```

```
lisp                 Locator ID Separation Protocol specific information
local-preference     BGP local preference path attribute
metric               Metric value for destination routing protocol
metric-type          Type of metric for destination routing protocol
mpls-label           Set MPLS label for prefix
nlri                 BGP NLRI type
omp-tag              OMP Tag value for destination routing protocol
origin               BGP origin code
overlay-summary      Set overlay summary
tag                  Tag value for destination routing protocol
traffic-index        BGP traffic classification number for accounting
vrf                  Define VRF name
weight               BGP weight for routing table
```

I would like to show you a couple of examples and suggest you do something similar in your lab or environment. I grabbed an arbitrary topology that will be used later in the chapter and created a quick scenario to modify. You can do the same.

In Example 4-5, notice all the IS-IS routes, particularly the one at the bottom that I chose and highlighted for your convenience. The network is 10.100.0.0, the third octet shows a connection between router 4 and 5, and the last octet shows the router number (it ends in 5, so it is router P5). This example shows the output of P4, where route 10.100.100.7/32 from P7 comes through two different interfaces (through PE6 and P5).

Example 4-5   *IS-IS Topology Before a Route Map Is Applied*

```
P4(config-router)# do show ip route isis
! Output omitted for brevity
      10.0.0.0/8 is variably subnetted, 17 subnets, 2 masks
i L2     10.100.23.0/24  [115/20] via 10.100.34.3, 00:00:24, GigabitEthernet2
i L2     10.100.35.0/24  [115/20] via 10.100.45.5, 00:00:24, GigabitEthernet1
i L2     10.100.57.0/24  [115/20] via 10.100.45.5, 00:00:24, GigabitEthernet1
i L2     10.100.67.0/24  [115/20] via 10.100.46.6, 00:00:24, GigabitEthernet3
i L2     10.100.100.3/32 [115/10] via 10.100.34.3, 00:00:24, GigabitEthernet2
i L2     10.100.100.5/32 [115/10] via 10.100.45.5, 00:00:24, GigabitEthernet1
i L2     10.100.100.6/32 [115/20] via 10.100.46.6, 00:00:24, GigabitEthernet3
i L2     10.100.100.7/32 [115/20] via 10.100.46.6, 00:00:24, GigabitEthernet3
                         [115/20] via 10.100.45.5, 00:00:24, GigabitEthernet1
```

Now you can test a couple of route maps. First, manipulate the routing table (RIB) to present P5 as the next hop for this route. You can match it with the route map in Example 4-6.

Example 4-6   *Applying a Route Map to IS-IS*

```
router isis
 net 49.0002.0101.0010.0004.00
 metric-style wide
 distribute-list route-map PREFER-P5 in
!
ip access-list standard 10
 10 permit 10.100.100.7
ip access-list standard 11
 10 permit 10.100.45.5
!
route-map PREFER-P5 permit 10
 match ip address 10
!
route-map PREFER-P5 permit 20
 match ip address 11
```

While looking at Example 4-6 and *before* looking at the output in Example 4-7, can you answer what this route map will accomplish? Take your time, you should not be in a hurry. After you have read it, you should realize that there are two access lists: one to select the 10.10.100.7 route from router PE7 and the second one to select where the route is coming from. It should be the next hop of 10.100.45.5, even though the same route is also advertised from 10.100.46.6. The route map should prefer P5 (10.100.45.5) because it is attached to the IS-IS distribute list that controls the IS-IS routing table. Is there anything else you can observe from what you have already learned today? Imagine what P4's routing table will look like.

Now, let's examine the result of applying the route map in Example 4-7.

Example 4-7   *The Results of Applying the Route Map*

```
P4(config-router)# do show ip route isis
! Output omitted for brevity
      10.0.0.0/8 is variably subnetted, 10 subnets, 2 masks
i L2     10.100.100.7/32 [115/20] via 10.100.46.6, 00:49:48, GigabitEthernet3
                         [115/20] via 10.100.45.5, 00:49:48, GigabitEthernet1
```

I wonder what routes you expected to see. It looks as though the route map had different results than I intended. Do not be alarmed if you got this wrong. It happens to all of us, even those who are skilled; that's why it's always good to test how a route map works. Routers do not think like humans, and we need to learn to think like routers. First, P5 is not preferred, and the route to PE7 shows up as before with two paths. Second, the rest of the IS-IS routes are gone. If you think about it, we told the router to do something, and it did so according to the rules described earlier. What went wrong? A couple of things. The route map for sequence 10 was processed, there was a match, and the route map exited execution. Based on that, the 10.100.100.7 got matched, but that is all. Sequence 20 was never read, and because the rest of the existing IS-IS routes in subsequent statements were not addressed, they all got removed. You can correct this issue to select only the route through P5.

Question: Which attempt in Example 4-8—the second or third—will select P5 as the only route to PE7?

Example 4-8   *Modifying the Route Map*

```
2nd Attempt
!
route-map PREFER-P5 permit 10
 match ip address 10
 continue
!
route-map PREFER-P5 permit 20
 match ip address 11

3rd Attempt
!
route-map PREFER-P5 permit 10
 match ip address 10 11
!
```

If you answered neither, you are correct. The output of **show ip route** is unchanged in both cases. Can you think this through and figure out why? The second attempt's sequence 10 matches the route from PE7, which includes both routes coming from PE6 and PE7. Because of the **continue** command, sequence 20 is examined, but it catches *nothing* because there is no route for 10.10.45.5 as defined in access-list 11. It is so easy to make such a rookie mistake when you are learning route maps. The third attempt fails as well because it is a Boolean **or**, and because **match ip address 10** is true, the router does not even bother to read **match ip address 11** (which does not work anyway because it is not a routing prefix that goes into the routing table via IS-IS).

How do you finally fix this? One possible solution to fix this issue would be to use a Boolean **and** operator, which you can engage by using two different types of matching. See Example 4-9.

Example 4-9   *Modifying the Route Map Further*

```
!
route-map PREFER-P5 permit 10
 match ip address 10
 match ip next-hop 11
!
P4(config-route-map)# do show ip route isis
! Output omitted for brevity
      10.0.0.0/8 is variably subnetted, 10 subnets, 2 masks
i L2    10.100.100.7/32 [115/20] via 10.100.45.5, 00:00:55, GigabitEthernet1
```

Finally, this example works correctly, but it is still missing the rest of the IS-IS routes. Now, let's look at another route map that shows how to change attributes of routes (see Example 4-10). Be aware that you are changing routers in this example.

Example 4-10 *Modifying Route Attributes*

```
P4(config-route-map)# do show ip interface brief | include Loopback
Loopback0                10.100.100.4      YES TFTP   up                       up
Loopback1                10.100.1.4        YES manual up                       up
Loopback2                10.100.2.4        YES manual up                       up
P4(config-route-map)# do show running-config | b route-map STATIC
route-map STATIC-->ISIS permit 10
 match interface Loopback1
 set metric 11
!
route-map STATIC-->ISIS permit 20
 match interface Loopback2
 set metric 22
!
P4(config-route-map)# router isis
P4(config-router)# redistribute connected route-map STATIC-->ISIS
P4(config-router)#
```

```
RP/0/RP0/CPU0:PE7# show ip route isis
! Output omitted for brevity
i L2 10.100.1.4/32   [115/31] via 10.100.67.6, 00:00:09, GigabitEthernet0/0/0/1
                     [115/31] via 10.100.57.5, 00:00:09, GigabitEthernet0/0/0/0
i L2 10.100.2.4/32   [115/42] via 10.100.67.6, 00:00:09, GigabitEthernet0/0/0/1
                     [115/42] via 10.100.57.5, 00:00:09, GigabitEthernet0/0/0/0
i L2 10.100.23.0/24  [115/40] via 10.100.67.6, 02:28:35, GigabitEthernet0/0/0/1
                     [115/40] via 10.100.57.5, 02:28:35, GigabitEthernet0/0/0/0
i L2 10.100.34.0/24  [115/30] via 10.100.67.6, 02:28:35, GigabitEthernet0/0/0/1
                     [115/30] via 10.100.57.5, 02:28:35, GigabitEthernet0/0/0/0
i L2 10.100.35.0/24  [115/20] via 10.100.57.5, 03:27:37, GigabitEthernet0/0/0/0
i L2 10.100.45.0/24  [115/20] via 10.100.57.5, 03:27:37, GigabitEthernet0/0/0/0
i L2 10.100.46.0/24  [115/20] via 10.100.67.6, 03:19:28, GigabitEthernet0/0/0/1
i L2 10.100.100.3/32 [115/30] via 10.100.67.6, 02:28:35, GigabitEthernet0/0/0/1
                     [115/30] via 10.100.57.5, 02:28:35, GigabitEthernet0/0/0/0
i L2 10.100.100.4/32 [115/30] via 10.100.67.6, 02:28:35, GigabitEthernet0/0/0/1
                     [115/30] via 10.100.57.5, 02:28:35, GigabitEthernet0/0/0/0
i L2 10.100.100.5/32 [115/10] via 10.100.57.5, 03:27:37, GigabitEthernet0/0/0/0
i L2 10.100.100.6/32 [115/20] via 10.100.67.6, 03:19:28, GigabitEthernet0/0/0/1
```

Example 4-10 redistributes interfaces Loopback1 and Loopback2 into IS-IS and sets different metrics for each route. The output from PE7 confirms the change was correctly done. Notice that the routes coming from the same router now have different metrics (+11 and +22). Compare these metrics to the rest of the routes.

I have some homework for you. Can you go to your network's P4 and add the rest of the IS-IS routes that were present before the change through the same route map? Similar skills will apply to OSPF, BGP, and most protocols you will encounter with route maps. It is worth your time to practice these on your own to build route-map-configuring skills.

I suggest you try a few BGP examples as well. Example 4-11 shows how to manipulate inbound and outbound routes. Notice that router P4 has a BGP neighbor PE6 (10.100.46.6), which shares the following three BGP routes (loopbacks on PE6). A side note: Instead of using the **show ip bgp** command, train yourself to use the **show bgp ipv4 unicast** command. It is clear, specific, and avoids output ambiguity in multi-address family environments, ensuring that you are querying only the IPv4 unicast address family.

Example 4-11 *BGP Routes from PE6*

```
P4(config-if)# do show bgp ipv4 unicast
BGP table version is 4, local router ID is 10.100.100.4
Status codes: s suppressed, d damped, h history, * valid, > best, i - internal,
              r RIB-failure, S Stale, m multipath, b backup-path, f RT-Filter,
              x best-external, a additional-path, c RIB-compressed,
              t secondary path, L long-lived-stale,
Origin codes: i - IGP, e - EGP, ? - incomplete
RPKI validation codes: V valid, I invalid, N Not found

     Network          Next Hop            Metric LocPrf Weight Path
*>   10.100.61.0/24   10.100.46.6              0             0 65006 i
*>   10.100.62.0/24   10.100.46.6              0             0 65006 i
*>   10.100.63.0/24   10.100.46.6              0             0 65006 i
```

Next, try using PE6 to control which routes are advertised to P4 by using a simple route map, as in Example 4-12.

Example 4-12 *Controlling BGP Outbound Routes with Route Maps*

```
PE6(config)# do show running-config
! Output omitted for brevity
router bgp 65006
 bgp log-neighbor-changes
 network 10.100.61.0 mask 255.255.255.0
 network 10.100.62.0 mask 255.255.255.0
 network 10.100.63.0 mask 255.255.255.0
 neighbor 10.100.46.4 remote-as 65004
 neighbor 10.100.46.4 route-map TO-P4 out
!
ip prefix-list 61-AND-62 seq 5 permit 10.100.61.0/24
ip prefix-list 61-AND-62 seq 10 permit 10.100.62.0/24
!
route-map TO-P4 permit 10
 match ip address prefix-list 61-AND-62

P4(config-if)# do show bgp ipv4 unicast
BGP table version is 11, local router ID is 10.100.100.4
Status codes: s suppressed, d damped, h history, * valid, > best, i - internal,
              r RIB-failure, S Stale, m multipath, b backup-path, f RT-Filter,
```

```
              x best-external, a additional-path, c RIB-compressed,
              t secondary path, L long-lived-stale,
Origin codes: i - IGP, e - EGP, ? - incomplete
RPKI validation codes: V valid, I invalid, N Not found


     Network          Next Hop          Metric LocPrf Weight Path
 *>  10.100.61.0/24   10.100.46.6            0             0 65006 i
 *>  10.100.62.0/24   10.100.46.6            0             0 65006 i
```

Example 4-12 uses route map TO-P4 to control which routes get advertised to PE6's neighbor, with P4 showing the immediate effect of the change because prefix 10.100.63.0/24 is no longer advertised. I suggest you go back to P4 and use a route map to add attributes to the two routes you received, as shown in Example 4-13.

Example 4-13 *Controlling BGP Inbound Routes with Route Maps*

```
PE4(config)# do show running-config
! Output omitted for brevity
router bgp 65004
 bgp log-neighbor-changes
 neighbor 10.100.46.6 remote-as 65006
 neighbor 10.100.46.6 route-map FROM-PE6 in
!
ip prefix-list 61-FROM-PE6 seq 5 permit 10.100.61.0/24
!
ip prefix-list 62-FROM-PE6 seq 5 permit 10.100.62.0/24
!
route-map FROM-PE6 permit 10
 match ip address prefix-list 61-FROM-PE6
 set as-path prepend 65006 65006
!
route-map FROM-PE6 permit 20
 match ip address prefix-list 62-FROM-PE6
 set local-preference 200
```

```
P4(config)# do show bgp ipv4 unicast
BGP table version is 14, local router ID is 10.100.100.4
Status codes: s suppressed, d damped, h history, * valid, > best, i - internal,
              r RIB-failure, S Stale, m multipath, b backup-path, f RT-Filter,
              x best-external, a additional-path, c RIB-compressed,
              t secondary path, L long-lived-stale,
Origin codes: i - IGP, e - EGP, ? - incomplete
RPKI validation codes: V valid, I invalid, N Not found


     Network          Next Hop          Metric LocPrf Weight Path
 *>  10.100.61.0/24   10.100.46.6            0             0 65006 65006 65006 i
 *>  10.100.62.0/24   10.100.46.6            0     200     0 65006 i
```

Here, the inbound route map FROM-PE6 prepends as-paths for 10.100.61.0/24 and sets a local preference of 200 for prefix 10.100.62.0/24.

Let's see how to use route maps with OSPF, as demonstrated in Example 4-14.

Example 4-14   *External Routes on PE2*

```
PE2# show ip route ospf
! Output omitted for brevity
        10.0.0.0/8 is variably subnetted, 22 subnets, 2 masks
O IA    10.10.34.0/24   [110/2] via 10.10.24.4, 00:31:04, GigabitEthernet1
                        [110/2] via 10.10.23.3, 00:20:05, GigabitEthernet2
O IA    10.10.35.0/24   [110/2] via 10.10.23.3, 00:20:05, GigabitEthernet2
O IA    10.10.36.0/24   [110/2] via 10.10.23.3, 00:20:05, GigabitEthernet2
O IA    10.10.45.0/24   [110/2] via 10.10.24.4, 00:31:04, GigabitEthernet1
O IA    10.10.46.0/24   [110/2] via 10.10.24.4, 00:31:04, GigabitEthernet1
O IA    10.10.56.5/32   [110/2] via 10.10.24.4, 00:21:04, GigabitEthernet1
                        [110/2] via 10.10.23.3, 00:20:05, GigabitEthernet2
O IA    10.10.56.6/32   [110/2] via 10.10.24.4, 00:28:17, GigabitEthernet1
                        [110/2] via 10.10.23.3, 00:20:05, GigabitEthernet2
O IA    10.10.57.0/24   [110/3] via 10.10.24.4, 00:21:03, GigabitEthernet1
                        [110/3] via 10.10.23.3, 00:20:05, GigabitEthernet2
O IA    10.10.67.0/24   [110/3] via 10.10.24.4, 00:28:17, GigabitEthernet1
                        [110/3] via 10.10.23.3, 00:20:05, GigabitEthernet2
O IA    10.10.100.3/32  [110/2] via 10.10.23.3, 00:20:05, GigabitEthernet2
O IA    10.10.100.4/32  [110/2] via 10.10.24.4, 00:31:04, GigabitEthernet1
O IA    10.10.100.5/32  [110/3] via 10.10.24.4, 00:21:04, GigabitEthernet1
                        [110/3] via 10.10.23.3, 00:20:05, GigabitEthernet2
O IA    10.10.100.6/32  [110/3] via 10.10.24.4, 00:28:17, GigabitEthernet1
                        [110/3] via 10.10.23.3, 00:20:05, GigabitEthernet2
O IA    10.10.100.7/32  [110/4] via 10.10.24.4, 00:21:45, GigabitEthernet1
                        [110/4] via 10.10.23.3, 00:20:05, GigabitEthernet2
O IA    10.10.101.0/24  [110/2] via 10.10.24.4, 00:31:04, GigabitEthernet1
O E1    10.10.111.0/24  [110/24] via 10.10.24.4, 00:21:45, GigabitEthernet1
                        [110/24] via 10.10.23.3, 00:20:05, GigabitEthernet2
O E2    10.10.222.0/24  [110/20] via 10.10.24.4, 00:21:45, GigabitEthernet1
                        [110/20] via 10.10.23.3, 00:20:05, GigabitEthernet2
```

In this example, look at the two external routes coming into router PE2 (you will encounter this setup later).

I suggest you create a route map to get rid of E1 routes. Example 4-15 shows one way to do this. In this example, as soon as you apply the route map, the route tagged as E1 disappears.

I cannot stress enough that you need to practice these scenarios before you see similar complexity on the exam. Question creators are clever in structuring questions in which the real answer lies beyond the first obvious solution.

Example 4-15   *Controlling OSPF External Routes with Route Maps*

```
PE2# show running-config
! Output omitted for brevity
router ospf 22
 network 10.10.0.0 0.0.255.255 area 100
 distribute-list route-map NO-E1-ROUTES in
!
route-map NO-E1-ROUTES deny 10
 match route-type external type-1
!
route-map NO-E1-ROUTES permit 20
!
PE2# show ip route ospf
! Output omitted for brevity

      10.0.0.0/8 is variably subnetted, 21 subnets, 2 masks
O IA     10.10.34.0/24    [110/2] via 10.10.24.4, 00:09:14, GigabitEthernet1
                          [110/2] via 10.10.23.3, 00:09:14, GigabitEthernet2
O IA     10.10.35.0/24    [110/2] via 10.10.23.3, 00:09:14, GigabitEthernet2
O IA     10.10.36.0/24    [110/2] via 10.10.23.3, 00:09:14, GigabitEthernet2
O IA     10.10.45.0/24    [110/2] via 10.10.24.4, 00:09:14, GigabitEthernet1
O IA     10.10.46.0/24    [110/2] via 10.10.24.4, 00:09:14, GigabitEthernet1
O IA     10.10.56.5/32    [110/2] via 10.10.24.4, 00:09:14, GigabitEthernet1
                          [110/2] via 10.10.23.3, 00:09:14, GigabitEthernet2
O IA     10.10.56.6/32    [110/2] via 10.10.24.4, 00:09:14, GigabitEthernet1
                          [110/2] via 10.10.23.3, 00:09:14, GigabitEthernet2
O IA     10.10.57.0/24    [110/3] via 10.10.24.4, 00:09:14, GigabitEthernet1
                          [110/3] via 10.10.23.3, 00:09:14, GigabitEthernet2
O IA     10.10.67.0/24    [110/3] via 10.10.24.4, 00:09:14, GigabitEthernet1
                          [110/3] via 10.10.23.3, 00:09:14, GigabitEthernet2
O IA     10.10.100.3/32   [110/2] via 10.10.23.3, 00:09:14, GigabitEthernet2
O IA     10.10.100.4/32   [110/2] via 10.10.24.4, 00:09:14, GigabitEthernet1
O IA     10.10.100.5/32   [110/3] via 10.10.24.4, 00:09:14, GigabitEthernet1
                          [110/3] via 10.10.23.3, 00:09:14, GigabitEthernet2
O IA     10.10.100.6/32   [110/3] via 10.10.24.4, 00:09:14, GigabitEthernet1
                          [110/3] via 10.10.23.3, 00:09:14, GigabitEthernet2
O IA     10.10.100.7/32   [110/4] via 10.10.24.4, 00:09:14, GigabitEthernet1
                          [110/4] via 10.10.23.3, 00:09:14, GigabitEthernet2
O IA     10.10.101.0/24   [110/2] via 10.10.24.4, 00:09:14, GigabitEthernet1
O E2     10.10.222.0/24   [110/20] via 10.10.24.4, 00:09:14, GigabitEthernet1
                          [110/20] via 10.10.23.3, 00:09:14, GigabitEthernet2
```

Route Policy Language (RPL)

In Cisco IOS, route maps are a series of instructions for handling routes. They're useful for deciding which routes to allow in or out, for example, or changing some details about how routes are handled. The examples I have shared with you so far in the chapter should give you a good idea of what is commonly possible and done.

In IOS XR, however, Cisco introduced something more powerful than route maps, called Route Policy Language (RPL). Think of RPL as upgrading from basic instructions to writing actual C-style if-then statement programs for manipulating routes. With route policies, you can do more than just follow a sequence of steps. You can also create reusable blocks of instructions, closely resembling functions in a computer program. Route policies can be put together like building blocks. You can call one policy from another, making it easy to build complex rules for how routes should be managed.

Here is the best part: Route policies are "compiled" into a runtime executable portion of code. This compilation process enhances performance and efficiency, ensuring that a significant number of routing policies can be executed fast.

Because it is a C-style program-like language, getting familiar with RPL might take a little time, but it is worth the effort. RPL is designed to be intuitive. When you start using it, you'll find that it's structured in a way that makes it easy to understand and figure out what you need. You won't have to rely on too many examples to get the hang of it. Once you get the basic approach, you'll enjoy working with RPL. I show you exactly where the stepping-stones are located. First, though, some background on RPL.

A route policy is a small program, and you can give it any name you like, the same as you have done with route maps. Within a route policy (shown hyphenated as *route-policy* in IOS XR), there are matches, conditional matches, and attribute modifications similar to what you have seen in route maps. What is unique are the actions taken within a route policy. Every route sent to the policy has to be examined, and a ticket (just like on a train) is required to pass the default "drop" action at the end of the policy. Table 4-2 shows the four primary actions that a route policy can contain.

Table 4-2   RPL Primary Actions

Action	Description
Pass	The route is granted a ticket to pass the default drop, and processing continues to the next RPL statement.
Set	The route is granted a ticket to pass the default drop, an attribute is modified, and processing continues to the next RPL statement.
Done	The route is granted a ticket to pass the default drop, but processing stops for the specified route.
Drop	A route is discarded, and processing stops.

If you are new to IOS XR, the first policy most people encounter is the one shown in Example 4-16.

Example 4-16 *Basic Route Policy*

```
RP/0/RP0/CPU0:PE3(config)# route-policy PASS-ALL
RP/0/RP0/CPU0:PE3(config-rpl)# pass
RP/0/RP0/CPU0:PE3(config-rpl)# end-policy
RP/0/RP0/CPU0:PE3(config)# route-policy DROP-ALL
RP/0/RP0/CPU0:PE3(config-rpl)# drop
RP/0/RP0/CPU0:PE3(config-rpl)# end-policy
RP/0/RP0/CPU0:PE3(config)# show
Building configuration...
!! IOS XR Configuration 7.7.1
!
route-policy DROP-ALL
  drop
end-policy
!
route-policy PASS-ALL
  pass
end-policy
!
end
```

This route policy is as basic as it gets. I named the route policy PASS-ALL, gave the ticket
pass for all routes (because nothing has been specified or "everything has been matched"),
and after the only component (the action **pass**) is provided, the policy is finalized with the
command **end-policy**. Then it specifies a drop policy (DROP-ALL) for comparison. When a
drop policy is not present, there is an implicit drop action. Adding a drop policy level is recommended because it makes it easier for less experienced engineers to read.

How do I know that most people encounter this simple policy first? Because I was a
victim of this experience myself when I could not get a BGP session to pass any routes
between two IOS XR routers a long time ago. By default, an XR router will drop BGP prefix
exchanges, and you must manually override this behavior. In IOS, by default, an external
BGP (EBGP) router propagates routes to and from an EBGP neighbor when you have not
configured inbound and outbound policies. Starting in version 17.2.1, however, this behavior
can be modified. When you configure **bgp safe-ebgp-policy**, if inbound and outbound
policies are not set, an EBGP router will not propagate routes to or from EBGP peers.

A BGP prefix exchange is common. Many network professionals get stumped when they
cannot get it to work while encountering IOS XR–based platforms. In Example 4-17, PE3
advertises networks 10.10.31.0/24, 10.10.32.0/24, and 10.10.33.0/24 to P5. P5 advertises networks 10.10.51.0/24, 10.10.52.0/24, and 10.10.53.0/24 to PE3. There is no way these routes
will get exchanged until you apply route policy PASS-ALL on *both* routers, as shown in this
example. Then you finally see P5's routes on PE3.

Example 4-17   *Basic BGP Route Policy to Exchange Routes*

```
RP/0/RP0/CPU0:PE3(config)# router bgp 65003
RP/0/RP0/CPU0:PE3(config-bgp)# neighbor 10.10.35.5
RP/0/RP0/CPU0:PE3(config-bgp-nbr)# address-family ipv4 unicast
RP/0/RP0/CPU0:PE3(config-bgp-nbr-af)# route-policy PASS-ALL in
RP/0/RP0/CPU0:PE3(config-bgp-nbr-af)# route-policy PASS-ALL out
RP/0/RP0/CPU0:PE3(config-bgp-nbr-af)# commit
RP/0/RP0/CPU0:PE3(config-bgp-nbr-af)# do show bgp ipv4 unicast
BGP router identifier 10.10.100.3, local AS number 65003
BGP generic scan interval 60 secs
Non-stop routing is enabled
BGP table state: Active
Table ID: 0xe0000000   RD version: 8
BGP main routing table version 8
BGP NSR Initial initsync version 2 (Reached)
BGP NSR/ISSU Sync-Group versions 0/0
BGP scan interval 60 secs


Status codes: s suppressed, d damped, h history, * valid, > best
              i - internal, r RIB-failure, S stale, N Nexthop-discard
Origin codes: i - IGP, e - EGP, ? - incomplete
   Network          Next Hop         Metric LocPrf Weight Path
*> 10.10.31.0/24    0.0.0.0               0        32768 i
*> 10.10.32.0/24    0.0.0.0               0        32768 i
*> 10.10.33.0/24    0.0.0.0               0        32768 i
*> 10.10.51.0/24    10.10.35.5            0            0 65005 i
*> 10.10.52.0/24    10.10.35.5            0            0 65005 i
*> 10.10.53.0/24    10.10.35.5            0            0 65005 i

Processed 6 prefixes, 6 paths
```

Next, you can modify the route policy attached to P5 to include a basic conditional statement to select only a single network, as demonstrated in Example 4-18.

Example 4-18   *Basic Conditional Statement in a Route Policy*

```
RP/0/RP0/CPU0:PE3(config)# show
Building configuration...
!! IOS XR Configuration 7.7.1
!
route-policy FROM-P5
  if destination in (10.10.51.0/24) then
    pass
  endif
end-policy
!
```

```
router bgp 65003
 neighbor 10.10.35.5
  address-family ipv4 unicast
   route-policy FROM-P5 in
  !
 !
!
end

RP/0/RP0/CPU0:PE3(config)# commit
RP/0/RP0/CPU0:PE3(config)# do show bgp ipv4 unicast
BGP router identifier 10.10.100.3, local AS number 65003
BGP generic scan interval 60 secs
Non-stop routing is enabled
BGP table state: Active
Table ID: 0xe0000000   RD version: 10
BGP main routing table version 10
BGP NSR Initial initsync version 2 (Reached)
BGP NSR/ISSU Sync-Group versions 0/0
BGP scan interval 60 secs


Status codes: s suppressed, d damped, h history, * valid, > best
              i - internal, r RIB-failure, S stale, N Nexthop-discard
Origin codes: i - IGP, e - EGP, ? - incomplete
   Network          Next Hop         Metric LocPrf Weight Path
*> 10.10.31.0/24    0.0.0.0               0         32768 i
*> 10.10.32.0/24    0.0.0.0               0         32768 i
*> 10.10.33.0/24    0.0.0.0               0         32768 i
*> 10.10.51.0/24    10.10.35.5            0             0 65005 i

Processed 4 prefixes, 4 paths
```

You can see the changes right before you commit them: the RPL policy FROM-P5 contains a single condition that only prefix 10.10.51.0/24 passes; everything else gets denied.

In Example, 4-19, you add a second condition to accept (pass) prefix 10.10.52.0/24 and set an attribute on that route. IOS XR allows you to directly edit a route policy without entering configuration mode. You can use this feature to modify your policy.

Example 4-19 *Conditional Statement with a Branching Option in a Route Policy*

```
RP/0/RP0/CPU0:PE3# edit route-policy FROM-P5 ?
  emacs  to use Emacs editor
  nano   to use nano editor
  vim    to use Vim editor
  <cr>
RP/0/RP0/CPU0:PE3# edit route-policy FROM-P5 vim
```

```
! Below is the old policy that opens up for editing
route-policy FROM-P5
  if destination in (10.10.51.0/24) then
pass
  endif
end-policy
!

! In VIM editor, I modified the following lines. If you have never touched a VI-style
! editor before, this will be a mildly frustrating exercise as you will have to learn
! how to work with this editing tool. My suggestion is to search for any VI tutorial
! on the Internet, they all show you similar things and it will not take you long to
! get the hang of it. In our case, I used the "j" keyboard key to navigate the cursor
! down to the "pass" line and press "o" to open a new line for editing. This allows
! you to type freehand and add the two lines just like you would in any other text
! editor. Once you are done, press ESC key on your keyboard to take you out of the
! editing mode and type in ":wq", which is a command to write and quit and you will
! see the confirmation line I show below.
route-policy FROM-P5
  if destination in (10.10.51.0/24) then
    pass
  else
    set local-preference 200
  endif
end-policy
!
~
~
~
"/tmp/rpl_edit.26914" 8 lines, 128 characters written
Proceed with commit (yes/no/cancel)? [cancel]: yes
Parsing.
128 bytes parsed in 1 sec (127)bytes/sec
Committing.
Prepared commit in 0 sec
.
1 items committed in 2 sec (0)items/sec
Updating.
Updated Commit database in 1 sec
RP/0/RP0/CPU0:PE3# show bgp ipv4 unicast
BGP router identifier 10.10.100.3, local AS number 65003
BGP generic scan interval 60 secs
Non-stop routing is enabled
BGP table state: Active
Table ID: 0xe0000000   RD version: 12
BGP main routing table version 12
BGP NSR Initial initsync version 2 (Reached)
BGP NSR/ISSU Sync-Group versions 0/0
```

```
BGP scan interval 60 secs

Status codes: s suppressed, d damped, h history, * valid, > best
              i - internal, r RIB-failure, S stale, N Nexthop-discard
Origin codes: i - IGP, e - EGP, ? - incomplete
   Network            Next Hop            Metric LocPrf Weight Path
*> 10.10.31.0/24      0.0.0.0                  0           32768 i
*> 10.10.32.0/24      0.0.0.0                  0           32768 i
*> 10.10.33.0/24      0.0.0.0                  0           32768 i
*> 10.10.51.0/24      10.10.35.5               0               0 65005 i
*> 10.10.52.0/24      10.10.35.5               0    200        0 65005 i
*> 10.10.53.0/24      10.10.35.5               0    200        0 65005 i

Processed 6 prefixes, 6 paths
```

This approach is slick. As you can see, you can edit this policy inline from the EXEC mode (not from the config mode). The **VIM** editor opens up, and you add an else branching statement to set the remaining prefixes to BGP local-preference 200. (**Nano** and **Emacs** editors, although present in this code, have been removed in the later IOS XR versions. If you learned **VI**, consider yourself lucky because you did not have to learn the other two editors.) Pay attention that, when you are done, IOS XR parses the RPL statement for grammatical correctness and successfully commits it to the desired result. I would show you what happens when you make syntactical errors but am rather confident you will get to see plenty of those on your own.

Example 4-20 demonstrates how to allow for more than a single decision.

Example 4-20   *Conditional Statement with Multiple Branching Options in a Route Policy*

```
route-policy FROM-P5
  if destination in (10.10.51.0/24) then
    pass
  elseif destination in (10.10.52.0/24) then
    set local-preference 200
  else
    set med 200
  endif
end-policy
!
~
~
~
~
"/tmp/rpl_edit.27606" 10 lines, 189 characters written
Proceed with commit (yes/no/cancel)? [cancel]: yes
Parsing.
189 bytes parsed in 1 sec (188)bytes/sec
Committing.
Prepared commit in 0 sec
```

```
1 items committed in 2 sec (0)items/sec
Updating.
Updated Commit database in 1 sec
RP/0/RP0/CPU0:PE3# show bgp ipv4 unicast
BGP router identifier 10.10.100.3, local AS number 65003
BGP generic scan interval 60 secs
Non-stop routing is enabled
BGP table state: Active
Table ID: 0xe0000000   RD version: 13
BGP main routing table version 13
BGP NSR Initial initsync version 2 (Reached)
BGP NSR/ISSU Sync-Group versions 0/0
BGP scan interval 60 secs


Status codes: s suppressed, d damped, h history, * valid, > best
              i - internal, r RIB-failure, S stale, N Nexthop-discard
Origin codes: i - IGP, e - EGP, ? - incomplete
   Network           Next Hop         Metric LocPrf Weight Path
*> 10.10.31.0/24     0.0.0.0               0         32768 i
*> 10.10.32.0/24     0.0.0.0               0         32768 i
*> 10.10.33.0/24     0.0.0.0               0         32768 i
*> 10.10.51.0/24     10.10.35.5            0             0 65005 i
*> 10.10.52.0/24     10.10.35.5            0   200       0 65005 i
*> 10.10.53.0/24     10.10.35.5          200             0 65005 i

Processed 6 prefixes, 6 paths
```

This example adds another branching statement, assigning the second network local-preference 200 and setting the metric for the third network to 200. The results are immediate.

Now that you are getting more comfortable with your knowledge, route policies also can contain policy "sets"—containers that store similar types of data. There are four main types of sets:

- Prefix-sets hold IPv4 or IPv6 prefix lists.

- Community sets hold community values.

- As-path-sets for AS path regular expressions that match against AS paths.

- Extcommunity-sets carry additional routing details.

Sets help organize and manage routing information efficiently. Let's look at a couple of examples that accomplish the same thing. Example 4-21 shows an *inline* set where all similar type entries are put into a single line—inline.

Example 4-21 *Route Policy with an Inline Set*

```
route-policy FROM-P5
  if destination in (10.10.51.0/24, 10.10.52.0/24) then
    pass
  else
    drop
  endif
end-policy
!
! Output omitted for brevity
   Network            Next Hop            Metric LocPrf Weight Path
*> 10.10.31.0/24      0.0.0.0                  0         32768 i
*> 10.10.32.0/24      0.0.0.0                  0         32768 i
*> 10.10.33.0/24      0.0.0.0                  0         32768 i
*> 10.10.51.0/24      10.10.35.5               0             0 65005 i
*> 10.10.52.0/24      10.10.35.5               0             0 65005 i

Processed 5 prefixes, 5 paths
RP/0/RP0/CPU0:PE3# show rpl route-policy FROM-P5 inline
route-policy FROM-P5
  if destination in (10.10.51.0/24, 10.10.52.0/24) then
    pass
  else
    drop
  endif
end-policy
!
```

Example 4-22 shows a *prefix* set approach that accomplishes exactly the same thing in this scenario. We discuss prefix sets in more detail in the section to follow.

Example 4-22 *Route Policy with a Prefix Set*

```
RP/0/RP0/CPU0:PE3# configure
RP/0/RP0/CPU0:PE3(config)# prefix-set PREFIXES-FROM-P5
RP/0/RP0/CPU0:PE3(config-pfx)# 10.10.51.0/24,10.10.52.0/24
RP/0/RP0/CPU0:PE3(config-pfx)# end-set
RP/0/RP0/CPU0:PE3(config)# show
Building configuration...
!! IOS XR Configuration 7.7.1
!
prefix-set PREFIXES-FROM-P5
  10.10.51.0/24,
  10.10.52.0/24
end-set
!
```

```
end

RP/0/RP0/CPU0:PE3(config)# commit
RP/0/RP0/CPU0:PE3(config)# end
RP/0/RP0/CPU0:PE3# edit route-policy FROM-P5 vim
route-policy FROM-P5
  if destination in PREFIXES-FROM-P5 then
    pass
  endif
end-policy
!
~
~
~
"/tmp/rpl_edit.29405" 6 lines, 93 characters written
Proceed with commit (yes/no/cancel)? [cancel]: yes
Parsing.
93 bytes parsed in 1 sec (92)bytes/sec
Committing.
Prepared commit in 0 sec
.
1 items committed in 2 sec (0)items/sec
Updating.
Updated Commit database in 1 sec
RP/0/RP0/CPU0:PE3# show ip bgp
BGP router identifier 10.10.100.3, local AS number 65003
BGP generic scan interval 60 secs
Non-stop routing is enabled
BGP table state: Active
Table ID: 0xe0000000   RD version: 15
BGP main routing table version 15
BGP NSR Initial initsync version 2 (Reached)
BGP NSR/ISSU Sync-Group versions 0/0
BGP scan interval 60 secs

Status codes: s suppressed, d damped, h history, * valid, > best
              i - internal, r RIB-failure, S stale, N Nexthop-discard
Origin codes: i - IGP, e - EGP, ? - incomplete
   Network          Next Hop            Metric LocPrf Weight Path
*> 10.10.31.0/24    0.0.0.0                  0         32768 i
*> 10.10.32.0/24    0.0.0.0                  0         32768 i
*> 10.10.33.0/24    0.0.0.0                  0         32768 i
*> 10.10.51.0/24    10.10.35.5               0             0 65005 i
*> 10.10.52.0/24    10.10.35.5               0             0 65005 i
```

```
Processed 5 prefixes, 5 paths
RP/0/RP0/CPU0:PE3# show rpl route-policy FROM-P5 detail
prefix-set PREFIXES-FROM-P5
  10.10.51.0/24,
  10.10.52.0/24
end-set
!
route-policy FROM-P5
  if destination in PREFIXES-FROM-P5 then
    pass
  endif
end-policy
!
```

Example 4-23 shows how to view which route policies are in use (active) and where they are attached (which module is using them).

Example 4-23   *Useful RPL Commands*

```
RP/0/RP0/CPU0:PE3# show rpl route-policy states
ACTIVE -- Referenced by at least one policy which is attached
INACTIVE -- Only referenced by policies which are not attached
UNUSED -- Not attached (directly or indirectly) and not referenced


The following policies are (ACTIVE)
-----------------------------------------
route-policy FROM-P5
  if destination in PREFIXES-FROM-P5 then
    pass
  endif
end-policy
!
route-policy PASS-ALL
  pass
end-policy
!
The following policies are (INACTIVE)
-----------------------------------------
None found with this status.
The following policies are (UNUSED)
-----------------------------------------
route-policy DROP-ALL
  drop
end-policy
!
RP/0/RP0/CPU0:PE3# show rpl route-policy FROM-P5 attachpoints
BGP Attachpoint: Neighbor
```

```
Neighbor/Group                           type  afi/safi      in/out  vrf name   bound by
---------------------------------------------------------------------------------------
10.10.35.5                                 --   IPv4/uni       in      default    FROM-P5

RP/0/RP0/CPU0:PE3# show rpl route-policy PASS-ALL attachpoints
Sat Apr  6 17:30:18.013 UTC


BGP Attachpoint: Neighbor

Neighbor/Group                           type  afi/safi      in/out  vrf name   bound by
---------------------------------------------------------------------------------------
10.10.35.5                                 --   IPv4/uni       out     default    PASS-ALL
```

Be aware that Boolean operators come into play in RPL as well. Example 4-24 inverts the
logic for the previous route policy and selects the *opposite* of the entries defined in the
prefix list.

Example 4-24   *Boolean Not Keyword Is Used*

```
route-policy FROM-P5
  if not destination in PREFIXES-FROM-P5 then
    pass
  endif
end-policy
!
~
~
~
"/tmp/rpl_edit.32104" 6 lines, 97 characters written
Proceed with commit (yes/no/cancel)? [cancel]: yes
Parsing.
97 bytes parsed in 1 sec (96)bytes/sec
Committing.
Prepared commit in 0 sec
.
1 items committed in 2 sec (0)items/sec
Updating.
Updated Commit database in 1 sec
RP/0/RP0/CPU0:PE3# show bgp ipv4 unicast
! Output omitted for brevity
   Network           Next Hop          Metric LocPrf Weight Path
*> 10.10.31.0/24     0.0.0.0                0          32768 i
*> 10.10.32.0/24     0.0.0.0                0          32768 i
*> 10.10.33.0/24     0.0.0.0                0          32768 i
*> 10.10.53.0/24     10.10.35.5             0              0 65005 i

Processed 4 prefixes, 4 paths
```

Example 4-25 shows how to use the conjunctive **and** keyword to combine statements. The final **show rpl** command shows the global systemwide configuration.

Example 4-25   *Boolean And Keyword Is Used*

```
route-policy FROM-P5
  if not destination in PREFIXES-FROM-P5 and as-path originates-from '65005' then
    pass
  endif
end-policy
!
"/tmp/rpl_edit.32603" 6 lines, 133 characters written
Proceed with commit (yes/no/cancel)? [cancel]: yes
Parsing.
133 bytes parsed in 1 sec (132)bytes/sec
Committing.
Prepared commit in 0 sec
.
1 items committed in 2 sec (0)items/sec
Updating.
Updated Commit database in 1 sec
RP/0/RP0/CPU0:PE3# show bgp ipv4 unicast
! Output omitted for brevity
   Network          Next Hop          Metric LocPrf Weight Path
*> 10.10.31.0/24    0.0.0.0                0            32768 i
*> 10.10.32.0/24    0.0.0.0                0            32768 i
*> 10.10.33.0/24    0.0.0.0                0            32768 i
*> 10.10.53.0/24    10.10.35.5             0                0 65005 i

Processed 4 prefixes, 4 paths
RP/0/RP0/CPU0:PE3# show rpl
Sat Apr  6 20:20:24.093 UTC
prefix-set PREFIXES-FROM-P5
  10.10.51.0/24,
  10.10.52.0/24
end-set
!
route-policy FROM-P5
  if not destination in PREFIXES-FROM-P5 and as-path originates-from '65005' then
    pass
  endif
end-policy
!
```

```
route-policy DROP-ALL
  drop
end-policy
!
route-policy PASS-ALL
  pass
end-policy
!
```

"Of showing many policies, there is no end" (to borrow an old expression). I could provide numerous examples of nesting and parameterization, but I must be mindful of your exam preparation and use our time together wisely. The last thing to know in this section is that you must exercise caution when working with route policies in the config mode. Example 4-26 shows a warning that you are about to erase the entire existing policy because you are not "editing" it, you are replacing it.

Example 4-26 *Working with Route Policies in the Configuration Mode*

```
RP/0/RP0/CPU0:PE3# configure
RP/0/RP0/CPU0:PE3(config)# route-policy FROM-P5
% WARNING: Policy object route-policy FROM-P5' exists! Reconfiguring it via CLI will
replace current definition. Use 'abort to cancel.!
```

Prefix Lists

If you have not encountered prefix lists before (other than earlier in Example 4-12), they're essential knowledge for the CCNP-level exam. They're not covered in the CCNA curriculum, which came as a surprise to me when I checked. The content in this section provides all the information you need to understand them thoroughly. Building on the principles we show you, you can engage your critical thinking skills to prepare for the exam questions.

Prefix lists are rules that filter traffic. They're more efficient than access lists, which can get complicated. Prefix lists can be more specific about what is allowed and are a better option for controlling traffic in networks. You can think of them as advanced filtering mechanisms used in networking to control the flow of traffic based on destination prefixes. By supporting more concise configuration syntax, such as IP addresses or subnets, prefix lists provide greater granularity and flexibility in traffic control. They are a superior alternative to access lists for implementing fine-grained traffic filtering and access control.

The prefix matching logic contains these match elements:

- High-order bit pattern (referred to as *network* in some documentation)

- High-order bit count (referred to as *mask length* in some documentation)

- matching length – ge (mnemonic for greater than or equal to, >=)

- matching length – le (mnemonic for less than or equal to, <=)

Consider the command **ip prefix-list FILTER-100 seq 5 permit 172.16.0.0/16 ge 24**. Which traffic will it match? The intent is to select a high-order bit pattern of 172.16.0.0 (network), high-order bit count of 16 (mask), and prefixes equal to or greater than /24. What does this mean exactly? The Cisco Press title *IP Routing on Cisco IOS, IOS XE, and IOS XR: An Essential Guide to Understanding and Implementing IP Routing Protocols* (ISBN-13: 978-1-58714-423-3) provides a detailed breakdown of how to understand this logic. Now consider Figure 4-1.

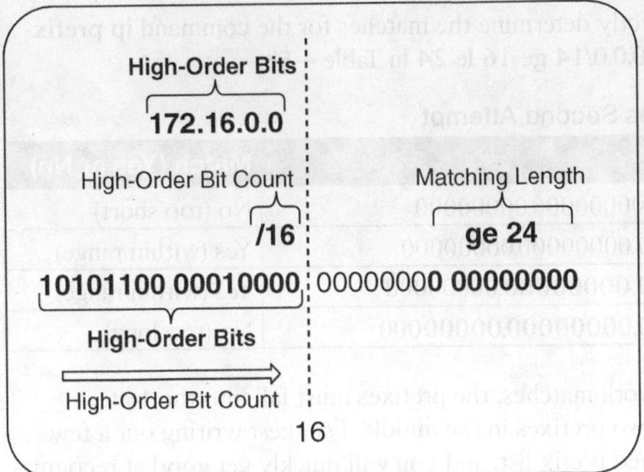

Figure 4-1 *Prefix Matching*

This prefix filter matches the following prefixes in binary:

- The first 16 bits must look exactly this way: 10101100 00010000.

- The prefix (network) must be /24 or greater (up to and including /32).

Let's practice. Table 4-3 challenges you to determine which prefixes the **ip prefix-list FILTER-200 seq 10 permit 10.48.0.0/14 ge 24** command will match. First, fill these out on your own. I provide a solution shortly.

Table 4-3 Determine Prefix Matches First Attempt

Prefix	Binary Calculation	Match (Yes or No)
10.48.0.0/14		
10.50.6.0/24		
10.51.0.0/26		
10.54.0.0/28		

Try to resist the temptation of looking at the answers in Table 4-4. If you're done with your attempt, let's examine it together. The 14 necessary bits are bold for clarity. The first network matches the network portion but fails the prefix length test. The second network matches the network portion, and its /24 prefix falls within the "greater than or equals 24" range; we have a match. The third network also matches the network portion and is /26—also a match. The fourth network matches the prefix length with /28 but has a problem with the network portion, which does not match in the 14th bit (it has a 1 instead of the necessary 0).

Table 4-4   Answers to Prefix Matches First Attempt

Prefix	Binary Calculation	Match (Yes or No)
10.48.0.0/14	00001010.00110000.00000000.00000000	No
10.50.6.0/24	00001010.00110010.00000110.00000000	Yes
10.51.0.0/26	00001010.00110011.00000000.00000000	Yes
10.54.0.0/28	00001010.00110110.00000000.00000000	No

Try one more time. Could you correctly determine the matches for the command **ip prefix-list FILTER-300 seq 15 permit 10.0.0.0/14 ge 16 le 24** in Table 4-5?

Table 4-5   Determine Prefix Matches Second Attempt

Prefix	Binary Calculation	Match (Yes or No)
10.0.0.0/8	00001010.00000000.00000000.00000000	No (too short)
10.0.0.0/16	00001010.00000000.00000000.00000000	Yes (within range)
10.0.0.0/24	00001010.00000000.00000000.00000000	Yes (within range)
10.0.0.0/30	00001010.00000000.00000000.00000000	No (too long)

In this table, although there are network matches, the prefixes must fall into the 16 to 24 range, which is only true of the two prefixes in the middle. I suggest writing out a few networks on your own for an imagined prefix list, and you will quickly get good at recognizing such matches.

Prefix lists, just like access lists, can contain multiple matching specification permit or deny entries and are processed in sequential order in a top-down fashion. The first prefix match processes with the appropriate permit or deny action. Prefix lists support sequencing—the deletion or addition of entries. If you do not provide a sequence value, the sequence entry will auto-increment by 5 based on the highest sequence number. Be aware that there is a slight difference in how prefix lists are configured in IOS and IOS XR.

- IOS prefix lists are configured with the global configuration command **ip prefix-list** *prefix-list-name* [**seq** *sequence-number*] {**permit** | **deny**} *high-order-bit-pattern/high-order-bit-count* [**ge** *ge-value*] [**le** *le-value*].

- IOS XR prefix lists are configured with the global configuration command **ipv4 prefix-list** *prefix-list-name* [**seq** *sequence-number*] {**permit** | **deny**} *high-order-bit-pattern/high-order-bit-count* [**ge** *ge-value*] [**le** *le-value*].

This difference is illustrated in Example 4-27. Go ahead and paste these into your routers.

Example 4-27   *Prefix List Examples from IOS and IOS XR*

```
IOS
ip prefix-list RFC1918 seq 5 permit 192.168.0.0/16 ge 32
ip prefix-list RFC1918 seq 10 deny 0.0.0.0/0 ge 32
ip prefix-list RFC1918 seq 15 permit 10.0.0.0/8 le 32
ip prefix-list RFC1918 seq 20 permit 172.16.0.0/12 le 32
ip prefix-list RFC1918 seq 25 permit 192.168.0.0/16 le 32
```

```
IOS XR

ipv4 prefix-list RFC1918 seq 5 permit 192.168.0.0/16 ge 32

ipv4 prefix-list RFC1918 seq 10 deny 0.0.0.0/0 ge 32

ipv4 prefix-list RFC1918 seq 15 permit 10.0.0.0/8 le 32

ipv4 prefix-list RFC1918 seq 20 permit 172.16.0.0/12 le 32

ipv4 prefix-list RFC1918 seq 25 permit 192.168.0.0/16 le 32
```

Which traffic do you think they match? You should be ready to put your knowledge
to the test at this point. The prefix list RFC1918 restricts the presence of /32 prefixes
within the RFC 1918 address ranges (10.0.0.0–10.255.255.255, 172.16.0.0–172.31.255.255,
192.168.0.0–192.168.255.255). Specifically, sequence 5 permits all /32 prefixes within the
192.168.0.0/16-bit pattern. Following this, sequence 10 denies all /32 prefixes in any bit
pattern. Subsequently, sequences 15, 20, and 25 permit routes in their respective network
ranges. This sequence order is crucial to ensure that only /32 prefixes exist (are matched)
within the 192.168.0.0 network range in the prefix list.

Prefix Sets

A prefix set is a component of IOS XR RPL that contains specifications for matching IPv4
or IPv6 prefixes; you saw one example earlier. Each specification has four components:
an address (required), a prefix length (optional), a minimum match length (optional), and a
maximum match length (optional). Example 4-28 shows what a prefix set looks like in the
running-configuration.

Example 4-28 *Prefix Sets in IOS XR*

```
RP/0/RP0/CPU0:PE3# show running-config | begin IPv4-EXAMPLE

prefix-set IPv4-EXAMPLE

  10.0.1.1,

  10.0.2.0/24,

  10.0.3.0/24 ge 26,

  10.0.4.0/24 le 26,

  10.0.5.0/24 ge 25 le 29,

  10.0.6.0/24 eq 27,

  10.0.7.10/32 ge 16 le 24,

  10.0.8.0/28 ge 8 le 16

end-set

!

prefix-set IPv6-EXAMPLE

  2001:1::/64,

  2001:2::/64 ge 96,

  2001:3::/64 ge 96 le 100,

  2001:4::/48 eq 100

end-set
```

Table 4-6 provides corresponding explanations for the IPv4 and IPv6 prefix set examples in
Example 4-28.

Table 4-6   Explanations for Example 4-28 Prefix Sets

Entry	Explanation
10.0.1.1	10.0.1.1/32 (the omission of mask length = /32), one possible host value
10.0.2.0/24	10.0.2.0/24, one possible value
10.0.3.0/24 ge 26	10.0.3.0/26 to 10.0.3.255/32, a range of prefix values
10.0.4.0/24 le 26	10.0.4.0/24 to 10.0.4.192/26, a range of prefix values
10.0.5.0/24 ge 25 le 29	10.0.5.0/25 to 10.0.5.248/29, a range of prefix values
10.0.6.0/24 eq 27	10.0.6.0/28 to 10.0.6.224/27, any /27 prefix in this range
10.0.7.10/32 ge 16 le 24	10.0.0.10 to 10.0.255.10, any /32 prefix in this range (this is tricky)
10.0.8.0/28 ge 8 le 16	10.0.8.0/26 to 10.255.8.0/26, any /26 prefix in this range
2001:1::/64	Matches a single IPv6 network
2001:2::/64 ge 96	Matches IPv6 prefixes within the range of 2001:2::/64 and longer, but with a minimum prefix length of /96
2001:3::/64 ge 96 le 100	Matches IPv6 prefixes within the range of 2001:3::/64 and longer, but with a minimum prefix length of /96 and a maximum prefix length of /100
2001:4::/48 eq 100	Matches IPv6 prefixes within the range of 2001:4::/48 with a prefix length exactly equal to /100

The purpose of these examples is not to make you practice valid combinations for the exam; they are here to help you understand how prefix sets work. The software will prompt you when you are misconfiguring prefixes and lengths.

Example 4-29 shows what happens when an invalid prefix set is constructed. Host 10.0.1.1 cannot have a prefix length of /24, and the parser is clear about ignoring the irrational instruction. XR allows you to commit the configuration, but notice that while the prefix set shows up in the configuration, the absurd entry is missing.

Example 4-29 *IOS XR Parser Checks Invalid Prefix Sets*

```
RP/0/RP0/CPU0:PE3# conf
RP/0/RP0/CPU0:PE3(config)# prefix-set INCORRECT-EXAMPLE
RP/0/RP0/CPU0:PE3(config-pfx)# 10.0.1.1/24
RP/0/RP0/CPU0:PE3(config-pfx)# end
RP/0/RP0/CPU0:Apr 22 18:01:25.470 UTC: parser[406]: %ROUTING-POLICY_REPOSITORY-
4-PARSER_VALIDATE : Policy parser DLL: Ignored inconsistent prefix definition:
10.0.1.1/24
RP/0/RP0/CPU0:PE3(config)# commit
RP/0/RP0/CPU0:PE3(config)# do show running-config | begin INCORRECT-EXAMPLE
Building configuration...
prefix-set INCORRECT-EXAMPLE
end-set
RP/0/RP0/CPU0:PE3(config)#
```

Example 4-30 shows how to apply a previous good example of a prefix set in an RPL policy.

Example 4-30 *Prefix Set Used in an RPL Policy*

```
RP/0/RP0/CPU0:PE3(config)# show
Building configuration...
!! IOS XR Configuration 7.7.1
!
route-policy DROP-IPv4-EXAMPLE
  if destination in IPv4-EXAMPLE then
    drop
  endif
end-policy
!
End
RP/0/RP0/CPU0:PE3(config)#
```

The most valuable advice I can offer is to practice configuring route maps and RPLs directly on routers in your lab environment. This hands-on approach will help you become proficient in using them effectively, enabling you to swiftly identify their proper usage during the exam and promptly detect any errors introduced by question scenarios.

Exam Preparation Tasks

As mentioned in the section "How to Use This Book" in the Introduction, you have a few choices for exam preparation: the exercises here, Chapter 23, "Final Preparation," and the exam simulation questions in the Pearson Test Prep Software Online.

Review All Key Topics

Review the most important topics in this chapter, noted with the Key Topic icon in the margin of the page. Table 4-7 lists a reference of these key topics and the page numbers on which each is found.

Table 4-7 Key Topics for Chapter 4

Key Topic Element	Description	Page Number
Table 4-2	RPL Primary Actions	88
List	Prefix Matching Logic	100
Figure 4-1	Prefix Matching	101
Table 4-4	Answers to Prefix Matches First Attempt	102
Table 4-5	Determine Prefix Matches Second Attempt	102
Table 4-6	Explanations for Example 4-28 Prefix Sets	104

Define Key Terms

Define the following key terms from this chapter and check the answers in the glossary:

Boolean, Emacs, Nano, TLV, VI, VIM

Command Reference to Check Your Memory

This section includes the most important configuration and EXEC commands covered in this chapter. You might not need to memorize the complete syntax of every command, but you should be able to remember the basic keywords that are needed.

To test your memory of the commands, cover the right side of Table 4-8 with a piece of paper, read the description on the left side, and then see how much of the command you can remember.

The 350-501 exam focuses on practical, hands-on skills that are used by networking professionals. Therefore, you should be able to identify the commands needed to configure and test. Note that not all commands are fully covered in the chapter, but their presence in the following table should lead you to investigate them further to understand this technology.

Table 4-8   CLI Commands to Know

Task	Command Syntax
Define conditions for redistributing routes from one routing protocol to another routing protocol, or to enable policy routing	**route-map** *map-tag* [**permit** | **deny**] [*sequence-number*] **ordering-seq** *sequence-name*
Match any routes that have a destination network number address that is permitted by a standard access list, an extended access list, or a prefix list	**match ip address** {*access-list-number* [*access-list-number . . .* | *access-list-name . . .*] | *access-list-name* [*access-list-number . . .* | *access-list-name*] | **prefix-list** *prefix-list-name* [*prefix-list-name . . .*]}
Match any routes that have a next hop router address passed by one of the access lists specified	**match ip next-hop** {*access-list-number* | *access-list-name*} [*. . . access-list-number* | *. . . access-list-name*]
Match routes that match a specific route tag	**match tag** {*tag-value* | *tag-value-dotted-decimal*} [*... tag-value* | *... tag-value-dotted-decimal*]
Indicate where to forward packets that pass a match clause of a route map for policy routing	**set interface** *type number* [*. . . type number*]
Indicate where to output packets that pass a match clause of a route map for policy routing	**set ip next-hop** {*ip-address* [*...ip-address*] | **dynamic dhcp** | **encapsulate l3vpn** *profile-name* | **peer-address** | **recursive** [**global** | **vrf** *vrf-name*] *ip-address* | **verify-availability** [*ip-address* **sequence** **track** *track-object-number*]}
Indicate where to forward packets that pass a match clause of a route map for policy routing when the next hop must be under a specified virtual routing and forwarding (VRF) name	**set ip vrf** *vrf-name* **next-hop** {*ip-address* [*. . . ip-address*] | **recursive** *ip-address*}

Task	Command Syntax
Specify a preference value for the autonomous system paths that pass the route map	**set local-preference** *number*
Define an RPL route policy and enter route-policy configuration mode	**route-policy** *name* [*(parameter1, parameter2, . . . , parameterN)*]
Decide which actions or dispositions should be taken for a given route; use the **if** command in route-policy configuration mode	**if** *conditional-expression* **then** *action-statement [action-statement]* [**elseif** *conditional-expression* **then** *action-statement [action-statement]*] [**else** *action-statement [action-statement]*] **endif**
Pass a route for further processing	**pass**
Discard a route	**drop**
Stop executing a policy and accept the route	**done**
Display systemwide RPL configuration	**show rpl**
Configure a prefix list in IOS	**ip prefix-list** *prefix-list-name* [**seq** *sequence-number*] {**permit** | **deny**} *high-order-bit-pattern/high-order-bit-count* [**ge** *ge-value*] [**le** *le-value*]
Configure a prefix list in IOS XR	**ipv4 prefix-list** *prefix-list-name* [**seq** *sequence-number*] {**permit** | **deny**} *high-order-bit-pattern/high-order-bit-count* [**ge** *ge-value*] [**le** *le-value*]

Review Questions

As a part of the review, we encourage you to provide *a single-sentence answer* (keep your answers as short as possible) to the following questions. If you struggle to complete this answer in a single sentence, this may indicate a lack of clarity or reveal gaps in your understanding. We have constructed these questions to help you consolidate this chapter's information and extract the essence of the covered content.

The answers to these questions appear in Appendix A. For more practice with exam format questions, use the Pearson Test Prep Software Online.

1.   What key advantage do path vector protocols offer over other routing protocols, particularly in terms of providing flexible policy-based routing and avoiding routing loops in complex network topologies?

2.   What is the primary advantage of using route maps in routing configurations, particularly in terms of enabling granular control over route redistribution and policy enforcement?

3.   What is the primary advantage of utilizing RPL in routing configurations?

CHAPTER 5

IS-IS

This chapter covers the following exam topics:

2.0 Networking

2.1 Implement IS-IS (IPv4 and IPv6)

- 2.1.a Route advertisement
- 2.1.b Area addressing
- 2.1.c Single/Multitopology
- 2.1.d Metrics

2.6 Troubleshoot routing protocols

- 2.6.a Neighbor adjacency (BGP, OSPF, IS-IS)
- 2.6.b Route advertisement (BGP, OSPF, IS-IS)

In the dynamic and expansive landscape of service provider environments, where scale, efficiency, and reliability are paramount, the role of routing protocols is critical. **Link-state routing protocols (LSPs)** emerge as a cornerstone in service providers' infrastructures, offering a sophisticated and adaptable mechanism for managing complex environments. These protocols provide a robust underlay, optimize routing decisions, enhance network responsiveness, and ensure smooth communication across vast and diverse service provider networks.

Service providers face unique challenges, such as diverse customer requirements, varying traffic patterns, and the need for rapid adaptation to changes in network topology. Link-state routing Protocols address these challenges by providing a decentralized and information-rich approach to routing. By disseminating detailed information about the state of network links, routers in service provider environments can construct and maintain an accurate map of the entire network. This comprehensive awareness empowers the network to dynamically adapt to changes, rerouting traffic efficiently and minimizing downtime.

The protocols we focus on in this chapter and the next are Intermediate System to Intermediate System (IS-IS) and Open Shortest Path First (OSPF). Unlike traditional distance-vector protocols, which focus on the distance or hops to reach a destination, IS-IS and OSPF prioritize the precise knowledge of the network's layout. Their ability to adapt has been the key factor in their enduring relevance. Five years can feel like an eternity in a digital landscape, yet both protocols have survived for decades. They excel at maintaining an accurate and up-to-date understanding of the network's topology and enable routers to make informed decisions about the most optimal paths for data transmission.

This chapter and the next examine the specific differences of IS-IS and OSPF. We have structured the chapters in a way that helps you rapidly acquire and retain practical knowledge of their underlying mechanics. Both of the protocols provide a good view into enhancing network efficiency, fault tolerance, and adaptability. By understanding the nuances of their implementation, you will appreciate the impact of Link-state routing protocols on the robustness and efficiency of routing within the intricate tapestry of service provider infrastructures.

One last thing: Extensive literature exists on IS-IS and OSPF, but our emphasis is on practical implementation for the exam. I (Brad) am trying to show you how to configure and deploy these protocols effectively within the limited pages available. Thus, I have prioritized the essential operational components while omitting detailed theoretical aspects to simplify content. Supplementing with additional resources outside this material can provide a comprehensive understanding. I encourage you to concentrate on the practical application; this will ensure success in demonstrating proficiency during the exam.

"Do I Know This Already?" Quiz

The "Do I Know This Already?" quiz allows you to assess whether you should read this entire chapter thoroughly or jump to the "Exam Preparation Tasks" section. If you are in doubt about your answers to these questions or your own assessment of your knowledge of the topics, read the entire chapter. Table 5-1 lists the major headings in this chapter and their corresponding "Do I Know This Already?" quiz questions. You can find the answers in Appendix A, "Answers to the 'Do I Know This Already?' Quizzes and Review Questions."

Table 5-1 "Do I Know This Already?" Section-to-Question Mapping

Foundation Topics Section	Questions
Implement IS-IS (IPv4 and IPv6)	1-4
Troubleshooting IS-IS	5

CAUTION   The goal of self-assessment is to gauge your mastery of the topics in this chapter. If you do not know the answer to a question or are only partially sure of the answer, you should mark that question as wrong for purposes of the self-assessment. Giving yourself credit for an answer you correctly guess skews your self-assessment results and might provide you with a false sense of security.

1. An IS-IS area is only used to regulate which of the following?

   a. Formation of adjacencies

   b. Scope of route advertisements

   c. LSA flooding

   d. LSP flooding

2. Which of the following statements accurately describes a characteristic of IS-IS? (Select all that apply.)

   a. A Level-1 router will never form adjacency with Level-2 only routers.

   b. Level-2 adjacencies must have the same area IDs.

   c. Level-1 routers will form adjacency with Level-2 only routers.

   d. Level-2 adjacencies can have different area IDs.

3. Which of the following are IPv6-related ISIS TVLs? (Select all that apply.)

    a. 232

    b. 233

    c. 234

    d. 237

4. Which protocol supports preemptive pseudonodes?

    a. OSPF

    b. IS-IS

    c. BGP

    d. BFD

5. What is the IS-IS LSP holdtime period in minutes?

    a. 10

    b. 20

    c. 30

    d. 60

Foundation Topics

Implement IS-IS (IPv4 and IPv6)

Intermediate System to Intermediate System (IS-IS) was originally developed for use in the Open Systems Interconnection (OSI) networking framework in the 1980s. However, its practicality and efficiency transcended its original OSI framework, leading to its adoption in Internet Protocol (IP) networks. These four key technical elements capture the essence of the IS-IS protocol:

- **SPF Algorithm:** This algorithm computes optimal routes based on the information collected about network link states.

- **CLNS Addressing:** Because it was originally designed for the OSI networking model, a **Connectionless Network Service (CLNS)** addressing scheme is employed. However, in IP networks, it smoothly integrates with IPv4 and IPv6, showcasing the protocol's adaptability.

- **Link-State Database (LSDB):** This database contains information about the state of each network link and forms the basis for informed routing decisions.

- **Hierarchical Design:** The design organizes routers into levels and areas. This hierarchical structure enhances scalability and facilitates efficient topology management.

Similar to OSPF, IS-IS is frequently used in both enterprise and service provider environments. It converges rapidly, scales remarkably well, and is particularly flexible for fine-tuning. Additionally, IS-IS is easily extensible through Type/Length/Value (**TLV**) extensions, simplifying the use of newer features, such as support for the IPv6 address family or Segment Routing. It is helpful to think of TLV extensions as train cars: The train does not care what load a car carries; it will transport coal, IPv6, or Segment Routing with these extensions anyway. This makes it a powerful attribute. Some argue that IS-IS is a straightforward protocol; a common sentiment is "If you are familiar with OSPF, discard half of your knowledge, and you're acquainted with IS-IS."

Remember that IS-IS is a Layer 2 protocol and is encapsulated in CLNS (not Layer 3 IP, like OSPF); each IS-IS router is uniquely identified with a Network Entity Title (NET) address.

Let's examine the following **NET address**: 49.0001.0000.0000.0001.00.

1. The first 8 bits (49) represent the address family identifier (AFI). Currently, 49 represents a locally defined format (suitable for private addressing, the operator is free to format to their liking). ISO used to assign AFI identifiers to different organizations that gave out addresses, but this no longer happens, and when it comes to IS-IS, most companies end up using 49. As an example, civilian departments within the U.S. government were designated with the code 47.0005, while the U.S. Department of Defense was identified by the code 47.0006.

2. The next 16 bits (0001) represent the area. This field can vary in length. You can just leave it "blank"—49.0000.0000.0001.00 (notice this differs from the highlighted example before this list). A better practice is to pick a number for this field (as I have done here) because you may want to add different areas in the future. This will become clear as we discuss this matter later in the chapter. In this case, I arbitrarily chose 0001, but I could have used 501 (the exam).

3. The next 48 bits identify the system ID. The formatting here may be confusing. It is 12 hex digits long with two dots in between (instead of three); notice that they are bold in the sample address. It is always the same fixed length. You can format this to what makes sense in your organization. Many examples in textbooks use a router number (in this example, router 1) in the last octet to produce the 0000.0000.0001 system ID. Frequently, network operators bake in the router's loopback address into this identifier; for example, 10.100.100.1 can be written as 0101.0010.0001 (highlighted for clarity), which I use in examples so that you become accustomed to looking at different formats. At first, the two-dotted notation may seem confusing because you usually see IP addresses with the three-dotted notation, but thinking of these as hex—that is, the MAC address notation—will help. You can even use a router's MAC address in this field (49.0001.5254.000d.f536), but the IP address approach described here makes most sense for troubleshooting issues. The bottom line is that you need a single ISO address per router, and a router's primary loopback interface is commonly adapted to fit this formatting.

4. Finally, the SEL field, also called an **NSAP** Selector or **NSEL** (the more commonly used abbreviation), is a 1-octet-long field. It identifies the service in or above the network layer on the destination node that processes the datagram. For IP, you use 00. In fact, if the device is a router, this field will always be 00.

Could you put it all together for an example of a NET address for a router using 192.168.1.1 for its loopback, which belongs to area 3? This exercise should not be hard. Tip: One of the answers could be 49.0003.1921.6800.1001.00.

IS-IS Topology

Consider the starting IS-IS network topology shown in Figure 5-1. To be able to work with IS-IS quickly (for the exam and otherwise), you should learn to visualize topologies like this in your head, without having to look up interfaces and their addresses (this is the reason I am deliberately not including them here on all interfaces). If you struggle to do this at first, you can mark up Figure 5-1 with what helps you get through tasks, but ideally, you should learn to do this in your head because being able to do so will make you a more careful, better engineer.

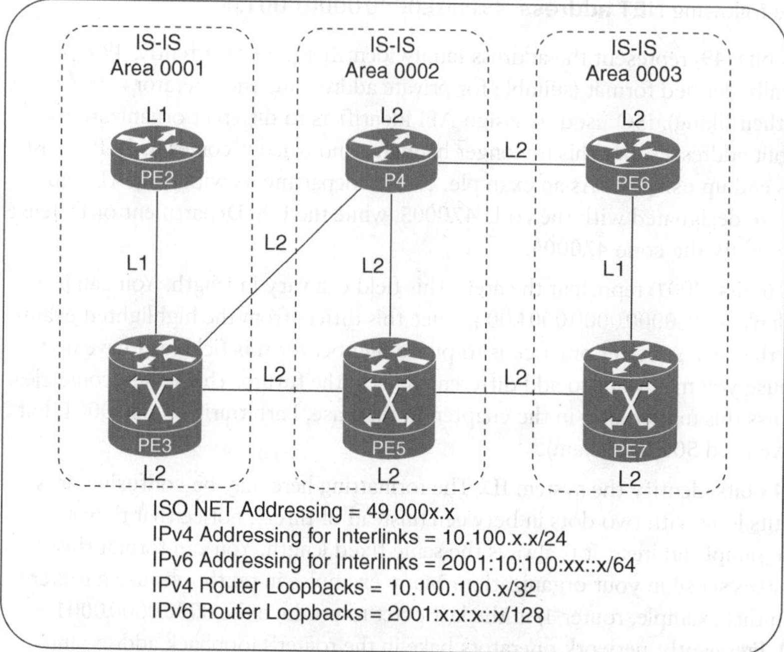

Figure 5-1   *Base IS-IS Topology*

Figure 5-1 includes everything you need to know about this topology. There are six routers in three areas. All links are Level-2 (L2), except for the ones in area 0001 and area 0003, which are Level-1 (L1). The networking domain is split into three areas, so you can easily remember which router is in which area. Consider router P4 as an example. Its ISO NET address will be 49.0002.0101.0010.0004.00 (you could zero out everything but the 4 at the end of the system ID, but you should get accustomed to recognizing these baked-in addresses). Its loopback address is 10.100.100.4/32. Its link to PE3 would have the IP address of 10.100.34.4/24 in this topology. If you understand these concepts, you already know the entire network in your head and can build and fix everything "from your head." Sometimes, you might have to look at the network diagram and draw things out, but by getting into the practice of doing this in your head, you will quickly become faster than your peers.

In this chapter, I give you the IS-IS portion for the configuration for routers PE3 and P4, but you must enable IS-IS on all other routers. Without having practiced this task on your own, you will struggle to answer exam questions, particularly when lablets (small lab simulation environments) are involved.

Basic IS-IS Configuration

IOS XE and IOS XR have minor differences when turning up IS-IS, as shown in Table 5-2.

Table 5-2 Configuring Basic IS-IS in IOS XE and IOS XR

Step #	IOS XE	IOS XR
1	Create IS-IS routing process	
2	Choose the IS-IS NET	
3	Activate IS-IS on the interfaces	Select the IS-IS interfaces
4		Activate the address family

Let's start with IOS in Example 5-1. I am deliberately drawing attention to the highlighted areas. You should learn to read these on your own throughout the book. If something stands out beyond the obvious, I will point it out further.

Example 5-1 *Basic IS-IS Configuration in IOS XE*

```
P4# configure terminal
Enter configuration commands, one per line.  End with CNTL/Z.
P4(config)# router isis net
P4(config-router)# net 49.0001.0101.0010.0004.00
P4(config-router)# log-adjacency-changes
P4(config-router)# exit
P4(config)# interface gigabitEthernet 2
P4(config-if)# ip router isis
P4(config-if)# end
P4# show isis protocol

IS-IS Router: <Null Tag> (0x10000)
  System Id: 0101.0010.0004.00    IS-Type: level-1-2
  Manual area address(es):
      49.0001
  Routing for area address(es):
      49.0001
  Interfaces supported by IS-IS:
      GigabitEthernet2 - IP
  Redistribute:
    static (on by default)
  Distance for L2 CLNS routes: 110
  RRR level: none
  Generate narrow metrics: level-1-2
  Accept narrow metrics:    level-1-2
  Generate wide metrics:    none
  Accept wide metrics:      none
P4# show clns
Global CLNS Information:
  1 Interfaces Enabled for CLNS
  Configuration Timer: 60, Default Holding Timer: 300, Packet Lifetime 64
```

```
      ERPDU's requested on locally generated packets
      Running IS-IS in IP-only mode (CLNS forwarding not allowed)
      NET: 49.0001.0101.0010.0004.00
 P4# show clns protocol

 IS-IS Router: <Null Tag> (0x10000)
   System Id: 0101.0010.0004.00  IS-Type: level-1-2
   Manual area address(es):
        49.0001
   Routing for area address(es):
        49.0001
   Interfaces supported by IS-IS:
        GigabitEthernet2 - IP
   Redistribute:
     static (on by default)
   Distance for L2 CLNS routes: 110
   RRR level: none
   Generate narrow metrics: level-1-2
   Accept narrow metrics:   level-1-2
   Generate wide metrics:   none
   Accept wide metrics:     none
 P4# show clns interface gigabitEthernet 2
 GigabitEthernet2 is up, line protocol is up
  Attached to: isis
    Checksums enabled, MTU 1497, Encapsulation SAP
    ERPDUs enabled, min. interval 10 msec.
    CLNS fast switching enabled
    CLNS SSE switching disabled
    DEC compatibility mode OFF for this interface
    Next ESH/ISH in 1 seconds
    Routing Protocol: IS-IS
      Circuit Type: level-1-2
      Interface number 0x0, local circuit ID 0x1
      Neighbor Extended Local Circuit ID: 0x0
      Level-1 Metric: 10, Priority: 64, Circuit ID: P4.01
      DR ID: 0000.0000.0000.00
      Level-1 IPv6 Metric: 10
      Number of active level-1 adjacencies: 0
      Level-2 Metric: 10, Priority: 64, Circuit ID: P4.01
      DR ID: 0000.0000.0000.00
      Level-2 IPv6 Metric: 10
      Number of active level-2 adjacencies: 0
      Next IS-IS LAN Level-1 Hello in 3 seconds
      Next IS-IS LAN Level-2 Hello in 3 seconds
```

What should you pick up on in this example? It enables IS-IS on a single Ethernet interface, verifies that the protocol is active for this interface, and uses narrow-metrics (not wide-metrics). The **show isis protocol** and **show clns protocol** command outputs look the same, the CLNS commands give you configuration and holding timers, and it uses a metric of 10. You can see the interface MTU, no adjacencies are present, IPv6 metrics are shown, and it sends out LAN Level-1 and Level-2 Hello messages every three seconds. The one command we would like to point out is **log-adjacency-changes**. By default, Cisco routers do not log IS-IS neighbor adjacencies forming or dissolving. It is good to get into the habit of using this command. You can see this on IOS XR, as demonstrated in Example 5-2.

Example 5-2 *Basic IS-IS Configuration in IOS XR*

```
RP/0/RP0/CPU0:PE3# configure
RP/0/RP0/CPU0:PE3(config)# router isis ?
  WORD  Process ID
RP/0/RP0/CPU0:PE3(config)# router isis CCNP
RP/0/RP0/CPU0:PE3(config-isis)# net 49.0001.0101.0010.0003.00
RP/0/RP0/CPU0:PE3(config-isis)# log adjacency changes
RP/0/RP0/CPU0:PE3(config-isis)# interface gigabitEthernet 0/0/0/2
RP/0/RP0/CPU0:PE3(config-isis-if)# address-family ?
  ipv4  IPv4 address family
  ipv6  IPv6 address family
RP/0/RP0/CPU0:PE3(config-isis-if)# address-family ipv4  ?
  multicast  multicast topology
  unicast    unicast topology
RP/0/RP0/CPU0:PE3(config-isis-if)# address-family ipv4 unicast
RP/0/RP0/CPU0:PE3(config-isis-if-af)# exit
RP/0/RP0/CPU0:PE3(config-isis-if)# address-family ipv6 unicast
RP/0/RP0/CPU0:PE3(config-isis-if-af)# commit
Thu Feb 15 13:26:43.365 UTC
RP/0/RP0/CPU0:PE3(config-isis-if-af)# end
RP/0/RP0/CPU0:PE3# show isis protocols
IS-IS Router: CCNP
  System Id: 0101.0010.0003
  Job Id: 1011
  Process Id: 18820
  Instance Id: 0
  IS Levels: level-1-2
  Manual area address(es):
    49.0001
  Routing for area address(es):
    49.0001
  LSP MTU: 1492
  LSP Full: level-1: No, level-2: No
  Non-stop forwarding: Disabled
  Most recent startup mode: Cold Restart
```

```
    TE connection status: Down
    XTC connection status: Down
    Overload Bit: not configured
    Maximum Metric: not configured
    Topologies supported by IS-IS:
      IPv4 Unicast
        Rib connected
        Level-1
          Metric style (generate/accept): Narrow/Narrow
          Metric: 10
        Level-2
          Metric style (generate/accept): Narrow/Narrow
          Metric: 10
        No protocols redistributed
        Distance: 115
        Advertise Passive Interface Prefixes Only: No
      IPv6 Unicast
        Rib connected
        Level-1
          Metric: 10
        Level-2
          Metric: 10
        No protocols redistributed
        Distance: 115
        Advertise Passive Interface Prefixes Only: No
Interfaces supported by IS-IS:
    GigabitEthernet0/0/0/2 is running actively (active in configuration)
RP/0/RP0/CPU0:PE3# show isis interface brief

IS-IS CCNP Interfaces
    Interface       All     Adjs     Adj Topos  Adv Topos  CLNS   MTU   Prio
                    OK      L1  L2    Run/Cfg    Run/Cfg                 L1  L2
    ---------------- ---  --------- ---------  --------- ---- ---- --------
Gi0/0/0/2           Yes   1   1       2/2        2/2       Up   1497  64  64
RP/0/RP0/CPU0:PE3# show isis neighbor

IS-IS CCNP neighbors:
System Id       Interface       SNPA             State Holdtime Type IETF-NSF
P4              Gi0/0/0/2       5254.0014.ec27 Up     9         L1L2 Capable

Total neighbor count: 1
RP/0/RP0/CPU0:PE3# show log
! Output omitted for brevity
RP/0/RP0/CPU0:Feb 15 13:26:46.608 UTC: isis[1011]: %ROUTING-ISIS-5-ADJCHANGE : ISIS
(CCNP): Adjacency to 49.0001.0101.0010.0004 (GigabitEthernet0/0/0/2) (L2) Up, New
adjacency
```

```
RP/0/RP0/CPU0:Feb 15 13:26:46.900 UTC: isis[1011]: %ROUTING-ISIS-5-ADJCHANGE : ISIS
(CCNP): Adjacency to 49.0001.0101.0010.0004 (GigabitEthernet0/0/0/2) (L1) Up, New
adjacency
RP/0/RP0/CPU0:PE3# show isis instance CCNP

IS-IS Router: CCNP
  System Id: 0101.0010.0003
  Job Id: 1011
  Process Id: 18820
  Instance Id: 0
  IS Levels: level-1-2
  Manual area address(es):
    49.0001
  Routing for area address(es):
    49.0001
  LSP MTU: 1492
  LSP Full: level-1: No, level-2: No
  Non-stop forwarding: Disabled
  Most recent startup mode: Cold Restart
  TE connection status: Down
  XTC connection status: Down
  Overload Bit: not configured
  Maximum Metric: not configured
  Topologies supported by IS-IS:
    IPv4 Unicast
      Rib connected
      Level-1
        Metric style (generate/accept): Narrow/Narrow
        Metric: 10
      Level-2
        Metric style (generate/accept): Narrow/Narrow
        Metric: 10
      No protocols redistributed
      Distance: 115
      Advertise Passive Interface Prefixes Only: No
    IPv6 Unicast
      Rib connected
      Level-1
        Metric: 10
      Level-2
        Metric: 10
      No protocols redistributed
      Distance: 115
      Advertise Passive Interface Prefixes Only: No
```

```
   Interfaces supported by IS-IS:
      GigabitEthernet0/0/0/2 is running actively (active in configuration)
RP/0/RP0/CPU0:PE3# show clns ?
  pcb          Display protocol control block information(cisco-support)
  statistics  Show CLNS statistics (local)
  trace        CLNS ltrace data(cisco-support)
RP/0/RP0/CPU0:PE3# show clns statistics
CLNS Statistics:
Last counter clear:                      6742 seconds ago
Total number of packets sent:            73
Total number of packets received:        219
Send packets dropped, total:             0
Send packets dropped, buffer overflow:   0
Send packets dropped, out of memory:     0
Send packets dropped, netio:             0
Send packets dropped, other:             0
Receive socket max queue size:           2
Receive packets dropped, total:          0
Receive packets dropped, other:          0
Receive packets dropped per pdu class:


Class     Overflow/Max   Rate Limit/Max
IIH           0/0             0/0
LSP           0/0             0/0
SNP           0/0             0/0
OTHER         0/0             0/0
Total         0               0
RP/0/RP0/CPU0:PE3# show isis interface GigabitEthernet 0/0/0/2

GigabitEthernet0/0/0/2      Enabled
  Adjacency Formation:      Enabled
  Prefix Advertisement:     Enabled
  IPv4 BFD:                 Disabled
  IPv6 BFD:                 Disabled
  BFD Min Interval:         150
  BFD Multiplier:           3
  Bandwidth:                1000000

  Circuit Type:             level-1-2
  Media Type:               LAN
  Circuit Number:           1
  Last IIH Received:        13:31:12 (0.93 sec ago), 1497 octets
  Last IIH Sent:            13:31:09 (4.34 sec ago), 1497 octets
```

```
Level-1
  Adjacency Count:         1
  LAN ID:                  P4.01
  Priority (Local/DIS):    64/64
  Next LAN IIH in:         2 s
  LSP Pacing Interval:     33 ms
  PSNP Entry Queue Size:   0
  Hello Interval:          10 s
  Hello Multiplier:        3
Level-2
  Adjacency Count:         1
  LAN ID:                  P4.01
  Priority (Local/DIS):    64/64
  Next LAN IIH in:         3 s
  LSP Pacing Interval:     33 ms
  PSNP Entry Queue Size:   0
  Hello Interval:          10 s
  Hello Multiplier:        3

CLNS I/O
  Protocol State:          Up
  MTU:                     1497
  SNPA:                    5254.000b.e465
  Layer-2 Multicast:
    All Level-1 ISs:       Listening
    All Level-2 ISs:       Listening

IPv4 Unicast Topology:     Enabled
  Adjacency Formation:     Running
  Prefix Advertisement:    Running
     Policy (L1/L2):       -/-
  Metric (L1/L2):          10/10
  Metric fallback:
    Bandwidth (L1/L2):     Inactive/Inactive
    Anomaly (L1/L2):       Inactive/Inactive
  Weight (L1/L2):          0/0
  MPLS Max Label Stack:    1/3/7/7 (PRI/BKP/SRTE/SRAT)
  MPLS LDP Sync (L1/L2):   Disabled/Disabled
  FRR (L1/L2):             L1 Not Enabled    L2 Not Enabled
    FRR Type:              None              None
IPv6 Unicast Topology:     Enabled
  Adjacency Formation:     Running
  Prefix Advertisement:    Running
     Policy (L1/L2):       -/-
```

```
    Metric (L1/L2):          10/10
    Metric fallback:
      Bandwidth (L1/L2):     Inactive/Inactive
       Anomaly (L1/L2):      Inactive/Inactive
    Weight (L1/L2):          0/0
    MPLS Max Label Stack:    1/3/7/7 (PRI/BKP/SRTE/SRAT)
    MPLS LDP Sync (L1/L2):   Disabled/Disabled
    FRR (L1/L2):             L1 Not Enabled     L2 Not Enabled
      FRR Type:              None               None

  IPv4 Address Family:       Enabled
    Protocol State:          Up
    Forwarding Address(es):  10.100.34.3
    Global Prefix(es):       10.100.34.0/24 (0)
  IPv6 Address Family:       Enabled
    Protocol State:          Up
    Forwarding Address(es):  fe80::5054:ff:fe0b:e465
    Global Prefix(es):       2001:10:100:34::/64 (0)

  LSP Transmission is:       idle
  LSP Transmit Timer in:     0 ms
  LSP Burst Size:            6 LSPs in the next 0 ms

  PME Link Delays and Loss: -

RP/0/RP0/CPU0:PE3# show isis neighbor detail

IS-IS CCNP neighbors:
System Id      Interface      SNPA            State Holdtime Type IETF-NSF
P4             Gi0/0/0/2      5254.0014.ec27 Up    9        L1L2 Capable
  Area Address(es): 49.0001
  IPv4 Address(es): 10.100.34.4*
  Topologies: 'IPv4 Unicast'
  Uptime: 00:03:26

Total neighbor count: 1
```

What were you able to glean from this example? (It's not enough to just glance through; be sure to read and consume the output.)

Example 5-2 does the same things in different ways: it has the MTU, Level-1/Level-2 are on by default, it names the IS-IS process, it activates address families, it has different CLNS commands, and adjacency is apparent in the log messages. There is nothing to memorize, but you need to understand how this works.

Repetition is the mother of learning. The best advice I can give you at this point for the exam is to configure Figure 5-1 to its full state. I am going to do this now. It is well worth your time and practice, so take some time to do it now. In the end, you should have something that looks like the output in Example 5-3. It doesn't have to match perfectly, but I am looking for the IPv4 and IPv6 host routes on, let's say, PE7.

Example 5-3 *Desired Configurations Results*

```
RP/0/RP0/CPU0:PE7# show route | include /32
L    10.100.57.7/32 is directly connected, 00:13:23, GigabitEthernet0/0/0/0
L    10.100.67.7/32 is directly connected, 00:13:23, GigabitEthernet0/0/0/1
i L2 10.100.100.2/32 [115/30] via 10.100.57.5, 00:07:54, GigabitEthernet0/0/0/0
i L2 10.100.100.3/32 [115/20] via 10.100.57.5, 00:10:38, GigabitEthernet0/0/0/0
i L2 10.100.100.4/32 [115/30] via 10.100.57.5, 00:13:11, GigabitEthernet0/0/0/0
i L2 10.100.100.5/32 [115/10] via 10.100.57.5, 00:13:18, GigabitEthernet0/0/0/0
i L2 10.100.100.6/32 [115/40] via 10.100.57.5, 00:13:11, GigabitEthernet0/0/0/0
L    10.100.100.7/32 is directly connected, 00:19:30, Loopback0
RP/0/RP0/CPU0:PE7# show route ipv6 | include /128
i L2 2001:2:2:2::2/128
i L2 2001:3:3:3::3/128
i L2 2001:4:4:4::4/128
i L2 2001:5:5:5::5/128
i L2 2001:6:6:6::6/128
L    2001:7:7:7::7/128 is directly connected,
L    2001:10:100:57::7/128 is directly connected,
L    2001:10:100:67::7/128 is directly connected,
```

How is it going? Do you have your routes from PE2, PE3, P4, P5, and PE6? If you do, great! If you do not and are missing some IPv6 routes, welcome to the CCNP 305-501 exam! You must make this function properly, and you are burning precious minutes. Do you move on and lose the points (there are no lookbacks on this exam), or do you spend more time to get this answer correct?

Here's a hint: RFC 5120. You did not misconfigure IPv6 or miss some interfaces from being included (you likely have been checking for this for at least several minutes now). RFC 5120 introduced a third IPv6 TLV—Multi Topology Reachable IPv6 Prefix (TLV 237)—to support multiple independent topologies and SPF calculations. Wait… What are the first two? (A pop-quiz from an omitted theoretical section.) If you answered TLV 232 (IPv6 addressing, Hello PDU, etc.) and TLV 236 (IPv6 prefix reachability information—metrics, up/down bits, etc.), you are doing well. Back to TLV 237 though… What does TLV 237 have to do with not getting all the IPv6 routes on PE7? Everything. If you followed through with the exercise instead of just continuing to read this chapter, you may have picked up that XR routers were not getting XE routes and vice versa. Now you're learning.

IS-IS Single Topology and Multitopology

Cisco routers support three IS-IS topology configuration modes:

- **Single Topology:** In this mode, IPv4 and IPv6 are in the same logical topology table, sharing a single SPF computation for best path selection. *This mode is the default IPv6 mode for IOS routers.*

- **Multitopology:** This mode separates IPv4 and IPv6 into independent topology tables. Different metrics can be assigned to an interface via address families to allow for diverse paths and SPF calculations for each protocol. This is great when your network does not have a 1:1 correlation for IPv4 and IPv6 addresses. It is the recommended mode for this very reason. *This is the default mode for IOS XR routers.* Now you should understand why the two operating systems were not getting each other's IPv6 routes into their RIBs. In the sample topology, IOS routers are on the top, and XR routers are on the bottom.

Can you think of how to solve the routing problem now? Try it before reading further.

- **Single-Topology Transition:** This is a hybrid mode for legacy routers with IPv6 in a single-topology mode that need to add IPv4 support without disrupting the existing IPv6 network. As you saw in the now-memorable trap that I set up for you in the network, single-topology IOS routers cannot interpret multitopology TLVs sent by IOS XR routers, and you certainly do not want to run into these issues during a migration. Instead, you can put the multitopology XR routers into a single-topology mode (exactly how I collected all the routes in Example 5-3). Then both single and multitopology TLVs are exchanged, and a single SPF calculation is performed. Once the older routers are removed, the network can be returned to the multitopology state.

Example 5-4 shows how to fix this issue with the full IS-IS configuration from PE7. We do not keep any secrets from you. You will need to do this on PE3 and P5 as well.

Example 5-4   *Fixing the Problem with a Single-Topology Conversion*

```
RP/0/RP0/CPU0:PE7# show run router isis
Sat Feb 17 13:26:39.381 UTC
router isis CCNP
 net 49.0003.0101.0010.0007.00
 address-family ipv4 unicast
  metric-style wide
 !
 address-family ipv6 unicast
  metric-style wide
  single-topology
 !
 interface Loopback0
  passive
  circuit-type level-2-only
  address-family ipv4 unicast
  !
  address-family ipv6 unicast
  !
 !
 interface GigabitEthernet0/0/0/0
  circuit-type level-2-only
```

```
address-family ipv4 unicast
!
address-family ipv6 unicast
 !
 !
interface GigabitEthernet0/0/0/1
 circuit-type level-1
 address-family ipv4 unicast
  !
 address-family ipv6 unicast
  !
 !
 !
```

How do you turn on IS-IS IPv6 single topology on IOS routers? Recall from Table 5-2 that there is one additional step: enable IPv6 on the interface. Example 5-5 demonstrates an example from PE2.

Example 5-5 *Enabling IS-IS IPv6 Single Topology on IOS*

```
PE2# show running-config interface GigabitEthernet1
Building configuration...

Current configuration : 218 bytes
!
interface GigabitEthernet1
 ip address 10.100.23.2 255.255.255.0
 negotiation auto
 ipv6 address 2001:10:100:23::2/64
 ipv6 router isis
isis circuit-type level-1
end

PE2# show running-config | section router isis
 ip router isis
 ipv6 router isis
 ip router isis
 ipv6 router isis
router isis
 net 49.0001.0101.0010.0002.00
 metric-style wide
 log-adjacency-changes
```

Now you know how a single-topology mode works on IOS and how multitopology and single-topology modes work on IOS XR. What about multitopology on IOS? If you tried to get the previous scenarios to work, you may have used or noticed the use of wide metrics, which I cover soon. This is the final piece of the puzzle for this scenario. Example 5-6 shows how to enable a multitopology mode for IOS.

Example 5-6 *Enabling IS-IS IPv6 Multitopology on IOS*

```
PE2(config-router-af)# multi-topology
PE2(config-router-af)# end
PE2# show running-config | section isis
! Output omitted for brevity
router isis
 net 49.0001.0101.0010.0002.00
 metric-style wide
 log-adjacency-changes
 !
 address-family ipv6
  multi-topology
 exit-address-family
```

Example 5-7 shows how to enable a single-topology transition mode for IOS routers.

Example 5-7 *Enabling IS-IS Single-Topology Transition Mode on IOS*

```
PE2# configure terminal
Enter configuration commands, one per line.  End with CNTL/Z.
PE2(config)# router isis
PE2(config-router)# metric-style ?
  narrow      Use old style of TLVs with narrow metric
  transition  Send and accept both styles of TLVs during transition
  wide        Use new style of TLVs to carry wider metric
PE2(config-router)# address-family ipv6
PE2(config-router-af)# multi-topology transition
PE2(config-router-af)# end
PE2# show running-config | section isis
! Output omitted for brevity
router isis
 net 49.0001.0101.0010.0002.00
 metric-style transition
 log-adjacency-changes
 !
 address-family ipv6
  multi-topology transition
 exit-address-family
```

Example 5-8 shows how to enable a single-topology transition mode for IOS XR routers.

Example 5-8 *Enabling IS-IS Single-Topology Transition Mode on IOS XR*

```
RP/0/RP0/CPU0:PE3# show running-config router isis
Sat Feb 17 17:51:39.296 UTC
router isis CCNP
 net 49.0001.0101.0010.0003.00
```

```
log adjacency changes
!
address-family ipv6 unicast
 metric-style transition
 single-topology
 !
```

I am deliberately using this approach to make you better remember how to make this technology work instead of providing you with structured screenshots of various outputs. You need to learn how the protocol works by breaking it down and putting it back together; there is no substitute to mastering these topics. On the exam, you will have to visualize what happens in each task, and no memorization of output will suffice if you do not know the mechanics of enabling a feature.

Can we verify this? Yes, in Example 5-9 notice how PE2 advertises two TLVs because it is configured to use the single-topology transition mode. Prefix 2001:10:100:23::/64 appears twice in the database (notice the MT-IPv6 reference at the bottom).

Example 5-9 *Enabling IS-IS Single-Topology Transition Mode on IOS XR Continued*

```
PE2# show isis database detail


IS-IS Level-1 Link State Database:
LSPID                 LSP Seq Num   LSP Checksum  LSP Holdtime/Rcvd    ATT/P/OL
PE2.00-00           * 0x00000025    0xACF5              580/*            0/0/0
  Area Address: 49.0001
  NLPID:        0xCC 0x8E
  Topology:     IPv4 (0x0)
                IPv6 (0x2)
  Hostname: PE2
  Metric: 10        IS PE3.01
  Metric: 10        IS-Extended PE3.01
  IP Address:   10.100.100.2
  Metric: 10        IP 10.100.23.0 255.255.255.0
  Metric: 10        IP 10.100.100.2 255.255.255.255
  Metric: 10        IP 10.100.23.0/24
  Metric: 10        IP 10.100.100.2/32
  IPv6 Address: 2001:2:2:2::2
  Metric: 10        IPv6 2001:2:2:2::2/128
  Metric: 10        IPv6 2001:10:100:23::/64
  Metric: 10        IPv6 (MT-IPv6) 2001:2:2:2::2/128
  Metric: 10        IPv6 (MT-IPv6) 2001:10:100:23::/64
```

When you are considering these different topology modes, I recommend that you understand what their behavior is and think through exam questions or network problems.

Now, let's examine an issue in Figure 5-2.

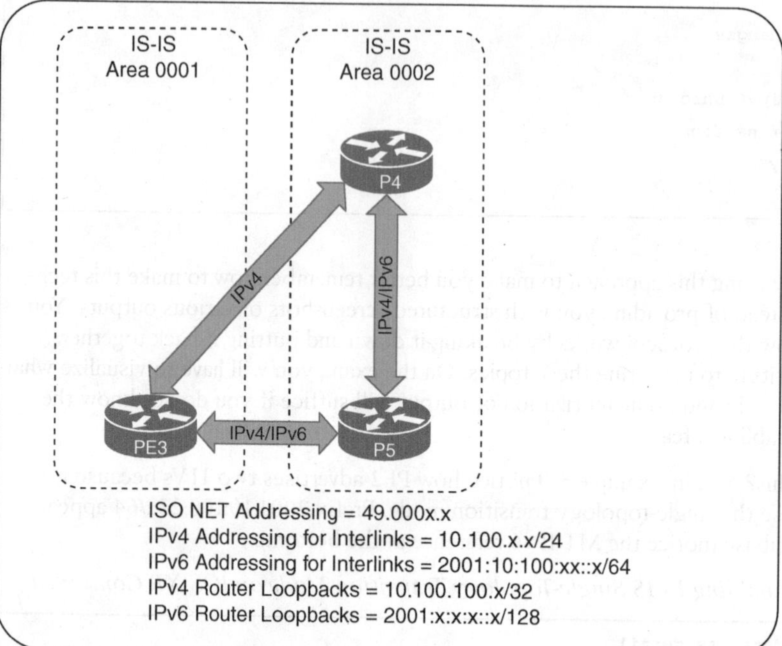

Figure 5-2 *Single-Topology Dual-Stack Network*

I simplified the starting topology by leaving only three routers that all run IOS; this removes any confusion regarding default IS-IS topology modes. (You should try to remove as many complexities as you can when you are learning something new.) So far, you've practiced on IOS and XR because you have to get used to the differences in platform configurations. These run single topology, but the links connecting to P5 are dual stacked, running IPv4 and IPv6. The link between PE3 and P4 runs IPv4 only. What can possibly go wrong here? Remember from our earlier discussion, the SPF calculation will be performed once for both IPv4 and IPv6. Because IS-IS is enabled on both links, PE3 and P4 think that PE3-P4 link will transport IPv6 traffic. To get a better understanding, look at what PE3 sees in Example 5-10.

Example 5-10 *IS-IS Single Topology for IPv6*

```
PE3# show isis database detail
! Output omitted for brevity
P4.00-00                    0x00000006    0x1B56                    1029/1199        0/0/0
  Area Address: 49.0002
  NLPID:        0xCC 0x8E
  Hostname: P4
  Metric: 10          IS-Extended P4.01
  Metric: 10          IS-Extended P4.02
  IP Address:   10.100.100.4
  Metric: 10          IP 10.100.34.0/24
  Metric: 10          IP 10.100.45.0/24
  Metric: 10          IP 10.100.100.4/32
```

```
IPv6 Address: 2001:4:4:4::4
  Metric: 10              IPv6 2001:4:4:4::4/128
  Metric: 10              IPv6 2001:10:100:45::/64
P4.01-00                  0x00000004   0xA2E7         595/1199        0/0/0
  Metric: 0              IS-Extended P4.00
  Metric: 0              IS-Extended PE3.00
P4.02-00                  0x00000003   0xC5C2        1197/1199        0/0/0
  Metric: 0              IS-Extended P4.00
  Metric: 0              IS-Extended P5.00
```

In its LSP database, PE3 sees P4 advertising the IPv6 loopback of 2001:4:4:4::4/128.
However, is this loopback reachable from PE3? You can test, as shown in Example 5-11.

Example 5-11 *PE3 Has No Reachability to P4's Loopback*

```
PE3# ping ipv6 2001:4:4:4::4
Type escape sequence to abort.
Sending 5, 100-byte ICMP Echos to 2001:4:4:4::4, timeout is 2 seconds:

% No valid route for destination
Success rate is 0 percent (0/1)
PE3# show ipv6 route
IPv6 Routing Table - default - 7 entries
Codes: C - Connected, L - Local, S - Static, U - Per-user Static route
       B - BGP, R - RIP, H - NHRP, I1 - ISIS L1
       I2 - ISIS L2, IA - ISIS interarea, IS - ISIS summary, D - EIGRP
       EX - EIGRP external, ND - ND Default, NDp - ND Prefix, DCE - Destination
       NDr - Redirect, RL - RPL, O - OSPF Intra, OI - OSPF Inter
       OE1 - OSPF ext 1, OE2 - OSPF ext 2, ON1 - OSPF NSSA ext 1
       ON2 - OSPF NSSA ext 2, la - LISP alt, lr - LISP site-registrations
       ld - LISP dyn-eid, lA - LISP away, le - LISP extranet-policy
       lp - LISP publications, a - Application, m - OMP
LC  2001:3:3:3::3/128 [0/0]
     via Loopback0, receive
I2  2001:5:5:5::5/128 [115/20]
       via FE80::5054:FF:FE0F:B9B0, GigabitEthernet3
C   2001:10:100:35::/64 [0/0]
       via GigabitEthernet3, directly connected
L   2001:10:100:35::3/128 [0/0]
       via GigabitEthernet3, receive
I2  2001:10:100:35::5/128 [115/20]
       via FE80::5054:FF:FE0F:B9B0, GigabitEthernet3
I2  2001:10:100:45::/64 [115/20]
       via FE80::5054:FF:FE0F:B9B0, GigabitEthernet3
L   FF00::/8 [0/0]
       via Null0, receive
```

Here, you can see that PE3 cannot ping it, and the route to this prefix is also missing! Because the single-topology mode was used, PE3 and P4 think that the link between them is usable for IPv6, which is not even running on that interface. One way to fix this issue is to enable IPv6 on this link to make it dual stack just as the links connecting to P5. Another way is to enable multitopology on all routers, as shown on PE3 in Example 5-12.

Example 5-12 *PE3 Obtains Reachability to P4's Loopback*

```
PE3(config)# router isis
PE3(config-router)# address-family ipv6
PE3(config-router-af)# multi-topology
PE3(config-router-af)# end
*Feb 17 20:16:10.802: %CLNS-5-ADJCHANGE: ISIS: Adjacency to P5 (GigabitEthernet3)
topology changed, TID (2) added, locally configured
PE3# ping ipv6 2001:4:4:4::4
Type escape sequence to abort.
Sending 5, 100-byte ICMP Echos to 2001:4:4:4::4, timeout is 2 seconds:
!!!!!
Success rate is 100 percent (5/5), round-trip min/avg/max = 1/1/2 ms
PE3# show ipv6 route 2001:4:4:4::4
Routing entry for 2001:4:4:4::4/128
  Known via "isis", distance 115, metric 30, type level-2
  Route count is 1/1, share count 0
  Routing paths:
    FE80::5054:FF:FE0F:B9B0, GigabitEthernet3
      From FE80::5054:FF:FE0F:B9B0
      Last updated 00:02:00 ago


P5# show ipv6 interface GigabitEthernet3
GigabitEthernet3 is up, line protocol is up
  IPv6 is enabled, link-local address is FE80::5054:FF:FE0F:B9B0
  No Virtual link-local address(es):
  Global unicast address(es):
    2001:10:100:35::5, subnet is 2001:10:100:35::5/128


RP/0/RP0/CPU0:PE3# show isis neighbor detail
Sat Feb 17 20:20:15.515 UTC


IS-IS CCNP neighbors:
System Id      Interface       SNPA          State Holdtime Type IETF-NSF
PE2            Gi0/0/0/1       *PtoP*        Up    26       L1   Capable
  Area Address(es): 49.0001
  IPv4 Address(es): 10.100.23.2*
  IPv6 Address(es): fe80::5054:ff:fe07:1d66*
  Topologies: 'IPv4 Unicast' 'IPv6 Unicast'
  Uptime: 00:02:12
```

```
P4              Gi0/0/0/2        *PtoP*          Up    26    L2   Capable
  Area Address(es): 49.0002
  IPv4 Address(es): 10.100.34.4*
  IPv6 Address(es): fe80::5054:ff:fe00:8de*
  Topologies: 'IPv4 Unicast' 'IPv6 Unicast'
  Uptime: 00:02:13
P5              Gi0/0/0/3        *PtoP*          Up    25    L2   Capable
  Area Address(es): 49.0002
  IPv4 Address(es): 10.100.35.5*
  IPv6 Address(es): fe80::5054:ff:fe08:a94c*
  Topologies: 'IPv4 Unicast' 'IPv6 Unicast'
  Uptime: 00:02:13

Total neighbor count: 3
```

Notice how PE3 uses GigabitEthernet3 (the link to P5) now. Also, notice that the **show isis neighbor detail** command reveals the supported topologies—IPv4 and IPv6.

Now that I've thrown you in at the deep end with this advanced multitopology topic, let's examine some of the basics. You might initially perceive the incremental buildup of IS-IS knowledge as a preferable approach. However, you'll come to appreciate this method in the long run. The approach of experimenting, encountering failure, and then striving to comprehend the reasons behind those failures ingrains knowledge more effectively. This approach contrasts with simply amassing theoretical knowledge beforehand, which often leads to forgetting key details during application.

IS-IS Adjacencies

In IS-IS networks, routing is organized into a two-level hierarchy of areas to provide scalability: Level-1 and Level-2. A contiguous collection of Level-2 routers forms the backbone. Non-backbone areas consist of Level-1 routers, and routers that handle both intra- and inter-area routing are classified as Level-1 and Level-2 routers. When no hierarchy is needed, all routers are treated as Level-2 routers (similar to a single Area 0 in OSPF). In fact, as routers have become more powerful, it has become very common to use a single IS-IS area for your entire domain.

Areas control *adjacencies, levels* create *topologies* (we discuss this more in the "Route Advertisement" section). You will appreciate this deceivingly simple wording because it is easy to get confused on the exam when questions about areas and levels between IS-IS and OSPF start blending in your mind and you start doubting your memory. Exam questions are deliberately built to confuse hesitating candidates. For now, remember that IS-IS areas affect only the formation of adjacencies between two routers; that is it.

- Areas control adjacency formation.

- A Level-1 router only forms an adjacency with another router in the same area.

- A Level-2 router forms an adjacency with a router in any area.

- Level-2 adjacencies must be contiguous and form the backbone area.

Memorize the preceding list and you will be able to quickly identify the right answer. Questions to solidify your knowledge include the following:

- Two routers are in the same area. Can they form Level-1 (L1) and Level-2 (L2) adjacencies at the same time? Yes, this is how Cisco routers work by default.

- Two routers are in different areas. Can they form an L2 adjacency? Yes.

- Two routers are in different areas. Can they form an L1 adjacency? No.

- If you want two routers to form a Level-1 adjacency, what should you do? Put them in the same area.

Refer to Figure 5-1 to solidify this knowledge. Then look at PE3's adjacencies in Example 5-13 because it has formed adjacencies in different areas.

Example 5-13 *PE3's IS-IS Adjacencies*

```
RP/0/RP0/CPU0:PE3# show isis adjacency


IS-IS CCNP Level-1 adjacencies:

System Id    Interface      SNPA             State Hold Changed   NSF IPv4 IPv6
                                                                      BFD  BFD

PE2          Gi0/0/0/1      5254.0012.8170 Up    7    00:03:16 Yes None None


Total adjacency count: 1


IS-IS CCNP Level-2 adjacencies:

System Id    Interface      SNPA             State Hold Changed   NSF IPv4 IPv6
                                                                      BFD  BFD

P4           Gi0/0/0/2      5254.000d.f536 Up    23   00:02:34 Yes None None
P5           Gi0/0/0/3      5254.0019.5442 Up    7    00:01:57 Yes None None


Total adjacency count: 2


RP/0/RP0/CPU0:PE3# show isis hostname
IS-IS CCNP hostnames

Level  System ID      Dynamic Hostname
 1     0101.0010.0002 PE2
 2     0101.0010.0004 P4
 2     0101.0010.0006 PE6
 1,2 * 0101.0010.0003 PE3
 2     0101.0010.0005 P5
 2     0101.0010.0007 PE7
```

Example 5-13 shows that PE3 has three adjacencies with one being an L1 adjacency. It is interesting that the System ID attribute references the router's hostname rather than the 6-byte system ID. This happens because the LSP exchange contains TLV 137, which provides a name-to-system-ID mapping during the LSP exchange. Additionally, notice the use of the **show isis hostname** command to quickly reveal router hostnames and adjacency levels.

I recommend you get in the lab and try changing levels and areas to have a solid understanding of this matter.

Example 5-14 shows how L1 areas must match for adjacencies to establish. PE2 is in area 1, but as soon as you put it in a different area, the adjacency no longer works.

Example 5-14 *Changing PE2 Level Area Adjacency*

```
PE2# configure terminal
Enter configuration commands, one per line.  End with CNTL/Z.
PE2(config)# router isis
PE2(config-router)# no net 49.0001.0101.0010.0002.00
PE2(config-router)#
15:51:54.025: %CLNS-5-ADJCLEAR: ISIS: All adjacencies cleared
PE2(config-router)# net 49.0002.0101.0010.0002.00
PE2(config-router)# end
PE2# debug isis adj-packets
IS-IS Adjacency related packets debugging is on for router process null
PE2#
15:52:21.241: ISIS-Adj: Rec L1 IIH from 5254.0006.5133 (GigabitEthernet1)
15:52:21.241: ISIS-Adj: cir type L1, cir id 0101.0010.0003.01, length 1497, ht(30)
15:52:21.241: ISIS-Adj: Area mismatch, level 1 IIH on GigabitEthernet1
15:52:26.975: ISIS-Adj: Sending L1 LAN IIH on GigabitEthernet1, length 1497
15:52:29.345: ISIS-Adj: Rec L1 IIH from 5254.0006.5133 (GigabitEthernet1)
15:52:29.345: ISIS-Adj: cir type L1, cir id 0101.0010.0003.01, length 1497, ht(30)
15:52:29.345: ISIS-Adj: Area mismatch, level 1 IIH on GigabitEthernet1
```

IS-IS Network Types

IS-IS has three possible adjacency states:

- **Down:** This is the initial state where no IS-IS Hellos (**IIH**s) have been received from the neighbor.

- **Initializing:** IIHs have been received from the neighbor, but there's uncertainty about whether the neighbor is properly receiving this router's IIHs.

- **Up:** IIHs have been received from the neighbor, confirming that the neighbor is properly receiving this router's IIHs.

IS-IS natively supports only *broadcast* (multiaccess, which is the default) and *point-to-point* network types. On broadcast networks, routers create adjacencies, synchronize their databases, and keep them synchronized. IS-IS elects one Designated Intermediate System (**DIS**) for each broadcast network. IS-IS has no concept of a backup DIS, and in fact, it does not need one. A DIS is elected based on these criteria:

1. The router with the highest interface priority.

2. In case of a tie, the router with the highest Subnetwork Point of Attachment (SNPA; data-link MAC address, an interface that attaches to a subnet) takes precedence.

3. In case the SNPAs cannot be compared, the router with the highest system ID will be declared the winner.

A DIS has two important functions:

- Helps routers on a broadcast segment to synchronize their network view.

- Assumes the role of a standalone object—the *pseudonode* (a virtual router) to represent the broadcast segment in the link-state database.

A pseudonode and DIS are present at each IS-IS level (L1 and L2); a broadcast network segment can have two pseudonodes and two DISs. The topology shown in Figure 5-1 does not have more than two routers on a network segment, but it does not matter, since by default Cisco routers create the broadcast networks on Ethernet segments.

Now, look at Example 5-15 to examine the network segment between routers PE3 (IOS XR) and P4 (IOS).

Example 5-15   *Viewing DIS Information in IOS and IOS XR*

```
RP/0/RP0/CPU0:PE3# show isis interface gigabitEthernet 0/0/0/2 | include "LAN|Priority"
  Media Type:              LAN
  LAN ID:                  PE3.03
  Priority (Local/DIS):    64/64
  Next LAN IIH in:         302 ms

P4# show clns interface gigabitEthernet 2 | include DR|Priority
  Level-2 Metric: 10, Priority: 64, Circuit ID: PE3.03
  DR ID: PE3.03
```

When you look at the two interfaces, which are facing each other, you can see that PE3 has won the DIS role. In IOS XR, it is under LAN ID on PE3 and under DR ID for the IOS-based P4, confirming that PE3 was elected. A priority value greater than the default value (64) will make the interface more preferable. In the topology, I left the priority values alone, so you should verify why PE3 was elected. To do so, compare the **SPNA**s (MAC addresses) on both routers in Example 5-16.

Example 5-16   *Changing IS-IS Interface Priority on P4*

```
RP/0/RP0/CPU0:PE3# show interface GigabitEthernet 0/0/0/2 | include bia
  Hardware is GigabitEthernet, address is 5254.0015.9b19 (bia 5254.0015.9b19)

P4# show interface GigabitEthernet 0/0/0/2 | include bia
  Hardware is CSR vNIC, address is 5254.000d.f536 (bia 5254.000d.f536)
```

It is easy to see that PE3 has a higher MAC address than P4 (15>0d). Since IS-IS DIS is preemptive (if a new router appears on the LAN with a higher interface priority, the new router becomes the DIS), the newcomer will purge the old pseudonode LSP and flood a new set of LSPs. Example 5-17 shows exactly that.

Example 5-17   *Configuring DIS Preemption and Verification*

```
P4# configure terminal
Enter configuration commands, one per line.  End with CNTL/Z.
P4(config)# interface GigabitEthernet2
P4(config-if)# isis priority 100
```

```
P4(config-if)# do show clns interface GigabitEthernet 2 | include DR|Priority
   Level-2 Metric: 10, Priority: 100, Circuit ID: P4.02
   DR ID: P4.02
```

```
RP/0/RP0/CPU0:PE3# show isis interface GigabitEthernet 0/0/0/2 | include "LAN|Priority"
   Media Type:                LAN
   LAN ID:                    P4.02
   Priority (Local/DIS):      64/100
   Next LAN IIH in:           874 ms
```

If you set IS-IS priority to the value of 0, it will *significantly lower* the probability of the router to become a DIS. What do IS-IS LSPs look like under the current network type of broadcast? As you can see in Example 5-18, there are quite a few of them.

Example 5-18   *IS-IS LSPs Under Network Type Broadcast*

```
RP/0/RP0/CPU0:PE3# show isis database

IS-IS CCNP (Level-1) Link State Database
LSPID              LSP Seq Num   LSP Checksum   LSP Holdtime/Rcvd   ATT/P/OL
PE2.00-00          0x00000025    0xa5c5         618   /1199         0/0/0
PE2.01-00          0x0000001e    0x5497         808   /1199         0/0/0
PE3.00-00        * 0x0000002b    0xb10a         943   /*            1/0/0

Total Level-1 LSP count: 3      Local Level-1 LSP count: 1


IS-IS CCNP (Level-2) Link State Database
LSPID              LSP Seq Num   LSP Checksum   LSP Holdtime/Rcvd   ATT/P/OL
PE3.00-00        * 0x0000002e    0x5f03         673   /*            0/0/0
P4.00-00           0x00000029    0xf816         721   /1199         0/0/0
P4.01-00           0x0000001e    0x96d7         1001  /1199         0/0/0
P4.02-00           0x00000003    0x9dec         679   /1199         0/0/0
P4.03-00           0x0000001e    0x9cce         617   /1199         0/0/0
P5.00-00           0x0000002b    0x79f0         399   /1200         0/0/0
P5.01-00           0x0000001e    0x6ffe         1091  /1200         0/0/0
P5.03-00           0x0000001e    0xb1b6         917   /1200         0/0/0
PE6.00-00          0x00000027    0x3bb5         903   /1198         0/0/0
PE7.00-00          0x00000029    0xb33e         432   /1200         0/0/0

Total Level-2 LSP count: 10     Local Level-2 LSP count: 1
```

You are going to love point-to-point interfaces where IS-IS expects a single neighbor, establishes an adjacency through a three-way handshake process, and subsequently synchronizes link-state databases. Unless you expect more than one neighbor on Ethernet segments, convert them to point-to-point network type because IS-IS routers will not benefit from the presence of a pseudonode. DIS elections waste resources, **CSNP**s (complete sequence number PDUs) are flooded into a segment, and the pseudonode LSP enters the LSP database for the routers in that level. I suggest you turn your broadcast interfaces into point-to-point interfaces, as in Example 5-19, where PE3 and P4 are shown. Please do this on all interfaces in the diagram.

Example 5-19 *IS-IS Network Goes Point-to-Point*

```
RP/0/RP0/CPU0:PE3# configure terminal
RP/0/RP0/CPU0:PE3(config)# router isis CCNP
RP/0/RP0/CPU0:PE3(config-isis)# interface gigabitEthernet 0/0/0/1
RP/0/RP0/CPU0:PE3(config-isis-if)# point-to-point

P4(config-if)# interface GigabitEthernet 2
P4(config-if)# isis network point-to-point
P4(config-if)#
```

I had to wait 20 minutes for the LSP holdtime of 1200 seconds to expire, and now there are only 7 LSPs instead of the 13 LSPs shown earlier in Example 5-18. The pseudonode objects are no longer advertised, as seen in Example 5-20.

Example 5-20 *IS-IS Database Under Point-to-Point Network Type*

```
RP/0/RP0/CPU0:PE3# show isis database

IS-IS CCNP (Level-1) Link State Database
LSPID                   LSP Seq Num  LSP Checksum  LSP Holdtime/Rcvd  ATT/P/OL
PE2.00-00                 0x0000002a   0x9acb         1138 /1199          0/0/0
PE3.00-00               * 0x00000032   0x298c         1123 /*             1/0/0

    Total Level-1 LSP count: 2     Local Level-1 LSP count: 1


IS-IS CCNP (Level-2) Link State Database
LSPID                   LSP Seq Num  LSP Checksum  LSP Holdtime/Rcvd  ATT/P/OL
PE3.00-00               * 0x00000036   0x411c          659 /*             0/0/0
P4.00-00                  0x00000031   0x5fab          566 /1200          0/0/0
P5.00-00                  0x00000033   0xa9bd          733 /1200          0/0/0
PE6.00-00                 0x0000002c   0xe509         1190 /1198          0/0/0
PE7.00-00                 0x0000002e   0xfef0          629 /1200          0/0/0

    Total Level-2 LSP count: 5     Local Level-2 LSP count: 1
```

What breaks IS-IS router adjacencies? If you slowed down and observed IS-IS adjacencies during cutting over to the point-to-point network types, you may have noticed network types break the adjacencies. However, try putting PE2 back to the broadcast network type. Example 5-21 shows a change in network type.

Example 5-21 *IS-IS Adjacency Not Coming Up*

```
PE2# debug isis adj-packets
IS-IS Adjacency related packets debugging is on for router process null
PE2# configure terminal
Enter configuration commands, one per line.  End with CNTL/Z.
PE2(config-if)# no isis network point-to-point
13:14:46.053: ISIS-Adj: Rec serial IIH from 5254.0018.5212 (GigabitEthernet1)
13:14:46.053: ISIS-Adj: cir type L1, cir id 00, length 1497
13:14:46.053: ISIS-Adj: rcvd state UP, old state UP, new state UP, nbr usable TRUE
13:14:46.053: ISIS-Adj: RCV:3way Adj. Local Ckt ID:0x8 Nghbr Ckt ID:0x1 Length:15
13:14:46.053: ISIS-Adj: Nghbr Ckt ID changed: FALSE
13:14:46.054: ISIS-Adj: received Neighbor System-ID (must be our) 0101.0010.0002
13:14:46.054: ISIS-Adj: received Neighbor ext.circuit ID (must be our) 0x1
13:14:46.054: ISIS-Adj: newstate:0, state_changed:0, going_up:0, going_down:0
13:14:46.054: ISIS-Adj: Action = ACCEPT
13:14:46.054: ISIS-Adj: ACTION_ACCEPT:
13:14:46.246: ISIS-Adj: L1 adj count 0
13:14:46.247: ISIS-Adj: Gi1: Current SYNC state: Normal(1)
13:14:46.247: ISIS-Adj: Event: No SYNC required(1)
13:14:46.247: ISIS-Adj: Gi1: New SYNC state: Normal(1)
13:14:46.247: ISIS-Adj: Gi1: Current SYNC state: Normal(1)
13:14:46.247: ISIS-Adj: Event: No SYNC required(1)
13:14:46.247: ISIS-Adj: Gi1: New SYNC state: Normal(1)
13:14:46.249: ISIS-Adj: Sending L1 LAN IIH on GigabitEthernet1, length 1497
13:14:49.247: ISIS-Adj: Run level-1 DR election for GigabitEthernet1
13:14:49.247: ISIS-Adj: No L1 adjacencies found for GigabitEthernet1
13:14:49.247: ISIS-Adj: Run level-2 DR election for GigabitEthernet1
13:14:49.247: ISIS-Adj: No L2 adjacencies found for GigabitEthernet1
13:14:55.429: ISIS-Adj: Sending L1 LAN IIH on GigabitEthernet1, length 1497
13:14:55.793: ISIS-Adj: Rec serial IIH from 5254.0018.5212 (GigabitEthernet1)
13:14:55.793: ISIS-Adj: cir type L1, cir id 00, length 1497
13:14:55.793: ISIS-Adj: Point-to-point IIH received on multi-point interface:
ignored IIH
PE2(config-if)# do show isis neighbor

System Id       Type Interface       IP Address      State Holdtime Circuit Id
PE2(config-if)# undebug all
PE2(config-if)#
```

As you can see in Example 5-21, the adjacency is immediately removed when network types
do not match. MTU mismatches can give you trouble as well. Observe Example 5-22.

Example 5-22 *IS-IS Interface MTU Mismatch*

```
PE2(config-if)# do debug isis adj-packets
IS-IS Adjacency related packets debugging is on for router process null
PE2(config-if)# mtu 1512
14:31:28.251: ISIS-Adj: Rec serial IIH from 5254.0018.5212 (GigabitEthernet1)
14:31:28.251: ISIS-Adj: cir type L1, cir id 00, length 1497
14:31:28.251: ISIS-Adj: rcvd state UP, old state UP, new state UP, nbr usable TRUE
14:31:28.251: ISIS-Adj: RCV:3way Adj. Local Ckt ID:0x8 Nghbr Ckt ID:0x1 Length:15
14:31:28.251: ISIS-Adj: Nghbr Ckt ID changed: FALSE
14:31:28.251: ISIS-Adj: received Neighbor System-ID (must be our) 0101.0010.0002
14:31:28.252: ISIS-Adj: received Neighbor ext.circuit ID (must be our) 0x1
14:31:28.252: ISIS-Adj: newstate:0, state_changed:0, going_up:0, going_down:0
14:31:28.252: ISIS-Adj: Action = ACCEPT
14:31:28.252: ISIS-Adj: ACTmtu 1512
PE2(config-if)#
14:31:32.708: %LINEPROTO-5-UPDOWN: Line protocol on Interface GigabitEthernet1,
changed state to down
14:31:32.718: ISIS-Adj: L1 adj count 0
14:31:42.013: %LINK-3-UPDOWN: Interface GigabitEthernet1, changed state to up
14:31:43.014: %LINEPROTO-5-UPDOWN: Line protocol on Interface GigabitEthernet1,
changed state to up
14:31:43.014: ISIS-Adj: Gi1: Current SYNC state: Normal(1)
14:31:43.015: ISIS-Adj: Event: No SYNC required(1)
14:31:43.015: ISIS-Adj: Gi1: New SYNC state: Normal(1)
14:31:43.015: ISIS-Adj: Gi1: Current SYNC state: Normal(1)
14:31:43.015: ISIS-Adj: Event: No SYNC required(1)
14:31:43.015: ISIS-Adj: Gi1: New SYNC state: Normal(1)
14:31:43.023: ISIS-Adj: SND:3way Adj. Local Ckt ID:0x1 Nghbr Ckt ID:0x0 Length:5
14:31:43.023: ISIS-Adj: Sending serial IIH on GigabitEthernet1, 3way state:DOWN,
length 1508
14:31:44.604: ISIS-Adj: Rec serial IIH from 5254.0018.5212 (GigabitEthernet1)
14:31:44.604: ISIS-Adj: cir type L1, cir id 00, length 1497
14:31:44.605: ISIS-Adj: RCV:3way Adj. Local Ckt ID:0x8 Nghbr Ckt ID:0x1 Length:15
14:31:44.605: ISIS-Adj: Nghbr Ckt ID changed: TRUE
14:31:44.605: ISIS-Adj: received Neighbor System-ID (must be our) 0101.0010.0002
14:31:44.605: ISIS-Adj: received Neighbor ext.circuit ID (must be our) 0x1
14:31:44.605: ISIS-Adj: newstate:2, state_changed:0, going_up:0, going_down:0
14:31:44.605: ISIS-Adj: Action = GOING UP, new type = L1
14:31:44.605: ISIS-Adj: New serial adjacency
14:31:44.605: ISIS-Adj: rcvd state UP, old state DOWN, new state DOWN, nbr usable TRUE
14:31:55.614: ISIS-Adj: Sending serial IIH on GigabitEthernet1, 3way state:INIT,
length 1508
14:32:03.633: ISIS-Adj: Rec serial IIH from 5254.0018.5212 (GigabitEthernet1)
14:32:03.633: ISIS-Adj: cir type L1, cir id 00, length 1497
14:32:03.633: ISIS-Adj: rcvd state DOWN, old state INIT, new state INIT,
nbr usable TRUE
14:32:03.633: ISIS-Adj: RCV:3way Adj. Local Ckt ID:0x8 Nghbr Ckt ID:0x1 Length:15
14:32:03.633: ISIS-Adj: Nghbr Ckt ID changed: FALSE
```

```
14:32:03.634: ISIS-Adj: received Neighbor System-ID (must be our) 0101.0010.0002
14:32:03.634: ISIS-Adj: received Neighbor ext.circuit ID (must be our) 0x1
14:32:03.634: ISIS-Adj: newstate:1, state_changed:0, going_up:0, going_down:0ii
14:32:03.634: ISIS-Adj: Action = ACCEPT
14:32:03.634: ISIS-Adj: ACTION_ACCEPTsis
14:32:05.582: ISIS-Adj: SND:3way Adj. Local Ckt ID:0x1 Nghbr Ckt ID:0x8 Length:15
14:32:05.582: ISIS-Adj: Sending serial IIH on GigabitEthernet1, 3way state:INIT,
length 1508
PE2(config-if)# do show isis neighbor

System Id          Type Interface      IP Address      State Holdtime Circuit Id
PE3                L1   Gi1             10.100.23.3     DOWN  29        00
PE2(config-if)# do show isis neighbor

System Id          Type Interface      IP Address      State Holdtime Circuit Id
PE3                L1   Gi1             10.100.23.3     DOWN  25        00
PE2(config-if)# do show isis neighbor

System Id          Type Interface      IP Address      State Holdtime Circuit Id
PE3                L1   Gi1             10.100.23.3     DOWN  22        00
PE2(config-if)# do show isis neighbor

System Id          Type Interface      IP Address      State Holdtime Circuit Id
PE3                L1   Gi1             10.100.23.3     DOWN  29        00
14:32:21.896: ISIS-Adj: Action = ACCEPT
14:32:21.896: ISIS-Adj: ACTION_ACCEPT:
PE2(config-if)# do show isis neighbor

System Id          Type Interface      IP Address      State Holdtime Circuit Id
PE3                L1   Gi1             10.100.23.3     DOWN  28        00
```

Setting one side's MTU to 1512 certainly kills the adjacency due to the difference in values, and you can observe how adjacency is kept in the DOWN state with the holdtime timer decrementing and then an IIH hello packet putting it back to the 30-second countdown.

Pop-quiz time: Do you know why I chose this specific MTU value? If the answer is no, you must study up on this topic. The short answer is every MPLS label takes 4 bytes, so adding the additional 12 bytes accounts for three additional labels in the label stack.

IS-IS Metrics

Cisco's IS-IS implementation sets a default metric of 10 for all interfaces, regardless of their bandwidth. Notice that I aim to steer clear of comparing IS-IS with OSPF features in contrast to many educational materials. The approach here avoids confusion during exam scenarios. Instead, I prefer separating the specifics of each protocol. This approach facilitates clearer understanding and quicker identification of knowledge gaps. It's preferable to maintain clarity rather than risk confusion during exams, especially with nuanced questions. However, everyone has their preferred study method, so choose what works best for you.

In IS-IS, administrators need to manually configure interface metrics if different values are required. The original IS-IS specification and RFC 1195 specify a 6-bit width for individual interface metrics (1–63) and a 10-bit width for complete path metrics (1–1023). While sufficient at the time of definition, modern requirements demand a broader metric range. Also, do not forget that vendors can implement RFCs differently. Think of the topology in Figure 5-1 (try to visualize this in your head). PE6 and PE7 are neighbors via L1, but their loopbacks are in L2; the path from PE7 to PE6's loopback 10.100.100.6 will have four links because it must travel through the contiguous L2 backbone. This should add up to the metric value of 40. I have quickly converted the wide metrics to the default narrow metrics on all routers (one command on IOS under the routing process, two commands on XR under each address family). You can see what happens in Example 5-23.

Example 5-23   *IS-IS Narrow Metrics Behavior*

```
RP/0/RP0/CPU0:PE7# show isis protocol | include Metric style
      Metric style (generate/accept): Narrow/Narrow
      Metric style (generate/accept): Narrow/Narrow
      Metric style (generate/accept): Narrow/Narrow
      Metric style (generate/accept): Narrow/Narrow
RP/0/RP0/CPU0:PE7# show ip route | include 100.6/32

i L2 10.100.100.6/32 [115/40] via 10.100.57.5, 00:01:33, GigabitEthernet0/0/0/0
RP/0/RP0/CPU0:PE7# traceroute 10.100.100.6

Type escape sequence to abort.
Tracing the route to 10.100.100.6

 1   10.100.57.5 6 msec   4 msec   5 msec
 2   10.100.45.4 6 msec   5 msec   5 msec
 3   10.100.46.6 7 msec   *   6 msec
```

Three links to get to PE6 plus the loopback add up to the metric value of 40, regardless of bandwidth. It doesn't matter if the links are 1 Mb or 400 Gb; they have the same path metric of 10. You can see how setting all interfaces to the same metric can lead to suboptimal routing and why designs may call for changing interface metrics. The IS-IS metric becomes similar to the hop count metric that is used by the distance-vector protocols. Then, there is the issue of correlating 1 Mb to 400 Gb. Now, you can attempt to change the PE6 loopback0 metric to 100 (you know that 63 is the maximum allowed under the narrow construct), as shown in Example 5-24.

Example 5-24   *IS-IS Narrow Metrics Changing Values*

```
PE6# configure terminal
Enter configuration commands, one per line.  End with CNTL/Z.
PE6(config)# interface loopback0
PE6(config-if)# isis metric 100
Warning: for metrics greater than 63, 'metric-style wide'  should be configured on
level-1-2, or it will be capped at 63.


RP/0/RP0/CPU0:PE7# show ip route | include 100.6/32
i L2 10.100.100.6/32 [115/93] via 10.100.57.5, 00:01:44, GigabitEthernet0/0/0/0
```

With a quick change on PE6, you can see that PE7 sees 93 (10 + 10 + 10 + 63). While the interface metric is limited to 63 and does not allow you to set 100, PE7 sees a path metric that exceeds 63 because the cost is added from the local LSP database. Now, try adding a metric on another router. Example 5-25 adds a metric of 20 (instead of 10) on P5.

Example 5-25   *IS-IS Narrow Metrics Changing Values on P5*

```
RP/0/RP0/CPU0:P5# configure
RP/0/RP0/CPU0:P5(config)# router isis CCNP
RP/0/RP0/CPU0:P5(config-isis)# interface gigabitEthernet 0/0/0/1
RP/0/RP0/CPU0:P5(config-isis-if)# address-family ipv4
RP/0/RP0/CPU0:P5(config-isis-if-af)# metric 20
RP/0/RP0/CPU0:P5(config-isis-if-af)# commit
RP/0/RP0/CPU0:P5(config-isis-if-af)#
```

```
RP/0/RP0/CPU0:PE7# show ip route | include 100.6/32
i L2 10.100.100.6/32 [115/103] via 10.100.57.5, 00:00:04, GigabitEthernet0/0/0/0
```

You can quickly see how this approach can become unmanageable on larger networks. This is why RFC 3784 (now RFC 5305) introduced wide metrics to address this issue, allowing for a 24-bit interface metric range and a 32-bit range for entire path metrics. It is highly recommended to utilize wide metrics, especially for Segment Routing support and why they are enabled at the beginning of this chapter. Remember that it is essential for all routers in an area to use the same metric type. Try getting on PE5 now and rolling back your configurations to wide metrics. You will achieve IS-IS adjacency, but you will not build the complete SPF tree. The reason is that you are sending different TLVs that are independent of each other. Example 5-26 clearly illustrates this from how PE6 views the topology.

Example 5-26   *IS-IS Incomplete SPF Tree Due to Mixed Narrow and Wide Metrics*

```
PE6# show isis topology

IS-IS TID 0 paths to level-1 routers
System Id            Metric      Next-Hop            Interface   SNPA
PE6                  --
PE7                  10          PE7                 Gi1         5254.0009.c33c


IS-IS TID 0 paths to level-2 routers
System Id            Metric      Next-Hop            Interface   SNPA
PE3                  20          P4                  Gi3         5254.0014.efed
P4                   10          P4                  Gi3         5254.0014.efed
P5                   **
PE6                  --
PE7                  **
```

PE6 can compute narrow metrics but has trouble with P5 and PE7, since P5 advertises wide metrics. *Both* routers' SPF trees are incomplete because the routers cannot reconcile 6-bit and 24-bit values—which is not possible. RFC 3787 specified the migration process from narrow to wide metrics without affecting the topology. Consult Example 5-27, where a transitional mode metric is applied to advertise both narrow and wide TLVs at the same time.

Once the network topology runs in the transitional state, the operator can gradually convert to wide metrics.

Example 5-27 *IS-IS Metrics Transitional State*

```
RP/0/RP0/CPU0:PE3(config-if)# router isis CCNP
RP/0/RP0/CPU0:PE3(config-isis)# address-family ipv4 unicast
RP/0/RP0/CPU0:PE3(config-isis-af)# metric-style ?
  narrow      Use old style of TLVs with narrow metric
  transition  Send and accept both styles of TLVs during transition
  wide        Use new style of TLVs to carry wider metric
RP/0/RP0/CPU0:PE3(config-isis-af)# metric-style transition ?
  level  Set metric-style for one level only
  <cr>
RP/0/RP0/CPU0:PE3(config-isis-af)# metric-style transition level ?
  <1-2>  Level
RP/0/RP0/CPU0:PE3(config-isis-af)# metric-style transition level 1 ?
  <cr>
RP/0/RP0/CPU0:PE3(config-isis-af)#
```

Also, observe that you can specify a different metric for different levels where you set the default metric of 100 for L1 interfaces and 1000 for L2 interfaces in Example 5-28. As you can see, metric 63 is still used for L1 connections even though you specify the default level of 100.

Example 5-28 *IS-IS Metrics Varying Level Metrics*

```
RP/0/RP0/CPU0:PE3(config-isis-af)# do show run router isis
router isis CCNP
 net 49.0001.0101.0010.0003.00
 log adjacency changes
 address-family ipv4 unicast
  metric-style narrow level 1
  metric-style wide level 2
  metric 100 level 1
  metric 1000 level 2
RP/0/RP0/CPU0:PE3(config-isis-af)# do show isis topology
Wed Feb 28 18:01:02.041 UTC


IS-IS CCNP paths to IPv4 Unicast (Level-1) routers
System Id        Metric    Next-Hop          Interface      SNPA
PE2                 63      PE2               Gi0/0/0/1      *PtoP*
PE3                 --


IS-IS CCNP paths to IPv4 Unicast (Level-2) routers
System Id        Metric    Next-Hop          Interface      SNPA
```

PE3	--			
P4	1000	P4	Gi0/0/0/2	*PtoP*
P5	1000	P5	Gi0/0/0/3	*PtoP*
PE6	1010	P4	Gi0/0/0/2	*PtoP*
PE7	1010	P5	Gi0/0/0/3	*PtoP*

Route Advertisement

As mentioned earlier, *areas* control *adjacencies*, *levels* create *topologies*. In IS-IS, levels control LSP flooding. Consider the following logic:

1. A Level-1 router looks at the destination address and compares the area address to its own area.

2. If the Level-1 area is equal, then flood within its Level-1 area (which is what normally happens).

3. If the Level-1 area is not equal, pass to the nearest Level-1-2 router.

4. At the Level-1-2 router, compare the area address to its own area. If the Level-1 area is equal, use the Level-1 database. If not equal, use the Level-2 database.

5. Level-2 LSPs are flooded across a contiguous set of Level-2 areas.

How can this be summarized in a single sentence so that you can remember it on the exam? *Use Level-1 if equal; if not equal, pass to Level-1-2; there, try Level-1 first, then use Level-2.* That's the best I have come up with thus far. Maybe you can come up with a better one.

Now, again consider Figure 5-1, where PE2 has only the Level-1 area routes. I got rid of all narrow metrics in the topology to make things cleaner. PE2 has two interfaces in the L1 area, one of these peering with PE3. Now, see what routes PE2 sees in Example 5-29.

Example 5-29 *PE2 Routes*

```
PE2# show ip route
! Output omitted for brevity
Gateway of last resort is 10.100.23.3 to network 0.0.0.0

i*L1  0.0.0.0/0 [115/10] via 10.100.23.3, 00:35:51, GigabitEthernet1
       10.0.0.0/8 is variably subnetted, 3 subnets, 2 masks
C        10.100.23.0/24 is directly connected, GigabitEthernet1
L        10.100.23.2/32 is directly connected, GigabitEthernet1
C        10.100.100.2/32 is directly connected, Loopback0
```

PE2 sees only L1 routes, and there are none coming from other routers at this time. L1 routers are aware only of the local area topology. The only route it receives is an L1 default route, which was never configured. It's interesting that Cisco routers do this on their own by default. This is not the behavior of non-Cisco routers, where you have to generate these manually. Now, see what routes PE3 sees in Example 5-30.

Example 5-30 *PE3 Routes*

```
RP/0/RP0/CPU0:PE3# show route isis

i L2 10.100.45.0/24 [115/20] via 10.100.34.4, 01:22:13, GigabitEthernet0/0/0/2
                    [115/20] via 10.100.35.5, 01:22:13, GigabitEthernet0/0/0/3
i L2 10.100.46.0/24 [115/20] via 10.100.34.4, 01:22:13, GigabitEthernet0/0/0/2
i L2 10.100.57.0/24 [115/20] via 10.100.35.5, 01:22:13, GigabitEthernet0/0/0/3
i L2 10.100.67.0/24 [115/30] via 10.100.34.4, 01:22:13, GigabitEthernet0/0/0/2
                    [115/30] via 10.100.35.5, 01:22:13, GigabitEthernet0/0/0/3
i L1 10.100.100.2/32 [115/20] via 10.100.23.2, 01:16:27, GigabitEthernet0/0/0/1
i L2 10.100.100.4/32 [115/20] via 10.100.34.4, 01:22:13, GigabitEthernet0/0/0/2
i L2 10.100.100.5/32 [115/10] via 10.100.35.5, 01:22:13, GigabitEthernet0/0/0/3
i L2 10.100.100.6/32 [115/30] via 10.100.34.4, 01:22:13, GigabitEthernet0/0/0/2
i L2 10.100.100.7/32 [115/20] via 10.100.35.5, 01:22:13, GigabitEthernet0/0/0/3
```

PE3, an L1-L2 router, on the other hand, sees the entire topology. It sees all L2 routes, which you can tell by the loopbacks of all five routers in the topology. It sees the L1 route 10.100.100.2 coming from PE2. It even sees the L1-level route from area 0003 (PE6 to PE7 link), but it comes in as an L2 route. Finally, let's look at an L2-only router; PE4 is a good example in Example 5-31.

Example 5-31 *PE4 Routes*

```
P4# show ip route
! Output omitted for brevity
Gateway of last resort is not set


      10.0.0.0/8 is variably subnetted, 16 subnets, 2 masks
i L2    10.100.23.0/24 [115/20] via 10.100.34.3, 00:42:04, GigabitEthernet2
C       10.100.34.0/24 is directly connected, GigabitEthernet2
L       10.100.34.4/32 is directly connected, GigabitEthernet2
i L2    10.100.35.0/24 [115/20] via 10.100.45.5, 00:42:04, GigabitEthernet1
                       [115/20] via 10.100.34.3, 00:42:04, GigabitEthernet2
C       10.100.45.0/24 is directly connected, GigabitEthernet1
L       10.100.45.4/32 is directly connected, GigabitEthernet1
C       10.100.46.0/24 is directly connected, GigabitEthernet3
L       10.100.46.4/32 is directly connected, GigabitEthernet3
i L2    10.100.57.0/24 [115/20] via 10.100.45.5, 10:51:27, GigabitEthernet1
i L2    10.100.67.0/24 [115/20] via 10.100.46.6, 10:50:46, GigabitEthernet3
i L2    10.100.100.2/32 [115/30] via 10.100.34.3, 00:36:19, GigabitEthernet2
i L2    10.100.100.3/32 [115/10] via 10.100.34.3, 10:51:59, GigabitEthernet2
C       10.100.100.4/32 is directly connected, Loopback0
i L2    10.100.100.5/32 [115/10] via 10.100.45.5, 10:51:27, GigabitEthernet1
i L2    10.100.100.6/32 [115/20] via 10.100.46.6, 10:50:46, GigabitEthernet3
i L2    10.100.100.7/32 [115/20] via 10.100.45.5, 10:50:20, GigabitEthernet1
```

Only L2 routes are seen. What is the conclusion? To put it into one exam-type statement: L1 routes are advertised into the L2 backbone, and L2 routes are not advertised into L1 areas by default, except for the default route.

Now, reread that last statement. What does it mean from a design perspective? *Configure the L1 areas to have a default route pointing to the L1-L2 router, or alternatively, place all routers within a single large L2 area.* The previous statement is *my opinion* (although an educated one based on experience). Wait, what is the point of having multiple L2 areas then? And why does Figure 5-1, the reference topology, have multiple L2 areas?

I constructed the diagram to illustrate how IS-IS behaves, not to make a design recommendation. Now that you know that PE1, which belongs to area 1, will still get area 2 and area 3 routes, why not run a single L2 area? That is what most ISPs try to do nowadays; simplicity is the key driving force. Unless you are running out of scale. Or if you run networks under different administrative governance. Or you are merging networks. Or you can dream up other corner case scenarios. And for those, there are discussions, differences of opinions, and "better" ways of doing things. If you are running out of scale, use BGP. Or use Cisco Unified MPLS, which bridges multiple IS-IS domains into a single LSP. Or use IS-IS prefix suppression to only advertise loopback interfaces. Or, depending on your topology, start summarizing routes, using IS-IS mesh-groups. (Look up mesh-groups when you have time.) … I have a headache coming on just thinking about this. We are here to see how the protocol works, and if I had my say, a single IS-IS Level-2 area for the network core is where I would start. But I am not you and I do not know your network and business. But I'm convinced I can charge a princely sum for my consultations, just like those trendy artisanal coffees… except I promise my advice won't leave a bitter taste in your mouth!

Back to something far more interesting. Where does PE2's default route in Example 5-28 come from? Yes, it comes from PE3, but how did PE3 know to advertise it? Remember, you did not configure the default route anywhere. Even more so, what is the IS-IS mechanism that advertised the default route to PE2? Meet the *attach bit* from RFC 3787, section 7. When a router is L1-L2, it will use the attach bit to advertise to the router in the same area how to exit the area to reach other destinations. Example 5-32 shows exactly that.

Example 5-32 *IS-IS Attach Bit*

```
RP/0/RP0/CPU0:PE3# show isis database detail PE3.00-00

IS-IS CCNP (Level-1) Link State Database
LSPID                 LSP Seq Num   LSP Checksum  LSP Holdtime/Rcvd  ATT/P/OL
PE3.00-00            * 0x00000009   0x71e8           856   /*         1/0/0
  Area Address:   49.0001
  NLPID:          0xcc
  NLPID:          0x8e
  IP Address:     10.100.100.3
  IPv6 Address:   2001:3:3:3::3
  Hostname:       PE3
  Metric: 10        IP-Extended 10.100.23.0/24
  Metric: 10        IPv6 2001:10:100:23::/64
  Metric: 10        IS-Extended PE2.00
```

```
IS-IS CCNP (Level-2) Link State Database
LSPID                  LSP Seq Num  LSP Checksum  LSP Holdtime/Rcvd  ATT/P/OL
PE3.00-00            * 0x0000000b   0xe0e8         820  /*            0/0/0
  Area Address:  49.0001
  NLPID:         0xcc
  NLPID:         0x8e
  IP Address:    10.100.100.3
  IPv6 Address:  2001:3:3:3::3
  Hostname:      PE3
  Metric: 10     IP-Extended 10.100.23.0/24
  Metric: 10     IP-Extended 10.100.34.0/24
  Metric: 10     IP-Extended 10.100.35.0/24
  Metric: 0      IP-Extended 10.100.100.3/32
  Metric: 20     IP-Extended 10.100.100.2/32
  Metric: 0      IPv6 2001:3:3:3::3/128
  Metric: 10     IPv6 2001:10:100:23::/64
  Metric: 10     IPv6 2001:10:100:34::/64
  Metric: 10     IPv6 2001:10:100:35::/64
  Metric: 20     IPv6 2001:2:2:2::2/128
  Metric: 10     IS-Extended P4.00
  Metric: 10     IS-Extended P5.00
RP/0/RP0/CPU0:PE3# show ip route
! Output omitted for brevity
Gateway of last resort is not set

C    10.100.23.0/24 is directly connected, 00:33:30, GigabitEthernet0/0/0/1
L    10.100.23.3/32 is directly connected, 00:33:30, GigabitEthernet0/0/0/1
C    10.100.34.0/24 is directly connected, 00:33:30, GigabitEthernet0/0/0/2
L    10.100.34.3/32 is directly connected, 00:33:30, GigabitEthernet0/0/0/2
C    10.100.35.0/24 is directly connected, 00:33:30, GigabitEthernet0/0/0/3
L    10.100.35.3/32 is directly connected, 00:33:30, GigabitEthernet0/0/0/3
i L2 10.100.45.0/24 [115/20] via 10.100.35.5, 00:33:26, GigabitEthernet0/0/0/3
                    [115/20] via 10.100.34.4, 00:33:26, GigabitEthernet0/0/0/2
i L2 10.100.46.0/24 [115/20] via 10.100.34.4, 00:33:29, GigabitEthernet0/0/0/2
i L2 10.100.57.0/24 [115/20] via 10.100.35.5, 00:33:26, GigabitEthernet0/0/0/3
i L2 10.100.67.0/24 [115/30] via 10.100.35.5, 00:33:26, GigabitEthernet0/0/0/3
                    [115/30] via 10.100.34.4, 00:33:26, GigabitEthernet0/0/0/2
i L1 10.100.100.2/32 [115/20] via 10.100.23.2, 00:33:30, GigabitEthernet0/0/0/1
L    10.100.100.3/32 is directly connected, 00:34:08, Loopback0
i L2 10.100.100.4/32 [115/20] via 10.100.34.4, 00:33:29, GigabitEthernet0/0/0/2
i L2 10.100.100.5/32 [115/10] via 10.100.35.5, 00:33:26, GigabitEthernet0/0/0/3
i L2 10.100.100.6/32 [115/30] via 10.100.34.4, 00:33:29, GigabitEthernet0/0/0/2
i L2 10.100.100.7/32 [115/20] via 10.100.35.5, 00:33:26, GigabitEthernet0/0/0/3
```

In PE3's LSP database Level-1 section, the ATT bit is flipped to the value of 1; this is what makes PE3 advertise this default route to this Level-1 area. What could be interesting is to look at PE6 and PE7, since they both belong to the same Level-1 area. How would their databases look for area 0003, I wonder? Example 5-33 shows this.

Example 5-33 *IS-IS Attach Bit on Multiple Routers*

```
PE6# show isis database detail

IS-IS Level-1 Link State Database:
LSPID                   LSP Seq Num  LSP Checksum  LSP Holdtime/Rcvd    ATT/P/OL
PE6.00-00             * 0x0000000B   0x8CE1                  1102/*      1/0/0
  Area Address: 49.0003
  NLPID:        0xCC 0x8E
  Hostname: PE6
  Metric: 10       IS-Extended PE7.00
  IP Address:   10.100.67.6
  Metric: 10       IP 10.100.67.0/24
  IPv6 Address: 2001:10:100:67::6
  Metric: 10       IPv6 2001:10:100:67::/64
PE7.00-00              0x0000000C   0x8C38                   599/1200    1/0/0
  Area Address: 49.0003
  NLPID:        0xCC 0x8E
  IP Address:   10.100.100.7
  IPv6 Address: 2001:7:7:7::7
  Hostname: PE7
  Metric: 10       IP 10.100.67.0/24
  Metric: 10       IPv6 2001:10:100:67::/64
  Metric: 10       IS-Extended PE6.00
```

Isn't that something? Both PE6 and PE7 advertise their own exits from area 0003. But back to PE3. In the lower output of Example 5-32, you should also observe that there is no default route on PE3; it just knows about all the IS-IS networks advertised in the topology. You can change this, however. You can hop on P4 and advertise the default route into the topology, as shown in Example 5-34.

Example 5-34 *IS-IS Default Route Origination*

```
P4# configure terminal
Enter configuration commands, one per line.  End with CNTL/Z.
P4(config)# router isis
P4(config-router)# default-information ?
  originate  Distribute a default route

P4(config-router)# default-information originate ?
  route-map  Route-map reference
  <cr>
```

```
P4(config-router)# default-information originate
P4(config-router)#
```

```
RP/0/RP0/CPU0:PE3# show ip route
! Output omitted for brevity
Gateway of last resort is 10.100.34.4 to network 0.0.0.0

i*L2 0.0.0.0/0 [115/10] via 10.100.34.4, 00:00:07, GigabitEthernet0/0/0/2
C    10.100.23.0/24 is directly connected, 00:52:00, GigabitEthernet0/0/0/1
L    10.100.23.3/32 is directly connected, 00:52:00, GigabitEthernet0/0/0/1
C    10.100.34.0/24 is directly connected, 00:52:00, GigabitEthernet0/0/0/2
L    10.100.34.3/32 is directly connected, 00:52:00, GigabitEthernet0/0/0/2
C    10.100.35.0/24 is directly connected, 00:52:00, GigabitEthernet0/0/0/3
L    10.100.35.3/32 is directly connected, 00:52:00, GigabitEthernet0/0/0/3
i L2 10.100.45.0/24 [115/20] via 10.100.35.5, 00:51:56, GigabitEthernet0/0/0/3
                    [115/20] via 10.100.34.4, 00:51:56, GigabitEthernet0/0/0/2
i L2 10.100.46.0/24 [115/20] via 10.100.34.4, 00:51:59, GigabitEthernet0/0/0/2
i L2 10.100.57.0/24 [115/20] via 10.100.35.5, 00:51:56, GigabitEthernet0/0/0/3
i L2 10.100.67.0/24 [115/30] via 10.100.35.5, 00:51:56, GigabitEthernet0/0/0/3
                    [115/30] via 10.100.34.4, 00:51:56, GigabitEthernet0/0/0/2
i L1 10.100.100.2/32 [115/20] via 10.100.23.2, 00:51:59, GigabitEthernet0/0/0/1
L    10.100.100.3/32 is directly connected, 00:52:38, Loopback0
i L2 10.100.100.4/32 [115/20] via 10.100.34.4, 00:51:59, GigabitEthernet0/0/0/2
i L2 10.100.100.5/32 [115/10] via 10.100.35.5, 00:51:56, GigabitEthernet0/0/0/3
i L2 10.100.100.6/32 [115/30] via 10.100.34.4, 00:51:59, GigabitEthernet0/0/0/2
i L2 10.100.100.7/32 [115/20] via 10.100.35.5, 00:51:56, GigabitEthernet0/0/0/3
```

Note the option to use a route map, but you just want the vanilla default route. It immediately shows up on PE3 as well. Again, P4 has no default route in its RIB. It doesn't matter, because it still advertises that route.

Overload Bit

The Overload bit is a good one to be aware of. Originally, it signified memory exhaustion on a router—a rare condition on modern routers. Operators cleverly use this technique to route the traffic around the router on which they plan to do maintenance. Example 5-36 shows this feature in action. I will take P5 out of service for "maintenance." But before we do, here is a good brainstorming activity to prepare you for the exam and professional work.

Look at Figure 5-1 again. When you take P5 out of service, what consequences will this have on the topology? Do not read the answer but think about this discussion on areas and levels. Will full reachability work between areas 1 and 3? Specifically, will PE3 be able to ping PE7's loopback 10.100.100.7?

The answer should be no, since PE7's loopback0 is in Level-2, which will be cut off from the contiguous connectivity to the backbone as soon as P5 is no longer a part of the path. By taking P5 out of service, you will break the rule of keeping the backbone fully connected and lose reachability. It is good to think ahead, and that is what I am trying to coach you on. Our suggestion is to convert the PE6-PE7 link to Level-2. Do this on your own. This task shouldn't be hard. If you do not do it, you will not be able to reach PE7 unless you come up with this or a different solution. Let's pick up in Example 5-35 before making the change.

Example 5-35 *Overload Bit Usage Part 1*

```
RP/0/RP0/CPU0:PE3# show ip route | include 10.100.100.7/32
i L2 10.100.100.7/32 [115/20] via 10.100.35.5, 00:00:36, GigabitEthernet0/0/0/3
RP/0/RP0/CPU0:PE3# trace 10.100.100.7

Type escape sequence to abort.
Tracing the route to 10.100.100.7

1  10.100.35.5 5 msec   3 msec   3 msec
2  10.100.57.7 6 msec   *   6 msec
```

Notice that PE3's route and trace to PE7 lie through P5. Now for some unscheduled maintenance window time...

Example 5-36 *Overload Bit Usage Part 2*

```
RP/0/RP0/CPU0:P5# configure
RP/0/RP0/CPU0:P5(config)# router isis CCNP
RP/0/RP0/CPU0:P5(config-isis)# se?
segment-routing  set-overload-bit
RP/0/RP0/CPU0:P5(config-isis)# set-overload-bit ?
  advertise    If overload-bit set advertise the following types of IP prefixes
  level        Set overload-bit for one level only
  on-startup   Set overload-bit temporarily after reboot
  <cr>
RP/0/RP0/CPU0:P5(config-isis)# set-overload-bit
RP/0/RP0/CPU0:P5(config-isis)# commit
RP/0/RP0/CPU0:P5(config-isis)# do show isis database P5.00-00

IS-IS CCNP (Level-1) Link State Database
LSPID                  LSP Seq Num  LSP Checksum  LSP Holdtime/Rcvd  ATT/P/OL
P5.00-00             * 0x00000011   0x46b8          1186 /*            0/0/1


IS-IS CCNP (Level-2) Link State Database
LSPID                  LSP Seq Num  LSP Checksum  LSP Holdtime/Rcvd  ATT/P/OL
P5.00-00             * 0x00000016   0xe798          1186 /*            0/0/1
```

After seeing the option to advertise the overload bit for different prefixes, levels, or on start-up, you can choose the road most traveled and see the OL bit flipped to 1 in the LSP database. In Example 5-37, you can confirm that PE3 now takes a different path.

Example 5-37   *Overload Bit Usage Part 3*

```
RP/0/RP0/CPU0:PE3# show ip route | include 10.100.100.7/32
i L2 10.100.100.7/32 [115/30] via 10.100.34.4, 00:06:11, GigabitEthernet0/0/0/2
RP/0/RP0/CPU0:PE3# trace 10.100.100.7

Type escape sequence to abort.
Tracing the route to 10.100.100.7

 1  10.100.34.4 3 msec  2 msec  3 msec
 2  10.100.46.6 37 msec  3 msec  3 msec
 3  10.100.67.7 9 msec  *  9 msec
```

Now you have all the time in the world to upgrade P5 to the image TAC wants you to load. What other things do I have in mind for you? Let's do a couple more before we move on to troubleshooting IS-IS.

Authentication

IS-IS supports plaintext and MD5 authentication on hello packets and LSPs. PE2 and PE3 peering desperately needs these, your manager tells you. For exam purposes, it's good to know that TLV 10 stores IS-IS authentication, which is present in IIH and PDUs. Example 5-38 shows one way to configure authentication.

Example 5-38   *IIH Plaintext Authentication IOS*

```
PE2# configure terminal
Enter configuration commands, one per line.  End with CNTL/Z.
PE2(config)# key chain IIH
PE2(config-keychain)# key 1
PE2(config-keychain-key)# key-string IKNOWISIS
PE2(config-keychain-key)# interface GigabitEthernet 1
PE2(config-if)# isis authentication mode ?
  md5    Keyed message digest
  text  Clear text password

PE2(config-if)# isis authentication mode text
PE2(config-if)# isis authentication key-chain IIH
PE2(config-if)# do show isis neighbor

System Id        Type Interface    IP Address      State Holdtime Circuit Id
PE3              L1   Gi1           10.100.23.3     UP    20       00

System Id        Type Interface    IP Address      State Holdtime Circuit Id
PE3              L1   Gi1           10.100.23.3     UP    11       00
PE2(config-if)# do show isis neighbor
```

```
System Id            Type Interface      IP Address          State Holdtime Circuit Id
PE3                  L1   Gi1            10.100.23.3          UP   2        00
PE2(config-if)# do show isis neighbor


System Id            Type Interface      IP Address          State Holdtime Circuit Id
PE3                  L1   Gi1            10.100.23.3          UP   005 ms   00
PE2(config-if)# do show isis neighbor


System Id            Type Interface      IP Address          State Holdtime Circuit Id
PE2(config-if)#
```

In this example, you enable the IOS side and can watch the peering dissolve in front of your eyes as the countdown timer expires. Now, you can fix the other side, as shown in Example 5-39.

Example 5-39 *IIH Plaintext Authentication IOS XR*

```
RP/0/RP0/CPU0:PE3# configure
RP/0/RP0/CPU0:PE3(config)# router isis CCNP
RP/0/RP0/CPU0:PE3(config-isis)# interface gigabitEthernet 0/0/0/1
RP/0/RP0/CPU0:PE3(config-isis-if)# hello-password ?
  WORD       The unencrypted (clear text) hello password
  accept     Use password for incoming authentication only
  clear      Specifies an unencrypted password will follow
  encrypted  Specifies an encrypted password will follow
  hmac-md5   Use HMAC-MD5 authentication
  keychain   Specifies a Key Chain name will follow
  text       Use cleartext password authentication
RP/0/RP0/CPU0:PE3(config-isis-if)# hello-password text IKNOWISIS
RP/0/RP0/CPU0:PE3(config-isis-if)# do show isis neighbor

IS-IS CCNP neighbors:
System Id    Interface    SNPA      State Holdtime Type IETF-NSF
PE2          Gi0/0/0/1    *PtoP*    Init  22       L1   Capable
P4           Gi0/0/0/2    *PtoP*    Up    26       L2   Capable
P5           Gi0/0/0/3    *PtoP*    Up    23       L2   Capable

Total neighbor count: 3
RP/0/RP0/CPU0:PE3(config-isis-if)# commit
RP/0/RP0/CPU0:PE3(config-isis-if)# do show isis neighbor

IS-IS CCNP neighbors:
System Id    Interface    SNPA      State Holdtime Type IETF-NSF
PE2          Gi0/0/0/1    *PtoP*    Up    29       L1   Capable
P4           Gi0/0/0/2    *PtoP*    Up    29       L2   Capable
P5           Gi0/0/0/3    *PtoP*    Up    28       L2   Capable
```

```
Total neighbor count: 3
```

```
PE2# show isis neighbors detail

System Id          Type Interface      IP Address        State Holdtime Circuit Id
PE3                L1   Gi1             10.100.23.3       UP    23       00
  Area Address(es): 49.0001
  SNPA: 5254.000e.c224
  IPv6 Address(es): FE80::5054:FF:FE0E:C224
  IPv6 Global Address: 2001:10:100:23::3
  State Changed: 00:15:56
  Format: Phase V
  Remote TID: 0
  Local TID:  0
  Interface name: GigabitEthernet1
  Neighbor Circuit Id: 7
  L1 Last Hello Authentication Type: Text
```

There are several authentication options. If you choose plaintext, right before hitting
commit, you see PE2 is in Init state. As you hit **commit**, it comes right back up.

What would be good homework at this point? Try getting this to work with key chains on
the XR side, because they do not support plaintext authentication.

The second task is to secure LSPs. You can take care of the IOS side first, as in Example 5-40.

Example 5-40 *LSP MD5 Authentication*

```
PE2# configure terminal
Enter configuration commands, one per line.  End with CNTL/Z.
PE2(config)# router isis
PE2(config-router)# authentication mode md5
PE2(config-router)# authentication key ?
  WORD  Name of key-chain

PE2(config-router)# authentication key LSP ?
  enable-poi  enable purge originator identification tlv
  level-1     ISIS authentication for level-1
  level-2     ISIS authentication for level-2
  <cr>        <cr>

PE2(config-router)# authentication key LSP
PE2(config-router)# exit
PE2(config)# key chain LSP
PE2(config-keychain)# key 1
PE2(config-keychain-key)# key-string AUTH-LSP
PE2(config-keychain-key)#
```

```
RP/0/RP0/CPU0:PE3# configure
RP/0/RP0/CPU0:PE3(config)# router isis CCNP
RP/0/RP0/CPU0:PE3(config-isis)# lsp-password ?
  WORD       The unencrypted (clear text) LSP/SNP password
  accept     Use password for incoming authentication only
  clear      Specifies an unencrypted password will follow
  encrypted  Specifies an encrypted password will follow
  hmac-md5   Use HMAC-MD5 authentication
  keychain   Specifies a Key Chain name will follow
  text       Use cleartext password authentication
RP/0/RP0/CPU0:PE3(config-isis)# lsp-password keychain LSP ?
  enable-poi  Enable purge originator identification
  level       Set lsp-password for one level only
  send-only   Authenticate outgoing LSPs/SNPs only
  snp         Specify SNP packets authentication mode
  <cr>
RP/0/RP0/CPU0:PE3(config-isis)# lsp-password keychain LSP
RP/0/RP0/CPU0:PE3(config-isis)# exit
RP/0/RP0/CPU0:PE3(config)# key chain LSP
RP/0/RP0/CPU0:PE3(config-LSP)# key 1
P/0/RP0/CPU0:PE3(config-LSP-1)# cryptographic-algorithm md5
RP/0/RP0/CPU0:PE3(config-LSP-1)# key-string AUTH-LSP
RP/0/RP0/CPU0:PE3(config-LSP-1)# commit
RP/0/RP0/CPU0:PE3(config-LSP-1)#
```

```
PE2# show isis database detail


IS-IS Level-1 Link State Database:
LSPID                    LSP Seq Num   LSP Checksum   LSP Holdtime/Rcvd    ATT/P/OL
PE2.00-00               * 0x00000026   0x2FC8              802/*            0/0/0
  Auth:          Algorithm MD5, Length: 17
  Area Address: 49.0001
  NLPID:         0xCC 0x8E
  Hostname: PE2
  Metric: 10        IS-Extended PE3.00
  IP Address:    10.100.100.2
  Metric: 10        IP 10.100.100.2/32
  Metric: 10        IP 10.100.23.0/24
  IPv6 Address: 2001:2:2:2::2
  Metric: 10        IPv6 2001:2:2:2::2/128
  Metric: 10        IPv6 2001:10:100:23::/64
PE3.00-00                0x00000024   0x6FB7          0 (802)/1200         1/0/0
  Auth:          Algorithm MD5, Length: 17
```

```
IS-IS Level-2 Link State Database:
LSPID                   LSP Seq Num  LSP Checksum  LSP Holdtime/Rcvd     ATT/P/OL
PE2.00-00               * 0x0000001E   0x272B                802/*         0/0/0
  Auth:                 Algorithm MD5, Length: 17
  Area Address: 49.0001
  NLPID:        0xCC 0x8E
  Hostname: PE2
  Metric: 10        IP 10.100.100.2/32
  Metric: 10        IP 10.100.23.0/24
  Metric: 10        IPv6 2001:2:2:2::2/128
  Metric: 10        IPv6 2001:10:100:23::/64
```

The task is now complete and verified. Note that I deliberately avoid the use of **show running-config** unless it is absolutely necessary. To excel in this exam and become a proficient engineer (as Cisco expects), hands-on learning is paramount—a belief I strongly uphold. Mere book knowledge falls short; I've encountered individuals adept at memorization yet unable to execute fundamental networking tasks. My aim is to pass invaluable skills on to you, those you'll appreciate profoundly if you embrace this method.

Back to IS-IS Areas

Would you like to do some "James Bond" networking before moving on to troubleshooting IS-IS? Look at Figure 5-3, where I propose making a couple of changes to the topology.

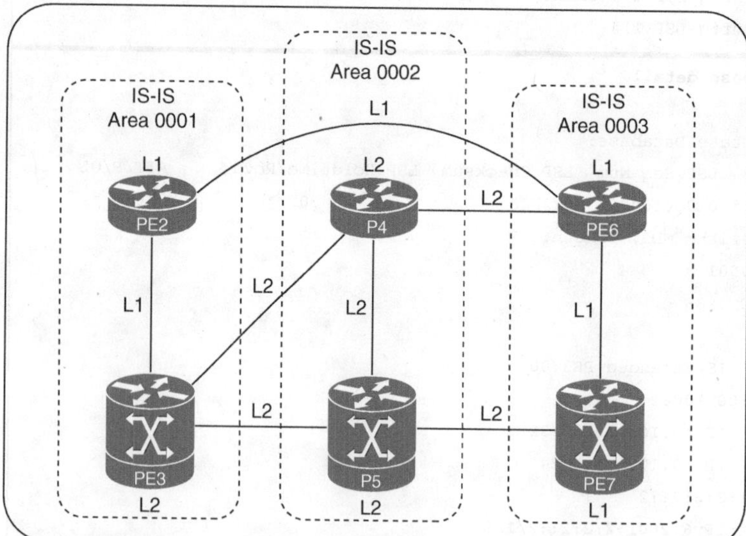

Figure 5-3 *IS-IS Topology Change*

To stage what I am about to show you next, you need to convert area 0003 to L1 links and add an additional L1 link between PE2 and PE6. If you are using CML or other virtualized platforms, this task should not take you long. I am going to power down the current lab to get interfaces added and will see you in a few minutes. You can also roll back the last change on P5 for the overload bit if you would like. Here is where you pick up in Example 5-41.

Example 5-41   *PE2-PE6 Connectivity Verified*

```
PE6(config-if)# do ping 10.100.26.2
Type escape sequence to abort.
Sending 5, 100-byte ICMP Echos to 10.100.26.2, timeout is 2 seconds:
.!!!!
Success rate is 80 percent (4/5), round-trip min/avg/max = 1/15/57 ms
```

Question: Can PE2 and PE6 exchange L1 routes? If you recall what we covered previously in
this chapter, the answer should be no. What is your explanation as to the reasons why? Here
are two. First, areas are not equal; therefore, the direct L1 adjacency is not possible. Second,
since L2 routes are not leaked to L1 areas by default, both PE2 and PE6 will be missing
routes from each other's areas. You can take a snapshot of what you see with Example 5-42.

Example 5-42   *PE6 Topology View*

```
PE6(config-if)# do show isis database

IS-IS Level-1 Link State Database:
LSPID                 LSP Seq Num   LSP Checksum  LSP Holdtime/Rcvd    ATT/P/OL
PE6.00-00           * 0x00000005    0x45D7                  1032/*       1/0/0
PE7.00-00             0x00000003    0xD768                  1027/1199    1/0/0
IS-IS Level-2 Link State Database:
LSPID                 LSP Seq Num   LSP Checksum  LSP Holdtime/Rcvd    ATT/P/OL
PE3.00-00             0x00000013    0x0C6C                  1032/1117    0/0/0
P4.00-00              0x0000000E    0xC616                  1031/1200    0/0/0
P5.00-00              0x00000011    0xED9B                  1032/645     0/0/0
PE6.00-00           * 0x00000015    0x8C88                  1036/*       0/0/0
PE7.00-00             0x00000017    0xA92C                  1032/1193    0/0/0
PE6(config-if)# do show ip route | include L1|L2
       i - IS-IS, su - IS-IS summary, L1 - IS-IS level-1, L2 - IS-IS level-2
i*L2  0.0.0.0/0 [115/10] via 10.100.46.4, 00:03:03, GigabitEthernet3
i L2     10.100.23.0/24 [115/30] via 10.100.46.4, 00:03:01, GigabitEthernet3
i L2     10.100.26.0/24 [115/40] via 10.100.46.4, 00:03:01, GigabitEthernet3
i L2     10.100.34.0/24 [115/20] via 10.100.46.4, 00:03:03, GigabitEthernet3
i L2     10.100.35.0/24 [115/30] via 10.100.46.4, 00:03:01, GigabitEthernet3
i L2     10.100.45.0/24 [115/20] via 10.100.46.4, 00:03:03, GigabitEthernet3
i L2     10.100.57.0/24 [115/30] via 10.100.46.4, 00:03:02, GigabitEthernet3
i L2     10.100.100.2/32 [115/40] via 10.100.46.4, 00:03:01, GigabitEthernet3
i L2     10.100.100.3/32 [115/20] via 10.100.46.4, 00:03:01, GigabitEthernet3
i L2     10.100.100.4/32 [115/20] via 10.100.46.4, 00:03:03, GigabitEthernet3
i L2     10.100.100.5/32 [115/20] via 10.100.46.4, 00:03:02, GigabitEthernet3
i L1     10.100.100.7/32 [115/10] via 10.100.67.7, 00:03:07, GigabitEthernet1
```

On PE6, notice the absence of PE2's peering (not in the LSP database) and the single L1
route from PE7. A critical question: How would you solve this "problem"? Think before
reading further.

If you understand the mechanics of IS-IS and what you need to know for the exam, a possible and quick solution should be to make their areas equal. I propose you convert area 0003 on PE6 and PE7 to area 0001. Example 5-43 shows PE6; PE7 needs this as well.

Example 5-43   *Changing Area 0003 to Area 0001*

```
PE6(config)# router isis
PE6(config-router)# no net 49.0003.0101.0010.0006.00
PE6(config-router)# net 49.0001.0101.0010.0006.00
PE6(config-router)#
```

Are you ready to see what happened? Take a look at Example 5-44.

Example 5-44   *Changing Area 0003 to Area 0001 results*

```
PE6(config-if)# do show isis database

IS-IS Level-1 Link State Database:
LSPID                 LSP Seq Num   LSP Checksum   LSP Holdtime/Rcvd     ATT/P/OL
PE2.00-00             0x00000012    0xFE7B            1192/1200          0/0/0
PE3.00-00             0x0000000F    0x7068            1193/527           1/0/0
PE6.00-00           * 0x0000000A    0xB524            1194/*             1/0/0
PE7.00-00             0x00000007    0xCF6C            1193/1200          1/0/0
IS-IS Level-2 Link State Database:
LSPID                 LSP Seq Num   LSP Checksum   LSP Holdtime/Rcvd     ATT/P/OL
PE3.00-00             0x00000014    0xC62E            1193/1199          0/0/0
P4.00-00              0x0000000E    0xC616             602/1200          0/0/0
P5.00-00              0x00000012    0xEB9C             927/1198          0/0/0
PE6.00-00           * 0x00000018    0x440A            1194/*             0/0/0
PE7.00-00             0x00000019    0xEEB1            1193/1199          0/0/0
PE6(config-if)# do sh ip route | i L1|L2
      i - IS-IS, su - IS-IS summary, L1 - IS-IS level-1, L2 - IS-IS level-2
i*L2  0.0.0.0/0 [115/10] via 10.100.46.4, 00:10:23, GigabitEthernet3
i L1      10.100.23.0/24 [115/20] via 10.100.26.2, 00:00:33, GigabitEthernet2
i L2      10.100.34.0/24 [115/20] via 10.100.46.4, 00:10:23, GigabitEthernet3
i L2      10.100.35.0/24 [115/30] via 10.100.46.4, 00:10:21, GigabitEthernet3
i L2      10.100.45.0/24 [115/20] via 10.100.46.4, 00:10:23, GigabitEthernet3
i L2      10.100.57.0/24 [115/30] via 10.100.46.4, 00:10:22, GigabitEthernet3
i L1      10.100.100.2/32 [115/20] via 10.100.26.2, 00:00:33, GigabitEthernet2
i L1      10.100.100.3/32 [115/20] via 10.100.26.2, 00:00:32, GigabitEthernet2
i L2      10.100.100.4/32 [115/20] via 10.100.46.4, 00:10:23, GigabitEthernet3
i L2      10.100.100.5/32 [115/20] via 10.100.46.4, 00:10:22, GigabitEthernet3
i L1      10.100.100.7/32 [115/10] via 10.100.67.7, 00:10:27, GigabitEthernet1
PE6(config-if)# do trace 10.100.100.3
Type escape sequence to abort.
Tracing the route to 10.100.100.3
VRF info: (vrf in name/id, vrf out name/id)
  1 10.100.26.2 2 msec 1 msec 0 msec
  2 10.100.23.3 20 msec 5 msec *
```

Voila! Notice that the peering is built, and L1 area 0001 contains routes from both PE3 and PE7. The adjacency completes, and the L1 routes dominate the pathing in the area as described at the beginning of IS-IS logical flow. The IS-IS jigsaw puzzle is finally complete. At this point, you should have a thorough understanding of how the protocol functions. When doing this "007" networking, it is easy to mess up the IS-IS database. Should this happen, clear the IS-IS processes and database, and the network will put itself back together.

Troubleshooting IS-IS

If you paced yourself and carefully examined the content in this chapter, you have climbed far on the IS-IS mountain and already have the most important aspect necessary for troubleshooting this protocol: you understand the mechanics of how it works. What you may be missing now are the commands to reveal where the problems lie. Table 5-3 summarizes the more important ones that you have seen throughout these discoveries.

Table 5-3   More Relevant IS-IS Troubleshooting Commands

Command	Clues It Provides
show isis neighbor	Shows level type, interfaces, state, holdtime
show isis neighbor detail	Displays SPNA, IPv4/IPv6 addresses, area address
show isis protocol	Displays interfaces, protocols and metrics, System ID
show isis database detail	Displays a detailed view of SPF tree and LSP database
show isis topology	Displays IS-IS paths to Intermediate Systems
show isis lsp-log	Displays LSP transitions
show ip route isis	Displays incoming IS-IS routes
show clns interface	Displays interface status and configuration, MTU
clear isis *	Clears all IS-IS data structures
clear isis lspfull	Clears LSP state
debug isis adj-packets	Debugs IS-IS adjacency information
debug isis authentication	Debugs IS-IS authentication events

Well, that is IS-IS for you. Stay confident in your understanding of this protocol and don't get bogged down in minutiae, because it's your grasp of the core principles that will prove most valuable during the exam. IS-IS is a robust protocol for running your network underlay. I suggest you go through the review section that follows and take a good break to let the knowledge settle for a few days before diluting it with OSPF, which we will tackle next.

Exam Preparation Tasks

As mentioned in the section "How to Use This Book" in the Introduction, you have a few choices for exam preparation: the exercises here, Chapter 23, "Final Preparation," and the exam simulation questions in the Pearson Test Prep Software Online.

Review All Key Topics

Review the most important topics in this chapter, noted with the Key Topic icon in the margin of the page. Table 5-4 lists a reference of these key topics and the page numbers on which each is found.

Table 5-4   Key Topics for Chapter 5

Key Topic Element	Description	Page Number
Paragraph	CLNS Addressing for IS-IS	111
Table 5-2	Configuring Basic IS-IS in IOS XE and IOS XR	113
Paragraph	Areas and Levels	129
Paragraph	Reasons for Broken Adjacencies	134
Section	Route Advertisement	141
Table 5-3	More Relevant IS-IS Troubleshooting Commands	155

Define Key Terms

Define the following key terms from this chapter and check the answers in the glossary:

Connectionless Network Service (CLNS), CSNP, DIS, IIH, Link-State Database (LSDB), link-state routing protocol (LSP), NET address, NSAP, NSEL, SPF Algorithm, SPNA, TLV

Command Reference to Check Your Memory

This section includes the most important configuration and EXEC commands covered in this chapter. You might not need to memorize the complete syntax of every command, but you should be able to remember the basic keywords that are needed.

To test your memory of the commands, cover the right side of Table 5-5 with a piece of paper, read the description on the left side, and then see how much of the command you can remember.

The 350-501 exam focuses on practical, hands-on skills that are used by networking professionals. Therefore, you should be able to identify the commands needed to configure and test. Note that not all commands are fully covered in the chapter, but their presence in the following table should lead you to investigate them further to understand this technology.

Table 5-5   CLI Commands to Know

Task	Command Syntax
Specify the type of authentication used in Intermediate System to Intermediate System (IS-IS) packets for the IS-IS instance	**authentication mode {md5	text} [level-1	level-2]**
Enable authentication IS-IS	**authentication key-chain** *name-of-chain* [level-1	level-2]
Globally change the metric value for all IS-IS interfaces	**metric** *default-value* [level-1	level-2]
Configure an IS-IS routing process for IP on an interface and to attach an area designator to the routing process	**ip router isis** *area-tag*

Task	Command Syntax
Configure a router running IS-IS so that it generates and accepts only new-style type, length, value objects (TLVs)	**metric-style wide [transition] [level-1 | level-2 | level-1-2]**
Display information about IS-IS neighbors	**show isis neighbors [detail]**
Display information regarding IS-IS nodes	**show isis node [link | prefix] [*node-name*]**
Display paths for a specific route or for all routes under a major network that are stored in the IP local Routing Information Base (RIB)	**show isis rib [*ip-address* | *ip-address-mask*]**
Display how often and why the router has run a full Shortest Path First (SPF) calculation	**show isis [*area-tag*] [ipv6 | *] spf-log [topology {ipv6 | *topology-name* | *}]**
Display a list of all connected routers in all areas	**show isis [*process-tag*] [ipv6 | *] topology [*hostname*] [level-1 | level-2 | l1 | l2]**

Review Questions

As a part of the review, we encourage you to provide *a single-sentence answer* (keep your answers as short as possible) to the following questions. If you struggle to complete this answer in a single sentence, this may indicate a lack of clarity or reveal gaps in your understanding. We have constructed these questions to help you consolidate this chapter's information and extract the essence of the covered content.

The answers to these questions appear in Appendix A. For more practice with exam format questions, use the Pearson Test Prep Software Online.

1. Can you explain the single key advantage of the IS-IS protocol over OSPF in a service provider network?

2. What is the difference between IS-IS areas and levels?

Bibliography

R. Callon. RFC 1195, *Use of OSI IS-IS for Routing in TCP/IP and Dual Environments*, IETF, https://tools.ietf.org/html/rfc1195, December 1990.

T. Li and H. Smit. RFC 3784, *Intermediate System to Intermediate System (IS-IS) Extensions for Traffic Engineering (TE)*, IETF, https://tools.ietf.org/html/rfc3784, June 2004.

T. Li and H. Smit. RFC 5305, *IS-IS Extensions for Traffic Engineering*, IETF, https://tools.ietf.org/html/5305, October 2008.

J. Parker. RFC 3787, *Recommendations for Interoperable IP Networks using Intermediate System to Intermediate System (IS-IS)*, IETF, https://tools.ietf.org/html/rfc3787, May 2004.

## CHAPTER 6

OSPF

This chapter covers the following exam topics:

2.2 Implement OSPF (v2 and v3)

- 2.2.a Neighbor adjacency
- 2.2.b Route advertisement
- 2.2.c Multiarea (addressing and types)
- 2.2.d Metrics

2.6 Troubleshoot routing protocols

- 2.6.a Neighbor adjacency (BGP, OSPF, IS-IS)
- 2.6.b Route advertisement (BGP, OSPF, IS-IS)

I (Brad) hope you took a break after the last chapter because you don't want to mix up the knowledge of OSPF with IS-IS. I strongly recommend that you avoid building your understanding of these protocols solely through comparisons because this method could hinder your ability to discern critical distinctions. I have been a victim of this approach and no longer support it for the reason I mention.

Recall from the preceding chapter on IS-IS that extensive literature exists on link-state routing protocols, but our emphasis is on practical implementation to quickly solve exam riddles. Thus, in this chapter, I prioritize the essential configuration components. Supplementing with additional resources outside this material can provide a comprehensive understanding. I encourage you to concentrate on practical applications; this will ensure success in demonstrating proficiency during the exam.

"Do I Know This Already?" Quiz

The "Do I Know This Already?" quiz allows you to assess whether you should read this entire chapter thoroughly or jump to the "Exam Preparation Tasks" section. If you are in doubt about your answers to these questions or your own assessment of your knowledge of the topics, read the entire chapter. Table 6-1 lists the major headings in this chapter and their corresponding "Do I Know This Already?" quiz questions. You can find the answers in Appendix A, "Answers to the 'Do I Know This Already?' Quizzes and Review Questions."

Table 6-1 "Do I Know This Already?" Section-to-Question Mapping

Foundation Topics Section	Questions
Implement OSPFv2	1–5
Implement OSPFv3	6
Troubleshooting OSPF	7

> **CAUTION**   The goal of self-assessment is to gauge your mastery of the topics in this chapter. If you do not know the answer to a question or are only partially sure of the answer, you should mark that question as wrong for purposes of the self-assessment. Giving yourself credit for an answer you correctly guess skews your self-assessment results and might provide you with a false sense of security.

1. Normal OSPF areas include all of these LSA types except for which of the following?

    a. 3

    b. 4

    c. 5

    d. 7

2. OSPFv3 supports which of the following? (Select all that apply.)

    a. IKE

    b. AH

    c. ESP

    d. Native OSPF encryption

3. Point-to-point interfaces generate which type routes?

    a. Host routes

    b. Network routes associated with the interface's subnet

    c. No routes are generated, because the router knows to send traffic to its subnet peer

    d. /31 network routes

4. Which of the following are true about OSPF area controls? (Select all that apply.)

    a. Storm updates that would cause routers to crash

    b. Pseudo node behavior for multi-access links

    c. Flooding scope of link-state advertisements

    d. Interval timers for hello packets

5. What does the presence of a router LSA E-bit indicate?

    a. The router is an ABR.

    b. The router is in NSSA.

    c. The router is an ASBR.

    d. The router is not in NSSA.

6. In an OSPFv3 network, you have configured multiple routers in a single OSPF area. Which of the following statements about the handling of link-local addresses and OSPFv3 LSA types is correct? (Select all that apply.)

    a. Link-local addresses are used for OSPFv3 neighbor discovery and adjacency formation.

    b. OSPFv3 uses the Link-LSA (Type 8) to advertise the IPv6 link-local addresses of the routers.

    c. OSPFv3 requires the manual configuration of the router ID for each router in the OSPF area.

    d. The Intra-Area-Prefix-LSA (Type 9) carries IPv6 prefixes associated with a specific OSPF area.

7. You are troubleshooting an OSPFv2 network where a router is not forming an OSPF adjacency with its neighbor. Which of the following could be a potential cause for this issue?

   a. The OSPF process IDs are different on the two routers.

   b. The OSPF Hello and Dead intervals are mismatched on the two routers.

   c. The OSPF area types (normal vs. stub) are different on the two routers.

   d. The router IDs are not manually configured on the routers.

Foundation Topics

Implement OSPFv2

Born out of the need for robustness and scalability, OSPF emerged in the late 1980s as a response to the limitations of earlier routing protocols like the Routing Information Protocol (RIP), which struggled to keep pace with the demands of burgeoning networks. Developed by the Internet Engineering Task Force (IETF), OSPF's link-state routing algorithm revolutionized the way routers exchanged information, paving the way for a more detailed and accurate view of network topology. As networks grew larger and more complex, OSPF proved its mettle time and again, becoming the "go-to choice" for interior gateway routing. It has been widely deployed in both service provider and enterprise markets, and its influence cannot be understated. So, whether you're a seasoned network engineer or an aspiring IT enthusiast, OSPF beckons with its promise of efficient routing and dynamic adaptability. *In my opinion*, OSPF's complexity dwarfs IS-IS in comparison. However, when it comes to the exam, complexity takes a backseat because your configuration prowess should steal the show.

To quote my university professor, "It is time to take off your diapers and put on your training pants." Do not proceed until you've committed Figure 6-1 and Table 6-2 to memory to the point where you could be woken up in the dead of night and still recite them flawlessly.

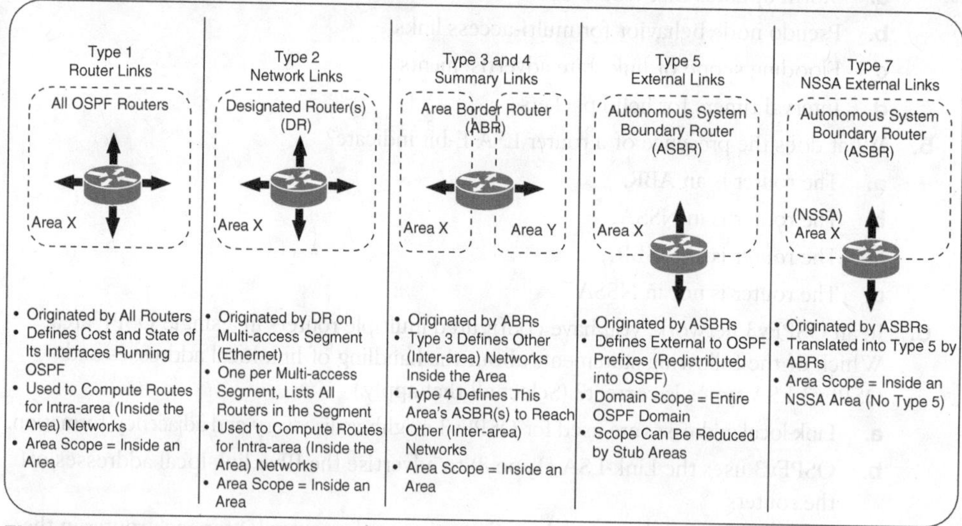

Figure 6-1 *OSPF LSA Types*

Table 6-2 OSPF Area Type and Corresponding LSAs

Area Type	Command (example)	LSAs Present	ASBR Support
Normal	area 100	1, 2, 3, 4, 5	Yes
Stub	area 100 stub	1, 2, 3	No
Totally stubby	area 100 stub no-summary	1, 2, 3 as only a default route supplied by ABR	No
Not so stubby	area 100 nssa	1, 2, 3, 7	Yes
Totally not so stubby	area 100 nssa no-summary	1, 2, 3 as only a default route supplied by ABR and can be changed to 7, 7	Yes

Just as we all have unforgettable visuals—like standing atop a mountain or witnessing the ocean for the first time—Figure 6-1 and Table 6-2 should be etched into your memory. I'm totally serious about this. Like the password to your bank account, which is not written down anywhere but in your mind, treat these two the same way. By the way, do you see why OSPF is more complex? The irony is that many of my customers are hesitant to touch IS-IS due to unfamiliarity. After you have memorized these elements, let me introduce you to the OSPF topology in Figure 6-2.

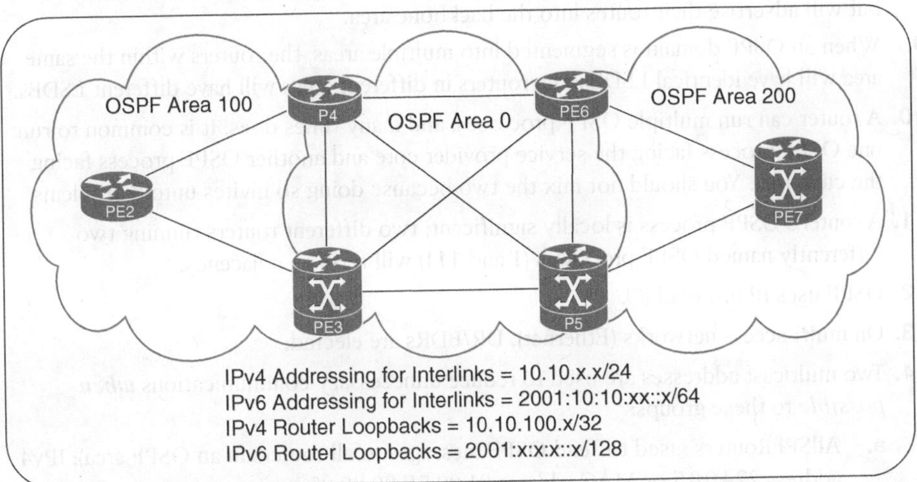

Figure 6-2 *OSPF Topology*

Study this topology, learn it, and attempt to work through the scenarios mostly "from your mind." I am constantly changing topologies (same topology, I just dragged our routers in the IS-IS topology to the sides) or changing the addressing a bit, and the router names are irrelevant. I have done this on purpose to get you to see that after a while, it should not take you long to consume the topology you see on the exam. Good engineers on my team can take literally 10 seconds to look at a complex customer drawing and jump straight into a heavy architectural conversation with zero preparation. How? They know what to look for in a diagram and so will you.

OSPF Overview

Books have been written on this subject, but my objective is to ramp up your knowledge fast. With this in mind, let's make complex simple:

1. OSPF uses link-state advertisements (**LSA**s) to flood link attributes (state and metrics) to neighboring routers.

2. Received LSAs are stored in each router's Link-State Database (LSDB) and are flooded *throughout the OSPF area* until *all routers in the area* have an identical copy of the LSDB.

3. Each router will run Dijkstra's **Shortest Path First (SPF) algorithm** (the same one I use to pick up groceries at the store) and will establish itself at the top or root of the computed SPF tree.

4. Each router's SPF *tree is different* while the *database is the same.*

5. The SPF tree shows the *shortest* path, and a common mistake is to assume there are no redundant or backup paths.

6. The SPF tree will get rebuilt when topology changes occur.

7. A two-tier hierarchical topology will consist of contiguous backbone area 0, which interconnects all other possible areas and advertises routes into nonbackbone areas.

8. Nonbackbone areas will not have a full view of OSPF topologies outside of their areas but will advertise their routes into the backbone area.

9. When an OSPF domain is segmented into multiple areas, the routers within the same area will have identical LSDBs; the routers in different areas will have different LSDBs.

10. A router can run multiple OSPF processes, and many times does. It is common to run one OSPF process facing the service provider core and another OSPF process facing the customer. You should not mix the two because doing so invites untold problems.

11. A router's OSPF process is locally significant; two different routers running two differently named OSPF processes (1 and 111) will form an adjacency.

12. OSPF uses IP protocol 89.

13. On multi-access networks (Ethernet), DR/BDRs are elected.

14. Two multicast addresses are used to reduce unnecessary communications *when possible* to these groups:

    a. AllSPFRouters (used to send OSPF messages to all routers in an OSPF area): IPv4 address 224.0.0.5 or MAC address 01:00:5E:00:00:05

    b. AllDRouters (used to send OSPF messages specifically to the designated router [DR] and backup designated router [BDR]): IPv4 address 224.0.0.6 or MAC address 01:00:5E:00:00:06

You must know the OSPF packet types described in Table 6-3 to understand and troubleshoot OSPF issues.

Table 6-3 OSPF Packet Types

Type	Name	Purpose
1	Hello	Sent out periodically to discover and maintain OSPF router adjacencies
2	Database Description (DBD)	Describes LSDB contents, exchanged upon adjacency
3	Link-State Request (LSR)	Requests a portion of a neighbor's LSDB when the local LSDB appears stale
4	Link-State Update (LSU)	Responds to a Type 3 request for a particular prefix
5	Link-State Acknowledgment	Responds to flooded LSAs, ensures the reliability of the flooding mechanism

You must know OSPF router adjacency stages and their purpose as described in Table 6-4 to understand and troubleshoot OSPF issues.

Table 6-4 OSPF Adjacency States and Stages

Stage	What Happens
Down	No OSPF Hello packets have been received.
Attempt	On nonbroadcast networks, the router attempts to communicate with a neighbor but does not see new information.
Init	A Hello packet has been received from another router, but there is no two-way communication.
2-Way	There is two-way communication and DR/BDR election if necessary.
ExStart	The router agrees on the master/slave relationship for LSDB synchronization.
Exchange	Links states and Type 2 DBD packets are exchanged.
Loading	LSRs are sent to update what was missed during the Exchange stage.
Full	Routers are fully adjacent.

NOTE Use of the terms *master* and *slave* is ONLY in association with the official terminology used in industry specifications and standards and in no way diminishes Pearson's commitment to promoting diversity, equity, and inclusion, and challenging, countering, and/or combating bias and stereotyping in the global population of the learners we serve.

This is OSPF in a nutshell. Reread this as many times as you need to cement this knowledge in your mind, but I strongly suggest not memorizing the preceding tables.

Now, let's configure OSPF, beginning with Example 6-1.

Example 6-1 *Starting OSPF on IOS XR*

```
RP/0/RP0/CPU0:PE3# configure
RP/0/RP0/CPU0:PE3(config)# router ospf 1
RP/0/RP0/CPU0:PE3(config-ospf)# area 0
RP/0/RP0/CPU0:PE3(config-ospf-ar)# interface loopback0
RP/0/RP0/CPU0:PE3(config-ospf-ar-if)# exit
RP/0/RP0/CPU0:PE3(config-ospf-ar)# interface gigabitEthernet 0/0/0/0
RP/0/RP0/CPU0:PE3(config-ospf-ar-if)# exit
RP/0/RP0/CPU0:PE3(config-ospf-ar)# interface gigabitEthernet 0/0/0/3
RP/0/RP0/CPU0:PE3(config-ospf-ar-if)# exit
RP/0/RP0/CPU0:PE3(config-ospf-ar)# interface gigabitEthernet 0/0/0/4
RP/0/RP0/CPU0:PE3(config)# commit
RP/0/RP0/CPU0:PE3(config)# end
RP/0/RP0/CPU0:PE3# show protocol ospf
Fri Mar  1 20:17:38.332 UTC
Routing Protocol OSPF 1
  Router Id: 10.10.35.3
  Distance: 110
  Non-Stop Forwarding: Disabled
  Redistribution:
    None
  Area 0
    Loopback0
    GigabitEthernet0/0/0/0
    GigabitEthernet0/0/0/3
    GigabitEthernet0/0/0/4
RP/0/RP0/CPU0:PE3#
```

With PE3 ready, let's turn up P4 in Example 6-2, which looks a bit different. Each **network** statement turns on OSPF on the interface with a specific IP address and associates it with OSPF Area 0. The 0.0.0.0 wildcard mask ensures OSPF is enabled precisely on the specified IP address rather than a range of IP addresses. Feel free to be specific or less exact with wildcard masks. I have shown how I do this to avoid confusion on *my* networks.

Example 6-2 *Starting OSPF on IOS*

```
P4# show ip interface brief
Interface              IP-Address      OK? Method Status                Protocol
GigabitEthernet1       10.10.24.4      YES manual up                    up
GigabitEthernet2       unassigned      YES unset  administratively down down
GigabitEthernet3       10.10.34.4      YES manual up                    up
GigabitEthernet4       10.10.46.4      YES manual up                    up
GigabitEthernet5       10.10.45.4      YES manual up                    up
Loopback0              10.10.100.4     YES manual up                    up
```

```
P4# configure terminal
Enter configuration commands, one per line.  End with CNTL/Z.
P4(config)# router ospf 1
P4(config-router)# network 10.10.100.4 0.0.0.0 area 0
P4(config-router)# network 10.10.34.4 0.0.0.0 area 0
P4(config-router)# network 10.10.46.4 0.0.0.0 area 0
P4(config-router)# network 10.10.45.4 0.0.0.0 area 0
P4(config-router)# do show ip ospf neighbor
Neighbor ID     Pri   State           Dead Time   Address        Interface
10.10.35.3        1   FULL/DR         00:00:32    10.10.34.3     GigabitEthernet3
P4(config-router)# end
P4# debug ip ospf adjacency
OSPF adjacency debugging is on
P4# clear ip ospf 1 process
Reset OSPF process 1? [no]: yes
20:25:12.057: OSPF-1 ADJ   Lo0: Interface going Down
20:25:12.057: OSPF-1 ADJ   Lo0: 10.10.100.4 address 10.10.100.4 is dead, state DOWN
20:25:12.059: OSPF-1 ADJ   Gi5: Interface going Down
20:25:12.059: OSPF-1 ADJ   Gi5: 10.10.100.4 address 10.10.45.4 is dead, state DOWN
20:25:12.059: OSPF-1 ADJ   Gi5: Neighbor change event
20:25:12.059: OSPF-1 ADJ   Gi5: DR/BDR election
20:25:12.059: OSPF-1 ADJ   Gi5: Elect BDR 0.0.0.0
20:25:12.060: OSPF-1 ADJ   Gi5: Elect DR 0.0.0.0
20:25:12.060: OSPF-1 ADJ   Gi5: Elect BDR 0.0.0.0
20:25:12.060: OSPF-1 ADJ   Gi5: Elect DR 0.0.0.0
20:25:12.060: OSPF-1 ADJ   Gi5: DR: none
20:25:12.061: OSPF-1 ADJ   Gi5:    BDR: none
20:25:12.061: OSPF-1 ADJ   Gi5: Flush network LSA immediately
20:25:12.061: OSPF-1 ADJ   Gi5: Remember old DR 10.10.100.4 (id)
20:25:12.061: OSPF-1 ADJ   Gi4: Interface going Down
20:25:12.061: OSPF-1 ADJ   Gi4: 10.10.100.4 address 10.10.46.4 is dead, state DOWN
20:25:12.061: OSPF-1 ADJ   Gi4: Neighbor change event
20:25:12.062: OSPF-1 ADJ   Gi4: DR/BDR election
20:25:12.062: OSPF-1 ADJ   Gi4: Elect BDR 0.0.0.0
20:25:12.062: OSPF-1 ADJ   Gi4: Elect DR 0.0.0.0
20:25:12.062: OSPF-1 ADJ   Gi4: Elect BDR 0.0.0.0
20:25:12.062: OSPF-1 ADJ   Gi4: Elect DR 0.0.0.0
20:25:12.062: OSPF-1 ADJ   Gi4: DR: none
20:25:12.063: OSPF-1 ADJ   Gi4:    BDR: none
20:25:12.063: OSPF-1 ADJ   Gi4: Flush network LSA immediately
20:25:12.063: OSPF-1 ADJ   Gi4: Remember old DR 10.10.100.4 (id)
20:25:12.063: OSPF-1 ADJ   Gi3: Interface going Down
20:25:12.063: OSPF-1.ADJ   Gi3: 10.10.35.3 address 10.10.34.3 is dead, state DOWN
```

```
20:25:12.064: %OSPF-5-ADJCHG: Process 1, Nbr 10.10.35.3 on GigabitEthernet3 from
FULL to DOWN, Neighbor Down: Interface down or detached
20:25:12.064: OSPF-1 ADJ    Gi3: Neighbor change event
20:25:12.064: OSPF-1 ADJ    Gi3: DR/BDR election
20:25:12.065: OSPF-1 ADJ    Gi3: Elect BDR 10.10.100.4
20:25:12.065: OSPF-1 ADJ    Gi3: Elect DR 10.10.100.4
20:25:12.066: OSPF-1 ADJ    Gi3: Elect BDR 0.0.0.0
20:25:12.066: OSPF-1 ADJ    Gi3: Elect DR 10.10.100.4
20:25:12.066: OSPF-1 ADJ    Gi3: DR: 10.10.100.4 (Id)
20:25:12.067: OSPF-1 ADJ    Gi3:     BDR: none
20:25:12.067: OSPF-1 ADJ    Gi3: Remember old DR 10.10.35.3 (id)
20:25:12.067: OSPF-1 ADJ    Gi3: 10.10.100.4 address 10.10.34.4 is dead, state DOWN
20:25:12.067: OSPF-1 ADJ    Gi3: Neighbor change event
20:25:12.067: OSPF-1 ADJ    Gi3: DR/BDR election
20:25:12.067: OSPF-1 ADJ    Gi3: Elect BDR 0.0.0.0
20:25:12.068: OSPF-1 ADJ    Gi3: Elect DR 0.0.0.0
20:25:12.068: OSPF-1 ADJ    Gi3: Elect BDR 0.0.0.0
20:25:12.068: OSPF-1 ADJ    Gi3: Elect DR 0.0.0.0
20:25:12.068: OSPF-1 ADJ    Gi3: DR: none
20:25:12.068: OSPF-1 ADJ    Gi3:     BDR: none
20:25:12.068: OSPF-1 ADJ    Gi3: Flush network LSA immediately
20:25:12.069: OSPF-1 ADJ    Gi3: Remember old DR 10.10.100.4 (id)
20:25:12.079: OSPF-1 ADJ    Lo0: Interface going Up
20:25:12.080: OSPF-1 ADJ    Gi5: Interface going Up
20:25:12.080: OSPF-1 ADJ    Gi4: Interface going Up
20:25:12.081: OSPF-1 ADJ    Gi3: Interface going Up
20:25:14.028: OSPF-1 ADJ    Gi3: Rcv pkt  src 10.10.34.3 dst 224.0.0.5 id 10.10.35.3
type 5 if_state 2 : ignored due to unknown neighbor
20:25:21.374: OSPF-1 ADJ    Gi3: 2 Way Communication to 10.10.35.3, state 2WAY
20:25:21.375: OSPF-1 ADJ    Gi3: Backup seen event before WAIT timer
20:25:21.375: OSPF-1 ADJ    Gi3: DR/BDR election
20:25:21.375: OSPF-1 ADJ    Gi3: Elect BDR 10.10.100.4
20:25:21.375: OSPF-1 ADJ    Gi3: Elect DR 10.10.35.3
20:25:21.375: OSPF-1 ADJ    Gi3: Elect BDR 10.10.100.4
20:25:21.375: OSPF-1 ADJ    Gi3: Elect DR 10.10.35.3
20:25:21.375: OSPF-1 ADJ    Gi3: DR: 10.10.35.3 (Id)
20:25:21.375: OSPF-1 ADJ    Gi3:     BDR: 10.10.100.4 (Id)
20:25:21.376: OSPF-1 ADJ    Gi3: Nbr 10.10.35.3: Prepare dbase exchange
20:25:21.376: OSPF-1 ADJ    Gi3: Send DBD to 10.10.35.3 seq 0xDAD opt 0x52
flag 0x7 len 32
20:25:21.383: OSPF-1 ADJ    Gi3: Rcv DBD from 10.10.35.3 seq 0x9085039 opt 0x52
flag 0x7 len 32  mtu 1500 state EXSTART
20:25:21.383: OSPF-1 ADJ    Gi3: First DBD and we are not SLAVE
20:25:21.384: OSPF-1 ADJ    Gi3: Rcv DBD from 10.10.35.3 seq 0xDAD opt 0x52
flag 0x2 len 52  mtu 1500 state EXSTART
20:25:21.384: OSPF-1 ADJ    Gi3: NBR Negotiation Done. We are the MASTER
```

```
20:25:21.384: OSPF-1 ADJ    Gi3: Nbr 10.10.35.3: Summary list built, size 1
20:25:21.384: OSPF-1 ADJ    Gi3: Send DBD to 10.10.35.3 seq 0xDAE opt 0x52
flag 0x1 len 52
20:25:21.388: OSPF-1 ADJ    Gi3: Rcv LS REQ from 10.10.35.3 length 36 LSA count 1
20:25:21.389: OSPF-1 ADJ    Gi3: Send LS UPD to 10.10.34.3 length 100 LSA count 1
20:25:21.389: OSPF-1 ADJ    Gi3: Rcv DBD from 10.10.35.3 seq 0xDAE opt 0x52
flag 0x0 len 32  mtu 1500 state EXCHANGE
20:25:21.389: OSPF-1 ADJ    Gi3: Exchange Done with 10.10.35.3
20:25:21.390: OSPF-1 ADJ    Gi3: Send LS REQ to 10.10.35.3 length 36
20:25:21.394: OSPF-1 ADJ    Gi3: Rcv LS UPD from Nbr ID 10.10.35.3 length 100 LSA
count 1
20:25:21.394: OSPF-1 ADJ    Gi3: Synchronized with 10.10.35.3, state FULL
20:25:21.395: %OSPF-5-ADJCHG: Process 1, Nbr 10.10.35.3 on GigabitEthernet3 from
LOADING to FULL, Loading Done
P4# undebug all
All possible debugging has been turned off
P4#
```

What am I trying to tell you here? You should reconcile Table 6-4 with Example 6-2. I did not cut anything out on purpose. How do you know you are ready to face this on the exam? You should be able to describe this process in detail without looking at any notes; that is when you know you got it right. There are plenty of pictures on the Internet and other books showing pictorials of how this relationship gets established and different states. Feel free to look them up. I am not a big fan of those tools. People review them for the exam, and the knowledge is gone two weeks later. When problems occur on the network, they have to go and find the picture. Cisco is asking for more from you on this specific exam. I view such diagrams as crutches that keep you from running when you easily can, but you are the captain of your fate.

What about the differences between IOS XR and IOS? IOS XR has a hierarchical command structure, as discussed in Chapter 2, so it allows for simpler configurations by nesting commands under one section, as you saw in Example 6-1. We included the interfaces we would like to participate in area 0—simple. In IOS, you need to either enable the interface with the **network** statement under the OSPF process or enable it under the interface itself with the **ip ospf** *process-id* **area** *area-id* command, which we do soon.

Look at how OSPF is configured on P4 in Example 6-2. First, you see what interfaces you need enabled and then use the **network** statement to match the IP addresses of the interfaces that will be advertised into OSPF through the link-state advertisement (LSA). It is a rookie mistake to think that this command advertises networks into OSPF (BGP does that). The proper command syntax is

network *ip-address wildcard-mask* **area** *area-id*

OSPF enables you to be as specific (what we did) or as vague as you would like to be. The example uses all 0s in the *wildcard-mask* portion, which means "match the exact values in the IP-address field." Using 255 would indicate that *any* value will be matched, and you have to do some easy subnetting math if you need something in between. I chose to be precise because in this topology P4's fifth interface GigabitEthernet1 with the IP address of 10.10.24.4 will be in area 100, not area 0. I could have done the math to find the perfect wildcard mask for the rest of the networks, but I will leave that up to the nerds and other exams. I am after getting the network going fast, along with your knowledge.

Now, let's hop on PE2 and use a less specific mask to enable all interfaces for area 100, as demonstrated in Example 6-3.

Example 6-3 *Starting OSPF on PE2 with a Larger Wildcard Mask*

```
PE2# show ip interface brief | exclude unassigned
Interface              IP-Address      OK? Method Status              Protocol
GigabitEthernet1       10.10.24.2      YES TFTP   up                  up
GigabitEthernet2       10.10.23.2      YES TFTP   up                  up
Loopback0              10.10.100.2     YES TFTP   up                  up
PE2(config)# router ospf 22
PE2(config-router)# network 10.10.0.0 0.0.255.255 area 100
PE2(config-router)# do show ip ospf interface brief
Interface    PID   Area          IP Address/Mask      Cost   State Nbrs F/C
Lo0          22    100           10.10.100.2/32       1      LOOP  0/0
Gi2          22    100           10.10.23.2/24        1      WAIT  0/0
Gi1          22    100           10.10.24.2/24        1      WAIT  0/0
PE2(config-router)#
```

Notice that OSPF process 22 has local significance and does not have to match P4's OSPF process 1; the routers will form a full relationship. A quick look at the interfaces in the up state reveals three interfaces we would like to run OSPF and enable that with a single statement. They are both in the "10.10" network (10.10.x.x/16 network range), so if we exactly match with 0.0 and leave the last two octets to be anything with 255.255, we will generate OSPF LSAs for all three desired interfaces and quicky validate our good work. If you ever want to blindly generate LSAs for all interfaces, using 0.0.0.0 255.255.255.255 will do the job. It's not the best practice if you ask me, because it will apply to all future interfaces. You are planting a landmine that someone (maybe even yourself) will step on one day.

Now, let's configure P4's IOS software to use an interface-specific command configuration to generate OSPF LSAs, as demonstrated in Example 6-4.

Example 6-4 *Starting OSPF on P4 with Interface-Specific Commands*

```
P4# show ip interface brief | exclude unassigned
Interface              IP-Address      OK? Method Status              Protocol
GigabitEthernet1       10.10.24.4      YES TFTP   up                  up
GigabitEthernet3       10.10.34.4      YES TFTP   up                  up
GigabitEthernet4       10.10.46.4      YES TFTP   up                  up
GigabitEthernet5       10.10.45.4      YES TFTP   up                  up
Loopback0              10.10.100.4     YES TFTP   up                  up
P4# show ip ospf interface brief
Interface    PID   Area          IP Address/Mask      Cost   State Nbrs F/C
Lo0          1     0             10.10.100.4/24       1      LOOP  0/0
Gi4          1     0             10.10.46.4/24        1      DR    0/0
Gi5          1     0             10.10.45.4/24        1      DR    0/0
Gi3          1     0             10.10.34.4/24        1      DR    1/1
```

```
P4# configure terminal
P4(config)# interface gigabitEthernet 1
P4(config-if)# ip ospf 1 area 100
P4(config-if)# do show ip ospf interface brief
Interface    PID    Area            IP Address/Mask    Cost   State  Nbrs F/C
Lo0          1      0               10.10.100.4/24     1      LOOP   0/0
Gi4          1      0               10.10.46.4/24      1      DR     0/0
Gi5          1      0               10.10.45.4/24      1      DR     0/0
Gi3          1      0               10.10.34.4/24      1      DR     1/1
Gi1          1      100             10.10.24.4/24      1      BDR    1/1
P4(config-if)# do show ip ospf neighbors

Neighbor ID      Pri   State        Dead Time   Address        Interface
10.10.100.3      1     FULL/BDR     00:00:32    10.10.34.3     GigabitEthernet3
10.10.100.2      1     FULL/DR      00:00:36    10.10.24.2     GigabitEthernet1
P4(config-if)#
```

If you're configuring this along with me, you should be feeling pretty fancy right now. Well, I am here to keep you humble and sane. This definitely works, but your P4 OSPF configuration is not centralized, and if you do this on too many routers or interfaces, the complexity of your network skyrockets because an unsuspecting Junior CCNA candidate may forget to check both places on all routers, and I will let your imagination finish the rest.

Pop-quiz time: What if you have both methods enabled on the same router—at the interface level and inside the OSPF process with the **network** command? Does this matter if the configurations are identical? Yes. What if the interface method specifies one area and the **network** command specifies another? Fun times. The interface method will prevail in such a hybrid configuration. Test this if you would like for your homework; it's a good way to burn this into your memory.

At this time, I suggest you save your work and pause your topology; we will come back to it shortly. We need to take a side trip into the world of DR and BDR routers.

Designated Router and Backup Designated Router

On multi-access networks (of which Ethernet is a good example), it is possible to have more than two routers on a network segment. The more routers you have forming adjacencies together, the more LSAs are generated and flooded to the segment. CPUs work harder to compute states, more memory is required to maintain adjacencies, and network bandwidth is used inefficiently. Examine Figure 6-3.

Four routers connected to the same Ethernet segment would need six adjacencies—the famous *n(n − 1)/2* formula tells us. 4(4 − 1)/2 = 12/2 = 6. 10(10 − 1)/2 = 45 adjacencies for 10 routers. There has to be a more efficient way. OSPF elects a leader. Designated router (DR) and OSPF routers on a segment will form adjacencies only with the DR, which will flood the updates to every router on the segment as they occur—requiring minimal effort. Should someone spill water on the DR, the election process will have to be repeated and routes will be lost in the process. Thus, a backup designated router (BDR) is elected alongside the DR (which you saw in the debug output) to minimize transition time because the BDR also forms relationships with all routers on a segment, ready to take over the leadership duties should the DR fail.

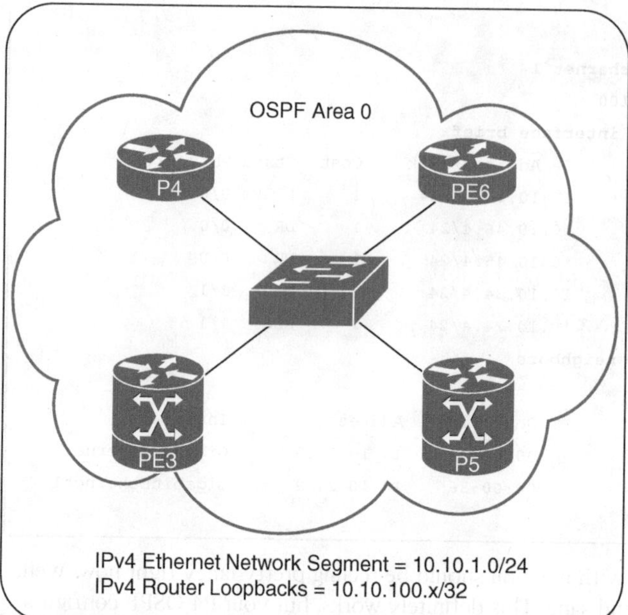

Figure 6-3 *Multi-Access Network Example*

I would like to repurpose the original diagram to Figure 6-3 and see what happens. Setting this up will not take you long; just do enough to get this to work. Example 6-5 shows the desired output.

Example 6-5 *OSPF DR and BDR on Multi-Access Ethernet*

```
RP/0/RP0/CPU0:P5# show ip ospf neighbors

* Indicates MADJ interface

# Indicates Neighbor awaiting BFD session up

Neighbors for OSPF 1

Neighbor ID     Pri   State        Dead Time   Address       Interface
10.10.10.3      1     2WAY/DROTHER 00:00:31    10.10.10.3
GigabitEthernet0/0/0/5

    Neighbor is up for 00:05:50

10.10.100.4     1     FULL/DR      00:00:31    10.10.10.4
GigabitEthernet0/0/0/5

    Neighbor is up for 00:05:53

10.10.100.6     1     FULL/BDR     00:00:38    10.10.10.6
GigabitEthernet0/0/0/5

    Neighbor is up for 00:05:54


Total neighbor count: 3
RP/0/RP0/CPU0:P5# show ip route
! Output omitted for brevity
```

```
Gateway of last resort is not set
C    10.10.10.0/24 is directly connected, 00:00:15, GigabitEthernet0/0/0/5
L    10.10.10.5/32 is directly connected, 00:00:15, GigabitEthernet0/0/0/5
O    10.10.100.3/32 [110/2] via 10.10.10.3, 00:00:08, GigabitEthernet0/0/0/5
O    10.10.100.4/32 [110/2] via 10.10.10.4, 00:00:08, GigabitEthernet0/0/0/5
L    10.10.100.5/32 is directly connected, 00:00:14, Loopback0
O    10.10.100.6/32 [110/2] via 10.10.10.6, 00:00:08, GigabitEthernet0/0/0/5
RP/0/RP0/CPU0:P5#
```

PE5 is the last router configured, and it demonstrates three roles on the multi-access segment: DR, BDR, and 2WAY/DROTHER (PE3 has formed a two-way hello-relationship with P5 and is also a "DR other," because it does not participate in DR elections). When PE3 is ready to announce a new network, it will send an LSA to AllDRouters 224.0.0.6 (as described previously in Step 14b in the "OSPF Overview" section) and the DR (P4 in this topology) will flood this LSA to AllSPFRouters 224.0.0.5 address. P5 is also a DROTHER.

Now, here is a good example of why I prefer studying RFCs and watching debug outputs to memorizing OSPF adjacency pictures and diagrams from the Internet or elsewhere. Those tend to leave this out. If you did not rush your way through Example 6-2 but thought about the peering process, you may have noticed that P4 got elected to the BDR role first and only then was promoted to DR (not "elect DR, add BDR after"). That is not an insignificant detail. This is done methodically to achieve an orderly and smooth transition of the BDR to DR role when a DR fails (think about that!). What is even more interesting is that RFC 2328 describes this very process, but this detail would be missed if you looked for visuals to quickly memorize for the exam. I would rather have you read that one RFC and lab up rather than consume several books on the subject. You do not have to understand everything or memorize it, but that RFC is one of the cleanest sources of OSPF knowledge.

I am going to do something cool; you can try this too. In the Figure 6-3 topology, an unmanaged switch interconnects the four routers. I will turn it off, but all the routers will remain up. In Example 6-6, I turn on debug on P4 and turn on the unmanaged switch, meaning we will see how these four routers elect DR and BDR roles.

Example 6-6 *OSPF DR and BDR Elections*

```
P4# debug ip ospf adjacency
OSPF adjacency debugging is on
P4#
19:42:45.719: OSPF-1 ADJ   Gi4: Rcv DBD from 10.10.10.5 seq 0x11CCBBFF opt 0x52 flag
0x7 len 32  mtu 1500 state INIT
19:42:45.719: OSPF-1 ADJ   Gi4: 2 Way Communication to 10.10.10.5, state 2WAY
19:42:45.719: OSPF-1 ADJ   Gi4: Neighbor change event
19:42:45.719: OSPF-1 ADJ   Gi4: DR/BDR election
19:42:45.719: OSPF-1 ADJ   Gi4: Elect BDR 0.0.0.0
19:42:45.719: OSPF-1 ADJ   Gi4: Elect DR 10.10.100.4
19:42:45.719: OSPF-1 ADJ   Gi4: DR: 10.10.100.4 (Id)
19:42:45.719: OSPF-1 ADJ   Gi4:    BDR: none
19:42:45.719: OSPF-1 ADJ   Gi4: Nbr 10.10.10.5: Prepare dbase exchange
```

```
19:42:45.719: OSPF-1 ADJ   Gi4: Send DBD to 10.10.10.5 seq 0xEC7 opt 0x52
flag 0x7 len 32

19:42:45.719: OSPF-1 ADJ   Gi4: First DBD and we are not SLAVE

19:42:45.721: OSPF-1 ADJ   Gi4: Rcv DBD from 10.10.10.5 seq 0xEC7 opt 0x52
flag 0x2 len 132  mtu 1500 state EXSTART

19:42:45.721: OSPF-1 ADJ   Gi4: NBR Negotiation Done. We are the MASTER

19:42:45.721: OSPF-1 ADJ   Gi4: Nbr 10.10.10.5: Summary list built, size 4

19:42:45.721: OSPF-1 ADJ   Gi4: Send DBD to 10.10.10.5 seq 0xEC8 opt 0x52
flag 0x1 len 72

19:42:45.722: OSPF-1 ADJ   Gi4: Rcv LS REQ from 10.10.10.5 length 36 LSA count 1

19:42:45.723: OSPF-1 ADJ   Gi4: Send LS UPD to 10.10.10.5 length 76 LSA count 1

19:42:45.723: OSPF-1 ADJ   Gi4: Rcv DBD from 10.10.10.5 seq 0xEC8 opt 0x52
flag 0x0 len 32  mtu 1500 state EXCHANGE

19:42:45.723: OSPF-1 ADJ   Gi4: Exchange Done with 10.10.10.5

19:42:45.723: OSPF-1 ADJ   Gi4: Send LS REQ to 10.10.10.5 length 48

19:42:45.724: OSPF-1 ADJ   Gi4: Rcv LS UPD from Nbr ID 10.10.10.5 length 116 LSA
count 2

19:42:45.724: OSPF-1 ADJ   Gi4: Synchronized with 10.10.10.5, state FULL

19:42:45.724: %OSPF-5-ADJCHG: Process 1, Nbr 10.10.10.5 on GigabitEthernet4 from
LOADING to FULL, Loading Done

19:42:45.728: OSPF-1 ADJ   Gi4: Rcv pkt  src 10.10.10.6 dst 224.0.0.5 id 10.10.100.6
type 4 if_state 5 : ignored due to unknown neighbor

19:42:45.772: OSPF-1 ADJ   Gi4: Rcv pkt  src 10.10.10.6 dst 224.0.0.5 id 10.10.100.6
type 4 if_state 5 : ignored due to unknown neighbor

19:42:45.805: OSPF-1 ADJ   Gi4: Rcv pkt  src 10.10.10.6 dst 224.0.0.5 id 10.10.100.6
type 4 if_state 5 : ignored due to unknown neighbor

19:42:50.775: OSPF-1 ADJ   Gi4: Rcv pkt  src 10.10.10.6 dst 224.0.0.5 id 10.10.100.6
type 4 if_state 5 : ignored due to unknown neighbor

19:42:53.224: OSPF-1 ADJ   Gi4: 2 Way Communication to 10.10.100.6, state 2WAY

19:42:53.225: OSPF-1 ADJ   Gi4: Neighbor change event

19:42:53.225: OSPF-1 ADJ   Gi4: DR/BDR election

19:42:53.225: OSPF-1 ADJ   Gi4: Elect BDR 0.0.0.0

19:42:53.225: OSPF-1 ADJ   Gi4: Elect DR 10.10.100.6

19:42:53.225: OSPF-1 ADJ   Gi4: Elect BDR 10.10.100.4

19:42:53.225: OSPF-1 ADJ   Gi4: Elect DR 10.10.100.6

19:42:53.225: OSPF-1 ADJ   Gi4: DR: 10.10.100.6 (Id)

19:42:53.225: OSPF-1 ADJ   Gi4:    BDR: 10.10.100.4 (Id)

19:42:53.225: OSPF-1 ADJ   Gi4: Nbr 10.10.100.6: Prepare dbase exchange

19:42:53.225: OSPF-1 ADJ   Gi4: Send DBD to 10.10.100.6 seq 0x203C opt 0x52
flag 0x7 len 32

19:42:53.225: OSPF-1 ADJ   Gi4: Set flush timer

19:42:53.225: OSPF-1 ADJ   Gi4: Remember old DR 10.10.100.4 (id)

19:42:53.225: OSPF-1 ADJ   Gi4: Rcv DBD from 10.10.100.6 seq 0x159C opt 0x52
flag 0x7 len 32  mtu 1500 state EXSTART

19:42:53.225: OSPF-1 ADJ   Gi4: NBR Negotiation Done. We are the SLAVE

19:42:53.225: OSPF-1 ADJ   Gi4: Nbr 10.10.100.6: Summary list built, size 6

19:42:53.225: OSPF-1 ADJ   Gi4: Send DBD to 10.10.100.6 seq 0x159C opt 0x52
flag 0x2 len 152
```

```
19:42:53.226: OSPF-1 ADJ   Gi4: Rcv DBD from 10.10.100.6 seq 0x159D opt 0x52
flag 0x1 len 52  mtu 1500 state EXCHANGE
19:42:53.226: OSPF-1 ADJ   Gi4: Exchange Done with 10.10.100.6
19:42:53.226: OSPF-1 ADJ   Gi4: Synchronized with 10.10.100.6, state FULL
19:42:53.226: %OSPF-5-ADJCHG: Process 1, Nbr 10.10.100.6 on GigabitEthernet4 from
LOADING to FULL, Loading Done
19:42:53.226: OSPF-1 ADJ   Gi4: Send DBD to 10.10.100.6 seq 0x159D opt 0x52
flag 0x0 len 32
19:42:54.383: OSPF-1 ADJ   Gi4: 2 Way Communication to 10.10.10.3, state 2WAY
19:42:54.383: OSPF-1 ADJ   Gi4: Neighbor change event
19:42:54.383: OSPF-1 ADJ   Gi4: DR/BDR election
19:42:54.383: OSPF-1 ADJ   Gi4: Elect BDR 10.10.100.4
19:42:54.383: OSPF-1 ADJ   Gi4: Elect DR 10.10.100.6
19:42:54.383: OSPF-1 ADJ   Gi4: DR: 10.10.100.6 (Id)
19:42:54.383: OSPF-1 ADJ   Gi4:    BDR: 10.10.100.4 (Id)
19:42:54.383: OSPF-1 ADJ   Gi4: Nbr 10.10.10.3: Prepare dbase exchange
19:42:54.383: OSPF-1 ADJ   Gi4: Send DBD to 10.10.10.3 seq 0x1C33 opt 0x52
flag 0x7 len 32
19:42:54.383: OSPF-1 ADJ   Gi4: Neighbor change event
19:42:54.383: OSPF-1 ADJ   Gi4: DR/BDR election
19:42:54.383: OSPF-1 ADJ   Gi4: Elect BDR 10.10.100.4
19:42:54.383: OSPF-1 ADJ   Gi4: Elect DR 10.10.100.6
19:42:54.383: OSPF-1 ADJ   Gi4: DR: 10.10.100.6 (Id)
19:42:54.383: OSPF-1 ADJ   Gi4:    BDR: 10.10.100.4 (Id)
19:42:54.401: OSPF-1 ADJ   Gi4: Rcv DBD from 10.10.10.3 seq 0x400CEAB7 opt 0x52
flag 0x7 len 32  mtu 1500 state EXSTART
19:42:54.401: OSPF-1 ADJ   Gi4: First DBD and we are not SLAVE
19:42:54.401: OSPF-1 ADJ   Gi4: Rcv DBD from 10.10.10.3 seq 0x1C33 opt 0x52
flag 0x2 len 132  mtu 1500 state EXSTART
19:42:54.401: OSPF-1 ADJ   Gi4: NBR Negotiation Done. We are the MASTER
19:42:54.401: OSPF-1 ADJ   Gi4: Nbr 10.10.10.3: Summary list built, size 6
19:42:54.401: OSPF-1 ADJ   Gi4: Send DBD to 10.10.10.3 seq 0x1C34 opt 0x52
flag 0x1 len 152
19:42:54.404: OSPF-1 ADJ   Gi4: Rcv LS REQ from 10.10.10.3 length 84 LSA count 5
19:42:54.404: OSPF-1 ADJ   Gi4: Send LS UPD to 10.10.10.3 length 252 LSA count 5
19:42:54.404: OSPF-1 ADJ   Gi4: Rcv DBD from 10.10.10.3 seq 0x1C34 opt 0x52
flag 0x0 len 32  mtu 1500 state EXCHANGE
19:42:54.404: OSPF-1 ADJ   Gi4: Exchange Done with 10.10.10.3
19:42:54.404: OSPF-1 ADJ   Gi4: Send LS REQ to 10.10.10.3 length 36
19:42:54.407: OSPF-1 ADJ   Gi4: Rcv LS UPD from Nbr ID 10.10.10.3 length 76 LSA
count 1
19:42:54.407: OSPF-1 ADJ   Gi4: Synchronized with 10.10.10.3, state FULL
19:42:54.407: %OSPF-5-ADJCHG: Process 1, Nbr 10.10.10.3 on GigabitEthernet4 from
LOADING to FULL, Loading Done
19:42:55.060: OSPF-1 ADJ   Gi4: Neighbor change event
19:42:55.061: OSPF-1 ADJ   Gi4: DR/BDR election
19:42:55.061: OSPF-1 ADJ   Gi4: Elect BDR 10.10.100.4
```

```
19:42:55.061: OSPF-1 ADJ   Gi4: Elect DR 10.10.100.6
19:42:55.061: OSPF-1 ADJ   Gi4: DR: 10.10.100.6 (Id)
19:42:55.061: OSPF-1 ADJ   Gi4:   BDR: 10.10.100.4 (Id)
19:42:55.061: OSPF-1 ADJ   Gi4: Neighbor change event
19:42:55.061: OSPF-1 ADJ   Gi4: DR/BDR election
19:42:55.061: OSPF-1 ADJ   Gi4: Elect BDR 10.10.100.4
19:42:55.061: OSPF-1 ADJ   Gi4: Elect DR 10.10.100.6
19:42:55.061: OSPF-1 ADJ   Gi4: DR: 10.10.100.6 (Id)
19:42:55.061: OSPF-1 ADJ   Gi4:   BDR: 10.10.100.4 (Id)
19:43:02.508: OSPF-1 ADJ   Gi4: Neighbor change event
19:43:02.508: OSPF-1 ADJ   Gi4: DR/BDR election
19:43:02.508: OSPF-1 ADJ   Gi4: Elect BDR 10.10.100.4
19:43:02.508: OSPF-1 ADJ   Gi4: Elect DR 10.10.100.6
19:43:02.508: OSPF-1 ADJ   Gi4: DR: 10.10.100.6 (Id)
19:43:02.508: OSPF-1 ADJ   Gi4:   BDR: 10.10.100.4 (Id)
19:43:03.895: OSPF-1 ADJ   Gi4: Neighbor change event
19:43:03.895: OSPF-1 ADJ   Gi4: DR/BDR election
19:43:03.895: OSPF-1 ADJ   Gi4: Elect BDR 10.10.100.4
19:43:03.895: OSPF-1 ADJ   Gi4: Elect DR 10.10.100.6
19:43:03.895: OSPF-1 ADJ   Gi4: DR: 10.10.100.6 (Id)
19:43:03.896: OSPF-1 ADJ   Gi4:   BDR: 10.10.100.4 (Id)
19:43:03.896: OSPF-1 ADJ   Gi4: Neighbor change event
19:43:03.896: OSPF-1 ADJ   Gi4: DR/BDR election
19:43:03.896: OSPF-1 ADJ   Gi4: Elect BDR 10.10.100.4
19:43:03.896: OSPF-1 ADJ   Gi4: Elect DR 10.10.100.6
19:43:03.896: OSPF-1 ADJ   Gi4: DR: 10.10.100.6 (Id)
19:43:03.896: OSPF-1 ADJ   Gi4:   BDR: 10.10.100.4 (Id)
19:43:25.723: OSPF-1 ADJ   Gi4: Nbr 10.10.10.5: Clean-up dbase exchange
19:43:33.226: OSPF-1 ADJ   Gi4: Nbr 10.10.100.6: Clean-up dbase exchange
19:43:34.404: OSPF-1 ADJ   Gi4: Nbr 10.10.10.3: Clean-up dbase exchange
P4# show ip ospf neighbors

Neighbor ID      Pri   State          Dead Time   Address       Interface
10.10.10.3        1    FULL/DROTHER   00:00:38    10.10.10.3    GigabitEthernet4
10.10.10.5        1    FULL/DROTHER   00:00:37    10.10.10.5    GigabitEthernet4
10.10.100.6       1    FULL/DR        00:00:33    10.10.10.6    GigabitEthernet4
P4#
```

```
RP/0/RP0/CPU0:PE3# show ip ospf neighbors
Sat Mar  2 19:53:39.453 UTC


* Indicates MADJ interface
# Indicates Neighbor awaiting BFD session up


Neighbors for OSPF 1
```

```
Neighbor ID     Pri   State        Dead Time   Address       Interface
10.10.10.5      1     2WAY/DROTHER 00:00:31    10.10.10.5    GigabitEthernet0/0/0/3
    Neighbor is up for 00:10:45
10.10.100.4     1     FULL/BDR     00:00:37    10.10.10.4    GigabitEthernet0/0/0/3
    Neighbor is up for 00:10:46
10.10.100.6     1     FULL/DR      00:00:36    10.10.10.6    GigabitEthernet0/0/0/3
    Neighbor is up for 00:10:46


Total neighbor count: 3
RP/0/RP0/CPU0:PE3#
```

```
RP/0/RP0/CPU0:P5# show ip ospf neighbors
Sat Mar  2 20:20:54.393 UTC


* Indicates MADJ interface
# Indicates Neighbor awaiting BFD session up

Neighbors for OSPF 1

Neighbor ID     Pri   State        Dead Time   Address       Interface
10.10.10.3      1     2WAY/DROTHER 00:00:34    10.10.10.3
GigabitEthernet0/0/0/5
    Neighbor is up for 00:38:01
10.10.100.4     1     FULL/BDR     00:00:34    10.10.10.4
GigabitEthernet0/0/0/5
    Neighbor is up for 00:38:10
10.10.100.6     1     FULL/DR      00:00:32    10.10.10.6
GigabitEthernet0/0/0/5
    Neighbor is up for 00:38:10


Total neighbor count: 3
RP/0/RP0/CPU0:P5#
```

```
PE6# show ip ospf neighbors

Neighbor ID     Pri   State          Dead Time   Address       Interface
10.10.10.3      1     FULL/DROTHER   00:00:38    10.10.10.3    GigabitEthernet6
10.10.10.5      1     FULL/DROTHER   00:00:32    10.10.10.5    GigabitEthernet6
10.10.100.4     1     FULL/BDR       00:00:38    10.10.10.4    GigabitEthernet6
PE6#
```

A couple of things are highlighted here to draw your attention. One of these is the use of 0.0.0.0 as the router ID (RID), which means that the router hasn't been explicitly configured with a RID, and it's using the highest IPv4 address of its active interfaces as the RID for the election process. Go through this unmodified output and interpret what is going on. Do not memorize it, but understand it. I have provided the views from all routers. Understand their relationships. For example, here is an exam question for you: Looking at the output from PE6 (and only PE6) at the bottom of Example 6-6, in what state is router PE6? This can be confusing until you realize that PE6 can only be the DR.

DR and BDR Priorities

Look at the output of **show ip ospf neighbors** in Example 6-6 again. When router IDs are not explicitly configured (which is true in our case), OSPF may generate them based on the highest IPv4 address among active interfaces. This can lead to unexpected or "jacked" neighbor IDs. Explicitly configuring router IDs is recommended for predictable OSPF neighbor relationships. In our example, IOS routers P4 and PE6 picked the highest loopbacks, while IOS XR router PE3 and P5 used the Ethernet interfaces (lower, but not lowest). I suggest that you always specify a router ID under the OSPF process, but do not do this to determine who will win the DR election. A far more elegant technique would be to modify the interface priority to that of a higher value than the current DR. By default, Cisco routers have an interface priority of 1, as seen in Example 6-7, and can be adjusted to values between 0 and 255, with greater values preferring election wins.

Example 6-7 *Determining OSPF Interface Priority for DR Placement*

```
PE6# show ip ospf interface | include Prio
 Transmit Delay is 1 sec, State DR, Priority 1
```

OSPF does not actively preempt the election, and even though you would only need to elevate the priority to greater than 1, nothing will happen until DR is taken out of service or the OSPF process gets restarted. On the other hand, as soon as you set the interface priority to 0, the interface will be immediately removed from DR/BDR elections.

To make things simple, let's watch what happens when setting PE3's interface priority to 3, P4's to 4, and P5's to 5. Observe the behavior and then set the current PE6's interface priority to 0, as in Example 6-8. I suggest you keep track of the differences in IOS and IOS XR.

Example 6-8 *Interface Priority Change on PE3*

```
RP/0/RP0/CPU0:PE3# configure
RP/0/RP0/CPU0:PE3(config)# router ospf 1
RP/0/RP0/CPU0:PE3(config-ospf)# area 0
RP/0/RP0/CPU0:PE3(config-ospf-ar)# interface gigabitEthernet 0/0/0/3
RP/0/RP0/CPU0:PE3(config-ospf-ar-if)# priority 3
RP/0/RP0/CPU0:PE3(config-ospf-ar-if)# commit
RP/0/RP0/CPU0:PE3(config-ospf-ar-if)# end
RP/0/RP0/CPU0:PE3# show ip ospf neighbor
* Indicates MADJ interface
# Indicates Neighbor awaiting BFD session up


Neighbors for OSPF 1


Neighbor ID    Pri  State         Dead Time   Address       Interface
10.10.10.5     1    2WAY/DROTHER  00:00:38    10.10.10.5    GigabitEthernet0/0/0/3
    Neighbor is up for 01:14:30
10.10.100.4    1    FULL/BDR      00:00:36    10.10.10.4    GigabitEthernet0/0/0/3
    Neighbor is up for 01:14:31
10.10.100.6    1    FULL/DR       00:00:36    10.10.10.6    GigabitEthernet0/0/0/3
    Neighbor is up for 01:14:31
```

```
Total neighbor count: 3
RP/0/RP0/CPU0:PE3# show ip ospf interface gigabitEthernet 0/0/0/3 | include Priority
  Transmit Delay is 1 sec, State DROTHER, Priority 3, MTU 1500, MaxPktSz 1500
```

Did PE3 evict PE6 from his DR status? No. Change P4 and P5 to 4 and 5, respectively.
Check P5 and find out that all is quiet on the OSPF front. Note that P4 runs IOS, and commands are under the interface section, not under the OSPF process. Example 6-9 shows how
to add these changes.

Example 6-9 *Interface Priority Change on P4 and P5*

```
P4# configure terminal
Enter configuration commands, one per line.  End with CNTL/Z.
P4(config)# interface gigabithEthernet 4
P4(config-if)# ip ospf priority 4
P4(config-if)#
```

```
RP/0/RP0/CPU0:P5# configure
RP/0/RP0/CPU0:P5(config)# router ospf 1
RP/0/RP0/CPU0:P5(config-ospf)# area 0
RP/0/RP0/CPU0:P5(config-ospf-ar)# interface gigabitEthernet 0/0/0/5
RP/0/RP0/CPU0:P5(config-ospf-ar-if)# priority 5
RP/0/RP0/CPU0:P5(config-ospf-ar-if)# commit
RP/0/RP0/CPU0:P5(config-ospf-ar-if)# end
RP/0/RP0/CPU0:P5# show ip ospf neighbors

* Indicates MADJ interface
# Indicates Neighbor awaiting BFD session up

Neighbors for OSPF 1

Neighbor ID     Pri  State        Dead Time  Address      Interface
10.10.10.3      3    2WAY/DROTHER 00:00:36   10.10.10.3   GigabitEthernet0/0/0/5
    Neighbor is up for 01:24:38
10.10.100.4     4    FULL/BDR     00:00:38   10.10.10.4   GigabitEthernet0/0/0/5
    Neighbor is up for 01:24:46
10.10.100.6     1    FULL/DR      00:00:39   10.10.10.6   GigabitEthernet0/0/0/5
    Neighbor is up for 01:24:46

Total neighbor count: 3
```

Get ready for the fireworks when you make the change on PE6 in Example 6-10. Now, place
your bets on which routers will become the DR/BDR!

Example 6-10 *Interface Priority Change on PE6*

```
PE6# configure terminal
Enter configuration commands, one per line.  End with CNTL/Z.
PE6(config)# interface gigabitEthernet 6
PE6(config-if)# ip ospf priority 0
PE6(config-if)#
21:13:10.566: OSPF-1 ADJ   Gi6: Neighbor change event
21:13:10.566: OSPF-1 ADJ   Gi6: DR/BDR election
21:13:10.566: OSPF-1 ADJ   Gi6: Elect BDR 10.10.100.4
21:13:10.566: OSPF-1 ADJ   Gi6: Elect DR 10.10.100.4
21:13:10.566: OSPF-1 ADJ   Gi6: Elect BDR 10.10.100.4
21:13:10.566: OSPF-1 ADJ   Gi6: Elect DR 10.10.100.4
21:13:10.566: OSPF-1 ADJ   Gi6: DR: 10.10.100.4 (Id)
21:13:10.566: OSPF-1 ADJ   Gi6:    BDR: 10.10.100.4 (Id)
21:13:10.566: OSPF-1 ADJ   Gi6: Reset adjacency with 10.10.10.3, state 2WAY
21:13:10.567: OSPF-1 ADJ   Gi6: Reset adjacency with 10.10.10.5, state 2WAY
21:13:10.567: OSPF-1 ADJ   Gi6: Set flush timer
21:13:10.567: OSPF-1 ADJ   Gi6: Remember old DR 10.10.100.6 (id)
21:13:18.597: OSPF-1 ADJ   Gi6: Neighbor change event
21:13:18.597: OSPF-1 ADJ   Gi6: DR/BDR election
21:13:18.597: OSPF-1 ADJ   Gi6: Elect BDR 10.10.100.4
21:13:18.597: OSPF-1 ADJ   Gi6: Elect DR 10.10.100.4
21:13:18.597: OSPF-1 ADJ   Gi6: DR: 10.10.100.4 (Id)
21:13:18.597: OSPF-1 ADJ   Gi6:    BDR: 10.10.100.4 (Id)
21:13:21.138: OSPF-1 ADJ   Gi6: Neighbor change event
21:13:21.138: OSPF-1 ADJ   Gi6: DR/BDR election
21:13:21.139: OSPF-1 ADJ   Gi6: Elect BDR 10.10.100.4
21:13:21.139: OSPF-1 ADJ   Gi6: Elect DR 10.10.100.4
21:13:21.139: OSPF-1 ADJ   Gi6: DR: 10.10.100.4 (Id)
21:13:21.139: OSPF-1 ADJ   Gi6:    BDR: 10.10.100.4 (Id)
21:13:21.837: OSPF-1 ADJ   Gi6: Neighbor change event
21:13:21.837: OSPF-1 ADJ   Gi6: DR/BDR election
21:13:21.837: OSPF-1 ADJ   Gi6: Elect BDR 10.10.10.5
21:13:21.837: OSPF-1 ADJ   Gi6: Elect DR 10.10.100.4
21:13:21.837: OSPF-1 ADJ   Gi6: DR: 10.10.100.4 (Id)
21:13:21.837: OSPF-1 ADJ   Gi6:    BDR: 10.10.10.5 (Id)
21:13:21.837: OSPF-1 ADJ   Gi6: Nbr 10.10.10.5: Prepare dbase exchange
21:13:21.837: OSPF-1 ADJ   Gi6: Send DBD to 10.10.10.5 seq 0xCE2 opt 0x52 flag 0x7
len 32
21:13:21.837: OSPF-1 ADJ   Gi6: Neighbor change event
21:13:21.837: OSPF-1 ADJ   Gi6: DR/BDR election
21:13:21.837: OSPF-1 ADJ   Gi6: Elect BDR 10.10.10.5
21:13:21.837: OSPF-1 ADJ   Gi6: Elect DR 10.10.100.4
21:13:21.837: OSPF-1 ADJ   Gi6: DR: 10.10.100.4 (Id)
21:13:21.837: OSPF-1 ADJ   Gi6:    BDR: 10.10.10.5 (Id)
```

```
21:13:21.839: OSPF-1 ADJ    Gi6: Rcv DBD from 10.10.10.5 seq 0x5388E47A opt 0x52 flag
0x7 len 32  mtu 1500 state EXSTART
21:13:21.839: OSPF-1 ADJ    Gi6: First DBD and we are not SLAVE
21:13:21.841: OSPF-1 ADJ    Gi6: Rcv DBD from 10.10.10.5 seq 0xCE2 opt 0x52 flag 0x2
len 152  mtu 1500 state EXSTART
21:13:21.841: OSPF-1 ADJ    Gi6: NBR Negotiation Done. We are the MASTER
21:13:21.841: OSPF-1 ADJ    Gi6: Nbr 10.10.10.5: Summary list built, size 6
21:13:21.841: OSPF-1 ADJ    Gi6: Send DBD to 10.10.10.5 seq 0xCE3 opt 0x52 flag 0x1
len 52
21:13:21.845: OSPF-1 ADJ    Gi6: Rcv DBD from 10.10.10.5 seq 0xCE3 opt 0x52 flag 0x0
len 32  mtu 1500 state EXCHANGE
21:13:21.845: OSPF-1 ADJ    Gi6: Exchange Done with 10.10.10.5
21:13:21.845: OSPF-1 ADJ    Gi6: Synchronized with 10.10.10.5, state FULLdo
21:13:21.845: %OSPF-5-ADJCHG: Process 1, Nbr 10.10.10.5 on GigabitEthernet6 from
LOADING to FULL, Loading D
21:13:28.544: OSPF-1 ADJ    Gi6: Neighbor change event
21:13:28.544: OSPF-1 ADJ    Gi6: DR/BDR election
21:13:28.544: OSPF-1 ADJ    Gi6: Elect BDR 10.10.10.5
21:13:28.544: OSPF-1 ADJ    Gi6: Elect DR 10.10.100.4
21:13:28.544: OSPF-1 ADJ    Gi6: DR: 10.10.100.4 (Id)
21:13:28.544: OSPF-1 ADJ    Gi6:   BDR: 10.10.10.5 (Id)
21:13:31.131: OSPF-1 ADJ    Gi6: Neighbor change event
21:13:31.131: OSPF-1 ADJ    Gi6: DR/BDR election
21:13:31.131: OSPF-1 ADJ    Gi6: Elect BDR 10.10.10.5
21:13:31.131: OSPF-1 ADJ    Gi6: Elect DR 10.10.100.4
21:13:31.131: OSPF-1 ADJ    Gi6: DR: 10.10.100.4 (Id)
21:13:31.131: OSPF-1 ADJ    Gi6:   BDR: 10.10.10.5 (Id)end
```

```
PE6# show ip ospf neighbors

Neighbor ID      Pri   State           Dead Time   Address       Interface
10.10.10.3         3   2WAY/DROTHER    00:00:30    10.10.10.3    GigabitEthernet6
10.10.10.5         5   FULL/BDR        00:00:33    10.10.10.5    GigabitEthernet6
10.10.100.4        4   FULL/DR         00:00:33    10.10.10.4    GigabitEthernet6
PE6#
```

Did you get this right, or did you get surprised? Did you think that P5 would be crowned
DR? Nope, P4 was BDR, so the OSPF electoral process promoted it to DR to "achieve an
orderly smooth transition," as described in the famed RFC, and P5 with the highest interface
priority became the BDR. Don't worry if you have lost points here; you will not lose them
on the exam, where they really count.

OSPF Timers

Back to our main topology in Figure 6-2, go ahead and unpause it. Let's look at router P4 in
Example 6-11 next.

Example 6-11 *Viewing Interface Timers on P4*

```
P4# show ip ospf interface gigabitEthernet 3
GigabitEthernet3 is up, line protocol is up
  Internet Address 10.10.34.4/24, Interface ID 9, Area 0
  Attached via Network Statement
  Process ID 1, Router ID 10.10.100.4, Network Type BROADCAST, Cost: 1
  Topology-MTID    Cost   Disabled    Shutdown      Topology Name
        0           1        no          no             Base
  Transmit Delay is 1 sec, State DR, Priority 1
  Designated Router (ID) 10.10.100.4, Interface address 10.10.34.4
  Backup Designated router (ID) 10.10.100.3, Interface address 10.10.34.3
  Timer intervals configured, Hello 10, Dead 40, Wait 40, Retransmit 5
    oob-resync timeout 40
    Hello due in 00:00:04
  Supports Link-local Signaling (LLS)
  Cisco NSF helper support enabled
  IETF NSF helper support enabled
  Can be protected by per-prefix Loop-Free FastReroute
  Can be used for per-prefix Loop-Free FastReroute repair paths
  Not Protected by per-prefix TI-LFA
  Index 1/1/2, flood queue length 0
  Next 0x0(0)/0x0(0)/0x0(0)
  Last flood scan length is 1, maximum is 1
  Last flood scan time is 0 msec, maximum is 0 msec
  Neighbor Count is 1, Adjacent neighbor count is 1
    Adjacent with neighbor 10.10.100.3   (Backup Designated Router)
  Suppress hello for 0 neighbor(s)
```

The OSPF network type is Broadcast (which we get to in a minute), but this network type
has Hello and Dead interval timers set to 10 and 40, respectively (Dead = 4 × Hello). These
are important because they have to match for OSPF neighbors to become adjacent. Cisco
gives you the option to set these to much lesser values. Observe Example 6-12 where the
Dead timer is set to 1 second on P4 (IOS) and PE3 (IOS XR).

Example 6-12 *Adjusting OSPF Timers to Subsecond Intervals*

```
P4# configure terminal
Enter configuration commands, one per line.  End with CNTL/Z.
P4(config)# interface gigabitEthernet 3
P4(config-if)# ip ospf dead-interval ?
  <1-65535>  Seconds
  minimal    Set to 1 second
P4(config-if)# ip ospf dead-interval minimal ?
  hello-multiplier  Set multiplier for Hellos
P4(config-if)# ip ospf dead-interval minimal hello-multiplier ?
  <3-20>  Number of Hellos sent within 1 second
```

```
P4(config-if)# ip ospf dead-interval minimal hello-multiplier 4
P4(config-if)# do show ip ospf interface gigabitEthernet 3 | include Timer
  Timer intervals configured, Hello 250 msec, Dead 1, Wait 1, Retransmit 5
```

```
RP/0/RP0/CPU0:PE3(config)# router ospf 1
RP/0/RP0/CPU0:PE3(config-ospf)# dead-interval minimal hello-multiplier 4
RP/0/RP0/CPU0:PE3(config-ospf)# commit
RP/0/RP0/CPU0:PE3(config-ospf)# do show ospf interface g0/0/0/3 | include
"Timer|Hello"
  Timer intervals configured, Hello 250ms, Dead 1, Wait 1, Retransmit 5
    Hello due in 00:00:00:108
RP/0/RP0/CPU0:PE3(config-ospf)# do show ospf neighbors
* Indicates MADJ interface
# Indicates Neighbor awaiting BFD session up

Neighbors for OSPF 1

Neighbor ID     Pri  State          Dead Time   Address       Interface
10.10.100.4     1    FULL/DR        -           10.10.34.4    GigabitEthernet0/0/0/3
    Neighbor is up for 00:01:38
Total neighbor count: 1
```

This example should be self-explanatory, but the one difference I would like to call your attention to is that in IOS you use the **show ip ospf interface** command instead of the **show ospf interface** command in IOS XR.

OSPF Network Types

To add to OSPF's growing complexity are multiple OSPF network types. You saw the mention of the Broadcast network type in Example 6-11. More than two routers can be present on multi-access networks such as Ethernet, and RFC 2328 specified the hello timer of 10 seconds. Prior to the industry's adoption of Ethernet as the current standard, various other technologies utilizing different media were explored and considered—X.25, Frame Relay, ATM, point-to-point serial links with PPP or HDLC encapsulation, and so on. OSPF supports five different network types to optimize its operations. What is the point of electing DR/BDR on a point-to-point segment, for example? You would just be wasting CPU cycles in this scenario. Table 6-5 lists the supported options.

Table 6-5   OSPF Network Types

Type	Notes	Timers	DR
Broadcast	Default for Ethernet	Hello = 10 Dead = 40	Yes
Nonbroadcast	Default on Frame-Relay main interfaces or Frame-Relay multipoint subinterfaces	Hello = 30 Dead = 120	Yes
Point-to-point	Default on Frame-Relay point-to-point subinterfaces	Hello = 10 Dead = 40	No
Point-to-multipoint	Used in hub-and-spoke topologies (DMVPN, L2VPN MPLS, etc.), generates a /32 host route	Hello = 30 Dead = 120	No
Loopback	Default on loopback interfaces, generates a /32 host route, regardless of subnet mask assigned to this interface	N/A	No

You will not see any references on the exam to Frame Relay, but how OSPF supports adjacencies over different media is on the exam. It may seem counterintuitive, but OSPF network types do not have to match for OSPF adjacencies and route exchanges. What has to match, though, are the hello timers and DR usage. In general, make everything consistent and you will avoid issues.

Now, let's grab PE6 and use its interfaces to set up these network types in Example 6-13.

Example 6-13 *Applying Different OSPF Network Types on PE6*

```
PE6# configure terminal
Enter configuration commands, one per line.  End with CNTL/Z.
PE6(config)# router ospf 1
PE6(config-router)# router-id 10.10.100.6
PE6(config-router)# neighbor 10.10.46.4
PE6(config-router)# interface loopback0
PE6(config-if)# ip ospf 1 area 0
PE6(config-if)# interface gigabitEthernet 4
PE6(config-if)# ip ospf 1 area 0
PE6(config-if)# ip ospf network ?
  broadcast              Specify OSPF broadcast multi-access network
  non-broadcast          Specify OSPF NBMA network
  point-to-multipoint    Specify OSPF point-to-multipoint network
  point-to-point         Specify OSPF point-to-point network
PE6(config-if)# ip ospf network non-broadcast
PE6(config-if)# interface gigabitEthernet 3
PE6(config-if)# ip ospf 1 area 0
PE6(config-if)# ip ospf network point-to-point
PE6(config-if)# interface gigabitEthernet 5
PE6(config-if)# ip ospf 1 area 0
PE6(config-if)# ip ospf network point-to-multipoint
PE6(config-if)# end
PE6# show ip ospf neighbor

Neighbor ID     Pri    State            Dead Time    Address         Interface
N/A              0     ATTEMPT/DROTHER    -           10.10.46.4      GigabitEthernet4
PE6#
```

There's a lot going on here, as I am deliberately making you multitask. I picked PE6 because it has no OSPF configurations, as seen in the first line. You turn on OSPF process 1 and properly assign it the router ID of the loopback interface (something we have not done on other routers). In my topology, PE6's interface numbers correspond to routers it is facing: interface GigabitEthernet4 faces router P4, interface GigabitEthernet5 faces router P5, and interface GigabitEthernet3 faces router PE3. I then bring each interface into OSPF process 1, show the available four options, and assign three remaining options to one of the interfaces (we deal with the fifth type of loopback soon). Note that PE6 has no neighbors; you only see an attempt to connect with P4 over the nonbroadcast medium where you do not have the luxury of multicast groups to send the packet to, but use the unicast address of P4 to establish the peering.

It's your turn now. Get on the P4, P5, and PE3 and complete the setup until you have proper peerings. You should see something like Example 6-14 on PE6 after you have completed your work. Be sure to take that subsecond dead interval confirmation off P4 and PE3; otherwise, you'll be chasing and correcting adjacency problems.

Example 6-14 *PE6 Different Network Type Adjacencies Confirmed*

```
PE6# show ip ospf neighbors


Neighbor ID       Pri   State        Dead Time   Address       Interface
10.10.100.3         0   FULL/ -      00:00:38    10.10.36.3    GigabitEthernet3
10.10.100.5         0   FULL/ -      00:01:58    10.10.56.5    GigabitEthernet5
10.10.100.4         1   FULL/DR      00:01:58    10.10.46.4    GigabitEthernet4
PE6# show ip ospf interfaces | include Type|Internet|Timer
  Internet Address 10.10.100.6/32, Interface ID 13, Area 0
  Process ID 1, Router ID 10.10.100.6, Network Type LOOPBACK, Cost: 1
  Internet Address 10.10.36.6/24, Interface ID 9, Area 0
  Process ID 1, Router ID 10.10.100.6, Network Type POINT_TO_POINT, Cost: 1
  Timer intervals configured, Hello 10, Dead 40, Wait 40, Retransmit 5
  Internet Address 10.10.56.6/24, Interface ID 11, Area 0
  Process ID 1, Router ID 10.10.100.6, Network Type POINT_TO_MULTIPOINT, Cost: 1
  Timer intervals configured, Hello 30, Dead 120, Wait 120, Retransmit 5
  Internet Address 10.10.46.6/24, Interface ID 10, Area 0
  Process ID 1, Router ID 10.10.100.6, Network Type NON_BROADCAST, Cost: 1
  Timer intervals configured, Hello 30, Dead 120, Wait 120, Retransmit 5
```

You must be able to reconcile this output with that one of Table 6-5. Notice how the P4 peering elects DR in nonbroadcast networks and does not in PE3 point-to-point and P5 point-to-multipoint peerings. Also, observe that we demonstrated OSPF network timers for each network type.

This leaves us with the network type Loopback (seen in Example 6-14), which is the default type for loopback interfaces. These are always advertised with a /32 host route, as you can see in Example 6-15 for the loopback interfaces coming from P4 (Loopback0 is configured with a /32 prefix and Loopback1 with a /24 prefix). Observe that, regardless of their native prefix, they are both advertised on PE6 as /32 routes.

Example 6-15 *OSPF Network Type Loopback*

```
P4# show running-config interface loopback 0
!
interface Loopback0
 ip address 10.10.100.4 255.255.255.255
 ipv6 address 2001:4:4:4::4/128
P4# show running-config interface loopback1
!
interface Loopback1
 ip address 10.10.101.4 255.255.255.0
end
```

```
PE6# show ip route | include 100.4|101.4
O       10.10.100.4/32 [110/2] via 10.10.46.4, 00:01:13, GigabitEthernet4
O       10.10.101.4/32 [110/2] via 10.10.46.4, 00:03:47, GigabitEthernet4
PE6#
```

If you would like to modify this default behavior, you should change network type **loopback** to type **point-to-point**, as seen in Example 6-16. PE6 now sees this loopback interface with a /24 route.

Example 6-16 *OSPF Network Type Loopback*

```
P4# configure terminal
P4(config)# interface loopback1
P4(config-if)# ip ospf network point-to-point
```

```
PE6# show ip route | include 100.4|101
O       10.10.100.4/32 [110/2] via 10.10.46.4, 00:08:37, GigabitEthernet4
O       10.10.101.0/24 [110/2] via 10.10.46.4, 00:01:45, GigabitEthernet4
PE6#
```

Let me conclude the section on OSPF adjacencies by showing how to authenticate neighbors. PE3 and PE6 use MD5 authentication in Example 6-17 even though plaintext authentication is also supported.

Example 6-17 *OSPF Adjacency Authentication on IOS XR*

```
RP/0/RP0/CPU0:PE3# configure terminal
16:58:03.471 UTC
RP/0/RP0/CPU0:PE3(config)# router ospf 1
RP/0/RP0/CPU0:PE3(config-ospf)# area 0
RP/0/RP0/CPU0:PE3(config-ospf-ar)# interface gigabitEthernet 0/0/0/4
RP/0/RP0/CPU0:PE3(config-ospf-ar-if)# authentication message-digest ?
  keychain   Specify keychain name
  <cr>
RP/0/RP0/CPU0:PE3(config-ospf-ar-if)# authentication message-digest
RP/0/RP0/CPU0:PE3(config-ospf-ar-if)# message-digest-key 1 md5 SPCOR
RP/0/RP0/CPU0:PE3(config-ospf-ar-if)# commit
16:59:59.195 UTC
RP/0/RP0/CPU0:PE3(config-ospf-ar-if)# do show ip ospf neighbors
Sun Mar  3 17:00:31.383 UTC
* Indicates MADJ interface
# Indicates Neighbor awaiting BFD session up


Neighbors for OSPF 1


Neighbor ID     Pri  State        Dead Time  Address       Interface
10.10.100.5     1    FULL/BDR     00:00:33   10.10.35.5    GigabitEthernet0/0/0/0
    Neighbor is up for 01:56:48
10.10.100.4     1    FULL/DR      00:00:33   10.10.34.4    GigabitEthernet0/0/0/3
    Neighbor is up for 01:59:30
```

```
10.10.100.6    1    FULL/  -        00:00:02      10.10.36.6      GigabitEthernet0/0/0/4
      Neighbor is up for 00:06:23


Total neighbor count: 3
RP/0/RP0/CPU0:PE3(config-ospf-ar-if)# do show ip ospf neighbors
17:00:34.175 UTC


* Indicates MADJ interface
# Indicates Neighbor awaiting BFD session up


Neighbors for OSPF 1


Neighbor ID    Pri  State        Dead Time   Address      Interface
10.10.100.5    1    FULL/BDR     00:00:30    10.10.35.5    GigabitEthernet0/0/0/0
      Neighbor is up for 01:56:51
10.10.100.4    1    FULL/DR      00:00:30    10.10.34.4    GigabitEthernet0/0/0/3
      Neighbor is up for 01:59:33


Total neighbor count: 2
```

Note that that I chose to authenticate under the interface subtree of the configuration. I could have chosen to do this under the area 0 option as well. I commit the changes, wait about 35 seconds, see 2 seconds left on the 40-second point-to-point dead interval time, and the neighbor is gone. Now, let's get on PE6 and configure the other side of this link. Example 6-18 captures the entire thing.

Example 6-18 *OSPF Adjacency Authentication on IOS*

```
PE6#
16:54:08.609: %OSPF-5-ADJCHG: Process 1, Nbr 10.10.100.3 on GigabitEthernet3 from
LOADING to FULL, Loading Done
*Mar  3 17:00:39.858: %OSPF-5-ADJCHG: Process 1, Nbr 10.10.100.3 on GigabitEthernet3
from FULL to DOWN, Neighbor Down: Dead timer expired
PE6# show ip ospf neighbors


Neighbor ID    Pri  State        Dead Time   Address      Interface
10.10.100.5    0    FULL/  -     00:01:45    10.10.56.5    GigabitEthernet5
10.10.100.4    1    FULL/DR      00:01:37    10.10.46.4    GigabitEthernet4
PE6# configure terminal
Enter configuration commands, one per line.  End with CNTL/Z.
PE6(config)# interface gigabitEthernet 3
PE6(config-if)# ip ospf authentication message-digest
PE6(config-if)# ip ospf message-digest-key 1 md5 SPCOR
PE6(config-if)#
17:13:03.413: %OSPF-5-ADJCHG: Process 1, Nbr 10.10.100.3 on GigabitEthernet3 from
LOADING to FULL, Loading Done
PE6(config-if)# do show ip ospf interface gigabitEthernet 3 | include auth|key
  Cryptographic authentication enabled
    Youngest key id is 1
```

Route Advertisement

Please complete the OSPF setup in Figure 6-2. You will have to turn up area 200. See you in a few minutes; this task should take you no time. I'm looking for the output from P5, as shown in Example 6-19.

Example 6-19 *Verify OSPF Setup*

```
RP/0/RP0/CPU0:P5# show ip route ospf
O IA 10.10.23.0/24 [110/3] via 10.10.45.4, 02:25:31, GigabitEthernet0/0/0/5
O IA 10.10.24.0/24 [110/2] via 10.10.45.4, 02:25:31, GigabitEthernet0/0/0/5
O    10.10.34.0/24 [110/2] via 10.10.45.4, 02:25:29, GigabitEthernet0/0/0/5
                   [110/2] via 10.10.35.3, 02:25:29, GigabitEthernet0/0/0/0
O    10.10.36.0/24 [110/2] via 10.10.56.6, 00:35:05, GigabitEthernet0/0/0/3
                   [110/2] via 10.10.35.3, 00:35:05, GigabitEthernet0/0/0/0
O    10.10.46.0/24 [110/2] via 10.10.56.6, 02:25:31, GigabitEthernet0/0/0/3
                   [110/2] via 10.10.45.4, 02:25:31, GigabitEthernet0/0/0/5
O    10.10.56.6/32 [110/1] via 10.10.56.6, 02:25:31, GigabitEthernet0/0/0/3
O    10.10.67.0/24 [110/2] via 10.10.57.7, 00:01:07, GigabitEthernet0/0/0/2
O IA 10.10.100.2/32 [110/3] via 10.10.45.4, 02:25:31, GigabitEthernet0/0/0/5
O    10.10.100.3/32 [110/2] via 10.10.35.3, 02:25:29, GigabitEthernet0/0/0/0
O    10.10.100.4/32 [110/2] via 10.10.45.4, 01:02:50, GigabitEthernet0/0/0/5
O    10.10.100.6/32 [110/2] via 10.10.56.6, 02:25:31, GigabitEthernet0/0/0/3
O    10.10.100.7/32 [110/2] via 10.10.57.7, 00:00:08, GigabitEthernet0/0/0/2
O    10.10.101.0/24 [110/2] via 10.10.45.4, 00:55:57, GigabitEthernet0/0/0/5
RP/0/RP0/CPU0:P5#
```

If you have all the loopbacks and interconnecting links, you have done this right. Notice that since P5 has a couple of links in the backbone area 0, most of the routes come with a "O" designation (OSPF intra-area). Three routes come in as "O IA" (OSPF inter-area); these are from area 100, and P5 does not participate in that area. Because P5 has one interface on area 200, the loopback 10.10.100.7 comes in an "O" intra-area route. P5 is an area border router (**ABR**), since it straddles a couple of areas.

Remember Figure 6-1 that I asked to you memorize? Let's learn how OSPF behaves in real life, not theoretically. Example 6-20 shows the contents of the OSPF database.

Example 6-20 *Type 1 Router Links*

```
RP/0/RP0/CPU0:P5# show ospf database
17:44:35.445 UTC

            OSPF Router with ID (10.10.100.5) (Process ID 1)

                Router Link States (Area 0)

Link ID         ADV Router      Age       Seq#        Checksum Link count
10.10.100.3     10.10.100.3     89        0x80000019 0x006825 5
10.10.100.4     10.10.100.4     400       0x8000002b 0x0096b4 5
10.10.100.5     10.10.100.5     1100      0x80000008 0x00301f 5
10.10.100.6     10.10.100.6     1061      0x8000001e 0x00dec7 6
```

Example 6-20 shows a partial output of the OSPF database, focusing on LSA Type 1. These are all the routers in Area 0 with their router IDs (Link ID); routers that advertised this LSA (ADV Router); age of the LSA (as these values get over 1800, they will soon be targeted to get refreshed); sequence number, which protects new information as it comes in; checksum to verify integrity during flooding; and the number of links in the Type 1 LSA.

Example 6-21 shows a different detailed view of the same Type 1 LSA. Three types of networks are mentioned:

- **Stub:** There is no neighbor adjacency on it (because it is a loopback interface on P5).

- **Transit:** An adjacency has formed with a DR election.

- **Point-to-point:** An adjacency has formed without a DR election.

Example 6-21   *Type 1 Router Links in the OSPF Database*

```
RP/0/RP0/CPU0:P5# show ospf database router
! Output omitted for brevity
  LS age: 1502
  Options: (No TOS-capability, DC)
  LS Type: Router Links
  Link State ID: 10.10.100.5
  Advertising Router: 10.10.100.5
  LS Seq Number: 80000009
  Checksum: 0x2e20
  Length: 84
  Area Border Router
  Number of Links: 5

    Link connected to: a Stub Network
      (Link ID) Network/subnet number: 10.10.100.5
      (Link Data) Network Mask: 255.255.255.255
      Number of TOS metrics: 0
        TOS 0 Metrics: 1
    Link connected to: a Transit Network
      (Link ID) Designated Router address: 10.10.35.3
      (Link Data) Router Interface address: 10.10.35.5
      Number of TOS metrics: 0
        TOS 0 Metrics: 1

    Link connected to: another Router (point-to-point)
      (Link ID) Neighboring Router ID: 10.10.100.6
      (Link Data) Router Interface address: 10.10.56.5
      Number of TOS metrics: 0
        TOS 0 Metrics: 1
```

```
   Link connected to: a Stub Network
     (Link ID) Network/subnet number: 10.10.56.5
     (Link Data) Network Mask: 255.255.255.255
      Number of TOS metrics: 0
       TOS 0 Metrics: 0


   Link connected to: a Transit Network
     (Link ID) Designated Router address: 10.10.45.4
     (Link Data) Router Interface address: 10.10.45.5
      Number of TOS metrics: 0
       TOS 0 Metrics: 1
```

Network LSA Type 2 comes next in Example 6-22. These are links on multi-access segments that use a DR. The output in this example shows the link between PE3 and P4 and the two routers participating in the DR election and the winner (P4).

Example 6-22   *Type 2 Router Links in the OSPF Database*

```
RP/0/RP0/CPU0:P5# show ospf database
! Output omitted for brevity

            Net Link States (Area 0)
Link ID          ADV Router        Age          Seq#        Checksum
10.10.34.4       10.10.100.4       1249         0x80000007 0x00e79d
10.10.35.3       10.10.100.3       931          0x80000007 0x00fe86
10.10.45.4       10.10.100.4       993          0x80000007 0x008aed
10.10.46.4       10.10.100.4       740          0x80000008 0x008be9
RP/0/RP0/CPU0:P5# show ospf database network
Sun Mar  3 18:35:59.550 UTC
            OSPF Router with ID (10.10.100.5) (Process ID 1)
            Net Link States (Area 0)
 Routing Bit Set on this LSA
 LS age: 950
 Options: (No TOS-capability, DC)
 LS Type: Network Links
 Link State ID: 10.10.34.4 (address of Designated Router)
 Advertising Router: 10.10.100.4
 LS Seq Number: 80000007
 Checksum: 0xe79d
 Length: 32
 Network Mask: /24
      Attached Router: 10.10.100.4
      Attached Router: 10.10.100.3
! Output omitted for brevity
```

While LSA Type 1 and 2 stay in the area, *ABRs* (router P5 is one) will not forward these into other areas. Type 3 LSAs, however, represent networks from other areas. Examine all entries; none of them are in from area 0. Duplicates indicate redundant paths and routers that advertised them. Example 6-23 shows these best. Note that PE3, P4, and PE6 are ABRs as well, and they advertise Type 3 LSAs into the backbone area.

Example 6-23   *Type 3 Summary Links in the OSPF Database*

```
RP/0/RP0/CPU0:P5# show ospf database
18:40:59.239 UTC
! Output omitted for brevity
            Summary Net Link States (Area 0)

Link ID         ADV Router       Age       Seq#        Checksum
10.10.23.0      10.10.100.3      443       0x80000002 0x001d77
10.10.23.0      10.10.100.4      1509      0x8000000c 0x000d7b
10.10.24.0      10.10.100.3      443       0x80000002 0x001c76
10.10.24.0      10.10.100.4      1509      0x8000000c 0x00f790
10.10.57.0      10.10.100.5      695       0x80000003 0x0097d7
10.10.57.0      10.10.100.6      333       0x80000003 0x009bd1
10.10.67.0      10.10.100.5      446       0x80000003 0x003331
10.10.67.0      10.10.100.6      583       0x80000003 0x002341
10.10.100.2     10.10.100.3      443       0x80000002 0x00c083
10.10.100.2     10.10.100.4      1509      0x8000000c 0x00a692
10.10.100.7     10.10.100.5      446       0x80000003 0x0080bb
10.10.100.7     10.10.100.6      333       0x80000003 0x007ac0
```

That is about what we have now. We are missing Type 4 and Type 5 LSAs, and the reason is that we do not have external to OSPF routes coming into the OSPF domain. Let's create a couple of loopback interfaces on PE7 and redistribute those into OSPF.

Example 6-24 shows a mildly complicated way of doing this on IOS XR, but you will have to deal with Route Policy Language (RPL) on the exam. You already had some practice in Chapter 4. Here, I show you the configuration that is about to go into PE7 (just copy-and-paste; it will work). This configuration

1. Creates interfaces Loopback111 and Loopback222.

2. Uses a route policy to match on those interface addresses.

3. Sets metric-type 1 for Loopback111.

4. Sets metric-type 2 for Loopback222.

5. Redistributes these into the OSPF process.

Next, let's commit and verify our work on P5, as demonstrated in Example 6-24.

Example 6-24   *Bringing in External Routes into OSPF on PE7*

```
RP/0/RP0/CPU0:PE7(config)# show
!! IOS XR Configuration 7.7.1
interface Loopback111
 ipv4 address 10.10.111.7 255.255.255.0
!
```

```
  interface Loopback222
   ipv4 address 10.10.222.7 255.255.255.0
   !
  route-policy EXTERNAL-ROUTES
    if destination in (10.10.111.0/24) then
      set metric-type type-1
    else
      if destination in (10.10.222.0/24) then
        set metric-type type-2
      endif
    endif
  end-policy
  !
  router ospf 1
   redistribute connected route-policy EXTERNAL-ROUTES
  !
  end

RP/0/RP0/CPU0:PE7(config)# commit
```

```
RP/0/RP0/CPU0:P5# show ip route | include "O E"
O E1 10.10.111.0/24 [110/21] via 10.10.57.7, 00:10:08, GigabitEthernet0/0/0/2
O E2 10.10.222.0/24 [110/20] via 10.10.57.7, 00:10:08, GigabitEthernet0/0/0/2
RP/0/RP0/CPU0:P5#
```

If you forgot what the differences are between E1 and E2 routes, refresh your CCNA
knowledge. E1 routes consider both the *external* cost and the *internal* cost to reach the
autonomous system boundary router (**ASBR**), while E2 routes only consider the *external*
cost advertised by the ASBR (21 and 20, respectively). Of paramount interest to us is the
Type-5 LSA that now shows up in the OSPF database in Example 6-25.

Example 6-25   *Type 5 External Links in the OSPF Database*

```
RP/0/RP0/CPU0:P5# show ospf database
! Output omitted for brevity
                Type-5 AS External Link States


Link ID          ADV Router       Age          Seq#        Checksum Tag
10.10.111.0      10.10.100.7      972          0x80000001  0x000c12 0
10.10.222.0      10.10.100.7      972          0x80000001  0x00c568 0
RP/0/RP0/CPU0:P5# show ospf database external
          OSPF Router with ID (10.10.100.5) (Process ID 1)
          Type-5 AS External Link States


Routing Bit Set on this LSA
  LS age: 1003
  Options: (No TOS-capability, DC)
```

```
LS Type: AS External Link
Link State ID: 10.10.111.0 (External Network Number)
Advertising Router: 10.10.100.7
LS Seq Number: 80000001
Checksum: 0xc12
Length: 36
Network Mask: /24
      Metric Type: 1 (Comparable directly to link state metric)
      TOS: 0
      Metric: 20
      Forward Address: 0.0.0.0
      External Route Tag: 0


Routing Bit Set on this LSA
LS age: 1003
Options: (No TOS-capability, DC)
LS Type: AS External Link
Link State ID: 10.10.222.0 (External Network Number)
Advertising Router: 10.10.100.7
LS Seq Number: 80000001
Checksum: 0xc568
Length: 36
Network Mask: /24
      Metric Type: 2 (Larger than any link state path)
      TOS: 0
      Metric: 20
      Forward Address: 0.0.0.0
      External Route Tag: 0
RP/0/RP0/CPU0:P5#
```

Did we miss LSA Type-4, ASBR Summary, which locates ASBRs for Type-5 LSAs? Not at all.
Example 6-26 shows exactly that.

Example 6-26 *Type 4 ASBR Summary in the OSPF Database*

```
RP/0/RP0/CPU0:P5# show ospf database
! Output omitted for brevity
            Summary ASB Link States (Area 0)


Link ID          ADV Router        Age       Seq#          Checksum
10.10.100.7      10.10.100.5       1376      0x80000001 0x006cd1
10.10.100.7      10.10.100.6       1377      0x80000001 0x0066d6
RP/0/RP0/CPU0:P5# show ospf data asbr-summary


          OSPF Router with ID (10.10.100.5) (Process ID 1)


          Summary ASB Link States (Area 0)
```

```
    LS age: 1527

    Options: (No TOS-capability, DC)

    LS Type: Summary Links (AS Boundary Router)

    Link State ID: 10.10.100.7 (AS Boundary Router address)

    Advertising Router: 10.10.100.5

    LS Seq Number: 80000001

    Checksum: 0x6cd1

    Length: 28

    Network Mask: /0

          TOS: 0   Metric: 1


    LS age: 1528

    Options: (No TOS-capability, DC)

    LS Type: Summary Links (AS Boundary Router)

    Link State ID: 10.10.100.7 (AS Boundary Router address)

    Advertising Router: 10.10.100.6

    LS Seq Number: 80000001

    Checksum: 0x66d6

    Length: 28

    Network Mask: /0

          TOS: 0   Metric: 1
RP/0/RP0/CPU0:P5#
```

Advertised by both P5 and PE6 with a metric of 1—now you don't have to wonder where that 1 in the E1 type route comes from (a Metric of 20 in Example 6-25 + Metric of 1 in Example 6-26 = E1 Metric of 21)!

There is also an interesting side note here. Both P5 and PE6 are ABRs for area 200, where these external routes are coming from. Look at P4's output in Example 6-27 because it sees the same routes coming from both ABRs yet chooses the router with the lower router ID as a tiebreaker for the best route. Remembering where things are lower and higher can be challenging—which is why I have attached our situations to them so that it will be easier to recall.

Example 6-27   *Tiebreaker for Equal-Cost External Routes*

```
P4# show ip route 10.10.111.0
Routing entry for 10.10.111.0/24
  Known via "ospf 1", distance 110, metric 22, type extern 1
  Last update from 10.10.46.6 on GigabitEthernet4, 00:01:28 ago
  Routing Descriptor Blocks:
    10.10.46.6, from 10.10.100.7, 00:01:28 ago, via GigabitEthernet4
      Route metric is 22, traffic share count is 1
  * 10.10.45.5, from 10.10.100.7, 00:01:36 ago, via GigabitEthernet5
      Route metric is 22, traffic share count is 1
P4#
```

A bit later in the chapter, I show the LSA Type-7 that deals with NSSA External Summaries, but let's save this until you learn about different area types first. For now, as you digest how OSPF constructs its OSPF database, memorize the following path selection logic and sequence (I have assumed the cost of the links is the same to simplify this sequence, making it suitable for memorization):

1. ECMP can install multiple OSPF paths. (If multiple equal-cost routes to a destination exist, they are all discovered and used. Keep in mind that each one of the multiple routes will be of the same type—intra-area, inter-area, type 1 external, or type 2 external).

2. Intra-area routes: if more than one, pick the path with the lowest total path metric.

3. Inter-area routes: if more than one, install and use both, but all must go through area 0.

4. N1 (What?!) Don't worry; it is the NSSA E1 route. But OSPF will prefer this route for its RIB when an equally good E1 route is present.

5. E1 (External Type 1, redistribution metric + total path metric). Pause here…and consider that the closer a router is to the originating ASBR, the lower its metric will be. Please make sure you understand what I just said. The further away the router is, the higher the total path metric will be. Think about this if you need clarity.

6. N2 is the NSSA E2 route. The same logic applies, and this route will be inserted into the RIB before E2.

7. E2 (External Type 2, redistribution metric alone). Here, you do not have a total path metric to compare, so the lower forwarding cost will be preferred.

Until I come up with a catchier name, I will call this section OSPF RIB Route Rush, RFC 13711— "Brad's OSPF Manifesto: The Oddly Uneven System for Route Rights and Protocol Privileges" (IETF proposal still pending). Why am I trying to call your attention to this section? This is rife with traps and pitfalls for exam questions to lose points on. Examples of which path will be selected:

- A slower intra versus faster inter?

- N1 versus E1?

- Closer E1 versus further E1?

- Two equal metric N1 routes?

- Area 0 versus ASBR in a different area?

You can figure these out by looking up the logic I outlined (but you won't be able to look at it on the exam), and I doubt you will see this clean format on the test. I would show you the outputs of configs and ask you the same question in a different form. You have to understand not only the configs but also how this logic applies. This can pose a challenge if your understanding of the topic isn't crystal clear. Bottom line: remember this OSPF RIB Route Rush (ORRR). By the way, have you started to appreciate the simplicity of IS-IS yet?

OSPF Stubby Areas

Thus far, I have shown you "normal" OSPF areas. Never quote me on this to Radia Perlman; she probably has the power to revoke my Cisco privileges. All OSPF areas are normal (legitimate), but there is a reason I had you memorize Table 6-2, because "non-normal" areas control LSA flooding. So, leaving all the technical insider ABR, ASBR, LSA "Type-X" inter-area mumbo-jumbo jargon behind, what does a stub area do?

A stub area filters out prefixes that did not natively originate in OSPF. Wow, that is a different way of thinking about Table 6-2. Let's look at Example 6-28, which shows the routing table or area 100's PE2, which at the moment sees a lot of different routes.

Example 6-28 *OSPF Area 100 Without Stub*

```
PE2# show ip route ospf
! Output omitted for brevity
      10.0.0.0/8 is variably subnetted, 22 subnets, 2 masks
O IA     10.10.34.0/24 [110/2] via 10.10.24.4, 09:52:49, GigabitEthernet1
                       [110/2] via 10.10.23.3, 04:00:05, GigabitEthernet2
O IA     10.10.35.0/24 [110/2] via 10.10.23.3, 04:00:05, GigabitEthernet2
O IA     10.10.36.0/24 [110/2] via 10.10.23.3, 04:00:05, GigabitEthernet2
O IA     10.10.45.0/24 [110/2] via 10.10.24.4, 09:52:39, GigabitEthernet1
O IA     10.10.46.0/24 [110/2] via 10.10.24.4, 09:52:49, GigabitEthernet1
O IA     10.10.56.5/32 [110/2] via 10.10.24.4, 06:59:24, GigabitEthernet1
                       [110/2] via 10.10.23.3, 04:00:05, GigabitEthernet2
O IA     10.10.56.6/32 [110/2] via 10.10.24.4, 07:26:09, GigabitEthernet1
                       [110/2] via 10.10.23.3, 04:00:05, GigabitEthernet2
O IA     10.10.57.0/24 [110/3] via 10.10.24.4, 04:36:50, GigabitEthernet1
                       [110/3] via 10.10.23.3, 04:00:05, GigabitEthernet2
O IA     10.10.67.0/24 [110/3] via 10.10.24.4, 04:36:10, GigabitEthernet1
                       [110/3] via 10.10.23.3, 04:00:05, GigabitEthernet2
O IA     10.10.100.3/32 [110/2] via 10.10.23.3, 04:00:05, GigabitEthernet2
O IA     10.10.100.4/32 [110/2] via 10.10.24.4, 05:36:42, GigabitEthernet1
O IA     10.10.100.5/32 [110/3] via 10.10.24.4, 06:59:24, GigabitEthernet1
                        [110/3] via 10.10.23.3, 04:00:05, GigabitEthernet2
O IA     10.10.100.6/32 [110/3] via 10.10.24.4, 07:28:32, GigabitEthernet1
                        [110/3] via 10.10.23.3, 04:00:05, GigabitEthernet2
O IA     10.10.100.7/32 [110/4] via 10.10.24.4, 04:34:00, GigabitEthernet1
                        [110/4] via 10.10.23.3, 04:00:05, GigabitEthernet2
O IA     10.10.101.0/24 [110/2] via 10.10.24.4, 05:29:50, GigabitEthernet1
O E1     10.10.111.0/24 [110/23] via 10.10.24.4, 02:37:05, GigabitEthernet1
                        [110/23] via 10.10.23.3, 02:37:05, GigabitEthernet2
O E2     10.10.222.0/24 [110/20] via 10.10.24.4, 02:37:05, GigabitEthernet1
                        [110/20] via 10.10.23.3, 02:37:05, GigabitEthernet2
PE2#
```

You can see a handful of inter-area routes and two external-to-OSPF routes coming in as E1 and E2 from "outside" the OSPF domain via redistribution accomplished earlier. If we had a ton of such routes brought in by LSA Type 5 but did not want them in area 100, we could filter these out individually, prefix by prefix, or we could accomplish this more simply by turning area 100 into a stub area that will filter out Type 5 LSAs. Let's try this in Example 6-29.

Example 6-29 *OSPF Area 100 Turned into Stub*

```
P4# configure terminal
Enter configuration commands, one per line.  End with CNTL/Z.
P4(config)# router ospf 1
P4(config-router)# area 100 stub
P4(config-router)#
```

```
RP/0/RP0/CPU0:PE3# configure
Sun Mar  3 22:17:58.512 UTC
RP/0/RP0/CPU0:PE3(config)# router ospf 1
RP/0/RP0/CPU0:PE3(config-ospf)# area 100
RP/0/RP0/CPU0:PE3(config-ospf-ar)# stub
RP/0/RP0/CPU0:PE3(config-ospf-ar)# commit
RP/0/RP0/CPU0:PE3(config-ospf-ar)#
```

```
PE2# configure terminal
Enter configuration commands, one per line.  End with CNTL/Z.
PE2(config)# router ospf 22
PE2(config-router)# area 100 stub
PE2(config-router)# do show ip route ospf
! Output omitted for brevity
O*IA  0.0.0.0/0 [110/2] via 10.10.24.4, 00:00:39, GigabitEthernet1
                [110/2] via 10.10.23.3, 00:00:44, GigabitEthernet2
      10.0.0.0/8 is variably subnetted, 20 subnets, 2 masks
O IA    10.10.34.0/24 [110/2] via 10.10.24.4, 00:00:39, GigabitEthernet1
                      [110/2] via 10.10.23.3, 00:00:44, GigabitEthernet2
O IA    10.10.35.0/24 [110/2] via 10.10.23.3, 00:00:44, GigabitEthernet2
O IA    10.10.36.0/24 [110/2] via 10.10.23.3, 00:00:44, GigabitEthernet2
O IA    10.10.45.0/24 [110/2] via 10.10.24.4, 00:00:39, GigabitEthernet1
O IA    10.10.46.0/24 [110/2] via 10.10.24.4, 00:00:39, GigabitEthernet1
O IA    10.10.56.5/32 [110/2] via 10.10.24.4, 00:00:39, GigabitEthernet1
                      [110/2] via 10.10.23.3, 00:00:44, GigabitEthernet2
O IA    10.10.56.6/32 [110/2] via 10.10.24.4, 00:00:39, GigabitEthernet1
                      [110/2] via 10.10.23.3, 00:00:44, GigabitEthernet2
O IA    10.10.57.0/24 [110/3] via 10.10.24.4, 00:00:39, GigabitEthernet1
                      [110/3] via 10.10.23.3, 00:00:44, GigabitEthernet2
O IA    10.10.67.0/24 [110/3] via 10.10.24.4, 00:00:39, GigabitEthernet1
                      [110/3] via 10.10.23.3, 00:00:44, GigabitEthernet2
O IA    10.10.100.3/32 [110/2] via 10.10.23.3, 00:00:44, GigabitEthernet2
O IA    10.10.100.4/32 [110/2] via 10.10.24.4, 00:00:39, GigabitEthernet1
O IA    10.10.100.5/32 [110/3] via 10.10.24.4, 00:00:39, GigabitEthernet1
                       [110/3] via 10.10.23.3, 00:00:44, GigabitEthernet2
O IA    10.10.100.6/32 [110/3] via 10.10.24.4, 00:00:39, GigabitEthernet1
                       [110/3] via 10.10.23.3, 00:00:44, GigabitEthernet2
O IA    10.10.100.7/32 [110/4] via 10.10.24.4, 00:00:39, GigabitEthernet1
                       [110/4] via 10.10.23.3, 00:00:44, GigabitEthernet2
```

6

```
O IA      10.10.101.0/24 [110/2] via 10.10.24.4, 00:00:39, GigabitEthernet1
PE2(config-router)# do show ip route ospf | include "E O"
//The routes are missing!!
PE2(config-router)# do show ip protocols | include stub
   Number of areas in this router is 1. 0 normal 1 stub 0 nssa
PE2(config-router)#
```

And magically, non-native to OSPF LSAs Type 5 are gone. I see inter-area routes; I see the default route. Can it be this simple? Yes.

OSPF Totally Stubby Areas

Fine, what do totally stubby areas do? They filter out prefixes that did not natively originate in *this area*. That means Type 3, Type 4, and Type 5 will be gone. Example 6-30 shows that we only need to append **no-summary** to our previous work. Right from where we were...

Example 6-30   *OSPF Area 100 Turned into Totally Stub*

```
P4(config-router)# area 100 stub no-summary

RP/0/RP0/CPU0:PE3(config-ospf-ar)# stub no-summary
RP/0/RP0/CPU0:PE3(config-ospf-ar)# commit

PE2(config-router)# area 100 stub no-summary
PE2(config-router)# do show ip route ospf
! Output omitted for brevity
Gateway of last resort is 10.10.24.4 to network 0.0.0.0

O*IA  0.0.0.0/0 [110/2] via 10.10.24.4, 00:01:29, GigabitEthernet1
                 [110/2] via 10.10.23.3, 00:01:29, GigabitEthernet2
PE2(config-router)#
```

Well, that is radical. All IA Type 3 routes except for the default IA route, Type 4, and Type 5 are gone! So, totally stubby filters out prefixes that did not natively originate in *this area, except for the default route.* This is a Cisco thing. On Juniper routers, you must manually generate the default route into totally stubby areas.

OSPF Not-So-Stubby Areas (NSSAs)

Here comes the NSSA area you were waiting for, but, seriously, what is it with these word games?! I told you OSPF can seem punishingly hard. Are you totally on board with me on IS-IS yet? Just wait until you realize what is going on. Stub areas (as you learned) filter LSAs Type 4 and Type 5, so you cannot bring in external-to-OSPF prefixes into stub areas. However, what if you wanted to? Why, you ask? Suppose you have a stub area that needs to have external BGP prefixes come in. Examine our modified Figure 6-4.

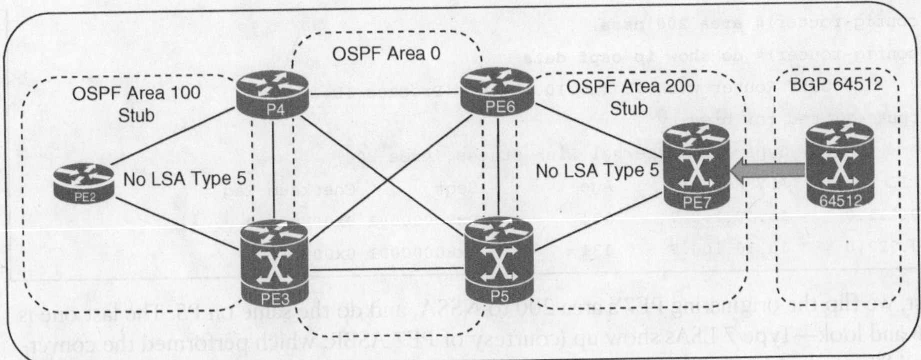

Figure 6-4 *How Would You Import BGP Routes into Stub?*

Why would external-to-OSPF routes coming from BGP need to be advertised into area 100? Why would you design this kind of network? Many times, network engineers do not get to choose and *must* solve connectivity issues with what they have. So, let's see what is going on here. When PE7 redistributes these into OSPF, they will come in as external-to-OSPF, LSA Type 5. *But* LSA Type 5 is a "no-no" for stub areas. *So*, the scenario is not as unreasonable as it first seemed.

To work around this "no LSA Type 5" rule, OSPF just imports LSAs Type 7 at the ASBR, and they are converted to LSAs Type 5 at the ABR. That is the essence of NSSA: using LSA Type 7 instead of Type 5 in a stub network. Once you follow this logic, you realize that NSSA is basically a hack to work around the "no LSAs Type 5" rule. NSSA is just like totally stubby + external routes.

I feel as if you are going to throw something at me right now. Restrain yourself. I am showing the stepping stones no one showed me. Time to see this in action on our topology in Example 6-31. To avoid confusion, remove all stub network references in area 100 (routers in area 100). Then, configure area 200 (routers in area 200) as NSSA and see what happens. You can pretend that redistributed routes have "come in from BGP"; no one will know any different anyway. Play close attention to what goes on here. I will give it to you play by play.

Example 6-31 *OSPF Area 200 Turned into NSSA*

```
RP/0/RP0/CPU0:PE7# configure
RP/0/RP0/CPU0:PE7(config)# router ospf 1
RP/0/RP0/CPU0:PE7(config-ospf)# area 200
RP/0/RP0/CPU0:PE7(config-ospf-ar)# nssa
RP/0/RP0/CPU0:PE7(config-ospf-ar)# commit

RP/0/RP0/CPU0:P5# configure terminal
RP/0/RP0/CPU0:P5(config)# router ospf 1
RP/0/RP0/CPU0:P5(config-ospf)# area 200
RP/0/RP0/CPU0:P5(config-ospf-ar)# nssa
RP/0/RP0/CPU0:P5(config-ospf-ar)# commit

PE6# configure terminal
Enter configuration commands, one per line.  End with CNTL/Z.
PE6(config)# router ospf 1
```

```
PE6(config-router)# area 200 nssa
PE6(config-router)# do show ip ospf data
            OSPF Router with ID (10.10.100.6) (Process ID 1)
! Output omitted for brevity

            Type-7 AS External Link States (Area 200)
Link ID         ADV Router       Age       Seq#        Checksum Tag
10.10.111.0     10.10.100.7      131       0x80000001 0x00D9BA 0
10.10.222.0     10.10.100.7      131       0x80000001 0x009311 0
```

First, we flip the originating PE7's area 200 to NSSA, and do the same on P5. The last one is
PE6 and look—Type 7 LSAs show up (courtesy of PE7 ASBR, which performed the conversion)! We worked around the stub limitation. As crucial as remembering to put on your pants
before leaving the house, look at the output of Example 6-32, which shows PE7's output of
show ip route.

Example 6-32 *LSA Type 7 Converted to Type 5 at ABRs*

```
RP/0/RP0/CPU0:PE7(config-ospf-ar)# do show ip route
! Output omitted for brevity
Gateway of last resort is 10.10.67.6 to network 0.0.0.0

O*IA 0.0.0.0/0 [110/2] via 10.10.67.6, 00:00:30, GigabitEthernet0/0/0/1
O  IA 10.10.23.0/24 [110/3] via 10.10.57.5, 00:00:30, GigabitEthernet0/0/0/2
O  IA 10.10.24.0/24 [110/3] via 10.10.57.5, 00:00:30, GigabitEthernet0/0/0/2
O  IA 10.10.34.0/24 [110/3] via 10.10.57.5, 00:00:30, GigabitEthernet0/0/0/2
O  IA 10.10.35.0/24 [110/2] via 10.10.57.5, 00:00:30, GigabitEthernet0/0/0/2
O  IA 10.10.36.0/24 [110/3] via 10.10.57.5, 00:00:30, GigabitEthernet0/0/0/2
O  IA 10.10.45.0/24 [110/2] via 10.10.57.5, 00:00:30, GigabitEthernet0/0/0/2
O  IA 10.10.46.0/24 [110/3] via 10.10.57.5, 00:00:30, GigabitEthernet0/0/0/2
O  IA 10.10.56.5/32 [110/1] via 10.10.57.5, 00:00:30, GigabitEthernet0/0/0/2
O  IA 10.10.56.6/32 [110/3] via 10.10.57.5, 00:00:30, GigabitEthernet0/0/0/2
C     10.10.57.0/24 is directly connected, 10:46:36, GigabitEthernet0/0/0/2
L     10.10.57.7/32 is directly connected, 10:46:36, GigabitEthernet0/0/0/2
C     10.10.67.0/24 is directly connected, 10:46:36, GigabitEthernet0/0/0/1
L     10.10.67.7/32 is directly connected, 10:46:36, GigabitEthernet0/0/0/1
O  IA 10.10.100.2/32 [110/4] via 10.10.57.5, 00:00:30, GigabitEthernet0/0/0/2
O  IA 10.10.100.3/32 [110/3] via 10.10.57.5, 00:00:30, GigabitEthernet0/0/0/2
O  IA 10.10.100.4/32 [110/3] via 10.10.57.5, 00:00:30, GigabitEthernet0/0/0/2
O  IA 10.10.100.5/32 [110/2] via 10.10.57.5, 00:00:30, GigabitEthernet0/0/0/2
O  IA 10.10.100.6/32 [110/4] via 10.10.57.5, 00:00:30, GigabitEthernet0/0/0/2
L     10.10.100.7/32 is directly connected, 11:37:11, Loopback0
O  IA 10.10.101.0/24 [110/3] via 10.10.57.5, 00:00:30, GigabitEthernet0/0/0/2
C     10.10.111.0/24 is directly connected, 11:37:11, Loopback111
L     10.10.111.7/32 is directly connected, 11:37:11, Loopback111
C     10.10.222.0/24 is directly connected, 11:37:11, Loopback222
L     10.10.222.7/32 is directly connected, 11:37:11, Loopback222
RP/0/RP0/CPU0:PE7(config-ospf-ar)#
```

```
PE6# show ip route
! Output omitted for brevity
Gateway of last resort is not set


O          10.10.101.0/24 [110/2] via 10.10.46.4, 00:01:42, GigabitEthernet4
O N1       10.10.111.0/24 [110/22] via 10.10.67.7, 00:03:41, GigabitEthernet1
O N2       10.10.222.0/24 [110/20] via 10.10.67.7, 00:03:41, GigabitEthernet1
PE6#
```

Do you see all those IA summary routes on PE7? Remember them well; you will need those
in a few minutes. Also, notice how on PE6 (and P5 for that matter), you finally see the N1,
N2 routes show up for the external networks. What are N1, N2 routes? They represent LSAs
Type 7 in an NSSA.

For now, we carry LSAs 1, 2, 3, and 7 in this NSSA area. Example 6-33 follows what
happens to LSA Type 7 throughout the rest of the network. PE6 and P5 ABRs will convert
this Type 7 into Type 5 to advertise into the backbone area 0 and into "normal" area 100
with ECMP paths. PE2 sees these as well as external routes.

Example 6-33 *LSA Type 7 Converted to Type 5 at ABRs*

```
P4# show ip ospf database
        OSPF Router with ID (10.10.101.4) (Process ID 1)
! Output omitted for brevity

            Type-5 AS External Link States

Link ID          ADV Router        Age          Seq#        Checksum Tag
10.10.111.0      10.10.100.6       166          0x80000001 0x00742B 0
10.10.222.0      10.10.100.6       166          0x80000001 0x002E81 0
P4#
```

```
PE2# show ip route ospf
! Output omitted for brevity
O E1     10.10.111.0/24 [110/24] via 10.10.24.4, 00:23:44, GigabitEthernet1
                        [110/24] via 10.10.23.3, 00:23:44, GigabitEthernet2
O E2     10.10.222.0/24 [110/20] via 10.10.24.4, 00:23:44, GigabitEthernet1
                        [110/20] via 10.10.23.3, 00:23:44, GigabitEthernet2
PE2#
```

Homework, you ask? Figure out how to originate the default route from NSSA area 200.
Hint: It is an additional option for the **nssa** command.

OSPF Totally Not-So-Stubby Areas

I am pretty sure even the hardcore OSPF defenders are beginning to see my point about
IS-IS simplicity. For the record, I have my preferences, but at the end of the day, it does not
matter. A good engineer sees these protocols as mere tools. I love Segment Routing, but if
you want to run RSVP-TE on your network, I will and I won't complain. IS-IS, sure. OSPF,
no problem. Totally not-so-stubby? I LIVE for it. They are the same as a totally stubby
area, but they filter out LSA Type 3 as well. Look again closely at the snipped output in

Example 6-32, which shows IA routes coming in. We will get rid of them in Example 6-34 as we convert to "TNSSA." Right from where we were on those routers with the **nssa no-summary** command…

Example 6-34   *Totally NSSA Type 4, Type 3 Blocked at ABRs*

```
RP/0/RP0/CPU0:P5(config-ospf-ar)# nssa no-summary
RP/0/RP0/CPU0:P5(config-ospf-ar)# commit


PE6(config-router)# area 200 nssa no-summary
PE6(config-router)#


RP/0/RP0/CPU0:PE7(config-ospf-ar)# nssa no-summary
RP/0/RP0/CPU0:PE7(config-ospf-ar)# commit
RP/0/RP0/CPU0:PE7(config-ospf-ar)# do show ip route
! Output omitted for brevity
Gateway of last resort is 10.10.57.5 to network 0.0.0.0
O*IA 0.0.0.0/0 [110/2] via 10.10.57.5, 00:00:25, GigabitEthernet0/0/0/2
               [110/2] via 10.10.67.6, 00:00:25, GigabitEthernet0/0/0/1
C    10.10.57.0/24 is directly connected, 10:58:17, GigabitEthernet0/0/0/2
L    10.10.57.7/32 is directly connected, 10:58:17, GigabitEthernet0/0/0/2
C    10.10.67.0/24 is directly connected, 10:58:18, GigabitEthernet0/0/0/1
L    10.10.67.7/32 is directly connected, 10:58:18, GigabitEthernet0/0/0/1
L    10.10.100.7/32 is directly connected, 11:48:52, Loopback0
C    10.10.111.0/24 is directly connected, 11:48:52, Loopback111
L    10.10.111.7/32 is directly connected, 11:48:52, Loopback111
C    10.10.222.0/24 is directly connected, 11:48:52, Loopback222
L    10.10.222.7/32 is directly connected, 11:48:52, Loopback222
RP/0/RP0/CPU0:PE7(config-ospf-ar)#
```

IA routes, present in Example 6-31, are gone. Only the single default route IA appears. To paraphrase Table 6-2, totally-not-so-stubby areas carry "LSA Types 1, 2, 3 as only a default route supplied by ABR and can be changed to 7, 7." It took us a long time to get here. Study Figure 6-1 and Table 6-2, and you will do fine.

OSPF Multi-Area Adjacencies

I have a significant task for you to complete if you are following this book alongside configuring, not just reading. Take the previous topology and convert it to what is shown in Figure 6-5. It will take you a while to complete this reconfiguration although the number of changes is not significant.

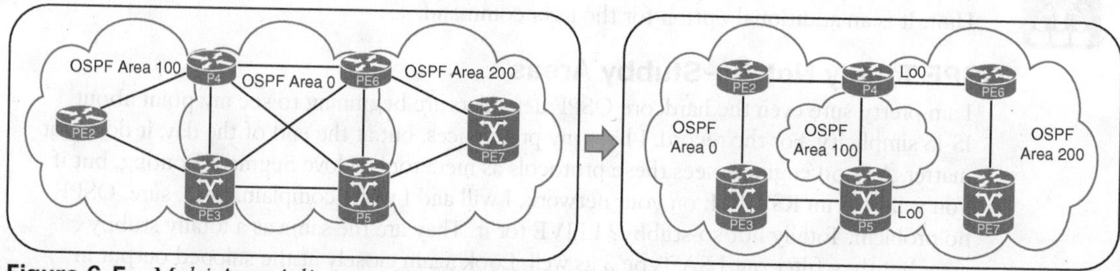

Figure 6-5   *Multi-Area Adjacency Topology*

First, remove the two interlinks between PE3-P4 and P5-PE6, and if you visually pull the topology to the right as if by a string, it will turn into the rectangle on the right. Clean up the configurations—OSPF process 22 on PE2, turn off all point-to-point/multipoint network types, turn off authentication, stubs, NSSAs, external loopback, RPL redistribution. Just make it clean. Change the OSPF areas to how they appear on the right, with loopback interfaces of P4 and P5 in area 200. This task may seem like a time-waster. Why not just stand up a new topology from scratch? Reconfiguring a network requires far more attention than building one, and your mind starts working differently. After a while, you do not pay attention to what the links are, what the names are (P/PE), or what the shapes look like as your mind becomes focused on the task at hand. Do you remember the engineers who can read diagrams correctly in a matter of a dozen seconds? They have done these reconfigurations often enough, and their minds have learned to see past the distractions. Do you know how to keep from running out of time on exams? By doing what I am suggesting. You will be able to look at any configuration, and your mind will quickly sort between the necessary and unimportant. I have taken enough exams to understand the desire to plow through the exam preparation content and pass it. There are many benefits to this. I have been there many times. Here's the best advice I can give you: take your time and go slow. It seems counterintuitive, but "slow is smooth, and smooth is fast." If you ever want to become fast, discipline your mind to learn slowly.

Enough philosophy. What am I cooking up for you in this topology? To reach P4's loopback, P5 will take a longer three-hop route through its own area 200 (intra-area) regardless of the presence of a direct hop through area 100 since the loopbacks belong to area 200. Welcome to Example 6-35.

Example 6-35 *Intra-Area Routing*

```
RP/0/RP0/CPU0:P5# show ip route | include 10.10.100.4
O    10.10.100.4/32 [110/4] via 10.10.57.7, 00:12:40, GigabitEthernet0/0/0/2
RP/0/RP0/CPU0:P5#
```

Do you see it going to 10.10.57.7 in area 200, not 10.10.45.5 in area 100? Imagine that on the links through area 200, PE6-PE7 has much lower bandwidth. We have not covered OSPF costs in this book, but if you do not know how this works, you need to brush up; this is so CCNA-basic. OSPF considers link cost in its SPF calculation, and the lower the speed of the link, the higher the cost—something we do not want. High-speed links—800G, 400G, 100G—have lower OSPF costs, so it can steer more of our traffic to them. Low-speed links cost more, making them less desirable. Imagine that the PE6-PE7 link is a lower-speed link for some reason, or configure the interfaces to simulate a higher, less desirable cost. But the direct link between P4-P5 is 400G. Are you tempted to use the 400G? My hands are itching to see if this can be done.

Before we do this, make sure you understand OSPF costs because this scenario can make you start pulling your hair out, and I highly recommend you do not skip this setup. This will work without adding the costs, but it is far more obvious that the reason I am having you do this is that we hit two birds with one stone. Dollars to donuts, you will lose points on the exam on this topic (both multi-area adjacency and costs) if you have not worked through this.

Crash course on costs. Default OSPF reference bandwidth is 100 Mbps. This means (CCNA) that anything higher than 100 Mbps will be treated as an OSPF cost of 1. Because we are dealing with 1 Gbps interfaces, the connection between P4-P5 loopback will be 4—one for each hop plus the loopback interface. How do you increase this reference bandwidth to account for higher-speed links? Go on all routers on the network, and under the OSPF process type shown in Example 6-36 from a random router, IOS XR works the same way (do not forget to **commit**, and I hope you're rolling your eyes at me at this point).

Example 6-36 *OSPF Auto-Cost Reference Bandwidth*

```
PE2(config)# router ospf 1
PE2(config-router)# auto-cost reference-bandwidth 1000
% OSPF: Reference bandwidth is changed.
        Please ensure reference bandwidth is consistent across all routers.
PE2(config-router)#
```

Even though we raised the reference bandwidth to 1 Gbps, we still have the same "hop-count" because we still have a cost of 1 through every link. Watch Example 6-37, where I pick out only the three loopbacks that are of interest to us from P4's and P5's perspectives. You can see that the remote loopbacks in area 200 are reachable via intra-area routes (not the direct link between P4 and P5) and observe the highlighted costs. Pay special attention to the P4 and P5 loopbacks.

Example 6-37 *OSPF Costs Examined*

```
P4# show ip route | include .5/|.6/|.7/
O        10.10.100.5/32 [110/4] via 10.10.46.6, 00:01:24, GigabitEthernet4
O        10.10.100.6/32 [110/2] via 10.10.46.6, 01:03:02, GigabitEthernet4
O        10.10.100.7/32 [110/3] via 10.10.46.6, 00:01:24, GigabitEthernet4
P4#

RP/0/RP0/CPU0:P5# show route | include ".4/|.6/|.7/"
O    10.10.100.4/32 [110/4] via 10.10.57.7, 00:05:38, GigabitEthernet0/0/0/2
O    10.10.100.6/32 [110/3] via 10.10.57.7, 00:05:38, GigabitEthernet0/0/0/2
O    10.10.100.7/32 [110/2] via 10.10.57.7, 00:27:49, GigabitEthernet0/0/0/2
RP/0/RP0/CPU0:P5#
```

I will increase the cost on PE6-P7. You should do the same on your network and make sure you do this on both routers! It is a rookie mistake to do this in one direction, since the costs will increase in only one direction, and the other directly will use the old math. This is an easy way to test someone's OSPF knowledge. Example 6-38 shows the change and the result. I like number 350 (our exam), so let's use that and examine the results on P4 and P5 but using the same commands.

Example 6-38 *OSPF Costs Examined (Continued)*

```
PE6# configure terminal
Enter configuration commands, one per line.  End with CNTL/Z.
PE6(config)# interface gigabitEthernet 1
PE6(config-if)# ip ospf cost 350

RP/0/RP0/CPU0:PE7# configure
RP/0/RP0/CPU0:PE7(config)# router ospf 1
RP/0/RP0/CPU0:PE7(config-ospf)# area 200
```

```
RP/0/RP0/CPU0:PE7(config-ospf-ar)# interface gigabitEthernet 0/0/0/1
RP/0/RP0/CPU0:PE7(config-ospf-ar-if)# cost 350
RP/0/RP0/CPU0:PE7(config-ospf-ar-if)# commit
```

```
P4# show ip route | include .5/|.6/|.7/
O        10.10.100.5/32 [110/353] via 10.10.46.6, 00:01:06, GigabitEthernet4
O        10.10.100.6/32 [110/2] via 10.10.46.6, 01:17:38, GigabitEthernet4
O        10.10.100.7/32 [110/352] via 10.10.46.6, 00:01:06, GigabitEthernet4
P4#
```

```
RP/0/RP0/CPU0:P5# show route | include ".4/|.6/|.7/"
O    10.10.100.4/32 [110/353] via 10.10.57.7, 00:00:34, GigabitEthernet0/0/0/2
O    10.10.100.6/32 [110/352] via 10.10.57.7, 00:00:34, GigabitEthernet0/0/0/2
O    10.10.100.7/32 [110/2] via 10.10.57.7, 00:39:00, GigabitEthernet0/0/0/2
RP/0/RP0/CPU0:P5#
```

We see the 350, so we have the costs out of the way and PE6-P7 is now a far less desirable link. The OSPF cost lesson is over. Remember that we have the imaginary direct 400G link between P4 and P5. How do we satisfy our itch and send the traffic across it? That is the main question of this section.

RFC 5185 allows OSPF point-to-point interfaces to become members of multiple areas. It doesn't matter what the physical interface type is. If you turn it into a point-to-point network, the routers will become adjacent in multiple areas. Can you believe this? Also, believe that you will see it on the exam. Example 6-39 takes us through this. Be thorough; this is *so easy to get wrong*. Starting with P4…

Example 6-39   *Multi-Area Adjacencies on IOS*

```
P4# show running-config | section ospf
 ip ospf multi-area 100
router ospf 1
 auto-cost reference-bandwidth 1000
 network 10.10.24.4 0.0.0.0 area 0
 network 10.10.45.4 0.0.0.0 area 100
 network 10.10.46.4 0.0.0.0 area 200
 network 10.10.100.4 0.0.0.0 area 200
P4# show running-config interface gigabithEthernet 5
interface GigabitEthernet5
 ip address 10.10.45.4 255.255.255.0
 negotiation auto
 ipv6 address 2001:10:10:45::4/64
 no mop enabled
 no mop sysid
P4# configure terminal
P4(config)# router ospf 1
P4(config-router)# network 10.10.45.4 0.0.0.0 area 200
```

```
P4(config-router)# exit
P4(config)# interface gigabitEthernet 5
P4(config-if)# ip ospf network point-to-point
P4(config-if)# ip ospf multi-area 100
P4(config-if)# end
P4#
```

On P4's IOS, under the router OSPF process, I switch GigabitEthernet5 to be in area 200, and then, under the interface, I enable network type point-to-point and make it a part of multi-area 100. Here comes P5, IOS XR (see Example 6-40).

Example 6-40 *Multi-Area Adjacencies on IOS XR*

```
RP/0/RP0/CPU0:P5# show running-config router ospf
router ospf 1
 router-id 10.10.100.5
 auto-cost reference-bandwidth 1000
 area 0
  interface GigabitEthernet0/0/0/0
 area 100
  interface GigabitEthernet0/0/0/5
 area 200
  interface Loopback0
  !
  interface GigabitEthernet0/0/0/2
RP/0/RP0/CPU0:P5# configure
RP/0/RP0/CPU0:P5(config)# router ospf 1
RP/0/RP0/CPU0:P5(config-ospf)# area 100
RP/0/RP0/CPU0:P5(config-ospf-ar)# int g0/0/0/5
RP/0/RP0/CPU0:P5(config-ospf-ar-if)# network point-to-point
RP/0/RP0/CPU0:P5(config-ospf-ar-if)# exit
RP/0/RP0/CPU0:P5(config-ospf-ar)# exit
RP/0/RP0/CPU0:P5(config-ospf)# area 200
RP/0/RP0/CPU0:P5(config-ospf-ar)# multi-area-interface g0/0/0/5
RP/0/RP0/CPU0:P5(config-ospf-ar-mif)# commit
RP/0/RP0/CPU0:P5(config-ospf-ar-mif)# end
RP/0/RP0/CPU0:P5#
```

Under the router process (the only place in IOS XR), in area 100, I changed the network type to point-to-point. Then, under area 200, I assigned interface GigabitEthernet0/0/0/5 as a multi-area interface. The results are stunning.

Now, examine Example 6-41, starting on P5 because that is where we were already anyway.

Example 6-41   *Multi-Area Adjacencies Verified on P5*

```
RP/0/RP0/CPU0:P5# show ospf interface brief
Tue Mar  5 16:44:23.947 UTC
* Indicates MADJ interface, (P) Indicates fast detect hold down state


Interfaces for OSPF 1


Interface          PID   Area              IP Address/Mask    Cost   State Nbrs F/C
Gi0/0/0/0          1     0                 10.10.35.5/24      1      BDR    1/1
Gi0/0/0/5          1     100               10.10.45.5/24      1      P2P    1/1
Lo0                1     200               10.10.100.5/32     1      LOOP   0/0
Gi0/0/0/5*         1     200               10.10.45.5/24      1      P2P    1/1
Gi0/0/0/2          1     200               10.10.57.5/24      1      BDR    1/1
RP/0/RP0/CPU0:P5# show route | include ".4/|.6/|.7/"
Tue Mar  5 16:45:23.197 UTC
O    10.10.100.4/32 [110/2] via 10.10.45.4, 00:07:46, GigabitEthernet0/0/0/5
O    10.10.100.6/32 [110/3] via 10.10.45.4, 00:07:46, GigabitEthernet0/0/0/5
O    10.10.100.7/32 [110/2] via 10.10.57.7, 01:08:55, GigabitEthernet0/0/0/2
RP/0/RP0/CPU0:P5#
```

First, P5's Gi0/0/0/5 now belongs to two different areas (100 and 200) with the multi-area interface indicated by an asterisk (*). Second, note that the route to P4's loopback now lies through a less costly (cost of 2, not 353) directly connected interface. Third, this change also affected the path to P6's loopback (and another P4-PE6 network I am not showing). Why? Because the cost to get to it through that link is 352! Example 6-42 shows P4, IOS.

Example 6-42   *Multi-Area Adjacencies Verified on P4*

```
P4# show ip ospf interface brief
Interface    PID   Area          IP Address/Mask    Cost   State Nbrs F/C
Gi1          1     0             10.10.24.4/24      1      BDR    1/1
MA0          1     100           Unnumbered Gi5     1      P2P    1/1
Lo0          1     200           10.10.100.4/32     1      LOOP   0/0
Gi5          1     200           10.10.45.4/24      1      P2P    1/1
Gi4          1     200           10.10.46.4/24      1      BDR    1/1
P4# show ip route | include .5/|.6/|.7/
O      10.10.100.5/32 [110/2] via 10.10.45.5, 00:16:19, GigabitEthernet5
O      10.10.100.6/32 [110/2] via 10.10.46.6, 01:56:24, GigabitEthernet4
O      10.10.100.7/32 [110/3] via 10.10.45.5, 00:16:19, GigabitEthernet5
P4#
```

No asterisk (*) here. Instead, you see interface MA0 (multiarea0) with interface Gigabit-Ethernet5 in both areas 100 and 200. Then, you see the paths to P5 and PE7 loopbacks going through area 100.

One last output for this section—let's look at what **show ip ospf neighbor** looks like in Example 6-43. I am super curious.

Example 6-43 *Multi-Area OSPF Neighbor Adjacencies*

```
P4# show ip ospf neighbors


Neighbor ID      Pri    State        Dead Time    Address        Interface
10.10.100.2       1     FULL/DR      00:00:38     10.10.24.2     GigabitEthernet1
10.10.100.5       0     FULL/ -      00:00:38     10.10.45.5     OSPF_MA3
10.10.100.5       0     FULL/ -      00:00:35     10.10.45.5     GigabitEthernet5
10.10.100.6       1     FULL/DR      00:00:38     10.10.46.6     GigabitEthernet4
P4#
```

```
RP/0/RP0/CPU0:P5# show ospf neighbors
Tue Mar  5 17:01:18.854 UTC


* Indicates MADJ interface
# Indicates Neighbor awaiting BFD session up


Neighbors for OSPF 1


Neighbor ID     Pri   State        Dead Time    Address        Interface
10.10.100.3      1    FULL/DR      00:00:36     10.10.35.3     GigabitEthernet0/0/0/0
    Neighbor is up for 01:24:53
10.10.100.4      1    FULL/ -      00:00:33     10.10.45.4     GigabitEthernet0/0/0/5
    Neighbor is up for 00:23:33
10.10.100.4      1    FULL/ -      00:00:38     10.10.45.4     GigabitEthernet0/0/0/5*
    Neighbor is up for 00:23:42
10.10.100.7      1    FULL/DR      00:00:34     10.10.57.7     GigabitEthernet0/0/0/2
    Neighbor is up for 01:24:51


Total neighbor count: 4
RP/0/RP0/CPU0:P5#
```

No explanation necessary—there are two adjacencies. This was a tough section, so take a break. It's probably one of the more difficult scenarios in the book.

OSPF Virtual Links

Now, let's reconfigure the network according to Figure 6-6.

Do you recall that OSPF needs backbone area 0 for nonbackbone areas to communicate with each other? A nonbackbone area must have connectivity to area 0's ABR. This is essential for maintaining OSPF's hierarchical structure, enabling efficient route summarization, facilitating inter-area communication, and preventing routing loops. Example 6-44 shows what P5 sees when not connected to area 0 (this happened to me once when my then-employer acquired a competitor based in Boston. Our network did not have area 0 in Boston at that time.)

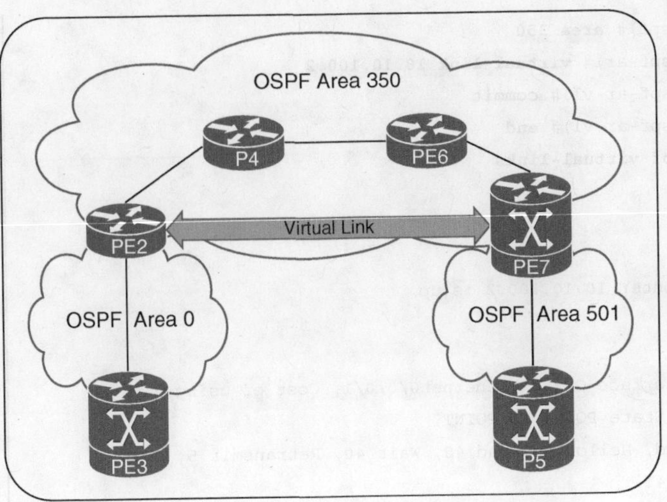

Figure 6-6 *OSPF Virtual Link Topology*

Example 6-44 *View from P5 When Not Connected to Backbone Area 0*

```
RP/0/RP0/CPU0:P5# show ospf neighbors
* Indicates MADJ interface
# Indicates Neighbor awaiting BFD session up


Neighbors for OSPF 1


Neighbor ID     Pri   State      Dead Time   Address        Interface
10.10.100.7     1     FULL/DR    00:00:32    10.10.57.7     GigabitEthernet0/0/0/2
    Neighbor is up for 00:09:00


Total neighbor count: 1
RP/0/RP0/CPU0:P5# show route ospf
% No matching routes found
RP/0/RP0/CPU0:P5#
```

Solution? Virtual links. Backbone partitions can be repaired by configuring virtual links.

Now, let's make area 350 a "tunnel" for area 501 to reach backbone area 0 in Example 6-45 and verifications.

Example 6-45 *Turning Area 350 into a Virtual Link*

```
PE2(config)# router ospf 1
PE2(config-router)# area 350 virtual-link 10.10.100.7
PE2(config-router)#
```

```
RP/0/RP0/CPU0:PE7# configure
RP/0/RP0/CPU0:PE7(config)# router ospf 1
```

```
RP/0/RP0/CPU0:PE7(config-ospf)# area 350
RP/0/RP0/CPU0:PE7(config-ospf-ar)# virtual-link 10.10.100.2
RP/0/RP0/CPU0:PE7(config-ospf-ar-vl)# commit
RP/0/RP0/CPU0:PE7(config-ospf-ar-vl)# end
RP/0/RP0/CPU0:PE7# show ospf virtual-links

Virtual Links for OSPF 1

Virtual Link OSPF_VL0 to router 10.10.100.2 is up
  Run as demand circuit
  DoNotAge LSA allowed.
  Transit area 350, via interface GigabitEthernet0/0/0/1, Cost of using 3
  Transmit Delay is 1 sec, State POINT_TO_POINT,
  Timer intervals configured, Hello 10, Dead 40, Wait 40, Retransmit 5
    Hello due in 00:00:09:041
    Adjacency State FULL (Hello suppressed)
    Number of DBD retrans during last exchange 0
    Index 1/3, retransmission queue length 0, number of retransmission 0
    First 0(0)/0(0) Next 0(0)/0(0)
    Last retransmission scan length is 0, maximum is 0
    Last retransmission scan time is 0 msec, maximum is 0 msec
RP/0/RP0/CPU0:PE7#
```

```
PE2# show ip ospf virtual-links
Virtual Link OSPF_VL0 to router 10.10.100.7 is up
  Run as demand circuit
  DoNotAge LSA allowed.
  Transit area 350, via interface GigabitEthernet1
Topology-MTID    Cost    Disabled    Shutdown    Topology Name
      0           3        no          no          Base
  Transmit Delay is 1 sec, State POINT_TO_POINT,
  Timer intervals configured, Hello 10, Dead 40, Wait 40, Retransmit 5
    Hello due in 00:00:06
    Adjacency State FULL (Hello suppressed)
    Index 1/2/3, retransmission queue length 0, number of retransmission 1
    First 0x0(0)/0x0(0)/0x0(0) Next 0x0(0)/0x0(0)/0x0(0)
    Last retransmission scan length is 1, maximum is 1
    Last retransmission scan time is 0 msec, maximum is 0 msec
PE2# show ip ospf neighbors

Neighbor ID     Pri   State       Dead Time   Address       Interface
10.10.100.7      0    FULL/  -        -        10.10.67.7    OSPF_VL0
10.10.100.3      1    FULL/BDR    00:00:34    10.10.23.3    GigabitEthernet2
10.10.100.4      1    FULL/BDR    00:00:34    10.10.24.4    GigabitEthernet1
PE2#
```

```
RP/0/RP0/CPU0:P5# show route ospf
O IA 10.10.23.0/24 [110/5] via 10.10.57.7, 00:05:05, GigabitEthernet0/0/0/2
O IA 10.10.24.0/24 [110/4] via 10.10.57.7, 00:05:14, GigabitEthernet0/0/0/2
O IA 10.10.46.0/24 [110/3] via 10.10.57.7, 00:05:14, GigabitEthernet0/0/0/2
O IA 10.10.67.0/24 [110/2] via 10.10.57.7, 00:05:14, GigabitEthernet0/0/0/2
O IA 10.10.100.2/32 [110/5] via 10.10.57.7, 00:05:14, GigabitEthernet0/0/0/2
O IA 10.10.100.3/32 [110/6] via 10.10.57.7, 00:05:05, GigabitEthernet0/0/0/2
O IA 10.10.100.4/32 [110/4] via 10.10.57.7, 00:05:14, GigabitEthernet0/0/0/2
O IA 10.10.100.6/32 [110/3] via 10.10.57.7, 00:05:14, GigabitEthernet0/0/0/2
O IA 10.10.100.7/32 [110/2] via 10.10.57.7, 00:05:14, GigabitEthernet0/0/0/2
RP/0/RP0/CPU0:P5#
```

This is easy to read, so don't miss P5 getting all the necessary routes now. Things to remember:

- Virtual links can be configured between any two backbone routers that have an interface to a common nonbackbone area.

- Virtual links are not supported with any OSPF stub areas.

- AS boundary routers (ASBRs) cannot be placed internal to stub areas.

- Virtual links are a temporary solution, so don't get carried away with them. Troubleshooting them can be fun, but I would not expect the exam to get into that. If you need a virtual link, it's a sign something's amiss in your OSPF design, and you're applying a band-aid fix. They are rarely seen in production networks.

Implement OSPFv3

Remember how IS-IS is protocol agnostic? Recall the passenger car train analogy. IS-IS TLV protocol extensions deliver whatever the load of the TLV is—thus allowing the protocol to carry IPv4 and IPv6 traffic natively. Not so with OSPF if you would like to work with IPv6. To support both the IPv6 address family, OSPFv3 (Open Shortest Path First Protocol Version 3) is needed. It is described in RFC 2740 (made obsolete by RFC 5340). I strongly suggest you consult the RFC for nuances of the standard. I will share with you my overview that will help you on the exam.

1. OSPFv3 is not backward compatible with OSPF (OSPFv2).
2. Protocol mechanisms you have learned in this book with OSPFv2 still apply with OSPFv3.
3. OSPFv3 supports both IPv4 and IPv6 address families.
4. OSPFv3 runs over IPv6; thus the packet format is different.
5. There has been a change to the LSA format, so I highly recommend that you read section 2.8, "LSA format changes," of RFC 2740.
6. There is a new LSA called the Link-LSA Type 8 that has a local-link flooding scope. These are never flooded beyond the link that they are associated with and have three purposes, they
    a. Provide the router's link-local address to all other routers attached to the link.

   b. Inform other routers attached to the link of a list of IPv6 prefixes to associate with the link.

   c. Allow the router to assert a collection of Options Field bits (this comes up later; standby) to associate with the Network-LSAs for the link.

This means that IP prefix information is no longer in the OSPF packet header; it is in the LSA payload.

7. The router ID is a must-configure field, which was not true (but recommended) in OSPFv2. The router ID is a 32-bit number with no relationship to an IPv6 address.

8. Neighbor authentication occurs natively in IPv6 packets through the IPsec extensions header, not in the OSPF protocol.

9. You can run multiple OSPFv3 processes in a link.

10. OSPFv3 mechanics:

   a. Protocol ID 89 is still used.

   b. FF02::5 address is used for OSPFv3 AllSPFRouters.

   c. FF02::6 address is used for OSPFv3 AllDRouters (DRs).

11. Lastly, know LSA packet types detailed in Table 6-6.

Table 6-6 OSPFv3 LSA Types

LSA Type	Description
0x2001	**Router-LSA:** Originated by the router to describe the state and cost of the router's interfaces to the area.
0x2002	**Network-LSA:** Originated by the link's designated router to describe all routers attached to the link, including the designated router itself.
0x2003	**Inter-area-prefix-LSAs:** The IPv6 equivalents of OSPFv2 for IPv4's type 3 summary-LSAs are originated by area border routers to describe routes to IPv6 address prefixes that belong to other areas.
0x2004	**Inter-area-router-LSAs:** The IPv6 equivalents of OSPFv2 for IPv4's type 4 summary-LSAs are originated by area border routers to describe routes to AS boundary routers in other areas.
0x2005	**AS-external-LSAs:** Originated by AS boundary routers to describe destinations external to the AS.
0x2006	Not used.
0x2007	**NSSA-LSAs:** Originated by AS boundary routers within an NSSA to describe destinations external to the AS that may or may not be propagated outside the NSSA.
0x2008	**Link-LSAs:** Originated by a router for a link-local flooding scope; they are never flooded beyond the associated link.
0x2009	**Intra-area-prefix-LSAs:** Advertise one or more IPv6 address prefixes that are associated with a local router address, an attached stub network segment, or an attached transit network segment.

Configuring OSPFv3

Enough theory. Recall Figure 6-2 with the topology you should know by heart by now. I have removed all—yes, all—IPv4 addressing. Thus, if you followed my instructions, you would have only IPv6 addresses left. Example 6-46 is your starting point.

Example 6-46   *IPv6 View of PE4 and P3*

```
P4# show ipv6 interface brief | exclude down|una
GigabitEthernet1          [up/up]
    FE80::5054:FF:FE19:A548
    2001:10:10:24::4
GigabitEthernet3          [up/up]
    FE80::5054:FF:FE02:A772
    2001:10:10:34::4
GigabitEthernet4          [up/up]
    FE80::5054:FF:FE16:368F
    2001:10:10:46::4
GigabitEthernet5          [up/up]
    FE80::5054:FF:FE1B:B3B3
    2001:10:10:45::4
Loopback0                 [up/up]
    FE80::21E:14FF:FEA4:D300
    2001:4:4:4::4

RP/0/RP0/CPU0:PE3# show ipv6 interface brief | exclude "down|una"
Loopback0                 [Up/Up]
    fe80::49b2:c6ff:fe6d:dcb2
    2001:3:3:3::3
GigabitEthernet0/0/0/0 [Up/Up]
    fe80::5054:ff:fe1c:b36a
    2001:10:10:35::3
GigabitEthernet0/0/0/2 [Up/Up]
    fe80::5054:ff:fe17:963d
    2001:10:10:23::3
GigabitEthernet0/0/0/3 [Up/Up]
    fe80::5054:ff:fe14:5069
    2001:10:10:34::3
GigabitEthernet0/0/0/5 [Up/Up]
    fe80::5054:ff:fe0c:cd68
    2001:10:10:36::3
```

Example 6-47 enables OSPFv3 on both routers. The verification should make sense for your topology (in case you used different interfaces than I did).

Example 6-47   *OSPFv3 Configuration*

```
P4# configure terminal
Enter configuration commands, one per line.  End with CNTL/Z.
P4(config)# router ospfv3 1
P4(config-router)# router-id 10.10.100.4
P4(config-router)# address-family ipv6 unicast
P4(config-router-af)# passive-interface loopback0
P4(config-router-af)# exit
P4(config-router)# exit
P4(config)# interface loopback0
P4(config-if)# ospfv3 1 ipv?

ipv4  ipv6
P4(config-if)# ospfv3 1 ipv6 area 0
P4(config-if)# interface gigabitEthernet 3
P4(config-if)# ospfv3 1 ipv6 area 0
P4(config-if)# interface gigabitEthernet 1
P4(config-if)# ospfv3 1 ipv6 area 100
P4(config-if)# end
P4# show ipv6 protocols
IPv6 Routing Protocol is "connected"
IPv6 Routing Protocol is "application"
IPv6 Routing Protocol is "omp"
  Redistribution:
    None
IPv6 Routing Protocol is "ND"
IPv6 Routing Protocol is "ospf 1"
  Router ID 10.10.100.4
  Area border router
  Number of areas: 2 normal, 0 stub, 0 nssa
  Interfaces (Area 0):
    Loopback0
    GigabitEthernet3
  Interfaces (Area 100):
    GigabitEthernet1
  Redistribution:
    None
P4#

RP/0/RP0/CPU0:PE3# configure
RP/0/RP0/CPU0:PE3(config)# router ospfv3 1
RP/0/RP0/CPU0:PE3(config-ospfv3)# router-id 10.10.100.3
RP/0/RP0/CPU0:PE3(config-ospfv3)# area 0
RP/0/RP0/CPU0:PE3(config-ospfv3-ar)# interface loopback0
RP/0/RP0/CPU0:PE3(config-ospfv3-ar-if)# passive
```

```
RP/0/RP0/CPU0:PE3(config-ospfv3-ar-if)# exit
RP/0/RP0/CPU0:PE3(config-ospfv3-ar)# interface gigabitEthernet 0/0/0/3
RP/0/RP0/CPU0:PE3(config-ospfv3-ar-if)# exit
RP/0/RP0/CPU0:PE3(config-ospfv3-ar)# exit
RP/0/RP0/CPU0:PE3(config-ospfv3)# area 100
RP/0/RP0/CPU0:PE3(config-ospfv3-ar)# interface gigabitEthernet 0/0/0/2
RP/0/RP0/CPU0:PE3(config-ospfv3-ar-if)# commit
RP/0/RP0/CPU0:PE3(config-ospfv3-ar-if)# end
RP/0/RP0/CPU0:PE3# show protocols ipv6


Routing Protocol OSPFv3 1
  Router Id: 10.10.100.3
  Distance: 110
  Graceful Restart: Disabled
  Redistribution:
    None
  Area 0
    GigabitEthernet0/0/0/3
    Loopback0
  Area 100
    GigabitEthernet0/0/0/2
RP/0/RP0/CPU0:PE3# show ospfv3 neighbors


# Indicates Neighbor awaiting BFD session up


Neighbors for OSPFv3 1


Neighbor ID    Pri  State        Dead Time   Interface ID    Interface
10.10.100.4    1    FULL/DR      00:00:35    9               GigabitEthernet0/0/0/3
    Neighbor is up for 00:02:58


Total neighbor count: 1
RP/0/RP0/CPU0:PE3# show route ipv6 ospf
O    2001:4:4:4::4/128
     [110/1] via fe80::5054:ff:fe02:a772, 00:06:33, GigabitEthernet0/0/0/3
O IA 2001:10:10:24::/64
     [110/2] via fe80::5054:ff:fe02:a772, 00:06:33, GigabitEthernet0/0/0/3
RP/0/RP0/CPU0:PE3#
```

Notice how much cleaner and shorter IOS XR configuration was. We verified from PE3 that
we have a neighbor relationship with P4, and we are getting the routes for the two interfaces
we turned up: an intra-area route from P4's loop back (O) and an inter-area route from the
area 100 interface that will lead to PE2 in a minute (O IA).

Example 6-48 verifies a completed configuration on PE2, which I have not supplied here.
That is a small task you have to undertake on your own. You see P4 and PE3's loopbacks and

the link that connects them together. This example should be self-explanatory in the highlighted sections if you followed the OSPFv2 examples thoroughly.

Example 6-48 *OSPFv3 Configuration Continues on PE2*

```
PE2# show ipv6 route ospf
IPv6 Routing Table - default - 9 entries
! Output omitted for brevity
OI  2001:3:3:3::3/128 [110/1]
     via FE80::5054:FF:FE17:963D, GigabitEthernet2
OI  2001:4:4:4::4/128 [110/1]
     via FE80::5054:FF:FE19:A548, GigabitEthernet1
OI  2001:10:10:34::/64 [110/2]
     via FE80::5054:FF:FE17:963D, GigabitEthernet2
     via FE80::5054:FF:FE19:A548, GigabitEthernet1
PE2# show ospfv3 interface gigabitEthernet 2
GigabitEthernet2 is up, line protocol is up
  Link Local Address FE80::5054:FF:FE08:87BD, Interface ID 8 (ios-if-index)
  Area 100, Process ID 1, Instance ID 0, Router ID 10.10.100.2
  Network Type BROADCAST, Cost: 1
  Transmit Delay is 1 sec, State BDR, Priority 1
  Designated Router (ID) 10.10.100.3, local address FE80::5054:FF:FE17:963D
  Backup Designated router (ID) 10.10.100.2, local address FE80::5054:FF:FE08:87BD
  Timer intervals configured, Hello 10, Dead 40, Wait 40, Retransmit 5
    Hello due in 00:00:00
  Graceful restart helper support enabled
  Index 1/2/2, flood queue length 0
  Next 0x0(0)/0x0(0)/0x0(0)
  Last flood scan length is 1, maximum is 1
  Last flood scan time is 0 msec, maximum is 1 msec
  Neighbor Count is 1, Adjacent neighbor count is 1
    Adjacent with neighbor 10.10.100.3  (Designated Router)
  Suppress hello for 0 neighbor(s)
```

Of specific interest for the purposes of the exam (and, of course, for your knowledge of OSPFv3) is the certain output of the OSPFv3 database shown in Example 6-49. This example shows the full output, since we have a small topology, and I would like for you to know what it may look like in real life.

Example 6-49 *OSPFv3 Option Bits Examined*

```
PE2# show ospfv3 database router


        OSPFv3 1 address-family ipv4 (router-id 10.10.100.2)


        OSPFv3 1 address-family ipv6 (router-id 10.10.100.2)


        Router Link States (Area 100)
```

```
LS age: 413
Options: (V6-Bit, E-Bit, R-Bit, DC-Bit)
LS Type: Router Links
Link State ID: 0
Advertising Router: 10.10.100.2
LS Seq Number: 80000006
Checksum: 0xBC99
Length: 56
Number of Links: 2

  Link connected to: a Transit Network
    Link Metric: 1
    Local Interface ID: 8
    Neighbor (DR) Interface ID: 8
    Neighbor (DR) Router ID: 10.10.100.3

  Link connected to: a Transit Network
    Link Metric: 1
    Local Interface ID: 7
    Neighbor (DR) Interface ID: 7
    Neighbor (DR) Router ID: 10.10.100.4


Routing Bit Set on this LSA
LS age: 470
Options: (V6-Bit, E-Bit, R-Bit, DC-Bit)
LS Type: Router Links
Link State ID: 0
Advertising Router: 10.10.100.3
LS Seq Number: 80000002
Checksum: 0xB342
Length: 40
Area Border Router
Number of Links: 1

  Link connected to: a Transit Network
    Link Metric: 1
    Local Interface ID: 8
    Neighbor (DR) Interface ID: 8
    Neighbor (DR) Router ID: 10.10.100.3


Routing Bit Set on this LSA
LS age: 480
Options: (V6-Bit, E-Bit, R-Bit, DC-Bit)
```

```
        LS Type: Router Links

        Link State ID: 0

        Advertising Router: 10.10.100.4

        LS Seq Number: 80000003

        Checksum: 0xA153

        Length: 40

        Area Border Router

        Number of Links: 1


          Link connected to: a Transit Network
            Link Metric: 1

            Local Interface ID: 7

            Neighbor (DR) Interface ID: 7

            Neighbor (DR) Router ID: 10.10.100.4
      PE2#
```

Remember I mentioned that Options Field bits would be coming up? Table 6-7 explains what these bits indicate.

Table 6-7   OSPFv3 Options Field Bits

Option	Description
V6-bit	If this bit is clear, the router/link should be excluded from IPv6 routing calculations. Not in our case. We are routing IPv6.
E-bit	This bit describes the way AS-external-LSAs are flooded. Not in our case. This bit will be cleared in stub areas, and mismatch E-bit values will prevent neighboring adjacencies.
R-bit	If you clear this bit (not in our case), then routes that transit this node cannot be computed. Used for router staging or disabling routing for non-locally addressed packets.
DC-bit	This bit describes the router's handling of demand circuits for Hello suppression. This is beyond the scope of the exam.
N-bit	This bit indicates whether or not the router is attached to an NSSA area.

Feel free to explore OSPFv3 on your own, but there is something else I would like to draw your attention to. Consider the output in Example 6-50.

Example 6-50   *OSPFv3 LSDB View*

```
PE2# show ospfv3 database


        OSPFv3 1 address-family ipv4 (router-id 10.10.100.2)


        OSPFv3 1 address-family ipv6 (router-id 10.10.100.2)


          Router Link States (Area 100)
```

```
ADV Router          Age         Seq#            Fragment ID  Link count  Bits

10.10.100.2         29          0x8000000D      0                2       None

10.10.100.3         137         0x80000009      0                1       B

10.10.100.4         301         0x8000000A      0                1       B


                    Net Link States (Area 100)


ADV Router          Age         Seq#            Link ID      Rtr count

10.10.100.3         137         0x80000008      8                2

10.10.100.4         301         0x80000008      7                2


                 Inter Area Prefix Link States (Area 100)


ADV Router          Age         Seq#            Prefix

10.10.100.3         891         0x80000008      2001:10:10:34::/64

10.10.100.3         891         0x80000008      2001:3:3:3::3/128

10.10.100.3         891         0x80000008      2001:4:4:4::4/128

10.10.100.4         1554        0x80000008      2001:4:4:4::4/128

10.10.100.4         1554        0x80000008      2001:10:10:34::/64

10.10.100.4         793         0x80000008      2001:3:3:3::3/128


                 Link (Type-8) Link States (Area 100)


ADV Router          Age         Seq#            Link ID      Interface

10.10.100.2         29          0x80000008      8            Gi2

10.10.100.3         891         0x80000008      8            Gi2

10.10.100.2         29          0x80000008      7            Gi1

10.10.100.4         1554        0x80000008      7            Gi1


                 Intra Area Prefix Link States (Area 100)


ADV Router          Age         Seq#            Link ID      Ref-lstype   Ref-LSID

10.10.100.2         29          0x80000008      0            0x2001       0

10.10.100.3         137         0x80000008      8192         0x2002       8

10.10.100.4         301         0x80000008      7168         0x2002       7

PE2#
```

First, notice the highlighted designations under router links on the top right. It lists "None" for PE2, and "B" for PE3 and P4. Basically, no bits are set for PE2; the B-bit is for ABR border routers. Now, consult Table 6-8.

Table 6-8   OSPFv3 Router LSA Bits

Value	Name	Description
0x01	B-bit	Indicates the router is an ABR
0x02	E-bit	Indicates the router is an ASBR
0x04	V-bit	Indicates the router is a virtual link endpoint
0x08	Not used	
0x10	Nt-bit	Indicates the router is an NSSA border router that translates LSA Type 7 into Type 5

Implementing OSPFv3 Authentication

I mentioned that OSPFv3 does not support native protocol authentication methods. Instead, the IP Security protocol (IPsec) is used to provide secure connections between routers. There are two available IPv6 extension header options:

- **Authentication Header (AH):** This one authenticates based on the header only.

- **Encapsulating Security Payload (ESP):** This one can add encryption on top of authentication.

Anytime IPsec, AH, and ESP are mentioned, minds drift to IPsec VPN tunnels, which many of us have done. Do not make this mistake. IPsec VPNs have a handy Internet Key Exchange (IKE) protocol that constructs security association (SA) values over an insecure medium, the Internet. OSPv3 does not have the luxury of the IKE, so the IPsec Security Parameter Index (SPI) hash algorithm and key must be manually specified. While we're on PE2, let's configure AH on the interface link to P4. Don't fret if you've never done this before; it's not that bad. We use the parameters supplied in Table 6-9.

Table 6-9   Security Components for OSPFv3 Authentication on IOS

Element	Value
Security Policy Index	350
Authentication Algorithm	SHA1
Authentication key	89a1c105a4720482e52ae423839ed97c693201ca
Encryption Algorithm	AES 256

Where did I get those key values? There are plenty of online key generators, but NEVER use them in production networks. There are far more secure ways available.

Now, let's look at Example 6-51.

Example 6-51   *OSPFv3 Interface Authentication*

```
PE2# configure terminal
Enter configuration commands, one per line.   End with CNTL/Z.
PE2(config)# interface gigabitEthernet 1
PE2(config-if)# ipv6 ospf authentication ?
  ipsec  Use IPsec authentication
  null   Use no authentication
```

```
PE2(config-if)# ipv6 ospf authentication ipsec spi ?
  <256-4294967295>  SPI

PE2(config-if)# ipv6 ospf authentication ipsec spi 350 ?
  md5   Use MD5 authentication
  sha1  Use SHA-1 authentication

PE2(config-if)# ipv6 ospf authentication ipsec spi 350 sha1 ?
  0           The key is not encrypted (plain text)
  7           The key is encrypted
  Hex-string  SHA-1 key (40 chars)

PE2(config-if)#ipv6 ospf authentication ipsec spi 350 sha1
89a1c105a4720482e52ae423839ed97c693201ca
PE2(config-if)# do show ipv6 ospf neighbors


            OSPFv3 Router with ID (10.10.100.2) (Process ID 1)


Neighbor ID     Pri   State          Dead Time   Interface ID    Interface
10.10.100.3      1    FULL/DR        00:00:38    8               GigabitEthernet2
10.10.100.4      1    FULL/DR        00:00:01    7               GigabitEthernet1
PE2(config-if)# do show ipv6 ospf neighbors


            OSPFv3 Router with ID (10.10.100.2) (Process ID 1)


Neighbor ID     Pri   State          Dead Time   Interface ID    Interface
10.10.100.3      1    FULL/DR        00:00:38    8               GigabitEthernet2
PE2(config-if)#
```

Observe that the neighbor adjacency quickly expires. Now, let's fix the other side. In
Example 6-52, I copy and paste the same command on P4, and the neighbor PE2 comes up.

Example 6-52 *Copying and Pasting on P4*

```
P4# show ipv6 ospf neighbors

            OSPFv3 Router with ID (10.10.100.4) (Process ID 1)


Neighbor ID     Pri   State          Dead Time   Interface ID    Interface
10.10.100.3      1    FULL/BDR       00:00:38    9               GigabitEthernet3
P4# configure terminal
Enter configuration commands, one per line.  End with CNTL/Z.
P4(config)# interface gigabitEthernet 1
P4(config-if)# ipv6 ospf authentication ipsec spi 350 sha1
89a1c105a4720482e52ae423839ed97c693201ca
P4(config-if)# end
```

```
P4# show ipv6 ospf neighbors


          OSPFv3 Router with ID (10.10.100.4) (Process ID 1)


Neighbor ID      Pri   State          Dead Time    Interface ID    Interface
10.10.100.3       1    FULL/BDR       00:00:37     9               GigabitEthernet3
10.10.100.2       1    FULL/BDR       00:00:39     7               GigabitEthernet1
P4# show ipv6 ospf interface gigabitEthernet 1 | include SHA-1
    SHA-1 authentication SPI 350, secure socket UP (errors: 0)
```

Are you ready to configure ESP encryption between PE3 and P5 (IOS XR)? See Table 6-10 and Example 6-53.

Table 6-10   Security Components for OSPFv3 Authentication and Encryption on IOS XR

Element	Value
Security Policy Index	501
Authentication Algorithm	SHA1
Authentication key	89a1c105a4720482e52ae423839ed97c693201ca
Encryption Algorithm	AES 192
Encryption key	75203A09B39AC50686BF2F32723FDD8091902AB85D7EC921

Example 6-53   *OSPFv3 Interface Authentication and Encryption*

```
RP/0/RP0/CPU0:P5# configure
RP/0/RP0/CPU0:P5(config)# router ospfv3 1
RP/0/RP0/CPU0:P5(config-ospfv3)# area 0
RP/0/RP0/CPU0:P5(config-ospfv3-ar)# interface gigabitEthernet 0/0/0/0
RP/0/RP0/CPU0:P5(config-ospfv3-ar-if)# encryption ipsec spi 501 esp aes
192 75203A09B39AC50686BF2F32723FDD8091902AB85D7EC921 authentication sha1
89a1c105a4720482e52ae423839ed97c693201ca
RP/0/RP0/CPU0:P5(config-ospfv3-ar-if)# commit
RP/0/RP0/CPU0:P5(config-ospfv3-ar-if)#


RP/0/RP0/CPU0:PE3(config-ospfv3-ar-if)# area 0
RP/0/RP0/CPU0:PE3(config-ospfv3-ar)# interface gigabitEthernet 0/0/0/0
RP/0/RP0/CPU0:PE3(config-ospfv3-ar-if)# encryption ipsec spi 501 esp aes
192 75203A09B39AC50686BF2F32723FDD8091902AB85D7EC921 authentication sha1
89a1c105a4720482e52ae423839ed97c693201ca
RP/0/RP0/CPU0:PE3(config-ospfv3-ar-if)# commit
RP/0/RP0/CPU0:PE3(config-ospfv3-ar-if)# end
RP/0/RP0/CPU0:PE3# show ospfv3 neighbors
# Indicates Neighbor awaiting BFD session up


Neighbors for OSPFv3 1


Neighbor ID      Pri   State          Dead Time    Interface ID    Interface
10.10.100.5       1    FULL/DR        00:00:36     6               GigabitEthernet0/0/0/0
  Neighbor is up for 00:00:08
```

```
10.10.100.4    1    FULL/BDR        00:00:33    9         GigabitEthernet0/0/0/3
     Neighbor is up for 01:41:26


Total neighbor count: 2
RP/0/RP0/CPU0:PE3# show ospfv3 interface gigabitEthernet 0/0/0/0
GigabitEthernet0/0/0/0 is up, line protocol is up, ipsec is up
   Link Local address fe80::5054:ff:fe1c:b36a, Interface ID 6
   Area 0, Process ID 1, Instance ID 0, Router ID 10.10.100.3
   Network Type BROADCAST, Cost: 1
   ESP Encryption AES-192, Authentication SHA1, SPI 501
   Bandwidth : 1000000
   RIB LC sync Yes
   Transmit Delay is 1 sec, State BDR, MTU 1500,  Priority 1
   Designated Router (ID) 10.10.100.5, local address fe80::5054:ff:fe16:f0f6
   Backup Designated router (ID) 10.10.100.3, local address fe80::5054:ff:fe1c:b36a
   Flush timer for old DR LSA due in 00:01:25
! Output omitted for brevity
```

Homework? Instead of getting this to work on the interfaces, make it work for the entire OSPF area. Also, use the rest of the lab environment to practice OSPFv3 freestyle. Try setting up stub or NSSA areas and observe different behaviors.

OSPFv3 Multiple Instances

In OSPFv3, neighbor adjacencies are formed with link-local IPv6 addressing. On shared links that have multiple routers, it may be desirable to form adjacencies only with specific routers. OSPFv3 has an Instance ID field that instructs routers to form adjacencies only with routers that have the same Instance ID. Remember the DR/BDR topology? I removed all of its IPv4 addresses and assigned IPv6 addresses that share the same multi-access LAN with their Ethernet interfaces. Figure 6-7 shows what the topology looks like now.

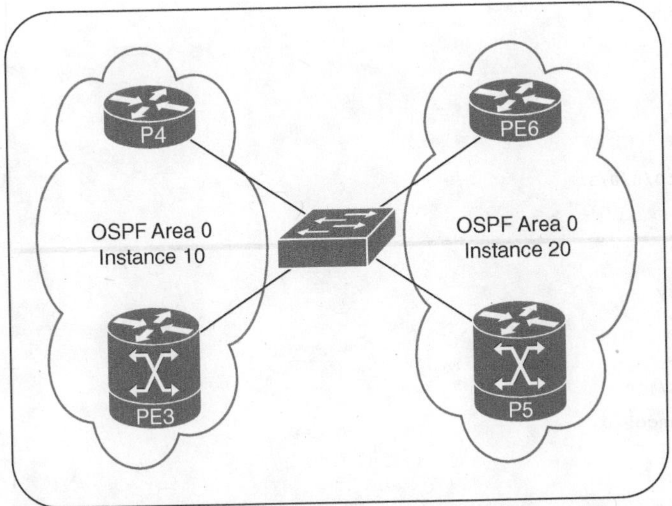

Figure 6-7 *OSPF Virtual Link Topology*

Example 6-54 shows the configuration you can stand up in your lab environment.

Example 6-54 *OSPFv3 Multiple Instances*

```
P4# show running-config
! Output omitted for brevity
interface Loopback0
 ipv6 address 2001:4:4:4::4/128
 ospfv3 1 ipv6 area 0 instance 10
!
interface GigabitEthernet4
 ipv6 address 2001:10:10:10::4/64
 ospfv3 1 ipv6 area 0 instance 10
!
router ospfv3 1
 router-id 10.10.100.4
 !
 address-family ipv6 unicast
 exit-address-family
 !

RP/0/RP0/CPU0:PE3# show running-config
! Output omitted for brevity
!
interface Loopback0
 ipv6 address 2001:3:3:3::3/128
 !
interface GigabitEthernet0/0/0/3
 ipv6 address 2001:10:10:10::3/64
 !
router ospfv3 1
 router-id 10.10.100.3
 area 0
  interface Loopback0
   instance 10
  !
  interface GigabitEthernet0/0/0/3
   instance 10

PE6# show running-config
! Output omitted for brevity
!
interface Loopback0
 ipv6 address 2001:6:6:6::6/128
 ospfv3 1 ipv6 area 0 instance 20
 !
```

```
interface GigabitEthernet6
 ipv6 address 2001:10:10:10::6/64
 ospfv3 1 ipv6 area 0 instance 20
!
router ospfv3 1
 router-id 10.10.100.6
 !
 address-family ipv6 unicast
 exit-address-family
 !
```

```
RP/0/RP0/CPU0:P5# show running-config
! Output omitted for brevity
!
interface Loopback0
 ipv6 address 2001:5:5:5::5/128
!
interface GigabitEthernet0/0/0/5
 ipv6 address 2001:10:10:10::5/64
!
router ospfv3 1
 router-id 10.10.100.5
 area 0
  interface Loopback0
   instance 20
  !
  interface GigabitEthernet0/0/0/5
   instance 20
  !
 !
!
end
```

Example 6-55 shows verifications from all routers to make sure they do not get wrong adjacencies or routes. P4 and PE3 are working together, and so are P5 and PE6—all happening on the same shared LAN!

Example 6-55 *OSPFv3 Multiple Instances Verified*

```
P4# show ipv6 ospf neighbors

            OSPFv3 Router with ID (10.10.100.4) (Process ID 1)


Neighbor ID     Pri   State           Dead Time    Interface ID    Interface
10.10.100.3       1   FULL/BDR        00:00:39     9               GigabitEthernet4
P4# show ipv6 route ospf
```

```
O    2001:3:3:3::3/128 [110/1]
        via FE80::5054:FF:FE1C:DBAB, GigabitEthernet4
```

```
RP/0/RP0/CPU0:PE3# show ospfv3 neighbors


# Indicates Neighbor awaiting BFD session up


Neighbors for OSPFv3 1


Neighbor ID     Pri   State          Dead Time    Interface ID    Interface
10.10.100.4     1     FULL/DR        00:00:36     10              GigabitEthernet0/0/0/3
     Neighbor is up for 00:22:05


Total neighbor count: 1
RP/0/RP0/CPU0:PE3# show route ipv6 ospf


O    2001:4:4:4::4/128
        [110/1] via fe80::5054:ff:fe16:289f, 00:22:37, GigabitEthernet0/0/0/3
RP/0/RP0/CPU0:PE3#
```

```
PE6# show ipv6 ospf neighbors


          OSPFv3 Router with ID (10.10.100.6) (Process ID 1)


Neighbor ID     Pri   State          Dead Time    Interface ID    Interface
10.10.100.5      1    FULL/BDR       00:00:31     11              GigabitEthernet6
PE6# sh ipv6 route ospf
O    2001:5:5:5::5/128 [110/1]
        via FE80::5054:FF:FE1B:9963, GigabitEthernet6
```

```
RP/0/RP0/CPU0:P5# show ospfv3 neighbors


# Indicates Neighbor awaiting BFD session up


Neighbors for OSPFv3 1


Neighbor ID     Pri   State          Dead Time    Interface ID    Interface
10.10.100.6     1     FULL/DR        00:00:34     12              GigabitEthernet0/0/0/5
     Neighbor is up for 00:21:07


Total neighbor count: 1
RP/0/RP0/CPU0:P5# show route ipv6 ospf


O    2001:6:6:6::6/128
        [110/1] via fe80::5054:ff:fe16:ddc, 00:21:13, GigabitEthernet0/0/0/5
```

Troubleshooting OSPF

After working through these scenarios, you should have a thorough understanding of where to look for OSPF issues and inconsistencies. Knowing the mechanics of a protocol is fundamental to locating and fixing OSPF problems. Table 6-11 includes the most useful OSPF commands for quickly diagnosing what needs to be corrected.

Table 6-11 More Relevant OSPF Troubleshooting Commands

Command	Clues It Provides
show ip protocol	Shows the global and interface-specific status of any configured Level 3 protocol in IOS
show protocol ospf	Displays general information about OSPF routing processes in IOS XR
debug ip ospf adjacency	Displays information regarding the formation of an OSPF neighbor relationship
clear ospf 1 process	Reloads the OSPF process
show ip ospf neighbor	Displays OSPF-related neighbor information
show ip ospf interface brief	Provides a summary of OSPF interfaces, including their interface ID, state, and IP addresses
show ip ospf interface	Displays information about all or specific OSPF-enabled interfaces
show ip route ospf	Displays the subset of IP routes in the routing table that were learned through OSPF
show ospf database	Displays the OSPF database for a specific router
show ospf virtual-links	Clears LSP state
show ip ospf events	Displays OSPF events information
show protocol ipv6	Displays information about the OSPFv3 process running on the router
show ospfv3 neighbor	Displays OSPFv3 neighbor information on an individual interface basis
show ospfv3 database	Displays the OSPF database for a specific router
show ipv6 ospf neighbor	Displays lists of information related to the OSPFv3 database for a specific router
show ospfv3 interface	Displays OSPFv3 interface information
show route ipv6 ospf	Displays OSPF information from the IPv6 routing table

And there you have it, folks! The grand finale of this rollercoaster ride of two chapters that focused on IGPs. We have held on tight, navigated challenging turns, and managed to keep our wits about us (mostly). It's been a wild ride, hasn't it? But hey, amidst the chaos, I hope you have discovered some of your hidden talents and practiced not giving up in the face of adversity. So, as we bid adieu to link-state protocols, let's throw confetti in the air and remind ourselves that if we can handle this, we can handle just about anything!

Exam Preparation Tasks

As mentioned in the section "How to Use This Book" in the Introduction, you have a few choices for exam preparation: the exercises here, Chapter 23, "Final Preparation," and the exam simulation questions in the Pearson Test Prep Software Online.

Review All Key Topics

Review the most important topics in this chapter, noted with the Key Topic icon in the margin of the page. Table 6-12 lists a reference of these key topics and the page numbers on which each is found.

Table 6-12   Key Topics for Chapter 6

Key Topic Element	Description	Page Number
Figure 6-1	OSPF LSA Types	160
Table 6-2	OSPF Area Type and Corresponding LSAs	161
Table 6-3	OSPF Packet Types	163
Table 6-4	OSPF Adjacency States and Stages	163
Table 6-5	OSPF Network Types	181
Table 6-6	OSPFv3 LSA Types	210
Table 6-7	OSPFv3 Options Field Bits	216
Table 6-8	OSPFv3 Router LSA Bits	218

Define Key Terms

Define the following key terms from this chapter and check the answers in the glossary:

ABR, AH, ASBR, ESP, LSA, Shortest Path First (SPF) algorithm

Command Reference to Check Your Memory

This section includes the most important configuration and EXEC commands covered in this chapter. You might not need to memorize the complete syntax of every command, but you should be able to remember the basic keywords that are needed.

To test your memory of the commands, cover the right side of Table 6-13 with a piece of paper, read the description on the left side, and then see how much of the command you can remember.

The 350-501 exam focuses on practical, hands-on skills that are used by networking professionals. Therefore, you should be able to identify the commands needed to configure and test. Note that not all commands are fully covered in the chapter, but their presence in the following table should lead you to investigate them further to understand this technology.

Table 6-13   CLI Commands to Know

Task	Command Syntax
Define an OSPF virtual link in router address family topology, router configuration, or address family configuration mode .	**area** *area-id* **virtual-link** *router-id* **authentication key-chain** *chain-name* [**hello-interval** *seconds*] [**retransmit-interval** *seconds*] [**transmit-delay** *seconds*] [**dead-interval** *seconds*] [**ttl-security hops** *hop-count*]

Task	Command Syntax
Generate a default external route into an OSPF routing domain	**default-information originate [always] [metric** *metric-value***] [metric-type** *type-value***] [route-map** *map-name***]**
Enable authentication in an OSPFv3 area	**area** *area-id* **authentication ipsec spi** *spi* *authentication-algorithm [key-encryption-type] key*
Explicitly specify the cost of sending a packet on an interface	**ip ospf cost** *interface-cost*
Configure multi-area adjacency on an interface that is configured with OSPF	**ip ospf multi-area** *multi-area-id*
Specify the cryptographic authentication keys for an OSPFv3 instance	**ospfv3 [***pid***] [ipv4**| **ipv6] authentication {key-chain** *chain-name* | **null}**

Review Questions

As a part of the review, we encourage you to provide *a single-sentence answer* (keep your answers as short as possible) to the following questions. If you struggle to complete this answer in a single sentence, this may indicate a lack of clarity or reveal gaps in your understanding. We have constructed these questions to help you consolidate this chapter's information and extract the essence of the covered content.

The answers to these questions appear in Appendix A. For more practice with exam format questions, use the Pearson Test Prep Software Online.

1. How can OSPF administrators effectively balance the trade-offs between the simplicity of a flat OSPF network design and the scalability benefits offered by hierarchical OSPF area structures?

2. How does OSPF calculate the cost of a route, and how do variations in link bandwidth, network delay, and interface type impact OSPF's decision-making process in selecting the best path for routing?

3. How does OSPFv3 address the limitations of OSPFv2 in IPv6 environments?

Bibliography

R. Coltun, D. Ferguson, and J. Moy. RFC 2740, *OSPF for IPv6*, IETF, https://tools.ietf.org/html/rfc2740, December 1999.

D. Ferguson, A. Lindem, and J. Moy. RFC 5340, *OSPF for IPv6*, IETF, https://tools.ietf.org/html/rfc5340, July 2008.

B. Hinden and S. E. Deering. RFC 2460, *Internet Protocol, Version 6 (IPv6) Specification*, IETF, https://tools.ietf.org/html/rfc2460, December 1998.

S. Kent and R. Atkinson. RFC 2406, *IP Encapsulating Security Payload (ESP)*, IETF, https://tools.ietf.org/html/rfc2406, June 2004.

A. Lindem, S. Mirtorabi, P. Psenak, and A. Oswal. RFC 5185, *OSPF Multi-Area Adjacency*, IETF, https://tools.ietf.org/html/rfc5185, May 2008.

J. Moy. RFC 2328, *OSPF Version 2*, IETF, https://tools.ietf.org/html/rfc2328, April 1998.

CHAPTER 7

BGP Fundamentals

This chapter covers the following exam topics:

2.3 Describe BGP path selection algorithm

2.4 Implement BGP (v4 and v6 for IBGP and EBGP)

- 2.4.a Neighbors
- 2.4.b Prefix advertisement
- 2.4.c Address family
- 2.4.d Path selection
- 2.4.e Attributes
- 2.4.f Redistribution

2.5 Implement routing policy language and route maps (BGP, OSPF, IS-IS)

2.6 Troubleshoot routing protocols

- 2.6.a Neighbor adjacency (BGP, OSPF, IS-IS)
- 2.6.b Route advertisement (BGP, OSPF, IS-IS)

The Border Gateway Protocol (BGP) is a standardized exterior gateway protocol that is designed to exchange routing and reachability information among autonomous systems (ASes) on the Internet. An autonomous system is a collection of IP networks and routers under the control of one entity that presents a common routing policy to the Internet.

BGP is the protocol used to make core routing decisions on the Internet. It works by maintaining a table of IP networks, or *prefixes*, which designate network reachability among autonomous systems. BGP routers exchange information about reachable networks with their neighboring routers and build a topology map of the Internet.

Overall, BGP plays a crucial role in ensuring the proper functioning and stability of the global Internet by facilitating the exchange of routing information among autonomous systems.

"Do I Know This Already?" Quiz

The "Do I Know This Already?" quiz allows you to assess whether you should read this entire chapter thoroughly or jump to the "Exam Preparation Tasks" section. If you are in doubt about your answers to these questions or your own assessment of your knowledge of the topics, read the entire chapter. Table 7-1 lists the major headings in this chapter and their corresponding "Do I Know This Already?" quiz questions. You can find the answers in Appendix A, "Answers to the 'Do I Know This Already?' Quizzes and Review Questions."

Table 7-1   "Do I Know This Already?" Section-to-Question Mapping

Foundation Topics Section	Questions
Introduction to BGP	1
BGP Address Families	8
BGP Prefix Advertisement	5
BGP Path Attributes	2
BGP Path Selection	4
Redistribution	9
Communities	3
Mitigating the Split-Horizon Rule with Route Reflection and Confederations	7
BGP Loop Prevention	6
Troubleshooting	10

CAUTION   The goal of self-assessment is to gauge your mastery of the topics in this chapter. If you do not know the answer to a question or are only partially sure of the answer, you should mark that question as wrong for purposes of the self-assessment. Giving yourself credit for an answer you correctly guess skews your self-assessment results and might provide you with a false sense of security.

1. If we want to establish an eBGP session between two BGP speakers using loopback interface as a source for BGP updates, what additional parameter will be required along with the **remote-as** statement for this session to come up? (Select all that apply.)

   a. eBGP TTL is 2 by default, so there is no need to configure any extra command.

   b. Routing must be sorted to ensure loopback-to-loopback connectivity.

   c. BGP automatically chooses the highest loopback as the source for BGP updates, so there is no need for extra configuration.

   d. eBGP-multihop must be explicitly configured to account for the actual number of hops between the source and destination.

2. The BGP ORIGIN attribute is best defined as which of the following?

   a. Well-known mandatory attribute

   b. Well-known discretionary attribute

   c. Optional transitive attribute

   d. Optional nontransitive attribute

3. Which community can be applied to solve the transit-AS (dual-homed) deployments?

   a. No-advertise

   b. Internet

   c. No-export

   d. local-as

4. What is true about the following output?

```
R4# show bgp ipv4 unicast | begin Network
Network              Next Hop        Metric LocPrf Weight Path
 *>  192.168.0.0/21   10.1.24.2                  0        0 200 {100,300} i
```

   a. Aggregate-address with no added configuration

   b. Aggregate-address with summary-only keyword

   c. Aggregate-address with summary-only and as-set

   d. Aggregate-address with advertise-map only

5. Which BGP table will store NLRIs before inbound route policies take place?

   a. Adj-RIB-In

   b. Adj-RIB-Out

   c. RIB

   d. Loc-RIB

6. Where is the **as-override** configuration applied?

   a. On the BGP speaker that refused the update and does its own AS within AS-PATH.

   b. On the BGP speaker that sent the update.

   c. On the BGP speaker that originated the update.

   d. It should be configured on all eBGP neighbors.

7. If an RR receives a prefix from an eBGP peer, it will advertise the prefix to which of the following?

   a. RR clients only.

   b. RR clients and non-RR clients.

   c. It will not advertise the prefix anywhere (acting as a no-advertise community).

   d. RR clients, non-RR clients, and other eBGP peers.

8. In BGP VPNv4 and VPNv6 address families, what information is included in the NLRI?

   a. IPv4/IPv6 prefix + Route target

   b. IPv4/IPv6 prefix + Route distinguisher

   c. Route distinguisher

   d. Route target

9. What does the following output from the **show bgp ipv4 unicast** command indicate? (Select all that apply.)

```
r>   10.1.100.2/32    10.1.12.2                  0        0 23 ?
```

   a. We have used a network statement to advertise this prefix.

   b. We have used redistribution to advertise this prefix.

   c. We have a better route to this destination installed in the RIB.

   d. No matching route exists for this prefix within the RIB.

10. What does the following log message indicate?

```
%TCP-6-BADAUTH: No MD5 digest
```

   a. No password is configured at the end of the BGP session.

   b. A password is configured at the end of the BGP session but mistakenly (it does not match).

   c. The local router does not support MD5 password capability.

   d. A TCP stack on the local router does not support MD5 password capability.

Foundation Topics

Introduction to BGP

The **Border Gateway Protocol (BGP)** enables core routing decisions on the Internet. It operates by maintaining a table of IP network prefixes and their associated routing information. BGP routers exchange information about reachable networks with their neighboring routers and build a topology map of the Internet.

Key features of BGP include

- **Path Vector Protocol:** BGP is a path vector protocol, meaning it includes the path information along with the destination network in its updates. This allows BGP to make routing decisions based not just on the destination but also on the characteristics of the path.

- **Policy-Based Routing:** BGP allows network administrators to implement various policies for traffic routing based on criteria such as AS-PATH, prefix length, and community attributes. This flexibility enables fine-grained control over routing decisions.

- **Path Selection:** BGP routers select the best path to a destination based on a combination of criteria, including the shortest AS-PATH, preference for certain neighboring autonomous systems, and local policies.

- **Reliability and Scalability:** BGP is designed for reliability and scalability, making it suitable for use in large-scale networks such as the Internet. It achieves this through mechanisms like route aggregation and incremental updates.

- **External and Internal BGP:** BGP can be configured to run either as external BGP (eBGP) between routers in different autonomous systems or as internal BGP (iBGP) within the same autonomous system. iBGP is typically used to distribute external routing information within an AS.

Autonomous System (AS)

An **autonomous system (AS)** is a collection of IP networks and routers under the control of one or more network operators that present a common routing policy to the Internet. Autonomous systems are identified by a unique number assigned by a **Regional Internet Registry (RIR)**. This number is known as an autonomous system number (ASN).

Autonomous systems are fundamental building blocks of the Internet's routing infrastructure. They are responsible for routing traffic between different parts of the Internet, ensuring that data packets are delivered efficiently and reliably to their destinations.

Key characteristics of an AS include the following:

- **Single Routing Policy:** An AS presents a single routing policy to the rest of the Internet. This policy defines how traffic is routed within the AS and how it interacts with other autonomous systems.

- **Border Routers:** An AS is connected to other autonomous systems through border routers. These routers exchange routing information with routers in neighboring autonomous systems using exterior gateway protocols such as Border Gateway Protocol.

- **Unique ASN:** Each AS is assigned a unique autonomous system number by an Internet registry. This number is used to identify the AS in routing updates exchanged between autonomous systems.

- **Internal Connectivity:** Within an AS, routers exchange routing information using interior gateway protocols (IGPs) such as Open Shortest Path First (OSPF) or Intermediate System to Intermediate System (IS-IS). This allows routers within the AS to dynamically learn and maintain routes to destinations within the AS. In some cases, iBGP can be used internally to exchange routes, such as DMVPN.

- **Peering Relationships:** Autonomous systems establish peering relationships with other autonomous systems to exchange traffic and routing information. Peering can be settlement-free, whereas traffic exchange is based on mutual agreement, or paid, where one AS pays another for the transit of its traffic.

Overall, autonomous systems play a critical role in the operation of the Internet by enabling the routing of traffic between different networks and ensuring the efficient and reliable delivery of data packets across the global Internet infrastructure.

AS numbers were defined as 16 bits, which allowed for a maximum of 65,535 assignments. Due to the exhaustion of ASN space, a new format of 32 bits was introduced to account for the demand.

In the 16-bit notation, the ASN range of 64,512–65,534 is reserved for private use within enterprise networks. Similarly, in the 32-bit notation, the 4,200,000,000–4,294,967,294 range also is reserved for private use. These ASNs are not definable on the public Internet.

A Regional Internet Registry is an organization responsible for the allocation and registration of Internet number resources within a specific geographic region. There are currently five RIRs worldwide, each serving a distinct region of the globe. These regions and their corresponding RIRs are as follows:

- **American Registry for Internet Numbers (ARIN):** ARIN serves the United States, Canada, and numerous Caribbean and North Atlantic islands.

- **Réseaux IP Européens Network Coordination Centre (RIPE NCC):** RIPE NCC serves Europe, the Middle East, and parts of Central Asia.

- **Asia-Pacific Network Information Centre (APNIC):** APNIC serves Asia, Australia, New Zealand, and the Pacific Islands.

- **Latin America and Caribbean Network Information Centre (LACNIC):** LACNIC serves Latin America and the Caribbean.

- **African Network Information Centre (AFRINIC):** AFRINIC serves Africa and parts of the Indian Ocean.

Each RIR is responsible for managing and distributing Internet number resources, which include IPv4 and IPv6 addresses as well as ASNs, within its respective region. These resources are allocated to Internet service providers (ISPs), organizations, and end users according to established policies and procedures.

In addition to resource allocation, RIRs also maintain public databases containing registration information for allocated IP addresses and ASNs. These databases provide transparency and facilitate the efficient coordination and management of Internet resources within each region.

RIRs also play a crucial role in policy development related to Internet number resource management. They facilitate community-driven processes through which policies are developed, reviewed, and updated to address emerging needs and challenges in the management of IP addresses and ASNs.

Overall, RIRs are essential organizations that contribute to the stable and sustainable operation of the Internet by ensuring the fair and equitable distribution of Internet number resources and fostering cooperation and coordination among stakeholders within their respective regions.

Internal Border Gateway Protocol (iBGP) and external Border Gateway Protocol (eBGP) are two variations of the Border Gateway Protocol used within autonomous systems to facilitate routing between routers. Here are the key differences between iBGP and eBGP:

- **iBGP:** Internal BGP is used for BGP peering between routers within the same autonomous system. iBGP sessions are established between routers within the AS to exchange routing information.

- **eBGP:** External BGP is used for BGP peering between routers in different autonomous systems. eBGP sessions are established between routers in different autonomous systems to exchange routing information between autonomous systems.

Figure 7-1 shows a basic topology to differentiate iBGP from eBGP from an AS perspective.

When we start configuring the BGP, the basic block will be the autonomous system. The router will use the **router bgp** *autonomous system* command from global configuration mode to start the BGP negotiation, and each router will use the AS it's located in within the command; for example, if R1 is in AS 100, it will start the process through **router bgp 100** commands. Next, it will use a neighbor statement to define the peer IP address to which it needs to communicate to establish the relation and then the remote autonomous system for which the peer router is located.

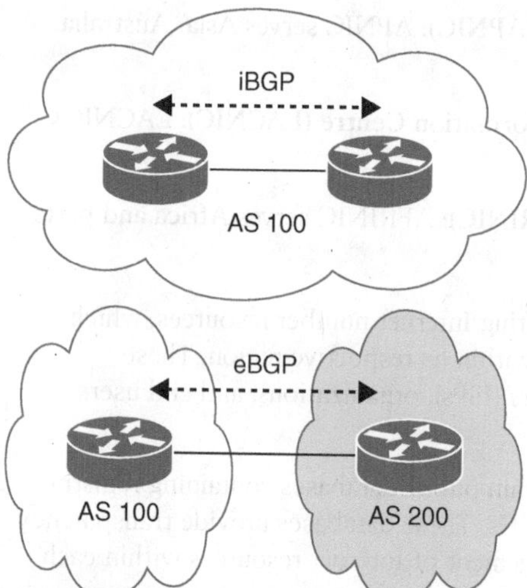

Figure 7-1 *iBGP vs. eBGP*

NOTE By default, Cisco routers automatically initialize the IPv4 unicast address family. When using the **no bgp default ipv4-unicast** command, we must explicitly add the needed configuration items under the IPv4 address family, and this applies for all address families supported by BGP.

For IOS XR, we cannot commit changes without initializing the address family first from the global BGP configuration mode and then activate it under the respective neighbor.

Example 7-1 shows basic configuration items (assuming direct connectivity between R1 [IOS] and R2 [IOS XR]) for which we will establish an eBGP session (no route advertisement for now).

Example 7-1 *BGP Basic Commands*

```
R1(config)# router bgp 100
R1(config-router)# no bgp default ipv4-unicast
R1(config-router)# neighbor 10.1.12.2 remote-as 200
R1(config-router)# address-family ipv4 unicast
R1(config-router-af)# neighbor 10.1.12.2 activate
```

```
RP/0/0/CPU0:R2(config)# router bgp 200
RP/0/0/CPU0:R2(config-bgp)# address-family ipv4 unicast
RP/0/0/CPU0:R2(config-bgp)# neighbor 10.1.12.1
RP/0/0/CPU0:R2(config-bgp-nbr)# remote-as 100
RP/0/0/CPU0:R2(config-bgp-nbr)# address-family ipv4 unicast
! If we did not enter the address-family ipv4 unicast command under the neighbor
! statement on R2 (IOS XR), the commit will be successful but R1 will keep producing
! the log message and the session will keep in the Idle state.
%BGP-5-NBR_RESET: Neighbor 10.1.12.2 active reset (Peer closed the session)
%BGP_SESSION-5-ADJCHANGE: neighbor 10.1.12.2 IPv4 Unicast topology base removed from
session Peer closed the session
```

When building an eBGP neighborship sourced from a loopback interface, we must instruct the BGP speaker that the neighbor is to be reached over multihop because usually eBGP sessions are built using direct physical interfaces (a **time to live [TTL]** of 1). This means if more than one hop is needed to reach the speaker, TTL is decremented to 0, and therefore, the packets will be discarded.

We can overcome this issue; we must increase the TTL using the **neighbor** *ip-address* **ebgp-multihop** *TTL-value* command on IOS and IOS XE software (the same syntax is used on IOS XR under the neighbor statement). Because we're speaking about multihop, that means we need to introduce some sort of routing to reach the loopback with which we will establish the eBGP peering, which could be exposed to denial-of-service (DoS) attacks (such as brute-force attacks) using forged source and destination IP addresses that eventually will exhaust CPU.

NOTE   Building eBGP peering using loopback interfaces is not common. One of the rare use cases for this is MPLS Inter-AS L3VPN option B, which we will encounter in Chapter 13, "Advanced MPLS Services."

If we already established the eBGP relation using multihop, we will have to remove the **neighbor** *ip-address* **ebgp-multihop** *TTL-value* command and replace it with **neighbor** *ip-address* **ttl-security hops** *hop-count*.

Let's check Example 7-2 for quick verification of how this will work in action. To clarify it, we have two directly connected routers: R2 (IOS XR) and R4 (IOS).

Example 7-2   *BGP TTL Security Example #1*

```
R4(config)# router bgp 400
R4(config-router)# bgp log-neighbor-changes
R4(config-router)# no bgp default ipv4-unicast
R4(config-router)# neighbor 10.1.100.2 remote-as 100
R4(config-router)# neighbor 10.1.100.2 ebgp-multihop 2
R4(config-router)# neighbor 10.1.100.2 update-source Loopback0
R4(config-router)# address-family ipv4
R4(config-router-af)# neighbor 10.1.100.2 activate

RP/0/0/CPU0:R2(config)# router bgp 100
RP/0/0/CPU0:R2(config-bgp)# address-family ipv4 unicast
RP/0/0/CPU0:R2(config-bgp-af)# neighbor 10.1.100.4
RP/0/0/CPU0:R2(config-bgp-nbr)# remote-as 400
RP/0/0/CPU0:R2(config-bgp-nbr)# ebgp-multihop 2
RP/0/0/CPU0:R2(config-bgp-nbr)# update-source Loopback0

R4# show bgp ipv4 unicast neighbors 10.1.100.2 | include TTL
Connection is ECN Disabled, Minimum incoming TTL 0, Outgoing TTL 2

R4(config)# router bgp 400
R4(config-router)# no neighbor 10.1.100.2 ebgp-multihop 2
R4(config-router)# neighbor 10.1.100.2 ttl-security hops 2
R4#show bgp ipv4 unicast neighbors 10.1.100.2 | include TTL
Connection is ECN Disabled, Minimum incoming TTL 253, Outgoing TTL 255
```

The **hop-count** argument is the number of hops between the local and remote peers. If the expected TTL value in the IP header is 254, then we will set up the hop-count argument for 1. This means BGP will accept IP packets (this is an IPv4-based example) with a TTL value equal to or greater than the expected TTL value. If packets are not accepted, they silently will be dropped.

As seen, we have changed the value only from the R4 perspective, which will cause neighborship to go down. Now let's examine Example 7-3 for verification of the status.

Example 7-3   *BGP TTL Security Example #2*

```
RP/0/0/CPU0:R2# show bgp summary | begin Neighbor
Neighbor        Spk   AS MsgRcvd MsgSent   TblVer   InQ OutQ  Up/Down   St/PfxRcd
10.1.100.4        0  400     16      17        0     0    0  00:04:57 OpenConfirm
! Turning on debugging on R4 (debug bgp ipv4 unicast events).
%BGP-3-BGP_NO_REMOTE_READ: 10.1.100.2 connection timed out - has not accepted a mes-
sage from us for 180000ms (hold time), 0 messages pending transmission.
%BGP-3-NOTIFICATION: sent to neighbor 10.1.100.2 active 4/0 (hold time expired) 0
bytes
%BGP-5-NBR_RESET: Neighbor 10.1.100.2 active reset (BGP Notification sent)
%BGP-5-ADJCHANGE: neighbor 10.1.100.2 active Down BGP Notification sent
%BGP_SESSION-5-ADJCHANGE: neighbor 10.1.100.2 IPv4 Unicast topology base removed
from session  BGP Notification sent

RP/0/0/CPU0:R2(config)# router bgp 100
RP/0/0/CPU0:R2(config-bgp)# neighbor 10.1.100.4
RP/0/0/CPU0:R2(config-bgp-nbr)# no ebgp-multihop 2
RP/0/0/CPU0:R2(config-bgp-nbr)# ttl-security

bgp[1060]: %ROUTING-BGP-5-ADJCHANGE : neighbor 10.1.100.4 Up (VRF: default) (AS: 400)
```

NOTE   The BGP **ttl-security** feature is designed for eBGP session protection; it is not supported on iBGP peering (or iBGP peer groups).

BGP ASN Representation

In the basic commands to operationalize the BGP neighborship, we use a 16-bit autonomous system number—in this case, **router bgp 100**. As we mentioned earlier, we now have two versions of the ASN: 16-bit and 32-bit.

To clarify, we have three methods to write ASN:

- Asplain

- Asdot

- Asdot+

Asplain is the simplest form of writing the ASN because they are regular decimal numbers. Asdot represents ASNs below 65,536 (the 16-bit ASN range ends with 65,536), whereas Asdot+ represents numbers above 65,536.

For ASNs higher than 65,536, the new higher-order bits start counting from 0 again. For example, ASN 65,536 counts for 1.0, ASN 65,537 counts for 1.1, and so on.

If a conversion is needed from an Asplain to an Asdot+ ASN, we will take the Asplain ASN and divide it by 65,536 and count to produce the high-order bits.

Consider the following conversion process and associated example for better clarity:

```
Integer (high order bits) = asplain/65536

Remainder (low order bits) = asplain - (integer * 65535)

Example #1: 1499547

Integer = 1499547 / 65536 = 22.8 -> 22

Remainder = 1499547 - (22 * 65536) = 57755

Asdot representation : 22.57755
```

The conversion is not easy, so we can use online converters to avoid making mistakes. One of the available tools we can utilize to conduct the same calculation is demonstrated in Figure 7-2; see https://baranoski.ca/BGP_4-Byte_ASN_Format_Converter.

BGP 4-Byte ASN Format Converter

This will let you convert 4-Byte Autonmous System Numbers between the ASDecimal (123456) and ASDdot (1.57920) formats.

Enter ASDot or ASDecimal [1499547]   [Submit]   22.57755

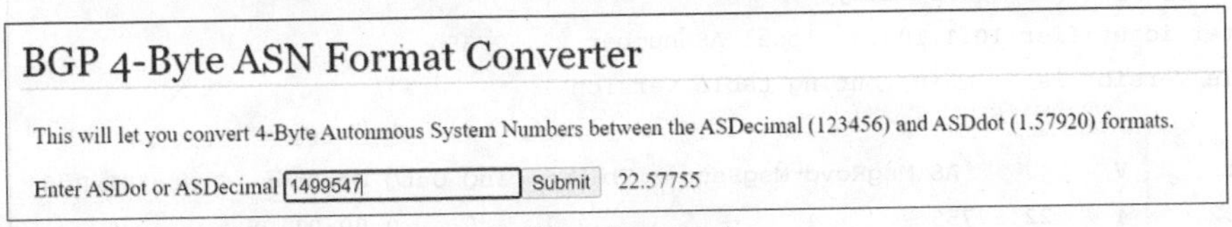

Figure 7-2 *Asplain to Asdot+ Online Conversion*

Now, let's use the same example (R1 [IOS] → R2 [IOS XR]) and see what options we have available from ASN, as shown in Example 7-4.

Example 7-4 *BGP AS Number Variations*

```
R1(config)# router bgp ?
<1-4294967295>  Autonomous system number
<1.0-XX.YY>     Autonomous system number

RP/0/0/CPU0:R2(config)# router bgp ?
  <1-65535>           2-byte AS number
  <1-65535>.          4-byte AS number in asdot (X.Y) format - first half (X)
  <65536-4294967295>  4-byte AS number in asplain format
```

Next, let's use the same AS for which we previously conducted calculations (1499547) and use the asplain format on IOS and the asdot format on IOS XR, as illustrated in Example 7-5.

Example 7-5 *BGP AS Number Configuration Using Asdot Format*

```
R1(config)# router bgp 1499547
R1(config-router)# no bgp default ipv4-unicast
R1(config-router)# neighbor 10.1.12.2 remote-as 1499547
R1(config-router)# address-family ipv4 unicast
R1(config-router-af)# neighbor 10.1.12.2 activate
```

```
RP/0/0/CPU0:R2(config)# router bgp 22.57755
RP/0/0/CPU0:R2(config-bgp)# address-family ipv4 unicast
RP/0/0/CPU0:R2(config-bgp)# neighbor 10.1.12.1
RP/0/0/CPU0:R2(config-bgp-nbr)# remote-as 22.57755
RP/0/0/CPU0:R2(config-bgp-nbr)# address-family ipv4 unicast
```

```
R1# show bgp ipv4 unicast summary
BGP router identifier 10.1.100.7, local AS number 1499547
BGP table version is 1, main routing table version 1

Neighbor        V         AS MsgRcvd MsgSent   TblVer  InQ OutQ Up/Down  State/PfxRcd
10.1.12.2       4    1499547        3       4        1    0    0 00:00:40           0
```

We can change the AS format to asdot from an IOS perspective by using the **bgp asnotation dot** command under the BGP global configuration mode, as illustrated in Example 7-6.

Example 7-6 *BGP AS Notation*

```
R1(config)# router bgp 1499547
R1(config-router)# bgp asnotation dot
```

```
R1# show bgp ipv4 unicast summary
BGP router identifier 10.1.100.7, local AS number 22.57755
BGP table version is 1, main routing table version 1


Neighbor        V         AS MsgRcvd MsgSent   TblVer  InQ OutQ Up/Down  State/PfxRcd
10.1.12.2       4   22.57755        4       5        1    0    0 00:01:25           0
```

As discussed in Chapter 5, "IS-IS" and Chapter 6, "OSPF," routing decisions are based on several factors, starting with the longest match criteria. Without repetitive information and focusing on administrative distance (AD), eBGP prefixes are assigned an AD of 20, whereas iBGP prefixes are assigned an AD of 200.

NOTE As a reminder about administrative distance, AD is a measure of trustworthiness of the source of the routing information. The smaller the value, the more reliable the protocol.

BGP Messages

Border Gateway Protocol uses various messages to exchange routing information and maintain the network topology. These messages help BGP routers communicate with each other, establish peering sessions, advertise routes, and perform various other functions. Here are some of the key BGP messages:

- **Open:** The Open message is the first message sent by a BGP router to initiate a BGP session with its neighbor. It contains parameters such as BGP version number, BGP router ID, and hold time.

- **Keepalive:** Keepalive messages are sent periodically to maintain the BGP session and indicate that the connection is still active. If a BGP router does not receive any Keepalive messages within the hold time interval, it assumes the connection with its neighbor has failed.

- **Update:** The Update message is used to advertise routing information. It contains information about new routes, withdrawn routes, and path attributes associated with the routes. Updates can include information about reachable prefixes, AS-PATH, next hop, and various other attributes.

- **Notification:** The Notification message is sent to indicate errors or abnormal conditions during the BGP session. It can be used to signal that a session is being terminated, report an error in a received message, or notify about a configuration issue.

These are the primary BGP message types used in the operation of the protocol. Each message serves a specific purpose in the establishment and maintenance of BGP sessions and the exchange of routing information.

BGP Neighbor States

Border Gateway Protocol operates using a finite state machine (FSM) model to manage the establishment and maintenance of BGP peering sessions between routers. The BGP finite state machine defines the various states that a BGP router can be in during the process of establishing and maintaining BGP sessions with its peers. Here are the main states of the BGP finite state machine:

- **Idle State (Idle):** This is the initial state of a BGP router. In this state, the BGP process is not running, and the router is not attempting to establish any BGP connections.

- **Connect State (Connect):** In this state, the BGP router is attempting to establish a TCP connection with its BGP neighbor. This state occurs after the router sends an Open message to its peer and is waiting for the TCP connection to be established.

- **Active State (Active):** If the TCP connection establishment fails in the Connect state, the BGP router moves to the Active state. In this state, the router retries establishing the TCP connection with its peer.

- **OpenSent State (OpenSent):** After the TCP connection is successfully established, the BGP router transitions to the OpenSent state. In this state, the router sends an Open message to its peer and waits for a response.

- **OpenConfirm State (OpenConfirm):** Once the BGP router receives an Open message from its peer and verifies that the message is correct, it moves to the OpenConfirm state. In this state, the router sends a Keepalive message to its peer and waits to receive one in return.

- **Established State (Established):** This is the final state of the BGP peering process. Once the BGP router receives a Keepalive message from its peer in the OpenConfirm state, it transitions to the Established state. In this state, BGP routing information exchange can occur, and the router is fully synchronized with its peer.

These are the primary states of the BGP finite state machine. BGP routers transition between these states based on events such as TCP connection establishment, receipt of BGP messages, or failure conditions. Proper management of the BGP finite state machine is crucial for establishing and maintaining stable BGP peering sessions and ensuring the reliable exchange of routing information. Figure 7-3 summarizes the BGP neighbor states.

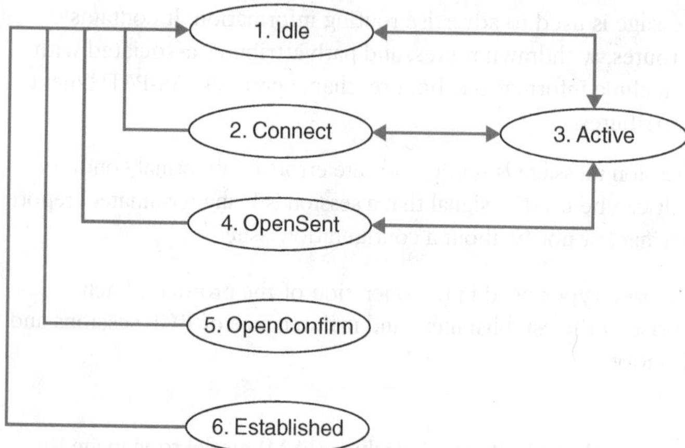

Figure 7-3 *BGP Neighbor States*

To make it more practical, we will use the sample topology in Figure 7-4 to clarify the neighbor states that BGP encounters once the negotiations start between BGP speakers.

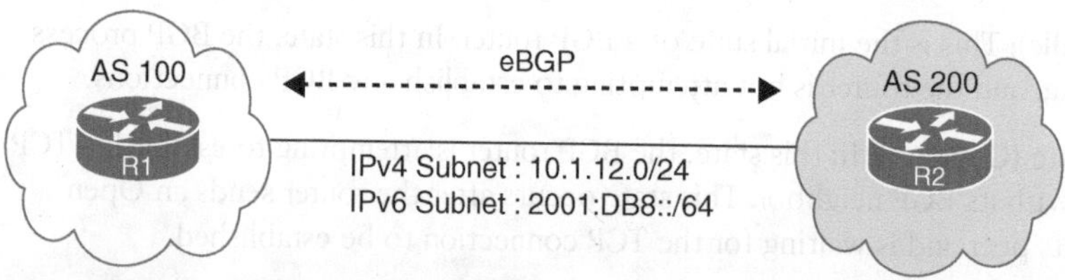

Figure 7-4 *BGP Messages Exchange, IPv4 and IPv6 Address Families*

To clarify the BGP operation and the messages exchange, let's turn on debugging for both IPv4 and IPv6 address families (we just want to confirm the same operations will take place for different address families). To do so, let's go through Example 7-7.

Example 7-7 *BGP Neighbor States*

```
! IPv4 address-family
R1# debug bgp ipv4 unicast
BGP debugging is on for address family: IPv4 Unicast

R1(config)# router bgp 100
R1(config-router)# no bgp default ipv4-unicast
R1(config-router)# neighbor 10.1.12.2 remote-as 200
R1(config-router)# address-family ipv4 unicast
R1(config-router)# neighbor 10.1.12.2 activate

BGP: 10.1.12.2 passive open to 10.1.12.1
BGP: Fetched peer 10.1.12.2 from tcb
BGP: 10.1.12.2 passive went from Idle to Connect
BGP: ses global 10.1.12.2 (0xD0E2718:0) pas Setting open delay timer to 60 seconds.
BGP: ses global 10.1.12.2 (0xD0E2718:0) pas read request no-op
BGP: 10.1.12.2 passive rcv message type 1, length (excl. header) 38
```

```
BGP: ses global 10.1.12.2 (0xD0E2718:0) pas Receive OPEN
BGP: 10.1.12.2 passive rcv OPEN, version 4, holdtime 180 seconds
BGP: 10.1.12.2 passive rcv OPEN w/ OPTION parameter len: 28
BGP: 10.1.12.2 passive rcvd OPEN w/ optional parameter type 2 (Capability) len 6
BGP: 10.1.12.2 passive OPEN has CAPABILITY code: 1, length 4
BGP: 10.1.12.2 passive OPEN has MP_EXT CAP for afi/safi: 1/1
BGP: 10.1.12.2 passive rcvd OPEN w/ optional parameter type 2 (Capability) len 2
BGP: 10.1.12.2 passive OPEN has CAPABILITY code: 128, length 0
BGP: 10.1.12.2 passive OPEN has ROUTE-REFRESH capability(old) for all address-families
BGP: 10.1.12.2 passive rcvd OPEN w/ optional parameter type 2 (Capability) len 2
BGP: 10.1.12.2 passive OPEN has CAPABILITY code: 2, length 0
BGP: 10.1.12.2 passive OPEN has ROUTE-REFRESH capability(new) for all address-families
BGP: 10.1.12.2 passive rcvd OPEN w/ optional parameter type 2 (Capability) len 2
BGP: 10.1.12.2 passive OPEN has CAPABILITY code: 70, length 0
BGP: ses global 10.1.12.2 (0xD0E2718:0) pas Enhanced Refresh cap received in
open message
BGP: 10.1.12.2 passive rcvd OPEN w/ optional parameter type 2 (Capability)
BGP: 10.1.12.2 passive OPEN has CAPABILITY code: 65, length 4
BGP: 10.1.12.2 passive OPEN has 4-byte ASN CAP for: 200
BGP: 10.1.12.2 passive rcvd OPEN w/ remote AS 200, 4-byte remote AS 200
BGP: ses global 10.1.12.2 (0xD0E2718:0) pas Adding topology IPv4 Unicast:base
BGP: ses global 10.1.12.2 (0xD0E2718:0) pas Send OPEN
BGP: ses global 10.1.12.2 (0xD0E2718:0) pas Building Enhanced Refresh capability
BGP: 10.1.12.2 passive went from Connect to OpenSent
BGP: 10.1.12.2 passive sending OPEN, version 4, my as: 100, holdtime 180 seconds,
ID A010C01
BGP: 10.1.12.2 passive went from OpenSent to OpenConfirm
BGP: 10.1.12.2 passive went from OpenConfirm to Established
BGP: ses global 10.1.12.2 (0xD0E2718:1) pas Assigned ID
BGP: nbr global 10.1.12.2 Stop Active Open timer as all topologies are allocated
BGP: ses global 10.1.12.2 (0xD0E2718:1) Up
%BGP-5-ADJCHANGE: neighbor 10.1.12.2 Up
```

```
! Before going through IPv6 related peer establishment and the associated
! messages, we turned off the ipv4-unicast default behavior which applies
! here. We will have to activate the neighbor under the respective
! address-family: IPv6.
! IPv6 address-family
R2(config)# router bgp 200
R2(config-router)# no bgp default ipv4-unicast
R2(config-router)# neighbor 2001:db8::1 remote-as 100
R2(config-router)# address-family ipv6 unicast
R2(config-router)# neighbor 2001:db8::1 activate
% IPv6 routing not enabled
! It is mandatory to enable IPv6 routing capabilities from global configuration mode.
R2(config)# ipv6 unicast-routing
```

```
R1(config)# router bgp 100
R1(config-router)# no bgp default ipv4-unicast
R1(config-router)# neighbor 2001:DB8::2 remote-as 200
R1(config-router)# address-family ipv6 unicast
R1(config-router-af)# neighbor 2001:DB8::2 activate
```

```
BGP: nbr global 2001:DB8::2 Open active delayed 10240ms (35000ms max, 60% jitter)
BGP: 2001:DB8::2 passive open to 2001:DB8::1
BGP: Fetched peer 2001:DB8::2 from tcb
BGP: 2001:DB8::2 passive went from Idle to Connect
BGP: ses global 2001:DB8::2 (0x11DAE9B8:0) pas Setting open delay timer to 60 seconds.
BGP: ses global 2001:DB8::2 (0x11DAE9B8:0) pas read request no-op
BGP: 2001:DB8::2 passive rcv message type 1, length (excl. header) 38
BGP: ses global 2001:DB8::2 (0x11DAE9B8:0) pas Receive OPEN
BGP: 2001:DB8::2 passive rcv OPEN, version 4, holdtime 180 seconds
BGP: 2001:DB8::2 passive rcv OPEN w/ OPTION parameter len: 28
BGP: 2001:DB8::2 passive rcvd OPEN w/ optional parameter type 2 (Capability) len 6
BGP: 2001:DB8::2 passive OPEN has CAPABILITY code: 1, length 4
BGP: 2001:DB8::2 passive OPEN has MP_EXT CAP for afi/safi: 2/1
BGP: 2001:DB8::2 passive rcvd OPEN w/ optional parameter type 2 (Capability) len 2
BGP: 2001:DB8::2 passive OPEN has CAPABILITY code: 128, length 0
: 2001:DB8::2 passive OPEN has ROUTE-REFRESH capability(old) for all address-families
BGP: 2001:DB8::2 passive rcvd OPEN w/ optional parameter type 2 (Capability) len 2
BGP: 2001:DB8::2 passive OPEN has CAPABILITY code: 2, length 0
BGP: 2001:DB8::2 passive OPEN has ROUTE-REFRESH capability(new) for all address-families
BGP: 2001:DB8::2 passive rcvd OPEN w/ optional parameter type 2 (Capability) len 2
BGP: 2001:DB8::2 passive OPEN has CAPABILITY code: 70, length 0
BGP: ses global 2001:DB8::2 (0x11DAE9B8:0) pas Enhanced Refresh cap received in
open message
BGP: 2001:DB8::2 passive rcvd OPEN w/ optional parameter type 2 (Capability) len 6
BGP: 2001:DB8::2 passive OPEN has CAPABILITY code: 65, length 4
BGP: 2001:DB8::2 passive OPEN has 4-byte ASN CAP for: 200
BGP: 2001:DB8::2 passive rcvd OPEN w/ remote AS 200, 4-byte remote AS 200
BGP: ses global 2001:DB8::2 (0x11DAE9B8:0) pas Adding topology IPv6 Unicast:base
BGP: ses global 2001:DB8::2 (0x11DAE9B8:0) pas Send OPEN
BGP: ses global 2001:DB8::2 (0x11DAE9B8:0) pas Building Enhanced Refresh capability
BGP: 2001:DB8::2 passive went from Connect to OpenSent
BGP: 2001:DB8::2 passive sending OPEN, version 4, my as: 100, holdtime 180 seconds,
ID A010C01
BGP: 2001:DB8::2 passive went from OpenSent to OpenConfirm
BGP: 2001:DB8::2 passive went from OpenConfirm to Established
BGP: ses global 2001:DB8::2 (0x11DAE9B8:1) pas Assigned ID
BGP: nbr global 2001:DB8::2 Stop Active Open timer as all topologies are allocated
BGP: ses global 2001:DB8::2 (0x11DAE9B8:1) Up
%BGP-5-ADJCHANGE: neighbor 2001:DB8::2 Up
```

As we can see from the output in Example 7-7, the neighborship is in place, which means ESTABLISHED in BGP language. We can verify the operation of this peering by checking the BGP neighbor table, as shown in Example 7-8, and we can check the TCP session.

BGP relies on TCP as a transport protocol to successfully establish the peering, which solely means a client/server model. BGP uses source and destination ports other than 179, depending on the initiation and origination of the session. When a router initiates a BGP session (the client), a request is sent to the server with a destination port of 179 and a random source port. The peering router to which we are trying to establish a BGP session (the server) responds with a source port of 179 and a random destination port. In summary, this means client-to-server traffic uses a destination port of 179, and server-to-client traffic uses a source port of 179.

Example 7-8 *BGP Neighbor States, Established*

```
R1# show bgp ipv4 unicast summary
BGP router identifier 10.1.100.8, local AS number 100
BGP table version is 1, main routing table version 1
Neighbor        V      AS MsgRcvd MsgSent   TblVer  InQ OutQ Up/Down   State/PfxRcd
10.1.12.2       4     200      4      4        1    0    0 00:00:37           0
! Even if the number of received prefixes is 0, the relation is established.
```

```
R1# show bgp ipv4 unicast neighbors 10.1.12.2 | include BGP state
BGP state = Established, up for 00:00:39
```

```
R1# show tcp brief
TCB        Local Address          Foreign Address        (state)
11DD00B0   10.1.12.1.179          10.1.12.2.18971        ESTAB
R2# show tcp brief
TCB        Local Address          Foreign Address        (state)
11DAD750   10.1.12.2.18971        10.1.12.1.179          ESTAB
```

Now, the question is, What could cause the neighborship to move into other nonoperational states?

If a route does not exist to the neighboring device, the state will turn Idle. (We have eBGP peering based on the physical interfaces, so changing the IP address on one of the interfaces will do the trick.) We can verify this by using Example 7-9.

Example 7-9 *BGP Neighbor States, Idle*

```
R1# show bgp ipv4 unicast summary
BGP router identifier 10.1.100.1, local AS number 100
BGP table version is 1, main routing table version 1
Neighbor        V      AS MsgRcvd MsgSent   TblVer  InQ OutQ Up/Down   State/PfxRcd
10.1.12.2       4     200      0      0        1    0    0 00:00:05        Idle
```

```
R1# show bgp ipv4 unicast neighbors 10.1.12.2 | include BGP state
BGP state = Idle
```

We can see the Idle state as well if we administratively shut down the neighbor from the global BGP configuration mode, as shown in Example 7-10.

Example 7-10 *BGP Neighbor States, Idle (Administratively)*

```
R1(config)# router bgp 100
R1(config-router)# neighbor 10.1.12.2 shutdown

R1# show bgp ipv4 unicast summary
BGP router identifier 10.1.100.1, local AS number 100
BGP table version is 1, main routing table version 1
Neighbor        V           AS MsgRcvd MsgSent   TblVer  InQ OutQ Up/Down  State/PfxRcd
10.1.12.2       4          200       0       0        1    0    0 00:00:40 Idle (Admin)

R1# show bgp ipv4 unicast neighbors 10.1.12.2 | include BGP state
BGP state = Idle
```

BGP Address Families

The invention of BGP was necessary to cover IPv4 deployments over the Internet. **Address Family Identifiers (AFIs)** (extensions) were introduced to account for new services, protocols, and applications. AFIs are used to support different types of network layer protocols and their associated address spaces such as IPv4 and IPv6. **Subsequent Address Family Identifiers (SAFIs)** were introduced to give more granularity to traffic types such as unicast and multicast.

With the support of path attributes, or PAs (such as MP_REACH_NLRI and MP_UNREACH_NLRI), which are carried in BGP update messages, different network reachability information can be transported for different address families.

Following are the most common address families in BGP:

- **IPv4 Unicast Address Family (AFI/SAFI 1/1):** This is the most widely used address family in BGP. It is used to exchange routing information for IPv4 unicast addresses. BGP speakers exchange IPv4 routing information using **Network Layer Reachability Information (NLRI)** encoded as IPv4 prefixes.

- **IPv6 Unicast Address Family (AFI/SAFI 2/1):** This address family is used to exchange routing information for IPv6 unicast addresses. As with IPv4, BGP speakers exchange IPv6 routing information using NLRI encoded as IPv6 prefixes.

- **IPv4 Multicast Address Family (AFI/SAFI 1/2):** This address family is used to exchange routing information for IPv4 multicast addresses. BGP speakers exchange information about IPv4 multicast routes using NLRI encoded as IPv4 multicast group prefixes.

- **IPv6 Multicast Address Family (AFI/SAFI 2/2):** Like IPv4 multicast, this address family is used to exchange routing information for IPv6 multicast addresses. BGP speakers exchange information about IPv6 multicast routes using NLRI encoded as IPv6 multicast group prefixes.

- **IPv4 and IPv6 Virtual Private Network (VPN) Address Families (AFI/SAFI 1/128 and 2/128):** These address families are used to support BGP/MPLS IP VPNs, which enable the exchange of routing information for VPN-IPv4 and VPN-IPv6 addresses.

BGP carries VPN routes in a special format where the NLRI includes both a route distinguisher (RD) and an IPv4 or IPv6 prefix.

- **Layer 2 Virtual Private Network (VPN) Address Families (AFI/SAFI 25/65 and 25/70):** These address families are used to support BGP/MPLS Layer 2 VPNs, which enable the exchange of routing information for Layer 2 VPNs. BGP carries Layer 2 VPN routes with NLRI encoded as Ethernet MAC addresses.

- **Multicast Virtual Private Network (MVPN) Address Families:** These address families are used to support BGP/MPLS Multicast Virtual Private Network (MVPN) deployments, which enable efficient multicast distribution over MPLS-based VPNs.

- **Link-State (LS) Address Family:** This address family is defined to carry the interior gateway protocol link-state database through BGP. It allows policy-base control for information hiding, abstraction, and aggregation.

These are some of the common address families supported by BGP. Each address family defines specific attributes and NLRI formats for exchanging routing information of the corresponding network layer protocol or VPN type.

Network engineers and vendors continue to add functionality and feature enhancements to BGP. BGP now provides a scalable control plane for signaling overlay technologies like MPLS VPNs, IPsec security associations, and Virtual Extensible LAN (VXLAN).

These overlays can provide Layer 3 connectivity via MPLS L3VPNs, or Layer 2 connectivity via MPLS L2VPNs (L2VPN), such as Virtual Private LAN Service (VPLS) or Ethernet VPNs (EVPNs).

Every address family maintains a separate database and configuration for each protocol (address family + sub-address family) in BGP. This allows for a routing policy in one address family to be different from a routing policy in a different address family even though the router uses the same BGP session to the other router. BGP includes an AFI and an SAFI with every route advertisement to differentiate between the AFI and SAFI databases. Table 7-2 provides a short list of common AFIs and SAFIs.

Table 7-2   BGP Address Families

Network Layer Information	AFI	SAFI
IPv4 Unicast	1	1
IPv4 Multicast	1	2
IPv4 Unicast with MPLS Label	1	4
MPLS L3VPN IPv4	1	128
IPv6	2	1
IPv6 Unicast with MPLS Label	2	4
MPLS L3VPN IPv6	2	128
Virtual Private LAN Service (VPLS), Virtual Private Wire Service (VPWS)	25	65
Ethernet VPN (EVPN)	25	70
BGP-LS	16388	71
BGP-LS-VPN	16388	72

Example 7-11 lists the **address-family** options we can encounter when entering BGP configuration mode for both IOS XE and IOS XR.

Example 7-11 *BGP Address Family Options*

```
! IOS and IOS XE
PE2(config)# router bgp 100
PE2(config-router)# address-family ?
  ipv4        Address family
  ipv6        Address family
  l2vpn       Address family
link-state  Address family
  nsap        Address family
  rtfilter    Address family
  vpnv4       Address family
  vpnv6       Address family

! IOS XR
RP/0/0/CPU0:P5(config)# router bgp 100
RP/0/0/CPU0:P5(config-bgp)# address-family ?
  ipv4        IPv4 Address Family
  ipv6        IPv6 Address Family
  l2vpn       L2VPN Address Family
link-state  Link-state Address Family
  vpnv4       VPNv4 Address Family
  vpnv6       VPNv6 Address Family
```

BGP Prefix Advertisement

BGP uses **network** statements to specify the prefixes to be installed in the BGP local routing information base (Loc-RIB). BGP searches the global RIB for a network prefix match after configuring the **network** statement. The prefix is then added to the BGP Loc-RIB if there is an exact match.

All routes in the Loc-RIB table are advertised to BGP peers using the following steps:

Step 1. Check validity to ensure Network Layer Reachability Information (NLRI) is valid and a next-hop address can be resolved in the global RIB. If the NLRI is invalid, processing stops.

Step 2. Process outbound neighbor route policies. If the outbound policies do not deny a route after processing, it is saved in adj-RIB-out.

Step 3. Advertise NLRI to BGP peers. If the next hop of the NLRI is 0.0.0.0, the next-hop address is set to the BGP session's IP address.

Figure 7-5 shows a high-level flow of the steps we have discussed to ensure proper route advertisement.

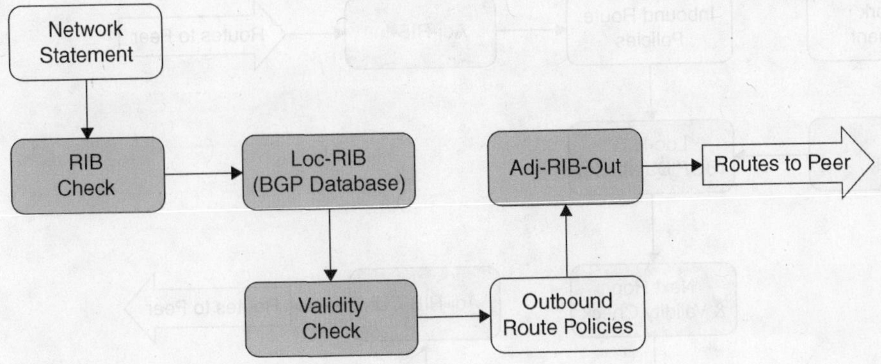

Figure 7-5 *BGP Prefix Advertisement*

BGP maintains the network prefix and path attributes of a route using the following tables:

- **Adj-RIB-In:** This table stores NLRIs in their original form before processing inbound route policies. After processing all policies, the table is cleared.

- **Loc-RIB:** All local and received NLRIs from BGP are stored in this table. BGP best path criteria will determine the best NLRI for a specific prefix after NLRIs passing the validity check and next-hop check. Also, routes within the IP routing table are presented here.

- **Adj-RIB-Out:** After outbound route policies are processed, routes are stored here.

However, not all prefixes in the Loc-RIB are advertised to BGP peers or installed in the global RIB. BGP carries out route processing actions as follows:

Step 1. Keep the route in the original state in the Adj-RIB-In table and apply inbound route policy based on the neighbor that sent the route.

Step 2. Update Loc-RIB with recent entries and clear the Adj-RIB-In table for resource reservation.

Step 3. Check validity passing to ensure the route is correct and the next hop is resolvable in the global RIB. If a route fails, it will stay in the Loc-RIB table with no further processing.

Step 4. Determine the best path, and only one path will be used.

Step 5. The best path will be added to the global RIB, the outbound route policy will be implemented, and nondiscarded routes will be saved in the Adj-RIB-Out table and eventually advertised to BGP peers.

Figure 7-6 shows the route processing flow and the interaction between the BGP tables to ensure successful installation of routes inside the global RIB.

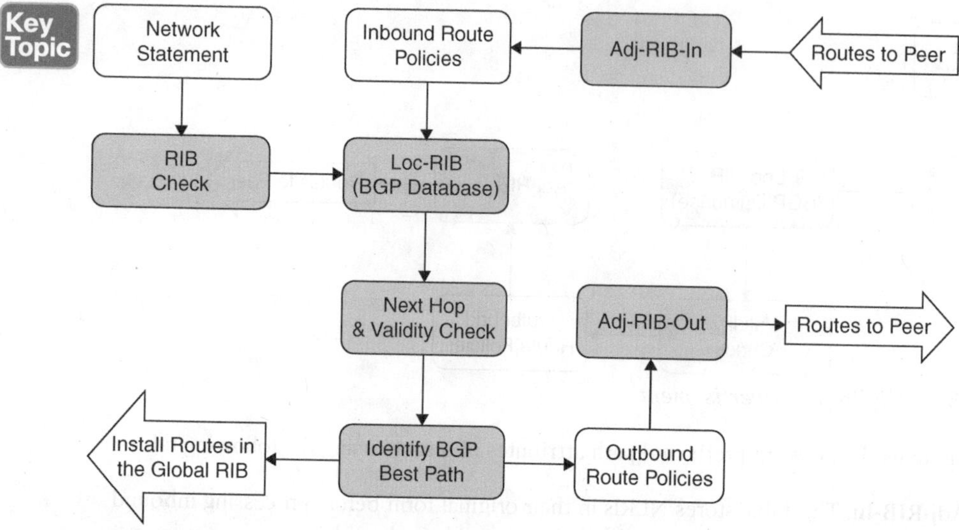

Figure 7-6 *BGP Prefix Advertisement, Installing Inside Global RIB*

BGP Path Attributes

Border Gateway Protocol path attributes are pieces of information attached to BGP routing updates that describe various characteristics of the route being advertised. These attributes help BGP routers make informed routing decisions and implement routing policies. There are several types of BGP path attributes, including

- **Well-Known Mandatory Attributes:** These attributes must be present in all BGP routing updates and are recognized by all BGP routers. They include

  - **Origin (ORIGIN):** This attribute indicates the origin of the route and can have one of three possible values:

    - **IGP (Interior Gateway Protocol):** The route was learned via an Interior Gateway Protocol such as OSPF or IS-IS.

    - **EGP (Exterior Gateway Protocol):** The route was learned via the legacy Exterior Gateway Protocol.

    - **Incomplete:** The origin of the route is unknown or not specified.

  - **Autonomous system Path (AS_PATH):** This attribute lists the sequence of autonomous systems that the route has traversed. It helps prevent routing loops and allows BGP routers to select the best path to a destination.

  - **Next Hop (NEXT_HOP):** This attribute specifies the IP address of the next-hop router to reach the destination network.

- **Well-Known Discretionary Attributes:** These attributes are recognized by all BGP routers but are not required to be present in BGP routing updates. They include

  - **Local Preference (LOCAL_PREF):** This attribute is used within an autonomous system to indicate the preferred exit point for traffic leaving the AS. Higher values indicate higher preference.

- **Optional Transitive Attributes:** These attributes may or may not be recognized by all BGP routers and are not required to be present in BGP routing updates. They include

  - **Community:** The community attribute is used to tag routes with community values that can be used for various purposes, such as route filtering and policy enforcement.

  - **Extended Community:** Like the community attribute, the extended community attribute allows for additional information to be carried along with the route.

  - **Multi-Exit Discriminator (MED):** The MED attribute is used to influence the path selection process between different autonomous systems. It is typically used to indicate the preferred exit point for traffic leaving an AS when multiple exit points exist.

These are some of the most common BGP path attributes used to describe routing information in BGP updates. Understanding these attributes is essential for network administrators and engineers to configure BGP routing policies effectively.

Figure 7-7 provides an overview of the path attributes.

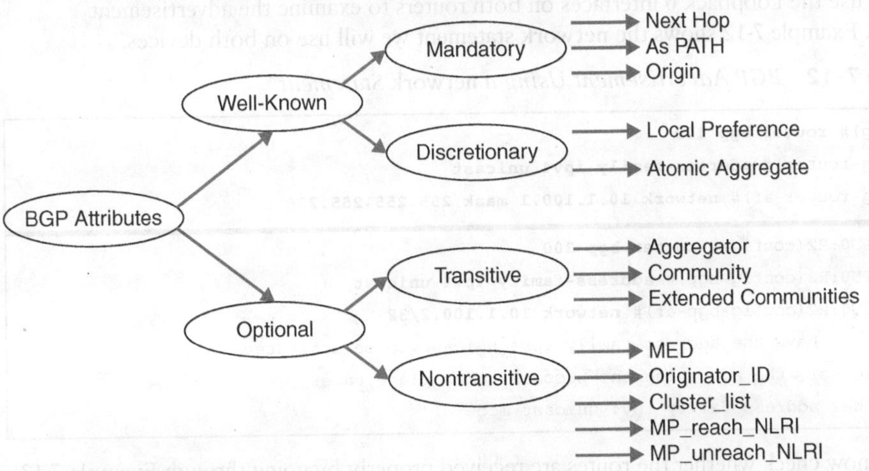

Figure 7-7 *BGP Path Attributes*

Before we go through the attributes and the path selection process of BGP, it's worth shedding some light on the advertisement process. When we dealt with IGP, we used the **network** statement solely to advertise a specific prefix. (After IOS and IOS XE software enhancements, we could also advertise a network through interface configuration mode, which is like the hierarchical structure of IOS XR.)

When we want to advertise a network in BGP, we use the **network** statement under the BGP configuration mode. (If we choose to specify which address family we need to activate, the advertisement takes place under the respective address-family configuration mode). The command to place is **network** *ip-address* **mask** *subnet-mask*. This applies for both iBGP and eBGP.

As we mentioned earlier, BGP has three tables to maintain the prefixes and associated path attributes. The **network** statement identifies a prefix to be installed in the Loc-RIB table and does not identify an interface. Once we configure the **network** statement, the BGP process will look up the global RIB for an exact match. Generally, the **network** statement will be for a connected network or a route from routing protocol. Once verification is done and the match is completed, the prefix will be installed in the Loc-RIB.

Let's use the topology in Figure 7-8 to investigate the advertisement process of BGP.

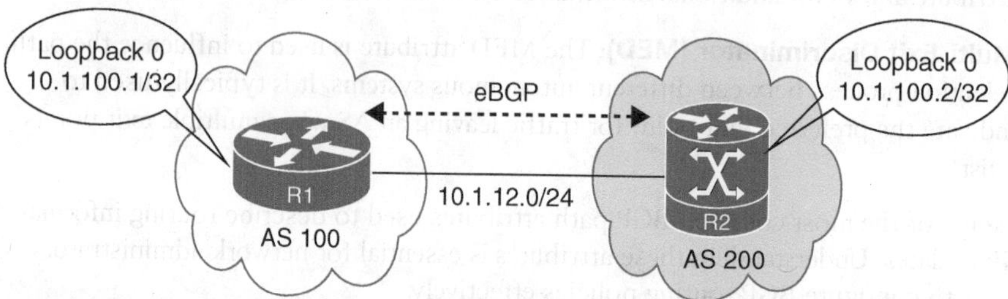

Figure 7-8 *BGP Prefix Advertisement Process*

We will use the Loopback 0 interfaces on both routers to examine the advertisement process. Example 7-12 shows the **network** statement we will use on both devices.

Example 7-12 *BGP Advertisement Using a **network** Statement*

```
R1(config)# router bgp 100
R1(config-router)# address-family ipv4 unicast
R1(config-router-af)# network 10.1.100.1 mask 255.255.255.255

RP/0/0/CPU0:R2(config)# router bgp 200
RP/0/0/CPU0:R2(config-bgp)# address-family ipv4 unicast
RP/0/0/CPU0:R2(config-bgp-af)# network 10.1.100.2/32
! Though, we have the address-family ipv4 unicast to be activated
! per neighbor, the advertisement process takes place under
! the global address-family ipv4 unicast mode.
```

We can now check whether the routes are received properly by going through Example 7-13.

Example 7-13 *BGP Table Validation*

```
R1# show bgp ipv4 unicast
BGP table version is 2, local router ID is 10.1.100.7
Status codes: s suppressed, d damped, h history, * valid, > best, i - internal,
r RIB-failure, S Stale, m multipath, b backup-path, f RT-Filter,
x best-external, a additional-path, c RIB-compressed,
t secondary path, L long-lived-stale,
Origin codes: i - IGP, e - EGP, ? - incomplete
RPKI validation codes: V valid, I invalid, N Not found
     Network          Next Hop            Metric LocPrf Weight Path
 *>   10.1.100.1/32    0.0.0.0                  0         32768 i
```

```
RP/0/0/CPU0:R2# show bgp
BGP router identifier 10.1.100.2, local AS number 200
BGP generic scan interval 60 secs
Non-stop routing is enabled
BGP table state: Active
Table ID: 0xe0000000   RD version: 3
BGP main routing table version 3
BGP NSR Initial initsync version 2 (Reached)
BGP NSR/ISSU Sync-Group versions 0/0
BGP scan interval 60 secs
Status codes: s suppressed, d damped, h history, * valid, > best
i - internal, r RIB-failure, S stale, N Nexthop-discard
Origin codes: i - IGP, e - EGP, ? - incomplete
   Network          Next Hop            Metric LocPrf Weight Path
*> 10.1.100.2/32    0.0.0.0                           32768 i
Processed 1 prefixes, 1 paths
```

As we can see, each router BGP table contains its own advertised route. Before going through the reasons, we can see that the next hop of each self-advertised route is set to 0.0.0.0, and the weight value (by default, for self-originated routes) is set to 32768.

Now the reason for not being able to receive routes is caused by IOS XR (don't forget that we are establishing an eBGP relation). IOS XR, by default, will prevent eBGP routes from being installed (inbound/outbound) without a route policy in which we control the prefixes to be imported or exported per neighbor. This can be achieved using Route Policy Language (RPL), which was extensively covered in Chapter 4, "Routing Fundamentals."

To ensure proper eBGP route advertisement following our example, we can define a general route policy just for the sake of route installation, as shown in Example 7-14, by turning on debugging.

Example 7-14   *BGP IOS XR, Route Policy*

```
RP/0/0/CPU0:R2# debug bgp update afi ipv4 unicast

RP/0/0/CPU0:R2(config)# route-policy eBGP_ROUTES
RP/0/0/CPU0:R2(config-rpl)# pass
RP/0/0/CPU0:R2(config-rpl)# exit

R1# debug ip bgp updates

RP/0/0/CPU0:R2(config)# router bgp 200
RP/0/0/CPU0:R2(config-bgp)# neighbor 10.1.12.1
RP/0/0/CPU0:R2(config-bgp-nbr)# address-family ipv4 unicast
RP/0/0/CPU0:R2(config-bgp-nbr-af)# route-policy ?
eBGP_ROUTES  Name of the policy
WORD         Name of the policy
! Once the route-policy is configured properly, we will see it listed automatically
! where applicable.
```

```
RP/0/0/CPU0:R2(config-bgp-nbr-af)# route-policy eBGP_ROUTES ?
  (      Specify parameter values for the policy
  in    Apply route policy to inbound routes
  out   Apply route policy to outbound routes
! We can apply the RPL either in the inbound direction or the outbound direction per
! neighbor under the respective address-family.
RP/0/0/CPU0:R2(config-bgp-nbr-af)# route-policy eBGP_ROUTES in
RP/0/0/CPU0:R2(config-bgp-nbr-af)# route-policy eBGP_ROUTES out
```

```
! R2 log output.
bgp[1060]: [default-upd] (ip4u): Adding neighbor 10.1.12.1 to new filter-group 0.2
in IPv4 Unicast sub-group 0.2 rtset size 0 in updgrp 0.1
bgp[1060]: [default-upd] (ip4u): Added neighbor 10.1.12.1 to update filter-group 0.2
in IPv4 Unicast sub-group 0.2
bgp[1060]: [default-upd] (ip4u): Added neighbor 10.1.12.1 to update sub-group 0.2 in
IPv4 Unicast update-group 0.1
bgp[1060]: [default-upd] (ip4u): Added neighbor 10.1.12.1 to update group 0.1 for
IPv4 Unicast
bgp[1060]: [default-upd] (ip4u): Permit UPDATE to filter-group 0.2 (Regular, pelem
Regular) for 10.1.100.2/32 (changedfl=0x0/0x0), path
```

```
! R1 log output.
BGP(0): (base) 10.1.12.2 send UPDATE (format) 10.1.100.1/32, next 10.1.12.1, metric
0, path Local
BGP(0): 10.1.12.2 rcvd UPDATE w/ attr: nexthop 10.1.12.2, origin i, metric 0, merged
path 200, AS_PATH
BGP(0): 10.1.12.2 rcvd 10.1.100.2/32
BGP(0): Revise route installing 1 of 1 routes for 10.1.100.2/32 -> 10.1.12.2(global)
to main IP table
```

```
R1# show bgp ipv4 unicast
BGP table version is 3, local router ID is 10.1.100.7
Status codes: s suppressed, d damped, h history, * valid, > best, i - internal,
r RIB-failure, S Stale, m multipath, b backup-path, f RT-Filter,
x best-external, a additional-path, c RIB-compressed,
t secondary path, L long-lived-stale,
Origin codes: i - IGP, e - EGP, ? - incomplete
RPKI validation codes: V valid, I invalid, N Not found

     Network          Next Hop            Metric LocPrf Weight Path
 *>   10.1.100.1/32    0.0.0.0                  0        32768 i
 *>   10.1.100.2/32    10.1.12.2                0            0 200 i
```

```
RP/0/0/CPU0:R2# show bgp
BGP router identifier 10.1.100.2, local AS number 200
BGP generic scan interval 60 secs
Non-stop routing is enabled
BGP table state: Active
Table ID: 0xe0000000   RD version: 4
BGP main routing table version 4
```

```
BGP NSR Initial initsync version 2 (Reached)
BGP NSR/ISSU Sync-Group versions 0/0
BGP scan interval 60 secs
Status codes: s suppressed, d damped, h history, * valid, > best
i - internal, r RIB-failure, S stale, N Nexthop-discard
Origin codes: i - IGP, e - EGP, ? - incomplete
   Network              Next Hop            Metric LocPrf Weight Path
*> 10.1.100.1/32        10.1.12.1                0          0 100 i
*> 10.1.100.2/32        0.0.0.0                  0            32768 i
Processed 2 prefixes, 2 paths
```

```
R1# show bgp ipv4 unicast neighbors 10.1.12.2 advertised-routes
BGP table version is 3, local router ID is 10.1.100.7
Status codes: s suppressed, d damped, h history, * valid, > best, i - internal,
r RIB-failure, S Stale, m multipath, b backup-path, f RT-Filter,
x best-external, a additional-path, c RIB-compressed,
t secondary path, L long-lived-stale,
Origin codes: i - IGP, e - EGP, ? - incomplete
RPKI validation codes: V valid, I invalid, N Not found
   Network              Next Hop            Metric LocPrf Weight Path
 *>   10.1.100.1/32     0.0.0.0                  0            32768 i
Total number of prefixes 1
```

We need to shed some light on the path denotation (i), which means we used the **network** statement to advertise that prefix to our BGP neighbor.

BGP will not advertise a route unless there is a match for it inside the routing table (RIB), so we must be careful of the subnet mask associated with the prefix when advertising it.

Now, let's move the other way to advertise the route, which is redistribution, as per the topology we're working on. Here, the loopback interfaces are directly connected, which means we will use the **redistribute connected** statement for advertising. To learn more, let's walk through Example 7-15.

Example 7-15 *BGP Advertisement Using Redistribution*

```
R1(config)# router bgp 100
R1(config-router)# address-family ipv4 unicast
R1(config-router-af)# redistribute connected
```

```
RP/0/0/CPU0:R2(config)# router bgp 200
RP/0/0/CPU0:R2(config-bgp)# address-family ipv4 unicast
RP/0/0/CPU0:R2(config-bgp-af)# redistribute connected
```

```
RP/0/0/CPU0:R2# show bgp
BGP router identifier 10.1.100.2, local AS number 200
BGP generic scan interval 60 secs
Non-stop routing is enabled
BGP table state: Active
```

```
Table ID: 0xe0000000   RD version: 13
BGP main routing table version 13
BGP NSR Initial initsync version 2 (Reached)
BGP NSR/ISSU Sync-Group versions 0/0
BGP scan interval 60 secs
Status codes: s suppressed, d damped, h history, * valid, > best
i - internal, r RIB-failure, S stale, N Nexthop-discard
Origin codes: i - IGP, e - EGP, ? - incomplete
   Network            Next Hop            Metric LocPrf Weight Path
*> 10.1.12.0/24       0.0.0.0                  0           32768   ?
*                     10.1.12.1                0            0  100 ?
*> 10.1.100.1/32      10.1.12.1                0            0  100 ?
*> 10.1.100.2/32      0.0.0.0                  0           32768   ?
*> 10.1.200.2/32      0.0.0.0                  0           32768   ?
Processed 4 prefixes, 5 paths
```

```
R1# show bgp ipv4 unicast neighbors 10.1.12.2 advertised-routes
BGP table version is 9, local router ID is 10.1.100.7
Status codes: s suppressed, d damped, h history, * valid, > best, i - internal,
r RIB-failure, S Stale, m multipath, b backup-path, f RT-Filter,
x best-external, a additional-path, c RIB-compressed,
t secondary path, L long-lived-stale,
Origin codes: i - IGP, e - EGP, ? - incomplete
RPKI validation codes: V valid, I invalid, N Not found

    Network          Next Hop            Metric LocPrf Weight Path
 *>   10.1.12.0/24    0.0.0.0                  0           32768   ?
 *>   10.1.100.1/32   0.0.0.0                  0           32768   ?
Total number of prefixes 2
```

```
R1(config)# route-map MAP permit 10
R1(config-route-map)# match ip address prefix-list R1_LOOP
R1(config)# router bgp 100
R1(config-router)# address-family ipv4 unicast
R1(config-router-af)# redistribute connected route-map MAP
```

```
RP/0/0/CPU0:R2(config)# route-policy MAP
RP/0/0/CPU0:R2(config-rpl)# if destination in R2_LOOP then pass endif
RP/0/0/CPU0:R2(config-rpl)# exit
RP/0/0/CPU0:R2(config)# commit
RP/0/0/CPU0:R2(config)# router bgp 200
RP/0/0/CPU0:R2(config-bgp)# address-family ipv4 unicast
RP/0/0/CPU0:R2(config-bgp-af)# redistribute connected route-policy MAP
```

```
R1# show bgp ipv4 unicast
BGP table version is 16, local router ID is 10.1.100.7
Status codes: s suppressed, d damped, h history, * valid, > best, i - internal,
```

```
r RIB-failure, S Stale, m multipath, b backup-path, f RT-Filter,
x best-external, a additional-path, c RIB-compressed,
t secondary path, L long-lived-stale,
Origin codes: i - IGP, e - EGP, ? - incomplete
RPKI validation codes: V valid, I invalid, N Not found
     Network          Next Hop          Metric LocPrf Weight Path
 *>  10.1.100.1/32    0.0.0.0                0         32768   ?
 *>  10.1.100.2/32    10.1.12.2              0            0  200 ?
```

BGP Path Selection

Now, we can start investigating the path selection process of BGP. BGP uses an attribute list to determine the best path to a destination. (Usually, within the big picture of BGP deployment, we could receive multiple paths to a destination.)

The BGP selection process relies on the following:

1. Prefer the path with the highest WEIGHT.
2. Prefer the path with the highest LOCAL PREFERENCE.
3. Prefer the path that was locally originated via a **network** or **redistribute** command.
4. Accumulated IGP (AIGP).
5. Prefer the path with the lowest AS_PATH.
6. Prefer the path with the lowest ORIGIN type.
7. Prefer the path with the lowest MULTI-EXIT DISCRIMINATOR (MED).
8. Prefer eBGP over iBGP.
9. Prefer the path with the lowest IGP metric to the BGP next hop.
10. When both paths are external, prefer the one that was received first.
11. Prefer the route that comes from the BGP router with the lowest router ID.
12. If the originator or router ID is the same for multiple paths, prefer the path with the minimum cluster list length.
13. Prefer the path that comes from the lowest neighbor address.

We will use the topology in Figure 7-9 to illustrate most of the attributes and how we can manipulate path selection.

We have a basic configuration implemented on all devices with each router advertising its loopback network as a **network** statement inside BGP. Now, we can start with the R1 BGP table and explore the output in Example 7-16.

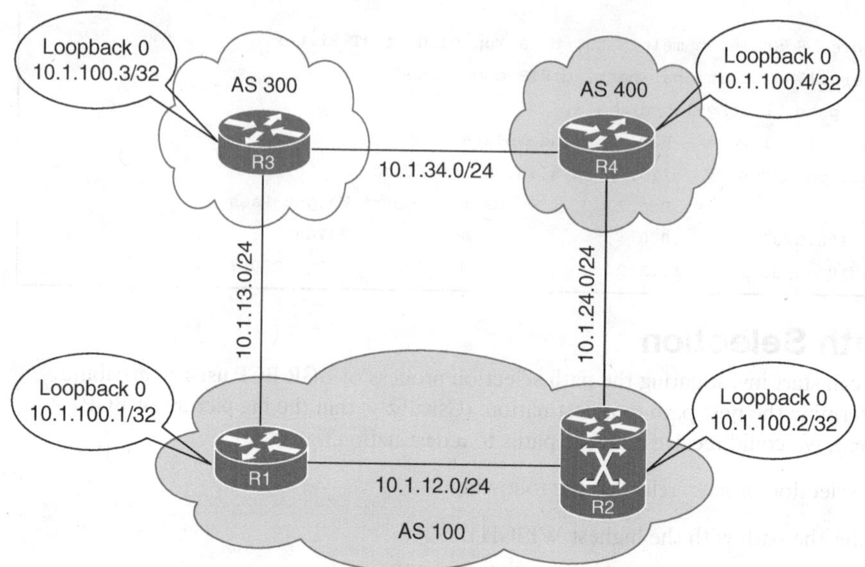

Figure 7-9 *BGP Path Attributes Demonstration Example*

Example 7-16 *R1's BGP IPv4 Table Validation*

```
R1# show bgp ipv4 unicast
BGP table version is 5, local router ID is 10.1.100.1
Status codes: s suppressed, d damped, h history, * valid, > best, i - internal,
              r RIB-failure, S Stale, m multipath, b backup-path, f RT-Filter,
              x best-external, a additional-path, c RIB-compressed,
              t secondary path,
Origin codes: i - IGP, e - EGP, ? - incomplete
RPKI validation codes: V valid, I invalid, N Not found
     Network          Next Hop            Metric LocPrf Weight Path
 *>   10.1.100.1/32    0.0.0.0                  0         32768 i
 r>i  10.1.100.2/32    10.1.100.2               0    100     0 i
 * i  10.1.100.3/32    10.1.24.4                     100     0 400 300 i
 *>                    10.1.13.3                0             0 300 i
 * i  10.1.100.4/32    10.1.24.4                0    100     0 400 i
 *>                    10.1.13.3                              0 300 400 i
```

If we take a quick look at the BGP routing table of R1, we can see that the prefix 192.168.1.0
has a next-hop value of 0.0.0.0, which means that it's locally advertised (generated). By
default, the locally generated routes have a weight value if 32768, and the letter **i** at the end
of the line refers to the **origin code**. In our case, this means IGP, which means it was generated using the **network** statement. If we had used the **redistribute** command, we would find
the **?** symbol instead of **i**.

Next, let's look at the prefixes 10.1.100.3/32 and 10.1.100.4/32 (which are the Loopback 0
networks of R3 and R4, respectively). The prefix 10.1.100.3/32 is learned through two
paths: either from the direct relation (through 10.1.13.3) or through R4 (through our iBGP
neighbor: R2). If we examine the next hop of the prefix learned through R2, the next hop is

set to 10.1.24.3. The next hop has not been changed by the iBGP peer, and for sure (because we did not perform any kind of redistribution), we do not recognize this next hop. Example 7-17 shows the R1 RIB output for both next hops.

Example 7-17 *R1's RIB Output for BGP Next Hops*

```
R1# show ip route 10.1.24.4
% Subnet not in table
```

```
R1# show ip route 10.1.13.3
Routing entry for 10.1.13.0/24
  Known via "connected", distance 0, metric 0 (connected, via interface)
  Routing Descriptor Blocks:
  * directly connected, via GigabitEthernet0/1
      Route metric is 0, traffic share count is 1
```

Now, to solve this issue, which we usually face when an iBGP peer advertises a route it learned from an eBGP peer to an iBGP peer, we will use a **next-hop-self** statement attached to the **neighbor** statement (for the iBGP peer) under the BGP configuration mode, as shown in Example 7-18.

Example 7-18 *BGP Next-Hop-Self*

```
R1(config)# router bgp 100
R1(config-router)# address-family ipv4 unicast
R1(config-router-af)# neighbor 10.1.100.2 next-hop-self
```

```
RP/0/0/CPU0:R2(config)# router bgp 100
RP/0/0/CPU0:R2(config-bgp)# neighbor 10.1.100.1
RP/0/0/CPU0:R2(config-bgp-nbr)# address-family ipv4 unicast
RP/0/0/CPU0:R2(config-bgp-nbr-af)# next-hop-self
```

```
R1# show bgp ipv4 unicast 10.1.100.4/32
BGP routing table entry for 10.1.100.4/32, version 9
Paths: (2 available, best #2, table default)
Advertised to update-groups:
6
Refresh Epoch 1
300 400
10.1.13.3 from 10.1.13.3 (10.1.100.3)
Origin IGP, localpref 100, valid, external
rx pathid: 0, tx pathid: 0
Updated on Aug 1 2024 13:08:16 UTC
Refresh Epoch 1
400
10.1.100.2 (metric 2) from 10.1.100.2 (10.1.100.2)
Origin IGP, metric 0, localpref 100, valid, internal, best
rx pathid: 0, tx pathid: 0x0
```

Suppose that we have a big network with a large number of iBGP speakers that also have eBGP relations. It would be massively resource-intensive to ensure that the next hop of the eBGP peers—which will not change when the route is propagated inside the AS (from eBGP to iBGP) for which we must import the prefix—will import all of these next hops inside the autonomous system.

Here is where the next-hop-self technique comes into play. We will alter the BGP next hop without having to import (redistribute) the peering link.

Moving through more details that we have captured through the BGP output, we can see from each prefix installed in the BGP table that it is associated with the AS-PATH it spanned to reach the destination. So, let's focus on an example to make it clearer (see Example 7-19).

Example 7-19   *BGP Table Output for 10.1.100.4/32*

```
R1# show bgp ipv4 unicast 10.1.100.4/32
BGP routing table entry for 10.1.100.4/32, version 9
Paths: (2 available, best #2, table default)
Advertised to update-groups:
6
Refresh Epoch 1
300 400
10.1.13.3 from 10.1.13.3 (10.1.100.3)
Origin IGP, localpref 100, valid, external
rx pathid: 0, tx pathid: 0
Refresh Epoch 1
400
10.1.100.2 (metric 2) from 10.1.100.2 (10.1.100.2)
Origin IGP, metric 0, localpref 100, valid, internal, best
rx pathid: 0, tx pathid: 0x0
```

We can see that R1 learns about 10.1.100.4/32 (as we mentioned) through two paths. The first one is through its direct eBGP neighbor 10.1.13.3 with AS-PATH 300 400 (the destination or originator AS will be the last one in the AS-PATH and then addition to the transit AS begins). The other one is through its iBGP neighbor 10.1.100.2, which appears as 400 (the last AS in the path; i.e., AS 100 will be removed because we already have iBGP in place).

The prefix 10.1.100.2/32 is also advertised into BGP and will be sent as a BGP update. The question then becomes: Is it logical to accept a prefix from our own AS (100) from another eBGP (R3)? The answer is no. This is the built-in loop prevention mechanism of BGP. Now, let's turn on **debug bgp ipv4 unicast updates** on R1 and check the output in Example 7-20 for better clarity.

Example 7-20   *R1 debug bgp ipv4 unicast updates Output*

```
R1# clear bgp ipv4 unicast * soft
BGP(0): (base) 10.1.13.3 send UPDATE (format) 10.1.100.4/32, next 10.1.13.1,
metric 0, path 400
BGP(0): 10.1.100.2 NEXT_HOP is set to self for net 10.1.100.3/32,
BGP(0): (base) 10.1.100.2 send UPDATE (format) 10.1.100.3/32, next 10.1.100.1,
metric 0, path 300
```

```
BGP(0): (base) 10.1.13.3 send UPDATE (format) 10.1.100.2/32, next 10.1.13.1,
metric 0, path Local
BGP(0): (base) 10.1.13.3 send UPDATE (format) 10.1.100.1/32, next 10.1.13.1,
metric 0, path Local
BGP(0): 10.1.100.2 NEXT_HOP is set to self for net 10.1.100.1/32,
BGP(0): (base) 10.1.100.2 send UPDATE (format) 10.1.100.1/32, next 10.1.100.1,
metric 0, path Local
BGP: nbr_topo global 10.1.13.3 IPv4 Unicast:base (0x7F80280A7C60:1) rcvd Refresh
Start-of-RIB
BGP: nbr_topo global 10.1.13.3 IPv4 Unicast:base (0x7F80280A7C60:1) refresh_epoch is 3
BGP(0): 10.1.13.3 rcvd UPDATE w/ attr: nexthop 10.1.13.3, origin i,
merged path 300 400, AS_PATH
BGP(0): 10.1.13.3 rcvd 10.1.100.4/32...duplicate ignored
BGP: 10.1.13.3 Next hop is our own address 10.1.13.1
BGP(0): 10.1.13.3 rcv UPDATE w/ attr: nexthop 10.1.13.1, origin i, originator 0.0.0.0,
merged path 300 100, AS_PATH , community , extended community , SSA attribute
BGPSSA ssacount is 0, Tunnel attribute
Tunnel encap type: 0, encap size: 0, Link-state attribute: {}, PrefixSid attribute:
BGP(0): 10.1.13.3 rcv UPDATE about 10.1.100.2/32 -- DENIED due to: AS-PATH contains
our own AS; NEXTHOP is our own address;
BGP: 10.1.13.3 Next hop is our own address 10.1.13.1
BGP(0): 10.1.13.3 rcv UPDATE w/ attr: nexthop 10.1.13.1, origin i, originator 0.0.0.0,
merged path 300 100, AS_PATH , community , extended community , SSA attribute
BGPSSA ssacount is 0, Tunnel attribute
Tunnel encap type: 0, encap size: 0, Link-state attribute: {}, PrefixSid attribute:
BGP(0): 10.1.13.3 rcv UPDATE about 10.1.100.1/32 -- DENIED due to: AS-PATH contains
our own AS; NEXTHOP is our own address;
BGP(0): 10.1.13.3 rcvd UPDATE w/ attr: nexthop 10.1.13.3, origin i, metric 0, merged
path 300, AS_PATH
BGP(0): 10.1.13.3 rcvd 10.1.100.3/32...duplicate ignored
BGP: nbr_topo global 10.1.13.3 IPv4 Unicast:base (0x7F80280A7C60:1) rcvd Refresh
End-of-RIB
BGP(0): 10.1.100.2 rcvd UPDATE w/ attr: nexthop 10.1.100.2, origin i, localpref 100,
metric 0, merged path 400, AS_PATH
BGP(0): 10.1.100.2 rcvd 10.1.100.4/32...duplicate ignored
BGP(0): 10.1.100.2 rcvd UPDATE w/ attr: nexthop 10.1.100.2, origin i, localpref 100,
metric 0
BGP(0): 10.1.100.2 rcvd 10.1.100.2/32...duplicate ignored
```

The BGP table will hold information about all possible paths compared to the routing table (RIB), for which only the best routes will be installed. If we check Example 7-21 for a quick comparison, we can see that we have one path to be used for each specific prefix we learned externally.

Example 7-21 *R1 BGP and RIB Table Output*

```
R1# show bgp ipv4 unicast
BGP table version is 6, local router ID is 10.1.100.1
Status codes: s suppressed, d damped, h history, * valid, > best, i - internal,
              r RIB-failure, S Stale, m multipath, b backup-path, f RT-Filter,
```

```
                 x best-external, a additional-path, c RIB-compressed,
                 t secondary path,
Origin codes: i - IGP, e - EGP, ? - incomplete
RPKI validation codes: V valid, I invalid, N Not found

     Network          Next Hop            Metric LocPrf Weight Path
 *>  10.1.100.1/32    0.0.0.0                  0          32768 i
 r>i 10.1.100.2/32    10.1.100.2               0    100       0 i
 *>  10.1.100.3/32    10.1.13.3                0              0 300 i
 *>i 10.1.100.4/32    10.1.100.2               0    100       0 400 i
 *                    10.1.13.3                               0 300 400 i
```

```
R1# show ip route bgp | begin Gateway
Gateway of last resort is not set
10.0.0.0/8 is variably subnetted, 8 subnets, 2 masks
B        10.1.100.3/32 [20/0] via 10.1.13.3, 05:27:15
B        10.1.100.4/32 [200/0] via 10.1.100.2, 05:27:15
```

What about the 10.1.100.2/32? It is marked as **r**, which will not be available in the RIB as
a BGP route if we go through the supportive statements at the beginning of the **show bgp
ipv4 unicast** output. We are running an OSPF flat area inside AS 100 to ensure proper
loopback network connectivity between R1 and R2 to successfully build the iBGP session
sourced from these loopback addresses. The **r** means we have another better source for a prefix, which is the Interior Gateway Protocol (OSPF in our case). If we check Example 7-22, we
can see it is learned as an OSPF route.

Example 7-22   *R1's RIB Output for 10.1.100.2/32*

```
R1# show ip route 10.1.100.2 255.255.255.255
Routing entry for 10.1.100.2/32
Known via "ospf 1", distance 110, metric 2, type intra area
Last update from 10.1.12.2 on GigabitEthernet2, 06:32:45 ago
Routing Descriptor Blocks:
*        10.1.12.2, from 10.1.100.2, 06:32:45 ago, via GigabitEthernet2
Route metric is 2, traffic share count is 1
```

To shed more light on the iBGP relations for which we built the relation using loopback interfaces rather than physical interfaces, BGP will use the outbound interface used to reach our
direct neighbor. If, for example, we lose this link and no alternative path exists, we will lose
our relation directly. An alternative solution would be to install a second link (physically, this
will involve an SP new circuit, which will increase the cost), or we can ensure the proper IGP
is in place (different paths) to ensure loopback interfaces, which we will then use to establish
that the relation is reachable to each other via different paths to account for possible failures.

The loopback interface is a virtual interface; therefore, it will not be impacted by physical
failure. Thus, IGP will be responsible for finding an alternate path to ensure proper loopback-
to-loopback connectivity. This will turn the BGP session from a one-hop to a multiple-hop
relation. Doing so will require use of the **neighbor** *ip-address* **update-source** *interface-type
interface-number* command to ensure that BGP is sourcing the packets from the default
physical interface to the new interface (loopback).

Now let's examine some of the attributes we have explained from a more technical point of view to understand how we can manipulate and control them.

Weight

Weight is a Cisco proprietary attribute that affects the outbound traffic; its effect is local to the router where it is configured. This attribute can be applied directly to a neighbor, which will affect all the outbound traffic. Alternatively, it can be set using a route map, which will give flexibility for controlling the outbound prefixes we want to reach. Higher is better. Example 7-23 shows how to check the current R3's vision of the R2 loopback network, 10.1.100.2/32.

Example 7-23 *R3 BGP Output for 10.1.100.2/32*

```
R3# show bgp ipv4 unicast 10.1.100.2/32 longer-prefixes | begin Network
     Network           Next Hop            Metric LocPrf Weight Path
 *     10.1.100.2/32     10.1.34.4                            0 400 100 i
 *>                      10.1.13.1                            0 100 i
```

NOTE The **show bgp ipv4 unicast** *network subnet-mask* **longer-prefixes** command allows us to see any subnets of the network we specified if they are present in the RIB.

From an R3 perspective, using the path through 10.1.13.1 is better to reach the prefix 10.1.100.2/32. Why? Because starting from weight, local preference, and origin, they are all tied, so now the AS-PATH attribute, which states that the shorter AS-PATH wins, holds true in our case because the path through 10.1.13.1 passes through 1 autonomous system (100), where through 10.1.3.4, it passes through 2 autonomous systems (400 100).

Now, we would like to change the weight value toward 10.1.34.4 to make it more preferred, as shown in Example 7-24.

Example 7-24 *BGP IOS Weight Attribute Configuration Using the* **weight** *Command*

```
R3(config)# router bgp 300
R3(config-router)# address-family ipv4 unicast
R3(config-router-af)# neighbor 10.1.34.4 weight ?
<0-65535>  default weight
R3(config-router-af)# neighbor 10.1.34.4 weight 100

R3# clear bgp ipv4 unicast * soft

R3# show bgp ipv4 unicast 10.1.100.2/32 longer-prefixes | begin Network
     Network           Next Hop            Metric LocPrf Weight Path
 *>    10.1.100.2/32     10.1.34.4                          100 400 100 i
 *                       10.1.13.1                            0 100 i
```

As we can see, we have applied the weight per neighbor. The weight value will affect only the local router, and this value will not be propagated outside the AS. Practically, the command will affect all prefixes in the outbound direction, and generally, we will be more specific by defining a route map that will do the same with stricter control. Example 7-25 demonstrates this approach via a route map.

Example 7-25 *BGP IOS Weight Attribute Configuration Using* **route-map**

```
R3(config)# ip prefix-list R2_LOOP seq 5 permit 10.1.100.2/32
R3(config)# route-map WEIGHT_MAP permit 10
R3(config-route-map)# match ip address prefix-list R2_LOOP
R3(config-route-map)# set weight 100

R3(config)# router bgp 300
R3(config-router)# address-family ipv4 unicast
R3(config-router-af)# neighbor 10.1.13.1 route-map WEIGHT_MAP out
% "WEIGHT_MAP" used as BGP outbound route-map, set weight not supported
! As can be seen, the route-map with weight attribute cannot be applied in the
! outbound direction. So we have to apply it in the inbound direction.
! Make sure to remove the command if you applied it by mistake because it
! will be kept within the configuration!
R3(config-router-af)# neighbor 10.1.13.1 route-map WEIGHT_MAP in

R3# clear bgp ipv4 unicast * soft

R3# show bgp ipv4 unicast 10.1.100.2/32 longer-prefixes | begin Network
     Network           Next Hop            Metric LocPrf Weight Path
 *    10.1.100.2/32    10.1.34.4
                                                         100 400 100 i
 *>                    10.1.13.1
                                                         100 100 i
```

The same applies from an IOS XR perspective. Example 7-26 shows what needs to be done to accomplish the same function.

Example 7-26 *BGP IOS XR Weight Attribute Configuration*

```
RP/0/0/CPU0:R2(config)# prefix-set R2_LOOP
RP/0/0/CPU0:R2(config-pfx)# 10.1.100.2/32
RP/0/0/CPU0:R2(config)# route-policy WEIGHT_POLICY
RP/0/0/CPU0:R2(config-rpl)# if destination in R2_LOOP then set weight ?
<0-65535>   16-bit decimal number
parameter   Identifier specified in the format: '$' followed by alphanumeric characters
RP/0/0/CPU0:R2(config-rpl)# if destination in R2_LOOP then set weight 100 else pass endif
```

Local preference is an attribute that affects traffic leaving the AS, that is, outbound traffic. Its effect is spread across the AS; higher is better. R1 prefers to reach the prefix 10.1.100.4/32 through 10.1.100.2 because it has a shorter AS-PATH. Now, we can manipulate this following the same syntax we used with weight (route-map), as illustrated in Example 7-27.

Example 7-27 *BGP IOS Local Preference Attribute Configuration*

```
R1(config)# ip prefix-list R4_LOOP seq 5 permit 10.1.100.4/32
R1(config)# route-map LP_MAP permit 10
R1(config-route-map)# match ip address prefix-list R4_LOOP
R1(config-route-map)# set local-preference ?
<0-4294967295>   Preference value
R1(config-route-map)# set local-preference 200
```

```
R1(config)# router bgp 100
R1(config-router)# address-family ipv4 unicast
R1(config-router-af)# neighbor 10.1.13.3 route-map LP_MAP in

R1# show bgp ipv4 unicast | begin Network
     Network           Next Hop           Metric LocPrf Weight Path
 *>  10.1.100.1/32     0.0.0.0                 0            32768 i
 r>i 10.1.100.2/32     10.1.100.2              0    100       0 i
 *>  10.1.100.3/32     10.1.13.3               0            0 300 i
 *>  10.1.100.4/32     10.1.13.3                    200     0 300 400 i
! Local Preference value is distributed to routers within the same AS, we can
! validate by checking the BGP table on R2.
RP/0/0/CPU0:R2# show bgp | begin Network
     Network           Next Hop           Metric LocPrf Weight Path
 *>i10.1.100.1/32      10.1.100.1              0    100       0 i
 *>  10.1.100.2/32     0.0.0.0                 0            32768 i
 *   10.1.100.3/32     10.1.24.4                             0 400 300 i
 *>i                   10.1.100.1              0    100     0 300 i
 *   10.1.100.4/32     10.1.24.4               0            0 400 i
 *>i                   10.1.100.1              0    200     0 300 400 i
Processed 4 prefixes, 6 paths
```

Locally Originated

The path that was locally originated via a **network** or **aggregate** BGP subcommand or through redistribution from an IGP is preferred. Local paths sourced by **network** or **redistribute** commands are preferred over local aggregates sourced by the **aggregate-address** command.

We mentioned that the prefixes will be installed in the Loc-RIB table and a matching process will take place against the global RIB. If a match is in place, the prefix will be installed in the BGP table and used for forwarding. The path attributes (PAs) of the installed prefix will change according to the type of prefix, as follows:

- **Connected Network:** The next hop for this prefix will be 0.0.0.0 from a BGP perspective, the origin set to i, and as mentioned, weight will be the default, which is 32,768.

- **Static Route or Routing Protocol:** The next hop for this prefix will be the RIB IP address (extracted from IGP); similarly, the weight will be 32,768, the origin set to i, and the MED value will be extracted from the IGP metric.

AS Path

As mentioned earlier, the shorter AS-PATH wins, but how can we manipulate this? We can accomplish this by using *as-path prepending*. We influence our AS to be longer through one of our uplinks. The AS-PATH affects inbound traffic. Let's check out what R3 sees in its BGP table in Example 7-28.

Example 7-28 *BGP AS-PATH Validation*

```
R3# show bgp ipv4 unicast 10.1.100.2/32 longer-prefixes | begin Network
Network            Next Hop          Metric LocPrf Weight Path
•10.1.100.2/32     10.1.34.4                          0 400 100 i
*>                 10.1.13.1                           0 100 i
```

So, the preferred inbound traffic for the prefix 10.1.100.2/32 located in ASN 100 is through 10.1.13.1, which has an AS-PATH of 100 compared to 10.1.34.4 ,which has a longer AS-PATH of 400 100. Let's change this path using **as-path prepending**, as demonstrated in Example 7-29.

Example 7-29 *BGP AS-PATH Prepending on IOS and IOS XE*

```
R1(config)# ip prefix-list R2_LOOP seq 5 permit 10.1.100.2/32
R1(config)# route-map PREPEND_MAP permit 10
R1(config-route-map)# match ip address prefix-list R2_LOOP
R1(config-route-map)# set as-path prepend ?
  <1-4294967295>  AS number
  <1.0-XX.YY>     AS number
  last-as         Prepend last AS to the as-path
R1(config-route-map)# set as-path prepend 100 100 100
R1(config)# router bgp 100
R1(config-router)# address-family ipv4 unicast
R1(config-router-af)# neighbor 10.1.13.3 route-map PREPEND_MAP out

R3# show bgp ipv4 unicast 10.1.100.2/32 longer-prefixes | begin Network
   Network         Next Hop          Metric LocPrf Weight Path
*>   10.1.100.2/32 10.1.34.4                        0  400 100 i
     10.1.13.1                                       0  100 100 100 100 i
! We have removed the weight relative configuration.
```

From an IOS XR perspective, it is the same, but here's a small caveat to watch for: we must define a separate route policy for the prepend value and then nest it to the route policy for which we have the prefix of concern and attach it to the target neighbor. To do so, let's go through Example 7-30.

Example 7-30 *BGP AS_PATH Prepending on IOS XR*

```
R4# show bgp ipv4 unicast | begin Network
   Network         Next Hop          Metric LocPrf Weight Path
*>   10.1.100.1/32 10.1.24.2                           0 100 i
*>   10.1.100.2/32 10.1.24.2          0                0 100 i
*    10.1.100.3/32 10.1.24.2                           0 100 300 i
*>                 10.1.34.3          0                0 300 i
*>   10.1.100.4/32 0.0.0.0            0            32768 i

RP/0/0/CPU0:R2(config)# prefix-set R1_LOOP
RP/0/0/CPU0:R2(config-pfx)# 10.1.100.1/32
RP/0/0/CPU0:R2(config)# route-policy PREPEND_POLICY
```

```
RP/0/0/CPU0:R2(config-rpl)# prepend as-path 100 2
RP/0/0/CPU0:R2(config)# route-policy PREPEND_POLICY_NEIGHBOR
RP/0/0/CPU0:R2(config-rpl)# if destination in R1_LOOP then apply PREPEND_POLICY else
pass endif
```

```
RP/0/0/CPU0:R2(config)# router bgp 100
RP/0/0/CPU0:R2(config-bgp)# neighbor 10.1.24.4
RP/0/0/CPU0:R2(config-bgp-nbr)# address-family ipv4 unicast
RP/0/0/CPU0:R2(config-bgp-nbr-af)# route-policy PREPEND_POLICY_NEIGHBOR out
```

```
R4# show bgp ipv4 unicast | begin Network
     Network          Next Hop          Metric LocPrf Weight Path
 *>  10.1.100.1/32    10.1.34.3                           0   300 100 i
 *       10.1.24.2                                        0   100 100 100 i
 *>  10.1.100.2/32    10.1.34.3                           0   300 100 i
 *>  10.1.100.3/32    10.1.34.3                           0   0 300 i
 *>  10.1.100.4/32    0.0.0.0                             0   32768 i
```

As we mentioned, R3 learns 10.1.100.2/32 through the shorter AS-PATH. We will repeat the
AS-PATH prepend process, but only with one extra AS to make the two available options
equal, as shown in Example 7-31.

Example 7-31   *BGP AS-PATH Prepending, One Hop (AS)*

```
R3# show bgp ipv4 unicast 10.1.100.2/32 longer-prefixes | begin Network
Network          Next Hop          Metric LocPrf Weight Path
 *   10.1.100.2/32    10.1.34.4                        0   400 100 i
 *>                   10.1.13.1                        0   100 100 i
```

In this case, the question that arises is: Why has the path been preferred through 10.1.13.1?
Let's try to shut down the neighbor with R1 and bring it up again, as in Example 7-32.

Example 7-32   *Shutdown R3 BGP Peering to R1*

```
R3(config)# router bgp 300
R3(config-router)# neighbor 10.1.13.1 shutdown
```

```
%BGP-3-NOTIFICATION: sent to neighbor 10.1.13.1 6/2 (Administrative Shutdown) 0 bytes
%BGP-5-NBR_RESET: Neighbor 10.1.13.1 reset (Admin. shutdown)
%BGP-5-ADJCHANGE: neighbor 10.1.13.1 Down Admin. shutdown
%BGP_SESSION-5-ADJCHANGE: neighbor 10.1.13.1 IPv4 Unicast topology base removed from
session  Admin. shutdown
```

```
R3# show bgp ipv4 unicast 10.1.100.2/32 longer-prefixes | begin Network
Network          Next Hop          Metric LocPrf Weight Path
 *   10.1.100.2/32    10.1.13.1                        0   100 100 i
 *>                   10.1.34.4                        0   400 100 i
```

AS-PATH prepending does not work on iBGP sessions.

The examples we have gone through are for outbound AS path prepending. In some cases we can utilize inbound AS-PATH prepending. It is possible to use AS-PATH prepending as the last-resort mechanism to influence global BGP routing policies where other tools such as MED, local preference, or communities are not available due to lack of support from the upstream provider.

We will use the topology in Figure 7-10 to demonstrate the effect of configuring AS-PATH prepending inbound versus outbound.

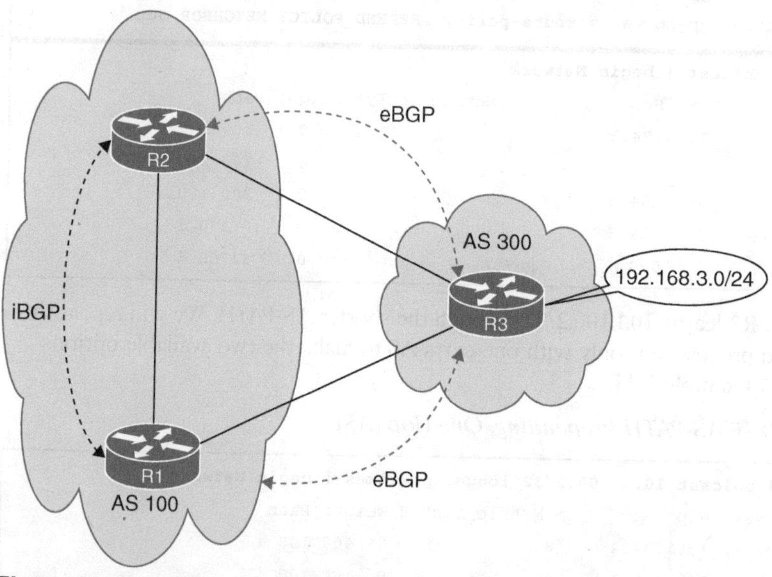

Figure 7-10 *BGP AS-PATH Prepending*

Let's start with prepending R3 AS three times and check the effect on both devices running inside AS 100 using R1 and R2, as shown in Example 7-33.

Example 7-33 *BGP Outbound AS-PATH Prepending*

```
R3(config)# route-map OUT_PREPEND permit 10
R3(config-route-map)# set as-path prepend 300 300 300
R3(config-route-map)# router bgp 300
R3(config-router)# address-family ipv4 unicast
R3(config-router-af)# neighbor 10.1.23.2 route-map OUT_PREPEND out

R2# show bgp ipv4 unicast | begin Network
     Network          Next Hop            Metric LocPrf Weight Path
 *>  192.168.3.0      10.1.23.3                0              0 300 300 300 300 i
 * i                  10.1.13.3                0    100      0 300 i

R1# show bgp ipv4 unicast | begin Network
     Network          Next Hop            Metric LocPrf Weight Path
 *>  192.168.3.0      10.1.13.3                0              0 300 i
```

R1 receives the original update from R3 with no prepend because it has a direct connection to it. To manipulate the traffic from an inbound perspective, we will configure R1 with the **set as-path prepend last-as** command. What differs from the previous command we used in the outbound direction is that the **last-as** keyword will copy the autonomous system of the neighbor that advertises the prefix and matches the route map. To learn more, let's check out Example 7-34.

Example 7-34   *BGP AS Path Inbound Prepending*

```
R1(config)# route-map IN_PREPEND permit 10
R1(config-route-map)# set as-path prepend last-as ?
 <1-10>  number of last-AS prepends
R1(config-route-map)# set as-path prepend last-as 2
R1(config-route-map)# router bgp 100
R1(config-router)# address-family ipv4 unicast
R1(config-router-af)# neighbor 10.1.13.3 route-map IN_PREPEND in

R1# show bgp ipv4 unicast | begin Network
     Network          Next Hop            Metric LocPrf Weight Path
 *>   192.168.3.0      10.1.13.3                0             0 300 300 300 i

R2# show bgp ipv4 unicast | begin Network
     Network          Next Hop            Metric LocPrf Weight Path
 *'   192.168.3.0      10.1.23.3                0             0 300 300 300 300 i
 *>i                   10.1.100.1               0    100      0 300 300 300 i
```

What we are trying to achieve *and* what BGP attribute is available to use are subjective to the use case. In this case, is the service provider applying any attributes from that end, and will the SP overwrite the configuration we are trying to deploy due to the best selection criteria? Do we have a dual-homed configuration, and are we trying to load share, or are we satisfied with active/backup deployment? All these questions will determine the deployment.

Origin

Because of the rule, we know that if a best path already exists, we prefer it over newer routes. As can be seen, origin codes listed in the supportive keywords at the beginning of the **show bgp ipv4 unicast** output list each symbol with the corresponding meaning. We are using the **network** statement to advertise prefixes, which means we will see the **i** symbol. At this point, we will change the origin code to see the effect on the path selection for 10.1.100.2/32. To do so, let's examine Example 7-35. (Because the next hop for the preferred prefix is 10.1.34.4, that means we have learned it through R2 → R4.)

Example 7-35   *BGP Origin Attribute Configuration in IOS XR*

```
RP/0/0/CPU0:R2# show run prefix-set R2_LOOP
prefix-set R2_LOOP
10.1.100.2/32
end-set

RP/0/0/CPU0:R2(config)# route-policy ORIGIN_POLICY
RP/0/0/CPU0:R2(config-rpl)# if destination in R2_LOOP then set origin incomplete
then pass endif
```

```
RP/0/0/CPU0:R2(config)# router bgp 100
RP/0/0/CPU0:R2(config-bgp)# neighbor 10.1.24.4
RP/0/0/CPU0:R2(config-bgp-nbr)# address-family ipv4 unicast
RP/0/0/CPU0:R2(config-bgp-nbr-af)# route-policy ORIGIN_POLICY out
RP/0/0/CPU0:R2(config-bgp-nbr-af)# route-policy PASS in
```

```
R3# show bgp ipv4 unicast 10.1.100.2/32 longer-prefixes | begin Network
     Network              Next Hop            Metric LocPrf Weight Path
 *>   10.1.100.2/32       10.1.13.1                          0 100 100 i
 *                        10.1.34.4                          0 400 100 ?
```

MED

Multi-Exit Discriminator (MED) is an optional nontransitive attribute that provides information to external neighbors showing how to enter our ASN. This attribute is at the opposite spectrum of the Local Preference (LP) attribute, which informs internal neighbors how to exit.

MED is an attribute applied in the outbound direction and suggests a best inbound traffic flow direction. The default MED value is 0. The lower the value, the better.

A local preference attribute is sent to internal neighbors (contained with an autonomous system), where MED is sent only between eBGP neighbors.

Let's look at the topology in Figure 7-11 to better understand the functionality of the MED attribute.

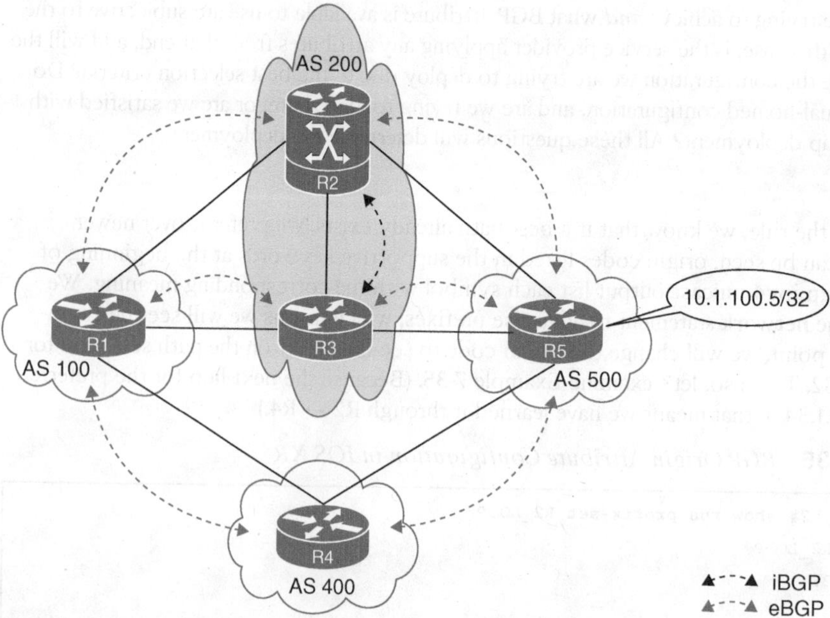

Figure 7-11 *BGP MED Attribute*

There's nothing special as of now. We're just advertising the 10.1.100.5/32 prefix, which will be received by all eBGP neighbors and eventually will reach out to R1 through three different paths, as shown in Example 7-36.

Example 7-36   *R1 BGP Table Output*

```
R1# show bgp ipv4 unicast | begin Network
     Network              Next Hop              Metric LocPrf Weight Path
 *>  10.1.100.5/32        10.1.12.2                            0 200 500 i
 *                        10.1.13.3                            0 200 500 i
 *                        10.1.14.4                            0 400 500 i
```

The first question that you might ask is, Why has this route been installed as the best through R2? When we walk through the selection criteria, are all attributes the same? We looked lower in the list because the oldest route will be installed according to the selection criteria.

Let's manipulate the MED value to see the effect. We know that the MED value is exchanged between eBGP neighbors. Consequently, we can instruct routers R2, R3, and R4 to advertise MED values of 200, 300, and 400, respectively, and then check what took place in the BGP routing table of R1. To see that configuration in effect, let's look at Example 7-37.

Example 7-37   *BGP MED Attribute Configuration*

```
R4(config)# ip prefix-list R5-LOOP seq 5 permit 10.1.100.5/32
R4(config)# route-map BGP_MED permit 10
R4(config-route-map)# match ip address prefix-list R5-LOOP
R4(config-route-map)# set metric 400
R4(config-route-map)# router bgp 400
R4(config-router)# address-family ipv4 unicast
R4(config-router-af)# neighbor 10.1.14.1 route-map BGP_MED out

RP/0/0/CPU0:R2(config)# prefix-set R5_LOOP
RP/0/0/CPU0:R2(config-pfx)# 10.1.100.5/32
RP/0/0/CPU0:R2(config)# route-policy MED_RPL
RP/0/0/CPU0:R2(config-rpl)# if destination in R5_LOOP then set med 200 else pass endif
RP/0/0/CPU0:R2(config)# router bgp 200
RP/0/0/CPU0:R2(config-bgp)# neighbor 10.1.12.1
RP/0/0/CPU0:R2(config-bgp-nbr)# address-family ipv4 unicast
RP/0/0/CPU0:R2(config-bgp-nbr-af)# route-policy MED_RPL out

R1# show bgp ipv4 unicast 10.1.100.5
BGP routing table entry for 10.1.100.5/32, version 5
Paths: (3 available, best #2, table default)
  Advertised to update-groups:
     2
  Refresh Epoch 1
  400 500
    10.1.14.4 from 10.1.14.4 (10.1.100.4)
      Origin IGP, metric 400, localpref 100, valid, external
      rx pathid: 0, tx pathid: 0
      Updated on Aug 22 2024 12:48:00 UTC
  Refresh Epoch 1
  200 500
```

```
     10.1.12.2 from 10.1.12.2 (10.1.100.2)
       Origin IGP, metric 200, localpref 100, valid, external, best
       rx pathid: 0, tx pathid: 0x0
       Updated on Aug 22 2024 12:47:26 UTC
   Refresh Epoch 3
   200 500
     10.1.13.3 from 10.1.13.3 (10.1.100.3)
       Origin IGP, metric 300, localpref 100, valid, external
       rx pathid: 0, tx pathid: 0
```

Here, the best path is chosen to be through R2, but why? Routes are compared in the order that they appear in the BGP table. (The order of routes is the newest at the top down to the oldest at the bottom.) That means we will compare the first R4 path with the R2 path, and then we will compare the winner with R3 at the bottom.

R4 and R2 have different AS-PATHs: the R4 path is 400 500, and the R2 path is 200 500. When the same prefix is used through different eBGP peers with different AS-PATHs, MED will be ignored, and therefore, the prefix through R2 will be the winner because it is the oldest. Now, after continuing with R2, we will compare it with R3. At this point, we have the same prefix through different eBGP peers but with the same AS-PATHs (200 500), and the MED comes into play here. As we have configured, the metric of R3 is 300, and the metric of R2 is 200. Consequently, the lowest wins, and this confirms what is shown in the output.

Now, to group the options together and allow a fair comparison for the MED value, we have the option of using the **bgp deterministic-med** feature command, for which we will rearrange the prefixes and rely on the MED value to determine the best path to follow. To see this in action, let's go through Example 7-38.

Example 7-38 *BGP deterministic-med Configuration*

```
R1(config)# router bgp 100
R1(config-router)# bgp deterministic-med

R1# show bgp ipv4 unicast 10.1.100.5/32
BGP routing table entry for 10.1.100.5/32, version 5
BGP Bestpath: deterministic-med
Paths: (3 available, best #1, table default)
  Advertised to update-groups:
     2
  Refresh Epoch 1
  200 500
    10.1.12.2 from 10.1.12.2 (10.1.100.2)
       Origin IGP, metric 200, localpref 100, valid, external, best
       rx pathid: 0, tx pathid: 0x0
       Updated on Aug 23 2024 12:50:02 UTC
  Refresh Epoch 4
  200 500
    10.1.13.3 from 10.1.13.3 (10.1.100.3)
       Origin IGP, metric 300, localpref 100, valid, external
```

```
      rx pathid: 0, tx pathid: 0
      Updated on Aug 23 2024 12:50:00 UTC
  Refresh Epoch 2
  400 500
    10.1.14.4 from 10.1.14.4 (10.1.100.4)
      Origin IGP, metric 400, localpref 100, valid, external
      rx pathid: 0, tx pathid: 0
```

To confirm that the old path is the winner and the tiebreaker, let's clear both R2 and R3 sessions and check the output again, as shown in Example 7-39.

Example 7-39 *R1 BGP Output Validation*

```
R1# clear bgp ipv4 unicast 10.1.12.2
R1# clear bgp ipv4 unicast 10.1.13.3
```

```
R1# show bgp ipv4 unicast 10.1.100.5/32
BGP routing table entry for 10.1.100.5/32, version 4
BGP Bestpath: deterministic-med
Paths: (3 available, best #3, table default)
  Advertised to update-groups:
    1
  Refresh Epoch 1
  200 500
    10.1.12.2 from 10.1.12.2 (10.1.100.2)
      Origin IGP, metric 200, localpref 100, valid, external
      rx pathid: 0, tx pathid: 0
  Refresh Epoch 1
  200 500
    10.1.13.3 from 10.1.13.3 (10.1.100.3)
      Origin IGP, metric 300, localpref 100, valid, external
      rx pathid: 0, tx pathid: 0
  Refresh Epoch 2
  400 500
    10.1.14.4 from 10.1.14.4 (10.1.100.4)
      Origin IGP, metric 400, localpref 100, valid, external, best
      rx pathid: 0, tx pathid: 0x0
```

Now, the comparison takes place again in sequential order (the available paths have been rearranged again). If we compare the path through R2 and the path through R3, they hold the same AS-PATH information (200 500). MED will be compared, and R2 will win because it has a lower MED. Next, we will compare the R2 path to the R4 path, and MED will not be considered for comparison because the AS-PATH is different; hence, the oldest route will win.

Can we force the MED to be compared even though the AS-PATH is different? Here comes the **bgp always-compare-med** command. The MED comparison will take place regardless of the AS-PATH. Example 7-40 shows the changes.

Example 7-40   *BGP* always-compare-med *Configuration*

```
R1(config)# router bgp 100
R1(config-router)# bgp always-compare-med
```

```
R1# show bgp ipv4 unicast 10.1.100.5/32
BGP routing table entry for 10.1.100.5/32, version 5
BGP Bestpath: deterministic-med
Paths: (3 available, best #1, table default)
  Advertised to update-groups:
    1
  Refresh Epoch 1
  200 500
    10.1.12.2 from 10.1.12.2 (10.1.100.2)
      Origin IGP, metric 200, localpref 100, valid, external, best
      rx pathid: 0, tx pathid: 0x0
  Refresh Epoch 2
  200 500
    10.1.13.3 from 10.1.13.3 (10.1.100.3)
      Origin IGP, metric 300, localpref 100, valid, external
      rx pathid: 0, tx pathid: 0
  Refresh Epoch 3
  400 500
    10.1.14.4 from 10.1.14.4 (10.1.100.4)
      Origin IGP, metric 400, localpref 100, valid, external
      rx pathid: 0, tx pathid: 0
```

Now, let's remove the two commands we have configured on R1: **bgp deterministic-med**
and **bgp always-compare-med**. Then we can clear the BGP process on R1 using the **clear
bgp ipv4 unicast * soft** command and check the output for the last time, as depicted in
Example 7-41.

Example 7-41   *R1 BGP Table Output, No MED*

```
R1# show ip bgp 10.1.100.5/32
BGP routing table entry for 10.1.100.5/32, version 6
Paths: (3 available, best #1, table default)
  Advertised to update-groups:
    1
  Refresh Epoch 1
  200 500
    10.1.12.2 from 10.1.12.2 (10.1.100.2)
      Origin IGP, metric 200, localpref 100, valid, external, best
      rx pathid: 0, tx pathid: 0x0
  Refresh Epoch 3
  200 500
    10.1.13.3 from 10.1.13.3 (10.1.100.3)
      Origin IGP, metric 300, localpref 100, valid, external
      rx pathid: 0, tx pathid: 0
```

```
Refresh Epoch 4
400 500
   10.1.14.4 from 10.1.14.4 (10.1.100.4)
      Origin IGP, metric 400, localpref 100, valid, external
      rx pathid: 0, tx pathid: 0
```

R2 is the winner. Why? Because R2 has the lowest router ID, and hence, the path through
R2 will be marked as the best path and be used for forwarding, as proven by Example 7-42.

Example 7-42   *R1 Routing Table Output*

```
R1# show ip route 10.1.100.5 255.255.255.255
Routing entry for 10.1.100.5/32
  Known via "bgp 100", distance 20, metric 200
  Tag 200, type external
  Last update from 10.1.12.2 00:02:29 ago
  Routing Descriptor Blocks:
  * 10.1.12.2, from 10.1.12.2, 00:02:29 ago
      Route metric is 200, traffic share count is 1
      AS Hops 2
      Route tag 200
      MPLS label: none
```

BGP Multipath

BGP Multipath enables the addition of several BGP routes to the IP routing table, all leading
to the same destination. These routes are included in the table alongside the optimal path
for distributing the load; however, BGP Multipath does not alter the best path selection.
For instance, a router continues to identify one route as the optimal path according to the
algorithm and broadcasts this optimal path to its neighboring routers.

The BGP multipath features are as follows:

- eBGP Multipath

- iBGP Multipath

- eiBGP Multipath

To qualify for multipath, the routes to the same goal must match or exceed the qualities of
the optimal route:

- Weight

- Local preference

- AS-PATH length

- Origin

- MED

- One of the following:

    - Neighboring AS or sub-AS (before the addition of the eiBGP Multipath feature)

    - AS-PATH (after the addition of the eiBGP Multipath feature)

Certain BGP Multipath functionalities impose extra criteria on multipath options. The extra criteria for eBGP multipath are as follows: the path needs to be acquired from an external or confederation-external neighbor (eBGP), and the IGP metric to the BGP next hop should match the metric of the best-path IGP.

For iBGP multipath, the path must originate from an internal neighbor. The IGP metric to the BGP next hop should match the metric of the best-path IGP, unless the router is set up to support the unequal-cost iBGP multipath.

NOTE   BGP inserts up to n most recently received paths from multipath candidates in the IP routing table. The maximum value of n is currently 6. When multipath is disabled, the default value is 1.

We can check the respective commands to activate these features, as shown in Example 7-43.

Example 7-43   *BGP Multipath Configuration Options*

```
! IOS

R3(config)# router bgp 300

R3(config-router)# address-family ipv4 unicast

R3(config-router-af)# maximum-paths ?

  <1-32>  Number of paths

  eibgp   Both eBGP and iBGP paths as multipath

  ibgp    iBGP-multipath

! IOS XR

RP/0/0/CPU0:R2(config)# router bgp 2

RP/0/0/CPU0:R2(config-bgp)# address-family ipv4 unicast

RP/0/0/CPU0:R2(config-bgp-af)# maximum-paths ?

  ebgp    eBGP-multipath

  eibgp   eiBGP-multipath

  ibgp    iBGP-multipath

! IOS XE

R3(config-router-af)# maximum-paths ?

  <1-32>  Number of paths

  eibgp   Both eBGP and iBGP paths as multipath

  ibgp    iBGP-multipath

  import  Maximum import paths
```

eBGP vs. iBGP

Continuing the list of best-path selection criteria, if we reach a tie in the previous attributes, then we will reach a point where we need to compare the prefixes according to the source. Is the prefix learned via an iBGP or an eBGP peer? From a reliability perspective, the iBGP and eBGP are treated differently with regard to administrative distance (AD). The lowest will be the winner: eBGP has an AD of 20, and iBGP has an AD of 200.

IGP Next Hop

If we receive a prefix via two peers for which the IGP metric to the BGP next hop is different, the lowest metric will win and the prefix from that lower metric next hop will be installed.

Oldest Route

If both paths are external, we will prefer the oldest route (which was learned first).

Router ID

The route that comes from the BGP router with the lowest router ID is the preferred route. The router ID is the highest IP address on the router, with preference given to loopback addresses. Also, we can use the **bgp router-id** command to manually set the router ID.

Accumulated IGP (AIGP)

The **Accumulated IGP (AIGP)** metric is a nontransitive optional BGP path attribute that is defined by RFC 7311. The AIGP Attribute value field definition is a collection of Type-Length-Value elements (TLVs). The Accumulated IGP metric is contained in the BGP AIGP TLV. (We postponed the discussion about this feature because it is deployed per specific use cases).

BGP is an inter-AS domain routing protocol, and there is no inter-AS metric that can be used for end-to-end shortest path selection.

The AIGP metric attribute for BGP enables deployment in which a single administration can run several contiguous BGP autonomous systems. Such deployments allow BGP to make routing decisions based on the IGP metric. In such networks, it is possible for BGP to select paths based on metrics, as done by IGPs. In this case, BGP chooses the shortest path between two nodes, even though the nodes might be in two different autonomous systems.

To make the problem and the solution clearer, let's look at the topology in Figure 7-12, where two autonomous systems (AS 100 and AS 200) belong to the same administration. The prefix for which we are trying to achieve an optimal end-to-end path is the R4 loopback network, 10.1.100.4/32. We have placed an arbitrary IGP cost value (here, we assume OSPF is in place, but any routing protocol could suffice to fulfill the requirement).

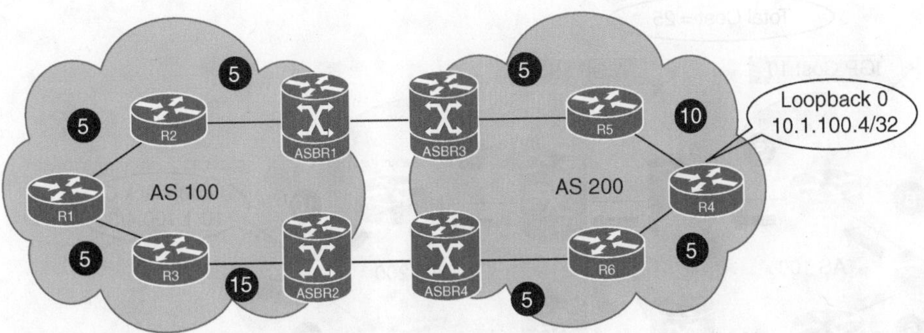

Figure 7-12 *BGP AIGP Demonstration Example #1*

The initial solution is to use MED to alter the traffic because it enters AS 100 by setting the MED to 100 on ASBR3, for example, and to 50 on ASBR4, which will make the optimal path flow through the path shown in Figure 7-13. R1 receives two paths and will prefer the update from ASBR2 because it has a next hop with a lower MED value. But the issue is in the end-to-end path, which will follow the upper path.

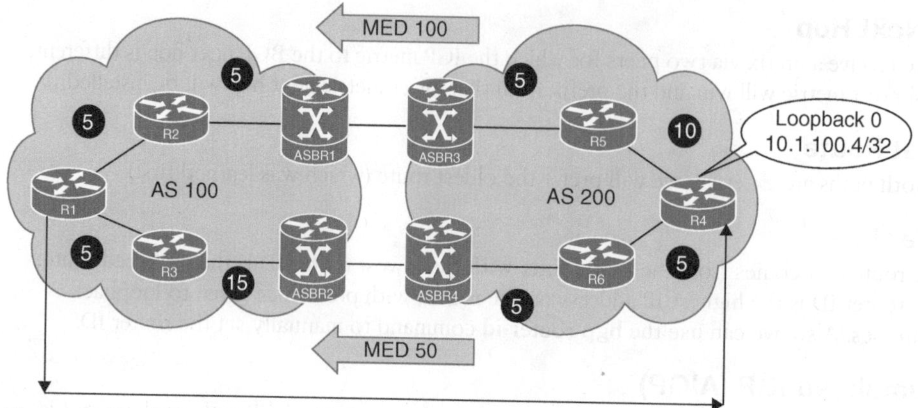

Figure 7-13 *BGP Path Control Using MED Attribute*

Now, AIGP will involve the IGP metric in the calculations to make sure the end-to-end path is influenced by the IGP metric rather than the MED value, which does not guarantee an optimal path as needed. The following steps illustrate the AIGP operation:

Step 1. BGP is running on all ASBR routers as well as on R1 and R4 (representing PE devices).

Step 2. We will enable the AIGP feature on all BGP speakers (eBGP and iBGP).

Step 3. ASBR3 and ASBR4 will advertise the 10.1.100.4/32 prefix to ASBR1 and ASBR2 in AS 100 with the AIGP metric, which includes the IGP metric to R4.

Step 4. When R1 receives the 10.1.100.4/32 prefix with the AIGP metric of 15 from ASBR3 and 10 from ASBR4, which represents the IGP cost to R4 inside AS 200, R1 will add the IGP cost to ASBR1 and ASBR2 and choose the BGP next hop based on the new formula, solely relying on the IGP metric, as shown in Figure 7-14.

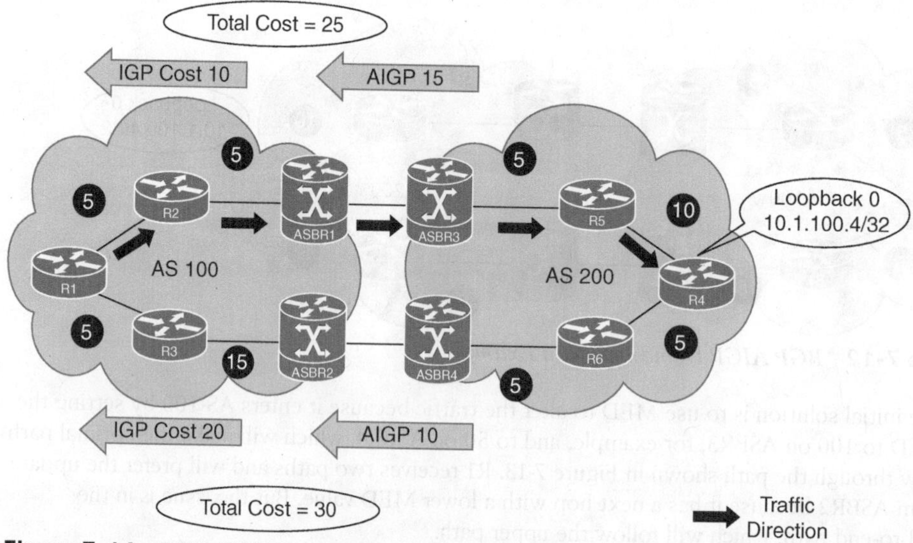

Figure 7-14 *BGP AIGP Demonstration Example #2*

Use Case: Seamless MPLS

One of the more common use cases for which AIGP can help optimize the traffic path is with seamless MPLS (covered in more detail in Chapter 13).

The transport network in large service providers is generally divided into several IGP islands and stitched together using iBGP-labeled unicast (end-to-end label-switched path, or LSP). In the topology in Figure 7-15, the network is divided into two IGP islands. The challenge is that the traffic from the core network toward the station connected to R1 is taking a suboptimal path compared to the upward traffic. Here, we can utilize the AIGP attribute to enforce an optimal path for inbound/outbound traffic (symmetrical routing).

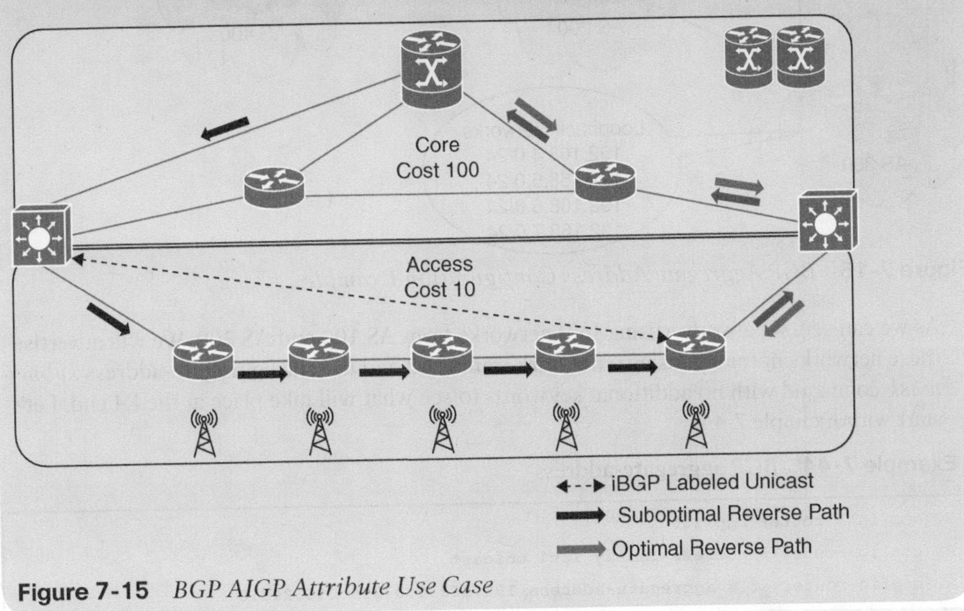

Figure 7-15 *BGP AIGP Attribute Use Case*

Aggregate Address

Route aggregation (summarization) is the ability to aggregate several routes together. These aggregated routes can be deployed for several reasons, such as RIB size minimization or backups for more specific routes. BGP summarization is similar to the concept of IGP, except that, by default, all *specific* routes also appear in the BGP table. Figure 7-16 demonstrates contiguous subnets chosen to make the summary more clear, because our focus is the behavior of BGP when aggregating routes.

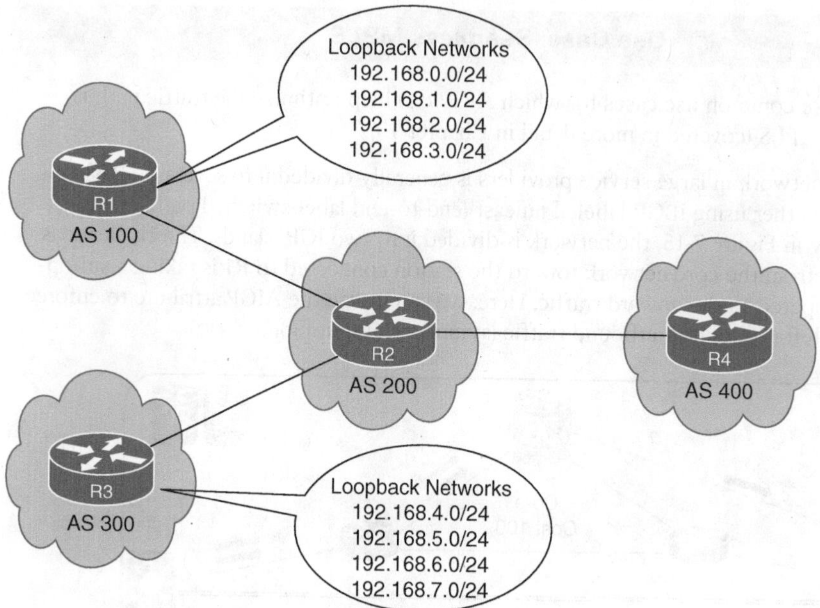

Figure 7-16 *BGP Aggregate Address Configuration Example*

As we can see, we are advertising four networks from AS 100 and AS 200. We will advertise these networks normally (using a **network** statement) and use the **aggregate-address** *subnet-mask* command with no additional keywords to see what will take place at the R4 end. Let's start with Example 7-44.

Example 7-44 *BGP* **aggregate-address**

```
R2(config)# router bgp 200
R2(config-router)# address-family ipv4 unicast
R2(config-router-af)# aggregate-address 192.168.0.0 255.255.248.0

R4# show bgp ipv4 unicast | begin Network
     Network          Next Hop          Metric LocPrf Weight Path
 *>  192.168.0.0      10.1.24.2                         0 200 100 i
 *>  192.168.0.0/21   10.1.24.2              0           0 200 i
 *>  192.168.1.0      10.1.24.2                         0 200 100 i
 *>  192.168.2.0      10.1.24.2                         0 200 100 i
 *>  192.168.3.0      10.1.24.2                         0 200 100 i
 *>  192.168.4.0      10.1.24.2                         0 200 300 i
 *>  192.168.5.0      10.1.24.2                         0 200 300 i
 *>  192.168.6.0      10.1.24.2                         0 200 300 i
 *>  192.168.7.0      10.1.24.2                         0 200 300 i
```

As discussed, individual prefixes appear along the summary route, which does not solve the issue of reducing the BGP table size. We can add the **summary-only** keyword to the **aggregate-address** command to make sure only the summary is available inside the BGP table, as demonstrated in Example 7-45.

Example 7-45 *BGP aggregate-address, summary-only*

```
R2(config-router-af)# aggregate-address 192.168.0.0 255.255.248.0 summary-only

R4# show bgp ipv4 unicast | begin Network
    Network           Next Hop          Metric LocPrf Weight Path
*>  192.168.0.0/21    10.1.24.2              0             0 200 i
```

Looking deeply into the output in Example 7-33, we can see that the AS-PATH associated with the summary route is marked with AS 200. It appears that the route was originated inside that ASN. This is not totally true because the routes originated from AS 100 and 200. To preserve the actual ASN for the aggregate address, we can attach the **as-set** keyword to the **aggregate-address** command, as shown in Example 7-46.

Example 7-46 *BGP aggregate-address, summary-only, and* **as-set**

```
R2(config-router-af)# aggregate-address 192.168.0.0 255.255.248.0 summary-only as-set

R4# show bgp ipv4 unicast | begin Network
    Network           Next Hop          Metric LocPrf Weight Path
*>  192.168.0.0/21    10.1.24.2              0             0 200 {100,300} i

! After we reserved AS-PATH, R1 started to produce the below
! log messages as it started to receive updates with its own AS within the AS-PATH.
BGP(0): 10.1.12.2 rcv UPDATE about 192.168.1.0/24 -- DENIED due to: AS-PATH contains
our own AS; NEXTHOP is our own address;
BGP(0): 10.1.12.2 rcv UPDATE about 192.168.2.0/24 -- DENIED due to: AS-PATH contains
our own AS; NEXTHOP is our own address;
BGP(0): 10.1.12.2 rcv UPDATE about 192.168.3.0/24 -- DENIED due to: AS-PATH contains
our own AS; NEXTHOP is our own address;
```

In some instances, you might need to control the ASN that will be associated with the summary route. In closed networks, aggregate information can be propagated through the autonomous system and back to one of the autonomous systems listed in **as-set**, which may create loops. The loop detection methodology of BGP notes that its own AS is within the **as-set** of the aggregate and drops the update and hence prevents the loop.

We can deploy an advertise map and associate it with the **aggregate-address** command. For example, let's assume we need only AS 100 to appear within the AS-PATH of the aggregate address. In that case, we will define an ACL that matches the routes originated from that AS, create a route map, and use it as an advertise map. Example 7-47 shows how this works.

Example 7-47 *BGP aggregate-address, advertise-map*

```
R2(config)# ip access-list standard R1_SUBNETS
R2(config-std-nacl)# permit 192.168.0.0 0.0.3.255
R2(config)# route-map AS100_MAP permit 10
R2(config-route-map)# match ip address R1_SUBNETS

R2(config)# router bgp 200
R2(config-router)# address-family ipv4 unicast
R2(config-router-af)# aggregate-address 192.168.0.0 255.255.248.0 summary-only
as-set advertise-map AS100_MAP
```

```
R4# show bgp ipv4 unicast | begin Network
     Network          Next Hop         Metric LocPrf Weight Path
 *>  192.168.0.0/21   10.1.24.2              0          0 200 {100} i
```

There are still more control configuration aspects we can deploy, such as controlling routes to be suppressed when an aggregate is advertised, what attributes we can associate with the aggregate, and so on. Table 7-3 summarizes all of these capabilities.

Table 7-3   BGP **aggregate-address** Additional Keywords

Configuration Tools Associated with aggregate-address Command	Description
summary-only	Stops specific routes from being advertised
as-set	Preserves originating autonomous systems
advertise-map (route-map)	Determines which routes will have attributes within the aggregate
suppress-map (route-map)	Determines which routes will be suppressed when the aggregate is advertised
attribute-map (route-map)	Sets attributes to the aggregate route
unsuppress-map (route-map)	Determines which routes will be unsuppressed when the aggregate is advertised

Redistribution

As with any other protocol, we can redistribute routes from and to BGP. There are several caveats associated with redistribution, but the main point to focus on is the metric of the redistributed routes. When we redistribute a route inside BGP, the metric from the original protocol from which we are redistributing routes will be maintained inside the BGP table.

We will use the topology in Figure 7-17 to illustrate the metric concept discussed here.

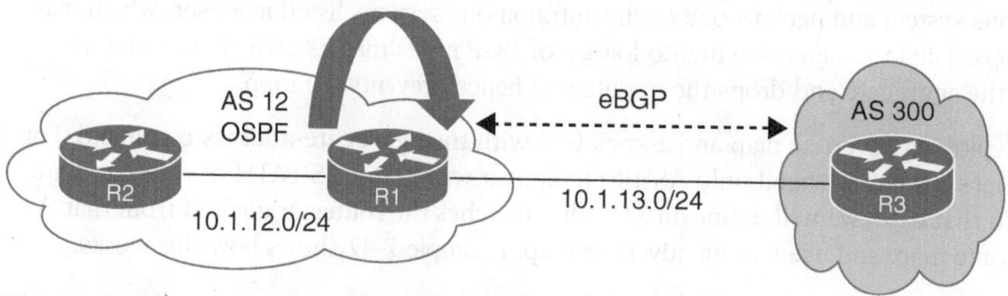

Figure 7-17   *BGP Redistribution Example*

We are simply establishing OSPF inside AS 12 and then redistributing the routes inside the BGP process on the ASBR (R1), as shown in Example 7-48. A simple loopback network is configured on R2 to test the redistribution to 192.168.0.0/24.

Example 7-48   *BGP and OSPF Mutual Redistribution*

```
R1(config)# router ospf 1
R1(config-router)# redistribute bgp 12 subnets
! A quick reminder about the subnets keyword when redistributing
! inside OSPF to reserve the actual subnet mask.
R1(config)# router bgp 12
R1(config-router)# address-family ipv4 unicast
R1(config-router-af)# redistribute ospf 1

R3# show bgp ipv4 unicast | include 192.168.0.0|Metric
      Network          Next Hop          Metric LocPrf Weight Path
 *>   192.168.0.0      10.1.13.1             33              0 12 ?
! We used a filter to focus on 192.168.0.0/24 network; however, the
! interconnection link between R1 and R2 which is used to establish
! the OSPF neighborship will also be redistributed by default.
```

We can restrict the redistribution to a specific prefix, define a route map to set the metric
value, and make sure the value will be propagated, as in Example 7-49.

Example 7-49   *BGP Redistribution, Metric Manipulation*

```
R1(config)# ip prefix-list R2_LOOPBACK seq 5 permit 192.168.0.0/24
R1(config)# route-map METRIC_MAP permit 10
R1(config-route-map)# set metric 33

R1(config)# router bgp 12
R1(config-router)# address-family ipv4 unicast
R1(config-router-af)# redistribute ospf 1 route-map METRIC_MAP

R3# show bgp ipv4 unicast | include 192.168.0.0|Metric
      Network          Next Hop          Metric LocPrf Weight Path
 *>   192.168.0.0      10.1.13.1             33      0      12   ?
```

There is one caveat to mention about how BGP behaves when redistributing OSPF into its
process. As we can see, the route that R1 learns from R2 (from an OSPF perspective) is the
intra-area route, which means it is from the same area and advertised using the **network**
command under the OSPF process or the **ip ospf** *process-id* **area** *area-number* command
under the interface level. What would happen if we redistributed a route that is external to
R1 (because it came from another routing process)? Let's check Example 7-50, where we
have used the **redistribute connected** command to simulate the external routing process and
make sure that the OSPF route is tagged with E (it will be E2 because we did not change the
default metric type of OSPF external routes).

Example 7-50   *OSPF Advertisement on IOS Using Redistribution*

```
R2(config)# interface loopback 2
R2(config-if)# ip address 172.16.2.2 255.255.255.0
R2(config-if)# ip ospf network point-to-point
```

```
! We configured the point-to-point network type as the OSPF will advertise it as
/32 and the actual subnet mask is 24 and therefore we can overcome this behavior by
changing the network type to point-to-point.
```

```
R2(config)# route-map EXTERNAL permit 10
R2(config-route-map)# match interface loopback 2
```

```
R2(config)# router ospf 1
R2(config-router)# redistribute connected subnets route-map EXTERNAL
```

```
R3# show bgp ipv4 unicast | include 172.16.2.0
R3#
```

Nothing appeared. The reason is that only OSPF inter-area and intra-area routes are redistributed by default if we use the **redistribute ospf** *process-id* command under the BGP **address-family ipv4** command with no extra keywords. We must be specific to the BGP process that we are going to send in external routes, so let's check Example 7-51 for the additional keywords.

Example 7-51 *OSPF to BGP Redistribution, Match External*

```
R1(config)# router bgp 12
R1(config-router)# address-family ipv4
R1(config-router-af)# redistribute ospf 1 match ?
  external       Redistribute OSPF external routes
  internal       Redistribute OSPF internal routes
  nssa-external  Redistribute OSPF NSSA external routes
R1(config-router-af)# redistribute ospf 1 match external
```

```
R3# show bgp ipv4 unicast | include Metric|172.16.2.0
     Network          Next Hop            Metric LocPrf Weight Path
 *>  172.16.2.0/24    10.1.13.1               20           0 12 ?
! We did not alter the metric of the redistributed route and therefore it will be an
! E2 route and will hold a metric value of 20 along the way.
```

Communities

The BGP community is an optional, transitive BGP attribute. BGP communities are simply values attached to a route sent to BGP peers. These values have special meanings to the peers and cause specific actions to be taken, depending on the values assigned. So, it is an effective way to affect path selection and gives granular control on prefix advertisement and filtering.

Customers can use BGP communities internally to mark a set of prefixes that share a common property and then apply a common routing policy such as filtering or assigning a specific attribute (for example, local preference). Service providers can make an agreement with customers on a specific policy to be applied to their prefixes using BGP communities.

Generally, there are three types of communities:

- Standard communities

- Extended communities

- Large communities

Table 7-4 highlights the types of communities and the structure of each community.

Table 7-4 BGP Community Types

Community	Size	Structure
Standard	32-bit, written in the form AS:Action	The first 16 bits define the AS, which defines the community. The second 16 bits define the action (local significance).
Extended	64-bits, written in the form Type:AS:Member	The first 16 bits define the purpose. The type of community is assigned by IANA. The remaining 48 bits define the policy.
Large	96-bits, Source AS:Action:Target AS	This community is split into three 32-bit values to give more granular identification to include 4-byte ASNs.

By default, BGP has the following four well-known communities (standard) that can be used to mark prefixes:

- **Internet:** Advertise these routes to all neighbors.

- **Local-as:** Prevent sending routes outside the local AS within the confederation.

- **No-Advertise:** Do not advertise this route to any peer, internal or external.

- **No-Export:** Do not advertise this route to external BGP peers.

Let's further examine the well-known communities, starting with the no-export community. Example 7-52 shows how this community works and what the effect is locally and in communication with another AS.

NOTE If you did not configure the **send-community** capability, the direct neighbor will not receive the prefix tagged with the community. However, other uplink routers will receive the community because the BGP community is an optional transitive community and can be recognized and passed to other BGP peers.

Example 7-52   *BGP No-Export Community, IOS and IOS XE*

```
R1# show bgp ipv4 unicast neighbors 10.1.100.2 advertised-routes | begin Network
      Network          Next Hop          Metric LocPrf Weight Path
 *>   10.1.100.1/32    0.0.0.0                0           32768 i
 *>   10.1.100.3/32    10.1.13.3              0               0 300 i
 *>   10.1.100.4/32    10.1.13.3                              0 300 400 i
Total number of prefixes 3

R1# show bgp ipv4 unicast neighbors 10.1.13.3 advertised-routes | begin Network
      Network          Next Hop          Metric LocPrf Weight Path
 *>   10.1.100.1/32    0.0.0.0                0           32768 i
 r>i  10.1.100.2/32    10.1.100.2             0     100       0 i
Total number of prefixes 2

R1(config)# route-map NO_EXPORT permit 10
R1(config-route-map)# match ip address prefix-list R1_LOOP
R1(config-route-map)# set community no-export

R1(config)# router bgp 100
R1(config-router)# address-family ipv4
R1(config-router-af)# network 10.1.100.1 mask 255.255.255.255 route-map NO_EXPORT

R1# show bgp ipv4 unicast neighbors 10.1.100.2 advertised-routes | begin Network
      Network          Next Hop          Metric LocPrf Weight Path
 *>   10.1.100.1/32    0.0.0.0                0           32768 i
 *>   10.1.100.3/32    10.1.13.3              0               0 300 i
 *>   10.1.100.4/32    10.1.13.3                              0 300 400 i
Total number of prefixes 3

R1# show bgp ipv4 unicast neighbors 10.1.13.3 advertised-routes | begin Network
      Network          Next Hop          Metric LocPrf Weight Path
 r>i  10.1.100.2/32    10.1.100.2             0     100       0 i
Total number of prefixes 1

R1# show bgp ipv4 unicast 10.1.100.1/32
BGP routing table entry for 10.1.100.1/32, version 7
Paths: (1 available, best #1, table default, not advertised to EBGP peer)
Advertised to update-groups:
16
Refresh Epoch 1
Local
0.0.0.0 from 0.0.0.0 (10.1.100.1)
Origin IGP, metric 0, localpref 100, weight 32768, valid, sourced, local, best
Community: no-export
rx pathid: 0, tx pathid: 0x0
```

Example 7-53 lists the same configuration aspect, but from the IOS XR perspective. Just as a reminder, with IOS XR, everything is done through a route policy.

Example 7-53 *BGP No-Export Community, IOS XR*

```
RP/0/0/CPU0:R2(config)# community-set NO_EXPORT_COMM
RP/0/0/CPU0:R2(config-comm)# no-export

RP/0/0/CPU0:R2(config)# route-policy NO_EXPORT_POLICY
RP/0/0/CPU0:R2(config-rpl)# set community NO_EXPORT_COMM

RP/0/0/CPU0:R2(config)# router bgp 100
RP/0/0/CPU0:R2(config-bgp)# address-family ipv4 unicast
RP/0/0/CPU0:R2(config-bgp-af)# network 10.1.100.2/32 route-policy NO_EXPORT_POLICY

RP/0/0/CPU0:R2# show bgp neighbor 10.1.100.1 advertised-routes
Network           Next Hop          From            AS Path
10.1.100.2/32     10.1.100.2        Local           i
10.1.100.3/32     10.1.24.4         10.1.24.4       400 300i
10.1.100.4/32     10.1.24.4         10.1.24.4       400i
Processed 3 prefixes, 3 paths

RP/0/0/CPU0:R2# show bgp neighbor 10.1.24.4 advertised-routes
Network           Next Hop          From            AS Path
10.1.100.1/32     10.1.24.2         10.1.100.1      100i
Processed 1 prefixes, 1 paths
```

Continuing through the well-known communities, we will now examine how to configure
the **no-advertise** community, which will prevent the prefix from being advertised to an internal or external peer, as illustrated in Example 7-54.

Example 7-54 *BGP no-advertise Community, IOS and IOS XE*

```
R1(config)# route-map NO_ADVERTISE permit 10
R1(config-route-map)# set community no-advertise

R1(config)# router bgp 100
R1(config-router)# address-family ipv4
R1(config-router-af)# network 10.1.100.1 mask 255.255.255.255 route-map NO_ADVERTISE

R1# show bgp ipv4 unicast neighbors 10.1.100.2 advertised-routes | begin Network
     Network          Next Hop          Metric LocPrf Weight Path
 *>  10.1.100.3/32     10.1.13.3              0             0 300 i
 *>  10.1.100.4/32     10.1.13.3                            0 300 400 i
Total number of prefixes 2

R1# show bgp ipv4 unicast 10.1.100.1/32
BGP routing table entry for 10.1.100.1/32, version 10
Paths: (1 available, best #1, table default, not advertised to any peer)
Not advertised to any peer
Refresh Epoch 1
Local
0.0.0.0 from 0.0.0.0 (10.1.100.1)
Origin IGP, metric 0, localpref 100, weight 32768, valid, sourced, local, best
```

```
Community: no-advertise
rx pathid: 0, tx pathid: 0x0
! We can specifically check the route that has the no-advertise community attached
! to it.
```

```
R1# show bgp ipv4 unicast community no-advertise | begin Network
     Network          Next Hop            Metric LocPrf Weight Path
 *>  10.1.100.1/32    0.0.0.0                  0            32768 i
```

Giant service providers have a predefined community value that they use to control traffic among themselves. Many large networks publish a list of communities that they set and honor, often in the routing registries, such as Level 3 communities in the RIPE database at https://apps.db.ripe.net/db-web-ui/lookup?source=ripe-nonauth&key=AS3356&type= aut-num. Also, you can check out the BGP community guides for major service providers and the attributes associated with each predefined community (effect on traffic) by visiting https://onestep.net/communities/.

One example is that, when you're utilizing two Internet connections, both will be employed for incoming and outgoing traffic. Nevertheless, in certain situations, it may be advantageous to designate one connection to manage all traffic while reserving the second connection as a backup that remains inactive until the primary connection experiences a failure.

Managing outgoing traffic is relatively straightforward: you can simply reduce the local preference for all prefixes acquired through the backup line. Conversely, for incoming traffic, it is necessary to decrease the local preference within the neighboring autonomous system. It is noteworthy that Level 3 offers three communities specifically designed to achieve this:

- **3356:70**: Set local preference to 70

- **3356:80**: Set local preference to 80

- **3356:90**: Set local preference to 90

We can also define communities to be used for path selection, filtering, and other related control aspects. Generally, the community format will be in the form *ASN:NN*, where *NN* is any arbitrary number. Example 7-55 shows how to implement user-defined communities.

Example 7-55 *BGP User-Defined Communities*

```
R1(config)# route-map COMM permit 10
R1(config-route-map)# set community 100:1

R1(config)# router bgp 100
R1(config-router)# address-family ipv4
R1(config-router-af)# network 10.1.100.1 mask 255.255.255.255 route-map COMM

R1# show bgp ipv4 unicast 10.1.100.1/32
BGP routing table entry for 10.1.100.1/32, version 12
Paths: (1 available, best #1, table default)
Advertised to update-groups:
15          16
```

```
Refresh Epoch 1
Local
  0.0.0.0 from 0.0.0.0 (10.1.100.1)
    Origin IGP, metric 0, localpref 100, weight 32768, valid, sourced, local, best
    Community: 6553601
    rx pathid: 0, tx pathid: 0x0
    Updated on Aug 1 2024 21:41:11 UTC
```

```
R3# show bgp ipv4 unicast 10.1.100.1/32
BGP routing table entry for 10.1.100.1/32, version 38
Paths: (2 available, best #1, table default)
  Advertised to update-groups:
     3
  Refresh Epoch 2
  100
  10.1.13.1 from 10.1.13.1 (10.1.100.1)
    Origin IGP, metric 0, localpref 100, valid, external, best
    rx pathid: 0, tx pathid: 0x0
  Refresh Epoch 7
  400 100
  10.1.34.4 from 10.1.34.4 (10.1.100.4)
    Origin IGP, localpref 100, valid, external
    rx pathid: 0, tx pathid: 0
```

```
! As can we see, R3 received the update from R1 but no community has been
! attached to the prefix. We must instruct the neighbor that a community
! is to be sent attached to the update.
R1(config)# router bgp 100
R1(config-router)# address-family ipv4 unicast
R1(config-router-af)# neighbor 10.1.13.3 send-community
```

```
R3# show bgp ipv4 unicast 10.1.100.1/32
BGP routing table entry for 10.1.100.1/32, version 39
Paths: (2 available, best #1, table default)
  Advertised to update-groups:
     3
  Refresh Epoch 2
  100
  10.1.13.1 from 10.1.13.1 (10.1.100.1)
    Origin IGP, metric 0, localpref 100, valid, external, best
    Community: 6553601
    rx pathid: 0, tx pathid: 0x0
  Refresh Epoch 7
  400 100
  10.1.34.4 from 10.1.34.4 (10.1.100.4)
    Origin IGP, localpref 100, valid, external
    rx pathid: 0, tx pathid: 0
```

```
! The community value appears in decimal format though we used the
! ASN:NN notation, we have to change the way the community is interpreted
! using the IOS/IOS XE command ip bgp-community new-format.
R3(config)# ip bgp-community new-format
```

```
R3# show bgp ipv4 unicast 10.1.100.1/32
BGP routing table entry for 10.1.100.1/32, version 39
Paths: (2 available, best #1, table default)
Advertised to update-groups:
3
Refresh Epoch 2
100
10.1.13.1 from 10.1.13.1 (10.1.100.1)
Origin IGP, metric 0, localpref 100, valid, external, best
Community: 100:1
rx pathid: 0, tx pathid: 0x0
Refresh Epoch 7
400 100
10.1.34.4 from 10.1.34.4 (10.1.100.4)
Origin IGP, localpref 100, valid, external
rx pathid: 0, tx pathid: 0
! IOS XR Community Configuration using ASN:NN Format.
RP/0/0/CPU0:R2(config)# community-set COMMUNITY_VALUE
RP/0/0/CPU0:R2(config-comm)# 100:20
```

```
RP/0/0/CPU0:R2(config)# route-policy COMM
RP/0/0/CPU0:R2(config-rpl)# if destination in R2_LOOP then set community
COMMUNITY_VALUE
RP/0/0/CPU0:R2(config-rpl)# exit
RP/0/0/CPU0:R2(config)# commit
```

```
RP/0/0/CPU0:R2(config)# router bgp 100
RP/0/0/CPU0:R2(config-bgp)# address-family ipv4 unicast
RP/0/0/CPU0:R2(config-bgp-af)# network 10.1.100.2/32 route-policy COMM
RP/0/0/CPU0:R2(config-bgp-af)# commit
```

```
RP/0/0/CPU0:R2# show bgp 10.1.100.2/32
BGP routing table entry for 10.1.100.2/32
Versions:
  Process           bRIB/RIB  SendTblVer
  Speaker              57         57
Last Modified: Aug  1 18:23:53.281 for 00:00:05
Paths: (1 available, best #1)
Advertised IPv4 Unicast paths to peers (in unique update groups):
10.1.100.1
Path #1: Received by speaker 0
```

```
Advertised IPv4 Unicast paths to peers (in unique update groups):
10.1.100.1
Local
0.0.0.0 from 0.0.0.0 (10.1.100.2)
Origin IGP, metric 0, localpref 100, weight 32768, valid, local, best, group-best
Received Path ID 0, Local Path ID 1, version 57
Community: 100:20
```

```
RP/0/0/CPU0:R2(config)# router bgp 100
RP/0/0/CPU0:R2(config-bgp)# neighbor 10.1.24.4
RP/0/0/CPU0:R2(config-bgp-nbr)# address-family ipv4 unicast
RP/0/0/CPU0:R2(config-bgp-nbr-af)# send-community-ebgp
```

```
R4# show bgp ipv4 unicast 10.1.100.2/32
BGP routing table entry for 10.1.100.2/32, version 31
Paths: (2 available, best #2, table default)
Advertised to update-groups:
2
Refresh Epoch 7
300 100
10.1.34.3 from 10.1.34.3 (10.1.100.3)
Origin IGP, localpref 100, valid, external
rx pathid: 0, tx pathid: 0
Refresh Epoch 1
100
10.1.24.2 from 10.1.24.2 (10.1.100.2)
Origin IGP, metric 0, localpref 100, valid, external, best
Community: 6553620
rx pathid: 0, tx pathid: 0x0
! No need for the new community command on IOS XR.
```

The same applies for the Internet community from a configuration perspective. It is a matter
of tagging, and it will deliver to all neighbors, whether internal or external, as shown in
Example 7-56.

Example 7-56   *BGP Communities, Internet*

```
R1(config)# ip prefix-list R1_LOOP seq 5 permit 10.1.100.1/32
R1(config)# route-map MAP permit 10
R1(config-route-map)# match ip address prefix-list R1_LOOP
R1(config-route-map)# route-map INET_COMM permit 10
R1(config-route-map)# set community internet
```

```
R1(config-route-map)# router bgp 100
R1(config-router)# address-family ipv4 unicast
R1(config-router-af)# network 10.1.100.1 mask 255.255.255.255 route-map INET_COMM
```

```
R1# show bgp ipv4 unicast 10.1.100.1/32 | include Community
Community: internet
```

Community Lists

BGP community lists are used to create groups of communities and attached to route maps to better control route transportation on the Internet. It will give autonomous systems the flexibility to control and filter routes away from IPv4/IPv6 addressing. The functionality is like an ACL, but with the introduction of the **ip community-list** command. Let's quickly check the basic configuration shown in Example 7-57.

Example 7-57   *BGP Community List*

```
R3(config)# ip community-list 1 deny ?
<1-4294967295>   community number
  aa:nn             community number
  gshut             Graceful Shutdown (well-known community)
  internet          Internet (well-known community)
  local-AS          Do not send outside local AS (well-known community)
  no-advertise      Do not advertise to any peer (well-known community)
  no-export         Do not export to next AS (well-known community)
  <cr>              <cr>
R3(config)# ip community-list 1 deny 100:1
R3(config)# ip community-list 1 permit

R3(config)# route-map COMMUNITY_DENY permit 10
R3(config-route-map)# match community 1

R3(config)# router bgp 300
R3(config-router)# address-family ipv4 unicast
R3(config-router-af)# neighbor 10.1.13.1 route-map COMMUNITY_DENY in

BGP(0): 10.1.13.1 rcvd UPDATE w/ attr: nexthop 10.1.13.1, origin i, metric 0, merged
path 100, AS_PATH , community 100:1
BGP(0): 10.1.13.1 rcvd 10.1.100.1/32 -- DENIED due to: route-map;
BGP(0): 10.1.13.1 rcvd UPDATE w/ attr: nexthop 10.1.13.1, origin i, merged path 100,
AS_PATH
```

NOTE   Another community worth mentioning is the well-known community GSHUT, which works in conjunction with BGP Graceful Restart (GR), which is covered in Chapter 8, "BGP Optimization and Convergence." This community is applied to a neighbor specified by the Graceful Restart (shutting down the link is expected within seconds).

To summarize the tools we have discussed and others available to manipulate prefixes and attach communities, Table 7-5 lists the available options to use from a configuration standpoint.

Table 7-5   BGP Community Configuration Options

Configuration	Description
network command	Attach the route map directly to the network statement
aggregate-address command	Set the attribute map to the aggregate address

Configuration	Description
neighbor command	Use the route map attached to the neighbor under the BGP configuration
Redistribution	Set the community for redistributed prefixes by using the route map

BGP Peer Templates

The intention of the peer templates feature is to reduce the CPU on devices where many neighbors have a large number of configuration lines of shared policy and thus are a management burden.

There are two types of templates:

- **Session Templates:** These templates affect the actual BGP session with peers. Examples are password, remote-as, timers, and update-source.

- **Policy Templates:** These templates affect protocol-specific (NLRI) policy. Examples are next-hop-self, send-community, and route-reflector-client.

To clarify what we mean in configuration language, we have four routers inside AS 100. R2 is the route reflector, and R1, R3, and R4 are route reflector clients. We will assume a need for the route reflector to send a community to the clients. (An example could be an MPLS L3VPN environment where route target is an extended community and must be explicitly sent to the neighbors via the **neighbor** *ip-address* **send-community** command under the respective address family to interpret the prefix, as we will encounter in Chapter 12.) Example 7-58 shows the configuration with and without peer groups; this example clearly shows the reduction in configuration lines.

Example 7-58 *BGP Peer Templates*

```
R2(config)# router bgp 100
R2(config-router)# neighbor 10.1.100.1 remote-as 100
R2(config-router)# neighbor 10.1.100.3 remote-as 100
R2(config-router)# neighbor 10.1.100.4 remote-as 100
R2(config-router)# address-family ipv4 unicast
R2(config-router-af)# neighbor 10.1.100.1 activate
R2(config-router-af)# neighbor 10.1.100.3 activate
R2(config-router-af)# neighbor 10.1.100.4 activate
R2(config-router-af)# neighbor 10.1.100.1 send-community
R2(config-router-af)# neighbor 10.1.100.3 send-community
R2(config-router-af)# neighbor 10.1.100.4 send-community
R2(config-router-af)# neighbor 10.1.100.1 route-reflector-client
R2(config-router-af)# neighbor 10.1.100.3 route-reflector-client
R2(config-router-af)# neighbor 10.1.100.4 route-reflector-client

R2(config)# router bgp 100
R2(config-router)# neighbor ?
  A.B.C.D    Neighbor address
  WORD       Neighbor tag
```

```
X:X:X:X::X  Neighbor IPv6 address
R2(config-router)# neighbor GROUP peer-group
R2(config-router)# neighbor GROUP remote-as 100
R2(config-router)# neighbor GROUP update-source loopback 0
R2(config-router)# address-family ipv4 unicast
R2(config-router-af)# neighbor GROUP route-reflector-client
R2(config-router-af)# neighbor GROUP send-community
R2(config-router-af)# neighbor GROUP activate
% Activation failed : configure "bgp listener range" before activating peergroup
R2(config-router-af)# end
R2(config-router)# bgp listen range 10.1.100.0/24 peer-group GROUP
R2(config-router)# address-family ipv4 unicast
R2(config-router-af)# neighbor GROUP activate
```

Cost Community

A BGP cost community is an extended community attribute passed to iBGP and confederation peers only (not to eBGP peers). This community assists in influencing the best path selection process by customizing local preference.

The syntax used for configuring this community is **set extcommunity** cost {*Community ID*} {*Cost Value*}. (This will be attached to a route map, and the route map will be applied internally on a neighbor basis.) If two paths have the same cost value, the lower-cost community ID will be preferred.

We will use the topology in Figure 7-18 to demonstrate the concept.

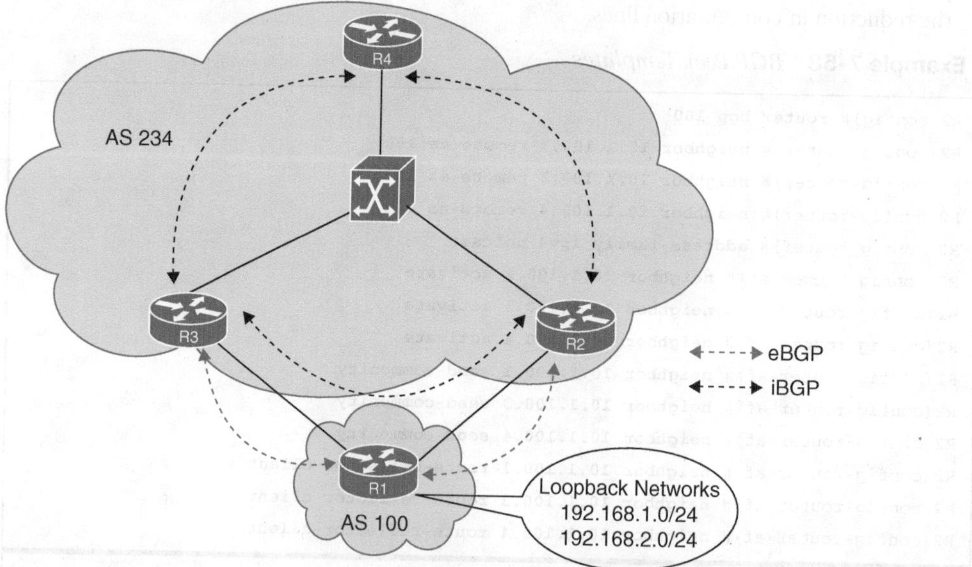

Figure 7-18 *BGP Cost Community Demonstration Example*

Before making any changes, let's see the output of the BGP table from an R4 perspective, as shown in Example 7-59.

Example 7-59   *BGP Table Output*

```
R4# show bgp ipv4 unicast | begin Network
Network             Next Hop            Metric LocPrf Weight Path
 i  192.168.1.0        10.1.100.3                  0    100      0 100 i
*>i                    10.1.100.2                  0    100      0 100 i
*i  192.168.2.0        10.1.100.3                  0    100      0 100 i
*>i                    10.1.100.2                  0    100      0 100 i
```

Now, we will define an ACL to match the target prefix for which R4 wants to adjust the cost community (192.168.1.0/24), define the route map, and then apply the route map per neighbor. Example 7-60 shows how to do this.

Example 7-60   *BGP Cost Community*

```
R4(config)# ip prefix-list R1_LOOP1 permit 192.168.1.0/24
R4(config)# route-map COMM_MAP permit 10
R4(config-route-map)# match ip add prefix R1_LOOP1
R4(config-route-map)# set extcommunity cost 1 1
R4(config-route-map)# route-map COMM_MAP permit 20
R4(config-route-map)# router bgp 234
R4(config-router)# neighbor 10.234.234.3 route-map COMM_MAP in

R4# show bgp ipv4 unicast | begin Network
Network             Next Hop            Metric LocPrf Weight Path
* i  192.168.1.0       10.1.100.2                  0    100      0 100 i
*>i                    10.1.100.3                  0    100      0 100 i
*>i  192.168.2.0       10.1.100.2                  0    100      0 100 i
* i                    10.1.100.3                  0    100      0 100 i

R4# show bgp ipv4 unicast 192.168.1.0
BGP routing table entry for 192.168.1.0/24, version 2
Paths: (2 available, best #2, table default)
Not advertised to any peer
Refresh Epoch 1
100
10.1.100.2 (metric 2) from 10.1.100.2 (10.1.100.2)
Origin IGP, metric 0, localpref 100, valid, internal
rx pathid: 0, tx pathid: 0
Refresh Epoch 1
100
10.1.100.3 (metric 2) from 10.1.100.3 (10.1.100.3)
Origin IGP, metric 0, localpref 100, valid, internal, best
Extended Community: Cost:igp:1:1
rx pathid: 0, tx pathid: 0x0
```

Regular Expressions

Regular expressions are strings of special characters that can be used to search and find character patterns. Regular expressions are used often for BGP route manipulation or filtering. We'll look at some useful regular expressions, but first let's look at the different characters that can be used, as depicted in Table 7-6.

Table 7-6   Regular Expression Characters

Character	Meaning
?	Repeats the previous character one or zero times.
*	Repeats the previous character zero or many times.
+	Repeats the previous character one or more times.
^	Matches the beginning of a string.
$	Matches the end of a string.
[]	Is a range.
_	Matches the space between AS numbers or the end of the AS-PATH list.
\	Is an escape character. You'll need this for BGP confederations.

Table 7-7 shows sample regular expressions and what output is associated with each expression.

Table 7-7   Regular Expression Examples

Regular Expression	Description
_51$	Matches prefixes that originated in AS 51. The $ ensures that it's the beginning of the AS-PATH.
^$	Matches locally originated routes.
^51_	Matches prefixes from AS 51 that are directly connected to our AS.
51	Matches prefixes that transit AS 51.

We will use Example 7-61 to examine some of these regular expressions to see the differences in output based on what has been placed in the command.

Example 7-61   *BGP Regular Expressions*

```
R1# show bgp ipv4 unicast regexp ^$ | begin Network
     Network          Next Hop            Metric LocPrf Weight Path
 *>    10.1.100.1/32    0.0.0.0                  0          32768 i
 r>i  10.1.100.2/32    10.1.100.2               0    100       0 i


R1# show bgp ipv4 unicast regexp _300$ | begin Network
 Network          Next Hop            Metric LocPrf Weight Path
 * i  10.1.100.3/32    10.1.24.4                       100     0 400 300 i
 *>                    10.1.13.3                0             0 300 i


R1# show bgp ipv4 unicast regexp 300 | begin Network
 Network          Next Hop            Metric LocPrf Weight Path
 * i  10.1.100.3/32    10.1.24.4                       100     0 400 300 i
```

```
 *>                 10.1.13.3                      0              0 300 i
 *>    10.1.100.4/32  10.1.13.3                                   0 300 400 i

R1# show bgp ipv4 unicast regexp .* | begin Network
       Network          Next Hop          Metric LocPrf Weight Path
 *>    10.1.100.1/32    0.0.0.0                 0              32768 i
 r>i   10.1.100.2/32    10.1.100.2              0      100       0 i
 * i   10.1.100.3/32    10.1.24.4                      100     0 400 300 i
 *>                     10.1.13.3               0              0 300 i
 * i   10.1.100.4/32    10.1.24.4               0      100     0 400 i
 *>                     10.1.13.3                              0 300 400 i
! Similar command is used on IOS XR: show bgp regexp regular expression.
```

Filter Lists

As we mentioned, one of the main use cases for using regular expressions is to precisely filter
output based on a certain criterion (for example, a prefix originated in an autonomous system
or prefix passing through an autonomous system). However, we could use these regular expressions in a filtering process and gain more granular control on the traffic entering or leaving an
autonomous system. We can accomplish this by defining an access list for a specific regular
expression (like an IP ACL but for regular expressions instead of IP addresses), creating a filter
list, and attaching it per neighbor under BGP configuration mode for the functional address
family. Let's examine a quick command set by going through Example 7-62.

Example 7-62 *BGP Filter List Using Regular Expressions*

```
R1# show bgp ipv4 unicast | begin Network
       Network          Next Hop          Metric LocPrf Weight Path
 *>    10.1.100.1/32    0.0.0.0                 0              32768 i
 r>i   10.1.100.2/32    10.1.100.2              0      100       0 i
 *>    10.1.100.3/32    10.1.13.3               0              0 300 i
 * i                    10.1.100.2                     100     0 400 300 i
 *>i   10.1.100.4/32    10.1.100.2              0      100     0 400 i
 *                      10.1.13.3                              0 300 400 i

R1(config)# ip as-path access-list 1 deny _300$
! We are denying the prefixes originated in AS 300 (as mentioned, the $ will
! ensure AS 300 is the beginning of the AS-PATH).
R1(config)# ip as-path access-list 1 permit .*
! Like an ACL, permit any any in simple words.
R1(config)# router bgp 100
R1(config-router)# address-family ipv4 unicast
R1(config-router-af)# neighbor 10.1.13.3 filter-list 1 in
R1# clear bgp ipv4 unicast * soft
! Do not forget to clear the session as filtering will not take place (until for
! sure the neighbor is down for some reason).

R1# show bgp ipv4 unicast | begin Network
       Network          Next Hop          Metric LocPrf Weight Path
 *>    10.1.100.1/32    0.0.0.0                 0              32768 i
```

```
r>i   10.1.100.2/32      10.1.100.2                    0     100      0 i
*>i   10.1.100.3/32      10.1.100.2                          100      0 400 300 i
*>i   10.1.100.4/32      10.1.100.2                    0     100      0 400 i
*                        10.1.13.3                                    0 300 400 i
! As we see, the prefix 10.1.100.3/32 which has the next-hop of 10.1.13.3 has gone
! (though, we learned it via a different path as AS 300 is not the beginning of the
! AS-PATH).

R1# show bgp ipv4 unicast regexp _300$ | begin Network
     Network            Next Hop          Metric LocPrf Weight Path
*>i  10.1.100.3/32      10.1.100.2                    100      0 400 300 i
```

Use Case: BGP Transit AS and no-export community

By default, eBGP neighbors will advertise prefixes learned from eBGP neighbors to other eBGP neighbors. Where could you face an issue like this, considering the big picture of the Internet and the interconnected autonomous systems? The answer is when you are multihomed to uplink providers for which they are going to use your own AS as a transit AS.

We have several techniques to deploy, such as filtering using distribute lists, filter lists, and so on. However, we can smoothly apply an easier community to avoid being a transit AS.

In the topology shown in Figure 7-19, R3 is multihomed to R1 and R2, and R1 and R2 can use R3 to communicate for certain destination prefixes, which could affect your uplink bandwidth, resources, and so on. In such a case any prefix received from R1 (Prefix 1) could be tagged with no-export community, which means it will not be advertised to other eBGP speakers such as R3. The same applies for Prefix 2, which also will be tagged once received from R2 and will not be sent to R1. Surely, we can control which prefixes that we can apply the no-export to in case some application requires a transit AS or direct peering.

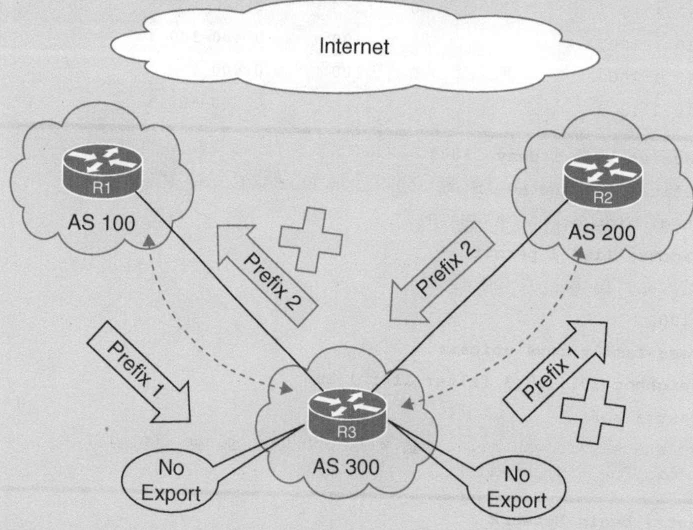

Figure 7-19 *BGP Transit AS*, **no-export community**

Mitigating the Split-Horizon Rule with Route Reflection and Confederations

> **NOTE**   While route reflection and confederations are not listed explicitly in the SPCOR 350-501 exam objectives, you will need to understand these concepts when encountering exam questions about exam objectives 2.6.a (Neighbor adjacency [BGP, OSPF, IS-IS] and 2.6.b (Route advertisement [BGP, OSPF, IS-IS]).

Within a single autonomous system, the BGP relations will be in the form of internal BGP sessions (iBGP). The assumption is that we have a full mesh of relations between the routers within the same AS. They will follow the formula of $n(n - 1)/2$, which will be of concern from a scalability perspective due to the number of established sessions as the number of routers grows.

Apart from design aspects (scalability), the advertisement of prefixes can cause confusion because the prefix learned from the iBGP peer will not be advertised to another iBGP peer in normal circumstances. The reason is that a full mesh of peering is in place. This is called the *split-horizon rule*, which is a built-in routing loop detection mechanism for BGP when running internally inside an autonomous system.

Figure 7-20 provides an illustrative overview of what we've discussed so far from a prefix advertisement perspective.

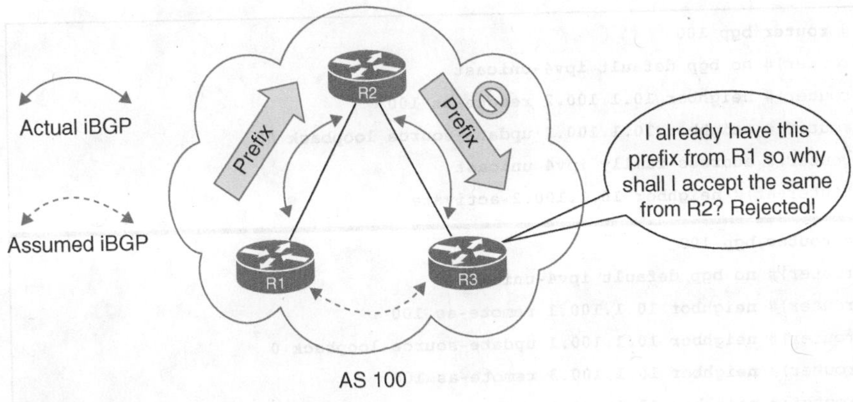

Figure 7-20   *BGP Route Reflection*

Route Reflection

RFC 1966 introduced the concept of iBGP peering to be able to reflect routes to another iBGP peer. The concept is simply including a route reflector (which is the router that will reflect the route/prefix received from iBGP peer to another iBGP peer), and the routers that use the assistance of the route reflector to reflect routes are called *route reflector clients*. It's like a client/server model.

Due to variations of deployments, three main rules apply to route reflection. Let's go through each one of these rules in detail.

Rule #1: If a route reflector receives a prefix from a non-RR client, the route reflector will advertise this prefix to the RR client but will not advertise it to the non-RR client.

We will use the sample topology in Figure 7-21 to clarify route reflector rule #1.

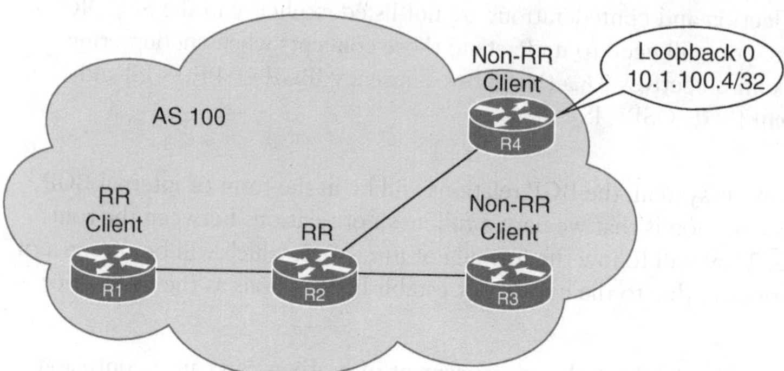

Figure 7-21 *Topology for BGP Route Reflection Rule #1*

Example 7-63 demonstrates where R2 is the route reflector, R1 is the RR client, and R2 and R3 are non-RR clients (as depicted from Figure 7-21). We will start the example with basic iBGP peering sourced from the Loopback 0 interface; we have flat OSPF area 0 within AS 100 to ensure proper loopback-to-loopback connectivity among the routers within the AS.

Example 7-63 *BGP Route Reflection Rule #1, Configuration*

```
R1(config)# router bgp 100
R1(config-router)# no bgp default ipv4-unicast
R1(config-router)# neighbor 10.1.100.2 remote-as 100
R1(config-router)# neighbor 10.1.100.2 update-source loopback 0
R1(config-router)# address-family ipv4 unicast
R1(config-router-af)# neighbor 10.1.100.2 activate

R2(config)# router bgp 100
R2(config-router)# no bgp default ipv4-unicast
R2(config-router)# neighbor 10.1.100.1 remote-as 100
R2(config-router)# neighbor 10.1.100.1 update-source loopback 0
R2(config-router)# neighbor 10.1.100.3 remote-as 100
R2(config-router)# neighbor 10.1.100.3 update-source loo0
R2(config-router)# neighbor 10.1.100.4 remote-as 100
R2(config-router)# neighbor 10.1.100.4 update-source loo0
R2(config-router)# address-family ipv4 unicast
R2(config-router-af)# neighbor 10.1.100.1 activate
R2(config-router-af)# neighbor 10.1.100.1 route-reflector-client
R2(config-router-af)# neighbor 10.1.100.3 activate
R2(config-router-af)# neighbor 10.1.100.4 activate

R3(config)# router bgp 100
R3(config-router)# no bgp default ipv4-unicast
R3(config-router)# neighbor 10.1.100.2 remote-as 100
```

```
R3(config-router)# neighbor 10.1.100.2 update-source loopback 0
R3(config-router)# address-family ipv4 unicast
R3(config-router-af)# neighbor 10.1.100.2 activate
```

```
R4(config)# router bgp 100
R4(config-router)# no bgp default ipv4-unicast
R4(config-router)# neighbor 10.1.100.2 remote-as 100
R4(config-router)# neighbor 10.1.100.2 update-source loopback 0
R4(config-router)# address-family ipv4 unicast
R4(config-router-af)# neighbor 10.1.100.2 activate
```

If we check Example 7-64, surely no routes will exist in the BGP or the RIB because we did not advertise any prefix using a network statement or redistribution.

Example 7-64   *BGP Route Reflection Rule #1, BGP Table Output*

```
R2# show bgp ipv4 unicast summary | begin Neighbor
Neighbor      V      AS MsgRcvd MsgSent    TblVer   InQ OutQ Up/Down   State/PfxRcd
10.1.100.1    4      100      4       4         1     0    0 00:00:07             0
10.1.100.3    4      100     12      12         1     0    0 00:07:46             0
10.1.100.4    4      100     12       9         1     0    0 00:07:12             0
```

Now, let's examine the first rule of BGP route reflection. To do so, we will advertise a prefix from R4 (non-RR) and check whether the RR client (R1) will receive it, as shown in Example 7-65.

Example 7-65   *BGP Route Reflection Rule #1, Network Advertisement and Debug Output*

```
R4(config)# router bgp 100
R4(config-router-af)# network 10.1.100.4 mask 255.255.255.255
```

```
R2# debug ip bgp updates
BGP(0): 10.1.100.4 rcvd UPDATE w/ attr: nexthop 10.1.100.4, origin i, localpref 100,
metric 0
BGP(0): 10.1.100.4 rcvd 10.1.100.4/32
BGP(0): Revise route installing 1 of 1 routes for 10.1.100.4/32 ->
10.1.100.4(global) to main IP table
BGP(0): (base) 10.1.100.1 send UPDATE (format) 10.1.100.4/32, next 10.1.100.4,
metric 0, path Local
```

```
R1# debug ip bgp updates
BGP(0): 10.1.100.2 rcvd UPDATE w/ attr: nexthop 10.1.100.4, origin i, localpref 100,
metric 0, originator 10.1.100.4, clusterlist 10.1.100.2
BGP(0): 10.1.100.2 rcvd 10.1.100.4/32
BGP(0): Revise route installing 1 of 1 routes for 10.1.100.4/32 ->
10.1.100.4(global) to main IP table
```

```
R3# show bgp ipv4 unicast
R3#
```

This output matches what was stated in route reflection rule #1: R1, which is the RR client, will receive the update through the RR (R2), whereas R3, the non-RR client, will not receive or install the update, as illustrated in Figure 7-22.

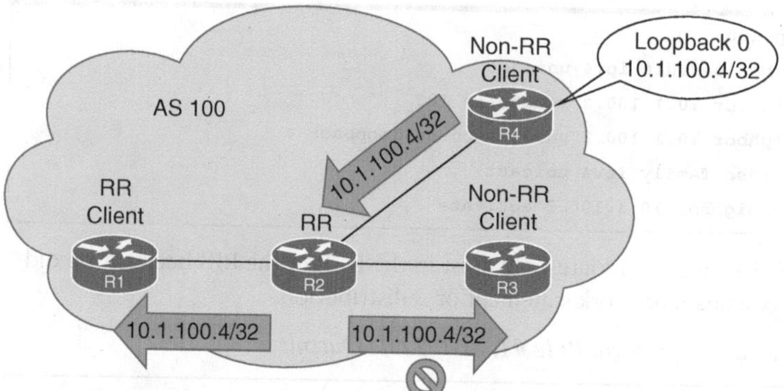

Figure 7-22 *BGP Route Reflection Rule #1*

Rule #2: If a route reflector receives a prefix from an RR client, it will advertise the prefix to the RR client(s) and non-RR client(s). However, the RR client that advertised the prefix will discard the update from the RR because it is the originator of the prefix.

Let's examine Example 7-66 for a better understanding of this rule (note that **debug bgp ipv4 unicast updates** is still in place).

Example 7-66 *BGP Route Reflection Rule #2*

```
R1(config)# router bgp 100
R1(config-router)# address-family ipv4 unicast
R1(config-router-af)# network 10.1.100.1 mask 255.255.255.255

! R1 debug output.
BGP(0): sourced route for 10.1.100.1/32 created
BGP(0): sourced route for 10.1.100.1/32 path 0xD14F234 id 0 gw 0.0.0.0 created
(weight 32768)
BGP(0): local route 10.1.100.1/32 added gw 0.0.0.0
BGP: topo global:IPv4 Unicast:base Remove_fwdroute for 10.1.100.1/32
BGP(0):  local route 10.1.100.1/32 modified rib-gw 0.0.0.0 path-gw 0.0.0.0
[0xD14F234:0]
BGP(0): redist event (4) request for 10.1.100.1/32
BGP(0) route 10.1.100.1/32 gw-1 0.0.0.0 src_proto (null) path-limit 1
BGP(0): redistributed local route 10.1.100.1/32 modified rib-gw 0.0.0.0 path-gw
0.0.0.0 [0xD14F234:0]
BGP(0): (base) 10.1.100.2 send UPDATE (format) 10.1.100.1/32, next 10.1.100.1,
metric 0, path Local

! R2 debug output.
BGP(0): 10.1.100.1 rcvd UPDATE w/ attr: nexthop 10.1.100.1, origin i, localpref 100,
metric 0
BGP(0): 10.1.100.1 rcvd 10.1.100.1/32
```

```
BGP(0): Revise route installing 1 of 1 routes for 10.1.100.1/32 ->
10.1.100.1(global) to main IP table

BGP(0): (base) 10.1.100.3 send UPDATE (format) 10.1.100.1/32, next 10.1.100.1,
metric 0, path Local
```

```
! R4 debug output.
BGP(0): 10.1.100.2 rcvd UPDATE w/ attr: nexthop 10.1.100.1, origin i, localpref 100,
metric 0, originator 10.1.100.1, clusterlist 10.1.100.2

BGP(0): 10.1.100.2 rcvd 10.1.100.1/32

BGP(0): Revise route installing 1 of 1 routes for 10.1.100.1/32 ->
10.1.100.1(global) to main IP table
```

```
! R3 debug output.
BGP(0): 10.1.100.2 rcvd UPDATE w/ attr: nexthop 10.1.100.1, origin i, localpref 100,
metric 0, originator 10.1.100.1, clusterlist 10.1.100.2

BGP(0): 10.1.100.2 rcvd 10.1.100.1/32

BGP(0): Revise route installing 1 of 1 routes for 10.1.100.1/32 ->
10.1.100.1(global) to main IP table
```

As expected, the prefix advertised by R1 (RR client) is installed in both R3 (non-RR client) and R4 (RR client). Figure 7-23 summarizes the updates we have logged.

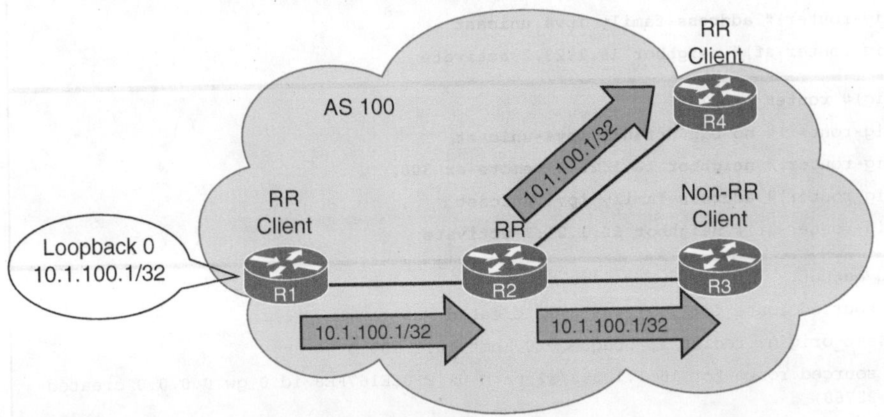

Figure 7-23 *BGP Route Reflection Rule #2*

Rule #3: If an RR receives a prefix from an eBGP peer, it will advertise the prefix to RR client(s) and non-RR client(s). We will use the topology in Figure 7-24 to validate the rule functionality.

Now, let's establish the eBGP relation between R3 (located in AS 300) and R2, which is the RR (located in AS 100), and advertise the network 10.1.100.3/32 from R3. Also, let's turn on the **debug bgp ipv4 updates**, as illustrated in Example 7-67.

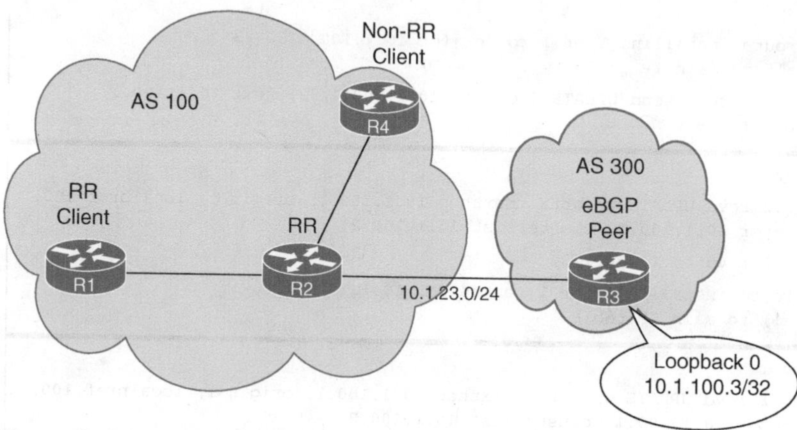

Figure 7-24 *BGP Route Reflection Rule #3*

Example 7-67 *Topology for BGP Route Reflection Rule #3*

```
R3(config)# router bgp 300
R3(config-router)# no bgp default ipv4-unicast
R3(config-router)# neighbor 10.1.23.2 remote-as 100
R3(config-router)# address-family ipv4 unicast
R3(config-router-af)# neighbor 10.1.23.2 activate
```

```
R2(config)# router bgp 100
R2(config-router)# no bgp default ipv4-unicast
R2(config-router)# neighbor 10.1.23.3 remote-as 300
R2(config-router)# address-family ipv4 unicast
R2(config-router-af)# neighbor 10.1.23.3 activate
```

```
! R3 log output.
BGP(0): sourced route for 10.1.100.3/32 created
bgp_ipv4set_origin: redist 1, opaque 0x0, net 10.1.100.3
BGP(0): sourced route for 10.1.100.3/32 path 0x7F10CE167FE8 id 0 gw 0.0.0.0 created
(weight 32768)
BGP(0): local route 10.1.100.3/32 added gw 0.0.0.0
BGP: topo global:IPv4 Unicast:base Remove_fwdroute for 10.1.100.3/32
bgp_ipv4update_origin: redist 0, opaque 0x0, net 10.1.100.3
BGP(0):  local route 10.1.100.3/32 modified rib-gw 0.0.0.0 path-gw 0.0.0.0
[0x7F10CE167FE8:0]
BGP(0): redist event (4) request for 10.1.100.3/32
BGP(0) route 10.1.100.3/32 gw-1 0.0.0.0 src_proto (null) path-limit 1
bgp_ipv4update_origin: redist 1, opaque 0x0, net 10.1.100.3
BGP(0): redistributed local route 10.1.100.3/32 modified rib-gw 0.0.0.0 path-gw
0.0.0.0 [0x7F10CE167FE8:0]
BGP(0): (base) 10.1.23.2 send UPDATE (format) 10.1.100.3/32, next 10.1.23.3, metric
0, path Local
```

```
! R1 log output.
BGP(0): 10.1.100.2 rcvd UPDATE w/ attr: nexthop 10.1.23.3, origin i, localpref 100,
metric 0, merged path 300, AS_PATH
BGP(0): 10.1.100.2 rcvd 10.1.100.3/32
BGP(0): Revise route installing 1 of 1 routes for 10.1.100.3/32 -> 10.1.23.3(global)
to main IP table
```

```
! R4 log output.
BGP(0): 10.1.100.2 rcvd UPDATE w/ attr: nexthop 10.1.23.3, origin i, localpref 100,
metric 0, merged path 300, AS_PATH
BGP(0): 10.1.100.2 rcvd 10.1.100.3/32
BGP(0): Revise route installing 1 of 1 routes for 10.1.100.3/32 -> 10.1.23.3(global)
to main IP table
```

To summarize, let's look at Figure 7-25.

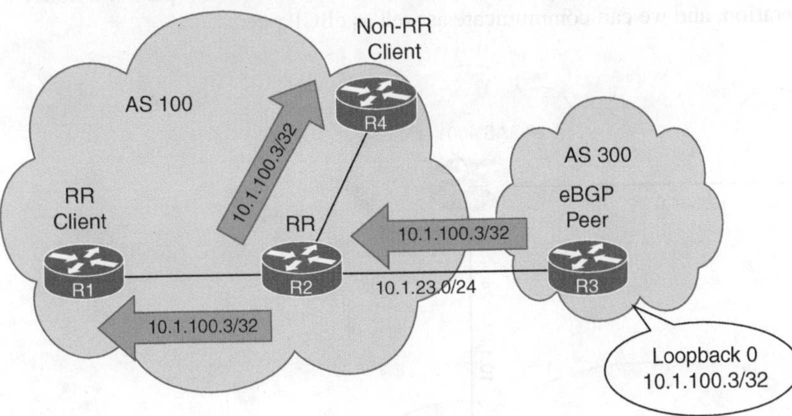

Figure 7-25 *BGP Route Reflection Rule #3*

Before moving on to the next section, let's briefly look at the configuration of BGP route reflection on IOS XR. Example 7-68 provides a reference sample of the main commands needed (assuming R5 and R6, where R5, which is IOS XR–based, is the route reflector).

Example 7-68 *BGP Route Reflection Rule #3*

```
RP/0/0/CPU0:P5(config)# router bgp 100
! As discussed, we must explicitly initialize the IPv4 address-family when dealing
! with IOS XR software.
RP/0/0/CPU0:P5(config-bgp)# address-family ipv4 unicast
RP/0/0/CPU0:P5(config-bgp)# neighbor 10.1.100.6
RP/0/0/CPU0:P5(config-bgp-nbr)# remote-as 100
RP/0/0/CPU0:P5(config-bgp-nbr)# update-source loopback 0
RP/0/0/CPU0:P5(config-bgp-nbr)# address-family ipv4 unicast
RP/0/0/CPU0:P5(config-bgp-nbr-af)# route-reflector-client
```

```
RP/0/0/CPU0:P5# show bgp neighbor 10.1.100.6 | begin For Address Family
For Address Family: IPv4 Unicast
```

```
BGP neighbor version 0

Update group: 0.1 Filter-group: 0.0  No Refresh request being processed
Route-Reflector Client
! Output omitted for brevity.
```

Confederations

Another methodology to avoid the split-horizon rule and the full mesh of iBGP sessions is confederation. The main idea is to segment the autonomous system for which we have internal BGP sessions into new sub-autonomous systems, which will show that new eBGP sessions are in place. However, no changes will be made from our eBGP sessions.

We will use the same topology as Figure 7-26 and conduct the confederation configuration on AS 100. We will segment it into two new sub-ASes: 1 and 2. We already have eBGP sessions in place from both R3 and R4 toward AS 100. Nothing will change from the perspective of R3 and R4, but we will tell our internal devices that we are now part of a newly created confederation, and we can communicate as well as eBGP peers.

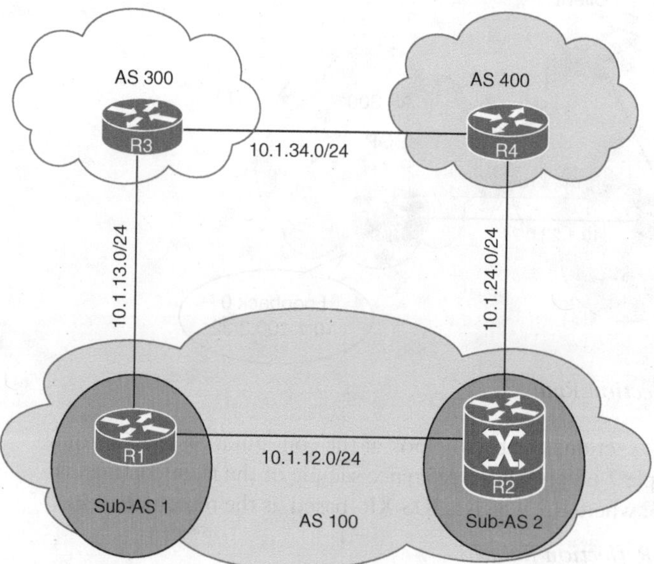

Figure 7-26 *BGP Confederation Example*

First, let's check R1 and R2 configurations, which are part of AS 100, in Example 7-69.

Example 7-69 *BGP Confederation Example, IOS*

```
R1(config)# no router bgp 100
R1(config)# router bgp 1
R1(config-router)# no bgp default ipv4-unicast
R1(config-router)# neighbor 10.1.100.2 remote-as 2
R1(config-router)# neighbor 10.1.100.2 update-source loopback 0
R1(config-router)# address-family ipv4 unicast
R1(config-router-af)# neighbor 10.1.100.2 activate
```

```
R1(config-router)# neighbor 10.1.13.3 remote-as 300
R1(config-router)# address-family ipv4 unicast
R1(config-router-af)# neighbor 10.1.13.3 activate
R1(config-router)# bgp confederation ?
identifier  Set routing domain confederation AS
peers       Peer ASs in BGP confederation
R1(config-router)# bgp confederation identifier 100
! The identified is the actual AS for which we are creating the confederation for.
R1(config-router)# bgp confederation peers 2
```

```
R1(config)# router bgp 1
R1(config-router)# neighbor 10.1.100.2 ebgp-multihop 2
! it is crucial to note that we are now establishing eBGP neighbor and sourcing the
! BGP packets from loopback and therefore ebgp-multihop command is needed.
RP/0/0/CPU0:R2(config)# no router bgp 100
RP/0/0/CPU0:R2(config)# router bgp 2
RP/0/0/CPU0:R2(config-bgp)# address-family ipv4 unicast
RP/0/0/CPU0:R2(config-bgp-af)# exit
RP/0/0/CPU0:R2(config-bgp)# neighbor 10.1.100.1
RP/0/0/CPU0:R2(config-bgp-nbr)# remote-as 1
RP/0/0/CPU0:R2(config-bgp-nbr)# update-source loopback 0
RP/0/0/CPU0:R2(config-bgp-nbr)# address-family ipv4 unicast
RP/0/0/CPU0:R2(config-bgp)# neighbor 10.1.24.4
RP/0/0/CPU0:R2(config-bgp-nbr)# remote-as 400
RP/0/0/CPU0:R2(config-bgp-nbr)# address-family ipv4 unicast
RP/0/0/CPU0:R2(config-bgp-nbr-af)# route-policy PASS in
RP/0/0/CPU0:R2(config-bgp-nbr-af)# route-policy PASS out
RP/0/0/CPU0:R2(config-bgp)# neighbor 10.1.100.1
RP/0/0/CPU0:R2(config-bgp-nbr)# address-family ipv4 unicast
RP/0/0/CPU0:R2(config-bgp-nbr)# ebgp-multihop 2
! R2 which is IOS XR based is peering with R1 as eBGP neighbor now,
! shall we define a route-policy? The answer is no. IOS XR does not
! require routers to have a route-policy in case of confederations
! even though it appears like an external peer.
RP/0/0/CPU0:R2(config-bgp-nbr-af)# commit
RP/0/0/CPU0:R2(config)# router bgp 2
RP/0/0/CPU0:R2(config-bgp)# bgp confederation identifier 100
RP/0/0/CPU0:R2(config-bgp)# bgp confederation peers 1
RP/0/0/CPU0:R2(config-bgp)# commit
```

```
R1# show bgp ipv4 unicast | begin Network
Network          Next Hop         Metric LocPrf Weight Path
*   10.1.100.3/32    10.1.24.4                  100      0 (2) 400 300 i
*>                   10.1.13.3             0             0 300 i
*   10.1.100.4/32    10.1.24.4             0    100      0 (2) 400 i
*>                   10.1.13.3                           0 300 400 i
```

```
! As we can see the AS-PATH appears like (2) 400 300
! (as an example for 10.1.100.3/32 received from 10.1.24.4).
! This value between parentheses is called AS_CONFED_SEQUENCE attribute.
! This value will be appended as the route passes from sub-AS to another
! sub-AS. Though, it will not be counted for AS-PATH best path considerations.
R1# show bgp ipv4 unicast | begin Network
     Network          Next Hop          Metric LocPrf Weight Path
 *>  10.1.100.1/32    0.0.0.0                0          32768 i
 r>  10.1.100.2/32    10.1.100.2             0    100       0 (2) i
 *   10.1.100.3/32    10.1.24.4                   100       0 (2) 400 300 i
 *>                   10.1.13.3              0              0 300 i
 *   10.1.100.4/32    10.1.24.4              0    100       0 (2) 400 i
 *>                   10.1.13.3                             0 300 400 i
! Also, the next-hop for routes (external) that passed from sub-as to
! another sub-as will have the next-hop unchanged.
```

MED and Local preference attributes are transitive to all sub-ASes but will not leave the confederation.

The AS_CONFED_SEQUENCE will be removed from the AS-PATH once the route is advertised outside the confederation, as shown in Example 7-70.

Example 7-70 *R3 BGP Table Output*

```
R3# show bgp ipv4 unicast | begin Network
     Network          Next Hop          Metric LocPrf Weight Path
 *   10.1.100.1/32    10.1.34.4                             0 400 100 i
 *>                   10.1.13.1              0              0 100 i
 *   10.1.100.2/32    10.1.34.4                             0 400 100 i
 *>                   10.1.13.1                             0 100 i
 *>  10.1.100.3/32    0.0.0.0                0          32768 i
 *>  10.1.100.4/32    10.1.34.4              0              0 400 i
```

BGP Loop Prevention

We have covered some of the built-in loop prevention mechanisms in both iBGP and eBGP environments. In iBGP, we talked about the full-mesh assumption within a single AS for which the iBGP speaker will not send an iBGP learned route to another iBGP neighbor. The reason is that an imaginary full mesh of internal BGP sessions is in place, and we showed that the solution is either to configure a full mesh of iBGP sessions—which will be considered from a scalability perspective due to the $n(n - 1)/2$ sessions produced, where n is the number of BGP speakers inside an AS—or to deploy a route reflector inside the autonomous system.

From an eBGP perspective, we have covered only the most important loop prevention mechanism in which the router will not accept a prefix where its own AS is attached. However, we intend to cover two quick techniques where we can encounter this rejection by using two tools: Allow AS, for which we will allow an update where an AS is within the AS-PATH, and AS override, where the BGP speaker will send the update (with our own AS in place) and instruct the receiver that the update came from it, not from another place.

We will use the sample topology in Figure 7-27 to demonstrate these two features.

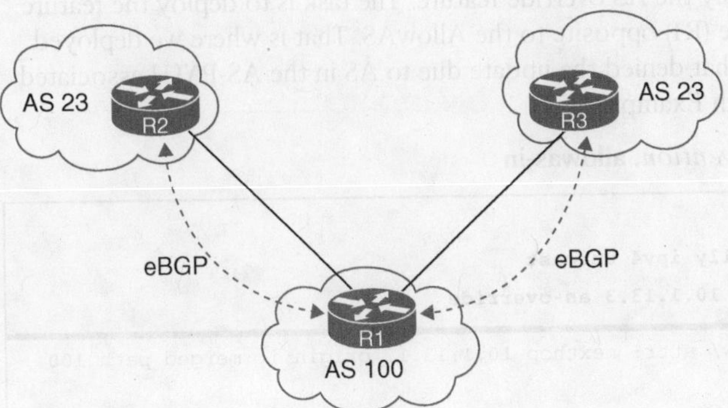

Figure 7-27 *BGP Loop Prevention Demonstration Example*

Allowas-in

R2 will advertise the prefix (10.1.100.2/32) using the **network** statement. We have turned on **debug bgp ipv4 unicast updates** on R3. Now, let's check what will take place by going through Example 7-71.

Example 7-71 *BGP Loop Prevention,* **allowas-in**

```
R2(config-router-af)# network 10.1.100.2 mask 255.255.255.255

R3# debug bgp ipv4 unicast updates
BGP updates debugging is on for address family: IPv4 Unicast
10.1.13.1 rcv UPDATE w/ attr: nexthop 10.1.13.1, origin i, originator 0.0.0.0,
merged path 100 23, AS_PATH , community , extended community , SSA attribute
BGPSSA ssacount is 0, Tunnel attribute
Tunnel encap type: 0, encap size: 0, Link-state attribute: {}, PrefixSid attribute:
BGP(0): 10.1.13.1 rcv UPDATE about 10.1.100.2/32 -- DENIED due to: AS-PATH contains
our own AS;
R3(config)# router bgp 23
R3(config-router)# address-family ipv4 unicast
R3(config-router-af)# neighbor 10.1.13.1 allowas-in
BGP: nbr_topo global 10.1.13.1 IPv4 Unicast:base (0x7F10CDE3F3F0:1) rcvd Refresh
Start-of-RIB
BGP: nbr_topo global 10.1.13.1 IPv4 Unicast:base (0x7F10CDE3F3F0:1) refresh_epoch is 4
BGP(0): 10.1.13.1 rcvd UPDATE w/ attr: nexthop 10.1.13.1, origin i, merged path 100
23, AS_PATH
BGP(0): 10.1.13.1 rcvd 10.1.100.2/32
BGP: nbr_topo global 10.1.13.1 IPv4 Unicast:base (0x7F10CDE3F3F0:1) rcvd Refresh
End-of-RIB
BGP(0): Revise route installing 1 of 1 routes for 10.1.100.2/32 -> 10.1.13.1(global)
to main IP table

R3# show bgp ipv4 unicast | begin Network
     Network          Next Hop            Metric LocPrf Weight Path
 *>  10.1.100.2/32    10.1.13.1                            0 100 23 i
```

AS Override

We will do the same now to apply the AS override feature. The task is to deploy the feature on the router sending the update (R1) opposite to the AllowAS. That is where we deployed the feature on the end speaker that denied the update due to AS in the AS-PATH associated with the update. Let's go through Example 7-72.

Example 7-72 *BGP Loop Prevention,* **allowas-in**

```
R1(config)# router bgp 100
R1(config-router)# address-family ipv4 unicast
R1(config-router-af)# neighbor 10.1.13.3 as-override

BGP(0): 10.1.13.1 rcvd UPDATE w/ attr: nexthop 10.1.13.1, origin i, merged path 100
100, AS_PATH
BGP(0): 10.1.13.1 rcvd 10.1.100.2/32
BGP(0): Revise route installing 1 of 1 routes for 10.1.100.2/32 -> 10.1.13.1(global)
to main IP table

R3# show bgp ipv4 unicast | begin Network
    Network          Next Hop            Metric LocPrf Weight Path
 *>   10.1.100.2/32    10.1.13.1                          0 100 100 i
! The AS-PATH appears as 100 100 which like we conducted prepending.
```

Troubleshooting

In this section, we examine the most common errors indicating that an unsuccessful BGP relation is in place. We rely heavily on log messages to give practical tips on how to analyze these messages and spot the workaround quickly.

ACL/Firewalls

Due to security concerns (even internally), it is possible to have a firewall that could possibly intercept BGP messages. Similarly, an ACL configured on an intermediate device could block the TCP port number that BGP uses for negotiations—in this case, it is 179.

To see this example in action, we can turn on **debug ip tcp packet** on R1 (direct BGP relation R1 → R2) and see the ports associated with the already established session, as demonstrated in Example 7-73.

Example 7-73 *BGP and TCP Interaction*

```
R1# debug ip tcp packet
tcp0: O ESTAB 10.1.100.2:179 10.1.100.1:14802 seq 1804580192
ACK 1028357032  WIN 16177
R1# show tcp brief
TCB        Local Address          Foreign Address           (state)
11DD9B28   10.1.100.1.14802       10.1.100.2.179            ESTAB

! We can configure a simple standard ACL to validate the TCP packets in action.
R1(config)# ip access-list extended DENY_BGP
R1(config-ext-nacl)# deny tcp any any eq bgp
```

```
R1(config-ext-nacl)# deny tcp any eq bgp any
R1(config)# interface GigabitEthernet0/0
R1(config-if)# ip access-group DENY_BGP in
```

```
R1# clear bgp ipv4 unicast * soft
```

```
R1# show access-lists
Extended IP access list DENY_BGP
10 deny tcp any any eq bgp (3 matches)
20 deny tcp any eq bgp any
R1# show access-lists
Extended IP access list DENY_BGP
10 deny tcp any any eq bgp (5 matches)
20 deny tcp any eq bgp any
```

As we can see, the ACL is counting after we applied the ACL on the interface that we used to build the BGP neighborship. This will simulate whether a firewall is placed in between and blocking port 179, where we will end up with a failed attempt to build a BGP peering. (BGP uses source and destination ports other than 179, depending on who originates the session. When the "client" router initiates the BGP session, it sends a request to the server with a destination port of 179 and a random source port.)

TTL

As previously established, when we try to establish an eBGP session, usually the physical interface is used as a source for BGP packets, which will automatically decrease the default TTL of 1 to 0. Don't worry; the packet has arrived due to a direct connection. However, if we decide to source the BGP packets from a loopback interface (for which we need some sort of routing to ensure loopback-to-loopback reachability), the TTL needs to be increased, made possible through the **eBGP-multihop** command. Let's check the log message we will encounter after we improperly configure the TTL value, as shown in Example 7-74.

Example 7-74   *BGP Loop Prevention,* **allowas-in**

```
R1(config)# router bgp 100
R1(config-router)# neighbor 10.1.100.2 ebgp-multihop 1

BGP: 10.1.100.1 active went from Idle to Active
BGP: 10.1.100.1 open active, local address 10.1.100.2
BGP: 10.1.100.1 open failed: Connection refused by remote host
BGP: 10.1.100.1 Active open failed - tcb is not available, open active delayed
9216ms (35000ms max, 60% jitter)
ses global 10.1.100.1 (0x7FC2B1D174D0:0) act Reset (Active open failed).
BGP: 10.1.100.1 active went from Active to Idle
BGP: nbr global 10.1.100.1 Active open failed - open timer running
BGP: nbr global 10.1.100.1 Active open failed - open timer running


R2# show bgp ipv4 unicast summary | begin Neighbor
Neighbor        V         AS MsgRcvd MsgSent   TblVer  InQ OutQ Up/Down  State/PfxRcd
10.1.100.1      4        100       0       0        1    0    0 never    Idle
```

Authentication

It is a common practice (for IGP, LDP, BGP, and so on) to have authentication to protect updates or messages. We can use the **neighbor** *ip-address* **password** *password* command to protect our BGP session. What will take place when we enable it from one place and not another or if we have mismatched passwords? Let's find out in Example 7-75.

Example 7-75 *BGP Authentication Troubleshooting*

```
R1(config-router)# neighbor 10.1.100.2 password SPCOR
%TCP-6-BADAUTH: No MD5 digest from 10.1.100.2(179) to 10.1.100.1(60769) tableid - 0
%TCP-6-BADAUTH: No MD5 digest from 10.1.100.2(179) to 10.1.100.1(60769) tableid - 0
! The No MD5 digest means the authentication is configured from one end and not
! the other.
R1# show bgp ipv4 unicast summary | include Neighbor
Neighbor        V        AS MsgRcvd MsgSent    TblVer   InQ OutQ Up/Down   State/PfxRcd
! If the authentication is configured for both peers and the Passwords do not match,
! the log message appears.
Invalid MD5 digest from 10.1.100.2(26735) to 10.1.100.1(179) tableid - 0
```

The log message will assist in determining what took place as highlighted. If we encounter the **Invalid MD5 digest** message, that means we have authentication configured at both ends, but no match. A **No MD5 digest** message indicates a missing password statement at one of the session ends.

Autonomous System

If we mistakenly configured BGP with the wrong **remote-as**, we will receive the log message generated in Example 7-76.

Example 7-76 *BGP AS Mismatch Troubleshooting*

```
%BGP-3-NOTIFICATION: sent to neighbor 10.1.100.1 passive 2/2 (peer in wrong AS)
2 bytes 0064
%BGP-4-MSGDUMP: unsupported or mal-formatted message received from 10.1.100.1:
FFFF FFFF FFFF FFFF FFFF FFFF FFFF FFFF 0039 0104 0064 00B4 0A01 6401 1C02 0601
```

Clearly, the log message indicates that the peer AS is wrong. When we use **router bgp 100** on the first BGP speaker, the **neighbor** *ip-address* **remote-as 100** should be configured on the second BGP speaker and vice versa.

Different Address Families

As we mentioned, the BGP session will try to come up using the IPv4 AF by default. If we disable the default behavior by using the **no bgp default ipv4-unicast** command from the global BGP configuration, then we must activate under the target address family on both peers. What message will we encounter if the address families at both ends are different? We'll see in Example 7-77.

Example 7-77 *BGP Different Address Family Troubleshooting*

```
R2(config-router)# address-family vpnv4 unicast
R2(config-router-af)# neighbor 10.1.100.1 activate
! R1 is configured with address-family ipv4 unicast
%BGP-5-NBR_RESET: Neighbor 10.1.100.1 passive reset (BGP Notification sent)
%BGP-5-ADJCHANGE: neighbor 10.1.100.1 passive Down AFI/SAFI not supported
%BGP_SESSION-5-ADJCHANGE: neighbor 10.1.100.1 VPNv4 Unicast topology base removed
from session  Capability changed
%BGP-3-NOTIFICATION: sent to neighbor 10.1.100.1 passive 2/8 (no supported AFI/SAFI)
3 bytes 000000
```

As discussed earlier in the chapter, the BGP AFI/SAFI associated attributes are carried inside the BGP update message. If different AFIs are present and do not match, we will face failure in building the BGP relationship.

MTU

A **maximum transmission unit (MTU)** is one of the most important aspects of the physical layer at which network devices initially start to communicate. The MTU is an interface-level aspect. These MTU values could change from device to device, depending on the software as well.

An excellent resource for troubleshooting this issue is *Troubleshoot BGP Neighbor Flaps with MTU*, available at https://www.cisco.com/c/en/us/support/docs/ip/border-gateway-protocol-bgp/116377-troubleshoot-bgp-mtu.html.

Exam Preparation Tasks

As mentioned in the section "How to Use This Book" in the Introduction, you have a few choices for exam preparation: the exercises here, Chapter 23, "Final Preparation," and the exam simulation questions in the Pearson Test Prep Software Online.

Review All Key Topics

Review the most important topics in this chapter, noted with the Key Topic icon in the margin of the page. Table 7-8 lists a reference of these key topics and the page numbers on which each is found.

Table 7-8 Key Topics for Chapter 7

Key Topic Element	Description	Page Number
Paragraph	BGP and eBGP TTL behavior interaction	235
Section	BGP ASN Representation	236
Section	BGP Neighbor States	239
Paragraph	BGP and TCP interaction	243
Section	BGP Address Families	244
List	BGP prefix advertisement	247
Figure 7-6	BGP Prefix Advertisement, Installing Inside Global RIB	248

Key Topic Element	Description	Page Number
Figure 7-7	BGP Path Attributes	249
Paragraph	IOS XR BGP RPL	251
List	BGP path selection criteria	255
Paragraph	iBGP neighborship establishment using loopback	260
Example 7-30	BGP AS-PATH Prepending on IOS XR	264
Section	MED	268
Section	Accumulated IGP (AIGP)	275
Table 7-3	BGP **aggregate-address** Additional Keywords	280
List	BGP well-known communities	283
Paragraph	Service provider predefined BGP communities	286
Table 7-6	Regular Expression Characters	294
Section	Mitigating the Split-Horizon Rule with Route Reflection and Confederations	297
Section	BGP Loop Prevention	306

Define Key Terms

Define the following key terms from this chapter and check the answers in the glossary:

Accumulated IGP (AIGP), Address Family Identifier (AFI), Autonomous System (AS), Border Gateway Protocol (BGP), maximum transmission unit (MTU), Multi-Exit Discriminator (MED), Network Layer Reachability Information (NLRI), Regional Internet Registry (RIR), Subsequent Address Family Identifier (SAFI), Time to Live (TTL)

Command Reference to Check Your Memory

This section includes the most important commands covered in this chapter. You might not need to memorize the complete syntax of every command, but you should be able to remember the basic keywords that are needed.

To test your memory of the commands, cover the right side of Table 7-9 with a piece of paper, read the description on the left side, and then see how much of the command you can remember.

The SPCOR 350-501 exam focuses on practical, hands-on skills that are used by networking professionals. Therefore, you should be able to identify the commands needed to configure and test. Note that not all commands are fully covered in the chapter, but their presence in the following table should lead you to investigate them further to understand this technology.

Table 7-9 BGP Commands to Know

Task	Command Syntax
Add any IPv4 unicast commands specifically under the IPv4 unicast family.	**no bgp default ipv4-unicast**
Define BGP neighbor IP address with the AS in which the neighbor is located	**neighbor** *ip-address* **remote-as** *as-number*

Task	Command Syntax
Change the TTL value for eBGP neighbors to account for the hops between eBGP neighbors when using loopback interfaces as a source for BGP packets	**neighbor** *ip-address* **ebgp-multihop** *TTL-value*
Specify that autonomous system (AS) numbers greater than 65535 be shown in dotted integer format for all **show** commands, including running-configuration	**bgp asnotation dot**
Display which routes are advertised to a specific neighbor	**show bgp ipv4 unicast neighbors** *ip-address* **advertised-routes**
Display any subnets of the network you specified to see if they are present in the routing table	**show bgp ipv4 unicast** *network subnet-mask* **longer-prefixes**
Use this local display command to change the 32-bit format in AA:NN format (4 bytes)	**ip bgp-community new-format**
Prepend the list of the configured AS numbers to the AS-PATH attribute of the routes	**set as-path prepend** *as-number*
Display routes matching the specified regular expression	**show bgp ipv4 unicast regexp ^$**
Match (permit) the AS patterns you want	**ip as-path access-list** *ACL-number*
Define a password (authentication) for the BGP speaker to protect BGP updates	**neighbor** *ip-address* **password** *password*
Enable BGP to establish a connection with external peers residing on networks that are not directly connected	**neighbor** *ip-address* **ttl-security hops** *number*
Copy the autonomous system of the neighbor that advertises the prefix and matches the route map to the AS-PATH	**set as-path prepend last-as** *number*
Ensure the comparison of the MED for paths from neighbors in different autonomous systems	**bgp deterministic-med**
Enable the comparison of the Multi-Exit Discriminator (MED) for paths from neighbors in different autonomous systems	**bgp always-compare-med**
Specify load sharing for the eBGP and iBGP features to configure multipath load balancing with both (eBGP) and (iBGP) paths in BGP networks	**Maximum-paths**
Redistribute OSPF with the possibility to determine the route type, whether internal or external	**redistribute ospf** *process-ID* **match** *route-type*
Identify the specified neighbor as a client and the local router as a route reflector	**neighbor** *ip-address* **route-reflector-client**

Task	Command Syntax
Specify the BGP process for the main AS of the confederation	**bgp confederation identifier** *as-number*
List all the autonomous systems that are part of the same confederation	**bgp confederation peers** *as-number*
Allow the BGP speaker to accept the BGP updates even if its own BGP AS is in the AS-Path attribute	**neighbor** *ip-address* **allowas-in**
Change the AS in outgoing BGP updates	**neighbor** *ip-address* **as-override**

Review Questions

As a part of the review, we encourage you to provide *a single-sentence answer* (keep your answers as short as possible) to the following questions. If you struggle to complete this in a single sentence, this answer may indicate a lack of clarity or reveal gaps in your understanding. We have constructed these questions to help you consolidate this chapter's information and extract the essence of the covered content.

The answers to these questions appear in Appendix A. For more practice with exam format questions, use the Pearson Test Prep Software Online.

1. What would be an issue to consider when implementing confederation from a neighborship perspective?

2. What would be a well-known way for large service providers to alter the traffic path and manipulate BGP path attributes?

3. What is the impact of inventing BGP address families?

4. What could be a valid use case for the BGP Accumulated IGP (AIGP) attribute?

5. Why would we choose loopback interfaces as a source for BGP sessions?

Bibliography

T. Bates and R. Chandra. RFC 1966, *BGP Route Reflection: An Alternative to Full Mesh IBGP*, IETF, https://www.ietf.org/rfc/rfc1966.txt, June 1996.

BGP MTU Troubleshooting. https://www.cisco.com/c/en/us/support/docs/ip/border-gateway-protocol-bgp/116377-troubleshoot-bgp-mtu.html, November 2023.

Cisco Systems. *How to Optimize BGP Path Using AIGP.* https://www.cisco.com/c/en/us/support/docs/multiprotocol-label-switching-mpls/mpls/221236-how-to-optimize-bgp-path-using-aigp.html, December 2023.

B. Edgeworth, A. Foss, and R. Garza Rios. *IP Routing on Cisco IOS, IOS XE, and IOS XR: An Essential Guide to Understanding and Implementing IP Routing Protocols.* Cisco Press, 2014.

V. Jain and B. Edgeworth. *Troubleshooting BGP: A Practical Guide to Understanding and Troubleshooting BGP.* Cisco Press, 2016.

P. Mohapatra, R. Fernando, E. Rosen, and J. Uttaro. RFC 7311, *The Accumulated IGP Metric Attribute for BGP*, IETF, https://www.ietf.org/rfc/rfc7311.txt, August 2014.

Y. Rekhter and T. Li. RFC 1654, *A Border Gateway Protocol 4 (BGP-4)*, IETF, https://www.ietf.org/rfc/rfc1654.txt, July 1994.

RIPE Database. https://apps.db.ripe.net/db-web-ui/lookup?source=ripe-nonauth&key=AS3356&type=aut-num

The 16-bit AS Number Report. https://www.potaroo.net/tools/asn16/, August 2024.

## CHAPTER 8

BGP Optimization and Convergence

This chapter covers the following exam topics:

2.4 Implement BGP (v4 and v6 for IBGP and EBGP)

- 2.4.d Path selection
- 2.4.g Additional paths
- 2.4.h PIC

When a change occurs in the reachability of one or more prefixes, routing protocols need to adapt to that change and reach a new stable state. This process is called *convergence*. How fast the Border Gateway Protocol (BGP) converges, and changes occur during the convergence process, depends on four conditions:

- How fast BGP detects that a neighbor has become unreachable
- How many routing changes BGP needs to go through before a new stable state is reached
- The time between iterations
- If backup paths are immediately available or need one or more iterations to become available

"Do I Know This Already?" Quiz

The "Do I Know This Already?" quiz allows you to assess whether you should read this entire chapter thoroughly or jump to the "Exam Preparation Tasks" section. If you are in doubt about your answers to these questions or your own assessment of your knowledge of the topics, read the entire chapter. Table 8-1 lists the major headings in this chapter and their corresponding "Do I Know This Already?" quiz questions. You can find the answers in Appendix A, "Answers to the 'Do I Know This Already?' Quizzes and Review Questions."

Table 8-1 "Do I Know This Already?" Section-to-Question Mapping

Foundation Topics Section	Questions
Minimum Route Advertisement Interval (MRAI)	1
Fast Peering Session Deactivation	2
Next-Hop Tracking	3–4
BGP Route Dampening	5

1. What is the default advertisement interval for eBGP speakers on IOS XR–based software?

   a.   0 seconds

   b.   30 seconds

   c.   15 seconds

   d.   60 seconds

2. By default, what is the holdtime for tearing down an eBGP session?

   a.   60 seconds

   b.   180 seconds

   c.   190 seconds

   d.   30 seconds

3. When negotiations take place to establish a BGP session, a timer is triggered with a default value of 120 seconds. What is the name of this timer?

   a.   Update-delay

   b.   Session-delay

   c.   Hold-time

   d.   Keepalive

4. BGP next-hop tracking aims to enhance the convergence time by

   a.   validating BGP next hop for routes installed in the FIB.

   b.   validating BGP next hop for routes installed in the RIB.

   c.   adjusting the metric for unavailable next hops to the maximum value.

   d.   manipulating the router ID of the BGP speaker that first discovered the nonavailable BGP next hop.

5. When a prefix is dampened, its state changed as which option:

   a.   History → Damp

   b.   Valid → Damp

   c.   History → Not available

   d.   History → Invalid

Foundation Topics

Minimum Route Advertisement Interval (MRAI)

The **Minimum Route Advertisement Interval (MRAI)** determines how much time should elapse before an advertisement or withdrawal of routes to a BGP neighbor occurs. This does not necessarily mean that periodic updates are tied to this timer. The idea is to wait for a proper time before sending a bunch of updates to a neighbor.

The default value for eBGP neighbors is 30 seconds, and for iBGP neighbors, it is 0 seconds. The purpose is to make the network more stable and less prone to flapping incidents. Instead of constantly sending updates (when you receive a number of prefixes), you wait for the interval after sending the first group of updates.

In this chapter, we will use the sample topology in Figure 8-1 to establish the iBGP neighborship between R1 and R2 (located in AS 12) and an eBGP neighborship between R2 and R3 (R3 located in AS 3) with no route advertisements. A flat OSPF area 0 is running inside AS 12 for proper loopback reachability and successful neighborship between R1 and R2.

NOTE We are using public autonomous systems for illustration purposes only. In production, your ISP will assign this number to you to establish proper connectivity.

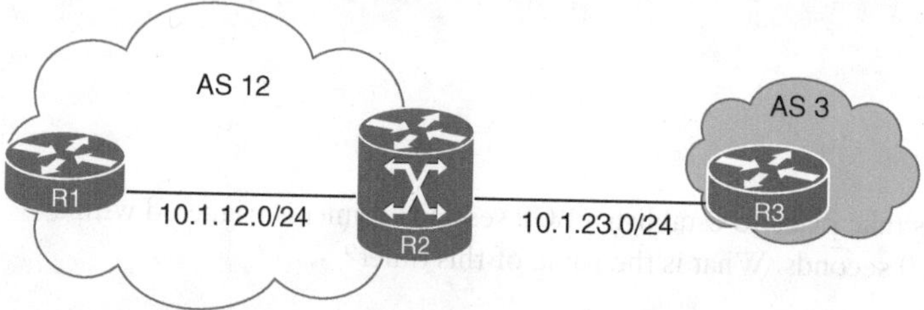

Figure 8-1 *MRAI Sample Topology*

We covered the basic configurations of BGP for both IOS and IOS XR operating systems in Chapter 7, "BGP Fundamentals." Now, let's examine the default values for both iBGP and eBGP, as discussed at the beginning of this section. Example 8-1 lists the needed command for validating the MRAI values.

Example 8-1 *Validating the BGP Advertisement-Interval Value*

```
R1# show bgp ipv4 unicast neighbors | include advertisement
  Default minimum time between advertisement runs is 0 seconds

RP/0/0/CPU0:R2# show bgp ipv4 unicast neighbors 10.1.100.1 | include advertisement
  Minimum time between advertisement runs is 0 secs

RP/0/0/CPU0:R2# show bgp ipv4 unicast neighbors 10.1.23.3 | include advertisement
  Minimum time between advertisement runs is 30 secs
  Policy for incoming advertisements is PASS
  Policy for outgoing advertisements is PASS
```

As can be confirmed from the output, the default advertisement interval for iBGP neighbors is 0, and for eBGP, it is 30 seconds. The MRAI value is configured per neighbor. Example 8-2 shows the command needed to alter the MRAI value.

Example 8-2   *BGP Advertisement-Interval Commands*

```
!IOS Advertisement-interval manipulation
R1(config)# router bgp 12
R1(config-router)# address-family ipv4 unicast
R1(config-router-af)# neighbor 10.1.100.2 advertisement-interval ?
  <0-600>  time in seconds
```

```
! IOS XR Advertisement-interval manipulation
RP/0/0/CPU0:R2(config)# router bgp 12
RP/0/0/CPU0:R2(config-bgp)# neighbor 10.1.100.1
RP/0/0/CPU0:R2(config-bgp-nbr)# advertisement-interval ?
  <0-600>  time in seconds
```

Next, let's configure a new loopback interface on R2 and advertise it under the IPv4 address family, as depicted in Example 8-3, and then check the time difference before and after the new route advertisement. Simultaneously, we will turn on debugging for BGP updates on R3 (which is the eBGP neighbor).

Example 8-3   *Testing the BGP Advertisement-Interval*

```
RP/0/0/CPU0:R2# configure terminal
RP/0/0/CPU0:R2(config)# interface loopback 1
RP/0/0/CPU0:R2(config-if)# ipv4 address 172.16.2.2/32
```

```
R3# show clock
*09:23:06.234
```

```
RP/0/0/CPU0:R2(config-bgp)# address-family ipv4 unicast
RP/0/0/CPU0:R2(config-bgp-af)# network 172.16.2.2/32
RP/0/0/CPU0:R2(config-bgp-af)# commit
```

```
09:23:36.433: BGP(0): 10.1.23.2 rcvd UPDATE w/ attr: nexthop 10.1.23.2, origin i,
metric 0, merged path 12, AS_PATH
09:23:36.433: BGP(0): 10.1.23.2 rcvd 172.16.2.2/32
09:23:36.433: BGP(0): Revise route installing 1 of 1 routes for 172.16.2.2/32 ->
10.1.23.2(global) to main IP table
! We committed the changes at 23:06 and we can see the changes take place at 23:36.
R3# show clock
*09:23:40.349
```

Fast Peering Session Deactivation

Usually, eBGP peering is built between direct neighbors using the IP addresses of physical interfaces. By default, the holdtime for tearing down the eBGP session is 180 seconds, and the keepalive messages are sent between neighbors every 60 seconds (Holdtime = Keepalive * 3).

We will refer to Figure 8-1 to demonstrate the functionality of this feature. The first thing to do is to validate the timer values, as depicted in Example 8-4.

Example 8-4   *BGP Hold and Keepalive Timers (Default)*

```
R3# show ip bgp neighbors | include hold
  Last read 00:00:34, last write 00:00:40, hold time is 180, keepalive interval is
60 seconds
minRTT: 21 ms, maxRTT: 1000 ms, ACK hold: 200 ms
```

```
RP/0/0/CPU0:R2# show bgp ipv4 unicast neighbors 10.1.23.3 | include hold
  Configured hold time: 180, keepalive: 60, min acceptable hold time: 3
  Threshold for warning message 75%, restart interval 0 min
```

Now, we will introduce a failure on R2 on the interface connected to R3 (which forms the eBGP peering) and track the neighborship by turning on the **debug ip routing** command on R3, as shown in Example 8-5.

Example 8-5   *BGP Hold and Keepalive Timers Tracking*

```
RP/0/0/CPU0:R2(config)# interface GigabitEthernet0/0/0/3
RP/0/0/CPU0:R2(config-if)# shutdown
RP/0/0/CPU0:R2(config-if)# commit
```

```
11:17:42.912: %BGP-3-NOTIFICATION: sent to neighbor 10.1.23.2 4/0 (hold time
expired) 0 bytes
11:17:42.912: %BGP-5-NBR_RESET: Neighbor 10.1.23.2 reset (BGP Notification sent)
11:17:42.913: BGP(0): no valid path for 172.16.2.2/32
11:17:42.913: %BGP-5-ADJCHANGE: neighbor 10.1.23.2 Down BGP Notification sent
11:17:42.913: %BGP_SESSION-5-ADJCHANGE: neighbor 10.1.23.2 IPv4 Unicast topology
base removed from session  BGP Notification sent
11:17:42.914: BGP: topo global:IPv4 Unicast:base Remove_fwdroute for 172.16.2.2/32
11:17:42.914: RT: del 172.16.2.2 via 10.1.23.2, bgp metric [20/0]
11:17:42.914: RT: delete subnet route to 172.16.2.2/32
```

The primary objective of the BGP **fast-external-fallover** command is to immediately terminate the eBGP session without waiting for the hold timer to expire when the directly connected link used for eBGP session establishment goes down.

Now, let's walk through the testing of this feature functionality by examining Example 8-6.

Example 8-6   *Disable BGP Fast-External-Fallover*

```
R3# debug bgp ipv4 unicast 10.1.23.2
BGP debugging is on for neighbor 10.1.23.2 for address family: IPv4 Unicast
R3(config)# router bgp 3
R3(config-router)# no bgp fast-external-fallover
R3(config)# interface GigabitEthernet0/0
R3(config-if)# shutdown
```

```
13:00:01.849: BGP: 10.1.23.2 resetting - interface GigabitEthernet0/0 down
13:00:01.849: %BGP-5-NBR_RESET: Neighbor 10.1.23.2 reset (Interface flap)
13:00:01.849: BGP: ses global 10.1.23.2 (0xE10A1D0:1) Reset (Interface flap).
13:00:01.851: BGP: nbr_topo global 10.1.23.2 IPv4 Unicast:base (0xE10A1D0:1) NSF
delete stale NSF not active
13:00:01.851: BGP: nbr_topo global 10.1.23.2 IPv4 Unicast:base (0xE10A1D0:1) NSF no
stale paths state is NSF not active
13:00:01.852: BGP: nbr_topo global 10.1.23.2 IPv4 Unicast:base (0xE10A1D0:1)
Resetting ALL counters.
13:00:01.852: BGP: 10.1.23.2 closing
* 13:00:01.852: BGP: ses global 10.1.23.2 (0xE10A1D0:1) Session close and reset
neighbor 10.1.23.2 topostate
13:00:01.852: BGP: nbr_topo global 10.1.23.2 IPv4 Unicast:base (0xE10A1D0:1)
Resetting ALL counters.
* 13:00:01.852: BGP: 10.1.23.2 went from Established to Idle
13:00:01.852: %BGP-5-ADJCHANGE: neighbor 10.1.23.2 Down Interface flap
13:00:01.853: %BGP_SESSION-5-ADJCHANGE: neighbor 10.1.23.2 IPv4 Unicast topology
base removed from session  Interface flap
13:00:01.853: BGP: ses global 10.1.23.2 (0xE10A1D0:1) Removed topology IPv4
Unicast:base
13:00:01.853: BGP: ses global 10.1.23.2 (0xE10A1D0:1) Removed last topology
13:00:01.853: BGP: nbr global 10.1.23.2 Open active delayed 12288ms (35000ms max,
60% jitter)
13:00:01.853: BGP: nbr global 10.1.23.2 Active open failed - open timer running
13:00:55.125: BGP: 10.1.23.2 Active open failed - update-source NULL is not
available, open active delayed 10240ms (35000ms max, 60% jitter)
```

The default behavior is that the **fast-external-fallover** is turned on by default, which means that there is no waiting for the holdtime to expire.

Next, let's disable the behavior by shutting down the interface serving the primary interconnection, as shown in Example 8-7. Then, we can see the difference by tracking the timestamps associated with the log messages generated after the **debug ip bgp 10.1.23.2** command.

Example 8-7   *BGP Fast-External-Fallover Tracking*

```
R3(config)# interface GigabitEthernet0
R3(config-if)# shutdown

13:38:46.657: %LINK-5-CHANGED: Interface GigabitEthernet0/0, changed state to admin-
istratively down
13:38:47.657: %LINEPROTO-5-UPDOWN: Line protocol on Interface GigabitEthernet0/0,
changed state to down
! The difference between the interface flap and the closing of the BGP session is
! around
! 180 seconds which is the default hold time.
13:41:40.427: BGP: 10.1.23.2 connection timed out 180669ms (last update) 180000ms
(hold time)
! Output omitted for brevity
```

NOTE This feature improves the convergence time for the BGP instance; however, if flapping links do exist in the network, they will cause instabilities in the BGP tables. Additionally, this feature is disabled by default for iBGP neighbors because iBGP sessions typically use loopback interfaces as the source. Since there is usually internal redundancy to ensure the loopbacks can reach each other, maintaining the iBGP session is more reliable.

Next-Hop Tracking

BGP uses a mechanism called a *scanner* to validate the next-hop addresses and conduct the best-path calculations. By default, this mechanism runs every 60 seconds.

What is the impact of a 60-second scan time? If the next hop has failed and we must wait this long, routing loops or black holes could be introduced before the problem is resolved.

The main goal of next-hop tracking is to enhance convergence time by validating the BGP next hop for the routes installed in the **routing information base (RIB)**. This process is event-driven, which means it will detect changes in the routing table and, accordingly, schedule a next-hop scan to adjust next hops.

The default delay for scan time after detecting a change is 5 seconds.

We will use Figure 8-2 to go through the details of this feature.

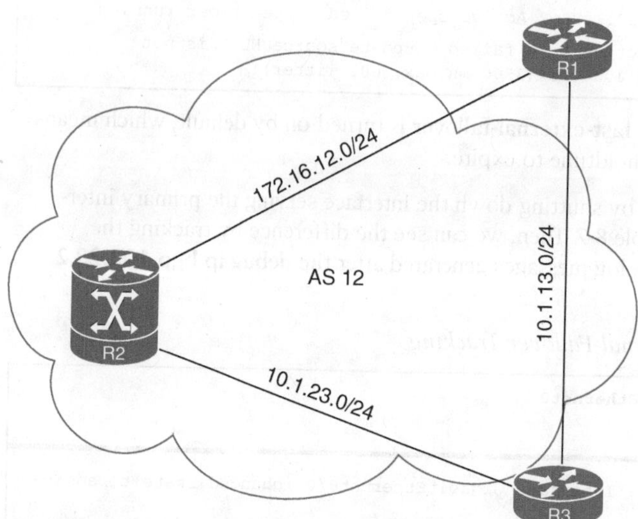

Figure 8-2 *BGP Next-Hop Tracking*

To shed some light on the topology, we are running iBGP inside AS 12 between R1, R2, and R3 with loopback interfaces advertised by OSPF (Area 0) and used as the source for iBGP sessions. From an advertisement perspective, we will track the link between R1 and R2 (172.16.12.0/24) and advertise it using a network statement inside BGP.

First, let's check the default scan time running every 60 seconds, as discussed earlier, by turning on **debug ip bgp** on R3 and checking the output logging messages, as Example 8-8 demonstrates.

Example 8-8   *BGP Scanning Process*

```
R3# debug bgp ipv4 unicast
BGP debugging is on for address family: IPv4 Unicast
08:55:55.194: BGP: topo global:IPv4 Unicast:base Scanning routing tables
08:55:55.194: BGP: topo global:IPv4 Multicast:base Scanning routing tables
08:55:55.194: BGP: topo global:L2VPN E-VPN:base Scanning routing tables
08:55:55.194: BGP: topo global:MVPNv4 Unicast:base Scanning routing tables
08:56:55.197: BGP: topo global:IPv4 Unicast:base Scanning routing tables
08:56:55.197: BGP: topo global:IPv4 Multicast:base Scanning routing tables
08:56:55.197: BGP: topo global:L2VPN E-VPN:base Scanning routing tables
08:56:55.197: BGP: topo global:MVPNv4 Unicast:base Scanning routing tables
```

We can validate the default behavior of the feature as well as the delay (5 seconds) by
examining Example 8-9.

Example 8-9   *BGP Scanning Process*

```
R3# show running-config all | include bgp nexthop
 bgp nexthop trigger enable
 bgp nexthop trigger delay 5
```

NOTE   For more output and defaults within the device configuration, we can issue the
show running-config all command.

Before diving into the details of next-hop tracking, let's check the BGP table for R3, as
shown in Example 8-10.

Example 8-10   *R3 BGP Table*

```
R3# show bgp ipv4 unicast | begin Network
    Network          Next Hop            Metric LocPrf Weight Path
 * i  172.16.12.0/24    10.1.100.2              0    100      0 i
 *>i                    10.1.100.1              0    100      0 i
```

Now, it's time to observe the actual behavior of the tracking mechanism; hence, we will turn
on two debug commands: **debug ip routing** for routing table changes detection and **debug ip
bgp events nexthop** for next-hop tracking functionality.

We can see that R3 receives 172.16.12.0/24 from both R1 and R2 with a preference for R1.
Additionally, when checking the next hop for both paths, we find that the next hop for the
prefix corresponds to the loopback interfaces of both R1 and R2, which were used to establish the iBGP session with R2.

Now, let's examine Example 8-11.

Example 8-11　*R3 BGP Table After Disabling the R1 Loopback Interface*

```
R1(config)# interface loopback 0
R1(config-if)# shutdown


11:02:28.587: RT: del 10.1.100.1 via 10.1.13.1, ospf metric [110/2]
11:02:28.587: RT: delete subnet route to 10.1.100.1/32
11:02:28.588: EvD: accum. penalty decayed to 0 after 553 second(s)
11:02:28.588: BGP(0): IPv4 Unicast::base nexthop modified, reuse in 00:00:19, 19000,
scheduling nexthop scan in 5 secs
11:02:33.588: BGP: BGP Event nhop timer
11:02:33.588: BGP: tbl IPv4 Unicast:base Nexthop walk
11:02:33.588: BGP(IPv4 Unicast): CHANGED Path metric 0 Path aigp-metric 0 nexthop:
10.1.100.1
11:02:33.588: RT: updating bgp 172.16.12.0/24 (0x0)  :
    via 10.1.100.2   0 1048577
11:02:33.588: RT: closer admin distance for 172.16.12.0, flushing 1 routes
11:02:33.588: RT: add 172.16.12.0/24 via 10.1.100.2, bgp metric [200/0]


R3# show bgp ipv4 unicast | begin Network
    Network           Next Hop          Metric LocPrf Weight Path
 *>i 172.16.12.0/24    10.1.100.2             0    100      0 i
 *  i                  10.1.100.1             0    100      0 i
! We still see the prefix learned through the two paths since the hold timer has not
! expired yet.
```

After the hold timer expires, we can verify that the path with the nonreachable next hop is
removed from the BGP table (and consequently from the routing table), as shown in
Example 8-12.

Example 8-12　*R3 BGP Table After Hold-Time Expiry*

```
R3# show bgp ipv4 unicast | begin Network
    Network           Next Hop          Metric LocPrf Weight Path
 *>i 172.16.12.0/24    10.1.100.2             0    100      0 i
```

We will continue to the R2 loopback interface, where we will shut it down and track the log
messages (the debug is still running on R3), as shown in Example 8-13.

Example 8-13　*R3 Logging Messages After Disabling R2 Loopback Interface*

```
11:05:11.309: %BGP-5-NBR_RESET: Neighbor 10.1.100.2 reset (Peer closed the session)
11:05:11.309: BGP: topo global:IPv4 Unicast:base Nexthop 10.1.100.2 removed
11:05:11.310: %BGP-5-ADJCHANGE: neighbor 10.1.100.2 Down Peer closed the session
11:05:11.310: %BGP_SESSION-5-ADJCHANGE: neighbor 10.1.100.2 IPv4 Unicast topology
base removed from session  Peer closed the session
```

```
11:05:11.310: RT: del 172.16.12.0 via 10.1.100.2, bgp metric [200/0]

11:05:11.310: RT: delete subnet route to 172.16.12.0/24

11:05:16.391: RT: del 10.1.100.2 via 10.1.23.2, ospf metric [110/2]

11:05:16.391: RT: delete subnet route to 10.1.100.2/32

11:05:16.392: EvD: accum. penalty decayed to 0 after 167 second(s)

11:05:16.392: BGP(0): IPv4 Unicast::base nexthop modified, reuse in 00:00:19, 19000
, scheduling nexthop scan in 5 secs

11:05:21.392: BGP: BGP Event nhop timer

11:05:21.392: BGP: tbl IPv4 Unicast:base Nexthop walk

! The loopback was removed (as a next hop) from BGP table and a penalty timer has
! been reset to 0.
```

In summary, BGP next-hop tracking determines whether the next hop is reachable, validates the next hop, and then verifies the reachability of neighbors after the outgoing next-hop calculation.

Now, a pertinent question arises: Will changes in the next-hop metric from the perspective of the IGP affect the behavior of the next hop? From an IOS perspective, it will not. The change of an IGP metric is not considered a critical event for IOS. On the other hand, IOS XR treats this differently, in that a change in the RIB is considered a critical event, a delay of 3 seconds is associated with the event, and the change of IGP metric is considered noncritical, although a different delay value is attached—in this case, 10 seconds. Example 8-14 verifies these values by examining the output of the **show bgp nexthops** command.

Example 8-14   *IOS XR Next-Hop Delays*

```
RP/0/0/CPU0:R2# show bgp nexthops | begin Gateway
Gateway Address Family: IPv4 Unicast

Table ID: 0xe0000000

Nexthop Count: 2

Critical Trigger Delay: 3000msec

Non-critical Trigger Delay: 10000msec

BGP Update Delay
```

When a BGP speaker or router initiates negotiations to establish a session or peering, it triggers a timer known as *update-delay*. This timer, by default, is set to 120 seconds.

Once the timer expires, best-path calculations take place and, consequently, the advertisement of prefixes to neighbors. Adjusting this timer can lead to complications because multiple paths to a destination may exist. Therefore, after a BGP speaker sends an advertisement based on its current best path, a better path might become available on the network, necessitating a new advertisement to reflect this improvement.

This approach enhances convergence time and optimizes resource usage (CPU cycles) by ensuring that the latest updates are promptly sent. This way, updates are not sent prematurely, and they do not need to be re-sent later due to the discovery of a better prefix.

Additionally, this behavior works well for production deployments because routers could receive a full routing table; however, for lab environments, such changes should be harmless.

Example 8-15 shows how to adjust this value.

Example 8-15 *BGP Update-Delay Configuration Command*

```
R1(config)# router bgp 12
R1(config-router)# bgp update-delay ?
  <1-3600>  Delay value (seconds)

RP/0/0/CPU0:R2(config)# router bgp 12
RP/0/0/CPU0:R2(config-bgp)# bgp update-delay ?
  <0-3600>  Delay value (seconds)
```

To make this scenario clearer, let's clear the BGP relation between R1 and R2 after manipulating the update-delay to 5 seconds, as shown in Example 8-16.

Example 8-16 *BGP Update-Delay and End-of-RIB*

```
R1(config)# router bgp 12
R1(config-router)# bgp update-delay 5

R1# debug bgp ipv4 unicast updates
BGP updates debugging is on for address family: IPv4 Unicast

R1# clear bgp ipv4 unicast * soft
07:04:47.942: BGP(0): (base) 10.1.100.3 send UPDATE (format) 172.16.12.0/24, next
10.1.100.1, metric 0, path Local
07:04:48.167: BGP: nbr_topo global 10.1.100.3 IPv4 Unicast:base (0x7F1096307BA8:1)
rcvd Refresh Start-of-RIB
07:04:48.167: BGP: nbr_topo global 10.1.100.3 IPv4 Unicast:base (0x7F1096307BA8:1)
refresh_epoch is 3
07:04:48.169: BGP: nbr_topo global 10.1.100.3 IPv4 Unicast:base (0x7F1096307BA8:1)
rcvd Refresh End-of-RIB
```

The BGP End-of-RIB (EoR) highlighted in Example 8-16 is a BGP update message with no NLRI needed for a Graceful Restart mechanism used when the BGP speaker needs to be restarted for some reason (for example, software code upgrade or maintenance activity). The BGP session will be preserved during the restart, and the forwarding plane will continue to function. With this functionality, network disruptions are minimized during planned outages. After the restart is completed, the BGP speaker will learn the prefixes again from its peers. The beneficial aspect of this feature is the fact that the peers will keep routing information unchanged for the router that was restarted for a period.

BGP and IGP Interaction

It is known that BGP is the slowest routing protocol, which means slower convergence. If BGP is to be aligned to the running IGP, convergence could be faster. To achieve faster convergence, we can manipulate or tune IGP. Most service providers run either OSPF or IS-IS as their underlying core routing protocol; they are almost similar in the way they converge.

NOTE   Something worth mentioning is that we use a loopback interface as a source for establishing iBGP sessions because what converges is the underlay, not the next hop, and therefore provides better convergence.

Another option to achieve fast convergence is to consider event-driven detection mechanisms such as Loss of Signal (LoS) or **Bidirectional Forwarding Detection (BFD)**.

BFD is a hello-protocol used for fast detection. The following set of BFD features makes it desirable for failure detection:

- Subsecond failure detection

- Capability to run over UDP

- Data protocol independent (IPv4, IPv6)

- Application independent (IGPs, tunnel liveliness, FRR triggers, and so on)

- Media independent (Ethernet, Serial, Packet over Sonet [POS])

BFD runs in two modes:

- **Asynchronous mode:** This is the primary mode of operation in which each device periodically sends BFD control packets with no dependency on request/response cycles.

- **Demand mode:** No control packets are exchanged after session establishment (with the assumption that another method of connectivity verification is in place).

On the other hand, we have a fast detection mechanism that runs on the physical layer, which is called *carrier delay*. The default behavior is to use a default value of 0 milliseconds (or ms) on all Ethernet interfaces. For critical interfaces, it is recommended to set the value of carrier delay to 0 ms. A sample of how to set the value of the carrier delay on an interface is shown in Example 8-17.

Example 8-17   *Carrier-Delay Configuration*

```
R2(config)# interface GigabitEthernet2
R2(config-if)# carrier-delay msec 0
```

Carrier delay is primarily a router feature, the main function of which is to filter up or down events on links and interfaces. Carrier delay is mainly a software feature compared to other features such as a debounce timer, which runs in firmware.

We can control the processing of hardware link notifications (down or up) by adjusting the timer through the **carrier-delay** command under the interface shown in Example 8-18.

Example 8-18 *Carrier-Delay Timer Configuration*

```
RP/0/0/CPU0:R2(config)# interface GigabitEthernet0/0/0/0
RP/0/0/CPU0:R2(config-if)# carrier-delay ?
  down   Set the carrier delay down value
  up     Set the carrier delay up value
RP/0/0/CPU0:R2(config-if)# carrier-delay down 2000 ?
  up     Set the carrier delay up value
RP/0/0/CPU0:R2(config-if)# carrier-delay down 2000 up ?
  <0-2147483647>  Delay in milliseconds
RP/0/0/CPU0:R2(config-if)# carrier-delay down 20000 up 20000
! As you can see, the delay value is in milliseconds which means if we need 20
! seconds, we have to configure the value as 20,000.
```

Another aspect to consider regarding the interaction between BGP and IGP is the fact that BGP does not discover routes and needs to import the routes discovered by IGP. When an **autonomous system boundary router (ASBR)** advertises routes or prefixes to another autonomous system (AS), ASBR needs to import routes to the BGP table.

We can utilize the tools we have, such as routing policies, to control or filter routes and manipulate their attributes when importing routes in both directions.

BGP Route Dampening

Stability and efficient resource allocation are among the critical aspects of network management. What will happen if we have a flapping route or interface within a network boundary? Every time a flap takes place, a BGP UPDATE message is sent. If the number of these flaps is very large, the **central processing unit (CPU)** would be impacted, causing slowness or service disruption.

BGP route dampening is used to prevent flapping routes from being installed and advertised to other neighbors or peers, which will positively impact the CPU by reducing the processing of flapping routes.

Before diving into the details of the BGP dampening process, let's examine the topology in Figure 8-3, where we will advertise a loopback interface on R3 and disable it while turning on **debug ip bgp updates** on R1, as shown in Example 8-19.

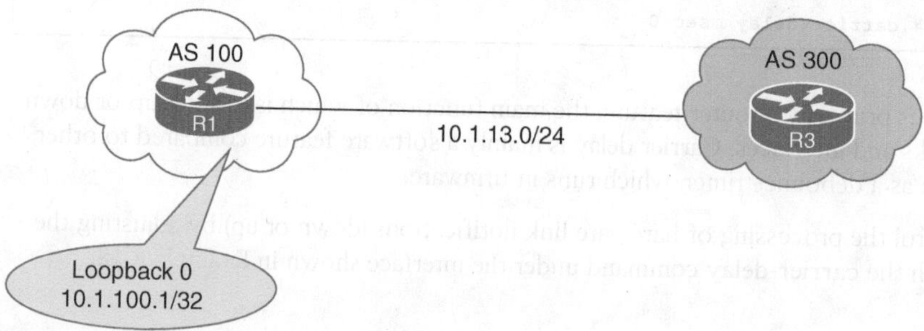

Figure 8-3 *BGP Dampening Example*

Example 8-19   *BGP Updated for a Flapping Route*

```
R3(config)# router bgp 12
R3(config-router)# address-family ipv4 unicast
R3(config-router-af)# network 3.3.3.3 mask 255.255.255.255

BGP updates debugging is on for address family: IPv4 Unicast
08:49:39.569: BGP(0): 10.1.100.3 rcvd UPDATE w/ attr: nexthop 10.1.100.3, origin i,
localpref 100, metric 0
08:49:39.578: BGP(0): 10.1.100.3 rcvd 3.3.3.3/32
08:49:39.603: BGP(0): Revise route installing 1 of 1 routes for 3.3.3.3/32 ->
10.1.100.3(global) to main IP table

R3(config-router-af)# no network 3.3.3.3 mask 255.255.255.255
08:49:59.406: BGP(0): 10.1.100.3 rcv UPDATE about 3.3.3.3/32 -- withdrawn
08:49:59.412: BGP(0): no valid path for 3.3.3.3/32
08:49:59.413: BGP: topo global:IPv4 Unicast:base Remove_fwdroute for 3.3.3.3/32

R3(config-router-af)# network 3.3.3.3 mask 255.255.255.255
08:50:05.819: BGP(0): 10.1.100.3 rcvd UPDATE w/ attr: nexthop 10.1.100.3, origin i,
localpref 100, metric 0
08:50:05.819: BGP(0): 10.1.100.3 rcvd 3.3.3.3/32
08:50:05.820: BGP(0): Revise route installing 1 of 1 routes for 3.3.3.3/32 ->
10.1.100.3(global) to main IP tableshow cp
```

The following parameters are associated with the dampening process:

- **Penalty:** When a route or prefix flaps, the penalty is increased by 1000.

- **Suppress-Limit:** If the penalty exceeds the suppress-limit, the route gets dampened. The default value is 2000. When the route is dampened, it will not be considered for best-path calculations, and its state changes from History to Damp. (The History entry is used to store flap information, to keep track of the oscillation. When a route gets stabilized, it will be flushed from the router.)

- **Half-Life:** The penalty of a route is decreased based on this period. The default value is 15 minutes.

- **Reuse Limit:** The route is unsuppressed if the penalty falls below the reuse limit. The default value is 750.

- **Maximum Suppress-Limit:** This is the maximum amount of time for which a route can be suppressed. The default value is 60 minutes, which equals half-life * 4.

Now, let's move into the configuration details to clarify all related aspects. Example 8-20 shows what we will get when trying to show the details of the parameters just discussed.

Example 8-20   *Enabling BGP Dampening*

```
R1# show bgp ipv4 unicast dampening parameters
% dampening not enabled for base

! We can turn on the dampening feature from the respective address-family we are
! testing for : IPv4 using the command bgp dampening.
R3(config)# router bgp 300
R3(config-router)# address-family ipv4 unicast
R3(config-router-af)# bgp dampening
21:22:24.452: BGP(0): Created dampening structures with halflife time 15,
reuse/suppress 750/2000
```

From the log messages generated after enabling BGP dampening under the IPv4 address family, we can observe the values of the parameters discussed earlier. We can list the parameters in a more tabular format by using the **show bgp ipv4 unicast dampening parameters** command after we issue the **bgp dampening** command under the IPv4 address family, as listed in Example 8-21.

Example 8-21   *BGP Dampening Parameters*

```
R3# show bgp ipv4 unicast dampening parameters
dampening 15 750 2000 60 (DEFAULT)
  Half-life time       : 15 mins    Decay Time        : 2320 secs
  Max suppress penalty: 12000       Max suppress time: 60 mins
  Suppress penalty     :  2000      Reuse penalty     : 750
```

Next, we can adjust the values according to our preferences using the same command, navigating through the available options, as demonstrated in Example 8-22.

Example 8-22   *BGP Dampening Parameters Configuration Options*

```
R3(config-router-af)# bgp dampening ?
  <1-45>      Half-life time for the penalty
  route-map  Route-map to specify criteria for dampening
  <cr>        <cr>

! The same applies when using route-map for modifying bgp dampening parameters.
R3(config)# route-map MAP permit 10
R3(config-route-map)# set dampening ?
  <1-45>  half-life time for the penalty
```

Now, let's get into more detail about the dampening process. We will use the sample topology in Figure 8-3, for which we established eBGP neighborship between R1 and R3.

We have advertised only the R1 loopback network into the BGP process, as shown in Example 8-23.

Example 8-23 *BGP Dampening Flapping Route Demonstration Example*

```
R3# show bgp ipv4 unicast | begin Network


     Network            Next Hop          Metric LocPrf Weight Path
 *>  10.1.100.1/32      10.1.13.1              0          0 100 i


! We will turn on debug bgp ipv4 unicast dampening on R3 and shutdown the loopback
! interface on R1.
R3# debug bgp ipv4 unicast dampening
BGP dampening debugging is on for all address families
```

```
R1(config)# interface loopback 0
R1(config-if)# shutdown
```

```
R3#
21:35:18.130: EvD: charge penalty 1000, new accum. penalty 1000, flap count 1
21:35:18.130: EvD: unsuppress item left in reuse timer array with penalty 1000
* 21:35:18.130: BGP(0): charge penalty for 10.1.100.1/32 path 100 with halflife-time
15 reuse/suppress 750/2000
21:35:18.130: BGP(0): flapped 1 times since 00:00:00. New penalty is 1000
R3#
21:35:24.495: EvD: accum. penalty decayed to 996 after 6 second(s)
```

```
! The flap that took place can be verified by using the command show bgp ipv4
! unicast dampening flap-statistics
R3# show bgp ipv4 unicast dampening flap-statistics | begin Network


     Network            From              Flaps Duration Reuse    Path
 h   10.1.100.1/32      10.1.13.1            1    00:00:43         100


! We still did not bring the interface up and log messages and delay continues to
! change.
21:36:24.498: EvD: accum. penalty decayed to 950 after 60 second(s)
21:37:24.502: EvD: accum. penalty decayed to 906 after 60 second(s)
21:38:14.727: EvD: accum. penalty decayed to 871 after 50 second(s)


! The route is still in the BGP table denoted as h: history.
```

```
R3# show bgp ipv4 unicast | begin Network


     Network            Next Hop          Metric LocPrf Weight Path
 h   10.1.100.1/32      10.1.13.1              0          0 100 i
```

```
R3# show bgp ipv4 unicast 10.1.100.1/32
BGP routing table entry for 10.1.100.1/32, version 3
Paths: (1 available, no best path)
  Not advertised to any peer
  Refresh Epoch 1
  100 (history entry)
    10.1.13.1 from 10.1.13.1 (10.1.100.1)
      Origin IGP, metric 0, localpref 100, external
      Dampinfo: penalty 871, flapped 1 times in 00:02:56
      rx pathid: 0, tx pathid: 0


! Let us now bring the interface up/down again and check the generated logging
! messages.

R1(config-if)# no shutdown
21:42:47.616: EvD: charge penalty 1000, new accum. penalty 1706, flap count 2
21:42:47.616: EvD: unsuppress item left in reuse timer array with penalty 1706
21:42:47.616: BGP(0): charge penalty for 10.1.100.1/32 path 100 with halflife-time
15 reuse/suppress 750/2000
! We can see the accumulated penalty.
```

```
R3# show bgp ipv4 unicast dampening flap-statistics | begin Network

   Network          From             Flaps Duration Reuse    Path
 h 10.1.100.1/32    10.1.13.1          2    00:08:17          100
```

```
! Keep flapping the interface will cause it to be suppressed.
21:47:07.836: BGP(0): suppress 10.1.100.1/32 path 100 for 00:24:30 (penalty 2334)
21:47:07.836: halflife-time 15, reuse/suppress 750/2000
21:47:07.836: EvD: accum. penalty 2334, now suppressed with a reuse intervals of 147
```

```
R3# show bgp ipv4 unicast dampening flap-statistics | begin Network

    Network          From             Flaps Duration Reuse    Path
*d  10.1.100.1/32    10.1.13.1          3    00:12:45 00:01:49 100
```

```
! If we wait for a long time, we can see that the prefix as back to play and got
! unsuppressed.
22:11:53.728: EvD: accum. penalty 747, now unsuppressed
```

NOTE The BGP dampening process affects only eBGP prefixes. iBGP prefixes are not affected by the flapping of a route or prefix. Also, the BGP dampening process works on a per-path basis. If a prefix is dampened on one path, the other path will still be available to eBGP peers.

Prefix Independent Convergence

Prefix Independent Convergence (PIC) aims primarily to enhance and speed up the convergence process in many different scenarios (spanning IP- and MPLS-enabled networks).

PIC primarily touches the **Forwarding Information Base (FIB)** table for which the next hop for a specific prefix is determined.

Typically, when route reflectors are deployed, they obscure the initial point of the best path because they advertise the best path based on their own perspective. Here, the PIC comes into play because it allows a BGP speaker to advertise the available options (paths) and it allows BGP receivers to expect different paths to account for better failover and hence enhanced convergence. This will touch high-load networks, for which plenty of routes are installed and communicate with each other, advertising a remarkable number of prefixes, which will eventually affect the intervening tables.

The PIC is tied to a capability called ADD-PATH, which can be configured per address family or can be configured per neighbor under the subjective address family, as illustrated by Example 8-24.

Example 8-24 *BGP Additional Path Configuration*

```
R5(config)# router bgp 100
R5(config-router)# address-family ipv4 unicast
R5(config-router-af)# bgp additional-paths select all
! We can control how many prefixes we can select; the option will range between 2
! to 3.
R5(config-router-af)# bgp additional-paths select best ?
  <2-3>  Number of best paths in additional paths to be selected
R5(config-router-af)# bgp additional-paths send
! We can control the capability of the BGP speaker to send or receive.
R5(config-router-af)# bgp additional-paths install

R5(config-router-af)# router bgp 100
R5(config-router)# address-family ipv4 unicast
R5(config-router-af)# neighbor 10.1.100.3 advertise additional-paths all
```

NOTE The **neighbor** *level* command has a higher preference over the **address-family** *level* command.

There are a lot of use cases and deployment modes for PIC, but we will focus on a use case (as shown in Figure 8-4) where we have an external route coming from R4 and advertise it to the routes running inside AS# 100. R5 acts as a route reflector for the IPv4 address family. (In the previous example, we focused on how the route reflector within an AS would advertise additional paths; the relative clients will handle this task.)

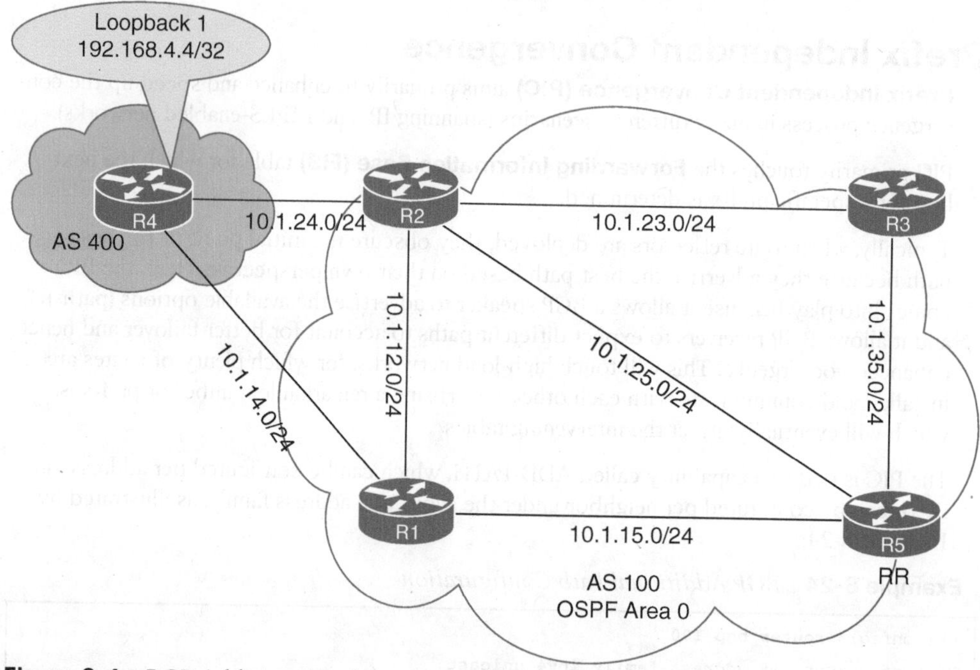

Figure 8-4 *BGP Additional Paths*

If we are going to examine what is taking place, R4 will advertise the 192.168.4.4/32 network to both R2 and R1 (acting as eBGP neighbors). R2 and R1 will advertise the prefix toward R5, which acts as a route reflector inside AS# 100, for which the BGP route reflector clients will accept the vision of their route reflector (R5) on how they should reach the 192.168.4.4/32 network. This scenario is depicted in Example 8-25.

Example 8-25 *BGP Table Output Verification*

```
R5# show bgp ipv4 unicast | begin Network
    Network          Next Hop            Metric LocPrf Weight Path
 * i  192.168.4.4/32   10.1.100.2               0    100      0 400 i
 *>i                   10.1.100.1               0    100      0 400 i


R5# show bgp ipv4 unicast neighbors 10.1.100.3 advertised-routes | begin Network

    Network          Next Hop            Metric LocPrf Weight Path
 *>i  192.168.4.4/32   10.1.100.1               .     0    100      0 400 i
Total number of prefixes 1
```

As we can see, R5 installs two routes (note that one of them is denoted as a backup because we did not enable the additional-paths capability. R3, which is one of the clients for the route reflector (R5), will learn about only one route that is the best path from an R5 (route reflector) perspective. Now, let's turn on the capability on R5, as shown in Example 8-26.

Example 8-26 *BGP Additional Paths Install*

```
R5(config)# router bgp 100
R5(config-router)# address-family ipv4 unicast
R5(config-router-af)# bgp additional-paths install
! Instructs the BGP speaker to install the additional paths available in the BGP
! table.

R5# show bgp ipv4 unicast | begin Network
    Network          Next Hop          Metric LocPrf Weight Path
 *bi  192.168.4.4/32  10.1.100.2             0    100      0 400 i
 *>i                  10.1.100.1             0    100      0 400 i


R5(config)# router bgp 100
R5(config-router)# address-family ipv4 unicast
R5(config-router-af)# bgp additional-paths send
! Enabling the BGP add-path capability will tear down the BGP relation as this
! capability is exchanged in BGP OPEN message.
%BGP-5-ADJCHANGE: neighbor 10.1.100.3 Down Capability changed
%BGP_SESSION-5-ADJCHANGE: neighbor 10.1.100.3 IPv4 Unicast topology base removed
from session  Capability changed

R5# show bgp ipv4 unicast | begin Network
    Network          Next Hop          Metric LocPrf Weight Path
 *>i  192.168.4.4/32  10.1.100.1             0    100      0 400 i
 *bia                 10.1.100.2             0    100      0 400 i

R5# show bgp ipv4 unicast neighbors 10.1.100.3 advertised-routes | begin Network
    Network          Next Hop          Metric LocPrf Weight Path
 *>i  192.168.4.4/32  10.1.100.1             0    100      0 400 i
Total number of prefixes 1
```

As can be seen, the additional path is still not advertised from R5 toward R3. So, let's turn on the feature from R3's perspective to enable it for receiving additional paths, as shown in Example 8-27.

Example 8-27 *BGP Additional Path Receive Capability*

```
R3(config)# router bgp 100
R3(config-router)# address-family ipv4 unicast
R3(config-router-af)# neighbor 10.1.100.5 additional-paths receive
11:18:18.845: BGP(0): Calculating bestpath (bump) for 192.168.4.4/32 flags
0000000000000000 :path_count:- 0/0, best-path =0.0.0.0, bestpath runtime :- 0 ms(or
98 usec) for net 192.168.4.4
11:18:18.845:  BGP(0): compare_member_policy regarding best-external for nbr
10.1.100.5 (nbr:F|group_policy:F)
11:18:18.846:  BGP(0): compare_member_policy regarding best-external for nbr
10.1.100.5 (nbr:F|group_policy:F)
11:18:18.846: %BGP-5-ADJCHANGE: neighbor 10.1.100.5 Down Capability changed
11:18:18.846: %BGP_SESSION-5-ADJCHANGE: neighbor 10.1.100.5 IPv4 Unicast topology
base removed from session  Capability changed
11:18:19.605: %BGP-5-ADJCHANGE: neighbor 10.1.100.5 Up
11:18:19.610: BGP(0): 10.1.100.5 rcvd NEW PATH UPDATE (bp/be - Deny)w/ prefix:
192.168.4.4/32, label 1048577, bp=N, be=N
11:18:19.610: BGP(0): 10.1.100.5 rcvd UPDATE w/ prefix: 192.168.4.4/32, - DO
BESTPATH
11:18:19.610: BGP(0): Calculating bestpath (no bump) for 192.168.4.4/32 flags
0000000000000000 :path_count:- 1/0, best-path =10.1.100.1, bestpath runtime :- 1
ms(or 136 usec) for net 192.168.4.4

R3# show bgp ipv4 unicast | begin Network
    Network          Next Hop         Metric LocPrf Weight Path
 *>i  192.168.4.4/32   10.1.100.1            0    100     0 400 i
```

No changes occurred, indicating that we need to instruct the route reflector to ensure that
this neighbor (R3) receives the additional paths, as shown in Example 8-28.

Example 8-28 *BGP Additional Path Send/Advertise Capability*

```
R5(config-router)# address-family ipv4 unicast
R5(config-router-af)# neighbor 10.1.100.3 additional-paths send
R5(config-router-af)# neighbor 10.1.100.3 advertise additional-paths all

R3# show bgp ipv4 unicast | begin Network
    Network          Next Hop         Metric LocPrf Weight Path
 * i  192.168.4.4/32   10.1.100.1            0    100     0 400 i
 *>i                   10.1.100.2            0    100     0 400 i

11:23:36.958: BGP(0): 10.1.100.5 rcvd NEW PATH UPDATE (bp/be - Deny)w/ prefix:
192.168.4.4/32, label 1048577, bp=N, be=N
11:23:36.958: BGP(0): 10.1.100.5 rcvd UPDATE w/ prefix: 192.168.4.4/32, - DO
BESTPATH
```

```
11:23:36.958: BGP(0): Calculating bestpath (no bump) for 192.168.4.4/32 flags
0000000000000000 :path_count:- 1/0, best-path =10.1.100.2, bestpath runtime :- 0
ms(or 235 usec) for net 192.168.4.4

11:23:36.959: BGP(0): 10.1.100.5 rcvd NEW PATH UPDATE (bp/be - Deny)w/ prefix:
192.168.4.4/32, label 1048577, bp=N, be=N

11:23:36.959: BGP(0): 10.1.100.5 rcvd UPDATE w/ prefix: 192.168.4.4/32, - DO
BESTPATH

11:23:36.959: BGP(0): Calculating bestpath (no bump) for 192.168.4.4/32 flags
0004000000004100 :path_count:- 2/0, best-path =10.1.100.2, bestpath runtime :- 0
ms(or 94 usec) for net 192.168.4.4

11:23:41.958: BGP(0): Calculating bestpath (no bump) for 192.168.4.4/32 flags
0000000000000000 :path_count:- 2/0, best-path =10.1.100.2, bestpath runtime :- 0
ms(or 141 usec) for net 192.168.4.4
```

```
R5# show bgp ipv4 unicast neighbors 10.1.100.3 advertised-routes | begin Network
     Network            Next Hop           Metric LocPrf Weight Path
 *>i 192.168.4.4/32     10.1.100.1              0    100      0 400 i
 *bia 192.168.4.4/32    10.1.100.2              0    100      0 400 i
```

```
R3# show bgp ipv4 unicast 192.168.4.4/32
BGP routing table entry for 192.168.4.4/32, version 8
Paths: (2 available, best #1, table default)
Flag: 0x100
  Not advertised to any peer
  Refresh Epoch 1
  400
    10.1.100.2 (metric 2) from 10.1.100.5 (10.1.100.5)
      Origin IGP, metric 0, localpref 100, valid, internal, best
      Originator: 10.1.100.2, Cluster list: 10.1.100.5
      rx pathid: 0x1, tx pathid: 0x0
  Refresh Epoch 1
  400
    10.1.100.1 (metric 3) from 10.1.100.5 (10.1.100.5)
      Origin IGP, metric 0, localpref 100, valid, internal
      Originator: 10.1.100.1, Cluster list: 10.1.100.5
      rx pathid: 0x0, tx pathid: 0
```

```
R3# show bgp ipv4 unicast | begin Network
     Network            Next Hop           Metric LocPrf Weight Path
 *>i 192.168.4.4/32     10.1.100.2              0    100      0 400 i
 *  i                   10.1.100.1              0    100      0 400 i
```

We can also check for this capability on a per-neighbor basis, as shown in Example 8-29.

Example 8-29 *BGP Additional Path Per-Neighbor Capability*

```
R3# show bgp ipv4 unicast neighbors 10.1.100.5 | include Additional
  Additional Paths send capability: received
  Additional Paths receive capability: advertised

R5# show bgp ipv4 unicast neighbors 10.1.100.3 | include Additional
  Additional Paths send capability: advertised
  Additional Paths receive capability: received
```

The same applies for eBGP deployment, where sometimes we need to make sure that we have a backup path for an outside prefix(es) for better convergence and faster reaction to failures. We will use the topology in Figure 8-5 for which all routers establish eBGP peering and advertise a loopback interface with the syntax 10.1.100.x/32, where x is the router number.

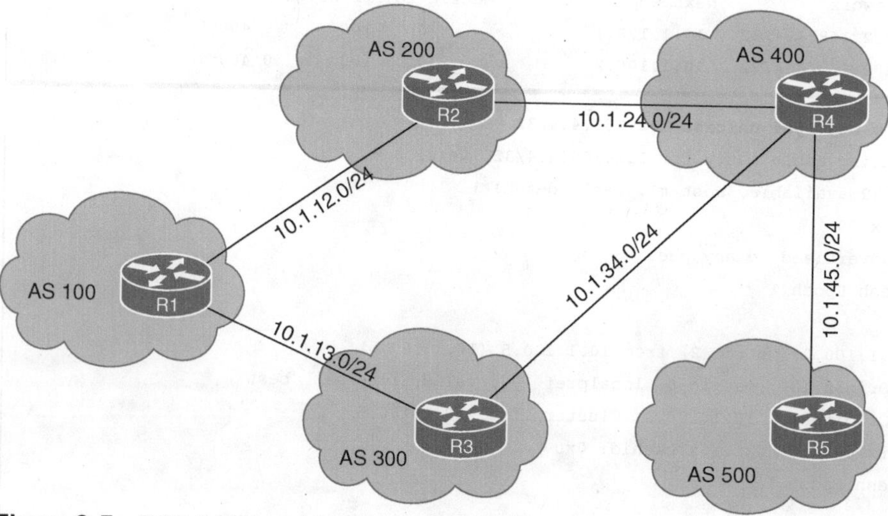

Figure 8-5 *BGP Additional Paths on eBGP Topology*

Now, as we check the BGP table on R1 after enabling the additional paths install feature, we can see the prefixes are denoted with *b*, which stands for backup-path. Example 8-30 validates the backup-path installation.

Example 8-30 *BGP Additional Path Using eBGP Topology*

```
R1(config)# router bgp 100
R1(config-router)# address-family ipv4 unicast
R1(config-router-af)# bgp additional-paths install

22:19:18.963:  Start bgp additional paths walker.
22:19:18.963:  Start bestpath(backup path) recalc timer
22:19:29.107: BGP: Start to walker BGP tables -1 for bestpath  recalc
```

```
22:19:29.107: BGP(0): Calculating bestpath (bump) for 10.1.100.1/32 flags
0000004400000000 :path_count:- 1/0, best-path =0.0.0.0, bestpath runtime :- 1 ms(or
0 usec) for net 10.1.100.1

22:19:29.108: BGP(0): Calculating bestpath (bump) for 10.1.100.3/32 flags
0000004400000000 :path_count:- 1/0, best-path =10.1.13.3, bestpath runtime :- 1
ms(or 0 usec) for net 10.1.100.3

22:19:29.109: BGP(0): Calculating bestpath (bump) for 10.1.100.4/32 flags
0000004400000000 :path_count:- 2/0, best-path =10.1.13.3, bestpath runtime :- 0
ms(or 0 usec) for net 10.1.100.4

22:19:29.110: BGP(0): Calculating Backup path::Backup-Path for 10.1.100.4/32:BUMP-
VERSION:, Updated backup-path:Backup-Path  is 10.1.12.2, backup path runtime :- 1 ms
(or 1000 usec)

22:19:29.114: BGP(0): Calculating bestpath (bump) for 10.1.100.5/32 flags
0000004400000000 :path_count:- 2/0, best-path =10.1.13.3, bestpath runtime :- 3 ms
(or 4000 usec) for net 10.1.100.5

22:19:29.115: BGP(0): Calculating Backup path::Backup-Path for 10.1.100.5/32:BUMP-
VERSION:, Updated backup-path:Backup-Path  is 10.1.12.2, backup path runtime :- 1 ms
(or 1000 usec)
```

```
R1# show bgp ipv4 unicast | begin Network


     Network          Next Hop              Metric LocPrf Weight Path
 *>  10.1.100.1/32    0.0.0.0                    0          32768 i
 *>  10.1.100.3/32    10.1.13.3                  0              0 300 i
 *b  10.1.100.4/32    10.1.12.2                                 0 200 400 i
 *>                   10.1.13.3                                 0 300 400 i
 *b  10.1.100.5/32    10.1.12.2                                 0 200 400 500 i
 *>                   10.1.13.3                                 0 300 400 500 i
```

```
R1# show bgp ipv4 unicast 10.1.100.5/32
BGP routing table entry for 10.1.100.5/32, version 9
Paths: (2 available, best #2, table default)
  Additional-path-install
  Advertised to update-groups:
     2
  Refresh Epoch 1
  200 400 500
    10.1.12.2 from 10.1.12.2 (10.1.100.2)
      Origin IGP, localpref 100, valid, external, backup/repair ,
recursive-via-connected
      rx pathid: 0, tx pathid: 0
      Updated on Jun 15 2024 22:17:14 UTC
  Refresh Epoch 2
  300 400 500
    10.1.13.3 from 10.1.13.3 (10.1.100.3)
      Origin IGP, localpref 100, valid, external, best , recursive-via-connected
```

```
        rx pathid: 0, tx pathid: 0x0

        Updated on Jun 15 2024 22:12:19 UTC
```

```
R1# show ip cef 10.1.100.5 255.255.255.255 detail
10.1.100.5/32, epoch 2, flags [rib only nolabel, rib defined all labels]
  recursive via 10.1.13.3
    attached to GigabitEthernet2
  recursive via 10.1.12.2, repair
    attached to GigabitEthernet1
```

When we're dealing with IOS XR–based software devices, the same approach applies; however, an additional step takes place from a configuration perspective. This step is about defining a route policy and attaching it to the address family, as shown in Example 8-31.

Example 8-31   *BGP Additional Path on IOS XR*

```
RP/0/0/CPU0:R2(config)# route-policy ADD_PATH
RP/0/0/CPU0:R2(config-rpl)# set path-selection ?
  all          BGP all paths
  backup       BGP backup path
  best-path    BGP best path
  group-best   BGP group best path
  multipath    BGP multipath
RP/0/0/CPU0:R2(config-rpl)# set path-selection all
```

```
RP/0/0/CPU0:R2(config)# router bgp 100
RP/0/0/CPU0:R2(config-bgp)# address-family ipv4 unicast
RP/0/0/CPU0:R2(config-bgp-af)# additional-paths selection route-policy ADD_PATH
```

NOTE   There are two flavors of BGP PIC:

BGP PIC Core: It will assist in decreasing the convergence time when a core node fails and the underlying IGP has to find a new path to the edge of the network.

BGP PIC Edge: It will assist in decreasing the convergence time when an edge device fails and moving to another edge device to overcome the failure (this is what has been discussed in the previous examples).

BGP Shadow Route Reflector

Following the same path diversity concern, let's look at another feature called a *shadow route reflector* for which we can add a shadow RR (also known as a *diverse-path route reflector*). This feature will advertise a diverse path to the route reflector clients (that is, a second-best path).

There are some design caveats to consider from a location perspective concerning the shadow RR (co-located vs. not co-located). In this case, the IGP metric needs to be considered, but this is out of the scope of this book.

Figure 8-6 shows a sample topology for two interconnected autonomous systems and how the shadow RR will advertise a backup (diverse) path to the clients.

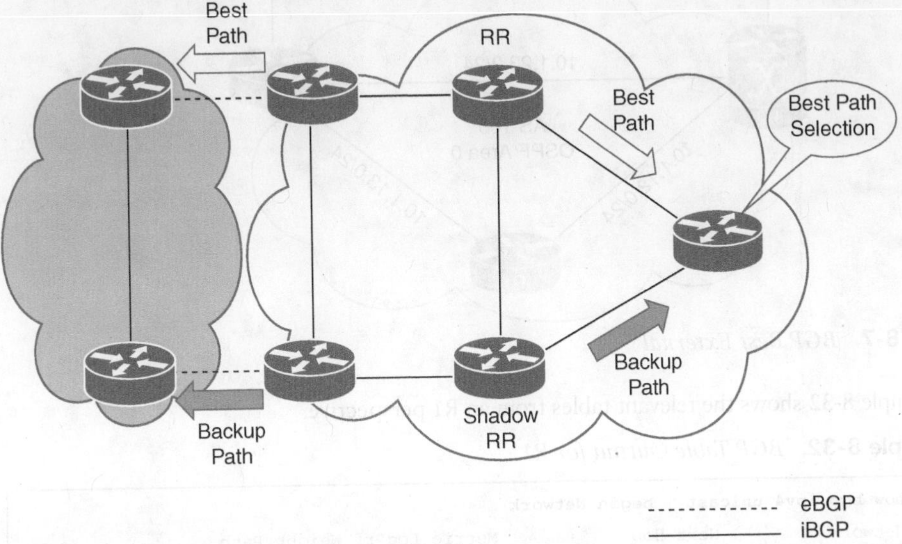

Figure 8-6   *BGP Shadow Route Reflector*

Although shadow route reflection is effective, it requires extra hardware (physical router) to be installed and hence extra capital expenditures.

To overcome the cost limitations associated with using a shadow route reflector, we can utilize the shadow sessions feature in which the route reflector (active/primary) will advertise both primary and backup paths. The limitation from a configuration perspective is that we cannot use the same BGP session with the same IP address, which will require configuring an extra loopback interface to create the shadow session.

BGP Best External

The main goal of the BGP External feature is to achieve subsecond convergence where we try to import an external prefix/route into an iBGP domain, for which we will get the same information from more than one path. Once a failure takes place, we will get the same information shortly through the other path.

We will use Figure 8-7 to demonstrate the functionality of the feature for which we have an iBGP domain (R1, R2, and R3 with full-mesh BGP relations in place), and we have eBGP peering between R2 → R4 and R3 → R5, respectively.

We are advertising the same prefix from both R4 and R5 (192.168.45.1/32), and per the routing decision and rules we discussed in Chapter 7, only one path will be installed in the BGP table and consequently the routing table.

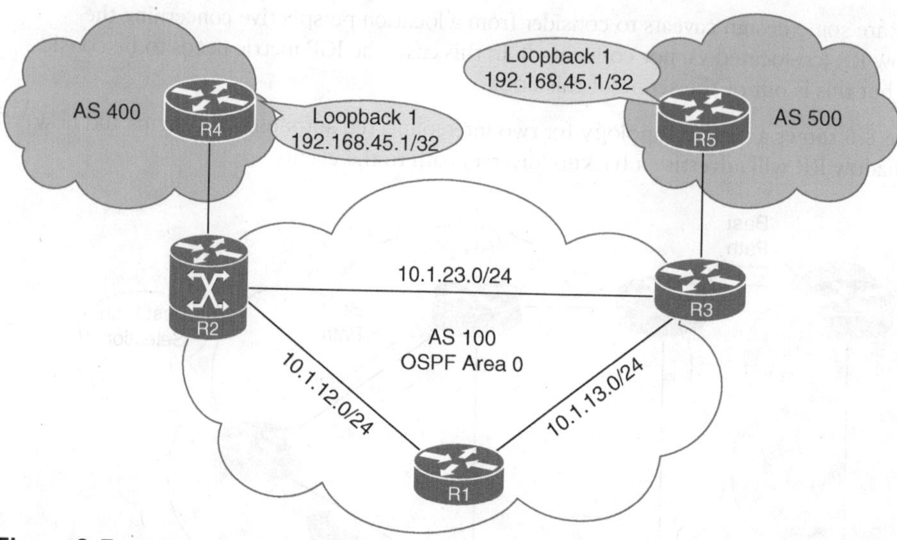

Figure 8-7 *BGP Best External*

Example 8-32 shows the relevant tables from an R1 perspective.

Example 8-32 *BGP Table Output for R1*

```
R1# show bgp ipv4 unicast | begin Network
     Network          Next Hop          Metric LocPrf Weight Path
 * i 192.168.45.1/32  10.1.35.5              0    100      0 500 i
 *>i                  10.1.24.4              0    100      0 400 i


R1# show ip route bgp | begin Gateway
Gateway of last resort is not set

      192.168.45.0/32 is subnetted, 1 subnets
B        192.168.45.1 [200/0] via 10.1.24.4, 00:02:23


R1# show bgp ipv4 unicast 192.168.45.1/32
BGP routing table entry for 192.168.45.1/32, version 4
Paths: (2 available, best #2, table default)
  Not advertised to any peer
  Refresh Epoch 2
  500
    10.1.35.5 (inaccessible) from 10.1.100.3 (10.1.100.3)
      Origin IGP, metric 0, localpref 100, valid, internal
      rx pathid: 0, tx pathid: 0
      Updated on Jun 20 2024 10:37:09 UTC
```

```
Refresh Epoch 1
400
  10.1.24.4 (metric 2) from 10.1.100.2 (10.1.100.2)
    Origin IGP, metric 0, localpref 100, valid, internal, best
    rx pathid: 0, tx pathid: 0x0
    Updated on Jun 20 2024 10:36:19 UTC
```

The question is why R1 chose the update from R4 (through the iBGP neighbor R2) rather than R5 (through the iBGP neighbor R3)? We did not influence any parameter, so going through the selection criteria, we will end up with the lowest router ID.

Let's not forget that we are running full-mesh iBGP peering inside AS 100, and therefore, a split-horizon rule will take place.

Now, let's create a failure on the connection between R2 and R4 and turn on the **debug ip routing** on R1. We can see what happens in Example 8-33.

Example 8-33 *BGP Best-External Feature*

```
R1# debug ip routing
IP routing debugging is on

R4(config)# router bgp 400
R4(config-router)# address-family ipv4 unicast
R4(config-router)# neighbor 10.1.24.2 shutdown
16:01:46.284: RT: updating bgp 192.168.45.1/32 (0x0) [local lbl/ctx:1048577/0x0]
omp-tag:0  :
    via 10.1.100.3   1 0 0x7F10CDFEABD8 1048577 0x100001
16:01:46.286: RT: closer admin distance for 192.168.45.1, flushing 1 routes
16:01:46.288: RT: add 192.168.45.1/32 via 10.1.100.3, bgp metric [200/0]

R2# show bgp ipv4 unicast neighbors 10.1.100.1 advertised-routes
Total number of prefixes 0

R3# show bgp ipv4 unicast neighbors 10.1.100.1 advertised-routes | begin Network

     Network          Next Hop         Metric LocPrf Weight Path
 *>  192.168.45.1/32  10.1.35.5             0           0 500 i
Total number of prefixes 1

16:04:05.929: RT: updating bgp 192.168.45.1/32 (0x0) [local lbl/ctx:1048577/0x0]
omp-tag:0  :
    via 10.1.100.2   1 0 0x7F10CDFEAD10 1048577 0x100001
```

```
16:04:05.941: RT: closer admin distance for 192.168.45.1, flushing 1 routes
16:04:05.943: RT: add 192.168.45.1/32 via 10.1.100.2, bgp metric [200/0]

R3# show bgp ipv4 unicast | begin Network


    Network            Next Hop            Metric LocPrf Weight Path
*bi  192.168.45.1/32   10.1.24.4                0    100      0 400 i
*>                     10.1.35.5                0             0 500 i
```

High Availability: BGP Graceful Restart

A **BGP Graceful Restart (GR)** allows a BGP speaker to preserve the forwarding state during a session failure or route processor (RP) failure. In other words, this capability, which is exchanged between BGP peers, enables them to conduct non-stop forwarding, which helps in minimizing the impact on the running services.

BGP Graceful Restart will dramatically reduce the impact of BGP peering failure or restart, especially in large-scale deployments due to the large number of prefixes handled by BGP. The impact will be remarkable in route reflection deployment (most of the deployments consider out-of-band), which will be responsible for prefix distribution and act as the brain of the BGP space.

When routers are running dual-route processors, it is highly recommended for the GR to be enabled for all routing protocols to conduct switchover in case of failure. As discussed earlier, BGP runs on TCP port 179, and by default, GR is enabled for non-TCP-based protocols such as Interior Gateway Protocols (IGPs), which will allow you to enable GR on both ends of the BGP peering.

BGP GR is an optional feature, and the GR capability will be exchanged through BGP Open messages. (Enabling BGP GR will cause the BGP peering to reset, so make sure that this is a green field or that a proper maintenance window is in place.) Within the OPEN messages, the following information is exchanged:

- **Restart Flag:** This bit indicates if the peer sending the GR capability got restarted; it is used to prevent situations where both peers restart at the same time.

- **Restart Time:** This is the time that the sender of the GR capability needs to complete a restart, which will eventually speed up the convergence process.

- **AFI/SAFI:** This is the address family for which we enabled GR.

- **AFI Flag:** This flag contains a bit indicating whether the peer sending the GR capability has preserved the forwarding state during a previous restart; this bit is called a forwarding state bit.

When RP failure takes place on the BGP peer, or RP switchover happens, the routes located in the forwarding table are marked as stable, which preserves the forwarding state because the independence of the control plane and forwarding plane is in action. On the restarting peer, the active RP starts to establish BGP sessions with all peers (configured). On the non-restarting peer, new connection requests are marked as coming, and the BGP state is already established, which is an indication for a non-restarting router that the peer is restarting. At this point, the restarting peer sends the GR capability with a restart state bit set to 1 as well as a forwarding state bit for AFIs and SAFIs.

Continually, the non-restarting peer will clear old (dead) BGP sessions and mark all routes in the BGP table (received from the restarting peer) as stale. If, for any reason, the BGP session does not successfully reestablish the BGP session, the non-restarting peer will remove all stale routes after the restart time expires. This will enable the non-restarting peer to send an initial RIB update followed by an End-of-RIB (EoR) marker.

GR can be configured either globally or on a per-neighbor basis. For global deployment, we can use the BGP **graceful-restart** command.

Let's examine the global configuration and the associated parameters going through Example 8-34, starting with IOS XR software.

Example 8-34 *BGP Graceful Restart, IOS XR Global Configuration*

```
RP/0/0/CPU0:R2(config)# router bgp 2
RP/0/0/CPU0:R2(config-bgp)# bgp graceful-restart
RP/0/0/CPU0:R2(config-bgp)# bgp graceful-restart ?
  graceful-reset  Reset gracefully if configuration change forces a peer reset
  purge-time      Time before stale routes are purged.
  restart-time    Restart time advertised to neighbors
  stalepath-time  Maximum time to wait for restart of GR capable peers
RP/0/0/CPU0:R2(config-bgp)# bgp graceful-restart restart-time ?
  <1-4095>  Max time (seconds)
RP/0/0/CPU0:R2(config-bgp)# bgp graceful-restart restart-time 200
! This value sets the GR restart timers.
RP/0/0/CPU0:R2(config-bgp)# bgp graceful-restart stalepath-time 300
RP/0/0/CPU0:R2(config-bgp)# bgp graceful-restart purge-time 400

RP/0/0/CPU0:R2# show bgp ipv4 unicast neighbors 10.1.100.1 | include Graceful
  Graceful restart is enabled
    Graceful Restart capability advertised
```

NOTE   The **bgp graceful-restart stalepath-timer** *value* command on IOS and IOS XE sets the maximum time for which the router will maintain the stale path entries in case no EoR is received from the restarting router. On IOS XR, the command sets the maximum time to wait for GR-capable peers to restart, and therefore, the **bgp graceful-restart purge-time** *value* command has been introduced on IOS XR to take care of removing stale paths from peers.

Now, let's examine a similar set of commands on IOS and IOS XE by checking Example 8-35.

Example 8-35   *BGP Graceful Restart, IOS and IOS XE Global Configuration*

```
R1(config)# router bgp 1
R1(config-router)# bgp graceful-restart
All BGP sessions must be reset to take the new GR config
! BGP sessions have to reset to enable GR capabilities so make sure to reserve
! maintenance window.
R1(config-router)# bgp graceful-restart ?
  all              Enable BGP GR for all platforms (even non-NSF capable ones)
  extended         Enable Graceful-Restart Extension
  restart-time     Set the max time needed to restart and come back up
  stalepath-time   Set the max time to hold onto restarting peer's stale paths
! As we can see, the purge-time option is not available as it is introduced in IOS
! XR as mentioned.
R1(config-router)# bgp graceful-restart restart-time 200
R1(config-router)# bgp graceful-restart stalepath-time 300
```

```
R1# show bgp ipv4 unicast neighbors 10.1.100.2 | include Graceful
   Graceful Restart Capability: advertised
   Graceful-Restart is enabled, restart-time 200 seconds, stalepath-time 300 seconds
```

```
RP/0/0/CPU0:R2# show bgp ipv4 unicast neighbors 10.1.100.1 | Begin Graceful
  Graceful restart is enabled
  Restart time is 200 seconds
  Stale path timeout time is 300 seconds
! Output omitted for brevity.
```

It might not always be the case where we must enable BGP GR for all peers or support is not in place. Here, we can enable the feature on a per-neighbor basis. Let's examine Example 8-36 for more details.

Example 8-36   *BGP Graceful Restart, per Neighbor Configuration*

```
! IOS XR
RP/0/0/CPU0:R2(config)# router bgp 2
RP/0/0/CPU0:R2(config-bgp)# neighbor 10.1.100.1
RP/0/0/CPU0:R2(config-bgp-nbr)# graceful-restart
```

```
! IOS and IOS XE
R1(config)# router bgp 1
R1(config-router)# neighbor 10.1.100.2 ha-mode graceful-restart
```

Cisco's deployment of GR assumes NSF is enabled; however, enabling GR does not explicitly mean that NSF is enabled. NSF is not configurable but is enabled by default when a router is running in Stateful Switchover (SSO) mode.

The GR restart timer, which defaults to 120 seconds, takes care of clearing stale information in case BGP does not get established within that time.

High Availability: BGP Non-Stop Routing

There might be some instances where GR is not a feasible solution due to the fact that a customer's equipment might not support the GR capability. **Non-stop routing (NSR)** comes into play because it is transparent to the customer, and this is one of the primary assets of this feature. NSR is a feature where routing protocols explicitly checkpoint state from active RP to the standby RP to maintain routing information across a switchover.

NSR sessions are established on the standby RP before the switchover takes place, and they stay established after the switchover.

NSR operation goes through three phases:

1. **Synchronization:** Session-state mirroring takes place between the active and the standby RP. TCP will get synchronized first and then BGP (representing the application) will sync after.

2. **NSR-Ready:** Incoming packets or updates are replicated to both RPs. Outgoing updates are sent out via active or standby RPs, depending on the platform. (In IOS and IOS XE, an active RP sends updates to peers, whereas in IOS XR, the update is sent via the standby RP.) Then this question arises: How do active and standby RPs get the information replicated? The answer is through a process called inter-process communication (IPC), which functions asynchronously.

3. **Switchover:** When the switchover happens, TCP activates the sockets based on an application trigger and restores keepalive to maintain the state of the sessions.

Example 8-37 shows the basic commands needed to operationalize the NSR feature.

Example 8-37   *BGP NSR Configuration*

```
! IOS configuration.
R1(config)# router bgp 1
R1(config-router)# bgp sso route-refresh-enable

! IOS XR configuration.
RP/0/0/CPU0:R2(config)# router bgp 2
RP/0/0/CPU0:R2(config-bgp)# nsr

R1# show bgp ipv4 unicast neighbors 10.1.100.2 | include (Stateful|refresh)
    Route refresh: advertised and received(new)
    Stateful switchover support enabled: NO for session 1

RP/0/0/CPU0:R2# show bgp ipv4 unicast neighbors 10.1.100.1 | include Non-stop
  Non-stop routing is enabled

RP/0/0/CPU0:R2# show bgp process | include Non-stop
Non-stop routing is enabled
```

To summarize the functional aspects of NSR, Figure 8-8 depicts the BGP NSR architecture from a functionality perspective.

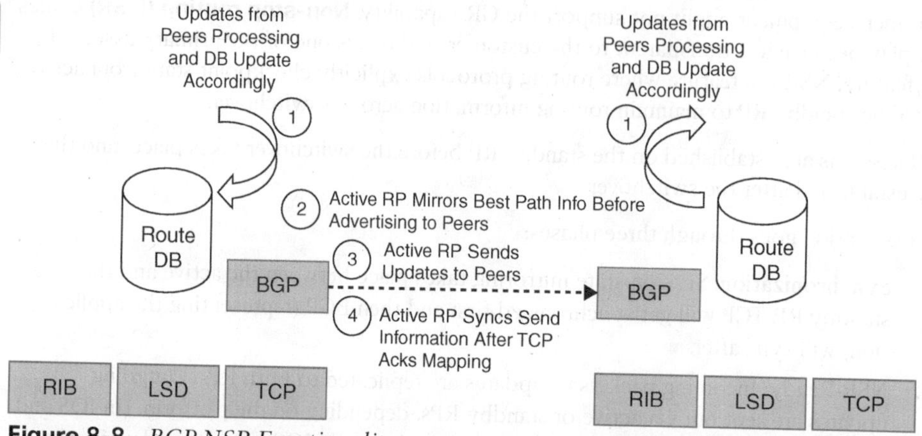

Figure 8-8 *BGP NSR Functionality*

Exam Preparation Tasks

As mentioned in the section "How to Use This Book" in the Introduction, you have a few choices for exam preparation: the exercises here, Chapter 23, "Final Preparation," and the exam simulation questions in the Pearson Test Prep Software Online.

Review All Key Topics

Review the most important topics in this chapter, noted with the Key Topic icon in the margin of the page. Table 8-2 lists a reference of these key topics and the page numbers on which each is found.

Table 8-2   Key Topics for Chapter 8

Key Topic Element	Description	Page Number
Paragraph	Fast-external-fallover importance	320
Paragraph	Next-hop-tracking functionality	322
Paragraph	Next-hop-tracking: IOS vs. IOS XR	325
Paragraph	BGP End-of-RIB	326
Paragraph	BGP route dampening functionality	328
Paragraph	Route reflectors path diversity	333
Paragraph	BGP Graceful Restart importance	344
Figure 8-8	BGP NSR Functionality	348

Define Key Terms

Define the following key terms from this chapter and check the answers in the glossary:

Autonomous System Boundary Router (ASBR), BGP Graceful Restart (GR), Bidirectional Forwarding Detection (BFD), central processing unit (CPU), forwarding information base (FIB), Minimum Route Advertisement Interval (MRAI), non-stop routing (NSR), Prefix Independent Convergence (PIC), routing information base (RIB)

Command Reference to Check Your Memory

This section includes the most important commands covered in this chapter. You might not need to memorize the complete syntax of every command, but you should be able to remember the basic keywords that are needed.

To test your memory of the commands, cover the right side of Table 8-3 with a piece of paper, read the description on the left side, and then see how much of the command you can remember.

The SPCOR 350-501 exam focuses on practical, hands-on skills that are used by networking professionals. Therefore, you should be able to identify the commands needed to configure and test. Note that not all commands are fully covered in the chapter, but their presence in the following table should lead you to investigate them further to understand this technology.

Table 8-3   BGP Commands to Know

Task	Command Syntax
Set the advertisement interval, which defines the length of time between transmission of BGP routing updates	**neighbor** *ip-address* **advertisement-interval** *value*
Terminate external BGP sessions of any directly adjacent peer if the link used to reach the peer goes down	**bgp fast-external-fallover**
Prevent the installation of flapping BGP routes and forwarding them to other BGP routers	**bgp dampening**
Display detailed BGP dampening information	**show ip bgp dampening parameters**
Display BGP flap statistics	**show ip bgp dampening flap-statistics**
Configure the BGP speaker to select all available additional paths	**bgp additional-paths select all**
Configure the BGP speaker to send additional paths	**bgp additional-paths send**
Configure the BGP speaker to install additional paths in the BGP table	**bgp additional-paths install**
Enable the graceful restart capability globally	**bgp graceful restart**

Review Questions

As a part of the review, we encourage you to provide *a single-sentence answer* (keep your answers as short as possible) to the following questions. If you struggle to complete this in a single sentence, this answer may indicate a lack of clarity or reveal gaps in your understanding. We have constructed these questions to help you consolidate this chapter's information and extract the essence of the covered content.

The answers to these questions appear in Appendix A. For more practice with exam format questions, use the Pearson Test Prep Software Online.

1. How does BGP next-hop tracking function?
2. Why is fast-failover for iBGP turned off by default?

Bibliography

A. Bashandy, Ed., C. Filsfils, and P. Mohapatra. *BGP Prefix Independent Convergence draft-ietf-rtgwg-bgp-pic-20.txt*, IETF, https://datatracker.ietf.org/doc/html/draft-ietf-rtgwg-bgp-pic-20, October 2023.

V. Jain and B. Edgeworth. *Troubleshooting BGP: A Practical Guide to Understanding and Troubleshooting BGP*, Cisco Press, December 2023, https://www.ciscopress.com/store/troubleshooting-bgp-a-practical-guide-to-understanding-9780134436548

S. Sangli, E. Chen, R. Fernando, J. Scudder, and Y. Rekhter. RFC 4724, *Graceful Restart Mechanism for BGP*, IETF, https://datatracker.ietf.org/doc/html/rfc4724, January 2007.

## CHAPTER 9

Multicast

This chapter covers the following exam topics:

4.4 Implement multicast services

- 4.4.a PIM (PIM-SM, PIM-SSM, and PIM-BIDIR, PIMv6)
- 4.4.b IGMP v1/v2/v3 and MLD

Multicast is a communication paradigm used in computer networks to efficiently distribute data from one sender to multiple recipients. Unlike unicast, where data is sent from one sender to one receiver, and broadcast, where data is sent from one sender to all recipients in the network, multicast enables a single sender to send data to multiple recipients who have expressed interest in receiving the data. This approach conserves network bandwidth and processing resources by minimizing duplicate transmissions and ensuring that only interested recipients receive the data. Multicast is commonly used for streaming media, real-time collaboration applications, content delivery networks (CDNs), and many other scenarios where data needs to be distributed to multiple recipients simultaneously. This chapter focuses on topics you are highly likely to see on the exam.

"Do I Know This Already?" Quiz

The "Do I Know This Already?" quiz allows you to assess whether you should read this entire chapter thoroughly or jump to the "Exam Preparation Tasks" section. If you are in doubt about your answers to these questions or your own assessment of your knowledge of the topics, read the entire chapter. Table 9-1 lists the major headings in this chapter and their corresponding "Do I Know This Already?" quiz questions. You can find the answers in Appendix A, "Answers to the 'Do I Know This Already?' Quizzes and Review Questions."

Table 9-1 "Do I Know This Already?" Section-to-Question Mapping

Foundation Topics Section	Questions
Multicast	1
IGMP	3
Multicast Routing Protocol Types	2, 4, 5, 6

CAUTION The goal of self-assessment is to gauge your mastery of the topics in this chapter. If you do not know the answer to a question or are only partially sure of the answer, you should mark that question as wrong for purposes of the self-assessment. Giving yourself credit for an answer you correctly guess skews your self-assessment results and might provide you with a false sense of security.

1. The 239.0.0.0/8 block of addresses is reserved for which of the following?
    a. Private use
    b. Source-specific multicast
    c. Internetwork control
    d. GLOP
2. Which of the following are mechanisms to achieve RP failover in PIM-SM? (Select all that apply.)
    a. Backup rendezvous points (RPs)
    b. Election Protocol for Rendezvous Points (EPRP)
    c. Multicast Failover Protocol (MFP)
    d. Backup Bootstrap Router (BSR)
3. What is the purpose of the Group-Specific Query message in IGMPv3?
    a. Sent by multicast routers to solicit membership reports from all group members in a specific multicast group
    b. Used by multicast routers to determine the number of group members interested in receiving traffic for a particular multicast group
    c. Used by the querier to query a multicast group member about its current group membership state
    d. Sent by multicast routers to identify and exclude specific group members from receiving multicast traffic for a particular group
4. Which of the following accurately describes the operation of Cisco Auto-RP?
    a. Relies on a designated mapping agent to dynamically assign RP addresses to multicast groups
    b. Uses a distributed mechanism where each router independently determines the RP for multicast groups
    c. Employs a centralized approach where a single router is elected as the rendezvous point for all (or groups of) multicast traffic
    d. Operates independently of any multicast routing protocol and is solely responsible for multicast group management
5. Which of the following accurately describes the BSR mechanism?
    a. Relies on a central mapping agent to dynamically assign RP addresses to multicast groups
    b. Uses a distributed approach where each router independently determines the RP for multicast groups
    c. Operates independently of any multicast routing protocol and is solely responsible for multicast group management
    d. Employs a distributed mechanism where multiple routers compete to become the rendezvous point for multicast traffic

6. In PIMv6, what is the role of the designated router (DR)?

   a. Dynamically assigns rendezvous point (RP) addresses to multicast groups

   b. Elected within each IPv6 multicast-enabled subnet to manage the exchange of multicast routing information

   c. A centralized router that maintains the Multicast Forwarding Information Base (MFIB) for the entire PIMv6 domain

   d. Forwarding multicast packets between IPv6 multicast-enabled subnets in the absence of a Multicast Border Router (MBR)

Foundation Topics

Multicast

Multicast, though a powerful communication technique, is often considered complex and is less often encountered in comparison to unicast and broadcast. Its implementation involves specialized protocols and network configurations, which can be challenging for network operators to learn and grasp. Additionally, troubleshooting multicast-related issues requires a deep understanding of underlying network principles and multicast-specific protocols like IGMP and PIM. Despite its complexity, multicast offers significant advantages in efficiently distributing data to multiple recipients, making it invaluable for applications such as video streaming, online gaming, and content delivery networks. Mastering multicast techniques can enhance network efficiency and enable scalable and robust communication infrastructures.

Note that this topic is vast in scope because multiple approaches have been tried. Some have withstood the test of time, whereas others have faded into occasional mentions in books and references. There are also new and emerging ideas, but these are yet to face customer scrutiny and monetization challenges. The exam is clear that it focuses mainly on *certain aspects* of Protocol-Independent Multicast (PIM, named this way because it supports *any* protocol for RPF checks as you will learn later, thus independent) and **Internet Group Management Protocol (IGMP)**, both of which are covered in the pages to follow. Please note that the blueprint emphasizes the importance of practical, hands-on skills, in addition to theoretical understanding. This means a candidate (you) must be adept at reading configurations and suggest which corrections must be made. Theoretical knowledge is already assumed.

What would I (Brad) have you know about multicast for this exam?

- While unicast traffic involves "one-to-one" communication and broadcast "one-to-all" (on a segment) communication, multicast communication enables a "one-to-many" (but not all) along with "many-to-many" traffic patterns.

- Multicast tries to deliver a single copy (or a stream) of data through the network to minimize bandwidth consumption.

- Once the packets get closer to the receivers (at the edge of the network), routers closest to the receivers will perform stream multiplication to deliver the same single stream to multiple listeners.

- Many multicast applications are UDP-based, which leads to obvious and at times more subtle drawbacks. Among the obvious are the lack of TCP congestion and retransmission controls. Less apparent ones include security, where unintended receivers can gain access to multicast-delivered sensitive financial data.

Table 9-2 lists several notable address ranges reserved by the Internet Assigned Numbers Authority (IANA) because they have relevance to the exam.

Table 9-2   Important Multicast Ranges

Addresses	Block Name	Relevant to Exam Usage
224.0.0/24	Local Network Control	Never forwarded off the local network; TTL set to 1 (do you recall AllSPFRouters?)
224.0.1.0/24	Internetwork Control	Control traffic forwarded through the Internet; Cisco RP-Announce (224.0.1.39) and Cisco RP-Discovery (224.0.1.40), which you will see soon enough
232.0.0.0/8	Source-Specific Multicast	Traffic for multicast sources explicitly requested by the receivers (SSM)
239.0.0.0/8	Organization-Local Scope	Private range (think of these as "RFC 1918 for Multicast"), which does not conflict with the same range being used by other organizations
233.0.0.0/8	GLOP	A block where the middle two octets are formed from assigned ASNs, giving any operator assigned 256 globally unique multicast group addresses

Recall that the first 25 bits of the multicast MAC address are fixed as 01-00-5E. This prefix indicates that the frame is a multicast frame. That only leaves 23 bits of the IPv4 multicast address to convert binary. The IEEE chose this structure to provide a balance between the need for uniqueness and the efficient use of address space. There are 23 bits available to identify a multicast group, and this number is typically sufficient for most networking needs. The downside of this approach is that there is not a one-to-one mapping between multicast MAC addresses and multicast IP addresses. In fact, there is a 1:32 address mapping: each unique multicast MAC address will share 32 multicast IP addresses. If you're wondering how this complication arose, it's the result of not being able to justify the purchase of a complete 28-bit range of MAC addresses for organizationally unique identifiers (OUIs), and we're obliged to live with it. Despite the complexity, there are plenty of calculators available on the Internet that will perform this conversion for you, but basically, since IEEE scrapped 5 bits of an IP address to accomplish the balance that I mentioned, 2^5 bits (0 or 1 in binary) =32 unique IP addresses were "sacrificed." Thus, the "first" multicast MAC address 01-00-5E-**00**-00-01 will represent IPv4 addresses of 224.0.0.1, 224.128.0.1, 225.0.0.1, 225.128.0.1, and so on until we get to the end of the multicast range of 239.255.255.255. Be careful here because these values will be different if we change the multicast MAC address to another value—01-00-5e-**64**-00-01 will become 224.**100**.0.1, 224.**228**.0.1, 225.**100**.0.1, 225.**228**.0.1, and so on. You should not see the exam asking you for these conversions, but you should understand this lack of one-to-one mapping.

On a given Layer 2 segment, when a receiver wants to receive a specific multicast feed, it will send a join-group message using the multicast IP group for that feed. It will also reprogram its interface for accepting the MAC address that represents that multicast IP group. This way, the receiver will ignore OSPF AllSPFRouters updates but will tune into a financial trader feed. This is good but also has implications for how you design multicast applications. The network may have LAN switches that are not IP-aware and only filter on MAC addresses. Thus, if you have two feeds with different IP addresses that map to the same MAC address, you may be delivering these feeds to undesired receivers—which can carry bandwidth or security implications.

Table 9-3 should help refresh your memory about reserved multicast addresses.

Table 9-3   Important Reserved Multicast Addresses

Multicast Addresses	Reserved for
224.0.0.1	All-hosts on a subnet
224.0.0.2	All-routers on a subnet
224.0.0.13	All PIM routers
224.0.0.22	IGMPv3-capable multicast routers
224.0.1.39	Cisco Auto-RP Announce
224.0.1.40	Cisco Auto-RP Discovery

When dealing with multicast, keep Figure 9-1 in mind. A source will send the stream to the **First Hop Router (FHR)**, which will take care of getting through Layer 3 "cloud." PIM is the protocol that will construct a Layer 3 path to deliver multicast traffic to the **Last Hop Router (LHR)**, which is closest to the receiver. LHR will multiply the stream to as many receivers on the Layer 2 LAN as have subscribed to the multicast group. IGMP will deliver this stream to the switch ports that are members of this multicast group. Notice the reference to "Querier."

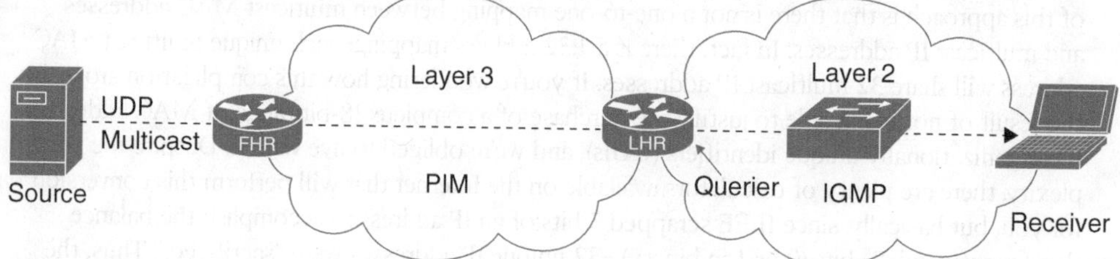

Figure 9-1   *Multicast Big Picture*

Let's look at the simpler of the two—IGMP, which is responsible for getting traffic to the right receivers on the LAN.

IGMP

Internet Group Management Protocol (IGMP) provides the means for the receivers of multicast traffic to express their interest in multicast traffic. In turn, LHR will join a multicast group and will start forwarding traffic to the LAN and, ultimately, the receiver. There have been three different versions of IGMP, with the last one coming out over 20 years ago—so this protocol has been around. Without IGMP snooping, a switch forwards a multicast frame to all switch ports (except the incoming port, of course). IGMP snooping changes this behavior, so the switch sends multicast frames *only* to those receivers that join a particular group by listening for report/leave messages. This is efficient and desired behavior.

IGMPv1

In the late 1980s, RFC 1112 described IGMPv1 with two types of IGMP messages:

- **Host Membership Query:** Multicast routers sent messages (every 60–120 seconds) to address 224.0.0.1 (all-hosts group) with the IP TTL of 1 (i.e., the LAN).

- **Host Membership Report:** Receivers (hosts) generated these messages to indicate their interest in multicast streams. Before responding, hosts would start a report delay timer for each group at random time intervals to space out the reports to not overwhelm the LAN.

Simple. There was very little to no coordination in this process. The router sent three successive IGMP queries, and if hosts were no longer interested in multicast traffic, the membership reports timed out. The router would notice three unanswered queries—indicating that it should stop delivering multicast traffic to the LAN. If the hosts became interested in multicast traffic again, they sent IGMP messages that the router heard, and the process would restart.

IGMPv2

Ten years later, RFC 2236 added several improvements while ensuring compatibility with IGMPv1 hosts. Consider the following enhancements:

- **Group-Specific Query:** In addition to the general query (described in IGMPv1), a router could now learn if a *specific multicast group* had any members (receivers) on an attached LAN. This optimized LAN operations, since now the router could query only the multicast hosts who participated in the mentioned group (G), rather than all multicast receivers (224.0.0.1) as was done in IGMPv1.

- **Leave Group Message:** When the last receiver left a multicast group, it sent this message to the All-Routers multicast group (224.0.0.2). This not only reduced the protocol traffic on a multicast-busy LAN but also improved *leave* latency because the protocol no longer depended on timing out multicast; there was a specific instruction of "we are done with multicast on this LAN for now."

- **Querier Election:** Imagine the LAN that has more than one router. IGMPv1 had no provisions for this. Now, there were two roles on the network—Querier and non-Querier. Every router would start as a Querier, but if a lower IP address Querier showed up, the router would become a non-Querier. If a router has not heard a Query message from another router, it would assume the role of Querier again.

- **Tunable Intervals:** Queries and query responses can be now fine-tuned to reduce the multicast's burstiness; queries and responses could be spread over larger intervals of time.

IGMPv3

Described in RFC 3376, IGMPv3 brought, among other things, the following major enhancements:

- A receiver could request a specific source for a particular multicast group. Now, routers running in PIM Sparse mode (this is all coming up in the PIM section) could build a *direct* multicast distribution tree between the source and receiver, avoiding the RP. As you may recall from your CCNA studies, routers build (*, G—Any, Group) joins to "any source" RPs. In Source-Specific Multicast (SSM), specific (S, G—Source, Group) joins are issued to bypass the RP. Recall that the 232.0.0.0/8 address block is used in SSM.

- IGMPv3 reports were sent with an IP destination address of 224.0.0.22—all IGMPv3-capable multicast routers. You could even now use IPsec to authenticate peers.

- Backward compatibility with IGMPv1 and IGMPv3 was made available.

- The ability to filter groups and sources was made available. This capability can become handy when an undesired source (a hacker?) begins to stream their multicast feed to your group.

Implementing IGMP

It's time to complement this theoretical understanding with practical skills. I have set up the following simple topology in CML. Figure 9-2 shows two routers (Last Hop Routers [LHRs]) and two multicast receivers connected to the same shared LAN.

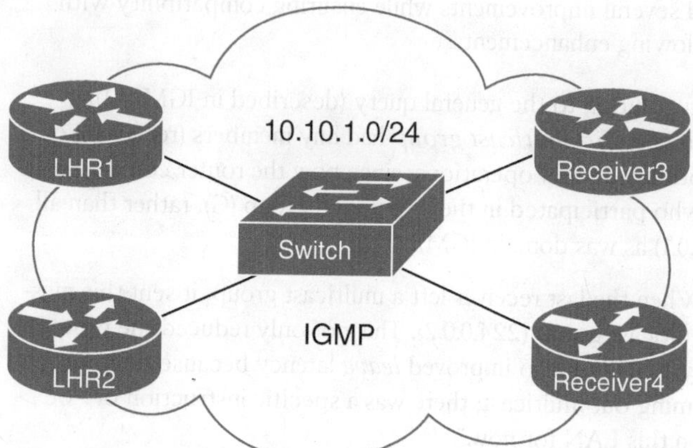

Figure 9-2 *IGMP Reference Diagram*

I have chosen to exclude all presently unnecessary components to focus only on understanding IGMP at this time. Presume the routers are connected or will be connected in the future to some sources or RPs; it doesn't really matter for the operation of IGMP. I am also using routers to represent multicast receivers (or hosts). Feel free to launch genuine multicast through your own lab if you feel it enhances your knowledge, but I do not believe this is necessary. There are VLC players and iperf testers running on slimmed-out Linux distributions, allowing you to quickly simulate multicast traffic. I am most interested in showing you how IGMP operates, and this topology is easily constructed—thus my attraction to it.

Example 9-1 shows a blank router (LHR1 in this case) configuration. We will not bring up LHR2 until later, but go ahead and configure the receivers. You should receive pings from Receiver3 and Receiver4 before you proceed, as shown in the example. We miss the first ping due to ARP, the second one succeeds, and there are only two hosts on this LAN.

Example 9-1   *Basic Routing Setup*

```
inserthostname-here# configure terminal
Enter configuration commands, one per line.  End with CNTL/Z.
inserthostname-here(config)# hostname LHR1
LHR1(config)# interface gigabitEthernet 1
LHR1(config-if)# ip address 10.10.1.254 255.255.255.0
LHR1(config-if)# no shutdown
LHR1(config-if)#
*Mar 12 13:44:36.337: %LINK-3-UPDOWN: Interface GigabitEthernet1, changed state to
up
*Mar 12 13:44:37.337: %LINEPROTO-5-UPDOWN: Line protocol on Interface
GigabitEthernet1, changed state to up
LHR1(config-if)# do show ip interface brief
Interface              IP-Address      OK? Method Status               Protocol
GigabitEthernet1       10.10.1.254     YES manual up                   up
GigabitEthernet2       unassigned      YES unset  administratively down down
GigabitEthernet3       unassigned      YES unset  administratively down down
GigabitEthernet4       unassigned      YES unset  administratively down down
LHR1(config-if)# do ping 10.10.1.255 repeat 2
Type escape sequence to abort.
Sending 2, 100-byte ICMP Echos to 10.10.1.255, timeout is 2 seconds:
.
Reply to request 1 from 10.10.1.4, 53 ms
Reply to request 1 from 10.10.1.3, 57 ms
LHR1(config-if)#
```

When it comes to multicast, let's first look at the switch in the middle of Figure 9-2 in Example 9-2.

Example 9-2   *IGMP Snooping Observations on the Switch*

```
Switch# show ip igmp snooping
Global IGMP Snooping configuration:
-------------------------------------------------
IGMP snooping            : Enabled
Global PIM Snooping      : Disabled
```

```
IGMPv3 snooping               : Enabled
Report suppression            : Enabled
TCN solicit query             : Disabled
TCN flood query count         : 2
Robustness variable           : 2
Last member query count       : 2
Last member query interval    : 1000


Vlan 1:
--------

IGMP snooping                     : Enabled
Pim Snooping                      : Disabled
IGMPv2 immediate leave            : Disabled
Explicit host tracking            : Enabled
Multicast router learning mode    : pim-dvmrp
CGMP interoperability mode        : IGMP_ONLY
Robustness variable               : 2
Last member query count           : 2
Last member query interval        : 1000


Switch# show interfaces status


Port          Name          Status      Vlan    Duplex  Speed Type
Gi1/0/1                     connected   1        a-full a-1000 unknown
Gi1/0/2                     connected   1        a-full a-1000 unknown
Gi1/0/3                     connected   1        a-full a-1000 unknown
Gi1/0/4                     connected   1        a-full a-1000 unknown
Gi1/0/5                     connected   1        a-full a-1000 unknown
Gi1/0/6                     connected   1        a-full a-1000 unknown
Gi1/0/7                     connected   1        a-full a-1000 unknown
Gi1/0/8                     connected   1        a-full a-1000 unknown
```

The only thing I configured on the blank switch is the hostname. We can see that IGMP snooping is enabled by default. (Globally, you can change this behavior by enabling or disabling it per VLAN under the appropriate interface VlanX configuration section. Let this be your homework.) It is running on Vlan 1, the four ports we are going to use are in Vlan 1, and this switch can run IGMPv3. Nothing else to configure on the switch at this time, it seems. I suggest we turn on debugging to see what will happen when we turn on multicast routing on LHR1. Example 9-3 observes IGMP behavior.

Example 9-3 *IGMP Protocol Between the Router and Switch*

```
Switch# configure terminal
Enter configuration commands, one per line.  End with CNTL/Z.
Switch(config)# logging console
Switch(config)# end
Switch# debug ip igmp snooping ?
  A.B.C.D       IPv4 group address
  ancp          igmp snooping ancp activity
  group         igmp snooping group activity
  management    igmp snooping management activity
  querier       igmp snooping querier events
  redundancy    igmp snooping redundancy events
  router        igmp snooping router activity
  timer         igmp snooping timer events
  <cr>          <cr>

Switch# debug ip igmp snooping router ?
  <cr>  <cr>

Switch# debug ip igmp snooping router
router debugging is on
Switch#
```

```
LHR1(config-if)# exit
LLHR1(config)# ip multicast-routing ?
  distributed  Distributed multicast switching
  vrf          Select VPN Routing/Forwarding instance

LHR1(config)# ip multicast-routing distributed
LHR1(config)# interface gigabitEthernet 1
LHR1(config-if)# ip pim sparse-mode
LHR1(config-if)#
*Mar 12 17:56:04.214: %PIM-5-DRCHG: DR change from neighbor 0.0.0.0 to 10.10.1.254
on interface GigabitEthernet1
```

```
Switch#
*Mar 12 17:56:02.220: IGMPSN: router: Received non igmp pak on Vlan 1, port Gi1/0/1
*Mar 12 17:56:02.220: IGMPSN: router: PIMV2 Hello packet received in 1
*Mar 12 17:56:02.220: IGMPSN: l2mc_mrd_learn_router_port_internal Gi1/0/1 on Vlan 1
*Mar 12 17:56:02.220: IGMPSN: router: Is not a router port on Vlan 1, port Gi1/0/1
*Mar 12 17:56:02.220: IGMPSN: router: Is not a router port on Vlan 1, port Gi1/0/1
*Mar 12 17:56:02.220: IGMPSN: router: Created router port on Vlan 1, port Gi1/0/1
*Mar 12 17:56:02.223: IGMPSN: After l2mcm_rport_add-1 Gi1/0/1 on Vlan 1
*Mar 12 17:56:02.223: IGMPSN: router: Calling HA mrouter sync Iport:Gi1/0/1 p_type:1
mrt_enable:0
```

```
*Mar 12 17:56:02.223: IGMPSN: router: Learning port: Gi1/0/1 as rport on Vlan 1
*Mar 12 17:56:02.226: IGMPSN: router: Received IGMP pak on Vlan 1, port Gi1/0/1
*Mar 12 17:56:02.226: IGMPSN: l2mc_mrd_learn_router_port_internal Gi1/0/1 on Vlan 1
*Mar 12 17:56:02.226: IGMPSN: router: Is a router port on Vlan 1, port Gi1/0/1
*Mar 12 17:56:02.226: IGMPSN: router: Learning port: Gi1/0/1 as rport on Vlan 1
Switch# show ip igmp snooping querier
Vlan      IP Address              IGMP Version  Port
------------------------------------------------------------------
1         10.10.1.254                 v2           Gi1/0/1


Switch# show ip igmp snooping groups
Vlan      Group              Type        Version     Port List
------------------------------------------------------------------
1         224.0.1.40         igmp          v2         Gi1/0/1
```

Lots to unpack here after we turned on debugging on the switch. Since we had IGMP already working on the switch by default, we only needed two commands on the LHR1 to enable multicast on the LAN. *Without* having any multicast sources or RPs, we used only two commands to turn on multicast routing globally and enabled **ip pim sparse-mode** on the interface facing the LAN. We could have used any other PIM mode, but as you will learn later in the PIM section, **PIM Sparse mode** is really what you should be using nowadays. **PIM Dense mode** and its variations were too inefficient, and pretty much no one has been using them for some time.

Then, looking at the switch's debug output, we saw a PIMv2 hello packet arrive, the switch mentioning that Gi1/0/1 (connected to LHR1) is not a router port, then seeing an IMGP packet and declaring this interface as a router port. What we learned here is that as soon as we turned on PIM Sparse mode on the interface, the router immediately started sending IGMP messages to the LAN (IGMP comes included when you turn on PIM).

Next, the **show ip igmp snooping querier** command is quite handy to know because it shows you the router is sending Membership Query messages (also recall seeing Querier in Figure 9-1). We can see the Vlan1, interface Gi1/0/1, the IP address of the Querier, and IGMPv2 being used. Note the multicast group 224.0.1.40 (Cisco RP-Discovery) showed up (a consequence of turning on PIM). Ignore it. It gets added by default.

I suggest we do the following. Let's turn off our debug, start another debug for an arbitrary multicast group from the private multicast address block, and observe what happens. Using 239.100.100.100 sounds like a reasonable choice because it will translate into the multicast MAC address of 01-00-5E-64-64-64. We will then make Receiver3 join this multicast group. Example 9-4 demonstrates this process. Pay special attention to the **ip igmp join-group** command, which causes the router to send an IGMP membership report.

Example 9-4   *Turning on Multicast Receiver3 (IGMPv2 Report Generation)*

```
Switch# undebug all
All possible debugging has been turned off
Switch# debug ip igmp snooping 239.100.100.100
group IP address debugging is on for 239.100.100.100
Switch#

Receiver3# configure terminal
Enter configuration commands, one per line.  End with CNTL/Z.
Receiver3(config)# interface gigabitEthernet 1
Receiver3(config-if)# ip igmp join-group 239.100.100.100
Receiver3(config-if)#

Switch#
*Mar 12 19:04:58.235: IGMPSN: Received IGMPv2 Report for group 239.100.100.100
received on Vlan 1, port Gi1/0/3
*Mar 12 19:04:58.235: IGMPSN: Group: Received IGMPv2 report for mcast group
239.100.100.100 from Client 10.10.1.3. Received on Vlan 1, port Gi1/0/3.
*Mar 12 19:04:58.235: L2MM: Add member: gda:0100.5e64.6464, adding Gi1/0/1
*Mar 12 19:04:58.235: IGMPSN: mgt: added port Gi1/0/1 on gce 0100.5e64.6464, Vlan 1
*Mar 12 19:04:58.235: IGMPSN: group: Created group 239.100.100.100
*Mar 12 19:04:58.235: IGMPSN: Add v2 group 239.100.100.100 member port Gi1/0/3, on
Vlan 1
*Mar 12 19:04:58.235: L2MM: Add member: gda:0100.5e64.6464, adding Gi1/0/3
*Mar 12 19:04:58.235: IGMPSN: mgt: added port Gi1/0/3 on gce 0100.5e64.6464, Vlan 1
*Mar 12 19:04:58.235: IGMPSN: notify_stdby_1 v2 group 239.100.100.100 member port
Gi1/0/3, on Vlan 1
*Mar 12 19:04:58.235: IGMPSN: notify_stdbyis set v2 group 239.100.100.100 member
port Gi1/0/3, on Vlan 1 msg_version 2
*Mar 12 19:04:58.235: IGMPSN: Call snoop_group_port_update v2 group 239.100.100.100
member port Gi1/0/3, on Vlan 1 version 2
*Mar 12 19:04:58.235: IGMPSN: group: Added port Gi1/0/3 to group 239.100.100.100
*Mar 12 19:04:58.235: IGMPSN: group: Forwarding 239.100.100.100 report to router
ports
Switch# show ip igmp snooping groups
Vlan      Group              Type        Version      Port List
-------------------------------------------------------------------
1         224.0.1.40         igmp        v2           Gi1/0/1
1         239.100.100.100    igmp        v2           Gi1/0/3
```

Read carefully through the output in Example 9-4. With a single interface command on
Receiver3, we join our multicast group and immediately see IGMPv2 report for this group on
interface Gi1/0/3. Note the multicast MAC address of 0100.5364.6464 being added to both
Gi1/0/1 (LHR1) and G1/0/3 (Receiver3). We finally see the host membership report being sent
to the router port, and the snooping group shows Receiver3's port added. Be sure you understand the big picture. Once done, we will add a second host, Receiver4, to the same multicast
group, 239.100.100.100, in Example 9-5.

Example 9-5 *Turning on Multicast Receiver4*

```
Receiver4# configure terminal
Enter configuration commands, one per line.  End with CNTL/Z.
Receiver4(config)# interface gigabitEthernet 1
Receiver4(config-if)# ip igmp join-group 239.100.100.100
Receiver4(config-if)#

Switch#
*Mar 12 22:34:49.039: IGMPSN: Received IGMPv2 Report for group 239.100.100.100
received on Vlan 1, port Gi1/0/4
*Mar 12 22:34:49.039: IGMPSN: Group: Received IGMPv2 report for mcast group
239.100.100.100 from Client 10.10.1.4. Received on Vlan 1, port Gi1/0/4.
*Mar 12 22:34:49.039: IGMPSN: Add v2 group 239.100.100.100 member port Gi1/0/4,
on Vlan 1
*Mar 12 22:34:49.039: L2MM: Add member: gda:0100.5e64.6464, adding Gi1/0/4
*Mar 12 22:34:49.039: IGMPSN: mgt: added port Gi1/0/4 on gce 0100.5e64.6464, Vlan 1
*Mar 12 22:34:49.039: IGMPSN: notify_stdby_1 v2 group 239.100.100.100 member port
Gi1/0/4, on Vlan 1
*Mar 12 22:34:49.039: IGMPSN: notify_stdbyis set v2 group 239.100.100.100 member
port Gi1/0/4, on Vlan 1 msg_version 2
*Mar 12 22:34:49.039: IGMPSN: Call snoop_group_port_update v2 group 239.100.100.100
member port Gi1/0/4, on Vlan 1 version 2
*Mar 12 22:34:49.039: IGMPSN: group: Added port Gi1/0/4 to group 239.100.100.100
*Mar 12 22:34:49.039: IGMPSN: .group: Forwarding 239.100.100.100 report to router
ports
Switch# show ip igmp snooping groups
Vlan      Group                     Type        Version      Port List
---------------------------------------------------------------------------
1         224.0.1.40                igmp        v2           Gi1/0/1
1         239.100.100.100           igmp        v2           Gi1/0/3, Gi1/0/4
```

Notice the same multicast group, the same multicast MAC address, but a different port
Gi1/0/4. This port is added to the multicast group, and a host membership report is sent to
router ports. Of interest to us is that now two ports—Gi1/0/3 and Gi1/0/4—show up in the
IGMP port group for our multicast group subscription in the output of the **show ip igmp
snooping group** command.

Without IGMP snooping enabled on the switch, not all receivers send membership reports.
When a receiver hears a Group-Specific Query, a receiver sets a delay timer to a random
value selected from the range (0, Max Response Time). If a receiver receives another host's
Report (version 1 or 2) while it has a timer running, it will cancel its own membership report
for the specified group and not send a Report, in order to suppress duplicate Reports. *With
IGMP snooping, all receivers send membership reports.*

This subtle but important difference is shown in Example 9-6, where I turn on debug on
LHR1, Receiver3, and Receiver4.

Example 9-6 *IGMP Snooping All Receivers Send Membership Reports*

```
LHR1# debug ip igmp
IGMP debugging is on
LHR1#
```

```
Receiver3# debug ip igmp
IGMP debugging is on
Receiver3#
```

```
Receiver4# debug ip igmp
IGMP debugging is on
Receiver4#
```

```
LHR1#
*Mar 13 12:26:39.801: IGMP(0): Send v2 general Query on GigabitEthernet1
*Mar 13 12:26:39.801: IGMP(0): Set report delay time to 3.0 seconds for 224.0.1.40
on GigabitEthernet1
*Mar 13 12:26:41.273: IGMP(0): Received v2 Report on GigabitEthernet1 from 10.10.1.4
for 239.100.100.100
*Mar 13 12:26:41.273: IGMP(0): Received Group record for group 239.100.100.100,
mode 2 from 10.10.1.4 for 0 sources
*Mar 13 12:26:41.273: IGMP(0): Updating EXCLUDE group timer for 239.100.100.100
*Mar 13 12:26:41.273: IGMP(0): MRT Add/Update GigabitEthernet1 for
(*,239.100.100.100) by 0
*Mar 13 12:26:42.841: IGMP(0): Send v2 Report for 224.0.1.40 on GigabitEthernet1
*Mar 13 12:26:42.841: IGMP(0): Received v2 Report on GigabitEthernet1 from
10.10.1.254 for 224.0.1.40
*Mar 13 12:26:42.841: IGMP(0): Received Group record for group 224.0.1.40, mode 2
from 10.10.1.254 for 0 sources
*Mar 13 12:26:42.841: IGMP(0): Updating EXCLUDE group timer for 224.0.1.40
*Mar 13 12:26:42.841: IGMP(0): MRT Add/Update GigabitEthernet1 for (*,224.0.1.40)
by 0
*Mar 13 12:27:39.802: IGMP(0): Send v2 general Query on GigabitEthernet1
*Mar 13 12:27:39.802: IGMP(0): Set report delay time to 7.3 seconds for 224.0.1.40
on GigabitEthernet1
*Mar 13 12:27:42.409: IGMP(0): Received v2 Report on GigabitEthernet1 from 10.10.1.3
for 239.100.100.100
*Mar 13 12:27:42.410: IGMP(0): Received Group record for group 239.100.100.100,
mode 2 from 10.10.1.3 for 0 sources
*Mar 13 12:27:42.410: IGMP(0): Updating EXCLUDE group timer for 239.100.100.100
*Mar 13 12:27:42.410: IGMP(0): MRT Add/Update GigabitEthernet1 for
(*,239.100.100.100) by 0
*Mar 13 12:27:47.142: IGMP(0): Send v2 Report for 224.0.1.40 on GigabitEthernet1
*Mar 13 12:27:47.142: IGMP(0): Received v2 Report on GigabitEthernet1 from
10.10.1.254 for 224.0.1.40
```

```
*Mar 13 12:27:47.142: IGMP(0): Received Group record for group 224.0.1.40, mode 2
from 10.10.1.254 for 0 sources
*Mar 13 12:27:47.142: IGMP(0): Updating EXCLUDE group timer for 224.0.1.40
*Mar 13 12:27:47.142: IGMP(0): MRT Add/Update GigabitEthernet1 for (*,224.0.1.40)
by 0
LHR1#
```

```
Receiver3#
*Mar 13 12:26:39.823: IGMP(0): Received v2 Query on GigabitEthernet1 from
10.10.1.254
*Mar 13 12:26:39.823: IGMP(0): Set report delay time to 7.2 seconds for
239.100.100.100 on GigabitEthernet1
*Mar 13 12:26:47.093: IGMP(0): Send v2 Report for 239.100.100.100 on
GigabitEthernet1
*Mar 13 12:27:39.819: IGMP(0): Received v2 Query on GigabitEthernet1 from
10.10.1.254
*Mar 13 12:27:39.820: IGMP(0): Set report delay time to 2.5 seconds for
239.100.100.100 on GigabitEthernet1
*Mar 13 12:27:42.393: IGMP(0): Send v2 Report for 239.100.100.100 on
GigabitEthernet1
Receiver3#
```

```
Receiver4#
*Mar 13 12:26:39.825: IGMP(0): Received v2 Query on GigabitEthernet1 from
10.10.1.254
*Mar 13 12:26:39.825: IGMP(0): Set report delay time to 1.4 seconds for
239.100.100.100 on GigabitEthernet1
*Mar 13 12:26:41.256: IGMP(0): Send v2 Report for 239.100.100.100 on
GigabitEthernet1
*Mar 13 12:27:39.824: IGMP(0): Received v2 Query on GigabitEthernet1 from
10.10.1.254
*Mar 13 12:27:39.824: IGMP(0): Set report delay time to 5.4 seconds for
239.100.100.100 on GigabitEthernet1
*Mar 13 12:27:45.256: IGMP(0): Send v2 Report for 239.100.100.100 on
GigabitEthernet1
Receiver4#
```

Pay attention to messages and timestamps. LHR1 sends a general query and receives back reports from *both* Receiver3 and Receiver4. Receiver3 receives the query from the router (LHR1), sets off a 7.2-second timer, waits, and sends the report. Same events on Receiver4 with different timers. Lesson here—there is no suppression of messages; all receivers send their own messaging reports.

Next, let's observe the behavior when one member of the existing IMGP group decides to leave the group, signaling the end of interest in multicast traffic, as demonstrated in Example 9-7. Be sure to have debugging turned on LHR1, Switch, and Receiver3.

Example 9-7   *Receiver3 Decides to Leave the Multicast Group*

```
Receiver3# configure terminal
Enter configuration commands, one per line.  End with CNTL/Z.
Receiver3(config)# interface gigabitEthernet 1
Receiver3(config-if)# no ip igmp join-group 239.100.100.100
Receiver3(config-if)#
*Mar 13 14:27:23.609: IGMP(0): IGMP delete group 239.100.100.100 on GigabitEthernet1
*Mar 13 14:27:23.636: IGMP(0): Send Leave for 239.100.100.100 on GigabitEthernet1
*Mar 13 14:27:23.638: IGMP(0): Deregistering IGMP with ipmulticast GIR
Receiver3(config-if)#


Switch#
*Mar 13 14:27:23.616: IGMPSN: Received IGMP Leave for group 239.100.100.100 received
on Vlan 1, port Gi1/0/3
*Mar 13 14:27:23.616: IGMPSN: group: Group exist - Leave for group 239.100.100.100
Client 10.10.1.3 received on Vlan 1, port Gi1/0/3, group state (1)
*Mar 13 14:27:23.616: IGMPSN: group: Created v2 leave port on port Gi1/0/3, for
group 239.100.100.100 on Vlan 1
*Mar 13 14:27:25.616: IGMPSN: group: Deleting leave port on port Gi1/0/3, for
239.100.100.100 on Vlan 1
*Mar 13 14:27:25.616: IGMPSN: Clearing all hosts on port Gi1/0/3 for group
239.100.100.100
*Mar 13 14:27:25.616: IGMPSN: Delete v2 group 239.100.100.100 member port Gi1/0/3,
on Vlan 1
*Mar 13 14:27:25.617: L2MM: Add member: gda:0100.5e64.6464, removing Gi1/0/3
*Mar 13 14:27:25.617: IGMPSN: mgt: deleted port Gi1/0/3 on gce 0100.5e64.6464, on
Vlan 1
*Mar 13 14:27:25.617: IGMPSN: group: Deleting port Gi1/0/3 from group
239.100.100.100 on Vlan 1
Switch#


LHR1#
LHR1#
```

Notice how Receiver3 sends an IGMP leave message. The Switch receives the leave message
for group 239.100.100.100 and deletes port G1/0/3 from the group. Observe that no leave
messages were sent to LHR1, and its debug output is silent to this event. Now let's remove
Receiver4, the last remaining multicast group member, and see what happens in Example 9-8.

Example 9-8   *The Remaining Receiver4 Decides to Leave the Multicast Group*

```
Switch# show ip igmp snooping groups
Vlan      Group               Type       Version    Port List
-----------------------------------------------------------------------
1         224.0.1.40          igmp       v2         Gi1/0/1
1         239.100.100.100     igmp       v2         Gi1/0/4


Switch#
```

```
Receiver4# configure terminal
Enter configuration commands, one per line.  End with CNTL/Z.
Receiver4(config)# interface gigabitEthernet 1
Receiver4(config-if)# no ip igmp join-group 239.100.100.100
Receiver4(config-if)#
*Mar 13 15:07:13.735: IGMP(0): IGMP delete group 239.100.100.100 on GigabitEthernet1
*Mar 13 15:07:13.759: IGMP(0): Send Leave for 239.100.100.100 on GigabitEthernet1
*Mar 13 15:07:13.761: IGMP(0): Deregistering IGMP with ipmulticast GIR
Receiver4(config-if)#
```

```
Switch#
*Mar 13 15:07:13.735: IGMPSN: Received IGMP Leave for group 239.100.100.100 received
on Vlan 1, port Gi1/0/4
*Mar 13 15:07:13.735: IGMPSN: group: Group exist - Leave for group 239.100.100.100
Client 10.10.1.4 received on Vlan 1, port Gi1/0/4, group state (1)
*Mar 13 15:07:13.735: IGMPSN: group: Created v2 leave port on port Gi1/0/4, for
group 239.100.100.100 on Vlan 1
*Mar 13 15:07:15.736: IGMPSN: group: Deleting leave port on port Gi1/0/4, for
239.100.100.100 on Vlan 1
*Mar 13 15:07:15.736: IGMPSN: Clearing all hosts on port Gi1/0/4 for group
239.100.100.100
*Mar 13 15:07:15.736: IGMPSN: Delete v2 group 239.100.100.100 member port Gi1/0/4,
on Vlan 1
*Mar 13 15:07:15.736: L2MM: Add member: gda:0100.5e64.6464, removing Gi1/0/4
*Mar 13 15:07:15.736: IGMPSN: mgt: deleted port Gi1/0/4 on gce 0100.5e64.6464, on
Vlan 1
*Mar 13 15:07:15.736: IGMPSN: group: Deleting port Gi1/0/4 from group
239.100.100.100 on Vlan 1
*Mar 13 15:07:15.736: IGMPSN: mgt: try to delete group 239.100.100.100, on Vlan 1
*Mar 13 15:07:15.736: IGMPSN: group: purge group 239.100.100.100 in vlan 1
*Mar 13 15:07:15.736: IGMPSN: mgt: deleting group 239.100.100.100, on Vlan 1
*Mar 13 15:07:15.736: IGMPSN: mgt: deleting gce 0100.5e64.6464, on Vlan 1
*Mar 13 15:07:15.759: IGMPSN: Received IGMP Query for group 239.100.100.100 received
on Vlan 1, port Gi1/0/1
*Mar 13 15:07:16.833: IGMPSN: Received IGMP Query for group 239.100.100.100 received
on Vlan 1, port Gi1/0/1
Switch# sh ip igmp snooping groups
Vlan      Group              Type          Version     Port List
---------------------------------------------------------------------------
1         224.0.1.40         igmp          v2          Gi1/0/1

Switch#
```

```
LHR1#
*Mar 13 15:06:41.672: IGMP(0): Received v2 Report on GigabitEthernet1 from 10.10.1.4
for 239.100.100.100
*Mar 13 15:06:41.672: IGMP(0): Received Group record for group 239.100.100.100, mode
2 from 10.10.1.4 for 0 sources
```

```
*Mar 13 15:06:41.672: IGMP(0): Updating EXCLUDE group timer for 239.100.100.100
*Mar 13 15:06:41.672: IGMP(0): MRT Add/Update GigabitEthernet1 for
(*,239.100.100.100) by 0
*Mar 13 15:07:15.774: IGMP(0): Received Leave from 10.10.1.4 (GigabitEthernet1) for
239.100.100.100
*Mar 13 15:07:15.775: IGMP(0): Received Group record for group 239.100.100.100, mode
3 from 10.10.1.4 for 0 sources
*Mar 13 15:07:15.775: IGMP(0): Lower expiration timer to 2000 msec for
239.100.100.100 on GigabitEthernet1
*Mar 13 15:07:15.775: IGMP(0): Send v2 Query on GigabitEthernet1 for group
239.100.100.100
*Mar 13 15:07:16.847: IGMP(0): Send v2 Query on GigabitEthernet1 for group
239.100.100.100
*Mar 13 15:07:17.846: IGMP(0): Switching to INCLUDE mode for 239.100.100.100 on
GigabitEthernet1
*Mar 13 15:07:17.846: IGMP(0): MRT delete GigabitEthernet1 for (*,239.100.100.100)
by 0
*Mar 13 15:07:39.822: IGMP(0): Send v2 general Query on GigabitEthernet1
*Mar 13 15:07:39.822: IGMP(0): Set report delay time to 6.8 seconds for 224.0.1.40
on GigabitEthernet1
*Mar 13 15:07:46.647: IGMP(0): Send v2 Report for 224.0.1.40 on GigabitEthernet1
*Mar 13 15:07:46.647: IGMP(0): Received v2 Report on GigabitEthernet1 from
10.10.1.254 for 224.0.1.40
*Mar 13 15:07:46.647: IGMP(0): Received Group record for group 224.0.1.40, mode 2
from 10.10.1.254 for 0 sources
*Mar 13 15:07:46.647: IGMP(0): Updating EXCLUDE group timer for 224.0.1.40
*Mar 13 15:07:46.647: IGMP(0): MRT Add/Update GigabitEthernet1 for (*,224.0.1.40) by
0
LHR1#
```

Observe that the only receiver left in the IGMP snooping port-list on Switch is on port
Gi1/0/4, which is Receiver4. As soon as we remove the subscription to multicast group
239.100.100.100, Switch purges group 239.100.100.100 from multicast subscriptions on
Vlan1. The port list is now empty for that group (only the RP-Discovery remains). Finally,
LHR1 receives the Leave message for its interface GigabitEthernet1 because there are no subscribers left on this segment. Example 9-9 demonstrates the effect of turning on multicast
on LHR2.

Example 9-9 *Adding LHR2 to the Network*

```
inserthostname-here#
inserthostname-here # debug ip igmp
IGMP debugging is on
inserthostname-here# configure terminal
Enter configuration commands, one per line.  End with CNTL/Z.
inserthostname-here(config)# hostname LHR2
```

```
LHR2(config)# loggin console
LHR2(config)# ip multicast-routing distributed
LHR2(config)# interface gigabitEthernet 1
LHR2(config-if)# ip add 10.10.1.250 255.255.255.0
LHR2(config-if)# ip pim sparse-mode
LHR2(config-if)# no shutdown
LHR2(config-if)#
*Mar 13 16:18:05.033: %PIM-5-DRCHG: DR change from neighbor 0.0.0.0 to 10.10.1.250
on interface GigabitEthernet1
*Mar 13 16:18:06.660: %LINK-3-UPDOWN: Interface GigabitEthernet1, changed state to up
*Mar 13 16:18:06.665: IGMP(0): WAVL Insert group: 224.0.1.40    interface:
GigabitEthernet1 Successful
*Mar 13 16:18:06.667: IGMP(0): Send v2 Report for 224.0.1.40 on GigabitEthernet1
*Mar 13 16:18:06.667: IGMP(0): Received v2 Report on GigabitEthernet1 from
10.10.1.250 for 224.0.1.40
*Mar 13 16:18:06.667: IGMP(0): Received Group record for group 224.0.1.40, mode 2
from 10.10.1.250 for 0 sources
*Mar 13 16:18:06.667: IGMP(0): Updating EXCLUDE group timer for 224.0.1.40
*Mar 13 16:18:06.667: IGMP(0): MRT Add/Update GigabitEthernet1 for (*,224.0.1.40)
by 0
*Mar 13 16:18:06.668: IGMP(0): MRT Add/Update GigabitEthernet1 for (*,224.0.1.40)
by 4
*Mar 13 16:18:06.668: IGMP(0): MRT Add/Update GigabitEthernet1 for (*,224.0.1.40)
by 4
*Mar 13 16:18:06.668: IGMP(0): Send v2 Report for 224.0.1.40 on GigabitEthernet1
*Mar 13 16:18:06.668: IGMP(0): Received v2 Report on GigabitEthernet1 from
10.10.1.250 for 224.0.1.40
*Mar 13 16:18:06.668: IGMP(0): Received Group record for group 224.0.1.40, mode 2
from 10.10.1.250 for 0 sources
*Mar 13 16:18:06.668: IGMP(0): Updating EXCLUDE group timer for 224.0.1.40
*Mar 13 16:18:06.669: IGMP(0): MRT Add/Update GigabitEthernet1 for (*,224.0.1.40)
by 0
*Mar 13 16:18:06.670: IGMP(0): Send v2 init  Query on GigabitEthernet1
*Mar 13 16:18:06.670: IGMP(0): Set report delay time to 2.4 seconds for 224.0.1.40
on GigabitEthernet1
*Mar 13 16:18:07.261: IGMP(0): Received v2 Report on GigabitEthernet1 from
10.10.1.254 for 224.0.1.40
*Mar 13 16:18:07.261: IGMP(0): Received Group record for group 224.0.1.40, mode 2
from 10.10.1.254 for 0 sources
*Mar 13 16:18:07.261: IGMP(0): Cancel report for 224.0.1.40 on GigabitEthernet1
*Mar 13 16:18:07.261: IGMP(0): Updating EXCLUDE group timer for 224.0.1.40
*Mar 13 16:18:07.261: IGMP(0): MRT Add/Update GigabitEthernet1 for (*,224.0.1.40)
by 0
*Mar 13 16:18:07.660: %LINEPROTO-5-UPDOWN: Line protocol on Interface
GigabitEthernet1, changed state to up
LHR2(config-if)#
```

```
LHR1#
*Mar 13 16:18:06.726: IGMP(0): Received v2 Report on GigabitEthernet1 from
10.10.1.250 for 224.0.1.40
*Mar 13 16:18:06.726: IGMP(0): Received Group record for group 224.0.1.40, mode 2
from 10.10.1.250 for 0 sources
*Mar 13 16:18:06.726: IGMP(0): Updating EXCLUDE group timer for 224.0.1.40
*Mar 13 16:18:06.726: IGMP(0): MRT Add/Update GigabitEthernet1 for (*,224.0.1.40)
by 0
*Mar 13 16:18:06.728: IGMP(0): Received v2 Report on GigabitEthernet1 from
10.10.1.250 for 224.0.1.40
*Mar 13 16:18:06.728: IGMP(0): Received Group record for group 224.0.1.40, mode 2
from 10.10.1.250 for 0 sources
*Mar 13 16:18:06.728: IGMP(0): Updating EXCLUDE group timer for 224.0.1.40
*Mar 13 16:18:06.728: IGMP(0): MRT Add/Update GigabitEthernet1 for (*,224.0.1.40)
by 0
*Mar 13 16:18:06.747: IGMP(0): Received v2 Query on GigabitEthernet1 from
10.10.1.250
*Mar 13 16:18:06.747: IGMP(0): Set report delay time to 0.5 seconds for 224.0.1.40
on GigabitEthernet1
*Mar 13 16:18:07.248: IGMP(0): Send v2 Report for 224.0.1.40 on GigabitEthernet1
*Mar 13 16:18:07.248: IGMP(0): Received v2 Report on GigabitEthernet1 from
10.10.1.254 for 224.0.1.40
*Mar 13 16:18:07.248: IGMP(0): Received Group record for group 224.0.1.40, mode 2
from 10.10.1.254 for 0 sources
*Mar 13 16:18:07.248: IGMP(0): Updating EXCLUDE group timer for 224.0.1.40
*Mar 13 16:18:07.249: IGMP(0): MRT Add/Update GigabitEthernet1 for (*,224.0.1.40)
by 0
LHR1#
```

```
Switch# show ip igmp snooping querier

Vlan      IP Address                    IGMP Version  Port
-------------------------------------------------------------------
1         10.10.1.250                   v2            Gi1/0/2

Switch#
```

```
LHR1# show ip igmp interface gigabitEthernet 1
GigabitEthernet1 is up, line protocol is up
  Internet address is 10.10.1.254/24
  IGMP is enabled on interface
  Current IGMP host version is 2
  Current IGMP router version is 2
  IGMP query interval is 60 seconds
  IGMP configured query interval is 60 seconds
  IGMP querier timeout is 120 seconds
```

```
IGMP configured querier timeout is 120 seconds
IGMP max query response time is 10 seconds
Last member query count is 2
Last member query response interval is 1000 ms
Inbound IGMP access group is not set
IGMP activity: 4 joins, 3 leaves
Multicast routing is enabled on interface
Multicast TTL threshold is 0
Multicast designated router (DR) is 10.10.1.254 (this system)
IGMP querying router is 10.10.1.250
Multicast groups joined by this system (number of users):
    224.0.1.40(1)
LHR1#
```

```
LHR2# show ip igmp interface gigabitEthernet 1 | include querying
  IGMP querying router is 10.10.1.250 (this system)
LHR2#
```

Do you recall that it is the lower IP address that will become the Querier for the subnet? We turn on LHR2, select the lower 10.10.1.250 address than the LHR1's 10.10.1.254, and use **no shutdown** on the interface. Watch the timestamps—as soon as LHR1 receives the report both routers set off delay timers, LHR2 cancels its report for RP-Discovery because it sees LHR1's messaging. Switch verifies that LHR2 is now the official Querier for this network segment. We also confirm this from LHR1 and LHR2's outputs. Note the IGMP query interval timers as well.

Now let's move to IGMPv3, which allows the receiver to specify sources and the ability to filter groups and sources. Let's see how this works in the following examples, beginning with Example 9-10, which shows us turning on IGMPv3 on LHR1.

Example 9-10 *Turning on IGMPv3 on LHR1*

```
LHR1# configure terminal
Enter configuration commands, one per line.  End with CNTL/Z.
LHR1(config)# ip pim ssm default
LHR1(config)# interface gigabitEthernet 1
LHR1(config-if)# ip igmp version 3
LHR1(config-if)# end
*Mar 14 00:00:50.561: %SYS-5-CONFIG_I: Configured from console by console
LHR1# debug ip packet
IP packet debugging is on
LHR1#
```

```
*Mar 14 00:01:09.735: IP: s=10.10.1.254 (local), d=224.0.0.13 (GigabitEthernet1),
len 58, sending broad/multicast
*Mar 14 00:01:09.735: IP: s=10.10.1.254 (local), d=224.0.0.13 (GigabitEthernet1),
len 58, output feature, feature skipped, MFIB Adjacency(93), rtype 0, forus FALSE,
sendself FALSE, mtu 0, fwdchk FALSE
*Mar 14 00:01:39.285: IP: s=10.10.1.254 (local), d=224.0.0.13 (GigabitEthernet1),
len 58, sending broad/multicast
*Mar 14 00:01:39.285: IP: s=10.10.1.254 (local), d=224.0.0.13 (GigabitEthernet1),
len 58, output feature, feature skipped, MFIB Adjacency(93), rtype 0, forus FALSE,
sendself FALSE, mtu 0, fwdchk FALSE
*Mar 14 00:01:48.951: IP: s=10.10.1.254 (local), d=224.0.0.1 (GigabitEthernet1),
len 36, sending broad/multicast
*Mar 14 00:01:48.951: IP: s=10.10.1.254 (local), d=224.0.0.1 (GigabitEthernet1),
len 36, output feature, feature skipped, MFIB Adjacency(93), rtype 0, forus FALSE,
sendself FALSE, mtu 0, fwdchk FALSE
*Mar 14 00:01:52.183: IP: s=10.10.1.254 (local), d=224.0.0.22 (GigabitEthernet1),
len 40, sending broad/multicast
*Mar 14 00:01:52.183: IP: s=10.10.1.254 (local), d=224.0.0.22 (GigabitEthernet1),
len 40, output feature, feature skipped, MFIB Adjacency(93), rtype 0, forus FALSE,
sendself FALSE, mtu 0, fwdchk FALSE
```

I turned on PIM Source-Specific Multicast (SSM) for the default range of 232/8 and enabled IGMPv3 on the interface facing the LAN. I turned on IP packet debugging (*do not do this in production this way!* I only have a couple of routers here with no traffic), waited a few moments, and saw packets to destination 224.0.0.13 (All PIM Routers), 224.0.0.1 (All Multicast Hosts), and finally 224.0.0.22 (All IGMPv3 Routers).

Now let's head to Receiver3 and turn on IGMPv3, along with a couple of SSM multicast groups requesting this traffic from specific sources in Example 9-11.

Example 9-11   *Turning on IGMPv3 on Receiver3*

```
Receiver3(config-if)# do debug ip igmp
IGMP debugging is on
Receiver3(config-if)# ip igmp version 3
*Mar 14 00:19:38.120: IGMP(0): Switching IGMP version from 2 to 3 on
GigabitEthernet1
*Mar 14 00:19:48.969: IGMP(0): Received v3 Query on GigabitEthernet1 from
10.10.1.254
Receiver3(config-if)# ip igmp join-group 232.100.100.100 source 10.254.254.254
*Mar 14 00:20:19.283: IGMP(0): WAVL Insert group: 232.100.100.100   interface: Giga-
bitEthernet1 Successful
*Mar 14 00:20:19.285: IGMP(0): Create source 10.254.254.254
*Mar 14 00:20:19.285: IGMP(0): Building v3 Report on GigabitEthernet1
*Mar 14 00:20:19.286: IGMP(0): Add Group Record for 232.100.100.100, type 5
*Mar 14 00:20:19.286: IGMP(0): Add Source Record 10.254.254.254
*Mar 14 00:20:19.286: IGMP(0): Add Group Record for 232.100.100.100, type 6
*Mar 14 00:20:19.286: IGMP(0): No sources to add, group record removed from report
```

```
*Mar 14 00:20:19.286: IGMP(0): Send unsolicited v3 Report with 1 group records on
int gig 1
*Mar 14 00:20:20.121: IGMP(0): Building v3 Report on GigabitEthernet1
*Mar 14 00:20:20.121: IGMP(0): Add Group Record for 232.100.100.100, type 5
*Mar 14 00:20:20.121: IGMP(0): Add Source Record 10.254.254.254
*Mar 14 00:20:20.122: IGMP(0): Add Group Record for 232.100.100.100, type 6
*Mar 14 00:20:20.122: IGMP(0): No sources to add, group record removed from report
*Mar 14 00:20:20.122: IGMP(0): Send unsolicited v3 Report with 1 group records on
GigabitEthernet1
Receiver3(config-if)# ip igmp join-group 232.100.100.101 source 10.100.100.100
Receiver3(config-if)#
*Mar 14 00:20:48.973: IGMP(0): Received v3 Query on GigabitEthernet1 from
10.10.1.254
*Mar 14 00:20:48.973: IGMP(0): Set report delay to 5.7 seconds to respond to General
Query on GigabitEthernet1
*Mar 14 00:20:50.412: IGMP(0): WAVL Insert group: 232.100.100.101   interface: Giga-
bitEthernet1 Successful
*Mar 14 00:20:50.413: IGMP(0): Create source 10.100.100.100
*Mar 14 00:20:50.413: IGMP(0): Building v3 Report on GigabitEthernet1
*Mar 14 00:20:50.413: IGMP(0): Add Group Record for 232.100.100.101, type 5
*Mar 14 00:20:50.413: IGMP(0): Add Source Record 10.100.100.100
*Mar 14 00:20:50.413: IGMP(0): Add Group Record for 232.100.100.101, type 6
*Mar 14 00:20:50.413: IGMP(0): No sources to add, group record removed from report
*Mar 14 00:20:50.413: IGMP(0): Send unsolicited v3 Report with 1 group records on
GigabitEthernet1
*Mar 14 00:20:51.121: IGMP(0): Building v3 Report on GigabitEthernet1
*Mar 14 00:20:51.121: IGMP(0): Add Group Record for 232.100.100.101, type 5
*Mar 14 00:20:51.121: IGMP(0): Add Source Record 10.100.100.100
*Mar 14 00:20:51.121: IGMP(0): Add Group Record for 232.100.100.101, type 6
*Mar 14 00:20:51.121: IGMP(0): No sources to add, group record removed from report
*Mar 14 00:20:51.121: IGMP(0): Send unsolicited v3 Report with 1 group records on
GigabitEthernet1
*Mar 14 00:20:54.721: IGMP(0): Building v3 Report on GigabitEthernet1
*Mar 14 00:20:54.721: IGMP(0): Add Group Record for 232.100.100.100, type 1
*Mar 14 00:20:54.721: IGMP(0): Add Source Record 10.254.254.254
*Mar 14 00:20:54.721: IGMP(0): Add Group Record for 232.100.100.101, type 1
*Mar 14 00:20:54.721: IGMP(0): Add Source Record 10.100.100.100
*Mar 14 00:20:54.721: IGMP(0): Send v3 Report with 2 group records on
GigabitEthernet1
Receiver3(config-if)#
```

```
LHR1#
*Mar 14 00:20:19.305: IGMP(0): Received v3 Report for 1 group on GigabitEthernet1
from 10.10.1.3
```

```
*Mar 14 00:20:19.305: IGMP(0): Received Group record for group 232.100.100.100,
mode 5 from 10.10.1.3 for 1 sources
*Mar 14 00:20:19.305: IGMP(0): WAVL Insert group: 232.100.100.100    interface:
GigabitEthernet1 Successful
*Mar 14 00:20:19.305: IGMP(0): Create source 10.254.254.254
*Mar 14 00:20:19.305: IGMP(0): Updating expiration time on (10.254.254.254,232.100.1
00.100)   to 180 secs
*Mar 14 00:20:19.305: IGMP(0): Setting source flags 4 on (10.254.254.254,232.100.100
.100)
*Mar 14 00:20:19.305: IGMP(0): MRT Add/Update GigabitEthernet1 for (10.254.254.254,2
32.100.100.100) by 0
*Mar 14 00:20:48.951: IGMP(0): Send v3 general Query on GigabitEthernet1
*Mar 14 00:20:48.951: IGMP(0): Set report delay to 0.8 seconds to respond to General
Query on GigabitEthernet1
*Mar 14 00:20:49.784: IGMP(0): Building v3 Report on GigabitEthernet1
*Mar 14 00:20:49.784: IGMP(0): Add Group Record for 224.0.1.40, type 2
*Mar 14 00:20:49.784: IGMP(0): Send v3 Report with 1 group records on
GigabitEthernet1
*Mar 14 00:20:49.784: IGMP(0): Received v3 Report for 1 group on GigabitEthernet1
from 10.10.1.254
*Mar 14 00:20:49.784: IGMP(0): Received Group record for group 224.0.1.40, mode 2
from 10.10.1.254 for 0 sources
*Mar 14 00:20:49.784: IGMP(0): Updating EXCLUDE group timer for 224.0.1.40
*Mar 14 00:20:49.784: IGMP(0): MRT Add/Update GigabitEthernet1 for (*,224.0.1.40)
by 0
*Mar 14 00:20:50.429: IGMP(0): Received v3 Report for 1 group on GigabitEthernet1
from 10.10.1.3
*Mar 14 00:20:50.429: IGMP(0): Received Group record for group 232.100.100.101, mode
5 from 10.10.1.3 for 1 sources
*Mar 14 00:20:50.429: IGMP(0): WAVL Insert group: 232.100.100.101    interface:
GigabitEthernet1 Successful
*Mar 14 00:20:50.429: IGMP(0): Create source 10.100.100.100
*Mar 14 00:20:50.429: IGMP(0): Updating expiration time on (10.100.100.100,232.100.1
00.101)   to 180 secs
*Mar 14 00:20:50.429: IGMP(0): Setting source flags 4 on (10.100.100.100,232.100.100
.101)
*Mar 14 00:20:50.430: IGMP(0): MRT Add/Update GigabitEthernet1 for (10.100.100.100,2
32.100.100.101) by 0
*Mar 14 00:20:54.734: IGMP(0): Received v3 Report for 1 group on GigabitEthernet1
from 10.10.1.3
*Mar 14 00:20:54.734: IGMP(0): Received Group record for group 232.100.100.100,
mode 1 from 10.10.1.3 for 1 sources
*Mar 14 00:20:54.734: IGMP(0): MRT Add/Update GigabitEthernet1 for (10.254.254.254,2
32.100.100.100) by 0
*Mar 14 00:20:54.735: IGMP(0): Updating expiration time on (10.254.254.254,232.100.1
00.100)   to 180 secs
LHR1# show ip igmp groups
IGMP Connected Group Membership
```

```
Group Address      Interface                 Uptime   Expires   Last Reporter   Group
Accounted
232.100.100.100   GigabitEthernet1          00:16:49  stopped   10.10.1.3
232.100.100.101   GigabitEthernet1          00:16:17  stopped   10.10.1.3
224.0.1.40        GigabitEthernet1          02:47:18  00:02:50  10.10.1.254

Switch# show ip igmp groups
IGMP Connected Group Membership
Group Address      Interface                 Uptime   Expires   Last Reporter   Group
Accounted
Switch#sh ip igmp snooping groups
Vlan       Group                   Type         Version      Port List
------------------------------------------------------------------------
1          224.0.1.40              igmp         v2,v3        Gi1/0/1
1          232.100.100.100         igmp         v3           Gi1/0/3
1          232.100.100.101         igmp         v3           Gi1/0/3
```

Interspersed with the debug output, we see how we turn on IGMPv3 on the interface and create two separate (S, G) groups—multicast group 232.100.100.**100** requested from source (imaginary) 10.254.254.254 and multicast group 232.100.100.**101** requested from source (imaginary) 10.100.100.100. Both of these groups are confirmed on LHR1 and Switch.

Next, let's filter out the second group because IGMPv3 allows for that. Watch Example 9-12. I will turn on debugging before I hit Enter with the last command.

Example 9-12   *IGMPv3 Group Filtering*

```
LHR1# configure terminal
Enter configuration commands, one per line.  End with CNTL/Z.
LHR1(config)# ip access-list extended FILTER-SSM
LHR1(config-ext-nacl)# deny igmp host 10.100.100.100 any
LHR1(config-ext-nacl)# permit igmp any any
LHR1(config-ext-nacl)# exit
LHR1(config)# int gig 1
LHR1(config-if)# do debug ip igmp
IGMP debugging is on
LHR1(config-if)# ip igmp access-group FILTER-SSM
LHR1(config-if)#
*Mar 14 00:44:48.953: IGMP(0): Send v3 general Query on GigabitEthernet1
*Mar 14 00:44:48.953: IGMP(0): Set report delay to 3.3 seconds to respond to General
Query on GigabitEthernet1
*Mar 14 00:44:51.341: IGMP(0): Received v3 Report for 2 groups on GigabitEthernet1
from 10.10.1.3
*Mar 14 00:44:51.342: IGMP(0): Received Group record for group 232.100.100.100, mode
1 from 10.10.1.3 for 1 sources
```

```
*Mar 14 00:44:51.342: IGMP(0): MRT Add/Update GigabitEthernet1 for (10.254.254.254,2
32.100.100.100) by 0
*Mar 14 00:44:51.342: IGMP(0): Updating expiration time on (10.254.254.254,232.100.1
00.100)   to 180 secs
*Mar 14 00:44:51.342: IGMP(*): Source: 10.100.100.100, Group 232.100.100.101 access
denied on GigabitEthernet1
*Mar 14 00:44:52.284: IGMP(0): Building v3 Report on GigabitEthernet1
*Mar 14 00:44:52.285: IGMP(0): Add Group Record for 224.0.1.40, type 2
*Mar 14 00:44:52.285: IGMP(0): Send v3 Report with 1 group records on
GigabitEthernet1
*Mar 14 00:44:52.285: IGMP(0): Received v3 Report for 1 group on GigabitEthernet1
from 10.10.1.254
*Mar 14 00:44:52.285: IGMP(0): Received Group record for group 224.0.1.40, mode 2
from 10.10.1.254 for 0 sources
*Mar 14 00:44:52.285: IGMP(0): Updating EXCLUDE group timer for 224.0.1.40
*Mar 14 00:44:52.285: IGMP(0): MRT Add/Update GigabitEthernet1 for (*,224.0.1.40)
by 0
*Mar 14 00:45:50.285: IGMP(0): Building v3 Report on GigabitEthernet1
*Mar 14 00:45:50.285: IGMP(0): Add Group Record for 224.0.1.40, type 2
*Mar 14 00:45:50.285: IGMP(0): Send v3 Report with 1 group records on
GigabitEthernet1
*Mar 14 00:45:50.285: IGMP(0): Received v3 Report for 1 group on GigabitEthernet1
from 10.10.1.254
*Mar 14 00:45:50.285: IGMP(0): Received Group record for group 224.0.1.40, mode 2
from 10.10.1.254 for 0 sources
*Mar 14 00:45:50.285: IGMP(0): Updating EXCLUDE group timer for 224.0.1.40
*Mar 14 00:45:50.285: IGMP(0): MRT Add/Update GigabitEthernet1 for (*,224.0.1.40)
by 0
*Mar 14 00:45:58.942: IGMP(0): Received v3 Report for 2 groups on GigabitEthernet1
from 10.10.1.3
*Mar 14 00:45:58.942: IGMP(0): Received Group record for group 232.100.100.100, mode
1 from 10.10.1.3 for 1 sources
*Mar 14 00:45:58.942: IGMP(0): MRT Add/Update GigabitEthernet1 for (10.254.254.254,2
32.100.100.100) by 0
*Mar 14 00:45:58.942: IGMP(0): Updating expiration time on (10.254.254.254,232.100.1
00.100)   to 180 secs
*Mar 14 00:45:58.942: IGMP(*): Source: 10.100.100.100, Group 232.100.100.101 access
denied on GigabitEthernet1
LHR1(config-if)# do show ip igmp groups
IGMP Connected Group Membership
Group Address     Interface                 Uptime     Expires    Last Reporter    Group
Accounted
232.100.100.100   GigabitEthernet1          00:26:19   stopped    10.10.1.3
232.100.100.101   GigabitEthernet1          00:25:48   stopped    10.10.1.3
224.0.1.40        GigabitEthernet1          02:56:49   00:02:11   10.10.1.254
LHR1(config-if)#
*Mar 14 00:46:48.953: IGMP(0): Send v3 general Query on GigabitEthernet1
```

```
*Mar 14 00:46:48.953: IGMP(0): Set report delay to 4.5 seconds to respond to General
Query on GigabitEthernet1

*Mar 14 00:46:52.040: IGMP(0): Received v3 Report for 2 groups on GigabitEthernet1
from 10.10.1.3

*Mar 14 00:46:52.040: IGMP(0): Received Group record for group 232.100.100.100, mode
1 from 10.10.1.3 for 1 sources

*Mar 14 00:46:52.040: IGMP(0): MRT Add/Update GigabitEthernet1 for (10.254.254.254,2
32.100.100.100) by 0

*Mar 14 00:46:52.040: IGMP(0): Updating expiration time on (10.254.254.254,232.100.1
00.100)   to 180 secs

*Mar 14 00:46:52.040: IGMP(*): Source: 10.100.100.100, Group 232.100.100.101 access
denied on GigabitEthernet1

*Mar 14 00:46:53.484: IGMP(0): Building v3 Report on GigabitEthernet1

*Mar 14 00:46:53.484: IGMP(0): Add Group Record for 224.0.1.40, type 2

*Mar 14 00:46:53.484: IGMP(0): Send v3 Report with 1 group records on
GigabitEthernet1

*Mar 14 00:46:53.484: IGMP(0): Received v3 Report for 1 group on GigabitEthernet1
from 10.10.1.254

*Mar 14 00:46:53.484: IGMP(0): Received Group record for group 224.0.1.40, mode 2
from 10.10.1.254 for 0 sources

*Mar 14 00:46:53.485: IGMP(0): Updating EXCLUDE group timer for 224.0.1.40

*Mar 14 00:46:53.485: IGMP(0): MRT Add/Update GigabitEthernet1 for (*,224.0.1.40)
by 0

*Mar 14 00:46:57.485: IGMP(0): Source timer expired for (10.100.100.100,232.100.100.
101) on GigabitEthernet1

*Mar 14 00:46:57.485: IGMP(0): MRT delete GigabitEthernet1 for (10.100.100.100,232.1
00.100.101) by 0

*Mar 14 00:46:57.485: IGMP(0): Deleting source (10.100.100.100,232.100.100.101)

*Mar 14 00:47:48.953: IGMP(0): Send v3 general Query on GigabitEthernet1

*Mar 14 00:47:48.953: IGMP(0): Set report delay to 4.2 seconds to respond to General
Query on GigabitEthernet1

*Mar 14 00:47:49.640: IGMP(0): Received v3 Report for 2 groups on GigabitEthernet1
from 10.10.1.3

*Mar 14 00:47:49.640: IGMP(0): Received Group record for group 232.100.100.100, mode
1 from 10.10.1.3 for 1 sources

*Mar 14 00:47:49.640: IGMP(0): MRT Add/Update GigabitEthernet1 for (10.254.254.254,2
32.100.100.100) by 0

*Mar 14 00:47:49.641: IGMP(0): Updating expiration time on (10.254.254.254,232.100.1
00.100)   to 180 secs

LHR1(config-if)#

*Mar 14 00:47:49.641: IGMP(*): Source: 10.100.100.100, Group 232.100.100.101 access
denied on GigabitEthernet1

LHR1(config-if)# do sh ip igmp groups

IGMP Connected Group Membership

Group Address     Interface               Uptime     Expires    Last Reporter    Group
Accounted

232.100.100.100  GigabitEthernet1        00:27:34   stopped    10.10.1.3
```

```
224.0.1.40        GigabitEthernet1        02:58:03  00:02:59  10.10.1.254
LHR1(config-if)#


Switch# show ip igmp snooping groups
Vlan      Group                         Type        Version     Port List
-----------------------------------------------------------------------------
1         224.0.1.40                    igmp        v2,v3       Gi1/0/1
1         232.100.100.100               igmp        v3          Gi1/0/3
1         232.100.100.101               igmp        v3          Gi1/0/3

Switch#
```

We create an extended access list to deny source 10.100.100.100 from multicasting to any group and permit the remaining IGMP traffic. We then turn on the debug to catch all activities and apply this to our LAN interface. The traffic gets denied and is marked for group deletion by the associated timer. For a while (watch the timestamps), the group still remains on the router, but then, once the timer expires, it is deleted from the IGMP groups. Note that it will be present on the Switch, since it still receives requests from Receiver3. I assumed here that the LAN we are experimenting on is a stub LAN and all multicast traffic will come in from somewhere beyond LHR1. I did turn off LHR2 to limit the debugging output.

For homework, I suggest you configure IGMP not globally, as I have done in our examples, but rather on any other VLAN than VLAN 1.

MLD

Multicast Listener Discovery (MLD), much like IGMP, also optimizes multicast traffic by not forwarding it out of all ports, but only out of ports where IPv6 receivers (hosts) subscribe to multicast streams. The good news, you already know how MLD functions because there are two versions of MLD: version 1 and version 2.

- MLDv1 of IPv6 works similar to IGMPv2 for IPv4.

- MLDv2 is comparable to IGMPv3. It is backward compatible with MLDv1 and adds support for SSM (the ability to choose sources for specific multicast groups).

RFC 2710 describes MLDv1 operations. There are three types of MLD messages, and they are identified in IPv6 packets by *type*, which is represented by the decimal format shown in Table 9-4.

Table 9-4   MLDv1 Messages

Name	Type	Description
Listener Query	decimal 130	Sent by router, there are two subtypes: **General Query** is used to learn which multicast addresses have listeners on an attached link; the Multicast Address field will be set to zero and will be sent to the all-nodes multicast address FF02::1. **Multicast-Address-Specific Query** is used if a particular multicast address has listeners on an attached link; the multicast address will be set to a specific IPv6 multicast address.

Name	Type	Description
Listener Report	decimal 131	A receiver/host/listener indicates interest in a specific IPv6 multicast address, and the report is sent to the multicast address group.
Listener Done	decimal 132	A receiver/host/listener stops listening to a specific IPv6 multicast address and MAY send a single Done message to the link-scope all-routers multicast address FF02::2 unless suppressed by hearing another Report message (see above).

MLDv2 is described in RFC 3810 and is a translation of the IGMPv3 protocol (described in RFC 3376) to accommodate IPv6 semantics. Are you glad you learned about Done messages in MLDv1? Good, because

- There are no Done messages in MLDv2; they have been eliminated.

- This leaves us with Query and Report messages.

- There is no host suppression either; all listeners send Report messages.

- It is backward compatible with MLDv1.

- MLDv2 Listener reports are sent with an IP destination address of FF02:0:0:0:0:0:0:16, to which all MLDv2-capable multicast routers listen.

- MLDv2 uses two filter modes to maintain records of the multicast state for each of its interfaces—INCLUDE and EXCLUDE.

  - In the INCLUDE mode, reception of packets for a specific multicast address is only enabled from the addresses in the source list.

  - In the EXCLUDE mode, reception of packets is enabled for any source, except for those listed in the source list.

The RFC has a lengthy discussion on this topic, and some RFCs can be notoriously hard to read and understand. Vendors may implement RFCs differently, but do not let this distract you from passing the exam or understanding this technology. Multicast is a complex topic and the reason that many of my customers are running from it. Others have embraced it, because for the time being, they cannot find a reasonable alternative. What does this mean for the exam? As you can see, this topic is a treasure hunt for "test torturers." Which address, include, exclude, in which version…? Don't get yourself worked up. I've given you enough information to recognize where the tester is coming from. Also, remember that there are only so many questions that can be asked on a particular topic, since there are so many topics on this exam.

I suggest we finish up by configuring MLDv2. Let's keep things simple here and involve IOS XR as well. To help you retain the technology, focus on the concepts rather than just examples from diagrams you can find outside of this book. Figure 9-3 illustrates our topology. I renamed our routers to the convention we used in the earlier chapters.

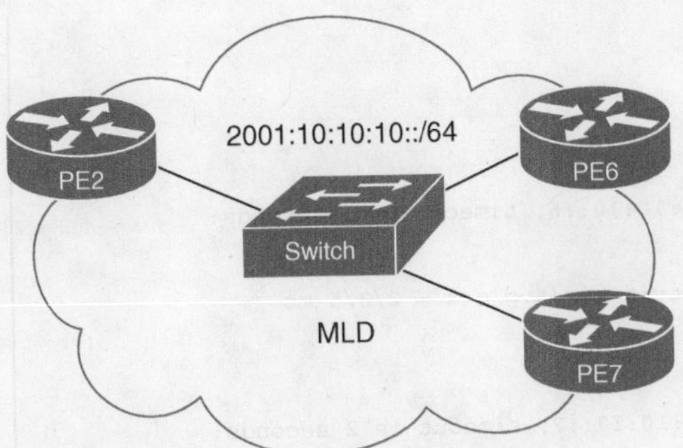

Figure 9-3 *MLD Reference Diagram*

We will use PE2 as our connection to the rest of the work. PE6 and PE7 will represent our listeners, as shown in Example 9-13.

Example 9-13 *Turning Up MLDv2 on IOS Routers*

```
PE6# configure terminal
Enter configuration commands, one per line.  End with CNTL/Z.
PE2(config)# ipv6 multicast-routing
PE6(config)# interface gigabitEthernet 1
PE6(config-if)# ipv6 address 2001:10:10:10::6/64
PE6(config-if)# no shutdown
PE6(config-if)#

RP/0/RP0/CPU0:PE7# configure
Fri Mar 15 10:52:20.921 UTC
RP/0/RP0/CPU0:PE7(config)# multicast-routing
RP/0/RP0/CPU0:PE7(config-mcast)# address-family ipv6
RP/0/RP0/CPU0:PE7(config-mcast-default-ipv6)# interface all enable
RP/0/RP0/CPU0:PE7(config-mcast-default-ipv6)# exit
RP/0/RP0/CPU0:PE7(config-mcast)# exit
RP/0/RP0/CPU0:PE7(config)# interface GigabitEthernet0/0/0/0
RP/0/RP0/CPU0:PE7(config-if)# ipv6 address 2001:10:10:10::7/64
RP/0/RP0/CPU0:PE7(config-if)# no shutdown
RP/0/RP0/CPU0:PE7(config-if)# commit
Fri Mar 15 10:53:21.977 UTC
RP/0/RP0/CPU0:PE7(config-if)#

PE2# configure terminal
Enter configuration commands, one per line.  End with CNTL/Z.
PE2(config)# ipv6 multicast-routing
PE2(config)# interface gigabitEthernet 1
PE2(config-if)# ipv6 address 2001:10:10:10::2/64
```

```
PE2(config-if)# no shutdown
PE2(config-if)# end
PE2# ping 2001:10:10:10::6
Type escape sequence to abort.
Sending 5, 100-byte ICMP Echos to 2001:10:10:10::6, timeout is 2 seconds:
!!!!!
Success rate is 100 percent (5/5), round-trip min/avg/max = 2/3/5 ms
PE2# ping 2001:10:10:10::7
Type escape sequence to abort.
Sending 5, 100-byte ICMP Echos to 2001:10:10:10::7, timeout is 2 seconds:
!!!!!
Success rate is 100 percent (5/5), round-trip min/avg/max = 2/6/25 ms
```

This way, you can see what you need to set up when you're practicing. Since we're using
MLDv2, let's turn on a couple of IPv6 groups, two of them specifically for SSM. Again,
these are "fake, nonpresent" sources (since it does not matter, we are learning how MLD
works at this time). Be aware (as this is not a course on IPv6) that address prefixes FF3X::/32
and FFBX::/32 are reserved for SSM, and RFC 3306 and RFC 4607 claim that FF3X::/96 is
the valid block of addresses for SSM. With that in mind, Example 9-14 shows us joining
specific multicast groups.

Example 9-14 *Turning Up SSM for IPv6*

```
PE6(config-if)# ipv6 mld join-group FF6E::6
PE6(config-if)# ipv6 mld join-group FF36::600 ?
  X:X:X:X::X    Switch to include mode using given address
  exclude       Switch to exclude mode
  include       Switch to include mode
  source-list   Specify a source-list
  <cr>          <cr>

PE6(config-if)# ipv6 mld join-group FF36::600 2001:10:100:100::100
PE6(config-if)#
```

```
RP/0/RP0/CPU0:PE7(config)# router mld
RP/0/RP0/CPU0:PE7(config-mld)# interface gigabitEthernet 0/0/0/0
RP/0/RP0/CPU0:PE7(config-mld-default-if)# join-group ff7e::7
RP/0/RP0/CPU0:PE7(config-mld-default-if)# join-group ff37::700 ?
  X:X::X    Source address to include
  exclude   Exclude the only following source address
  include   Include only the following source address
  <cr>
RP/0/RP0/CPU0:PE7(config-mld-default-if)# join-group ff37::700 2001:10:254:254::254
RP/0/RP0/CPU0:PE7(config-mld-default-if)# root
```

```
RP/0/RP0/CPU0:PE7(config)# show
Fri Mar 15 16:14:24.910 UTC
Building configuration...
!! IOS XR Configuration 7.7.1
interface GigabitEthernet0/0/0/0
!
router mld
 interface GigabitEthernet0/0/0/0
  join-group ff37::700 2001:10:254:254::254
  join-group ff7e::7
 !
!
router mld
!
end

RP/0/RP0/CPU0:PE7(config)# commit
Fri Mar 15 16:14:27.559 UTC
RP/0/RP0/CPU0:PE7(config)#
```

```
PE2# show ipv6 mld groups
No groups found.
PE2# debug ipv6 mld
MLD debugging is on
PE2#
*Mar 15 16:14:00.336: MLD: [0x0] Received v2 Report for 1 group on GigabitEthernet1
from FE80::5054:FF:FE0E:9470
*Mar 15 16:14:00.337: MLD: [0x0] group_db: add new group FF6E::6 on GigabitEthernet1
*Mar 15 16:14:00.337: MLD: [0x0] MRIB updated (*,FF6E::6) : Success on
GigabitEthernet1
*Mar 15 16:14:00.337: MLD: [0x0] MRIB updated (*,FF6E::6) : Success on
GigabitEthernet1
*Mar 15 16:14:00.337: MLD: [0x0] Switching to EXCLUDE mode for FF6E::6 on
GigabitEthernet1
*Mar 15 16:14:00.337: MLD: [0x0] Updating EXCLUDE group timer for FF6E::6
*Mar 15 16:14:00.339: MLD: [0x0] (*,FF6E::6/128) MRIB update (t=1).
*Mar 15 16:14:00.339: MLD: [0x0] (*,FF6E::6/128) GigabitEthernet1 MRIB update
(f=109,c=1).
*Mar 15 16:14:01.120: MLD: [0x0] Received v2 Report for 1 group on GigabitEthernet1
from FE80::5054:FF:FE0E:9470
*Mar 15 16:14:01.120: MLD: [0x0] Updating EXCLUDE group timer for FF6E::6
*Mar 15 16:14:05.342: MLD: [0x0] Received v2 Report for 1 group on GigabitEthernet1
from FE80::5054:FF:FE0E:9470
```

```
*Mar 15 16:14:05.342: MLD: [0x0] group_db: add new group FF36::600 on
GigabitEthernet1
*Mar 15 16:14:05.342: MLD: [0x0] MRIB updated (*,FF36::600) : Success on
GigabitEthernet1
*Mar 15 16:14:05.342: MLD: [0x0] group_db: add new source (2001:10:100:100::100,FF36
::600) on GigabitEthernet1
*Mar 15 16:14:05.342: MLD: [0x0] MRIB updated (2001:10:100:100::100,FF36::600) :
Success on GigabitEthernet1
*Mar 15 16:14:05.342: MLD: [0x0] Update expiration time on (2001:10:100:100::100,FF3
6::600) to 260 secs
*Mar 15 16:14:05.342: MLD: [0x0] Set source flags 4 on (2001:10:100:100::100,FF36::6
00)
*Mar 15 16:14:05.342: MLD: [0x0] MRIB updated (2001:10:100:100::100,FF36::600) :
Success on GigabitEthernet1
*Mar 15 16:14:05.344: MLD: [0x0] (2001:10:100:100::100,FF36::600/128) MRIB update
(t=1).
*Mar 15 16:14:05.344: MLD: [0x0] (2001:10:100:100::100,FF36::600/128) GigabitEther-
net1 MRIB update (f=109,c=1).
*Mar 15 16:14:05.345: MLD: [0x0] Processing group timers for FF36::600 on
GigabitEthernet1
*Mar 15 16:14:05.868: MLD: [0x0] Received v2 Report for 1 group on GigabitEthernet1
from FE80::5054:FF:FE0E:9470
*Mar 15 16:14:05.868: MLD: [0x0] Update expiration time on (2001:10:100:100::100,FF3
6::600) to 260 secs
PE2#
*Mar 15 16:14:28.852: MLD: [0x0] Received v2 Query on GigabitEthernet1 from
FE80::5054:FF:FE07:D323
*Mar 15 16:14:28.852: MLD: [0x0] Set GigabitEthernet1 General report delay timer to
7.936 seconds
*Mar 15 16:14:28.905: MLD: [0x0] Received v2 Query on GigabitEthernet1 from
FE80::5054:FF:FE07:D323
*Mar 15 16:14:28.907: MLD: [0x0] Received v2 Query on GigabitEthernet1 from
FE80::5054:FF:FE07:D323
*Mar 15 16:14:28.908: MLD: [0x0] Received v2 Report for 1 group on GigabitEthernet1
from FE80::5054:FF:FE07:D323
*Mar 15 16:14:28.908: MLD: [0x0] group_db: add new group FF37::700 on
GigabitEthernet1
*Mar 15 16:14:28.908: MLD: [0x0] MRIB updated (*,FF37::700) : Success on
GigabitEthernet1
*Mar 15 16:14:28.908: MLD: [0x0] group_db: add new source (2001:10:254:254::254,FF37
::700) on GigabitEthernet1
*Mar 15 16:14:28.908: MLD: [0x0] MRIB updated (2001:10:254:254::254,FF37::700) :
Success on GigabitEthernet1
*Mar 15 16:14:28.908: MLD: [0x0] Update expiration time on (2001:10:254:254::254,FF3
7::700) to 260 secs
*Mar 15 16:14:28.908: MLD: [0x0] Set source flags 4 on (2001:10:254:254::254,FF37::7
00)
*Mar 15 16:14:28.908: MLD: [0x0] MRIB updated (2001:10:254:254::254,FF37::700) :
Success on GigabitEthernet1
```

```
*Mar 15 16:14:28.910: MLD: [0x0] (2001:10:254:254::254,FF37::700/128) MRIB update
(t=1).
*Mar 15 16:14:28.910: MLD: [0x0] (2001:10:254:254::254,FF37::700/128) GigabitEther-
net1 MRIB update (f=109,c=1).
*Mar 15 16:14:28.910: MLD: [0x0] Received v2 Report for 1 group on GigabitEthernet1
from FE80::5054:FF:FE07:D323
*Mar 15 16:14:28.910: MLD: [0x0] group_db: add new group FF7E::7 on GigabitEthernet1
*Mar 15 16:14:28.911: MLD: [0x0] MRIB updated (*,FF7E::7) : Success on
GigabitEthernet1
*Mar 15 16:14:28.911: MLD: [0x0] MRIB updated (*,FF7E::7) : Success on
GigabitEthernet1
*Mar 15 16:14:28.911: MLD: [0x0] Switching to EXCLUDE mode for FF7E::7 on
GigabitEthernet1
*Mar 15 16:14:28.911: MLD: [0x0] Updating EXCLUDE group timer for FF7E::7
*Mar 15 16:14:28.913: MLD: [0x0] (*,FF7E::7/128) MRIB update (t=1).
*Mar 15 16:14:28.913: MLD: [0x0] (*,FF7E::7/128) GigabitEthernet1 MRIB update
(f=109,c=1).
*Mar 15 16:14:29.054: MLD: [0x0] Received v2 Report for 5 groups on GigabitEthernet1
from FE80::5054:FF:FE07:D323
*Mar 15 16:14:29.054: MLD: [0x0] Ignoring report for group address FF02::2
*Mar 15 16:14:29.054: MLD: [0x0] Ignoring report for group address FF02::D
*Mar 15 16:14:29.054: MLD: [0x0] Ignoring report for group address FF02::16
*Mar 15 16:14:29.054: MLD: [0x0] Update expiration time on (2001:10:254:254::254,FF3
7::700) to 260 secs
*Mar 15 16:14:29.054: MLD: [0x0] Updating EXCLUDE group timer for FF7E::7
*Mar 15 16:14:29.271: MLD: [0x0] Processing group timers for FF37::700 on
GigabitEthernet1
*Mar 15 16:14:29.553: MLD: [0x0] Received v2 Report for 1 group on GigabitEthernet1
from FE80::5054:FF:FE07:D323
*Mar 15 16:14:29.553: MLD: [0x0] Updating EXCLUDE group timer for FF7E::7
*Mar 15 16:14:29.852: MLD: [0x0] Received v2 Report for 1 group on GigabitEthernet1
from FE80::5054:FF:FE07:D323
*Mar 15 16:14:29.852: MLD: [0x0] Update expiration time on (2001:10:254:254::254,FF3
7::700) to 260 secs
*Mar 15 16:14:32.370: MLD: [0x0] Received v2 Report for 5 groups on GigabitEthernet1
from FE80::5054:FF:FE0E:9470
*Mar 15 16:14:32.370: MLD: [0x0] Ignoring report for group address FF02::2
*Mar 15 16:14:32.370: MLD: [0x0] Ignoring report for group address FF02::1:FF00:6
*Mar 15 16:14:32.370: MLD: [0x0] Ignoring report for group address FF02::1:FF0E:9470
*Mar 15 16:14:32.370: MLD: [0x0] Update expiration time on (2001:10:100:100::100,FF3
6::600) to 260 secs
*Mar 15 16:14:32.370: MLD: [0x0] Updating EXCLUDE group timer for FF6E::6
PE2#
*Mar 15 16:14:37.021: MLD: [0x0] Building v2 response to General Query on
GigabitEthernet1
*Mar 15 16:14:37.021: MLD: [0x0] Send v2 aggregate Report on GigabitEthernet1
```

```
*Mar 15 16:14:37.022: MLD: [0x0] Received v2 Report for 5 groups on GigabitEthernet1
from FE80::5054:FF:FE0B:3E11
*Mar 15 16:14:37.022: MLD: [0x0] Ignoring report for group address FF02::2
*Mar 15 16:14:37.022: MLD: [0x0] Ignoring report for group address FF02::D
*Mar 15 16:14:37.022: MLD: [0x0] Ignoring report for group address FF02::16
*Mar 15 16:14:37.022: MLD: [0x0] Ignoring report for group address FF02::1:FF00:2
*Mar 15 16:14:37.022: MLD: [0x0] Ignoring report for group address FF02::1:FF0B:3E11
PE2# undebug all
All possible debugging has been turned off
PE2#
```

All four groups are added to the Multicast RIB (MRIB). Note the membership reports, (*, G), and (S, G) entries; all of this should make sense to you. Observe Example 9-15 for the current state of MLD groups on IOS XR and IOS.

Example 9-15   *State of MLDv2 Groups*

```
RP/0/RP0/CPU0:PE7(config)# end
RP/0/RP0/CPU0:PE7# show mld groups
Fri Mar 15 16:28:21.655 UTC
MLD Connected Group Membership

GigabitEthernet0/0/0/0

Group Address : ff02::2
Last Reporter : fe80::5054:ff:fe0e:9470
        Uptime : 05:34:59
       Expires : never
Group Address : ff02::d
Last Reporter : fe80::5054:ff:fe0b:3e11
        Uptime : 05:34:59
       Expires : never
Group Address : ff02::16
Last Reporter : fe80::5054:ff:fe0b:3e11
        Uptime : 05:34:59
       Expires : never
Group Address : ff02::1:ff00:2
Last Reporter : fe80::5054:ff:fe0b:3e11
        Uptime : 05:34:53
       Expires : 00:03:30
Group Address : ff02::1:ff00:6
Last Reporter : fe80::5054:ff:fe0e:9470
        Uptime : 05:34:50
       Expires : 00:03:34
```

```
Group Address : ff02::1:ff0b:3e11
Last Reporter : fe80::5054:ff:fe0b:3e11
        Uptime : 05:34:53
       Expires : 00:03:30
Group Address : ff02::1:ff0e:9470
Last Reporter : fe80::5054:ff:fe0e:9470
        Uptime : 05:34:50
       Expires : 00:03:34
Group Address : ff36::600
Last Reporter : fe80::5054:ff:fe0e:9470
        Uptime : 00:14:17
       Expires : not used
Group Address : ff37::700
Last Reporter : fe80::5054:ff:fe07:d323
        Uptime : 00:13:54
       Expires : never
Group Address : ff6e::6
Last Reporter : fe80::5054:ff:fe0e:9470
        Uptime : 00:14:22
       Expires : 00:03:34
Group Address : ff7e::7
Last Reporter : fe80::5054:ff:fe07:d323
        Uptime : 00:13:54
       Expires : never
RP/0/RP0/CPU0:PE7#
```

```
PE2# show ipv6 mld groups
MLD Connected Group Membership
Group Address                      Interface
Uptime     Expires
FF36::600                          GigabitEthernet1
00:00:47   not used
FF37::700                          GigabitEthernet1
00:00:23   not used
FF6E::6                            GigabitEthernet1
00:00:52   00:03:59
FF7E::7                            GigabitEthernet1
00:00:23   00:03:57
```

The last thing I would like to show you is similar filtering you can do on these groups. In
Example 9-16, I assign an IPv6 access list on PE2 to drop two of the groups. Let's pick on
IOS, since I am partial to XR after all.

Example 9-16 *State of MLDv2 Groups*

```
PE2# configure terminal
Enter configuration commands, one per line.  End with CNTL/Z.
PE2(config)# ipv6 access-list MLD-FILTER
PE2(config-ipv6-acl)# deny ?
  <0-255>              An IPv6 protocol number
  X:X:X:X::X           IPv6 source address x:x::y
  X:X:X:X::X/<0-128>   IPv6 source prefix x:x::y/<z>
  ahp                  Authentication Header Protocol
  any                  Any source prefix
  esp                  Encapsulation Security Payload
  hbh                  Hop by Hop options header
  host                 A single source host
  icmp                 Internet Control Message Protocol
  ipv6                 Any IPv6
  object-group         Service object group
  pcp                  Payload Compression Protocol
  sctp                 Streams Control Transmission Protocol
  tcp                  Transmission Control Protocol
  udp                  User Datagram Protocol

PE2(config-ipv6-acl)# deny any host FF6E::6
PE2(config-ipv6-acl)# deny any host FF36::600
PE2(config-ipv6-acl)# permit any any
PE2(config-ipv6-acl)# interface gigabitEthernet 1
PE2(config-if)# ipv6 mld ?
  access-group             source, group membership access
  explicit-tracking        explicit host tracking
  join-group               join multicast group
  limit                    Membership limit
  query-interval           host query interval
  query-max-response-time  max query response value
  query-timeout            previous querier timeout
  router                   Disable membership tracking
  static-group             static multicast group
  v2-report-type           MLDv2 Report Type
  version                  version

PE2(config-if)# ipv6 mld access-group ?
  WORD  Named access list specifying access group range

PE2(config-if)# ipv6 mld access-group MLD-FILTER
```

```
PE2(config-if)# do debug ipv6 mld
MLD debugging is on
PE2(config-if)#
*Mar 15 16:35:48.751: MLD: [0x0] Received v2 Query on GigabitEthernet1 from
FE80::5054:FF:FE07:D323
*Mar 15 16:35:48.751: MLD: [0x0] Set GigabitEthernet1 General report delay timer to
1.587 seconds
*Mar 15 16:35:50.522: MLD: [0x0] Building v2 response to General Query on
GigabitEthernet1
*Mar 15 16:35:50.522: MLD: [0x0] Send v2 aggregate Report on GigabitEthernet1
*Mar 15 16:35:50.522: MLD: [0x0] Received v2 Report for 5 groups on GigabitEthernet1
from FE80::5054:FF:FE0B:3E11
*Mar 15 16:35:50.522: MLD: [0x0] Ignoring report for group address FF02::2
*Mar 15 16:35:50.522: MLD: [0x0] Ignoring report for group address FF02::D
*Mar 15 16:35:50.522: MLD: [0x0] Ignoring report for group address FF02::16
*Mar 15 16:35:50.522: MLD: [0x0] Ignoring report for group address FF02::1:FF00:2
*Mar 15 16:35:50.522: MLD: [0x0] Ignoring report for group address FF02::1:FF0B:3E11
*Mar 15 16:35:56.452: MLD: [0x0] Received v2 Report for 5 groups on GigabitEthernet1
from FE80::5054:FF:FE07:D323
*Mar 15 16:35:56.452: MLD: [0x0] Ignoring report for group address FF02::2
*Mar 15 16:35:56.452: MLD: [0x0] Ignoring report for group address FF02::D
*Mar 15 16:35:56.452: MLD: [0x0] Ignoring report for group address FF02::16
*Mar 15 16:35:56.453: MLD: [0x0] Update expiration time on (2001:10:254:254::254,FF3
7::700) to 260 secs
*Mar 15 16:35:56.453: MLD: [0x0] Updating EXCLUDE group timer for FF7E::7
*Mar 15 16:35:58.118: MLD: [0x0] Received v2 Report for 5 groups on GigabitEthernet1
from FE80::5054:FF:FE0E:9470
*Mar 15 16:35:58.118: MLD: [0x0] Ignoring report for group address FF02::2
*Mar 15 16:35:58.118: MLD: [0x0] Ignoring report for group address FF02::1:FF00:6
*Mar 15 16:35:58.118: MLD: [0x0] Ignoring report for group address FF02::1:FF0E:9470
*Mar 15 16:35:58.119: MLD: [0x0] Source 2001:10:100:100::100, Group FF36::600:
denied on GigabitEthernet1
*Mar 15 16:35:58.119: MLD: [0x0] Group FF6E::6 access denied on GigabitEthernet1
PE2(config-if)# do show ipv6 mld groups
MLD Connected Group Membership
Group Address              Interface            Uptime      Expires
FF36::600                  GigabitEthernet1     00:22:06    not used
FF37::700                  GigabitEthernet1     00:21:43    not used
FF6E::6                    GigabitEthernet1     00:22:11    00:02:01
FF7E::7                    GigabitEthernet1     00:21:43    00:04:04
```

```
PE2(config-if)#

*Mar 15 16:37:53.753: MLD: [0x0] Received v2 Query on GigabitEthernet1 from
FE80::5054:FF:FE07:D323

*Mar 15 16:37:53.753: MLD: [0x0] Set GigabitEthernet1 General report delay timer to
8.571 seconds

*Mar 15 16:37:55.368: MLD: [0x0] Received v2 Report for 5 groups on GigabitEthernet1
from FE80::5054:FF:FE0E:9470

*Mar 15 16:37:55.369: MLD: [0x0] Ignoring report for group address FF02::2

*Mar 15 16:37:55.369: MLD: [0x0] Ignoring report for group address FF02::1:FF00:6

*Mar 15 16:37:55.369: MLD: [0x0] Ignoring report for group address FF02::1:FF0E:9470

*Mar 15 16:37:55.369: MLD: [0x0] Source 2001:10:100:100::100, Group FF36::600:
denied on GigabitEthernet1

*Mar 15 16:37:55.369: MLD: [0x0] Group FF6E::6 access denied on GigabitEthernet1

PE2(config-if)#

*Mar 15 16:38:01.952: MLD: [0x0] Received v2 Report for 5 groups on GigabitEthernet1
from FE80::5054:FF:FE07:D323

*Mar 15 16:38:01.952: MLD: [0x0] Ignoring report for group address FF02::2

*Mar 15 16:38:01.953: MLD: [0x0] Ignoring report for group address FF02::D

*Mar 15 16:38:01.953: MLD: [0x0] Ignoring report for group address FF02::16

*Mar 15 16:38:01.953: MLD: [0x0] Update expiration time on (2001:10:254:254::254,FF3
7::700) to 260 secs

*Mar 15 16:38:01.953: MLD: [0x0] Updating EXCLUDE group timer for FF7E::7

*Mar 15 16:38:02.522: MLD: [0x0] Building v2 response to General Query on
GigabitEthernet1

*Mar 15 16:38:02.522: MLD: [0x0] groupsSend v2 aggregate Report on GigabitEthernet1

*Mar 15 16:38:02.522: MLD: [0x0] Received v2 Report for 5 groups on GigabitEthernet1
from FE80::5054:FF:FE0B:3E11

*Mar 15 16:38:02.522: MLD: [0x0] Ignoring report for group address FF02::2

*Mar 15 16:38:02.522: MLD: [0x0] Ignoring report for group address FF02::D

*Mar 15 16:38:02.522: MLD: [0x0] Ignoring report for group address FF02::16

*Mar 15 16:38:02.522: MLD: [0x0] Ignoring report for group address FF02::1:FF00:2

*Mar 15 16:38:02.522: MLD: [0x0] Ignoring report for group address FF02::1:FF0B:3E11

*Mar 15 16:38:13.521: MLD: [0x0] Processing source timers for (2001:10:100:100::100,
FF36::600) on GigabitEthernet1

*Mar 15 16:38:13.521: MLD: [0x0] Source timer expired for (2001:10:100:100::100,FF36
::600) on GigabitEthernet1

*Mar 15 16:38:13.521: MLD: [0x0] MRIB updated (2001:10:100:100::100,FF36::600) :
Success on GigabitEthernet1

*Mar 15 16:38:13.521: MLD: [0x0] MRIB updated (2001:10:100:100::100,FF36::600) :
Success on GigabitEthernet1

*Mar 15 16:38:13.522: MLD: [0x0] group_db: delete source (2001:10:100:100::100,FF36:
:600) on GigabitEthernet1

*Mar 15 16:38:13.522: MLD: [0x0] Processing group timers for FF6E::6 on
GigabitEthernet1

*Mar 15 16:38:13.522: MLD: [0x0] EXCLUDE mode expired for FF6E::6 on
GigabitEthernet1
```

```
*Mar 15 16:38:13.522: MLD: [0x0] MRIB updated (*,FF6E::6) : Success on
GigabitEthernet1
*Mar 15 16:38:13.522: MLD: [0x0] MRIB updated (*,FF6E::6) : Success on
GigabitEthernet1
*Mar 15 16:38:13.522: MLD: [0x0] group_db: delete group FF6E::6 on GigabitEthernet1
*Mar 15 16:38:13.537: MLD: [0x0] (2001:10:100:100::100,FF36::600/128) MRIB update
(t=1).
*Mar 15 16:38:13.538: MLD: [0x0] (2001:10:100:100::100,FF36::600/128) GigabitEther-
net1 MRIB update (f=0,c=1).
*Mar 15 16:38:13.538: MLD: [0x0] (*,FF6E::6/128) MRIB update (t=1).
*Mar 15 16:38:13.538: MLD: [0x0] (*,FF6E::6/128) GigabitEthernet1 MRIB update
(f=0,c=1).
*Mar 15 16:38:13.538: MLD: [0x0] Processing group timers for FF36::600 on
GigabitEthernet1
*Mar 15 16:38:13.538: MLD: [0x0] MRIB updated (*,FF36::600) : Success on
GigabitEthernet1
*Mar 15 16:38:13.539: MLD: [0x0] group_db: delete group FF36::600 on
GigabitEthernet1
PE2(config-if)# do show ipv6 mld groups
MLD Connected Group Membership
Group Address                        Interface             Uptime    Expires
FF37::700                            GigabitEthernet1      00:23:55  not used
FF7E::7                              GigabitEthernet1      00:23:55  00:03:57

PE2(config-if)# do show ipv6 mld interface gigabitEthernet 1
GigabitEthernet1 is up, line protocol is up
  Internet address is FE80::5054:FF:FE0B:3E11/10
  MLD is enabled on interface
  Current MLD version is 2
  MLD query interval is 125 seconds
  MLD querier timeout is 255 seconds
  MLD max query response time is 10 seconds
  Last member query response interval is 1 seconds
  Inbound MLD access group is: MLD-FILTER
  MLD activity: 14 joins, 7 leaves
  MLD querying router is FE80::5054:FF:FE07:D323

PE2(config-if)# do undebug all
All possible debugging has been turned off
PE2(config-if)#
```

Notice how I applied the access list and the location where you can change the MLD version. You will have to wait a few seconds until the timer kicks in after you supply the access list, so be patient when you try this on your own. The output might be lengthy, but I've intentionally left it unedited so you can review it in its entirety and gain a thorough understanding of actual MLD operations, without any omissions. You can see a couple of denies for the multicast groups from PE6 I was targeting, and finally, they both get purged from PE2's MLD compute state. I also include the output of showing MLD running on PE2's only interface in the "up" state. You can observe various timers and the applied access list. Keep in mind that I'm demonstrating how to use these tools, so it's crucial for you to grasp exam questions and apply your knowledge effectively.

To summarize, what have you learned in this section? *That a crucial aspect in multicast packet flow involves delivering packets from the Last Hop Router to the receiver.* In IPv4 environments, this multicast portion of the multicast domain is regulated by the Internet Group Management Protocol (IGMP), while in IPv6 networks, the Multicast Listener Discovery (MLD) protocol takes charge of this responsibility.

Multicast Routing Protocol Types

There are two types of multicast routing protocols—Dense and Sparse. Note that exam focuses only on the Sparse mode, so we will not discuss Dense mode too much, but I will give you a short healthy perspective here:

- **Dense type** protocols use the push model where multicast traffic is flooded to all branches of the distribution tree because it assumed a dense distribution of multicast clients throughout the network. Branches without multicast receivers will get pruned (removed from the tree), and this cycle will repeat every three minutes or so. The examples of this type are MOSPF (based on OSPF extensions), DVMRP, and PIM-DM (PIM Dense-Mode). I don't know anyone who uses these anymore, particularly in service provider environments; the overhead and inefficiencies are too great.

- **Sparse type** protocols assume a sparse distribution of receivers and use the pull model (do you remember using **join** commands in the previous sections?), where Last Hop Routers will pull the traffic from either the meeting point (RP) or directly from the source. In this type, branches of the multicast distribution tree that have no receivers will never get multicast traffic. PIM-SM (Sparse Mode) is a good example and is efficient for pretty much any kind or size of network. Over the years, several enhancements have been introduced, including Bidirectional PIM (BiDir-PIM) and Source-Specific Multicast (SSM), which further optimize multicast routing for diverse network scenarios. These variations are the objects of subsequent pages.

PIM-SM Multicast Distribution Trees

In multicast networking, trees define the paths along which multicast traffic flows from the sender to the receivers. These paths are structured hierarchically, resembling tree structures, hence the name *multicast trees*. If you think of Layer 2 Spanning Tree Protocol, which is constructed to avoid traffic loops, you realize you have seen network tree structures before. There are two primary types of multicast trees:

- **Source-Based Trees:** These trees are rooted at the multicast sources and branch out toward the receivers. Each receiver joins the tree at a point closest to itself (recall

IGMP or MLD). There are different variations of source-based trees, such as the shortest-path tree (SPT) and the reverse path forwarding (RPF) tree.

- **Shared Trees:** Shared trees have a single common root shared among all sources and receivers—a rendezvous point (RP). Traffic is forwarded along branches from the RP (root) to the receivers.

These trees are dynamically constructed and maintained by multicast routing protocols (like PIM) to ensure that multicast packets are delivered efficiently to all interested receivers while minimizing network traffic.

Figure 9-4 shows an example of a multicast source-based tree. Some textbooks prefer to visualize trees "standing up vertically" with sources on top, or root them from the bottom, or vice versa, but it's all just a matter of perspective. My multicast source-based tree is casually sprawled out on the ground.

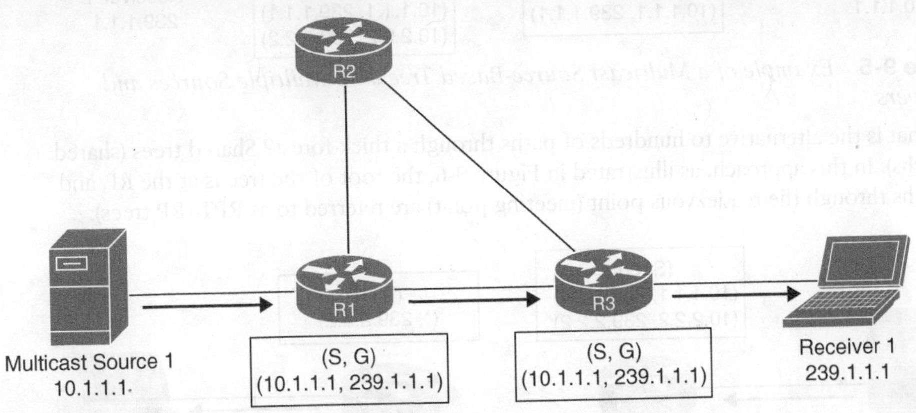

Figure 9-4 *Example of a Multicast Source Tree*

In Figure 9-4, a server 10.1.1.1 is the source of a multicast stream for group 239.1.1.1. The First Hop Router (FHR) happens to be R1, since it is closest to the source. The Last Hop Router (LHR) is R3, since it happens to be closest to Receiver 1, which is *pulling down* the 239.1.1.1 multicast stream by subscribing to it via IGMP. The "pull-down" is called an "explicit join" (remember that we had to subscribe to multicast groups in earlier examples)? PIM-SM has constructed this tree *through the shortest path*, not through R2, which sits on the longer path. Thus, source-based trees are shortest-path trees (SPTs). R1 and R3 build this shortest path with a notation of (S, G), pronounced "S comma G." S refers to the source, and G refers to the multicast group that Receiver 1 joins. What is important here? Since the source is root, every source must build its own tree through the network—100 sources, 100 paths. When sources are scattered across different locations or subnets, these trees form a "thick multicast forest" on the network. Figure 9-5 provides a visualization for when another pair of sources and receivers is added to the network with R3 having to keep path state for multiple paths.

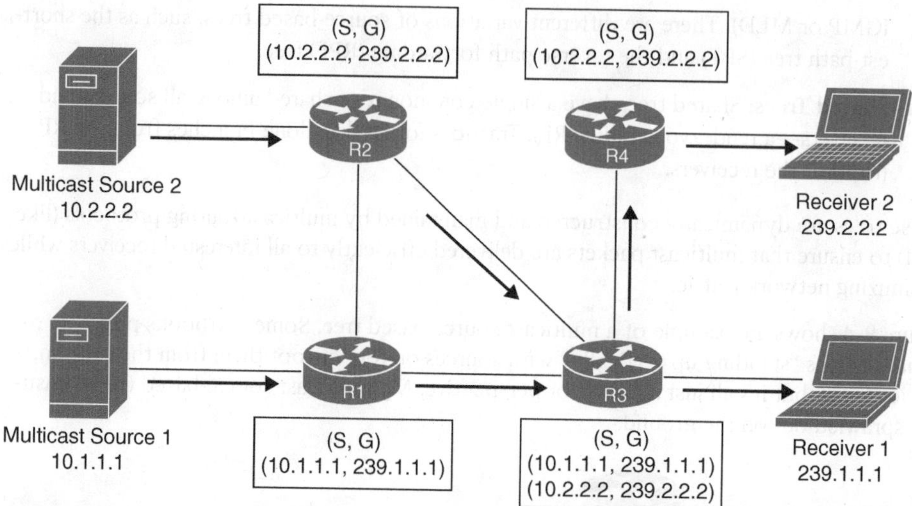

Figure 9-5 *Example of a Multicast Source-Based Tree with Multiple Sources and Receivers*

What is the alternative to hundreds of paths through a thick forest? Shared trees (shared paths). In this approach, as illustrated in Figure 9-6, the root of the tree is at the RP, and paths through the rendezvous point (meeting point) are referred to as RPT (RP trees).

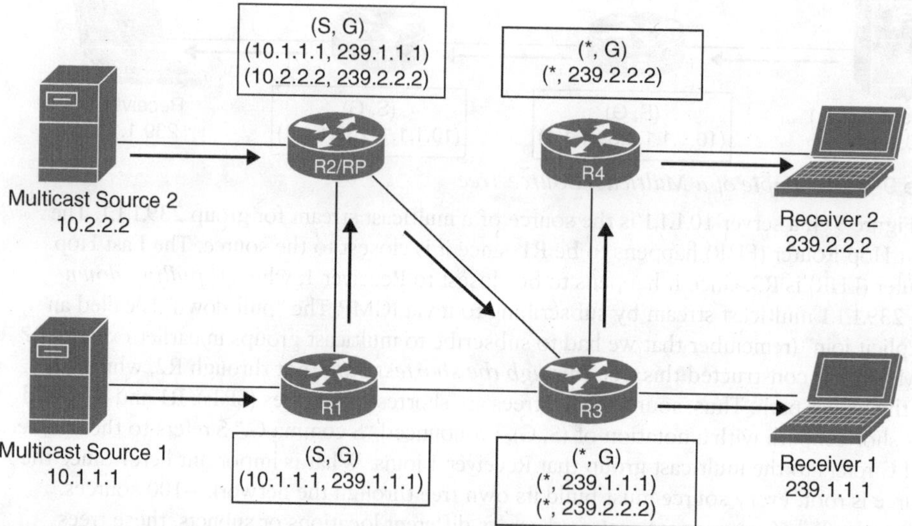

Figure 9-6 *Example of a Multicast RP Tree with Multiple Sources and Receivers*

Notice the shared tree rooted at R2 that is configured as the RP. The shared path through the "forest" is through the R2-R3. For now, all multicast paths *have to* cross R2 (you will soon see how shared trees are gradually replaced by shorter, source-oriented trees). A notion of (*, G)—pronounced "Star, comma, G"—indicates the multicast state created between the RP and LHRs.

Notice that, in the case of RP trees, two trees are constructed:

- **RP Tree:** Receivers initiate IGMP joins to their closest LHRs. LHRs send PIM joins to the RP.

- **Source-Based Tree:** RP sends PIM joins to the sources.

Let's learn step by step by understanding how these trees are built and changed. Consider our setup in Figure 9-7.

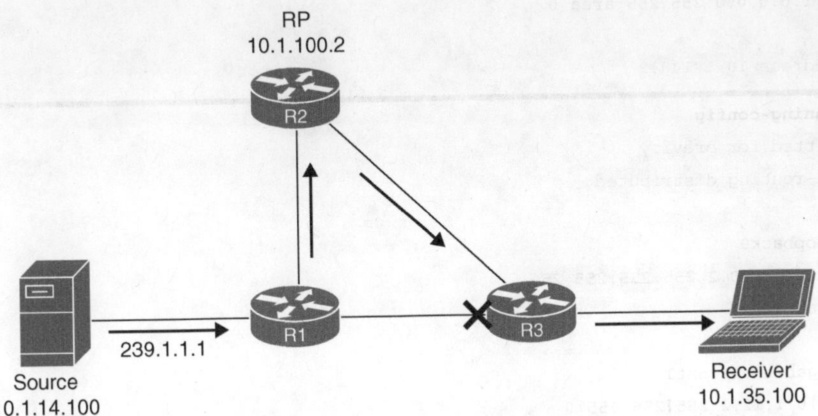

Figure 9-7 *Building a Shared RP-Based Multicast Tree*

The link connections between routers follow our numbering convention. There is a multicast source of 10.1.14.100 and receiver 10.1.35.100; both are routers I will use to simulate multicast traffic. We will configure R2 as the RP with the IP address of 10.1.100.2. This small network has full reachability (I am running OSPF on R1, R2, and R3, and the source and receiver have only a single interface enabled with a default route toward neighboring routers). We have full reachability; the source should be able to ping the receiver. One small detail: I have temporarily shut down R3's interface toward R1. You will soon learn why. I will build a shared tree going through R2. Example 9-17 shows the relevant configurations from R1–R3 to start our testing.

Example 9-17 *Turning Up MLDv2 on IOS Routers*

```
R1# show running-config
! Output omitted for brevity
ip multicast-routing distributed
!
interface GigabitEthernet1
 ip address 10.1.14.1 255.255.255.0
 ip pim sparse-mode
!
interface GigabitEthernet2
 ip address 10.1.13.1 255.255.255.0
```

```
  ip pim sparse-mode
 !
interface GigabitEthernet3
 ip address 10.1.12.1 255.255.255.0
 ip pim sparse-mode
 !
router ospf 1
 router-id 10.1.100.1
 network 10.1.0.0 0.0.255.255 area 0
 !
ip pim rp-address 10.1.100.2
```

```
R2# show running-config
! Output omitted for brevity
ip multicast-routing distributed
 !
interface Loopback0
 ip address 10.1.100.2 255.255.255.255
 ip pim sparse-mode
 !
interface GigabitEthernet1
 ip address 10.1.12.2 255.255.255.0
 ip pim sparse-mode
 !
interface GigabitEthernet2
 ip address 10.1.23.2 255.255.255.0
 ip pim sparse-mode
 !
router ospf 1
 router-id 10.1.100.2
 network 10.1.0.0 0.0.255.255 area 0
 !
ip pim rp-address 10.1.100.2
```

```
R3# show running-config
! Output omitted for brevity
ip multicast-routing distributed
 !
interface GigabitEthernet1
 ip address 10.1.23.3 255.255.255.0
 ip pim sparse-mode
 !
```

```
interface GigabitEthernet2
 ip address 10.1.13.3 255.255.255.0
 ip pim sparse-mode
 shutdown
!
interface GigabitEthernet3
 ip address 10.1.35.3 255.255.255.0
 ip pim sparse-mode
!
router ospf 1
 router-id 10.1.100.3
 network 10.1.0.0 0.0.255.255 area 0
!
ip pim rp-address 10.1.100.2
```

I have turned on **ip multicast-routing**, configured **ip pim sparse-mode** (which turns on PIM-SM and IGMP), configured R2's loopback0 as the RP, and *statically* pointed R1 and R3 to the RP (you will learn there are other ways of doing this). *There are no sources and no receivers.* Look at what we can observe from R1 (FHR, future First Hop Router) in Example 9-18.

Example 9-18   *R1 FHR Observations*

```
R1# show ip pim neighbor
PIM Neighbor Table
Mode: B - Bidir Capable, DR - Designated Router, N - Default DR Priority,
      P - Proxy Capable, S - State Refresh Capable, G - GenID Capable,
      L - DR Load-balancing Capable
Neighbor          Interface                Uptime/Expires    Ver    DR
Address                                                             Prio/Mode
10.1.12.2         GigabitEthernet3         11:09:42/00:01:39 v2     1 / DR S P G
R1# show ip pim tunnel
Tunnel0
   Type        : PIM Encap
   RP          : 10.1.100.2
   Source      : 10.1.12.1
   State       : UP
   Last event : Created (00:11:14)
R1# show ip pim rp
Group: 224.0.1.40, RP: 10.1.100.2, uptime 01:19:42, expires never
R1#
R1# show ip mroute
! Output omitted for brevity
(*, 224.0.1.40), 01:19:29/00:02:47, RP 10.1.100.2, flags: SJCL
   Incoming interface: GigabitEthernet3, RPF nbr 10.1.12.2
   Outgoing interface list:
       GigabitEthernet1, Forward/Sparse, 01:19:29/00:02:47
```

Because of our configuration in Example 9-17, R1 has a single PIM neighbor, R2, to which it has built a PIM tunnel, which will be used to send Register messages when Source finally sends its multicast stream. Notice that only a single default group 224.0.1.40 (Cisco RP-Discovery) is available. Also, the **show ip mroute** command (a very useful one) shows that the RPF path toward this RP group lies through GigabitEthernet3, and the outgoing interface is GigabitEthernet1 (this just happens to be where Source will connect). In multicast, RPF stands for Reverse Path Forwarding. It's a technique used to ensure that multicast traffic flows along the most efficient path within a network. RPF works by checking the incoming interface of multicast packets against the unicast routing table to verify if the packet arrived via the shortest path back to the source of the multicast traffic. If the incoming interface matches the route back to the source, the packet is forwarded; otherwise, it is dropped. This process helps prevent loops and ensures that multicast traffic follows the correct path through the network. Recall the mention of different types of multicast trees? The RPF tree leads back to the source.

Let's connect just the Source to group 239.1.1.1 and observe the behavior on routers R1, R2, and R3. In Example 9-19, we trace from Source just to be sure that the R1→R3 connection does not work, turn on debugging on all multicast routers, and launch a multicast stream.

Example 9-19   *Connecting the Multicast Source*

```
R1# debug ip pim 239.1.1.1
PIM debugging is on
R1#
```

```
R2# debug ip pim 239.1.1.1
PIM debugging is on
R2#
```

```
R3# debug ip pim 239.1.1.1
PIM debugging is on
R3#
```

```
Source# trace 10.1.35.100
Type escape sequence to abort.
Tracing the route to 10.1.35.100
VRF info: (vrf in name/id, vrf out name/id)
  1 10.1.14.1 35 msec 1 msec 0 msec
  2 10.1.12.2 33 msec 1 msec 1 msec
  3 10.1.23.3 34 msec 2 msec 1 msec
  4 10.1.35.100 49 msec 3 msec *
Source# configure terminal
Enter configuration commands, one per line.  End with CNTL/Z.
Source(config)# ip sla 1
```

```
Source(config-ip-sla)# udp-echo 239.1.1.1 5000 source-ip 10.1.14.100 control disable
Source(config-ip-sla-udp)# frequency 5
Source(config-ip-sla-udp)# ip sla schedule 1 start-time now
Source(config)# end
Source# show ip sla summary
IPSLAs Latest Operation Summary
Codes: * active, ^ inactive, ~ pending
All Stats are in milliseconds. Stats with u are in microseconds


ID          Type        Destination       Stats        Return      Last
                                                        Code        Run

----------------------------------------------------------------------------

*1          udp-echo    239.1.1.1         -            Timeout     8 seconds ago
```

Now let's examine what happened in the multicast world in Example 9-20.

Example 9-20 *Connecting the Multicast Source Continued (Multicast Register Messages)*

```
R1#
*Mar 19 10:38:37.733: PIM(0): Re-check RP 10.1.100.2 into the (*, 239.1.1.1) entry
*Mar 19 10:38:37.733: PIM(0): Building Triggered (*,G) Join / (S,G,RP-bit) Prune
message for 239.1.1.1
*Mar 19 10:38:37.733: PIM(0): Adding register encap tunnel (Tunnel0) as forwarding
interface of (10.1.14.100, 239.1.1.1).
*Mar 19 10:38:37.795: PIM(0): Received v2 Register-Stop on GigabitEthernet3 from
10.1.100.2
*Mar 19 10:38:37.795: PIM(0):  for source 10.1.14.100, group 239.1.1.1
*Mar 19 10:38:37.795: PIM(0): Removing register encap tunnel (Tunnel0) as forwarding
interface of (10.1.14.100, 239.1.1.1).
*Mar 19 10:38:37.796: PIM(0): Clear Registering flag to 10.1.100.2 for
(10.1.14.100/32, 239.1.1.1)
*Mar 19 10:39:37.579: PIM(0): Building Periodic (*,G) Join / (S,G,RP-bit) Prune mes-
sage for 239.1.1.1
*Mar 19 10:40:37.078: PIM(0): Building Periodic (*,G) Join / (S,G,RP-bit) Prune mes-
sage for 239.1.1.1
*Mar 19 10:40:37.779: PIM(0): Send v2 Data-header Register to 10.1.100.2 for
10.1.14.100, group 239.1.1.1
*Mar 19 10:40:37.780: PIM(0): Received v2 Register-Stop on GigabitEthernet3 from
10.1.100.2
*Mar 19 10:40:37.780: PIM(0):  for source 10.1.14.100, group 239.1.1.1
*Mar 19 10:40:37.780: PIM(0): Clear Registering flag to 10.1.100.2 for
(10.1.14.100/32, 239.1.1.1)

R2(config)#
*Mar 19 10:38:37.774: PIM(0): Received v2 Register on GigabitEthernet1 from
10.1.12.1
```

```
*Mar 19 10:38:37.774:              for 10.1.14.100, group 239.1.1.1
*Mar 19 10:38:37.774: PIM(0): Re-check RP 10.1.100.2 into the (*, 239.1.1.1) entry
*Mar 19 10:38:37.774: PIM(0): Adding register decap tunnel (Tunnel1) as accepting
interface of (*, 239.1.1.1).
*Mar 19 10:38:37.783: PIM(0): Adding register decap tunnel (Tunnel1) as accepting
interface of (10.1.14.100, 239.1.1.1).
*Mar 19 10:38:37.794: PIM(0): Send v2 Register-Stop to 10.1.12.1 for 10.1.14.100,
group 239.1.1.1
*Mar 19 10:39:36.796: PIM(0): Building Periodic (*,G) Join / (S,G,RP-bit) Prune mes-
sage for 239.1.1.1
*Mar 19 10:39:36.796: PIM: rp our address
*Mar 19 10:40:36.096: PIM(0): Building Periodic (*,G) Join / (S,G,RP-bit) Prune mes-
sage for 239.1.1.1
*Mar 19 10:40:36.096: PIM: rp our address
*Mar 19 10:40:37.782: PIM(0): Received v2 Register on GigabitEthernet1 from
10.1.12.1
*Mar 19 10:40:37.782:          (Data-header) for 10.1.14.100, group 239.1.1.1
*Mar 19 10:40:37.782: PIM(0): Send v2 Register-Stop to 10.1.12.1 for 10.1.14.100,
group 239.1.1.1
*Mar 19 10:41:35.895: PIM(0): Building Periodic (*,G) Join / (S,G,RP-bit) Prune mes-
sage for 239.1.1.1
*Mar 19 10:41:35.895: PIM: rp our address
```

I suggest you read this thoroughly; it reads like a novel. This is not an attempt at humor. If you want to understand multicast and answer exam questions correctly, it is going to take you slowing down and visualizing what is going on in routers. Read the above on your own.

Now, here's my summary. As soon as Source sent a UDP multicast stream packet to the network, FHR (R1) *registered* this source to the RP (R2), requesting the RP to build a tree back to Source. To do that, FHR encapsulated the multicast data from the source in a PIM-SM message called the *register* message and unicasted this data to the RP via the tunnel we saw in Example 9-18. The RP received the register message, decapsulated the multicast data inside the message, and sent a *register stop* back to the FHR directly, outside the tunnel, asking it to stop sending register messages. Why? There are no interested receivers; therefore, there is no active shared tree.

Let's continue. I had zero output on R3. All was quiet, since there were no multicast group subscribers. (Remember that PIM-SM is a *pull* model?) I suggest we turn on the listener (Receiver) to complete the multicast conversation and watch what happens again, as shown in Example 9-21.

Example 9-21   *Connecting the Multicast Receiver*

```
Receiver# configure terminal
Enter configuration commands, one per line.  End with CNTL/Z.
Receiver(config)# interface gigabitEthernet 1
Receiver(config-if)# ip igmp join-group 239.1.1.1
Receiver(config-if)#
```

```
R3#
*Mar 19 11:01:04.683: PIM(0): Re-check RP 10.1.100.2 into the (*, 239.1.1.1) entry
*Mar 19 11:01:04.685: PIM(0): Building Triggered (*,G) Join / (S,G,RP-bit) Prune
message for 239.1.1.1
*Mar 19 11:01:04.687: PIM(0): Building Triggered (*,G) Join / (S,G,RP-bit) Prune
message for 239.1.1.1
*Mar 19 11:01:04.687: PIM(0): Upstream mode for (*, 239.1.1.1) changed from 0 to 1
*Mar 19 11:01:04.688: PIM(0): Insert (*,239.1.1.1) join in nbr 10.1.23.2's queue
*Mar 19 11:01:04.690: PIM(0): Building Join/Prune packet for nbr 10.1.23.2
*Mar 19 11:01:04.690: PIM(0):  Adding v2 (10.1.100.2/32, 239.1.1.1), WC-bit, RPT-
bit, S-bit Join
*Mar 19 11:01:04.691: PIM(0): Send v2 join/prune to 10.1.23.2 (GigabitEthernet1)
*Mar 19 11:01:07.776: PIM(0): Insert (10.1.14.100,239.1.1.1) join in nbr 10.1.23.2's
queue
*Mar 19 11:01:07.777: PIM(0): Building Join/Prune packet for nbr 10.1.23.2
*Mar 19 11:01:07.777: PIM(0):  Adding v2 (10.1.14.100/32, 239.1.1.1), S-bit Join
*Mar 19 11:01:07.777: PIM(0): Send v2 join/prune to 10.1.23.2 (GigabitEthernet1)
R3#
```

```
R2(config)#
*Mar 19 11:01:04.695: PIM(0): Received v2 Join/Prune on GigabitEthernet2 from
10.1.23.3, to us
*Mar 19 11:01:04.695: PIM(0): Join-list: (*, 239.1.1.1), RPT-bit set, WC-bit set,
S-bit set
*Mar 19 11:01:04.695: PIM(0): Add GigabitEthernet2/10.1.23.3 to (*, 239.1.1.1), For-
ward state, by PIM *G Join
*Mar 19 11:01:04.695: PIM(0): Add GigabitEthernet2/10.1.23.3 to (10.1.14.100,
239.1.1.1), Forward state, by PIM *G Join
*Mar 19 11:01:04.695: PIM(0): Insert (10.1.14.100,239.1.1.1) join in nbr 10.1.12.1's
queue
*Mar 19 11:01:04.695: PIM(0): Building Join/Prune packet for nbr 10.1.12.1
*Mar 19 11:01:04.695: PIM(0):  Adding v2 (10.1.14.100/32, 239.1.1.1), S-bit Join
*Mar 19 11:01:04.696: PIM(0): Send v2 join/prune to 10.1.12.1 (GigabitEthernet1)
*Mar 19 11:01:07.735: PIM(0): Removing register decap tunnel (Tunnel1) as accepting
interface of (10.1.14.100, 239.1.1.1).
*Mar 19 11:01:07.735: PIM(0): Installing GigabitEthernet1 as accepting interface for
(10.1.14.100, 239.1.1.1).
*Mar 19 11:01:07.735: PIM(0):  Prune to 0.0.0.0 on  for (10.1.14.100, 239.1.1.1),
Ignored.
*Mar 19 11:01:07.780: PIM(0): Received v2 Join/Prune on GigabitEthernet2 from
10.1.23.3, to us
*Mar 19 11:01:07.783: PIM(0): Join-list: (10.1.14.100/32, 239.1.1.1), S-bit set
*Mar 19 11:01:07.783: PIM(0): Update GigabitEthernet2/10.1.23.3 to (10.1.14.100,
239.1.1.1), Forward state, by PIM SG Join
*Mar 19 11:01:14.096: PIM(0): Insert (10.1.14.100,239.1.1.1) join in nbr 10.1.12.1's
queue
*Mar 19 11:01:14.096: PIM(0): Building Join/Prune packet for nbr 10.1.12.1
```

```
*Mar 19 11:01:14.096: PIM(0):  Adding v2 (10.1.14.100/32, 239.1.1.1), S-bit Join
*Mar 19 11:01:14.096: PIM(0): Send v2 join/prune to 10.1.12.1 (GigabitEthernet1)
*Mar 19 11:01:18.396: PIM(0): Building Periodic (*,G) Join / (S,G,RP-bit) Prune mes-
sage for 239.1.1.1
*Mar 19 11:01:18.396: PIM: rp our address
```

```
R1#
*Mar 19 11:00:37.779: PIM(0): Send v2 Data-header Register to 10.1.100.2 for
10.1.14.100, group 239.1.1.1
*Mar 19 11:00:37.782: PIM(0): Received v2 Register-Stop on GigabitEthernet3 from
10.1.100.2
*Mar 19 11:00:37.783: PIM(0):   for source 10.1.14.100, group 239.1.1.1
*Mar 19 11:00:37.783: PIM(0): Clear Registering flag to 10.1.100.2 for
(10.1.14.100/32, 239.1.1.1)
*Mar 19 11:01:04.694: PIM(0): Received v2 Join/Prune on GigabitEthernet3 from
10.1.12.2, to us
*Mar 19 11:01:04.694: PIM(0): Join-list: (10.1.14.100/32, 239.1.1.1), S-bit set
*Mar 19 11:01:04.695: PIM(0): Add GigabitEthernet3/10.1.12.2 to (10.1.14.100,
239.1.1.1), Forward state, by PIM SG Join
*Mar 19 11:01:04.695: PIM(0):  Join to 0.0.0.0 on GigabitEthernet1 for (10.1.14.100,
239.1.1.1), Ignored.
*Mar 19 11:01:14.095: PIM(0): Received v2 Join/Prune on GigabitEthernet3 from
10.1.12.2, to us
*Mar 19 11:01:14.095: PIM(0): Join-list: (10.1.14.100/32, 239.1.1.1), S-bit set
*Mar 19 11:01:14.095: PIM(0): Update GigabitEthernet3/10.1.12.2 to (10.1.14.100,
239.1.1.1), Forward state, by PIM SG Join
*Mar 19 11:01:15.678: PIM(0): Building Periodic (*,G) Join / (S,G,RP-bit) Prune
message for 239.1.1.1
*Mar 19 11:01:21.778: PIM(0):  Join to 0.0.0.0 on GigabitEthernet1 for (10.1.14.100,
239.1.1.1), Ignored.
R1#
```

I again suggest reading this example thoroughly because I can highlight only so much until it loses its impact; thus I am highlighting the most obvious elements. My version of what happened: Receiver subscribed to the 239.1.1.1 stream (you should know all this from our extensive study on IGMP). LHR (R3) immediately checked in with the RP and added a join for R2's multicast queue. RP received the join and constructed a shortest-path tree on the interface going to FHR. There are some cryptic messages about an S-bit. In PIM, the S-bit, or S-flag, stands for the "Sparse" flag. This flag is used in PIM Join/Prune messages to indicate the type of multicast distribution tree being requested. When the S-bit is set to 0, it indicates that the receiver is interested in joining the (*, G) shared tree, where * represents all sources and G represents a specific multicast group. When the S-bit is set to 1, it indicates that the receiver is interested in joining the (S, G) source-based tree, where S represents a specific source and G represents a specific multicast group. This flag helps control the construction of multicast distribution trees based on the requirements of the receivers. FHR is ready for the (S, G) group now, and the multicast traffic flows freely.

Example 9-22 looks at the **show ip mroute** command, which helps you make sense of what goes on in multicast networks. It has the output explaining the multicast flags I mentioned (I will remove it from the other routers to save pages). I do not say "memorize the table," but you have to keep referring to it to understand what the network is trying to tell you (or the exam is trying to ask you).

Example 9-22 *Mroute Tables on R3, R2, and R1*

```
R3# show ip mroute
IP Multicast Routing Table
Flags: D - Dense, S - Sparse, B - Bidir Group, s - SSM Group, C - Connected,
       L - Local, P - Pruned, R - RP-bit set, F - Register flag,
       T - SPT-bit set, J - Join SPT, M - MSDP created entry, E - Extranet,
       X - Proxy Join Timer Running, A - Candidate for MSDP Advertisement,
       U - URD, I - Received Source Specific Host Report,
       Z - Multicast Tunnel, z - MDT-data group sender,
       Y - Joined MDT-data group, y - Sending to MDT-data group,
       G - Received BGP C-Mroute, g - Sent BGP C-Mroute,
       N - Received BGP Shared-Tree Prune, n - BGP C-Mroute suppressed,
       Q - Received BGP S-A Route, q - Sent BGP S-A Route,
       V - RD & Vector, v - Vector, p - PIM Joins on route,
       x - VxLAN group, c - PFP-SA cache created entry,
       * - determined by Assert, # - iif-starg configured on rpf intf,
       e - encap-helper tunnel flag, l - LISP Decap Refcnt Contributor
Outgoing interface flags: H - Hardware switched, A - Assert winner, p - PIM Join
 Timers: Uptime/Expires
 Interface state: Interface, Next-Hop or VCD, State/Mode

(*, 239.1.1.1), 00:01:00/stopped, RP 10.1.100.2, flags: SJC
  Incoming interface: GigabitEthernet1, RPF nbr 10.1.23.2
  Outgoing interface list:
    GigabitEthernet3, Forward/Sparse, 00:01:00/00:01:59

(10.1.14.100, 239.1.1.1), 00:00:57/00:02:02, flags: JT
  Incoming interface: GigabitEthernet1, RPF nbr 10.1.23.2
  Outgoing interface list:
    GigabitEthernet3, Forward/Sparse, 00:00:57/00:02:02

(*, 224.0.1.40), 00:35:03/00:02:32, RP 10.1.100.2, flags: SJPCL
  Incoming interface: GigabitEthernet1, RPF nbr 10.1.23.2
  Outgoing interface list: Null

R2# sh ip mroute
! Output omitted for brevity
```

```
(*, 239.1.1.1), 00:23:57/00:02:58, RP 10.1.100.2, flags: S
  Incoming interface: Null, RPF nbr 0.0.0.0
  Outgoing interface list:
    GigabitEthernet2, Forward/Sparse, 00:01:31/00:02:58

(10.1.14.100, 239.1.1.1), 00:23:57/00:01:01, flags: T
  Incoming interface: GigabitEthernet1, RPF nbr 10.1.12.1
  Outgoing interface list:
    GigabitEthernet2, Forward/Sparse, 00:01:31/00:03:00

(*, 224.0.1.40), 00:44:03/00:03:17, RP 10.1.100.2, flags: SJCL
  Incoming interface: Null, RPF nbr 0.0.0.0
  Outgoing interface list:
    GigabitEthernet2, Forward/Sparse, 00:34:53/00:03:17
    GigabitEthernet1, Forward/Sparse, 00:35:22/00:02:55
    Loopback0, Forward/Sparse, 00:44:01/00:02:57
```

```
R1# sh ip mroute
! Output omitted for brevity
(*, 239.1.1.1), 00:23:43/stopped, RP 10.1.100.2, flags: SPF
  Incoming interface: GigabitEthernet3, RPF nbr 10.1.12.2
  Outgoing interface list: Null

(10.1.14.100, 239.1.1.1), 00:23:43/00:01:16, flags: FT
  Incoming interface: GigabitEthernet1, RPF nbr 0.0.0.0
  Outgoing interface list:
    GigabitEthernet3, Forward/Sparse, 00:01:16/00:03:21

(*, 224.0.1.40), 00:36:41/00:02:19, RP 10.1.100.2, flags: SJCL
  Incoming interface: GigabitEthernet3, RPF nbr 10.1.12.2
  Outgoing interface list:
    GigabitEthernet1, Forward/Sparse, 00:36:41/00:02:19
```

Ignore anything in the group 224.0.1.40 for now. Follow the logic here:

- On LHR (R3), for both (*, G) and (S, G) entries, the incoming interface is toward the RP, and the outgoing interface is toward Receiver. Different flags are set for these entries. The (*, G) entry has SJC flags. They are

  - S: This flag indicates that it runs in Sparse mode.

  - J: The Join SPT flag suggests that the next (S, G) received packet will trigger a PIM shortest path switchover. For that to occur, C flags must be present.

  - C: A multicast group member is present on a directly connected interface.

- The (S, G) entry has FT flags. They are

  - **F:** This flag indicates that register messages are sent to the RP for the multicast source.

  - **T:** The SPT-bit set indicates that the packets have been received on the shortest-path tree.

  Note that the RPF paths are both through the RP (RP is the neighbor).

- On RP (R2), the (*, G) entry leads to the Null interface on this router with 0.0.0.0 as the RPF neighbor—meaning it is the RP and the outgoing interface points toward R3. The (S, G) entry shows that the incoming interface is from GHR (R1), and the outgoing interface is toward LHR (R3). Think about the flags shown here.

- On FHR (R1), the (*, G) entry is stopped. It is coming from the RP but not going anywhere, because the P flag indicates that it has been pruned—not used because of the (S, G) entry, but the R1 keeps this (*, G) entry in case a downstream member wants to join the source. The (S, G) entry shows the incoming interface from the Source (the RFP neighbor is 0.0.0.0) and the outgoing interface is toward the RP.

If you understand the preceding list, you are doing well because you know exactly how this multicast tree was built. If there was a problem, you know where to check for a broken path, and the flags should give you clues on what the issue could be.

What I would like to show you next is a PIM SPT (shortest path) switchover. PIM-SM will build a shortest-path tree *away from the RP when such a path is available.* PIM-SM allows LHRs to switch from *shared to shortest* paths (and you control this for specific sources with access-list). Lucky for us, our LHR (R3) will have a shorter path available as soon as we "no shutdown" the interface leading directly to FHR (R1—refer to Figure 9-8 where I have removed the black X next to R3).

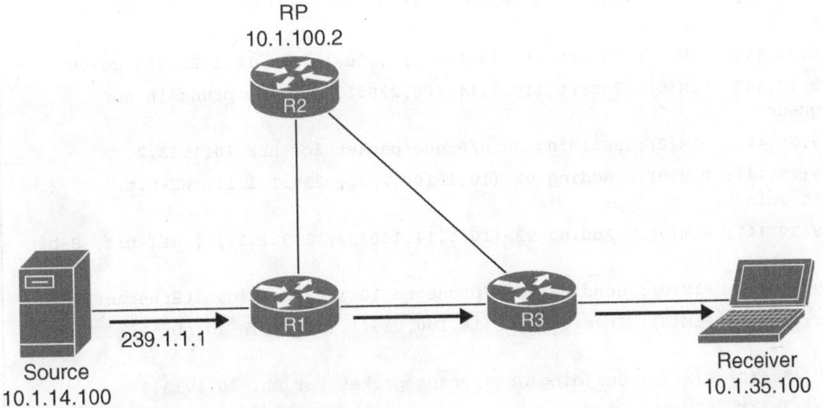

Figure 9-8 *PIM SPT Switchover*

Let's see what happens in Example 9-23.

Example 9-23   *Observing the PIM SPT Switchover*

```
R3# configure terminal
Enter configuration commands, one per line.  End with CNTL/Z.
R3(config)# interface gigabitEthernet 2
R3(config-if)# no shutdown
*Mar 19 13:29:19.231: PIM(0): Check DR after interface: GigabitEthernet2 came up!
*Mar 19 13:29:19.231: PIM(0): Changing DR for GigabitEthernet2, from 0.0.0.0 to
10.1.13.3 (this system)
*Mar 19 13:29:19.232: %PIM-5-DRCHG: DR change from neighbor 0.0.0.0 to 10.1.13.3 on
interface GigabitEthernet2
*Mar 19 13:29:21.161: %LINK-3-UPDOWN: Interface GigabitEthernet2, changed state to
up
*Mar 19 13:29:21.166: %PIM-5-NBRCHG: neighbor 10.1.13.1 UP on interface
GigabitEthernet2
*Mar 19 13:29:22.161: %LINEPROTO-5-UPDOWN: Line protocol on Interface
GigabitEthernet2, changed state to up
*Mar 19 13:29:22.231: PIM(0): Check DR after interface: GigabitEthernet2 came up!
*Mar 19 13:29:29.342: %OSPF-5-ADJCHG: Process 1, Nbr 10.1.100.1 on GigabitEthernet2
from LOADING to FULL, Loading Done
*Mar 19 13:29:29.398: PIM(0): Insert (10.1.14.100,239.1.1.1) join in nbr 10.1.13.1's
queue
*Mar 19 13:29:29.398: PIM(0): Insert (10.1.14.100,239.1.1.1) prune in nbr
10.1.23.2's queue
*Mar 19 13:29:29.398: PIM(0): Building Join/Prune packet for nbr 10.1.23.2
*Mar 19 13:29:29.399: PIM(0):  Adding v2 (10.1.14.100/32, 239.1.1.1), S-bit Prune
*Mar 19 13:29:29.399: PIM(0): Send v2 join/prune to 10.1.23.2 (GigabitEthernet1)
*Mar 19 13:29:29.399: PIM(0): Building Join/Prune packet for nbr 10.1.13.1
*Mar 19 13:29:29.399: PIM(0):  Adding v2 (10.1.14.100/32, 239.1.1.1), S-bit Join
*Mar 19 13:29:29.399: PIM(0): Send v2 join/prune to 10.1.13.1 (GigabitEthernet2)
*Mar 19 13:29:29.440: PIM(0): Building Periodic (*,G) Join / (S,G,RP-bit) Prune
message for 239.1.1.1
*Mar 19 13:29:29.440: PIM(0): Insert (*,239.1.1.1) join in nbr 10.1.23.2's queue
*Mar 19 13:29:29.440: PIM(0): Insert (10.1.14.100,239.1.1.1) sgr prune in nbr
10.1.23.2's queue
*Mar 19 13:29:29.441: PIM(0): Building Join/Prune packet for nbr 10.1.23.2
*Mar 19 13:29:29.441: PIM(0):  Adding v2 (10.1.100.2/32, 239.1.1.1), WC-bit,
RPT-bit, S-bit Join
*Mar 19 13:29:29.441: PIM(0):  Adding v2 (10.1.14.100/32, 239.1.1.1), RPT-bit, S-bit
Prune
*Mar 19 13:29:29.441: PIM(0): Send v2 join/prune to 10.1.23.2 (GigabitEthernet1)
*Mar 19 13:29:43.440: PIM(0): Insert (10.1.14.100,239.1.1.1) join in nbr 10.1.13.1's
queue
*Mar 19 13:29:43.440: PIM(0): Building Join/Prune packet for nbr 10.1.13.1
*Mar 19 13:29:43.441: PIM(0):  Adding v2 (10.1.14.100/32, 239.1.1.1), S-bit Join
*Mar 19 13:29:43.441: PIM(0): Send v2 join/prune to 10.1.13.1 (GigabitEthernet2)
```

```
R3(config-if)# do show ip mroute
! Output omitted for brevity
(*, 239.1.1.1), 02:28:58/stopped, RP 10.1.100.2, flags: SJC
  Incoming interface: GigabitEthernet1, RPF nbr 10.1.23.2
  Outgoing interface list:
    GigabitEthernet3, Forward/Sparse, 02:28:58/00:02:00

(10.1.14.100, 239.1.1.1), 00:03:16/00:02:43, flags: JT
  Incoming interface: GigabitEthernet2, RPF nbr 10.1.13.1
  Outgoing interface list:
    GigabitEthernet3, Forward/Sparse, 00:03:16/00:02:00

(*, 224.0.1.40), 03:03:01/00:02:31, RP 10.1.100.2, flags: SJPCL
  Incoming interface: GigabitEthernet1, RPF nbr 10.1.23.2
  Outgoing interface list: Null
```

```
R2#
*Mar 19 13:28:54.498: PIM(0): Insert (10.1.14.100,239.1.1.1) join in nbr 10.1.12.1's
queue
*Mar 19 13:28:54.498: PIM(0): Building Join/Prune packet for nbr 10.1.12.1
*Mar 19 13:28:54.498: PIM(0):  Adding v2 (10.1.14.100/32, 239.1.1.1), S-bit Join
*Mar 19 13:28:54.498: PIM(0): Send v2 join/prune to 10.1.12.1 (GigabitEthernet1)
*Mar 19 13:29:29.402: PIM(0): Received v2 Join/Prune on GigabitEthernet2 from
10.1.23.3, to us
*Mar 19 13:29:29.402: PIM(0): Prune-list: (10.1.14.100/32, 239.1.1.1)
*Mar 19 13:29:29.402: PIM(0): Prune GigabitEthernet2/239.1.1.1 from (10.1.14.100/32,
239.1.1.1)
*Mar 19 13:29:29.402: PIM(0): Insert (10.1.14.100,239.1.1.1) prune in nbr
10.1.12.1's queue - deleted
*Mar 19 13:29:29.402: PIM(0): Building Join/Prune packet for nbr 10.1.12.1
*Mar 19 13:29:29.402: PIM(0):  Adding v2 (10.1.14.100/32, 239.1.1.1), S-bit Prune
*Mar 19 13:29:29.402: PIM(0): Send v2 join/prune to 10.1.12.1 (GigabitEthernet1)
*Mar 19 13:29:29.444: PIM(0): Received v2 Join/Prune on GigabitEthernet2 from
10.1.23.3, to us
*Mar 19 13:29:29.444: PIM(0): Join-list: (*, 239.1.1.1), RPT-bit set, WC-bit set,
S-bit set
*Mar 19 13:29:29.444: PIM(0): Update GigabitEthernet2/10.1.23.3 to (*, 239.1.1.1),
Forward state, by PIM *G Join
*Mar 19 13:29:29.444: PIM(0): Prune-list: (10.1.14.100/32, 239.1.1.1) RPT-bit set
R2# show ip mroute
! Output omitted for brevity
(*, 239.1.1.1), 02:53:33/00:02:45, RP 10.1.100.2, flags: S
  Incoming interface: Null, RPF nbr 0.0.0.0
  Outgoing interface list:
```

```
    GigabitEthernet2, Forward/Sparse, 02:31:06/00:02:45


(10.1.14.100, 239.1.1.1), 00:05:24/00:01:34, flags: PT
  Incoming interface: GigabitEthernet1, RPF nbr 10.1.12.1
  Outgoing interface list: Null


(*, 224.0.1.40), 03:13:39/00:03:21, RP 10.1.100.2, flags: SJCL
  Incoming interface: Null, RPF nbr 0.0.0.0
  Outgoing interface list:
    GigabitEthernet2, Forward/Sparse, 03:04:28/00:03:21
    GigabitEthernet1, Forward/Sparse, 03:04:57/00:02:58
    Loopback0, Forward/Sparse, 03:13:37/00:02:21

R1#
*Mar 19 13:28:54.497: PIM(0): Received v2 Join/Prune on GigabitEthernet3 from
10.1.12.2, to us
*Mar 19 13:28:54.498: PIM(0): Join-list: (10.1.14.100/32, 239.1.1.1), S-bit set
*Mar 19 13:28:54.498: PIM(0): Update GigabitEthernet3/10.1.12.2 to (10.1.14.100,
239.1.1.1), Forward state, by PIM SG Join
*Mar 19 13:29:21.166: %PIM-5-NBRCHG: neighbor 10.1.13.3 UP on interface
GigabitEthernet2
*Mar 19 13:29:21.167: PIM(0): Changing DR for GigabitEthernet2, from 10.1.13.1 to
10.1.13.3
*Mar 19 13:29:21.167: %PIM-5-DRCHG: DR change from neighbor 10.1.13.1 to 10.1.13.3
on interface GigabitEthernet2
*Mar 19 13:29:29.342: %OSPF-5-ADJCHG: Process 1, Nbr 10.1.100.3 on GigabitEthernet2
from LOADING to FULL, Loading Done
*Mar 19 13:29:29.400: PIM(0): Received v2 Join/Prune on GigabitEthernet2 from
10.1.13.3, to us
*Mar 19 13:29:29.400: PIM(0): Join-list: (10.1.14.100/32, 239.1.1.1), S-bit set
*Mar 19 13:29:29.400: PIM(0): Add GigabitEthernet2/10.1.13.3 to (10.1.14.100,
239.1.1.1), Forward state, by PIM SG Join
*Mar 19 13:29:29.401: PIM(0): Received v2 Join/Prune on GigabitEthernet3 from
10.1.12.2, to us
*Mar 19 13:29:29.401: PIM(0): Prune-list: (10.1.14.100/32, 239.1.1.1)
*Mar 19 13:29:29.402: PIM(0): Prune GigabitEthernet3/239.1.1.1 from (10.1.14.100/32,
239.1.1.1) - deleted
*Mar 19 13:29:43.081: PIM(0): Building Periodic (*,G) Join / (S,G,RP-bit) Prune
message for 239.1.1.1
*Mar 19 13:29:43.442: PIM(0): Received v2 Join/Prune on GigabitEthernet2 from
10.1.13.3, to us
*Mar 19 13:29:43.442: PIM(0): Join-list: (10.1.14.100/32, 239.1.1.1), S-bit set
*Mar 19 13:29:43.442: PIM(0): Update GigabitEthernet2/10.1.13.3 to (10.1.14.100,
239.1.1.1), Forward state, by PIM SG Join
*Mar 19 13:29:45.381: PIM(0):  Join to 0.0.0.0 on GigabitEthernet1 for (10.1.14.100,
239.1.1.1), Ignored.
```

```
*Mar 19 13:30:21.081: PIM(0): Adding register encap tunnel (Tunnel0) as forwarding
interface of (10.1.14.100, 239.1.1.1).
R1# show ip mroute
! Output omitted for brevity
(*, 239.1.1.1), 00:05:59/stopped, RP 10.1.100.2, flags: SPF
  Incoming interface: GigabitEthernet3, RPF nbr 10.1.12.2
  Outgoing interface list: Null

(10.1.14.100, 239.1.1.1), 00:05:59/00:03:10, flags: FT
  Incoming interface: GigabitEthernet1, RPF nbr 0.0.0.0
  Outgoing interface list:
    GigabitEthernet2, Forward/Sparse, 00:03:16/00:03:24

(*, 224.0.1.40), 03:07:05/00:02:57, RP 10.1.100.2, flags: SJCL
  Incoming interface: GigabitEthernet3, RPF nbr 10.1.12.2
  Outgoing interface list:
    GigabitEthernet1, Forward/Sparse, 03:07:05/00:02:57

R1#
```

At this point, I would like for you to have read through the example and derived the following.

On LHR (R3), as soon as I unshut the interface with the shortest path to FHR (R1), PIM neighborship comes up. This leads to the insertion of join messages toward R1 and insertion of prune messages toward the RP. The output from **show ip mroute** shows that the RPF tree now leads directly to R1, bypassing the RP. This transition signifies a shift from the shared tree to the shortest-path tree.

On the RP (R2), the interface to LHR (R3) is pruned because there are no other listeners on this interface. The outgoing interface list of Null also provides a clue for that. Additionally, a WC-bit is mentioned in the debug output. In PIM, the WC-bit stands for the "Wild Card" bit. This bit is used in PIM Join/Prune messages to indicate whether the receiver is willing to accept traffic from any source for a specific multicast group (i.e., a (*, G) join) when building the shared tree. When the WC-bit is set to 1, it signifies that the receiver is willing to accept traffic from any source for the specified group, allowing the router to join the shared tree without specifying particular source information. If the WC-bit is set to 0, it means that the receiver is not willing to accept traffic from any source and prefers to join the shared tree only for traffic originating from specific sources. This bit helps control the flexibility of multicast group memberships and tree construction in PIM networks.

FHR (R1) has a PIM designated router (DR) election on its link to LHR (R3), which R3 wins because it has a higher IP address. The DR is elected to avoid sending duplicate multicast traffic to the LAN or the RP (which happened on all connections earlier; I just did not draw your attention to these events). By default, the DR priority is set to the value of 1, and you can adjust it by using the **ip pim dr-priority** *priority-value* command under interface configuration mode and with the **dr-priority** *priority-value* command under PIM or PIM interface configuration mode in IOS XR. This topic can be a question on the exam.

Back to our scenario, RP (R2) sends a message to prune the interface leading to itself from this group. The (S, G) entry contains a single interface in its outgoing list (toward listeners)—GigabitEthernet2, leading to LHR (R3).

My suggestion? Consider taking a break from the book for a couple of days. It's important to give yourself time to absorb this knowledge without it becoming jumbled with other information.

Rendezvous Points

In our previous example, I had you configure static RP mapping on all routers. It is a straight-forward task, especially in networks with few and stable (they do not change frequently) RPs. In smaller networks, this approach may be considered the most efficient.

Example 9-24 shows that you can control multicast groups for specific RPs via access lists.

Example 9-24   *Static RP Configuration Options*

```
R1(config)# ip pim rp-address ?
  A.B.C.D  IP address of Rendezvous-point for group


R1(config)# ip pim rp-address 10.1.100.2 ?
  <1-99>       Access-list reference for group
  <1300-1999>  Access-list reference for group (expanded range)
  WORD         IP Named Standard Access list
  override     Overrides dynamically learnt RP mappings
  <cr>         <cr>

R1(config)#
```

Also, notice the **override** option. Because static RPs can co-exist with a couple of "auto-magic" options (which I'll introduce shortly) that typically take precedence over a stati-cally configured RP, the override option ensures that the router disregards those automatic options and exclusively uses the static mappings. But back to more important things. Once you have more than a few routers on the network, making changes to RPs would require touching and reconfiguring every router in your multicast domain. Plus, what about failovers if our statically configured RP fails? Or if we wanted to split the load between RPs? Well, you have a couple of options, and one is from Cisco.

PIM Auto-RP

When you get tired of configuring RPs manually, Cisco has a proprietary mechanism to distribute group-to-RP mappings, making it easier to administer and update RP information. You can manipulate different RPs to service different multicast groups, load-share multi-cast traffic between them, and make them back up each other for fault-tolerance. To look at how these function, in Figure 9-9 I have added another router to our topology, R6 (since Source and Receiver took up "4" and "5" addressing). I suggest you make R6 an XR device so that you can practice multicast on these devices as well. I added it to OSPF and have full reachability. I'm including it in this setup because our multicast configuration is already functional, making it convenient for you to practice. This setup already has both a source and a receiver, providing an opportunity for hands-on practice if you wish to do so.

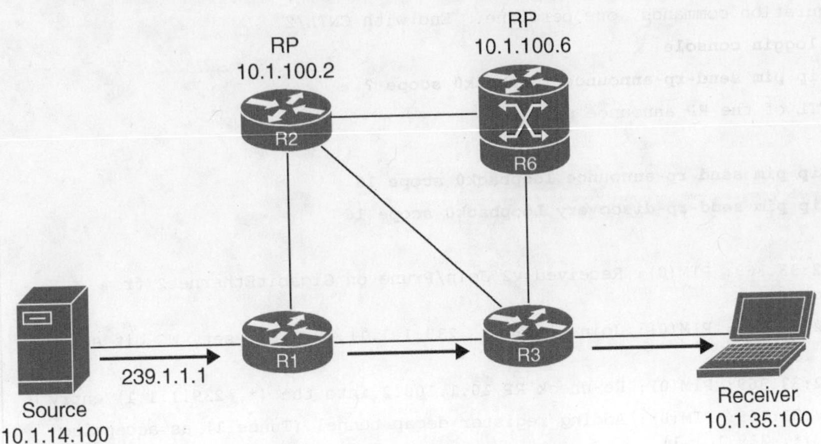

Figure 9-9 *Introducing a Second RP to the Topology*

When dealing with Auto-RPs, you have to be mindful of two components:

- **Candidate RPs:** Because you have more than one router for this role, candidate routers advertise their intent to be an RP by using an RP announcement message. These messages are sent every 60 seconds (by default) to the well-known reserved multicast group 224.0.1.39 (Cisco RP-Announce). A candidate RP with the highest IP address will become the RP.

- **RP Mapping Agents:** These agents join multicast group 224.0.1.39 to listen to the RP announcements and advertise the elected RPs and their group-to-RP mappings to the rest of the multicast domain via the 224.0.1.40 (Cisco-RP-Discovery) address you have seen before in our outputs. All PIM-enabled routers join multicast group 224.0.1.40 and store the elected RP along with the group-to-RP mappings in their local cache.

You will need to remove all static RP references and proceed to Example 9-25. R2 is ready to become the RP. You need two commands highlighted here. The **send-rp-announce** command causes the router to send an Auto-RP announcement message to the well-known group CISCO-RP-ANNOUNCE (224.0.1.39). This message announces the router as a candidate RP for the groups in the range defined by the access list. We do not use an access list in this example, so the announcement will be for 244.0.0.0/4 (224.0.0.0 to 239.255.255.255). The scope limits how many TTL hops the announcement can go through. We definitely have fewer than 16 hops in our topology. The **send-rp-discovery** command configures the mapping agent (you can co-locate this function on the RP or choose another router; it doesn't matter). Mapping agents listen on the well-known group address Cisco-RP-Announce (224.0.1.39) and send RP-to-group mappings in an Auto-RP discovery message to the well-known group Cisco-RP-Discovery (224.0.1.40) to all PIM DR routers so that they can figure out which RPs to use.

Example 9-25 *Auto-RP Configuration*

```
R2# configure terminal
Enter configuration commands, one per line.  End with CNTL/Z.
R2(config)# loggin console
R2(config)# ip pim send-rp-announce loopback0 scope ?
  <1-255>  TTL of the RP announce packet

R2(config)# ip pim send-rp-announce loopback0 scope 16
R2(config)# ip pim send-rp-discovery Loopback0 scope 16
R2(config)#
*Mar 22 11:32:33.369: PIM(0): Received v2 Join/Prune on GigabitEthernet2 from
10.1.23.3, to us
*Mar 22 11:32:33.369: PIM(0): Join-list: (*, 239.1.1.1), RPT-bit set, WC-bit set,
S-bit set
*Mar 22 11:32:33.369: PIM(0): Re-check RP 10.1.100.2 into the (*, 239.1.1.1) entry
*Mar 22 11:32:33.369: PIM(0): Adding register decap tunnel (Tunnel1) as accepting
interface of (*, 239.1.1.1).
*Mar 22 11:32:33.370: PIM(0): Add GigabitEthernet2/10.1.23.3 to (*, 239.1.1.1), For-
ward state, by PIM *G Join
R2(config)# end
R2# show ip pim rp
*Mar 22 11:32:37.853: %SYS-5-CONFIG_I: Configured from console by console
Group: 239.1.1.1, RP: 10.1.100.2
R1#
*Mar 22 11:09:59.501: PIM(0): Building Periodic (*,G) Join / (S,G,RP-bit) Prune mes-
sage for 239.1.1.1
*Mar 22 11:10:00.000: PIM(0):  Join to 0.0.0.0 on GigabitEthernet1 for (10.1.14.100,
239.1.1.1), Ignored.
*Mar 22 11:10:00.678: PIM(0): Received v2 Join/Prune on GigabitEthernet2 from
10.1.13.3, to us
*Mar 22 11:10:00.678: PIM(0): Join-list: (10.1.14.100/32, 239.1.1.1), S-bit set
*Mar 22 11:10:00.678: PIM(0): Update GigabitEthernet2/10.1.13.3 to (10.1.14.100,
239.1.1.1), Forward state, by PIM SG Join
R1# show ip pim rp
Group: 239.1.1.1, RP: 0.0.0.0
R1# show ip pim rp
R1#
```

Our debug captures the register message from our ever-streaming source, and R2 even shows that it is the RP for the 239.1.1.1 group. All is good, although something is not quite right on R1, where the debug was running as well. First off, the RP address is not R2. Then, after a while the information seems to time out, and there is no RP present at all. And where are all the joins and PIM messages? What do you think the problem is?

Welcome to the world of multicast. You have just met the "sparse-mode problem." In Auto-RP, messages are transmitted to multicast group addresses 224.0.1.39 and 224.0.1.40, requiring routers to join these groups. However, to establish the multicast tree in Sparse mode, a rendezvous point (RP) address is necessary. This creates a circular dependency where an RP address is needed to obtain an RP address. What?! It is hard to keep calm here. We can use a static RP address for 224.0.1.39 and 224.0.1.40, but the purpose of Auto-RP should be to avoid the need for static configurations. There are a couple of ways to solve this:

- Put all interfaces into **pim sparse-dense** mode instead of the "normal" **pim sparse** mode I have instructed you to use. This would cause Dense mode forwarding for .39 and .40. This also has the side effect of any group that doesn't have an RP address using Dense mode. You can be playing with fire here if all RPs fail, because then all groups will use Dense mode, effectively eating network bandwidth and leading to inefficient routing. (You can fix this behavior with the **no ip pim dm-fallback** global command.)

- Use the **ip pim autorp listener** command to run Sparse mode, although .39 and .40 are still in Dense mode. We will put this command on R1 to the test and, once it works, on the rest of your testbed, except the RPs.

Example 9-26 shows the effect of adding **autorp listener**.

Example 9-26 *Auto-RP Listener Configuration*

```
R1# configure terminal
Enter configuration commands, one per line.  End with CNTL/Z.
R1(config)# ip pim autorp listener
R1(config)#
*Mar 22 12:05:06.800: PIM(0): Building Graft message for 224.0.1.40, GigabitEther-
net3: no entries
*Mar 22 12:05:06.800: PIM(0): Building Graft message for 224.0.1.40, GigabitEther-
net2: no entries
*Mar 22 12:05:06.801: PIM(0): Building Graft message for 224.0.1.40, GigabitEther-
net1: no entries
R1(config)# end
R1#
*Mar 22 12:05:20.631: %SYS-5-CONFIG_I: Configured from console by console
*Mar 22 12:05:22.000: PIM(0): Building Graft message for 224.0.1.39,
GigabitEthernet3:
     10.1.100.2/32 count 1
*Mar 22 12:05:22.000: PIM(0): Send v2 Graft to 10.1.12.2 (GigabitEthernet3)
*Mar 22 12:05:22.001: PIM(0): Building Graft message for 224.0.1.39, GigabitEther-
net2: no entries
*Mar 22 12:05:22.003: PIM(0): Received v2 Graft-Ack on GigabitEthernet3 from
10.1.12.2
*Mar 22 12:05:22.003:        Group 224.0.1.39:
     10.1.100.2/32
*Mar 22 12:06:03.040: PIM(0): Initiating register encapsulation tunnel creation for
RP 10.1.100.2
*Mar 22 12:06:03.040: PIM(0): Initial register tunnel creation succeeded for RP
10.1.100.2
```

```
*Mar 22 12:06:03.064: PIM(0): pim_reg_tun_comingup Tunnel0 RP 10.1.100.2 previous
event 0

*Mar 22 12:06:03.064: PIM(0): pim_ipv4_reg_tun_event_set Tunnel0 RP 10.1.100.2
previous event 0 new event 2

*Mar 22 12:06:03.101: PIM(0): Building Graft message for 224.0.1.40,
GigabitEthernet3:

     10.1.100.2/32 count 1

*Mar 22 12:06:03.101: PIM(0): Send v2 Graft to 10.1.12.2 (GigabitEthernet3)

*Mar 22 12:06:03.101: PIM(0): Building Graft message for 224.0.1.40,
GigabitEthernet2: no entries

*Mar 22 12:06:03.101: PIM(0): Building Graft message for 224.0.1.40,
GigabitEthernet1: no entries

*Mar 22 12:06:03.103: PIM(0): Received v2 Graft-Ack on GigabitEthernet3 from
10.1.12.2

*Mar 22 12:06:03.103:          Group 224.0.1.40:

     10.1.100.2/32

*Mar 22 12:06:04.042: %LINEPROTO-5-UPDOWN: Line protocol on Interface Tunnel0,
changed state to up

*Mar 22 12:06:04.042: PIM(0): pim_reg_tun_comingup Tunnel0 RP 10.1.100.2 previous
event 0

*Mar 22 12:06:04.042: PIM(0): pim_ipv4_reg_tun_event_set Tunnel0 RP 10.1.100.2
previous event 0 new event 2

*Mar 22 12:06:12.913: PIM(0): Re-check RP 10.1.100.2 into the (*, 239.1.1.1) entry

*Mar 22 12:06:12.913: PIM(0): Building Triggered (*,G) Join / (S,G,RP-bit) Prune
message for 239.1.1.1

*Mar 22 12:06:12.913: PIM(0): Adding register encap tunnel (Tunnel0) as forwarding
interface of (10.1.14.100, 239.1.1.1).

*Mar 22 12:06:12.937: PIM(0): Received v2 Join/Prune on GigabitEthernet3 from
10.1.12.2, to us

*Mar 22 12:06:12.937: PIM(0): Join-list: (10.1.14.100/32, 239.1.1.1), S-bit set

*Mar 22 12:06:12.937: PIM(0): Add GigabitEthernet3/10.1.12.2 to (10.1.14.100,
239.1.1.1), Forward state, by PIM SG Join

*Mar 22 12:06:12.938: PIM(0):  Join to 0.0.0.0 on GigabitEthernet1 for (10.1.14.100,
239.1.1.1), Ignored.

*Mar 22 12:06:12.961: PIM(0): Received v2 Join/Prune on GigabitEthernet2 from
10.1.13.3, to us

*Mar 22 12:06:12.961: PIM(0): Join-list: (10.1.14.100/32, 239.1.1.1), S-bit set

*Mar 22 12:06:12.961: PIM(0): Add GigabitEthernet2/10.1.13.3 to (10.1.14.100,
239.1.1.1), Forward state, by PIM SG Join

*Mar 22 12:06:22.914: PIM(0): Received v2 Join/Prune on GigabitEthernet3 from
10.1.12.2, to us

*Mar 22 12:06:22.915: PIM(0): Prune-list: (10.1.14.100/32, 239.1.1.1)

*Mar 22 12:06:22.915: PIM(0): Prune GigabitEthernet3/239.1.1.1 from (10.1.14.100/32,
239.1.1.1) - deleted

*Mar 22 12:06:32.905: PIM(0): Received v2 Register-Stop on GigabitEthernet3 from
10.1.100.2

*Mar 22 12:06:32.905: PIM(0):   for source 10.1.14.100, group 239.1.1.1
```

```
*Mar 22 12:06:32.905: PIM(0): Removing register encap tunnel (Tunnel0) as forwarding
interface of (10.1.14.100, 239.1.1.1).
*Mar 22 12:06:32.905: PIM(0): Clear Registering flag to 10.1.100.2 for
(10.1.14.100/32, 239.1.1.1)
R1# show ip pim rp
Group: 239.1.1.1, RP: 10.1.100.2, uptime 00:00:40, expires 00:02:17
R1# show ip pim rp mapping
PIM Group-to-RP Mappings

Group(s) 224.0.0.0/4
  RP 10.1.100.2 (?), v2v1
    Info source: 10.1.100.2 (?), elected via Auto-RP
         Uptime: 00:12:43, expires: 00:02:05
R1#
```

I suggest that you read the output on your own (without my highlights), but R1 has the correct RP now, auto-magically distributed—less work for everyone. Time to get IOS XR involved with R6.

Now let's add another RP to the mix and see what the network does. Did you add autorp listener on R3? I knew you did. You may find it surprising that in our setup R3 keeps getting the RP information anyway. The reason is that a connected Receiver keeps sending multicast requests to R3. Example 9-27 shows us turning on multicast on all interfaces for the IPv4 address family and announcing RP candidacy.

Example 9-27 *Adding a Second RP to the Network*

```
RP/0/RP0/CPU0:R6# configure
Fri Mar 22 12:34:09.222 UTC
RP/0/RP0/CPU0:R6(config)# multicast-routing
RP/0/RP0/CPU0:R6(config-mcast)# address-family ipv4
RP/0/RP0/CPU0:R6(config-mcast-default-ipv4)# interface all enable
RP/0/RP0/CPU0:R6(config-mcast-default-ipv4)# router pim
RP/0/RP0/CPU0:R6(config-pim)# address-family ipv4
RP/0/RP0/CPU0:R6(config-pim-default-ipv4)# auto-rp candidate-rp loopback0 scope 16
RP/0/RP0/CPU0:R6(config-pim-default-ipv4)# commit
RP/0/RP0/CPU0:R6(config-pim-default-ipv4)#

R1# show ip pim rp
Group: 239.1.1.1, RP: 10.1.100.6, uptime 00:10:48, expires 00:02:02
R1#

R3# show ip pim rp mapping
PIM Group-to-RP Mappings
```

```
Group(s) 224.0.0.0/4
  RP 10.1.100.6 (?), v2
    Info source: 10.1.100.2 (?), elected via Auto-RP
          Uptime: 00:15:51, expires: 00:02:00
R3#
```

On R6, the commands are under address families. I turned on multicast routing for all interfaces and announced the RP candidacy. In my lab, I got a massive debug output, which I cannot show here due to prime real estate for each page. Basically, R6 takes over the RP role, since it has a higher IP address than R2. The results are clear on R1 and R3, with R6 being the winner. R3 shows that it received this mapping from R2.

PIM Bootstrap Router (BSR)

RFC 5059 describes a standards-based, nonproprietary, fault-tolerant, and automated RP discovery and distribution mechanism. It is included in PIM version 2. BSR performs the same function as Cisco's Auto-RP but floods BSR messages from the RP to intermediate routers hop by hop. The All PIM Routers address 224.0.0.13 with a TTL of 1 is used for messaging. Typically, multiple BSRs are deployed to avoid a single point of failure. An election takes place with a router with highest configured priority declared a winner or the highest IP address in case of a priority tie.

Among the unique differences from the Auto-RP method, there is no mapping agent in BSR to declare the active RP as you saw in the previous example. Each router will use a well-known algorithm to elect the active RP for a specific group range. Since the list of candidate RPs for particular groups and the algorithm are the same, the same RP will be elected. Lower-priority RPs are preferred, but the highest IP address will win in case of a tie (low, high, high, low—how to remember all this?).

Two commands are necessary to turn on BSR on IOS R2 and IOS XR R6. Notice the verification on R1 as demonstrated by Example 9-28.

Example 9-28   *Enabling BSR*

```
R2(config)# ip pim bsr-candidate loopback0
R2(config)# ip pim rp-candidate loopback0 ?
  group-list  group-list
  interval    RP candidate advertisement interval
  priority    RP candidate priority
  <cr>        <cr>

R2(config)# ip pim rp-candidate lo0 priority ?
  <0-255>  Priority value

R2(config)# ip pim rp-candidate lo0 priority 192
R2(config)#
```

```
RP/0/RP0/CPU0:R6# configure
Fri Mar 22 14:54:10.782 UTC
RP/0/RP0/CPU0:R6(config)# router pim
RP/0/RP0/CPU0:R6(config-pim)# address-family ipv4
RP/0/RP0/CPU0:R6(config-pim-default-ipv4)# bsr candidate-rp ?
  A.B.C.D  IP address of BSR Candidate-RP
RP/0/RP0/CPU0:R6(config-pim-default-ipv4)# bsr candidate-rp 10.1.100.6 priority
192 ?
  bidir       To specify group ranges as Bidir
  group-list  Group List access-list
  interval    C-RP Advertisement interval
  <cr>
RP/0/RP0/CPU0:R6(config-pim-default-ipv4)# bsr candidate-rp 10.1.100.6 priority 192
RP/0/RP0/CPU0:R6(config-pim-default-ipv4)# bsr candidate-bsr 10.1.100.6  priority
100
RP/0/RP0/CPU0:R6(config-pim-default-ipv4)# commit
Fri Mar 22 14:55:53.407 UTC
RP/0/RP0/CPU0:R6(config-pim-default-ipv4)#
```

```
R1# show ip pim rp mapping
PIM Group-to-RP Mappings


Group(s) 224.0.0.0/4
  RP 10.1.100.6 (?), v2
    Info source: 10.1.100.6 (?), via bootstrap, priority 192, holdtime 150
      Uptime: 00:30:38, expires: 00:02:03
  RP 10.1.100.2 (?), v2
    Info source: 10.1.100.6 (?), via bootstrap, priority 192, holdtime 150
      Uptime: 01:42:43, expires: 00:01:58
R1#
```

A note on priorities: I chose candidate RP-Priority of 192 for a good reason. Cisco IOS implementations of PIM BSR use the value 0 as the default priority for candidate RPs and BSRs. This implementation predates the draft-ietf-pim-sm-bsr IETF draft, the first IETF draft to specify 192 as the default priority value. The Cisco IOS and Cisco IOS XE implementations, thus, deviate from the IETF draft. To comply with the default priority value specified in the draft, you must explicitly set the priority value to 192. IOS XR, on the other hand, uses the value 192 for candidate RPs and 1 for candidate BSRs. As you can see, I changed the last value to 100 to draw your attention to this topic. Be mindful of these differences from Cisco's Auto-RP.

On the exam, you might encounter common questions regarding mapping certain multicast groups to certain RPs for failover, redundancy, or load-splitting. As long as you understand the basic method, you should be able to decipher what the exam is asking. Example 9-29 shows a simple memorable approach you should be able to appropriate for your own or exam needs.

Example 9-29 *Mapping a Group to a Certain RP*

```
R2(config)# ip access-list standard GROUP-239
R2(config-std-nacl)# permit 239.1.1.1 0.0.0.0
R2(config-std-nacl)# exit
R2(config)# ip pim rp-candidate lo0 ?
  group-list  group-list
  interval    RP candidate advertisement interval
  priority    RP candidate priority
  <cr>        <cr>

R2(config)# ip pim rp-candidate lo0 group-list GROUP-239
R2(config)#
```

```
R1# show ip pim rp mapping
PIM Group-to-RP Mappings


Group(s) 224.0.0.0/4
  RP 10.1.100.6 (?), v2
    Info source: 10.1.100.6 (?), via bootstrap, priority 192, holdtime 150
      Uptime: 00:53:06, expires: 00:02:06
Group(s) 239.1.1.1/32
  RP 10.1.100.2 (?), v2
    Info source: 10.1.100.6 (?), via bootstrap, priority 0, holdtime 150
      Uptime: 00:00:23, expires: 00:02:02
R1#
```

I mapped our 239.1.1.1 multicast group to R2 via the access list. Then, I used R1 to verify and see that R2 is now responsible for this group. Observe that since I omitted priority 192 when assigning the group list on R2, R1 now sees it with a priority of 0. This is my way to draw your attention to recognize it in the exam outputs. I highly suggest practicing this in different ways to build familiarity.

Bidirectional PIM

Bidirectional PIM (BiDir-Pim) is a very different approach to multicast than you have seen up till now. Traditional multicast routing protocols, such as PIM Sparse Mode (PIM-SM) or PIM Dense Mode (PIM-DM), are optimized for unidirectional traffic flows. In contrast, BiDir-PIM is specifically tailored for applications where traffic flows in both directions between sources and receivers. In BiDir-PIM, there's no need for a rendezvous point or explicit join messages from receivers. Instead, all routers in the multicast domain participate in the delivery of multicast traffic and use a shared tree for both upstream and downstream traffic. This shared tree minimizes the need for state maintenance and reduces overhead compared to source-specific trees used in other multicast protocols.

BiDir-PIM achieves efficiency by constructing a bidirectional shared distribution tree rooted at the source. This tree encompasses all group members, allowing data to flow bidirectionally between the source and receivers without the need for additional signaling. This simplifies the multicast routing process and reduces the complexity of managing multicast traffic flows. Why such a drastic change from what you have learned already? In all our examples, we have assumed one source or few sources with many receivers. Think of a live multicast video stream that launches at a central point and is distributed to all employees at a company's branches—a "one-to-many" approach.

Multicast streams can have a "many-to-many" flavor as well. You can think of video conferencing meetings where several participants are engaging with each other as one of the examples. What does this have to do with us? Consider what you have learned about PIM-SM in our examples. You clearly saw that sparse-mode builds two trees. The first tree has (S, G) from FHR to RP. The second tree has (*, G) along with (S, G) entries from RP to LHR (look at Example 9-22 on R3, which clearly shows both built and directed toward the RP if you need to refresh your memory). When you have many multicast sources, many (S, G) entries can be present on the FHRs and then, when SPT cutover takes place, many will bypass the RP, creating a larger burden on all routers in the network. Some of this behavior can be remedied. For one, we can improve the first tree I mentioned by disabling SPT switchover on the LHRs; this will force routers to always use the shared tree to the RP and can be somewhat helpful. However, the bigger issue lies with the second tree, which still has (S, G) entries along the RP-LHR path and inefficiency persists.

Here is what you need to know to be technically competent and clear exam topics:

- BiDir-PIM will never build (S, G) entries.

- Only (*, G) entries are allowed on the shared tree.

- Recall that in PIM-SM, the downstream (away from the source) tree can be different from the upstream (toward the source) tree because the RPF check sends it on the shortest path back to the source. There's no such thing in BiDir-PIM; the traffic flows up and down the shared tree.

- Furthermore, RPF check does not exist. Loop prevention is handled with designated forwarders (DFs). Only one DF is allowed per segment; no loops are possible.

- There are no register or register stop messages or mechanisms in BiDir. Each source sends traffic to the RP at will.

What does this mean for network design decisions? RPs have to be somewhere in the middle between sources and receivers; otherwise, multicast paths will be "suboptimal" at best. The best way to consolidate this knowledge is to make it functional. Example 9-30 picks up with the BiDir-PIM enabled on all routers except R1. Here comes R1.

Example 9-30 *BiDir-PIM (Closer to Source)*

```
R1# show ip pim rp
R1# configure terminal
Enter configuration commands, one per line.  End with CNTL/Z.
R1(config)# ip pim bidir-enable
R1(config)# ip pim rp-address 10.1.100.2 bidir
R1(config)#
```

```
*Mar 22 20:47:04.313: PIM(0): Re-check RP 10.1.100.2 into the (*, 224.0.1.40) entry
*Mar 22 20:47:04.314: PIM(0): Building Triggered Join/Prune message for 224.0.1.40
*Mar 22 20:47:04.316: PIM(0): Received v2 DF on GigabitEthernet2 from 10.1.13.3
*Mar 22 20:47:04.316: PIM(0): Received v2 DF on GigabitEthernet2 from 10.1.13.3
*Mar 22 20:47:04.462: PIM(0): Building Triggered Join/Prune message for 224.0.1.40
*Mar 22 20:47:07.015: PIM(0): Received v2 DF on GigabitEthernet3 from 10.1.12.2
*Mar 22 20:47:07.051: PIM(0): Received v2 DF on GigabitEthernet3 from 10.1.12.2
*Mar 22 20:47:07.101: PIM(0): Received v2 DF on GigabitEthernet3 from 10.1.12.2
*Mar 22 20:47:07.150: PIM(0): Received v2 DF on GigabitEthernet3 from 10.1.12.2
*Mar 22 20:47:07.165: PIM(0): Received v2 DF on GigabitEthernet2 from 10.1.13.3
*Mar 22 20:47:07.188: PIM(0): Received v2 DF on GigabitEthernet2 from 10.1.13.3
*Mar 22 20:47:07.201: PIM(0): Received v2 DF on GigabitEthernet3 from 10.1.12.2
*Mar 22 20:47:07.662: PIM(0):  Prune to 0.0.0.0 on GigabitEthernet3 for (10.1.100.2,
224.0.1.40), Ignored.
*Mar 22 20:47:07.662: PIM(0): Building Triggered Join/Prune message for 224.0.1.40
*Mar 22 20:47:07.662: PIM(0): Upstream mode for (*, 224.0.1.40) changed from 0 to 1
*Mar 22 20:47:07.662: PIM(0): Insert (*,224.0.1.40) join in nbr 10.1.12.2's queue
*Mar 22 20:47:07.662: PIM(0): Building Join/Prune packet for nbr 10.1.12.2
*Mar 22 20:47:07.663: PIM(0):  Adding v2 (10.1.100.2/32, 224.0.1.40), WC-bit,
RPT-bit, S-bit Join
*Mar 22 20:47:07.663: PIM(0): Send v2 join/prune to 10.1.12.2 (GigabitEthernet3)
*Mar 22 20:47:10.065: PIM(0): Received v2 DF on GigabitEthernet2 from 10.1.13.3
*Mar 22 20:47:12.550: PIM(0): Received v2 DF on GigabitEthernet3 from 10.1.12.2
*Mar 22 20:47:12.914: PIM(0): Received v2 DF on GigabitEthernet2 from 10.1.13.3
*Mar 22 20:47:15.865: PIM(0): Received v2 DF on GigabitEthernet2 from 10.1.13.3
*Mar 22 20:47:18.137: PIM(0): Received v2 DF on GigabitEthernet2 from 10.1.13.3
*Mar 22 20:47:18.501: PIM(0): Received v2 DF on GigabitEthernet3 from 10.1.12.2
*Mar 22 20:47:21.064: PIM(0): Received v2 DF on GigabitEthernet2 from 10.1.13.3
*Mar 22 20:47:23.137: PIM(0): Received v2 DF on GigabitEthernet2 from 10.1.13.3
*Mar 22 20:47:24.451: PIM(0): Received v2 DF on GigabitEthernet3 from 10.1.12.2
*Mar 22 20:47:26.064: PIM(0): Received v2 DF on GigabitEthernet2 from 10.1.13.3
*Mar 22 20:47:28.137: PIM(0): Received v2 DF on GigabitEthernet2 from 10.1.13.3
*Mar 22 20:47:29.304: PIM(0): Building Periodic Join/Prune message for 224.0.1.40
*Mar 22 20:47:29.304: PIM(0): Insert (*,224.0.1.40) join in nbr 10.1.12.2's queue
*Mar 22 20:47:29.304: PIM(0): Building Join/Prune packet for nbr 10.1.12.2
*Mar 22 20:47:29.305: PIM(0):  Adding v2 (10.1.100.2/32, 224.0.1.40), WC-bit,
RPT-bit, S-bit Join
*Mar 22 20:47:29.305: PIM(0): Send v2 join/prune to 10.1.12.2 (GigabitEthernet3)
*Mar 22 20:47:29.450: PIM(0): Received v2 DF on GigabitEthernet3 from 10.1.1end
*Mar 22 20:47:31.064: PIM(0): Received v2 DF on GigabitEthernet2 from 10.1.13.3
*Mar 22 20:47:32.016: %SYS-5-CONFIG_I: Configured from console by console
*Mar 22 20:47:33.138: PIM(0): Received v2 DF on GigabitEthernet2 from 10.1.13.3
*Mar 22 20:47:34.451: PIM(0): Received v2 DF on GigabitEthernet3 from 10.1.12.2
```

```
*Mar 22 20:47:35.964: PIM(0): Received v2 DF on GigabitEthernet2 from 10.1.13.3
R1# show ip pim rp
Group: 224.0.1.40, RP: 10.1.100.2, uptime 00:01:14, expires never
R1# show ip pim rp map
PIM Group-to-RP Mappings

Group(s): 224.0.0.0/4, Static, Bidir Mode
    RP: 10.1.100.2 (?)
R1# show ip mroute
IP Multicast Routing Table
Flags: D - Dense, S - Sparse, B - Bidir Group, s - SSM Group, C - Connected,
       L - Local, P - Pruned, R - RP-bit set, F - Register flag,
       T - SPT-bit set, J - Join SPT, M - MSDP created entry, E - Extranet,
       X - Proxy Join Timer Running, A - Candidate for MSDP Advertisement,
       U - URD, I - Received Source Specific Host Report,
       Z - Multicast Tunnel, z - MDT-data group sender,
       Y - Joined MDT-data group, y - Sending to MDT-data group,
       G - Received BGP C-Mroute, g - Sent BGP C-Mroute,
       N - Received BGP Shared-Tree Prune, n - BGP C-Mroute suppressed,
       Q - Received BGP S-A Route, q - Sent BGP S-A Route,
       V - RD & Vector, v - Vector, p - PIM Joins on route,
       x - VxLAN group, c - PFP-SA cache created entry,
       * - determined by Assert, # - iif-starg configured on rpf intf,
       e - encap-helper tunnel flag, l - LISP Decap Refcnt Contributor
Outgoing interface flags: H - Hardware switched, A - Assert winner, p - PIM Join
 Timers: Uptime/Expires
 Interface state: Interface, Next-Hop or VCD, State/Mode

(*,224.0.0.0/4), 00:03:44/-, RP 10.1.100.2, flags: B
  Bidir-Upstream: GigabitEthernet3, RPF nbr: 10.1.12.2
  Incoming interface list:
    GigabitEthernet1, Accepting/Sparse
    GigabitEthernet3, Accepting/Sparse

(*, 224.0.1.40), 00:05:17/00:02:05, RP 10.1.100.2, flags: BCL
  Bidir-Upstream: GigabitEthernet3, RPF nbr 10.1.12.2
  Outgoing interface list:
    GigabitEthernet1, Forward/Sparse, 00:03:44/00:02:05
    GigabitEthernet3, Bidir-Upstream/Sparse, 00:03:44/stopped
R1# sh ip pim interface df
* implies this system is the DF
Interface          RP              DF Winner       Metric    Uptime
GigabitEthernet1   10.1.100.2      *10.1.14.1        2        00:03:52
```

```
GigabitEthernet2                10.1.100.2          10.1.13.3           2          00:03:52
GigabitEthernet3                10.1.100.2          10.1.12.2           0          00:03:49
R1#
```

```
RP/0/RP0/CPU0:R6(config)# router pim
RP/0/RP0/CPU0:R6(config-pim)# address-family ipv4
RP/0/RP0/CPU0:R6(config-pim-default-ipv4)# rp-address 10.1.100.2 ?
  WORD        Access list of groups that should map to given RP
  bidir       Specify keyword bidir to configure a bidir RP
  override    Static RP config overrides auto-rp and BSR
  <cr>
RP/0/RP0/CPU0:R6(config-pim-default-ipv4)# rp-address 10.1.100.2 bidir
RP/0/RP0/CPU0:R6(config-pim-default-ipv4)# commit
Fri Mar 22 20:56:00.418 UTC
RP/0/RP0/CPU0:R6(config-pim-default-ipv4)# do show pim interfaces
Fri Mar 22 20:56:37.418 UTC


PIM interfaces in VRF default
Address             Interface               PIM  Nbr    Hello  DR     DR
                                                 Count  Intvl  Prior

10.1.100.6          Loopback0               on   1      30     1      this system
10.1.26.6           GigabitEthernet0/0/0/0  on   2      30     1      this system
10.1.36.6           GigabitEthernet0/0/0/1  on   2      30     1      this system
RP/0/RP0/CPU0:R6(config-pim-default-ipv4)#
```

I encourage you to read through the highlighted items. They explain what is taking place far better than any words. I enabled BiDir-PIM, and DF messages start rolling in. Reasonably quickly, BiDir entries show up in the mroute table. The last command shows DF winners on all segments—R1 losing them all except the interface facing source. Ending in .1 does not help in becoming a winner, but it does not matter, since we have no loops in the network. R6's output shows how to turn on BiDir-PIM on IOS XR-based platforms. Look at how R6 wins all the elections due to having the highest value in the last octet. Example 9-31 shows multicast router states on R3 and RP.

Example 9-31 *BiDir-PIM on RP and R3 (Closer to Receiver)*

```
R3# show ip pim interface df
* implies this system is the DF
Interface            RP               DF Winner        Metric    Uptime
GigabitEthernet1     10.1.100.2       10.1.23.2        0         00:11:19
GigabitEthernet2     10.1.100.2       *10.1.13.3       2         00:03:53
```

```
GigabitEthernet3          10.1.100.2          *10.1.35.3          2          00:11:19
GigabitEthernet4          10.1.100.2          *10.1.36.3          2          00:11:10
R3# show ip mroute
IP Multicast Routing Table
Flags: D - Dense, S - Sparse, B - Bidir Group, s - SSM Group, C - Connected,
       L - Local, P - Pruned, R - RP-bit set, F - Register flag,
       T - SPT-bit set, J - Join SPT, M - MSDP created entry, E - Extranet,
       X - Proxy Join Timer Running, A - Candidate for MSDP Advertisement,
       U - URD, I - Received Source Specific Host Report,
       Z - Multicast Tunnel, z - MDT-data group sender,
       Y - Joined MDT-data group, y - Sending to MDT-data group,
       G - Received BGP C-Mroute, g - Sent BGP C-Mroute,
       N - Received BGP Shared-Tree Prune, n - BGP C-Mroute suppressed,
       Q - Received BGP S-A Route, q - Sent BGP S-A Route,
       V - RD & Vector, v - Vector, p - PIM Joins on route,
       x - VxLAN group, c - PFP-SA cache created entry,
       * - determined by Assert, # - iif-starg configured on rpf intf,
       e - encap-helper tunnel flag, l - LISP Decap Refcnt Contributor
Outgoing interface flags: H - Hardware switched, A - Assert winner, p - PIM Join
 Timers: Uptime/Expires
 Interface state: Interface, Next-Hop or VCD, State/Mode


(*,224.0.0.0/4), 00:24:31/-, RP 10.1.100.2, flags: B
  Bidir-Upstream: GigabitEthernet1, RPF nbr: 10.1.23.2
  Incoming interface list:
    GigabitEthernet2, Accepting/Sparse
    GigabitEthernet3, Accepting/Sparse
    GigabitEthernet1, Accepting/Sparse

(*, 239.1.1.1), 00:24:30/00:02:03, RP 10.1.100.2, flags: BC
  Bidir-Upstream: GigabitEthernet1, RPF nbr 10.1.23.2
  Outgoing interface list:
    GigabitEthernet3, Forward/Sparse, 00:24:30/00:02:03
    GigabitEthernet1, Bidir-Upstream/Sparse, 00:24:30/stopped

(*, 224.0.1.40), 08:43:21/00:02:55, RP 10.1.100.2, flags: BPL
  Bidir-Upstream: GigabitEthernet1, RPF nbr 10.1.23.2
  Outgoing interface list:
    GigabitEthernet1, Bidir-Upstream/Sparse, 00:24:31/stopped

R3#
```

```
R2# show ip mroute
```

```
! Output omitted for brevity
(*,224.0.0.0/4), 00:53:34/-, RP 10.1.100.2, flags: B
   Bidir-Upstream: Loopback0, RPF nbr: 10.1.100.2
   Incoming interface list:
      GigabitEthernet1, Accepting/Sparse
      GigabitEthernet2, Accepting/Sparse
      GigabitEthernet3, Accepting/Sparse
      Loopback0, Accepting/Sparse

(*, 239.1.1.1), 00:50:48/00:02:59, RP 10.1.100.2, flags: B
   Bidir-Upstream: Null, RPF nbr 0.0.0.0
   Outgoing interface list:
      GigabitEthernet2, Forward/Sparse, 00:50:48/00:02:59

(*, 224.0.1.40), 00:53:34/00:03:10, RP 10.1.100.2, flags: BCL
   Bidir-Upstream: Null, RPF nbr 0.0.0.0
   Outgoing interface list:
      GigabitEthernet1, Forward/Sparse, 00:42:59/00:03:10
      GigabitEthernet2, Forward/Sparse, 00:50:59/00:02:41
      Loopback0, Forward/Sparse, 00:53:34/00:02:27

R2#
```

Notice the flags in R3's mroute table. All multicast groups point toward R2, the RP. The most interesting output is the group entry for (*, 239.1.1.1): the BiDir tree is on GigabitEthernet1, toward the RP, and GigabitEthernet3 is forwarding toward our Receiver. On R2, the RP is on the Loopback0 interface, accepting traffic from all interfaces. Currently, group (*, 239.1.1.1) has the outgoing list built for only GigabitEthernet2, which faces R3, where our Receiver is connected. That is BiDir-PIM.

Source-Specific Multicast (SSM)

Everything I discussed previously in the PIM sections has been about multicast service models that became collectively known as *Any Source Multicast* (ASM). ASM, the original multicast, allowed for both one-to-many and many-to-many models. If someone asked you what these models have in common, how would you answer? At least one way to think this would be that any ASM network must have a *source discovery function* to locate sources of multicast traffic when interested receivers are present.

In every scenario, including those not covered in the exam, such as PIM Dense mode, the multicast receiver remains unaware of the multicast source—a problem that the network must resolve. PIM Dense mode addressed this by flooding source information to every router in the network (a *push*-to-network model), resulting in significant scalability issues and high network resource utilization. PIM Sparse mode achieved source discovery without flooding (a *pull*-from-network model), but this introduced considerable complexity because RPs were responsible for constructing intricate shared distribution trees. ASM had other not-so-obvious challenges as well. For instance, receivers accepted traffic coming from *any* network source transmitting to a specific group. Is that acceptable? Maybe, maybe not. You could filter out the unwanted traffic on the receivers themselves (which many applications did), but the *network* still had to absorb this unnecessary bandwidth.

For these and other reasons, RFC 4607 defined *PIM Source-Specific Multicast (SSM)* as one of the alternative options for running PIM. It is a simpler one-to-many model, which you already encountered when you observed the shortest-path tree (SPT) cut-over. **PIM SSM** bypasses the RP connection phase by directly establishing shortest-path trees rooted at the source instead of relying on shared distribution trees. No shared trees, no RPs, no RP mappings. The identification of a multicast stream is based on the channel (the *unicast* address of the source and the *multicast* group address).

What is the simplest, most memorable, technical way to describe SSM? SSM is a subset of PIM Sparse mode that uses IGMPv3 routers to allow clients to receive multicast traffic directly from the source without an RP's assistance. Earlier in the IGMP section, you already encountered SSM. Since a well-known range 232.0.0.0/8 has been assigned by IANA to SSM, routers support SSM by default. You can also use any multicast group in the 224.0.0.0/4 group except the Local Network Control Block 224.0.0.0/24 (224.0.0.0-224.0.0.255). Also, recall and make a connection to the MLD section (along with IGMPv3) in this chapter's discussion on exclude and include modes. In SSM, only include mode reports are accepted to the LHR (last hop router). Let's look at our network, where I strongly suggest (for multiple reasons) you remove any relics of ASM multicast from the previous sections. After you're done, we'll pick up at R3, closest to our Receiver. Example 9-32 shows what happens when we turn on SSM on R3.

Example 9-32 *Turning on SSM on R3*

```
R3# show ip igmp interface gigabitEthernet 3
GigabitEthernet3 is up, line protocol is up
  Internet address is 10.1.35.3/24
  IGMP is enabled on interface
  Current IGMP host version is 2
  Current IGMP router version is 2
  IGMP query interval is 60 seconds
  IGMP configured query interval is 60 seconds
  IGMP querier timeout is 120 seconds
  IGMP configured querier timeout is 120 seconds
  IGMP max query response time is 10 seconds
  Last member query count is 2
  Last member query response interval is 1000 ms
  Inbound IGMP access group is not set
  IGMP activity: 1 joins, 0 leaves
  Multicast routing is enabled on interface
  Multicast TTL threshold is 0
  Multicast designated router (DR) is 10.1.35.3 (this system)
  IGMP querying router is 10.1.35.3 (this system)
  No multicast groups joined by this system
```

```
R3# configure terminal
Enter configuration commands, one per line.  End with CNTL/Z.
R3(config)# ip pim ssm ?
  default  Use 232/8 group range for SSM
  range    ACL for group range to be used for SSM

R3(config)# ip pim ssm default ?
  <cr>  <cr>


R3(config)# ip pim ssm default
R3(config)# interface gigabitEthernet 3
R3(config-if)# ip igmp ?
  access-group                 IGMP group access group
  explicit-tracking            Enable/Disable IGMP explicit-tracking
  helper-address               IGMP helper address
  iif-starg                    IGMP update incoming interface field of starg
  immediate-leave              Leave groups immediately without sending last member
query, use for one host network only
  join-group                   IGMP join multicast group
  last-member-query-count      IGMP last member query count
  last-member-query-interval   IGMP last member query interval
  limit                        IGMP limit
  mroute-proxy                 Mroute to IGMP proxy
  proxy-report-interval        IGMP proxy report interval
  proxy-service                Enable IGMP mroute proxy service
  querier-timeout              IGMP previous querier timeout
  query-interval               IGMP host query interval
  query-max-response-time      IGMP max query response value
  static-group                 IGMP static multicast group
  tcn                          IGMP TCN configuration
  unidirectional-link          IGMP unidirectional link multicast routing
  upstream-proxy               IGMP upstream IGMP proxy
  v3-query-max-response-time   IGMP v3 max query response value
  v3lite                       Enable/disable IGMPv3 Lite
  version                      IGMP version

R3(config-if)# ip igmp version 3 ?
  <cr>  <cr>


R3(config-if)# ip igmp version 3
R3(config-if)# do show ip igmp interface gigabitEthernet 3
GigabitEthernet3 is up, line protocol is up
```

```
Internet address is 10.1.35.3/24
IGMP is enabled on interface
Current IGMP host version is 3
Current IGMP router version is 3
IGMP query interval is 60 seconds
IGMP configured query interval is 60 seconds
IGMP querier timeout is 120 seconds
IGMP configured querier timeout is 120 seconds
IGMP max query response time is 10 seconds
Last member query count is 2
Last member query response interval is 1000 ms
Inbound IGMP access group is not set
IGMP activity: 1 joins, 0 leaves
Multicast routing is enabled on interface
Multicast TTL threshold is 0
Multicast designated router (DR) is 10.1.35.3 (this system)
IGMP querying router is 10.1.35.3 (this system)
No multicast groups joined by this system
R3(config-if)#
```

Here, we run IGMPv2 initially. Then we configure SSM globally on the router through the
ip pim ssm default command. Observe that we can change this group by specifying a different range with an ACL. There is nothing below the default option in the configuration tree.
Notice the change to IGMPv3 under the interface command, and notice the v3lite option. IGMP
v3lite was a Cisco-developed transitional solution for application developers to immediately start
programming SSM applications on hosts that do not yet support IGMPv3 in their operating system kernel. Next, we verify that the interface facing the receiver is now running IGMPv3. Then
we can configure the same on R1, R2, and R6. (You will find IOS XR very easy because everything you need has already been turned on and IGMPv3 is already running.)

I am going to give you a task to complete on the Receiver. Let's start there because that is
where the SSM conversation originates (the pull-from-network model). The **show run** command reveals we are still using the old 239 group. Could you join this interface to SSM group
239.100.100.100, the same one used at the beginning of this chapter? I will wait for you.
Example 9-33 demonstrates how to initialize SSM on the Receiver.

Example 9-33 *Initializing SSM*

```
Receiver# show running-config interface gigabitEthernet 1
Building configuration...

Current configuration : 194 bytes
!
```

```
interface GigabitEthernet1
 ip address 10.1.35.100 255.255.255.0
 ip igmp join-group 239.1.1.1
 negotiation auto
 no mop enabled
 no mop sysid
end
```

Are you done? On R3, please issue the **show ip igmp groups** command. Then, you should see the group as I show it in Example 9-34.

Example 9-34   *R3 IGMP Groups*

```
R3# show ip igmp groups
IGMP Connected Group Membership
Group Address      Interface                Uptime     Expires    Last Reporter   Group
Accounted
232.100.100.100   GigabitEthernet3         00:00:22   stopped    10.1.35.100
224.0.1.40        GigabitEthernet1         03:00:35   00:02:17   10.1.23.3
```

Do you have the same output? Or do you only see the 224.0.1.40 group? Hm…*Did you just lose exam points?* My best advice is to turn on debugging on R3 and collect clues. Let's unpack this. You "should have done" the following:

1. You should have specified IGMPv3 on Receiver because you need version 3 reports. Without the **ip igmp version 3** interface command, my output looked like Example 9-35.

Example 9-35   *R3 Debug Output Without IGMPv3 on Receiver*

```
R3# debug ip pim 232.100.100.100
*Mar 23 13:58:04.701: IGMP(0): Received v3 Query on GigabitEthernet1 from 10.1.23.2
PIM debugging is on
R3#
*Mar 23 13:58:46.548: IGMP(0): Received v3 Query on GigabitEthernet2 from 10.1.13.1
*Mar 23 13:59:04.701: IGMP(0): Received v3 Query on GigabitEthernet1 from 10.1.23.2
*Mar 23 13:59:16.705: IGMP(0): Send v3 general Query on GigabitEthernet3
*Mar 23 13:59:18.554: IGMP(0): Received v2 Report on GigabitEthernet3 from
10.1.35.100 for 232.100.100.100
*Mar 23 13:59:18.554: IGMP(0): Received Group record for group 232.100.100.100, mode
2 from 10.1.35.100 for 0 sources
*Mar 23 13:59:18.554: IGMP(0): Group Record mode 2 for SSM group 232.100.100.100
from 10.1.35.100 on GigabitEthernet3, ignored
```

We are getting IGMPv3 queries from R1 and R2 and sending IGMPv3 query to Receiver on GigabitEthernet3, but what comes back is ignored because it is in group mode 2! Please fix this. If you have the output in Example 9-36 after fixing the IGMP version, you will need to look at the second item after the example.

Example 9-36 *R3 Debug Output with IGMPv3 on Receiver, Still Not Working*

```
*Mar 23 14:01:46.548: IGMP(0): Received v3 Query on GigabitEthernet2 from 10.1.13.1
*Mar 23 14:02:04.701: IGMP(0): Received v3 Query on GigabitEthernet1 from 10.1.23.2
*Mar 23 14:02:13.079: IGMP(0): Received v3 Report for 1 group on GigabitEthernet3
from 10.1.35.100
*Mar 23 14:02:13.079: IGMP(0): Received Group record for group 232.100.100.100, mode
4 from 10.1.35.100 for 0 sources
*Mar 23 14:02:13.079: IGMP(0): Group Record mode 4 for SSM group 232.100.100.100
from 10.1.35.100 on GigabitEthernet3, ignored
```

Now we are getting group record mode 4. Still ignoring though.

2. Did you specify the source for the multicast group? That is the premise of SSM. You should have specified the source!

Observe Example 9-37, where we finally get R3 working.

Example 9-37 *R3 Finally Working*

```
Receiver(config-if)# do sh running-config interface gigabitEthernet 1
Building configuration...

Current configuration : 194 bytes
!
interface GigabitEthernet1
 ip address 10.1.35.100 255.255.255.0
 ip igmp join-group 232.100.100.100 source 10.1.14.100
 ip igmp version 3
 negotiation auto
 no mop enabled
 no mop sysid
end

R3#
*Mar 23 14:33:16.708: IGMP(0): Send v3 general Query on GigabitEthernet3
*Mar 23 14:33:19.355: IGMP(0): Received v3 Report for 1 group on GigabitEthernet3
from 10.1.35.100
*Mar 23 14:33:19.355: IGMP(0): Received Group record for group 232.100.100.100, mode
2 from 10.1.35.100 for 0 sources
*Mar 23 14:33:19.355: IGMP(0): Group Record mode 2 for SSM group 232.100.100.100
from 10.1.35.100 on GigabitEthernet3, ignored
*Mar 23 14:33:27.858: IGMP(0): Send v2 general Query on GigabitEthernet4
*Mar 23 14:33:30.230: IGMP(0): Received v3 Report for 1 group on GigabitEthernet3
from 10.1.35.100
*Mar 23 14:33:30.230: IGMP(0): Received Group record for group 232.100.100.100,
mode 5 from 10.1.35.100 for 1 sources
```

```
*Mar 23 14:33:30.230: IGMP(0): WAVL Insert group: 232.100.100.100   interface:
GigabitEthernet3 Successful
*Mar 23 14:33:30.230: IGMP(0): Create source 10.1.14.100
*Mar 23 14:33:30.231: IGMP(0): Updating expiration time on
(10.1.14.100,232.100.100.100)   to 180 secs
*Mar 23 14:33:30.231: IGMP(0): Setting source flags 4 on
(10.1.14.100,232.100.100.100)
*Mar 23 14:33:30.231: IGMP(0): MRT Add/Update GigabitEthernet3 for
(10.1.14.100,232.100.100.100) by 0
*Mar 23 14:33:30.232: PIM(0): Insert (10.1.14.100,232.100.100.100) join in nbr
10.1.13.1's queue
*Mar 23 14:33:30.232: PIM(0): Building Join/Prune packet for nbr 10.1.13.1
*Mar 23 14:33:30.232: PIM(0): Adding v2 (10.1.14.100/32, 232.100.100.100), S-bit
Join
*Mar 23 14:33:30.232: PIM(0): Send v2 join/prune to 10.1.13.1 (GigabitEthernet2)
*Mar 23 14:33:30.763: IGMP(0): Received v3 Report for 1 group on GigabitEthernet3
from 10.1.35.100
*Mar 23 14:33:30.763: IGMP(0): Received Group record for group 232.100.100.100, mode
5 from 10.1.35.100 for 1 sources
*Mar 23 14:33:30.763: IGMP(0): MRT Add/Update GigabitEthernet3 for
(10.1.14.100,232.100.100.100) by 0
*Mar 23 14:33:30.763: IGMP(0): Updating expiration time on
(10.1.14.100,232.100.100.100)   to 180 secs
*Mar 23 14:33:32.636: IGMP(0): v3 report on interface configured for v2, ignored
R3#
*Mar 23 14:33:46.550: IGMP(0): Received v3 Query on GigabitEthernet2 from 10.1.13.1
R3# show ip igmp groups
IGMP Connected Group Membership
Group Address     Interface             Uptime     Expires   Last Reporter   Group
Accounted
232.100.100.100   GigabitEthernet3      00:00:22   stopped   10.1.35.100
224.0.1.40        GigabitEthernet1      03:00:35   00:02:17  10.1.23.3
R3# show ip mroute
! Output omitted for brevity
(10.1.14.100, 232.100.100.100), 00:06:54/00:01:52, flags: sTI
  Incoming interface: GigabitEthernet2, RPF nbr 10.1.13.1
  Outgoing interface list:
    GigabitEthernet3, Forward/Sparse, 00:06:54/00:01:52

(*, 224.0.1.40), 01:32:54/00:02:43, RP 0.0.0.0, flags: DCL
  Incoming interface: Null, RPF nbr 0.0.0.0
  Outgoing interface list:
    GigabitEthernet1, Forward/Sparse, 01:32:54/00:02:43
```

Finally, things are working and R3 points to R1 for the source of this multicast group. In
Example 9-38, let's see what is going on with R1, our FHR, closest to Source 10.1.14.100,
which is NOT transmitting anything at the moment.

Example 9-38 *R1's State*

```
R1# show ip igmp groups
IGMP Connected Group Membership
Group Address     Interface                Uptime    Expires    Last Reporter    Group
Accounted
224.0.1.40        GigabitEthernet1         03:17:55  00:02:04   10.1.14.1
R1# show ip mroute
! Output omitted for brevity
(10.1.14.100, 232.100.100.100), 00:15:26/00:02:48, flags: sT
  Incoming interface: GigabitEthernet1, RPF nbr 0.0.0.0
  Outgoing interface list:
    GigabitEthernet2, Forward/Sparse, 00:15:26/00:02:48

(*, 224.0.1.40), 01:40:15/00:02:45, RP 0.0.0.0, flags: DCL
  Incoming interface: Null, RPF nbr 0.0.0.0
  Outgoing interface list:
    GigabitEthernet1, Forward/Sparse, 01:39:19/00:02:45

R1#
```

R1 knows that Source is connected to the incoming interface GigabitEthernet1 and will send the traffic to the outgoing interface GigabitEthernet2, which leads to R3. Example 9-39 initiates a multicast stream to our 232.100.100.100 SSM group. Feel free to use a VLC player or an iperf multicast tester. I am choosing the simplest of tools this time—a ping of 10 counts. "Give me 10 pings, Vasili, 10 pings only…" (a *Hunt for Red October* reference).

Example 9-39 *Launching Traffic from Source*

```
Source# ping 232.100.100.100 repeat 10
Type escape sequence to abort.
Sending 10, 100-byte ICMP Echos to 232.100.100.100, timeout is 2 seconds:
..........
Source#
```

```
R1# sh ip mroute count
Use "show ip mfib count" to get better response time for a large number of mroutes.

IP Multicast Statistics
2 routes using 2572 bytes of memory
2 groups, 0.50 average sources per group
Forwarding Counts: Pkt Count/Pkts per second/Avg Pkt Size/Kilobits per second
Other counts: Total/RPF failed/Other drops(OIF-null, rate-limit etc)
```

```
Group: 232.100.100.100, Source count: 1, Packets forwarded: 10, Packets received: 10
   Source: 10.1.14.100/32, Forwarding: 10/0/114/0, Other: 10/0/0


Group: 224.0.1.40, Source count: 0, Packets forwarded: 0, Packets received: 0
R1#
```

```
R3# show ip mroute count
Use "show ip mfib count" to get better response time for a large number of mroutes.

IP Multicast Statistics
2 routes using 2572 bytes of memory
2 groups, 0.50 average sources per group
Forwarding Counts: Pkt Count/Pkts per second/Avg Pkt Size/Kilobits per second
Other counts: Total/RPF failed/Other drops(OIF-null, rate-limit etc)

Group: 232.100.100.100, Source count: 1, Packets forwarded: 10, Packets received: 10
   Source: 10.1.14.100/32, Forwarding: 10/0/114/0, Other: 10/0/0


Group: 224.0.1.40, Source count: 0, Packets forwarded: 0, Packets received: 0
R3# show ip mfib
Entry Flags:    C - Directly Connected, S - Signal, IA - Inherit A flag,
                ET - Data Rate Exceeds Threshold, K - Keepalive
                DDE - Data Driven Event, HW - Hardware Installed
                ME - MoFRR ECMP entry, MNE - MoFRR Non-ECMP entry, MP - MFIB
                MoFRR Primary, RP - MRIB MoFRR Primary, P - MoFRR Primary
                MS  - MoFRR  Entry in Sync, MC - MoFRR entry in MoFRR Client,
                e   - Encap helper tunnel flag.
I/O Item Flags: IC - Internal Copy, NP - Not platform switched,
                NS - Negate Signalling, SP - Signal Present,
                A - Accept, F - Forward, RA - MRIB Accept, RF - MRIB Forward,
                MA - MFIB Accept, A2 - Accept backup,
                RA2 - MRIB Accept backup, MA2 - MFIB Accept backup

Forwarding Counts: Pkt Count/Pkts per second/Avg Pkt Size/Kbits per second
Other counts:      Total/RPF failed/Other drops
I/O Item Counts:   HW Pkt Count/FS Pkt Count/PS Pkt Count   Egress Rate in pps
Default
 (*,224.0.0.0/4) Flags: HW
   SW Forwarding: 0/0/0/0, Other: 0/0/0
   HW Forwarding:   0/0/0/0, Other: 0/0/0
 (*,224.0.1.40) Flags: C HW
```

```
 SW Forwarding: 0/0/0/0, Other: 0/0/0
 HW Forwarding:    0/0/0/0, Other: 0/0/0
 GigabitEthernet1 Flags: F IC NS
   Pkts: 0/0/0     Rate: 0 pps
(*,232.0.0.0/8) Flags: HW
 SW Forwarding: 0/0/0/0, Other: 0/0/0
 HW Forwarding:    0/0/0/0, Other: 4/4/0
(10.1.14.100,232.100.100.100) Flags: HW
 SW Forwarding: 0/0/0/0, Other: 0/0/0
 HW Forwarding:    10/0/114/0, Other: 0/0/0
 GigabitEthernet2 Flags: A
 GigabitEthernet3 Flags: F NS
   Pkts: 0/0/0     Rate: 0 pps


R3# clear ip mroute *
R3# show ip mroute count
Use "show ip mfib count" to get better response time for a large number of mroutes.


IP Multicast Statistics
1 routes using 1110 bytes of memory
1 groups, 0.00 average sources per group
Forwarding Counts: Pkt Count/Pkts per second/Avg Pkt Size/Kilobits per second
Other counts: Total/RPF failed/Other drops(OIF-null, rate-limit etc)


Group: 224.0.1.40, Source count: 0, Packets forwarded: 0, Packets received: 0
R3#
```

The **show ip mroute count** and **show ip mfib** commands are great to have because they can validate traffic flowing through the infrastructure and what is the multicast forwarding table. A = accepting on GigabitEthernet2 coming from R1, and F = forwarding to Receiver on GigabitEthernet3. The **clear ip mroute** * command will reset these counters so you can test over and over again.

And with that, I have given you the world of multicast—a vast landscape with endless possibilities. While exam questions may vary infinitely, I have equipped you with the foundational knowledge and tools to grasp the essence of this complex technology. On the exam and professional endeavors, remember to pause and reflect on what you have learned here. With this understanding, you will confidently navigate questions and solve multicast challenges.

PIMv6

Much of the multicast principles you have already learned apply to **PIMv6** (PIM for IPv6). In the topology shown in Figure 9-10, all multicast routers run IOS XR, and the source and receiver are simulated with IOS routers. I have hard-coded IPv6 addresses a certain way; this makes it easy to understand to facilitate faster learning for those who are new to IPv6.

I employed full reachability and chose IS-IS as the routing protocol. Both source and receiver have static default routes toward the network.

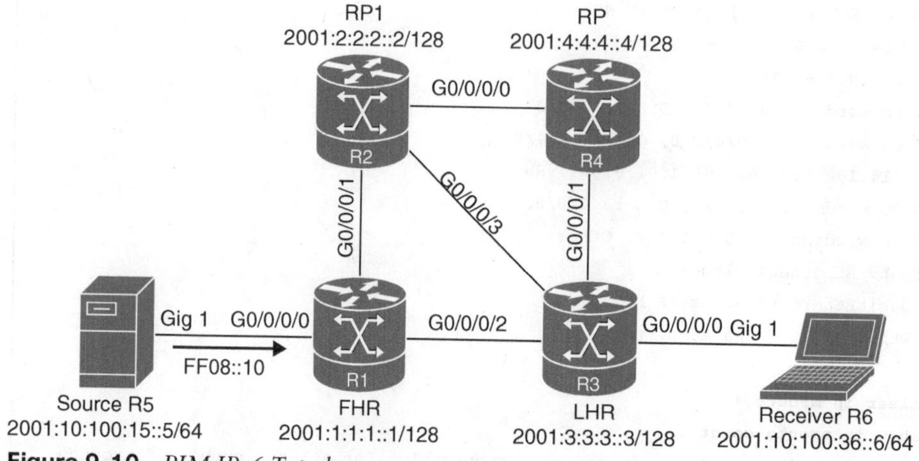

Figure 9-10 *PIM IPv6 Topology*

MLD

In Example 9-40, I confirm receiver-to-source reachability and turn on MLDv2. Notice Receiver R6 has this highlighted link-local address ending in 643F.

Example 9-40 *Turning on Multicast on the Receiver R6*

```
R6# ping ipv6 2001:10:100:15::5 source 2001:10:100:36::6
Type escape sequence to abort.
Sending 5, 100-byte ICMP Echos to 2001:10:100:15::5, timeout is 2 seconds:
Packet sent with a source address of 2001:10:100:36::6
!!!!!
Success rate is 100 percent (5/5), round-trip min/avg/max = 2/2/4 ms
R6# configure terminal
Enter configuration commands, one per line.  End with CNTL/Z.
R6(config)# interface GigabitEthernet1
R6(config-if)# ipv6 mld join-group FF08::10
R6(config-if)# ipv6 mld version ?
  <1-2>  version number

R6(config-if)# ipv6 mld version 2
R6(config-if)#
R6# show ipv6 interface GigabitEthernet1
GigabitEthernet1 is up, line protocol is up
  IPv6 is enabled, link-local address is FE80::5054:FF:FE05:643F
```

It is time to turn on multicast routers on R1, R2, R3, and R4. Example 9-41 shows only R3; you will have to repeat the highlighted steps on R1, R2, and R4.

Example 9-41 *Turning on Multicast on IOS XR*

```
RP/0/RP0/CPU0:R3# configure
Tue Apr 23 12:24:17.435 UT
RP/0/RP0/CPU0:R3(config)# multicast-routing
RP/0/RP0/CPU0:R3(config-mcast)# address-family ipv6
RP/0/RP0/CPU0:R3(config-mcast-default-ipv6)# interface all enable
RP/0/RP0/CPU0:R3(config-mcast-default-ipv6)# commit
Tue Apr 23 12:24:39.750 UTC
RP/0/RP0/CPU0:R3(config-mcast-default-ipv6)# end
RP/0/RP0/CPU0:R3# show mld groups
Tue Apr 23 12:24:50.237 UTC
MLD Connected Group Membership

Loopback0

Group Address : ff02::2
Last Reporter : fe80::8c2b:e1ff:fe3f:d42b
        Uptime : 00:00:10
       Expires : never
Group Address : ff02::d
Last Reporter : fe80::8c2b:e1ff:fe3f:d42b
        Uptime : 00:00:10
       Expires : never
Group Address : ff02::16
Last Reporter : fe80::8c2b:e1ff:fe3f:d42b
        Uptime : 00:00:10
       Expires : never


GigabitEthernet0/0/0/0

Group Address : ff02::2
Last Reporter : fe80::5054:ff:fe16:2fc2
        Uptime : 00:00:10
       Expires : never
Group Address : ff02::d
Last Reporter : fe80::5054:ff:fe16:2fc2
        Uptime : 00:00:10
       Expires : never
Group Address : ff02::16
Last Reporter : fe80::5054:ff:fe16:2fc2
        Uptime : 00:00:10
       Expires : never
```

```
 Group Address : ff02::1:ff00:6
 Last Reporter : fe80::5054:ff:fe05:643f
         Uptime : 00:00:02
        Expires : 00:04:17
 Group Address : ff02::1:ff05:643f
 Last Reporter : fe80::5054:ff:fe05:643f
         Uptime : 00:00:02
        Expires : 00:04:17
 Group Address : ff08::10
 Last Reporter : fe80::5054:ff:fe05:643f
         Uptime : 00:00:02
        Expires : 00:04:17

GigabitEthernet0/0/0/1

 Group Address : ff02::2
 Last Reporter : fe80::5054:ff:fe0f:d514
         Uptime : 00:00:10
        Expires : never
 Group Address : ff02::d
 Last Reporter : fe80::5054:ff:fe0f:d514
         Uptime : 00:00:10
        Expires : never
 Group Address : ff02::16
 Last Reporter : fe80::5054:ff:fe0f:d514
         Uptime : 00:00:10
        Expires : never

GigabitEthernet0/0/0/2

 Group Address : ff02::2
 Last Reporter : fe80::5054:ff:fe0c:f89b
         Uptime : 00:00:10
        Expires : never
 Group Address : ff02::d
 Last Reporter : fe80::5054:ff:fe0c:f89b
         Uptime : 00:00:10
        Expires : never
 Group Address : ff02::16
 Last Reporter : fe80::5054:ff:fe0c:f89b
         Uptime : 00:00:10
        Expires : never
```

```
GigabitEthernet0/0/0/3

Group Address : ff02::2
Last Reporter : fe80::5054:ff:fe00:ea27
       Uptime : 00:00:10
      Expires : never
Group Address : ff02::d
Last Reporter : fe80::5054:ff:fe00:ea27
       Uptime : 00:00:10
      Expires : never
Group Address : ff02::16
Last Reporter : fe80::5054:ff:fe00:ea27
       Uptime : 00:00:10
      Expires : never
RP/0/RP0/CPU0:R3#
```

First, notice the three multicast groups under the Loopback0 interface (also present under other interfaces). Do you recognize these groups? In IPv4 multicast, the addressing is 32-bit, based on the Class D range of 224.0.0.0/8 (224.0.0.0–239.255.255.255). In IPv6 multicast, the addresses are 128-bit (112-bit group) in the range of ff::/8. FF tips you off that these are multicast. Recall that ff02::2 is a group reserved for all routers, ff02::16 is a group for MLDv2 Listener Reports messages, and ff02::d (13) is for the All PIM Routers group. Also, observe in the lower output that our 643F MLD receiver only shows up on interface GigabitEthernet0/0/0/0 as "last reporter," which faces the receiver, no other interface. By default, routers do not actively track the state of each MLD listener but rather confirm the presence of a single active listener. If you needed to track individual listeners, Example 9-42 shows you how this is enabled.

Example 9-42 *Enabling Explicit MLD Tracking*

```
RP/0/RP0/CPU0:R3# configure
Tue Apr 23 15:31:51.093 UTC
RP/0/RP0/CPU0:R3(config)# router mld
RP/0/RP0/CPU0:R3(config-mld)# interface gigabitEthernet 0/0/0/0
RP/0/RP0/CPU0:R3(config-mld-default-if)# explicit-tracking ?
  WORD     Access list specifying tracking group range
  disable  Disable MLD explicit host tracking
  <cr>
RP/0/RP0/CPU0:R3(config-mld-default-if)#
```

PIMv2

Once you have turned on multicast, PIM comes up, and Example 9-43 shows PIM neighbors as seen from R3. IPv6 routers use PIMv2 for signaling, so the same PIMv2 message types you saw in IPv4 apply here, although PIM Dense mode and the Auto-RP announcement mechanism are absent. Example 9-43 shows the result of turning on multicast. Designated routers (DRs) are elected by the highest IPv6 address on a segment, and R3 "won some, lost some," as you can see by comparing the link-local addresses.

Example 9-43 *PIM Neighbors Are Up*

```
RP/0/RP0/CPU0:R3# show pim ipv6 neighbor
Tue Apr 23 13:33:37.865 UTC


PIM neighbors in VRF default
Flag: B - Bidir capable, P - Proxy capable, DR - Designated Router,
      S - Sticky DR Neighbor
      * indicates the neighbor created for this router


Loopback0


Neighbor Address                             Uptime    Expires  DR pri  DR  Flags
fe80::8c2b:e1ff:fe3f:d42b*                   01:08:58  00:01:43 1       (DR) B


GigabitEthernet0/0/0/0


Neighbor Address                             Uptime    Expires  DR pri  DR  Flags
fe80::5054:ff:fe16:2fc2*                     01:08:58  00:01:39 1       (DR) B


GigabitEthernet0/0/0/3


Neighbor Address                             Uptime    Expires  DR pri  DR  Flags
fe80::5054:ff:fe00:ea27*                     01:08:58  00:01:25 1            B
fe80::5054:ff:fe08:ee4f                      00:00:42  00:01:18 1       (DR) B


GigabitEthernet0/0/0/2


Neighbor Address                             Uptime    Expires  DR pri  DR  Flags
fe80::5054:ff:fe07:8985                      00:01:20  00:01:36 1            B
fe80::5054:ff:fe0c:f89b*                     01:08:58  00:01:35 1       (DR) B


GigabitEthernet0/0/0/1


Neighbor Address                             Uptime    Expires  DR pri  DR  Flags
fe80::5054:ff:fe03:4d6f                      00:00:26  00:01:40 1            B
fe80::5054:ff:fe0f:d514*                     01:08:58  00:01:40 1       (DR) B
RP/0/RP0/CPU0:R3#show ipv6 interface | utility egrep 'Gi|link'
Tue Apr 23 14:57:02.978 UTC
  IPv6 is enabled, link-local address is fe80::8c2b:e1ff:fe3f:d42b
  IPv6 is disabled, link-local address unassigned
GigabitEthernet0/0/0/0 is Up, ipv6 protocol is Up, Vrfid is default (0x60000000)
  IPv6 is enabled, link-local address is fe80::5054:ff:fe16:2fc2
```

```
GigabitEthernet0/0/0/1 is Up, ipv6 protocol is Up, Vrfid is default (0x60000000)
  IPv6 is enabled, link-local address is fe80::5054:ff:fe0f:d514
GigabitEthernet0/0/0/2 is Up, ipv6 protocol is Up, Vrfid is default (0x60000000)
  IPv6 is enabled, link-local address is fe80::5054:ff:fe0c:f89b
GigabitEthernet0/0/0/3 is Up, ipv6 protocol is Up, Vrfid is default (0x60000000)
  IPv6 is enabled, link-local address is fe80::5054:ff:fe00:ea27
RP/0/RP0/CPU0:R3#
```

Static RP

I don't know about you, but I am ready to get some RPs going. Example 9-44 shows the
router PIM tunnel state (remember this one from IPv4) before and after turning up static RP
mapping on all XR routers (obviously, R2 becomes the RP).

Example 9-44 *Statically Mapping RPs in PIMv6*

```
RP/0/RP0/CPU0:R3# show pim ipv6 tunnel info all
Tue Apr 23 16:12:45.366 UTC
No tunnel interface(s) information found.
RP/0/RP0/CPU0:R3# conf
Tue Apr 23 16:12:58.460 UTC
RP/0/RP0/CPU0:R3(config)# router pim
RP/0/RP0/CPU0:R3(config-pim)# address-family ipv6
RP/0/RP0/CPU0:R3(config-pim-default-ipv6)# rp-address 2001:2:2:2::2
RP/0/RP0/CPU0:R3(config-pim-default-ipv6)# commit
Tue Apr 23 16:13:04.482 UTC
RP/0/RP0/CPU0:R3(config-pim-default-ipv6)# end
RP/0/RP0/CPU0:R3# show pim ipv6 tunnel info all
Tue Apr 23 16:13:08.620 UTC

Interface          RP Address      Source Address

Encaps6tunnel0     2001:2:2:2::2   2001:10:100:23::3
RP/0/RP0/CPU0:R3#
```

To test whether the control plane comes up, you can use a VLC player, iperf, or a multicast
streamer of your choice. I will issue a ping to see if PIM will "light up the path" for this
group. Example 9-45 starts out with empty PIM topology, a ping from Source R5, and full
verification of the outgoing interfaces down the multicast tree until Receiver R6 is reached.

Example 9-45 *Verifying Multicast Traffic Path Through Static RP*

```
RP/0/RP0/CPU0:R1# show pim ipv6 topology
Tue Apr 23 20:11:14.099 UTC
No PIM topology table entries found.
```

```
RP/0/RP0/CPU0:R1#
```

```
R5# ping ipv6 ff08::10 repeat 100
Output Interface: GigabitEthernet1
Type escape sequence to abort.
Sending 100, 100-byte ICMP Echos to FF08::10, timeout is 2 seconds:
Packet sent with a source address of 2001:10:100:15::5

Request 0 timed out
Request 1 timed out
Request 2 timed out
Request 3 timed out
Request 4 timed out
Request 5 timed out
! Output omitted for brevity, 100 pings continue
```

```
RP/0/RP0/CPU0:R1# show pim ipv6 topology
Tue Apr 23 20:25:57.387 UTC

IP PIM Multicast Topology Table
Entry state: (*/S,G)[RPT/SPT] Protocol Uptime Info
Entry flags: KAT - Keep Alive Timer, AA - Assume Alive, PA - Probe Alive
    RA - Really Alive, IA - Inherit Alive, LH - Last Hop
    DSS - Don't Signal Sources,  RR - Register Received
    SR - Sending Registers, SNR - Sending Null Registers
    E - MSDP External, EX - Extranet
    MFA - Mofrr Active, MFP - Mofrr Primary, MFB - Mofrr Backup
    DCC - Don't Check Connected, ME - MDT Encap, MD - MDT Decap
    MT - Crossed Data MDT threshold, MA - Data MDT Assigned
    SAJ - BGP Source Active Joined, SAR - BGP Source Active Received,
    SAS - BGP Source Active Sent, IM - Inband mLDP, X - VxLAN
Interface state: Name, Uptime, Fwd, Info
Interface flags: LI - Local Interest, LD - Local Dissinterest,
    II - Internal Interest, ID - Internal Dissinterest,
    LH - Last Hop, AS - Assert, AB - Admin Boundary, EX - Extranet,
    BGP - BGP C-Multicast Join, BP - BGP Source Active Prune,
    MVS - MVPN Safi Learned, MV6S - MVPN IPv6 Safi Learned

(2001:10:100:15::5,ff08::10)
SM Up: 00:01:20 JP: Null(never) Flags: KAT(00:02:12) RA DCC
  RPF: GigabitEthernet0/0/0/0,fe80::5054:ff:fe18:7135*
```

```
  No interfaces in immediate olist
RP/0/RP0/CPU0:R1#
```

```
RP/0/RP0/CPU0:R2# show pim ipv6 topology
Tue Apr 23 20:26:41.954 UTC
! Output omitted for brevity, this is the RP


(*,ff08::10)
SM Up: 04:13:37 JP: Join(never) Flags:
RP: 2001:2:2:2::2*
RPF: Decaps6tunnel0,2001:2:2:2::2
   GigabitEthernet0/0/0/3       04:13:37   fwd Join(00:02:35)
RP/0/RP0/CPU0:R2#
```

```
RP/0/RP0/CPU0:R3# show pim ipv6 topology
Tue Apr 23 20:27:38.968 UTC
! Output omitted for brevity
(*,ff08::10)
SM Up: 08:02:50 JP: Join(00:00:39) Flags: LH
RP: 2001:2:2:2::2
RPF: GigabitEthernet0/0/0/3,fe80::5054:ff:fe08:ee4f
   GigabitEthernet0/0/0/0       08:02:50   fwd LI AS(self,00:01:52) LH
RP/0/RP0/CPU0:R3# show mrib ipv6 route
Tue Apr 23 20:28:39.477 UTC


IP Multicast Routing Information Base
Entry flags: L - Domain-Local Source, E - External Source to the Domain,
    C - Directly-Connected Check, S - Signal, IA - Inherit Accept,
    IF - Inherit From, D - Drop, ME - MDT Encap, EID - Encap ID,
    MD - MDT Decap, MT - MDT Threshold Crossed, MH - MDT interface handle
    CD - Conditional Decap, MPLS - MPLS Decap, EX - Extranet
    MoFE - MoFRR Enabled, MoFS - MoFRR State, MoFP - MoFRR Primary
    MoFB - MoFRR Backup, RPFID - RPF ID Set, X - VXLAN
Interface flags: F - Forward, A - Accept, IC - Internal Copy,
    NS - Negate Signal, DP - Don't Preserve, SP - Signal Present,
    II - Internal Interest, ID - Internal Disinterest, LI - Local Interest,
    LD - Local Disinterest, DI - Decapsulation Interface
    EI - Encapsulation Interface, MI - MDT Interface, LVIF - MPLS Encap,
    EX - Extranet, A2 - Secondary Accept, MT - MDT Threshold Crossed,
    MA - Data MDT Assigned, LMI - mLDP MDT Interface, TMI - P2MP-TE MDT Interface
    IRMI - IR MDT Interface, TRMI - TREE SID MDT Interface, MH - Multihome Interface
```

```
(*,ff00::/8)
  RPF nbr: fe80::5054:ff:fe08:ee4f Flags: C RPF P
  Up: 04:18:34

(*,ff00::/15)
  Flags: D P
  Up: 08:06:59

(*,ff02::/16)
  Flags: D P
  Up: 08:06:59

(*,ff08::10)
  RPF nbr: fe80::5054:ff:fe08:ee4f Flags: C RPF
  Up: 08:06:51
  Incoming Interface List
    GigabitEthernet0/0/0/3 Flags: A NS, Up: 04:18:34
  Outgoing Interface List
    GigabitEthernet0/0/0/0 Flags: F NS LI, Up: 08:06:51

(*,ff10::/15)
  Flags: D P
  Up: 08:06:59
! Output omitted for brevity
```

What would I have you notice?

- The FF08::10 group is on all routers.

- R1's RFP check is toward the source.

- RP R2's outgoing interface list is GigabitEthernet0/0/0/3—toward R3.

- RP R2's RFP check is toward itself; it is the RP, after all.

- R3's outgoing interface list is GigabitEthernet0/0/0/0, which leads to Receiver R6 and is marked LH (Last Hop router).

- The **show mrib ipv6 route** command (do you remember its equivalent for IPv4?) is useful to see the outgoing and incoming (toward the RP) interfaces.

BSR

Recall that the BSR is a way to create RP redundancy. Remove static RPs on all routers (not shown, so complete on your own) and configure BSR (please review the logic in the IPv4 multicast section) on R2 and R4, as shown in Example 9-46. Notice how RP-priority gets added by IOS XR, since I did not specify it.

Example 9-46 *Configuring BSR on R2 and R4*

```
RP/0/RP0/CPU0:R2# configure
Tue Apr 23 21:27:32.445 UTC
RP/0/RP0/CPU0:R2(config)# router pim
RP/0/RP0/CPU0:R2(config-pim)# address-family ipv6
RP/0/RP0/CPU0:R2(config-pim-default-ipv6)# bsr candidate-bsr 2001:2:2:2::2
RP/0/RP0/CPU0:R2(config-pim-default-ipv6)# bsr candidate-rp 2001:2:2:2::2
RP/0/RP0/CPU0:R2(config-pim-default-ipv6)# commit
Tue Apr 23 21:28:29.258 UTC
RP/0/RP0/CPU0:R2(config-pim-default-ipv6)# end
RP/0/RP0/CPU0:R2# show running-config router pim
Tue Apr 23 21:29:56.643 UTC
router pim
 address-family ipv6
  bsr candidate-bsr 2001:2:2:2::2 hash-mask-len 126 priority 1
  bsr candidate-rp 2001:2:2:2::2 priority 192 interval 60
 !
!

RP/0/RP0/CPU0:R2#
```

```
RP/0/RP0/CPU0:R4# conf
Tue Apr 23 21:28:38.333 UTC
RP/0/RP0/CPU0:R4(config)# router pim
RP/0/RP0/CPU0:R4(config-pim)# address-family ipv6
RP/0/RP0/CPU0:R4(config-pim-default-ipv6)# bsr candidate-bsr 2001:4:4:4::4
RP/0/RP0/CPU0:R4(config-pim-default-ipv6)# bsr candidate-rp 2001:4:4:4::4
RP/0/RP0/CPU0:R4(config-pim-default-ipv6)# commit
Tue Apr 23 21:29:12.199 UTC
RP/0/RP0/CPU0:R4(config-pim-default-ipv6)# end
RP/0/RP0/CPU0:R4# show running-config router pim
Tue Apr 23 21:29:43.662 UTC
router pim
 address-family ipv6
  bsr candidate-bsr 2001:4:4:4::4 hash-mask-len 126 priority 1
  bsr candidate-rp 2001:4:4:4::4 priority 192 interval 60
 !
!

RP/0/RP0/CPU0:R4#
```

What are the results? Let's examine them in Example 9-47.

Example 9-47   *Which Router Wins BSR Election?*

```
RP/0/RP0/CPU0:R4# show pim ipv6 bsr election
Tue Apr 23 21:30:30.611 UTC
PIM BSR Election State


Cand/Elect-State          Uptime   BS-Timer BSR                            C-BSR

Elected/Accept-Pref          00:01:18 00:00:56 2001:4:4:4::4 [1, 126]    2001:4:4:4::4
[1, 126]
RP/0/RP0/CPU0:R4# show pim ipv6 bsr rp-cache
Tue Apr 23 21:31:47.022 UTC
PIM BSR Candidate RP Cache


Group(s) ff00::/8, RP count 2
RP-addr           Proto Priority Holdtime(s) Uptime    Expires
2001:4:4:4::4     SM     192      150          00:02:34 00:01:55
2001:2:2:2::2     SM     192      150          00:02:34 00:01:55


RP/0/RP0/CPU0:R4# show pim ipv6 bsr candidate-rp
Tue Apr 23 21:32:05.032 UTC
PIM BSR Candidate RP Info


Cand-RP           mode  scope priority uptime    group-list
2001:4:4:4::4     SM    16    192      00:02:52  ff00::/8
RP/0/RP0/CPU0:R4#

RP/0/RP0/CPU0:R2# show pim ipv6 bsr election
Tue Apr 23 21:30:48.053 UTC
PIM BSR Election State


Cand/Elect-State          Uptime   BS-Timer BSR                            C-BSR

Not-Elected/Accept-Pref 00:01:35 00:01:49 2001:4:4:4::4 [1, 126]    2001:2:2:2::2 [1,
126]
RP/0/RP0/CPU0:R2# show pim ipv6 bsr rp-cache
Tue Apr 23 21:31:19.298 UTC
PIM BSR Candidate RP Cache


RP/0/RP0/CPU0:R2# show pim ipv6 bsr candidate-rp
Tue Apr 23 21:32:18.912 UTC
PIM BSR Candidate RP Info
```

```
Cand-RP             mode  scope priority uptime    group-list
2001:2:2:2::2       SM    16    192       00:03:06  ff00::/8
RP/0/RP0/CPU0:R2#
```

```
RP/0/RP0/CPU0:R1# show pim ipv6 rp mapping
Tue Apr 23 21:33:11.121 UTC
PIM Group-to-RP Mappings
Group(s) ff00::/8
  RP 2001:4:4:4::4 (?), v2
    Info source: fe80::5054:ff:fe0c:f89b (?), elected via bsr, priority 192, hold-
time 150
       Uptime: 00:03:59, expires: 00:01:45
Group(s) ff00::/8
  RP 2001:2:2:2::2 (?), v2
    Info source: fe80::5054:ff:fe0c:f89b (?), elected via bsr, priority 192, hold-
time 150
       Uptime: 00:03:59, expires: 00:01:45
RP/0/RP0/CPU0:R1#
```

What would I have you remember?

- R4 wins the election.

- Only the elected RP has the list of candidates (in its cache via **show pim ipv6 bsr rp-cache**); note this is absent of R2.

- R1 has both RPs. I did not have to configure anything on it or R3.

What else do you need to know about PIM v6? SSM is on by default, and the presence of
SSM groups on the router confirms it. You already know the mechanics of how it functions
from the IPv4 section. In IPv6, the currently permitted SSM destination addresses are delineated by the prefix ff3x::/96, wherein the hexadecimal character "x" denotes the scope. Look
at Example 9-48 for confirmation.

Example 9-48   *PIM v6 SSM*

```
RP/0/RP0/CPU0:R3# show pim ipv6 group-map
Wed Apr 24 09:52:03.885 UTC

IP PIM Group Mapping Table
(* indicates group mappings being used)
(+ indicates BSR group mappings active in MRIB)

Group Range                              Proto Client   Groups
ff02::/16*                               NO    perm     0
```

```
    RP: ::

  ff12::/16*                                            NO      perm    0
    RP: ::

  ff22::/16*                                            NO      perm    0
    RP: ::

! Output omitted for brevity, these groups continue to increment

  fff0::/15*                                            NO      perm    0
    RP: ::

  ff70::/12*                                            SM      embd    0
    RP: ::
    RPF: Null,::

  fff0::/12*                                            NO      embd    0
    RP: ::
!My comment (not a part of the actual output), observe SSM groups ff3x showing up

  ff33::/32*                                            SSM     config  0
    RP: ::

  ff34::/32*                                            SSM     config  0
    RP: ::

  ff35::/32*                                            SSM     config  0
    RP: ::

  ff36::/32*                                            SSM     config  0
    RP: ::

  ff37::/32*                                            SSM     config  0
    RP: ::

  ff38::/32*                                            SSM     config  0
    RP: ::

  ff39::/32*                                            SSM     config  0
    RP: ::

  ff3a::/32*                                            SSM     config  0
    RP: ::
```

```
ff3b::/32*                                                       SSM    config   0
  RP: ::

ff3c::/32*                                                       SSM    config   0
  RP: ::

ff3d::/32*                                                       SSM    config   0
  RP: ::

ff3e::/32*                                                       SSM    config   0
  RP: ::

ff3f::/32*                                                       SSM    config   0
  RP: ::

ff00::/8*                                                        SM     static   0
  RP: ::
  RPF: Null,::

RP/0/RP0/CPU0:R3#
```

There is another option for IPv6, which is called the "Embedded RP." In it, the multicast group address is structured to include details about the RP's location, enabling routers to establish the rendezvous point tree (RPT) directly to the RP when group members join. In our topology, if we needed to create a stream for group FF7E:0A0A, then the address of our R2 RP would be embedded in the group and would become FF7E:0A0A:2001:2:2:2::2. The only thing left is to hard-code the RP on R2 itself, and all the other routers in the network would dynamically learn the RP address from the group address.

Based on my observations, many customers have transitioned from using static RPs to adopting Source-Specific Multicast (SSM) as their preferred multicast approach. It's essential to strike a balance between dedicating time to academic exercises for exam preparation and focusing on practical applications of multicast technologies. I'll leave it to you to determine the optimal allocation of time for these pursuits.

Exam Preparation Tasks

As mentioned in the section "How to Use This Book" in the Introduction, you have a few choices for exam preparation: the exercises here, Chapter 23, "Final Preparation," and the exam simulation questions in the Pearson Test Prep Software Online.

Review All Key Topics

Review the most important topics in this chapter, noted with the Key Topic icon in the margin of the page. Table 9-5 lists a reference of these key topics and the page numbers on which each is found.

Table 9-5 Key Topics for Chapter 9

Key Topic Element	Description	Page Number
List	Multicast basics	354
Table 9-2	Important Multicast Ranges	355
Table 9-3	Important Reserved Multicast Addresses	356
Paragraph	Last Hop Router (LHR) connects L3 PIM and L2 IGMP domains	356
Figure 9-1	Multicast Big Picture	356
Example 9-4	Turning on Multicast Receiver3 (IGMPv2 Report Generation)	363
Paragraph	Membership reports with IGMP snooping	364
Table 9-4	MLDv1 Messages	379
Paragraph	Last Hop Router (LHR) IMGP and MLD reports	392
List	RP Tree construction	395
Example 9-20	Connecting the Multicast Source Continued (Multicast Register Messages)	399
Paragraph	Auto-RP and BSR differences	416
List	BiDiR-PIM details	419
Paragraph	SSM details	425

Define Key Terms

Define the following key terms from this chapter and check the answers in the glossary:

First Hop Router (FHR), Internet Group Management Protocol (IGMP), Last Hop Router (LHR), Multicast Listener Discovery (MLD), PIM Dense Mode, PIM Sparse Mode, PIM SSM, PIMv6

Command Reference to Check Your Memory

This section includes the most important configuration and EXEC commands covered in this chapter. You might not need to memorize the complete syntax of every command, but you should be able to remember the basic keywords that are needed.

To test your memory of the commands, cover the right side of Table 9-6 with a piece of paper, read the description on the left side, and then see how much of the command you can remember.

The 350-501 exam focuses on practical, hands-on skills that are used by networking professionals. Therefore, you should be able to identify the commands needed to configure and test. Note that not all commands are fully covered in the chapter, but their presence in the following table should lead you to investigate them further to understand this technology.

Table 9-6 CLI Commands to Know

Task	Command Syntax
Enable IP multicast routing in global configuration mode. To disable IP multicast routing, use the **no** form of this command.	**ip multicast-routing**

Task	Command Syntax
Globally enable Internet Group Management Protocol (IGMP) snooping with an option to enable it on a per-VLAN basis.	**ip igmp snooping** [**vlan** *vlan-id*]
Globally enable the IGMP querier function in Layer 2 networks.	**ip igmp snooping** [**vlan** *vlan-id*] **querier** [**address** *ip-address* | **max-response-time** *response-time* | **query-interval** *interval-count* | **tcn query** {**count** *count* | **interval** *interval*} |**timer expiry** *expiry-time* | **version** *version*]
Display the Internet Group Management Protocol (IGMP) snooping configuration.	**show ip igmp snooping** [**groups** | **mrouter** | **querier**] [**vlan** *vlan-id*] [**detail**]
Configure an interface on the router to join the specified group or channel.	**ip igmp join-group** *group-address* [**source** *source-address*]
Display the Internet Group Management Protocol (IGMP) snooping multicast table and information.	**show ip igmp snooping groups** [**vlan** *vlan-id*] [[**count**] | *ip_address*]
Configure which version of Internet Group Management Protocol (IGMP) the router uses.	**ip igmp version** {**1** | **2** | **3**}
Enable multicast routing using Protocol-Independent Multicast (PIM) and Multicast Listener Discovery (MLD) on all IPv6-enabled interfaces of the router and to enable multicast forwarding.	**ipv6 multicast-routing** [**vrf** *vrf-name*]
Configure MLD reporting for a specified group and source.	**ipv6 mld join-group** [*group-address*] [**include** | **exclude**] {*source-address* | **source-list** *acl*}
Display the multicast groups that are directly connected to the router and that were learned through MLD.	**show ipv6 mld** [**vrf** *vrf-name*] **groups** [**link-local**] [*group-name* | *group-address*] [*interface-type interface-number*] [**detail** | **explicit**]
Display PIM packets received and transmitted, as well as PIM-related events.	**debug ip pim** [**vrf** *vrf-name*] [*ip-address* | **atm** | **auto-rp** | **bfd** | **bsr** | **crimson** | **df** *rp-address* | **drlb** | **hello** | **timers**]
Enable IGMP snooping and to statically add a Layer 2 port as a member of a multicast group.	**ip igmp snooping vlan** *vlan-id* **static** *ip-address* **interface** *interface-id*
Configure a candidate BSR in global configuration mode.	**ip pim** [**vrf** *vrf-name*] **bsr-candidate** *interface-id* [*ash-mask-length*] [*priority*]
Statically configure the address of a PIM rendezvous point (RP) for multicast groups.	**ip pim** [**vrf** *vrf-name*] **rp-address** *rp-address* [*access-list*] [**override**] [**bidir**]
Configure the router to advertise itself to the BSR as a PIM version 2 (PIMv2) candidate rendezvous point (C-RP).	**ip pim** [**vrf** *vrf-name*] **rp-candidate** *interface-id* [**group-list** *access-list-number*]

Task	Command Syntax
Use Auto-RP to configure groups for which the device will act as an RP.	**ip pim** [**vrf** *vrf-name*] **send-rp-announce** *interface-id* **scope** *ttl-value* [**group-list** *access-list-number*] [**interval** *seconds*] [**bidir**]
Specify the threshold that must be reached before moving to shortest-path tree (SPT).	**ip pim spt-threshold** {*kbps* | **infinity**} [**group-list** *access-list*]
Display the contents of the multicast routing (mroute) table.	**show ip mroute** [**vrf** { *vrf-name* | ***** }]
Enable PIM Sparse mode on an interface.	**ip pim sparse-mode**
Enable PIM Sparse-Dense mode on an interface.	**ip pim sparse-dense-mode**
Cause IP multicast traffic to PIM Dense mode flooded across interfaces operating in PIM Sparse mode.	**ip pim autorp listener**
Prevent PIM Dense mode fallback.	**no ip pim dm-fallback**
Enable multicast routing on all IPv6-enabled interfaces and enable multicast forwarding for PIM and MLD on all enabled interfaces of the device.	**ipv6 multicast-routing**
Display the contents of the IPv6 multicast routing table.	**show mrib ipv6 route**

Review Questions

As a part of the review, we encourage you to provide *a single-sentence answer* (keep your answers as short as possible) to the following questions. If you struggle to complete this answer in a single sentence, this may indicate a lack of clarity or reveal gaps in your understanding. We have constructed these questions to help you consolidate this chapter's information and extract the essence of the covered content.

The answers to these questions appear in Appendix A. For more practice with exam format questions, use the Pearson Test Prep Software Online.

1. How can PIM Sparse mode effectively address multicast state explosion, packet loss, and convergence delays in dynamic and heterogeneous network topologies while minimizing resource consumption and operational complexity?

2. How does IGMPv3 effectively handle Source-Specific Multicast (SSM) communication in large-scale networks with dynamic membership changes and heterogeneous receiver capabilities, while ensuring efficient utilization of network resources and minimal overhead?

3. Can you comprehensively detail the role and function of the rendezvous point (RP) in facilitating multicast traffic delivery?

Bibliography

N. Bhaskar, A. Gall, J. Lingard, and S. Venaas. RFC 5059, *Bootstrap Router (BSR) Mechanism for Protocol Independent Multicast (PIM)*, IETF, https://datatracker.ietf.org/doc/html/rfc5059, January 2008.

B. Cain, S. Deering, I. Kouvelas, B. Fenner, and A. Thyagarajan. RFC 3376, *Internet Group Management Protocol, Version 3*, IETF, https://www.ietf.org/rfc/rfc3376.txt, October 2002.

S. Deering. RFC 1112, *Host Extensions for IP Multicasting*, IETF, https://www.ietf.org/rfc/rfc1112.txt, August 1989.

S. Deering, W. Fenner, and B. Haberman. RFC 2710, *Multicast Listener Discovery (MLD) for IPv6*, IETF, https://www.ietf.org/rfc/rfc2710.txt, October 1999.

W. Fenner. RFC 2236, *Host Extensions for IP Multicasting*, IETF, https://www.ietf.org/rfc/rfc2236.txt, November 1997.

B. Haberman and D. Thaler. RFC 3306, *Unicast-Prefix-Based IPv6 Multicast Addresses*, IETF, https://www.ietf.org/rfc/rfc3306.txt, August 2002.

H. Holbrook and B. Cain. RFC 4607, *Source-Specific Multicast for IP*, IETF, https://datatracker.ietf.org/doc/html/rfc4607.txt, August 2006.

IPv4 Multicast Address Space Registry. https://www.iana.org/assignments/multicast-addresses/multicast-addresses.xhtml

D. Meyer and P. Lothberg. RFC 3180, *GLOP Addressing in 233/8*, IETF, https://www.ietf.org/rfc/rfc3180.txt, September 2001.

R. Vida and L. Costa. RFC 3810, *Multicast Listener Discovery Version 2 (MLDv2) for IPv6*, IETF, https://www.ietf.org/rfc/rfc3810.txt, June 2004.

## CHAPTER 10

MPLS Fundamentals

This chapter covers the following exam topics:

3.1 Implement MPLS

- 3.1.a LDP sync
- 3.1.b LDP session protection
- 3.1.c LDP neighbors
- 3.1.e MPLS OAM

Multiprotocol Label Switching (MPLS) constructs the core network of most if not all service providers. Due to the flexibility of the transport mechanism and the associated services or applications, it now extends to form the core of Enterprise networks. In Chapters 11 to 14, we expand the discussion of MPLS into support of services and applications.

"Do I Know This Already?" Quiz

The "Do I Know This Already?" quiz allows you to assess whether you should read this entire chapter thoroughly or jump to the "Exam Preparation Tasks" section. If you are in doubt about your answers to these questions or your own assessment of your knowledge of the topics, read the entire chapter. Table 10-1 lists the major headings in this chapter and their corresponding "Do I Know This Already?" quiz questions. You can find the answers in Appendix A, "Answers to the 'Do I Know This Already?' Quizzes and Review Questions."

Table 10-1 "Do I Know This Already?" Section-to-Question Mapping

Foundation Topics Section	Questions
MPLS Fundamentals	1–3
MPLS LDP Session Protection	4
MPLS LDP IGP Synchronization	5–7
MPLS OAM	8

CAUTION The goal of self-assessment is to gauge your mastery of the topics in this chapter. If you do not know the answer to a question or are only partially sure of the answer, you should mark that question as wrong for purposes of the self-assessment. Giving yourself credit for an answer you correctly guess skews your self-assessment results and might provide you with a false sense of security.

1. How many bytes are there in an MPLS header?

   a. 32

   b. 8

   c. 4

   d. 2

2. How many LDP sessions will come up between R1 and R2 (with two links connected over GigabitEthernet interfaces), taking into consideration that OSPF is running on the Ethernet segments and the loopback networks are advertised properly?

   a. One.

   b. LDP does not operate on Ethernet (ARPA encapsulation).

   c. An LDP session will not establish on broadcast media.

   d. Two.

3. What will be the impact of the following configuration on LDP Hello messages?

```
PE2(config)# access-list 100 deny udp any any eq 646
PE2(config)# access-list 100 permit ip any any
PE2(config)# interface gigabitEthernet 2
PE2(config)# ip access-group 100 in
```

   a. The LDP session will remain up because the access list should be applied in the outbound direction to take effect.

   b. The LDP session will be down.

   c. The LDP session will remain up because the UDP port should be associated with the source address within the access list.

   d. All traffic between PE2 and its directly connected neighbors will go down.

4. What is the state of the LDP session protection after the IGP fails?

   a. Ready

   b. Protecting

   c. Protected

   d. Converged

5. Which of the following options are correct about the following output?

```
PE2# show mpls ldp igp sync
    GigabitEthernet2:
        LDP configured; LDP-IGP Synchronization enabled.
        Sync status: sync achieved; peer reachable.
        Sync delay time: 0 seconds (0 seconds left)
        IGP holddown time: infinite.
        Peer LDP Ident: 10.1.100.4:0
        IGP enabled: OSPF 1
```

```
GigabitEthernet3:
    LDP configured; LDP-IGP Synchronization enabled.
    Sync status: sync not achieved; peer reachable.
    Sync delay time: 0 seconds (0 seconds left)
    IGP holddown time: infinite.
    IGP enabled: OSPF 1
```

   a. PE2 has two active LDP neighbors.

   b. PE2 is running OSPF PID 2 as the underlying IGP.

   c. MPLS LDP sync is running only on GigabitEthernet2.

   d. PE2 has only one LDP neighbor.

6. Which of the following is correct with respect to the MPLS LDP IGP sync feature?

   a. MPLS LDP IGP sync will work only with link-state protocols.

   b. MPLS LDP IGP sync is an interface-level feature.

   c. MPLS LDP IGP sync ensures proper traffic rerouting by increasing the cost across the segment where LDP is not functional.

   d. MPLS LDP IGP sync ensures proper traffic rerouting by increasing the cost across the segment where the IGP neighbor(s) is down.

7. When an MPLS LDP IGP synchronization feature is enabled and a fault takes place on the labeled path, which of the following is true?

   a. The AD of the routing protocol will go infinite for the unlabeled path.

   b. The AD of the routing protocol will go infinite for the labeled path.

   c. The metric of the route that the labeled path is using will go very high.

   d. The metric of the route that the unlabeled path is using will go very high.

8. Which of the following is true regarding MPLS ping?

   a. MPLS ping uses ICMP packets.

   b. MPLS ping uses echo packets over UDP port 3503.

   c. MPLS ping uses echo packets over TCP port 3503.

   d. MPLS ping uses new IP packets with new reserved labels.

Foundation Topics

MPLS Fundamentals

Multiprotocol Label Switching (MPLS) evolved to improve the packet forwarding process across packet-switched networks. From an OSI perspective, MPLS relies on L2.5 between L2 (Data Link layer) and L3 (Network layer), resulting in a more flexible network fabric with increased performance and stability.

If MPLS is turned on within a Cisco core network, performance is not actually enhanced because both the Forwarding Information Base (FIB) and the introduced Label Forwarding Information Base (LFIB) are handled with Cisco Express Forwarding (CEF). Figure 10-1 illustrates the placement of MPLS within an Ethernet header and the constructional elements of the MPLS header (sometimes referred to as a Shim header).

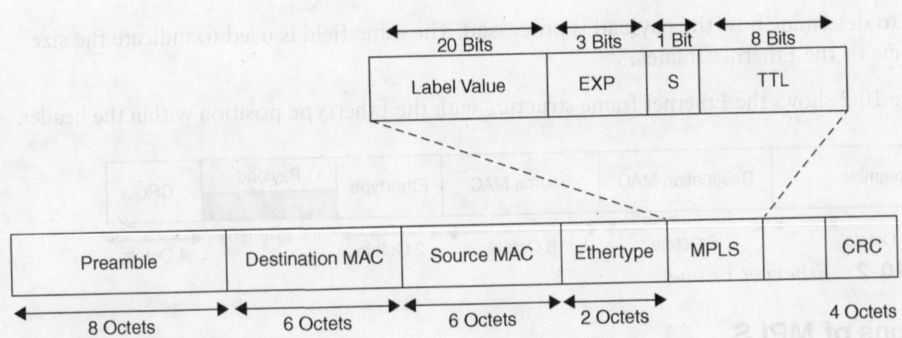

Figure 10-1 *MPLS Header*

An MPLS **label** has local significance, and each router within the MPLS core will assign the label independently (no global assignment). As can be seen from Figure 10-1, the label value is 20 bits, and it ranges from 16 to 1,048,475 because the 0–15 range is reserved for special purposes (this applies to IOS and IOS XE; for IOS XR, the label assignment starts from 16,000). RFC 3032 specifies the label stack entries and the size (in bits) for each subjective field.

MPLS uses labels instead of network addresses to route traffic optimally via shorter pathways. MPLS is protocol-agnostic and can speed up and shape traffic flows across WANs and service provider networks.

The label header fields are interpreted as follows:

- **Label Value (20 bits):** Used for forwarding decisions (it determines the next hop and the action to be taken on the packet).

- **EXP (3 bits):** Refers to the experimental bits used solely for quality of service (QoS), that is, traffic classes.

- **S (1 bit):** Refers to the bottom of the stack (indicating the last label).

- **TTL (8 bits):** Refers to the Time to Live field that prevents packets from looping indefinitely.

Reserved Labels

MPLS has five reserved label values that each have a predefined meaning and function. Label 0 is the IPv4 explicit null label, and it indicates that the packet should be forwarded as an IPv4 packet with the label removed at the egress **label switch router (LSR)**. Label 1, the router alert label, is used to signal that the packet contains information requiring attention from the LSR, such as an OAM or RSVP message.

Label 2 is the IPv6 explicit null label, indicating that the packet should be forwarded as an IPv6 packet and the label removed before reaching the egress LSR. Label 3, known as implicit null or **penultimate hop popping (PHP)**, is used by the ingress LSR to inform the penultimate LSR to remove the label and forward the packet based on its IP header. Finally, Label 4 is reserved for future use and should not be assigned to any packet.

Ethertype

Ethertype is a two-octet field in the Ethernet frame; it is used to indicate which protocol is encapsulated in the payload of the frame and is used at the receiving end by the Data Link layer to determine how the payload is processed. The same field is used to indicate the size of some of the Ethernet frames.

Figure 10-2 shows the Ethernet frame structure with the Ethertype position within the header.

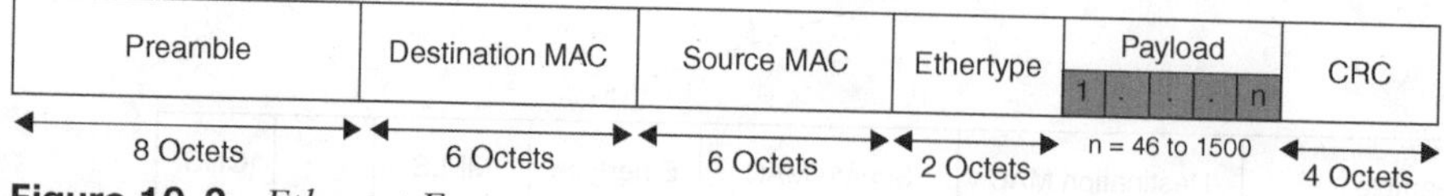

Figure 10-2 *Ethernet Frame*

Additions of MPLS

As mentioned previously, MPLS was not intended only for packet transport within a core network. The associated services and applications are what makes MPLS an evolving technology. The following are examples of the services and applications that MPLS provides:

- **VPNs:** A wide variety of virtual private networks (ranging from Layer 2 to Layer 3) assist customers in carrying distributed traffic across a unified infrastructure or backbone that usually resides in a service provider network.

- **Traffic Engineering:** MPLS explicitly provides the capability to control traffic based on a certain criterion that legacy protocols such as Policy-Based Routing (PBR) and static routes are limited to handle, which results in enhanced utilization of unused links as well as a long-term strategic solution for traffic distribution.

- **Quality of Service (QoS):** MPLS ensures proper QoS treatment for customers through several classes of service.

MPLS Label Operations

To clarify the MPLS operations, let's look at the interworking devices or protocols that construct the MPLS backbone, as illustrated in Figure 10-3.

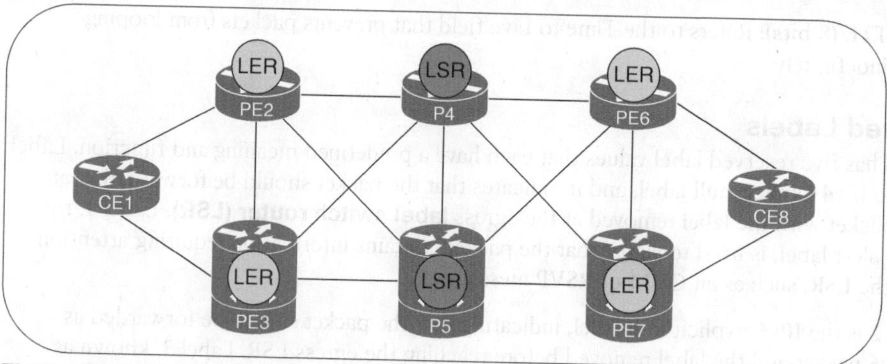

Figure 10-3 *MPLS Main Components*

CE, LER, and LSR in this figure are defined as follows:

- **CE:** Stands for customer edge device, which resides at the customer premises. There are two models from a deployment perspective: managed CE, in which the service provider is responsible for managing the CE; and unmanaged CE, in which the customer is responsible for managing the device with proper SLAs in place.

- **LER:** Stands for label edge router (also known as PE, or provider edge), which is located at the service provider premises, and it is the first interface (attachment point) for the customer traffic coming from the CE device. The first label insertion/imposition takes place at this point with proper classification of packets coming from the CE.

- **LSR:** Stands for label switch router (also known as P, or Provider), which is located at the core of the MPLS backbone and does not interact directly with customer traffic. The label swapping takes place at this element to validate service class and destination.

MPLS Label Types

When the packet arrives at the ingress **label edge router (LER)**, the LER will push two labels onto the packet: a **label switched path (LSP)** label and a VPN label. This is referred to as a label stack. For example, let's look at an Ethernet frame with L3VPN in mind, as depicted in Figure 10-4.

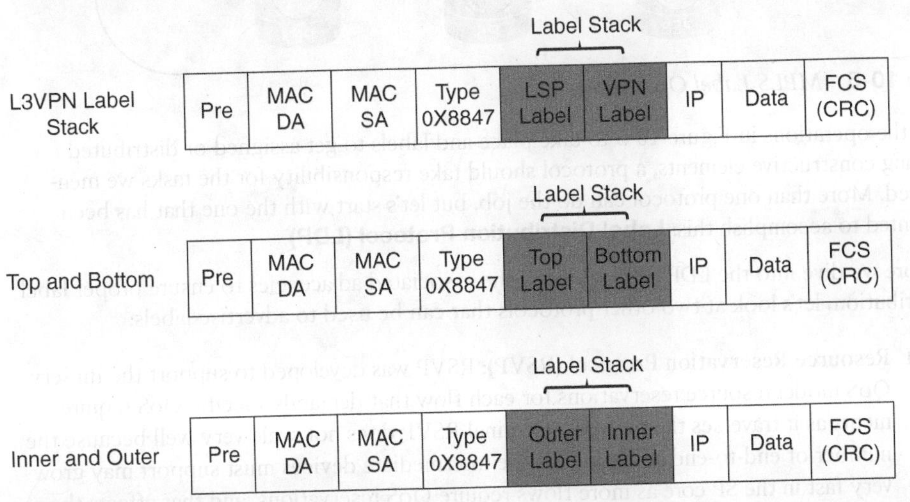

Figure 10-4   *MPLS Label Types*

The arrangement is that the LSP label is adjacent to the Ethertype field, and the VPN label follows that, adjacent to the IP header. Label positions are commonly referred to as *top* and *bottom*, or sometimes referred to as *inner* and *outer*. Thus, when implementing MPLS L3VPN service, you use two labels:

- Top = Outer = LSP Label (LDP, RSVP)

- Bottom = inner = VPN label (mBGP)

Label stacking is a technique that allows multiple labels to be attached to a packet, forming a label stack. The label stack is read from top to bottom, and each label corresponds to a different level of hierarchy or context. For example, a packet can have a label stack that consists of a VPN label, a TE label, and an LDP label, indicating that the packet belongs to a VPN service, follows a TE path, and uses LDP for label distribution. Label stacking enables MPLS to support various applications and features, such as VPNs, TE, pseudowires, and hierarchical LSPs.

Figure 10-5 illustrates the basic operations of MPLS from the packet transport perspective and where the label insertion, swapping, and removal take place.

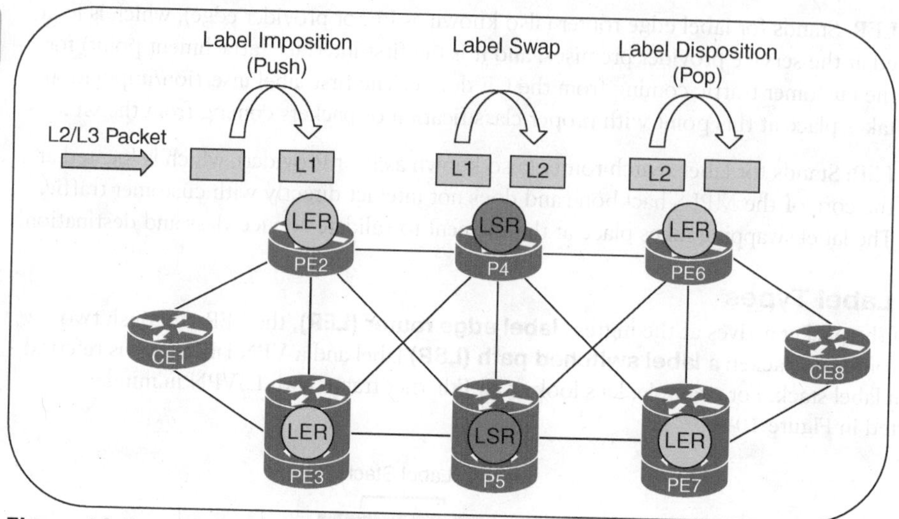

Figure 10-5 *MPLS Label Operations*

For the operations in Figure 10-5 to take place and labels to get assigned or distributed among constructive elements, a protocol should take responsibility for the tasks we mentioned. More than one protocol can do the job, but let's start with the one that has been invented to accomplish this: **Label Distribution Protocol (LDP).**

Before we dive into the LDP operation and the associated adjacencies to ensure proper label distribution, let's look at two other protocols that can be used to advertise labels:

■ **Resource Reservation Protocol (RSVP):** RSVP was developed to support the IntServ QoS model resource reservations for each flow that demands specific QoS requirements as it traverses the network. Original RSVP does not scale very well because the number of end-to-end sessions that the intermediate devices must support may grow very fast in the SP core as more flows require QoS reservations, and that affects the control plane state that devices must support.

RSVP was extended to support the creation and maintenance of LSPs and to be able to make bandwidth reservations for the signaled LSPs.

■ **Border Gateway Protocol (BGP):** For the specific case of MPLS VPNs, BGP is used to distribute VPN label information between PE routers, enabling MPLS VPN services over BGP. The key reason behind this is control and flexibility. BGP allows more control over path selection based on policy (as opposed to just shortest path) and allows the network to scale to larger sizes.

Label Assignment

There are two main methods for assigning labels to packets in MPLS: downstream unsolicited (DU) and downstream on demand (DoD). In the DU method, an LSR assigns a label to a destination prefix and advertises it to its upstream neighbors without waiting for a request. In the DoD method, an LSR assigns a label to a destination prefix only when it receives a request from its upstream neighbor. The request and the advertisement are done using a Label Distribution Protocol (LDP), which is a protocol that enables LSRs to exchange label information and establish label switched paths (LSPs).

The first step in getting this functional is to establish a successful peering (session) between LSRs and LERs (which are responsible for label imposition/disposition). As with link-state protocols, Hello messages are exchanged between directly connected neighbors for them to validate proper parameters in between that will bring the session up. LDP Hello messages are UDP messages sent on the interconnection to the multicast address 224.0.0.2 on Layer 4 port 646.

Hello messages contain a hold time (by default, 15 seconds) for which the LDP speaking router will remove the neighbor from the discovered list in case of absence of hello packets passing this interval.

Figure 10-6 illustrates the exchange of Hello messages at the start of building the LDP session between the directly connected neighbors (10.1.100.x represents the loopback address of routers, where x is the router number for which OSPF area 0 is configured to ensure proper loopback address exchange between PE2 and P4).

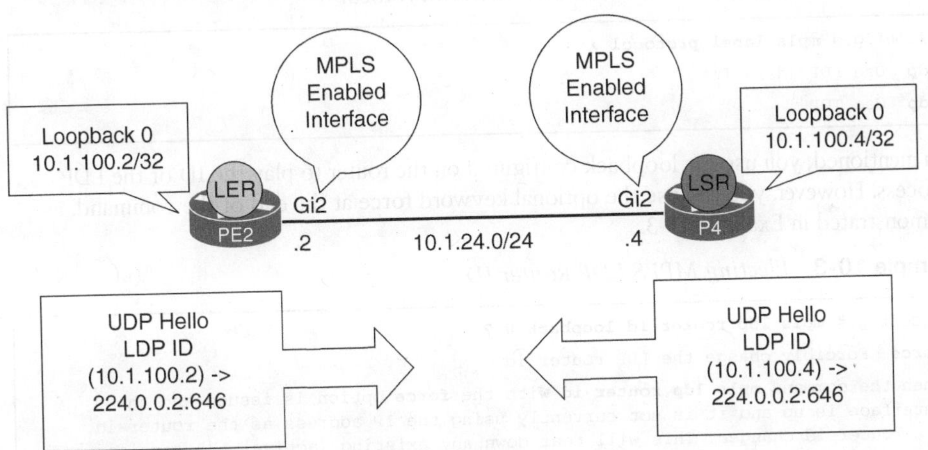

Figure 10-6 *MPLS LDP Session Establishment*

To enable MPLS on a specific interface, you use the command **mpls ip** under the interface configuration mode, as demonstrated in Example 10-1.

NOTE   In older IOS versions, **mpls ip** was used globally to enable hop-by-hop forwarding. However, enabling it globally will not enable it on the interfaces. The interfaces must be configured separately with the **mpls ip** command.

Example 10-1   *Enable MPLS on a Physical Interface*

```
PE2(config)# interface GigabitEthernet3
PE2(config-if)# mpls ip

PE2# debug mpls ldp messages sent
ldp: Sent init msg to 10.1.100.4:0 (pp 0x0)
ldp: Sent keepalive msg to 10.1.100.4:0 (pp 0x0)
%LDP-5-NBRCHG: LDP Neighbor 10.1.100.4:0 (1) is UP
ldp: Sent address msg to 10.1.100.4:0 (pp 0x7F3D55B7C910)
```

You can specifically determine the label distribution protocol using the **mpls label protocol** command from global configuration mode, as demonstrated in Example 10-2.

NOTE   As depicted, the old Tag Switching Protocol (TDP) is still an option to consider. However, at the time of writing, TDP is almost obsolete due to the development and innovation in software code. The default keyword clarifies LDP is the default label distribution protocol in case you do not use the preceding command.

Example 10-2   *Configure the Label Distribution Protocol*

```
PE2(config)# mpls label protocol ¿
  ldp  Use LDP (default)
  tdp  Use TDP
```

As mentioned, you use the loopback configured on the router to play the ID of the LDP process. However, you can use the optional keyword **force** at the end of the command, as demonstrated in Example 10-3.

Example 10-3   *Electing MPLS LDP Router ID*

```
PE2(config)# mpls ldp router-id loopback 0 ?
  force  Forcibly change the LDP router id
! When the command mpls ldp router-id with the force option is issued and the
! interface is up and it is not currently using the IP address as the router-id,
! the router-id changes. This will tear down any existing (active) LDP sessions and
! interrupt the MPLS forwarding.
```

For the LDP neighbor/session to establish successfully, an operating routing protocol should be in place for the loopback of each LDP speaking device to communicate properly. Usually, you configure the loopback interfaces with a /32 subnet mask.

Something to watch for when using OSPF as the **Interior Gateway Protocol (IGP)** for proper loopback exchange is that if you advertised the loopback interface in the OSPF with a /24 subnet mask, OSPF will advertise this network as a host route (/32) regardless of the actual subnet mask. If, for specific requirement, you must configure the loopback interface with a /24 subnet mask, then you must change the OSPF network type from LOOP to point-to-point by using the **ip ospf network point-to-point** command under the interface loopback configuration mode to make sure the subnet mask is advertised as a /32. As with OSPF (a link-state protocol), a router ID is assigned to each LDP speaking router.

From a configuration perspective, you can ensure to have the router ID hard-coded. For the Hello messages to start exchanging, you can enable MPLS (LDP) on the directly connected interfaces between the devices for which you want to establish an LDP session.

The reason for the option is that if a router ID was not assigned for the LDP process, the router will check all the operational interfaces; if any of the operational interfaces are loopback type, the highest one will be elected as the router ID. If no loopback interfaces exist, then the highest physical interface will be elected as the router ID. Changing the router ID after it has been selected will cause the LDP sessions to close down, which will impact a production environment.

Example 10-4 shows the MPLS LDP discovery output that clarifies the LDP ID and the interface used for discovering the neighbor and building the associated neighborship.

Example 10-4   *Check LDP Discovery Parameters*

```
PE2# show mpls ldp discovery
Local LDP Identifier:
    10.1.100.2:0
    Discovery Sources:
    Interfaces:
        GigabitEthernet2 (ldp): xmit/recv
            LDP Id: 10.1.100.4:0
```

Example 10-5 demonstrates how to forcibly change the LDP router ID, which will cause the current active neighbor to close down and build again using the newly configured router ID.

Example 10-5   *Manipulating the LDP Router ID with a New Address*

```
PE2(config)# interface loopback 1
PE2(config-if)# ip address 10.2.100.2 255.255.255.0
PE2(config-if)# exit
PE2(config)# mpls ldp router-id loopback 1 force

%LDP-5-INFO: default: LDP ID removed
%LDP-5-NBRCHG: LDP Neighbor 10.1.100.4:0 (1) is DOWN (LDP Router ID changed)
```

The LDP will never go up because you did not actually advertise the new loopback network in the OSPF (IGP).

Example 10-6 demonstrates how to advertise the loopback network into OSPF using the interface-level configuration mode, which you also can use in addition to the **network** statement under the OSPF global configuration mode.

Example 10-6   *OSPF Configuration from the Interface Level*

```
PE2(config)# interface loopback 1
PE2(config-if)# ip ospf 1 area 0
%LDP-5-NBRCHG: LDP Neighbor 10.1.100.4:0 (1) is UP
```

Example 10-7 demonstrates how the LDP discovery output changed after successfully advertising the loopback network into the OSPF process.

Example 10-7 *Verifying LDP Discovery*

```
PE2# show mpls ldp discovery
Local LDP Identifier:
    10.2.100.2:0
    Discovery Sources:
    Interfaces:
        GigabitEthernet2 (ldp): xmit/recv
            LDP Id: 10.1.100.4:0
```

It is obvious from the log message in Example 10-6 that the LDP neighbor is up. What, then, is the actual impact related to the /24 subnet mask under the loopback interfaces and the /32 subnet mask for the OSPF advertised route?

The impact can be depicted from the new table created for LDP, which is the Label Forwarding Information Protocol (LFIB). Each learned route from the IGP will be assigned a label according to the default range mentioned earlier (unless explicitly changed for illustration purposes).

NOTE A packet that comes to the label edge router (LER) will be examined and forwarded to the appropriate label, based on the Ethertype field, to determine the protocol in payload of the Ethernet frame.

0X0800 – IPv4: Lookup in FIB

0X8847 – MPLS Unicast: Lookup in LFIB

Table 10-2 lists the interworking tables with a brief description about their functionality and the relative commands used to show them.

Table 10-2 Routing and Forwarding Tables

Table Name	Description	Command used to show the table
Routing Information Base (RIB)	This is the routing table.	#show ip route
Forwarding Information Base (FIB)	The FIB is an optimized version of the RIB, or more correctly, it's the table that a router looks at when deciding where to forward traffic. In Cisco, the CEF table is an FIB.	#show ip cef
Label Information Base (LIB)	The LIB is an MPLS table. This is the place where the router will keep all known MPLS labels.	#show mpls ldp bindings
Label Forwarding Information Base (LFIB)	The LFIB is another MPLS table. This is the table that the router uses to forward labeled packets going through the network. Much like the RIB uses the FIB to forward traffic, the LIB uses the LFIB to forward traffic.	#show mpls forwarding-table

NOTE   A router may have many separate RIBs if you are running VRFs with customers, which will entitle a separate RIB for each VRF. The command used for showing the RIB output in this case is the same, except the VRF name is associated with the **show ip route vrf** {*vrf name*} command.

The same applies for the FIB: **show ip cef vrf** {*vrf name*}.

Now going back to the configuration example we started with, the interesting piece is the new loopback (1) configured on PE2 for the LDP router-ID demonstration. Checking the direct neighbor PE3's LFIB indicates that no label is assigned to network 10.2.100.0/24, which is the actual subnet mask configured under the loopback interface.

Example 10-8 demonstrates the output of the Label Forwarding Information Base. The output displays separate columns for incoming and outgoing labels associated with the target Forwarding Equivalence Class (FEC) and the next-hop to reach the prefix.

NOTE   *FEC* is a term used in MPLS networks to describe a set of incoming packets with similar characteristics, allowing those packets to be allocated the same label and forwarded down the same label-switched path.

Example 10-8   *Verifying LFIB Output*

```
RP/0/0/CPU0:PE3# show mpls forwarding-table
Wed Jan  3 06:55:03.406 UTC
Local   Outgoing    Prefix              Outgoing      Next Hop        Bytes
Label   Label       or ID               Interface                     Switched

------  ----------  ------------------  ------------  --------------- -----------
16300   16500       10.1.100.2/32       Gi0/0/0/3     10.1.35.5       98
16301   16502       10.1.100.4/32       Gi0/0/0/3     10.1.35.5       186
16302   16503       10.1.100.6/32       Gi0/0/0/3     10.1.35.5       0
16303   16506       10.1.24.0/24        Gi0/0/0/3     10.1.35.5       0
16304   Pop         10.1.45.0/24        Gi0/0/0/3     10.1.35.5       0
16305   16507       10.1.46.0/24        Gi0/0/0/3     10.1.35.5       0
16306   16508       10.1.67.0/24        Gi0/0/0/3     10.1.35.5       0
16307   Pop         10.1.57.0/24        Gi0/0/0/3     10.1.35.5       0
16308   Pop         10.1.100.5/32       Gi0/0/0/3     10.1.35.5       6541992
16309   16509       10.1.100.7/32       Gi0/0/0/3     10.1.35.5       0
16310   16504       10.2.100.2/32       Gi0/0/0/3     10.1.35.5       0
```

Now, you can change the OSPF network type to point-to-point for the loopback 1 interface on PE2, as demonstrated in Example 10-9.

Example 10-9 *OSPF Point-to-Point Network Type and Label Assignment*

```
PE2# show ip ospf interface brief | include (State|LOOP)
Interface    PID   Area          IP Address/Mask     Cost  State Nbrs F/C
Lo0          1     0             10.1.100.2/32       1     LOOP  0/0
Lo1          1     0             10.2.100.2/24       1     LOOP  0/0

PE2(config)# interface loopback 1
PE2(config-if)# ip ospf network point-to-point

RP/0/0/CPU0:PE3# show mpls forwarding | include 10.2.100.
16311  16510         10.2.100.0/24     Gi0/0/0/3    10.1.35.5        0
```

Now, the label is assigned properly, and the LDP data plane is maintained for end-to-end connectivity, as illustrated in Figure 10-7.

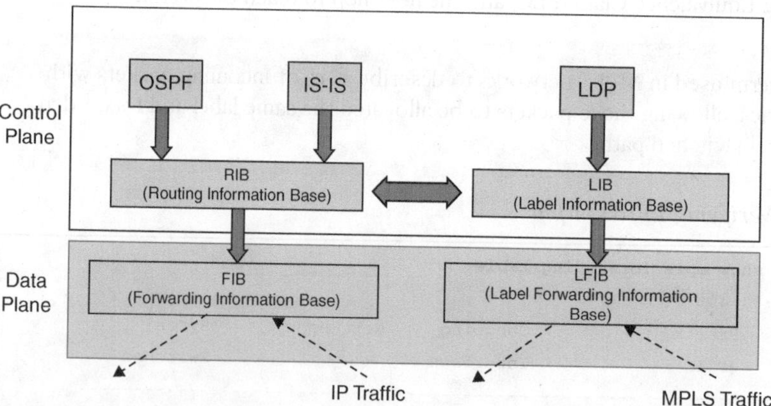

Figure 10-7 *Data Plane and Control Plane*

Usually, IP routing relies on destination-based lookup, which solely depends on both RIB (the routing table) and FIB (the forwarding table). Example 10-10 verifies that PE2 can properly install the PE3 loopback 0 network in both RIB and FIB.

Example 10-10 *RIB and FIB Output*

```
PE2# show ip route 10.1.100.3
Routing entry for 10.1.100.3/32
  Known via "ospf 1", distance 110, metric 22, type intra area
  Last update from 10.1.24.4 on GigabitEthernet2, 00:06:39 ago
  Routing Descriptor Blocks:
  * 10.1.24.4, from 10.1.100.3, 00:06:39 ago, via GigabitEthernet2
      Route metric is 22, traffic share count is 1

PE2# show ip cef 10.1.100.3
10.1.100.3/32
  nexthop 10.1.24.4 GigabitEthernet2
```

The next hop for PE2 to reach the loopback network of PE3 is through 10.1.24.4 using GigabitEthernet2 as an exit interface to reach that destination.

The same will apply after you configure the **mpls ip** command under the core interfaces and establish LDP sessions successfully.

You can use the **show mpls forwarding-table** command to check the LFIB and the assigned labels.

MPLS LDP Autoconfig

Another useful feature to reduce the configuration burden is to use the **mpls ldp autoconfig** feature under the global routing process (this example uses OSPF).

You already have **mpls ip** configured under each interface.

Example 10-11 demonstrates the LDP/IGP interaction on an enabled interface for both protocols and the associated main parameters.

Example 10-11   *Display MPLS LDP/IGP-Enabled Interface Output Command*

```
PE2# show ip ospf mpls ldp interface
Loopback0
  Process ID 1, Area 0
  LDP is not configured through LDP autoconfig
  LDP-IGP Synchronization : Not required
  Holddown timer is disabled
  Interface is up
GigabitEthernet3
  Process ID 1, Area 0
  LDP is not configured through LDP autoconfig
  LDP-IGP Synchronization : Not required
  Holddown timer is disabled
  Interface is up
GigabitEthernet2
  Process ID 1, Area 0
  LDP is not configured through LDP autoconfig
  LDP-IGP Synchronization : Not required
  Holddown timer is disabled
  Interface is up
```

As depicted, LDP is explicitly not configured using this feature. The **mpls ldp autoconfig area** *{area-id}* command under the **router OSPF** *{process-id}* checks all interfaces enabled for IGP and in an Up state and enables MPLS (LDP session establishment capabilities), as demonstrated in Example 10-12 and confirmed in Example 10-13.

Example 10-12   *Enable LDP Autoconfig*

```
PE2(config)# router ospf 1
PE2(config-router)# mpls ldp autoconfig ?
  area  Configure an OSPF area to run MPLS LDP
! We can explicitly determine the OSPF area for which we need to enable LDP on
! active interfaces on active interfaces.
```

```
! The same methodology is used on IOS XR based software with minor difference due to
! hierarchical structure of the IOS XR
RP/0/0/CPU0:PE3(config)# router ospf 1
RP/0/0/CPU0:PE3(config-ospf)# mpls ldp auto-config
```

You can verify the functionality of enabling LDP autoconfig on the respective interfaces by using the **show ip ospf ldp interface** command on IOS-based software, as shown in Example 10-13.

Example 10-13 *Check LDP Autoconfig for IGP-Enabled Interface*

```
PE2# show ip ospf mpls ldp interface
Loopback0
  Process ID 1, Area 0
  LDP is not configured through LDP autoconfig
  LDP-IGP Synchronization : Not required
  Holddown timer is disabled
  Interface is up
GigabitEthernet3
  Process ID 1, Area 0
  LDP is configured through LDP autoconfig
  LDP-IGP Synchronization : Not required
  Holddown timer is disabled
  Interface is up
GigabitEthernet2
  Process ID 1, Area 0
  LDP is configured through LDP autoconfig
  LDP-IGP Synchronization : Not required
  Holddown timer is disabled
  Interface is up
! A similar command is used on IOS XR based software as shown below:
RP/0/0/CPU0:PE3# show mpls ldp interface
Interface GigabitEthernet0/0/0/2 (0x80)
  VRF: 'default' (0x60000000)
  Enabled via config: IGP Auto-config
Interface GigabitEthernet0/0/0/3 (0xa0)
  VRF: 'default' (0x60000000)
  Enabled via config: IGP Auto-config
Interface GigabitEthernet0/0/0/4 (0xc0)
  VRF: 'default' (0x60000000)
  Enabled via config: LDP interface, IGP Auto-config
```

Even if the **mpls ip** command is removed from interface-level configuration mode, the MPLS functionality will remain in place due to the autoconfig feature enabled under the OSPF process, as demonstrated in Example 10-14.

Example 10-14 *LDP via Interface Level vs. Autoconfig*

```
PE2(config)# interface GigabitEthernet2
PE2(config-if)# no mpls ip
% LDP remains enabled on interface Gi2 by autoconfig.
 Autoconfig can be removed from Gi2 with 'no mpls ldp igp autoconfig.'

PE2# show ip ospf mpls ldp interface gigabitEthernet 2
 Process ID 1, Area 0
 LDP is configured through LDP autoconfig
 LDP-IGP Synchronization : Not required
 Holddown timer is disabled
 Interface is up
```

MPLS Label Assignment

Next, you can change the label range for each device within the domain you are working on to make it clearer when analyzing label assignments and distribution, as demonstrated in Example 10-15.

Example 10-15 *MPLS LDP Label Range Configuration*

```
! Before we issue the command for changing the MPLS label range, let us check what
! currently is available by default.
PE2# show mpls label range
Downstream Generic label region: Min/Max label: 16/1048575

PE2(config)# mpls label range 200 299
PE6# show mpls label range
Downstream Generic label region: Min/Max label: 200/299

! The same context is used for IOS XR based software.
RP/0/0/CPU0:P5(config)# mpls label range 16500 16599
```

You can verify the local label assignments per the label range you have adjusted using the **show mpls ldp bindings local** command, as shown in Example 10-16.

Example 10-16 *MPLS LDP Label Range Command*

```
PE2# show mpls ldp bindings local
  lib entry: 10.1.24.0/24, rev 2
        local binding:  label: imp-null
  lib entry: 10.1.46.0/24, rev 4
        local binding:  label: 200
  lib entry: 10.1.67.0/24, rev 6
        local binding:  label: 201
  lib entry: 10.1.100.2/32, rev 8
        local binding:  label: imp-null
  lib entry: 10.1.100.4/32, rev 10
        local binding:  label: 202
```

```
    lib entry: 10.1.100.6/32, rev 12
          local binding:  label: 203
    lib entry: 10.1.100.7/32, rev 14
          local binding:  label: 204
! Again, the label will take place for the routes installed in the routing table
! with the assist of the running routing protocol.

! We can also verify the number of assigned labels from the pool using the show mpls
! ldp bindings summary
PE2# show mpls ldp bindings summary
Total number of prefixes: 7
Generic label bindings

                      assigned          learned
         prefixes     in labels       out labels
             7            7               7
Total tib route info allocated: 7
Previous tib remote label entries allocated Current/Total: 0/0
Previous tib remote label queues allocated Current/Total: 0/0
```

For clarification, Table 10-3 contains the range value for labels that the core MPLS devices will assign.

Table 10-3 MPLS Label Range

Device Hostname	Label Range
PE2	200–299
PE3	16,300–16,399
P4	400–499
P5	16,500–16,599
PE6	600–699
PE7	16,700–16,799

The main MPLS network in place will be as shown in Figure 10-8.

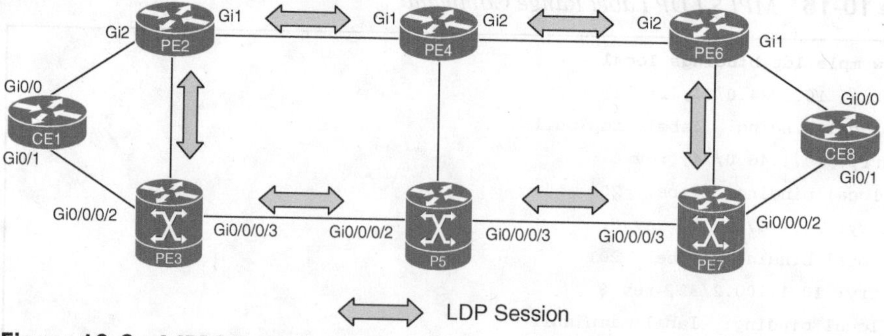

Figure 10-8 *MPLS Domain*

MPLS Advertise Labels

As mentioned in the previous section, LDP will assign labels to every prefix learned through the IGP and installed in the routing table.

You can control which prefixes get a label tagged to it either in the inbound or the outbound direction by simply defining an access list (you can also use a prefix list to gain more granular control).

Example 10-17 demonstrates a regular LFIB output.

Example 10-17   *LFIB Output*

```
P4# show mpls forwarding-table
Local       Outgoing    Prefix          Bytes Label   Outgoing    Next Hop
Label       Label       or Tunnel Id    Switched      interface
400         Pop Label   10.1.23.0/24    0             Gi1         10.1.24.2
401         Pop Label   10.1.35.0/24    0             Gi3         10.1.45.5
402         604         10.1.57.0/24    0             Gi2         10.1.46.6
403         Pop Label   10.1.67.0/24    0             Gi2         10.1.46.6
404         Pop Label   10.1.100.2/32   0             Gi1         10.1.24.2
405         205         10.1.100.3/32   0             Gi1         10.1.24.2
406         Pop Label   10.1.100.5/32   0             Gi3         10.1.45.5
407         Pop Label   10.1.100.6/32   0             Gi2         10.1.46.6
408         609         10.1.100.7/32   0             Gi2         10.1.46.6
```

Example 10-18 shows the same table after attaching an access list to control which prefixes are eligible for tagging.

Example 10-18   *Outbound LDP Label Control*

```
PE2(config)# access-list 5 permit host 10.1.100.2
PE2(config)# no mpls ldp advertise-labels
PE2(config)# mpls ldp advertise-labels for 5

P4# show mpls forwarding-table
Local       Outgoing    Prefix          Bytes Label   Outgoing    Next Hop
Label       Label       or Tunnel Id    Switched      interface
400         No Label    10.1.23.0/24    0             Gi1         10.1.24.2
401         Pop Label   10.1.35.0/24    0             Gi3         10.1.45.5
402         604         10.1.57.0/24    0             Gi2         10.1.46.6
403         Pop Label   10.1.67.0/24    0             Gi2         10.1.46.6
404         Pop Label   10.1.100.2/32   0             Gi1         10.1.24.2
405         No Label    10.1.100.3/32   0             Gi1         10.1.24.2
406         Pop Label   10.1.100.5/32   0             Gi3         10.1.45.5
407         Pop Label   10.1.100.6/32   0             Gi2         10.1.46.6
408         609         10.1.100.7/32   0             Gi2         10.1.46.6

PE2# show access-lists
Standard IP access list 5
    10 permit 10.1.100.2 (5 matches)
```

The debug output in Example 10-19 shows the implicit null associated with prefixes excluded using the access list configured in Example 10-18.

Example 10-19 *Debug LDP Advertisements Output*

```
PE2# debug mpls ldp advertisements prefix-acl 5
LDP label and address advertisements debugging is on for prefix ACL 5

lcon: peer 10.1.100.3:0 (pp 0x7F3D55C63D10): advertise 10.1.100.2/32, label 3
(imp-null) (#205)
lcon: peer 10.1.100.4:0 (pp 0x7F3D55B7C910): advertise 10.1.100.2/32, label 3
(imp-null) (#205)
```

The preceding examples focus on outbound label advertisement. Keep in mind that influencing the label tagging on inbound direction is also possible.

You can create another access list that will match the prefixes for which you need to access inbound tagging and associate it with the neighbor that sent the tagged packet, as demonstrated in Example 10-20.

Example 10-20 *LFIB Output*

```
PE2# show mpls forwarding-table
Local      Outgoing     Prefix            Bytes Label    Outgoing     Next Hop
Label      Label        or Tunnel Id      Switched       interface
200        Pop Label    10.1.35.0/24      0              Gi3          10.1.23.3
201        Pop Label    10.1.45.0/24      0              Gi2          10.1.24.4
202        Pop Label    10.1.46.0/24      0              Gi2          10.1.24.4
203        402          10.1.57.0/24      0              Gi2          10.1.24.4
204        403          10.1.67.0/24      0              Gi2          10.1.24.4
205        Pop Label    10.1.100.3/32     0              Gi3          10.1.23.3
206        Pop Label    10.1.100.4/32     0              Gi2          10.1.24.4
207        406          10.1.100.5/32     0              Gi2          10.1.24.4
208        407          10.1.100.6/32     0              Gi2          10.1.24.4
209        408          10.1.100.7/32     0              Gi2          10.1.24.4

PE2# show access-lists 7
Standard IP access list 7
    10 deny    10.1.100.7 (1 match)
    20 permit any (12 matches)
```

LDP will assign labels for all prefixes installed in the RIB through the underlying routing protocol. You also can control what prefixes you would like to be filtered from being assigned a label by using an access list (these examples use a standard access list) and attaching the access list to the neighbor from which you learned the target prefix, as shown in Example 10-21.

Example 10-21 *Inbound LDP Label Control*

```
PE2(config)# access-list 7 deny host 10.1.100.7
PE2(config)# mpls ldp neighbor 10.1.100.4 labels accept 7
```

```
PE2# show mpls forwarding-table
```

Local Label	Outgoing Label	Prefix or Tunnel Id	Bytes Label Switched	Outgoing interface	Next Hop
200	Pop Label	10.1.35.0/24	0	Gi3	10.1.23.3
201	Pop Label	10.1.45.0/24	0	Gi2	10.1.24.4
202	Pop Label	10.1.46.0/24	0	Gi2	10.1.24.4
203	402	10.1.57.0/24	0	Gi2	10.1.24.4
204	403	10.1.67.0/24	0	Gi2	10.1.24.4
205	Pop Label	10.1.100.3/32	0	Gi3	10.1.23.3
206	Pop Label	10.1.100.4/32	0	Gi2	10.1.24.4
207	406	10.1.100.5/32	0	Gi2	10.1.24.4
208	407	10.1.100.6/32	0	Gi2	10.1.24.4
209	No Label	10.1.100.7/32	0	Gi2	10.1.24.4

NOTE   From a design perspective, the goal of an advertise label is to reduce the size of the local label space and limit the advertisements to the neighbors. This will increase the scalability in large-scale networks.

Now, LDP will assign a label for each prefix learned through the underlying IGP (which is OSPF in this case). Referring to Example 10-22, look through the RIB (routing table) and focus on the IGP learned routes; then compare it to the MPLS forwarding table (LFIB).

Example 10-22 *LFIB and OSPF RIB Outputs*

```
PE2# show mpls forwarding-table
```

Local Label	Outgoing Label	Prefix or Tunnel Id	Bytes Label Switched	Outgoing interface	Next Hop
200	Pop Label	10.1.35.0/24	0	Gi3	10.1.23.3
201	Pop Label	10.1.45.0/24	0	Gi2	10.1.24.4
202	Pop Label	10.1.46.0/24	0	Gi2	10.1.24.4
203	402	10.1.57.0/24	0	Gi2	10.1.24.4
204	403	10.1.67.0/24	0	Gi2	10.1.24.4
205	Pop Label	10.1.100.3/32	0	Gi3	10.1.23.3
206	Pop Label	10.1.100.4/32	0	Gi2	10.1.24.4
207	406	10.1.100.5/32	0	Gi2	10.1.24.4
208	407	10.1.100.6/32	0	Gi2	10.1.24.4
209	408	10.1.100.7/32	0	Gi2	10.1.24.4

```
PE2# show ip route ospf
! Output omitted for brevity


Gateway of last resort is not set
```

```
                    10.0.0.0/8 is variably subnetted, 17 subnets, 2 masks
O          10.1.35.0/24 [110/20] via 10.1.23.3, 00:22:05, GigabitEthernet3
O          10.1.45.0/24 [110/11] via 10.1.24.4, 00:22:41, GigabitEthernet2
O          10.1.46.0/24 [110/2] via 10.1.24.4, 1d23h, GigabitEthernet2
O          10.1.57.0/24 [110/13] via 10.1.24.4, 00:22:05, GigabitEthernet2
O          10.1.67.0/24 [110/3] via 10.1.24.4, 1d23h, GigabitEthernet2
O          10.1.100.3/32 [110/11] via 10.1.23.3, 00:22:41, GigabitEthernet3
O          10.1.100.4/32 [110/2] via 10.1.24.4, 1d23h, GigabitEthernet2
O          10.1.100.5/32 [110/12] via 10.1.24.4, 00:22:05, GigabitEthernet2
O          10.1.100.6/32 [110/3] via 10.1.24.4, 1d23h, GigabitEthernet2
O          10.1.100.7/32 [110/4] via 10.1.24.4, 12:57:12, GigabitEthernet2
```

Example 10-23 lists all available options from the PE2 routing perspective to reach the PE7 loopback network.

Example 10-23 *Specific Route Output*

```
PE2# show ip route 10.1.100.7 255.255.255.255
Routing entry for 10.1.100.7/32
  Known via "ospf 1", distance 110, metric 4, type intra area
  Last update from 10.1.24.4 on GigabitEthernet2, 12:24:07 ago
  Routing Descriptor Blocks:
    10.1.24.4, from 10.1.100.7, 12:24:07 ago, via GigabitEthernet2
      Route metric is 4, traffic share count is 1
  * 10.1.23.3, from 10.1.100.7, 12:24:07 ago, via GigabitEthernet3
      Route metric is 4, traffic share count is 1
```

From a metric perspective, both routes are equal and can be used for traffic forwarding; however, one of the routes will be elected as the best one and will be used for traffic forwarding and maintaining end-to-end connectivity between the loopback networks.

To make it simple from an output and verification perspective, you can adjust the OSPF cost (increment the cost to make the target path less preferred) and choose the PE2 → P4 → PE6 → PE7 path as the preferred path (see Example 10-24).

Example 10-24 *OSPF Cost*

```
PE2# show ip ospf interface GigabitEthernet3 | include Cost
  Process ID 1, Router ID 10.1.100.2, Network Type POINT_TO_POINT, Cost: 1
  Topology-MTID    Cost    Disabled    Shutdown    Topology Name
PE2(config)# interface GigabitEthernet3
PE2(config-if)# ip ospf cost 10

PE2# show ip ospf interface GigabitEthernet3 | include Cost
  Process ID 1, Router ID 10.1.100.2, Network Type POINT_TO_POINT, Cost: 10
  Topology-MTID    Cost    Disabled    Shutdown    Topology Name
```

Because we have changed the cost for one of the paths, we have eliminated the possibility to have equal cost paths available, so one path should be available in the PE2 routing table. See Example 10-25.

Example 10-25 *LSP Path Visibility*

```
PE2# show ip route 10.1.100.7
Routing entry for 10.1.100.7/32
  Known via "ospf 1", distance 110, metric 4, type intra area
  Last update from 10.1.24.4 on GigabitEthernet2, 12:35:15 ago
  Routing Descriptor Blocks:
  * 10.1.24.4, from 10.1.100.7, 12:35:15 ago, via GigabitEthernet2
      Route metric is 4, traffic share count is 1

PE2# traceroute 10.1.100.7 source loopback 0 numeric
VRF info: (vrf in name/id, vrf out name/id)
  1 10.1.24.4 [MPLS: Label 408 Exp 0] 6 msec 4 msec 5 msec
  2 10.1.46.6 [MPLS: Label 609 Exp 0] 3 msec 2 msec 3 msec
  3 10.1.67.7 8 msec *  5 msec
```

To validate the next hop and outgoing interface that PE2 will use to reach the destination (which is 10.1.100.7/32 as an example), you can check the CEF table (FIB), as demonstrated in Example 10-26.

Example 10-26 *FIB Output*

```
PE2# show ip cef 10.1.100.7 255.255.255.255
10.1.100.7/32
  nexthop 10.1.24.4 GigabitEthernet2 label 407-(local:209)
```

In Figure 10-9, a packet is being transmitted from PE2 toward PE7. Notice that there is no label for the packet destined to PE7 from PE6, which is ultimately the last hop in the LSP. This is called penultimate hop popping (PHP) in MPLS environments. The process functions by removing the outermost label of the tagged MPLS packet before the packet is passed to the last device in the LSP (which will be LER usually because the LSP path usually starts with an LER and ends with a similar one).

Outgoing Interface	Next Hop	Local Label	Remote Label
Gi2	10.1.24.4	209	408
Gi2	10.1.46.6	408	609
Gi3	10.1.67.7	609	No Label / Pop

Figure 10-9 *MPLS Label Swapping*

To confirm the output again, you can check the LFIB from the router before the last hop, which is PE6, as shown in Example 10-27.

Example 10-27 *LFIB Output*

```
PE6# show mpls forwarding-table 10.1.100.7 32
Local        Outgoing    Prefix           Bytes Label    Outgoing    Next Hop
Label        Label       or Tunnel Id     Switched       interface
609          Pop Label   10.1.100.7/32    5336           Gi3         10.1.67.7
```

How did PE6 know that a label pop operation should take place? This is done using implicit null (removing the outermost label). PE7 tells PE6 through the implicit null label that it is the last router on the LSP and there is no need to do extra label lookup. Ultimately, the goal is to reserve the extra lookup and speed up the packet transport to the destination.

Going through the reverse direction will yield similar output using a different label stack.

Example 10-28 demonstrates the relevant LFIB outputs for tracking the label assignment reaching to the pop operation before reaching the destination.

Example 10-28 *Check Label Assignments*

```
RP/0/0/CPU0:PE7# show mpls forwarding prefix 10.1.100.2/32
Local  Outgoing   Prefix              Outgoing      Next Hop        Bytes
Label  Label      or ID               Interface                     Switched
------ ---------- ------------------- ------------- --------------- ------------
16700  605        10.1.100.2/32       Gi0/0/0/4     10.1.67.6       1436

PE6# show mpls forwarding-table 10.1.100.2 255.255.255.255
Local        Outgoing    Prefix           Bytes Label    Outgoing    Next Hop
Label        Label       or Tunnel Id     Switched       interface
605          404         10.1.100.2/32    0              Gi2         10.1.46.4

P4# show mpls forwarding-table 10.1.100.2 255.255.255.255
Local        Outgoing    Prefix           Bytes Label    Outgoing    Next Hop
Label        Label       or Tunnel Id     Switched       interface
404          Pop Label   10.1.100.2/32    3770           Gi1         10.1.24.2
```

Figure 10-10 illustrates the implicit null operation and the outermost label removal. To further investigate the label operation (pushing and popping), a trace has been issued from PE7 toward PE2, as can be depicted from Example 10-28. Figure 10-10 clearly demonstrates the implicit null operation that will take place close to the destination per the example.

You can change the default PHP behavior by enforcing the explicit null label to be sent to the upstream LSR that performs the PHP function.

The implicit null label is used by default and works well when the network has no QoS requirements, or if the QoS is end-to-end between customer edges. On the other hand, explicit null is used when the MPLS core network needs to know the QoS values, as demonstrated in Example 10-29.

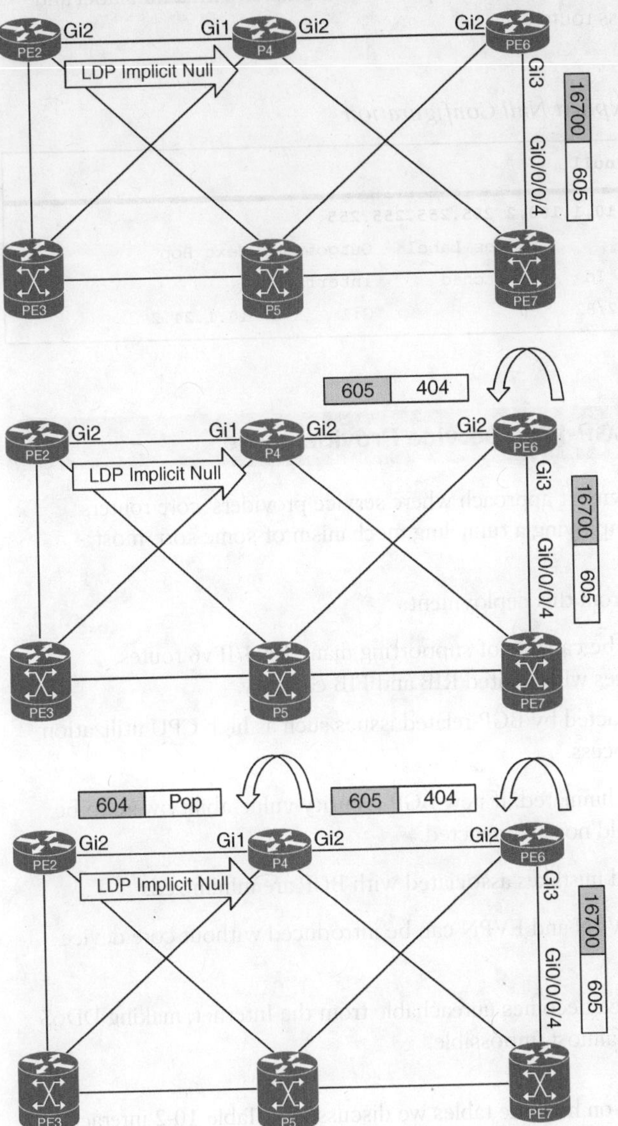

Figure 10-10 *MPLS PHP*

NOTE   Per RFC 3032, implicit null and explicit null labels have reserved values (0 and 3, respectively). It is recommended for the implicit null and the subsequent PHP operation to take place to reserve the lookup process. With explicit null, which is used in signaling protocols and label headers, the penultimate router swaps the MPLS label with a null label and sends a labeled packet to the egress router.

Example 10-29   *MPLS LDP Explicit Null Configuration*

```
PE2(config)# mpls ldp explicit-null

P4# show mpls forwarding-table 10.1.100.2 255.255.255.255
Local      Outgoing   Prefix          Bytes Label   Outgoing    Next Hop
Label      Label      or Tunnel Id    Switched      interface
404        explicit-n 10.1.100.2/32   0             Gi1         10.1.24.2
```

Use Case: BGP-Free Service Provider Core

BGP-Free Core is a network deployment approach where service providers' core routers do not run BGP. This is done by employing a tunneling mechanism of some sort, most commonly MPLS.

Several advantages can be gained from this deployment:

- Core devices do not need to be capable of supporting many IPv4/IPv6 routes, allowing you to deploy devices with limited RIB and FIB capacity.

- Core devices will not be impacted by BGP-related issues such as high CPU utilization during the reconvergence process.

- One of the attack vectors is eliminated. If new BGP security vulnerability were to be discovered, core devices would not be impacted.

- The configuration burden and mistakes associated with BGP are minimized.

- New services such as MPLS VPN and EVPN can be introduced without core device modification.

- If deployed properly, BGP-Free becomes unreachable from the Internet, making DDoS attacks against core elements almost impossible.

Figure 10-11 shows final thoughts on how the tables we discussed in Table 10-2 interact and outputs intervene in a meaningful way to construct the forwarding process of IP packets and labeled packets.

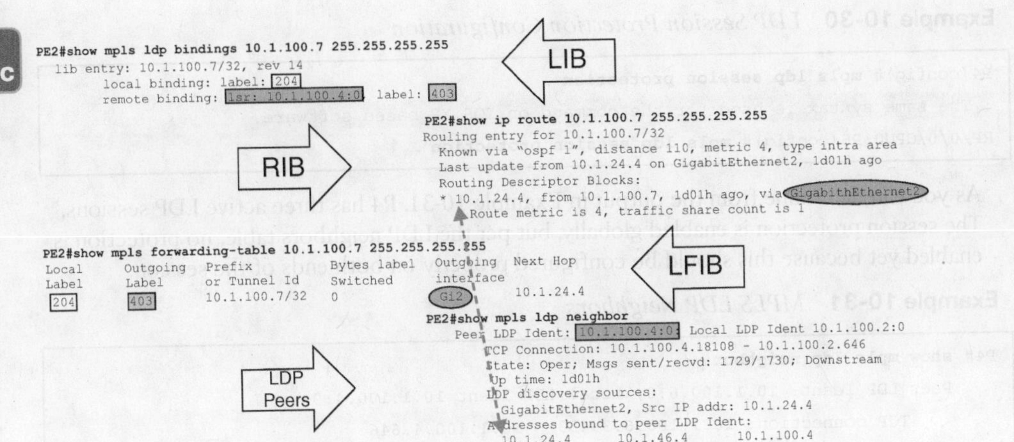

Figure 10-11 *MPLS Tables Interaction*

MPLS LDP Session Protection

Due to the interaction between LDP and IGP, flapping links (link failures in general) could affect dramatically the performance of labeled traffic forwarding. The reason is that when two LDP neighbors (LSRs) lose their direct connectivity, the LDP session will go down, which means the session needs to be rebuilt again and, accordingly, LDP bindings to be exchanged/distributed again.

To avoid such scenarios, LDP session protection plays a significant role in convergence because it encounters the situation by building a targeted LDP session between the two directly affected LSRs (which have an LDP session functional in between), which will solely preserve the session state.

Figure 10-12 illustrates a targeted LDP session establishment after the directly connected LDP neighbor is torn down.

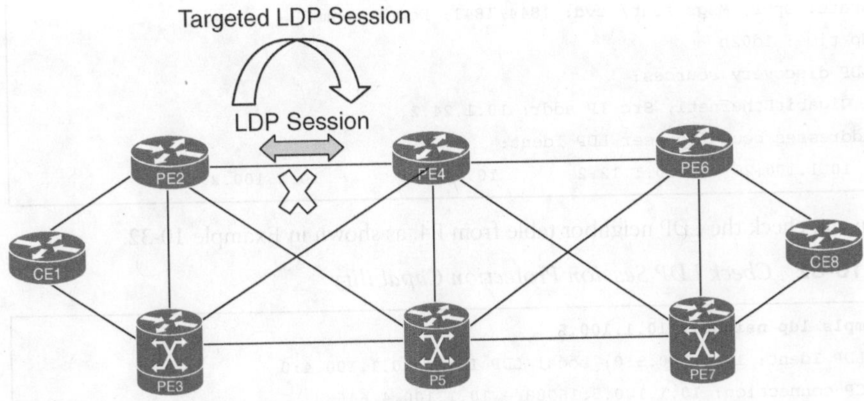

Figure 10-12 *MPLS LDP Session Protection*

To enable session protection for LDP, you can configure it globally by using the command demonstrated in Example 10-30.

Example 10-30 *LDP Session Protection Configuration*

```
P4(config)# mpls ldp session protection
! The same syntax is used for the command on IOS XR based software.
RP/0/0/CPU0:P5(config)# mpls ldp session protection
```

As you can determine from the output in Example 10-31, P4 has three active LDP sessions. The session protection is enabled globally, but per the LDP neighbors table, no protection is enabled yet because this should be configured properly on both ends of the session.

Example 10-31 *MPLS LDP Neighbors*

```
P4# show mpls ldp neighbor
    Peer LDP Ident: 10.1.100.6:0; Local LDP Ident 10.1.100.4:0
        TCP connection: 10.1.100.6.39433 - 10.1.100.4.646
        State: Oper; Msgs sent/rcvd: 11705/11698; Downstream
        Up time: 1w0d
        LDP discovery sources:
          GigabitEthernet2, Src IP addr: 10.1.46.6
        Addresses bound to peer LDP Ident:
          10.1.46.6       10.1.67.6       10.1.100.6       10.1.68.6
    Peer LDP Ident: 10.1.100.5:0; Local LDP Ident 10.1.100.4:0
        TCP connection: 10.1.100.5.16988 - 10.1.100.4.646
        State: Oper; Msgs sent/rcvd: 11694/11707; Downstream
        Up time: 1w0d
        LDP discovery sources:
          GigabitEthernet3, Src IP addr: 10.1.45.5
        Addresses bound to peer LDP Ident:
          10.1.100.5      10.1.45.5       10.1.35.5        10.1.57.5
    Peer LDP Ident: 10.2.100.2:0; Local LDP Ident 10.1.100.4:0
        TCP connection: 10.2.100.2.33709 - 10.1.100.4.646
        State: Oper; Msgs sent/rcvd: 1844/1841; Downstream
        Up time: 1d02h
        LDP discovery sources:
          GigabitEthernet1, Src IP addr: 10.1.24.2
        Addresses bound to peer LDP Ident:
          10.1.100.2      10.1.12.2       10.1.24.2        10.2.100.2
```

Now, you can check the LDP neighbor table from P4, as shown in Example 10-32.

Example 10-32 *Check LDP Session Protection Capability*

```
P4# show mpls ldp neighbor 10.1.100.5
    Peer LDP Ident: 10.1.100.5:0; Local LDP Ident 10.1.100.4:0
        TCP connection: 10.1.100.5.16988 - 10.1.100.4.646
        State: Oper; Msgs sent/rcvd: 11696/11708; Downstream
        Up time: 1w0d
        LDP discovery sources:
```

```
        GigabitEthernet3, Src IP addr: 10.1.45.5
        Targeted Hello 10.1.100.4 -> 10.1.100.5, active, passive
    Addresses bound to peer LDP Ident:
        10.1.100.5      10.1.45.5       10.1.35.5       10.1.57.5
```

```
P4# show mpls ldp neighbor 10.1.100.5 detail | include Protection
    LDP Session Protection enabled, state: Ready
```

The other configuration alternative to enable session protection for LDP is to use the **mpls ldp discovery targeted-hello accept** command from the global configuration command, as Example 10-33 demonstrates.

Example 10-33 *Check LDP Session Protection Capability Details*

```
PE2(config)# mpls ldp discovery targeted-hello accept
```

```
P4# show mpls ldp neighbor 10.1.100.2 detail | include Protection
    LDP Session Protection enabled, state: Ready
```

Next, to verify the establishment of the targeted LDP session, you can simulate a failure on the IGP by disabling the interface GigabitEthernet2, as demonstrated in Example 10-34.

Example 10-34 *LDP Session Protection State*

```
PE2(config)# interface GigabitEthernet2
PE2(config-if)# shutdown
```

```
P4# show mpls ldp neighbor 10.1.100.2 detail | include Protection
    LDP Session Protection enabled, state: Protecting
```

The debug in Example 10-35 shows the state change for the LDP protection from Ready to Protecting, ensuring the feature is functional as desired.

Example 10-35 *Debug MPLS LDP Session Protection*

```
P4# debug mpls ldp session protection
LDP session protection events debugging is on
LDP SP: 10.1.100.2:0: last primary adj lost; starting session protection holdup
timer
LDP SP: 10.1.100.2:0: LDP session protection holdup timer started, 86400 seconds
LDP SP: 10.1.100.2:0: state change (Ready -> Protecting)
%LDP-5-SP: 10.1.100.2:0: session hold up initiated
```

You can control which LDP peer you want to enable session protection for by associating an access list with the command shown in Example 10-36.

Example 10-36 *Control MPLS LDP Session Protection*

```
P4(config)# access-list 1 permit host 10.1.100.5
P4(config)# mpls ldp session protection for 1
```

```
LDP SP: 10.1.100.2:0: disabling session protection: configuration change
LDP SP: 10.1.100.2:0: state change (Ready -> None)
```

```
P4# show mpls ldp neighbor 10.1.100.5 detail | begin LDP Session
      LDP Session Protection enabled, state: Ready
          acl: 1, duration: 86400 seconds
```

You also can control the period for which the session protection will be functional, as demonstrated in Example 10-37.

Example 10-37 *MPLS LDP Session Protection Timer*

```
P4(config)# mpls ldp session protection duration 1440
LDP SP: 10.1.100.2:0: enabling session protection: configuration change
LDP SP: 10.1.100.2:0: state change (None -> Incomplete)
LDP SP: 10.1.100.6:0: enabling session protection: configuration change
LDP SP: 10.1.100.6:0: state change (None -> Incomplete)
LDP SP: 10.1.100.2:0: state change (Incomplete -> Ready)

P4# show mpls ldp neighbor 10.1.100.5 detail | begin LDP Session
      LDP Session Protection enabled, state: Ready
          duration: 1440 seconds
      NSR: Not Ready
      Capabilities Sent:
        [ICCP (type 0x0405) MajVer 1 MinVer 0]
        [Dynamic Announcement (0x0506)]
        [mLDP Point-to-Multipoint (0x0508)]
        [mLDP Multipoint-to-Multipoint (0x0509)]
        [Typed Wildcard (0x050B)]
      Capabilities Received:
        [mLDP Point-to-Multipoint (0x0508)]
        [mLDP Multipoint-to-Multipoint (0x0509)]
        [Typed Wildcard (0x050B)]
```

MPLS LDP Session Authentication

LDP sessions are TCP sessions, which means they can be targeted by spoofed TCP segments. To make sure you protect these sessions from such attacks, you can configure authentication on these sessions. Example 10-38 shows the current established TCP sessions, and as you can see, port 646 associated with listed IP addresses clearly identifies these sessions as LDP sessions.

Example 10-38 *TCP Connections Verification*

```
PE2# show tcp brief
TCB          Local Address          Foreign Address        (state)
7F3D8895C6E8 10.1.100.2.646         10.1.100.3.37460       ESTAB
7F3D88A89580 10.1.100.2.646         10.1.100.4.11028       ESTAB
```

You can enable the enforcement of an LDP password to be configured by using the **mpls ldp password required** command, as demonstrated in Example 10-39.

Example 10-39 *MPLS LDP Neighbor Authentication*

```
PE2(config)# mpls ldp password required
ldp: Sent notif msg to 10.1.100.3:0 (pp 0x7F3D88A9AC40)
ldp: Sent notif msg to 10.1.100.3:0 (pp 0x7F3D88A9AC40)
ldp: Sent notif msg to 10.1.100.4:0 (pp 0x7F3D55B7C910)
ldp: Sent notif msg to 10.1.100.4:0 (pp 0x7F3D55B7C910)
%LDP-5-NBRCHG: LDP Neighbor 10.1.100.3:0 (2) is DOWN (Session's MD5 password changed)
%LDP-5-NBRCHG: LDP Neighbor 10.1.100.4:0 (1) is DOWN (Session's MD5 password changed)
%LDP-4-PWD: MD5 protection is required for peer 10.1.100.4:0, no password configured
```

As a result, all active LDP sessions will go down because you only enabled the command
from one end of the sessions. What you need to do is to enable a password for each session
individually, as demonstrated in Example 10-40 and confirmed in Example 10-41.

Example 10-40 *MPLS LDP Neighbor Authentication*

```
PE2(config)# mpls ldp neighbor 10.1.100.4 password SPCOR
P4(config)# mpls ldp neighbor 10.1.100.2 password SPCOR
%LDP-5-NBRCHG: LDP Neighbor 10.1.100.4:0 (1) is UP
```

After you have turned on authentication on both ends (P4 → PE2), you can see the authentication type marked as MD5, with the keyword required attached to the password field in
the **show mpls ldp neighbor detail** output, as shown in Example 10-41.

Example 10-41 *MPLS LDP Neighbor Detail Output*

```
P4# show mpls ldp neighbor detail
    Peer LDP Ident: 10.1.100.2:0; Local LDP Ident 10.1.100.4:0
        TCP connection: 10.1.100.2.646 - 10.1.100.4.49994; MD5 on
        Password: required, neighbor, in use
        State: Oper; Msgs sent/rcvd: 17/18; Downstream; Last TIB rev sent 44
        Up time: 00:00:56; UID: 12; Peer Id 0
        LDP discovery sources:
          GigabitEthernet1; Src IP addr: 10.1.24.2
            holdtime: 15000 ms, hello interval: 5000 ms
        Addresses bound to peer LDP Ident:
          10.1.100.2      10.1.12.2      10.1.24.2      10.1.23.2
        Peer holdtime: 180000 ms; KA interval: 60000 ms; Peer state: estab
```

You can specify what neighbors need to get authenticated by creating an access list matching the neighbor ID and then attaching it to a password, as demonstrated in Example 10-42.

Example 10-42 *Controlling LDP Authentication with an ACL and Password*

```
P4(config)# access-list 10 permit host 10.1.100.5
P4(config)# mpls ldp password option 1 for 10 SPCOR
%TCP-6-BADAUTH: No MD5 digest from 10.1.100.5(44634) to 10.1.100.4(646) tableid - 0
RP/0/0/CPU0:P5# configure terminal
```

```
RP/0/0/CPU0:P5(config)# mpls ldp neighbor 10.1.100.4:0 password clear SPCOR
RP/0/0/CPU0:P5(config)# commit
%LDP-5-NBRCHG: LDP Neighbor 10.1.100.5:0 (2) is UP
```

```
P4# show mpls ldp neighbor 10.1.100.5 detail
  Peer LDP Ident: 10.1.100.5:0; Local LDP Ident 10.1.100.4:0
    TCP connection: 10.1.100.5.53703 - 10.1.100.4.646; MD5 on
    Password: required, option 1, in use
    State: Oper; Msgs sent/rcvd: 19/19; Downstream; Last TIB rev sent 44
    Up time: 00:03:06; UID: 13; Peer Id 1
    LDP discovery sources:
      GigabitEthernet3; Src IP addr: 10.1.45.5
        holdtime: 15000 ms, hello interval: 5000 ms
    Addresses bound to peer LDP Ident:
      10.1.100.5      10.1.45.5       10.1.35.5      10.1.57.5
    Peer holdtime: 180000 ms; KA interval: 60000 ms; Peer state: estab
    NSR: Not Ready
    Capabilities Sent:
      [ICCP (type 0x0405) MajVer 1 MinVer 0]
      [Dynamic Announcement (0x0506)]
      [mLDP Point-to-Multipoint (0x0508)]
      [mLDP Multipoint-to-Multipoint (0x0509)]
      [Typed Wildcard (0x050B)]
    Capabilities Received:
      [mLDP Point-to-Multipoint (0x0508)]
      [mLDP Multipoint-to-Multipoint (0x0509)]
      [Typed Wildcard (0x050B)]
```

Let's now examine the same configuration statements from an IOS XR perspective by exploring a sample topology where (PE3(IOS XR) and P5(IOS XE)) are connected point-to-point with OSPF in place to ensure proper loopback-to-loopback reachability.

Turning on the same command used in Example 10-43 to enable LDP neighbor authentication, you can explore logging messages generated from PE3, informing you that you lack authentication for the established LDP session.

Example 10-43   *MPLS LDP Neighbor Authentication*

```
P5(config)# mpls ldp neighbor 10.1.100.3 password SPCOR
```

```
tcp[399]: %IP-TCP-3-NOAUTH : Authentication info not programmed for the packet
received from 10.1.100.5:42597 to 10.1.100.3:646
```

When you are examining the equivalent command from an IOS XR perspective, there are two notes to watch for. The first one is the LDP router ID when completing the command. When issuing the command on IOS XE, you simply place the IP address you identified for the LDP router ID process. Using IOS XR, you are asked to enter it as shown in the LDP neighbor details, as shown in Example 10-44.

Example 10-44 *MPLS LDP Identifier, IOS XR*

```
RP/0/0/CPU0:PE3# show mpls ldp neighbor
Peer LDP Identifier: 10.1.100.5:0

RP/0/0/CPU0:PE3(config)# mpls ldp neighbor 10.1.100.5:?
  <0-0>  Label Space Id of neighbor
```

The second aspect is the authentication options you have available for protecting the LDP session from an IOS XR perspective, as in Example 10-45.

Example 10-45 *MPLS LDP Authentication, IOS XR*

```
RP/0/0/CPU0:PE3(config)# mpls ldp neighbor 10.1.100.5:0 password ?
  clear      Specifies an UNENCRYPTED password will follow
  disable    Disables the global password from this neighbor
  encrypted  Specifies an ENCRYPTED password will follow

RP/0/0/CPU0:PE3(config)# mpls ldp neighbor 10.1.100.5:0 password SPCOR
```

You can choose the **clear** keyword, as in Example 10-46, and check for the relative **show** command.

Example 10-46 *MPLD LDP Protection Verification*

```
RP/0/0/CPU0:PE3# show mpls ldp neighbor 10.1.100.5:0 detail | include MD5
  TCP connection: 10.1.100.5:11107 - 10.1.100.3:646; MD5 on
```

MPLS LDP IGP Synchronization

Routing protocols play the main role for building the necessary underlying data plane for LDP to operate properly and distribute functional labels that will ensure the traffic path will follow the unidirectional LSP. This means that the two protocols—IGP and LDP—will operate synchronously to maintain end-to-end connectivity over a labeled path.

If the LDP fails for some reason over any segment along the labeled switched path (LSP), IGP will still report the necessary route to follow to maintain end-to-end connection between desired elements; however, the traffic mostly will follow a new unlabeled path that ultimately will not serve the intended MPLS operation for traffic transportation.

Recall from the previous sections that we have altered the OSPF cost to make the path through PE2 → P4 → PE6 → PE7 the preferred path, and this can be shown by checking the routing table output for that specific route (which, in this example, is the PE7 loopback 0 interface: 10.1.100.7/32). Example 10-47 validates the insertion of PE7 loopback address 10.1.100.7/32 in PE2 RIB.

Example 10-47 *Routing Table Output*

```
PE2# show ip route 10.1.100.7 255.255.255.255
Routing entry for 10.1.100.7/32
  Known via "ospf 1", distance 110, metric 4, type intra area
  Last update from 10.1.24.4 on GigabitEthernet2, 3d23h ago
```

```
Routing Descriptor Blocks:
* 10.1.24.4, from 10.1.100.7, 3d23h ago, via GigabitEthernet2
    Route metric is 4, traffic share count is 1
```

Example 10-48 validates the label assignment for PE7 loopback 0 address 10.1.100.7/32, the outgoing interface to be used by PE2 to reach this destination (PE7 loopback 0 address), and the next hop to use for reaching it.

Example 10-48 *Specific Prefix LFIB Output*

```
PE2# show mpls forwarding-table 10.1.100.7
Local       Outgoing    Prefix          Bytes Label   Outgoing    Next Hop
Label       Label       or Tunnel Id    Switched      interface
209         408         10.1.100.7/32      0           Gi2         10.1.24.4
```

Figure 10-13 shows the primary LSP to be used for end-to-end traffic (because we manipulated the IGP cost) as well as the secondary/backup path in case of failures.

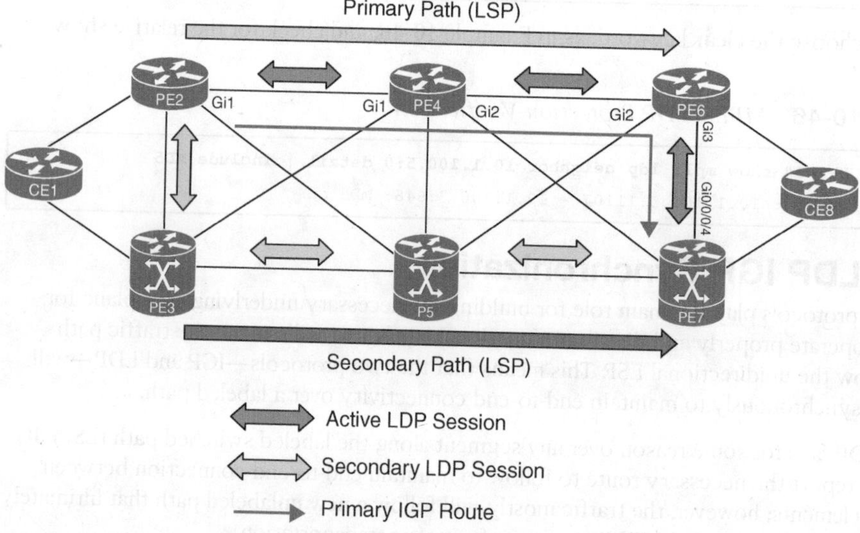

Figure 10-13   *MPLS LDP IGP Synchronization*

You can enable the MPLS LDP sync feature on the segment between PE2 and PE4. The command takes place under the OSPF routing process, as Example 10-49 demonstrates.

Example 10-49   *IOS MPLS LDP IGP Synchronization Configuration*

```
PE2(config)# router ospf 1
PE2(config-router)# mpls ldp sync
```

This command will enable the feature (MPLS LDP IGP synchronization) on all OSPF-speaking interfaces, as confirmed by the output in Example 10-50.

Example 10-50 *LDP IGP Synchronization Verification*

```
PE2# show mpls ldp igp sync
   GigabitEthernet2:
        LDP configured; LDP-IGP Synchronization enabled.
        Sync status: sync achieved; peer reachable.
        Sync delay time: 0 seconds (0 seconds left)
        IGP holddown time: infinite.
        Peer LDP Ident: 10.1.100.4:0
        IGP enabled: OSPF 1
   GigabitEthernet3:
        LDP configured; LDP-IGP Synchronization enabled.
        Sync status: sync achieved; peer reachable.
        Sync delay time: 0 seconds (0 seconds left)
        IGP holddown time: infinite.
        Peer LDP Ident: 10.1.100.3:0
        IGP enabled: OSPF 1
```

You can specifically disable the feature from interface-level configuration mode by using the
no mpls ldp igp sync command, which will override the global command configured under
the OSPF process, as demonstrated in Example 10-51.

Example 10-51 *LDP IGP Synchronization Verification*

```
PE2(config)# interface gigabitEthernet 3
PE2(config-if)# no mpls ldp igp sync

PE2# show mpls ldp igp sync
   GigabitEthernet2:
        LDP configured; LDP-IGP Synchronization enabled.
        Sync status: sync achieved; peer reachable.
        Sync delay time: 0 seconds (0 seconds left)
        IGP holddown time: infinite.
        Peer LDP Ident: 10.1.100.4:0
        IGP enabled: OSPF 1
   GigabitEthernet3:
        LDP configured; LDP-IGP Synchronization not enabled.
```

The command is similar using IOS XR software, as demonstrated in Example 10-52.

Example 10-52 *IOS XR MPLS LDP IGP Synchronization Configuration*

```
RP/0/0/CPU0:PE3(config)# router ospf 1
RP/0/0/CPU0:PE3(config-ospf)# area 0
RP/0/0/CPU0:PE3(config-ospf-ar)# mpls ldp sync
RP/0/0/CPU0:PE3(config-ospf-ar)# commit
```

```
RP/0/0/CPU0:PE3# show mpls ldp igp sync
GigabitEthernet0/0/0/3:
  VRF: 'default' (0x60000000)
  Sync delay: Disabled
  Sync status: Ready
    Peers:
      10.1.100.5:0
GigabitEthernet0/0/0/4:
  VRF: 'default' (0x60000000)
  Sync delay: Disabled
  Sync status: Ready
    Peers:
      10.1.100.2:0
```

Even if you removed the command from interface configuration mode, the command would not show explicitly under the interface because it will be cloned from the previous global configuration command. Example 10-53 demonstrates.

Example 10-53 *LDP IGP Synchronization Verification*

```
PE2(config)# interface gigabitEthernet 3
PE2(config-if)# no mpls ldp igp sync

PE2# show running-config interface GigabitEthernet3
interface GigabitEthernet3
 ip address 10.1.23.2 255.255.255.0
 ip ospf network point-to-point
 ip ospf cost 10
 mpls ip
```

Before testing the feature functionality (altering the operation LDP session), you can shut down the interface (which is used by the CEF table for forwarding) to check the alternative path, as Example 10-54 demonstrates.

Example 10-54 *Interface Shutdown Command*

```
PE2(config)# interface GigabitEthernet2
PE2(config-if)# shutdown
```

As expected, the alternative path will use PE3 as the next hop to reach the PE7 loopback 0 network, as Example 10-55 demonstrates.

Example 10-55   *RIB and Traceroute Verification Outputs*

```
PE2# show ip route 10.1.100.7 255.255.255.255
Routing entry for 10.1.100.7/32
  Known via "ospf 1", distance 110, metric 31, type intra area
  Last update from 10.1.23.3 on GigabitEthernet3, 00:00:17 ago
  Routing Descriptor Blocks:
  * 10.1.23.3, from 10.1.100.7, 00:00:17 ago, via GigabitEthernet3
      Route metric is 31, traffic share count is 1

PE2# traceroute 10.1.100.7 numeric
VRF info: (vrf in name/id, vrf out name/id)
  1 10.1.23.3 [MPLS: Label 16309 Exp 0] 10 msec 9 msec 11 msec
  2 10.1.35.5 [MPLS: Label 16509 Exp 0] 10 msec 8 msec 8 msec
  3 10.1.57.7 9 msec *  11 msec
```

Now, if you turned off MPLS LDP on the interface going from PE2 to P4, the alternative path will take place going through PE3, as the output in Example 10-56 confirms.

Example 10-56   *RIB Table Output*

```
PE2# show ip route 10.1.100.7 255.255.255.255
Routing entry for 10.1.100.7/32
  Known via "ospf 1", distance 110, metric 31, type intra area
  Last update from 10.1.23.3 on GigabitEthernet3, 00:00:08 ago
  Routing Descriptor Blocks:
  * 10.1.23.3, from 10.1.100.7, 00:00:08 ago, via GigabitEthernet3
      Route metric is 31, traffic share count is 1
```

To see the actual effect of the feature, you can turn on the current active path through PE3 to see what change is taking place from the PE2 perspective, as demonstrated in Example 10-57.

Example 10-57   *RIB Table Output*

```
PE2# show ip route 10.1.100.7 255.255.255.255
Routing entry for 10.1.100.7/32
  Known via "ospf 1", distance 110, metric 65538, type intra area
  Last update from 10.1.24.4 on GigabitEthernet2, 00:00:01 ago
  Routing Descriptor Blocks:
  * 10.1.24.4, from 10.1.100.7, 00:00:01 ago, via GigabitEthernet2
      Route metric is 65538, traffic share count is 1
```

As you can see, the metric is high, which means it is extremely less desirable for the unlabeled path to be used under the status of LDP operation. Figure 10-14 illustrates.

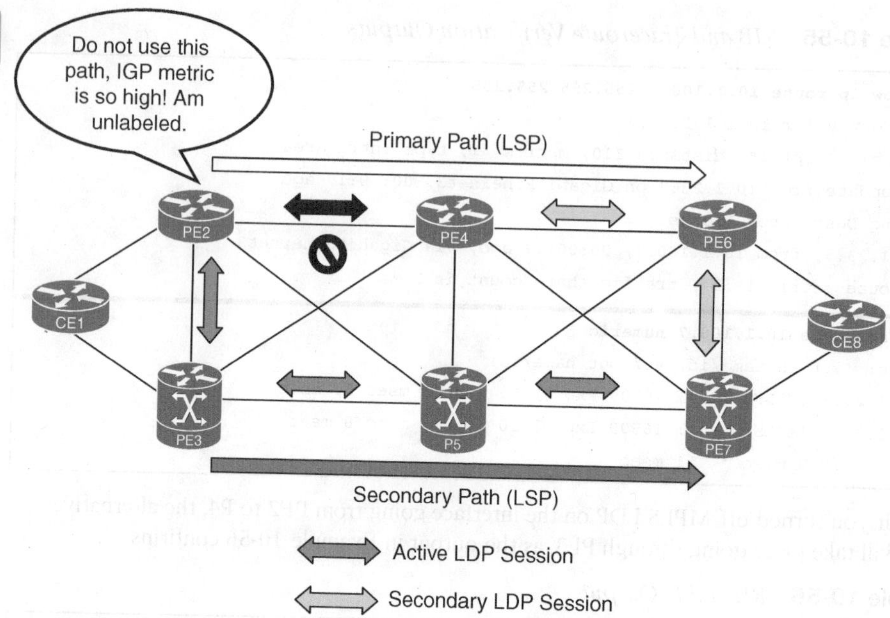

Figure 10-14 *MPLS LDP IGP Synchronization Traffic Redirection*

MPLS OAM

MPLS **Operation, Administration, and Maintenance (OAM)** helps service providers to maintain operationality and functionality of label switched paths to quickly isolate forwarding issues and increase fault detection rate. Briefly, these tools are used for reactive and proactive troubleshooting MPLS core environments.

The two main techniques of concern are

- **MPLS LSP ping:** Used for testing end-to-end connectivity and validating reachability of LDP-signaled LSPs. MPLS LSP ping uses echo request and echo reply packets for LSP validation, which uses UDP packets with both the source and destination port set to 3503.

- **MPLS LSP trace:** Used for hop-by-hop tracing of MPLS-enabled paths and path tracing for LDP-signaled LSPs. MPLS LSP trace uses echo request and echo reply packets for LSP validation, which uses UDP packets with both the source and destination port set to 3503.

Let's start with verifying MPLS LSP ping and its associated statistics. Let's use the active LSP (which we used mainly in the previous configuration examples: PE2 → P4 → PE6 → PE7.)

Before we start going into the statistics, let's start with the **ping mpls ipv4 10.1.100.7/32** command (the LSP ping starts from PE2 [IOS XE] and ends at PE7 [IOS XR]). Example 10-58 demonstrates.

Example 10-58 *MPLS ping Command*

```
PE2# ping mpls ipv4 10.1.100.7/32
Sending 5, 72-byte MPLS Echos to 10.1.100.7/32,
     timeout is 2 seconds, send interval is 0 msec:
Codes: '!' - success, 'Q' - request not sent, '.' - timeout,
  'L' - labeled output interface, 'B' - unlabeled output interface,
  'D' - DS Map mismatch, 'F' - no FEC mapping, 'f' - FEC mismatch,
  'M' - malformed request, 'm' - unsupported tlvs, 'N' - no label entry,
  'P' - no rx intf label prot, 'p' - premature termination of LSP,
  'R' - transit router, 'I' - unknown upstream index,
  'l' - Label switched with FEC change, 'd' - see DDMAP for return code,
  'X' - unknown return code, 'x' - return code 0
Type escape sequence to abort.
.....
Success rate is 0 percent (0/5)
 Total Time Elapsed 9520 ms
```

The output reveals that MPLS ping is not successful. The reason is that MPLS OAM should
be enabled globally on the IOS XR device. Example 10-59 shows how to enable this feature
on IOS XR–enabled devices.

Example 10-59 *MPLS OAM on IOS XR*

```
RP/0/0/CPU0:PE7(config)# mpls oam
RP/0/0/CPU0:PE7(config)# commit
```

```
PE2# ping mpls ipv4 10.1.100.7 255.255.255.255
Sending 5, 72-byte MPLS Echos to 10.1.100.7/32,
     timeout is 2 seconds, send interval is 0 msec:
Codes: '!' - success, 'Q' - request not sent, '.' - timeout,
  'L' - labeled output interface, 'B' - unlabeled output interface,
  'D' - DS Map mismatch, 'F' - no FEC mapping, 'f' - FEC mismatch,
  'M' - malformed request, 'm' - unsupported tlvs, 'N' - no label entry,
  'P' - no rx intf label prot, 'p' - premature termination of LSP,
  'R' - transit router, 'I' - unknown upstream index,
  'l' - Label switched with FEC change, 'd' - see DDMAP for return code,
  'X' - unknown return code, 'x' - return code 0
Type escape sequence to abort.
!!!!!
Success rate is 100 percent (5/5), round-trip min/avg/max = 5/5/5 ms
 Total Time Elapsed 38 ms
```

```
PE2# show mpls oam echo statistics summary
Cisco TLV version: RFC 4379 Compliant
Echo Requests: sent (5)/received (0)/timedout (0)/unsent (0)
Echo Replies: sent (0)/received (5)/unsent (0)
```

In the same way, you can issue the trace command associated with the MPLS keyword and analyze the output in Example 10-60.

Example 10-60   *MPLS Trace Output*

```
PE2# traceroute mpls ipv4 10.1.100.7/32
Tracing MPLS Label Switched Path to 10.1.100.7/32, timeout is 2 seconds

Codes: '!' - success, 'Q' - request not sent, '.' - timeout,
  'L' - labeled output interface, 'B' - unlabeled output interface,
  'D' - DS Map mismatch, 'F' - no FEC mapping, 'f' - FEC mismatch,
  'M' - malformed request, 'm' - unsupported tlvs, 'N' - no label entry,
  'P' - no rx intf label prot, 'p' - premature termination of LSP,
  'R' - transit router, 'I' - unknown upstream index,
  'l' - Label switched with FEC change, 'd' - see DDMAP for return code,
  'X' - unknown return code, 'x' - return code 0
Type escape sequence to abort.
  0 10.1.24.2 MRU 1500 [Labels: 408 Exp: 0]
L 1 10.1.24.4 MRU 1500 [Labels: 609 Exp: 0] 14 ms
L 2 10.1.46.6 MRU 1500 [Labels: implicit-null Exp: 0] 331 ms
! 3 10.1.67.7 6 ms
```

Example 10-61 introduces an error within the LSP by removing MPLS forwarding on a peer link to check the implication on the output in Example 10-60.

Example 10-61   *MPLS Ping Verification*

```
P4(config)# interface GigabitEthernet2
P4(config-if)# no mpls ip

PE2# traceroute mpls ipv4 10.1.100.7/32
Tracing MPLS Label Switched Path to 10.1.100.7/32, timeout is 2 seconds
Codes: '!' - success, 'Q' - request not sent, '.' - timeout,
  'L' - labeled output interface, 'B' - unlabeled output interface,
  'D' - DS Map mismatch, 'F' - no FEC mapping, 'f' - FEC mismatch,
  'M' - malformed request, 'm' - unsupported tlvs, 'N' - no label entry,
  'P' - no rx intf label prot, 'p' - premature termination of LSP,
  'R' - transit router, 'I' - unknown upstream index,
  'l' - Label switched with FEC change, 'd' - see DDMAP for return code,
  'X' - unknown return code, 'x' - return code 0

Type escape sequence to abort.
  0 10.1.24.2 MRU 1500 [Labels: 408 Exp: 0]
p 1 10.1.24.4 14 ms
. 2 *
. 3 *
B 4 10.1.24.4 MRU 1500 [No Label] 5 ms
B 5 10.1.24.4 MRU 1500 [No Label] 4 ms
B 6 10.1.24.4 MRU 1500 [No Label] 4 ms
! Output omitted for brevity
```

For LSP/Ping packets used in MPLS OAM to be treated as control packets, the same label stack is used as the one used for the target LSP, which will cause the echo to be switched in band of the LSP (see Figure 10-15). The destination address (DA) of echo request is 127.0.0.0/8 with the source address (SA) being the IP address of the originating IP packet. The reason is to be able to punt the packet for local processing and force the packet to be processed by the route processor at the egress router.

NOTE *Punt a packet* refers to a situation in which a network device is unable to process a packet normally (from a forwarding plane perspective) and sends it to the control plane or CPU for processing. This could take place in cases such as fragmentation or encryption.

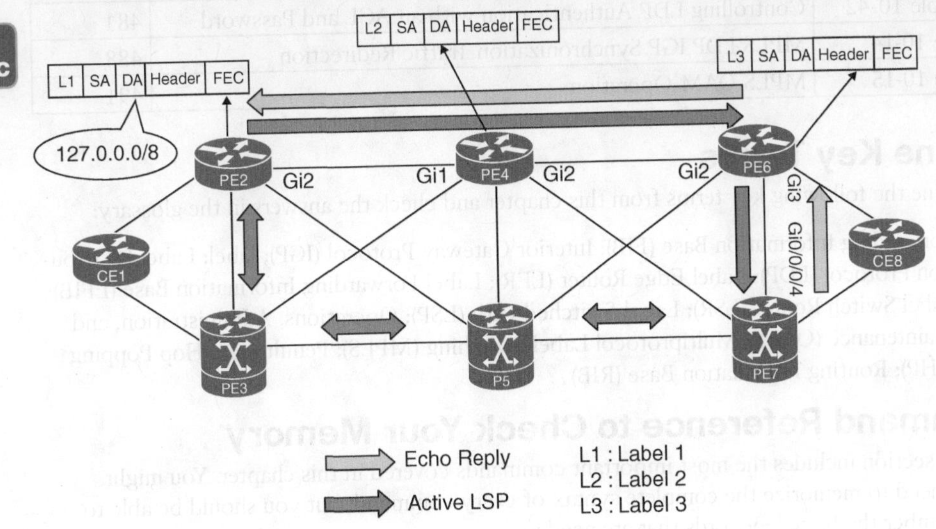

Figure 10-15 *MPLS OAM Operation*

NOTE The destination address is set to 127.0.0.0/8 address so that the packet will not be dropped in case of any LSP failure. The echo reply destination address is copied from the echo request's source address, and it is returned as IP or MPLS traffic.

Exam Preparation Tasks

As mentioned in the section "How to Use This Book" in the Introduction, you have a few choices for exam preparation: the exercises here, Chapter 23, "Final Preparation," and the exam simulation questions in the Pearson Test Prep Software Online.

Review All Key Topics

Review the most important topics in this chapter, noted with the Key Topic icon in the margin of the page. Table 10-4 lists a reference of these key topics and the page numbers on which each is found.

Table 10-4 Key Topics for Chapter 10

Key Topic Element	Description	Page Number
Section	MPLS Label Operations	456
Figure 10-5	MPLS Label Operations	458
Paragraph	LDP neighborship establishment	460
Table 10-2	Routing and Forwarding Tables	462
Example 10-15	MPLS LDP Label Range Configuration	467
Paragraph	Penultimate Hop Popping (PHP)	473
Figure 10-11	MPLS Tables Interaction	477
Example 10-42	Controlling LDP Authentication with an ACL and Password	481
Figure 10-14	MPLS LDP IGP Synchronization Traffic Redirection	488
Figure 10-15	MPLS OAM Operation	491

Define Key Terms

Define the following key terms from this chapter and check the answers in the glossary:

Forwarding Information Base (FIB); Interior Gateway Protocol (IGP); label; Label Distribution Protocol (LDP); Label Edge Router (LER); Label Forwarding Information Base (LFIB); Label Switch Router (LSR); Label-Switched Path (LSP); Operations, Administration, and Maintenance (OAM); Multiprotocol Label Switching (MPLS); Penultimate Hop Popping (PHP); Routing Information Base (RIB)

Command Reference to Check Your Memory

This section includes the most important commands covered in this chapter. You might not need to memorize the complete syntax of every command, but you should be able to remember the basic keywords that are needed.

To test your memory of the commands, cover the right side of Table 10-5 with a piece of paper, read the description on the left side, and then see how much of the command you can remember.

The SPCOR 350-501 exam focuses on practical, hands-on skills that are used by networking professionals. Therefore, you should be able to identify the commands needed to configure and test. Note that not all commands are fully covered in the chapter, but their presence in the following table should lead you to investigate them further to understand this technology.

Table 10-5 MPLS Commands

Task	Command Syntax
Enable Multiprotocol Label Switching (MPLS) forwarding of IPv4 and IPv6 packets from interface level	**mpls ip**
Globally enable LDP on every interface associated with an IGP instance	**mpls ldp autoconfig [area]** *area ID*

Task	Command Syntax
Reconfigure the range used for dynamically assigned labels	**mpls label range** *minimum maximum*
Protect all LDP sessions	**mpls ldp session protection**
Configure the router to accept targeted hello requests coming from other router	**mpls ldp discovery targeted-hello accept**
Configure LDP authentication (clear text, encrypted)	**mpls ldp neighbor** *ip-address* **password** {0 | 7} *password*
Display the contents of the MPLS Label Forwarding Information Base (LFIB)	**show mpls forwarding-table**
Display information about all LDP neighbors in the entire routing domain	**show mpls ldp neighbors**
Display LDP-IGP synchronization information	**show mpls ldp igp sync**

Review Questions

As a part of the review, we encourage you to provide *a single-sentence answer* (keep your answers as short as possible) to the following questions. If you struggle to complete this in a single sentence, this answer may indicate a lack of clarity or reveal gaps in your understanding. We have constructed these questions to help you consolidate this chapter's information and extract the essence of the covered content.

The answers to these questions appear in Appendix A. For more practice with exam format questions, use the Pearson Test Prep Software Online.

1. What is the actual impact of advertising a /24 mask for a loopback interface in a network running OSPF from an LDP operation perspective?

2. How does PhP work, and what design aspect does it add to the network?

3. How does implicit null interact with QoS?

Bibliography

L. Andersson, I. Minei, and B. Thomas, eds. RFC 5036, *LDP Specification*, IETF, https://datatracker.ietf.org/doc/html/rfc5036, October 2007.

Designing IP VPNs: https://www.ciscolive.com/c/dam/r/ciscolive/global-event/docs/2022/pdf/BRKMPL-2102.pdf

Introduction to MPLS: https://www.ciscolive.com/c/dam/r/ciscolive/us/docs/2020/pdf/DGTL-BRKMPL-1100.pdf

M. Leelanivas and Y. Rekhter. RFC 3478, *Graceful Restart Mechanism for Label Distribution Protocol*, IETF, https://datatracker.ietf.org/doc/html/rfc3478, February 2003.

MPLS Command Reference: https://www.cisco.com/c/en/us/td/docs/optical/cpt/r9_3/command/reference/cpt93_cr/cpt93_cr_chapter_010.html#wp1254011620.

E. Rosen, D. Tappan, and G. Fedorkow. RFC 3032, *MPLS Label Stack Encoding*, IETF, https://datatracker.ietf.org/doc/html/rfc3032, January 2001.

CHAPTER 11

MPLS L2VPNs

This chapter covers the following exam topics:

1.1 Describe service provider architectures

- 1.1.a Core architectures (Metro Ethernet, MPLS, unified MPLS, SR, SRTE, SRv6)

4.1 Describe VPN services

- 4.1.a EVPN

4.2 Configure L2VPN and Carrier Ethernet

- 4.2.a Ethernet services (E-Line, E-Tree, E-Access, E-LAN)

- 4.2.b IEEE 802.1ad, IEEE 802.1ah, and ITU G.8032

- 4.2.c Ethernet OAM

- 4.2.d VLAN tag manipulation

Layer 2 MPLS virtual private networks provide a flexible and scalable solution for extending Layer 2 connectivity between multiple sites over an MPLS-enabled service provider network. They offer the benefits of a traditional LAN environment while leveraging the capabilities and features of MPLS for efficient and reliable service delivery in addition to the direct point-to-point connectivity.

"Do I Know This Already?" Quiz

The "Do I Know This Already?" quiz allows you to assess whether you should read this entire chapter thoroughly or jump to the "Exam Preparation Tasks" section. If you are in doubt about your answers to these questions or your own assessment of your knowledge of the topics, read the entire chapter. Table 11-1 lists the major headings in this chapter and their corresponding "Do I Know This Already?" quiz questions. You can find the answers in Appendix A, "Answers to the 'Do I Know This Already?' Quizzes and Review Questions."

Table 11-1 "Do I Know This Already?" Section-to-Question Mapping

Foundation Topics Section	Questions
Metro Ethernet	1
MPLS AToM	2
VPLS	3, 4
Provider Bridges (802.1ad)	5
EVPN	6

1. Which Carrier Ethernet service provides multipoint-to-multipoint service?

    a.   E-Line

    b.   E-LAN

    c.   E-Tree

    d.   E-Access

2. What is the purpose of the inner label assigned to packets in MPLS AToM terminology?

    a.   Transport label

    b.   Pseudowire label

    c.   Intermediate P Loopback IP address

    d.   Preserved for QoS along the LSP

3. In VPLS architecture, which term represents data encapsulation?

    a.   Virtual Forwarding Instance (VFI)

    b.   Attachment circuit (AC)

    c.   Virtual circuit (VC)

    d.   Bridge domain

4. In VPLS architecture, the tunnel label is distributed by means of which protocols? (Choose two.)

    a.   LDP

    b.   Targeted LDP

    c.   BGP

    d.   RSVP

5. In 802.1ad, which of the following is not a valid port type?

    a.   C-UNI

    b.   S-UNI

    c.   S-NNI

    d.   NNI

6. Which of the following statements about EVPN is true in regards to functionality?

    a.   EVPN uses BGP as the control plane protocol to exchange MAC address reachability information between provider edge routers.

    b.   EVPN uses BGP as the control plane protocol to exchange IP address reachability information between provider edge routers.

    c.   EVPN uses BGP as the signaling protocol to exchange IP address reachability information between provider edge routers.

    d.   EVPN uses LDP as the control plane protocol to exchange MAC address reachability information between provider edge routers.

Foundation Topics

Metro Ethernet

In the early days of Ethernet's development, it was primarily confined to local area network (LAN) deployments, which imposed restrictions on both bandwidth and transmission distances. As standards evolved and technology advanced, carriers and providers began incorporating Ethernet into their networks for metropolitan area networks (MANs) and wide area networks (WANs). This high-capacity Ethernet is called *carrier Ethernet*.

In Metro Ethernet technology, there are four different service types:

- Ethernet Line Services (E-Line)

- Ethernet LAN Services (E-LAN)

- Ethernet Tree Services (E-Tree)

- Ethernet Access Services (E-Access)

The deployment can support either a single circuit per interface or multiple circuits per interface. Table 11-2 outlines the available options from a termination perspective (interface versus VLAN).

Table 11-2   Metro Ethernet Services Deployment

Service	Interface Based	VLAN Based
E-Line	Ethernet Private Line (EPL)	Ethernet Virtual Private Line (EVPL)
E-LAN	Ethernet Private LAN (EP-LAN)	Ethernet Virtual Private LAN (EVP-LAN)
E-Tree	Ethernet Private Tree (EP-Tree)	Ethernet Virtual Private Tree (EVP-Tree)
E-Access	Access Ethernet Private Line (Access EPL)	Access Ethernet Virtual Private Line (Access EVPL)

E-Line (Ethernet Line Services)

E-Line service, often referred to as Ethernet Line or Ethernet Virtual Private Line (EVPL), is a type of Ethernet service that establishes a point-to-point Ethernet connection between two locations; exactly two user network interfaces (UNIs) can communicate with each other. This service is commonly used to provide a dedicated and transparent communication channel between different sites. It uses Ethernet, thus providing a familiar and widely used networking protocol and making it compatible with various types of Ethernet-enabled devices. Its transparent nature allows customers to run any networking protocol over established Ethernet connections. Supporting high-bandwidth speeds makes it suitable for applications that require significant data transfer rates. Figure 11-1 shows basic connectivity for an E-Line service for which you can use one Ethernet Virtual Circuit (EVC) per interface

(Ethernet Private Line [EPL]), or you can use more than one EVC where you need 802.1q to jump in to allow for multiple EVCs to operate simultaneously (Ethernet Virtual Private Line [EVPL]).

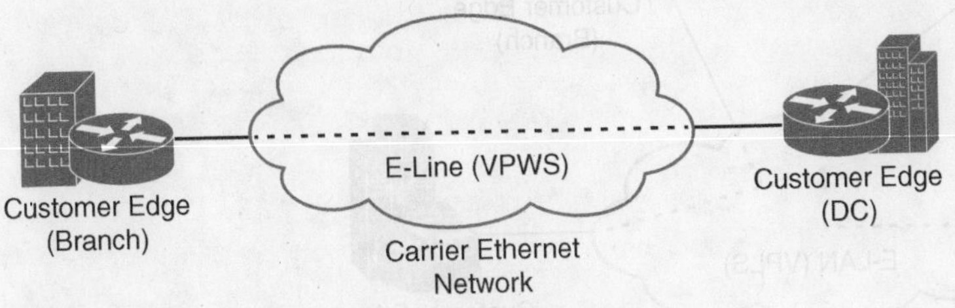

Figure 11-1 *Ethernet Private Line (E-Line)*

E-LAN (Ethernet LAN Services)

In Figure 11-2, we expand our network and introduce a couple more routers in the service provider network. We also add another site. In this offering, the EVC connects all sites with a full-mesh interconnect because they share the same local area network. Distance-wise, these sites long ago exhausted the limits of LAN Ethernet reach, but this service removes this physical limitation. Sometimes, it helps to think of the service provider's network as one giant switch that provides multipoint-to-multipoint services. If a service provider is running **Multiprotocol Label Switching (MPLS)**, this EVC would be referred to as a Virtual Private LAN Service (VPLS), which is created on several vendors, such as Cisco and Juniper, with bridge domains.

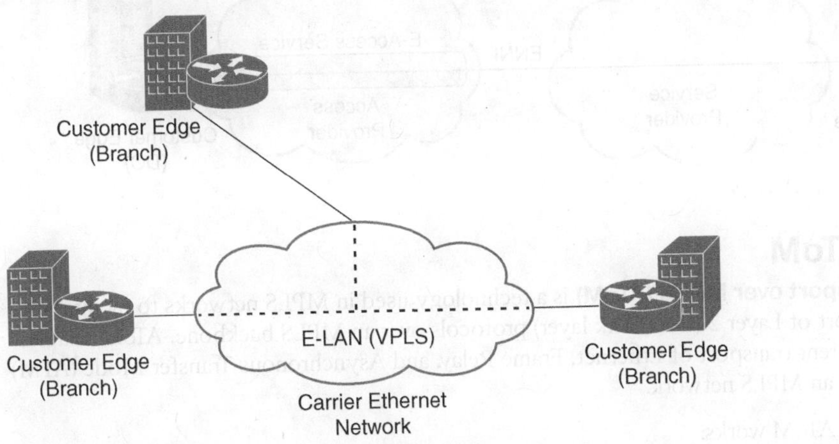

Figure 11-2 *Ethernet LAN Services (E-LAN)*

E-Tree (Ethernet Tree Services)

E-Tree services are likely to connect multiple sites to the central site (point-to-multipoint) to access shared resources at that site. You can think of this topology as like hub-and-spoke, where the spokes can still communicate with each other, but not directly, only going through the central site. Figure 11-3 shows a basic topology that reflects the connectivity model for the point-to-multipoint service provided by E-Tree.

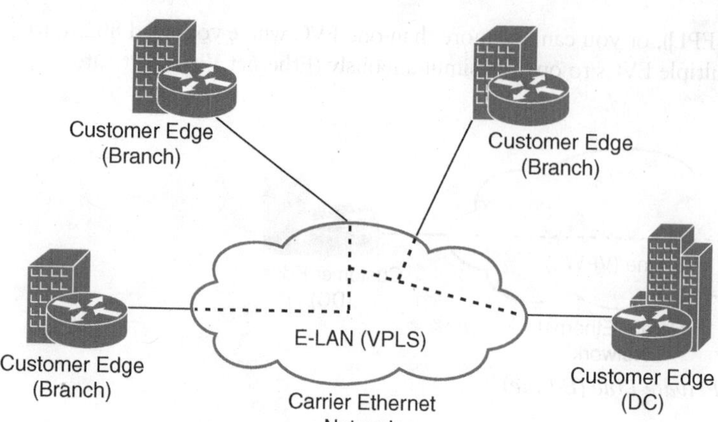

Figure 11-3 *Ethernet Tree Services (E-Tree)*

E-Access

E-Access is a service composed of a data tunnel that allows transport of an EVC across an access provider's network to reach an out-of-franchise subscriber location. This configuration uses the help of the External Network to Network Interface (ENNI), as shown in Figure 11-4, which represents a reference point as a boundary between two operators acting as separate administrative domains.

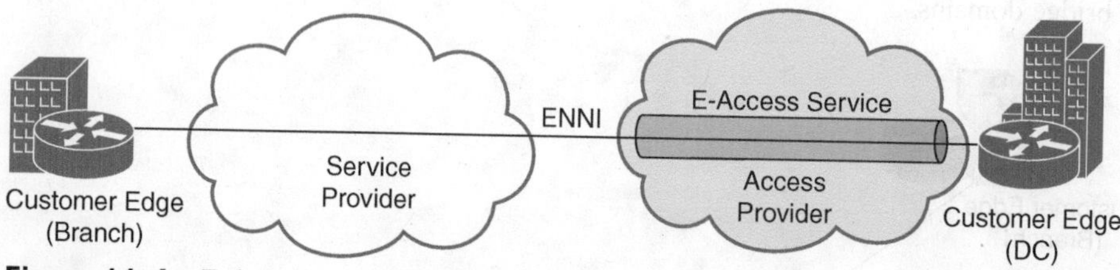

Figure 11-4 *E-Access*

MPLS AToM

Any Transport over MPLS (AToM) is a technology used in MPLS networks to facilitate the transport of Layer 2 (Data Link layer) protocols over an MPLS backbone. AToM enables the transparent transport of Ethernet, Frame Relay, and Asynchronous Transfer Mode (ATM) traffic over an MPLS network.

Here's how AToM works:

1. **Pseudowire Emulation:** AToM employs the concept of pseudowires to emulate the behavior of a point-to-point connection between two endpoints over the MPLS network. A pseudowire is essentially a logical connection that emulates the characteristics of a specific Layer 2 protocol.

2. **Label Distribution:** Label distribution protocols, such as **Label Distribution Protocol (LDP)** or Resource Reservation Protocol-Traffic Engineering (RSVP-TE), are used to distribute labels between MPLS routers. These protocols ensure that all routers in the MPLS network have the necessary label bindings to forward traffic along the correct LSPs.

3. **Label Stack:** When traffic enters the MPLS network, the ingress router assigns two labels to the packet: one for the outer MPLS label and another for the pseudowire label. The outer label is used for MPLS forwarding within the network, while the inner label is used for pseudowire emulation.

4. **Label Switching:** In an MPLS network, routers use labels to forward packets based on predetermined paths called label-switched paths (LSPs). Each packet entering the MPLS network is assigned a label by the ingress router.

5. **Forwarding and Encapsulation:** As traffic traverses the MPLS network, routers swap the outer MPLS labels based on the forwarding table entries. When the traffic reaches the egress router, the outer MPLS label is removed, and the packet is forwarded based on the inner pseudowire label. The egress router then strips off the pseudowire label and forwards the original Layer 2 frame to its destination.

AToM is commonly used in service provider networks to provide Layer 2 VPN services to customers. It allows service providers to offer point-to-point and point-to-multipoint Layer 2 connectivity across their MPLS networks, enabling customers to seamlessly extend their Layer 2 networks over wide distances. This capability is particularly useful for enterprises with multiple branch locations or for connecting remote data centers. Figure 11-5 shows the different encapsulation types supported to be transported over the point-to-point virtual Layer 2 connection.

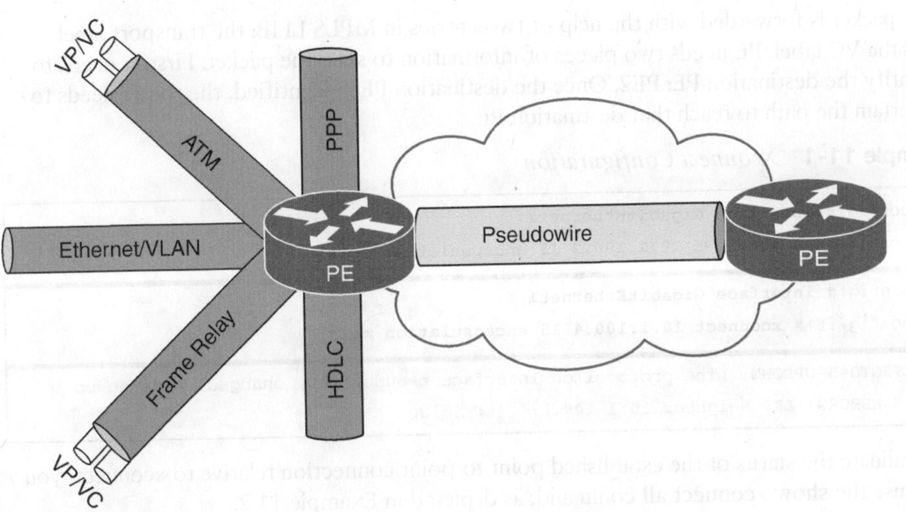

Figure 11-5 *AToM*

We use Figure 11-6 to explain how AToM works; here, we use Ethernet as the transport type between CE and PE.

Example 11-1 lists the basic command to establish LDP neighborship through the establishment of a Layer 2 connection (point-to-point) using the **xconnect** *peer-ip-address vc-id* **encapsulation mpls** [*pw-type*] command.

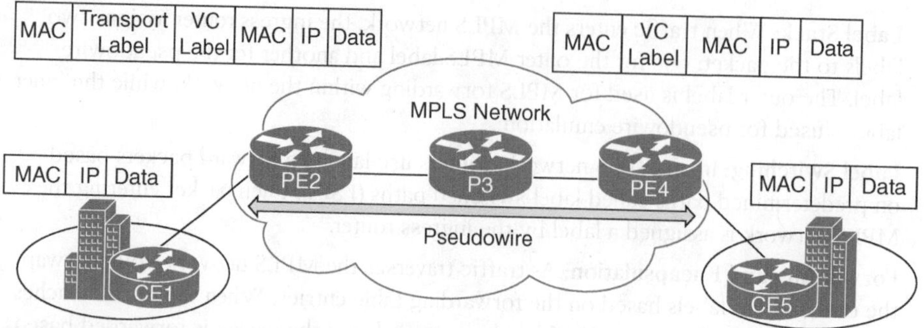

Figure 11-6 *AToM Example*

At CE1, the packet typically includes IP/MAC and Data fields, with the possibility of also containing an 802.1Q field. When the packet reaches PE2 (where the xconnect is configured), two more labels are added to the original packet: the transport label and the virtual circuit (VC) label. The transport label is used to switch the packet in the MPLS network. The VC label is used when the packet reaches destination PE. At the same time, a new Layer 2 (MAC address) header is added to the packet to be used for hop-to-hop forwarding. When the packet moves from the P3 router to the PE2 router, MPLS penultimate hop popping (PHP) occurs, and the transport label is removed from the packet. However, the VC label remains on the packet that is used by PE2 to identify the virtual circuit (ckt) for which the packet is destined.

The packet is forwarded with the help of two entries in MPLS LFIB: the transport label and the VC label. PE needs two pieces of information to send the packet. First, it needs to identify the destination PE: PE2. Once the destination PE is identified, the router needs to ascertain the path to reach that destination PE.

Example 11-1 *Xconnect Configuration*

```
PE4(config)# interface GigabitEthernet2
PE4(config-if)# xconnect 10.1.100.2 15 encapsulation mpls

PE2(config)# interface GigabitEthernet1
PE2(config-if)# xconnect 10.1.100.4 15 encapsulation mpls

%LINEPROTO-5-UPDOWN: Line protocol on Interface pseudowire0, changed state to up
%LDP-5-NBRCHG: LDP Neighbor 10.1.100.2:0 (2) is Up
```

To validate the status of the established point-to-point connection relative to xconnect, you can use the **show xconnect all** command, as depicted in Example 11-2.

Example 11-2 *VPWS Validation*

```
PE4# show xconnect all
Legend:    XC ST=Xconnect State  S1=Segment1 State  S2=Segment2 State
  UP=Up        DN=Down           AD=Admin Down      IA=Inactive
  SB=Standby  HS=Hot Standby     RV=Recovering      NH=No Hardware
XC ST   Segment 1                          S1 Segment 2                       S2
------+----------------------------------+--+----------------------------------+--
UP pri   ac Gi2:8(Ethernet)                 UP mpls 10.1.100.2:15              UP
```

```
PE4# show mpls ldp neighbor
    Peer LDP Ident: 10.1.100.3:0; Local LDP Ident 10.1.100.4:0
        TCP connection: 10.1.100.3.646 - 10.1.100.4.27329
        State: Oper; Msgs sent/rcvd: 12159/12142; Downstream
        Up time: 1w0d
        LDP discovery sources:
            GigabitEthernet1, Src IP addr: 10.1.34.3
        Addresses bound to peer LDP Ident:
            10.1.23.3        10.1.34.3        10.1.100.3
    Peer LDP Ident: 10.1.100.2:0; Local LDP Ident 10.1.100.4:0
        TCP connection: 10.1.100.2.646 - 10.1.100.4.25941
        State: Oper; Msgs sent/rcvd: 10/9; Downstream
        Up time: 00:00:46
        LDP discovery sources:
            Targeted Hello 10.1.100.4 -> 10.1.100.2, active, passive
        Addresses bound to peer LDP Ident:
            10.1.100.2       10.1.23.2
```

To check the label assignments and the detailed status of the xconnect (**pseudowire [PW]**), you can use Example 11-3. At this point, you need to check the xconnect (XC) state for both segments as well as label assignments (local and remote for termination points of the pseudowire: provider edges [PEs]) to ensure service functionality.

Example 11-3   *Xconnect Detailed Status*

```
PE4# show xconnect interface gigabitEthernet 2 detail
Legend:    XC ST=Xconnect State  S1=Segment1 State  S2=Segment2 State
  UP=Up        DN=Down            AD=Admin Down      IA=Inactive
  SB=Standby  HS=Hot Standby     RV=Recovering      NH=No Hardware
XC ST  Segment 1                             S1 Segment 2                              S2
------+-------------------------------------+--+-------------------------------------+--
UP pri   ac Gi2:8(Ethernet)                 UP mpls 10.1.100.2:15                     UP
             Interworking: none                Local VC label 404
                                               Remote VC label 201
```

Example 11-4 shows the relevant Label Forwarding table. As discussed in Chapter 10, "MPLS Fundamentals," the LFIB table will bind the IGP learned routes to labels. You can see the PoP label associated with prefixes where penultimate hop popping takes place.

Example 11-4   *LFIB Output of PE4*

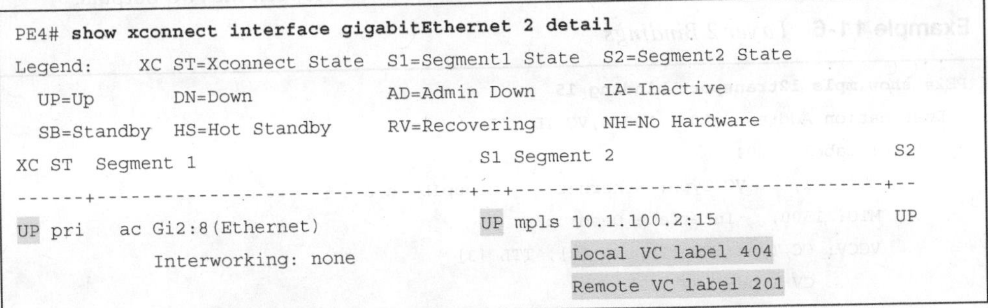

```
PE4# show mpls forwarding-table
Local      Outgoing    Prefix          Bytes Label  Outgoing    Next Hop
Label      Label       or Tunnel Id    Switched     interface
400        Pop Label   10.1.100.3/32   0            Gi1         10.1.34.3
401        300         10.1.100.2/32   0            Gi1         10.1.34.3
402        Pop Label   10.1.23.0/24    0            Gi1         10.1.34.3
404        No Label    l2ckt(1)        2214         Gi2         point2point
```

LFIB outputs from the PE2 and PE4 can be verified, as shown in Example 11-5, which clearly shows the local labels assigned for this Layer 2 connection (as denoted by the Next Hop field: point2point) where the Prefix or Tunnel-Id field is marked with l2ckt, denoting you are implementing an MPLS Layer 2 connection.

Example 11-5 *LFIB Output Xconnect Endpoints: PE2 and PE4*

```
PE2# show mpls forwarding-table
Local       Outgoing    Prefix          Bytes Label   Outgoing    Next Hop
Label       Label       or Tunnel Id    Switched      interface
200         301         10.1.100.4/32   0             Gi2         10.1.23.3
202         Pop Label   10.1.34.0/24    0             Gi2         10.1.23.3
203         Pop Label   10.1.100.3/32   0             Gi2         10.1.23.3
204         No Label    l2ckt(2)        66895         Gi1         point2point

PE4# sh mpls forwarding-table
Local       Outgoing    Prefix          Bytes Label   Outgoing    Next Hop
Label       Label       or Tunnel Id    Switched      interface
400         Pop Label   10.1.100.3/32   0             Gi1         10.1.34.3
401         300         10.1.100.2/32   0             Gi1         10.1.34.3
402         Pop Label   10.1.23.0/24    0             Gi1         10.1.34.3
403         No Label    l2ckt(2)        67219         Gi2         point2point
```

You can dive deeper in validating the Layer 2 connection by checking the binding to the VC ID, as shown in Example 11-6, taking into consideration the previous output (the LFIB table from both PE2 and PE4) where the local label values match between the two outputs.

Example 11-6 *Layer 2 Bindings*

```
PE2# show mpls l2transport binding 15
  Destination Address: 10.1.100.4,VC ID: 15
    Local Label:  204
        Cbit: 1,    VC Type: Ethernet,    GroupID: n/a
        MTU: 1500,    Interface Desc: n/a
        VCCV: CC Type: CW [1], RA [2], TTL [3]
            CV Type: LSPV [2]
    Remote Label: 403
        Cbit: 1,    VC Type: Ethernet,    GroupID: 0
        MTU: 1500,    Interface Desc: n/a
        VCCV: CC Type: CW [1], RA [2], TTL [3]
            CV Type: LSPV [2]
```

VPLS

Virtual Private LAN Services (VPLS) is a service provider service that enables customers with distributed Ethernet LAN segments to connect with each other in a full-mesh fashion.

It will appear to end customers that they are connected to a big Ethernet switch; however, from a business perspective, service providers can utilize the infrastructure to provide a seamless service with no major capital expenditure (CAPEX).

VPLS is primarily sought after for its scalability, as opposed to **Virtual Private Wire Services (VPWS)**; in this case, xconnect-based services or EoMPLS, which are limited to point-to-point connections and may not scale effectively. With VPLS, each pair of PE devices will have label-switched paths forming a pseudowire (one in each direction as the LSP is unidirectional). If the PE devices are not interconnected in a fully meshed configuration (and considering you are operating at the Layer 2 service level), Spanning Tree Protocol (STP) is required to prevent loops in the switched environment. Implementing a full mesh of pseudowires, PE devices will rely on split horizon during the Layer 2 forwarding process to detect loops. Figure 11-7 shows a high-level topology illustrating how the connectivity model will typically look, connecting several sites belonging to different customers using the same service provider backbone emulating a large Layer 2 switch.

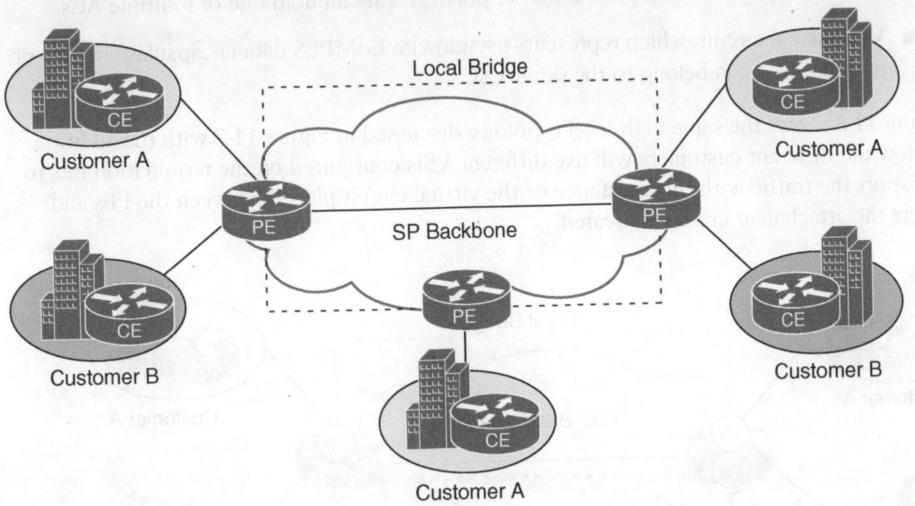

Figure 11-7 *Ethernet Tree Services (E-Tree) Connectivity Model.*

NOTE *Split horizon* here means that a flooded frame that is received on one pseudowire will never be forwarded to other pseudowires.

Like conventional switch environments, MAC addresses will expire or age out after a certain period.

VPLS setup starts with creating a **Virtual Forwarding Instance (VFI)** on each participating PE. VFI specifies

- The VPN ID of a VPLS domain

- The addresses of neighboring PE routers within the VPL domain

- Tunnel signaling and encapsulation mechanisms for each neighboring PE

PE routers will use the VFI to establish a full-mesh LSP of emulated virtual circuits (VCs). The set of VFIs formed by interconnecting emulated VCs is called a *VPLS instance*.

The full-mesh configuration allows the PE router to maintain a single broadcast domain. Thus, when the PE router receives a broadcast, multicast, or unknown unicast packet on an attachment circuit, it sends the packet out on all other attachment circuits and emulated circuits to all other CE devices participating in that VPLS instance. The CE devices see the VPLS instance as an emulated LAN.

After successful definition of VFI, bounding to an **attachment circuit (AC)** should take place on the CE devices.

- **VSI:** Virtual Switching Instance, which emulates an L2 broadcast domain among VCs and ACs. It is unique per device, and multiple VSIs can exist on the same provider edge.

- **AC:** Attachment circuit, which is the connection to the customer edge device (which could be a physical or logical Ethernet port). A VSI can hold one or multiple ACs.

- **VC:** Virtual circuit, which represents pseudowire EoMPLS data encapsulation. One or multiple VCs can belong to the same VSI.

Figure 11-8 shows the same high-level topology discussed in Figure 11-7 with the addition of how the different customers will use different VSIs configured on the termination PEs to transport the traffic with the assistance of the virtual circuit placed between the PEs and where the attachment circuit is located.

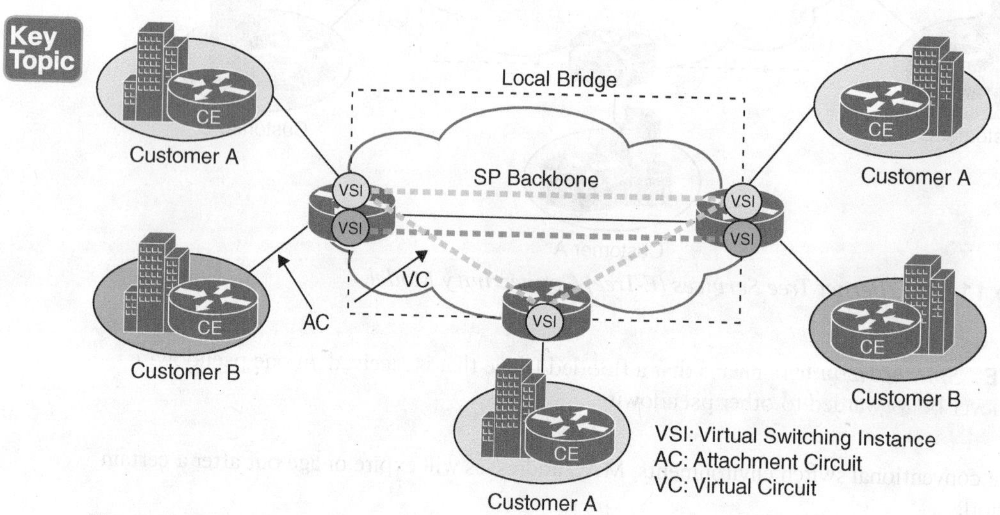

Figure 11-8 *VPLS Architecture*

The packet forwarding decision is made by looking up the Layer 2 Virtual Forwarding Instance (VFI) of a particular VPLS domain.

NOTE Virtual Switching Instance (VSI) in Cisco terminology is called Virtual Forwarding Instance (VFI).

A VPLS instance on a particular PE router receives Ethernet frames that enter on specific physical or logical ports and populates a MAC table similarly to how an Ethernet switch works. The PE router can use the MAC address to switch those frames into the appropriate LSP for delivery to another PE router at a remote site.

If the MAC address is not in the MAC address table, the PE router replicates the Ethernet frame and floods it to all logical ports associated with that VPLS instance, except the ingress port where it just entered. The PE router updates the MAC table as it receives packets on specific ports and removes addresses that haven't been used for specific periods.

MPLS is a mandatory component when implementing VPLS. You use MPLS for VPLS the same way you use it for L3VPNs. A stack of two labels is added to traffic received from a CE on the ingress PE. One label (the top label) determines the transport in the SP core toward the egress PE. This is equivalent to how the Loopback interface of a PE in L3VPNs is reached. Also, a VPN label is used to determine which VPLS the egress PE must use to forward the traffic to the correct CE.

The outer label is distributed by LDP (it can also be distributed using Border Gateway Protocol [BGP] or Resource Reservation Protocol [RSVP]), while the inner (VC or service) label is distributed by targeted LDP or BGP. Packets switched between PEs use a tunnel label, whereas a VC label identifies PW (the VC label signaled between PEs).

Discovery and Signaling

We have several options for signaling and discovery inside the VPLS domain. Figure 11-9 illustrates the available options.

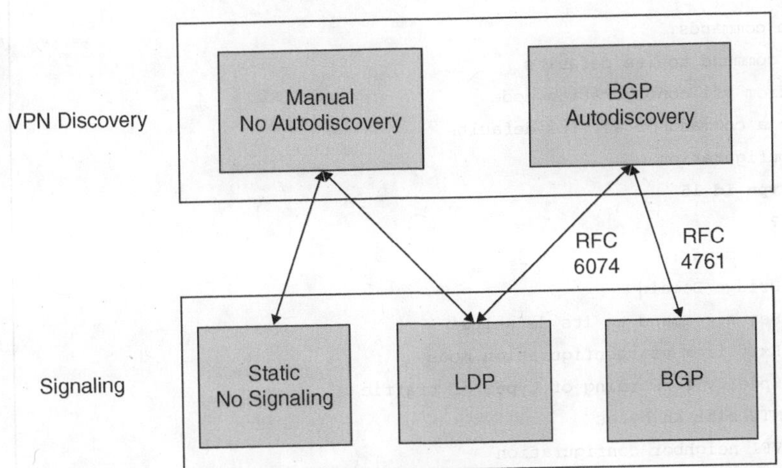

Figure 11-9 *VPLS Discovery and Signaling*

PEs require communication with each other, and one option is to manually configure the addresses of remote PEs. However, manual configuration is unnecessary if autodiscovery is used. Autodiscovery allows PE devices to automatically discover other PE devices that have an association with a particular VPLS instance. Once the PEs have discovered other PEs for a VPLS instance, they can then signal connections to interconnect the PEs.

VPLS Signaled with LDP (Manual)

Figure 11-10 shows the establishment of the pseudowire across the serving PEs with the definition of VSI on each PE to fulfill the requirement of manual VPLS service.

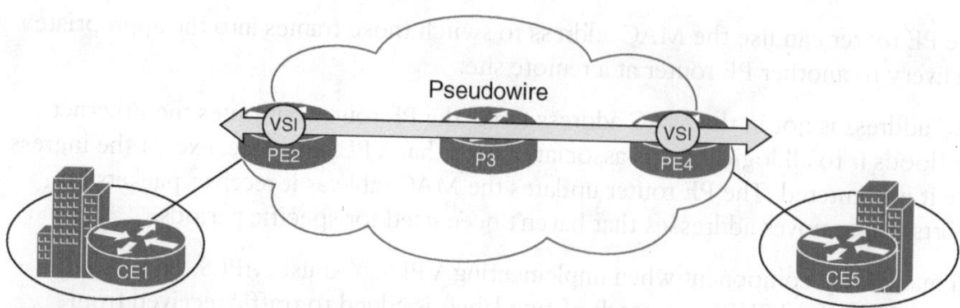

Figure 11-10 *VPLS with Manual LDP*

Example 11-7 starts by establishing the L2 VFI, associated VPN ID, bridge domain, and manual definition of the target neighbors. The bridge domain is a set of logical ports sharing the same broadcast (flooding) characteristics. The VPN ID should be unique within a VPLS domain, which means the same value should be configured on all participating PEs serving a unique customer.

Example 11-7 *VPLS VFI Definition*

```
PE2(config)# l2 vfi CONN manual
! If we check the options available once we issue the above command, the vpn id will
! appear and bridge-domain will not which clearly means we have to define vpn id at
! the first place.
PE2(config-vfi)# ?
VFI configuration commands:
  default  Set a command to its defaults
  exit     Exit from vfi configuration mode
  no       Negate a command or set its defaults
  vpn      VPN configuration
PE2(config-vfi)# vpn id 15
PE2(config-vfi)# ?
VFI configuration commands:
  bridge-domain  Bridge Domain
  default        Set a command to its defaults
  exit           Exit from vfi configuration mode
  forward        Specify forwarding of types of traffic
  mtu            MTU size in bytes
  neighbor       VFI neighbor configuration
  no             Negate a command or set its defaults
  shutdown       Shutdown VFI
  status         Pseudowire status capabilities
  vpn            VPN configuration
PE2(config-vfi)# bridge-domain 10
PE2(config-vfi)# neighbor 10.1.100.4 encapsulation mpls
PE2(config-vfi)# neighbor 10.1.100.4 encapsulation mpls
```

Example 11-8 shows the necessary configuration items needed to associate the service instance to the interface connected to the customer edge (CE) and the bridge domain for service establishment.

Example 11-8   *Bridge Domain Association Under Interface*

```
PE2(config)# interface gigabitEthernet 1
PE2(config-if)# service instance 10 ethernet
PE2(config-if-srv)# encapsulation untagged
PE2(config-if-srv)# bridge-domain 10
```

NOTE   Service instance could be considered as a way to use a single port as a combination of Layer 2 and Layer 3 ports. Multiple service instances can be created under one physical interface.

You can verify LDP targeted peers (LDP sessions are targeted in this case like a unicast session established between the PEs), as shown in Example 11-9.

Example 11-9   *LDP Discovery Output*

```
PE2# show mpls ldp discovery
Local LDP Identifier:
    10.1.100.2:0
    Discovery Sources:
    Interfaces:
        GigabitEthernet2 (ldp): xmit/recv
            LDP Id: 10.1.100.3:0
    Targeted Hellos:
        10.1.100.2 -> 10.1.100.4 (ldp): active/passive, xmit/recv
            LDP Id: 10.1.100.4:0
```

To verify the VC status for the deployed VPLS instance, you can use the **show mpls l2transport vc** command, as shown in Example 11-10.

Example 11-10   *Layer 2 Transport per VC Output*

```
PE2# show mpls l2transport vc 15
Local intf      Local circuit             Dest address      VC ID      Status
-------------   -----------------------   ---------------   --------   ----------

VFI CONN        vfi                       10.1.100.4        15         UP
```

Example 11-11 demonstrates how to get more verification for the connection from signaling to state perspective.

Example 11-11   *VFI Connection State*

```
PE2# show vfi name CONN
Legend: RT=Route-target, S=Split-horizon, Y=Yes, N=No
VFI name: CONN, state: up, type: multipoint, signaling: LDP
    VPN ID: 15
    Bridge-Domain 10 attachment circuits:
    Neighbors connected via pseudowires:
    Peer Address      VC ID        S
    10.1.100.4        15           Y
```

Example 11-12 demonstrates how to use the **show mpls l2transport binding** command to get detailed verification about the bindings (labels, VC IDs, and destination IP addresses).

Example 11-12 *Layer 2 Bindings*

```
PE2# show mpls l2transport binding
  Destination Address: 10.1.100.4,VC ID: 15
    Local Label:  205
        Cbit: 1,     VC Type: Ethernet,     GroupID: n/a
      MTU: 1500,    Interface Desc: n/a
      VCCV: CC Type: RA [2], TTL [3]
            CV Type: LSPV [2]
    Remote Label: 404
        Cbit: 1,     VC Type: Ethernet,     GroupID: 0
      MTU: 1500,    Interface Desc: n/a
      VCCV: CC Type: RA [2], TTL [3]
            CV Type: LSPV [2]
```

Finally, Example 11-13 demonstrates how to ensure successful MAC address learning of the destination CE.

Example 11-13 *MAC Address Learning*

```
PE2# show bridge-domain
Bridge-domain 10 (2 ports in all)
State: UP                          Mac learning: Enabled
Aging-Timer: 300 second(s)
Maximum address limit: 65536
   GigabitEthernet1 service instance 10
   vfi CONN neighbor 10.1.100.4 15
   AED MAC address      Policy Tag      Age  Pseudoport
   0   5081.9800.4100 forward dynamic   299  GigabitEthernet1.EFP10
```

To add some variety to the operating systems we're dealing with, let's look at another example to illustrate the concept of MPLS VPLS functioning on IOS XR using the topology in Figure 11-11.

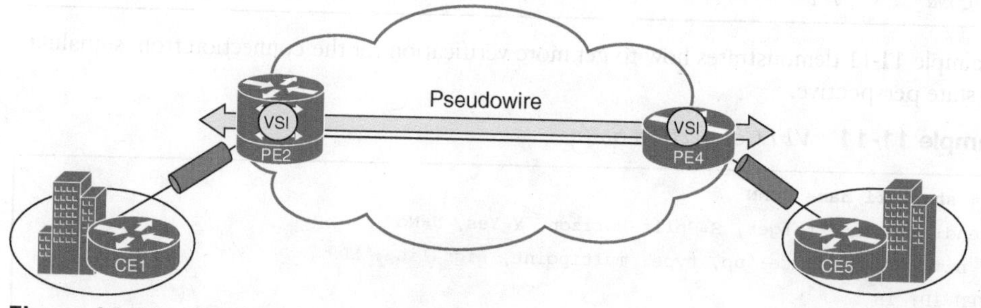

Figure 11-11 *VPLS with Manual LDP, IOS XR*

IOS XR introduces a parent configuration element per the hierarchical structure, and because we are dealing with a Layer 2 VPN kind of technology, the main parent command starts with the **l2vpn** keyword, as shown in Example 11-14.

Example 11-14 *IOS XR VPLS L2VPN Configuration*

```
RP/0/0/CPU0:R2(config)# l2vpn
RP/0/0/CPU0:R2(config-l2vpn)# bridge group GROUP
RP/0/0/CPU0:R2(config-l2vpn-bg)# bridge-domain 15
RP/0/0/CPU0:R2(config-l2vpn-bg-bd)# interface GigabitEthernet0/0/0/2.15
RP/0/0/CPU0:R2(config-l2vpn-bg-bd-ac)# vfi CONN
RP/0/0/CPU0:R2(config-l2vpn-bg-bd-vfi)# neighbor 10.1.100.4 pw-id 15
```

Another caveat introduced here is the subinterface, for which you will send tagged traffic by configuring VLAN 15 to be transported across the MPLS network to serve end-to-end Layer 2 reachability. On IOS XR, you use the **l2transport** keyword associated with the subinterface, as shown in Example 11-15. The **l2transport** command identifies a subinterface, a physical port, as an Ethernet flow point (EFP).

Example 11-15 *IOS XR l2transport Interface Configuration*

```
RP/0/0/CPU0:R2(config)# interface GigabitEthernet0/0/0/2.15 l2transport
RP/0/0/CPU0:R2(config-subif)# encapsulation dot1q 15
```

Several commands can be used to validate the operationality, as depicted in Example 11-16, by focusing on the state of the attachment circuit (AC) and pseudowires (PWs) within the created VFI.

Example 11-16 *IOS XR VPLS Validation*

```
RP/0/0/CPU0:R2# show l2vpn bridge-domain
Legend: pp = Partially Programmed.
Bridge group: GROUP, bridge-domain: 15, id: 0, state: up, ShgId: 0, MSTi: 0
  Aging: 300 s, MAC limit: 4000, Action: none, Notification: syslog
  Filter MAC addresses: 0
  ACs: 1 (1 up), VFIs: 1, PWs: 1 (1 up), PBBs: 0 (0 up), VNIs: 0 (0 up)
  List of ACs:
    Gi0/0/0/2.15, state: up, Static MAC addresses: 0
  List of Access PWs:
  List of VFIs:
    VFI CONN (up)
      Neighbor 10.1.100.4 pw-id 15, state: up, Static MAC addresses: 0
  List of Access VFIs:
```

VPLS Signaled with LDP (Autodiscovery)

LDP signaling requires that each PE is identified and a targeted LDP session is active for autodiscovery; it has no inherent autodiscovery, so the pseudowires must be manually configured or some external autodiscovery mechanism must be used. The overall scalability is poor because a PE must be associated with all other PEs for LDP discovery to work, which can lead to many targeted LDP sessions.

LDP is used for the signaling of pseudowires that interconnect the VPLS instance of a given customer on the PEs. To signal a full mesh of pseudowires, a full mesh of targeted LDP (T-LDP) sessions is required between the PEs. In the absence of autodiscovery, these sessions must be manually configured on each PE router. The LDP session communicates the *inner label* or *VC label* that must be used for each pseudowire. The network operator assigns a *VC ID* to identify a particular pseudowire. The same value for a particular VPLS instance must be present on all PE routers.

In Example 11-17, you configure the L2 instance using the context keyword on the respective PEs and determine the discovery protocol as well as the signaling protocol. As mentioned before, you must first define the VPN ID (the auto-discovery option will not be available until you define the VPN ID). After you have configured the VPN ID, you can see the auto-discovery option and the associated signaling available to be configured. The auto-discovery using BGP as a protocol will eventually require you to define the BGP process and the associated neighbors under the respective address family (**address-family l2vpn vpls**) using the command **neighbor** *ip-address* **activate** and **neighbor** *ip-address* **send-community** (that is why the route-target import/export values are configured as part of the l2vpn context, as you may recall; the route-target is an extended community transported using BGP).

Example 11-17 *L2 Instance Definition*

```
PE2(config)# l2vpn vfi context SPCOR_VPLS
PE2(config-vfi)# vpn id 15
PE2(config-vfi)# ?
L2VPN vfi configuration commands:
  autodiscovery  Auto Discovery mode
  default        Set a command to its defaults
  evc            EVC Name
  exit           Exit from L2VPN vfi configuration mode
  forward        Specify forwarding of types of traffic
  l2protocol     Configure l2 control protocol processing
  member         VFI member configuration
  mtu            set Maximum Transmission Unit
  no             Negate a command or set its defaults
  shutdown       Shutdown VFI
  status         Pseudowire status capabilities
  vpn            VPN configuration
! We can see that for the autodiscovery we have only one protocol to choose which is
! BGP. However, for signaling we have two options which we are going to go through.
R1(config-vfi)# autodiscovery bgp signaling ?
  bgp  Use BGP signaling and discovery
  ldp  Use LDP signaling
PE2(config-vfi)# autodiscovery bgp signaling ldp
PE2(config-vfi-autodiscovery)# vpls-id 100:1
PE2(config-vfi-autodiscovery)# route-target export 100:1
PE2(config-vfi-autodiscovery)# route-target import 100:1
```

Next, you establish the BGP peering under the respective address-family: L2VPN VPLS, as shown in Example 11-18. You are establishing iBGP peering, and loopback interfaces are used to source the BGP packets. Because you turned on the default IPv4 address-family establishment, you need to activate the neighbors under the target address-family. Also, you need to make sure the community is sent using the **neighbor** *ip-address* **send-community [standard|extended|both]** command. As mentioned previously, the route-target is part of the L2VPN context and route-target is an extended community.

Example 11-18 *BGP Peering Under L2VPN VPLS AF*

```
PE2(config)# router bgp 100
PE2(config-router)# neighbor 10.1.100.4 remote-as 100
PE2(config-router)# neighbor 10.1.100.4 update-source Loopback0
PE2(config-router)# neighbor 10.1.100.6 remote-as 100
PE2(config-router)# neighbor 10.1.100.6 update-source Loopback0
PE2(config-router)# address-family l2vpn vpls
PE2(config-router-af)# neighbor 10.1.100.4 activate
PE2(config-router-af)# neighbor 10.1.100.4 send-community both
PE2(config-router-af)# neighbor 10.1.100.6 activate
PE2(config-router-af)# neighbor 10.1.100.6 send-community both
```

For the attachment (binding) to take place, you define the bridge domain and associate both the interface connected to the customer edge and the L2 instance (VF), as demonstrated in Example 11-19.

Example 11-19 *Bridge Domain Definition*

```
PE2(config)# bridge-domain 10
PE2(config-bdomain)# member GigabitEthernet1 service-instance 10
PE2(config-bdomain)# member vfi SPCOR_VPLS
```

In this case, we have bound the interface to the service instance, and for illustration purposes, we chose the encapsulation to be untagged although we have several options to choose from; usually, this is the case when you're dealing with production customers who could be assigned VLAN IDs from the service provider end or, upon agreement, could propose from their end. Example 11-20 illustrates the process.

Example 11-20 *Service Instance Interface Association*

```
PE2(config)# interface GigabitEthernet1
PE2(config-if)# no ip address
PE2(config-if)# service instance 10 ethernet
PE2(config-if-srv)# encapsulation untagged
```

Example 11-21 validates the LDP peering (targeted) because of the successful result for LDP signaling with the BGP discovery process through neighborship under the L2VPN BGP AF.

Example 11-21 *LDP Discovery Output*

```
PE2# show mpls ldp discovery
 Local LDP Identifier:
    10.1.100.2:0
 Discovery Sources:
  Interfaces:
      GigabitEthernet2 (ldp): xmit/recv
         LDP Id: 10.1.100.3:0
  Targeted Hellos:
      10.1.100.2 -> 10.1.100.4 (ldp): active/passive, xmit/recv
         LDP Id: 10.1.100.4:0
      10.1.100.2 -> 10.1.100.6 (ldp): active/passive, xmit/recv
         LDP Id: 10.1.100.6:0
```

Now, you can use the **show mpls l2transport vc** command (associated with the virtual circuit number) to validate the operational status of the L2 instances, as shown in Example 11-22.

Example 11-22 *MPLS L2 Instances Validation*

```
PE2# show mpls l2transport vc 15
Local intf      Local circuit              Dest address    VC ID     Status
------------    ----------------------     --------------  --------  ----------
VFI SPCOR_VPLS  \
                vfi                        10.1.100.4      15        UP
VFI SPCOR_VPLS  \
                vfi                        10.1.100.6      15        UP
```

You can use an alternative command to validate the pseudowire status by using the **show vfi** command associated with the instance name that you configured, as shown in Example 11-23.

Example 11-23 *VFI Status*

```
PE2# show vfi name SPCOR_VPLS
Legend: RT=Route-target, S=Split-horizon, Y=Yes, N=No
VFI name: SPCOR_VPLS, state: up, type: multipoint, signaling: LDP
  VPN ID: 15, VPLS-ID: 100:1
  RD: 100:15, RT: 100:15, 100:1,
  Bridge-Domain 10 attachment circuits:
  Neighbors connected via pseudowires:
  Peer Address     VC ID      Discovered Router ID    S
  10.1.100.6       15         10.1.100.6              Y
  10.1.100.4       15         10.1.100.4              Y
```

Example 11-24 displays the BGP output, showing learned networks in a format equivalent to /96 prefix lengths, analogous to VPNv4 prefixes.

Example 11-24 *BGP VPLS Learned Routes*

```
PE2# show bgp l2vpn vpls all
! Output omitted for brevity
   Network            Next Hop            Metric LocPrf Weight Path
Route Distinguisher: 100:15
 *>  100:15:10.1.100.2/96
                      0.0.0.0                              32768 ?
 *>i 100:15:10.1.100.4/96
                      10.1.100.4               0    100     0 ?
 *>i 100:15:10.1.100.6/96
                      10.1.100.6               0    100     0 ?
```

Now, you can validate the label learnings (MPLS is in place) through the **l2transport binding** validation, as shown in Example 11-25.

Example 11-25 *L2 Bindings and Learnings*

```
PE2# show mpls l2transport binding
  Destination Address: 10.1.100.4,VC ID: 15
    Local Label:  203
        Cbit: 1,    VC Type: Ethernet,    GroupID: n/a
        MTU: 1500,    Interface Desc: n/a
        VCCV: CC Type: RA [2], TTL [3]
            CV Type: LSPV [2]
    Remote Label: 405
        Cbit: 1,    VC Type: Ethernet,    GroupID: n/a
        MTU: 1500,    Interface Desc: n/a
        VCCV: CC Type: RA [2], TTL [3]
            CV Type: LSPV [2]
  Destination Address: 10.1.100.6,VC ID: 15
    Local Label:  208
        Cbit: 1,    VC Type: Ethernet,    GroupID: n/a
        MTU: 1500,    Interface Desc: n/a
        VCCV: CC Type: RA [2], TTL [3]
            CV Type: LSPV [2]
    Remote Label: 608
        Cbit: 1,    VC Type: Ethernet,    GroupID: n/a
        MTU: 1500,    Interface Desc: n/a
        VCCV: CC Type: RA [2], TTL [3]
            CV Type: LSPV [2]
```

VPLS Signaled with BGP

BGP can be used as the signaling protocol to transmit Layer 2 information and VE labels between PEs. BGP was chosen as the means for exchanging L2VPN information for two reasons: it offers mechanisms for both autodiscovery and signaling, and it allows for operational convergence.

The BGP NLRI takes care of autodiscovery and signaling at the same time; the NLRI is generated by a given PE containing the necessary information required by any other PE. These components enable the automatic setting up of a full mesh of pseudowires for each VPLS.

On each PE, a route distinguisher (RD) and a router target (RT) are configured for each VPLS, like L3VPN and L2VPN. The RT value is the same for a particular VPLS across all PEs and is used to identify a specific VPLS instance. The RD is used to disambiguate routes. On a given PE, each VPLS instance is configured with an identifier—a VPLS edge identifier (VE ID). Each PE participating in the same VPLS instance must be configured with a different VE ID. BGP is used to advertise the VE IDs to other PEs. This, along with other information in NLRI, is used to calculate the value of the pseudowire label required to reach the advertising PE.

For a given VPLS, a PE requires that each remote PE use a different pseudowire label to send traffic to that PE. This is necessary to facilitate the MAC learning process. This way, the receiving PE can learn which PE is associated with the source MAC address of the frame. A PE could send a list of pseudowire labels required to reach it, one per remote VPLS edge in that VPLS instance. However, this would mean that a PE sends a long list of labels if there are many PEs. Instead, the necessary information is carried in BGP NLRI. This allows all remote PEs to calculate the pseudowire label expected by the advertising PE.

A BGP update message contains the following items:

- An extended community route-target allows the receiving PE to determine the specific VPN.

- Layer 2 information is automatically generated by the sending PE and contains the following:

    - Control flags to indicate whether a control word is included

    - Encapsulation type (Ethernet or VLAN tagged)

    - MTU

    - Other BGP attributes like AS Path, Origin, and so on

- The NLRI contains the following information:

    - Route distinguisher

    - VE ID

    - Label base

    - VE block offset

    - VE block size

The label base, VE block offset, and VE block size are the elements that the receiving PE requires to calculate the pseudowire label when sending traffic for VPLS to the advertising PE. A PE allocates blocks of labels. Each block is a contiguous set of label values. The PE advertises the value of the first label (label base) and the number of labels in the block (block size). The label value to reach the advertising PE is computed as

label value = label base + VE ID − 1

We use the topology in Figure 11-12 to illustrate the concepts behind which BGP is used for both discovery and signaling for the VPLS service. Here, three sites are connected to different PEs to verify point-to-multipoint capability.

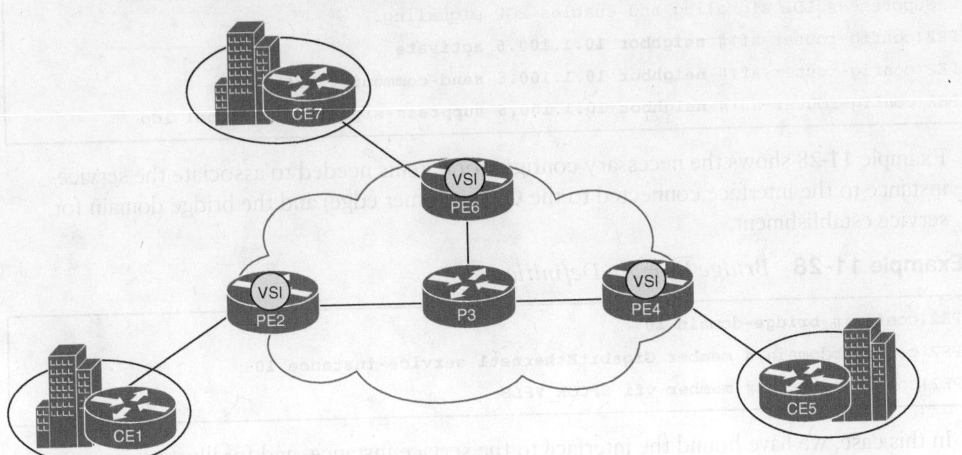

Figure 11-12   *VPLS Demonstration Example*

In Example 11-26, you configure the L2 instance using the context keyword on the respective PEs and determine the discovery protocol as well as the signaling protocol. The addition to this example is the extra parameters associated with using BGP as a signaling protocol, such as the endpoint ID and range.

Example 11-26   *L2VPN Context Using BGP as a Signaling Protocol*

```
PE2(config)# l2vpn vfi context SPCOR_VPLS
PE2(config-vfi)# vpn id 15
PE2(config-vfi)# autodiscovery bgp signaling bgp
PE2(config-vfi-autodiscovery)# ve id 2
! Specifies VPLS Endpoint Device ID.
PE2(config-vfi-autodiscovery)# ve range 50
! Specifies the VE Device ID range value, it is label block size.
! route-target export ASN:NN can be configured next , though can be generated
! automatically.
```

Next, you establish the BGP peering under the respective address-family, L2VPN VPLS, as shown in Example 11-27. Here, we have introduced the **suppress-signaling-protocol ldp** command to suppress LDP from being used as a signaling protocol and to solely depend on BGP.

Example 11-27   *BGP Peering Establishment with BGP Signaling*

```
PE2(config)# router bgp 100
PE2(config-router)# neighbor 10.1.100.4 remote-as 100
PE2(config-router)# neighbor 10.1.100.4 update-source Loopback0
PE2(config-router)# neighbor 10.1.100.6 remote-as 100
PE2(config-router)# neighbor 10.1.100.6 update-source Loopback0
PE2(config-router)# address-family l2vpn vpls
```

```
PE2(config-router-af)# neighbor 10.1.100.4 activate
PE2(config-router-af)# neighbor 10.1.100.4 send-community both
PE2(config-router-af)# neighbor 10.1.100.4 suppress-signaling-protocol ldp
! Suppresses LDP signaling and enables BGP signaling.
PE2(config-router-af)# neighbor 10.1.100.6 activate
PE2(config-router-af)# neighbor 10.1.100.6 send-community both
PE2(config-router-af)# neighbor 10.1.100.6 suppress-signaling-protocol ldp
```

Example 11-28 shows the necessary configuration items needed to associate the service instance to the interface connected to the CE (customer edge) and the bridge domain for service establishment.

Example 11-28 *Bridge Domain Definition*

```
PE2(config)# bridge-domain 10
PE2(config-bdomain)# member GigabitEthernet1 service-instance 10
PE2(config-bdomain)# member vfi SPCOR_VPLS
```

In this case, we have bound the interface to the service instance, and for illustration purposes, we chose the encapsulation to be untagged although we have several options to choose from; usually, this is the case when you are dealing with production customers who could be assigned VLAN IDs from the service provider end or upon agreement could propose from their end. Example 11-29 provides a concise overview of the process.

Example 11-29 *Service Instance Interface Association*

```
PE2(config)# interface GigabitEthernet1
PE2(config-if)# service instance 10 ethernet
PE2(config-if-srv)# encapsulation untagged
```

Example 11-30 lists the BGP output with learned network statements in the format of a prefix that contains a route-target and a virtual endpoint.

Example 11-30 *BGP Learned Routes, BGP Signaling*

```
PE2# show bgp l2vpn vpls all
! Output omitted for brevity
     Network           Next Hop            Metric LocPrf Weight Path
Route Distinguisher: 100:15
 *>   100:15:VEID-2:Blk-1/136
                       0.0.0.0                             32768 ?
 *>i  100:15:VEID-4:Blk-1/136
                       10.1.100.4              0    100       0 ?
 *>i  100:15:VEID-6:Blk-1/136
                       10.1.100.6              0    100       0 ?
! 100:15 is the automatically generated RD (autonomous system number & VPN ID),
! VEID-4 specifies VEID. Blk-1 specifies the label block offset.
```

To get more details about the prefix, you can issue the command (associated with the RD, VE ID, and label block offset) shown in Example 11-31. The RD value and the RT are automatically generated in the example and extracted from both the BGP autonomous system number (here, you use 100) and the VPN ID (15), which forms the 100:15 value.

Example 11-31 *BGP Detailed Output*

```
PE2# show bgp l2vpn vpls rd 100:15 ve-id 4 block-offset 1
BGP routing table entry for 100:15:VEID-4:Blk-1/136, version 55
Paths: (1 available, best #1, table L2VPN-VPLS-BGP-Table)
  Not advertised to any peer
  Refresh Epoch 1
  Local
    10.1.100.4 (metric 3) from 10.1.100.4 (10.1.100.4)
      Origin incomplete, metric 0, localpref 100, valid, internal, best
      AGI version(0), VE Block Size(50) Label Base(409)
      Extended Community: RT:100:15 L2VPN L2:0x0:MTU-1500
      mpls labels in/out exp-null/409
      rx pathid: 0, tx pathid: 0x0

PE2# show bgp l2vpn vpls rd 100:15 ve-id 6 block-offset 1
BGP routing table entry for 100:15:VEID-6:Blk-1/136, version 56
Paths: (1 available, best #1, table L2VPN-VPLS-BGP-Table)
  Flag: 0x100
  Not advertised to any peer
  Refresh Epoch 1
  Local
    10.1.100.6 (metric 3) from 10.1.100.6 (10.1.100.6)
      Origin incomplete, metric 0, localpref 100, valid, internal, best
      AGI version(0), VE Block Size(50) Label Base(609)
      Extended Community: RT:100:15 L2VPN L2:0x0:MTU-1500
      mpls labels in/out exp-null/609
      rx pathid: 0, tx pathid: 0x0
```

Another handy command to use to verify the VFI state is **show l2vpn vfi**, which is associated with the L2 instance name, as demonstrated in Example 11-32.

Example 11-32 *L2 Instance Verification*

```
PE2# show l2vpn vfi name SPCOR_VPLS
Legend: RT=Route-target, S=Split-horizon, Y=Yes, N=No
VFI name: SPCOR_VPLS, state: up, type: multipoint, signaling: BGP
  VPN ID: 15, VE-ID: 2, VE-SIZE: 50
  RD: 100:15, RT: 100:15,
  Bridge-Domain 10 attachment circuits:
  Pseudo-port interface: pseudowire100019
  Interface          Peer Address    VE-ID   Local Label   Remote Label   S
  pseudowire100021   10.1.100.6      6       214           610            Y
  pseudowire100020   10.1.100.4      4       212           410            Y
```

To make it clearer from a label assignment perspective, let's go through an example of how the label values are calculated and placed in the output, as shown in Example 11-30. As mentioned, we chose to get the RT value automatically generated, which equals 100:15. The relevant calculations follow the output in Example 11-33.

Example 11-33 *BGP Output and Label Assignment*

```
PE2# show bgp l2vpn vpls rd 100:15 ve-id 4 block-offset 1
BGP routing table entry for 100:15:VEID-4:Blk-1/136, version 55
Paths: (1 available, best #1, table L2VPN-VPLS-BGP-Table)
  Not advertised to any peer
  Refresh Epoch 1
  Local
    10.1.100.4 (metric 3) from 10.1.100.4 (10.1.100.4)
      Origin incomplete, metric 0, localpref 100, valid, internal, best
      AGI version(0), VE Block Size(50) Label Base(409)
      Extended Community: RT:100:15 L2VPN L2:0x0:MTU-1500
      mpls labels in/out exp-null/409
      rx pathid: 0, tx pathid: 0x0

PE4# show bgp l2vpn vpls rd 100:15 ve-id 4 block-offset 1
BGP routing table entry for 100:15:VEID-4:Blk-1/136, version 46
Paths: (1 available, best #1, table L2VPN-VPLS-BGP-Table)
  Advertised to update-groups:
     27
  Refresh Epoch 1
  Local
    0.0.0.0 from 0.0.0.0 (10.1.100.4)
      Origin incomplete, localpref 100, weight 32768, valid, sourced, local, best
      AGI version(0), VE Block Size(50) Label Base(409)
      Extended Community: RT:100:15 L2VPN L2:0x0:MTU-1500
      mpls labels in/out exp-null/409
      rx pathid: 0, tx pathid: 0x0

PE4# show bgp l2vpn vpls rd 100:15 ve-id 2 block-offset 1
BGP routing table entry for 100:15:VEID-2:Blk-1/136, version 47
Paths: (1 available, best #1, table L2VPN-VPLS-BGP-Table)
  Not advertised to any peer
  Refresh Epoch 2
  Local
    10.1.100.2 (metric 3) from 10.1.100.2 (10.1.100.2)
      Origin incomplete, metric 0, localpref 100, valid, internal, best
      AGI version(0), VE Block Size(50) Label Base(209)
      Extended Community: RT:100:15 L2VPN L2:0x0:MTU-1500
      mpls labels in/out exp-null/209
      rx pathid: 0, tx pathid: 0x0
```

The label values are calculated and placed as follows:

- On PE2, the local label for VE-ID 4 on PE4: Local Label 209 (Label Base) + 4 (Remote VE-ID) – 1 (Offset) = 212

- On PE2, the local label for VE-ID 6 on PE6: Local Label 209 (Label Base) + 6 (Remote VE-ID) – 1 (Offset) = 214

- On PE4, the local label for VE-ID 2 on PE2: Local Label 409 (Label Base) + 2 (Remote VE-ID) – 1 (Offset) = 410

Example 11-34 proves the preceding calculations from a label-creating and assignment perspective.

Example 11-34 *Label Assignment*

```
PE2# show l2vpn vfi name SPCOR_VPLS
Legend: RT=Route-target, S=Split-horizon, Y=Yes, N=No
VFI name: SPCOR_VPLS, state: up, type: multipoint, signaling: BGP
  VPN ID: 15, VE-ID: 2, VE-SIZE: 50
  RD: 100:15, RT: 100:15,
  Bridge-Domain 10 attachment circuits:
  Pseudo-port interface: pseudowire100019
  Interface         Peer Address   VE-ID  Local Label  Remote Label    S
  pseudowire100021  10.1.100.6      6      214          610             Y
  pseudowire100020  10.1.100.4      4      212          410             Y
```

H-VPLS

Hierarchical VPLS (H-VPLS) reduces signaling and replication overhead by using both full-mesh and hub-and-spoke configurations. Hub-and-spoke configurations operate with split horizon to allow packets to be switched between pseudowires (PWs), effectively reducing the number of PWs between PEs.

H-VPLS is an extension of traditional VPLS technology designed to address scalability challenges in large-scale service provider networks. VPLS is a Layer 2 VPN technology that enables the emulation of a multipoint Ethernet network over a service provider's MPLS network. It allows multiple sites to appear as if they are connected to the same LAN segment, providing transparent connectivity for Ethernet-based services.

In a traditional VPLS deployment, all provider edge (PE) routers in the service provider's network participate in a single VPLS instance. As the number of customer sites and VPLS subscribers grows, the control plane and data plane overhead associated with maintaining full-mesh connectivity between all PE routers can become significant, leading to scalability challenges.

H-VPLS addresses these scalability challenges by introducing a hierarchical structure to the VPLS network, typically consisting of two layers:

- **Core Layer:** This layer comprises a set of core PE routers that are responsible for interconnecting multiple VPLS edge networks. The core PE routers participate only in the core VPLS instance and are not directly connected to customer sites.

- **Edge Layer:** This layer consists of multiple VPLS edge networks, each managed by a set of edge PE routers. The edge PE routers connect directly to customer sites and participate in the VPLS instance serving those sites.

Hierarchical VPLS operates as follows:

- Each edge PE router maintains full-mesh connectivity with other edge PE routers within its own VPLS edge network.

- Core PE routers establish a mesh of connections between each other, forming a core VPLS instance.

- Edge PE routers maintain connections only with core PE routers, not with each other.

- Customer traffic is encapsulated and forwarded between edge PE routers through the core VPLS instance.

By dividing the VPLS network into core and edge layers, hierarchical VPLS reduces the number of full-mesh connections required between all PE routers, improving scalability and reducing control plane overhead. This hierarchical structure allows service providers to support larger numbers of VPLS subscribers and customer sites while maintaining efficient network operation. Additionally, hierarchical VPLS enhances network resiliency and facilitates traffic engineering capabilities within the core layer.

H-VPLS provides a solution for VPLS for improved pseudowire scalability. This improvement is achieved by reducing the number of PE devices connected in full-mesh topology and thus improves control plane scalability. It reduces the burden on core devices presented by frame replication. However, there are better ways to address scalability problems than those defined by LDP-based H-VPLS. For instance, H-VPLS does not offer a better solution to efficiently address multicast traffic. BGP-based VPLS with point-to-multipoint LSPs can be a better option for service providers.

There are two fundamental scale-limiting factors of plain or flat VPLS architectures:

- Signaling overhead

- Packet replication

There is no hierarchical scalability in a flat VPLS design because a full mesh of directed LDP sessions is required between PE devices. That means that you need (N*(N−1))/2 PW for N-PE devices in the network, and that represents a lot of signaling overhead. Clearly, that represents a scalability problem in the control plane as the number of PEs grows.

Packet replication overhead is another scale-limiting factor of VPLS because packet replication consumes CPU resources, and a lot of bandwidth may be needed to support packet replication (unknown unicast, multicast, or broadcast) over the same physical interface.

Let's look at the topology in Figure 11-13, which illustrates the required protocols for the needed functionality.

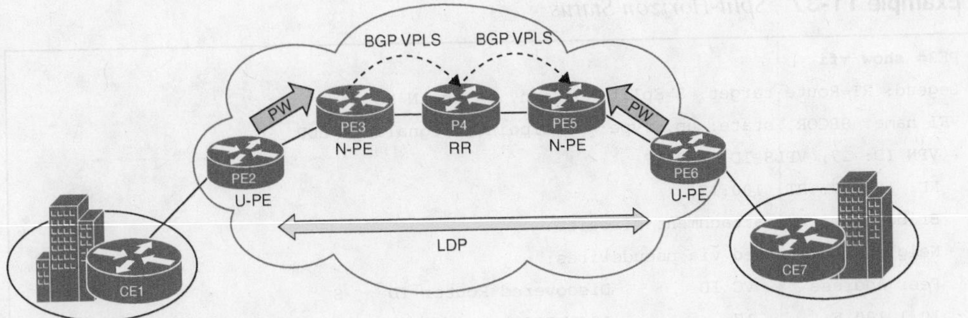

Figure 11-13 *H-VPLS*

Let's start by configuring the VFI on the N-PE routers, as demonstrated by Example 11-35.

Example 11-35 *N-PE VFI Definition*

```
PE3(config)# l2vpn vfi context SPCOR
PE3(config-vfi)# vpn id 17
PE3(config-vfi)# autodiscovery bgp signaling ldp
PE3(config-vfi-autodiscovery)# vpls-id 100:17
```

Notice that this example specifies a VPN ID. In fact, you must specify the VPN ID before you can configure anything else under the VFI. The VPN ID is essential because it defines the ID of this l2vpn service. It is also used as part of the RD in this format: ASN:VPN_ID.

With the VFI BGP AD default configuration, **auto-route-target** is enabled. This makes the RT the same value as the RD, as shown in the output in Example 11-36.

Example 11-36 *BGP L2VPN VPLS Output*

```
PE3# show bgp l2vpn vpls rd 100:17 10.1.100.5
BGP routing table entry for 100:17:10.1.100.5/96, version 6
Paths: (1 available, best #1, table L2VPN-VPLS-BGP-Table)
  Not advertised to any peer
  Refresh Epoch 2
  Local
    10.1.100.5 (metric 3) from 10.1.100.4 (10.1.100.4)
      Origin incomplete, metric 0, localpref 100, valid, internal, best, AGI
version(4043309058)
      Extended Community: RT:100:17 L2VPN AGI:100:17
      Originator: 10.1.100.5, Cluster list: 10.1.100.4
      mpls labels in/out exp-null/3179258
      rx pathid: 0, tx pathid: 0x0
```

To verify split horizon, you can look at the VFI (generally), as shown in Example 11-37.

Example 11-37   *Split-Horizon Status*

```
PE3# show vfi
Legend: RT=Route-target, S=Split-horizon, Y=Yes, N=No
VFI name: SPCOR, state: up, type: multipoint, signaling: LDP
  VPN ID: 17, VPLS-ID: 100:17
  RD: 100:17, RT: 100:17,
  Bridge-Domain 1 attachment circuits:
  Neighbors connected via pseudowires:
  Peer Address      VC ID          Discovered Router ID    S
  10.1.100.5        17             10.1.100.5              Y
  10.1.100.2        17             n/a                     N
```

The split horizon is enabled toward the other N-PE, R5. It is disabled, however, toward the U-PE, R2.

Next, you need a bridge domain to tie all the pieces together. A bridge domain represents an L2 broadcast domain consisting of interfaces that share the same forwarding characteristics. You need it to be able to bridge traffic between both PWs and physical interfaces. The former is used only on the U-PE. Example 11-38 provides a concise overview of the bridge domain configuration.

Example 11-38   *Bridge Domain Definition*

```
PE3(config)# bridge-domain 1
PE3(config-bdomain)# member vfi SPCOR
PE3(config-bdomain)# member 10.1.100.2 17 encapsulation mpls
```

This configuration is like configuring PEs manually under a VFI. You configure the U-PEs under the bridge domain instead of under the VFI to disable split horizon for loop prevention. You want traffic to be forwarded further downstream toward the egress PE, the U-PE. Had you configured the U-PE under the VFI, traffic would not be sent out to any neighbors in that VFI once received. You can, however, "bridge it out of an interface," or to other PWs. This is essentially what makes VPLS hierarchical. Figure 11-14 shows the construal topology and the main concepts associated with H-VPLS deployments for which an RR is also added inside the AS to clarify the use of BGP VPLS in a cascaded fashion. Also, this configuration demonstrates the hub pseudowire and spoke pseudowire among the PEs, with each functioning as either N-PE or U-PE according to the placement in the network from a customer termination perspective.

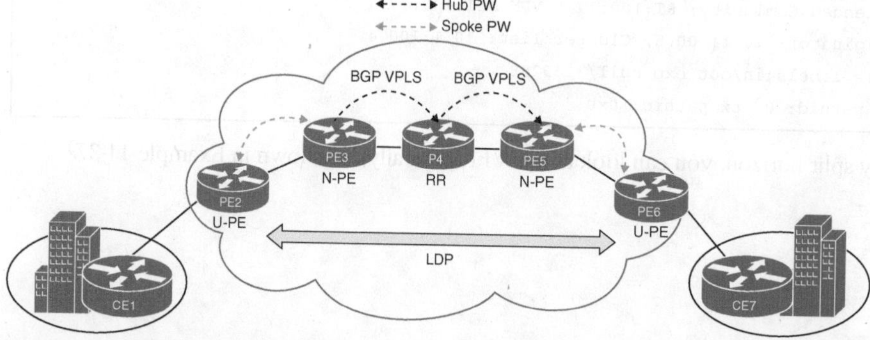

Figure 11-14   *H-VPLS Architecture*

To finalize how to configure H-VPLS, let's look at the U-PEs and the associated configurations as listed in Example 11-39.

Example 11-39 *L2 VFI Instance Configuration*

```
PE2(config)# l2vpn vfi context SPCOR
PE2(config-vfi)# vpn id 17
PE2(config-vfi)# member 10.1.100.3 encapsulation mpls

PE2(config)# bridge-domain 1
PE2(config-bdomain)# member GigabitEthernet1 service-instance 1
PE2(config-bdomain-efp)# member vfi SPCOR

PE2(config)# interface GigabitEthernet1
PE2(config-if)# service instance 1 ethernet
PE2(config-if-srv)# encapsulation default
```

To verify the MAC address learning, you can check the bridge domain statistics on the N-PE, as shown in Example 11-40.

Example 11-40 *Bridge Domain Analysis*

```
PE3# show bridge-domain 1
Bridge-domain 1 (2 ports in all)
State: UP                       Mac learning: Enabled
Aging-Timer: 300 second(s)
Maximum address limit: 65536
    vfi SPCOR neighbor 10.1.100.2 17
    vfi SPCOR neighbor 10.1.100.5 17
  AED MAC address    Policy Tag      Age  Pseudoport
   0  5081.9800.4100 forward dynamic  167  SPCOR.404010
```

Example 11-41 shows how to check the VC **l2transport** output from both hub-and-spoke PEs using the **show mpls l2transport** command associated with the virtual circuit (VC) ID.

Example 11-41 *MPLS* **L2transport** *Output*

```
PE2# show mpls l2transport vc 17

Local intf     Local circuit              Dest address    VC ID     Status
-------------  -------------------------  --------------  --------  ----------
VFI SPCOR      vfi                        10.1.100.3      17        UP

PE3# show mpls l2transport vc 17
Local intf     Local circuit              Dest address    VC ID     Status
-------------  -------------------------  --------------  --------  ----------
VFI SPCOR      vfi                        10.1.100.2      17        UP
VFI SPCOR      vfi                        10.1.100.5      17        UP
```

Now, you can check the label assignments with a detailed show output (targeting the egress PE), as shown in Example 11-42.

Example 11-42 *Label Assignment*

```
PE3# show mpls l2transport vc destination 10.1.100.5 detail | include labels
      MPLS VC labels: local 307, remote 509

PE3# show mpls forwarding-table
Local     Outgoing    Prefix          Bytes Label   Outgoing   Next Hop
Label     Label       or Tunnel Id    Switched      interface
300       Pop Label   10.1.100.2/32   428058        Gi1        10.1.23.2
301       Pop Label   10.1.100.4/32   459766        Gi2        10.1.34.4
302       Pop Label   10.1.45.0/24    0             Gi2        10.1.34.4
303       403         10.1.100.5/32   0             Gi2        10.1.34.4
304       404         10.1.56.0/24    0             Gi2        10.1.34.4
305       405         10.1.100.6/32   0             Gi2        10.1.34.4
306       No Label    l2ckt(1)        0             none       point2point
307       No Label    l2ckt(2)        0             none       point2point

PE5# show mpls forwarding-table
Local     Outgoing    Prefix          Bytes Label   Outgoing   Next Hop
Label     Label       or Tunnel Id    Switched      interface
500       Pop Label   10.1.100.4/32   0             Gi2        10.1.45.4
501       400         10.1.100.3/32   0             Gi2        10.1.45.4
502       401         10.1.100.2/32   0             Gi2        10.1.45.4
503       Pop Label   10.1.34.0/24    0             Gi2        10.1.45.4
504       402         10.1.23.0/24    0             Gi2        10.1.45.4
505       Pop Label   10.1.100.6/32   0             Gi1        10.1.56.6
508       No Label    l2ckt(3)        0             none       point2point
509       No Label    l2ckt(2)        0             none       point2point

PE3# show mpls l2transport vc destination 10.1.100.5 detail | include imposed
      Output interface: Gi2, imposed label stack {403 509}

P4# show mpls forwarding-table 10.1.100.5 32
Local     Outgoing    Prefix          Bytes Label   Outgoing   Next Hop
Label     Label       or Tunnel Id    Switched      interface
403       Pop Label   10.1.100.5/32   1046596       Gi1        10.1.45.5

PE3# show ip cef 10.1.100.5/32
10.1.100.5/32
    nexthop 10.1.34.4 GigabitEthernet2 label 403-(local:303)
```

Finally, the end-to-end connectivity test between CEs is shown in Example 11-43.

Example 11-43 *CE-to-CE Connectivity*

```
CE1# ping 172.16.17.1
Type escape sequence to abort.
Sending 5, 100-byte ICMP Echos to 172.16.17.1, timeout is 2 seconds:
!!!!!
Success rate is 100 percent (5/5), round-trip min/avg/max = 1/1/1 ms
```

```
CE1# traceroute 172.16.17.7 numeric
VRF info: (vrf in name/id, vrf out name/id)
  1 172.16.17.7 6 msec 6 msec 7 msec
```

ITU-T G.8032 Ethernet Ring Protection Switching

The ITU-T G.8032 Ethernet ring protection switching function implements the protection-switching mechanism of the Ethernet layer ring topology. This feature leverages the G.8032 Ethernet Ring Protection (ERP) protocol defined in ITU-T G.8032 to protect Ethernet traffic in ring topologies while ensuring that no loops exist within the ring at the Ethernet layer. You can prevent loops by blocking traffic on a given link or a failed link. An Ethernet ring consists of multiple Ethernet ring nodes. Each Ethernet ring node is connected to adjacent Ethernet ring nodes via two independent ring connections. Ring connections prevent the formation of loops that can affect your network. Ethernet rings use specific connections to protect the entire Ethernet ring. This special link is called a **ring protection link (RPL)**. A ring link is connected by two adjacent Ethernet ring nodes and ring link ports (also called *ring ports*). There must be at least two Ethernet ring nodes in an Ethernet ring.

The Ethernet ring protection functionality includes the following:

- Loop avoidance

- The use of learning, forwarding, and filtering database (FDB) mechanisms

Loop avoidance in an Ethernet ring is achieved by ensuring that, at any time, traffic flows on all but the ring protection link.

The following are RPL types (or RPL nodes) and their functions:

- **RPL Owner:** The owner is responsible for blocking traffic over the RPL so that no loops are formed in the Ethernet traffic. There can be only one RPL owner in a ring.

- **RPL Neighbor Node:** This Ethernet ring node is adjacent to the RPL. It is responsible for blocking its end of the RPL under normal conditions. This node type is optional and prevents RPL usage when protected.

- **RPL Next-Neighbor Node:** Next-neighbor node is an Ethernet ring node adjacent to an RPL owner node or RPL neighbor node. It is mainly used for FDB flush optimization on the ring. This node is also optional.

Figure 11-15 illustrates the G.8032 Ethernet ring topology.

Nodes on the ring use control messages called Ring Automatic Protection Switching (R-APS) messages to coordinate the activities of switching the ring protection link on and off. Any failure along the ring triggers an R-APS Signal Failure (R-APS SF) message in both directions of the nodes adjacent to the failed link, after the nodes have blocked the port facing the failed link. On obtaining this message, the RPL owner unblocks the RPL port.

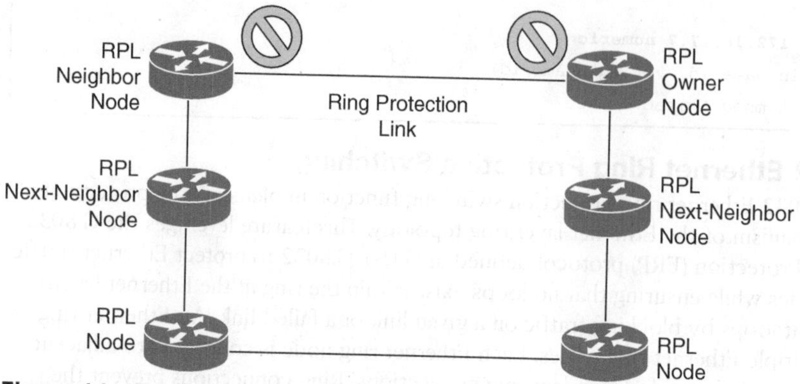

Figure 11-15 *G.8032 Ethernet Ring*

CFM Protocols and Link Failures

Connectivity Fault Management (CFM) and line status messages are used to detect ring link and node failures. During the recovery phase, when the failed link is restored, nodes send Ring Automatic Protection Switching (R-APS) No Request (R-APS NR) messages along the restored link. Upon receiving these messages, the ring protection link owner blocks the RPL port and sends R-APS NR and R-APS RPL (Route Blocking: RB) messages. These messages cause all nodes in the ring except the RPL owner to unblock all blocked ports. The Ethernet Ring Protection (ERP) protocol handles unidirectional failures and multilink failures in ring topologies.

A G.8032 ring can support multiple instances. An instance is a logical ring running on a physical ring. There are several reasons for using such instances, such as load-balancing VLANs across a ring. For example, odd-numbered VLANs can run in one direction of the ring, and even-numbered VLANs can run in the other direction of the ring. Some VLANs can be configured under only one instance. You cannot overlap multiple instances. Otherwise, traffic or R-APS messages may cross the logical ring, which is undesirable.

Ethernet Connectivity Fault Management

Ethernet Connectivity Fault Management (CFM) is an end-to-end per-service-instance Ethernet layer OAM protocol that includes proactive connectivity monitoring, fault verification, and fault isolation. End-to-end can mean PE to PE or customer edge (CE) to CE. *Per-service-instance* means per VLAN.

The advent of Ethernet as a MAN and WAN technology imposes a new set of **Operations, Administration, and Maintenance (OAM)** requirements on Ethernet's traditional operations, which were centered on enterprise networks only. The expansion of Ethernet technology into the domain of service providers, where networks are substantially larger and more complex than enterprise networks and the user base is wider, which makes the operational management of link uptime crucial. More importantly, timeliness in isolating and responding to a failure becomes mandatory for normal day-to-day operations, and OAM translates directly to the competitiveness of the service provider.

Being an end-to-end technology is the distinction between CFM and other metro-Ethernet OAM protocols. For example, MPLS, ATM, and SONET OAM help in debugging Ethernet wires but are not always end-to-end. IEEE 802.3ah OAM is a single-hop and per-physical-wire protocol. It is not end-to-end or service-aware. Ethernet Local Management Interface (E-LMI) is confined between the PE and CE and relies on CFM for reporting status of the metro-Ethernet network to the CE.

Troubleshooting carrier networks offering Ethernet Layer 2 services is challenging. Customers contract with service providers for end-to-end Ethernet service, and service providers may subcontract with operators to provide equipment and networks. Compared to enterprise networks, where Ethernet traditionally has been implemented, these constituent networks belong to distinct organizations or departments, are substantially larger and more complex, and have a wider user base. Ethernet CFM provides a competitive advantage to service providers for which the operational management of link uptime and timeliness in isolating and responding to failures is crucial to daily operations.

Some of the benefits of Ethernet CFM as described by Cisco include

- End-to-end service-level OAM technology

- Reduced operating expense for service provider Ethernet networks

- Competitive advantage for service providers

- Support for both distribution and access network environments with the outward-facing maintenance endpoint (MEP) enhancement

Customer Service Instance

A customer service instance is an Ethernet Virtual Connection (EVC), which is identified by an S-VLAN within an Ethernet island and is identified by a globally unique service ID (the C-VLAN is the VLAN used by the customer on the private network, whereas the S-VLAN is the VLAN used by the provider to transmit the customer-tagged traffic). A customer service instance can be point-to-point or multipoint-to-multipoint. Figure 11-16 shows two customer service instances. Service Instance Green is point-to-point, and Service Instance Blue is multipoint-to-multipoint.

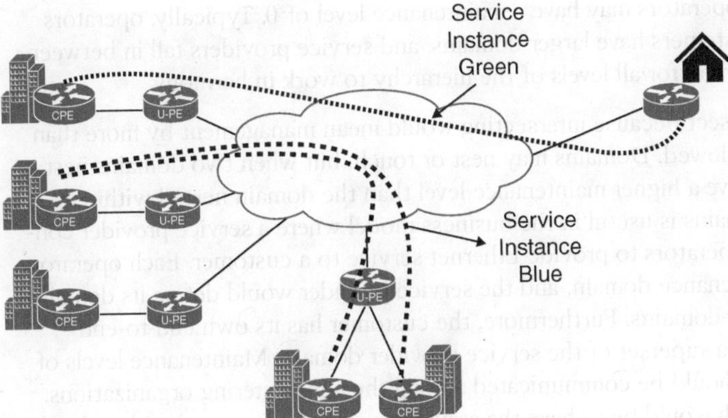

Figure 11-16   *Customer Service Instance*

Maintenance Domain

A maintenance domain is a management space for the purpose of managing and administering a network. A domain is owned and operated by a single entity and defined by the set of ports internal to it and at its boundary. Figure 11-17 illustrates a typical maintenance domain.

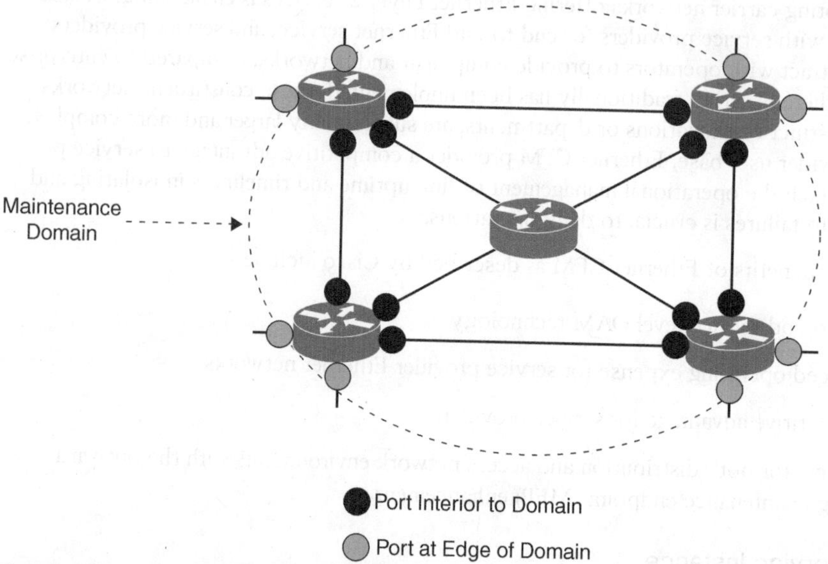

Figure 11-17 *CFM Maintenance Domain*

Ethernet CFM Maintenance Domain

A network administrator assigns a maintenance level ranging from 0 to 7 to each domain. These levels, along with domain names, help establish the hierarchical relationship among domains. This relationship mirrors the structure of customer, service provider, and operator. The larger the domain, the higher the level assigned to it. For instance, a customer domain would have a higher maintenance level than an operator domain. Customers may have a maintenance level of 7, while operators may have a maintenance level of 0. Typically, operators have smaller domains, customers have larger domains, and service providers fall in between in terms of size. It is essential for all levels of the hierarchy to work in harmony.

Domains should not intersect because intersecting would mean management by more than one entity, which is not allowed. Domains may nest or touch, but when two domains nest, the outer domain must have a higher maintenance level than the domain nested within it. Nesting maintenance domains is useful in the business model where a service provider contracts with one or more operators to provide Ethernet service to a customer. Each operator would have its own maintenance domain, and the service provider would define its domain— a superset of the operator domains. Furthermore, the customer has its own end-to-end domain, which is, in turn, a superset of the service provider domain. Maintenance levels of various nesting domains should be communicated among the administering organizations. For example, one approach would be to have the service provider assign maintenance levels to operators.

CFM exchanges messages and performs operations on a per-domain basis. For example, running CFM at the operator level does not allow discovery of the network by the higher provider and customer levels.

Maintenance Point

A maintenance point refers to a demarcation point on an interface (port) that actively engages in CFM within a maintenance domain. These points, located on device ports, function as filters that restrict CFM frames within the limits of a domain by discarding frames that do not pertain to the appropriate level. It is essential to explicitly configure maintenance points on Cisco devices. There are two categories of maintenance points: MEPs and MIPs.

Maintenance Association

A maintenance association (MA) is a set of MEPs that have the same MA identifier and MD level within one service instance to verify the integrity of the service. Figure 11-18 shows the different CFM domains across a network.

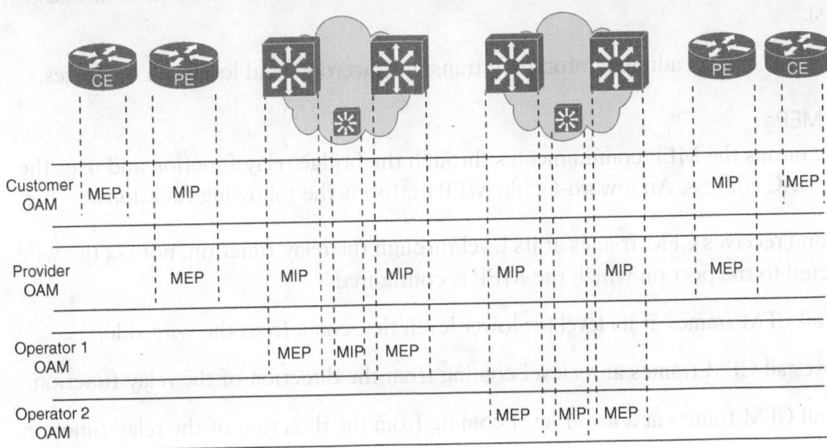

Figure 11-18 *Maintenance Association*

The following rules apply to CFM message processing:

- If the MD level of the CFM message is higher than the MD level of the MEP/MIP, the MEP/MIP transparently passes the CFM message.

- If the MD level of the CFM message is lower than the MD level of the MEP/MIP, the MEP/MIP discards the CFM message.

- If the MD level of the CFM message is equal to the MD level of the MEP/MIP, the MEP/MIP processes the CFM message. Depending on the type of CFM message, the MEP/MIP responds to, transports to, or accepts the message.

An MEP/MIP with a particular MD level generates a CFM message only at that level. Therefore, the MA has a high MD level (for example, MD = 7). The MEPs/MIPs in provider and operator networks transparently pass customers CFM messages. The provider is interested in the health of the service it provides. Therefore, the MA has a higher MD level (for example, MD = 5) than the operator's MD level but lower than the customer's MD level. So, the

MEPs/MIPs in an operator network transparently pass the provider's CFM messages. The operators are interested only in the health of their own networks. Therefore, their MAs have the lowest MD level (for example, MD = 0). So, the CFM messages are confined to their own network.

Maintenance Endpoints

Maintenance endpoints (MEPs) have the following characteristics:

- They constrict frames within the domain boundary for the maintenance domain (level) and service provider VLAN (S-VLAN) or EVC, and remove frames that do not belong to the correct level.

- At the edge of a domain, they define the boundary.

- Within the bounds of a maintenance domain, they confine CFM messages.

- When configured to do so, they proactively transmit CFM continuity check messages (CCMs).

- At the request of an administrator, they transmit traceroute and loopback messages.

Inward-Facing MEPs

Inward facing means the MEP communicates through the bridge relay function and uses the bridge-brain MAC address. An inward-facing MEP performs the following functions:

- Sends and receives CFM frames at its level through the relay function, not via the wire connected to the port on which the MEP is configured.

- Drops all CFM frames at its level (or lower level) that come from the wire side.

- Processes all CFM frames at its level coming from the direction of the relay function.

- Drops all CFM frames at a lower level coming from the direction of the relay function.

- Transparently forwards all CFM frames at a higher level, independent of whether they come in from the relay function side or the wire side.

Outward-Facing MEPs

Outward facing means that the MEP communicates through the wire. Outward-facing MEPs use the port MAC address, not the bridge-brain MAC address used by inward-facing MEPs. Outward-facing MEPs can be configured only on routed ports. An MIP configuration at a level higher than the level of the outward-facing MEP is not required.

An outward-facing MEP performs the following functions:

- Sends and receives CFM frames at its level via the wire connected to the port where the MEP is configured.

- Drops all CFM frames at its level (or at a lower level) that come from the relay function side.

- Processes all CFM frames at its level coming from the direction of the wire.

- Drops all CFM frames at a lower level coming from the direction of the wire.

■ Transparently forwards all CFM frames at levels higher than the level of the outward-facing MEP, independent of whether they come in from the relay function side or the wire side (not applicable to routed ports).

■ If the port on which the outward-facing MEP is configured is blocked by the Spanning Tree Protocol, the MEP can still transmit and receive CFM messages via the wire.

Maintenance Intermediate Points

Maintenance intermediate points (MIPs) have the following characteristics:

■ All S-VLANs that are enabled or allowed on a port are governed by a maintenance domain level.

■ They are internal to a domain, not at the boundary (as opposed to maintenance points, which reside on the edge and form the boundary).

■ CFM frames received from MEPs and other MIPs are cataloged and forwarded, using both the wire and the relay function.

■ All CFM frames at a lower level are stopped and dropped, independent of whether they originate from the wire or relay function.

■ All CFM frames at a higher level are forwarded, independent of whether they arrive from the wire or relay function.

■ Passive points respond only when triggered by CFM traceroute and loopback messages.

■ Bridge-brain MAC addresses are used.

If the port on which an MIP is configured is blocked by Spanning Tree Protocol, the MIP cannot receive CFM messages or relay them toward the relay function side. The MIP can, however, receive and respond to CFM messages from the wire.

An MIP has only one level associated with it, and the command-line interface (CLI) does not allow you to configure an MIP for a domain that does not exist.

CFM Messages

Connectivity Fault Management uses standard Ethernet frames. CFM frames are distinguishable by Ethertype and for multicast messages by MAC address. CFM frames are sourced, terminated, processed, and relayed by bridges. Routers can support only limited CFM functions.

Bridges that cannot interpret CFM messages forward them as normal data frames. All CFM messages are confined to a maintenance domain and to an S-VLAN (PE-VLAN or Provider-VLAN). Three types of messages are supported:

■ Continuity check

■ Loopback

■ Traceroute

Continuity Check Messages

CFM continuity check messages (CCMs) are multicast heartbeat messages exchanged periodically among MEPs. They allow MEPs to discover other MEPs within a domain and allow MIPs to discover MEPs. CCMs are confined to a domain and S-VLAN.

CFM CCMs have the following characteristics:

- Transmitted at a configurable periodic interval by MEPs. The interval can be from 10 seconds to 65,535 seconds; the default is 30.

- Contain a configurable hold-time value to indicate to the receiver the validity of the message. The default is 2.5 times the transmit interval.

- Catalogued by MIPs at the same maintenance level.

- Terminated by remote MEPs at the same maintenance level.

- Unidirectional and do not solicit a response.

- Carry the status of the port on which the MEP is configured.

Loopback Messages

CFM loopback messages are unicast frames that an MEP transmits, at the request of an administrator, to verify connectivity to a particular maintenance point. A reply to a loopback message indicates whether a destination is reachable but does not allow hop-by-hop discovery of the path. A loopback message is similar in concept to an Internet Control Message Protocol (ICMP) Echo (ping) message.

A CFM loopback message can be generated on demand using the CLI. The source of a loopback message must be an MEP; the destination may be an MEP or an MIP. CFM loopback messages are unicast; replies to loopback messages also are unicast. CFM loopback messages specify the destination MAC address, VLAN, and maintenance domain.

Traceroute Messages

CFM traceroute messages are multicast frames that an MEP transmits, at the request of an administrator, to track the path (hop-by-hop) to a destination MEP. They allow the transmitting node to discover vital connectivity data about the path and allow the discovery of all MIPs along the path that belong to the same maintenance domain. For each visible MIP, traceroute messages indicate ingress action, relay action, and egress action. Traceroute messages are similar in concept to User Datagram Protocol (UDP) traceroute messages.

Traceroute messages include the destination MAC address, VLAN, and maintenance domain and they have a time to live (TTL) to limit propagation within the network. They can be generated on demand using the CLI. Traceroute messages are multicast; reply messages are unicast.

Cross-Check Function

The cross-check function is a timer-driven post-provisioning service verification between dynamically discovered MEPs (via CCMs) and expected MEPs (via configuration) for a service. The cross-check function verifies that all endpoints of a multipoint or point-to-point service are operational. The function supports notifications when the service is operational; otherwise, it provides alarms and notifications for unexpected endpoints or missing endpoints.

The cross-check function is performed one time. You must initiate the cross-check function from the CLI every time you want a service verification.

Ethernet CFM and Ethernet OAM Interaction

To understand how CFM and OAM interact, you should understand the following concepts:

- Ethernet Virtual Circuit

- OAM Manager

Ethernet Virtual Circuit

An Ethernet Virtual Circuit (EVC), as defined by the Metro Ethernet Forum, is a port-level point-to-point or multipoint-to-multipoint Layer 2 circuit. EVC status can be used by a CE device either to find an alternative path into the service provider network or, in some cases, to fall back to a backup path over Ethernet or over another alternative service such as Frame Relay or ATM.

OAM Manager

The OAM manager is an infrastructure element that streamlines interaction between OAM protocols. The OAM manager requires two interworking OAM protocols—in this case, Ethernet CFM and Ethernet OAM. Interaction is unidirectional from the OAM manager to the CFM protocol, and the only information exchanged is the user network interface (UNI) port status. Additional port status values available include

- **REMOTE_EE:** Remote excessive errors

- **LOCAL_EE:** Local excessive errors

- **TEST:** Either remote or local loopback

After CFM receives the port status, it communicates that status across the CFM domain.

Finally, Figure 11-19 shows the CFM terminology.

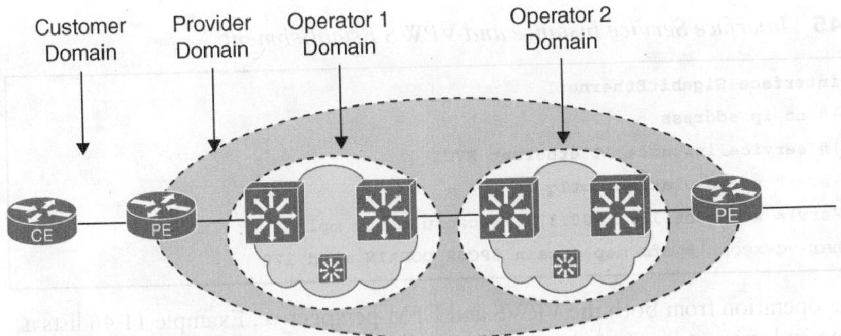

Figure 11-19   *CFM Terminology*

Let's use the sample topology in Figure 11-20 to deploy basic CFM functionality for an active xconnect (VPWS) between two customers for which we need to deploy fault management.

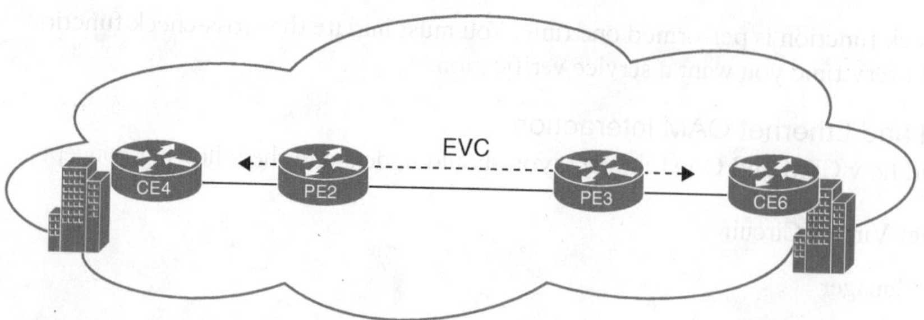

Figure 11-20   *CFM over VPWS Connection*

Example 11-44 lists the needed CFM-related configuration items to start the process.

Example 11-44   *Ethernet CFM Configuration*

```
PE2(config)# ethernet cfm ieee
PE2(config)# ethernet cfm global
PE2(config)# ethernet cfm traceroute cache
PE2(config)# ethernet cfm mip auto-create level 7 evc EVC1
PE2(config)# ethernet cfm alarm notification all
PE2(config)# ethernet cfm domain SPCOR_DOMAIN level 7
PE2(config-ecfm)# service EVC_SRVC evc EVC1
PE2(config-ecfm-srv)# mep mpid 170
PE2(config-ecfm-srv)# mip auto-create

PE2(config-ecfm-srv)# ethernet evc EVC1
PE2(config-evc)# oam protocol cfm domain SPCOR_DOMAIN
```

On the interface connected to the customer (CE4), you can define the service instance (as we did in VPWS and VPLS in the previous section) and attach the EVC to that service instance and accordingly establish the VPWS using the xconnect command, as shown in Example 11-45.

Example 11-45   *Interface Service Instance and VPWS Establishment*

```
PE2(config)# interface GigabitEthernet1
PE2(config-if)# no ip address
PE2(config-if)# service instance 10 ethernet EVC1
PE2(config-if-srv)# encapsulation dot1q 20
PE2(config-if-srv)# xconnect 10.1.100.3 17 encapsulation mpls
PE2(cfg-if-ether-vc-xconn)# cfm mep domain SPCOR_DOMAIN mpid 170
```

To validate the operation from both the VPWS and CFM perspective, Example 11-46 lists a couple of commands you can use.

Example 11-46   *VPWS and CFM Validation Outputs*

```
PE2# show xconnect all
Legend:     XC ST=Xconnect State  S1=Segment1 State  S2=Segment2 State
   UP=Up       DN=Down            AD=Admin Down       IA=Inactive
   SB=Standby  HS=Hot Standby     RV=Recovering       NH=No Hardware
```

```
XC ST  Segment 1                                    S1 Segment 2                                       S2
-------+----------------------------------------+--+-------------------------------------+--
UP pri    ac Gi1:10(Eth VLAN)                      UP mpls 10.1.100.3:17                              UP

PE2# show ethernet cfm maintenance-points local
Local MEPs:
----------------------------------------------------------------------------
MPID Domain Name                                    Lvl   MacAddress       Type  CC
Ofld Domain Id                                      Dir   Port             Id
     MA Name                                              SrvcInst         Source
     EVC name
----------------------------------------------------------------------------
170  SPCOR_DOMAIN                                   7     001e.f636.e6bf XCON  I
No   SPCOR_DOMAIN                                   Up    Gi1              N/A
     EVC_SRVC                                             10               Static
     EVC1
Total Local MEPs: 1
Local MIPs: None

PE2# show ethernet cfm domain brief
Domain Name                                         Index Level Services Archive(min)
SPCOR_DOMAIN                                         2     7     1        100
```

Provider Bridges (802.1ad)

IEEE 802.1ad, also known as *provider bridges* or *Q-in-Q*, is a standard for Ethernet virtual bridged networks, specifying a method for implementing virtual local area network (VLAN) stacking or VLAN tagging within an Ethernet frame. It extends the original IEEE 802.1Q standard by adding a second VLAN tag, allowing for the encapsulation of multiple VLANs within a single Ethernet frame (as discussed earlier in the "ITU-T G.8032 Ethernet Ring Protection Switching" section).

Here are the key features and aspects of IEEE 802.1ad:

- **VLAN Stacking:**

  - 802.1ad enables the stacking of VLAN tags within Ethernet frames, allowing multiple VLANs to be encapsulated and transported over a single Ethernet link.

  - It introduces a new field in the Ethernet frame header, called the *Service Provider Tag* or *Outer VLAN tag*, which contains information about the outer VLAN.

- **Q-in-Q Encapsulation:**

  - Q-in-Q encapsulation involves adding an additional VLAN tag to an Ethernet frame, creating a hierarchical VLAN structure.

  - The outer VLAN tag (Service Provider Tag) identifies the customer VLAN, while the inner VLAN tag (Customer VLAN) identifies the specific VLAN within the customer's network.

- **Service Provider Tag (S-Tag):**

  - The Service Provider Tag is added to the Ethernet frame header by service provider equipment (such as switches or routers) at the network edge.

  - It identifies the customer VLAN (C-VLAN) associated with the frame and is used for VLAN identification and isolation within the service provider network.

- **Customer VLAN (C-VLAN):**

  - The Customer VLAN is the inner VLAN tag that carries the original VLAN information from the customer's network.

  - It remains intact within the Ethernet frame and is not modified by the service provider equipment.

- **VLAN Identification and Isolation:**

  - 802.1ad allows service providers to transport multiple customer VLANs (C-VLANs) over a single network infrastructure while maintaining VLAN isolation and separation.

  - Each customer VLAN is identified and isolated based on the Service Provider Tag added by the service provider equipment.

- **Scalability and Efficiency:**

  - 802.1ad improves scalability and efficiency in service provider networks by reducing the number of VLANs required within the provider's network infrastructure.

  - It allows service providers to aggregate multiple customer VLANs onto a single VLAN trunk, simplifying network management and reducing configuration overhead.

- **Backward Compatibility:** Devices that support IEEE 802.1ad are backward compatible with devices that only support IEEE 802.1Q, allowing for interoperability and gradual deployment of Q-in-Q technology in existing networks.

Overall, IEEE 802.1ad (provider bridges or Q-in-Q) provides a standardized method for VLAN stacking and encapsulation, enabling service providers to efficiently transport and isolate multiple customer VLANs over a shared Ethernet infrastructure. It is widely used in service provider networks, data center interconnects, and Metro Ethernet deployments to support multitenant environments and VLAN-based network segmentation.

IEEE 802.1ad enables the service providers to use the architecture and protocols of IEEE 802.1Q to offer separate LANs, bridged local area networks, or virtual bridged local area networks to several customers, with minimal cooperation or no cooperation between each customer and the service provider.

IEEE 802.1ad implements standard protocols for double tagging of data. The data traffic coming from the customer side is double tagged in the provider network where the inner tag is the customer-tag (C-tag), and the outer tag is the provider-tag (S-tag). The control packets are tunneled by changing the destination MAC address in the provider network.

A service provider's Layer 2 network transports the subscriber's Layer 2 protocols transparently. A provider bridge allows the service provider switches to transparently carry customer Layer 2 control frames, such as spanning tree Bridge Protocol Data Units (BPDUs) or Cisco proprietary protocol frames such as Cisco Discovery Protocol (CDP) without mixing the service provider's own traffic with other customer traffic in the service provider's network. A provider bridge is just like a standard 802.1Q bridge, but it imposes a set of requirements, defined by IEEE 802.1ad standards, on a port in a provider bridge that interfaces with a customer. This port is a UNI port. The 802.1ad provider bridge thus achieves the same functionality as being addressed with L2PT and Q-in-Q.

For 802.1Q VLANs and 802.1ad Q-in-Q VLANs, the Ethertype is a tag protocol identifier (TPID) that, along with other tagging information, is inserted after the frame's source MAC address field. Because this TPID is at the same byte offset as the original Ethertype field, it is common to refer to this field as an *Ethertype field* when discussing VLANs. Figure 11-21 illustrates the distinction. Each tag adds 4 bytes of data to the Ethernet frame.

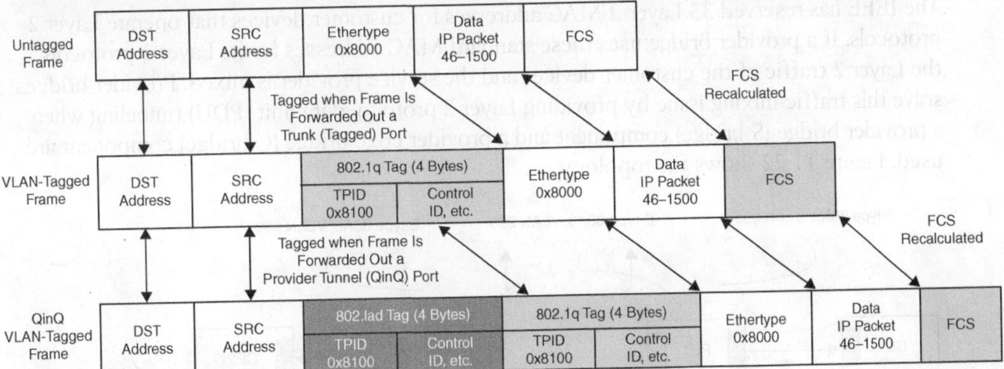

Figure 11-21 *Ethertypes and Frame Tagging*

As per Figure 11-21, the frame size is increased by 4 bytes per each added tag. Table 11-3 shows the size implications.

Table 11-3 MTU Implications

Use	Header Size	Tag Size	MTU	FCS	Total Frame Size
Standard Ethernet	14	0	1500	4	1518
802.1q VLAN trunk	14	+4	1500	4	1522
802.1ad (QinQ) VLAN	14	+4 +4	1500	4	1526

802.1ad Ports

In 802.1ad, a port is configured as either a customer user-network interface (C-UNI), a service-provider UNI (S-UNI), or a network-to-network interface (NNI). Only Layer 2 interfaces can be 802.1ad ports.

- **C-UNI:** This can be either an access port or an 802.1Q trunk port. The port uses the customer bridge addresses. To configure a C-UNI port, enter the **ethernet dot1ad uni c-port interface** configuration command.

- **S-UNI:** This is an access port that provides the same service to all customer VLANs entering the interface, marking all C-VLANs entering the port with the same S-VLAN. In this mode, the customer's port is configured as a trunk port, and traffic entering the S-UNI is tagged. You can use the **ethernet dot1ad uni s-port interface** configuration command on an access port with an access VLAN.

- **NNI:** Entering the **ethernet dot1ad nni interface** command on a trunk port creates the 802.1ad Ethertype (0x88a8) and uses S-bridge addresses for CPU-generated Layer 2 protocol PDUs.

Service Provider Bridges

Provider bridges pass the network traffic of multiple customers. The traffic flow of each customer must be isolated from one another. For Layer 2 protocols within customer domains to function properly, geographically separated customer sites must appear to be connected via a LAN, and the provider network must be transparent.

The IEEE has reserved 33 Layer 2 MAC addresses for customer devices that operate Layer 2 protocols. If a provider bridge uses these standard MAC addresses for its Layer 2 protocols, the Layer 2 traffic of the customer devices and the service provider is mixed. Provider bridges solve this traffic-mixing issue by providing Layer 2 protocol data unit (PDU) tunneling when a provider bridge (S-bridge) component and a provider edge bridge (C-bridge) component are used. Figure 11-22 shows the topology.

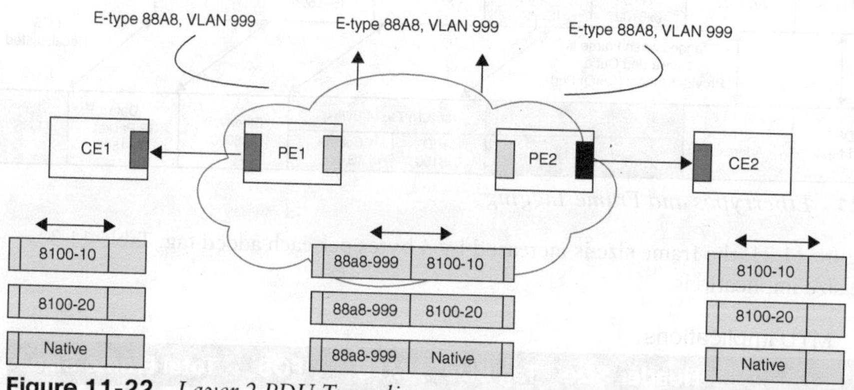

Figure 11-22 *Layer 2 PDU Tunneling*

S-Bridge Component

The S-bridge component can insert or remove a service provider VLAN (S-VLAN) for all traffic on a particular port. IEEE 802.1ad adds a new tag called a Service tag (S-tag) to all ingress frames traveling from the customer to the service provider.

The VLAN in the S-tag is used for forwarding the traffic in the service provider network. Different customers use different S-VLANs, which results in isolation of traffic of each customer. In the S-tag, provider bridges do not understand the standard Ethertype. Hence, they use an Ethertype value that is different from the standard 802.1Q Ethertype value. This difference makes customer traffic that is tagged with the standard Ethertype appear as untagged in the provider network. The customer traffic is tunneled in the port VLAN of the provider port. The 802.1ad service provider user-network interfaces (S-UNIs) and network-to-network interfaces (NNIs) implement the S-bridge component.

For example, a VLAN tag has a VLAN ID of 1, the C-tag Ethertype has a value of 8100 0001, the S-tag Ethertype has a value of 88A8 0001, and the class of service (CoS) has a value of zero.

C-Bridge Component

All customer VLANs (C-VLANs) that enter a user-network interface (UNI) port in an S-bridge component receive the same service (marked with the same S-VLAN). C-VLAN components are not supported, but a customer may want to tag a particular C-VLAN packet separately to differentiate between services. Provider bridges allow C-VLAN packet tagging with a provider edge bridge, called the *C-bridge component* of the provider bridge. C-bridge components are C-VLAN aware and can insert or remove a C-VLAN 802.1Q tag. The C-bridge UNI port can identify the customer 802.1Q tag and insert or remove an S-tag on the packet on a per-service instance or C-VLAN basis. A C-VLAN tagged service instance allows service instance selection and identification by C-VLAN. The 801.1ad customer user-network interfaces (C-UNIs) implement the C-component.

NNI Port

Dot1ad NNI ports are core-facing ports. This port dot1ad (0x88A8) uses Ethertype. The customer-facing S-bridge port is identified by using the **ethernet dot1ad nni** command. The frames forwarded on this port are double tagged with the S-tag Ethertype set at 0x88a8.

The distinction between the different types of VLANs requires a discussion of the Ethernet's frame Ethertype field.

An Ethernet frame's header uses an Ethertype field to specify what type of data is contained within the frame. For VLANs, the value in the field is mostly determined by the port's configuration. Table 11-4 describes different use cases and port types with the impact on the Ethertype values.

Table 11-4 Ethertype and Ports Combinations

VLAN Type	Ethertype Value	Tag Port	Port Type	Note
None	Per Protocol	Untagged Frame	Access port	IP = 0x800, ARP = 0x0806, etc.
Customer	0x8100	Tagged Frame	802.1Q trunk port	802.1Q VLAN tagging
Service	0x88a8	QinQ tagged Frame	802.1ad (QinQ) VLAN trunk port	802.1ad provider tunnel

Provider Backbone Bridging (PBB)

Provider Backbone Bridging Ethernet VPN (PBB-EVPN) is an advanced networking technology that combines Provider Backbone Bridging (PBB) with Ethernet Virtual Private Network (EVPN) to create scalable and efficient Layer 2 (L2) and Layer 3 (L3) VPN services in large-scale service provider networks. PBB-EVPN is designed to address the limitations of traditional Ethernet VPNs and provide enhanced scalability, multitenancy support, and traffic engineering capabilities.

Here are the key components and features of PBB-EVPN:

- **Provider Backbone Bridging (PBB):**

    - PBB is an extension of the IEEE 802.1Q Ethernet bridging standard designed to overcome the limitations of VLAN-based networks, such as scalability and VLAN ID space exhaustion.

    - PBB uses a two-layer MAC-in-MAC encapsulation scheme, where customer MAC addresses (C-MACs) are encapsulated within provider MAC addresses (P-MACs) for transport across the provider network.

    - PBB introduces a service instance identifier (i-SID) to uniquely identify each customer service instance, allowing for efficient and scalable service multiplexing.

- **Ethernet VPN (EVPN):**

    - EVPN is a next-generation VPN technology that leverages Border Gateway Protocol (BGP) to provide scalable and flexible Layer 2 and Layer 3 VPN services over MPLS networks.

    - EVPN uses BGP for MAC address learning, advertisement, and distribution, allowing for efficient and dynamic MAC address mobility across the network.

    - EVPN supports both Ethernet segment (ES) and IP Prefix (IP-VRF) routes, providing seamless integration of Layer 2 and Layer 3 VPN services.

- **Integration of PBB and EVPN:**

    - PBB-EVPN integrates PBB with EVPN to combine the scalability and multitenancy capabilities of PBB with the flexibility and control plane benefits of EVPN.

    - PBB-EVPN uses PBB encapsulation for efficient transport of customer MAC addresses across the provider network and leverages EVPN for MAC address distribution and control plane signaling.

- **Service Multiplexing and Scalability:**

    - PBB-EVPN allows service providers to multiplex multiple customer services onto a single provider network infrastructure using the I-SID field in the PBB header.

    - This enables efficient utilization of network resources and improves scalability by reducing the number of VLANs required in the provider network.

- **Traffic Engineering and Traffic Isolation:**

    - PBB-EVPN provides traffic engineering capabilities through MPLS Traffic Engineering (MPLS TE) or Segment Routing (SR), allowing for optimized traffic routing and resource utilization.

    - It also ensures traffic isolation and segmentation between different customer services using PBB encapsulation and separate I-SIDs.

- **Interoperability and Standards Compliance:** PBB-EVPN is based on industry standards such as IEEE 802.1ah (PBB) and RFC 7432 (EVPN), ensuring interoperability with existing networking equipment and compatibility with other network protocols and technologies.

Overall, Provider Backbone Bridging Ethernet VPN is a powerful and scalable solution for delivering Layer 2 and Layer 3 VPN services in large-scale service provider networks. It combines the best features of PBB and EVPN to provide efficient, flexible, and resilient VPN services while addressing the challenges of scalability, multitenancy, and traffic engineering.

Figure 11-23 shows the components that make up the PBB-EVPN.

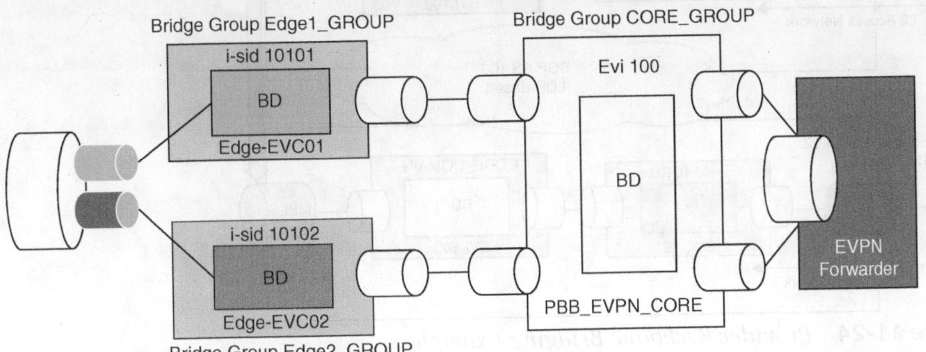

Figure 11-23 *Provider Edge Router*

PBB-EVPN Components

For the PBB-EVPN to function properly and to take advantage of both PBB and Ethernet VPN, some basic elements are included in the solution.

- **Bridge Group:** This is a group of one or more bridge domains. It follows the same concept and applicability as VPLS.

- **BD:** A bridge domain is nothing new here (it is like the traditional VPLS type of BD). When it comes to PBB-EVPN, though, there are two types of BDs: the edge bridge domain and the core bridge domain. Edge-BD is where the attachment circuits (interfaces connected toward customers) are included as part of the BD. That means all the Customer-MAC (C-MAC) addresses are part of this broadcast domain. Core-BD mainly contains the B-MAC—basically the MAC addresses of each provider edge device (for reachability purposes) within the same MPLS network.

- **EVI:** This EVPN instance identifies a VPN service on an IP/MPLS-based network. Here, you can import or export routes or MAC addresses based on route targets (like L3VPN services).

- **i-SID:** This service instance identifier, as its name implies, identifies the service instance. It is a best practice to keep the i-SID values unique per customer service instance.

Let's see how PBB-EVPN is implemented on an IOS XR–based network device. Here, we use four PE routers as part of the same MPLS-based network, as shown in Figure 11-24, and our focus is only on the L2VPN service based on PBB-EVPN. This example assumes a customer needs to connect four different locations (geographically apart), and the service provider is here to connect those locations to the same E-LAN (referring to the Metro Ethernet Forum naming convention).

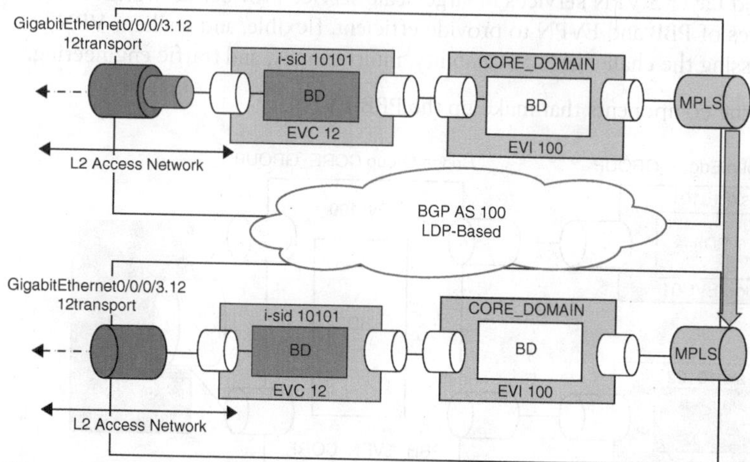

Figure 11-24 *Provider Backbone Bridging Example*

An MPLS network is already up and running (based on LDP). Example 11-47 shows the relative configuration.

Example 11-47 *Provider Backbone Bridging Configuration*

```
RP/0/0/CPU0:PE5(config)# interface GigabitEthernet0/0/0/3.12 12transport

! 12transport identifies a sub-interface, physical port pr bundle interface as
! Ethernet Flow Point (EFP). (EFP is a logical sub-interface used to identify or
! classify traffic under a physical or a bundle interface).

RP/0/0/CPU0:PE5(config-subif)# encapsulation dot1q 12

RP/0/0/CPU0:PE5(config-subif)# rewrite ingress tag pop 1 symmetric

! This command means if we received a frame from customer end with tag, the tag will
! be popped, and the frame will be sent to the provider network with no 802.1q tag.
! Symmetric keyword means if we are going to send the traffic toward the customer
! (Egress direction), tag will be imposed.


RP/0/0/CPU0:PE5(config)# 12vpn

RP/0/0/CPU0:PE5(config-12vpn)# bridge group GROUP

RP/0/0/CPU0:PE5(config-12vpn-bg)# bridge-domain EDGE_DOMAIN

RP/0/0/CPU0:PE5(config-12vpn-bg-bd)# interface GigabitEthernet0/0/0/3.12

RP/0/0/CPU0:PE5(config-12vpn-bg-bd-ac)# pbb edge i-sid 10101 core-bridge CORE_DOMAIN

RP/0/0/CPU0:PE5(config-12vpn-bg-bd-pbb-edge)# bridge group GROUP2

RP/0/0/CPU0:PE5(config-12vpn-bg)# bridge-domain CORE_DOMAIN

RP/0/0/CPU0:PE5(config-12vpn-bg-bd)# pbb core

RP/0/0/CPU0:PE5(config-12vpn-bg-bd-pbb-core)# evi 100


RP/0/0/CPU0:PE5(config)# router bgp 100

RP/0/0/CPU0:PE5(config-bgp)# address-family 12vpn evpn
```

```
RP/0/0/CPU0:PE5(config-bgp-af)# neighbor 10.1.100.6
RP/0/0/CPU0:PE5(config-bgp-nbr)# remote-as 100
RP/0/0/CPU0:PE5(config-bgp-nbr)# update-source Loopback0
RP/0/0/CPU0:PE5(config-bgp-nbr)# address-family l2vpn evpn
```

You can simply validate the BGP route advertisement through the respective address family—in this case, EVPN, as can be seen in Example 11-48.

Example 11-48 *Provider Backbone Bridging Validation*

```
RP/0/0/CPU0:PE5# show bgp l2vpn evpn summary
! Output omitted for brevity
Process          RcvTblVer   bRIB/RIB   LabelVer   ImportVer   SendTblVer   StandbyVer
Speaker              4           4          4           4           4            0

Neighbor       Spk     AS MsgRcvd MsgSent    TblVer  InQ OutQ  Up/Down   St/PfxRcd
10.1.100.6       0    100     56      56         4    0    0  00:52:42           1
```

```
RP/0/0/CPU0:PE5# show bgp l2vpn evpn
! Output omitted for brevity
Status codes: s suppressed, d damped, h history, * valid, > best
              i - internal, r RIB-failure, S stale, N Nexthop-discard
Origin codes: i - IGP, e - EGP, ? - incomplete
  Network          Next Hop           Metric LocPrf Weight Path
Route Distinguisher: 10.1.100.5:100 (default for vrf CORE_DOMAIN)
*> [2][0][48][02a3.406c.a405][0]/104
                   0.0.0.0                              0 i
*>i[2][0][48][02a8.ecbd.0c05][0]/104
                   10.1.100.6                    100    0 i
Route Distinguisher: 10.1.100.6:100
*>i[2][0][48][02a8.ecbd.0c05][0]/104
                   10.1.100.6                    100    0 i
Processed 3 prefixes, 3 paths
```

EVPN

Ethernet Virtual Private Network (EVPN) is a Layer 2 VPN technology that combines the scalability and flexibility of Ethernet with the capabilities and benefits of Multiprotocol Label Switching to provide advanced multihoming, traffic engineering, and integrated capabilities to deliver modern networking. EVPN is widely used in data center networks, service provider networks, and enterprise networks to support efficient and flexible connections of virtual machines, containers, and physical devices.

Here are the key features and components of EVPN:

- **MAC Address Learning and Forwarding:**

  - EVPN uses Border Gateway Protocol as the control plane protocol to exchange Media Access Control address reachability information between provider edge routers.

- PE routers learn MAC addresses associated with customer endpoints and use this information to build MAC address tables for forwarding Ethernet frames within the EVPN domain.

- **BGP Signaling:**

  - BGP is used as the signaling protocol in EVPN to exchange MAC address reachability information, route targets, and other attributes between PE routers.

  - BGP extended communities are utilized to carry EVPN-specific information, such as route distinguishers (RDs) and route targets (RTs), to differentiate between VPN instances and control the distribution of MAC addresses.

- **Multihoming and Redundancy:**

  - EVPN supports multihoming, allowing customer devices to connect to multiple PE routers for redundancy and load-balancing purposes.

  - All-active multihoming allows traffic to be load-balanced across multiple links, while single-active multihoming designates one PE router as the primary path and others as standby paths.

- **Integrated Layer 2 and Layer 3 Services:**

  - EVPN can be integrated with MPLS for seamless integration of Layer 2 and Layer 3 services, allowing customers to access both Layer 2 VPN and Layer 3 VPN services over the same infrastructure.

  - MPLS labels are used to encapsulate and forward traffic across the MPLS backbone, providing traffic engineering capabilities and efficient routing.

- **VXLAN Data Plane:**

  - EVPN often utilizes Virtual Extensible LAN as the data plane encapsulation method for transmitting Ethernet frames over an IP network.

  - VXLAN provides a scalable and flexible way to extend Layer 2 networks across Layer 3 boundaries, enabling overlay networks and virtualized environments.

- **Interoperability and Standards Compliance:**

  - EVPN is based on industry standards and interoperability frameworks, ensuring compatibility with a wide range of networking equipment and software implementations.

  - It is defined and standardized by the Internet Engineering Task Force (IETF) in RFC 7432, with additional extensions and enhancements introduced in subsequent RFCs.

Overall, EVPN offers a powerful and versatile solution for building scalable, resilient, and feature-rich Layer 2 VPNs in modern networking environments. Its support for multihoming, traffic engineering, integration with MPLS, and interoperability make it a popular choice for organizations seeking efficient and flexible connectivity solutions.

Next-Generation Solutions for L2VPN

EVPN is a more recent technology that aims to overcome some limitations associated with VPLS deployments, such as signaling protocols, multihoming, and MAC learning. At the end of the day, EVPN might not replace VPLS for several reasons, such as

- Less control plane consumption from a VPLS perspective

- Less service label utilization

We highlight some of the most spotted limitations from VPLS deployments.

CE Multihoming

Existing VPLS solutions do not offer an all-active per-flow redundancy. VPLS implements only a single active solution, in addition to looping of traffic flooded from the PE, as shown in Figure 11-25.

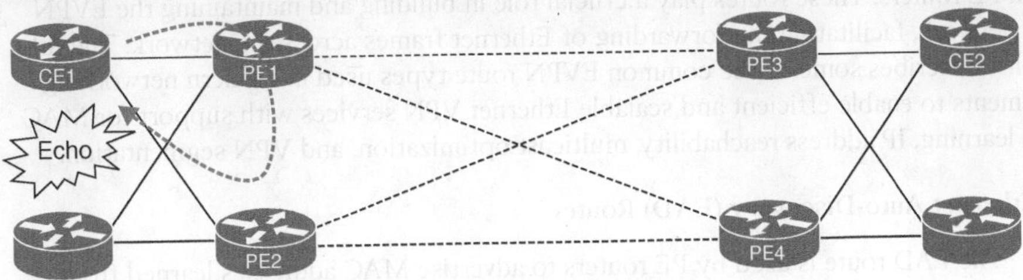

Figure 11-25   *VPLS Limitation: Per-flow Redundancy*

Frame Duplication

Duplicate frames flood from the core due to the full-mesh deployment model used especially in large-scale implementations, as illustrated in Figure 11-26.

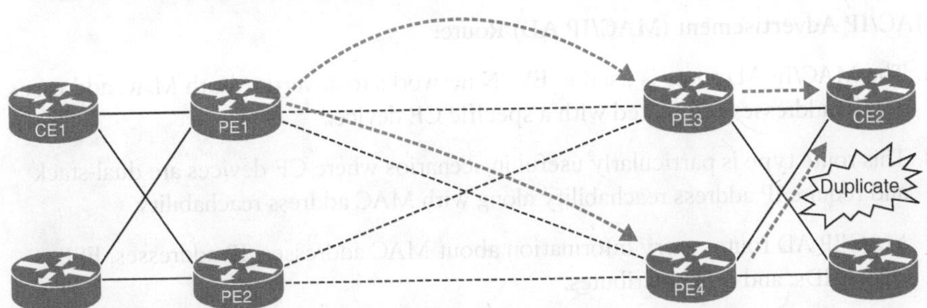

Figure 11-26   *VPLS Limitation: Frames Duplication*

MAC Flip-Flopping

MAC flip-flopping over pseudowire occurs because VPLS does not support all active multihoming, as demonstrated by Figure 11-27. VPLS supports MAC learning only on the data plane level on local ACs, which can cause a stale forwarding state, where EVPN relies on control plane MAC learning between PEs.

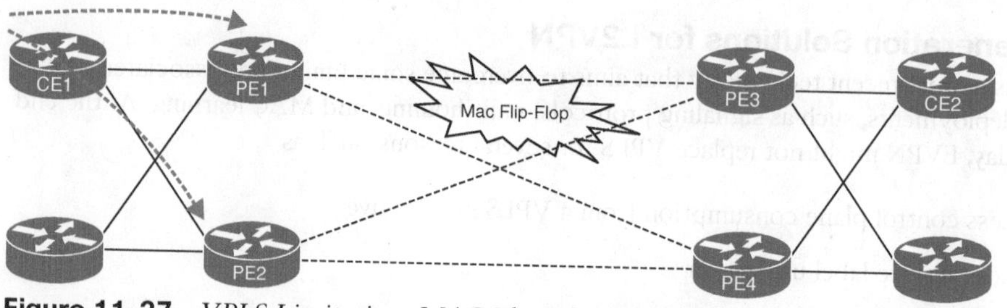

Figure 11-27 *VPLS Limitation: MAC Flip-Flopping*

Again, a business's drivers and vision of technology will control the selection of technology. Another factor is the experience of the staff (also depending on a managed versus unmanaged service model) that will administer the network.

In EVPN, different types of routes are used to exchange routing and forwarding information between PE routers. These routes play a crucial role in building and maintaining the EVPN overlay network, facilitating the forwarding of Ethernet frames across the network. The following list describes some of the common EVPN route types used in modern networking environments to enable efficient and scalable Ethernet VPN services with support for MAC address learning, IP address reachability, multicast optimization, and VPN segmentation.

- **Ethernet Auto-Discovery (EAD) Route:**

  - The EAD route is used by PE routers to advertise MAC addresses learned from customer edge devices within the EVPN instance.

  - Each EAD route carries information about a specific MAC address along with its associated Ethernet segment identifier (ESI) and VLAN ID.

  - EAD routes are used for MAC address reachability within the EVPN domain.

- **MAC/IP Advertisement (MAC/IP AD) Route:**

  - The MAC/IP AD route is used in EVPN networks to advertise both MAC addresses and IP addresses associated with a specific CE device.

  - This route type is particularly useful in scenarios where CE devices are dual-stack and require IP address reachability along with MAC address reachability.

  - MAC/IP AD routes carry information about MAC addresses, IP addresses, ESIs, VLAN IDs, and other attributes.

- **Inclusive Multicast Ethernet Tag Route (IMET) and Selective Multicast Ethernet Tag Route (SMET):**

  - IMET and SMET routes are used for multicast traffic optimization in EVPN networks.

  - IMET routes are used for inclusive multicast distribution, where multicast traffic is flooded to all receivers within the same EVPN instance.

  - SMET routes are used for selective multicast distribution, where multicast traffic is forwarded only to specific receivers based on MAC or IP addresses.

- **BGP Prefix Route:**

  - The BGP Prefix route is a standard BGP route used to advertise reachability information for IP prefixes within the EVPN network.

  - BGP Prefix routes are typically used for Layer 3 routing purposes, allowing PE routers to exchange IP routing information and reachability.

- **Route Target (RT) Route:**

  - RT routes are used in EVPN networks to carry information about VPN membership and VPN-specific policies.

  - RT routes help PE routers determine which EVPN routes should be imported and exported between different virtual private networks or Virtual Routing and Forwarding (VRF) instances.

- **Inclusive Multicast Ethernet Tag Route with No Route Target (IMET-NULL) and Selective Multicast Ethernet Tag Route with No Route Target (SMET-NULL):**

  - IMET-NULL and SMET-NULL routes are used for multicast optimization when route target filtering is applied.

  - These routes carry multicast group membership information without including route target attributes, allowing for more granular control over multicast traffic distribution.

MPLS-Based Data Plane EVPN

Next, we use the sample topology in Figure 11-28 to demonstrate the main blocks for establishing a successful end-to-end connectivity between CEs for which we will rely on LDP-based core.

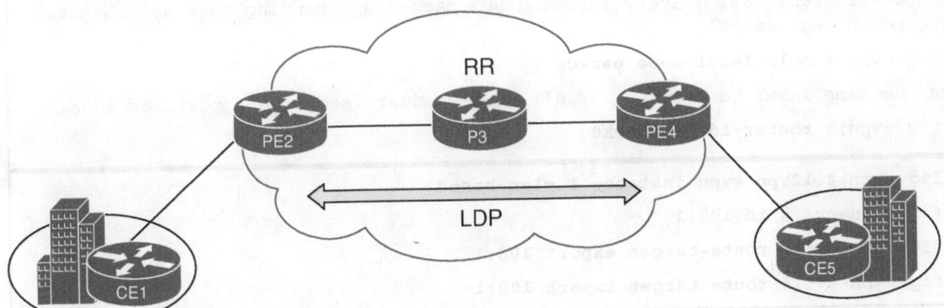

Figure 11-28 *EVPN Example*

You can start by establishing a BGP session (with route reflector in place) with the use of an EVPN address-family, as shown in Example 11-49.

Example 11-49 *BGP Configuration, EVPN AF*

```
RP/0/0/CPU0:P3(config)# router bgp 100
RP/0/0/CPU0:P3(config-bgp)# address-family l2vpn evpn
RP/0/0/CPU0:P3(config-bgp-af)# retain route-target all
RP/0/0/CPU0:P3(config-bgp-af)# neighbor 10.1.100.2
```

```
RP/0/0/CPU0:P3(config-bgp-nbr)# remote-as 100
RP/0/0/CPU0:P3(config-bgp-nbr)# update-source Loopback0
RP/0/0/CPU0:P3(config-bgp-nbr)# address-family l2vpn evpn
RP/0/0/CPU0:P3(config-bgp-nbr-af)# route-reflector-client
RP/0/0/CPU0:P3(config-bgp-nbr-af)# neighbor 10.1.100.4
RP/0/0/CPU0:P3(config-bgp-nbr)# remote-as 100
RP/0/0/CPU0:P3(config-bgp-nbr)# update-source Loopback0
RP/0/0/CPU0:P3(config-bgp-nbr)# address-family l2vpn evpn
RP/0/0/CPU0:P3(config-bgp-nbr-af)# route-reflector-client
```

```
PE2(config)# router bgp 100
PE2(config-router)# neighbor 10.1.100.3 remote-as 100
PE2(config-router)# neighbor 10.1.100.3 update-source Loopback0
PE2(config-router)# address-family l2vpn evpn
PE2(config-router-af)# neighbor 10.1.100.3 activate
PE2(config-router-af)# neighbor 10.1.100.3 send-community both
```

NOTE   You need to disable the default behavior of denying routes due to unconfigured route-target values by enabling the **retain route-target all** command (IOS XR).

Next, you can create the L2 EVPN instances and the associated parameters, as shown in Example 11-50.

Example 11-50   *EVPN L2 Instance Definition*

```
PE2(config)# l2vpn evpn
PE2(config-evpn)# replication-type ingress
! Ingress device replicating every incoming BUM packet and sending them as separate
! unicast to the egress PE.
PE2(config-evpn)# mpls label mode per-ce
! Allows the same label to be used for all routes advertised from a customer edge.
PE2(config-evpn)# router-id Loopback0
```

```
PE2(config-evpn)# l2vpn evpn instance 1 vlan-based
PE2(config-evpn-evi)# rd 100:1
PE2(config-evpn-evi)# route-target export 100:1
PE2(config-evpn-evi)# route-target import 100:1
```

Here, like the previous VPLS examples, you create a bridge domain and associate the service instance to the customer-facing interface, as shown in Example 11-51.

Example 11-51   *Bridge Domain Definition*

```
PE2(config)# bridge-domain 1
PE2(config-bdomain)# member GigabitEthernet1 service-instance 1
PE2(config-bdomain)# member evpn-instance 1
```

```
PE2(config)# interface GigabitEthernet1
PE2(config-if)# service instance 1 ethernet
PE2(config-if-srv)# encapsulation untagged
```

Next, you verify L2VPN EVPN neighborship from a BGP perspective, as shown in Example 11-52.

Example 11-52 *BGP EVPN AF Validation*

```
PE2# show bgp l2vpn evpn summary
BGP router identifier 10.1.100.2, local AS number 100
BGP table version is 20, main routing table version 20
4 network entries using 1536 bytes of memory
4 path entries using 896 bytes of memory
4/4 BGP path/bestpath attribute entries using 1152 bytes of memory
1 BGP rrinfo entries using 40 bytes of memory
1 BGP extended community entries using 24 bytes of memory
0 BGP route-map cache entries using 0 bytes of memory
0 BGP filter-list cache entries using 0 bytes of memory
BGP using 3648 total bytes of memory
BGP activity 10/6 prefixes, 10/6 paths, scan interval 60 secs
6 networks peaked at 23:34:21 Mar 16 2024 UTC (23:40:39.547 ago)
Neighbor        V         AS MsgRcvd MsgSent   TblVer  InQ OutQ Up/Down  State/PfxRcd
10.1.100.3      4        100    1437    1576       20    0    0 23:44:09         2
```

You can check if the routes (MAC addresses) are exchanged between the EVPN peers successfully by investigating the bridge domain as in Example 11-53.

Example 11-53 *Bridge Domain Validation*

```
PE2# show bridge-domain
Bridge-domain 1 (2 ports in all)
State: UP                        Mac learning: Enabled
Aging-Timer: 300 second(s)
Maximum address limit: 65536
    GigabitEthernet1 service instance 1
    EVPN Instance 1
    AED MAC address    Policy Tag       Age  Pseudoport
    -   5081.9800.4100 forward dynamic_c 292  GigabitEthernet1.EFP1
    -   5016.C200.4200 forward static_r   0   OCE_PTR:0xe8f66020

PE2# show l2vpn evpn mac
MAC Address      EVI  BD   ESI                               Ether Tag  Next Hop(s)
---------------- ---- ---- --------------------------------- ---------  -----------
5016.c200.4200   1    1    0000.0000.0000.0000.0000 0                   10.1.100.4
5081.9800.4100   1    1    0000.0000.0000.0000.0000 0                   Gi1:1

PE2# show l2fib bridge-domain 1 detail
Bridge Domain : 1
  Reference Count : 15
  Replication ports count : 2
```

```
Unicast Address table size : 3
IP Multicast Prefix table size : 4

Flood List Information :
  Olist: 1025, Ports: 2

Port Information :
  BD_PORT   Gi1:1
  MPLS_IR   PL:4(1) T:MPLS_IR [IR]404@10.1.100.4

Unicast Address table information :
  5016.c200.4200  MPLS_UC   PL:5(1) T:MPLS_UC [MAC]403@10.1.100.4
  5081.9800.4100  BD_PORT   Gi1:1
  ffff.ffff.fffe  Olist: 10242, Ports: 2

IP Multicast Prefix table information :
  Source: *, Group: 224.0.0.0/4, IIF: Null, Adjacency: Olist: 10243, Ports: 0
  Source: *, Group: 224.0.0.0/24, IIF: Null, Adjacency: Olist: 1025, Ports: 2
  Source: *, Group: 224.0.1.39, IIF: Null, Adjacency: Olist: 1025, Ports: 2
  Source: *, Group: 224.0.1.40, IIF: Null, Adjacency: Olist: 1025, Ports: 2
```

Finally, you can verify end-to-end connectivity between the CEs, as shown in Example 11-54.

Example 11-54 *CE-to-CE Communication*

```
CE1# show interface GigabitEthernet0/0 | include address
  Hardware is iGbE, address is 5081.9800.4100 (bia 5081.9800.4100)
  Internet address is 172.16.15.1/24

CE1# ping 172.16.15.5
Type escape sequence to abort.
Sending 5, 100-byte ICMP Echos to 172.16.15.5, timeout is 2 seconds:
!!!!!
Success rate is 100 percent (5/5), round-trip min/avg/max = 5/6/8 ms
```

Exam Preparation Tasks

As mentioned in the section "How to Use This Book" in the Introduction, you have a few choices for exam preparation: the exercises here, Chapter 23, "Final Preparation," and the exam simulation questions in the Pearson Test Prep Software Online.

Review All Key Topics

Review the most important topics in this chapter, noted with the Key Topic icon in the margin of the page. Table 11-5 lists a reference of these key topics and the page numbers on which each is found.

Table 11-5   Key Topics for Chapter 11

Key Topic Element	Description	Page Number
Paragraph	MPLS AToM	499
Example 11-3	Xconnect Detailed Status	501
Figure 11-8	VPLS Architecture	504
Figure 11-9	VPLS Discovery and Signaling	505
Figure 11-13	H-VPLS	521
Figure 11-19	CFM Terminology	533
Figure 11-21	Ethertypes and Frame Tagging	537
Table 11-4	Ethertype and Port Combinations	539

Define Key Terms

Define the following key terms from this chapter and check the answers in the glossary:

Any Transport over MPLS (AToM); Attachment Circuit (AC); Connectivity Fault Management (CFM); Label Distribution Protocol (LDP); Multiprotocol Label Switching (MPLS); Operations, Administration, and Maintenance (OAM); Pseudowire (PW); Ring Protection Link (RPL); Virtual Forwarding Instance (VFI); Virtual Private LAN Services (VPLS); Virtual Private Wire Services (VPWS)

Command Reference to Check Your Memory

This section includes the most important commands covered in this chapter. You might not need to memorize the complete syntax of every command, but you should be able to remember the basic keywords that are needed.

To test your memory of the commands, cover the right side of Table 11-6 with a piece of paper, read the description on the left side, and then see how much of the command you can remember.

The SPCOR 350-501 exam focuses on practical, hands-on skills that are used by networking professionals. Therefore, you should be able to identify the commands needed to configure and test. Note that not all commands are fully covered in the chapter, but their presence in the following table should lead you to investigate them further to understand this technology.

Table 11-6   Command Reference

Task	Command Syntax
All received VPN IPv4 routes are accepted. If the router is an autonomous system border or customer edge router, this is the desired behavior.	**no bgp default route-target filter**
Command applied to the VPN address-family under BGP and affects all VPN peers advertising VPN routes to this ASBR (iBGP and eBGP) on IOS-XR.	**retain route-target all**

Task	Command Syntax
Display Layer 2 virtual private network (L2VPN) address family information from the Border Gateway Protocol table	**show bgp l2vpn vpls all**
Define a CFM domain, set the domain level, and enter ethernet-cfm configuration mode for the domain. The maintenance level number range is 0 to 7.	**ethernet cfm domain** *domain-name* **level** *level-id*

Review Questions

As a part of the review, we encourage you to provide *a single-sentence answer* (keep your answers as short as possible) to the following questions. If you struggle to complete this in a single sentence, this answer may indicate a lack of clarity or reveal gaps in your understanding. We have constructed these questions to help you consolidate this chapter's information and extract the essence of the covered content.

The answers to these questions appear in Appendix A. For more practice with exam format questions, use the Pearson Test Prep Software Online.

1. What aspects did EVPN solve compared to VPLS from a Layer 2 Ethernet VPN services functionality perspective?

2. What limitations did H-VPLS address compared to VPLS?

3. What are two fundamental scale-limiting factors of plain/flat VPLS architecture?

Bibliography

Configuring Ethernet Connectivity Fault Management in a Service Provider Network, https://www.cisco.com/c/en/us/td/docs/ios/cether/configuration/guide/ce_cfm.html

Configuring Ethernet OAM, CFM, and E-LMI, https://www.cisco.com/en/US/docs/switches/metro/me3600x_3800x/trash/swoam.html

Configuring IEEE 802.1ad, https://www.cisco.com/c/en/us/td/docs/routers/asr920/configuration/guide/ce/16-12-1/b-ce-xe-16-12-asr920/b-ce-xe-16-11-asr920_chapter_01111.pdf

K. Kompella and Y. Rekhter. RFC 4761, *Virtual Private LAN Service (VPLS) Using BGP for Auto-Discovery and Signaling*, IETF, https://www.ietf.org/rfc/rfc4761.txt, October 2008.

E. Rosen, B. Davie, V. Radoaca, and W. Luo. RFC 6074, *Provisioning, Auto-Discovery, and Signaling in Layer 2 Virtual Private Networks (L2VPNs)*, IETF, https://www.ietf.org/rfc/rfc6074.txt, October 2008.

MPLS L3VPNs

This chapter covers the following exam topics:

4.0 Services

- 4.1.d mVPN
- 4.3 Configure L3VPN
- 4.3.b Shared services (extranet and Internet)

MPLS L3VPN is a type of PE-based L3VPN technology for service provider virtual private network solutions. It uses BGP to advertise VPN routes and uses MPLS to forward VPN packets on service provider backbones.

MPLS L3VPN provides flexible networking modes, excellent scalability, and convenient support for MPLS QoS and MPLS TE.

"Do I Know This Already?" Quiz

The "Do I Know This Already?" quiz allows you to assess whether you should read this entire chapter thoroughly or jump to the "Exam Preparation Tasks" section. If you are in doubt about your answers to these questions or your own assessment of your knowledge of the topics, read the entire chapter. Table 12-1 lists the major headings in this chapter and their corresponding "Do I Know This Already?" quiz questions. You can find the answers in Appendix A, "Answers to the 'Do I Know This Already?' Quizzes and Review Questions."

Table 12-1 "Do I Know This Already?" Section-to-Question Mapping

Foundation Topics Section	Questions
MPLS L3VPN	1, 2
MPLS L3VPN OSPF PE-CE Routing	3
MPLS L3VPN EIGRP PE-CE Routing	4
MPLS L3VPN BGP PE-CE Routing	5
Route Target Filtering Mechanisms	6
Multicast VPN	7

CAUTION The goal of self-assessment is to gauge your mastery of the topics in this chapter. If you do not know the answer to a question or are only partially sure of the answer, you should mark that question as wrong for purposes of the self-assessment. Giving yourself credit for an answer you correctly guess skews your self-assessment results and might provide you with a false sense of security.

1. Which technology allows multiple routing and forwarding tables to exist on a device in MPLS L3VPN technology?

    a. RIB

    b. VRF

    c. LIB

    d. FIB

2. Which protocol carries the VPN label in MPLS L3VPNs?

    a. RSVP

    b. LSR

    c. MP-BGP

    d. OSPF

3. When OSPF (Area 0) is used as the PE-CE routing protocol in MPLS L3VPN, how will routes appear in the CE routing table?

    a. O E2

    b. O E1

    c. O

    d. O IA

4. When EIGRP is used as the PE-CE routing protocol in MPLS L3VPN (with a backdoor in place between CEs), if a route is sent or received on an interface that has the SoO value set but does not match the one configured on an interface,

    a. the route is discarded.

    b. the route is preserved.

    c. a new route for this prefix toward null 0 is created automatically.

    d. a routing loop will take place.

5. If a customer is using BGP as MPLS L3VPN with the same AS number among all sites, what will be the status of traffic transport end to end between CE devices? If there is an issue, what could be deployed from the customer end if the service is unmanaged CE?

    a. BGP loop prevention takes place only in eBGP environments.

    b. Routes will not be imported due to the loop prevention mechanism, and BGP **allowas-in** should be configured.

    c. Routes will not be imported due to the loop prevention mechanism, and BGP **AS-override** should be configured.

    d. Redistribution between IGP and MP-BGP will manipulate the loop prevention mechanism of BGP, so routes will be imported successfully.

6. Which command can you use on IOS software under route-map to define the route-target value and be able to control whether prefixes are imported or exported?

    a. set route-target *ASN:NN*

    b. set community *ASN:NN*

   c.   set extcommunity *ASN:NN*

   d.   set community route-target *ASN:NN*

7. In the Draft-Rosen Multicast VPN solution, which protocol is used as the control plane to carry customer multicast information across the service provider network?

   a.   PIM

   b.   BGP

   c.   SSM

   d.   RSVP

Foundation Topics

MPLS L3VPN

As the name implies, the **Multiprotocol Label Switching (MPLS)** Layer 3 virtual private network (L3VPN) service is a Layer 3 service, which means the customer will participate in the routing process with the service provider.

For sure, this participation will depend on customer requirements and capabilities. Mentioning the capabilities is very important from a network design perspective and for business needs. For example, if the network staff at the customer end are not properly prepared to manage routing complexity, other options can arise from a management perspective, such as pushing for a managed L3VPN option for which the provider is responsible for managing the customer device, which eventually will impact the service cost. Or, the option will move with the Layer 2 option, which will have its own implications in general. So, customer requirements will determine which solution will fit.

The question is: What routing protocols can be implemented between the provider and the customer? Practically all routing protocols can be deployed, and each has its pros and cons. Generally speaking, BGP and static routing protocols are deployed the most often.

Before we get into the details of L3VPN configuration, let's review some points from the preceding chapter. Figure 12-1 illustrates the rough architecture of a normal service provider network.

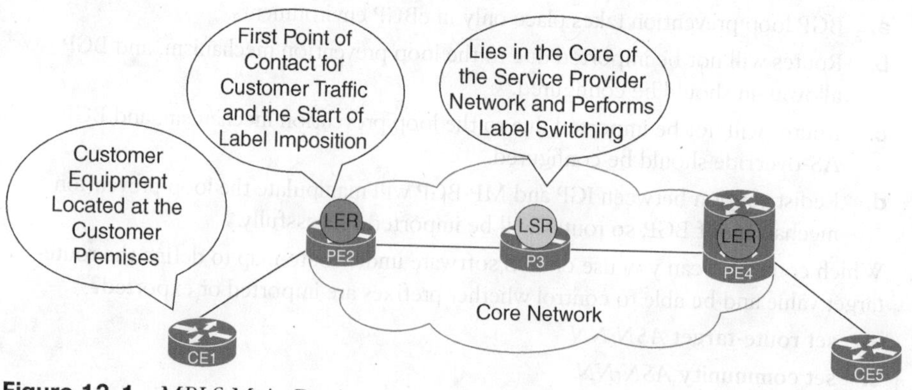

Figure 12-1 *MPLS Main Devices*

Virtual Routing and Forwarding (VRF)

The first step in implementing the MPLS L3VPN service is to ensure the proper traffic isolation/separation is in place to guarantee that no traffic leakage will occur because the provider should be able to support and serve several customers simultaneously using a single unified infrastructure.

The idea of **Virtual Routing and Forwarding (VRF)** is to create a new logical routing and forwarding table for each participating customer. We usually deal with one routing table, which is referred to as a global routing table (GRT), where the routing protocol is running. The idea is to make the routing device a group of logical routing tables, each serving a specific customer with no traffic leak by default (unless we need that on purpose). The high-level diagram in Figure 12-2 shows a routing device for which the GRT is built in and the new routing tables (VRFs) are created to handle different customers.

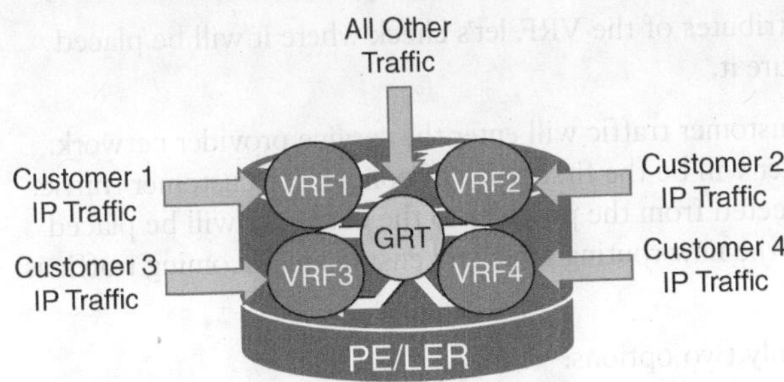

Figure 12-2   *GRT and VRF*

The main components of the VRF are as follows:

- **Route Distinguisher (RD):** This 64-bit value is represented as ASN:NN, where ASN is the autonomous system number and NN is a random number that represents a customer.

  The main idea of the RD (as the name implies) is to distinguish customer traffic from each other. For example, if two customers use the same internal IP space and normal routing is in place, one of them will be served, and the incoming packets will be transported per the general routing paradigm. By defining the RD, we are able to distinguish when we introduce a new packet in the form, as shown in Figure 12-3.

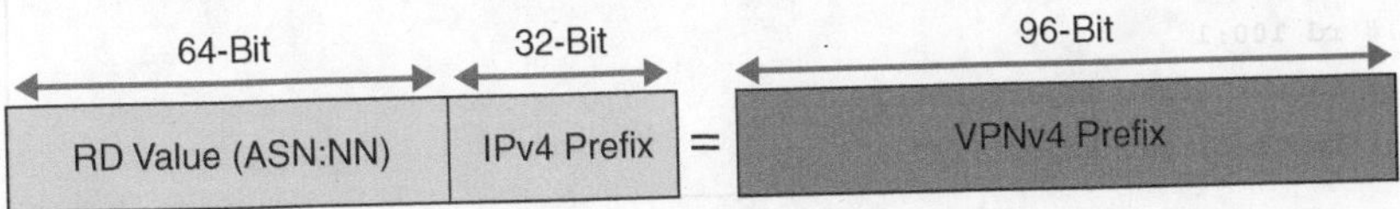

Figure 12-3   *Route Distinguisher and VPNv4*

The newly introduced prefix is called VPNv4 (it is VPN because the goal is to provide VPN service to customers and v4 because it handles IPv4 traffic). The new prefix will be different among customers because we are able to differentiate it due to the RD.

The important question now is: Which routing protocol will be able to transport and handle this prefix? The only protocol that supports it is Border Gateway Protocol through the introduction of Multi-Protocol BGP (MP-BGP).

NOTE MP-BGP uses a new Network Layer Reachability Information (NLRI) format with the following attributes:

- RD
- IPv4 prefix
- Next hop
- VPN label

- **Route Target (RT):** This value (which has the same format as the RD) introduces control capabilities for each VRF: what prefixes will be allowed to be accepted and what prefixes will be allowed to be advertised.

Now that we have listed the main attributes of the VRF, let's check where it will be placed and what options we have to configure it.

The VRF will be placed where the customer traffic will enter the service provider network. As discussed previously, the PE router will be the first point of contact for customer traffic, which means that the interface connected from the provider to the customer will be placed in a particular VRF, which will build the new routing table and ensure any incoming traffic is placed there.

For the VRF, we must configure mainly two options:

- **Option 1:** We can use the command **ip vrf {}** and list the VRF attributes underneath, as illustrated by Example 12-1.

NOTE The **ip vrf vrf-name** command is an IPv4-only command (as well as the **ip forwarding vrf** *vrf-name* command used under the interface). This command will not be able to serve coming IPv6 deployments. Cisco recommends using the multiprotocol VRF **vrf definition** and **vrf forwarding** (under the interface) commands.

Example 12-1 *VRF Configuration (Option 1)*

```
P3(config)# ip vrf SPCOR
P3(config-vrf)# rd 100:1
P3(config-vrf)# route-target import 100:1
P3(config-vrf)# route-target export 100:1
```

- **Option 2:** We can use the command **vrf definition {}** and list the VRF attributes. The main difference is that with the **vrf definition {}** command, we must specify which address family we are serving: IPv4 or IPv6. Example 12-2 shows the command syntax.

Example 12-2   *VRF Configuration (Option 2)*

```
PE2(config)# vrf definition SPCOR
PE2(config-vrf)# rd 100:1
PE2(config-vrf)# address-family ipv4 unicast
PE2(config-vrf-af)# route-target import 100:1
PE2(config-vrf-af)# route-target export 100:1
```

In both scenarios, we must reconfigure the IP address associated with the interface (if configured) once the VRF is tightened to the interface because the routing process aims to ensure the admin's decision by removing the interface from GRT and placing it in a VRF, as denoted by the log messages (which are shown in Example 12-3).

Example 12-3   *Attaching an Interface to VRF*

```
P3(config-vrf)# interface GigabitEthernet3
P3(config-if)# vrf forwarding SPCOR
% Use 'ip vrf forwarding' command for VRF SPCOR
! We must use the command ip vrf forwarding SPCOR
```

However, the syntax will slightly differ between the two flavors, as denoted by Example 12-4.

Example 12-4   *Attaching an Interface to VRF*

```
PE2(config)# interface GigabitEthernet1
PE2(config-if)# vrf forwarding SPCOR
% Interface GigabitEthernet1 IPv4 disabled and address(es) removed due to enabling
VRF SPCOR
! The preceding line means that the IP address is removed due to inserting this
! interface in the VRF as the router is making sure of the decision you made by
! moving this interface from the Global Routing Table (GRT) to a new routing table
! (VRF) called SPCOR.
PE2(config-if)# ip address 172.16.12.2 255.255.255.0
```

Now all communications between the provider edge (PE) and the customer edge (CE) will be within that VRF, even from management, troubleshooting, and routing.

Example 12-5 verifies the connectivity from PE2 to CE1 over the VRF-enabled interface.

Example 12-5   *Verifying Connectivity for the VRF-Enabled Interface*

```
PE2# ping vrf SPCOR 172.16.12.1
Type escape sequence to abort.
Sending 5, 100-byte ICMP Echos to 172.16.12.1, timeout is 2 seconds:
.!!!!
Success rate is 80 percent (4/5), round-trip min/avg/max = 1/1/2 ms
```

We can validate the interface membership into a specific VRF, as shown in Example 12-6. This example goes through the details for each VRF.

Example 12-6   show vrf *Output Details*

```
PE2# show vrf SPCOR
  Name                            Default RD          Protocols   Interfaces
  SPCOR                           100:1               ipv4        Gi1

PE2# show vrf ipv4 unicast SPCOR
  Name                            Default RD          Protocols   Interfaces
  SPCOR                           100:1               ipv4        Gi1

PE2# show vrf ipv4 unicast detail SPCOR
VRF SPCOR (VRF Id = 1); default RD 100:1; default VPNID <not set>
  New CLI format, supports multiple address-families
  Flags: 0x180C
  Interfaces:
    Gi1
Address family ipv4 unicast (Table ID = 0x1):
  Flags: 0x0
  Export VPN route-target communities
    RT:100:1
  Import VPN route-target communities
    RT:100:1
  No import route-map
  No global export route-map
  No export route-map
  VRF label distribution protocol: not configured
  VRF label allocation mode: per-prefix
```

VRF configuration on IOS XR is almost the same, with only minor differences in the
command syntax, as shown in Example 12-7.

Example 12-7   *VRF Configuration on IOS XR*

```
RP/0/0/CPU0:PE4(config)# vrf SPCOR
RP/0/0/CPU0:PE4(config-vrf)# rd 100:1
RP/0/0/CPU0:PE4(config-vrf)# address-family ipv4 unicast
RP/0/0/CPU0:PE4(config-vrf-af)# import route-target 100:1
RP/0/0/CPU0:PE4(config-vrf-af)# export route-target 100:1
```

Applying the VRF to the interface directly will produce an error message in IOS XR (with an
IPv4 address in place already), as illustrated by Example 12-8.

Example 12-8   *Attaching an Interface to VRF, IOS XR*

```
RP/0/0/CPU0:PE4(config)# interface GigabitEthernet0/0/0/2
RP/0/0/CPU0:PE4(config-if)# vrf SPCOR
RP/0/0/CPU0:PE4(config-if)# commit
```

```
% Failed to commit one or more configuration items during a pseudo-atomic operation.
All changes made have been reverted. Please issue 'show configuration failed [inher-
itance]' from this session to view the errors
```

```
RP/0/0/CPU0:PE4(config-if)# show configuration failed
!! SEMANTIC ERRORS: This configuration was rejected by
!! the system due to semantic errors. The individual
!! errors with each failed configuration command can be
!! found below.
RP/0/0/CPU0:PE4(config)# interface GigabitEthernet0/0/0/2
RP/0/0/CPU0:PE4(config-if)# vrf SPCOR
!!% 'RSI' detected the 'fatal' condition 'The interface's numbered and unnumbered
IPv4/IPv6 addresses must be removed prior to changing or deleting the VRF'
RP/0/0/CPU0:PE4(config-if)# no ipv4 address
RP/0/0/CPU0:PE4(config-if)# vrf SPCOR
RP/0/0/CPU0:PE4(config-if)# ipv4 address 172.16.45.4/24
RP/0/0/CPU0:PE4(config-if)# commit
```

For each created VRF, we can verify which interface is now part of that VRF and what attributes are attached to it (RD and RT), as illustrated in Example 12-9.

Example 12-9 *VRF Membership*

```
! IOS XR
RP/0/0/CPU0:R2# show vrf SPCOR detail
VRF SPCOR; RD 100:1; VPN ID not set
VRF mode: Regular
Description not set
Interfaces:
  GigabitEthernet0/0/0/2
Address family IPV4 Unicast
  Import VPN route-target communities:
    RT:100:1
  Export VPN route-target communities:
    RT:100:1
  No import route policy
  No export route policy
Address family IPV6 Unicast
  No import VPN route-target communities
  No export VPN route-target communities
  No import route policy
  No export route policy

! IOS
R1# show vrf SPCOR
```

```
Name                       Default RD          Protocols   Interfaces
SPCOR                      100:1               ipv4        Gi3
```

```
R1# show vrf detail
VRF SPCOR (VRF Id = 1); default RD 100:1; default VPNID <not set>
  New CLI format, supports multiple address-families
  Flags: 0x180C
  Interfaces:
    Gi3
Address family ipv4 unicast (Table ID = 0x1):
  Flags: 0x0
  Export VPN route-target communities
    RT:100:1
  Import VPN route-target communities
    RT:100:1
  No import route-map
  No global export route-map
  No export route-map
  VRF label distribution protocol: not configured
  VRF label allocation mode: per-prefix
Address family ipv6 unicast not active
Address family ipv4 multicast not active
Address family ipv6 multicast not active
```

MPLS LDP

Label Distribution Protocol (LDP) will be running within the interconnections in the core to ensure a functional **label-switched path (LSP)** end to end between the core device and will properly assign the labels (transport) for the edge devices to move the labeled packets.

As in Chapter 10, "MPLS Fundamentals," we will change the label range among the core devices for clarification purposes. From an IGP perspective, we will choose OSPF area 0 as the underlying internal protocol to make sure that router IDs are reachable, and therefore, that LDP neighborships are built as desired.

Example 12-10 briefly covers the previously mentioned aspects from a configuration perspective, particularly PE, P devices on IOS, and IOS XR operating systems.

Example 12-10 *PE2 LDP and IGP Configuration on IOS*

```
PE2(config)# mpls label protocol ldp
PE2(config)# mpls ldp router-id lo0 force
PE2(config)# mpls label range 200 299

PE2(config)# interface GigabitEthernet2
```

```
PE2(config-if)# mpls ip
```

```
PE2(config)# router ospf 1
PE2(config-router)# router-id 10.1.100.2
PE2(config-router)# network 10.1.23.2 0.0.0.0 area 0
PE2(config-router)# network 10.1.100.2 0.0.0.0 area 0
```

Example 12-11 applies the same exact configuration as implemented on PE2, except that it accounts for extra links due to the placement of P3 (acting as P/LSR) within the core network.

Example 12-11   *P3 LDP and IGP Configuration on IOS*

```
P3(config)# mpls label protocol ldp
P3(config)# mpls ldp router-id lo0 force
P3(config)# mpls label range 300 399
```

```
P3(config)# interface GigabitEthernet1
P3(config-if)# mpls ip
P3(config-if)# interface GigabitEthernet2
P3(config-if)# mpls ip
```

```
PE2(config)# router ospf 1
PE2(config-router)# router-id 10.1.100.3
PE2(config-router)# network 10.1.23.3 0.0.0.0 area 0
PE2(config-router)# network 10.1.34.3 0.0.0.0 area 0
PE2(config-router)# network 10.1.100.3 0.0.0.0 area 0
```

Example 12-12 lists the functional commands needed to activate LDP and associate the interface on which we will exchange Hello messages. As can be seen, on IOS XR, we enable the protocol and then associate the needed interfaces.

Example 12-12   *LDP and IGP Configuration on IOS XR*

```
RP/0/0/CPU0:PE4(config)# mpls ldp
RP/0/0/CPU0:PE4(config-ldp)# router-id 10.1.100.4
RP/0/0/CPU0:PE4(config-ldp)# interface GigabitEthernet0/0/0/3
RP/0/0/CPU0:PE4(config-ldp)# exit
RP/0/0/CPU0:PE4(config)# mpls label range 16400 16499
```

```
RP/0/0/CPU0:PE4(config)# router ospf 1
RP/0/0/CPU0:PE4(config-ospf)# router-id 10.1.100.4
RP/0/0/CPU0:PE4(config-ospf)# area 0
RP/0/0/CPU0:PE4(config-ospf-ar)# interface loopback 0
RP/0/0/CPU0:PE4(config-ospf-ar-if)# exit
RP/0/0/CPU0:PE4(config-ospf-ar)# interface GigabitEthernet0/0/0/3
RP/0/0/CPU0:PE4(config-ospf-ar)# commit
```

Table 12-2 shows the selected label ranges defined on the core devices (P and PEs) to clarify when tracing the label assignments.

Table 12-2 MPLS Label Range

Device Hostname	Label Range
PE2	200–299
P3	300–399
PE4	16400–16499

Multiprotocol-BGP (MP-BGP)

As discussed in the preceding chapter, LDP is responsible for allocating labels within the core network. These *transport labels* are responsible for assigning labels for the core devices for the packet to be transported to the correct device, which will be able to send it along the path to the destination.

The BGP comes into play because we are providing VPN services to our customers, for which we need to maintain separation, and therefore, new labels, called *VPN labels*, are introduced by BGP. Figure 12-4 shows the label stacking (we discussed the LSP/Transport label in Chapter 10 and now are introducing the VPN label).

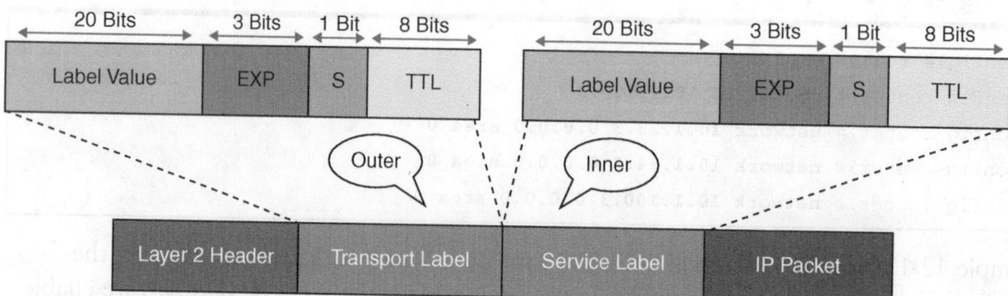

Figure 12-4 *MPLS Labels*

For the customer traffic to be transported from one edge device to another over the backbone, we need to establish a functional BGP session with a proper address family (VPNv4) that will be able to successfully exchange VPNv4 and VPNv6 prefixes.

Because the customer traffic is terminated at the PE devices, the session must be established only between these devices because the P/LSR does not actually hold any customer traffic, which, from a design aspect, will reserve resources. However, when we're dealing with large networks, P devices could play the role of route reflector for the respective address family.

The service provider network is a single autonomous system (AS), which means the BGP session will be an internal BGP session (iBGP), as discussed in Chapter 7, "BGP Fundamentals." Usually, iBGP sessions will be built using loopback addresses (loopback interfaces are logical interfaces, and therefore, they are up and will not suffer from incidents like physical interfaces; this approach also will be better for path diversity and availability [an alternative path through the core]). Consequently, reachability should be in place in between (we already achieved that by using OSPF as IGP, and Example 12-13 validates that by exploring the route table on PE2).

Example 12-13 *OSPF Routing Table Output*

```
PE2# show ip route ospf
! Output omitted for brevity
     10.0.0.0/8 is variably subnetted, 6 subnets, 2 masks
O        10.1.34.0/24 [110/2] via 10.1.23.3, 21:40:01, GigabitEthernet2
O        10.1.100.3/32 [110/2] via 10.1.23.3, 21:38:55, GigabitEthernet2
O        10.1.100.4/32 [110/3] via 10.1.23.3, 01:15:40, GigabitEthernet2
```

Reachability is conducted, as shown in Example 12-14, by sending ICMP packets sourced from a loopback 0 interface to ensure end-to-end connectivity.

Example 12-14 *ICMP Connectivity*

```
PE2# ping 10.1.100.4 source loopback 0
Type escape sequence to abort.
Sending 5, 100-byte ICMP Echos to 10.1.100.4, timeout is 2 seconds:
Packet sent with a source address of 10.1.100.2
!!!!!
Success rate is 100 percent (5/5), round-trip min/avg/max = 2/3/6 ms
```

Example 12-15 lists the needed configuration statements for establishing the BGP VPNv4 session. (We used AS 100 for the configuration illustrations.)

Example 12-15 *BGP VPNv4 Configuration on IOS*

```
PE2(config)# router bgp 100
PE2(config-router)# no bgp default ipv4-unicast
! By default, BGP will assume the session will be built for IPv4 address-family
! though we have turned off this default behavior for better control on the sessions
! that need to be established.
PE2(config-router)# neighbor 10.1.100.4 remote-as 100
! The remote-as statement is under the global BGP process.
PE2(config-router)# neighbor 10.1.100.4 update-source loopback 0
! As mentioned, the source of BGP packets will be through loopback interface. We
! must explicitly define it as BGP (Due to nature of protocol for handling external
! relations will assume the source as the direct physical interface).
PE2(config-router)# address-family vpnv4 unicast
PE2(config-router-af)# neighbor 10.1.100.4 activate
```

Before we move on to the IOS XR flavor and back to the VRF definition command, let's look at the Route Target, which is an extended community that should be explicitly configured to be successfully sent or received between the BGP neighbors. Example 12-16 lists the available options associated with the **send-community** keyword under the BGP VPNv4 **address-family** configuration command associated with the neighbor with which we are trying to establish a session.

Example 12-16 *VRF Definition and Interface Interaction on IOS XR*

```
PE2(config)# vrf definition SPCOR
PE2(config-vrf)# address-family ipv4 unicast
PE2(config-vrf-af)# ?
! Output omitted for brevity
  route-target        Specify Target VPN Extended Communities
```

```
PE2(config)# router bgp 100
PE2(config-router)# address-family vpnv4 unicast
PE2(config-router-af)# neighbor 10.1.100.4 send-community ?
  both       Send Standard and Extended Community attributes
  extended   Send Extended Community attribute
  standard   Send Standard Community attribute
PE2(config-router-af)# neighbor 10.1.100.4 send-community extended
```

From an IOS XR perspective, the approach is the same, but with minor changes. Example 12-17 displays the relative configuration in Example 12-16 but focuses on IOS XR.

Example 12-17 *BGP VPNv4 Configuration on IOS XR*

```
RP/0/0/CPU0:PE4(config)# router bgp 100
RP/0/0/CPU0:PE4(config-bgp)# address-family vpnv4 unicast
RP/0/0/CPU0:PE4(config-bgp-af)# exit
RP/0/0/CPU0:PE4(config-bgp)# neighbor 10.1.100.2
RP/0/0/CPU0:PE4(config-bgp-nbr)# remote-as 100
RP/0/0/CPU0:PE4(config-bgp-nbr)# update-source loopback 0
RP/0/0/CPU0:PE4(config-bgp-nbr)# address-family vpnv4 unicast
RP/0/0/CPU0:PE4(config-bgp-nbr-af)# commit
```

To check the BGP relation (VPNv4) from both PE devices, we can use the **show bgp vpnv4 unicast all summary** command on PE2 (IOS based) and the same command excluding the **all** keyword, as shown in Example 12-18.

Example 12-18 *BGP VPNv4 Table Output*

```
! IOS
PE2# show bgp vpnv4 unicast all summary
BGP router identifier 10.1.100.2, local AS number 100
BGP table version is 1, main routing table version 1
Neighbor        V    AS MsgRcvd MsgSent   TblVer  InQ OutQ Up/Down   State/PfxRcd
10.1.100.4      4    100 12      14        1       0   0    00:09:58  0
! The number of received prefixes is 0 which means we have a successful BGP neigh
! borship with no routes received yet.
```

```
! IOS XR
```

```
RP/0/0/CPU0:PE4# show bgp vpnv4 unicast summary
BGP router identifier 10.1.100.4, local AS number 100
BGP generic scan interval 60 secs
Non-stop routing is enabled
BGP table state: Active
Table ID: 0x0   RD version: 0
BGP main routing table version 1
BGP NSR Initial initsync version 1 (Reached)
BGP NSR/ISSU Sync-Group versions 0/0
BGP scan interval 60 secs
BGP is operating in STANDALONE mode.
Process       RcvTblVer   bRIB/RIB   LabelVer   ImportVer   SendTblVer   StandbyVer
Speaker       1           1          1          1           1            0
Neighbor    Spk         AS MsgRcvd MsgSent   TblVer      InQ OutQ  Up/Down    St/PfxRcd
10.1.100.2  0           100        15        13          1    0    0 00:10:33         0
```

Now that we have everything ready from a configuration perspective for the main functional elements to handle customer traffic, let's start examining different routing instances between PE and CE.

MPLS L3VPN Static PE-CE Routing

We are ready to start configuring static routing between PE and CE. As discussed, we are now dealing with the CE through its own routing instance (VRF), and therefore, anything from a routing perspective should fall under that VRF. So, in our example, the CE1 loopback interface represents the customer internal network, and therefore, we will reach it through VRF SPCOR, defined earlier. Figure 12-5 shows the topology that we use to demonstrate the concepts associated with establishing MPLS L3VPN.

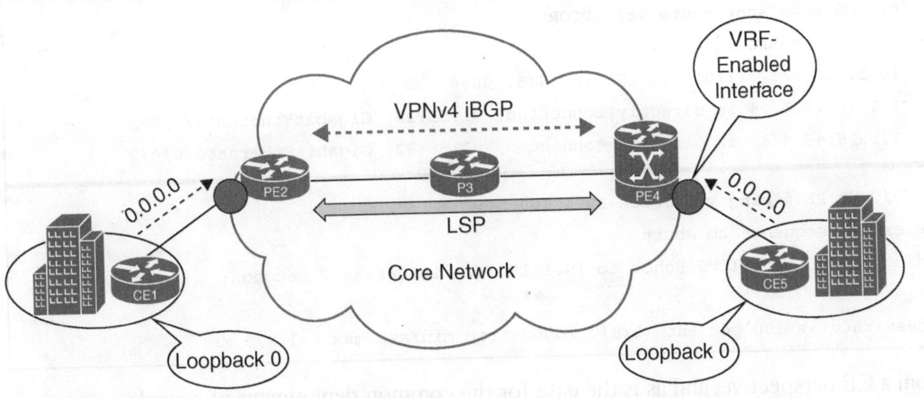

Figure 12-5 *MPLS L3VPN Static PE-CE*

Example 12-19 shows the normal static route configuration statement with a minor change. Here, the VRF is associated with the command because the destination we are trying to reach is through a VRF-enabled interface and the learned route will be installed into the VRF instead of the global routing table.

Example 12-19 *Static Route Under VRF Configuration*

```
PE2(config)# ip route vrf SPCOR 10.1.100.1 255.255.255.255 172.16.12.1
```

```
RP/0/0/CPU0:PE4(config)# router static
RP/0/0/CPU0:PE4(config-static)# vrf SPCOR
RP/0/0/CPU0:PE4(config-static-vrf-afi)# 10.1.100.5/32 172.16.45.5
RP/0/0/CPU0:PE4(config-static-vrf-afi)# commit
```

We can check the respective VRF routing table and validate connectivity, as shown in Example 12-20. As listed, all troubleshooting commands also are associated with the VRF.

Example 12-20 *Verifying Connectivity Through VRF*

```
PE2# sh ip route vrf SPCOR
Routing Table: SPCOR
! Output omitted for brevity
      10.0.0.0/32 is subnetted, 1 subnets
S        10.1.100.1 [1/0] via 172.16.12.1
      172.16.0.0/16 is variably subnetted, 2 subnets, 2 masks
C        172.16.12.0/24 is directly connected, GigabitEthernet1
L        172.16.12.2/32 is directly connected, GigabitEthernet1
```

```
PE2# ping vrf SPCOR 10.1.100.1
Type escape sequence to abort.
Sending 5, 100-byte ICMP Echos to 10.1.100.1, timeout is 2 seconds:
!!!!!
Success rate is 100 percent (5/5), round-trip min/avg/max = 2/4/11 ms
```

```
RP/0/0/CPU0:PE4# show route vrf SPCOR
! Output omitted for brevity
S    10.1.100.5/32 [1/0] via 172.16.45.5, 00:03:02
C    172.16.45.0/24 is directly connected, 01:55:32, GigabitEthernet0/0/0/2
L    172.16.45.4/32 is directly connected, 01:55:32, GigabitEthernet0/0/0/2
```

```
RP/0/0/CPU0:PE4# ping vrf SPCOR 10.1.100.5
Type escape sequence to abort.
Sending 5, 100-byte ICMP Echos to 10.1.100.5, timeout is 2 seconds:
!!!!!
Success rate is 100 percent (5/5), round-trip min/avg/max = 1/2/9 ms
```

From a CE perspective, and as is the case for the common deployment of a single exit point, a default route should be enough for connectivity, as shown in Example 12-21. Obviously, we do not need to associate the VRF with the command on the CE devices because the customer edges are not aware of any VRF.

Example 12-21 *Default Route Configuration*

```
CE1(config)# ip route 0.0.0.0 0.0.0.0 172.16.12.2
CE5(config)# ip route 0.0.0.0 0.0.0.0 172.16.45.4
```

The last question in the configuration is: How are we going to make the two islands (static with a VRF, MP-BGP) communicate? The answer is redistribution! When we have two different domains and route leaking is needed, redistribution is needed for the routes to be exchanged among the two domains.

For a static route, we do not have the ability to redistribute within (not like dynamic protocols, which have a process running and we can redistribute within).

However, the BGP process is running, and we can redistribute the static routes inside. Figure 12-6 shows where on the topology the redistribution will take place and the default routes from the CEs pointing directly to their next-hop: PEs.

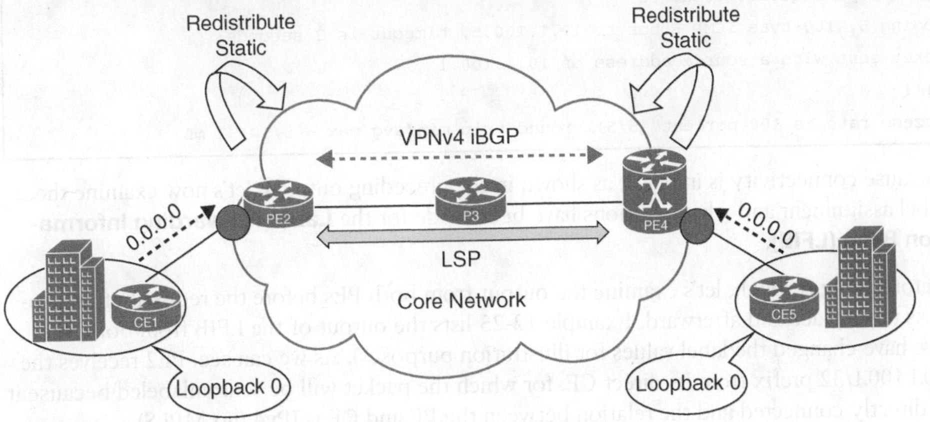

Figure 12-6 *MPLS L3VPN Static PE-CE, Redistribution Process*

Eventually, we will deal with IPv4 traffic coming from the customer end, but it will be sent inside the VRF. This means that, for the BGP process to interpret properly, we must define the IPv4 address-family support but for the VRF of concern, as demonstrated in Example 12-22.

Example 12-22 *Redistribution Under BGP for a Specific VRF*

```
PE2(config)# router bgp 100
PE2(config-router)# address-family ipv4 vrf SPCOR
PE2(config-router-af)# redistribute static

RP/0/0/CPU0:PE4(config)# router bgp 100
RP/0/0/CPU0:PE4(config-bgp)# vrf SPCOR
RP/0/0/CPU0:PE4(config-bgp-vrf)# address-family ipv4 unicast
RP/0/0/CPU0:PE4(config-bgp-vrf-af)# redistribute static
```

We can see that the prefix is now transported as needed from one end to the other by examining the route table (focused on BGP learned routes), as depicted in Example 12-23.

Example 12-23 *RIB Output*

```
PE2# show ip route vrf SPCOR bgp
! Output omitted for brevity
     10.0.0.0/32 is subnetted, 2 subnets
B       10.1.100.5 [200/0] via 10.1.100.4, 00:01:07


RP/0/0/CPU0:PE4# show route vrf SPCOR bgp
B    10.1.100.1/32 [200/0] via 10.1.100.2 (nexthop in vrf default), 00:01:22
```

Example 12-24 verifies connectivity from the CE1 loopback address to the CE2 loopback address by using ICMP.

Example 12-24 *Connectivity Verification*

```
CE1# ping 10.1.100.5 source loopback 0
Type escape sequence to abort.
Sending 5, 100-byte ICMP Echos to 10.1.100.5, timeout is 2 seconds:
Packet sent with a source address of 10.1.100.1
!!!!!
Success rate is 100 percent (5/5), round-trip min/avg/max = 5/10/32 ms
```

Because connectivity is in place, as shown in the preceding outputs, let's now examine the label assignment and what additions have been made for the **Label Forwarding Information Base (LFIB)**.

Before going through, let's examine the output from both PEs before the redistribution process takes place and afterward. Example 12-25 lists the output of the LFIB from both PEs (we have changed the label values for illustration purposes). As we can see, PE2 receives the 10.1.100.1/32 prefix from its direct CE, for which the packet will be sent unlabeled because it is directly connected and the relation between the PE and CE is IPv4 (no MPLS).

Example 12-25 *PE2 LFIB Output*

```
! Before redistribution
PE2# show mpls forwarding-table
Local       Outgoing    Prefix          Bytes Label   Outgoing    Next Hop
Label       Label       or Tunnel Id    Switched      interface
200         Pop Label   10.1.34.0/24    0             Gi2         10.1.23.3
201         Pop Label   10.1.100.3/32   0             Gi2         10.1.23.3
202         301         10.1.100.4/32   0             Gi2         10.1.23.3


! After redistribution
PE2# show mpls forwarding-table
Local       Outgoing    Prefix          Bytes Label   Outgoing    Next Hop
Label       Label       or Tunnel Id    Switched      interface
200         Pop Label   10.1.34.0/24    0             Gi2         10.1.23.3
201         Pop Label   10.1.100.3/32   0             Gi2         10.1.23.3
202         301         10.1.100.4/32   0             Gi2         10.1.23.3
203         No Label    10.1.100.1/32[V] 570          Gi1         172.16.12.1
```

Similarly, Example 12-26 lists the output of the MPLS forwarding table on PE4, which will be similar in functionality to what we examined in the previous example on PE2.

Example 12-26 *PE4 LFIB Output*

```
! Before redistribution
RP/0/0/CPU0:PE4# show mpls forwarding

Local   Outgoing    Prefix               Outgoing       Next Hop         Bytes
Label   Label       or ID                Interface                       Switched
------  ----------  -------------------  ------------   --------------   ------------
16400   300         10.1.100.2/32        Gi0/0/0/3      10.1.34.3        9832
16401   Pop         10.1.100.3/32        Gi0/0/0/3      10.1.34.3        13465
16402   Pop         10.1.23.0/24         Gi0/0/0/3      10.1.34.3        283140
```

```
! After redistribution
RP/0/0/CPU0:PE4# show mpls forwarding

Local   Outgoing    Prefix               Outgoing       Next Hop         Bytes
Label   Label       or ID                Interface                       Switched
------  ----------  -------------------  ------------   --------------   ------------
16400   300         10.1.100.2/32        Gi0/0/0/3      10.1.34.3        24493
16401   Pop         10.1.100.3/32        Gi0/0/0/3      10.1.34.3        28193
16402   Pop         10.1.23.0/24         Gi0/0/0/3      10.1.34.3        2860
16403   Unlabelled  10.1.100.5/32[V]     Gi0/0/0/2      172.16.45.5      500
```

Now let's trace the outputs for a step-by-step label assignment verification from a BGP perspective (BGP VPNv4 is used for packet transport among the core network). Example 12-27 lists the output of BGP VPNv4 output for the prefix of concern from a PE2 perspective.

Example 12-27 *BGP VPNv4 Output Verification*

```
PE2# show bgp vpnv4 unicast all 10.1.100.1 255.255.255.255
BGP routing table entry for 100:1:10.1.100.1/32, version 2
Paths: (1 available, best #1, table SPCOR)
  Advertised to update-groups:
    1
  Refresh Epoch 1
  Local
    172.16.12.1 (via vrf SPCOR) from 0.0.0.0 (10.1.100.2)
      Origin incomplete, metric 0, localpref 100, weight 32768, valid, sourced, best
      Extended Community: RT:100:1
      mpls labels in/out 203/nolabel
      rx pathid: 0, tx pathid: 0x0
      Updated on Jan 8 2024 12:11:48 UTC
```

We can confirm the label assignment by checking the FIB output from PE2, as shown in Example 12-28 (ensuring that the VRF is associated with the command).

Example 12-28 *FIB Output Details*

```
PE2# show ip cef vrf SPCOR 10.1.100.1 255.255.255.255 detail
10.1.100.1/32, epoch 0
  dflt local label info: other/203 [0x2]
  recursive via 172.16.12.1
    attached to GigabitEthernet1
```

Next, let's move to PE4 (IOS XR based) to validate the label assignments, as shown in Example 12-29.

Example 12-29 *Label Assignment for VPNv4*

```
RP/0/0/CPU0:PE4# show bgp vpnv4 unicast labels
! Output omitted for brevity
   Network             Next Hop          Rcvd Label       Local Label
Route Distinguisher: 100:1 (default for vrf SPCOR)
*>i10.1.100.1/32      10.1.100.2        203              nolabel
*> 10.1.100.5/32      172.16.45.5       nolabel          16403
```

We can continue the validation of label assignments and end with tracing from an edge through another edge, as depicted in Example 12-30.

Example 12-30 *LFIB Verification for a Certain Prefix*

```
RP/0/0/CPU0:PE4# show mpls forwarding prefix 10.1.100.2/32
Local   Outgoing   Prefix            Outgoing      Next Hop      Bytes
Label   Label      or ID             Interface                   Switched
------  ---------  ----------------  ------------  ------------  ----------
16400   300        10.1.100.2/32     Gi0/0/0/3     10.1.34.3     25412

RP/0/0/CPU0:PE4# show route vrf SPCOR 10.1.100.1 255.255.255.255 detail
Routing entry for 10.1.100.1/32
  Known via "bgp 100", distance 200, metric 0, type internal
  Installed Jan  8 12:12:20.462 for 00:12:44
  Routing Descriptor Blocks
    10.1.100.2, from 10.1.100.2
      Nexthop in Vrf: "default", Table: "default", IPv4 Unicast, Table Id:
0xe0000000
      Route metric is 0
      Label: 0xcb (203)
      Tunnel ID: None
      Binding Label: None
      Extended communities count: 0
      Source RD attributes: 0x0000:100:1
      NHID:0x0(Ref:0)
  Route version is 0x3 (3)
  No local label
  IP Precedence: Not Set
```

```
QoS Group ID: Not Set
Flow-tag: Not Set
Fwd-class: Not Set
Route Priority: RIB_PRIORITY_RECURSIVE (12) SVD Type RIB_SVD_TYPE_REMOTE
Download Priority 3, Download Version 8
No advertising protos.
```

Example 12-31 shows the FIB output for the prefix 10.1.100.1/32 within the VRF SCPOR and highlights the label's imposition.

Example 12-31 *FIB Output for VRF SPCOR*

```
RP/0/0/CPU0:PE4# show cef vrf SPCOR 10.1.100.1/32 detail
10.1.100.1/32, version 8, internal 0x5000001 0x0 (ptr 0xa142970c) [1], 0x0 (0x0),
0x208 (0xa1757108)
Prefix Len 32, traffic index 0, precedence n/a, priority 3
  gateway array (0xa1362800) reference count 1, flags 0x2038, source rib (7), 0
backups
                [1 type 1 flags 0x48441 (0xa1773358) ext 0x0 (0x0)]
  LW-LDI[type=0, refc=0, ptr=0x0, sh-ldi=0x0]
  gateway array update type-time 1 Jan  8 12:12:20.482
LDI Update time Jan  8 12:12:20.482
  via 10.1.100.2/32, 3 dependencies, recursive [flags 0x6000]
   path-idx 0 NHID 0x0 [0xa17cb70c 0x0]
   recursion-via-/32
   next hop VRF - 'default', table - 0xe0000000
   next hop 10.1.100.2/32 via 16400/0/21
   next hop 10.1.34.3/32 Gi0/0/0/3        labels imposed {300 203}
   Load distribution: 0 (refcount 1)
   Hash  OK  Interface               Address
   0     Y   Unknown                 16400/0
```

The traceroute in Example 12-32 verifies the labels imposed along the path (LSP) as we run through the core network intermediate devices: LER and LSR.

Example 12-32 *Traceroute Output*

```
CE5# traceroute 10.1.100.1 source loopback 0 numeric
VRF info: (vrf in name/id, vrf out name/id)
  1 172.16.45.4 5 msec 1 msec 2 msec
  2 10.1.34.3 [MPLS: Labels 300/203 Exp 0] 126 msec 10 msec 322 msec
  3 172.16.12.2 [MPLS: Label 203 Exp 0] 44 msec 6 msec 6 msec
  4 172.16.12.1 6 msec 4 msec 5 msec
```

Figure 12-7 shows how the label assignment takes place (transport and VPN) and where the label removal will take place (PHP), ending with CE1 receiving a pure IPv4 prefix. We did not encounter the swapping of labels across the core (P3) because this was demonstrated in Chapter 10.

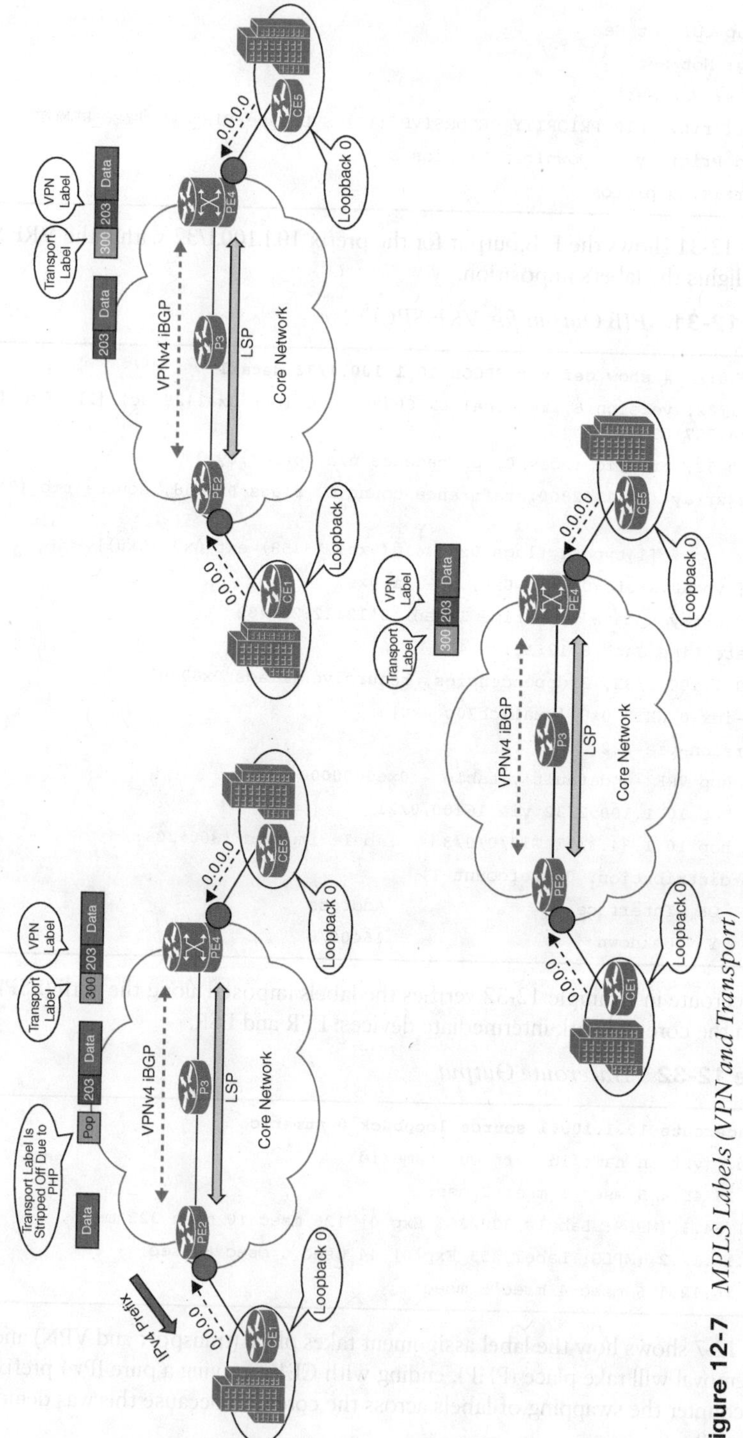

Figure 12-7 *MPLS Labels (VPN and Transport)*

Now as can be seen, we have started with static routing as the running protocol between PE and CE. This ensures that (because we are targeting the CE's loopback network) reachability is in place from loopback to loopback. Suppose we need to ping directly (as a test for the connectivity); the router will, by default, use the ICMP packet source as the physical interface (connected to the PE). Example 12-33 shows the ICMP failure.

Example 12-33 *ICMP Failure (Using Physical Interface)*

```
CE1# ping 10.1.100.5
Type escape sequence to abort.
Sending 5, 100-byte ICMP Echos to 10.1.100.5, timeout is 2 seconds:
.....
Success rate is 0 percent (0/5)
```

We have two options to isolate the issue and ensure proper connectivity. Either we use **redistribute connected** under the **address-family ipv4 vrf** {*vrf-name*} or we can advertise the PE-to-CE link into the BGP under the same address family. (Connecting is the simplest form of routing, so it can be redistributed into any dynamic routing protocol but not in a mutual fashion).

Let's look at the first option, the **redistribute connected** command, and check the connectivity, as illustrated in Example 12-34.

Example 12-34 *The* **redistribute connected** *Related Verification Outputs*

```
PE2# show ip route vrf SPCOR connected | begin Gateway
Gateway of last resort is not set
      172.16.0.0/16 is variably subnetted, 3 subnets, 2 masks
C         172.16.12.0/24 is directly connected, GigabitEthernet2
L         172.16.12.2/32 is directly connected, GigabitEthernet2

PE2# show bgp vpnv4 all neighbors 10.1.100.4 advertised-routes | include 172.16.12.1
 *>   10.1.100.1/32    172.16.12.1            0         32768 ?

PE2(config)# router bgp 100
PE2(config-router)# address-family ipv4 vrf SPCOR
PE2(config-router-af)# redistribute connected

PE2# show bgp vpnv4 unicast all neighbors 10.1.100.4 advertised-routes | include
172.16.12.0
 *>   172.16.12.0/24   0.0.0.0               0         32768 ?

RP/0/0/CPU0:PE4(config)# router bgp 100
RP/0/0/CPU0:PE4(config-bgp)# vrf SPCOR
RP/0/0/CPU0:PE4(config-bgp-vrf)# address-family ipv4 unicast
RP/0/0/CPU0:PE4(config-bgp-vrf-af)# redistribute connected
```

```
RP/0/0/CPU0:PE4# show bgp vpnv4 unicast neighbors 10.1.100.2 advertised-routes |
include 172.16.45.0
  172.16.45.0/24      10.1.100.4      Local        ?
```

```
CE1# debug ip icmp
CE1# ping 10.1.100.5
Type escape sequence to abort.
Sending 5, 100-byte ICMP Echos to 10.1.100.5, timeout is 2 seconds:
!!!!!
Success rate is 100 percent (5/5), round-trip min/avg/max = 6/9/12 ms
CE1#
ICMP: echo reply rcvd, src 10.1.100.5, dst 172.16.12.1, topology BASE, dscp 0 topoid
0
ICMP: echo reply rcvd, src 10.1.100.5, dst 172.16.12.1, topology BASE, dscp 0 topoid
0
ICMP: echo reply rcvd, src 10.1.100.5, dst 172.16.12.1, topology BASE, dscp 0 topoid
0
ICMP: echo reply rcvd, src 10.1.100.5, dst 172.16.12.1, topology BASE, dscp 0 topoid
0
ICMP: echo reply rcvd, src 10.1.100.5, dst 172.16.12.1, topology BASE, dscp 0 topoid
0
```

The other option is to use the **network** statement, as shown in Example 12-35.

Example 12-35   *Network Statement to Advertise Routes*

```
PE2(config)# router bgp 100
PE2(config-router)# address-family ipv4 vrf SPCOR
PE2(config-router-af)# network 172.16.12.0 mask 255.255.255.0
```

```
RP/0/0/CPU0:PE4(config)# router bgp 100
RP/0/0/CPU0:PE4(config-bgp)# vrf SPCOR
RP/0/0/CPU0:PE4(config-bgp-vrf)# address-family ipv4 unicast
RP/0/0/CPU0:PE4(config-bgp-vrf-af)# network 172.16.45.0/24
RP/0/0/CPU0:PE4(config-bgp-vrf-af)# commit
```

```
CE1# ping 10.1.100.5
Type escape sequence to abort.
Sending 5, 100-byte ICMP Echos to 10.1.100.5, timeout is 2 seconds:
!!!!!
Success rate is 100 percent (5/5), round-trip min/avg/max = 7/10/17 ms
```

The steps that follow summarize the process of transporting the traffic from one CE to another by passing through the MPLS core network (taking into consideration that the basic IP addressing is already in place and IGP is running inside the core network to make sure PE loopback reachability is in place).

Step 1. Define the VRF on the PE devices with an RD value to make sure the prefixes received from the CE devices are distinguished and the RT value controls the import/export action.

Step 2. Place the interface (subinterface) connected to the CE into the target VRF to make sure all customer traffic will be installed into the newly created routing table (VRF).

Step 3. Run the routing protocol between the CE and the PE to make sure all customer internal routes are learned dynamically and placed into the VRF.

Step 4. Enable MPLS LDP within the core network to make sure the LSP is built to handle the traffic (Labeled).

Step 5. Once the LDP is running and the neighborship between the core devices is up and functional, proper transport (outer) labels will be assigned, which will build the forwarding plane for transporting the labeled customer traffic.

Step 6. Once the IPv4 prefix is received within the VRF on the respective PE, the RD will be attached to the IPv4 prefix producing the VPNv4 prefix.

Step 7. The MP-BGP will be established between the PEs servicing the customer in order to interpret the VPNv4 prefixes and transport it across the MPLS domain.

Step 8. A new inner unique label (VPN) will be assigned to the customer traffic to identify the VRF to which the customer belongs.

Step 9. The receiving PE will check the RT values to make sure it is allowed to be imported inside the VRF.

Step 10. Once the receiving PE receives the VPNv4, it will strip the label and send a pure IPv4 prefix to the other CE.

MPLS L3VPN OSPF PE-CE Routing

Let's move now to a new protocol that can be deployed as the PE-CE routing protocol; however, it is worth mentioning that it is not usually used for this case because the goal is to use OSPF within service provider core networks or large enterprises due to its hierarchical structure and scalability.

We already have deployed OSPF per our example as the core network for maintaining end-to-end reachability within the core and hence building a successful labeled path (LSP). We are using a flat area design (Area 0) and process ID (PID) of 1. In this example, we deploy the same configuration, and referring to the previous section, we have VRFs configured, and so all communications will be through this VRF. Figure 12-8 shows the topology for this deployment.

Let's start from the CE devices and configure OSPF PID 1 normally, as we did with the original OSPF in the core. Example 12-36 lists the necessary commands to enable OSPF as a routing protocol on the edge devices, replacing the static process demonstrated in the previous section.

NOTE For clarification purposes, we changed the PE4 from IOS XR to IOS based.

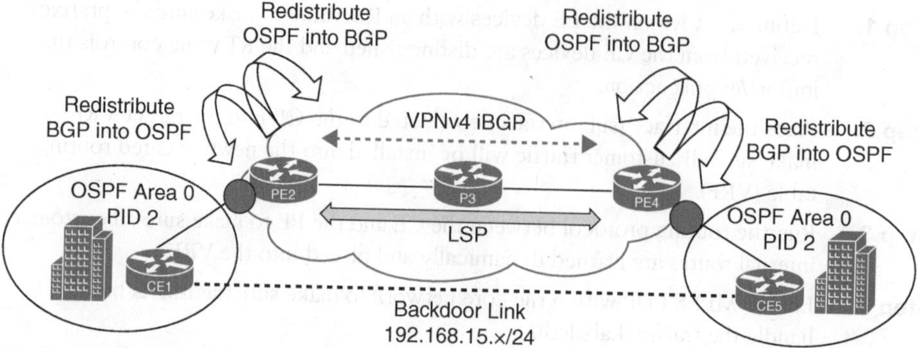

Figure 12-8 *OSPF as PE-CE Routing Protocol*

Example 12-36 *OSPF Basic Configuration*

```
CE1(config)# router ospf 1
CE1(config-router)# router-id 10.1.100.1
CE1(config-router)# network 10.1.100.1 0.0.0.0 area 0
CE1(config-router)# network 172.16.12.1 0.0.0.0 area 0
CE1(config-router)# interface GigabitEthernet0/0
CE1(config-if)# ip ospf network point-to-point
```

```
CE5(config)# router ospf 1
CE5(config-router)# router-id 10.1.100.5
CE5(config-router)# network 10.1.100.5 0.0.0.0 area 0
CE5(config-router)# network 172.16.45.5 0.0.0.0 area 0
CE5(config-router)# interface GigabitEthernet0/0
CE5(config-if)# ip ospf network point-to-point
```

Clearly, we cannot use the same PID on the PE device because we already used PID for
the global routing communication. However, the most important piece we need is the VRF
attachment to the OSPF process, as shown in Example 12-37.

Example 12-37 *OSPF Instance per VRF Definition*

```
PE2(config)# router ospf 2 vrf SPCOR
PE2(config-router)# network 172.16.45.4 0.0.0.0 area 0
PE2(config)# interface GigabitEthernet1
PE2(config-if)# ip ospf network point-to-point
%OSPF-5-ADJCHG: Process 2, Nbr 10.1.100.1 on GigabitEthernet1 from LOADING to FULL,
Loading Done
```

As previously mentioned, we must link the VRF to the relevant **show** command to validate
the route's installment, as shown in Example 12-38.

Example 12-38 *VRF-Related Verification Commands*

```
PE2# show ip route vrf SPCOR ospf
! Output omitted for brevity
      10.0.0.0/32 is subnetted, 2 subnets
O        10.1.100.1 [110/2] via 172.16.12.1, 00:01:18, GigabitEthernet1
```

```
PE2# ping vrf SPCOR 10.1.100.1
Type escape sequence to abort.
Sending 5, 100-byte ICMP Echos to 10.1.100.1, timeout is 2 seconds:
!!!!!
Success rate is 100 percent (5/5), round-trip min/avg/max = 1/1/2 ms
```

With a similar configuration on PE4, the initial connectivity is in place (PE-CE interconnection). We should now conduct the redistribution process again. What differs now is that we use a dynamic protocol, and therefore, a mutual redistribution process should take place.

The same applies from a VRF perspective: all routing updates and communications should go through the VRF. Example 12-39 shows the OSPF configuration linked to a VRF (a new PID = 2 has been introduced), as well as a redistribution statement under the OSPF process for the BGP protocol, which brings the target routes.

Example 12-39 *Mutual Redistribution for VRF SPCOR*

```
PE2(config)# router ospf 2 vrf SPCOR
PE2(config-router)# redistribute bgp 100 subnets
! It is crucial to use the subnets keyword when redistributing inside OSPF domain
! for the subnets to hold actual subnet mask.
PE2(config-router)# router bgp 100
PE2(config-router)# address-family ipv4 vrf SPCOR
PE2(config-router-af)# redistribute ospf 2 vrf SPCOR
```

NOTE   It is important to use the **subnets** keyword when redistributing inside the OSPF process because OSPF, by default, will only advertise classful networks. You need to add the **subnets** keyword at the end of the redistribution to enable advertisement of classless subnets.

Now let's start analyzing the routes sent and received from a CE1 perspective, as shown in Example 12-40.

Example 12-40 *Connectivity Verification*

```
CE1# show ip route ospf
! Output omitted for brevity
      10.0.0.0/32 is subnetted, 2 subnets
O IA     10.1.100.5 [110/3] via 172.16.12.2, 00:58:03, GigabitEthernet0/0
```

```
         172.16.0.0/16 is variably subnetted, 3 subnets, 2 masks
O E2        172.16.45.0/24 [110/1] via 172.16.12.2, 00:58:17, GigabitEthernet0/0
```

```
CE1# ping 10.1.100.5 source loopback 0
Type escape sequence to abort.
Sending 5, 100-byte ICMP Echos to 10.1.100.5, timeout is 2 seconds:
Packet sent with a source address of 10.1.100.1
!!!!!
Success rate is 100 percent (5/5), round-trip min/avg/max = 5/9/23 ms
```

As we can see, the routes have been received successfully. The received routes are denoted as inter-area (IA) routes because we are using the redistribution process. The reason is that an attribute called the OSPF Domain Identifier (ID) is defined as the BGP extended community and carried over the VPNv4 update between PEs.

If the route is from the same domain as the OSPF instance into which it has been redistributed and originally advertised as an inter-area route, it will be treated as an inter-area route delivered to the end CE in a **link-state advertisement (LSA)** Type 3.

Next, let's examine what really is taking place through the route advertisement going through the redistribution. Example 12-41 highlights the OSPF process ID from both CE1 and PE2 with clear output for the domain ID value.

Example 12-41 *OSPF Process ID and Domain ID Verification*

```
CE1# show ip ospf | include ID
 Routing Process "ospf 1" with ID 10.1.100.1
```

```
PE1# show ip ospf 2 | include ID
 Routing Process "ospf 2" with ID 172.16.12.2
   Domain ID type 0x0005, value 0.0.0.2
```

If you recall, we did not explicitly define the router-ID for the VRF OSPF process (#2), and therefore, it was elected as the highest IP address within the VRF.

The OSPF domain ID is 42 bytes, and the domain ID is encoded in a 2-byte type field. Cisco IOS, by default, uses 0X0005. The next 2 bytes carry the actual domain ID, which is extracted from the process ID. The last 4 bytes are not used. Checking the BGP VPNv4 output for the target prefix, as illustrated in Example 12-42, will shed light on the domain ID.

Example 12-42 *BGP VPNv4 Output*

```
PE1# show bgp vpnv4 unicast all 10.1.100.1 255.255.255.255
BGP routing table entry for 100:1:10.1.100.1/32, version 2
Paths: (1 available, best #1, table SPCOR)
  Advertised to update-groups:
     1
```

```
Refresh Epoch 1
Local
   172.16.12.1 (via vrf SPCOR) from 0.0.0.0 (10.1.100.2)
      Origin incomplete, metric 2, localpref 100, weight 32768, valid, sourced, best
      Extended Community: RT:100:1 OSPF DOMAIN ID:0x0005:0x000000020200
         OSPF RT:0.0.0.0:2:0 OSPF ROUTER ID:172.16.12.2:0
      mpls labels in/out 18/nolabel
      rx pathid: 0, tx pathid: 0x0
! The same applies for PE4 for the prefix received from CE5.
```

```
PE4# show bgp vpnv4 unicast all 10.1.100.5 255.255.255.255
BGP routing table entry for 100:1:10.1.100.5/32, version 7
Paths: (1 available, best #1, table SPCOR)
  Advertised to update-groups:
     1
Refresh Epoch 1
Local
   172.16.45.5 (via vrf SPCOR) from 0.0.0.0 (10.1.100.4)
      Origin incomplete, metric 2, localpref 100, weight 32768, valid, sourced, best
      Extended Community: RT:100:1 OSPF DOMAIN ID:0x0005:0x000000020200
         OSPF RT:0.0.0.0:2:0 OSPF ROUTER ID:172.16.45.4:0
      mpls labels in/out 20/nolabel
      rx pathid: 0, tx pathid: 0x0
```

Both domain IDs match on both PEs, which means the route will be delivered to the CE devices as an inter-area route that can be verified from the OSPF database in Example 12-43.

Example 12-43 *OSPF Database Output*

```
CE1# show ip ospf database summary


              OSPF Router with ID (10.1.100.1) (Process ID 1)


                 Summary Net Link States (Area 0)


  LS age: 924
  Options: (No TOS-capability, DC, Downward)
  LS Type: Summary Links(Network)
  Link State ID: 10.1.100.5 (summary Network Number)
  Advertising Router: 172.16.12.2
  LS Seq Number: 80000003
  Checksum: 0xE6B
  Length: 28
  Network Mask: /32
        MTID: 0          Metric: 2
```

Now what will take place if we change the area from 0 to 1 (Normal area)? Does it change the route sent from the CE to the PE from intra-area to inter-area? Example 12-44 verifies the origin of the route as IA.

Example 12-44 *Route Table for OSPF Output*

```
CE5# show ip route ospf
! Output omitted for brevity
      10.0.0.0/32 is subnetted, 2 subnets
O IA     10.1.100.1 [110/3] via 172.16.45.4, 00:00:07, GigabitEthernet0/0
      172.16.0.0/16 is variably subnetted, 3 subnets, 2 masks
O IA     172.16.12.0/24 [110/2] via 172.16.45.4, 00:00:07, GigabitEthernet0/0
```

Nothing happened, so either the inter-area or intra-area route will not affect it as long as the domain ID is the same on both end-to-end connections.

NOTE   You can check the available domain ID types by examining the **domain-id type {}** command under the OSPF configuration, as follows:

```
PE2(config-router)# domain-id type ?
  0005   Type 0x0005
  0105   Type 0x0105
  0205   Type 0x0205
  8005   Type 0x8005
```

Now let's change the domain ID on one of the PE devices to validate the impact on the routes delivered to the CE devices by modifying the domain ID. Example 12-45 shows how the domain ID value can be changed.

Example 12-45 *OSPF Domain ID Manipulation*

```
PE2(config)# router ospf 2 vrf SPCOR
PE2(config-router)# domain-id type 0005 value 000000030200
! We need to clear the OSPF process for the above command to take effect.

PE2# show bgp vpnv4 unicast all 10.1.100.1 255.255.255.255
BGP routing table entry for 100:1:10.1.100.1/32, version 22
Paths: (1 available, best #1, table SPCOR)
  Advertised to update-groups:
    1
  Refresh Epoch 1
  Local
    172.16.12.1 (via vrf SPCOR) from 0.0.0.0 (10.1.100.2)
      Origin incomplete, metric 2, localpref 100, weight 32768, valid, sourced, best
      Extended Community: RT:100:1 OSPF DOMAIN ID:0x0005:0x000000030200
        OSPF RT:0.0.0.1:2:0 OSPF ROUTER ID:172.16.12.2:0
      mpls labels in/out 18/nolabel
```

```
           rx pathid: 0, tx pathid: 0x0
```

```
CE1# show ip route ospf
! Output omitted for brevity
      10.0.0.0/32 is subnetted, 2 subnets
O E2     10.1.100.5 [110/2] via 172.16.12.2, 00:00:13, GigabitEthernet0/0
      172.16.0.0/16 is variably subnetted, 3 subnets, 2 masks
O E2     172.16.45.0/24 [110/1] via 172.16.12.2, 00:00:13, GigabitEthernet0/0
```

Next, let's put the IOS XR in its place (PE4) again to track the behavior compared to IOS. Figure 12-9 shows the topology used to illustrate the mutual redistribution process between OSPF as a routing protocol between CE and PE and BGP for transporting the prefixes across the core.

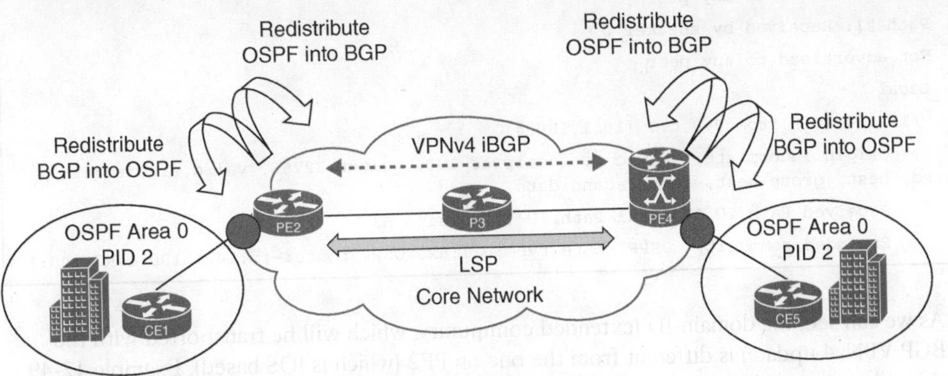

Figure 12-9 *MPLS L3VPN OSPF PE-CE, IOS XR*

Example 12-46 shows the output of the CE1 routing table after performing the redistribution from BGP (VPNv4) into OSPF on the PE, which yields OSPF learned as O E2 (external).

Example 12-46 *Route Table OSPF Output Verification*

```
CE1# show ip route ospf
! Output omitted for brevity
      10.0.0.0/32 is subnetted, 2 subnets
O E2     10.1.100.5 [110/2] via 172.16.12.2, 00:00:09, GigabitEthernet0/0
      172.16.0.0/16 is variably subnetted, 3 subnets, 2 masks
O E2     172.16.45.0/24 [110/1] via 172.16.12.2, 00:00:09, GigabitEthernet0/0
```

The routes are delivered as external routes, as can be verified by Example 12-42. Now let's check the behavior of IOS XR compared to IOS. Example 12-47 verifies the process ID.

Example 12-47 *OSPF Process ID Verification*

```
RP/0/0/CPU0:PE4# show ospf 2
 Routing Process "ospf 2" with ID 0.0.0.0
```

The IOS XR box does not allocate the router ID (OSPF process 2 has a valid IP address, which is the IP address used to interface with the CE inside the VRF). Example 12-48 shows how the OSPF route type is interpreted from an IOS XR perspective.

Example 12-48 *BGP Routing Table for VRF SPCOR*

```
RP/0/0/CPU0:PE4# show bgp vrf SPCOR 10.1.100.5
BGP routing table entry for 10.1.100.5/32, Route Distinguisher: 100:1
Versions:
  Process              bRIB/RIB   SendTblVer
  Speaker                 53             53
  Local Label: 16403
Last Modified: Jan 10 07:23:33.352 for 00:00:22
Paths: (1 available, best #1)
  Not advertised to any peer
  Path #1: Received by speaker 0
  Not advertised to any peer
  Local
    172.16.45.5 from 0.0.0.0 (10.1.100.4)
      Origin incomplete, metric 2, localpref 100, weight 32768, valid, redistrib-
uted, best, group-best, import-candidate
      Received Path ID 0, Local Path ID 1, version 53
      Extended community: OSPF route-type:0:1:0x0 OSPF router-id:10.1.100.4 RT:100:1
```

As we can see, the domain-ID (extended community, which will be transported with the BGP VPNv4 update) is different from the one on PE2 (which is IOS based). Example 12-49 shows how to set the router-id for the new process (between PE and CE) and how to clear the OSPF process for the ID to take effect.

Example 12-49 *OSPF Router-ID Configuration*

```
RP/0/0/CPU0:PE4(config)# router ospf 2
RP/0/0/CPU0:PE4(config-ospf)# router-id 172.16.45.4
RP/0/0/CPU0:PE4(config-ospf)# commit

RP/0/0/CPU0:PE4# clear ospf process
Reset ALL OSPF processes? [no]: yes

RP/0/0/CPU0:PE4# show ospf 2 | inc ID
Routing Process "ospf 2" with ID 172.16.45.4
```

We must manually set the domain ID on IOS XR–based devices to change the behavior of importing routes from the MPLS (super area) as LSA Type-3 or LSA Type-5. We can now manually change the domain ID on IOS XR, as demonstrated in Example 12-50.

Example 12-50 *OSPF Domain-ID Configuration on IOS XR*

```
RP/0/0/CPU0:PE4(config)# router ospf 2
RP/0/0/CPU0:PE4(config-ospf)# router-id 172.16.45.4
RP/0/0/CPU0:PE4(config-ospf)# vrf SPCOR
RP/0/0/CPU0:PE4(config-ospf-vrf)# domain-id type 0005 value 000000020200
```

```
RP/0/0/CPU0:PE4# show bgp vrf SPCOR 10.1.100.5
BGP routing table entry for 10.1.100.5/32, Route Distinguisher: 100:1
Versions:
  Process           bRIB/RIB   SendTblVer
  Speaker              59          59
    Local Label: 16403
Last Modified: Jan 10 07:45:02.352 for 00:00:31
Paths: (1 available, best #1)
  Not advertised to any peer
  Path #1: Received by speaker 0
  Not advertised to any peer
  Local
    172.16.45.5 from 0.0.0.0 (10.1.100.4)
      Origin incomplete, metric 2, localpref 100, weight 32768, valid, redistrib-
uted, best, group-best, import-candidate
      Received Path ID 0, Local Path ID 1, version 59
      Extended community: OSPF domain-id:0x5:0x000000020200 OSPF route-type:0:1:0x0
OSPF router-id:10.1.100.4 RT:100:1
```

```
CE1# show ip route ospf
! Output omitted for brevity
      10.0.0.0/32 is subnetted, 2 subnets
O IA    10.1.100.5 [110/3] via 172.16.12.2, 00:00:12, GigabitEthernet0/0
      172.16.0.0/16 is variably subnetted, 3 subnets, 2 masks
O IA    172.16.45.0/24 [110/2] via 172.16.12.2, 00:00:12, GigabitEthernet0/0
```

MPLS L3VPN OSPF Routing, Backdoor Link

Let's continue with OSPF as the routing protocol between PE and CE. We will add a new
link between the CEs (direct connectivity) and check the behavior for importing the routes
to the CE devices. Figure 12-10 shows the introduction of a backdoor link (a direct
link between CEs) to the same topology for which OSPF is used as a PE-to-CE routing
protocol.

Example 12-51 simply shows the addition of the new introduced link in the current OSPF
process between the CE and the PE.

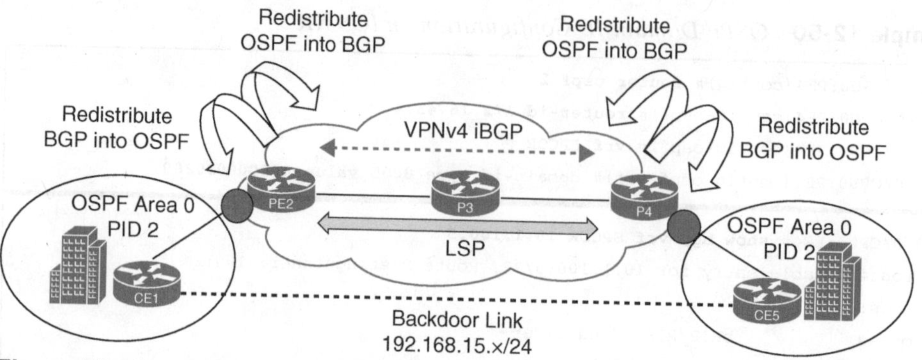

Figure 12-10 *MPLS PE-CE OSPF, Backdoor Link*

Example 12-51 *OSPF Network Advertisement*

```
CE1(config)# interface GigabitEthernet0/1
CE1(config-if)# ip address 192.168.15.1 255.255.255.0
CE1(config)# router ospf 1
CE1(config-router)# network 192.168.15.1 0.0.0.0 area 0

CE1# show ip route ospf
! Output omitted for brevity
      10.0.0.0/32 is subnetted, 2 subnets
O        10.1.100.5 [110/2] via 192.168.15.5, 00:00:04, GigabitEthernet0/1
      172.16.0.0/16 is variably subnetted, 3 subnets, 2 masks
O        172.16.45.0/24 [110/2] via 192.168.15.5, 00:00:04, GigabitEthernet0/1
```

As we can see, the routes are installed but preferred through the new introduced link. Generally, this is not undesirable because, from a business perspective, we pay for the MPLS circuit with reliable throughput and place the backdoor link for redundancy and failover. So, what can be done to force the traffic to use the backbone of the provider and utilize the MPLS service properly?

Before we jump to the technical solution, let's look at the routes. The routes now are learned as intra-area routes (denoted by O), and per the route selection criteria of OSPF, intra-area routes are preferred over inter-area routes. Consequently, the solution to be proposed should account for this. Figure 12-11 shows how the selection criteria will take place from a CE perspective because the comparison is now between receiving routes denoted as O (intra-area) or receiving routes denoted as O IA (inter-area). By referring to selection criteria, O-denoted routes will be preferred over O IA–denoted routes.

The solution is to use a so-called *sham-link*, as demonstrated in Example 12-52. The sham-link is a virtual link placed at the edges (PE devices) within the OSPF process associated with the VRF to simulate a new link that will manipulate the topology virtually to act as a direct point-to-point connection, and therefore, an extended area 0 is provided. The sham-link can be considered as a bridge with a /32 endpoint IP address that will produce an inter-area link that will make the MPLS backbone (super backbone) preferred. The command syntax for configuring the sham-link is **area** *area-id* **sham-link** *source-address destination-address* (we can associate cost with the command).

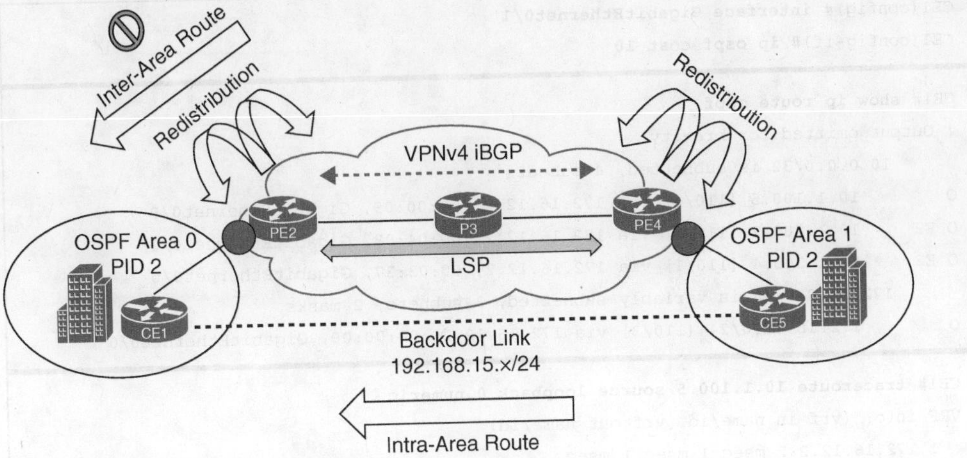

Figure 12-11 *OSPF Backdoor Link Intra-Area Routes*

Example 12-52 *OSPF Sham-Link Establishment*

```
PE2(config)# interface loopback 1
PE2(config-if)# vrf forwarding SPCOR
PE2(config-if)# ip address 10.1.200.2 255.255.255.255
PE2(config)# router ospf 2 vrf SPCOR
PE2(config-router)# area 0 sham-link 10.1.200.2 10.1.200.4

PE2(config)# router bgp 100
PE2(config-router)# address-family ipv4 vrf SPCOR
PE2(config-router-af)# network 10.1.200.2 mask 255.255.255.255

%OSPF-5-ADJCHG: Process 2, Nbr 172.16.45.4 on OSPF_SL0 from LOADING to FULL, Loading
Done
```

Now a new adjacency is established between the PE devices over the new virtual link, as shown in the output in Example 12-53.

Example 12-53 *OSPF Neighbors Output*

```
PE2# show ip ospf neighbor
Neighbor ID     Pri   State       Dead Time   Address        Interface
10.1.100.3       0    FULL/ -     00:00:36    10.1.23.3      GigabitEthernet0/1
172.16.45.4      0    FULL/ -     -           10.1.200.4     OSPF_SL0
10.1.100.1       0    FULL/ -     00:00:35    172.16.12.1    GigabitEthernet0/0
```

Adjusting the cost is illustrated in Example 12-54 to ensure a proper path end to end.

Example 12-54 *OSPF Metric Manipulation*

```
CE1(config)# interface GigabitEthernet0/1
CE1(config-if)# ip ospf cost 10

CE1# show ip route ospf
! Output omitted for brevity
      10.0.0.0/32 is subnetted, 4 subnets
O        10.1.100.5 [110/4] via 172.16.12.2, 00:00:09, GigabitEthernet0/0
O E2     10.1.200.2 [110/1] via 172.16.12.2, 00:04:08, GigabitEthernet0/0
O E2     10.1.200.4 [110/1] via 172.16.12.2, 00:03:37, GigabitEthernet0/0
      172.16.0.0/16 is variably subnetted, 3 subnets, 2 masks
O        172.16.45.0/24 [110/3] via 172.16.12.2, 00:00:09, GigabitEthernet0/0

CE1# traceroute 10.1.100.5 source loopback 0 numeric
VRF info: (vrf in name/id, vrf out name/id)
  1 172.16.12.2 2 msec 1 msec 1 msec
  2 10.1.23.3 [MPLS: Labels 17/20 Exp 0] 3 msec 3 msec 3 msec
  3 172.16.45.4 [MPLS: Label 20 Exp 0] 3 msec 3 msec 2 msec
  4 172.16.45.5 3 msec 3 msec 3 msec
```

Figure 12-12 shows a high-level overview of the same topology we have worked on after deploying the sham-link and manipulating the cost to make sure we utilize the MPLS backbone again instead of using the backdoor, which usually will be a backup (used when failure takes place from the service provider end).

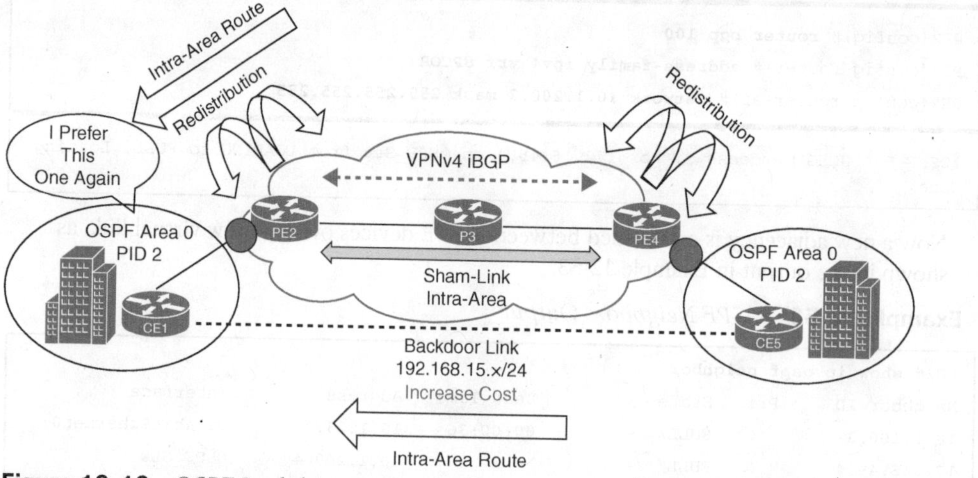

Figure 12-12 *OSPF Backdoor*

OSPF Down Bit

Another important caveat is that a loop prevention mechanism takes place in scenarios where OSPF is used as the PE-to-CE routing protocol and the CE is multihomed. As discussed, mutual redistribution is performed on the PEs between the OSPF and BGP and vice versa.

We use the topology in Figure 12-13 to demonstrate the concept of this down bit loop prevention mechanism.

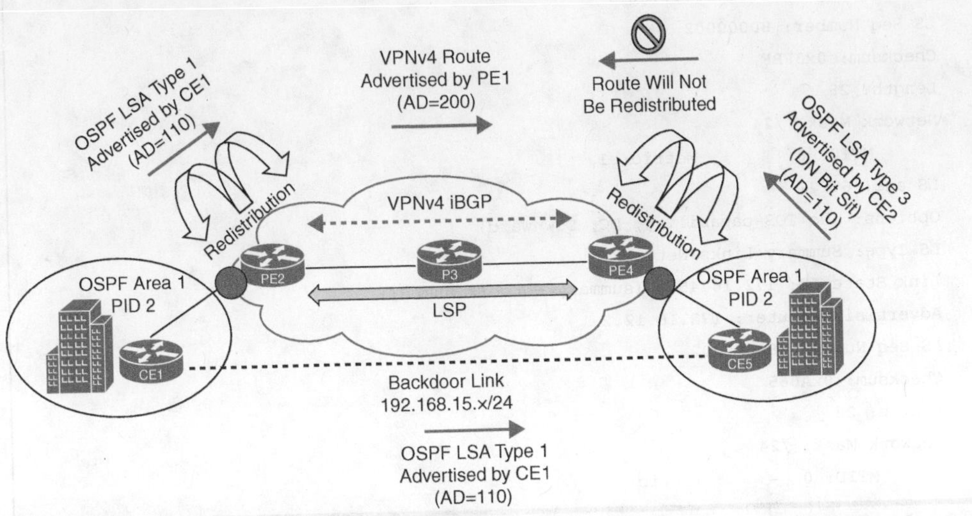

Figure 12-13 *OSPF MPLS L3VPN, Down Bit*

When the PE sends LSA Type-3 to the CE, the down bit (DN) will be set. If the CE sends this prefix to the other PE (with the DN set), the route will not be eligible for redistribution inside the MPLS backbone.

We can check the down bit association through the OSPF database (it will be written backward), as shown in Example 12-55.

Example 12-55 *PE2 and CE1 OSPF Database Output*

```
PE2# show ip ospf database summary
            OSPF Router with ID (10.1.100.2) (Process ID 1)
            OSPF Router with ID (172.16.12.2) (Process ID 2)
                Summary Net Link States (Area 0)

LS age: 672
Options: (No TOS-capability, DC, Downward)
LS Type: Summary Links(Network)
Link State ID: 10.1.100.5 (summary Network Number)
Advertising Router: 172.16.12.2
LS Seq Number: 80000002
Checksum: 0x106A
Length: 28
```

```
      Network Mask: /32
          MTID: 0           Metric: 2
      LS age: 677
      Options: (No TOS-capability, DC, Upward)
      LS Type: Summary Links(Network)
      Link State ID: 192.1681.15.0 (summary Network Number)
      Advertising Router: 10.1.100.1
      LS Seq Number: 80000002
      Checksum: 0x3FBF
      Length: 28
      Network Mask: /24
          MTID: 0           Metric: 1
      LS age: 672
      Options: (No TOS-capability, DC, Downward)
      LS Type: Summary Links(Network)
      Link State ID: 172.16.45.0 (summary Network Number)
      Advertising Router: 172.16.12.2
      LS Seq Number: 80000002
      Checksum: 0xA065
      Length: 28
      Network Mask: /24
          MTID: 0           Metric: 1
```

```
CE1# show ip ospf database summary

            OSPF Router with ID (10.1.100.1) (Process ID 1)

            Summary Net Link States (Area 0)

  LS age: 1501
  Options: (No TOS-capability, DC, Downward)
  LS Type: Summary Links(Network)
  Link State ID: 10.1.100.5 (summary Network Number)
  Advertising Router: 172.16.12.2
  LS Seq Number: 80000004
  Checksum: 0xC6C
  Length: 28
  Network Mask: /32
      MTID: 0           Metric: 2

  LS age: 1424
  Options: (No TOS-capability, DC, Upward)
  LS Type: Summary Links(Network)
  Link State ID: 172.16.15.0 (summary Network Number)
  Advertising Router: 10.1.100.1
  LS Seq Number: 80000004
  Checksum: 0x3BC1
```

```
Length: 28
Network Mask: /24
      MTID: 0          Metric: 1


LS age: 1501
Options: (No TOS-capability, DC, Downward)
LS Type: Summary Links(Network)
Link State ID: 172.16.45.0 (summary Network Number)
Advertising Router: 172.16.12.2
LS Seq Number: 80000004
Checksum: 0x9C67
Length: 28
Network Mask: /24
      MTID: 0          Metric: 1
```

MPLS L3VPN EIGRP PE-CE Routing

Continuing through the routing protocol options we can configure between PE and CE, let's now dive into EIGRP.

We will use AS#10 at customer ends, and for sure, this AS does not have to do with the BGP AS# configured for BGP within the service provider core. Example 12-56 lists the basic command to operationalize the EIGRP protocol as PE-CE.

Example 12-56 *EIGRP Configuration*

```
CE1(config)# router eigrp 10
CE1(config-router)# no auto-summary
CE1(config-router)# network 10.1.100.1 0.0.0.0
CE1(config-router)# network 172.16.12.1 0.0.0.0
PE2(config)# router eigrp 10
PE2(config-router)# address-family ipv4 vrf SPCOR autonomous-system 10
PE2(config-router-af)# redistribute bgp 100 metric 100 10 1 1 1500
PE2(config-router-af)# network 172.16.12.2 0.0.0.0
```

We can verify the impact of the configuration listed in Example 12-56 by checking the EIGRP route table, as shown in Example 12-57.

Example 12-57 *EIGRP Routing Table Output*

```
CE1# show ip route eigrp
! Output omitted for brevity
      10.0.0.0/32 is subnetted, 2 subnets
D        10.1.100.5 [90/131072] via 172.16.12.2, 00:00:25, GigabitEthernet0/0
      172.16.0.0/16 is variably subnetted, 3 subnets, 2 masks
D        172.16.45.0/24
```

```
                [90/3072] via 172.16.12.2, 00:00:25, GigabitEthernet0/0
```

```
CE1# ping 10.1.100.5 source loopback 0
Type escape sequence to abort.
Sending 5, 100-byte ICMP Echos to 10.1.100.5, timeout is 2 seconds:
Packet sent with a source address of 10.1.100.1
!!!!!
Success rate is 100 percent (5/5), round-trip min/avg/max = 4/66/317 ms
```

There's nothing remarkable about the output in Example 12-57. The routes are received successfully as internal EIGRP (AD = 90, as shown in the routing table output).

The main aspect of this scenario is the backdoor link (single multihomed deployment for CE) that we will add in between direct CEs and enable EIGRP on it, which will allow for a new adjacency establishment.

Usually, mutual redistribution of protocols could cause loops, especially where a backdoor link is linked to a race condition. The main reason for this is that locally redistributed routes (using a backdoor link) will be assigned a value of 32768, but routes received from VPNv4 are not given any weight values.

Now let's check what we have from a CE perspective by validating the EIGRP topology table as depicted in Example 12-58.

Example 12-58 *EIGRP Topology Output*

```
CE1# show ip eigrp topology 10.1.100.5 255.255.255.255
EIGRP-IPv4 Topology Entry for AS(10)/ID(10.1.100.1) for 10.1.100.5/32
  State is Passive, Query origin flag is 1, 1 Successor(s), FD is 130816
  Descriptor Blocks:
  192.168.15.5 (GigabitEthernet0/1), from 192.168.15.5, Send flag is 0x0
    Composite metric is (130816/128256), route is Internal
    Vector metric:
      Minimum bandwidth is 1000000 Kbit
      Total delay is 5010 microseconds
      Reliability is 255/255
      Load is 1/255
      Minimum MTU is 1500
      Hop count is 1
      Originating router is 10.1.100.5
  172.16.12.2 (GigabitEthernet0/0), from 172.16.12.2, Send flag is 0x0
    Composite metric is (131072/130816), route is Internal
    Vector metric:
      Minimum bandwidth is 1000000 Kbit
      Total delay is 5020 microseconds
      Reliability is 255/255
      Load is 1/255
      Minimum MTU is 1500
      Hop count is 2
      Originating router is 10.1.100.5
```

Surely, both paths are available from a topological perspective. However, from a routing perspective, only the route through the backdoor link will be used for traffic.

In such scenarios, we can use an option called EIGRP **Site of Origin (SoO)** to simplify the redistribution loops. SoO is an extended community of BGP (we already have the community send/receive capability turned on to accept RT from both PE devices). The two rules are

- If a route is sent or received on the same interface as the same SoO value was configured, the route is discarded.

- If a route is sent or received on an interface that has an SoO value set but does not match the one configured on an interface, the route is preserved.

EIGRP SoO is applied on an interface level using the sitemap construct. All EIGRP routes learned over that interface will carry the SoO extended community, and therefore, all BGP routes redistributed into EIGRP over this interface will have the SoO attached to it.

There are two options to deploy SoO, and each has implications, as highlighted in Table 12-3.

Table 12-3   SoO Deployment Options

Deployment	Aspect
PE-CE Interconnection	More stable, less redundant
PE-CE Interconnection, backdoor link	Less stable, more redundant

To verify, let's configure the relevant configuration and apply it on the interface connecting the PE to CE to check how the community is carried with the update, as shown in Example 12-59.

Example 12-59   *SOO Configuration and Association*

```
PE2(config)# route-map SOO permit 10
PE2(config-route-map)# set extcommunity soo 100:1
PE2(config)# interface GigabitEthernet 0/0
PE2(config-if)# ip vrf sitemap SOO
```

```
PE2# show bgp vpnv4 unicast all 10.1.100.1 255.255.255.255
BGP routing table entry for 100:1:10.1.100.1/32, version 52
Paths: (1 available, best #1, table SPCOR)
  Advertised to update-groups:
    4
Refresh Epoch 1
Local
    172.16.12.1 (via vrf SPCOR) from 0.0.0.0 (10.1.100.2)
      Origin incomplete, metric 130816, localpref 100, weight 32768, valid, sourced, best
        Extended Community: SoO:100:1 RT:100:1 Cost:pre-bestpath:128:130816
          0x8800:32768:0 0x8801:10:128256 0x8802:65281:2560 0x8803:65281:1500
```

```
        0x8806:0:167863297

  mpls labels in/out 25/nolabel

  rx pathid: 0, tx pathid: 0x0
```

```
CE5# show ip eigrp topology 10.1.100.1 255.255.255.255
EIGRP-IPv4 Topology Entry for AS(10)/ID(10.1.100.5) for 10.1.100.1/32
  State is Passive, Query origin flag is 1, 1 Successor(s), FD is 130816
  Descriptor Blocks:
  192.168.15.1 (GigabitEthernet0/1), from 192.168.15.1, Send flag is 0x0
      Composite metric is (130816/128256), route is Internal
      Vector metric:
        Minimum bandwidth is 1000000 Kbit
        Total delay is 5010 microseconds
        Reliability is 255/255
        Load is 1/255
        Minimum MTU is 1500
        Hop count is 1
        Originating router is 10.1.100.1
 172.16.45.4 (GigabitEthernet0/0), from 172.16.45.4, Send flag is 0x0
      Composite metric is (131072/130816), route is Internal
      Vector metric:
        Minimum bandwidth is 1000000 Kbit
        Total delay is 5020 microseconds
        Reliability is 255/255
        Load is 1/255
        Minimum MTU is 1500
        Hop count is 2
        Originating router is 10.1.100.1
      Extended Community: SoO:100:1
```

Figure 12-14 shows the options available from a deployment perspective for Site of
Origin (SoO).

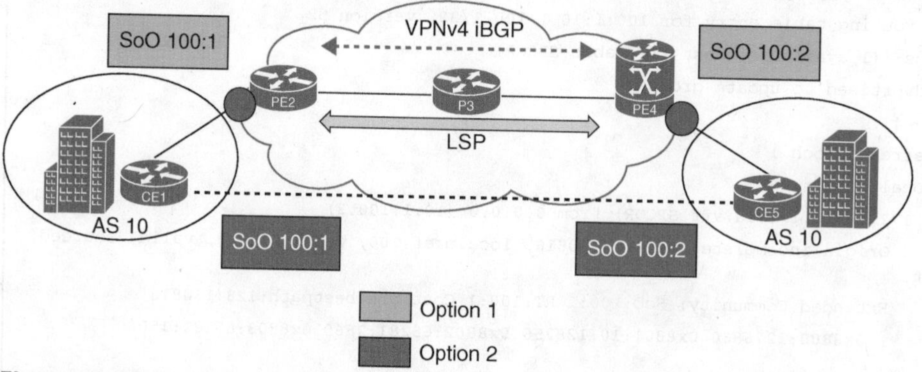

Figure 12-14   *MPLS L3VPN EIGRP, Backdoor Link*

MPLS L3VPN BGP PE-CE Routing

BGP is one of the most selected options for PE-CE deployment due to its flexibility and traffic manipulation capabilities. CE devices will peer with their respective PE devices over the eBGP session and advertise prefixes naturally, as is the case with any external BGP relation. Figure 12-15 shows the same topology used to describe the L3VPN MPLS service with BGP now in place for PE-to-CE routing. This figure also highlights the BGP session placement because we do not have two types of address families in play: IPv4 and VPNv4.

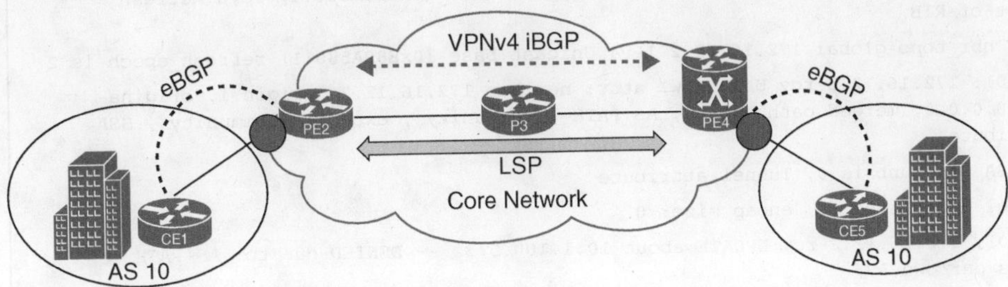

Figure 12-15 *MPLS L3VPN, BGP PE-CE*

End customers will use a single AS for connecting all the distributed branches; this will result in a small caveat that the traffic not be delivered due to the built-in loop prevention mechanism, which clearly states that a BGP speaker will not accept an update with its own autonomous system within the AS-PATH attribute associated with the update. There are two options to isolate this behavior and ensure update delivery between sites:

- **Allowas-in:** Allows the BGP router to accept updates even if its own autonomous system is in the AS-PATH.

- **AS Override:** Replaces the autonomous system of the originating router with the AS# of the sending BGP router.

Let's see this behavior in action. We start with Example 12-60, which provides an overview of the necessary commands to activate BGP as PE-CE considering the address families of concern.

Example 12-60 *BGP Configuration as PE-CE*

```
CE1(config)# router bgp 10
CE1(config-router)# no bgp default ipv4-unicast
CE1(config-router)# neighbor 172.16.12.2 remote-as 100
CE1(config-router)# address-family ipv4 unicast
CE1(config-router-af)# neighbor 172.16.12.2 activate
CE1(config-router-af)# network 10.1.100.1 mask 255.255.255.255

PE2(config)# router bgp 100
PE2(config-router)# address-family ipv4 vrf SPCOR
PE2(config-router-af)# neighbor 172.16.12.1 remote-as 10
```

As we can see from the logging messages in Example 12-61, the updates are denied due to the AS-PATH loop prevention mechanism of BGP.

Example 12-61 *AS-PATH Loop Prevention in BGP*

```
CE1# clear ip bgp * soft

BGP(0): (base) 172.16.12.2 send UPDATE (format) 10.1.100.1/32, next 172.16.12.1,
metric 0, path Local

BGP: nbr_topo global 172.16.12.2 IPv4 Unicast:base (0xE89A580:1) rcvd Refresh
Start-of-RIB

BGP: nbr_topo global 172.16.12.2 IPv4 Unicast:base (0xE89A580:1) refresh_epoch is 2

BGP(0): 172.16.12.2 rcv UPDATE w/ attr: nexthop 172.16.12.2, origin i, origina-
tor 0.0.0.0, merged path 100 10, AS_PATH , community , extended community , SSA
attribute

BGPSSA ssacount is 0, Tunnel attribute

Tunnel encap type: 0, encap size: 0

BGP(0): 172.16.12.2 rcv UPDATE about 10.1.100.5/32 -- DENIED due to: AS-PATH con-
tains our own AS;

BGP: nbr_topo global 172.16.12.2 IPv4 Unicast:base (0xE89A580:1) rcvd Refresh
End-of-RIB
```

Figure 12-16 shows the terminologies available to overcome the AS-PATH loop prevention. Each feature will turn at a different end of the network, allow-as-in will be applied from a CE perspective, and as-override will be applied from a PE perspective.

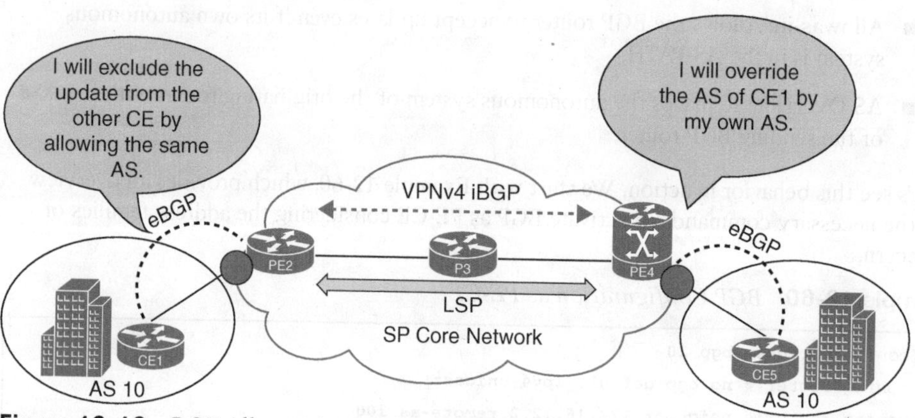

Figure 12-16 *BGP Allowas-in and AS Override*

BGP Allowas-in

Now let's apply the first option (allowas-in), which is configured from the CE side, as shown in Example 12-62.

Example 12-62 *BGP Allowas-in Configuration*

```
CE1(config)# router bgp 10
CE1(config-router)# address-family ipv4 unicast
CE1(config-router-af)# neighbor 172.16.12.2 allowas-in

BGP: nbr_topo global 172.16.12.2 IPv4 Unicast:base (0xE89A580:1) rcvd Refresh
Start-of-RIB
BGP: nbr_topo global 172.16.12.2 IPv4 Unicast:base (0xE89A580:1) refresh_epoch is 3
BGP(0): 172.16.12.2 rcvd UPDATE w/ attr: nexthop 172.16.12.2, origin i, merged path
100 10, AS_PATH
BGP(0): 172.16.12.2 rcvd 10.1.100.5/32
BGP: nbr_topo global 172.16.12.2 IPv4 Unicast:base (0xE89A580:1) rcvd Refresh
End-of-RIB
BGP(0): Revise route installing 1 of 1 routes for 10.1.100.5/32 ->
172.16.12.2(global) to main IP table
```

BGP AS-Override

Example 12-63 lists the necessary command to deploy the AS-override option from a PE
perspective. This feature replaces the autonomous system of the originating BGP speaker
with the autonomous system of the sending BGP speaker.

Example 12-63 *BGP AS-Override Configuration*

```
PE4(config)# router bgp 100
PE4(config-router)# address-family ipv4 vrf SPCOR
PE4(config-router-af)# neighbor 172.16.45.5 as-override
BGP(0): 172.16.45.4 rcv UPDATE about 10.1.100.5/32 -- withdrawn
BGP(0): 172.16.45.4 rcvd UPDATE w/ attr: nexthop 172.16.45.4, origin i, merged path
100 100, AS_PATH
BGP(0): 172.16.45.4 rcvd 10.1.100.1/32
BGP(0): Revise route installing 1 of 1 routes for 10.1.100.1/32 ->
172.16.45.4(global) to main IP table

CE1# ping 10.1.100.5 source loopback 0
Type escape sequence to abort.
Sending 5, 100-byte ICMP Echos to 10.1.100.5, timeout is 2 seconds:
Packet sent with a source address of 10.1.100.1
!!!!!
Success rate is 100 percent (5/5), round-trip min/avg/max = 2/2/3 ms

CE5# show ip bgp ipv4 unicast
! Output omitted for brevity
    Network          Next Hop        Metric LocPrf Weight Path
 *>   10.1.100.1/32    172.16.45.4                         0 100 100 i
 *>   10.1.100.5/32    0.0.0.0              0           32768 i
```

Route Target Filtering Mechanisms

As we discussed, Route Target is an extended BGP community configured under the VRF to control what prefixes are imported inside the customer routing table or exported out of the customer routing table. The main goal is to provide a layer of security for which we will add an extra layer of control to prevent route leakage between customers' routing tables, as well as allow leakage where appropriate for cases such as shared services.

We use the same topology from earlier (shown in Figure 12-17) for more clarity.

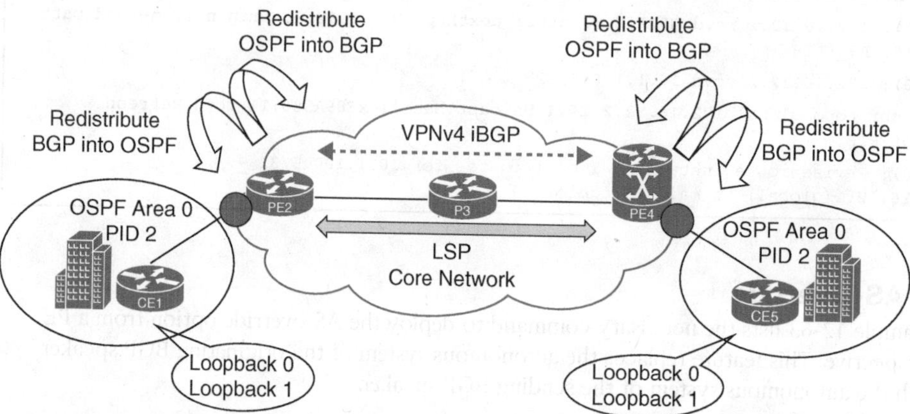

Figure 12-17   *Route Target Filtering*

Let's start with basic concepts to check the behavior. As depicted in Figure 12-17, we are running OSPF as the PE-to-CE routing protocol for which we are advertising two loopback networks from both CE devices.

Now, the first thing we want to examine is: What if we configured the VRF with only RD and no import or export values? To do so, we turn on debug on PE2 and check, as shown in Example 12-64.

Example 12-64   *Debug BGP VPNv4 Updates Output*

```
PE2# debug bgp vpnv4 unicast updates
BGP(4): 10.1.100.4 rcvd 100:1:10.1.100.5/32, label 16401 -- DENIED due to:  extended
community not supported;
BGP(4): 10.1.100.4 rcvd 100:1:192.168.5.5/32, label 16405 -- DENIED due to:
extended community not supported;
```

As we can see, prefixes are not allowed to be imported due to a lack of configured extended community.

What can we do? We can explicitly configure route-target import and export values to allow for the proper installation of routes. Or we can turn off the default behavior of route-target filtering on the PEs. To do so, we can use the **no bgp route-target filter** command built into the IOS and IOS XE operating systems, as illustrated in Example 12-65.

Example 12-65 *Turning Off BGP Default Route-Target Filter*

```
PE2(config)# router bgp 100
PE2(config-router)# no bgp default route-target filter
```

```
PE2# clear bgp vpnv4 unicast * soft
BGP(4): (base) 10.1.100.4 send UPDATE (format) 100:1:10.1.100.1/32, next
10.1.100.2, label 22, metric 2, path Local, extended community OSPF DOMAIN
ID:0x0005:0x000000020200 OSPF RT:0.0.0.0:2:0 OSPF ROUTER ID:172.16.12.2:0
BGP(4): (base) 10.1.100.4 send UPDATE (format) 100:1:172.16.12.0/24, next
10.1.100.2, label 21, metric 0, path Local, extended community OSPF DOMAIN
ID:0x0005:0x000000020200 OSPF RT:0.0.0.0:2:0 OSPF ROUTER ID:172.16.12.2:0
BGP(4): 10.1.100.4 rcvd UPDATE w/ attr: nexthop 10.1.100.4, origin ?, local-
pref 100, metric 2, extended community RT:100:1 OSPF RT:0.0.0.0:1:0 OSPF ROUTER
ID:172.16.45.4:0
BGP(4): 10.1.100.4 rcvd 100:1:10.1.100.5/32, label 16401
BGP(4): 10.1.100.4 rcvd 100:1:192.168.5.5/32, label 16405
BGP(4): 10.1.100.4 rcvd UPDATE w/ attr: nexthop 10.1.100.4, origin i, localpref 100,
metric 0, extended community RT:100:1
BGP(4): 10.1.100.4 rcvd 100:1:172.16.45.0/24, label 16402
```

Now, we can apply the same command to the IOS XR–based software with different syntax,
as shown in Example 12-66.

Example 12-66 *IOS XR BGP Retain Route Target*

```
RP/0/0/CPU0:PE4(config)# router bgp 100
RP/0/0/CPU0:PE4(config-bgp)# address-family vpnv4 unicast
RP/0/0/CPU0:PE4(config-bgp-af)# retain route-target all
```

However, the behavior differs because the routes will not be installed even with the **retain
route-target filter** applied.

We still did not configure PE2 to export routes with 100:1 RT, and therefore, no routes will
be accepted. To solve that issue, let's turn on debugging on PE4 (IOS XR) and configure
export on PE2, as shown in Example 12-67.

Example 12-67 *PE4 BGP VPNv4 Debugging Output*

```
RP/0/0/CPU0:PE4# debug bgp update afi vpnv4 unicast
```

```
PE2(config)# vrf definition SPCOR
PE2(config-vrf)# address-family ipv4
PE2(config-vrf-af)# route-target export 100:1
```

```
RP/0/0/CPU0:PE4# clear bgp vpnv4 unicast * soft in
```

```
bgp[1060]: [default-event] (vpn4u): Sending REFRESH_REQ to 10.1.100.2 for address
family TBL:default (1/128)
```

```
bgp[1060]: [default-upd] (vpn4u): No unreachable (not advertising to sender:
10.1.100.2) sent to sub-group 0.1 (Regular) with 2ASN:100:1:172.16.12.0/24 - already
withdrawn

bgp[1060]: [default-upd] (vpn4u): No unreachable (not advertising to sender:
10.1.100.2) sent to sub-group 0.1 (Regular) with 2ASN:100:1:192.168.1.1/32 - already
withdrawn

bgp[1060]: [default-upd] (vpn4u): No unreachable (not advertising to sender:
10.1.100.2) sent to sub-group 0.1 (Regular) with 2ASN:100:1:10.1.100.1/32 - already
withdrawn
```

```
RP/0/0/CPU0:PE4# show bgp vpnv4 unicast neighbors 10.1.100.2 routes | begin Network
   Network                Next Hop            Metric LocPrf Weight Path
Route Distinguisher: 100:1 (default for vrf SPCOR)
*>i10.1.100.1/32         10.1.100.2               2    100      0 ?
*>i172.16.12.0/24        10.1.100.2               0    100      0 ?
*>i192.168.1.1/32        10.1.100.2               2    100      0 ?
```

As shown, we are establishing the BGP VPNv4 session between PEs directly. Now, let's change the setup a little bit and deploy a route reflector (P3), as illustrated in Example 12-68.

Example 12-68 *BGP VPNv4 Neighborships Establishment*

```
P3(config)# router bgp 100
P3(config-router)# no bgp default ipv4-unicast
P3(config-router)# neighbor 10.1.100.2 remote-as 100
P3(config-router)# neighbor 10.1.100.2 update-source loopback 0
P3(config-router)# neighbor 10.1.100.4 remote-as 100
P3(config-router)# neighbor 10.1.100.4 update-source loopback 0
P3(config-router)# address-family vpnv4 unicast
P3(config-router-af)# neighbor 10.1.100.2 activate
P3(config-router-af)# neighbor 10.1.100.2 send-community both
P3(config-router-af)# neighbor 10.1.100.4 activate
P3(config-router-af)# neighbor 10.1.100.4 send-community both
```

Now, the default behavior is that the Route Target filtering is turned on. Will that affect transporting the prefixes among the core from one CE to another? Actually no. The RR, by default, will take routes from all VRFs even though no VRFs have been created on the RR : P3.

Another aspect to discuss and affect the route exchange is the **send-community** capability configured under the BGP VPNv4 address family. What will take place if we remove this capability? Let's check and verify by going through Example 12-69.

Example 12-69 *BGP VPNv4 Send-Community Configuration*

```
P3(config)# router bgp 100
P3(config-router)# address-family vpnv4 unicast
P3(config-router-af)# no neighbor 10.1.100.2 send-community both
```

```
PE2# show bgp vpnv4 unicast all 10.1.100.5/32
```

```
BGP routing table entry for 100:1:10.1.100.5/32, version 2
Paths: (1 available, best #1, no table)
Flag: 0x4100
  Not advertised to any peer
  Refresh Epoch 1
  Local
    10.1.100.4 (metric 3) (via default) from 10.1.100.3 (192.168.4.4)
      Origin incomplete, metric 2, localpref 100, valid, internal, best
      Originator: 10.1.100.4, Cluster list: 192.168.4.4
      mpls labels in/out nolabel/16401
      rx pathid: 0, tx pathid: 0x0
! As can be seen, there is no RT extended community attached to the prefix.

CE1# show ip route ospf | begin Gateway
Gateway of last resort is not set
```

Import and Export Maps

Now let's examine another handy tool to control RT attachment and prefix transportation on a prefix level by using a feature called import and export maps.

To make it easier, let's change the import/export values on PE2 and PE4, as shown in Table 12-4.

Table 12-4 Import/Export Values

Device/Control	Import	Export
PE2	200:1	100:1
PE4	100:1	200:1

Example 12-70 shows how to quickly check these values from a BGP perspective.

Example 12-70 *Route-Target Import/Export Validation*

```
PE2# show bgp vpnv4 unicast all 10.1.100.5/32 | include RT
    Extended Community: RT:200:1 OSPF RT:0.0.0.0:1:0


RP/0/0/CPU0:PE4# show bgp vpnv4 unicast vrf SPCOR 10.1.100.1/32
BGP routing table entry for 10.1.100.1/32, Route Distinguisher: 100:2
Versions:
  Process           bRIB/RIB  SendTblVer
  Speaker                 12          12
Last Modified: Jul 16 05:58:13.281 for 00:00:41
Paths: (1 available, best #1)
  Not advertised to any peer
  Path #1: Received by speaker 0
  Not advertised to any peer
```

```
  Local
    10.1.100.2 (metric 3) from 10.1.100.3 (10.1.100.2)
      Received Label 22
      Origin incomplete, metric 2, localpref 100, valid, internal, best, group-best,
import-candidate, imported
      Received Path ID 0, Local Path ID 1, version 12
      Extended community: OSPF domain-id:0x5:0x000000020200 OSPF route-type:0:2:0x0
OSPF router-id:172.16.12.2 RT:100:1
      Originator: 10.1.100.2, Cluster list: 192.168.4.4
      Source AFI: VPNv4 Unicast, Source VRF: default, Source Route Distinguisher:
100:1
```

This example advertises two networks from each CE. First, we change the route-target value
for one of these loopback networks using **route-map** in which we can set the RT value
using the **set extcommunity rt** [*ASN:NN*] command under the route map, as shown in
Example 12-71. For prefix classification, we can use a simple prefix list to match the prefix
for which we will change the RT value when exported.

Example 12-71 *Prefix List and* **route-map** *Definition*

```
PE2(config)# ip prefix-list CE1_LOOP1 seq 5 permit 192.168.1.0/24

PE2(config)# route-map ROUTE_TARGET permit 10
PE2(config-route-map)# set extcommunity ?
  cost               Cost extended community
  rt                 Route Target extended community
  soo                Site-of-Origin extended community
  vpn-distinguisher  VPN Distinguisher
PE2(config-route-map)# set extcommunity rt 300:1
PE2(config-route-map)# match ip address prefix-list CE1_LOOP1

RP/0/0/CPU0:PE4# show bgp vpnv4 unicast vrf SPCOR
BGP router identifier 10.1.100.4, local AS number 100
BGP generic scan interval 60 secs
Non-stop routing is enabled
BGP table state: Active
Table ID: 0x0   RD version: 0
BGP main routing table version 20
BGP NSR Initial initsync version 1 (Reached)
BGP NSR/ISSU Sync-Group versions 0/0
BGP scan interval 60 secs

Status codes: s suppressed, d damped, h history, * valid, > best
              i - internal, r RIB-failure, S stale, N Nexthop-discard
Origin codes: i - IGP, e - EGP, ? - incomplete
  Network          Next Hop            Metric LocPrf Weight Path
```

```
Route Distinguisher: 100:2 (default for vrf SPCOR)
*>i10.1.100.1/32        10.1.100.2              2    100      0 ?
*>  10.1.100.5/32       172.16.45.5             2         32768 ?
*>i172.16.12.0/24       10.1.100.2              0    100      0 ?
*>  172.16.45.0/24      0.0.0.0                 0         32768 i
*>  192.168.5.0/24      172.16.45.5             2         32768 ?
```

As Example 12-71 confirms, the route is not installed because we do not have a matching
route-target (import) that will allow this prefix with modified RT to be installed. Once we
allow the RT to be installed, we will have the route available with the new RT value, as shown
in Example 12-72.

Example 12-72 *Route-Target Import/Export Configuration and Verification*

```
RP/0/0/CPU0:PE4# configure terminal
RP/0/0/CPU0:PE4(config)# vrf SPCOR
RP/0/0/CPU0:PE4(config-vrf)# address-family ipv4 unicast
RP/0/0/CPU0:PE4(config-vrf-af)# import route-target
RP/0/0/CPU0:PE4(config-vrf-import-rt)# 300:1
```

```
RP/0/0/CPU0:PE4# show bgp vpnv4 unicast vrf SPCOR 192.168.1.0/24
BGP routing table entry for 192.168.1.0/24, Route Distinguisher: 100:2
Versions:
  Process           bRIB/RIB    SendTblVer
  Speaker              21           21
Last Modified: Jul 16 06:09:39.281 for 00:00:09
Paths: (1 available, best #1)
  Not advertised to any peer
  Path #1: Received by speaker 0
  Not advertised to any peer
  Local
    10.1.100.2 (metric 3) from 10.1.100.3 (10.1.100.2)
      Received Label 23
      Origin incomplete, metric 2, localpref 100, valid, internal, best, group-best,
import-candidate, imported
      Received Path ID 0, Local Path ID 1, version 21
      Extended community: OSPF domain-id:0x5:0x000000020200 OSPF route-type:0:2:0x0
OSPF router-id:172.16.12.2 RT:300:1
      Originator: 10.1.100.2, Cluster list: 192.168.4.4
      Source AFI: VPNv4 Unicast, Source VRF: default, Source Route Distinguisher:
100:1
```

The same applies for IOS XR–based software (PE4) for which we have to first define a route
policy and then attach the export map to the VRF, as shown in Example 12-73.

Example 12-73 *Export-Map Configuration Example, IOS XR*

```
RP/0/0/CPU0:PE4(config)# route-policy IMPORT_RT
RP/0/0/CPU0:PE4(config-rpl)# if destination in CE2_LOOP2 then set extcommunity rt
(400:1)
```

```
RP/0/0/CPU0:PE4(config)# vrf SPCOR
RP/0/0/CPU0:PE4(config-vrf)# address-family ipv4 unicast
RP/0/0/CPU0:PE4(config-vrf-af)# export route-policy IMPORT_RT
```

```
PE2# show bgp vpnv4 unicast all 192.168.5.0/24
BGP routing table entry for 100:2:192.168.5.0/24, version 33
Paths: (1 available, best #1, no table)
  Not advertised to any peer
  Refresh Epoch 3
  Local
    10.1.100.4 (metric 3) (via default) from 10.1.100.3 (192.168.4.4)
      Origin incomplete, metric 2, localpref 100, valid, internal, best
      Extended Community: RT:400:1 OSPF RT:0.0.0.0:1:0
        OSPF ROUTER ID:172.16.45.4:0
      Originator: 10.1.100.4, Cluster list: 192.168.4.4
      mpls labels in/out nolabel/16406
      rx pathid: 0, tx pathid: 0x0
```

As we can see, there is a difference between IOS and IOS XR. The route is installed in the BGP table (RIB) of PE2 (in the previous example, we had to explicitly define the RT value to be imported). However, the end CE (CE1) will not have this route installed into its routing table, as shown in Example 12-74.

Example 12-74 *CE1 RIB Output*

```
CE1# show ip route 192.168.5.5 255.255.255.0
% Network not in table
```

Route Target Constraint

Another technical piece to discuss that touches on route-target filtering is something called Route Target Constraint (RTC). When we went through route reflection for the VPNv4 AF, all VPNv4 traffic will be allowed to get to the destination PE for which the traffic will be either imported if there is a matching route-policy or route-map depending on the operating system or will be denied due to the extended community not being supported: no matching RT is configured.

The goal of RTC is to reduce the VPNv4 updates from being sent directly to the target PEs and filtering these unmatched prefixes at the RR level. This will be achieved by introducing a new address family under the BGP called *rtfilter*, as specified in RFC 4684. The filtering information will be gathered from filtering lists from all VRFs on the PE routers. The PE will send the filtering information in a BGP UPDATE message in the address-family rtfilter, and this information will be encoded in the Network Layer Reachability Information (NLRI) of MP_REACH_NLRI and MP_UNREACH_NLRI attributes.

We use a simple topology, as demonstrated in Figure 12-18, in which we simulate CEs by defining loopback interfaces (for simplification purposes).

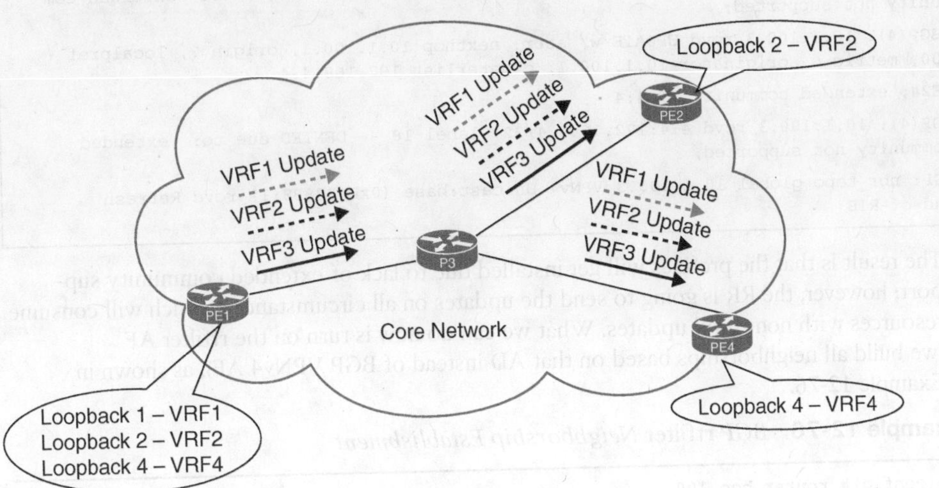

Figure 12-18 *Route Target Constraint*

For now, let's use the same configuration commands and P3 acts as a route reflector. We can clear the BGP session on PE2 (which is configured to import only RT of 2:2) and turn on **debug bgp vpnv4 unicast update**, as in Example 12-75.

Example 12-75 *Debug BGP VPNv4 Unicast Update Output*

```
PE2# clear bgp vpnv4 unicast * soft in
BGP: nbr_topo global 10.1.100.3 VPNv4 Unicast:base (0xD4378B8:1) rcvd Refresh
Start-of-RIB
BGP: nbr_topo global 10.1.100.3 VPNv4 Unicast:base (0xD4378B8:1) refresh_epoch is 4
BGP(4): 10.1.100.3 rcvd UPDATE w/ attr: nexthop 10.1.100.1, origin ?, localpref 100,
metric 0, originator 10.1.100.1, clusterlist 192.168.4.4, extended community RT:2:2
BGP(4): 10.1.100.3 rcvd 2:2:172.16.2.2/32, label 17...duplicate ignored
: 10.1.100.3 Next hop is our own address 10.1.100.2
BGP: 10.1.100.3 Local router is the Originator; Discard update
BGP(4): 10.1.100.3 rcv UPDATE w/ attr: nexthop 10.1.100.2, origin ?, localpref 100,
metric 0, originator 10.1.100.2, clusterlist 192.168.4.4, merged path , AS_PATH ,
community , extended community RT:2:2, SSA attribute
BGPSSA ssacount is 0, Tunnel attribute
Tunnel encap type: 0, encap size: 0
BGP(4): 10.1.100.3 rcv UPDATE about 2:2:10.1.2.2/32 -- DENIED due to: ORIGINATOR is
us; MP_REACH NEXTHOP is our own address;, label 16
BGP(4): 10.1.100.3 rcvd UPDATE w/ attr: nexthop 10.1.100.1, origin ?, localpref 100,
metric 0, originator 10.1.100.1, clusterlist 192.168.4.4, extended community RT:1:1
```

```
BGP(4): 10.1.100.3 rcvd 1:1:172.16.1.1/32, label 16 -- DENIED due to:  extended
community not supported;
BGP(4): 10.1.100.3 rcvd UPDATE w/ attr: nexthop 10.1.100.4, origin ?, localpref 100,
metric 0, originator 10.1.100.4, clusterlist 192.168.4.4, extended community RT:4:4
BGP(4): 10.1.100.3 rcvd 4:4:10.10.4.4/32, label 22 -- DENIED due to:  extended com-
munity not supported;
*BGP(4): 10.1.100.3 rcvd UPDATE w/ attr: nexthop 10.1.100.1, origin ?, localpref
100, metric 0, originator 10.1.100.1, clusterlist 192.168.4.4
PE2#, extended community RT:4:4
BGP(4): 10.1.100.3 rcvd 4:4:172.16.4.4/32, label 18 -- DENIED due to:  extended
community not supported;
BGP: nbr_topo global 10.1.100.3 VPNv4 Unicast:base (0xD4378B8:1) rcvd Refresh
End-of-RIB
```

The result is that the prefixes will get installed due to lack of extended community support; however, the RR is going to send the updates on all circumstances, which will consume
resources with nonuseful updates. What we can do now is turn on the rtfilter AF
(we build all neighborships based on that AD instead of BGP VPNv4 AF), as shown in
Example 12-76.

Example 12-76 *BGP rtfilter Neighborship Establishment*

```
P3(config)# router bgp 100
P3(config-router)# address-family rtfilter unicast
P3(config-router-af)# neighbor 10.1.100.1 activate
P3(config-router-af)# neighbor 10.1.100.1 send-community extended
P3(config-router-af)# neighbor 10.1.100.1 route-reflector-client
P3(config-router-af)# neighbor 10.1.100.2 activate
P3(config-router-af)# neighbor 10.1.100.2 send-community extended
P3(config-router-af)# neighbor 10.1.100.2 route-reflector-client
P3(config-router-af)# neighbor 10.1.100.4 activate
P3(config-router-af)# neighbor 10.1.100.4 send-community extended
P3(config-router-af)# neighbor 10.1.100.4 route-reflector-client
```

```
PE2# debug bgp rtfilter unicast updates
BGP(11): 10.1.100.3 NEXT_HOP self is set for sourced RT Filter for net 100:2:2:2
BGP(11): (base) 10.1.100.3 send UPDATE (format) 100:2:2:2, next 10.1.100.2, metric
0, path Local
BGP(11): 10.1.100.3 NEXT_HOP self is set for sourced RT Filter for net
100:258:10.1.100.2:0
BGP: nbr_topo global 10.1.100.3 RT Filter:base (0xD483728:1) rcvd Refresh
Start-of-RIB
BGP: nbr_topo global 10.1.100.3 RT Filter:base (0xD483728:1) refresh_epoch is 3
BGP(11): 10.1.100.3 rcvd UPDATE w/ attr: nexthop 10.1.100.4, origin i, localpref
100, metric 0, originator 192.168.4.4, clusterlist 192.168.4.4
BGP(11): 10.1.100.3 rcvd 100:258:10.1.100.4:0...duplicate ignored
BGP: 10.1.100.3 Next hop is our own address 10.1.100.2
```

```
BGP(11): 10.1.100.3 rcv UPDATE w/ attr: nexthop 10.1.100.2, origin i, localpref 100,
metric 0, originator 192.168.4.4, clusterlist 192.168.4.4, merged path , AS_PATH ,
community , extended community , SSA attribute

BGPSSA ssacount is 0, Tunnel attribute

Tunnel encap type: 0, encap size: 0

BGP(11): 10.1.100.3 rcv UPDATE about 100:258:10.1.100.2:0 -- DENIED due to: MP_REACH
NEXTHOP is our own address;

BGP(11): 10.1.100.3 rcvd UPDATE w/ attr: nexthop 10.1.100.1, origin i, localpref
100, metric 0, originator 192.168.4.4, clusterlist 192.168.4.4

BGP(11): 10.1.100.3 rcvd 100:2:1:1...duplicate ignored

BGP(11): 10.1.100.3 rcvd 100:2:2:2...duplicate ignored

BGP(11): 10.1.100.3 rcvd 100:2:4:4...duplicate ignored

BGP(11): 10.1.100.3 rcvd 100:258:10.1.100.1:0...duplicate ignored

BGP(11): 10.1.100.3 rcvd UPDATE w/ attr: nexthop 10.1.100.3, origin i, localpref
100, metric 0, commun

PE2#ity no-export

BGP(11): 10.1.100.3 rcvd 0:0:0:0...duplicate ignored

BGP(11): 10.1.100.3 rcvd UPDATE w/ attr: nexthop 10.1.100.3, origin i, localpref
100, metric 0

BGP(11): 10.1.100.3 rcvd 100:258:10.1.100.3:0...duplicate ignored

BGP: nbr_topo global 10.1.100.3 RT Filter:base (0xD483728:1) rcvd Refresh End-of-RIB
```

MPLS L3VPN Route Reflector Deployment

In most of the examples, we have established direct connectivity between PEs serving the
customers to transport the traffic over the MPLS backbone using MP-BGP. We introduced
route reflection in one of the examples but will shed some light on how the route reflection
will perform from a data plane and a control plane perspective.

We use the topology in Figure 12-19, where P2 acts as a route reflector for the BGP VPNv4
address family.

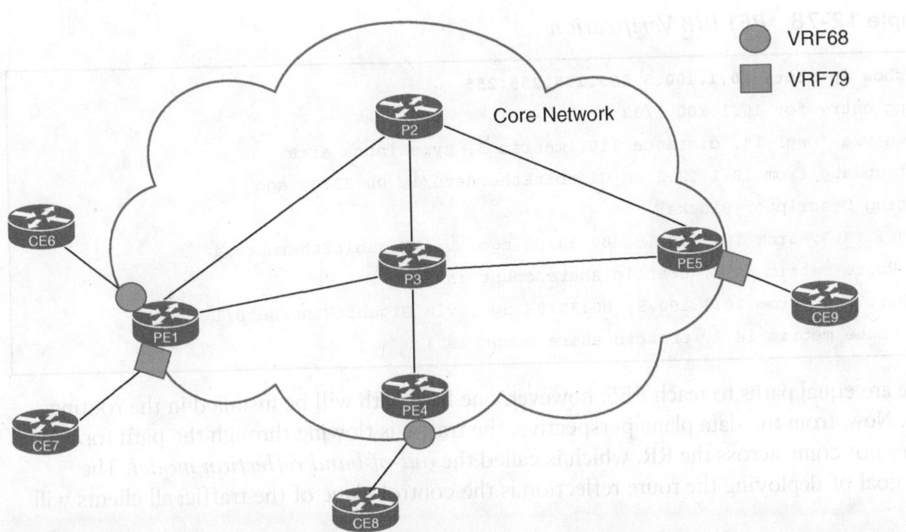

Figure 12-19 *MPLS L3VPN Route Reflectors*

Two VRFs are configured:

- VRF68 to serve the communications between CE6 and CE8

- VRF79 to service the communications between CE7 and CE9

P2 is the route reflector of the BGP VPNv4 domain for which it will reflect the prefixes received for both VRFs from one PE to another. There are no VRFs configured on the RR; however, as per our discussion about how IOS and IOS XE works, they will pass the traffic but will not install any related information (customer traffic). Let's test connectivity among both VRFs to see how the traffic is transported across the MPLS core network, as shown in Example 12-77.

Example 12-77 *Path Validation via* traceroute

```
CE6# traceroute 192.168.8.8 source loopback 0 numeric
VRF info: (vrf in name/id, vrf out name/id)
 1 172.16.16.1 1 msec 1 msec 1 msec
 2 10.1.13.3 [MPLS: Labels 201/23 Exp 0] 18 msec 33 msec 6 msec
 3 172.16.48.4 [MPLS: Label 23 Exp 0] 3 msec 3 msec 3 msec
 4 172.16.48.8 3 msec 4 msec 6 msec

CE7# traceroute 192.168.9.9 source loopback 0 numeric
VRF info: (vrf in name/id, vrf out name/id)
 1 172.16.17.1 1 msec 1 msec 1 msec
 2 10.1.13.3 [MPLS: Labels 200/23 Exp 0] 5 msec 6 msec 10 msec
 3 172.16.59.5 [MPLS: Label 23 Exp 0] 6 msec 3 msec 6 msec
 4 172.16.59.9 3 msec 3 msec 4 msec
```

As Example 12-77 shows, the traffic is flowing through PE1 → P3 → PE5 → CE9 (for VRF68), which follows the IGP best path. Let's check how PE2 is reaching PE5 from an OSPF perspective (OSPF Area 0 is running inside the core), as shown in Example 12-78.

Example 12-78 *PE1 RIB Verification*

```
PE1# show ip route 10.1.100.5 255.255.255.255
Routing entry for 10.1.100.5/32
  Known via "ospf 1", distance 110, metric 3, type intra area
  Last update from 10.1.12.2 on GigabitEthernet0/1, 00:33:07 ago
  Routing Descriptor Blocks:
  * 10.1.13.3, from 10.1.100.5, 00:33:52 ago, via GigabitEthernet0/4
      Route metric is 3, traffic share count is 1
    10.1.12.2, from 10.1.100.5, 00:33:07 ago, via GigabitEthernet0/1
      Route metric is 3, traffic share count is 1
```

There are equal paths to reach PE5; however, one best path will be installed in the routing table. Now, from the data plane perspective, the traffic is flowing through the path for which it does not come across the RR, which is called the *out-of-band reflection model*. The main goal of deploying the route reflection is the control plane of the traffic; all clients will communicate with the RR on the control plane level and will leave the data plane purely to IGP to handle.

· Next, let's change the OSPF cost manually on the PE1 interface connected to P3 and check the relevant changes after, as shown in Example 12-79.

Example 12-79 *CE6 to CE8 Path After OSPF Cost Manipulation*

```
PE1# configure terminal
PE1(config)# interface GigabitEthernet0/4
PE1(config-if)# ip ospf cost 50

PE1# show ip ospf interface brief
Interface   PID   Area        IP Address/Mask      Cost   State  Nbrs F/C
Lo0         1     0           10.1.100.1/32        1      LOOP   0/0
Gi0/4       1     0           10.1.13.1/24         50     P2P    1/1
Gi0/1       1     0           10.1.12.1/24         1      P2P    1/1

PE1# show ip route 10.1.100.5 255.255.255.255
Routing entry for 10.1.100.5/32
  Known via "ospf 1", distance 110, metric 3, type intra area
  Last update from 10.1.12.2 on GigabitEthernet0/1, 00:35:21 ago
  Routing Descriptor Blocks:
  * 10.1.12.2, from 10.1.100.5, 00:35:21 ago, via GigabitEthernet0/1
      Route metric is 3, traffic share count is 1

CE6# traceroute 192.168.8.8 source loopback 0 numeric
VRF info: (vrf in name/id, vrf out name/id)
  1 172.16.16.1 2 msec 2 msec 2 msec
  2 10.1.12.2 [MPLS: Labels 21/23 Exp 0] 7 msec 8 msec 6 msec
  3 10.1.25.5 [MPLS: Labels 16/23 Exp 0] 6 msec 5 msec 6 msec
  4 10.1.35.3 [MPLS: Labels 201/23 Exp 0] 21 msec 5 msec 7 msec
  5 172.16.48.4 [MPLS: Label 23 Exp 0] 3 msec 3 msec 3 msec
  6 172.16.48.8 6 msec 7 msec 4 msec
```

See how many hops we have to traverse to reach out to the target destination? Also, the RR is now in the path of data traffic (although it does not recognize the customer traffic).

All interfaces within the network are GigabitEthernet interfaces, which, following the OSPF default auto-cost calculation, yields a cost of 1. If we have higher interfaces (with adjusting the OSPF reference bandwidth), as the interfaces/speeds are evolving rapidly to account for the trends and needs, we could end up with a different situation without manipulation.

What could be done on the RR is to relate to the IGP, which will inform its neighbors that it is not likely to be a transit node for traffic. We can accomplish this by using the **max-metric router-lsa** command under the OSPF configuration mode. The feature is called a *stub router advertisement*, but don't confuse this with stub areas.

Eventually, this will affect large-scale networks, and changing the cost in lab environments will do the trick. Now, we can enable this command and check the path again, as demonstrated in Example 12-80.

Example 12-80 *OSPF* **max-metric router-lsa** *Configuration*

```
P2(config)# router ospf 1
P2(config-router)# max-metric router-lsa

CE6# traceroute 192.168.8.8 source loopback 0 numeric
VRF info: (vrf in name/id, vrf out name/id)
  1 172.16.16.1 2 msec 2 msec 2 msec
  2 10.1.13.3 [MPLS: Labels 201/23 Exp 0] 8 msec 8 msec 5 msec
  3 172.16.48.4 [MPLS: Label 23 Exp 0] 3 msec 5 msec 3 msec
  4 172.16.48.8 3 msec 3 msec 5 msec
! And we are back again to the same path and RR is excluded from the data plane.
```

Multicast VPN

Multicast VPN (MVPN) is a technology used in MPLS networks to enable efficient and scalable distribution of multicast traffic across a virtual private network. MVPN is particularly beneficial for applications that require multicast capabilities, such as video streaming, IPTV, online gaming, and real-time data dissemination.

Here are the key components and concepts of MVPN:

- **Multicast Distribution Trees:** MVPN uses multicast distribution trees to efficiently deliver multicast traffic to multiple receivers within the VPN. Two main types of multicast distribution trees are used in MVPN:

  - **Shared Trees:** Shared trees, also known as multicast distribution trees or multicast trees, are rooted at a designated point in the network, such as a rendezvous point (RP) or a multicast core. Receivers join the shared tree to receive multicast traffic, and the traffic is replicated and forwarded along the shared tree to reach all receivers.

  - **Source-Specific Trees:** Shortest Path Tree (SPTs) are rooted at the source of the multicast traffic, creating a direct path from the source to the receivers. Receivers explicitly signal their interest in receiving traffic from specific multicast sources, and the network establishes source-specific trees to deliver traffic.

- **Multicast Distribution Protocols:** MVPN utilizes multicast distribution protocols such as Protocol-Independent Multicast (PIM) or Multiprotocol Label Switching (MPLS) Multicast to manage and control multicast traffic within the VPN. PIM Sparse Mode (PIM-SM), PIM Dense Mode (PIM-DM), and PIM Source-Specific Multicast (PIM-SSM) are commonly used multicast routing protocols in MVPN deployments.

- **Multicast VPN Models:** Several MVPN models or approaches are used to deliver multicast traffic across VPNs:

- **Rosen Draft Model (Draft-Rosen):** This model uses MPLS labels to create multicast distribution trees within the VPN, providing a scalable and efficient way to deliver multicast traffic.

- **Draft-Rosen with PIM-SM:** This model combines the Draft-Rosen approach with PIM-SM for dynamic multicast routing and tree creation.

- **Next-Generation MVPN (NG-MVPN):** NG-MVPN introduces additional functionalities and enhancements to MVPN, including support for hierarchical multicast trees, multicast flow identification, and optimized multicast traffic delivery.

Multicast VPN Service Types

MVPN supports various multicast VPN service types, including Any Source Multicast (ASM) and Source-Specific Multicast (SSM), depending on the requirements of the application and the nature of the multicast traffic.

ASM allows receivers to join multicast groups without specifying the exact source of the traffic, while SSM requires receivers to specify both the multicast group and the specific source of the traffic.

Overall, Multicast VPN enables organizations to efficiently distribute multicast traffic across their MPLS-based VPNs, providing a scalable, secure, and reliable solution for delivering multicast services to multiple recipients within the VPN environment. MVPN plays a critical role in supporting applications that rely on multicast communication while maintaining isolation and privacy within VPNs.

Multicast Distribution Trees

Multicast distribution trees (MDTs) are multicast tunnels that transport customer multicast traffic by encapsulating it in GRE tunnels that will be part of the same multicast domain. There are two flavors of the MDT:

- **Default MDT:** Used by mVRF to send low-bandwidth multicast traffic to a distributed set of receivers. Usually, this MDT is used for multicast control traffic between PEs.

  PE routers always build a Default-MDT to peer PE routers, which have mVRF with the same MDT group address. MDT is maintained in the core network using PIM mechanisms like PIM SM.

- **Data MDT:** Used to tunnel high-bandwidth traffic destined to interested PEs. Unnecessary traffic is avoided in this type of MDT.

Any traffic offered to the Default-MDT is distributed to all PE routers that are part of the same multicast domain, regardless of whether active receivers are in an mVRF at a specific PE router, which could raise an issue from a utilization perspective, and therefore, this is solved by Data-MDT.

Draft-Rosen

The *Draft-Rosen model*, also known as the *Rosen Draft*, refers to a specific approach or methodology for implementing Multicast VPN services in Multiprotocol Label Switching networks. Draft-Rosen is one of the early models proposed to address the efficient distribution of multicast traffic across VPNs while leveraging MPLS for traffic engineering and scalability. It is based on the work described in the Internet Engineering Task Force (IETF) RFC 6037 drafts authored by Eric Rosen and Yakov Rekhter.

Here are the key aspects and characteristics of the Draft-Rosen model:

- **Multicast Distribution Trees:** Draft-Rosen utilizes shared multicast distribution trees within the MPLS network to efficiently deliver multicast traffic across the VPN. The model employs a technique called the *Rendezvous Point (RP) Tree* to establish a shared distribution tree rooted at a designated RP for each multicast group.

- **Multicast Signaling and Label Assignment:** Multicast traffic is signaled and assigned MPLS labels using the Protocol-Independent Multicast (PIM) protocol, typically in its Sparse Mode (PIM-SM) variant. PIM signaling is used to establish the RP Tree and to forward multicast traffic along the tree to reach receivers within the VPN.

- **Provider Tunnel and Customer Tunnel:** In the Draft-Rosen model, the MPLS provider network establishes a Provider Tunnel (P-Tunnel) for carrying multicast traffic across the network. Within each VPN, a separate Customer Tunnel (C-Tunnel) is established for delivering multicast traffic to VPN customers while maintaining isolation between VPNs.

- **MPLS Label Stacking:** MPLS label stacking is used to differentiate between multicast groups and to forward multicast traffic along the appropriate RP Tree within the MPLS network. Each multicast group is assigned a unique MPLS label stack, allowing routers to identify and forward traffic to the correct destination.

- **Scalability and Efficiency:** The Draft-Rosen model provides scalability and efficiency by using shared distribution trees and MPLS label switching to minimize replication and reduce network overhead. It supports large-scale multicast deployments across VPNs without requiring per-source or per-group state information in the core network.

- **Deployment Flexibility:** Draft-Rosen offers deployment flexibility by allowing multiple VPNs to share common RP Trees for multicast traffic, enabling efficient resource utilization and network optimization. It supports both Any Source Multicast (ASM) and Source-Specific Multicast (SSM) service models, depending on the requirements of the application and the nature of the multicast traffic.

Overall, the Draft-Rosen model is a widely adopted approach for implementing MVPN services in MPLS networks, providing efficient and scalable multicast distribution across VPNs while leveraging MPLS features for traffic engineering, isolation, and resource optimization.

The original solution for multicast in BGP/MPLS VPNs is often referred to as *draft-rosen*, after the name of the IETF draft [DRAFT-ROSEN] that first described it, or PIM/GRE mVPN, after the technologies used for the exchange of routing information and traffic forwarding. Note that although implementations of this solution were deployed by some of the largest networks in the industry, the draft itself never gained working group status in the IETF. However, the working group draft describing the architectural solution for multicast [VPN-MCAST] is a superset of draft-rosen, allowing all the functionality available in the original draft.

Although targeted to multicast traffic in a BGP/MPLS VPN setup, the draft-rosen solution departs from the BGP/MPLS VPN model for unicast traffic described in previous chapters. Nevertheless, some of the elements of BGP/MPLS VPNs are reused: the interface between PE and CE in the multicast solution is still based on the VRF concept of BGP/MPLS VPNs, and customer traffic is still tunneled through the provider core between the PEs (the VPN tunnel concept of BGP/MPLS VPNs). Despite these high-level similarities, the PIM/GRE multicast solution is very different from the unicast one. Exactly how different we will see in the remainder of this section by looking at the mechanisms used for carrying multicast mVPN routing information and data traffic. These will be discussed separately.

PIM/GRE mVPN: Routing Information Distribution Using PIM C-instances

Like the unicast VPN case, where the customer's CE routers maintain a routing adjacency only with the local PE router, the distribution of the PIM state among the customer sites is also based on a model where CE routers only require a PIM adjacency with their local PE router (rather than with all other CEs in the VPN). Again, like the unicast case, the PE must process the PIM messages exchanged with the CE in the context of the VRF to which the CE belongs.

To propagate the PIM information among the PE routers and onward to other VPN sites, PIM adjacencies are set up among the PEs that have sites in the same VPN. Because the PIM information exchanged among PEs is relevant only in the customer's VPN context, it is necessary to set up these PIM adjacencies among PEs on a per-VPN basis. These per-VPN PIM adjacencies ensure that the necessary multicast trees can be set up within each customer VPN. The need for per-VPN PIM adjacencies contrasts with the unicast case, where a PE uses a single BGP session to exchange routes belonging to all VPNs present on the PE.

The PIM sessions set up at PE1 are shown in Figure 12-20. Note that PE1 maintains not one but *two* separate PIM adjacencies with PE2—one for VPNA and the other for VPNB. It also maintains a PIM adjacency with PE3 for VPNA and a PIM adjacency with PE4 for VPNB. These VPN-specific PIM instances are referred to as a PIM C-instance (where C stands for customer).

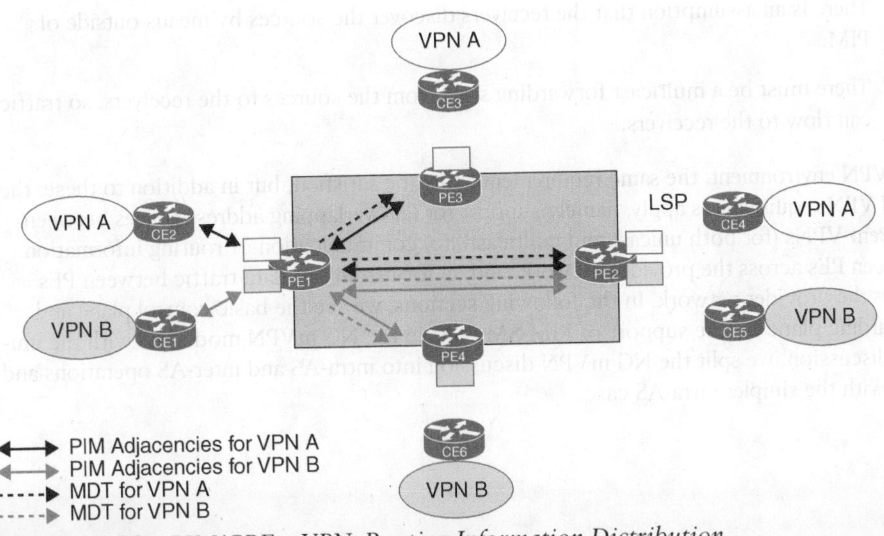

Figure 12-20 *PIM/GRE mVPN: Routing Information Distribution*

To summarize, the control plane of the draft-rosen mVPN solution uses PIM to carry customer multicast information across the service provider network. It does so by setting up per-VPN PIM adjacencies, called PIM C-instances, between the PEs that have sites of that VPN connected to them. In doing so, it diverges from the unicast model in (a) the choice of control protocol used and (b) the need to have per-VPN per PE routing peerings.

NG Multicast for L3VPN–BGP/MPLS mVPN (NG mVPN)

The NG mVPN approach brings the mVPN solution back into the framework and architecture of unicast BGP/MPLS VPNs by using BGP for the distribution of the routing information among PEs and MPLS for carrying the customer multicast traffic across the service provider network. This section presents the details of how this is done by looking at various flavors of multicast deployments.

Requirements for Support of PIM-SM SSM in an mVPN

Protocol-Independent Multicast (PIM) Sparse Mode (SM) is documented in RFC 4601. PIM-SM has two modes of operations: Source Specific Multicast (SSM) and Any Source Multicast (ASM). In the SSM mode of operation, PIM-SM provides a service model where there is a single multicast source and multiple receivers. An example of an application using this model is video distribution from one (well-known) source to several receivers. Although PIM-SM in SSM mode is less widely deployed than PIM-SM in ASM mode, in the context of the mVPN discussion, we will start by presenting it first as a customer mVPN deployment for two reasons: (1) it is simpler both in the customer domain and the service provider network, and (2) the mechanisms used to support it in an mVPN deployment form the foundation for supporting PIM-SM in ASM mode in an mVPN.

To understand what is required to support mVPNs running PIM-SM in SSM mode, let's start by looking at the requirements to support multicast in the SP infrastructure (global routing table):

- The multicast sources must know that there are multicast receivers. This is accomplished by the receivers informing the sources that they are interested in receiving traffic, using PIM join messages.

- There is an assumption that the receivers discover the sources by means outside of PIM.

- There must be a multicast forwarding state from the sources to the receivers, so traffic can flow to the receivers.

In a VPN environment, the same requirements must be satisfied, but in addition to these, the usual VPN requirements apply, namely support for (a) overlapping address spaces between different VPNs (for both unicast and multicast), (b) communication of routing information between PEs across the provider network, and (c) forwarding of data traffic between PEs across the provider network. In the following sections, we see the basic control plane and forwarding plane for the support of PIM-SM SSM in the NG mVPN model. As with the unicast discussion, we split the NG mVPN discussion into intra-AS and inter-AS operations and start with the simpler intra-AS case.

BGP/MPLS mVPN: Carrying Multicast mVPN Routing Information Using C-Multicast Routes

In an L3VPN, customer routing information is propagated between two sites in a VPN by advertising it between the remote PEs servicing these sites. In the case of unicast, the information is the prefix reachability, while in the case of multicast, it is the multicast group membership information that PEs obtain from the PIM join and prune messages that PEs receive from the CE routers. One of the major innovations of NG mVPN was to recognize that these join and prune messages are simply customer routing information, and thus, we could use BGP rather than PIM for carrying this information across the provider network by encoding it as a special customer multicast (C-multicast) route using BGP Multiprotocol Extensions (RFC 4760).

mVPN-BGP-ENC defines the encodings and procedures for using BGP to advertise C-multicast routes across the provider network. In a nutshell, this is accomplished by defining new BGP Network Layer Reachability Information (NLRI), the MCAST-VPN NLRI. When a PE receives a PIM join message from an attached CE, indicating the presence of a receiver for a particular multicast group and source in the customer site, the PE converts it to a BGP update containing the multicast group and source. As a result, the information received by the local PE in the PIM join is advertised to the remote PEs as a C-multicast route carried in BGP. At the remote PE, the information carried in the C-multicast route is converted back into a PIM join message that is propagated using PIM to the remote CE. Note that the CE devices are completely oblivious of what mechanism was used to propagate the information among the PEs across the provider network and simply continue to run PIM to the PEs they are attached to.

As with unicast, the BGP advertisement for a C-multicast route is made unique by attaching an RD to it (to deal with a situation where different VPNs use the same address space for unicast or multicast, or both) and is tagged with a Route Target (RT) extended community that will identify the correct VRF into which to import it.

By default, in the unicast VPN case, all VPN routing information for a particular VPN—for example, VPN X—is propagated to all PEs connected to sites belonging to VPN X and imported in the VRFs of VPN X present on all these PEs. In contrast, in the mVPN case, a C-multicast route carrying multicast routing information representing an (S, G) membership originated at a PE connected to a receiver, PE_R, should be propagated only to the PE connected to the site that contains the source, PE_S, and need not be propagated to any other PE. At PE_S, this route must be imported only in the VRF of VPN X, where the information carried by the route will be converted back into a PIM message and propagated to the CE.

To control the import of C-multicast routes into the VRF, each VRF has, in addition to the import RTs used for controlling other types of VPN routing information (such as unicast routes), an additional import RT extended community, called the C-multicast Import RT. An important property of the C-multicast Import RT is that it is unique across all VRFs and all PEs. The uniqueness property is accomplished by embedding the PE's IP address and a locally assigned number into the RT (the PE assigns a distinct number for each VRF present on the PE). This ensures not only that different mVPNs have different values but also that different VRFs within the same mVPN have different values.

The C-multicast Import RT, which is internally generated by the PE as explained previously, is automatically included in the filtering policy that is applied to incoming BGP advertisements. Since the PE that includes in its filtering policy a particular C-multicast Import RT expects C-multicast routes intended for the PE to be tagged with this autogenerated RT, the value of this RT must be known to other PEs. This is done by sending the value of this RT in a new extended community, called VRF Route Import, along with the unicast advertisement of the reachability to the source. In the earlier example for VPN X, PE_S sends the VRF Route Import constructed from its address and a locally unique number along with the unicast advertisement for S. Based on PE_S's unicast route advertisement for the source S, PE_R will know what RT to attach to its C-multicast routes, such that these routes will be imported into the VRF of VPN X at PE_S.

Let's look at the distribution of multicast routing information in the example in Figure 12-21.

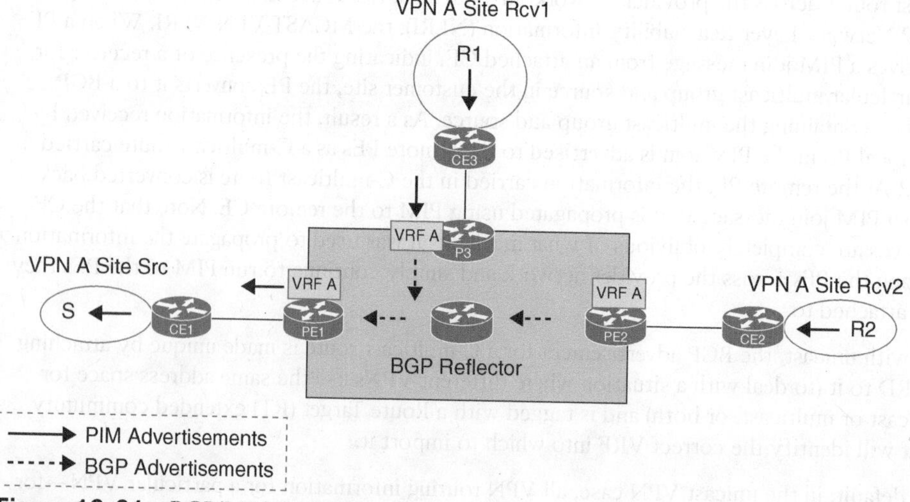

Figure 12-21 *BGP/MPLS mVPN*

Two receivers, R1 and R2, exist in sites (branch1 and branch2) of the VPN, serviced by PE2 and PE3, respectively. The source S is in site Src, serviced by PE1. Receivers R1 and R2 know about the existence of the source S. R1 and R2 advertise their interest in receiving multicast traffic from S by sending IGMP messages for an (S, G) to their designated routers, which, in turn, send PIM join messages for that (S, G) toward S. Let's continue the discussion from the point of view of R2 only, since the processing for R1 will be identical. The PIM join message for (S, G) is propagated within site Rcv2 that contains R2 toward CE2, which, in turn, propagates it to PE2. Note that on that PE, the PIM adjacency toward the CE is VRF-aware, and this is why the advertisement is shown in the figure as arriving at the VRF for VPN A.

When PE2 receives a PIM join from CE2, it uses the information carried in this PIM join to construct and originate a C-multicast route as follows:

1. PE2 finds in the VRF associated with VPN A the unicast VPN-IPv4 route to S and extracts from this route the RD and the VRF Route Import extended community.

2. PE2 builds a BGP C-multicast route that carries the source and group (S, G) information from the PIM join message received from the CE, the RD from the VPN-IPv4 route for S, and an RT constructed from the VRF Route Import of the VPN-IPv4

route. Note that PE2 does not attach to the C-multicast route the "regular" unicast RT associated with VPN A (the RT used by VPN-IPv4 routes).

3. PE2 sends the C-multicast advertisement to its BGP peers. In Figure 12-17, the advertisement is sent toward the route reflector shown in the middle of the provider network.

4. The route reflector receives the C-multicast advertisement from PE2, and the one similarly produced by PE3, aggregates them, and propagates the aggregated advertisement to PE1. On receipt of the C-multicast route advertisement, the following actions are taken on PE1:

5. PE1 accepts the C-multicast route into the VRF for VPN A because the C-multicast Import RT (which was automatically generated on this PE and automatically included in the import policy for the VRF) matches the RT attached to the route. Any other PE receiving the route ignores it because it does not match its C-multicast Import RT, and the "regular" unicast RT for VPN A is not attached to the route either.

6. As a result of accepting the C-multicast route advertisement, PE1 creates (S, G) state in the VRF and propagates the (S, G) join toward CE1 (attached to the site that contains the source S), using PIM as the PE-CE routing protocol. Note that this is the PIM instance running within the VRF on the PE1. (This is why in Figure 12.21 the advertisement is shown as originating in the VRF.)

Exam Preparation Tasks

As mentioned in the section "How to Use This Book" in the Introduction, you have a few choices for exam preparation: the exercises here, Chapter 23, "Final Preparation," and the exam simulation questions in the Pearson Test Prep Software Online.

Review All Key Topics

Review the most important topics in this chapter, noted with the Key Topic icon in the margin of the page. Table 12-5 lists a reference of these key topics and the page numbers on which each is found.

Table 12-5 Key Topics for Chapter 12

Key Topic Element	Description	Page Number
Section	Virtual Routing and Forwarding (VRF)	557
Section	Multiprotocol-BGP (MP-BGP)	564
Figure 12-7	MPLS Labels (VPN and Transport)	574
Steps	CE-to-CE traffic propagation	577
Paragraph	OSPF Domain-ID	580
Paragraph	OSPF sham-link	586
Figure 12-11	OSPF Backdoor Link Intra-Area Routes	587
Paragraph	OSPF down bit	589
Paragraph	Loops caused by mutual redistribution of protocols	592

Key Topic Element	Description	Page Number
Paragraph	EIGRP SoO	593
Paragraph	MPLS L3VPN BGP PE-CE routing	595
Section	Import and Export Maps	601
Example 12-76	BGP **rtfilter** Neighborship Establishment	606
Paragraph	**max-metric router-lsa**	609
Section	Draft-Rosen	611
Paragraph	Controlling the import of C-multicast routes into the VRF	615

Define Key Terms

Define the following key terms from this chapter and check the answers in the glossary:

Label Distribution Protocol (LDP), Label Forwarding Information Base (LFIB), label-switched path (LSP), link-state advertisement (LSA), Multiprotocol Label Switching (MPLS), Site of Origin (SoO), Virtual Routing and Forwarding (VRF)

Command Reference to Check Your Memory

This section includes the most important commands covered in this chapter. You might not need to memorize the complete syntax of every command, but you should be able to remember the basic keywords that are needed.

To test your memory of the commands, cover the right side of Table 12-6 with a piece of paper, read the description on the left side, and then see how much of the command you can remember.

The SPCOR 350-501 exam focuses on practical, hands-on skills that are used by networking professionals. Therefore, you should be able to identify the commands needed to configure and test. Note that not all commands are fully covered in the chapter, but their presence in the following table should lead you to investigate them further to understand this technology.

Table 12-6 CLI Commands to Know

Task	Command Syntax
On the interface level, use the **vrf forwarding** command to assign the interface to the correct VRF (VRF creation method is through the VRF **definition** command)	**vrf forwarding** *VRF_Name*
Configure the router to exchange VPNv4 routes for use with MPLS VPNs. This includes support for encoding Route Targets and route distinguishers within the updates for customer VPN prefixes.	**address-family vpnv4 unicast**
Display BGP neighbor status for the VPNv4 family, including VRF information	**show bgp vpnv4 unicast all**

Task	Command Syntax
Show all VPNv4 entries in the BGP routing table with the assigned labels	**show bgp vpnv4 unicast labels**
Display the content of the LSDB and verify information about specific LSAs. The output reveals the presence of different LSA types.	**show ip ospf database**
Configure extended community for Site of Origin (SoO), which will be applied to an interface using **ip vrf sitemap Route_map_name**	**set extcommunity soo ASN:NN**
Configure an unnumbered point-to-point intra-area link and advertise it as a Type-1 link in router-LSA	**area** *Area_Number* **sham-link** *Source Destination*
Allow the BGP speaker to accept the BGP updates even if its own BGP AS number is in the AS-Path attribute	**neighbor** *ip-address* **allowas-in**
Replace the AS number of the originating router with the AS number of the sending BGP router	**neighbor** *ip-address* **as-override**
All received VPN IPv4 routes are accepted. If the router is an autonomous system border or customer edge router, this is the desired behavior	**no bgp default route-target filter**
Apply to the VPN address-family under BGP; it affects all VPN peers advertising VPN routes to this ASBR (iBGP and eBGP) on IOS XR	**retain route-target all**
Distribute MPLS labels without a specific address family (VPNv4/VPNv6 unicast/multicast) per neighbor	**allocate-label all**

Review Questions

As a part of the review, we encourage you to provide *a single-sentence answer* (keep your answers as short as possible) to the following questions. If you struggle to complete this answer in a single sentence, this may indicate a lack of clarity or reveal gaps in your understanding. We have constructed these questions to help you consolidate this chapter's information and extract the essence of the covered content.

The answers to these questions appear in Appendix A. For more practice with exam format questions, use the Pearson Test Prep Software Online.

1. What is the purpose of a route distinguisher (RD)?

2. What additional functionalities did NG-MVPN introduce as enhancements to MVPN?

3. How can you ensure different mVPNs with different values and different VRFs within the same mVPN?

Bibliography

Y. Rekhter and E. Rosen. RFC 3107, *Carrying Label Information in BGP-4*, IETF, https://www.ietf.org/rfc/rfc3107.txt, May 2001.

E. Rosen and Y. Rekhter. RFC 4364, *BGP/MPLS IP Virtual Private Networks (VPNs)*, IETF, https://www.ietf.org/rfc/rfc4364.txt, February 2006.

E. Rosen, P. Psenak, and P. Pilley-Esnault. RFC 4577, *OSPF as the Provider/Customer Edge Protocol for BGP/MPLS IP Virtual Private Networks (VPNs)*, IETF, https://www.ietf.org/rfc/rfc4577.txt, June 2006.

E. Rosen, B. Davie, V. Radoaca, and W. Luo. RFC 6074, *Provisioning, Auto-Discovery, and Signaling in Layer 2 Virtual Private Networks (L2VPNs)*, IETF, https://www.ietf.org/rfc/rfc6074.txt, January 2011.

Advanced MPLS Services

This chapter covers the following exam topics:

1.4 Describe QoS architecture

- 1.4.a MPLS QoS models (Pipe, Short Pipe, and Uniform)
- 1.4.c DiffServ and IntServ QoS models
- 1.4.d Trust boundaries between enterprise and SP environments

4.1 Describe VPN services

- 4.1.b Inter-AS VPN
- 4.1.c CSC

One of the most important aspects of **Multiprotocol Label Switching (MPLS)** is the flexibility it provides that aligns to customer requirements. The main deployment of MPLS is related to VPN connectivity, but what about other services that could be requested, such as Internet access, in addition to the VPN? What are the Quality of Service (QoS) options the customer has in both managed and unmanaged MPLS deployment?

"Do I Know This Already?" Quiz

The "Do I Know This Already?" quiz allows you to assess whether you should read this entire chapter thoroughly or jump to the "Exam Preparation Tasks" section. If you are in doubt about your answers to these questions or your own assessment of your knowledge of the topics, read the entire chapter. Table 13-1 lists the major headings in this chapter and their corresponding "Do I Know This Already?" quiz questions. You can find the answers in Appendix A, "Answers to the 'Do I Know This Already?' Quizzes and Review Questions."

Table 13-1 "Do I Know This Already?" Section-to-Question Mapping

Foundation Topics Section	Questions
Unified MPLS	1
MPLS L3VPN Shared Services (Internet)	2
MPLS Inter-AS L3VPN	3, 4
Carrier Supporting Carrier (CsC)	5
MPLS QoS	6

1. In unified MPLS architecture, transport labels for egress PE reachability are assigned through which protocol?

    a. BGP

    b. LDP

    c. T-LDP

    d. RSVP

2. Which MPLS L3VPN Internet access option is more complex from an ASBR manageability perspective?

    a. VRF-specific default route

    b. Separate PE-CE interface

    c. Extranet with Internet-VRF

    d. VRF-aware NAT

3. In which MPLS L3VPN Inter-AS option is there a broken end-to-end LSP?

    a. Option A

    b. Option B

    c. Option C

    d. Option D

4. When you are designing for MPLS L3VPN Inter-AS Option C, which device should you choose with higher resources to account for seamless service?

    a. CE

    b. RR

    c. PE

    d. ASBR

5. What is the MPLS edge device located at the edge of the backbone carrier called?

    a. Backbone carrier

    b. Customer carrier

    c. CsC-PE

    d. CsC-CE

6. Which of the following MPLS QoS deployment modes is suitable for customer-managed deployments?

    a. Uniform mode

    b. Short pipe

    c. Long pipe

    d. None of the available options are suitable because the service provider will not be able to alter customer markings.

Foundation Topics

Unified MPLS

Unified MPLS, which is also known as *hierarchical MPLS*, is a model for ensuring a scalable large provider network in which multiple IGP islands exist.

The main goal, from a scalability perspective, is to segment the large network into several domains (aggregation, core), considering that these domains run IGPs for communication of internal network elements. Now we are in the process of deploying MPLS across all segments, which will basically require a functional **label-switched path (LSP)** across all elements. To make sure this is in place, we need to determine whether redistribution is available among routing devices to maintain the LSP state. However, redistribution, in general, will increase the management burden of the network, in addition to other issues. Here, we are targeting a network (regardless of the intervening domains) with fewer touch points.

To address the concept of unified MPLS, RFC 3107 introduced the use of BGP for label assignment/distribution functionality (inter-domain). That does not mean that the **Label Distribution Protocol (LDP)** will not be used, but it will be contained within a single domain and handle the intra-domain labels responsible for BGP (a transport label for egress PEs).

As we can see from the diagram in Figure 13-1, we will rely on BGP and the send-label capability associated with BGP neighborship to ensure that we have end-to-end LSP. Also, we will not perform any kind of redistribution within the IGP domains, which would minimize configuration touchpoints.

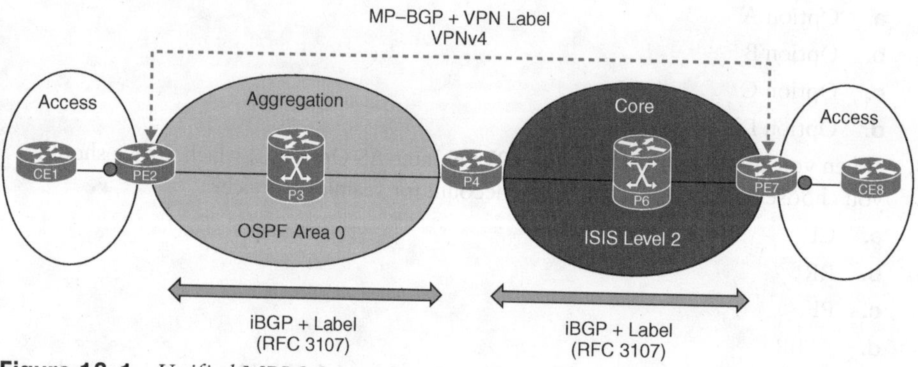

Figure 13-1 *Unified MPLS Structure*

P4 will act as an autonomous system boundary router (ASBR), which is a router that runs different protocols simultaneously. The main session is the VPNv4 session, which will be established between the edge PEs carrying traffic for customers. Example 13-1 lists the BGP configuration commands considering route reflection.

Example 13-1 *BGP Configuration*

```
P4(config)# router bgp 100
P4(config-router)# no bgp default ipv4-unicast
P4(config-router)# neighbor 10.1.100.2 remote-as 100
P4(config-router)# neighbor 10.1.100.2 update-source Loopback0
```

```
P4(config-router)# neighbor 10.1.100.7 remote-as 100
P4(config-router)# neighbor 10.1.100.7 update-source Loopback0
P4(config-router)# address-family ipv4
P4(config-router-af)# neighbor 10.1.100.2 activate
P4(config-router-af)# neighbor 10.1.100.2 route-reflector-client
P4(config-router-af)# neighbor 10.1.100.2 next-hop-self all
P4(config-router-af)# neighbor 10.1.100.2 send-label
P4(config-router-af)# neighbor 10.1.100.7 activate
P4(config-router-af)# neighbor 10.1.100.7 route-reflector-client
P4(config-router-af)# neighbor 10.1.100.7 next-hop-self all
P4(config-router-af)# neighbor 10.1.100.7 send-label
```

The route reflector (which is the ASBR in our case) is mandatory because the default loop prevention (split horizon) is in place; the reason is that we are running all BGP sessions inside the same autonomous system. The main idea is simplicity, and therefore, without route reflection capabilities, we would end up with several iBGP sessions (depending on the network size).

NOTE   Because we are not performing any redistribution among the IGP islands, we configured the next-hop-self option associated with BGP sessions. However, the default BGP next-hop-self functions regularly when we advertise an eBGP learned route to an iBGP neighbor. In our case, we are only talking about iBGP, which requires all options to be added at the end of the command statement:

```
P4(config-router-af)# neighbor 10.1.100.7 next-hop-self ?

all    Enable next-hop-self for both eBGP and iBGP received paths
```

To clarify the label bindings, let's trace the packet sourced from CE1 (10.1.100.1/32) going toward CE8 (10.1.100.8/32), as shown in Example 13-2.

Example 13-2   *Traceroute Output*

```
CE1# traceroute 10.1.100.8 source loopback 0 numeric
VRF info: (vrf in name/id, vrf out name/id)
  1 172.16.12.2 170 msec 0 msec 0 msec
  2 10.1.23.3 [MPLS: Labels 16300/405/700 Exp 0] 10 msec 9 msec 9 msec
  3 10.1.34.4 [MPLS: Labels 405/700 Exp 0] 8 msec 10 msec 9 msec
  4 10.1.46.6 [MPLS: Labels 16601/700 Exp 0] 8 msec 10 msec 11 msec
  5 172.16.78.7 [MPLS: Label 700 Exp 0] 10 msec 10 msec 10 msec
  6 172.16.78.8 14 msec 20 msec 11 msec
```

CE1 will send the packet for its directly connected PE (PE2). Example 13-3 shows how PE2 inspects the target FEC.

Example 13-3 *BGP VPNv4 Output*

```
PE2# show bgp vpnv4 unicast all 10.1.100.8
BGP routing table entry for 100:1:10.1.100.8/32, version 10
Paths: (1 available, best #1, table SPCOR)
  Not advertised to any peer
  Refresh Epoch 1
  Local
    10.1.100.7 (metric 3) (via default) from 10.1.100.7 (10.1.100.7)
      Origin incomplete, metric 0, localpref 100, valid, internal, best
      Extended Community: RT:100:1
      mpls labels in/out nolabel/700
      rx pathid: 0, tx pathid: 0x0
      Updated on Jan 23 2024 11:07:14 UTC
```

This update comes from PE7 (10.1.100.7). Now, let's check label binding for this PE loopback
address by examining the BGP table, as shown in Example 13-4.

Example 13-4 *BGP Table Output*

```
PE2# show bgp ipv4 unicast 10.1.100.7
BGP routing table entry for 10.1.100.7/32, version 4
Paths: (1 available, best #1, table default)
  Not advertised to any peer
  Refresh Epoch 1
  Local
    10.1.100.4 (metric 3) from 10.1.100.4 (10.1.100.4)
      Origin IGP, metric 0, localpref 100, valid, internal, best
      Originator: 10.1.100.7, Cluster list: 10.1.100.4
      mpls labels in/out nolabel/405
      rx pathid: 0, tx pathid: 0x0
      Updated on Jan 23 2024 11:07:09 UTC
```

As we can see, the next-hop to reach this end PE is via P4, which acts as the route
reflector and handles the iBGP + send-label functionality, as can be proven from the
Label Forwarding Information Base (LFIB) output in Example 13-5.

Example 13-5 *LFIB Output*

```
PE2# show mpls forwarding-table
Local    Outgoing    Prefix          Bytes Label   Outgoing    Next Hop
Label    Label       or Tunnel Id    Switched      interface
200      16300       10.1.100.4/32   0             Gi2         10.1.23.3
201      Pop Label   10.1.100.3/32   0             Gi2         10.1.23.3
202      Pop Label   10.1.34.0/24    0             Gi2         10.1.23.3
203      No Label    10.1.100.1/32[V] 3012         Gi1         172.16.12.1
```

So, the outgoing label 16300 mapped for 10.1.100.4 (P4) will be the last label to be pushed
on the stack.

The intermediate P3 will pop the label because it is directly connected to P4, as shown in Example 13-6.

Example 13-6   *LFIB Output*

```
RP/0/0/CPU0:P3# show mpls forwarding-table
Local   Outgoing    Prefix          Outgoing     Next Hop      Bytes
Label   Label       or ID           Interface                  Switched
------  ----------  --------------  -----------  ------------  ------------
16300   Pop         10.1.100.4/32   Gi0/0/0/3    10.1.34.4     507415
16301   Pop         10.1.100.2/32   Gi0/0/0/2    10.1.23.2     500725
```

Moving to our ASBR, we can see that the incoming packet with a label of 405 should be swapped to 16601, as in Example 13-7.

Example 13-7   *LFIB Output*

```
P4# show mpls forwarding-table
Local     Outgoing    Prefix          Bytes Label   Outgoing    Next Hop
Label     Label       or Tunnel Id    Switched      interface
400       Pop Label   10.1.100.3/32   0             Gi0/0       10.1.34.3
401       Pop Label   10.1.23.0/24    0             Gi0/0       10.1.34.3
402       Pop Label   10.1.100.6/32   0             Gi0/1       10.1.46.6
403       Pop Label   10.1.67.0/24    0             Gi0/1       10.1.46.6
404       16301       10.1.100.2/32   221700        Gi0/0       10.1.34.3
405       16601       10.1.100.7/32   229916        Gi0/1       10.1.46.6
```

P6 will receive the packet with a label of 16601, and the pop action will take place. It is directly connected to P7 (the other end of the LSP), as shown in Example 13-8.

Example 13-8   *LFIB Output*

```
RP/0/0/CPU0:P6# show mpls forwarding
Local   Outgoing    Prefix          Outgoing     Next Hop      Bytes
Label   Label       or ID           Interface                  Switched
------  ----------  --------------  -----------  ------------  ------------
16600   Pop         10.1.100.4/32   Gi0/0/0/3    10.1.46.4     497237
16601   Pop         10.1.100.7/32   Gi0/0/0/2    10.1.67.7     504365
```

PE7 will finally receive the packet and strip off the label because it will send an IP packet to the destination, which is CE8, as detailed in the output in Example 13-9.

Example 13-9   *BGP VPNv4 Output*

```
PE7# show bgp vpnv4 unicast all 10.1.100.8
BGP routing table entry for 100:1:10.1.100.8/32, version 6
Paths: (1 available, best #1, table SPCOR)
  Advertised to update-groups:
     2
  Refresh Epoch 1
  Local
```

```
172.16.78.8 (via vrf SPCOR) from 0.0.0.0 (10.1.100.7)
   Origin incomplete, metric 0, localpref 100, weight 32768, valid, sourced, best
   Extended Community: RT:100:1
   mpls labels in/out 700/nolabel
   rx pathid: 0, tx pathid: 0x0
   Updated on Jan 22 2024 20:14:49 UTC
```

Figure 13-2 shows label stacking (transport and VPN) along the LSP (through the intermediate devices, proving the functionality of BGP of assigning/distributing labels between the virtualized islands we created for scalability).

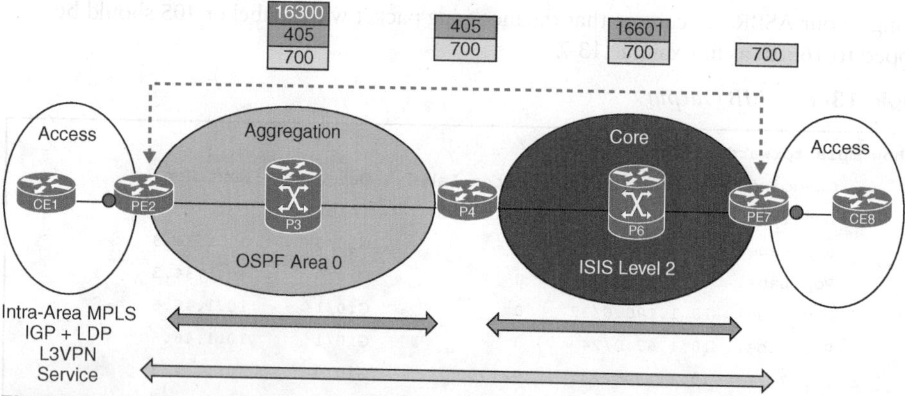

Figure 13-2 *Unified MPLS Label Operation*

Use Case: Unified MPLS Mobile Transport (UMMT)

Generally, service in transport platforms must be configured or provisioned at every network element, and this must be reflected in the management platforms.

With the deployment of MPLS across the aggregation, a number of operational points decreased. However, with an integration between MPLS islands, the operational burden is minimized more.

There are several deployment scenarios for which unified MPLS comes into play to minimize the operational touchpoints. One of these models is an extended MPLS to the access; it uses BGP + send-label capabilities to connect different islands (LDP is still running within each domain):

- Core and aggregation form a relatively small IGP/LDP domain.

- MPLS is enabled within the access. Each access network forms a separate IGP domain.

- Core/aggregation and RAN access networks are integrated through labeled BGP LSP.

- Access nodes learn only required service destinations.

Figure 13-3 shows a production use case of unified MPLS in telecom networks where the access node (where customers will terminate eventually) and the aggregation node are running LDP separately, with a common LSP spanning the network using BGP for label assignment and distribution.

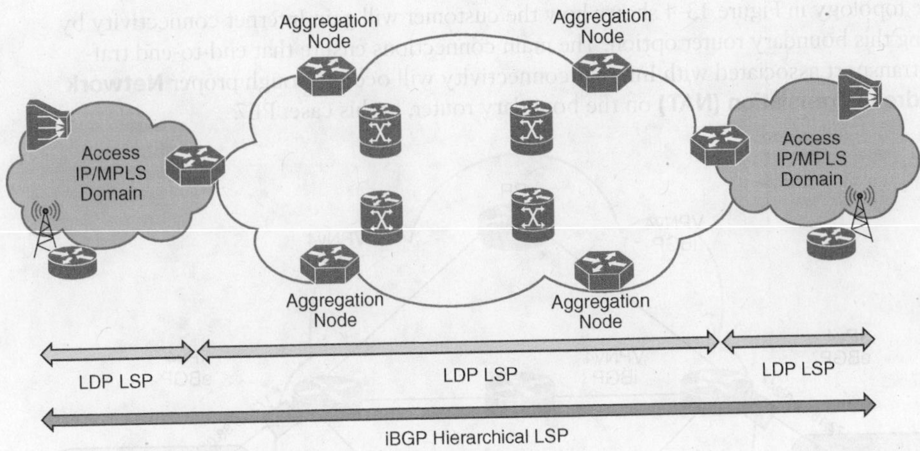

Figure 13-3 *Unified MPLS Use Case*

MPLS L3VPN Shared Services (Internet)

One of the applications that MPLS provides is WAN connectivity for enterprises (generally speaking) that seek secure communication among their entities and remote locations.

Customer demands expand beyond just WAN connectivity to gain Internet access utilizing the same last mile (last mile is the physical part of the network that serves as the final leg connecting the service provider's network to the customer/user), but is the service provider infrastructure capable of supporting such a setup? Sure, it can, so one of the main design aspects that MPLS technology supports is flexibility.

Now, because we have ensured that MPLS supports Internet access over the provided service (MPLS L3VPN), let's examine the available options from a technical perspective and highlight some design concerns among the available options.

Before we dive into the available options, let's categorize the options from a high level into

- MP-BGP

- Non-MP-BGP

MPLS L3VPN Internet Access Option 1: VRF-Specific Default Route

This option is based on using the static route to redirect traffic from customer **Virtual Routing and Forwarding (VRF)** to the Internet Gateway (boundary router) using the global routing table (GRT). If the L3VPN service relies solely on establishing a VPNv4 session between the serving PEs, where will we get the Internet routes? Usually through our GW (a boundary router).

How will this device be connected? The answer varies from one network to another. In our case, we will place the boundary router so that it is directly connected to the P5-INET device, which will provide the Internet routes. Also, we will place P9 to act as an out-of-band route reflector for the VPNv4 address family.

The topology in Figure 13-4 shows how the customer will gain Internet connectivity by using this boundary router option. The main connections ensure that end-to-end traffic transport associated with Internet connectivity will occur through proper **Network Address Translation (NAT)** on the boundary router, in this case, PE7.

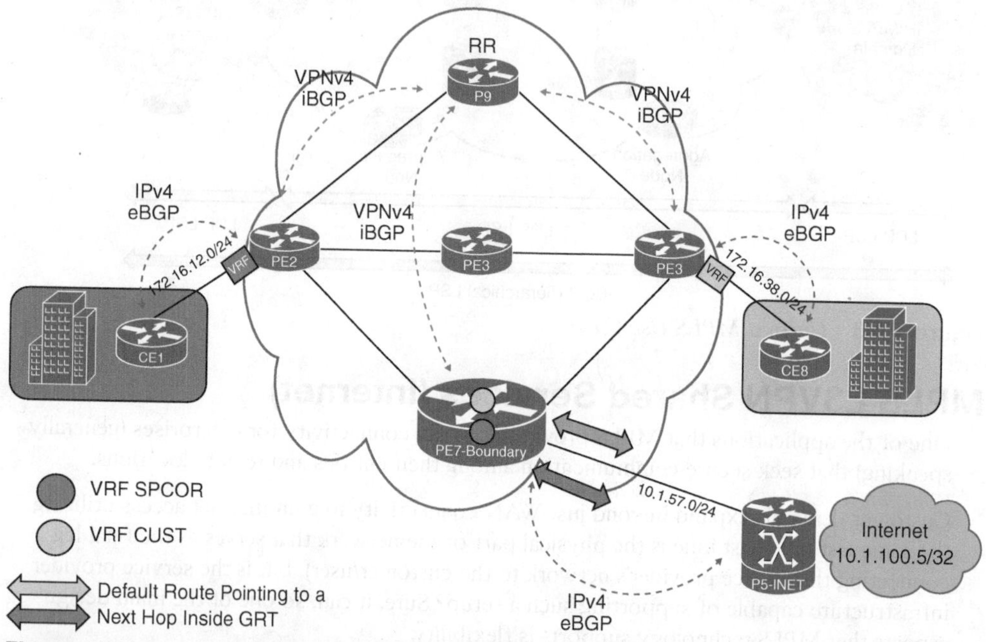

Figure 13-4 *MPLS L3VPN Internet Access Option 1*

The PE-CE routing protocol is eBGP, and OSPF is the IGP inside the network.

The Internet destination is represented by a loopback interface configured on the P5-INET router, which is advertised to the boundary router via BGP IPv4 unicast.

As the customers need Internet access (currently, they are using a private IP addressing scheme for WAN connectivity), some public IP addressing scheme should be implemented.

For the sake of this document, we will use the Carrier Grade NAT (CGNAT) reserved IP space for simulating the subnets to be used for NATting and therefore Internet connectivity.

NOTE The Carrier Grade NAT reserved IP address space is 100.64.0.0/16 to 100.127.255.255/16.

The main device of concern (from a configuration perspective) will be PE7 (the boundary router) because it will handle several functions.

For the NAT process, we will define NAT pools for which each VRF will be NATted for Internet connectivity, and the NAT directions will be placed properly to ensure private-to-public translation. Example 13-10 demonstrates these aspects of the boundary router NAT configuration.

Example 13-10 *Boundary Router NAT Configuration*

```
PE7-Boundary(config)# ip nat pool SPCOR_POOL 100.64.1.0 100.64.1.254 prefix-length 24
PE7-Boundary(config)# ip nat pool CUST_POOL 100.64.2.0 100.64.2.254 prefix-length 24

! We must define the interesting traffic (the customer traffic which will be the
source of the packets destined to the Internet).
PE7-Boundary(config)# ip access-list standard SPCOR_ACL
PE7-Boundary(config-std-nacl)# 5 permit host 10.1.100.1
PE7-Boundary(config)# ip access-list standard CUST_ACL
PE7-Boundary(config-std-nacl)# 5 permit host 10.1.100.2

PE7-Boundary(config)# ip nat inside source list CUST_ACL pool CUST_POOL vrf CUST
PE7-Boundary(config)# ip nat inside source list SPCOR_ACL pool SPCOR_POOL vrf SPCOR
! As can be seen, the NAT statement is associated not only with the interesting
! traffic (defined in the access-lists) and the NAT pools, but also associated with
! the VRF which will require these VRFs to be explicitly defined on the boundary
! router).

! We can verify the NAT statements in each respective direction by checking the
! interfaces to which each is connected.
PE7-Boundary# show running-config interface GigabitEthernet2 | include
(description|nat)
 description P5-INET
 ip nat outside
PE7-Boundary# show running-config interface GigabitEthernet3 | include
(description|nat)
 description PE2
 ip nat inside
PE7-Boundary# show running-config interface GigabitEthernet4 | include
(description|nat)
 description PE3
 ip nat inside
```

With regard to BGP advertisements, we use eBGP to advertise the NAT-purposed prefixes
to our P5-INET router. We do not have these routes installed in our RIB, and therefore, BGP
will not advertise it by default. We will inject two static routes pointing to Null 0 to allow
BGP to advertise the routes and therefore be accepted by P5-INET. (Do not forget that
P5-INET is IOS XR–based, so we must define route policy per the nature of the relation—in
this case, eBGP.) Example 13-11 goes through the route advertisement process.

Example 13-11 *BGP Advertisement and Null Routes*

```
PE7-Boundary(config)# ip route 100.64.1.0 255.255.255.0 Null0
PE7-Boundary(config)# ip route 100.64.2.0 255.255.255.0 Null0

PE7-Boundary(config)# router bgp 100
PE7-Boundary(config-router)# address-family ipv4
PE7-Boundary(config-router-af)# network 100.64.1.0 mask 255.255.255.0
PE7-Boundary(config-router-af)# network 100.64.2.0 mask 255.255.255.0
```

```
PE7-Boundary# show bgp ipv4 unicast neighbors 10.1.57.5 advertised-routes |
begin Network

       Network          Next Hop          Metric LocPrf Weight Path
  *>    100.64.1.0/24    0.0.0.0                     0          32768 i
  *>    100.64.2.0/24    0.0.0.0                     0          32768 i
Total number of prefixes 2
```

```
RP/0/0/CPU0:P5-INET# show bgp | begin Network | include 100.64
 *> 100.64.1.0/24      10.1.57.7                0          0 100 i
 *> 100.64.2.0/24      10.1.57.7                0          0 100 i
```

But how will the routes be imported into the specific VRFs? In design option 1, we are
relying on the global routing table to gain Internet access, so a static route points to the
Gateway (P5-INET) inside the respective VRF, as shown in Example 13-12.

Example 13-12 *VRF Static Routes with Next-Hop in GRT*

```
PE7-Boundary(config)# ip route vrf SPCOR 0.0.0.0 0.0.0.0 10.1.57.5 global
PE7-Boundary(config)# ip route vrf CUST 0.0.0.0 0.0.0.0 10.1.57.5 global
```

Now, as mentioned earlier, we have the IP subnet per VRF (in our demonstration example,
we have two VRFs), and the NAT process will be configured on the boundary router; here, it
is the PE7-Boundary. How will the respective PE devices receive the default route we created
on the PE7-Boundary pointing to the gateway using the global routing table? We will use the
established BGP VPNv4 session we have in place from the PE7-Boundary to the PEs; we are
using an out-of-band route reflector, following the most adopted route reflection deployment
model. Now, let's check Example 13-13 for default route delivery to the respective PEs.

Example 13-13 *Default Route Propagation Inside BGP (VRF Specific)*

```
PE7-Boundary(config)# router bgp 100
PE7-Boundary(config-router)# address-family ipv4 vrf CUST
PE7-Boundary(config-router-af)# network 0.0.0.0
PE7-Boundary(config-router)# address-family ipv4 vrf SPCOR
PE7-Boundary(config-router-af)# network 0.0.0.0
```

```
PE2# show bgp vpnv4 unicast all neighbors 10.1.100.9 routes | begin Network
       Network          Next Hop          Metric LocPrf Weight Path
Route Distinguisher: 100:1 (default for vrf SPCOR)
 *>i 0.0.0.0            10.1.100.7               0    100      0 i
Total number of prefixes 1
```

```
PE3# show bgp vpnv4 unicast all neighbors 10.1.100.9 routes | begin Network
       Network          Next Hop          Metric LocPrf Weight Path
Route Distinguisher: 200:1 (default for vrf CUST)
 *>i 0.0.0.0            10.1.100.7               0    100      0 i
Total number of prefixes 1
```

We have eBGP between CE and PE devices for both VRFs (as discussed, eBGP is one of the most adopted routing protocols between CE and PE for a more granular traffic control). Example 13-14 shows the installation of the default route inside each CE BGP table.

Example 13-14 *CEs Default Route Installation Verification*

```
CE1# show bgp ipv4 unicast 0.0.0.0/0
BGP routing table entry for 0.0.0.0/0, version 19
Paths: (1 available, best #1, table default)
  Not advertised to any peer
  Refresh Epoch 1
  100
    172.16.12.2 from 172.16.12.2 (10.1.100.2)
      Origin IGP, localpref 100, valid, external, best
      rx pathid: 0, tx pathid: 0x0
```

```
CE1# show ip route bgp | begin Gateway
Gateway of last resort is 172.16.12.2 to network 0.0.0.0
B*    0.0.0.0/0 [20/0] via 172.16.12.2, 1d11h
```

Finally, we will test connectivity from the CE toward the Internet prefix (10.1.100.5) sourced from each CE loopback, and consequently, the NAT translation on the PE7-Boundary, as shown in Example 13-15.

Example 13-15 *Connectivity Test and NAT Verification*

```
CE1# ping 10.1.100.5 source loopback 0
Type escape sequence to abort.
Sending 5, 100-byte ICMP Echos to 10.1.100.5, timeout is 2 seconds:
Packet sent with a source address of 10.1.100.1
!!!!!
Success rate is 100 percent (5/5), round-trip min/avg/max = 4/9/26 ms
```

```
CE8# ping 10.1.100.5 source loopback 0
Type escape sequence to abort.
Sending 5, 100-byte ICMP Echos to 10.1.100.5, timeout is 2 seconds:
Packet sent with a source address of 10.1.100.8
!!!!!
Success rate is 100 percent (5/5), round-trip min/avg/max = 2/3/6 ms
```

```
PE7-Boundary# show ip nat translations
Pro  Inside global     Inside local      Outside local     Outside global
---  100.64.2.0        10.1.100.8        ---               ---
---  100.64.1.0        10.1.100.1        ---               ---
icmp 100.64.2.0:6      10.1.100.8:6      10.1.100.5:6      10.1.100.5:6
icmp 100.64.1.0:29     10.1.100.1:29     10.1.100.5:29     10.1.100.5:29
Total number of translations: 4
```

NOTE   P9 acts as a route reflector for VPNv4; however, for the prefixes to be transported (the default route per our case), there is no need for the VRFs to be configured on the RR: P9. Using **no bgp default route-target filter** (IOS and IOS XE) or **retain route-target all** (IOS XR) under the BGP process will be enough to allow prefixes to pass through.

MPLS L3VPN Internet Access Option 2: Separate PE-CE Interface

The second option is still utilizing the non-MP-BGP relationship between our edge device (ASBR) and the serving PE, as depicted in Figure 13-5.

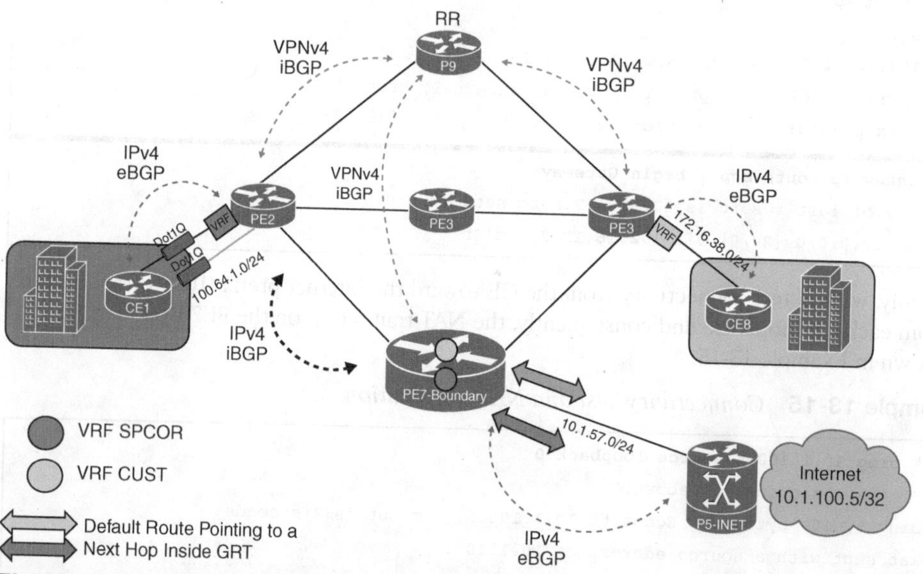

Figure 13-5   *MPLS L3VPN Internet Access Option 2*

This option is all about having multiple connections (logical or physical) between the CE and the PE. One of them still provides WAN connectivity to other branches/HQ, and the other one is a non-VRF link that is used solely for Internet access, which will entitle us to keep what we have implemented in option 1 while adding a new IPv4 session (iBGP) between the PE (we chose PE2 for illustration) and PE7. An important aspect to consider is that we configured the subnet 100.64.1.0/24 in the previous section for NAT (we had to configure a Null 0 route and advertise it from a PE7-Boundary perspective). The new setup will force us to remove that because now PE2 has a directly connected subinterface for which it will advertise to the boundary router. Example 13-16 shows the relevant commands.

Example 13-16   *MPLS L3VPN Internet Access Option 2 Relative Configuration*

```
PE2(config)# router bgp 100
PE2(config-router)# neighbor 10.1.100.7 remote-as 100
PE2(config-router)# neighbor 10.1.100.7 update-source Loopback0
PE2(config-router)# address-family ipv4
PE2(config-router-af)# network 100.64.1.0 mask 255.255.255.0
PE2(config-router-af)# neighbor 10.1.100.7 activate
```

```
PE2(config)# interface GigabitEthernet1.1
PE2(config)# encapsulation dot1Q 10
PE2(config)# vrf forwarding SPCOR
PE2(config)# ip address 172.16.12.2 255.255.255.0
```

```
PE2(config)# interface GigabitEthernet1.2
PE2(config)# encapsulation dot1Q 20
PE2(config)# ip address 62.215.1.2 255.255.255.0
```

```
CE1# ping 10.1.100.5 source 10.1.100.1
Type escape sequence to abort.
Sending 5, 100-byte ICMP Echos to 10.1.100.5, timeout is 2 seconds:
Packet sent with a source address of 10.1.100.1
!!!!!
Success rate is 100 percent (5/5), round-trip min/avg/max = 3/43/204 ms
```

```
CE1# ping 10.1.100.5 source 100.64.1.1
Type escape sequence to abort.
Sending 5, 100-byte ICMP Echos to 10.1.100.5, timeout is 2 seconds:
Packet sent with a source address of 100.64.1.1
.!!!!
Success rate is 80 percent (4/5), round-trip min/avg/max = 3/4/5 ms
```

```
PE7-Boundary# show ip nat translations
Pro  Inside global    Inside local    Outside local    Outside global
---  100.64.2.0       10.1.100.8      ---              ---
---  100.64.1.0       10.1.100.1      ---              ---
Total number of translations: 2
```

MPLS L3VPN Internet Access Option 3: Extranet with Internet-VRF

Now we will establish an MP-BGP session between our boundary router and our serving PEs to transport the Internet prefixes of concern inside the desired VRF.

What happens is like having so-called shared services VRF, in which the spokes can communicate with something common inside the HQ network.

Manipulating the route-target values will open the desired line of communication between the customer network and the Internet cloud.

What we will do is configure a new VRF on our boundary router and place the uplink in that specific VRF and then establish an eBGP session with the P5-INET router or using static routing.

Figure 13-6 shows the topology for options 1 and 2, along with the addition of the new VRF (INET). The figure shows how this VRF will be placed virtually on each PE from a route-target import perspective to allow for the routes to be installed successfully and connectivity to be maintained.

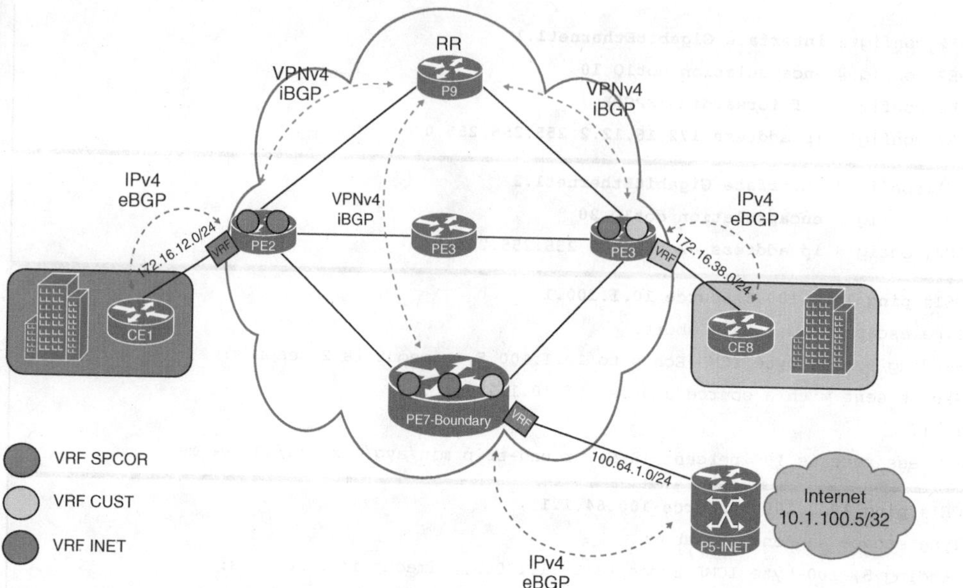

Figure 13-6   *MPLS L3VPN Internet Access Option 3*

NOTE   The route-target value is used to control the import/export mechanism inside a VRF, as discussed in Chapter 12, "MPLS L3VPNs," essentially establishing which prefixes are allowed to go out and which prefixes are allowed to move in.

Basically, what will happen in our scenario here is that the route distinguisher (RD) value for the new VRF will be allowed to enter the customer VRF, and the customer VRF RD will be allowed to enter the new VRF to allow bidirectional communication through the import function, as illustrated in Example 13-17.

Example 13-17   *VRF Definition*

```
PE7-Boundary(config)# vrf definition INET
PE7-Boundary (config-vrf)# rd 300:1
PE7-Boundary (config-vrf)# address-family ipv4
PE7-Boundary (config-vrf-af)# route-target export 300:1
PE7-Boundary (config-vrf-af)# route-target import 300:1
PE7-Boundary (config-vrf-af)# route-target import 100:1
PE7-Boundary (config-vrf-af)# route-target import 200:1

PE2(config)# vrf definition SPCOR
PE2(config-vrf)# rd 100:1
PE2(config-vrf)# address-family ipv4
PE2(config-vrf-af)# route-target export 100:1
PE2(config-vrf-af)# route-target import 100:1
PE2(config-vrf-af)# route-target import 300:1
```

Example 13-18 illustrates the relevant BGP configuration extracted from Figure 13-6.

Example 13-18 *BGP Configuration*

```
PE7-Boundary (config-vrf-af)# router bgp 100
PE7-Boundary (config-router)# no bgp default ipv4-unicast
PE7-Boundary (config-router)# neighbor 10.1.100.2 remote-as 100
PE7-Boundary (config-router)# neighbor 10.1.100.2 update-source Loopback0
PE7-Boundary (config-router)# address-family ipv4
PE7-Boundary (config-router-af)# neighbor 10.1.100.4 activate
PE7-Boundary (config-router-af)# neighbor 10.1.100.4 next-hop-self
PE7-Boundary (config-router-af)# address-family vpnv4
PE7-Boundary (config-router-af)# neighbor 10.1.100.2 activate
PE7-Boundary (config-router-af)# neighbor 10.1.100.2 send-community extended
PE7-Boundary (config-router)# address-family ipv4 vrf INET
PE7-Boundary (config-router-af)# neighbor 100.64.1.5 remote-as 200
PE7-Boundary (config-router-af)# neighbor 100.64.1.5 activate

PE2(config)# router bgp 100
PE2(config-router)# no bgp default ipv4-unicast
PE2(config-router)# neighbor 10.1.100.7 remote-as 100
PE2(config-router)# neighbor 10.1.100.7 update-source Loopback0
PE2(config-router)# address-family ipv4
PE2(config-router-af)# network 100.64.2.0 mask 255.255.255.0
PE2(config-router)# address-family vpnv4
PE2(config-router-af)# neighbor 10.1.100.7 activate
PE2(config-router-af)# neighbor 10.1.100.7 send-community both
```

We can verify the route import through analyzing the BGP VPNv4 output in Example 13-19.

Example 13-19 *BGP VPNv4 Output*

```
PE2# show bgp vpnv4 unicast all | begin Network
    Network          Next Hop            Metric LocPrf Weight Path
Route Distinguisher: 100:1 (default for vrf SPCOR)
 *>   10.1.100.1/32    172.16.12.1              1          32768 ?
 *>i  10.1.100.5/32    10.1.100.7               0    100     0 200 i
 *>   172.16.12.0/24   0.0.0.0                  0          32768 ?
Route Distinguisher: 300:1
 *>i  10.1.100.5/32    10.1.100.7               0    100     0 200 i
```

Checking connectivity, as in Example 13-20, will ensure successful deployment.

Example 13-20 *ICMP Connectivity*

```
CE1# ping 10.1.100.5 source loopback 0
Packet sent with a source address of 10.1.100.1
!!!!!
Success rate is 100 percent (5/5), round-trip min/avg/max = 2/3/4 ms
```

Something to notice with this deployment of MPLS L3VPN Internet access is the label assignment. By default, the label assignment will take place *per prefix*, which means a new label will be assigned for each advertised prefix. Example 13-21 shows the label assignment for the current prefixes.

Example 13-21 *Label Assignment Verification*

```
PE7-Boundary# show ip bgp vpnv4 vrf INET labels
   Network            Next Hop        In label/Out label
Route Distinguisher: 300:1 (INET)
   10.1.100.1/32      10.1.100.2        nolabel/205
   10.1.100.5/32      100.64.1.5      605/nolabel
   172.16.12.0/24     10.1.100.2        nolabel/206
```

Now let's introduce a new prefix under the BGP IPv4 address-family, as in Example 13-22.

Example 13-22 *BGP IPv4 New Prefix Advertisement*

```
RP/0/0/CPU0:P5-INET(config)# router bgp 200
RP/0/0/CPU0:P5-INET(config-bgp)# address-family ipv4 unicast
RP/0/0/CPU0:P5-INET(config-bgp-af)# network 10.1.200.5/32
```

Example 13-23 shows how to validate the label assignment after the creation and advertising of the new prefix.

Example 13-23 *Label Assignment Verification*

```
PE7-Boundary# show ip bgp vpnv4 vrf INET labels
   Network            Next Hop        In label/Out label
Route Distinguisher: 300:1 (INET)
   10.1.100.1/32      10.1.100.2        nolabel/205
   10.1.100.5/32      100.64.1.5      605/nolabel
   10.1.200.5/32      100.64.1.5      606/nolabel
   172.16.12.0/24     10.1.100.2        nolabel/206
```

To preserve the state of the ASBR from a design perspective and ensure that allocation is conducted per VRF instead of on a per-prefix basis, we can change the allocation mode, as depicted in Example 13-24.

Example 13-24 *Changing Label Allocation Mode*

```
PE7-Boundary(config)# mpls label mode vrf INET protocol bgp-vpnv4 per-vrf

PE7-Boundary# show ip bgp vpnv4 vrf INET labels
   Network            Next Hop        In label/Out label
Route Distinguisher: 300:1 (INET)
   10.1.100.1/32      10.1.100.2        nolabel/205
   10.1.100.5/32      100.64.1.5      IPv4 VRF Aggr:607/nolabel
   10.1.200.5/32      100.64.1.5      IPv4 VRF Aggr:607/nolabel
   172.16.12.0/24     10.1.100.2        nolabel/206
```

MPLS L3VPN Internet Access Option 4: VRF-Aware NAT

In our fourth and last option for providing customers with Internet access, we will establish a VPNv4 BGP session between the boundary router and the INET routers.

This scenario is usually called *VRF-Aware NAT*, which means that the customers' VRFs are also configured on the ASBR, and each VRF is injected with a default route that has the capability to perform NAT on the ASBR itself.

Some implementations use VRF where the interface connected to the INET router is placed in it, and some do not (however, this VRF will not have the route-target values manipulated like the one used in option 3).

In our scenario here, we will not deploy VRF, but we will rely on the global routing table. (As a rule of thumb, everything in the network field is doable; it's the design requirements, implications, and business drivers that really matter.)

The boundary router will inject a default route inside each of the target VRFs. The route will be injected through MP-BGP because the BGP VPNv4 session is already established between the boundary router and the serving PEs.

Because the NAT is done on the boundary router, overlapping IP address space can be served, and this is one of the advantages of this option.

Example 13-25 lists the configuration statements that operationalize MPLS L3VPN Internet access option 4.

Example 13-25   *MPLS L3VPN Internet Access Option 4–Related Configuration*

```
PE7-Boundary(config)# vrf definition SPCOR
PE7-Boundary (config-vrf)# rd 100:1
PE7-Boundary (config-vrf)# address-family ipv4
PE7-Boundary (config-vrf-af)# route-target export 100:1
PE7-Boundary (config-vrf-af)# route-target import 100:1

PE7-Boundary (config)# access-list 10 permit host 10.1.100.1

PE7-Boundary (config)# ip nat pool POOL 100.64.1.100 100.64.1.200 prefix-length 24
PE7-Boundary (config)# ip nat inside source list 10 pool POOL vrf SPCOR

PE7-Boundary (config)# interface GigabitEthernet1
PE7-Boundary (config-if)# ip nat inside

PE7-Boundary (config)# interface GigabitEthernet2
PE7-Boundary (config-if)# ip nat outside

PE7-Boundary (config)# ip route vrf SPCOR 0.0.0.0 0.0.0.0 212.118.67.6 global
```

We can verify the NAT translations (simulating successful Internet access to the destination) and the associated BGP output, as illustrated in Example 13-26.

Example 13-26 *Validating Internet Access Option 4*

```
PE7-Boundary# show ip nat translations
Pro   Inside global        Inside local          Outside local          Outside global
---   100.64.1.100         10.1.100.1            ---                    ---
icmp 100.64.1.100:18       10.1.100.1:18         10.1.100.6:18          10.1.100.6:18
Total number of translations: 2

PE2# show bgp vpnv4 unicast all | begin Route
Route Distinguisher: 100:1 (default for vrf SPCOR)
 *>i  0.0.0.0             10.1.100.7                       0   100     0 i
 *>   10.1.100.1/32       172.16.12.1                      1           32768 ?
 *>   172.16.12.0/24      0.0.0.0                          0           32768 ?
```

Figure 13-7 shows the propagation of the default routes from the ASBR inside each respective VRF through BGP VPNv4 sessions and the manipulation of the customers' VRF route-target import to allow for the Internet routes and therefore maintain connectivity.

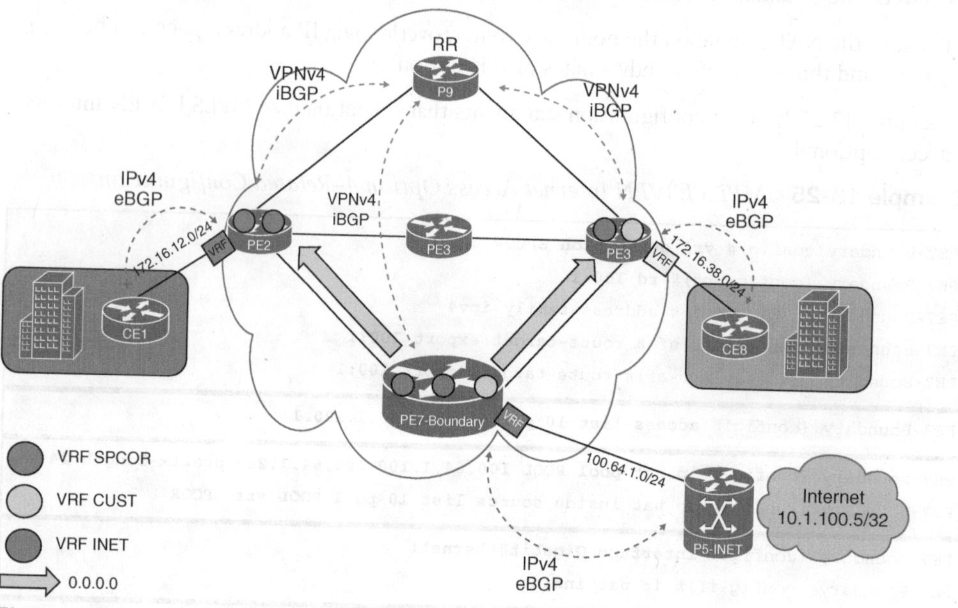

Figure 13-7 *MPLS L3VPN Internet Access Option 4*

MPLS Inter-AS L3VPN

Sometimes a customer needs an L3 VPN between two locations where the same service provider is not present. This can be on a national or international basis. It would be possible to buy an Internet circuit and run an overlay such as DMVPN, but what if the customer wants to buy an MPLS VPN circuit?

The customer could buy a VPN from SP1 in location1 and a VPN from SP2 in location2. The two service providers would then have to exchange traffic somehow to make the customer circuit end to end. Another reason is that the SP could do the NNI connection with faster speeds than pulling a circuit to DC where the first circuit resides, where they provide the NNI. Doing so also provides less overhead with support contracts.

The customer connects to the PE of each of the SPs. The SPs need to interconnect at some common point, either through a public peering place, such as an IX, or with a private interconnect at a common location. The routers that connect to each other are called *autonomous system border routers (ASBRs)* in some references, but we refer to them as *boundary routers* through the coming sections. There are three main options and a fourth option that combines two of the others.

Inter-AS Option A

MPLS VPNs are the most deployed VPN connection types due to the adaptability they provide to network administrators and the great movement over the legacy VPN technologies such as Frame Relay and ATM.

Usually, MPLS VPNs (either L3 or L2) are provided to enterprises utilizing the service provider network; that is, MPLS main components reside within the service provider cloud.

Connecting branches (or remote offices) to the headquarters within a served geographical area will not be an issue to the service provider (assuming the coverage is in place).

Inter-AS MPLS VPN Option A relies on the fact that every provider treats the other provider as a customer; that is, the VRF will be configured on the ASBR for each provider and advertise the necessary information through a connection (either an interface or subinterface) that is part of this respective VRF.

Any routing protocol could be used on the respective VRF to exchange the necessary routing information to maintain the connectivity needed. Usually, BGP is the choice for connecting customers to the SP infrastructure due to the capability to enforce policies at the edge of the SP network (traffic engineering using BGP communities is a flexible and scalable approach, which is harder to achieve when using IGPs).

Figure 13-8 shows relevant BGP sessions needed to ensure that proper prefixes transport from the customer edge to the ASBR (each in its respective autonomous system). Also, VRFs are extended toward the ASBR, where we placed the Inter-AS into the respective VRF, where we can turn on any routing to ensure successful route exchange (we used BGP as an example).

As discussed earlier, we can choose any routing protocol to participate in the interconnection between PE-CE. The same applies for the inter-AS connection within the extended VRF (between PE4 and PE5, which act as the ASBRs between the two autonomous systems). Example 13-27 lists the needed commands for a successful BGP operation. We used PE5 as an example to show how the IOS XR handles the eBGP session between the ASBRs within the VRF.

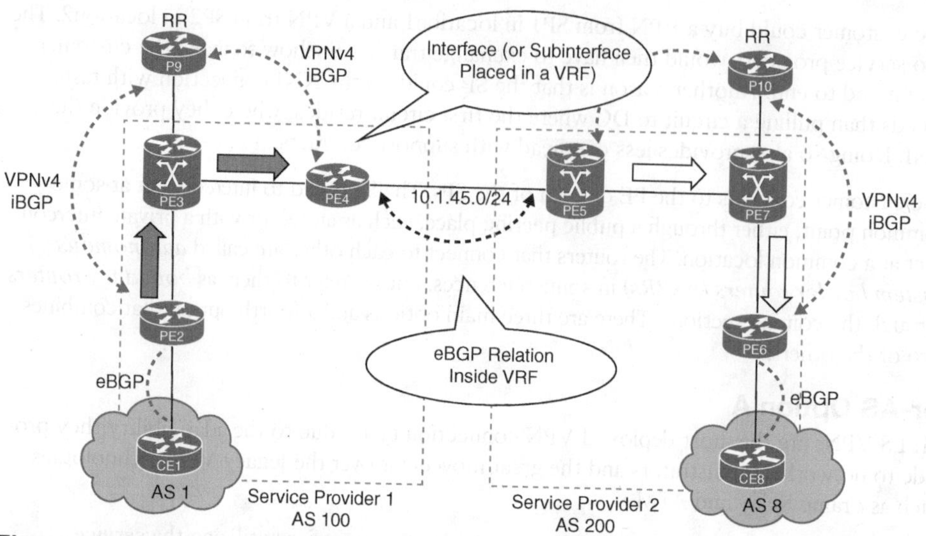

Figure 13-8   *MPLS L3VPN Inter-AS Option A*

Example 13-27   *BGP Configuration*

```
RP/0/0/CPU0:PE5(config)# router bgp 200
RP/0/0/CPU0:PE5(config-bgp)# address-family vpnv4 unicast
RP/0/0/CPU0:PE5(config-bgp-af)# exit
RP/0/0/CPU0:PE5(config-bgp)# neighbor 10.1.100.10
RP/0/0/CPU0:PE5(config-bgp-nbr)# update-source Loopback0
RP/0/0/CPU0:PE5(config-bgp-nbr)# address-family vpnv4 unicast
RP/0/0/CPU0:PE5(config-bgp-nbr-af)# vrf SPCOR
RP/0/0/CPU0:PE5(config-bgp-vrf)# rd 200:1
RP/0/0/CPU0:PE5(config-bgp-vrf)# address-family ipv4 unicast
RP/0/0/CPU0:PE5(config-bgp-vrf-af)# neighbor 10.1.45.4
RP/0/0/CPU0:PE5(config-bgp-vrf-nbr)# remote-as 100
RP/0/0/CPU0:PE5(config-bgp-vrf-nbr)# address-family ipv4 unicast
RP/0/0/CPU0:PE5(config-bgp-vrf-nbr-af)# route-policy ALLOW in
RP/0/0/CPU0:PE5(config-bgp-vrf-nbr-af)# route-policy ALLOW out
```

NOTE   Just a reminder about IOS XR behavior when it comes to eBGP relation and traffic insertion: we must define a route-policy (RPL) for which we explicitly permit or pass the traffic because the default behavior is to deny:

```
route-policy ALLOW
  pass
end-policy
```

It is well known that this Inter-AS option is called back-to-back VRF, as can be depicted from the deployment, because the ASBRs are connected to each other via a VRF participating interface (or subinterface to account for several customers).

We can control which traffic is passed by using the route-target extended community, which will add more security to the traffic. However, we can see that ASBRs carry the traffic of each customer, which, from a resource perspective, will increase the traffic state on the ASBRs. Example 13-28 shows the BGP VPNv4 output.

Example 13-28   *BGP VPNv4 Output*

```
PE4# show bgp vpnv4 unicast all
! Output omitted for brevity
     Network              Next Hop          Metric LocPrf Weight Path
Route Distinguisher: 100:1 (default for vrf SPCOR)
  *>i  10.1.100.1/32       10.1.100.9                 0    100      0 ?
  *>   10.1.100.8/32       10.1.45.5                                0 200 ?
```

Inter-AS Option B

A design consideration with Inter-AS Option A is that all VRF information is located at the boundary routers, which means, from a resource perspective, that utilization could be an issue if the number of customers supported is high.

Additionally, the LSP we have established to maintain connectivity is not contiguous, because the peering link between ASBRs is not MPLS enabled.

In Option B, we will extend the LSP end to end by establishing a labeled path through the assistance of BGP this time. (LDP is still running internally and is responsible for the label distribution/assignment process through the internal core for each of the providers.) We do so by establishing a VPNv4 session between the providers (eBGP) and activating the labeling capabilities, as depicted in Figure 13-9.

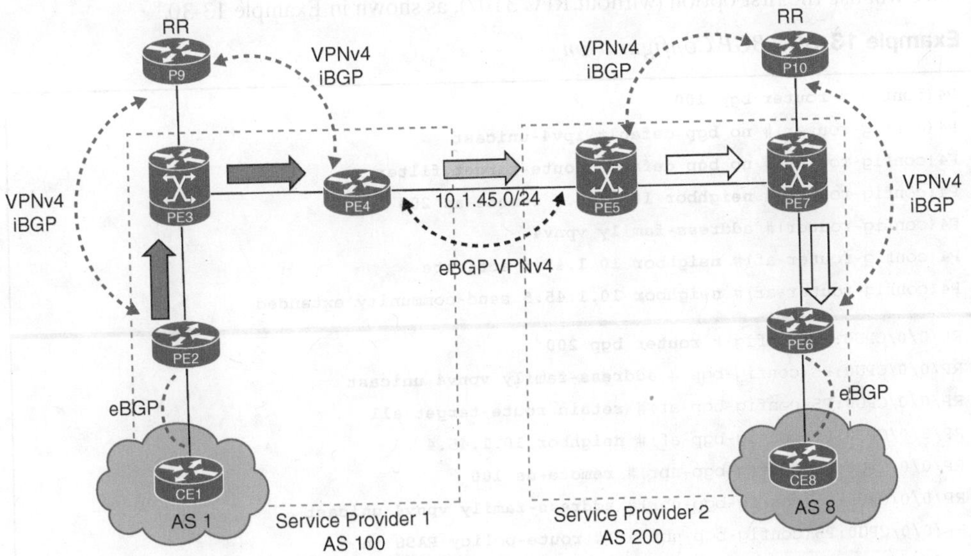

Figure 13-9   *MPLS L3VPN Inter-AS Option B*

We use BGP to advertise labels between the boundary routers instead of LDP (as we do with the core) following RFC 3107, although we have another option of using LDP on the interconnection link between the boundary routers.

Example 13-29 lists the functional commands for BGP under the VPNv4 address family (which we have listed in a remarkable number of examples, but we are trying to remind you about it).

Example 13-29 *BGP Configuration*

```
PE2(config)# router bgp 100
PE2(config-router)# bgp log-neighbor-changes
PE2(config-router)# no bgp default ipv4-unicast
PE2(config-router)# neighbor 10.1.100.9 remote-as 100
PE2(config-router)# neighbor 10.1.100.9 update-source Loopback0
PE2(config-router)# address-family vpnv4
PE2(config-router-af)# neighbor 10.1.100.9 activate
PE2(config-router-af)# neighbor 10.1.100.9 send-community extended
```

The most important part of the configuration is the BGP neighborship between the boundary routers. Mainly, we will have two flavors, as mentioned previously:

- We will follow RFC 3107 exactly so that BGP will be used for label allocation for the boundary router's loopback interfaces, and clearly, we will establish an eBGP VPNv4 multihop neighborship.

- We can establish the eBGP VPNv4 using the directly connected interface.

We will use the first option (without RFC 3107), as shown in Example 13-30.

Example 13-30 *BGP Configuration*

```
P4(config)# router bgp 100
P4(config-router)# no bgp default ipv4-unicast
P4(config-router)# no bgp default route-target filter
P4(config-router)# neighbor 10.1.45.5 remote-as 200
P4(config-router)# address-family vpnv4
P4(config-router-af)# neighbor 10.1.45.5 activate
P4(config-router-af)# neighbor 10.1.45.5 send-community extended

RP/0/0/CPU0:P5(config)# router bgp 200
RP/0/0/CPU0:P5(config-bgp)# address-family vpnv4 unicast
RP/0/0/CPU0:P5(config-bgp-af)# retain route-target all
RP/0/0/CPU0:P5(config-bgp-af)# neighbor 10.1.45.4
RP/0/0/CPU0:P5(config-bgp-nbr)# remote-as 100
RP/0/0/CPU0:P5(config-bgp-nbr)# address-family vpnv4 unicast
RP/0/0/CPU0:P5(config-bgp-nbr-af)# route-policy PASS in
RP/0/0/CPU0:P5(config-bgp-nbr-af)# route-policy PASS out
! Do not forget the neighborship between the boundary routers is eBGP and though a
! route-policy should be in place for the routes to be installed.
```

```
bgp[1060]: %ROUTING-BGP-6-NBR_NOPOLICY : No inbound VPNv4 Unicast policy is
configured for eBGP neighbor 10.1.45.4. No VPNv4 Unicast prefixes will be accepted
from the neighbor until inbound policy is configured.

bgp[1060]: %ROUTING-BGP-6-NBR_NOPOLICY : No outbound VPNv4 Unicast policy is
configured for eBGP neighbor 10.1.45.4. No VPNv4 Unicast prefixes will be sent to
the neighbor until outbound policy is configured.
```

Now the missing requirement is related to a well-known BGP behavior when an eBGP speaker advertises a route to an iBGP neighbor, which is the next hop. eBGP will advertise a route without changing a next hop. Example 13-31 verifies the next-hop behavior.

Example 13-31   *BGP VPNv4 Output and Next-Hop Behavior*

```
PE2# show bgp vpnv4 unicast all
! Output omitted for brevity
     Network          Next Hop            Metric LocPrf Weight Path
Route Distinguisher: 100:1 (default for vrf SPCOR)
 *>   10.1.100.1/32   172.16.12.1              0             32768 ?
 * i  10.1.100.8/32   10.1.45.5                0     100       0 200 ?
```

We must change the next hop on the ASBRs for the routes to be delivered successfully because eBGP received a prefix from another eBGP when advertised to an iBGP neighbor. The next hop will not change and will be kept as an IP address of the eBGP neighbor. We could work around this situation by conducting a sort of redistribution, but we have the next-hop-self feature available for similar scenarios without going through redistribution. (PE2 does not know anything about the interconnection link between P4 and P5: 10.1.45.0/24.) Example 13-32 shows how to change the next hop by introducing the **next-hop-self** command associated with the neighbor.

Example 13-32   *BGP next-hop-self Command*

```
PE4(config)# router bgp 100
PE4(config-router)# address-family vpnv4
PE4(config-router-af)# neighbor 10.1.100.9 next-hop-self

RP/0/0/CPU0:PE5(config)# router bgp 200
RP/0/0/CPU0:PE5(config-bgp)# neighbor 10.1.100.10
RP/0/0/CPU0:PE5(config-bgp-nbr)# address-family vpnv4 unicast
RP/0/0/CPU0:PE5(config-bgp-nbr-af)# next-hop-self

PE2# show bgp vpnv4 unicast all
! Output omitted for brevity
     Network          Next Hop            Metric LocPrf Weight Path
Route Distinguisher: 100:1 (default for vrf SPCOR)
 *>   10.1.100.1/32   172.16.12.1              0             32768 ?
 *>i  10.1.100.8/32   10.1.100.9               0     100       0 200 ?
```

Example 13-33 shows how the interface on the interconnection is MPLS enabled through BGP and how the **mpls bgp forwarding** command is automatically inserted under the interface. Once we activate the neighborship between the boundary routers under the VPNv4 address family, we will get a message that the **mpls bgp forwarding** command is injected under the interface for which we connect to the peer boundary router.

Example 13-33   *MPLS Enabled Interfaces Output*

```
PE4(config)# router bgp 100
PE4(config-router)# neighbor 10.1.45.5 remote-as 200
PE4(config-router)# address-family vpnv4 unicast
PE4(config-router-af)# neighbor 10.1.45.5 activate
PE4(config-router-af)# neighbor 10.1.45.5 send-community extended

%BGP-5-ADJCHANGE: neighbor 10.1.45.5 Up
%BGP_LMM-6-AUTOGEN1: The mpls bgp forwarding command has been configured on interface:
GigabitEthernet0/1
P4# show run interface GigabitEthernet0/1 | include mpls
interface GigabitEthernet0/1
 mpls bgp forwarding

PE4# show mpls interfaces
Interface            IP          Tunnel  BGP Static Operational
GigabitEthernet0/0   Yes (ldp)   No      No  No     Yes
GigabitEthernet0/1   No          No      Yes No     Yes
```

Moving down to path validation, we still do not have end-to-end reachability. Turning on debugging for BGP VPNv4 updates will yield a result indicating that we do have a denial for the traffic because the extended community (which, in this case, is the route target associated with the VRF) is not supported. The reason obviously is that we do not have the VRF defined or configured on the ASBRs. Example 13-34 lists the logging messages associated with the denial of traffic import.

Example 13-34   *Logging Message, Extended Community Support*

```
BGP(4): 10.1.45.5 rcvd UPDATE w/ attr: nexthop 10.1.45.5, origin ?, merged path 200,
AS_PATH , extended community RT:100:1
BGP(4): 10.1.45.5 rcvd 100:1:10.1.100.8/32, label 16504 -- DENIED due to:  extended
community not supported;
BGP(4): no valid path for 100:1:10.1.100.8/32
BGP: topo SPCOR:VPNv4 Unicast:base Remove_fwdroute for 100:1:10.1.100.8/32
BGP(4): (base) 10.1.100.2 send unreachable (format) 100:1:10.1.100.8/32
```

And we can see the extended community attached to the prefix of the customer in Example 13-35.

Example 13-35   *BGP VPNv4 Output, Extended Community*

```
PE2# show bgp vpnv4 unicast all 10.1.100.1/32
BGP routing table entry for 100:1:10.1.100.1/32, version 2
Paths: (1 available, best #1, table SPCOR)
  Advertised to update-groups:
     1
  Refresh Epoch 1
  Local
```

```
172.16.12.1 (via vrf SPCOR) from 0.0.0.0 (10.1.100.2)
  Origin incomplete, metric 0, localpref 100, weight 32768, valid, sourced, best
  Extended Community: RT:100:1
  mpls labels in/out 203/nolabel
  rx pathid: 0, tx pathid: 0x0
  Updated on Jan 14 2024 20:45:13 UTC
```

We can adjust this behavior by disabling the default behavior of BGP; to do so, we can disallow the prevention of prefixes where extended communities are attached, as shown in Example 13-36.

Example 13-36   *Disabling default route-target filter*

```
P4(config)# router bgp 100
P4(config-router)# no bgp default route-target filter
*Jan 15 11:36:09.478: BGP(4): (base) 10.1.45.5 send UPDATE (format)
100:1:10.1.100.1/32, next 10.1.45.4, label 404
P4#, metric 0, path Local, extended community RT:100:1
```

NOTE   The **no bgp default route-target filter** command is for IOS/IOS XE–based devices. For IOS XR, the similar command is **retain route-target all** under the VPNv4 address family.

However, this is not a practical experience; this will take place effectively on our out-of-band route reflectors, which are P9 and P10. Usually, we can alter the VRF configuration to allow the target RT to be imported inside the VRF, and vice versa, if mutual communication will take place, as demonstrated in Example 13-37.

Example 13-37   *Route-Target Manipulation*

```
PE2(config)# vrf definition SPCOR
PE2(config-vrf)# address-family ipv4
PE2(config-vrf-af)# route-target import 200:1
```

The other option we have is to use a rewrite option in which we can replace the unallowed RT (200:1) with the value that matches what we have in the import list—in this case, 100:1.

This is accomplished using the following steps:

Step 1.   Define the **extcommunity-list** to match what we need to rewrite.

Step 2.   Create a route map for which we are going to match the predefined **extcommunity-list** we have configured.

Step 3.   Define the rewrite RT value, which will match the RT that we have within the VRF definition.

Step 4.   Apply the route map in the outbound direction under the respective address-family (VPNv4) under the BGP configuration.

Example 13-38 lists these steps with the associated output to verify the rewrite operation and allow the route to be installed.

Example 13-38 *Route-Target Rewrite*

```
P9(config)# route-map REWRITE_MAP permit 10

P9(config-route-map)# match extcommunity 1
P9(config-route-map)# set extcomm-list 1 delete
P9(config-route-map)# set extcommunity rt 100:1 additive

P9(config)# router bgp 100
P9(config-router)# address-family vpnv4 unicast
P9(config-router-af)# neighbor 10.1.100.2 route-map REWRITE_MAP out

P9# clear bgp vpnv4 unicast * soft out

PE2# show bgp vpnv4 unicast all 10.1.100.8/32 | include RT
      Extended Community: RT:100:1
```

As we spotted, the **mpls bgp forwarding** command was automatically attached to the interface (ASBR-to-ASBR interconnection), which will make the router create a /32 host route for the peering interface. XR will not label switch traffic to a next hop that is not learned the same way. (BGP allocates a label for a /32 route to that peer and performs a NULL label rewrite. When forwarding a labeled packet to the peer, the router removes the top label from the label stack.) So, we can create a static route pointing to the neighboring interface as /32 to isolate the issue and behave similarly. Therefore, we can manipulate the peering relation by introducing eBGP-Multihop (however, we are peering using physical interfaces, not loopback interfaces). Penultimate hop popping (PHP) must take place for directly connected peers. Example 13-39 shows how to overcome the behavior of IOS XR.

Example 13-39 *Creating a /32 Host Route on IOS XR*

```
RP/0/0/CPU0:PE5(config)# router static
RP/0/0/CPU0:PE5(config-static)# address-family ipv4 unicast
RP/0/0/CPU0:PE5(config-static-afi)# 10.1.45.4/32 GigabitEthernet0/0/0/3

RP/0/0/CPU0:PE5# show mpls forwarding | include 10.1.45.4/32
16504   Pop         10.1.45.4/32      Gi0/0/0/3      10.1.45.4          10281744
```

Now, we can conduct a trace route to validate connectivity as well as LSP and label assignment, as shown in Example 13-40.

Example 13-40 *Traceroute Output*

```
CE1# traceroute 10.1.100.8 source loopback 0 numeric
VRF info: (vrf in name/id, vrf out name/id)
  1 172.16.12.2 1 msec 1 msec 0 msec
  2 10.1.23.3 [MPLS: Labels 16300/407 Exp 0] 25 msec 14 msec 13 msec
  3 10.1.34.4 [MPLS: Label 407 Exp 0] 13 msec 13 msec 13 msec
  4 10.1.45.5 [MPLS: Label 16504 Exp 0] 130 msec 39 msec 14 msec
  5 10.1.57.7 [MPLS: Labels 16702/600 Exp 0] 15 msec 13 msec 14 msec
  6 172.16.68.6 [MPLS: Label 600 Exp 0] 13 msec 14 msec 13 msec
  7 172.16.68.8 14 msec 13 msec 12 msec
```

Inter-AS Option C

After going through both options, A and B, we can see that these options meet the requirements for Inter-AS communications. The main drawback is the state on the ASBR because
the ASBRs need to distribute VPNv4 routes and exchange, accordingly, a noticed number of
prefixes.

The most common deployments for Option C are

- The PE devices in both service provider networks will establish an eBGP session
  (multihop), which is basically not scalable from the perspective that several PEs could
  be serving distributed customers.

- By using inter-provider with RR, we can specify an RR in each network that will be
  responsible for storing VPNv4 routes and exchanging these routers with local PE
  devices. These RRs will establish an MP-eBGP session to successfully build the
  relation and exchange the prefixes accordingly.

Figure 13-10 shows the main constructs needed to implement MPLS L3VPN Inter-AS
Option C for which we have now established the eBGP VPNv4 session between the route
reflectors (located in both autonomous systems).

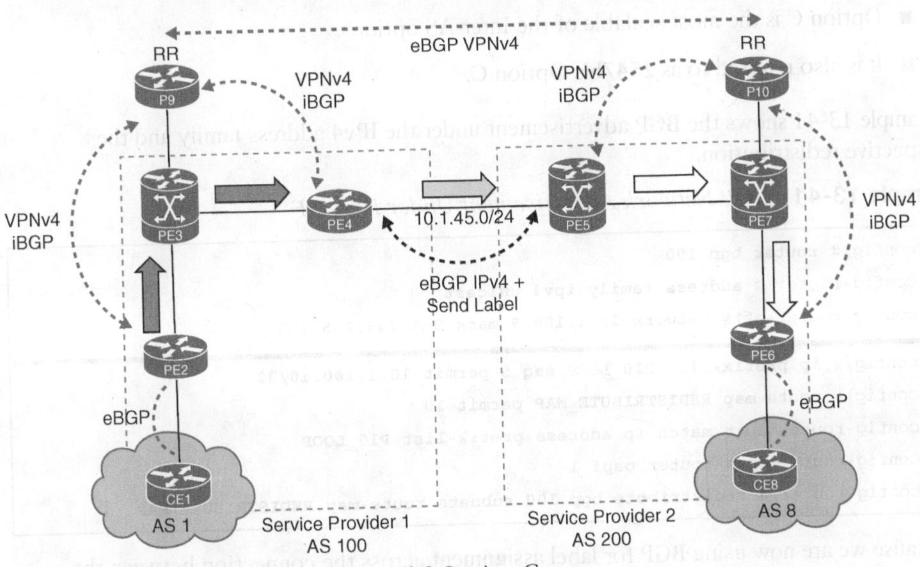

Figure 13-10   *MPLS L3VPN Inter-AS Option C*

The main role for the ASBRs is to exchange the loopback networks for each RR to achieve
connectivity and hence be able to build up the target eBGP neighborship. Label exchange is
another detail conducted by the session between ASBRs (creating transport labels), which
means eventually that the LSP is not broken and extended end to end, and the VPN label
will be maintained along the path because the VPNv4 next hop is not changed per the
characteristics of Option C.

The RR loopback network will be advertised as we do normally with BGP under the IPv4
address family and then redistributed in the IGP (which is OSPF in our demonstration
example).

In Inter-AS Option C, VPNv4 updates are either sent between PEs or more likely between RRs in the different ASes. It is the most scalable solution but also the least secure. It has the following characteristics:

- Option C takes away the heavy reliance on ASBRs. In this option, the ASBRs are only used to exchange the PE loopback routes using eBGP IPv4 sessions.

- To maintain the end-to-end LSP, labels are sent using BGP instead of LDP or RSVP. For other PEs to have reachability to the next hops, they redistribute these labeled prefixes into IGP.

- ASBRs only contain the addresses of remote PEs for BGP next-hop reachability of VPN routes.

- Usually, Option C is implemented with a multihop eBGP VPN session between route reflectors, but it doesn't have to be only RR; it could also be PEs. PEs from one carrier can have sessions with other PEs in the other carrier using a full mesh.

- The major scalability improvement of using Option C is that now the ASBRs don't have to keep labels for all VPNv4 prefixes, but rather move them to the route reflectors. These should already have the scalability to hold that many routes.

- Option C is the most scalable of the Inter-AS options.

- It is also referred to as 2547bis Option C.

Example 13-41 shows the BGP advertisement under the IPv4 address family and the respective redistribution.

Example 13-41   *BGP Network Advertisement Under IPv4 AF*

```
PE4(config)# router bgp 100
PE4(config-router)# address-family ipv4 unicast
PE4(config-router-af)# network 10.1.100.9 mask 255.255.255.255

PE4(config)# ip prefix-list P10_LOOP seq 5 permit 10.1.100.10/32
PE4(config)# route-map REDISTRIBUTE_MAP permit 10
PE4(config-route-map)# match ip address prefix-list P10_LOOP
PE4(config-route-map)# router ospf 1
PE4(config-router)# redistribute bgp 100 subnets route-map REDISTRIBUTE_MAP
```

Because we are now using BGP for label assignment across the connection between the boundary routers instead of LDP, the send-label capability is a per neighbor capability, as shown in Example 13-42.

Example 13-42   *BGP Send-Label Per Neighbor Capability, IOS*

```
PE4(config)# router bgp 100
PE4(config)# address-family ipv4 unicast
PE4(config)# neighbor 10.1.45.5 send-label
```

NOTE   The send-label capabilities are deployed as a new AF for IOS XR (using **address-family ipv4 labeled-unicast**). This must be associated with the **allocate-label-all** command under the IPv4 address family. BGP uses the **allocate-label-all** command to allocate labels. For clarity, Example 13-43 shows the relative configuration on IOS XR.

Example 13-43   *BGP Labeled-Unicast AF, IOS XR*

```
RP/0/0/CPU0:PE5(config)# router bgp 200
RP/0/0/CPU0:PE5(config-bgp)# address-family ipv4 unicast
RP/0/0/CPU0:PE5(config-bgp-af)# allocate-label all
RP/0/0/CPU0:PE5(config-bgp-af)# neighbor 10.1.45.4
RP/0/0/CPU0:PE5(config-bgp-nbr)# remote-as 100
RP/0/0/CPU0:PE5(config-bgp-nbr)# address-family ipv4 labeled-unicast
RP/0/0/CPU0:PE5(config-bgp-nbr-af)# route-policy PASS in
RP/0/0/CPU0:PE5(config-bgp-nbr-af)# route-policy PASS out

RP/0/0/CPU0:PE5(config)# prefix-set P9_LOOP_SET
RP/0/0/CPU0:PE5(config-pfx)# 10.1.100.9/32
RP/0/0/CPU0:PE5(config)# route-policy P9_LOOP
RP/0/0/CPU0:PE5(config-rpl)# if destination in P9_LOOP_SET then pass endif
RP/0/0/CPU0:PE5(config-rpl)# exit
RP/0/0/CPU0:PE5(config)# router ospf 1
RP/0/0/CPU0:PE5(config-ospf)# redistribute bgp 200 route-policy P9_LOOP

%BGP-5-ADJCHANGE: neighbor 10.1.100.9 Up
```

As discussed, we must establish an eBGP VPNv4 session between the RR on each service provider network to transport the VPNv4 prefixes of the customer. Surely, we will change the default source for BGP packets from physical to logical (loopback) across several hops, which means we need to explicitly configure the **ebgp-multihop**. To reserve the VPN labels and the associated next-hop, we will implement the **next-hop-unchanged** command under the respective address-family (VPNv4) within the BGP process. Example 13-44 shows how to configure the **next-hop-unchanged** command under the respective address family.

Example 13-44   *BGP Next-Hop-Unchanged Configuration*

```
P9# configure terminal
P9(config)# router bgp 100
P9(config-router)# neighbor 10.1.100.10 remote-as 200
P9(config-router)# neighbor 10.1.100.10 ebgp-multihop 255
P9(config-router)# neighbor 10.1.100.10 update-source Loopback0
P9(config-router)# address-family vpnv4 unicast
P9(config-router-af)# neighbor 10.1.100.10 activate
P9(config-router-af)# neighbor 10.1.100.10 send-community extended
P9(config-router-af)# neighbor 10.1.100.10 next-hop-unchanged
```

To validate the consistency of the VPN label along the LSP where the transport label changes (swaps) at each node, Figure 13-11 demonstrates the label assignment.

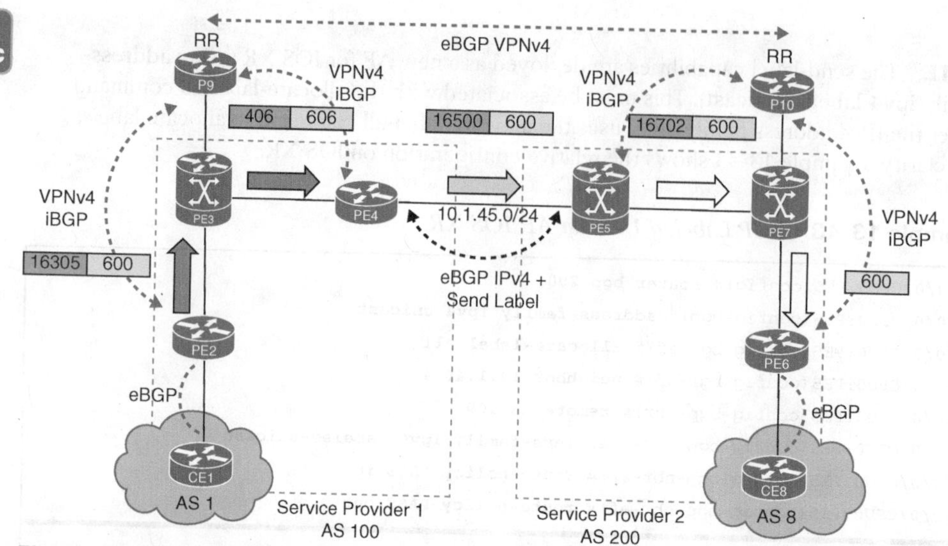

Figure 13-11 *Inter-AS Option C VPN Label Assignment*

Inter-AS Option AB

Although Option C is more scalable from a state perspective, it is the less secure option due to information leakage between the two providers to make sure connectivity/reachability between the BGP endpoints is in place. This kind of solution is appropriate for acquisitions or mergers in which all move under the same administration umbrella.

Option A might be better for granular QoS support compared to other options, but this option is limited to VRF support on the ASBR interconnection. Also, ASBRs are involved in customer traffic, which might be a shift in these devices' roles generally. Plus, there are design constraints to be considered when selecting the solution and the associated devices.

In contrast, Option B offers enhanced scalability because one eBGP session handles all labeled packets to be exchanged between the two autonomous systems; however, there is a lack of VRF isolation and the QoS approach is more difficult to follow.

Cisco released a hybrid solution (called Option AB and known as Option D) in which a combination of solution aspects for Option A and Option B are presented.

The only BGP session to be established is an eBGP VPNv4 session between the ASBRs over the subinterface placed in the global routing table, which is the same as Option B.

For each customer (VRF), a dedicated subinterface needs to be established between the two autonomous systems (forwarding plane), with no extra BGP sessions configured because all traffic will be sent over the unlabeled interfaces.

Figure 13-12 shows the combination of Option A (from the VRF extension up to the ASBRs) and Option B (from using eBGP VPNv4 in between the ASBRs for route exchange). Option AB sends unlabeled packets between the ASBRs, which helps it retain the positive attributes of Option A, such as per VRF policies and QoS markings. It does, however, use a single BGP session that was used in Option B for better scalability. The VRFs on the ASBR need to be enabled for Option AB and the peer under the eBGP VPNv4 session on the ASBR. This means that the ASBR needs one logical interface per VRF between the ASBRs and one global interface for the eBGP VPNv4 session. Another positive aspect of Option AB is that the ASBR acts as a PE in that it can import a certain RT value and export with another RT value. In Option B, no local VRF is configured, meaning that the RT values of the other AS get carried in the update.

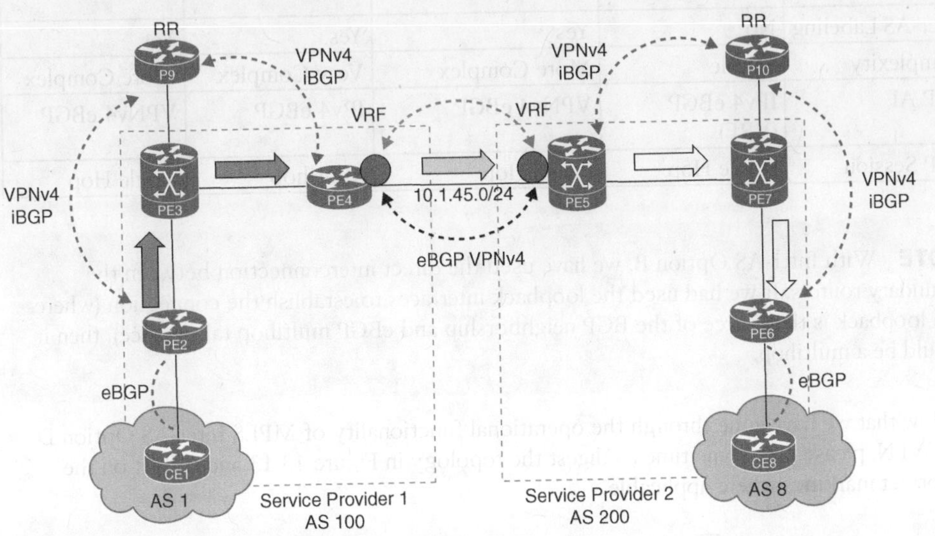

Figure 13-12   *MPLS L3VPN Inter-AS Option D (AB)*

We can summarize the forwarding operation that will take place when generating end-to-end traffic between CE1 and CE2:

1. The CE sends an IPv4 packet destined for the other CE to the serving PE.

2. The serving PE encapsulates the packet with a VPN label (Inner label) assigned by the local ASBR.

3. The P router will assign the IGP label (the outside label or transport label) to tunnel the packet to the local ASBR.

4. The local ASBR receives the packets, pops the VPN label, and sends the packet of concern unlabeled using the Inter-AS VRF interface.

5. The remote ASBR receives the packet (IPv4 packet) and encapsulates it with a VPN label assigned by the remote PE.

6. The remote P router assigns the needed transport label to tunnel the packet to the remote PE.

7. The remote PE receives the packet, pops the VPN label, and sends the unlabeled IPv4 packet to the receiving CE.

Now that we have gone through all the details related to MPLS Inter-AS L3VPN options, it is worth shedding some light on the major differences when it to comes to solution constraints, as outlined in Table 13-2.

Table 13-2 MPLS Inter-AS L3VPN Comparison

Aspect/Option	Option A	Option B	Option C	Option D
Scalability	Least Scalable	Less Scalable	Most Scalable	Scalable
Security	Most Secure	Less Secure	Least Secure	Less Secure
Resource Utilization	Highest	Moderate	Lowest	Higher
Inter-AS Labeling	No	Yes	Yes	Yes
Complexity	Simple	More Complex	Very Complex	More Complex
BGP AF	IPv4 eBGP (VRF)	VPNv4 eBGP	IPv4 eBGP	VPNv4 eBGP
BGP Session	Single Hop	Single Hop	Multihop	Single Hop

NOTE With Inter-AS Option B, we have used the direct interconnection between the boundary routers. If we had used the loopback interfaces to establish the connection (where the loopback is the source of the BGP neighborship and eBGP multihop takes place), then it would be a multihop.

Now that we have gone through the operational functionality of MPLS Inter-AS Option D L3VPN, please take some time to digest the topology in Figure 13-13 and reflect on the correct markings where applicable.

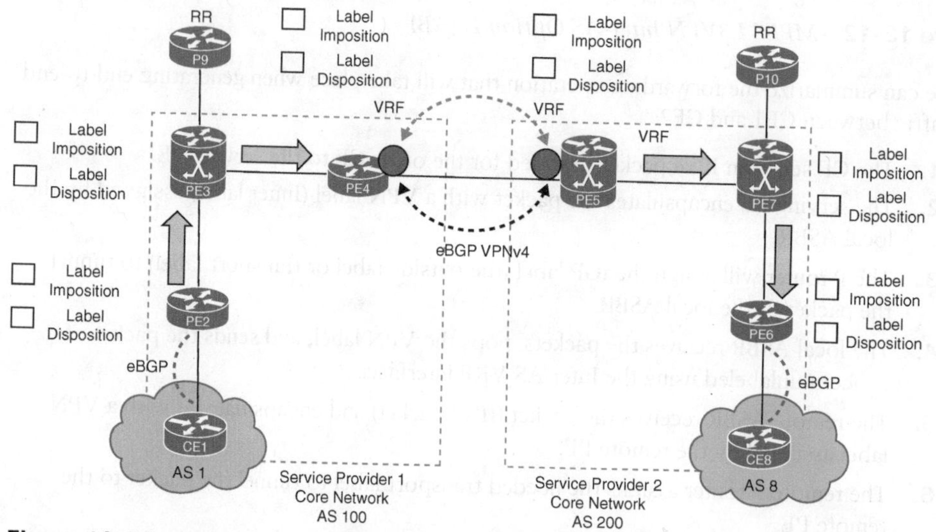

Figure 13-13 *Brainstorm (MPLS L3VPN Inter-AS Option D)*

Carrier Supporting Carrier (CsC)

We have gone through the available options for customers who buy different VPN services from two providers. Sometimes the situation could be business driven—that is, driven by the fact that the customer will provide VPN services to another end customer (like a chain). This is called **Carrier Supporting Carrier (CsC)** and sometimes referred to as

Carrier of Carrier. The reason for this name is that the service provider that is mainly offering the service is called a *backbone carrier*, and the customer (provider) that is using this to provide the service to an end customer is called a *customer carrier*. Due to the chaining of the VPN service, it also is sometimes called a *hierarchical VPN*. The main goal, from a design perspective and a business driver, is the ability of the service provider to expand the geographical diameter of the services it offers.

In terms of MPLS service (VPN), we already went through the label operations in a normal L3VPN service. The question now is: How will the label process be accomplished? We have two options:

- IGP + LDP

- Labeled BGP

To clarify, let's look at the terminology associated with CsC, including naming conventions for the participating devices, as illustrated in Figure 13-14.

- **Backbone carrier:** The service provider that provides the L3VPN to the other provider (customer).

- **Customer carrier:** The provider (customer) that provides the same service (roughly) to the end customer.

- **CsC-PE:** The MPLS edge device that is located at the edge of the backbone carrier.

- **CsC-CE:** The MPLS edge device that is located at the edge of the customer carrier.

- **C:** The customer edge device located at the end customer network.

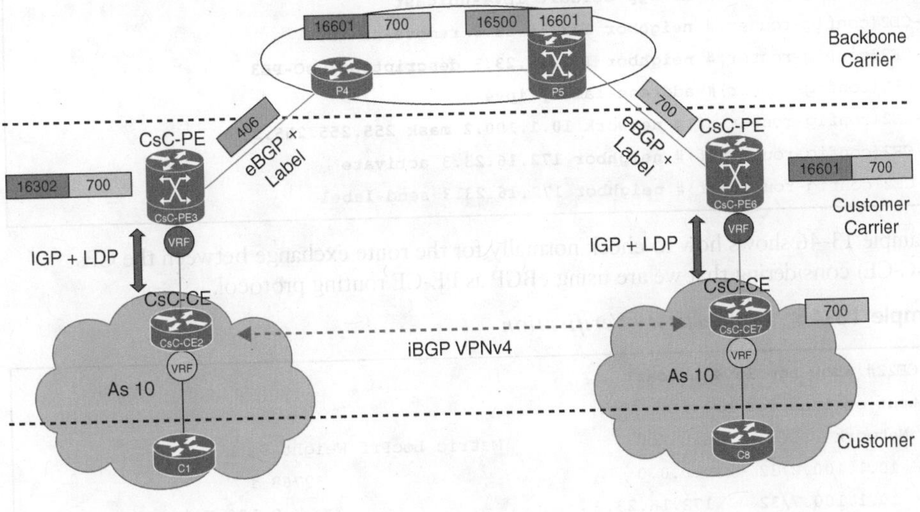

Figure 13-14 *MPLS Carrier Supporting Carrier (CsC)*

Here, we have chosen BGP as the routing protocol between CsC-PE and CsC-CE. Different autonomous systems are in play; however, usually we will use the same AS for the same customer, but that is not always the case.

NOTE   When using the same autonomous system for BGP running CEs, do not forget that the routes will be denied from being imported into their respective tables due to the loop prevention (updates from the same autonomous system are in the AS-PATH). In this case, **AS-override** or **allowas-in** should be implemented.

Example 13-45 lists the functional configuration statements to ensure proper functional configuration of BGP considering the aspects.

Example 13-45   *BGP Configuration from PE and CE*

```
RP/0/0/CPU0:CsC-PE3(config)# router bgp 100

RP/0/0/CPU0:CsC-PE3(config-bgp)# vrf SPCOR

RP/0/0/CPU0:CsC-PE3(config-bgp-vrf)# rd 100:1

RP/0/0/CPU0:CsC-PE3(config-bgp-vrf)# address-family ipv4 unicast

RP/0/0/CPU0:CsC-PE3(config-bgp-vrf-af)# allocate-label all

RP/0/0/CPU0:CsC-PE3(config-bgp-vrf-af)# neighbor 172.16.23.2

RP/0/0/CPU0:CsC-PE3(config-bgp-vrf-af)# description CsC-CE2

RP/0/0/CPU0:CsC-PE3(config-bgp-vrf-nbr)# remote-as 10

RP/0/0/CPU0:CsC-PE3(config-bgp-vrf-nbr)# address-family ipv4 labeled-unicast
! To remind that this command is needed to enable IPv4 labelled unicast for the
! BGP session.

RP/0/0/CPU0:CsC-PE3 (config-bgp-vrf-nbr-af)# route-policy ALLOW in

RP/0/0/CPU0:CsC-PE3 (config-bgp-vrf-nbr-af)# route-policy ALLOW out
! IOS-XR eBGP session requires a route-policy to allow the traffic to be imported.

CsC-CE2(config)# router bgp 10

CsC-CE2(config-router)# no bgp default ipv4-unicast

CsC-CE2(config-router)# neighbor 172.16.23.3 remote-as 100

CsC-CE2(config-router)# neighbor 172.16.23.3 description CsC-PE3

CsC-CE2(config-router)# address-family ipv4

CsC-CE2(config-router-af)# network 10.1.100.2 mask 255.255.255.255

CsC-CE2(config-router-af)# neighbor 172.16.23.3 activate

CsC-CE2(config-router-af)# neighbor 172.16.23.3 send-label
```

Example 13-46 shows how to check normally for the route exchange between the CEs (CsC-CE) considering that we are using eBGP as PE-CE routing protocol.

Example 13-46   *Connectivity Verification*

```
CsC-CE22# show bgp ipv4 unicast
! Output omitted for brevity
     Network          Next Hop            Metric LocPrf Weight Path
 *>  10.1.100.2/32    0.0.0.0                  0          32768 i
 *>  10.1.100.7/32    172.16.23.3                         0 100 7 i

CsC-CE2# ping 10.1.100.7 source loopback 0
Packet sent with a source address of 10.1.100.2
!!!!!
Success rate is 100 percent (5/5), round-trip min/avg/max = 13/29/95 ms
```

Now, we must build the eBGP VPNv4 between the CsC-CEs to serve the VPN traffic for the Cs, as depicted in Example 13-47.

Example 13-47   *eBGP Neighborship Building*

```
CsC-CE2(config)# router bgp 10
CsC-CE2(config-router)# neighbor 10.1.100.7 remote-as 7
CsC-CE2(config-router)# neighbor 10.1.100.7 ebgp-multihop 5
! Do not forget we are building eBGP session using loopbacks!
CsC-CE2(config-router)# neighbor 10.1.100.7 update-source Loopback0
CsC-CE2(config-router)# address-family vpnv4
CsC-CE2(config-router-af)# neighbor 10.1.100.7 activate
CsC-CE2(config-router-af)# neighbor 10.1.100.7 send-community extended
CsC-CE2(config-router-af)# address-family ipv4 vrf CUST
CsC-CE2(config-router-af)# redistribute static
```

We are using IOS XR for PE3, which means that we should configure /32 host route for the interconnection opposite the interface. Also, that static route should be part of the respective VRF. Example 13-48 validates host route /32 addition.

Example 13-48   *IOS XR Host Route*

```
RP/0/0/CPU0:CsC-PE3(config)# router static
RP/0/0/CPU0:CsC-PE3(config-static)# vrf SPCOR
RP/0/0/CPU0:CsC-PE3(config-static-vrf)# address-family ipv4 unicast
RP/0/0/CPU0:CsC-PE3(config-static-vrf-afi)# 172.16.23.2/32 GigabitEthernet0/0/0/2
```

Now we should have an operating BGP VPNv4 session between the CsC-CEs. Example 13-49 validates the BGP route exchange.

Example 13-49   *BGP VPNv4 Output*

```
CsC-CE2# show bgp vpnv4 unicast all
! Output omitted for brevity
     Network          Next Hop          Metric LocPrf Weight Path
Route Distinguisher: 200:1 (default for vrf CUST)
 *>  10.1.100.1/32    192.168.12.1                0           32768 ?
 *>  10.1.100.8/32    10.1.100.7                  0             0 7 ?
```

We have used the second option for ensuring proper label exchange and maintaining LSP end to end. As you may recall from previous sections, once we enabled the **send-label** command, that means BGP will be responsible for assigning labels. On IOS and IOS XE, the **mpls bgp forwarding** command will be automatically injected within the interface configuration. Example 13-50 validates the interface MPLS functionality through BGP.

NOTE The **mpls bgp forwarding** command was introduced in IOS 12.0(29)S: https://www.cisco.com/c/en/us/td/docs/ios/mpls/command/reference/mp_m1.html#wp1044109

Example 13-50 *Interface MPLS Functionality*

```
CsC-CE2# show running-config interface GigabitEthernet 2 | include bgp
 mpls bgp forwarding

CsC-CE2# show mpls interfaces
Interface            IP            Tunnel  BGP Static Operational
GigabitEthernet2     No            No      Yes No     Yes
```

We have another option to enable the LDP functionality between the CsC-PE and CsC-CE. Example 13-51 shows how to enable MPLS for a specific interface on IOS XR.

Example 13-51 *Enabling MPLS on Interface, IOS XR*

```
RP/0/0/CPU0:CsC-PE3(config)# mpls ldp
RP/0/0/CPU0:CsC-PE3(config-ldp-if)# vrf SPCOR
RP/0/0/CPU0:CsC-PE3(config-ldp-vrf)# router-id 172.16.23.3
RP/0/0/CPU0:CsC-PE3(config-ldp-vrf)# address-family ipv4
RP/0/0/CPU0:CsC-PE3(config-ldp-vrf-af)# interface GigabitEthernet0/0/0/2
RP/0/0/CPU0:CsC-PE3(config-ldp-vrf-if)# address-family ipv4

CsC-CE2(config)# interface GigabitEthernet2
CsC-CE2(config-if)# mpls ip
%LDP-5-NBRCHG: LDP Neighbor 172.16.23.3:0 (1) is UP
```

In CsC, two VPN services are running, which means an extra label will be produced from a transport perspective because we have two VPNv4 sessions, each serving a different VPN. Example 13-52 analyzes the label assignment through the trace output.

Example 13-52 *Traceroute Output and Label Assignment*

```
C1# traceroute 10.1.100.8 source loopback 0 numeric
VRF info: (vrf in name/id, vrf out name/id)
 1 192.168.12.2 1 msec 1 msec 1 msec
 2 172.16.23.3 [MPLS: Labels 16302/700 Exp 0] 14 msec 13 msec 13 msec
 3 10.1.34.4 [MPLS: Labels 406/16601/700 Exp 0] 12 msec 12 msec 13 msec
 4 10.1.45.5 [MPLS: Labels 16500/16601/700 Exp 0] 13 msec 13 msec 13 msec
 5 10.1.56.6 [MPLS: Labels 16601/700 Exp 0] 12 msec 13 msec 13 msec
 6 192.168.78.7 [MPLS: Label 700 Exp 0] 12 msec 14 msec 15 msec
 7 192.168.78.8 13 msec 12 msec 13 msec
```

Figure 13-15 illustrates the label imposition/disposition at each node along the LSP, simulating a packet originating from C1 and ending at C8.

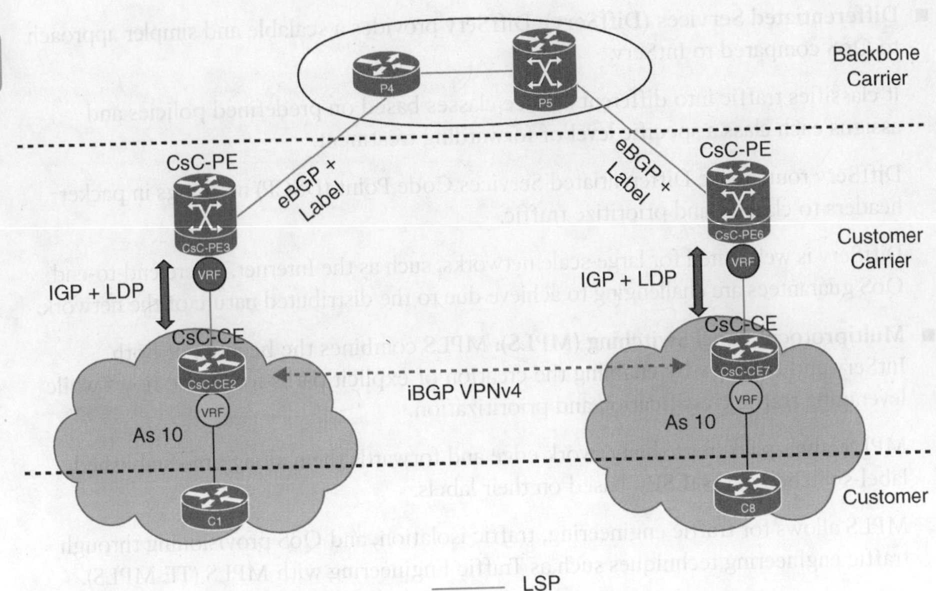

Figure 13-15 *MPLS CsC Label Operation*

Quality of Service (QoS)

Quality of Service (QoS) architecture models provide frameworks for implementing QoS mechanisms in computer networks to ensure that critical traffic receives preferential treatment over less critical traffic. Several QoS architecture models have been developed to address the diverse requirements of different network environments. Some common QoS architecture models include

- **Best Effort:** The Best Effort (BE) QoS model is the simplest model. It is the default QoS model used for the Internet, and it doesn't implement any QoS mechanism at all. That is the reason why there isn't any complexity associated with this QoS model.

  BE does not allow for resource reservation or any other mechanism related to asking for some kind of special treatment to the network. For this reason, the BE model does not work very well with any emerging application with real-time traffic demands.

  This model should not be used when the network resources are not enough to fulfill the QoS application requirements in terms of the main indicators, such as bandwidth, delay, and jitter. In these cases, with applications competing for resources, the quality of the end-user experience could be very poor if there is no other mechanism in place to manage the unfairness.

- **Integrated Services (IntServ):** The IntServ model offers fine-grained control over QoS by setting up individual reservations for each flow in the network.

  It requires signaling mechanisms such as Resource Reservation Protocol (RSVP) to establish and maintain reservations across network devices.

  IntServ is suitable for networks with relatively low traffic volume and known QoS requirements, such as small-scale enterprise networks or multimedia applications.

- **Differentiated Services (DiffServ):** DiffServ provides a scalable and simpler approach to QoS compared to IntServ.

  It classifies traffic into different service classes based on predefined policies and assigns each class a specific level of forwarding treatment.

  DiffServ routers use Differentiated Services Code Point (DSCP) markings in packet headers to classify and prioritize traffic.

  DiffServ is well suited for large-scale networks, such as the Internet, where end-to-end QoS guarantees are challenging to achieve due to the distributed nature of the network.

- **Multiprotocol Label Switching (MPLS):** MPLS combines the benefits of both IntServ and DiffServ by enabling the creation of explicit paths for traffic flows while leveraging traffic classification and prioritization.

  MPLS labels packets at the network edge and forwards them along pre-established label-switched paths (LSPs) based on their labels.

  MPLS allows for traffic engineering, traffic isolation, and QoS provisioning through traffic engineering techniques such as Traffic Engineering with MPLS (TE-MPLS).

- **Policy-Based QoS:** Policy-based QoS models allow administrators to define QoS policies based on specific criteria, such as source/destination addresses, applications, or traffic characteristics.

  Policies are implemented through the configuration of routers and switches to apply QoS mechanisms such as traffic shaping, policing, queuing, and prioritization.

  Policy-based QoS is flexible and adaptable to various network environments but may require more manual configuration and management compared to other models.

- **Software-Defined Networking (SDN):** SDN separates the control plane from the data plane and centralizes network control in a software-based controller.

  QoS policies can be defined and enforced centrally through the SDN controller, which communicates with network devices to configure QoS parameters dynamically.

  SDN offers programmability, automation, and scalability in QoS provisioning, making it suitable for dynamic and agile network environments.

These QoS architecture models provide different approaches to implementing QoS in networks, each with its own advantages and limitations. The choice of model depends on factors such as network size, traffic characteristics, scalability requirements, and administrative preferences.

MPLS QoS

Because we have gone through the deployment models of services and applications provided through MPLS VPNs, now it is time to analyze QoS behavior along the CE-to-CE path and how the service provider core treats the packets transporting through its domain.

Why do we need QoS in the first place? There are a lot of high-bandwidth and delay-sensitive traffic applications that sometimes need preferential treatment over less important traffic.

RFC 3270 comprehensively illustrates the models supported for QoS over MPLS VPNs. The models, in brief, are as follows:

- Uniform model

- Pipe model

- Short Pipe model

Figure 13-16 illustrates the topology we use to analyze all options.

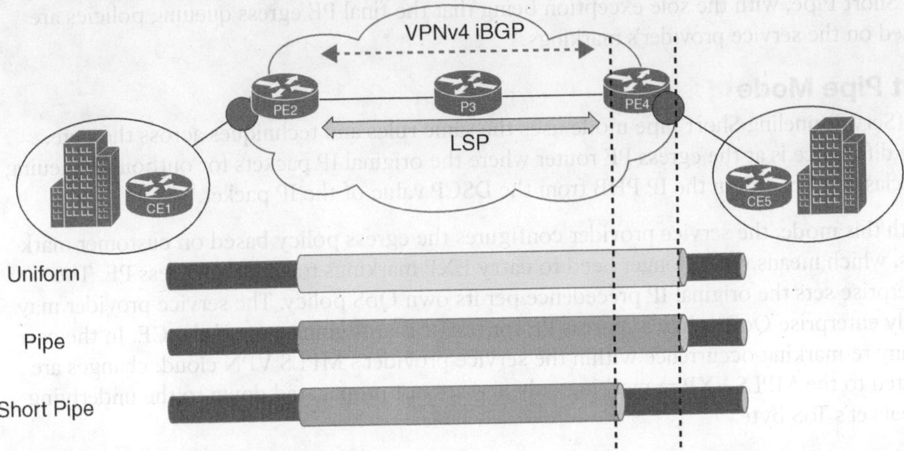

Figure 13-16 *MPLS QoS Models*

Uniform Mode

The Uniform mode is for customers who own their MPLS backbone. Usually, MPLS services are offered through providers. However, we currently see that big enterprises have their own backbone, infrastructure, and therefore control on the underlay/overlay.

This mode also can be used when the customer and the service provider share the same DiffServ domain. The ingress PE router copies the DSCP from the incoming IP packet into the MPLS EXP bits of the imposed labels.

As the EXP bits travel through the core, they may or may not be modified by intermediate P routers. At the egress P router, the EXP bits are copied to the EXP bits of the newly exposed label. Finally, at the egress PE router, the EXP bits are copied to the DSCP bits of the original IP packet. There's no guarantee that the ToS of customers' packets will remain intact, but the EXP and IP ToS fields of a data packet will always show the same.

Pipe Mode

In Pipe mode, the service provider will not modify or manipulate customer markings. The QoS policy is based on the service provider markings throughout the backbone network. Also, the policy on the edge toward the customer is based on MPLS EXP bits. What we can accomplish with this mode is enforcing the policy inbound on the PE and setting the EXP bits (on all imposed labels), which will eventually direct the customer on how to mark traffic that will be mapped to the classes structured by the service provider.

The DiffServ Tunneling Pipe mode uses two layers of QoS: an underlying QoS for the data, which remains unchanged when traversing the core; and a per-core QoS, which is separate from that of the underlying IP packets. This per-core QoS PHB remains transparent to end users. When a packet reaches the edge of the MPLS core, the egress PE router classifies the exposed IP packets for outbound queuing based on the MPLS PHB from the EXP bits of the recently removed label. The end-to-end MPLS bits, especially at the PHP, are maintained over the Explicit Null/Label 0 signaled from the egress PER to P.

This implementation avoids the additional operational overhead of per-customer configurations on each egress interface on the egress PE router. Pipe mode operation is identical to the Short Pipe, with the sole exception being that the final PE egress queuing policies are based on the service provider's markings.

Short Pipe Mode

DiffServ Tunneling Short Pipe mode uses the same rules and techniques across the core. The difference is at the egress PE router where the original IP packets for outbound queuing are classified based on the IP PHB from the DSCP value of the IP packet.

With this mode, the service provider configures the egress policy based on customer markings, which means we no longer need to carry EXP markings toward the egress PE. The enterprise sets the original IP precedence per its own QoS policy. The service provider may apply enterprise QoS policy at egress PE for traffic that is going toward the CE. In the case of any re-marking occurrence within the service provider's MPLS VPN cloud, changes are limited to the MPLS EXP re-marking only and are not propagated down to the underlying IP packet's ToS byte.

Short Pipe Tunneling mode is used when the customer and the service provider are in different DiffServ domains. Short Pipe mode is useful when the service provider wants to enforce its own DiffServ policy, while maintaining DiffServ transparency.

Exam Preparation Tasks

As mentioned in the section "How to Use This Book" in the Introduction, you have a few choices for exam preparation: the exercises here, Chapter 23, "Final Preparation," and the exam simulation questions in the Pearson Test Prep Software Online.

Review All Key Topics

Review the most important topics in this chapter, noted with the Key Topic icon in the margin of the page. Table 13-3 lists a reference of these key topics and the page numbers on which each is found.

Table 13-3 Key Topics for Chapter 13

Key Topic Element	Description	Page Number
Figure 13-1	Unified MPLS Structure	624
Paragraph	BGP advertisement, MPLS L3VPN Internet Access Option 1	631
Section	MPLS L3VPN Internet Access Option 3: Extranet with Internet-VRF	635

Key Topic Element	Description	Page Number
Figure 13-6	MPLS L3VPN Internet Access Option 3	636
Paragraph	VRF-Aware NAT	639
Paragraph	Back-to-back VRF	642
Paragraph	RFC 3107, BGP label allocation in MPLS Inter-AS VPN	644
Paragraph	MPLS Inter-AS Option C characteristics	650
Figure 13-11	Inter-AS Option C VPN Label Assignment	652
Table 13-2	MPLS Inter-AS L3VPN Comparison	654
Figure 13-14	MPLS Carrier Supporting Carrier (CsC)	655
Figure 13-15	MPLS CsC Label Operation	659

Define Key Terms

Define the following key terms from this chapter and check the answers in the glossary:

Carrier supporting Carrier (CsC), Label Distribution Protocol (LDP), Label Forwarding Information Base (LFIB), Label Switched Path (LSP), Multiprotocol Label Switching (MPLS), Network Address Translation (NAT), Quality of Service (QoS), Unified MPLS Mobile Transport (UMMT), Virtual Routing and Forwarding (VRF)

Command Reference to Check Your Memory

This section includes the most important commands covered in this chapter. You might not need to memorize the complete syntax of every command, but you should be able to remember the basic keywords that are needed.

To test your memory of the commands, cover the right side of Table 13-4 with a piece of paper, read the description on the left side, and then see how much of the command you can remember.

The SPCOR 350-501 exam focuses on practical, hands-on skills that are used by networking professionals. Therefore, you should be able to identify the commands needed to configure and test. Note that not all commands are fully covered in the chapter, but their presence in the following table should lead you to investigate them further to understand this technology.

Table 13-4   MPLS Commands to Know

Task	Command Syntax
On the interface level, use the **vrf forwarding** command to assign the interface to the correct VRF (the VRF creation method is through the **VRF definition** command).	**vrf forwarding** *VRF_Name*
Configure the router to exchange VPNv4 routes for use with MPLS VPNs. This includes support for encoding route targets and route distinguishers within the updates for customer VPN prefixes.	**address-family vpnv4 unicast**

Task	Command Syntax
Display BGP neighbor status for the VPNv4 family, including VRF information.	**show bgp vpnv4 unicast all**
Show all VPNv4 entries in the BGP routing table with the assigned labels.	**show bgp vpnv4 unicast labels**
Allow the BGP speaker to accept the BGP updates even if its own BGP AS number is in the AS-Path attribute.	**neighbor** *ip-address* **allowas-in**
Replace the AS number of the originating router with the AS number of the sending BGP router.	**neighbor** *ip-address* **as-override**
All received VPN IPv4 routes are accepted. If the router is an autonomous system border or customer edge router, this is the desired behavior.	**no bgp default route-target filter**
Apply this command to the VPN address-family under BGP; it affects all VPN peers advertising VPN routes to this ASBR (iBGP and eBGP) on IOS XR.	**retain route-target all**
Distribute MPLS labels without a specific address family (vpnv4/vpnv6 unicast/ multicast) per neighbor.	**allocate-label all**
Allow the advertisement of a single virtual private network (VPN) label for local routes throughout the entire VRF.	**mpls label mode vrf** *VRF_Name* **protocol bgp-vpnv4 per-vrf**

Review Questions

As a part of the review, we encourage you to provide *a single-sentence answer* (keep your answers as short as possible) to the following questions. If you struggle to complete this answer in a single sentence, this may indicate a lack of clarity or reveal gaps in your understanding. We have constructed these questions to help you consolidate this chapter's information and extract the essence of the covered content.

The answers to these questions appear in Appendix A. For more practice with exam format questions, use the Pearson Test Prep Software Online.

1. When you design for MPLS Inter-AS deployment, what aspects should you consider (generally)?

2. How can you ensure end-to-end LSP across a unified MPLS deployment?

Bibliography

M. Chen, R. Zhang, and X. Duan. RFC 5316, *ISIS Extensions in Support of Inter-Autonomous System (AS) MPLS and GMPLS Traffic Engineering*, IETF, https://www.ietf.org/rfc/rfc5316.txt, December 2008.

Configuring Ethernet Connectivity Fault Management in a Service Provider Network. https://www.cisco.com/c/en/us/td/docs/ios/cether/configuration/guide/ce_cfm.html. Accessed August 6, 2024.

K. Kompella and Y. Rekhter. RFC 2370, *The OSPF Opaque LSA Option*, IETF, https://www.ietf.org/rfc/rfc2370.txt, July 1998.

K. Kompella and Y. Rekhter. RFC 4761, *Virtual Private LAN Service (VPLS) Using BGP for Auto-Discovery and Signaling*, IETF, https://www.ietf.org/rfc/rfc4761.txt, January 2007.

F. Le Faucheru, L. Wu, B. Davie, S. Davara, P. Vaananen, R. Krishnan, P. Cheval, and J. Heinanen. RFC 3270, *Multi-Protocol Label Switching (MPLS) Support of Differentiated Services*, IETF, https://www.ietf.org/rfc/rfc3270.txt, May 2002.

Y. Rekhter and E. Rosen. RFC 3107, *Carrying Label Information in BGP-4*, IETF, https://www.ietf.org/rfc/rfc3107.txt, May 2001.

Y. Rekhter and E. Rosen. Internet Draft, *BGP/MPLS VPNs*, IETF, https://datatracker.ietf.org/doc/draft-rosen-vpn-mpls/01/, March 2013.

E. Rosen, B. Davie, V. Radoaca, and W. Luo. RFC 6074, *Provisioning, Auto-Discovery, and Signaling in Layer 2 Virtual Private Networks (L2VPNs)*, IETF, https://www.ietf.org/rfc/rfc6074.txt, January 2011.

E. Rosen, P. Psenak, and P. Pilley-Esnault. RFC 4577, *OSPF as the Provider/Customer Edge Protocol for BGP/MPLS IP Virtual Private Networks (VPNs)*, IETF, https://www.ietf.org/rfc/rfc4577.txt, June 2006.

E. Rosen and Y. Rekhter. RFC 4364, *BGP/MPLS IP Virtual Private Networks (VPNs)*, IETF, https://www.ietf.org/rfc/rfc4364.txt, February 2006.

Unified MPLS Functionality, Features, and Configuration Example. https://www.cisco.com/c/en/us/support/docs/multiprotocol-label-switching-mpls/mpls/118846-config-mpls-00.html. Accessed August 6, 2024.

CHAPTER 14

MPLS Traffic Engineering

This chapter covers the following exam topics:

- 1.4.b MPLS TE QoS (MAM, RDM, CBTS, PBTS, and DS-TE)

3.2 Describe traffic engineering

- 3.2.a ISIS and OSPF extensions
- 3.2.b RSVP functionality
- 3.2.c FRR

Multiprotocol Label Switching (MPLS) finds utility in traffic engineering (TE), which facilitates custom management of traffic to align with specific network needs. TE bypasses standard routing tables and is important for service providers to efficiently use their backbones and provide high resiliency.

Prior to MPLS TE, traffic engineering was performed either by IP or by ATM, depending on the protocol in use between two edge routers in a network. Consequently, the term *traffic engineering* has attained popularity and is used more in the context of MPLS TE today.

"Do I Know This Already?" Quiz

The "Do I Know This Already?" quiz allows you to assess whether you should read this entire chapter thoroughly or jump to the "Exam Preparation Tasks" section. If you are in doubt about your answers to these questions or your own assessment of your knowledge of the topics, read the entire chapter. Table 14-1 lists the major headings in this chapter and their corresponding "Do I Know This Already?" quiz questions. You can find the answers in Appendix A, "Answers to the 'Do I Know This Already?' Quizzes and Review Questions."

Table 14-1 "Do I Know This Already?" Section-to-Question Mapping

Foundation Topics Section	Questions
MPLS Traffic Engineering Fundamentals	1–3
MPLS TE QoS	4–5

CAUTION The goal of self-assessment is to gauge your mastery of the topics in this chapter. If you do not know the answer to a question or are only partially sure of the answer, you should mark that question as wrong for purposes of the self-assessment. Giving yourself credit for an answer you correctly guess skews your self-assessment results and might provide you with a false sense of security.

1. What is the Record Route Object in the RSVP used for?

   a. QoS requirements

   b. Loop avoidance

   c. Label assignment

   d. Database updates

2. When you are establishing traffic engineering tunnels for three distinct traffic flows to the same PE, which combination is needed?

   a. One RSVP session, three LSPs

   b. One RSVP session, one LSP

   c. Three RSVP sessions, one LSP

   d. Three RSVP sessions, three LSPs

3. Which method for directing traffic of interest through a tunnel involves treating the tunnel as an integral component of the underlying Interior Gateway Protocol (IGP)?

   a. Autoroute announce

   b. Forwarding adjacency

   c. Static routes

   d. Policy-Based Routing (PBR)

4. In an MPLS DiffServ-TE solution, what do you call the percentage of a link's bandwidth that a class type can take up?

   a. Bandwidth constraint (BC)

   b. Bandwidth class (BC)

   c. Bucket class (BC)

   d. Bucket constraint (BC)

5. Policy-Based Tunnel Selection (PBTS) serves the same goal as Class-Based Tunnel Selection (CBTS) on IOS software but is designed for which of the following?

   a. IOS XE operating system

   b. IOS XR operating system

   c. IOS and IOS XE operating systems

   d. PBTS and CBTS and can be configured on the IOS XR operating system

Foundation Topics

MPLS Traffic Engineering Fundamentals

MPLS Traffic Engineering (MPLS TE) is a set of techniques and strategies used in MPLS networks to optimize and control the routing of traffic flows based on specific criteria such as bandwidth, latency, and network resource utilization. MPLS TE enables network operators to engineer the paths that traffic takes through the network, ensuring efficient utilization of network resources and meeting **Quality of Service (QoS)** requirements.

The key components and features of MPLS Traffic Engineering are as follows:

- **Constraint-Based Routing:** MPLS TE allows network operators to define traffic engineering constraints and requirements, such as minimum bandwidth, maximum latency, and link utilization thresholds.

  Routers use constraint-based routing algorithms to compute optimal paths for traffic flows that satisfy these constraints, considering the current network topology and resource availability.

- **Traffic Engineering Tunnels:** MPLS TE establishes traffic engineering tunnels, also known as TE tunnels or label-switched paths (LSPs), to carry traffic along predefined paths through the network. MPLS TE tunnels are built from one headend to a tailend in a unidirectional fashion (the headend is the router where the tunnel initiates, and the tailend is the router where the tunnel terminates). This means traffic will be controlled in one direction of the flow.

  To implement bidirectional TE deployment, you need to configure a pair of tunnels. These tunnels are set up based on explicit routing paths that meet the specified constraints, such as shortest path, least congested path, or path with specified resource attributes.

- **Path Computation Element (PCE):** MPLS TE can leverage a Path Computation Element (PCE) to centrally compute and optimize traffic engineering paths across the network.

  The PCE is responsible for path computation, considering network topology, link metrics, traffic demands, and traffic engineering constraints.

- **Resource Reservation:** MPLS TE allows for the reservation of network resources along traffic engineering paths to ensure that sufficient bandwidth and resources are available for the traffic flows.

- **Fast Reroute (FRR):** MPLS TE supports FRR mechanisms to provide rapid backup paths in case of link or node failures along traffic engineering tunnels.

  FRR techniques such as link protection and node protection enable quick recovery and minimize service disruption in the event of network failures.

- **Scalability and Optimization:** MPLS TE is scalable and can be applied in large-scale networks with complex topologies and diverse traffic requirements.

  Optimization algorithms within MPLS TE help in efficient utilization of network resources, load balancing, and congestion avoidance.

- **Integration with QoS and SLA:** QoS policies can be applied to traffic engineering tunnels to prioritize and differentiate traffic based on application requirements.

MPLS TE is widely used by service providers, enterprises, and cloud providers to improve network performance, reliability, and scalability. It plays a critical role in optimizing traffic flows, managing network congestion, and delivering predictable performance for mission-critical applications.

The challenge with destination-based least-cost routing is that alternate links are often underutilized, as shown in Figure 14-1.

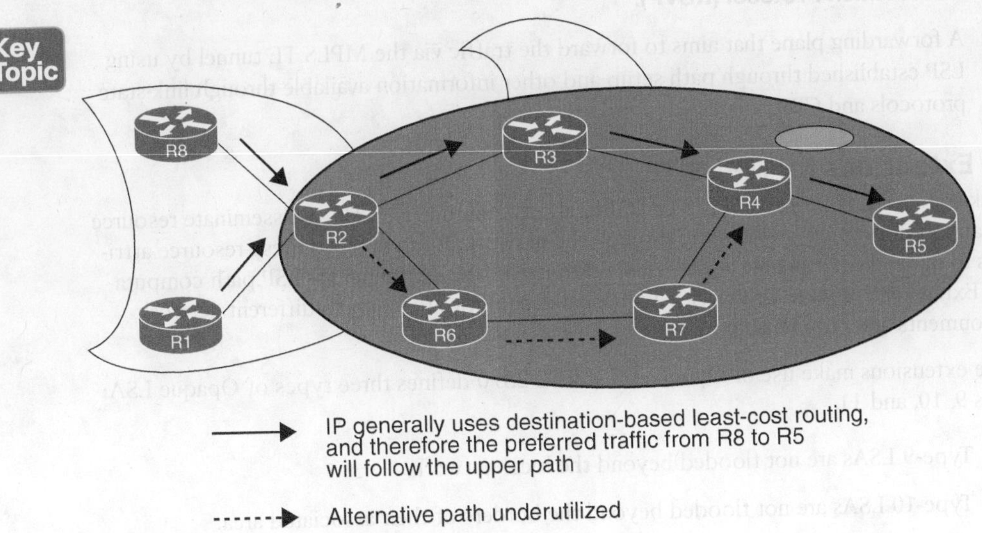

Figure 14-1   *IP Routing and the Fish*

Traditional IP routing (IGP) aims to efficiently forward traffic to its destination while adhering to established routing protocols and network configurations. As a result, the routing protocols usually discover the shortest path to the destination based on the cost of the link (also called the *metric*) that the packet is forwarded. Additionally, IP packets are forwarded on a per-hop basis, meaning each router (hop) forwards the packet based on the destination IP address.

Traditional IP routing does not consider the available bandwidth of the link. This can cause some links to be overutilized compared to others. This limitation in traditional IP routing can be addressed using *Policy-Based Routing (PBR)*. However, it requires policies to be implemented on every router along the path to the destination. This can result in massive configurations on every router. MPLS TE helps to solve this problem.

MPLS TE provides an efficient way of forwarding traffic throughout the network, by learning the topology and the available resources available to map traffic flows to a specific path based on the resources required by the traffic flow.

The main components that work together to make MPLS TE functional and work to adapt to traffic flow requirements are as follows:

- Link-state protocols (IS-IS or OSPF) that have been enhanced to carry additional information related to TE, such as available bandwidth and other aspects that are represented by Type-Length-Value (TLV).

- Path Calculation via Constrained-Based Routing (CBR) to find the shortest path to a specific network that matches the traffic flow resource requirements.

- Path setup for reservation (signaling) of resources for a specific traffic flow and to establish the label-switched path (LSP) that will be accomplished via **Resource Reservation Protocol (RSVP)**.

- A forwarding plane that aims to forward the traffic via the MPLS TE tunnel by using LSP established through path setup and other information available through link-state protocols and CBR.

OSPF Extensions for MPLS TE

A link-state routing protocol (IS-IS or OSPF) is required in MPLS TE to disseminate resource allocation information by flooding through the network. Routers flood these resource attributes to make them available at the headend router of the TE tunnel for LSP path computation. Extensions provide OSPF with additional capabilities to adapt to different network environments and requirements.

These extensions make use of Opaque LSA. RFC 2370 defines three types of Opaque LSA: Types 9, 10, and 11.

- Type-9 LSAs are not flooded beyond the local network.

- Type-10 LSAs are not flooded beyond the borders of their associated area.

- Type-11 LSAs are flooded throughout the autonomous system (AS). Opaque LSAs are not flooded to non-opaque-capable routers.

Opaque capability is learned at the beginning of the OSPF DBD exchange where opaque-capable routers set the O-bit in the Options field of the DBD packets.

An Opaque LSA is called a Traffic Engineering LSA (TE LSA). It carries additional attributes related to TE links, and standard link-state database flooding mechanisms are used to distribute TE LSAs. A TE LSA describes routers, point-to-point links, and connections to multi-access networks (like the Router LSA).

The LSA payload consists of one or more nested TLV triplets for extensibility. The Length field defines the length of the value portion (TLV with no value has a length of 0). Nested TLVs are 32 bits aligned.

There are two types of TE LSAs:

- **Router Address TLV (Type 1):** This TLV specifies a stable IP address (usually the Loopback interface) of the advertising router. The key attribute is that the address does not become unusable if an interface is down. This is usually known as router ID. The Router Address TLV is type 1 with a length of 4 octets and appears in one Traffic Engineering LSA originated by a router.

- **Link TLV (Type 2):** This TLV describes a TE link. It is constructed of a set of the following sub-TLVs that specify the link attributes:

  - **Link Type:** This 1-byte sub-TLV indicates whether the link is point-to-point or multi-access.

- **Link ID:** This 4-byte sub-TLV identifies the other end of the link. If the link is a point-to-point link, this field is the router ID of the neighbor. For a multi-access link, this field is the IP address of the DR.

- **Local Interface IP Address:** This 4-byte sub-TLV specifies the IP address(es) of the interface corresponding to this link. If there are multiple IP addresses, they are all listed.

- **Remote Interface IP Address:** This 4-byte sub-TLV specifies the IP address(es) of the neighbor's interface corresponding to this link. If the link type is multi-access, this field is set to 0.0.0.0.

- **Traffic Engineering Metric:** This 4-byte sub-TLV specifies the link metric for TE purposes. This metric is configurable (using the **mpls traffic-eng administrative-weight** interface configuration command) and hence can be different to the OSPF metric.

- **Maximum Bandwidth:** This 4-byte sub-TLV specifies the maximum bandwidth that can be used on this link from this router to the neighbor. This can be configured using the **bandwidth** *<value>* interface configuration command, or the default interface bandwidth is accepted.

- **Maximum Reservable Bandwidth:** This 4-byte sub-TLV specifies the maximum reservable bandwidth on this link in this direction. It can be configured using the **ip rsvp bandwidth** *<value>* interface configuration command.

- **Unreserved Bandwidth:** This 32-byte sub-TLV specifies the total bandwidth not reserved yet at each of eight priority levels (0–7).

- **Administrative Group:** This is also called Resource (link) color. This 4-byte sub-TLV contains a 4-byte bit mask assigned by the network administrator. Each set bit corresponds to one administrative group assigned to the interface. The least significant bit is referred to as *group 0*, and the most significant bit is referred to as *group 31*. It can be configured using the **mpls traffic-eng attribute-flags** interface configuration command.

IS-IS Extensions for MPLS TE

The Intermediate System to Intermediate System (IS-IS) protocol is specified in ISO 10589 (ISO-10589), with extensions for supporting IPv4 specified in RFC 1195. Each IS (router) advertises one or more IS-IS link-state protocol (LSP) data units with routing information. Each LSP is composed of a fixed header and several tuples, each consisting of a Type, a Length, and a Value. Such tuples are commonly known as TLVs and are a good way of encoding information in a flexible and extensible format.

Like OSPF, IS-IS can also be used as the link-state protocol of choice in the TE domain. IS-IS with extensions and newly defined TLVs can be used to propagate information pertaining to resource allocation in an MPLS TE domain. The following TLVs have been defined for the use of IS-IS as the link-state IGP in an MPLS TE domain:

- **TLV22: Extended IS reachability:** This TLV propagates information about the state of links in the network and allows the use of "wide" metrics. In addition, this TLV provides information on resource availability, like link bandwidths.

- **Administration Group:** If the link or interface has been colored (from a traffic engineering point of view), that information is carried by this TLV.

- **IPv4 Interface Address:** This interface IP address is used for traffic engineering purposes.

- **IPv4 Neighbor Address:** This neighbor interface IP address is used for traffic engineering purposes.

- **Maximum Link Bandwidth:** This is the maximum link bandwidth of the interface in question (for traffic engineering purposes).

- **Maximum Reservable Link Bandwidth:** This is the maximum amount of bandwidth that can be reserved on the interface in question.

- **Unreserved Bandwidth:** This is the amount of bandwidth that is not yet reserved on the interface.

- **Traffic Engineering Default Metric:** This metric is administratively assigned for traffic engineering purposes.

- **TLV134: Router ID:** This TLV is used to identify the router with a distinct IP address, usually a loopback address. The source and destination IP addresses used to identify and define the tunnel endpoints must match the router ID.

- **TLV135: Extended IP reachability:** This TLV uses "wide" metrics and determines whether a prefix is a level-1 or level-2 prefix. It also allows the flagging of routes when a prefix is leaked from level 2 into level 1.

- **Administration Group:** This sub-TLV associates a tag with an IP prefix. Some examples of this tag include controlling redistribution between levels and areas, different routing protocols, or on an interface.

Sub-TLVs use the same concepts as TLVs. The difference is that TLVs exist inside IS-IS packets, whereas sub-TLVs exist inside TLVs. TLVs are used to add extra information to IS-IS packets. Sub-TLVs are used to add extra information to TLVs. Each sub-TLV consists of three fields.

Constrained Shortest Path First

In the SPF calculation process for link-state protocols, a router places itself at the root of the tree with shortest paths to each of the destinations, only considering least metric (cost) to the destination.

The method used to determine the path for a traffic engineering (TE) tunnel differs from the conventional Shortest Path First (SPF) process. **Constrained Shortest Path First** uses more than link cost to identify the probable paths that can be used for TE LSP paths. CSPF determines the best path to only the tunnel tailend router, not to all routers. Rather than relying solely on a single cost metric for the link between two neighboring routers, the TE tunnel path computation considers additional factors such as bandwidth, link attributes, and administrative weights.

Before initiating the path computation, CSPF takes the input from both user-specified path constraints and the information in the TE database.

At the headend router, the selection of a path for establishing a TE LSP occurs following the exclusion of all links that fail to meet the bandwidth prerequisites, alongside an evaluation of the link cost. The result of the CSPF calculation is an ordered list of IP addresses that map to the next-hop addresses of routers that form the TE LSP.

Figure 14-2 highlights the relationship between SPF and CSPF and the interaction with RSVP. The following section describes RSVP in more detail.

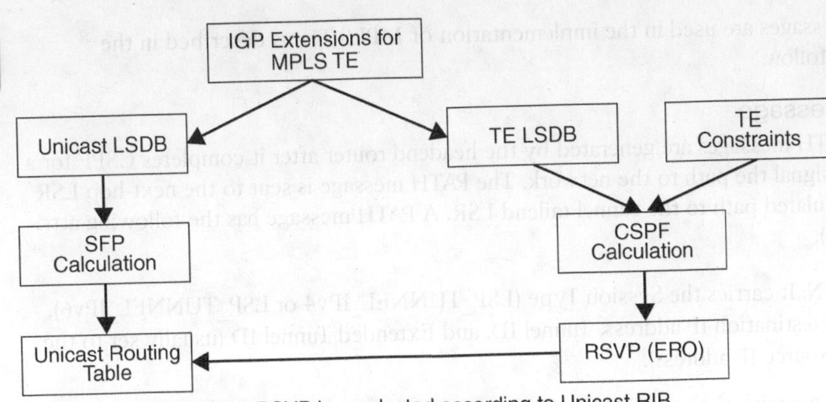

Figure 14-2   *RSVP Operation in MPLS TE*

Resource Reservation Protocol (RSVP) Operation in MPLS TE

The Resource Reservation Protocol (RSVP) enables hosts and applications to gain special treatment for their flows by reserving bandwidth for applications. RSVP is not a routing protocol but rather acts as a control protocol that works with a routing protocol.

Constrained Shortest Path First (CSPF) is an advanced form of the SFP algorithm described in Chapter 6, "OSPF." CSPF is used in the computation of LSP paths that are subject to multiple constraints. Once a CSPF calculation is completed, the path needs to be signaled across the network to establish a TE LSP and to consume resources along that path. RSVP (protocol type 46) is used to reserve resources throughout the network.

Extensions have been implemented in RSVP to enable it to transport MPLS labels and accommodate other TE specifics. RSVP tries to signal the TE tunnel along the path from headend to tailend LSR. RSVP relies on signaling to communicate and configure label information at each LSR along the path. It also reserves bandwidth along the path.

RSVP messages are sent by the headend router to identify resource availability along the path, as demonstrated in Figure 14-3.

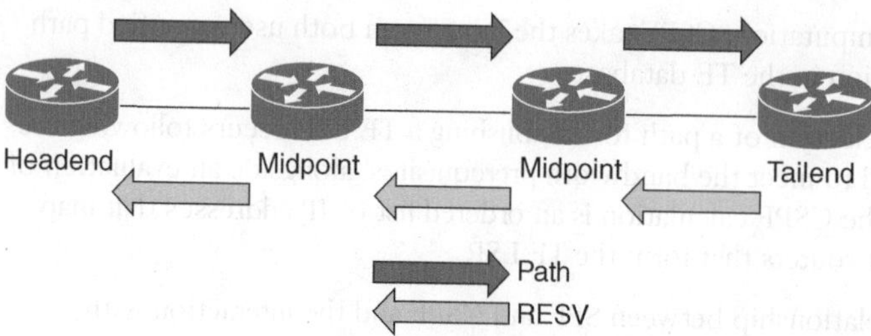

Figure 14-3 *RSVP Main Messages*

Four main messages are used in the implementation of MPLS TE, as described in the sections that follow.

RSVP PATH Message

The RSVP PATH messages are generated by the headend router after it completes CSPF for a TE tunnel to signal the path to the network. The PATH message is sent to the next-hop LSR along the calculated path to the tunnel tailend LSR. A PATH message has the following attributes (objects):

- **SESSION:** It carries the Session Type (LSP_TUNNEL_IPv4 or LSP_TUNNEL_IPv6), Tunnel Destination IP address, Tunnel ID, and Extended Tunnel ID (usually set to the Tunnel Source IP address).

- **HOP:** It contains the upstream LSR's interface IP address (previous HOP–PHOP).

- **TIME VALUES:** It is a refresh period (in milliseconds, or ms) used to send PATH or RESV messages. The default value is 30000 ms.

- **EXPLICIT ROUTE (ERO):** It defines the path that an MPLS TE tunnel takes. It is a collection of subobjects. Cisco IOS and IOS XR use only IPv4 subobjects containing IP addresses to which the router should forward this PATH message.

- **LABEL REQUEST:** It requests a label. It contains the Layer 3 Protocol ID (L3PID) that is carried in the label. The L3PID is always 0x0800 for IPv4. It requests the tailend router to provide a label for this IPv4 TE tunnel.

- **SESSION ATTRIBUTE:** It contains the setup and holding priorities of the LSP tunnel. It also contains the local protection flag (0x01 for link protection and 0x10 for node protection).

- **SENDER TEMPLATE:** It carries the Tunnel Sender IP address, which is the router ID of the TE tunnel headend router, and an LSP ID, which is the tunnel's LSP ID. The LSP ID changes when the tunnel's properties change, like bandwidth or path.

- **SENDER TSPEC:** It defines the traffic characteristics of the sender's data flow. It carries the requested bandwidth for the LSP tunnel.

- **ADSPEC:** It describes a reservation model in which PATH messages sent downstream gather information that the receivers can use to predict end-to-end service.

- **RECORD ROUTE:** This is optional and must be configured. It is used to collect detailed path information and is useful for loop detection and diagnostics. Essentially, it keeps track of a list of LSRs that the PATH message has traversed. It may be present in the RESV message.

- **FAST REROUTE:** It specifies the preferred FRR technique (facility backup or one-to-one backup) and the preferred attributes (priority, bandwidth, characteristics, etc.) of the backup TE LSP.

RSVP RESV Message

The RSVP Reservation (RESV) messages are generated by the TE tunnel tailend router and confirm the reservation request sent using PATH messages. The RSVP RESV message performs the function of label assignment for a particular LSP mapping to the TE tunnel. The tailend router first generates a label for the TE tunnel and sends it upstream. This process is followed at each hop where local label mapping to the TE tunnel is assigned and propagated upstream until the headend router is reached. A RESV message has the following attributes (objects):

- **SESSION:** It carries the same information as the PATH message.

- **HOP:** It contains the downstream LSR's interface IP address (next hop, or NHOP).

- **TIME VALUES:** It is a refresh period (in milliseconds) used to send PATH or RESV messages. The default value is 30000 ms.

- **STYLE:** The sender flags the reservation style in the PATH message. The receiver can choose one different style; each RSVP session must have a reservation style. There are three different reservation styles:

  - **Fixed Filter (FF) Style:** This style creates a distinct reservation for traffic from each sender that is not shared by other senders. Since each sender has its own reservation, a unique label is assigned to each sender. This results in P2P LSP between every sender–receiver pair.

  - **Wildcard Filter (WF) Style:** With this style, a single shared reservation is used for all senders to a session. A single multipoint-to-point (MP2P) LSP is created for all sessions to the sender. A single label value is allocated to the session.

  - **Shared Explicit (SE) Style:** This style allows a receiver to explicitly specify the senders to allow in a reservation. Because each sender is explicitly listed in the RESV message, different labels are assigned to different senders, creating a separate LSP for each sender.

- **FLOWSPEC:** It specifies the desired QoS. It also specifies the tunnel bandwidth in bytes/sec.

- **FILTERSPEC:** It carries the Tunnel Sender IP address, which is the router ID of the TE tunnel headend router, and an LSP ID, which is the tunnel's LSP ID. The LSP ID changes when a tunnel's properties change, like bandwidth or path. It is exactly the same as the SENDER TEMPLATE object in the PATH message.

- **LABEL:** It carries a label value that the PHOP should use for a particular tunnel.

RSVP Error Messages

When resources are not available, the router generates RSVP error messages and sends them to the router from which the request or reply was received. There are two types of RSVP error messages: PATHERR and RESVERR messages. PATHERR messages are sent upstream to the sender that created the error, whereas RESVERR messages are sent downstream. Both error messages contain the ERROR SPEC object along with other objects.

The ERROR SPEC object contains the error code and error value, which are used to decode the error types. The most common error code and error value are 00. This value indicates confirmation sent in response to receive a confirmation object. Another common error code is 24, but there are 10 different error values for this code. Figure 14-4 illustrates the possible RSVP error messages.

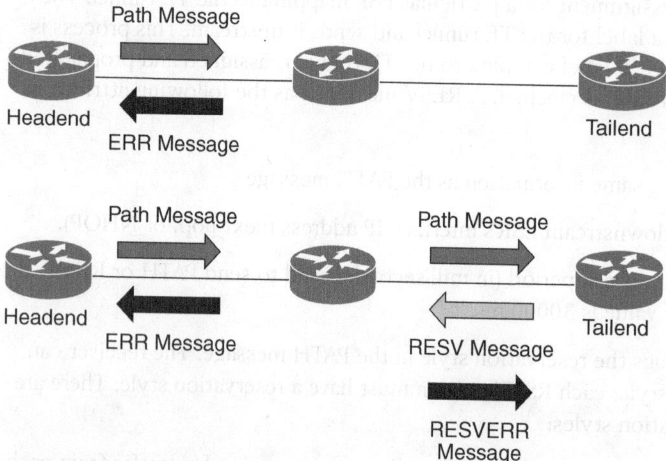

Figure 14-4 *RSVP Error Message*

RSVP Tear Messages

RSVP has two types of tear messages: PATHTEAR and RESVTEAR. The PATHTEAR message travels toward all receivers downstream from its point of initiation, whereas the RESVTEAR message travels toward all senders upstream from its point of initiation. These messages immediately clear the reservation states on the router. This enables the reuse of resources on the router for other requests. The teardown request may be initiated by the router because of state timeout or tunnel preemption.

NOTE FAST_REROUTE, RECORD_ROUTE and SESSION_ATTRIBUTE are RSVP objects used in MPLS TE FRR.

To shed some light on the messages that construct the core of RSVP operation, Example 14-1 shows the messages after turning on **debug ip rsvp dump-messages path**.

Example 14-1 *RSVP Messages, Debug Output*

```
PE2# debug ip rsvp dump-messages path
RSVP message dump debugging is on

PE2# configure terminal
PE2(config)# interface GigabitEthernet2
PE2(config-if)# shutdown
Incoming Path:
version:1 flags:0000 cksum:1D73 ttl:253 reserved:0 length:196
SESSION              type 7 length 16:
Tun Dest:   10.1.100.2  Tun ID: 0  Ext Tun ID: 10.1.100.6
HOP                  type 1 length 12:
Hop Addr: 10.1.23.3 LIH: 0x00000007
TIME_VALUES          type 1 length 8 :
Refresh Period (msec): 30000
* EXPLICIT_ROUTE      type 1 length 20:
10.1.23.2 (Strict IPv4 Prefix, 8 bytes, /32)
10.1.100.2 (Strict IPv4 Prefix, 8 bytes, /32)
LABEL_REQUEST        type 1 length 8 :
Layer 3 protocol ID: 2048
SESSION_ATTRIBUTE    type 7 length 28:
Setup Prio: 7, Holding Prio: 7
Flags: (0x7) Local Prot desired, Label Recording, SE Style
Session Name: PE6_t0
SENDER_TEMPLATE      type 7 length 12:
Tun Sender: 10.1.100.6  LSP ID: 8
SENDER_TSPEC         type 2 length 36:
version=0, length in words=7
Token bucket fragment (service_id=1, length=6 words
parameter id=127, flags=0, parameter length=5
average rate=0 bytes/sec, burst depth=1000 bytes
peak rate   =0 bytes/sec
min unit=40 bytes, max pkt size=500 bytes
ADSPEC               type 2 length 48:
version=0  length in words=10
General Parameters  break bit=0  service length=8
* IS Hops:3
Minimum Path Bandwidth (bytes/sec):0
Path Latency (microseconds):0
Path MTU:1500
Controlled Load Service  break bit=0  service length=0
```

How to Place Traffic into a TE Tunnel

For the MPLS TE tunnels to function properly, we have to tighten the tunnel to our internal routing paradigm. The following are some of the mostly adopted options to place traffic into TE tunnels, with each having its own interaction with IGP and accordingly processing to steer traffic:

- **Autoroute Announce:** By default, the shortest path is used for the destination prefix, and next-hop resolution is done for the next direct connection. When the autoroute feature is implemented, the next hop automatically becomes the destination address of the tunnel tailend (the tunnel destination).

  The drawback of this approach is that there is no traffic classification or separation, so all the traffic, regardless of importance, is sent through the LSP. Once MPLS traffic engineering is enabled and autoroute is used, traffic can be inserted only from the ingress node (the label-switched router).

  Any LSR other than the ingress point is unable to insert traffic into the Traffic Engineering LSP. Thus, the autoroute can only affect the path selection of the ingress LSR.

- **Forwarding Adjacency:** The MPLS Traffic Engineering Forwarding Adjacency feature allows a network administrator to handle a traffic engineering (TE) label-switched path (LSP) tunnel as a link in an Interior Gateway Protocol (IGP) network based on the Shortest Path First (SPF) algorithm.

Looking at an example to make it clearer and inspect all the related aspects of traffic engineering would be beneficial. Here, we use the topology illustrated in Figure 14-5.

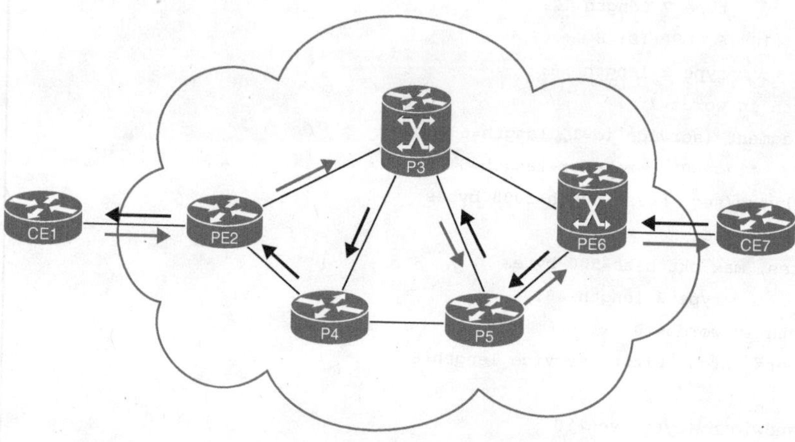

Figure 14-5 *MPLS Traffic Engineering Example*

Without going through the legacy configuration we went through in Chapter 12, "MPLS L3VPNs" (LDP, MP-BGP, VRF, VPNv4, etc.), we have put connectivity in place, as shown in Example 14-2.

Example 14-2   *End-to-End Connectivity*

```
CE1# traceroute 10.1.100.7 source loopback 0 numeric
VRF info: (vrf in name/id, vrf out name/id)
  1 172.16.12.2 22 msec 1 msec 2 msec
  2 10.1.23.3 [MPLS: Labels 16304/16609 Exp 0] 30 msec 9 msec 19 msec
  3 10.1.36.6 [MPLS: Label 16609 Exp 0] 13 msec 8 msec 8 msec
  4 172.16.67.7 9 msec 11 msec 9 msec
```

Because we did not alter any cost- or metric-related parameters across the core (OSPF area 0), naturally the traffic will follow the shortest path according to the OSPF default selection criteria, which is the PE2 → P3 → PE6 → CE7 path.

Now, we come to the TE-related tools by which we can force the traffic to follow a specific path according to certain conditions (using BW utilization as an example and distributing load on unutilized circuits). Also, we will go through the different options to place the desired traffic into the tunnel we will create.

RSVP is generally enabled from interface level mode (on the core links). We will instruct the router to use these core interfaces for assisting traffic engineering tunnels, as depicted in Example 14-3.

Example 14-3   *MPLS TE Tunnels and RSVP Configurations*

```
PE2(config)# interface GigabitEthernet2
PE2(config-if)# ip rsvp bandwidth
PE2(config-if)# mpls traffic-eng tunnels
LSP tunnels are not enabled on this router.
```

As seen, the **mpls traffic-eng tunnels** command generates a warning (log) message because the underlying IGP (OSPF) running on the interface is not ready to handle MPLS traffic engineering. (We did not instruct the IGP to use the necessary LSAs.) Also, the router itself should be able to terminate/initiate LSP traffic engineering tunnels. Example 14-4 shows how to enable the TE process over the target area under the running IGP by using OSPF.

Example 14-4   *IGP TE–Related Commands*

```
PE2(config)# mpls traffic-eng tunnels
PE2(config)# router ospf 1
PE2(config-router)# mpls traffic-eng area 0
PE2(config-router)# mpls traffic-eng router-id loopback 0
```

As mentioned, the traffic engineering tunnels that will be established are unidirectional, meaning we must establish two tunnels (each in a separate direction) if we need to control the traffic in both directions. The tunnel usually initiates at a node called the *head-end* and terminates on a device that is called the *tailend*. Figure 14-3 illustrates the main terminologies.

Now, we will force the traffic in one direction and then force it in another direction to achieve the necessary output. How will we place the traffic into the tunnel? First, we'll examine the autoroute announce option, which announces the tunnel to the running IGP (OSPF Area 0 in our case). Then we'll force the traffic between CE1 to CE7.

Let's start the tunnel configuration (which is a unidirectional tunnel) by defining the strict path option using the **ip explicit-path** command, as shown in Example 14-5, and then bind it to the tunnel interface using the **path-option** command.

Example 14-5   *Interface Tunnel with Explicit Path, IOS and IOS XE*

```
PE2(config)# ip explicit-path name PATH
PE2(cfg-ip-expl-path)# index 1 next-address 10.1.23.3
PE2(cfg-ip-expl-path)# index 2 next-address 10.1.35.5
PE2(cfg-ip-expl-path)# index 3 next-address 10.1.56.6

PE2(config)# interface Tunnel0
PE2(config-if)# ip unnumbered Loopback0
PE2(config-if)# tunnel mode mpls traffic-eng
PE2(config-if)# tunnel destination 10.1.100.6
PE2(config-if)# tunnel mpls traffic-eng autoroute announce
PE2(config-if)# tunnel mpls traffic-eng path-option 1 explicit name PATH
```

NOTE   The command on IOS XE does not explicitly force you to choose one of these options (**index 1 next-address** *{Loose | Strict}*, but it will choose *strict* by default.

Strict means that the next address in the explicit path belongs to an adjacent router to the router in the sequence. Loose means that the next address can belong to a router that is not necessarily adjacent.

On the other end of our topology (PE6), we will also build another unidirectional tunnel but with a different path to follow, as shown in Example 14-6.

Example 14-6   *Interface Tunnel with Explicit Path, IOS XR*

```
RP/0/0/CPU0:P6(config)# explicit-path name REVERSEPATH
RP/0/0/CPU0:P6(config-expl-path)# index 1 next-address strict ipv4 unicast 10.1.56.5
RP/0/0/CPU0:P6(config-expl-path)# index 2 next-address strict ipv4 unicast 10.1.35.3
RP/0/0/CPU0:P6(config-expl-path)# index 3 next-address strict ipv4 unicast 10.1.34.4
RP/0/0/CPU0:P6(config-expl-path)# index 4 next-address strict ipv4 unicast 10.1.24.2

RP/0/0/CPU0:P6(config)# interface tunnel-te0
RP/0/0/CPU0:P6(config-if)# ipv4 unnumbered Loopback0
RP/0/0/CPU0:P6(config-if)# autoroute announce
RP/0/0/CPU0:P6(config-if-tunte-aa)# destination 10.1.100.2
RP/0/0/CPU0:P6(config-if)# path-option 1 explicit name REVERSEPATH
```

If we now check the relevant output starting from end CEs to validate the path, we can ascertain the paths created through the network for the traffic to maintain reachability with the autoroute announce functionality that is confirmed, which can be validated through Example 14-7.

Example 14-7 *Connectivity Validation Between CEs*

```
CE1# traceroute 10.1.100.7 source loopback 0 numeric
VRF info: (vrf in name/id, vrf out name/id)
  1 172.16.12.2 2 msec 1 msec 1 msec
  2 10.1.23.3 [MPLS: Labels 16308/16609 Exp 0] 14 msec 12 msec 14 msec
  3 10.1.35.5 [MPLS: Labels 505/16609 Exp 0] 18 msec 14 msec 12 msec
  4 10.1.56.6 [MPLS: Label 16609 Exp 0] 10 msec 10 msec 12 msec
  5 172.16.67.7 14 msec 13 msec 11 msec


CE7# traceroute 10.1.100.1 source loopback 0 numeric
VRF info: (vrf in name/id, vrf out name/id)
  1 172.16.67.6 2 msec 1 msec 1 msec
  2 10.1.56.5 [MPLS: Labels 507/207 Exp 0] 16 msec 12 msec 20 msec
  3 10.1.35.3 [MPLS: Labels 16307/207 Exp 0] 13 msec 21 msec 20 msec
  4 10.1.34.4 [MPLS: Labels 401/207 Exp 0] 29 msec 30 msec 17 msec
  5 172.16.12.2 [MPLS: Label 207 Exp 0] 31 msec 13 msec 13 msec
  6 172.16.12.1 10 msec 11 msec 9 msec
```

Example 14-8 lists comprehensive output for the traffic engineering tunnels created on PE2 with all associated aspects.

Example 14-8 *Traffic Engineering Tunnel Details*

```
PE2# show mpls traffic-eng tunnels
P2P TUNNELS/LSPs:


Name: PE2_t0                              (Tunnel0) Destination: 10.1.100.6
  Status:
    Admin: up        Oper: up      Path: valid      Signalling: connected
    path option 1, type explicit PATH (Basis for Setup, path weight 3)
  Config Parameters:
    Bandwidth: 0         kbps (Global)  Priority: 7  7    Affinity: 0x0/0xFFFF
    Metric Type: TE (default)
    Path-selection Tiebreaker:
      Global: not set    Tunnel Specific: not set    Effective: min-fill (default)
    Hop Limit: disabled [ignore: Explicit Path Option with all Strict Hops]
    Cost Limit: disabled
    Path-invalidation timeout: 10000 msec (default), Action: Tear
    AutoRoute: enabled  LockDown: disabled Loadshare: 0 [0] bw-based
```

```
    auto-bw: disabled
   Fault-OAM: disabled, Wrap-Protection: disabled, Wrap-Capable: No
  Active Path Option Parameters:
   State: explicit path option 1 is active
   BandwidthOverride: disabled  LockDown: disabled  Verbatim: disabled
  Node Hop Count: 3
  InLabel  : -
  OutLabel : GigabitEthernet2, 16308
  Next Hop : 10.1.23.3
  RSVP Signalling Info:
      Src 10.1.100.2, Dst 10.1.100.6, Tun_Id 0, Tun_Instance 309
   RSVP Path Info:
    My Address: 10.1.23.2
    Explicit Route: 10.1.23.3 10.1.35.5 10.1.56.6 10.1.100.6
    Record   Route:   NONE
    Tspec: ave rate=0 kbits, burst=1000 bytes, peak rate=0 kbits
   RSVP Resv Info:
    Record   Route:   NONE
    Fspec: ave rate=0 kbits, burst=1000 bytes, peak rate=0 kbits
  History:
   Tunnel:
    Time since created: 1 days, 3 hours, 45 minutes
    Time since path change: 1 days, 12 minutes
    Number of LSP IDs (Tun_Instances) used: 309
   Current LSP: [ID: 309]
    Uptime: 1 days, 12 minutes
    Selection: reoptimization
   Prior LSP: [ID: 308]
    ID: path option unknown
    Removal Trigger: configuration changed (severe)
LSP Tunnel P6_t0 is signalled, connection is up
  InLabel  : GigabitEthernet3, implicit-null
  Prev Hop : 10.1.24.4
  OutLabel : -
  RSVP Signalling Info:
      Src 10.1.100.6, Dst 10.1.100.2, Tun_Id 0, Tun_Instance 2
   RSVP Path Info:
    My Address: 10.1.100.2
    Explicit Route: NONE
    Record   Route:   NONE
    Tspec: ave rate=0 kbits, burst=1000 bytes, peak rate=0 kbits
   RSVP Resv Info:
    Record   Route:   NONE
    Fspec: ave rate=0 kbits, burst=1000 bytes, peak rate=0 kbits
```

As we can see, a number is associated with the **tunnel mpls traffic-eng path-option** command, which is the preference for the path to be used. In our example here, we have only one available path. What we will examine now is the backup for this primary path with less preference.

NOTE   As we can see from the following command, several options can be used as backup (and, in fact, as the primary option).

```
PE2(config-if)# tunnel mpls traffic-eng path-option 2 ?
  dynamic          setup based on dynamically calculated path
  explicit         setup based on preconfigured path
  old-explicit     setup based on preconfigured tsp-hop path
  segment-routing  setup based on destination segment
  static           setup based on static next hop
```

For this example, we will choose the dynamic option. Example 14-9 shows the command added (with higher preference).

Example 14-9   *MPLS TE Path Options*

```
PE2(config)# interface Tunnel0
PE2(config-if)# tunnel mpls traffic-eng path-option 2 dynamic

PE2# show mpls traffic-eng tunnels tunnel 0 detail | include path option
    path option 1, type explicit PATH (Basis for Setup, path weight 3)
    path option 2, type dynamic
    State: explicit path option 1 is active
      ID: path option unknown
```

To validate the preference and traffic redirection using the dynamic path, we will create a failure along the primary path (LSP). Example 14-10 shows the output after disabling the interface connecting P3 to P5.

Example 14-10   *MPLS TE Tunnel Details*

```
PE2# show mpls traffic-eng tunnels tunnel 0 detail | include path option
    path option 2, type dynamic (Basis for Setup, path weight 2)
    path option 1, type explicit PATH
    State: dynamic path option 2 is active
      ID: path option unknown
```

When we check the connectivity after the dynamic path took over, traffic from both CEs will follow the dynamic path relying on the IGP metric. Let's validate this and check the output in Example 14-11.

Example 14-11 *MPLS TE Path Option Manipulation*

```
RP/0/0/CPU0:P6(config)# interface tunnel-te0
RP/0/0/CPU0:P6(config-if)# path-option 2 dynamic

CE1# traceroute 10.1.100.7 source loopback 0 numeric
VRF info: (vrf in name/id, vrf out name/id)
  1 172.16.12.2 1 msec 1 msec 1 msec
  2 10.1.23.3 [MPLS: Labels 16308/16609 Exp 0] 12 msec 14 msec 12 msec
  3 10.1.36.6 [MPLS: Label 16609 Exp 0] 8 msec 9 msec 9 msec
  4 172.16.67.7 11 msec 9 msec 8 msec

CE7# traceroute 10.1.100.1 source loopback 0 numeric
VRF info: (vrf in name/id, vrf out name/id)
  1 172.16.67.6 3 msec 1 msec 2 msec
  2 10.1.36.3 [MPLS: Labels 16307/207 Exp 0] 9 msec 18 msec 9 msec
  3 172.16.12.2 [MPLS: Label 207 Exp 0] 24 msec 25 msec 9 msec
  4 172.16.12.1 8 msec 14 msec 12 msec
```

It could take some time for the convergence process to take place, depending on the hardware box being used, so we can force soft optimization, as shown in Example 14-12.

Example 14-12 *MPLS TE Optimization*

```
PE2# mpls traffic-eng reoptimize tunnel 0

CE1# traceroute 10.1.100.7 source loopback 0 numeric
VRF info: (vrf in name/id, vrf out name/id)
  1 172.16.12.2 1 msec 0 msec 2 msec
  2 10.1.23.3 [MPLS: Labels 16310/16609 Exp 0] 11 msec 12 msec 11 msec
  3 10.1.35.5 [MPLS: Labels 504/16609 Exp 0] 19 msec 13 msec 19 msec
  4 10.1.56.6 [MPLS: Label 16609 Exp 0] 11 msec 11 msec 117 msec
  5 172.16.67.7 11 msec 10 msec 11 msec
```

Now, let's examine the other available options for placing the traffic into the tunnel. By using static routes, we flattened the topology to a single area. We can quickly check the route table at the end CE, as demonstrated by Example 14-13.

Example 14-13 *OSPF Learned Routes*

```
CE1# show ip route ospf | include 10.1.100.7
O       10.1.100.7/32 [110/5] via 10.1.12.2, 00:07:29, GigabitEthernet0/0
```

The only statement we have removed from the tunnel interface is the autoroute announce, as depicted in Example 14-14.

Example 14-14   *MPLS TE Tunnel Configuration, Without **autoroute announce***

```
PE2# show running-config interface tunnel0
interface Tunnel0
 ip unnumbered Loopback0
 tunnel mode mpls traffic-eng
 tunnel destination 10.1.100.6
 tunnel mpls traffic-eng path-option 1 explicit name PATH
```

Checking the trace route from both options, as in Example 14-15, will clearly show that we are solely depending on the routing table (OSPF as an IGP with a default metric because we did not manipulate any cost-related values).

Example 14-15   *Traceroute Outputs Between CEs*

```
CE1# traceroute 10.1.100.7 source loopback 0 numeric
VRF info: (vrf in name/id, vrf out name/id)
  1 10.1.12.2 0 msec 0 msec 0 msec
  2 10.1.23.3 3 msec 4 msec 3 msec
  3 10.1.36.6 5 msec 5 msec 6 msec
  4 10.1.67.7 5 msec 7 msec 7 msec


CE7# traceroute 10.1.100.1 source loopback 0 numeric
VRF info: (vrf in name/id, vrf out name/id)
  1 10.1.67.6 2 msec 1 msec 1 msec
  2 10.1.36.3 5 msec 9 msec 6 msec
  3 10.1.23.2 16 msec 20 msec 6 msec
  4 10.1.12.1 7 msec 6 msec 6 msec
```

Now, we will force the traffic to use the tunnel interfaces created on both PE2 and PE6 to use the predefined explicit path we used with the autoroute announce option and check the relevant path followed, as shown in Example 14-16.

Example 14-16   *Static Routes for Placing Traffic on the Tunnel*

```
PE2(config)# ip route 10.1.100.7 255.255.255.255 Tunnel0


RP/0/0/CPU0:P6(config)# router static
RP/0/0/CPU0:P6(config-static)# address-family ipv4 unicast
RP/0/0/CPU0:P6(config-static-afi)# 10.1.100.1/32 tunnel-te0


CE1# traceroute 10.1.100.7 source loopback 0 numeric
VRF info: (vrf in name/id, vrf out name/id)
  1 10.1.12.2 1 msec 2 msec 1 msec
  2 10.1.23.3 [MPLS: Label 16310 Exp 0] 35 msec 6 msec 8 msec
```

```
  3 10.1.35.5 [MPLS: Label 502 Exp 0] 9 msec 9 msec 9 msec
  4 10.1.56.6 9 msec 8 msec 11 msec
  5 10.1.67.7 10 msec 12 msec 12 msec
```

```
CE7# traceroute 10.1.100.1 source loopback 0 numeric
VRF info: (vrf in name/id, vrf out name/id)
  1 10.1.67.6 2 msec 1 msec 1 msec
  2 10.1.56.5 [MPLS: Label 503 Exp 0] 10 msec 16 msec 11 msec
  3 10.1.35.3 [MPLS: Label 16311 Exp 0] 16 msec 14 msec 25 msec
  4 10.1.34.4 [MPLS: Label 407 Exp 0] 23 msec 12 msec 13 msec
  5 10.1.24.2 9 msec 13 msec 8 msec
  6 10.1.12.1 9 msec 17 msec 10 msec
```

The tunnels use static routes for placing the traffic into the tunnels, as proved by
Example 14-17.

Example 14-17 *MPLS Traffic Engineering Tunnels Brief*

```
PE2# show mpls traffic-eng tunnels tunnel 0 brief
Signalling Summary:
    LSP Tunnels Process:            running
    Passive LSP Listener:           running
    RSVP Process:                   running
    Forwarding:                     enabled
    auto-tunnel:
        p2p    Disabled (0), id-range:62336-64335
    Periodic reoptimization:        every 3600 seconds, next in 541 seconds
    Periodic FRR Promotion:         Not Running
    Periodic auto-bw collection:    every 300 seconds, next in 245 seconds
    SR tunnel max label push:       13 primary path labels (13 repair path labels)
TUNNEL NAME                    DESTINATION      UP IF    DOWN IF   STATE/PROT
PE2_t0                         10.1.100.6       -        Gi2       up/up
```

```
PE2# show mpls forwarding-table detail
Local     Outgoing   Prefix         Bytes Label   Outgoing    Next Hop
Label     Label      or Tunnel Id   Switched      interface
201       Pop Label  0/1[TE-Bind]   0             Tu0         point2point
        MAC/Encaps=14/18, MRU=1500, Label Stack{16310}, via Gi2
        506A8300430350518400370188847 03FB6000
        No output feature configured
```

As we can see from Example 14-18, we can inspect the label assignments associated with the
tunnel interface.

Example 14-18   *MPLS Forwarding Table Output*

```
PE2# show mpls forwarding-table
Local        Outgoing   Prefix          Bytes Label   Outgoing    Next Hop
Label        Label      or Tunnel Id    Switched      interface
201     [T]  Pop Label  0/1[TE-Bind]    0             Tu0         point2point
207          No Label   10.1.100.1/32[V] 4812          Gi1         172.16.12.1

PE2# show mpls traffic-eng tunnels tunnel 0 | include Label
  InLabel  : -
  OutLabel : GigabitEthernet2, 16310

PE2# show mpls traffic-eng tunnels source-id 10.1.100.2 destination 10.1.100.6 |
include Label
  InLabel  : -
  OutLabel : GigabitEthernet2, 16310
```

With autoroute and static route, MPLS-TE provides for unequal-cost load balancing. Static routes inherit unequal-cost load sharing when recursing through a tunnel. IP routing has equal-cost load balancing but not unequal-cost. Unequal-cost load balancing is difficult to implement while guaranteeing a loop-free topology. Therefore, because MPLS does not forward based on the IP header, permanent routing loops do not occur. Further, 16 hash buckets are available for the next hop, and these are shared in rough proportion to the configured tunnel bandwidth or load-share value.

Forwarding Adjacency

The MPLS Traffic Engineering Forwarding Adjacency feature allows a network administrator to handle a traffic engineering (TE) label-switched path (LSP) tunnel as a link in an Interior Gateway Protocol (IGP) network based on the Shortest Path First (SPF) algorithm.

The IGP database grows when the MPLS Traffic Engineering Forwarding Adjacency feature is used, since it advertises a TE tunnel as a link, which is often taken into consideration during design. Additionally, because TE tunnels are unidirectional by nature, we need to configure two tunnels for each direction.

In the IGP network, TE tunnel interfaces are advertised in the exact same manner as traditional links. Then, even if they are not the headend of any TE tunnels, routers may use these advertisements in their IGPs for calculating the SPF.

Let's look at the topology (the global routing table in place from CE1 to CE7) in Figure 14-6 to demonstrate the forwarding adjacency functionality. Typically, CE1 will use the lower path (P4 → P5 → CE2) because it has lower OSPF cost by default, as depicted in Example 14-19 and shown in the figure.

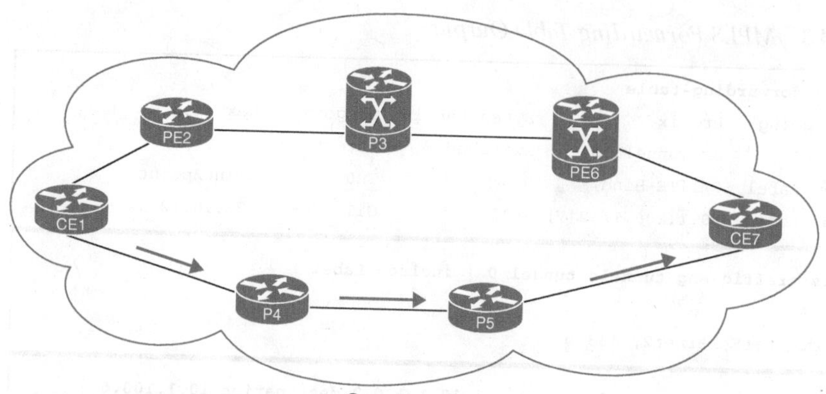

Figure 14-6 *MPLS TE Forwarding Adjacency*

In Example 14-19, we start investigating the forwarding adjacency list for the trace output between the CEs.

Example 14-19 *Traceroute Output*

```
CE1# traceroute 10.1.100.7 source loopback 0 numeric
VRF info: (vrf in name/id, vrf out name/id)
  1 10.1.14.4 2 msec 1 msec 0 msec
  2 10.1.45.5 1 msec 2 msec 1 msec
  3 10.1.57.7 2 msec 2 msec 3 msec
```

Enabling autoroute won't help here because this only changes the routing table of the PE routers. Autoroute doesn't advertise anything to other routers.

Therefore, we will fix this by having two TE tunnels—one from PE2 to PE6 and the other one from P4 to P5, as shown in Figure 14-7. The goal is to be able to utilize both links simultaneously and gain redundancy.

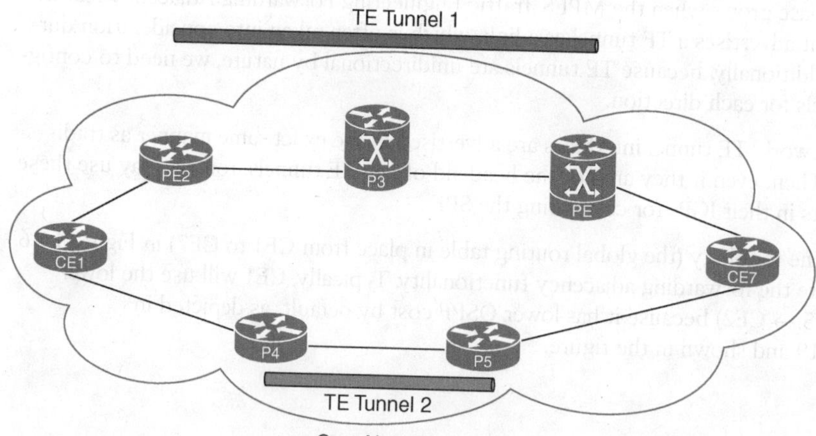

Figure 14-7 *MPLS Traffic Engineering Forwarding Adjacency*

MPLS TE tunnels are unidirectional but IS-IS or OSPF assume links are bidirectional. Because forwarding adjacency advertises the TE tunnel as a link in your IGP, we need tunnels in both directions.

Example 14-20 shows the commands needed to operationalize the forwarding adjacency using the **tunnel mpls traffic-end forwarding-adjacency** command from the interface tunnel configuration mode.

Example 14-20 *Forwarding Adjacency Configuration*

```
PE2(config)# interface Tunnel0
PE2(config-if)# tunnel mode mpls traffic-eng
PE2(config-if)# tunnel destination 10.1.100.6
PE2(config-if)# tunnel mpls traffic-eng forwarding-adjacency
PE2(config-if)# tunnel mpls traffic-eng path-option 1 dynamic
```

NOTE   We will have to adjust the cost of the IGP (OSPF in our demonstration example) to make the tunnels attractive to the traffic between CE1 and CE7. (All that the links cost is 1 from an OSPF perspective, and therefore, we will have to choose a value less than 4 in our example, because it is the calculated metric, as shown in Example 14-21.)

Example 14-21 *Adjusting OSPF Cost*

```
CE1# show ip route 10.1.100.7
Routing entry for 10.1.100.7/32
  Known via "ospf 1", distance 110, metric 4, type intra area
  Last update from 10.1.14.4 on GigabitEthernet0/1, 09:38:40 ago
  Routing Descriptor Blocks:
  * 10.1.14.4, from 10.1.100.7, 09:46:16 ago, via GigabitEthernet0/1
      Route metric is 4, traffic share count is 1
```

```
PE2(config)# interface Tunnel0
PE2(config-if)# ip ospf cost 1
```

```
CE1# show ip route 10.1.100.7
Routing entry for 10.1.100.7/32
  Known via "ospf 1", distance 110, metric 4, type intra area
  Last update from 10.1.12.2 on GigabitEthernet0/0, 00:01:04 ago
  Routing Descriptor Blocks:
  * 10.1.14.4, from 10.1.100.7, 09:52:17 ago, via GigabitEthernet0/1
      Route metric is 4, traffic share count is 1
    10.1.12.2, from 10.1.100.7, 00:01:04 ago, via GigabitEthernet0/0
      Route metric is 4, traffic share count is 1
```

Before we go through the more detailed convergence aspect of the forwarding adjacency, Example 14-22 lists **show** commands we can use to validate the operational functionality.

Example 14-22   *Forwarding Adjacency Detailed Output*

```
PE2# show mpls traffic-eng forwarding-adjacency
  destination 10.1.100.6, area ospf 1  area 0, has 1 tunnels
    Tunnel0      (load balancing metric 0, nexthop 10.1.100.6)
                 (flags: Forward-Adjacency holdtime 0)

PE2# show ip ospf database opaque-area type traffic-engineering adv-router
10.1.100.2

            OSPF Router with ID (10.1.100.2) (Process ID 1)


              Type-10 Opaque Area Link States (Area 0)


  LS age: 559
  Options: (No TOS-capability, DC)
  LS Type: Opaque Area Link
  Link State ID: 1.0.0.0
  Opaque Type: 1 (Traffic Engineering)
  Opaque ID: 0
  Advertising Router: 10.1.100.2
  LS Seq Number: 800000FC
  Checksum: 0x193A
  Length: 28
  Fragment number : 0

    MPLS TE router ID : 10.1.100.2

    Number of Links : 0


  LS age: 559
  Options: (No TOS-capability, DC)
  LS Type: Opaque Area Link
  Link State ID: 1.0.0.2
  Opaque Type: 1 (Traffic Engineering)
  Opaque ID: 2
  Advertising Router: 10.1.100.2
  LS Seq Number: 800000DC
  Checksum: 0x8C66
  Length: 132
```

```
Fragment number : 2

   Link connected to Point-to-Point network
      Link ID : 10.1.100.3
      Interface Address : 10.1.23.2
      Neighbor Address : 10.1.23.3
      Admin Metric : 1
      Maximum bandwidth : 125000000
      Maximum reservable bandwidth : 93750000
      Number of Priority : 8
      Priority 0 : 93750000      Priority 1 : 93750000
      Priority 2 : 93750000      Priority 3 : 93750000
      Priority 4 : 93750000      Priority 5 : 93750000
      Priority 6 : 93750000      Priority 7 : 93750000
      Affinity Bit : 0x0
      IGP Metric : 1
   Number of Links : 1
```

When we configure the forwarding adjacency, we can control the time that a TE tunnel waits after going down before informing the network, as shown in Example 14-23.

Example 14-23 *Forwarding Adjacency Holdtime*

```
PE2(config-if)# tunnel mpls traffic-eng forwarding-adjacency holdtime ?
  <0-4294967295>  Holdtime on MPLS TE Down.
```

If the link fails, the tunnel might go down and come back up quickly as it finds a new path. This is not the sort of thing you want to advertise into your IGP because the link would be removed and readvertised, causing unnecessary IGP churn. The holdtime is how long the TE tunnel must be down before its status is advertised in the IGP. The default forwarding adjacency holdtime is 0 ms.

Let's check using a couple of commands and turn on debugging, as shown in Example 14-24.

Example 14-24 *Forwarding Adjacency Debug Output*

```
PE2# debug mpls traffic-eng forwarding-adjacency detail
MPLS traffic-eng forwarding-adjacency over tunnels debugging is on

PE2(config-if)# tunnel mpls traffic-eng forwarding-adjacency holdtime 4000

TE-FAdj: FA Tunnel0 [353] (hold up), start hold up timer (4000 ms)
TE-FAdj: FA Tunnel0 [353] (hold up), set output i/f to null0
TE-FAdj: FA Tunnel0 [353] (hold up), not connected
%OSPF-5-ADJCHG: Process 1, Nbr 10.1.100.3 on GigabitEthernet2 from FULL to DOWN,
Neighbor Down: Interface down or detached
```

```
TE-FAdj: FA Tunnel0 [353] (hold up), verify, setup flags 0x1000A009
TE-FAdj: FA Tunnel0 [353] (hold up), tear down failed LSP
TE-FAdj: FA Tunnel0 [353] (hold up), verify, setup flags 0x1001A00D
TE-Auto: routing protocol get: destination 10.1.100.6, area ospf 1  area 0, has 1
tunnels
Tunnel0      (load balancing metric 0, nexthop 10.1.100.6)
 (flags: Forward-Adjacency holdtime 4000)
TE-Auto: routing protocol get: destination 10.1.100.6, area ospf 1  area 0, has 1
tunnels
Tunnel0      (load balancing metric 0, nexthop 10.1.100.6)
 (flags: Forward-Adjacency holdtime 4000)
%LINK-5-CHANGED: Interface GigabitEthernet2, changed state to administratively down
%LINEPROTO-5-UPDOWN: Line protocol on Interface GigabitEthernet2, changed state to
down
TE-FAdj: FA Tunnel0 [353] (hold up), hold timer fired while in hold up
TE-FAdj: FA Tunnel0 [353] (hold up), not connected
TE-FAdj: FA Tunnel0 [353] (up), clear hold up
%LINEPROTO-5-UPDOWN: Line protocol on Interface Tunnel0, changed state to down
```

```
PE2(config)# interface GigabitEthernet2
PE2(config-if)# no shutdown
%LINK-3-UPDOWN: Interface GigabitEthernet2, changed state to up
%LINEPROTO-5-UPDOWN: Line protocol on Interface GigabitEthernet2, changed state to
up
%OSPF-5-ADJCHG: Process 1, Nbr 10.1.100.3 on GigabitEthernet2 from LOADING to FULL,
Loading Done
%LINEPROTO-5-UPDOWN: Line protocol on Interface Tunnel0, changed state to up
TE-Auto: announcement that destination 10.1.100.6, area ospf 1  area 0, has 1
tunnels
Tunnel0      (load balancing metric 0, nexthop 10.1.100.6)
 (flags: Forward-Adjacency holdtime 4000)
TE-Auto: routing protocol get: destination 10.1.100.6, area ospf 1  area 0, has 1
tunnels
Tunnel0      (load balancing metric 0, nexthop 10.1.100.6)
 (flags: Forward-Adjacency holdtime 4000)
TE-Auto: routing protocol get: destination 10.1.100.6, area ospf 1  area 0, has 1
tunnels
Tunnel0      (load balancing metric 0, nexthop 10.1.100.6)
 (flags: Forward-Adjacency holdtime 4000)
! As can be seen from the flag denoted as Forward-Adjacency, the holdtime value
! shows as 4000 as per the configuration statement.
```

Use Case: Per VRF MPLS Traffic Engineering

As we mentioned previously, one of the main goals of traffic engineering is to properly utilize unused links. One of the use cases that we can utilize within service provider networks is to create traffic engineering tunnels and associate them with customers' VRFs.

This means that we can send **Virtual Routing and Forwarding (VRF)** traffic into a tunnel and send another VRF's traffic to another tunnel. From a BW utilization perspective, these tunnels eventually will have a specific path to follow (how we placed the traffic into the tunnel).

Figure 14-8 shows the topology used to demonstrate this feature. The following are the most important aspects of this use case that need to be clarified:

- We control traffic on a VRF basis and steer the traffic across the tunnels to provide redundancy and to improve BW utilization.

- We look at the behavior of the traffic engineering tunnels compared to BGP VPNv4 sessions.

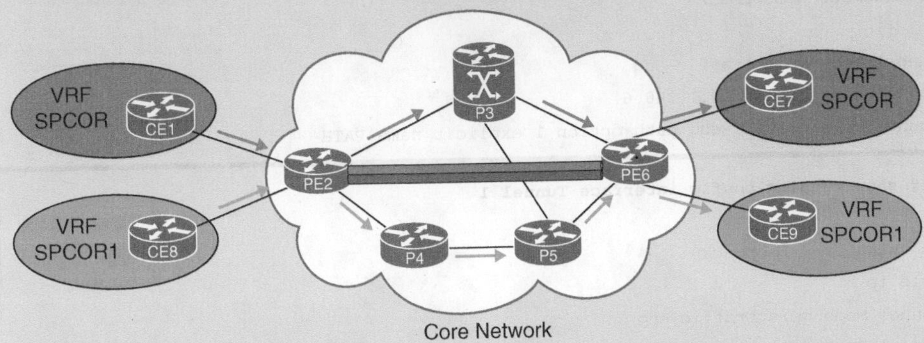

Figure 14-8 *Per-VRF MPLS TE Tunnels*

Prefixes are carried between distinct PEs over MP-BGP (regarding L3VPN), and we still need MP-BGP to carry labeled VPNv4 and labeled VPNv6 prefixes. A traffic engineering tunnel by itself doesn't create an end-to-end LSP; the LSP is created between the two iBGP loopbacks.

For traffic traversing the TE tunnel, the label stack will contain three labels: the tunnel label, which is the top label; the IGP label; and the VPN label, which is the bottom label. That's why we still need the customer VPN prefixes to be carried over the MP-BGP even though we have a tunnel, but we can force the traffic to traverse the tunnel to reach the egress LSR that terminates the LSP.

However, if you have a TE tunnel and you would like only specific VRFs to traverse through that tunnel, you will need to influence the BGP NEXT-HOP and force the IGP traffic to use this tunnel to reach the BGP next hop.

You would need to create a new loopback interface on the egress PE, and in the ingress PE, you would create a static route for that loopback pointing to the tunnel interface. You do this so that when BGP tries to establish an end-to-end LSP, it uses the TE tunnel interface to reach the BGP next hop.

Example 14-25 lists the main configuration aspects of the previously discussed use case with supporting **show** commands verifying what we have deployed.

Example 14-25 *MPLS TE Per-VRF Configuration*

```
PE2# show ip explicit-paths
PATH PATH (strict source route, path complete, generation 17)
    1: next-address 10.1.23.3
    2: next-address 10.1.36.6
PATH PATH2 (strict source route, path complete, generation 22)
    1: next-address 10.1.24.4
    2: next-address 10.1.45.5
    3: next-address 10.1.56.6

PE2# show running-config interface Tunnel 0
interface Tunnel0
 ip unnumbered Loopback0
 mpls ip
 tunnel mode mpls traffic-eng
 tunnel destination 10.1.100.6
 tunnel mpls traffic-eng path-option 1 explicit name PATH

PE2# show running-config interface Tunnel 1
interface Tunnel1
 ip unnumbered Loopback0
 mpls ip
 tunnel mode mpls traffic-eng
 tunnel destination 10.1.100.6
 tunnel mpls traffic-eng path-option 1 explicit name PATH2

PE2# show ip interface brief | include Loop
Loopback0          10.1.100.2        YES NVRAM  up         up
Loopback1          172.16.2.2        YES manual up         up
Loopback2          192.168.2.2       YES manual up         up

PE2# show running-config | section ip (route|Tunnel)
ip route 172.16.6.6 255.255.255.255 Tunnel0
ip route 192.168.6.6 255.255.255.255 Tunnel1

CE1# traceroute 10.1.100.7 source loopback0 numeric
VRF info: (vrf in name/id, vrf out name/id)
  1 172.16.12.2 1 msec 1 msec 1 msec
  2 10.1.23.3 [MPLS: Labels 16304/402 Exp 0] 8 msec 5 msec 111 msec
  3 172.16.67.6 [MPLS: Label 402 Exp 0] 8 msec 6 msec 9 msec
  4 172.16.67.7 9 msec 15 msec 6 msec

CE8# traceroute 10.1.100.9 source loopback0 numeric
```

```
VRF info: (vrf in name/id, vrf out name/id)
 1 172.16.28.2 2 msec 1 msec 2 msec
 2 10.1.24.4 [MPLS: Labels 400/409 Exp 0] 8 msec 9 msec 4 msec
 3 10.1.45.5 [MPLS: Labels 505/409 Exp 0] 4 msec 5 msec 7 msec
 4 172.16.69.6 [MPLS: Label 409 Exp 0] 12 msec 7 msec 5 msec
 5 172.16.69.9 7 msec 6 msec 3 msec
```

MPLS Fast Reroute (FRR)

MPLS Fast Reroute (FRR) is a mechanism used to protect LSPs in MPLS Traffic Engineering deployments from both link and node failures. FRR repairs the protected LSPs locally by rerouting the LSPs over backup tunnels bypassing either the failed link or node.

- **Link Protection:** Backup tunnels that bypass a single link on the LSP's route offer link protection by redirecting traffic to the next hop in the case of a link failure. These backup tunnels, known as next-hop (NHOP) backup tunnels, end at the next hop of the LSP after the failure point.

- **Node Protection:** FRR offers node protection for LSPs by utilizing next-next-hop (NNHOP) backup tunnels. These backup tunnels are designed to bypass the next-hop nodes along the LSP paths and terminate at the node following the next-hop node. This allows them to effectively bypass any potential failures at the next-hop node and protect the LSPs. In the event of a node failure along the path, the node upstream of the failure can reroute the LSPs and their traffic around the failed node to the next-next-hop. Additionally, FRR leverages RSVP Hellos to expedite the detection of node failures. Furthermore, NNHOP backup tunnels also provide protection against link failures because they can bypass both the failed link and the node.

Figure 14-9 demonstrates the basic terminologies that construct the main components of MPLS FRR.

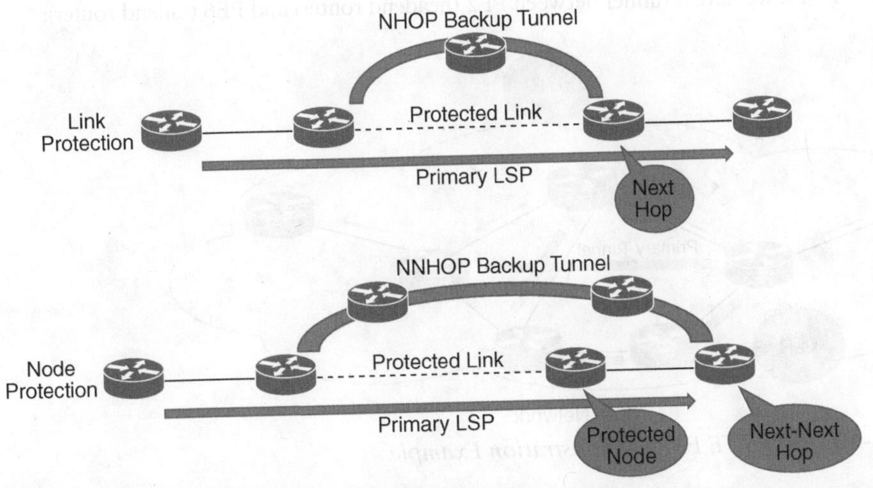

Figure 14-9 *MPLS TE FRR: Link and Node Protection*

Here are key aspects of MPLS Fast Reroute:

- Overall, MPLS FRR is a critical feature in MPLS networks, providing rapid fault recovery and ensuring high availability for real-time applications, voice services, and mission-critical data traffic. It enhances network resilience and minimizes the impact of network failures on the end-user experience.

- The default behavior of MPLS Traffic Engineering is that when something happens with a tunnel's LSP, the headend router calculates a best new path to the tailend router. This works, but it takes time. It could be too slow for delay-sensitive applications like VoIP, depending on the network size.

- MPLS supports FRR link and node protection. This provides recovery against link and node failures under ~50 ms.

FRR Terminology

Within the context of FRR, some naming conventions are associated with the routers within the core network that actually reflect the role of each in an FRR environment. The same applies to the tunnels that will be established across the intervening routers to functionalize the FRR and recovery.

- **Point of Local Repair (PLR):** This router is directly connected to a failed link or a failed node, where the backup tunnel starts.

- **Merge Point (MP):** This is the end of the backup tunnel, where the detour or facility backup joins the regular LSP path, from a failed state.

- **Next-Hop (NHOP) Backup Tunnels:** These backup tunnels bypass only a single link of the LSP's path providing link protection.

- **Next-Next-Hop (NNHOP) Backup Tunnels:** These backup tunnels bypass next-hop nodes along LSP paths providing node protection.

In Figure 14-10, we have a tunnel between PE2 (headend router) and PE6 (tailend router):

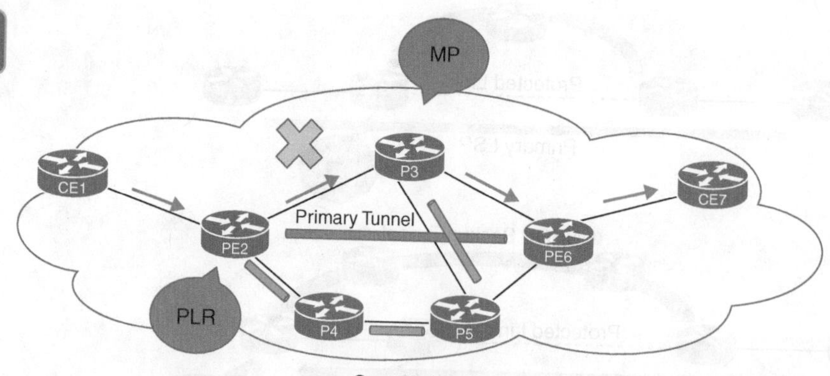

Figure 14-10 *MPLS TE FRR Demonstration Example*

Let's call this tunnel the "primary" tunnel. It's the tunnel that we want to protect. When something happens with the LSP because of a link or node failure, PE2 will calculate a new path.

With MPLS TE FRR, we configure a backup tunnel. When something happens with the LSP of the primary tunnel, instead of taking it down, we use the backup tunnel to forward the traffic.

This way, we repair the LSP at the point of failure, allowing traffic to continue. The headend router of the backup tunnel is PE2, and PE6 is the tailend. When we talk about the backup tunnel, we call the headend router the point of local repair (PLR) because this is where we repair the LSP. The tailend router is the merge point (MP) because this is where the traffic from the backup tunnel rejoins the LSP of the primary tunnel.

Once we use the backup tunnel, P3 will inform PE2 about this. PE2 will then recalculate a best new path for its tunnel. Once that is completed, we won't use the backup tunnel anymore.

As previously mentioned, MPLS TE fast reroute offers two protection options:

- Link protection

- Node protection

Link Protection

With link protection, we have a backup tunnel that bypasses only a single link of the LSP, as shown in Figure 14-11.

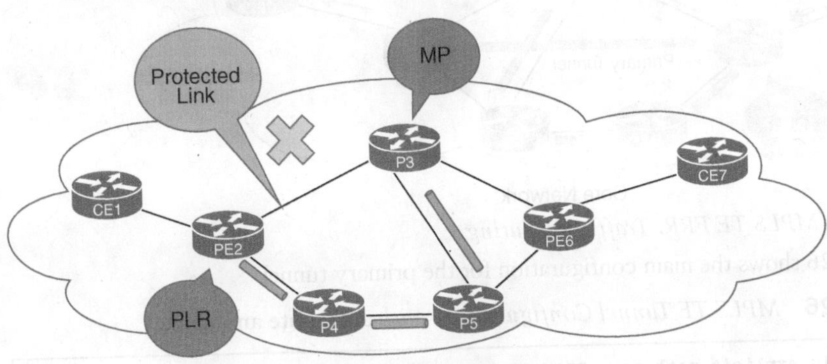

Figure 14-11 *MPLS TE FRR: Link Protection*

PE2 protects the link that connects to P3. We bypass this link by building a backup tunnel that goes through P4 and terminates at PE6. We call this backup tunnel a next-hop (NHOP) tunnel because it's a tunnel to the next hop (from P3's perspective), only bypassing the link.

Node Protection

With node protection, we have a backup tunnel that bypasses a next-hop node (router), as demonstrated in Figure 14-12.

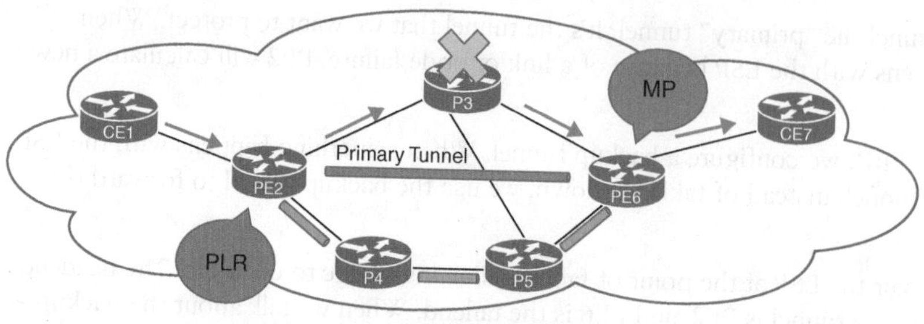

Figure 14-12 *MPLS TE FRR: Node Protection*

This backup tunnel starts at PE2 and terminates at P3. We call this backup tunnel a next-next-hop (NNHOP) tunnel because it's a tunnel to the next hop of the next-hop router. From P4's perspective, P5 is the next hop behind its next hop, P3. Node protection also offers link protection because we bypass both the link and the next-hop router.

Let's look at an example for link protection and see how the reroute process takes place. As illustrated in Figure 14-13, the primary path for CE1 to CE7 traffic will go over the PE2 → P3 → PE6 path.

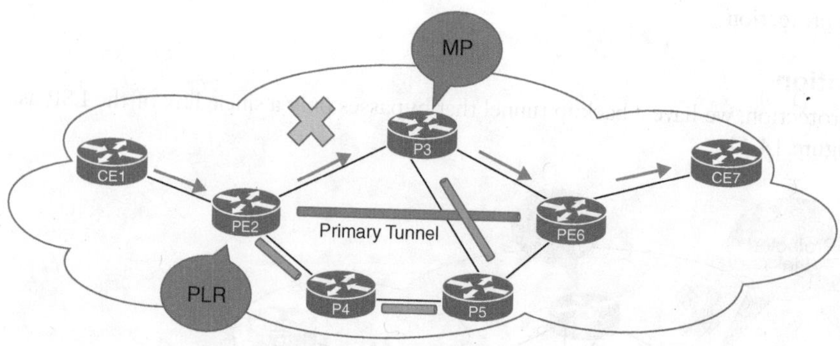

Figure 14-13 *MPLS TE FRR: Traffic Rerouting*

Example 14-26 shows the main configuration for the primary tunnel.

Example 14-26 *MPLS TE Tunnel Configuration, with* **autoroute announce**

```
PE2(config)# ip explicit-path name PRIMARY
PE2(cfg-ip-expl-path)# next-address 10.1.100.3
PE2(cfg-ip-expl-path)# next-address 10.1.100.6

PE2(config)# interface Tunnel0
PE2(config-if)# ip unnumbered Loopback0
PE2(config-if)# tunnel mode mpls traffic-eng
PE2(config-if)# tunnel destination 10.1.100.6
PE2(config-if)# tunnel mpls traffic-eng autoroute announce
PE2(config-if)# tunnel mpls traffic-eng path-option 1 explicit name PRIMARY
PE2(config-if)# tunnel mpls traffic-eng fast-reroute
```

Example 14-27 clarifies the functionality of the tunnel as well as the trace, as mentioned.

Example 14-27   *Traceroute Output*

```
CE1# traceroute 10.1.100.7 source loopback 0 numeric
VRF info: (vrf in name/id, vrf out name/id)
  1 10.1.12.2 2 msec 2 msec 1 msec
  2 10.1.23.3 [MPLS: Label 17 Exp 0] 4 msec 3 msec 3 msec
  3 10.1.36.6 4 msec 7 msec 4 msec
  4 10.1.67.7 4 msec 3 msec 3 msec
```

Now, we will build the backup tunnel that will take the path through PE2 → P4 → P5 → P3 (ending at P3, which is the merge point). Example 14-28 shows the command statements.

Example 14-28   *Backup MPLS TE Tunnel Configuration*

```
PE2(config)# ip explicit-path name REPAIR
PE2(cfg-ip-expl-path)# next-address 10.1.24.4
PE2(cfg-ip-expl-path)# next-address 10.1.45.5
PE2(cfg-ip-expl-path)# next-address 10.1.35.3

PE2(config)# interface Tunnel1
PE2(config-if)# ip unnumbered Loopback0
PE2(config-if)# tunnel mode mpls traffic-eng
PE2(config-if)# tunnel destination 10.1.100.3
PE2(config-if)# tunnel mpls traffic-eng path-option 1 explicit name REPAIR

P3(config)# ip explicit-path name REPAIR
P3(cfg-ip-expl-path)# next-address 10.1.35.5
P3(cfg-ip-expl-path)# next-address 10.1.45.4
P3(cfg-ip-expl-path)# next-address 10.1.24.2

P3(config)# interface Tunnel1
P3(config-if)# ip unnumbered Loopback0
P3(config-if)# tunnel mode mpls traffic-eng
P3(config-if)# tunnel destination 10.1.100.2
P3(config-if)# tunnel mpls traffic-eng path-option 1 explicit name REPAIR
```

The main concern is the PE2 → P3 link, for which we will associate the backup tunnels for the recovery to take place after any failure occurs.

Example 14-29 shows the command needed for the association.

Example 14-29 *Backup Tunnel for Reroute*

```
PE2(config)# interface GigabitEthernet0/1
PE2(config-if)# mpls traffic-eng backup-path Tunnel1
```

```
P3(config)# interface GigabitEthernet0/0
P3(config-if)# mpls traffic-eng backup-path Tunnel1
```

Example 14-30 verifies the status of the backup tunnel and how the database of the traffic engineering is updated with the new tunnel created for recovery.

Example 14-30 *MPLS TE FRR Database*

```
PE2# show mpls traffic-eng fast-reroute database
Headend frr information:
Protected tunnel          In-label Out intf/label   FRR intf/label   Status
Tunnel0                   Tun hd   Gio/1:17          Tu1:17           ready

LSP midpoint frr information:
LSP identifier            In-label Out intf/label   FRR intf/label   Status
```

```
PE2# show mpls traffic-eng tunnels backup
PE2_t1
  LSP Head, Tunnel1, Admin: up, Oper: up
  Src 10.1.100.2, Dest 10.1.100.3, Instance 6
  Fast Reroute Backup Provided:
    Protected i/fs: Gi0/1
    Protected lsps: 1 Active lsps: 0
    Backup BW: any pool unlimited; inuse: 0 kbps
```

```
P3# show mpls traffic-eng tunnels backup
P3_t1
  LSP Head, Tunnel1, Admin: up, Oper: up
  Src 10.1.100.3, Dest 10.1.100.2, Instance 5
  Fast Reroute Backup Provided:
    Protected i/fs: Gi0/0
    Protected lsps: 0 Active lsps: 0
    Backup BW: any pool unlimited; inuse: 0 kbps
```

Now we will disable one of the interfaces between PE2 and P3 to check how the recovery will take place and check the traffic redirection through the backup tunnel ending at the MP and continue to the destination, which is CE7. Example 14-31 shows the relevant output.

Example 14-31 *MPLS TE FRR Traffic Reroute*

```
PE2(config)# interface GigabitEthernet 0/1
PE2(config-if)# shutdown

PE2# show mpls traffic-eng fast-reroute database
Headend frr information:
Protected tunnel        In-label Out intf/label   FRR intf/label   Status
Tunnel0                 Tun hd   Gi0/1:17         Tu1:17           active


LSP midpoint frr information:
LSP identifier          In-label Out intf/label   FRR intf/label   Status

PE2# show mpls traffic-eng tunnels backup
PE2_t1
  LSP Head, Tunnel1, Admin: up, Oper: up
  Src 10.1.100.2, Dest 10.1.100.3, Instance 6
  Fast Reroute Backup Provided:
    Protected i/fs: Gi0/1
    Protected lsps: 1 Active lsps: 1
    Backup BW: any pool unlimited; inuse: 0 kbps

PE2# show ip rsvp reservation detail
Reservation:
  Tun Dest:   10.1.100.2  Tun ID: 0  Ext Tun ID: 10.1.100.6
  Tun Sender: 10.1.100.6  LSP ID: 150
  Next Hop: none
  Label: 1 (outgoing)
  Reservation Style is Shared-Explicit, QoS Service is Controlled-Load
  Resv ID handle: 0100040B.
  Created: 16:58:45 UTC Fri Mar 29 2024
  Average Bitrate is 0 bits/sec, Maximum Burst is 1K bytes
  Min Policed Unit: 0 bytes, Max Pkt Size: 1500 bytes
  Status: Proxied
  Policy: Accepted. Policy source(s): MPLS/TE
Reservation:
  Tun Dest:   10.1.100.2  Tun ID: 1  Ext Tun ID: 10.1.100.3
  Tun Sender: 10.1.100.3  LSP ID: 5
  Next Hop: none
  Label: 1 (outgoing)
  Reservation Style is Shared-Explicit, QoS Service is Controlled-Load
  Resv ID handle: 03000415.
```

```
  Created: 17:19:53 UTC Fri Mar 29 2024
  Average Bitrate is 0 bits/sec, Maximum Burst is 1K bytes
  Min Policed Unit: 0 bytes, Max Pkt Size: 1500 bytes
  Status: Proxied
  Policy: Accepted. Policy source(s): MPLS/TE
Reservation:
  Tun Dest:   10.1.100.3  Tun ID: 1  Ext Tun ID: 10.1.100.2
  Tun Sender: 10.1.100.2  LSP ID: 6
  Next Hop: 10.1.24.4 on GigabitEthernet0/2
  Label: 19 (outgoing)
  Reservation Style is Shared-Explicit, QoS Service is Controlled-Load
  Resv ID handle: 04000412.
  Created: 17:19:25 UTC Fri Mar 29 2024
  Average Bitrate is 0 bits/sec, Maximum Burst is 1K bytes
  Min Policed Unit: 0 bytes, Max Pkt Size: 1500 bytes
  Status:
  Policy: Accepted. Policy source(s): MPLS/TE
Reservation:
  Tun Dest:   10.1.100.6  Tun ID: 0  Ext Tun ID: 10.1.100.2
  Tun Sender: 10.1.100.2  LSP ID: 182
  FRR is in progress: (we are PLR)
   Bkup Next Hop is  10.1.35.3 on GigabitEthernet0/2
       Label     is  17 (outgoing)
   Orig Next Hop was 10.1.23.3 on GigabitEthernet0/1
       Label     was 17 (outgoing)
  Reservation Style is Shared-Explicit, QoS Service is Controlled-Load
  Resv ID handle: 0300040D.
  Created: 17:35:33 UTC Fri Mar 29 2024
  Average Bitrate is 0 bits/sec, Maximum Burst is 1K bytes
  Min Policed Unit: 0 bytes, Max Pkt Size: 1500 bytes
  RRO:
    10.1.100.3/32, Flags:0x20 (No Local Protection, Node-id)
      Label subobject: Flags 0x1, C-Type 1, Label 17
    10.1.100.6/32, Flags:0x20 (No Local Protection, Node-id)
      Label subobject: Flags 0x1, C-Type 1, Label 0
  Status:
  Policy: Accepted. Policy source(s): MPLS/TE
```

```
CE1# traceroute 10.1.100.7 source loopback 0 numeric
VRF info: (vrf in name/id, vrf out name/id)
  1 10.1.12.2 1 msec 1 msec 1 msec
  2 10.1.24.4 [MPLS: Labels 19/17 Exp 0] 4 msec 3 msec 4 msec
  3 10.1.45.5 [MPLS: Labels 19/17 Exp 0] 3 msec 3 msec 3 msec
  4 10.1.35.3 [MPLS: Label 17 Exp 0] 4 msec 3 msec 4 msec
  5 10.1.36.6 4 msec 4 msec 4 msec
  6 10.1.67.7 5 msec 5 msec 7 msec
```

Here's a quick snippet regarding the label assignment: if we check the MPLS tunnel 1 (which is the backup tunnel), as shown in Example 14-32, and the trace output from CE1, we can spot the label.

Example 14-32   *MPLS TE Label Tracking*

```
PE2# show mpls traffic-eng tunnels tunnel 1 | include Label
  InLabel  :  -
  OutLabel : GigabitEthernet0/2, 19
```

```
CE1# traceroute 10.1.100.7 source loopback 0 numeric
VRF info: (vrf in name/id, vrf out name/id)
  1 10.1.12.2 2 msec 1 msec 1 msec
  2 10.1.24.4 [MPLS: Labels 19/17 Exp 0] 3 msec 2 msec 3 msec
  3 10.1.45.5 [MPLS: Labels 19/17 Exp 0] 3 msec 3 msec 4 msec
  4 10.1.35.3 [MPLS: Label 17 Exp 0] 4 msec 3 msec 3 msec
  5 10.1.36.6 3 msec 4 msec 3 msec
  6 10.1.67.7 4 msec 4 msec 4 msec
```

FRR on IOS XR

Now, we will examine the same scenario by replacing PE6 (running on IOS XE) with a box running IOS XR to examine how the IOS XR functions with respect to FRR. Also, we will shed more light about the label assignment from an MPLS TE and FRR perspective.

Figure 14-14 shows the topology used to investigate the MPLS FRR capability and some configuration aspects from an IOS XR perspective.

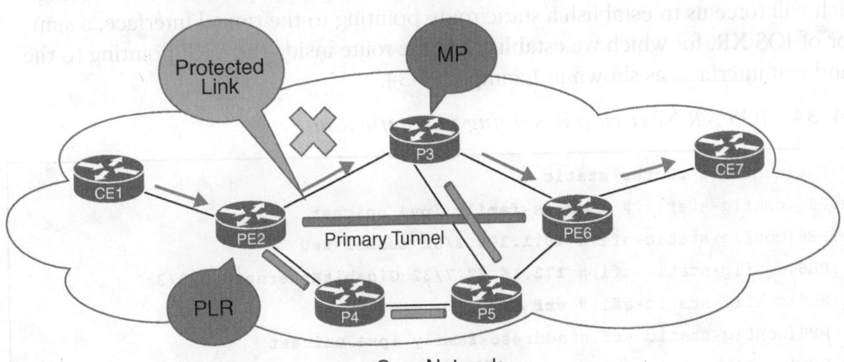

Figure 14-14   *MPLS TE FRR: Link Protection, IOS XR*

Because we already discussed how to configure the tunnel from an IOS XE perspective (PE2), let's focus on PE6 (which is IOS XR based). Example 14-33 lists the main configurations needed to establish a tunnel between PE2 and PE6 which the traffic from CE1 to CE7 will follow. What we have added to the previous example is an L3VPN service (with static routing in between PE to CE) to validate the label stacking as well.

Example 14-33 *IOS XR MPLS TE Configuration*

```
RP/0/0/CPU0:PE6(config)# mpls traffic-eng
RP/0/0/CPU0:PE6(config-mpls-te)# interface GigabitEthernet0/0/0/2
RP/0/0/CPU0:PE6(config-mpls-te)# interface GigabitEthernet0/0/0/4

RP/0/0/CPU0:PE6(config)# rsvp
RP/0/0/CPU0:PE6(config-rsvp)# interface GigabitEthernet0/0/0/2
RP/0/0/CPU0:PE6(config-rsvp)# interface GigabitEthernet0/0/0/4

RP/0/0/CPU0:PE6(config)# interface tunnel-te0
RP/0/0/CPU0:PE6(config-if)# ipv4 unnumbered Loopback0
RP/0/0/CPU0:PE6(config-if)# autoroute announce
RP/0/0/CPU0:PE6(config-if-tunte-aa)# destination 10.1.100.2
RP/0/0/CPU0:PE6(config-if)# path-option 1 dynamic

RP/0/0/CPU0:PE6(config)# router ospf 1
RP/0/0/CPU0:PE6(config-ospf)# router-id 10.1.100.6
RP/0/0/CPU0:PE6(config-ospf)# area 0
RP/0/0/CPU0:PE6(config-ospf-ar)# mpls traffic-eng
RP/0/0/CPU0:PE6(config-ospf-ar-if)# mpls traffic-eng router-id Loopback0
```

Here's what is interesting after establishing this tunnel: an explicit path has been defined in the previous example on PE2, where we examined link protection following the path CE1 → PE2 → P3 → PE6 → CE7. The autoroute announce functionality should be able to find the FEC of concern and establish the TE path. However, RIB entries are prevented from being found, which will force us to establish a static route pointing to the tunnel interface, a similar behavior of IOS XR, for which we establish a static route inside the VRF pointing to the next hop and exit interface, as shown in Example 14-34.

Example 14-34 *IOS XR Next Hop Resolving via Static Route*

```
RP/0/0/CPU0:PE6(config)# router static
RP/0/0/CPU0:PE6(config-static)# address-family ipv4 unicast
RP/0/0/CPU0:PE6(config-static-afi)# 10.1.100.2/32 tunnel-te0
RP/0/0/CPU0:PE6(config-static-afi)# 172.16.67.7/32 GigabitEthernet0/0/0/3
RP/0/0/CPU0:PE6(config-static-afi)# vrf SPCOR
RP/0/0/CPU0:PE6(config-static-vrf)# address-family ipv4 unicast
RP/0/0/CPU0:PE6(config-static-vrf-afi)# 10.1.100.7/32 172.16.67.7
```

As mentioned, now we are deploying the MPLS L3VPN service, for which we will rely solely on RSVP as a protocol for label distribution instead of LDP (which we did not initialize). However, LDP will be essential for LFIB initializing (although no interfaces must be mapped for LDP), as in Example 14-35.

Example 14-35   *IOS XR MPLS LDP Enable*

```
RP/0/0/CPU0:PE6# configure terminal
RP/0/0/CPU0:PE6(config)# mpls ldp
```

Now, let's examine connectivity between CE1 and CE7 in both directions and see the path from both ends, as in Example 14-36.

Example 14-36   *CEs Connectivity via Traceroute*

```
! Just to remind that we configured an explicit path on PE2.
CE1# traceroute 10.1.100.7 source loopback 0 numeric
VRF info: (vrf in name/id, vrf out name/id)
  1 172.16.12.2 1 msec 2 msec 1 msec
  2 10.1.23.3 [MPLS: Labels 23/16700 Exp 0] 12 msec 12 msec 24 msec
  3 10.1.36.6 [MPLS: Label 16700 Exp 0] 13 msec 12 msec 28 msec
  4 172.16.67.7 15 msec 46 msec 7 msec
! From PE6 perspective, we configured the path-option to be dynamic though following
! the IGP best path selection (OSPF Cost).
CE7# traceroute 10.1.100.1 source loopback 0 numeric
VRF info: (vrf in name/id, vrf out name/id)
  1 172.16.67.6 3 msec 2 msec 2 msec
  2 10.1.36.3 [MPLS: Labels 25/22 Exp 0] 12 msec 13 msec 16 msec
  3 172.16.12.2 [MPLS: Label 22 Exp 0] 10 msec 28 msec 23 msec
  4 172.16.12.1 6 msec 9 msec 10 msec
```

Now, let's track the labels we have spotted from the trace outputs and the relevant tables, as in Example 14-37.

Example 14-37   *MPLS TE Tunnel Label Assignment Verification*

```
PE2# show mpls traffic-eng tunnels detail | include Label
  InLabel  :  -
  OutLabel : GigabitEthernet2, 23
  FRR OutLabel : Tunnel1, 23
  InLabel  :  -
  OutLabel : GigabitEthernet1, 22
  InLabel  : GigabitEthernet2, implicit-null
  OutLabel :  -

RP/0/0/CPU0:PE6# show mpls traffic-eng tunnels detail | include Label
    Outgoing Interface: GigabitEthernet0/0/0/2, Outgoing Label: 25
  InLabel: GigabitEthernet0/0/0/2, implicit-null
```

We have VPN labels assigned to the prefixes we are transporting across the core network, as can be shown in Example 14-38.

Example 14-38 *LFIB Validation*

```
PE2# show mpls forwarding-table | include 10.1.100.1/32
22         No Label    10.1.100.1/32[V]  126474      Gi3        172.16.12.1
```

```
RP/0/0/CPU0:PE6# show mpls forwarding | include 10.1.100.7/32
16700  Unlabelled  10.1.100.7/32[V]   Gi0/0/0/3   172.16.67.7    122974
```

Figure 14-15 shows the label stacking—in this case, VPN and Tunnel. Clearly, the transport label is now assigned by MPLS TE and attached to the tunnel interfaces we created on both ends of the LSP.

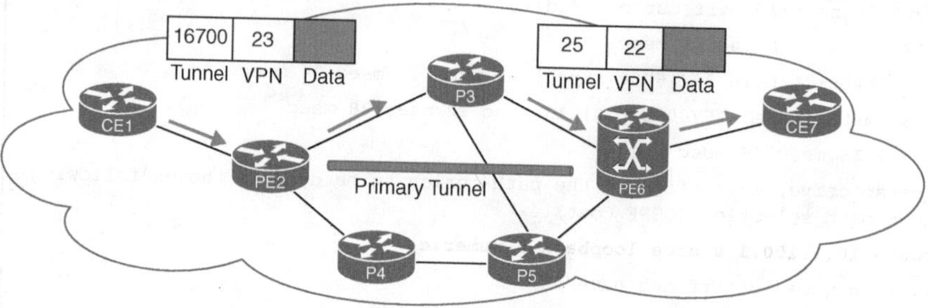

Figure 14-15 *MPLS TE FRR Labels*

Now, we will introduce a failure on the link between PE2 and P3 (protected link) to check for the new label produced to account for the FRR functionality, as demonstrated in Example 14-39.

Example 14-39 *MPLS TE FRR Backup Tunnel Interface Configuration*

```
PE2(config)# ip explicit-path name REPAIR enable
PE2(cfg-ip-expl-path)# index 1 next-address 10.1.24.4
PE2(cfg-ip-expl-path)# index 2 next-address 10.1.45.5
PE2(cfg-ip-expl-path)# index 3 next-address 10.1.35.3
Explicit Path name REPAIR:
    1: next-address 10.1.24.4
    2: next-address 10.1.45.5
    3: next-address 10.1.35.3
```

```
PE2(config)# interface tunnel 1
PE2(config-if)# ip unnumbered Loopback0
PE2(config-if)# tunnel mode mpls traffic-eng
PE2(config-if)# tunnel destination 10.1.100.3
PE2(config-if)# tunnel mpls traffic-eng path-option 1 explicit name REPAIR
```

```
PE2(config)# interface GigabitEthernet2
PE2(config-if)# mpls traffic-eng backup-path Tunnel1
```

Next, we will shut down the link between PE2 and P3 from the PE2 end and check the FRR database, as shown in Example 14-40.

Example 14-40   *MPLS TE FRR Database*

```
PE2# show mpls traffic-eng fast-reroute database
P2P Headend FRR information:
Protected tunnel                   In-label Out intf/label      FRR intf/label   Status
--------------------------------   -------- ---------------      --------------   ------
Tunnel0                            Tun hd   Gi2:23               Tu1:23           active

! Output omitted for brevity
```

Now, we will examine the label stacking by using the trace route utility, as shown in Example 14-41.

Example 14-41   *CE1 to CE7 Traceroute Output*

```
CE1# traceroute 10.1.100.7 source loopback 0 numeric
VRF info: (vrf in name/id, vrf out name/id)
  1 172.16.12.2 1 msec 1 msec 1 msec
  2 10.1.24.4 [MPLS: Labels 26/23/16700 Exp 0] 15 msec 66 msec 28 msec
  3 10.1.45.5 [MPLS: Labels 18/23/16700 Exp 0] 7 msec 9 msec 11 msec
  4 10.1.35.3 [MPLS: Labels 23/16700 Exp 0] 60 msec 23 msec 22 msec
  5 10.1.36.6 [MPLS: Label 16700 Exp 0] 26 msec 9 msec 18 msec
  6 172.16.67.7 15 msec 13 msec 12 msec
```

The backup tunnel is working as expected, and as we can see from the trace output, an extra label—an FRR label—has been added to the stack, as can be validated from the output in Example 14-42.

Example 14-42   *MPLS TE FRR Label*

```
PE2# show mpls traffic-eng tunnels detail | include Label
  InLabel  :  -
  OutLabel : GigabitEthernet2, 23
  FRR OutLabel : Tunnel1, 23 (in use)
  InLabel  :  -
  OutLabel : GigabitEthernet1, 26
  InLabel  : GigabitEthernet1, implicit-null
  OutLabel :  -

PE2# show mpls traffic-eng fast-reroute database backup-interface tunnel 1 detail
FRR Database Summary:
  Protected interfaces    : 1
  Protected LSPs/Sub-LSPs : 1
  Backup tunnels          : 1
```

```
   Active interfaces          : 1
   FRR Active tunnels         : 1


 P2P LSPs:


  Tun ID: 0, LSP ID: 2432, Source: 10.1.100.2
  Destination: 10.1.100.6
   State        : active
   InLabel      : Tunnel Head
   OutLabel     : Gi2:23
  FRR OutLabel  : Tu1:23
```

We introduced a new hop in the LSP due to the backup tunnel passing through a different path, which is now through PE2 → P4 → P5 → PE6, which also means that extra labels have been added and need to be validated. Let's check the output in Example 14-43.

Example 14-43 *MPLS TE FRR Label Stack*

```
P4# show mpls traffic-eng tunnels
P2P TUNNELS/LSPs:
LSP Tunnel PE2_t1 is signalled, connection is up
  InLabel   : GigabitEthernet1, 26
  Prev Hop : 10.1.24.2
  OutLabel : GigabitEthernet2, 18
  Next Hop : 10.1.45.5
  RSVP Signalling Info:
       Src 10.1.100.2, Dst 10.1.100.3, Tun_Id 1, Tun_Instance 3
    RSVP Path Info:
     My Address: 10.1.45.4
     Explicit Route: 10.1.45.5 10.1.35.3 10.1.100.3
     Record   Route:   NONE
     Tspec: ave rate=0 kbits, burst=1000 bytes, peak rate=0 kbits
    RSVP Resv Info:
     Record   Route:   NONE
     Fspec: ave rate=0 kbits, burst=1000 bytes, peak rate=0 kbits

LSP Tunnel PE6_t0 is signalled, connection is up
  InLabel   : GigabitEthernet2, 22
  Prev Hop : 10.1.45.5
  OutLabel : GigabitEthernet1, implicit-null
  Next Hop : 10.1.24.2
  RSVP Signalling Info:
       Src 10.1.100.6, Dst 10.1.100.2, Tun_Id 0, Tun_Instance 6
    RSVP Path Info:
```

```
      My Address: 10.1.24.4

      Explicit Route: 10.1.24.2 10.1.100.2

      Record   Route:   NONE

      Tspec: ave rate=0 kbits, burst=1000 bytes, peak rate=0 kbits

    RSVP Resv Info:

      Record   Route:   NONE

      Fspec: ave rate=0 kbits, burst=1000 bytes, peak rate=0 kbits


P2MP TUNNELS:


P2MP SUB-LSPS:


P5# show mpls traffic-eng tunnels
LSP Tunnel PE2_t1 is signalled, connection is up
  InLabel   : GigabitEthernet0/1, 18
  OutLabel : GigabitEthernet0/2, implicit-null
  RSVP Signalling Info:
       Src 10.1.100.2, Dst 10.1.100.3, Tun_Id 1, Tun_Instance 3
    RSVP Path Info:
      My Address: 10.1.35.5
      Explicit Route: 10.1.35.3 10.1.100.3
      Record   Route:   NONE
      Tspec: ave rate=0 kbits, burst=1000 bytes, peak rate=0 kbits
    RSVP Resv Info:
      Record   Route:   NONE
      Fspec: ave rate=0 kbits, burst=1000 bytes, peak rate=0 kbits


LSP Tunnel PE6_t0 is signalled, connection is up
  InLabel   : GigabitEthernet0/0, 16
  OutLabel : GigabitEthernet0/1, 22
  RSVP Signalling Info:
       Src 10.1.100.6, Dst 10.1.100.2, Tun_Id 0, Tun_Instance 6
    RSVP Path Info:
      My Address: 10.1.45.5
      Explicit Route: 10.1.45.4 10.1.24.2 10.1.100.2
      Record   Route:   NONE
      Tspec: ave rate=0 kbits, burst=1000 bytes, peak rate=0 kbits
    RSVP Resv Info:
      Record   Route:   NONE
      Fspec: ave rate=0 kbits, burst=1000 bytes, peak rate=0 kbits
```

Eventually, we will end up with a packet passing through the core network using the backup tunnel, with FRR in place for rapid convergence and maintaining connectivity with a proper label stack, as demonstrated in Figure 14-16.

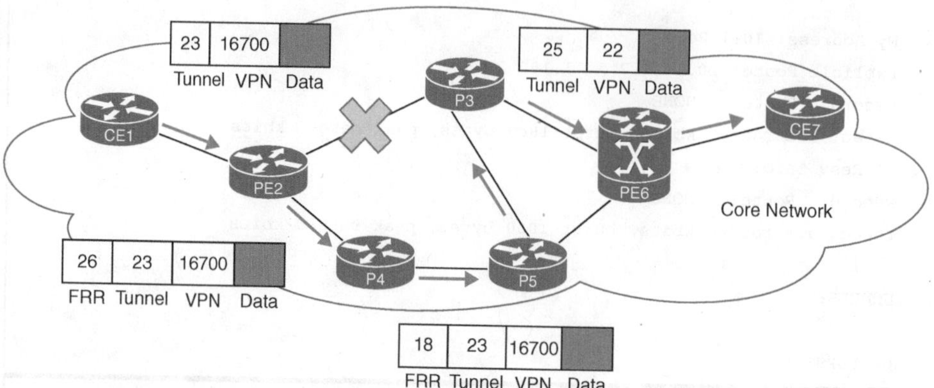

Figure 14-16 *MPLS TE FRR, Label Stacking*

The same applies from an IOS XR perspective: we will do the same to investigate the configuration commands needed. We will configure a backup tunnel following the path PE6 → P5 → P4 → PE2. Example 14-44 shows the applicable commands.

Example 14-44 *MPLS TE FRR IOS XR*

```
RP/0/0/CPU0:PE6(config)# explicit-path name PATH

RP/0/0/CPU0:PE6(config-expl-path)# index 1 next-address strict ipv4 unicast
10.1.36.3

RP/0/0/CPU0:PE6(config-expl-path)# index 2 next-address strict ipv4 unicast
10.1.23.2

RP/0/0/CPU0:PE6(config-expl-path)# explicit-path name REPAIR

RP/0/0/CPU0:PE6(config-expl-path)# index 1 next-address strict ipv4 unicast
10.1.56.5

RP/0/0/CPU0:PE6(config-expl-path)# index 2 next-address strict ipv4 unicast
10.1.45.4

RP/0/0/CPU0:PE6(config-expl-path)# index 3 next-address strict ipv4 unicast
10.1.24.2

RP/0/0/CPU0:PE6(config)# interface tunnel-te0

RP/0/0/CPU0:PE6(config-if)# fast-reroute

RP/0/0/CPU0:PE6(config)# interface tunnel-te1

RP/0/0/CPU0:PE6(config-if)# ipv4 unnumbered Loopback0

RP/0/0/CPU0:PE6(config-if)# autoroute announce

RP/0/0/CPU0:PE6(config-if)# destination 10.1.100.2

RP/0/0/CPU0:PE6(config-if)# path-option 1 explicit name REPAIR

RP/0/0/CPU0:PE6(config)# mpls traffic-eng

RP/0/0/CPU0:PE6(config-mpls-te)# interface GigabitEthernet0/0/0/1

RP/0/0/CPU0:PE6(config-mpls-te-if)# backup-path tunnel-te 1
```

Example 14-45 shows how to check the MPLS traffic-eng FRR database to spot the difference before and after the failure on the link between PE6 → P3.

Example 14-45 *MPLS FRR Database*

```
! Before the failure
RP/0/RP0/CPU0:PE6# show mpls traffic-eng fast-reroute database

Tunnel head FRR information:

Tunnel        Out Intf : Label    FRR Intf : Label    Status
-----------   -----------------   ------------------  -------
tt0           Gi0/0/0/1:17        tt1:ExpNull4        Ready
! After the failure
RP/0/RP0/CPU0:PE6# show mpls traffic-eng fast-reroute database

Tunnel head FRR information:

Tunnel        Out Intf : Label    FRR Intf : Label    Status
-----------   -----------------   ------------------  -------
tt0           tt1:ExpNull4                            Active
```

The extra label added by FRR can be differentiated by comparing the trace route from CE7 to CE1 before and after the failure. (We already have an active tunnel on both PEs: PE2 and PE6 for transporting the VPNv4 prefixes because no LDP is currently running inside the core network.) Example 14-46 clarifies the difference.

Example 14-46 *Trace Route Outputs Before and After Failure*

```
! Before the failure
CE7# traceroute 10.1.100.1 source loopback 0 numeric

VRF info: (vrf in name/id, vrf out name/id)
  1 10.1.67.6 3 msec 2 msec 2 msec
  2 10.1.36.3 [MPLS: Labels 16/16 Exp 0] 3 msec 3 msec 3 msec
  3 10.1.12.2 [MPLS: Label 16 Exp 0] 3 msec 3 msec 3 msec
  4 10.1.12.1 6 msec *  4 msec
! After the failure
CE7# traceroute 10.1.100.1 source loopback 0 numeric

VRF info: (vrf in name/id, vrf out name/id)
  1 10.1.67.6 3 msec 4 msec 2 msec
  2 10.1.56.5 [MPLS: Labels 16/0/16 Exp 0] 5 msec 6 msec 5 msec
  3 10.1.45.4 [MPLS: Labels 16/0/16 Exp 0] 5 msec 6 msec 5 msec
  4 10.1.12.2 [MPLS: Labels 0/16 Exp 0] 4 msec 6 msec 5 msec
  5 10.1.12.1 4 msec *  6 msec
```

In the context of MPLS FRR link protection and taking into consideration the protected link in the dashed line and the traffic path illustrated by the arrows, please assign the respective MPLS FRR terms on Figure 14-17.

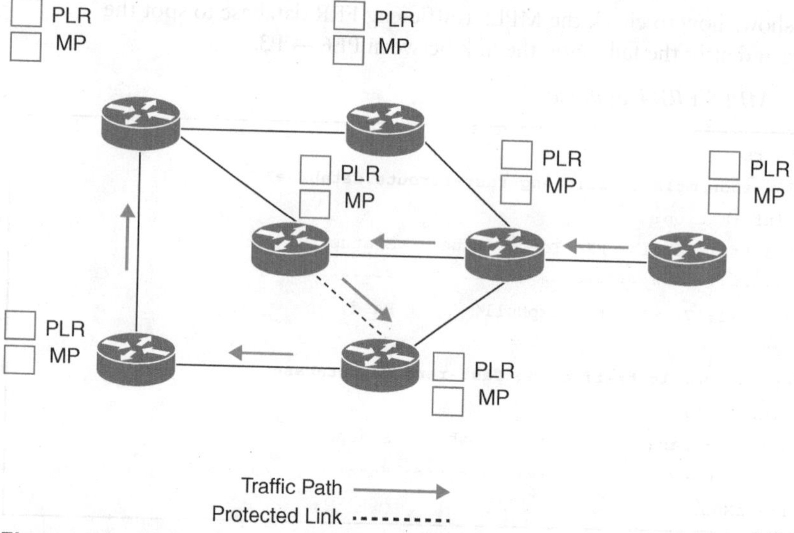

Figure 14-17   *Brainstorm: MPLS TE FRR Roles*

MPLS TE QoS

MPLS DiffServ TE (DS-TE) makes MPLS TE (also called aggregate MPLS TE) QoS aware, allowing resource reservation with QoS granularity. DS-TE delivers QoS guarantees for sensitive traffic, such as voice. To achieve QoS optimization, traffic engineering is done at the per-class level instead of at the aggregate (global) level. When a specific DiffServ class of service's traffic is mapped onto a distinct LSP, it enables the traffic to make use of resources allocated to that class on routes that satisfy constraints unique to that class.

The DiffServ-TE Solution

The fundamental requirement of DS-TE is to be able to enforce different bandwidth constraints for different sets of DS-TE tunnels. RFC 3564 introduces the concept of class types. The main components of the MPLS DS-TE that overcome the limitations of the traditional DS-TE are as follows:

1. **Class Types (CT):** DS-TE must be able to keep track of the available bandwidth for each class of traffic. For keeping track of available bandwidth for each type of traffic, class types are defined. There are no rules that govern what traffic maps to which CT. A given DS-TE tunnel belongs to the same CT on all links.

   Eight CTs are defined—CT0 through CT7. A DS-TE LSP can carry traffic from only one CT. Suppose a network supports voice and data traffic, with voice being EF PHB (EF queue) and data being best-effort (BE queue). In this case, CT1 can be mapped to the EF queue, and CT0 can be mapped to the BE queue. Separate TE LSPs are established with separate bandwidth requirements from CT0 and from CT1.

2. **CSPF in DS-TE:** In aggregate MPLS TE, CSPF computes a path based on user-defined constraints such as bandwidth and link attributes (setup and hold priority). DS-TE adds available bandwidth at each of the eight CTs as a constraint that can be applied

to a path. Therefore, CSPF is enhanced to consider a CT-specific bandwidth at a given priority as a constraint when computing a path.

This means, ideally, that the IGP must carry bandwidth information of eight CTs at eight priority levels (i.e., 64 values) for each link in LSAs. However, only eight values are advertised. A TE class is a combination of CT and setup priority. The IGPs advertise the available bandwidth for each of the TE classes defined. DS-TE supports a maximum of eight TE classes, TE0 through TE7, which are chosen from a possible 64 different CT-priority combinations through configuration. The combination chosen depends on the classes and priorities that the network supports.

The IGP carries the TE class information in the Unreserved Bandwidth sub-TLV, which is present in the Link Information TLV of TE LSA. CSPF uses this information, including user-defined constraints, to calculate a path. This information is passed to RSVP for signaling.

3. **RSVP in DS-TE:** Once a path is calculated, it is signaled using RSVP-TE, and admission control is performed at each hop. RFC 4124 defines a new RSVP object for carrying CT information. This object is called a CLASSTYPE object. It is carried in RSVP PATH messages, including the SESSION TEMPLATE and LABEL REQUEST objects to establish a TE LSP. The CLASSTYPE object carries CT values from 1 through 7; 0 is the default for the global TE tunnel.

    If the LSP is to be established for a CT value of 0, the CLASSTYPE object is not carried in the PATH message. This allows backward compatibility with non-DS-TE capable/configured LSRs.

    Each LSR along the path records the CLASSTYPE object. During the establishment of LSP for a particular CT, the LSR performs admission control, considering the bandwidth available for that particular CT. If an LSR does not support DS-TE extensions for RSVP (i.e., a CLASSTYPE object), it rejects the path establishment.

4. **Bandwidth Constraint Models:** The percentage of a link's bandwidth that a CT can take up is called bandwidth constraint (BC). A BC model defines a set of rules:

    - The maximum number of BCs

    - Which CTs each BC applies to and how

    A CT can be applied to either a BC or a set of BCs. Several BC models exist, and the most common ones are described in the sections that follow.

Maximum Allocation Model (MAM)

The Maximum Allocation Model (MAM) maps one BC to one CT; that is, BC n defines the maximum amount of reservable bandwidth for CT n. The use of preemption does not affect the amount of bandwidth that a CT receives. This model does not allow sharing of unused bandwidth by other CTs.

Each CT has its BC, and you can't share bandwidth between CTs. The advantage is that each CT is isolated because it has its own "reservation." You'll never run into a scenario where the LSP of one CT preempts the LSP of another CT. The disadvantage of MAM is that we waste bandwidth. A single CT cannot access any unused bandwidth that is not utilized by other CTs.

What you'll see when you use MAM is that sometimes LSPs won't be able to select the most optimal path in the network. Figure 14-18 shows three CTs (CT0, CT1, and CT2). Each CT has its BC. If you use all eight CTs, you will have the BCs described in Table 14-2.

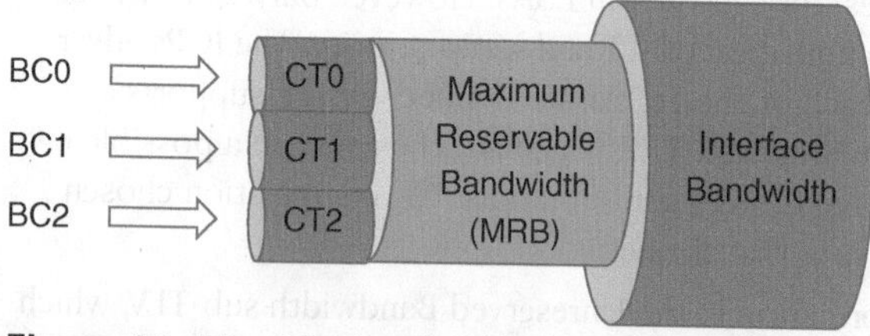

Figure 14-18 *Maximum Allocation Model*

Table 14-2   MPLS Label Range

Bandwidth Constraint	Maximum Bandwidth Allocation For
BC7	CT7
BC6	CT6
BC5	CT5
BC4	CT4
BC3	CT3
BC2	CT2
BC1	CT1
BC0	CT0

Russian Dolls Model (RDM)

The Russian Dolls Model (RDM) improves bandwidth efficiency over the MAM model by allowing CTs to share bandwidth. In this model, CT7 has the strictest QoS requirements, and CT0 has the best-effort QoS requirements. BC7 has a fixed percentage of link bandwidth that is reserved for CT7 only. BC6 accommodates traffic from CT7 and CT6; BC5 accommodates CT7, CT6, and CT5, and so on. So, BC0 represents the entire link bandwidth and is shared among all CTs. Figure 14-19 shows three CTs (CT0, CT1, and CT2).

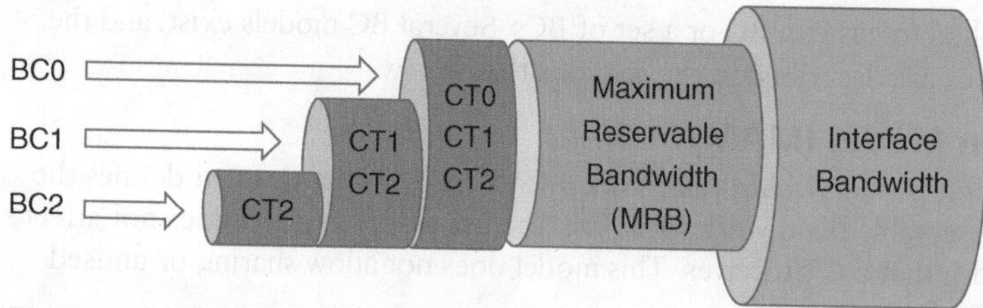

Figure 14-19 *Russian Dolls Model*

The global pool (BC0) equals the MRB of the interface. Here's how it works:

1.   BC2 limits CT2 to a small portion of the bandwidth.

2.   BC1 limits CT1 + CT2 to a larger portion of the bandwidth.

3.   BC0 limits CT1 + CT2 + CT3 to the MRB.

Table 14-3 outlines the maximum bandwidth allocation per bandwidth constraint in RDM, where CT0 is best-effort traffic and CT7 has the strictest requirements.

Table 14-3 RDM Maximum Bandwidth Allocation

Bandwidth Constraint	Maximum Bandwidth Allocation For
BC7	CT7
BC6	CT6 + CT7
BC5	CT5 + CT6 + CT7
BC4	CT4 + CT5 + CT6 + CT7
BC3	CT3 + CT4 + CT5 + CT6 + CT7
BC2	CT2 + CT3 + CT4 + CT5 + CT6 + CT7
BC1	CT1 + CT2 + CT3 + CT4 + CT5 + CT6 + CT7
BC0	CT0 + CT1 + CT2 + CT3 + CT4 + CT5 + CT6 + CT7

DiffServ for DS-TE

After LSPs are set up for each CT, the correct scheduler queue must be mapped for each LSP. RFC 3270 defines a solution using two types of LSPs:

- **EXP-inferred LSP (E-LSP):** Set the EXP bits appropriately at the LSP ingress. This allows eight PHBs due to the 3-bit field of EXP. The EXP field conveys to the LSR the PHB to be applied to the packet about the packet's queuing treatment and drop precedence.

- **LSP-inferred LSP (L-LSP):** Encode the scheduling behavior in the label installed for the LSP and use the EXP field to convey the drop precedence for the traffic. Any number of PHBs can be supported in this way.

Thus, DiffServ provides correct scheduling behavior for each traffic type. Cisco IOS only supports E-LSPs.

DS-TE Modes

MPLS networks may accomplish DS-TE in three different combinations or modes with the addition of the IETF-standard. These modes are

- **Prestandard Mode:** This is the default mode in Cisco IOS. This mode describes networks that already operate DS-TE.

- **Migration Mode:** The networks that wish to upgrade to the IETF standard must first configure the routers to migration mode. This allows the tunnel to continue to operate without being torn down. Further, the IGP and RSVP-TE will continue to signal as in prestandard mode, but the routers will add TE class mapping and continue to accept advertisements in prestandard and IETF standard form.

- **Liberal IETF Mode:** The networks that are in migration mode can then move into IETF formats by reconfiguring the routers into this mode, thus allowing the routers to generate IGP advertisements and RSVP-TE signaling according to the IETF standard. This mode also allows backward compatibility with the previous two modes.

Example 14-47 shows the options (modes) we have from both IOS– and IOS XR–based software.

Example 14-47 *IOS XE and IOS XR DS-TE Modes*

```
PE2(config)# mpls traffic-eng ds-te mode ?
  ietf          Configure DS-TE standard mode
  migration     Configure DS-TE migration mode
  pre-standard  Configure default mode

RP/0/0/CPU0:PE7(config)# mpls traffic-eng ds-te mode ?
  ietf  IETF Standard Mode
```

Table 14-4 demonstrates a few key differences between prestandard and standard DS-TE modes.

Table 14-4 DS-TE Standards

Prestandard DS-TE	Standard DS-TE
Enabled by default.	Configured using **mpls traffic-eng ds-te mode** *{migration | ietf}* global configuration command.
Only supports the RDM bandwidth constraint model; enabled by default.	Supports MAM and RDM bandwidth constraint models.
No RSVP extensions; sub-pool signaled as guaranteed service; global pool signaled as controlled-load service.	Uses RSVP extensions—CLASSTYPE object.
Bandwidth constraints and BC-model information not included in IGP link advertisement.	Bandwidth constraints and BC-model information included in IGP link advertisement.

Class-Based Tunnel Selection (CBTS)

Class-Based Tunnel Selection (CBTS) is a technique used in Multiprotocol Label Switching networks to select and assign traffic to specific traffic engineering tunnels based on predefined classes or criteria. It allows network operators to apply different policies and routing decisions to different classes of traffic, optimizing network resource utilization and meeting Quality of Service requirements for various traffic types.

By implementing Class-Based Tunnel Selection, MPLS networks can achieve efficient traffic engineering, QoS provisioning, and network optimization by aligning routing decisions with the specific requirements and characteristics of different classes of traffic. This approach improves network performance, resource utilization, and service delivery for diverse traffic types within the network.

You can forward traffic with certain EXP values into different TE tunnels. You can assign one or more EXP values to a tunnel and assign a TE tunnel as the default. This way, you don't have to assign all EXP values separately.

CBTS is a local mechanism on the headend router and only works for TE tunnels between the same headend and tailend router. We call this "set" of TE tunnels a *bundle*. There is one master tunnel that bundles the member tunnels, as depicted in Figure 14-20.

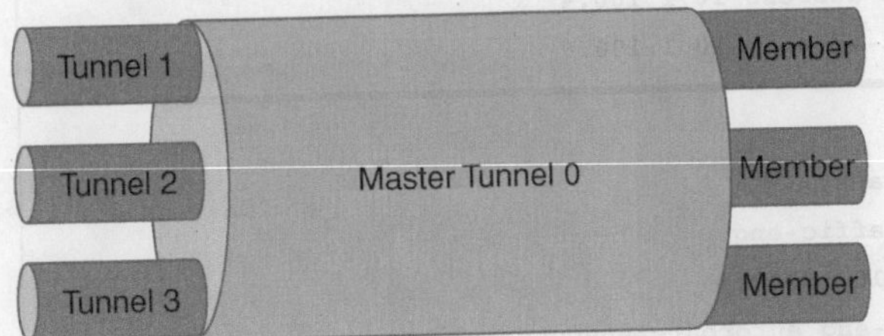

Figure 14-20   *CBTS Master Tunnel and Tunnel Members*

CBTS is not a routing solution. You still need something like a static route or autoroute to send traffic down the master tunnel interface. When the headend router receives traffic in the master tunnel interface, it will automatically select the correct member tunnel interface based on the EXP value of the packet. That's the only thing CBTS does.

NOTE   Packets can enter the headend router through multiple incoming interfaces, and not all packets may be marked correctly if you deal with different customers. When you configure MQC to (re)mark packets on the headend router, CBTS will use the new EXP values to decide what TE tunnel to use.

Figure 14-21 shows the related configuration items associated with CBTS and associated functionality.

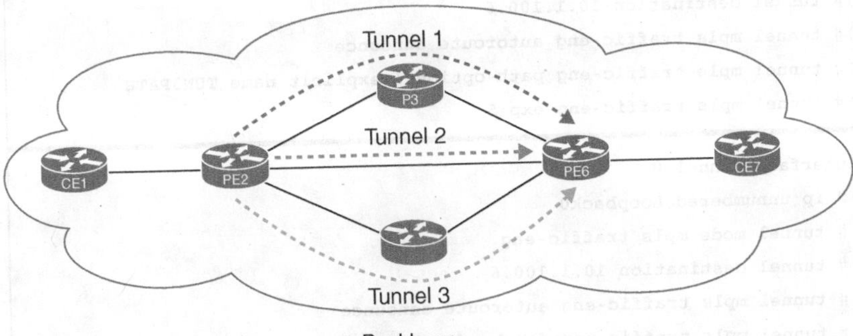

Figure 14-21   *Policy-Based Tunnel Selection*

Example 14-48 lists the configuration of the master tunnel, tunnel members, and the association of different QoS EXP values (randomly) with each tunnel member.

Example 14-48   *Policy-Based Tunnel Selection Configuration*

```
PE2(config)# ip explicit-path name TUN1PATH
PE2(cfg-ip-expl-path)# index 1 next-address 10.1.100.3
PE2(cfg-ip-expl-path)# index 2 next-address 10.1.100.6

PE2(config)# ip explicit-path name TUN2PATH
```

```
PE2(cfg-ip-expl-path)# index 1 next-address 10.1.100.6
```

```
PE2(config)# ip explicit-path name TUN3PATH
PE2(cfg-ip-expl-path)# index 1 next-address 10.1.100.4
PE2(cfg-ip-expl-path)# index 2 next-address 10.1.100.6
```

```
PE2(config)# interface tunnel 1
PE2(config-if)# ip unnumbered Loopback0
PE2(config-if)# tunnel mode mpls traffic-eng
PE2(config-if)# tunnel destination 10.1.100.6
PE2(config-if)# tunnel mpls traffic-eng autoroute announce
PE2(config-if)# tunnel mpls traffic-eng path-option 1 explicit name TUN1PATH
PE2(config-if)# tunnel mpls traffic-eng exp 0
```

```
PE2(config)# interface tunnel 2
PE2(config-if)# ip unnumbered Loopback0
PE2(config-if)# tunnel mode mpls traffic-eng
PE2(config-if)# tunnel destination 10.1.100.6
PE2(config-if)# tunnel mpls traffic-eng autoroute announce
PE2(config-if)# tunnel mpls traffic-eng path-option 1 explicit name TUN2PATH
PE2(config-if)# tunnel mpls traffic-eng exp 3
```

```
PE2(config)# interface tunnel 3
PE2(config-if)# ip unnumbered Loopback0
PE2(config-if)# tunnel mode mpls traffic-eng
PE2(config-if)# tunnel destination 10.1.100.6
PE2(config-if)# tunnel mpls traffic-eng autoroute announce
PE2(config-if)# tunnel mpls traffic-eng path-option 1 explicit name TUN3PATH
PE2(config-if)# tunnel mpls traffic-eng exp 5
```

```
PE2(config)# interface tunnel 0
PE2(config-if)# ip unnumbered Loopback0
PE2(config-if)# tunnel mode mpls traffic-eng
PE2(config-if)# tunnel destination 10.1.100.6
PE2(config-if)# tunnel mpls traffic-eng autoroute announce
PE2(config-if)# tunnel mpls traffic-eng exp-bundle master
PE2(config-if)# tunnel mpls traffic-eng exp-bundle member Tunnel1
PE2(config-if)# tunnel mpls traffic-eng exp-bundle member Tunnel2
PE2(config-if)# tunnel mpls traffic-eng exp-bundle member Tunnel3
```

We can investigate the EXP values and the association (per configuration) to each tunnel member and then trace the packets following a certain tunnel by using predefined explicit paths, as in Example 14-49.

Example 14-49 *MPLS Traffic Engineering EXP Values Validation*

```
PE2# show mpls traffic-eng exp
Destination: 10.1.100.6
   Master: Tunnel0            Status:  up
   Members        Status           Conf Exp              Actual Exp
   Tunnel1        up  (Active)         0                   0 1 2 4 6 7
   Tunnel2        up  (Active)         3                   3
   Tunnel3        up  (Active)         5                   5
(D) : Destination is different
(NE): Exp values not configured on tunnel

PE2# traceroute mpls traffic-eng tunnel 1 exp 0
Tracing MPLS TE Label Switched Path on Tunnel1, timeout is 2 seconds

Codes: '!' - success, 'Q' - request not sent, '.' - timeout,
   'L' - labeled output interface, 'B' - unlabeled output interface,
   'D' - DS Map mismatch, 'F' - no FEC mapping, 'f' - FEC mismatch,
   'M' - malformed request, 'm' - unsupported tlvs, 'N' - no label entry,
   'P' - no rx intf label prot, 'p' - premature termination of LSP,
   'R' - transit router, 'I' - unknown upstream index,
   'X' - unknown return code, 'x' - return code 0

Type escape sequence to abort.
  0 10.1.23.2 MRU 1500 [Labels: 17 Exp: 0]
L 1 10.1.23.3 MRU 1504 [Labels: implicit-null Exp: 0] 3 ms
! 2 10.1.36.6 3 ms

PE2# traceroute mpls traffic-eng tunnel 2 exp 3
Tracing MPLS TE Label Switched Path on Tunnel2, timeout is 2 seconds
Codes: '!' - success, 'Q' - request not sent, '.' - timeout,
   'L' - labeled output interface, 'B' - unlabeled output interface,
   'D' - DS Map mismatch, 'F' - no FEC mapping, 'f' - FEC mismatch,
   'M' - malformed request, 'm' - unsupported tlvs, 'N' - no label entry,
   'P' - no rx intf label prot, 'p' - premature termination of LSP,
   'R' - transit router, 'I' - unknown upstream index,
   'X' - unknown return code, 'x' - return code 0
Type escape sequence to abort.
```

```
  0 10.1.26.2 MRU 1500 [Labels: implicit-null Exp: 3]
! 1 10.1.26.6 2 ms
```

```
PE2# traceroute mpls traffic-eng tunnel 3 exp 5
Tracing MPLS TE Label Switched Path on Tunnel3, timeout is 2 seconds
Codes: '!' - success, 'Q' - request not sent, '.' - timeout,
  'L' - labeled output interface, 'B' - unlabeled output interface,
  'D' - DS Map mismatch, 'F' - no FEC mapping, 'f' - FEC mismatch,
  'M' - malformed request, 'm' - unsupported tlvs, 'N' - no label entry,
  'P' - no rx intf label prot, 'p' - premature termination of LSP,
  'R' - transit router, 'I' - unknown upstream index,
  'X' - unknown return code, 'x' - return code 0
Type escape sequence to abort.
  0 10.1.24.2 MRU 1500 [Labels: 17 Exp: 5]
L 1 10.1.24.4 MRU 1504 [Labels: implicit-null Exp: 5] 3 ms
! 2 10.1.46.6 3 ms
```

Policy-Based Tunnel Selection

Policy-Based Tunnel Selection (PBTS) provides a mechanism that lets you direct traffic into specific TE tunnels based on different criteria. PBTS will benefit Internet service providers (ISPs) that carry voice and data traffic through their MPLS and MPLS/VPN networks and want to route this traffic to provide an optimized voice service.

Policy-Based Tunnel Selection serves the same goal as Class-Based Tunnel Selection on IOS software but is designed for IOS XR. It will provide a mechanism for directing traffic into specific RSVP TE tunnels based on different QoS criteria (EXP, DSCP, and Precedence values).

The following steps show how to configure PBTS on IOS XR:

Step 1. Classify/mark the traffic using class maps.

Step 2. Create a rule for classified traffic using the forward class through the policy map.

Step 3. Configure a service policy on each core interface that will be part of the PBTS path.

Step 4. Create two traffic engineering tunnels: one for carrying high-priority traffic (VoIP) and a second tunnel for low-priority traffic (data).

In PBTS, a class map is defined for various types of packets and for associating this class map with a forward class. The class map defines the matching criteria for classifying a particular type of traffic, while the forward class defines the forwarding path these packets should take. Once a class map is associated with a forwarding class in the policy map, all the packets that match the class map are forwarded as defined in the policy map. When the TE interfaces are associated with the forward class, they can be exported to the routing protocol module using the **autoroute** command, which will then associate the route in the FIB database with these tunnels. If the TE interface is not explicitly associated with a forward class, it gets associated with a default class (0). All non-TE interfaces that were learned through the destination route will be pushed down by the routing protocol to the forwarding plane with the forwarding class set to the default class.

When PBR is configured, TE tunnel interfaces are selected to forward traffic based on matching class types in a policy map. When a forward class value for a TE tunnel is configured, that TE process passes to the LSD process as part of the label rewrite for the tunnel head. The TE allows one 32-bit value for a forward class per tunnel that is opaque to the TE, and the TE will use it to program the tunnel for forwarding.

PBTS supports a maximum of eight forward class and eight TE tunnels within each forward class. A maximum of 32 TE tunnels can be associated with the destination route.

Forward class configuration does not apply to the FRR backup tunnels and will be ignored. The forward class configuration is not supported for the auto-backup tunnels and P2MP-TE (MTE) tunnels.

Figure 14-22 illustrates a high-level example of a use case for which we can deploy PBTS.

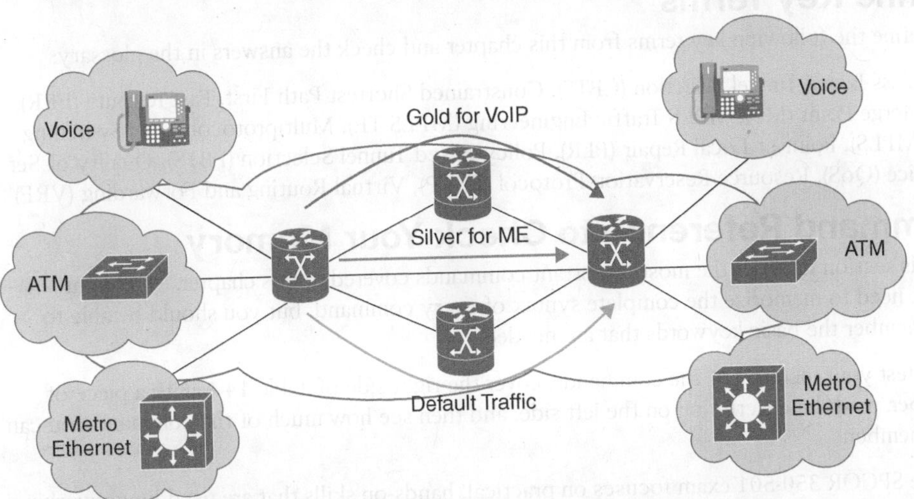

Figure 14-22 *Policy-Based Tunnel Selection Deployment Examples*

Exam Preparation Tasks

As mentioned in the section "How to Use This Book" in the Introduction, you have a few choices for exam preparation: the exercises here, Chapter 23, "Final Preparation," and the exam simulation questions in the Pearson Test Prep Software Online.

Review All Key Topics

Review the most important topics in this chapter, noted with the Key Topic icon in the margin of the page. Table 14-5 lists a reference of these key topics and the page numbers on which each is found.

Table 14-5 Key Topics for Chapter 14

Key Topic Element	Description	Page Number
Figure 14-1	IP Routing and the Fish	699
Paragraph	Traditional IP routing	699
Figure 14-2	RSVP Operation in MPLS TE	673
Section	Resource Reservation Protocol (RSVP) Operation in MPLS TE	673
Section	How to Place Traffic into a TE Tunnel	678
Section	MPLS Fast Reroute (FRR)	695
List	MPLS FRR Aspects	696
Figure 14-10	MPLS TE FRR	696
Figure 14-16	MPLS TE FRR, Label Stacking	710
Example 14-47	IOS XE and IOS XR DS-TE Modes	716
Table 14-4	DS-TE Standards	716

Define Key Terms

Define the following key terms from this chapter and check the answers in the glossary:

Class-Based Tunnel Selection (CBTS), Constrained Shortest Path First, Fast Reroute (FRR), Merge Point (MP), MPLS Traffic Engineering (MPLS TE), Multiprotocol Label Switching (MPLS), Point of Local Repair (PLR), Policy-Based Tunnel Selection (PBTS), Quality of Service (QoS), Resource Reservation Protocol (RSVP), Virtual Routing and Forwarding (VRF)

Command Reference to Check Your Memory

This section includes the most important commands covered in this chapter. You might not need to memorize the complete syntax of every command, but you should be able to remember the basic keywords that are needed.

To test your memory of the commands, cover the right side of Table 14-6 with a piece of paper, read the description on the left side, and then see how much of the command you can remember.

The SPCOR 350-501 exam focuses on practical, hands-on skills that are used by networking professionals. Therefore, you should be able to identify the commands needed to configure and test. Note that not all commands are fully covered in the chapter, but their presence in the following table should lead you to investigate them further to understand this technology.

Table 14-6 CLI Commands to Know

Task	Command Syntax
On the interface level, we use the **vrf forwarding** command to assign the interface to the correct VRF (the VRF creation method is through the **VRF definition** command).	**vrf forwarding** *VRF_Name*

Task	Command Syntax
Configure the router to exchange VPNv4 routes for use with MPLS VPNs. This includes support for encoding route targets and route distinguishers within the updates for customer VPN prefixes.	**address-family vpnv4 unicast**
Display BGP neighbor status for the VPNv4 family, including VRF information.	**show bgp vpnv4 unicast all**
Reserve resources along the communication path; by default, 75 percent will be preserved.	**ip rsvp bandwidth**
Install traffic engineering tunnels as the next hop in the headend router's routing table.	**tunnel mpls traffic-eng autoroute announce**
Display the contents of the fast reroute database.	**show mpls traffic-eng fast-reroute database**
Forward traffic down a backup tunnel when there is a link or node failure in the LSP of the primary tunnel.	**tunnel mpls traffic-eng fast-reroute**

Review Questions

As a part of the review, we encourage you to provide *a single-sentence answer* (keep your answers as short as possible) to the following questions. If you struggle to complete this answer in a single sentence, this may indicate a lack of clarity or reveal gaps in your understanding. We have constructed these questions to help you consolidate this chapter's information and extract the essence of the covered content.

The answers to these questions appear in Appendix A. For more practice with exam format questions, use the Pearson Test Prep Software Online.

1. How is the RSVP distinguished from LDP when it comes to forwarding?

2. What controls the selection of MAM versus RDM in an MPLS TE–enabled network?

3. How does MPLS Traffic Engineering work?

Bibliography

R. Coltun. RFC 2370, *The OSPF Opaque LSA Option*, IETF, https://www.rfc-editor.org/rfc/rfc2370, July 1998.

F. Le Faucheur, Ed. RFC 3564, *Requirements for Support of Differentiated Services-Aware MPLS Traffic Engineering*, IETF, https://datatracker.ietf.org/doc/html/rfc3564, July 2003.

F. Le Faucheur, Ed. RFC 4124, *Protocol Extensions for Support of Diffserv-Aware MPLS Traffic Engineering*, IETF, https://datatracker.ietf.org/doc/html/rfc4124, June 2005.

T. Li. RFC 5305, *IS-IS Extensions for Traffic Engineering*, IETF, https://datatracker.ietf.org/doc/html/rfc5305, October 2008.

S. Previdi, Ed., Internet Draft, *IS-IS Traffic Engineering (TE) Metric Extensions*, IETF, https://datatracker.ietf.org/doc/html/draft-ietf-isis-te-metric-extensions-03, April 25, 2014.

E. Rosen. RFC 4363, *BGP/MPLS IP Virtual Private Networks (VPNs)*, IETF, https://datatracker.ietf.org/doc/html/rfc4364, February 2006.

R. Zhang. RFC 5316, *ISIS Extensions in Support of Inter-Autonomous System (AS) MPLS and GMPLS Traffic Engineering*, IETF, https://datatracker.ietf.org/doc/rfc5316/, December 2008.

CHAPTER 15

Segment Routing

This chapter covers the following exam topics:

3.3 Describe segment routing

- 3.3.a Segment types
- 3.3.b SR control plane (BGP, OSPF, IS-IS)
- 3.3.c Segment routing traffic engineering
- 3.3.d TI-LFA
- 3.3.e PCE-PCC architectures
- 3.3.f Flexible algorithm
- 3.3.g SRv6 (locator, micro-segment, encapsulation, interworking gateway)

Segment Routing represents a cutting-edge technology designed to enhance and optimize the use of MPLS-based and IPv6 networks. This innovative approach introduces a suite of tools and concepts that not only simplify network operations but also significantly enhance the flexibility available to network operators. By allowing for more granular control over packet paths, Segment Routing empowers network operators to efficiently navigate the intricacies of modern networks, adapt to dynamic requirements, and minimize the challenges associated with traditional MPLS-based architectures.

In essence, Segment Routing is a beacon of progress in the networking realm, offering a robust set of solutions to meet the most demanding network requirements. Its advent marks a transformative shift in how networks are managed, providing operators with a versatile toolkit to navigate the complexities of traffic engineering, and ensuring that networks can dynamically respond to changing conditions in real time. By simplifying the routing paradigm and enhancing the scalability of MPLS-based networks, Segment Routing emerges as a pivotal technology, poised to play a crucial role in the evolution of modern network architectures.

"Do I Know This Already?" Quiz

The "Do I Know This Already?" quiz allows you to assess whether you should read this entire chapter thoroughly or jump to the "Exam Preparation Tasks" section. If you are in doubt about your answers to these questions or your own assessment of your knowledge of the topics, read the entire chapter. Table 15-1 lists the major headings in this chapter and their corresponding "Do I Know This Already?" quiz questions. You can find the answers in Appendix A, "Answers to the 'Do I Know This Already?' Quizzes and Review Questions."

Table 15-1   "Do I Know This Already?" Section-to-Question Mapping

Foundation Topics Section	Questions
Segment Types	1–2
Segment Routing Control Plane	3–4
Segment Routing Traffic Engineering	5–8
PCE-PCC Architecture	9–10

CAUTION   The goal of self-assessment is to gauge your mastery of the topics in this chapter. If you do not know the answer to a question or are only partially sure of the answer, you should mark that question as wrong for purposes of the self-assessment. Giving yourself credit for an answer you correctly guess skews your self-assessment results and might provide you with a false sense of security.

1. Which of the following are viable options for assigning SRGB ranges? (Select all that apply.)

   a. Globally

   b. Per IGP

   c. Dynamically

   d. Statically

2. Which labels cannot be a part of SRGB? (Select all that apply.)

   a. 15999

   b. 16000

   c. 24999

   d. 1,048,576

3. Which TLVs play an important role in Segment Routing? (Select all that apply.)

   a. 22

   b. 41

   c. 135

   d. 163

4. Which of the following is not an option for the SR Control Plane?

   a. RSVP-TE

   b. IS-IS

   c. OSPF

   d. BGP

5. Which of the following is not a viable option to supply SR policy to the ingress router?

   a. NETCONF

   b. FIB

   c. CLI

   d. PCEP

6. Which behavior properly describes an SR policy?

   a. An SR policy uses Network Service Orchestrator (NSO) to program its data plane.

   b. SR-PCE will use BGP-LS to program an SR policy into the ingress node.

   c. An SR policy encodes the list of constraints into the MPLS headers.

   d. An SR policy will use BSID entries to program its forwarding table.

7. Which of the following describes TI-LFA functionality? (Select all that apply.)

   a. TI-LFA must rely on LDP functionality to provide double-segment protection.

   b. TI-LFA uses next-hop neighbor as the point of local repair.

   c. TI-LFA preprograms the post-convergence path into a router's data plane.

   d. TI-LFA can use P space to calculate the post-convergence path.

8. Viable repair tunnel endpoints are found at which intersections?

   a. At midpoints of extended spaces

   b. At the intersection of point of local repair and double segments

   c. At the intersection of PQ nodes

   d. At the intersection of P and Q spaces

9. Which component serves the needs of long-term network engineering and capacity planning?

   a. Crosswork Network Controller

   b. Crosswork Optimization Engine

   c. WAN Automation Engine

   d. Crosswork Cloud

10. Which of the following protocols are used by PCEP to calculate network paths? (Select all that apply.)

   a. IS-IS

   b. BGP-LS

   c. RSVP-TE

   d. OSPF

Foundation Topics

Over time, a skilled engineer learns to make the most of the available resources. Over the past three decades, various strategies have been explored to maximize the potential of computer networks. The traditional approach to steering network traffic has been to manipulate the Interior Gateway Protocol (IGP) and rely solely on destination-based routing strategies. This only provided a restricted range of options for directing traffic within the network. The main limitation of using IGP metrics has been the "all or nothing" approach. Some of the links inevitably become congested while other links remain underutilized even though they are high bandwidth or low latency. IGP metrics simply lack optimization capabilities because they do not allow you to map different services to different paths. Despite years of featured improvements, such challenges persist and remain unsolvable with conventional IGP manipulations and destination-based routing strategies.

Thus, in the 1990s, the development of the **Label Distribution Protocol (LDP)** and Resource Reservation Protocol with Traffic Engineering extensions (RSVP-TE) marked a significant advancement in networking. These capable adjunct protocols effectively addressed specific challenges and provided network operators with crucial Traffic Engineering tools to overcome a wide variety of traffic-steering issues. Network operators could now manipulate how traffic flowed through the network to make the most of the available paths. Nevertheless, while providing network optimization, these protocols also introduced intricate challenges.

In the case of LDP, an additional process had to be created and maintained on the network, which led to a complex interaction with the Interior Gateway Protocol. LDP-IGP synchronization problems would cause traffic disruptions until these two protocols could settle on an agreement regarding the best way to forward traffic.

When dealing with RSVP-TE, reserving bandwidth accurately involves placing traffic within RSVP-TE tunnels. While this approach is feasible in smaller networks with minimal traffic engineering needs, it becomes exceedingly intricate on a larger scale. Managing hundreds of tunnels, their backup paths, and upkeep of a pertinent set of rules in the face of a dynamically evolving network posed formidable challenges, demanding considerable time and effort. Such scaling issues led many operators to limit their RSVP-TE deployments to the fast reroute (FRR) use cases. RSVP-TE is also not "ECMP-friendly," so it can never use all IGP-derived paths, forcing the operator to create more tunnels. An additional aspect to consider is that RSVP-TE generates a persistent "always-on" network state where every router must account for available bandwidth and that state must be constantly monitored. This incurs a cost in terms of network compute resources and the hardware required to sustain this continuous state irrespective of whether the network experiences congestion or not.

Could network optimization be further improved? These were the experiences and thoughts of the designers behind Segment Routing. They proposed that a properly designed network should have enough capacity to effectively handle an expected volume of traffic without congestion, even in the presence of a probable set of independent failures. IGP coupled with ECMP can competently absorb the majority of the traffic volume. In less frequent instances of congestion, traffic engineering tools would address applications intolerant of such network bottlenecks. This represented a simpler and more resource-efficient approach, both in terms of hardware and human efforts.

They proposed that it is better to distribute labels associated with IGP-signaled prefixes within the IGP framework itself, rather than relying on a separate protocol such as LDP to perform this task. This would solve the LDP-IGP synchronization problem during network failures because there now would be a single source of truth (IGP) to find available network paths. The network would precalculate such paths even before the failure occurred. IGP can have such "preknowledge"—think of an EIGRP-feasible successor—which is aware of the best available network route even before the failure occurs.

Second, why not give the network operator the power to direct any packet to any path at the ingress router only (where the packet enters the network), without having to maintain the expensive and complex "always-on" state throughout the entire network domain? This would lower control plane pressure, conserve network resources, and give the operator the full flexibility to force any packet anywhere.

Cisco engineers formulated the Segment Routing concept, obtained approval from their management in 2012, presented the idea to IETF in March 2013, authored numerous IETF drafts, and significantly influenced the industry in 2015 with the introduction of Segment Routing on IOS XR platforms (IOS and NX-OS carry some of the SR features). The market positively responded with other vendors supporting this capable technology. It is also referred to as Source Routing outside of Cisco. As of the present moment, Cisco alone has documented more than 1200 operational Segment Routing production deployments.

Segment Routing can be deployed on two data planes:

- MPLS data plane where segments will be encoded with MPLS labels.

- IPv6 data plane where segments will be encoded with IPv6 addresses.

Segment Types

Think of segments as a set of instructions. In Segment Routing, a source (an ingress router, as an example) chooses a certain path through the network and encodes the path in the packet header as an ordered list of instructions. These instructions are termed *segments* because they describe components of a divided whole.

In **SR-MPLS (Segment Routing based on MPLS data plane)**, such an identifier refers to an ordered list of segments represented by a stack of MPLS labels. When you instruct routers to follow these labels in a given sequence, the packets will take this path through the network. In **SRv6 (Segment Routing based on IPv6 data plane)**, it refers to an ordered list of segments encoded into a routing extension header. When you instruct routers to follow this list, the packets will flow via this path. In Figure 15-1, assigning such identifiers to routers can provide instructions for a specific path to send packets.

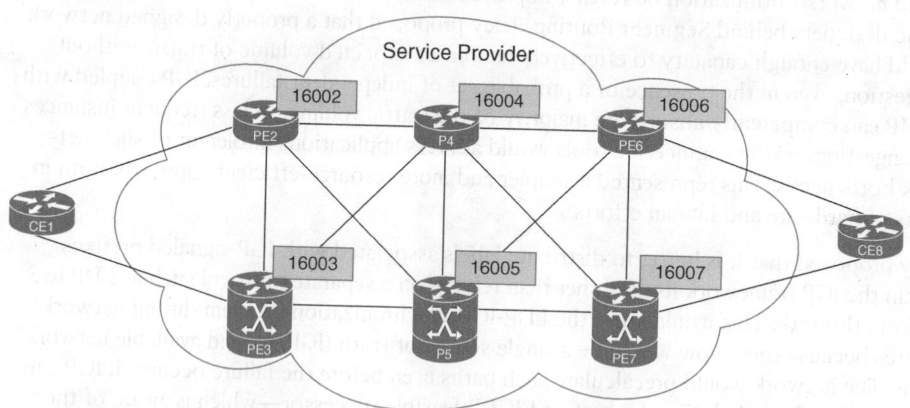

Figure 15-1 *Assigning Segments to Network*

Global Segments

Every router in a Segment Routing, or SR, domain understands such instruction and installs it in its forwarding table. This instruction is a domain-wide (watch the misleading name *global* because it is not known globally around the world) unique label value (a numerical number) that comes from the **Segment Routing Global Block (SRGB)** database. Table 15-2 shows how the **Label Switching Database (LSD)** carves the following default ranges (some can be changed) on Cisco routers running Segment Routing–capable software.

Table 15-2 LSD Label Ranges

Label Range	Reserved for	Examples
0–15	Base special-purpose MPLS labels	0—IPv4 Explicit NULL 3—Implicit NULL
16–15,999	Static MPLS labels	LDP assigned
16,000–23,999	SRGB	Global Segments (i.e., SR)
24,000–1,048,575	Dynamic allocation	Adjacency Segments

In Figure 15-1, every node in the domain knows that label 16002 always and uniquely represents Router PE2, 16003 always represents Router PE3, and so on. These are referred to as Node SIDs (Segment Identifiers).

A Node SID is a type of Prefix SID, as it represents any prefix linked to a node. To send a set of segment routing instructions is to specify these labels (Node SIDs); 16002, 16003 literally means "send this traffic via shortest ECMP path to PE2, then same to PE3." If the "uniqueness" rule is broken (two distinct routers are assigned the same label value), there will be an issue on your network because the nodes will not be able to accurately determine the appropriate path for routing traffic. (Technically, what happens is that IS-IS will prioritize the "first programmed" label and ignore the "second" one. This can get complex as to what "first programmed" means, as in when a router reboots or has failed, which router becomes "first programmed"? OSPF, on the other hand, will withdraw both SIDs. Don't worry about this because this topic is highly unlikely to show up on the exam, but good to know.)

Global Segments are always distributed as a unique value via IGP (remember that SR no longer relies on LDP as the label distribution mechanism). This value must be unique and comes from a combination of a label range (SRGB) + index. The default SRGB range for Cisco routers is 16000–23999 (notice how it does not overlap with the LDP range) and the index is zero based (the first index = 0). In our scenario, we start adding index values to our routers (index 2 for PE2, index 3 for PE3), so we will come up with globally known unique values of 16002 and 16003 for these routers. Cisco gives an option to also define these as an absolute value. There is no difference in daily operations whether absolute or relative indexes are used.

There are two minimum requirements to enable Segment Routing:

- Configure the Segment Routing Global Block (SRGB)

- Enable Segment Routing and Node SID in the IGP (shown later in the chapter under respective protocols)

Example 15-1 demonstrates SRGB assignment on both IOS XE as well as IOS XR operating systems.

Example 15-1 *SRGB Verification on IOS XE and IOS XR*

```
IOS
PE2# show running-config segment routing
!
```

```
 segment-routing
  global-block 16000 23999
 !
PE2#
```

```
IOS XR
RP/0/0/CPU0:PE4# show running-config segment-routing
 !
segment-routing
 global-block 16000 23999
 !
RP/0/0/CPU0:PE4#
```

When you're configuring an SRGB block, the recommendation is to configure it globally (again misleading, in the global, i.e., router-wide configuration), not per individual IGP; this way, all IGP instances as well as BGP can use the global (i.e., router-wide) SRGB. This is important because, later on, if you choose to add another protocol and the SRGB range has to change, you will have to reload the router. To avoid this, it is better to assign the SRGB block globally in the router so that multiple protocols (including BGP) can use it, not just a specific IGP. You should have a homogenous SRGB block (same SRGB range) on all routers on the network. If you do not, you will have fun times building end-to-end LSPs.

Local Segments

This instruction is allocated and understood by the originating node. It is locally significant only (which aligns with the intended meaning regarding the local router). A locally allocated MPLS label would be a good example of a **local segment**. Sometimes a router has more than a single link for forwarding traffic. The operator can prefer one of these paths over the other. In Figure 15-2, a packet arrives at PE3 (via label 16003). PE3 intends to send this packet to PE6, and there are two shortest available paths—through P4 and P5. These links are identified with local labels 24100 and 24150. Selecting one of them will instruct the local router to pick the appropriate link.

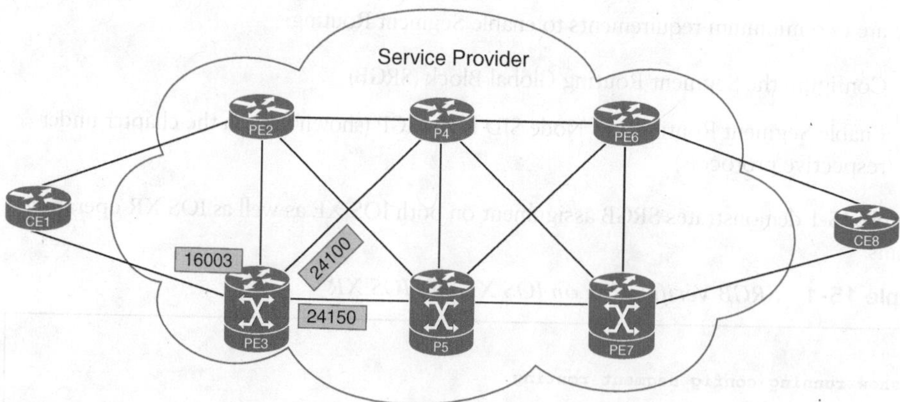

Figure 15-2 *Assigning Local Segments to Network*

IGP Segments

Segments construct a path through a network. There are two building blocks distributed by IGP: Prefix Segments and Adjacency Segments.

IGP Prefix Segments

Think of an **IGP Prefix Segment** as a shortest path to the IGP prefix. Note that it is

- Known as Prefix-SID

- Associated with an IP prefix

- Represents an ECMP (Equal Cost Multi-Path)-aware shortest path to a prefix

- Likely a multihop path

- A Global Segment—known uniquely on the SR domain

- A Label (16000 + Index) that is advertised as an index

- Distributed via IGP (ISIS/OSPF)

Observe this behavior in Figure 15-3 (note that we removed two links to better illustrate our example), where different routers are used to forward traffic to P5 based on label 16005, destined to the loopback address of 10.1.100.5. For this Segment Routing domain, PE3, P4, PE6, and PE7 send traffic directly to P5 because when these routers look at the MPLS forwarding table, label 16005 will be associated with the one interface directly connecting to P5. The only exception is PE2 which will have two equal paths available due to ECMP. How did all the routers learn that prefix 10.1.100.5/32 is associated with label 16005? R5 has generated this value from the combination of the SRGB label base 16000, added its operator assigned index +5, and advertised this label via IGP.

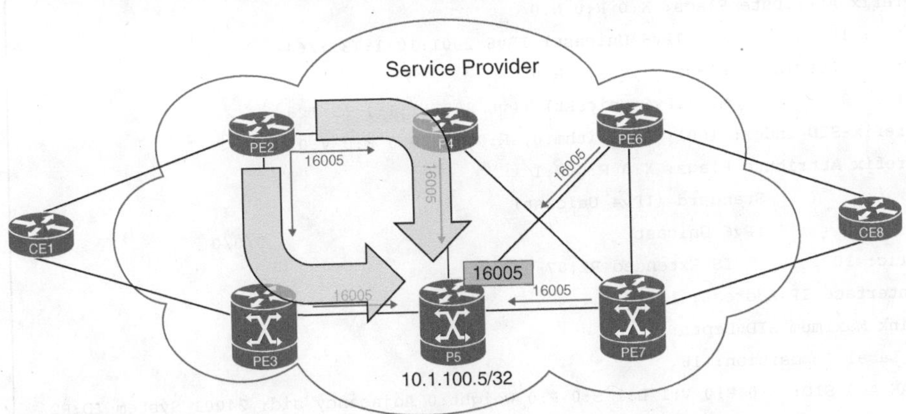

Figure 15-3 *IGP Prefix Segment Behavior*

I need to point something out here. Technically, there is a difference between a Node SID (which we just showed you) and a Prefix SID. A Node SID points to a router that can be a visiting point on the network. A Prefix SID is a label for a network prefix that is advertised by a router. This causes a point of confusion at times. Note that a special N flag is set to indicate that a SID represents a router (node) on the network. This is advanced and is unlikely to show up on the exam, but we include Example 15-2 to clear up any confusion regarding the difference.

Example 15-2 *Node SID and the N Flag*

```
RP/0/0/CPU0:R2# show isis database R1.00-00 detail verbose
Thu May  9 13:03:44.757 UTC
IS-IS lab (Level-1) Link State Database
LSPID                   LSP Seq Num  LSP Checksum  LSP Holdtime/Rcvd  ATT/P/OL
The requested LSP R1.00-00 was not found in the IS-IS lab Level-1 LSP Database
IS-IS lab (Level-2) Link State Database
LSPID                   LSP Seq Num  LSP Checksum  LSP Holdtime/Rcvd  ATT/P/OL
R1.00-00                0x00000007   0xf6b7        1108 /1199         0/0/0
  Area Address:   49.0001
  NLPID:          0xcc
  NLPID:          0x8e
  IP Address:     1.1.1.1
  Metric: 10         IP-Extended 10.1.12.0/24
    Prefix Attribute Flags: X:0 R:0 N:0
  Metric: 10         IP-Extended 10.1.13.0/24
    Prefix Attribute Flags: X:0 R:0 N:0
  Metric: 0          IP-Extended 1.1.1.1/32
   Prefix-SID Index: 1, Algorithm:0, R:0 N:1 P:0 E:0 V:0 L:0
    Prefix Attribute Flags: X:0 R:0 N:1
  Hostname:       R1
  IPv6 Address:   2001:1:1:1::1
  Metric: 10         MT (IPv6 Unicast) IPv6 2001:10:1:12::/64
    Prefix Attribute Flags: X:0 R:0 N:0
  Metric: 10         MT (IPv6 Unicast) IPv6 2001:10:1:13::/64
    Prefix Attribute Flags: X:0 R:0 N:0
  Metric: 0          MT (IPv6 Unicast) IPv6 2001:1:1:1::1/128
    Prefix-SID Index: 1001, Algorithm:0, R:0 N:1 P:0 E:0 V:0 L:0
    Prefix Attribute Flags: X:0 R:0 N:1
  MT:             Standard (IPv4 Unicast)
  MT:             IPv6 Unicast                              0/0/0
  Metric: 10         IS-Extended R2.07
   Interface IP Address: 10.1.12.1
   Link Maximum SID Depth:
    Label Imposition: 10
   LAN-ADJ-SID: F:0 B:0 V:1 L:1 S:0 P:0 weight:0 Adjacency-sid: 24001 System ID:R2
  Metric: 10         MT (IPv6 Unicast) IS-Extended R2.07
   Interface IPv6 Address: 2001:10:1:12::1
Link Maximum SID Depth:
    Label Imposition: 10
   LAN-ADJ-SID: F:1 B:0 V:1 L:1 S:0 P:0 weight:0 Adjacency-sid: 24003 System ID:R2
  Router Cap:     1.1.1.1 D:0 S:0
```

```
  Segment Routing: I:1 V:1, SRGB Base: 16000 Range: 8000
  SR Local Block: Base: 15000 Range: 1000
  SR Algorithm:
    Algorithm: 0
    Algorithm: 1
  Node Maximum SID Depth:
    Label Imposition: 10
RP/0/0/CPU0:R2#
```

This example from IS-IS shows the R2 is receiving SR information from R1, which has IPv4 (1.1.1.1/32) and IPv6 (2001:1:1:1::1/128) prefixes advertised with the N (Node) flag set to 1—a Node SID, not a Prefix SID.

IGP Adjacency Segment

An **IGP Adjacency Segment** is an identifier that describes a particular link between two routers. It is used to direct traffic over a specific link within the IGP routing domain. Routers can be given an instruction to forward based on the IGP adjacency. Note that adjacency segment is

- Known as Adj-SID

- Represents a hop over a specific link between two IGP-speaking routers

- Likely a one-hop path

- A Local Segment—significant only on a particular router

- Advertised as a label value

- Distributed via IGP (ISIS/OSPF)

Figure 15-4 illustrates this. Now, the packet has arrived at P5 and needs to travel further to PE6 (10.1.100.6). The operator has a choice to impose a local decision on P5 on which links to use—the direct link to PE6 or two-hop link via PE7. In this case, the link to PE7 is preferred (higher bandwidth, lower latency, encryption—take your pick), and label 24150 steers the traffic toward PE7.

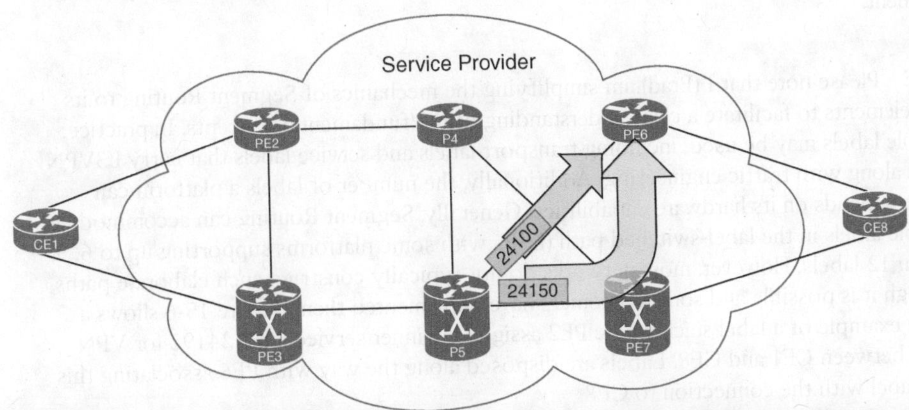

Figure 15-4 *IGP Prefix Segment Behavior with Adjacency Segments*

Combining IGP Segments

By combining segment IDs, you can groom traffic on any path in the network:

1. Specify the sequential list of segment IDs in the packet header, known as a label stack with the top label being read first.

2. Path is *not* signaled, and per flow state is not created (as in RSVP-TE).

3. A single protocol (IS-IS, OSPF, BGP) distributes this instruction.

In Figure 15-5, a network operator instructs PE2 to steer traffic to PE6 by sending it to P5 first via two available ECMP paths. Once P5 gets the packet, the top label 16005 is removed, and P5 uses the direct link to PE6 by looking up this interface in the forwarding table where it is associated with the dynamic adjacency label 24100.

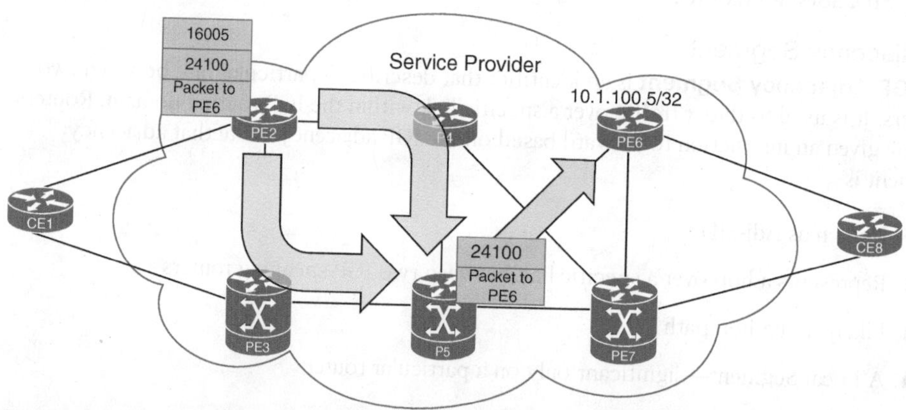

Figure 15-5 *Combining IGP Segment IDs for Traffic Steering*

By combining segment IDs (Prefix-SID and Adj-SID) in this way, you can put a packet on any path through the network, no matter how complex or unnatural this path may be. That is the power and essence of Segment Routing. At each hop, the top segment identifies the next hop. Segment IDs are stacked in sequential order at the top of the packet header. When the top segment ID contains the identity of another router, the receiving node uses equal cost multipaths (ECMP) to move the packet to the next hop. When the identity is the receiving router itself, the router will pop the top segment and perform the task required by the next segment.

NOTE Please note that I (Brad) am simplifying the mechanics of Segment Routing to its basic elements to facilitate a clear understanding of the fundamental concepts. In practice, multiple labels may be used, including transport labels and service labels that carry L3VPN traffic along with traffic engineering. Additionally, the number of labels a platform can handle depends on its hardware capabilities. Generally, Segment Routing can accommodate multiple labels in the label-switched path (LSP), with some platforms supporting up to 6, 9, or even 12 labels. However, most networks do not typically construct such elaborate paths, although it is possible and some customers have implemented them. Figure 15-6 shows a simple example of a label stack where PE2 assigns the inner service label 24192 for VPN traffic between CE1 and CE8. Labels are disposed along the way with PE6 associating this VPN label with the connection to CE8.

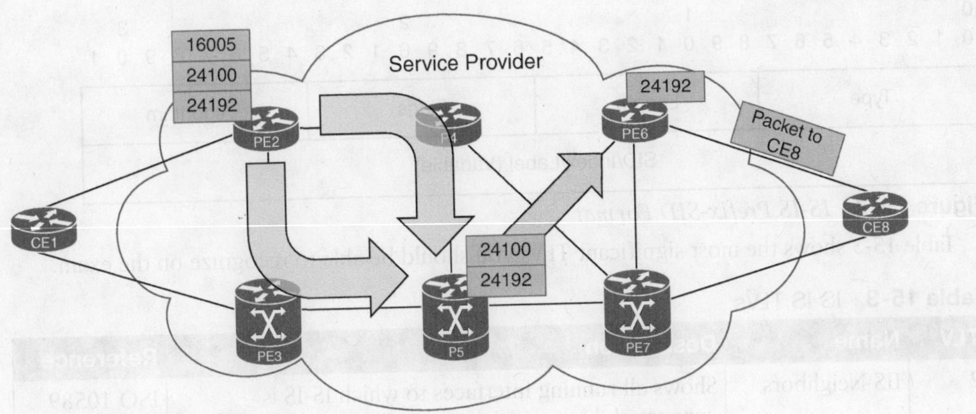

Figure 15-6 *Label Stack Example*

Segment Routing Control Plane

The control plane in Segment Routing (SR) plays a crucial role in managing how segment ID information is shared among network devices. Link-state Interior Gateway Protocol mechanisms distribute segment IDs on Segment Routing networks. Both OSPF and IS-IS include protocol extensions to support the distribution of segment IDs. These extensions enable routers to maintain a comprehensive database containing information about all nodes and adjacency segments. Because IGPs are now responsible for distributing segment IDs, and labels in the case of the MPLS data plane, there's no need for a separate label distribution protocol, as mentioned earlier. Our control plane has become far simpler because it is working with only one source of truth—IGP—instead of having to reconcile both IGP and LDP information during failure events. It is important to note that the **Segment Routing control plane** can be applied to both MPLS and IPv6 data planes. In Cisco's documentation, this is referred to as SR-MPLS and SRv6, the former running on MPLS labels and the latter on IPv6 routing. Let's start by examining SR-MPLS and learn the details behind protocols that provide this unified well-organized improvement.

IS-IS Control Plane

The **IS-IS control plane** disseminates Segment Routing information within an autonomous system. Because LDP is not necessary, IS-IS will distribute both the prefixes and labels in the extensions built into IS-IS itself. This allows for seamless deployment of Segment Routing in existing MPLS networks. Rather than modifying the protocol itself, the designers "extended" its use by providing these additional protocol add-ons to carry information not originally intended by protocol designers. Think of a train of railway cars where the locomotive does not know the load being carried inside each car it is pulling. This way, new functionalities can be added to the protocol by adding new TLVs. IS-IS works exactly this way, because it understands how to transport such values for the use of Segment Routing. It uses Type-Length-Value (TLV) triplets along with sub-TVLs to encapsulate various information in its advertisements. It can support both IPv4 and IPv6 control planes and extends its reach to level-1, level-2, and multilevel routing. It is capable of providing MPLS penultimate hop popping (PHP) and explicit-null signaling as well. Several RFCs, including RFC 8667 and RFC 8402, describe the process of how Prefix-SID and Adj-SID are carried in sub-TLVs in great detail. Figure 15-7 shows the format of the Prefix-SID sub-TLV.

```
 0                   1                   2                   3
 0 1 2 3 4 5 6 7 8 9 0 1 2 3 4 5 6 7 8 9 0 1 2 3 4 5 6 7 8 9 0 1
+-------------------+-------------------+-------------------+-------------------+
|       Type        |      Length       |       Flags       |     Algorithm     |
+-------------------+-------------------+-------------------+-------------------+
|                        SID/Index/Label (Variable)                             |
+-------------------------------------------------------------------------------+
```

Figure 15-7 *IS-IS Prefix-SID Format*

Table 15-3 shows the most significant TLVs you should be able to recognize on the exam.

Table 15-3 IS-IS TLVs

TLV	Name	Description	Reference
2	IIS Neighbors	Shows all running interfaces to which IS-IS is connected, has a maximum metric of 6 with only 6 out of 8 bits used.	ISO 10589
10	Authentication	The information is used to authenticate IS-IS PDUs.	ISO 10589
22	Extended IS Reachability	Increases the maximum metric to 3 bytes (24 bits), addressing TLV 2 metric limitation.	RFC 5305
134	TE Router ID	MPLS Traffic Engineering router ID.	RFC 5305
135	Extended IP Reachability	Provides a 32-bit metric with an "up/down" bit for the route-leaking of L2 Ð L1.	RFC 5305
149	Segment Identifier/Label Binding	Advertises prefixes to SID/Label mappings. This functionality is called the Segment Routing Mapping Server (SRMS).	RFC 8867
222	MT-ISN	Allows for multiple-topology adjacencies.	RFC 5120
236	IPv6 Reachability	Describes network reachability through the specification of a routing prefix.	RFC 5308
242	IS-IS Router CAPABILITY	Allows a router to announce its capabilities within an IS-IS level or the entire routing domain.	RFC 7981

IS-IS allocates the SRGB along with the Adjacency-SIDs and advertises both in IS-IS for the enabled address-families. IS-IS enables MPLS forwarding for all non-passive interfaces. Example 15-3 shows commands necessary to turn on Segment Routing in IS-IS.

Example 15-3 *Commands to Turn on Segment Routing in IS-IS*

```
IOS XR
RP/0/0/CPU0:PE4# show running-config router isis
router isis CCNP
 set-overload-bit on-startup 300
 is-type level-2-only
 net 49.0001.0000.0000.0004.00
 distribute link-state
 nsf ietf
```

```
log adjacency changes
lsp-gen-interval maximum-wait 10000 initial-wait 20 secondary-wait 200 level 2
lsp-refresh-interval 65000
max-lsp-lifetime 65535
address-family ipv4 unicast
 metric-style wide
 metric 100 level 2
 microloop avoidance
 mpls traffic-eng level-2-only
 mpls traffic-eng router-id Loopback0
 spf-interval maximum-wait 2000 initial-wait 50 secondary-wait 200
 router-id Loopback0
 segment-routing mpls
!
address-family ipv6 unicast
 metric-style wide
 spf-interval maximum-wait 2000 initial-wait 50 secondary-wait 200
!
interface Loopback0
 passive
 address-family ipv4 unicast
  prefix-sid index 4
!
!
mpls traffic-eng
RP/0/0/CPU0:PE4#
```

OSPFv2 Control Plane

Much like in IS-IS, OSPF does not rely on LDP to transmit prefix label information. It uses protocol extensions to distribute Segment Routing labels in the **OSPFv2 control plane**. OSPF relies on fixed-length link-state advertisements (LSAs) for its fundamental operations. Later, Opaque LSAs were introduced to expand to new protocol capabilities, accommodating features like Segment Routing and Traffic Engineering. These advertisements are flooded to OSPF neighbors opaquely, implying that even if a transit router lacks comprehension of this information (perhaps due to running older software), it will nonetheless indiscriminately transmit it to its neighboring routers. Multi-area functionality is supported, host loopback prefixes are advertised as IPv4 Prefix Segment IDs (Prefix-SIDs), and Adjacency Segment IDs (Adj-SIDs) are used for adjacencies. MPLS penultimate hop popping (PHP) and explicit-null signaling are also supported.

Note the format of Opaque LSAs in Figure 15-8.

Figure 15-8 *Opaque LSA Format*

Opaque LSA types are identified by the topology flooding scope in Table 15-4. The most known of these (when it comes to Segment Routing) is type 10 LSAs, which distribute Traffic Engineering (TE) link attributes. It is often referred to as the *TE LSA*, yet it has other applications as well.

Table 15-4 OSPF Opaque LSAs

LSA type	LSA Scope	Topology Flooding Scope	Reference
9	Link-local	Local network only	RFC 5250
10	Area-local	Only within an area	RFC 5250
11	Autonomous System	Domain-wide, same as AS-External type-5 LSAs	RFC 5250

Similar to IS-IS, OSPF will allocate and advertise the SRGB to its neighbors. It activates MPLS forwarding on all OSPF interfaces, excluding loopback interfaces, and assigns Adjacency-SIDs to these interfaces. Example 15-4 shows commands necessary to turn on OSPF for Segment Routing.

Example 15-4 *Commands to Turn on OSPF for Segment Routing*

```
IOS XR
RP/0/0/CPU0:PE4# show running-config router ospf
router ospf CCNP
 nsr
 distribute link-state
 log adjacency changes detail
 router-id 10.1.100.10
 segment-routing mpls
 segment-routing forwarding mpls
 fast-reroute per-prefix
```

```
fast-reroute per-prefix ti-lfa enable
affinity-map
 RED bit-position 0
!
nsf ietf
! Output omitted for brevity
address-family ipv4 unicast
area 0
 mpls traffic-eng
 segment-routing mpls
 interface Loopback0
  passive enable
  prefix-sid index 10
!
 interface HundredGigE0/0/0/0
 bfd minimum-interval 20
 bfd fast-detect
 bfd multiplier 3
  cost 200
 network point-to-point
 !
 interface HundredGigE0/0/0/1
 bfd minimum-interval 20
 bfd fast-detect
 bfd multiplier 3
  cost 200
 network point-to-point
 !
 !
mpls traffic-eng
RP/0/0/CPU0:PE4#
```

What about OSPFv3? While OSPFv3 has the potential to accommodate Segment Routing for IPv6 and utilize a native IPv6 data plane, specific extensions outlined in an IETF draft are required for implementation. It's worth noting that, at press time, these extensions have not been integrated into Cisco IOS XR and IOS XE.

BGP Control Plane

BGP also has the capability to function as the control plane for Segment Routing (SR), enabling prefix distribution throughout the network. In the context of Segment Routing, the **BGP control plane** distributes segment routing information between routers, enabling them to make forwarding decisions based on predefined segments. While seen less frequently than IS-IS and OSPF, BGP has been effectively used in practice in multiple large-scale web data centers. Such data centers can support over 100,000 services, profoundly influencing and challenging the scalability and operational efficiency of the underlying network architectures. To meet the demands of high-intensity east-west traffic found in these compute clusters, operators frequently opt for variations of Clos or Fat-tree topologies. In these massive data center networks, symmetrical topologies with numerous parallel paths connecting two server-attachment points are common. It is in this context that BGP excels and arguably surpasses the IGP approach. The assertion that "BGP is a better IGP" challenges traditional viewpoints and has sparked conversations.

What would make BGP an attractive choice? Remember that these massive data centers seek maximum bandwidth to be transferred across the midpoint of the system. Such network structures are designed to be both highly scalable, cost-effective, and are constructed from affordable, low-end access-level switches. To maintain this level of scale, the designs call for a single protocol with simple behavior and wide vendor support. With the above in mind, when it comes to simplicity, BGP certainly has its advantages because it has less of a state machine and fewer data structures. This may not appear intuitive at first glance, but it does not take long to realize that the BGP RIB structure is simpler than those of Link-State Databases (LSDBs). There is a very clear picture of "which routing information is sent where." There is a RIB-In and RIB-Out, a far easier construct for tracing exact routing paths than following link-state topology constraints with areas and levels. When it comes to operational troubleshooting, this is definitely a strength. Also, event propagation is more constrained in BGP because link failures have limited propagation scope. We can argue that BGP has more stability due to the reduced "event-flooding" domains. When it comes to traffic steering, BGP allows for per-hop Traffic Engineering that can be used for unequal cost Anycast load-balancing. In addition, BGP is widely supported by practically all vendors, so from the perspective of interoperability, BGP beats IGPs. We have been conditioned to perceive BGP as slow and suitable primarily for inter-domain routing, but it has no issues with demonstrating its adaptability and effectiveness in modern topologies. Therefore, it is advisable to approach BGP with an open mind, recognizing its potential to perform as well as, or even better than, traditional IGP alternatives in contemporary implementations.

BGP will advertise a BGP Prefix-SID associated with a prefix via BGP Labeled Unicast (BGP-LU) IPv4/IPv6 Labeled Unicast address-families. BGP Prefix-SID is a global SID, and the instruction forwards the packet over the ECMP-aware BGP best path to the associated prefix. RFC 8277 specifies that Label-Index TLV must be present in the BGP Prefix-SID attribute attached to IPv4/IPv6 Labeled Unicast prefixes. This 32-bit value represents the index value in the SRGB space and has the format illustrated in Figure 15-9.

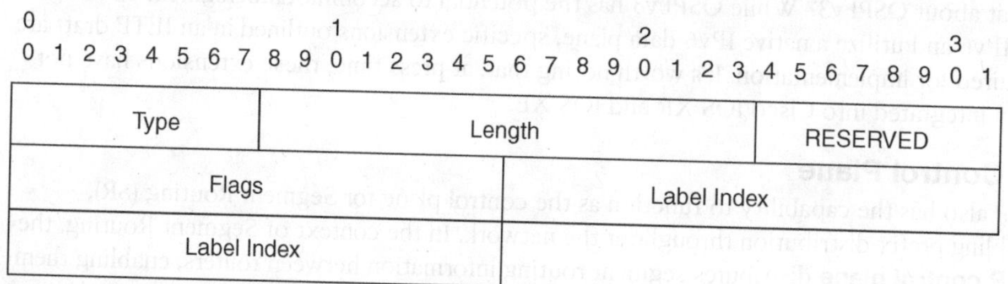

Figure 15-9 *BGP Prefix SID Advertised Format*

The Prefix-SID for a locally originated BGP route can be set with a route-policy.
Example 15-5 shows how to attach a label-index with **network** and **redistribute** commands.

Example 15-5   *Attaching a Label-Index via a Route-Policy*

```
IOS XR configuration with network command


route-policy SIDs($SID)
  set label-index $SID
end-policy
!
router bgp 100
 address-family ipv4 unicast
  network 10.1.100/4/32 route-policy SID(1)
  allocate-label all


IOS XR configuration with redistribute command


route-policy SIDs
 if destination in (10.1.100.4/32) then
  set label-index 1
 endif end-policy
!
router bgp 100
 address-family ipv4 unicast
  redistribute connected route-policy SIDs
  allocate-label all
```

One last thing regarding having BGP for a Segment Routing control plane. Remember the
Anycast load-balancing I mentioned earlier in this section? Anycast allows different nodes to
advertise the same BGP prefix. It is an application of Prefix SIDs to achieve anycast operations. Look at Figure 15-10, where I again moved some links around to represent a data
center's spine-and-leaf architectures, with spines located at the top. PE2 and P4, while advertising their individual BGP Prefix-SIDs (16002 and 16004, respectively), have been made
members of the same unicast set. Both of them advertise anycast prefix 10.1.100.24/32 with
BGP-Anycast SID 20001. PE3 wants to send traffic to PE7 but would like to exclude spine
PE6. BGP-Anycast SID 20001 will load-balance the traffic to any member of the Anycast set
and then forward it to PE7.

Additionally, due to BGP Prefix-SID global label usage, BGP-LU local labels are going to
be the same across all of the network's ASBRs. As a result, these Anycast loopbacks can be
used as the next-hop for BGP-LU prefixes. That is pretty good resiliency! Nothing to scoff
at, for sure.

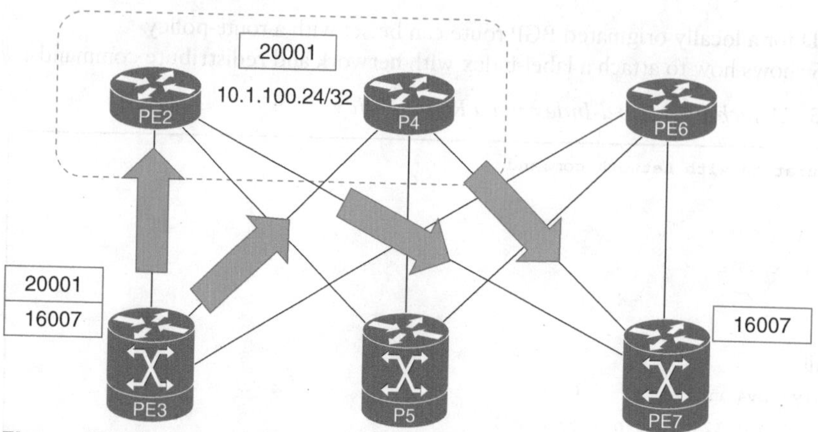

Figure 15-10   *BGP-SR Anycast Load-Balancing*

SRv6 Control Plane

The **SRv6 control plane** manages the signaling, routing, and forwarding information for Segment Routing over IPv6 (SRv6) networks. It serves as the Segment Routing architecture tailored for the IPv6 data plane and extends to the value of IPv6, influencing future IP infrastructure deployments, whether in data centers, large-scale aggregation, or backbone networks. SRv6 functions as an extension of the Segment Routing architecture specifically designed for IPv6 networks. It introduces a source-routing mechanism by encoding instructions within the IPv6 packet header.

The use of IPv6 addresses to identify objects, content, or functions applied to objects opens up significant possibilities, particularly in the realm of chaining microservices within distributed architectures or optimizing content networking. Notably, stable networks, particularly in the Asia-Pacific region, have embraced SRv6, boasting tens of thousands of nodes on a single network as of the time of writing this book.

Fundamentally, SRv6 encodes topological and services paths into the packet header. The SRv6 domain does not hold any per-flow state for Traffic Engineering or network function virtualization (NFV). Sub-50ms path protection is delivered with TI-LFA. It natively delivers all services in the packet header, without any shims or overlays. IPv4's limitations have forced the industry to create extra tools to deal with its challenges. When IPv4 lacked sufficient address space, NAT was created to hide and conserve addresses. For engineered load-balancing, we have had to invent MPLS Entropy Label and VxLAN UDP. For separating discrete networks, MPLS VPNs along VxLAN were created. Since Traffic Engineering functions were missing in IPv4, RSVP-TE and SR-TE MPLS appeared. Network Service Header (NSH) overcame IPv4 service chaining limitations. All of the above is done natively in IPv6 and why so many service providers are turning to this technology.

SRv6 (Segment Routing over IPv6) Header

At the heart of SRv6 is the IPv6 Segment Routing Header (SRH). Figure 15-11 shows the IPv6 SRH replicated from RFC 8754. This header is added to IPv6 packets to implement Segment Routing on the IPv6 forwarding plane. SRH specifies an IPv6 explicit path, listing one or more intermediate nodes the packet should visit on the way to its final destination. The Segment Left field provides the number of transit nodes before traffic reaches its destination. Then, the Segment List fields indicate the sequence of nodes in 128-bit IPv6 addresses to be visited from bottom to top. Segment List [n] shows the first node in the path; Segment List [0] shows the last node in the path.

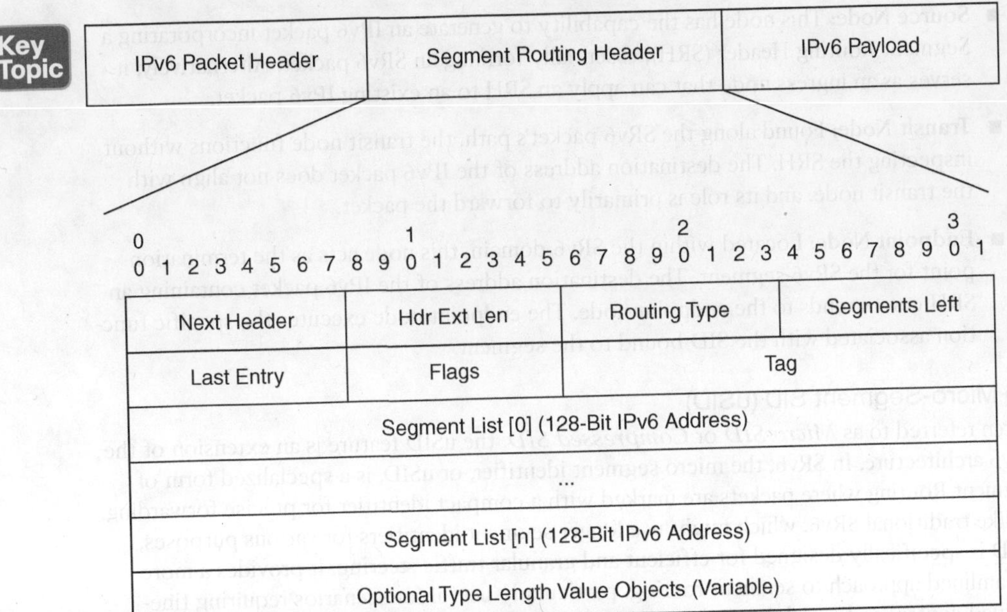

Figure 15-11   *IPv6 Segment Routing Header Format*

In SRv6, each segment is represented by an IPv6 address known as a segment identifier (SID). These SIDs play a crucial role in defining specific paths or instructions for forwarding packets throughout the network. It looks a lot like a 128-bit IPv6 address, but has different semantics because it consists of two parts, with Figure 15-12 providing the visualization:

- **Locator:** Represents an address of a specific SRv6 node performing the function.

- **Function:** Represents any possible network instruction bound to the node that generates the SRv6 SID (network instruction) and is executed locally on that particular node, specified by the locator bits.

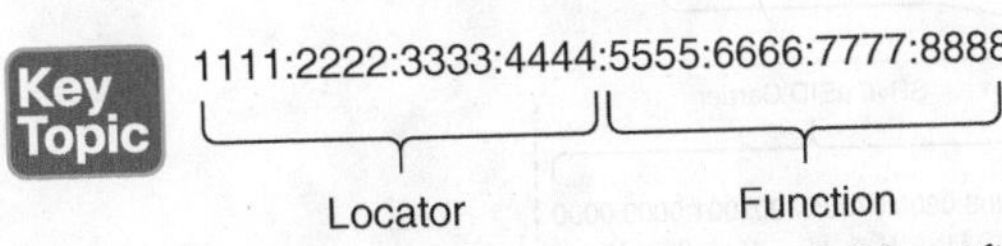

Figure 15-12   *IPv6 Segment Identifier*

You now have the ability to send packets to a node (locator) and then instruct the node to execute an action (function). This is not a subtle difference! In SR-MPLS, IGP with extensions advertised the transport mechanism, and services (L2VPNs, L3VPNs) were signaled *independently* via LDP or MP-BGP. You could change your transport (from MPLS to SR) without affecting the upper protocols that ran on top of it. For the first time in the industry, transport and services instructions are coupled and signaled in the SID. You will see an example of this coming up shortly where an L3VPN is written into the SID.

SRv6 Node Roles

In the context of SRv6 (Segment Routing over IPv6) networks, different nodes play distinct roles in facilitating packet forwarding and processing. These roles include

- **Source Node:** This node has the capability to generate an IPv6 packet incorporating a Segment Routing Header (SRH), essentially forming an SRv6 packet. Alternatively, it serves as an ingress node that can apply an SRH to an existing IPv6 packet.

- **Transit Node:** Found along the SRv6 packet's path, the transit node functions without inspecting the SRH. The destination address of the IPv6 packet does not align with the transit node, and its role is primarily to forward the packet.

- **Endpoint Node:** Located within the SRv6 domain, this node acts as the termination point for the SRv6 segment. The destination address of the IPv6 packet containing an SRH corresponds to the endpoint node. The endpoint node executes the specific function associated with the SID bound to the segment.

SRv6 Micro-Segment SID (uSID)

Often referred to as *Micro-SID* or *Compressed SID*, the uSID feature is an extension of the SRv6 architecture. In SRv6, the micro segment identifier, or uSID, is a specialized form of Segment Routing where packets are marked with a compact identifier for precise forwarding. Unlike traditional SRv6, which might use longer segment identifiers for various purposes, uSID is specifically designed for efficient and granular traffic steering. It provides a more streamlined approach to segment routing, particularly useful for scenarios requiring fine-grained control and scalability enhancements.

Using the established SRv6 Network Programming framework, it can encode up to six SRv6 Micro-SID (uSID) instructions within a singular 128-bit SID address, termed a *uSID Carrier*. Moreover, this extension seamlessly integrates with the existing SRv6 data plane and control plane, requiring no modifications. Notably, it ensures minimal MTU overhead. For instance, when incorporating six uSIDs within a uSID carrier, it yields 18 source-routing waypoints with just 40 bytes of overhead in the Segment Routing Header. Look at Figure 15-13, which illustrates the usage of uSID. Pay attention to how the highlighted uSIDs correspond to router numbering/naming.

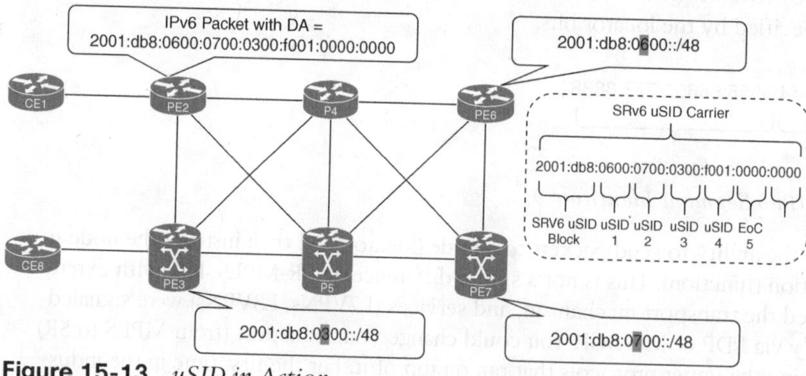

Figure 15-13   *uSID in Action*

The customer at CE1 is using the VPNv4 SP service to connect to a remote site CE8. Router PE2 sends traffic to VPNv4 CE8 to router PE3 via a traffic-engineered path visiting routers

PE6 and PE7 using a single (!) SRv6 SID (note that without uSID, a sequential Segment List would have to be specified). Let's unpack this:

1. PE2, PE6, PE7, and PE3 are SRv6 capable and are configured with 32-bit SRv6 block 2001:db8.

2. P4 and P5 run classic IPv6 forwarding and do not change the Destination Address.

3. PE6, PE7, and PE3 advertise their corresponding 2001:db8:0600::/48, 2001:db8:0700::/48, and 2001:db8:0300::/48 routes.

4. PE2 receives an IPv4 packet from CE1, encapsulates it, and sends an IPv6 packet with the destination address 2001:db8:0600:0700:0300:f001:0000:0000. This is an SRv6 uSID Carrier that contains a sequence of micro-SIDs (instructions 0600, 0700, 0300, f001, and 0000).

5. The 0600, 0700, and 0300 uSIDs are used to construct a traffic engineering path to PE3 with two stops along the way—PE6 and PE7. uSID f001 is a BGP-signaled instruction sent by PE3 indicating the VPNv4 service. uSID 0000 indicates the end of instructions.

6. What happens at P4? P4, running only classic IPv6, forwards the packet along the shortest path to PE6.

7. PE6 receives the packet, pops its own uSID 0600, and advances the micro-program by looking up the shortest path to the next Destination Address (DA) 2001:db8:0700::/48. Now the DA is 2001:db8:0700:0300:f001:0000:0000:0000. This behavior is called *shift and forward*.

8. PE7 receives the packet, pops its own uSID 0700, and advances the micro-program by looking up the shortest path to the next Destination Address (DA) 2001:db8:0300::/48. Now the DA is 2001:db8:0300:f001:0000:0000:0000:0000. Shift and forward again.

9. P5 forwards the packet to PE3, just like P4 did.

10. PE2 receives the packet and executes the VPNv4 function based on this own instruction f001. It decapsulates the IPv6 packet, performs IPv4 table lookup, and forwards the IPv4 packet to CE8.

SRv6/MPLS L3 Service Interworking Gateway

The SRv6/MPLS L3 Service Interworking Gateway facilitates the seamless extension of L3 services between MPLS and SRv6 domains, ensuring continuity in service delivery across both control and data planes. This feature enables interoperability between SRv6 L3VPN and existing MPLS L3VPN domains, offering a pathway for transitioning from MPLS to SRv6 L3VPN.

At the gateway node, the SRv6/MPLS L3 Service Interworking Gateway performs both transport and service termination tasks. It generates SRv6 VPN SIDs and MPLS VPN labels for all prefixes within the configured VRF for re-origination, as illustrated in Figure 15-14. The gateway supports traffic forwarding from the MPLS domain to the SRv6 domain by removing the MPLS VPN label, performing a destination prefix lookup, and applying the appropriate SRv6 encapsulation. Conversely, for traffic from the SRv6 domain to the MPLS domain, the gateway removes the outer IPv6 header, performs a destination prefix lookup, and applies the VPN and next-hop MPLS labels.

PE3 is the interworking gateway that has one leg in the SR-MPLS domain and the other in the SRv6 domain. It performs a translation service by popping the MPLS VPN label and looking up the destination prefix in the SRv6 domain. It encapsulates the payload in the outer IPv6 header with P4's destination address. In the opposite direction, PE3 removes the outer IPv6 header, looks up the destination prefix, and pushes MPLS label 16002 for the BGP next-hop of PE2.

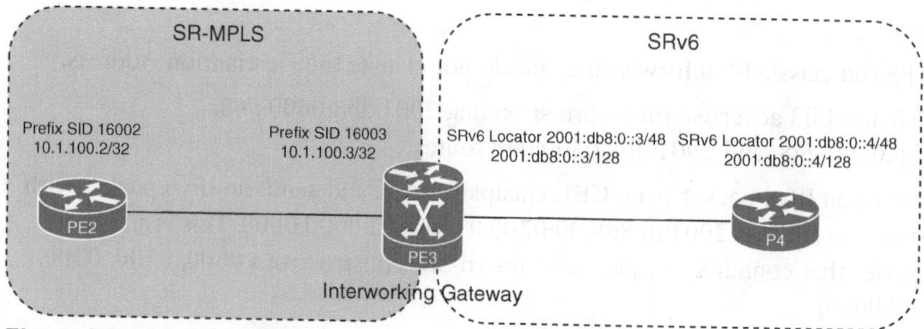

Figure 15-14 *SR-MPLS SRv6 Interworking Gateway*

Co-existence with LDP

It would be nice to never worry about LDP and RSVP, but the reality is that many of today's engineers will have to touch these older MPLS networks. A Segment Routing control plane can co-exist with the label-switched paths (LSPs) constructed with LDP or RSVP. The MPLS architecture allows for the simultaneous use of multiple label distribution protocols, including LDP, RSVP-TE, and others. The SR control plane can coexist alongside these protocols without any interaction. In Figure 15-15, we have removed some links in our network and have thus completely flattened it. This network runs a mix of both Segment Routing (SR) and Label Distribution Protocol (LDP). It is possible to establish an end-to-end seamless Multiprotocol Label Switching (MPLS) LSP, which will ensure interoperability between these two domains. To accomplish this, one or more nodes function as Segment Routing Mapping Servers (SRMS). These SRMS entities take on the responsibility of advertising SID mappings on behalf of nodes that are not SR-capable. This mechanism enables SR-capable nodes to learn about the SIDs assigned to non-SR-capable nodes without the need for explicit individual node configurations. Let's unpack this.

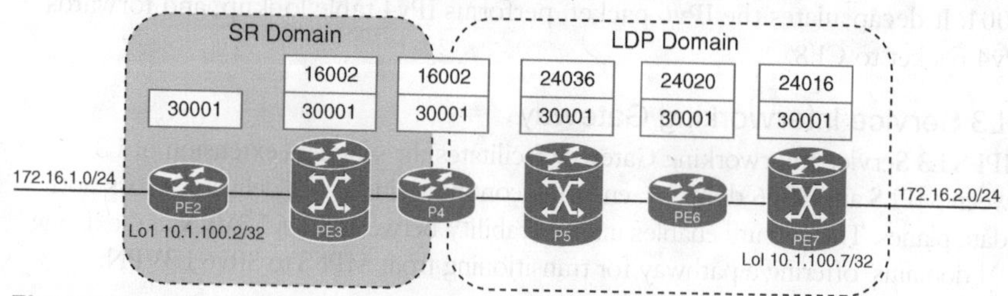

Figure 15-15 *SR and LDP Domain Interoperability*

Notice that this network runs both SR and LDP, which can be typical during network transitions and upgrades. PE2 and PE7 are exchanging BGP VPNv4 routes. PE2, PE3, and P4 are SR-capable. PE4, P5, P6, and PE7 use LDP. How do these two domains talk to each other end to end? First, let's start from the LDPÐSR direction, which is quite easy because SR-capable routers will automatically translate between LDP- and SR-based labels:

1. PE7 learns a service route (L3VPN route, for example) for customer prefix 172.16.1.0/24 with a service/VPN label of 30001.

2. PE7's BGP next-hop for this service label is associated with PE2's lol 10.1.100.2/32.

3. PE7 finds LDP label binding 24016 from its neighbor PE6 for PE2's Forwarding Equivalence Class (FEC) of 10.10.100.2/32 and forwards the packet to PE6.

4. PE6 finds LDP label binding 24020 from its neighbor PE5 for PE2's FEC of 10.10.100.2/32, swaps 24016 for 24020, and forwards the packet to PE5.

5. PE5 finds LDP label binding 24036 from its neighbor PE4 for PE2's FEC of 10.10.100.2/32, swaps 24020 for 24046, and forwards the packet to P4.

6. P4 lacks an LDP binding originating from its next-hop PE3 for the FEC associated with PE1. What it does carry, though, is an SR node segment pointing to an IGP route leading to PE2. P4 engages in label merging, wherein it replaces its local LDP label (24036) for FEC PE2 with the corresponding SR node segment label, which is 16002.

7. PE3 pops label 16002 (assuming penultimate hop popping function is used) and forwards the packet to PE2.

8. PE2 receives the packet, looks up its service label of 30001, and drops the packet into the appropriate customer VRF.

We now have an end-to-end LDPÐSR path. Simple. What about in the opposite direction? This is where we will encounter a problem going from SRÐLDP. Can you take a moment to think what the problem would be by looking at Figure 15-14 before you examine Figure 15-15? PE2 needs to send traffic to 172.16.2.0/24 with service label 40001 that it received with the BGP next-hop of 10.1.100.7/32. Since PE2 only speaks SR, when it looks up the node segment for 10.1.100.7/32, what will it find in its label database? Nothing. Why? Because such label mapping does not exist on the network, since the operator has never configured it; therefore, no router advertises or receives this label mapping. There must be something to associate PE7's loopback with SR label mapping. The better answer here is Segment Routing Mapping Server (SRMS). All analogies finally break down, but it is possible to think of SRMS as a sort of route reflector for SR labels. Just as in BGP, we can centrally instruct all routers in our SR domain. Look at Figure 15-16.

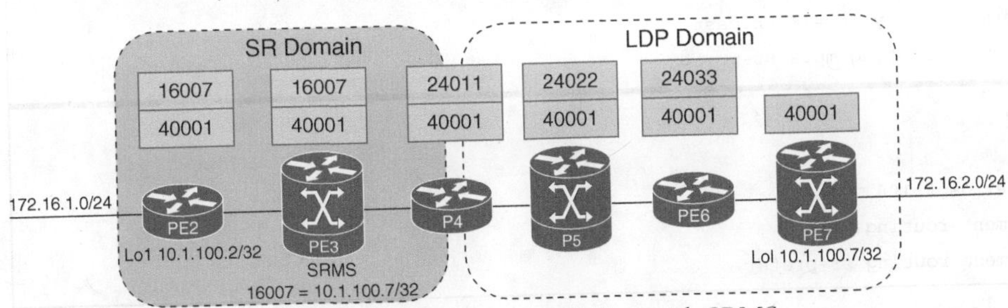

Figure 15-16   *SR and LDP Domain Interoperability with SRMS*

Walking back in the opposite direction looks like this:

1. PE3 is chosen as a Segment Routing Mapping Server (SRMS). In practice, it is recommended to have a redundant SRMS.

2. As PE7 lacks Segment Routing (SR) capability, you must create a mapping policy on the SRMS, which associates label 16007 with PE7's lo1 10.1.100.7/32.

3. Now, PE2 learns a service route (L3VPN route via BGP) for customer prefix 172.16.1.0/24 with a service/VPN label of 40001 with the BGP next-hop of 10.1.100.7/32.

4. PE2 finds an SR label binding 16007 it has received from the SRMS PE3 for PE7's FEC of 10.10.100.7/32 and forwards the packet to PE3 as the IGP next-hop.

5. PE3 finds an SR label binding 16007 pointing to its neighbor P4 as the IGP next-hop, swaps 16007 for 16007, and forwards to P4.

6. P4 does not have an SR label for PE7's IGP route, but it holds LDP label 24011 for this FEC. It swaps 16007 for 24011 (remember the process is called *label merge*) and forwards to P5.

7. P5 swaps 24011 for 24022 and forwards to PE6.

8. PE6 pops the label (due to PHP in this setup) and forwards to PE7.

9. PE7 receives the packet, looks up its service label of 40001, and drops the packet into the appropriate customer VRF.

What should you remember here? Segment Routing Mapping Server labels are only necessary in the SRÐLDP direction. SR and LDP labels come from separate label database ranges (16000–23999 for SR and 24000+ for LDP), so unless the operator has deliberately violated this guidance, there is not a chance the network will be in a state of confusion, since the SR and LDP labels do not overlap each other. The network must maintain continuous SR connectivity in the SR domain. The network must also maintain continuous LDP connectivity in the LDP domain. If you understood the packet walkthrough, these points should be clear.

One last thing to know for completeness. By default, Cisco routers prefer LDP as the label imposition mechanism when the MPLS features are turned on. The way to enable SR for label imposition is shown in Example 15-6.

Example 15-6 *Segment Routing Label Imposition Preferred*

```
IS-IS

router isis 100
 address-family ipv4|6 unicast
  segment-routing mpls sr-prefer

OSPF

router ospf 100
 segment-routing mpls
 segment-routing sr-prefer
```

Segment Routing Traffic Engineering

RSVP-TE, despite its powerful Traffic Engineering capabilities, poses challenges in practical deployments due to its complexity. Managing backup tunnels, intricate configurations at scale, the absence of seamless inter-domain intelligence, and the complexities of steering traffic through methods like PBR or autoroute have resulted in various issues and limited widespread adoption. Simplifying these aspects is crucial for enhancing the usability and deployment scope of Traffic-Engineered networks. Enter Segment Routing policies. They are simple, automated, scalable, and carry support for a wide variety of functionalities including multidomain intelligence, which is provided by Path Computation Element (PCE) and Binding-SID (BSID)—more on this later.

Segment Routing Policies

In Segment Routing, there are no tunnels (the closest possible thing is Circuit-Style Segment Routing, which has policies to put traffic on the same A–Z path, akin to bidirectional co-routed LSPs—this is outside of the current exam's scope). Instead, Segment Routing introduces the concept of Segment Routing Policies. These are typically deployed at ingress routers at the edge of the network and can force the packet to follow any desired path.

An SR Policy is fundamentally a sequence of segments. In its most basic structure, it is a sequence of IP waypoints presented in either SR-MPLS or SRv6 format (SID list), with the initial entry as the first destination to be visited. An SR Policy is uniquely identified by these attributes:

- **Headend:** An ingress router where the policy is implemented.

- **Tailend:** An egress router where the policy ends.

- **Color:** A numeric value that uniquely identifies multiple SR Traffic Engineering policies between the same pair of routers.

Figure 15-17 illustrates this best. PE2 needs to send traffic for prefixes 172.16.100.0/24 and 172.16.200.0/24 to the same PE7 router, since it is the egress point connecting these two networks. However, traffic destined for 172.16.100.0/24 must follow the top low-delay path due to latency requirements, and traffic for 172.16.200/24 must take the bottom low-cost path because the customer is not paying for the premium service. Try doing this with IGP alone! SR policies, on the other hand, easily differentiate traffic between the same pair of routers by steering them into differently colored policies (different numeric values) that properly groom traffic onto the desired paths.

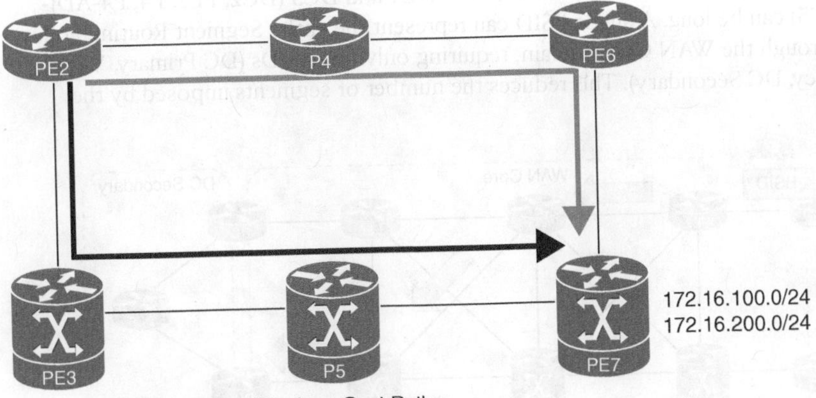

Figure 15-17 *Segment Routing Policy Places Traffic on Diverse Paths*

SR Policies and Candidate Paths

An SR Policy consists of one or more **Candidate Paths**. Each Candidate Path has a single SID-list or a set of weighted SID-list. Things to consider regarding a Candidate Path (the order is not important here):

1. Can be explicitly defined. The operator will provide the exact sequence of SIDs to be visited along the way to the destination.

2. Can be dynamically defined. The operator will provide optimization objectives (select only encrypted links) and constraints, a set of rules to follow (exclude links certain attributes, such as not meeting minimum delay).

3. Has a preference value (numeric, higher is preferred).

4. Is associated with a single Binding-SID (BSID, more on this later).

5. Can be supplied to the headend via

   a. CLI

   b. NETCONF

   c. PCEP (Path Computation Element Protocol)

   d. BGP

6. An SR Policy will select a single best Candidate Path and program it via BSID into the router's RIB/FIB forwarding table.

Binding-SID (BSID)

Binding Segment Identifier (BSID) is a SID value that is an opaque representation of a Segment Routing Policy. BSID shows a chosen path to upstream routers. It provides isolation and decoupling between distinct source-routed domains while increasing overall network scalability. Do not forget that SR Policies use BSID to program a router's forwarding table (just mentioned in point 6).

Note how in Figure 15-18 different routing/SR domains are involved. The list of SIDs to steer traffic onto the imagined low-delay path between DC1 and DC5 (DC2, PE2, P4, P4-ADJ-SID, PE7, DC5) can be long. A single BSID can represent the entire Segment Routing Policy sending it through the WAN Core domain, requiring only three SIDs (DC Primary, WAN Core SR Policy, DC Secondary). This reduces the number of segments imposed by the source.

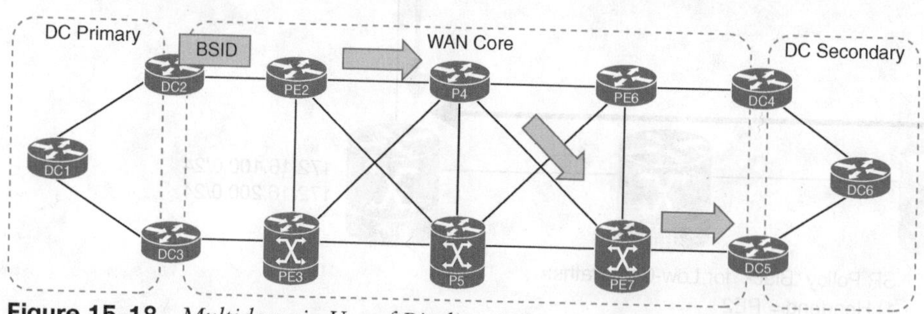

Figure 15-18   *Multidomain Use of Binding-SID*

Additionally, this approach keeps one domain unaffected by routing changes in another domain, since BSID does not change during these events. Domain internal operations can be thus hidden (opaque) from each other, which can be beneficial to service providers who do not want to disclose the details of how they provide services to their customers.

Flex-Algo

Flex-Algo is the best way to do traffic engineering today. Flex-Algo, short for Flexible Algorithm, enhances Segment Routing Traffic Engineering (SRTE) by introducing additional segments with distinct properties compared to the Interior Gateway Protocol Prefix segments. It expands the SRTE capabilities by including customizable, user-defined segments in the toolbox. It can also use Segment Routing on-demand next hop (ODN) and Automated Steering to create traffic-engineered paths based on user intentions; these are outside of the scope of this book.

IETF has standardized algorithms 0 through 127. Routers run the default algorithm 0 as the IGP shortest path derived from the IGP metric. Additional algorithms 128 through 255 can be customized by network operators. They are known as *SR IGP Flexible Algorithms*, or Flex-Algo as the shorter version. It is called *flexible* because you can decide which metric you want to use in your intent.

In our earlier discussion of Prefix-SID in this chapter, we focused solely on explaining the default aspect of Prefix-SID behavior, specifically the one linked to algorithm 0. When you read (you really should) RFC 8867 and RFC 8665, you will notice that both IS-IS and OSPF include Prefix-SID sub-TLV algorithm field in the formats illustrated in Figure 15-19 and Figure 15-20.

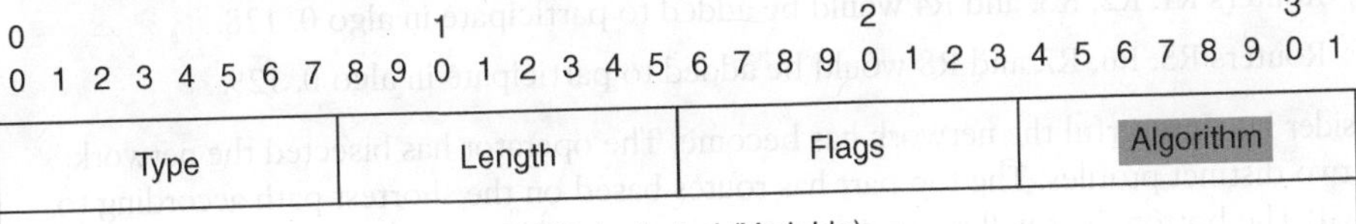

Figure 15-19 *Algorithm Field in Prefix-SID Sub-TLV for IS-IS*

Figure 15-20 *Algorithm Field in Prefix-SID Sub-TLV for OSPF*

This means that the operator can change the default algorithm 0 (IGP shortest-path) behavior on routers that are assigned to use a different algorithm (128–255) as different constraints (logical rules) will be imposed on the part of the network that participates in this algorithm. Let's look at Figure 15-21, where we break from the familiar-to-us topology.

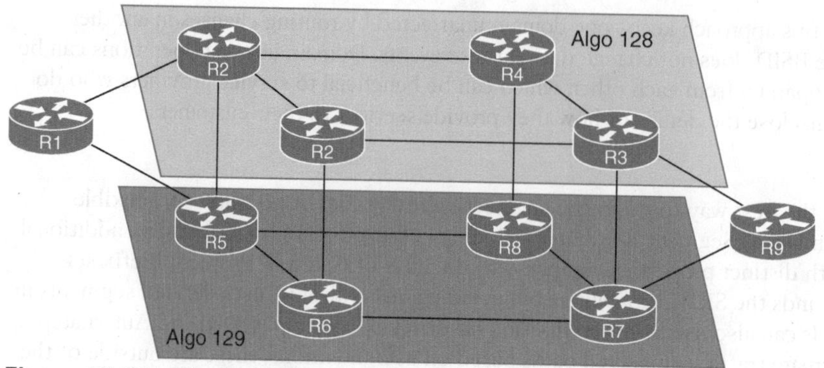

Figure 15-21   *Flex-Algo Network Slicing*

Suppose the operator wanted to impose different type behaviors on this network. Instead of using the default algo 0 (IGP shortest-path), the operator can define other algorithms that can minimize metrics other than shortest path, such as delay, for example. The operator can also combine this with rules to exclude links with certain properties (link-affinity, SRLG, encryption, etc.). Here is one example of what can be done:

1. The operator can define Flex-Algo 128 to prioritize IGP metric and avoid link-affinity "dark-gray" on the bottom.

2. The operator can define Flex-Algo 129 to delay metric and avoid link-affinity "light-gray" on the top.

3. Routers R1 and R9 would be added to participate in algo 0, 128, and 129.

4. Routers R1, R2, R3, and R4 would be added to participate in algo 0, 128.

5. Routers R5, R6, R7, and R8 would be added to participate in algo 0, 129.

Consider how powerful the network has become. The operator has bisected the network into two distinct profiles. The top part has routes based on the shortest path according to the IGP. The bottom half will route delay-sensitive traffic through the part of the network that uses dynamic link-delay measurement, which will be advertised by the IGP. Someone reroutes your optical underlay path? Does not matter. Someone moves a circuit without bothering to notify your department? Does not matter. The network will recalculate the best path according to the intent you had in mind. If you see the beauty of this approach, you will understand that the limitation of what can be done on a network at scale exists only in the minds of its architects. Low-cost delay-optimized paths (my personal SP operator nirvana, because this is where I make money) have now become a reality because we can now finally differentiate services on our infrastructure. It is my opinion that while SR policies are effective for carving dynamic paths on the network, the simplicity and flexibility of Flex-Algo allow the operator to easily slice the network into multiple planes that can be used to carry encrypted, application-dependent, dynamic delay-based, low-cost, and other intent-based traffic. You can even drain all network traffic to the bottom dark-gray plane of the network, run upgrades on the top light-gray plane of the network, and repeat the process again in the other direction—accomplishing zero downtime for your customers.

That is the power of Flex-Algo—operational simplicity and scale. You can finally manage massive networks with a simple picture in mind, rather than constructing hundreds of SR Policies for individual applications. Flex-Algo is applicable to SR-MPLS and SRv6. In the case of SR-MPLS, you will get an extra label for the router's loopback. In SRv6, you get a different locator (recall our earlier discussion on this topic). SP operators are really beginning to heavily use this approach with SRv6 (IPv6).

Something you need to be aware of that is directly called out in the exam blueprint is *encapsulation*. SR-MPLS uses SRTE policies (on-demand or manual) to steer traffic into Flex-Algo. If you want traffic to follow a particular path, you specify a list of SIDs. When you specify the SID associated with Flex-Algo, the traffic takes that specific Flex-Algo plane. In contrast, SRv6 does not use policies. In SRv6, the ingress PE will directly encapsulate traffic based on the Service SID advertised in BGP. That Service SID (remember locator + function?) is a combination for the Algo locator and decapsulation function. Transport and Service become blended and are encoded into the transport intent (Algo locator). Transport intent and Service function are *encapsulated* into the same instruction. SRv6 is a much simpler approach to driving traffic intent.

TI-LFA

To date, TI-LFA is the number one reason why network operators deploy SR: they want an automated way to compute a backup path by IGP. No need to do MPLS-TE (traffic engineering tunnels) for fast reroute (FRR). **Topology-independent loop-free alternate (TI-LFA)** provides a simple, automatic, optimal, and topology-independent sub-50ms per-prefix protection to the network. It can protect Segment Routing, LDP, and IP traffic without relying on the construction of backup tunnels of any sort, as is the case in RSVP-TE. Whether IS-IS or OSPF is used, these protocols precompute a backup path for each active path per IP prefix destination. They run an SPF algorithm for the primary path and then automatically run the SPF again, *excluding* the primary path—deriving the backup path. IGP pre-installs this path in the data plane and immediately uses it once the active destination path is impacted. Be careful with analogies, because they all finally breakdown, but it can be helpful to think of how an EIGRP-feasible successor works. The router already knows what the post-convergence path will look like even before the failure occurs.

Figure 15-22 shows a fundamental TI-LFA operation from router PE2's perspective; once the protected PE4–P2 link fails, traffic is rerouted over the post-convergence path, which is known and preprogrammed before the link failure occurs. The recommendation is to enable this functionality on all routers in your Segment Routing domain. This approach creates automatic backup paths throughout the network without the burden of manually provisioning backup tunnel paths.

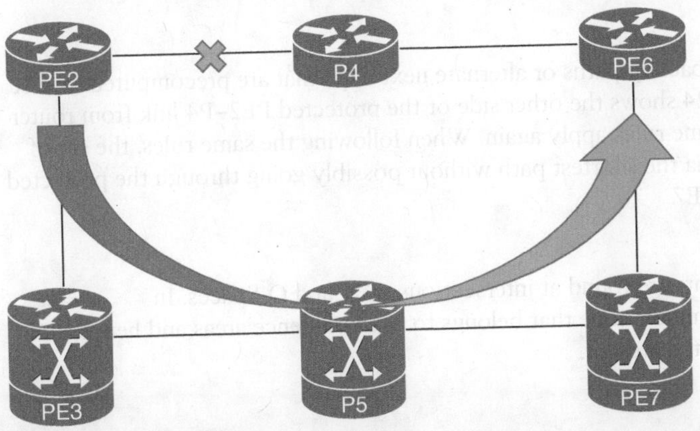

Figure 15-22 *TI-LFA Operation*

Terms from Remote LFA Technology

RFC 7490 describes the following architectural reference areas to understand repair tunnel endpoints for link protection. While there is no concept of tunnels in Segment Routing (they have been replaced by policies), the same reference areas apply and are important for this exam.

P-Space

In Figure 15-23, we return to our topology and remove some of the internal links to create a ring topology to better understand these reference areas.

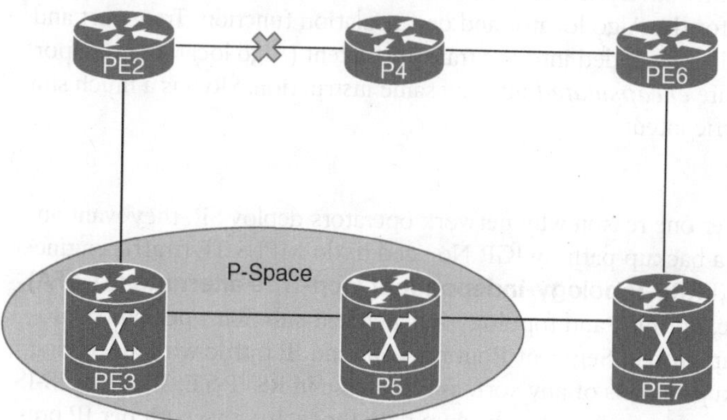

Figure 15-23 *P-Space Reference Area*

Reference areas are always seen from a perspective of a certain router with respect to a particular failed link. The way to look at reference areas depends on which router we're considering and the specific link it is protecting. In this example, router PE2 would like to protect the link between itself and router P4. The protected space (**P-Space**) of a router concerning a protected link refers to routers that PE2 can reach through the shortest paths without having to use the protected link. Which routers would those be? All link costs being equal here, only PE3 and P5 will be in P-Space. What about PE7? Not quite, as it is possible, due to ECMP, that PE2 can send a packet to PE7 through the top of the diagram through the protected link, thus disqualifying from being the shortest path. What would be the point of using a link that can potentially fail? Expressed in cost terms, P-Space contains a set of routers found on a shorter path than the path cost going through the protected link. In the case of PE7, it is equal and not shortest—thus, not a part of P-Space.

Q-Space

Q-space refers to a set of backup paths or alternate next hops that are precomputed for use during a failure. Figure 15-24 shows the other side of the protected PE2–P4 link from router P4's perspective, and the same rules apply again. When following the same rules, the set of routers reachable from P4 via the shortest path without possibly going through the protected link only include PE6 and PE7.

PQ Node

Viable repair tunnel endpoints are found at intersections of P- and Q-Spaces. In Figure 15-25, there is no common node that belongs to both reference areas and hence no viable repair tunnel endpoint is present.

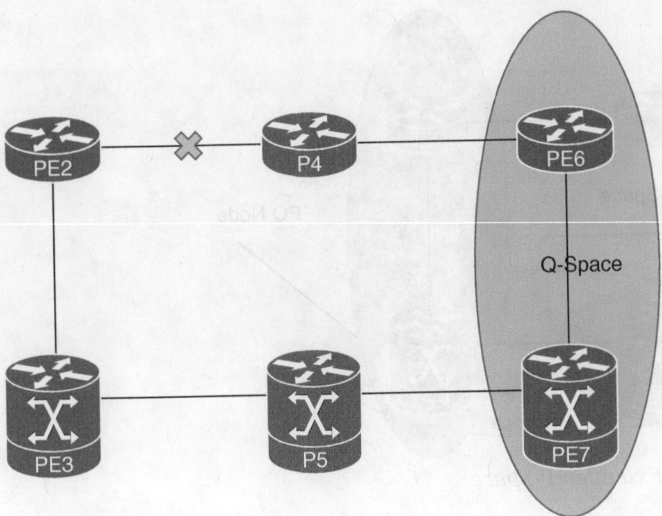

Figure 15-24   *Q-Space Reference Area*

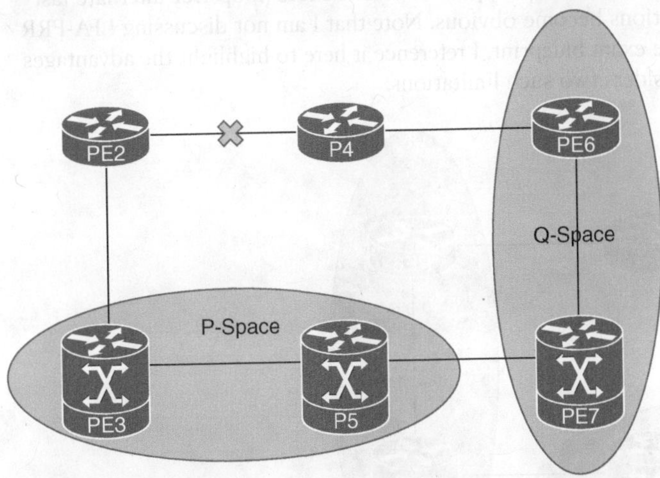

Figure 15-25   *P-Space and Q-Space Reference Area*

Extended P-Space

Because PE4 needs to repair the protected PE4–P2 link and reach any router in this ring topology without using the protected link, the concept of **Extended P-Space** was introduced. Extended P-Space is the union of each of PE4's neighbors. In this case, this is router PE3 in Figure 15-26, whose P-Space contains routers P5 and PE7. By combining P-Spaces of PE2 and PE3, we extend PE2's reach, and PE7 becomes a common point for P- and Q-Spaces. A **PQ node** of a node PE2, in relation to a protected link PE2–P4, is a node that belongs to both the P-space (or extended P-space) of PE2 for that link and the Q-space of P4 for the same link. PE7 is chosen as the repair tunnel endpoint. Why? Because repair tunnels are chosen from a set of PQ nodes.

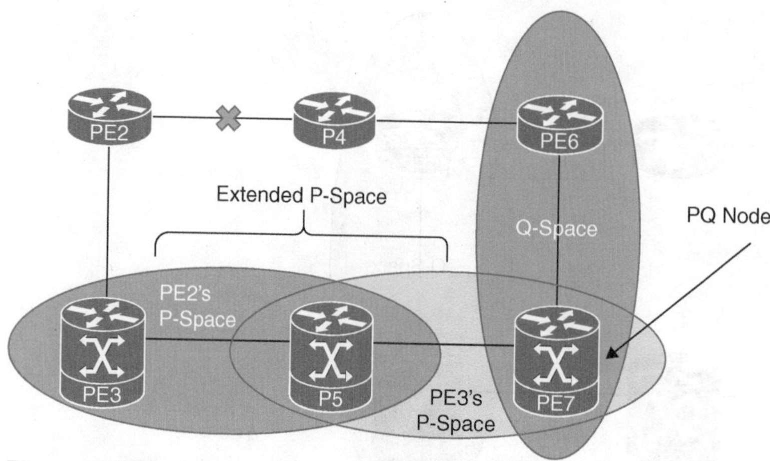

Figure 15-26 *PQ Node and Extended P-Space*

Classic LFA Limitations

Now, with the understanding of the reference points, Classic LFA's (loop-free alternate fast reroute, aka LFA-FRR) limitations become obvious. Note that I am not discussing LFA-FRR because it is not a part of the exam blueprint. I reference it here to highlight the advantages of TI-LFA. Figure 15-27 considers two such limitations.

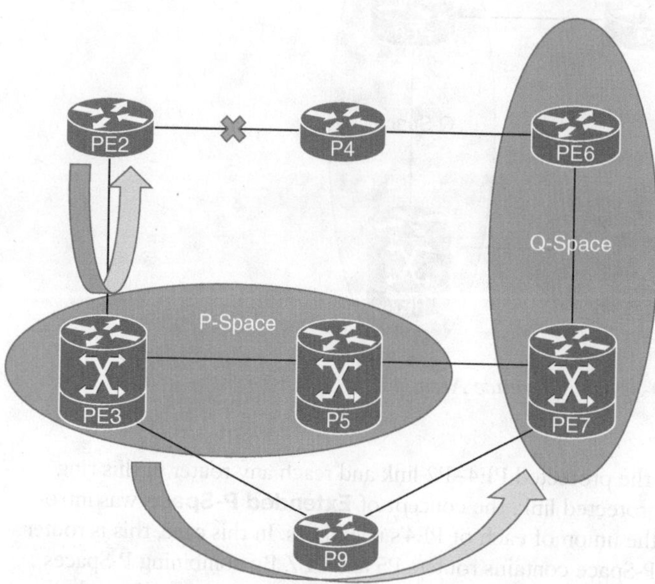

Figure 15-27 *Classic LFA Limitations Examples*

First, LFA-FRR suffers from incomplete coverage, which makes it topology dependent (as opposed to TI-LFA, which is topology independent). Recall our discussion about the PQ node. PE2 protects the PE2–P4 link and sends traffic to PE6. When the PE2–P4 link fails, PE2 will send traffic to PE3. Before the network converges via IGP, PE3 has a problem, since the shortest path to PE8 is still through the failed PE2–P4 link and PE3 will send the traffic back to PE2, looping the doomed packets. This is a real problem that, in the rLFA (Remote LFA) cases, can sometimes be solved by a Targeted LDP session, where PE2 would establish a remote LDP session with PE7, but this approach also has limitations that are outside of the scope of this exam. TI-LFA handles this topology though a "double-segment" coverage, where two labels are pushed (PE3, PE3-R5 ADJ-SID) to overcome this problem.

Second, notice the additional P9 router. Let's suppose it is not a part of the network core or planned for capacity. Classic LFA will steer the traffic on this suboptimal backup path. Additional case-specific operator involvement would be necessary to avoid such undesired backup paths.

In contrast, a topology-independent loop free alternate (TI-LFA) provides 100 percent coverage and uses the post-convergence path as the fast reroute (FRR) backup path.

TI-LFA delivers significant improvements over the traditional loop-free alternate fast reroute (LFA-FRR) approach. TI-LFA uses a post-convergence path after a link failure occurs. This path is known before a failure occurs and is preprogrammed into the data plane. TI-LFA uses PQ nodes, or a combination of P and Q nodes located on the post-convergence path to compute backup paths. Traffic will be rerouted in sub-50ms on any topology.

While the blueprint does not focus on configuration of Segment Routing features, you need to know how to configure TI-LFA. So, here is your homework for this section: return to Example 15-3, which I took from a massive production lab we have within Cisco to show the latest technologies. Study it and locate the two highlighted commands that start with **fast-reroute**. I recommend you enable this on all provider facing links; they will provide "automagic" protection mechanisms for your entire network without having to build backup tunnels. Know that TI-LFA works seamlessly with Flex-Algo we discussed in the previous section.

NOTE   One last thing that will not come up on the exam (as TI-LFA is positioned as a better alternative). Be aware that the TI-LFA concept is not new. RFC 4090 (*Fast Reroute Extensions to RSVP-TE for LSP Tunnels*) described this very technique in 2005, 10 years before Segment Routing hit the street) in Section 3.1 (One-to-one Backup method), albeit RSVP used signaling for tunnels and Segment Routing uses a label stack to guide the packet onto the new path. I'm here to assist you in preparing for your exam and provide valuable background information, without engaging in debates over differing viewpoints.

PCE-PCC Architecture

PCE-PCC architecture involves a Path Computation Element (PCE) that centrally computes optimal network paths and a Path Computation Client (PCC) that requests these paths, enabling efficient and scalable traffic engineering across the network. To take a step back, Segment Routing Traffic Engineering (SRTE) allows the network operator to force a packet anywhere on the network. The ingress router will contain the policy containing the operator's intent. If the network is small like the basic topology we have been using for our examples, there are only a handful for routers that we have to individually configure with such policies. A great majority of service provider networks you are likely to encounter in your career will contain dozens, hundreds, or maybe thousands of nodes. The task of deploying a uniform policy on such a distributed network domain becomes laborious and operationally costly. How do you scale this type of rollout? There are many other limitations operators have encountered on distributed SR (or RSVP-TE for that matter) networks. Among the more notable ones is stale policies, in which operators define a set of policies and in six months traffic patterns change, which leads to continuous "rinse-and-repeat" of policy redeployment. Another one would be applications requesting the best available path in real time—not something that can by automatically done with the SRTE approach we have described thus far. What about being able to offer paths that meet certain SLAs? There are many other ones.

From the beginning of Traffic Engineering, the need for a centralized optimization element that can dynamically adjust policies based on current network conditions was apparent. Enter Path Computation Element Protocol (PCEP). It was initially specified to support the classic RSVP-TE protocol. With the introduction of Segment Routing, PCEP has been extended to support SRTE. RFC 4655 defines multiple terms that support PCEP-based architecture. Of immediate interest to us are the following terms:

- **Path Computation Element (PCE)**, which is "an entity that can compute a network path or route based on a network graph, and of applying computational constraints during the computation. The PCE entity is an application that can be located within a network node or component, on an out-of-network server, etc...." (RFC 4655)

- **Path Computation Client (PCC)**, which is "a client application requesting a path computation to be performed by the Path Computation Element..." (RFC 4655)

- **Path Computation Element Protocol (PCEP)**, which is north-bound API capable, meaning that it can ingest information coming from the network routers (via BGP-LS updates, for example) and make real-time Traffic Engineering decisions based on current network conditions. This is extremely powerful and desired on modern networks.

Notice that you can run PCE on the router itself or can rely on another adjunct processor to perform this function. In the case of Cisco products, that would be the Crosswork Network Controller, which provides a wide assortment of functionalities that helps customers to simplify and automate intent-based network service provisioning, visualization, monitoring, and optimization in a multivendor network environment with a common GUI and API. In Cisco's documentation, you will often encounter references to SR-PCE. When you see these, it will either be a router running PCE or the Crosswork Network Controller. It can also think of PCE as a BGP Route-Reflector for Segment Routing and associated services. The following is a partial list of its capabilities (get the overall picture, do not memorize these for the exam):

- Segment Routing (SR) policy provisioning with explicit intent (for example, bandwidth constraints, latency minimization, etc.).

- Services provisioning (for example, L2VPN, L3VPN services with associated segment routing policy).

- Collection of real-time performance information and network optimization to maintain the intent of the associated segment routing policy.

- Tactical optimization of the network during times of congestion.

- Assistance with migration to next-generation networks and technologies (for example, migration from RSVP-TE to SR-TE, implementing multicast with SR Tree-SID, embracing 5G network slicing, etc.).

- Monitoring and troubleshooting the health of L2VPN and L3VPN services through empirical data plane verification.

- Streamlining and automating network-focused Method of Procedure (MOP) for remediation and maintenance tasks.

What makes the SR-PCE controller so powerful is that it provided centralized SRTE visibility into multidomain topologies, something that SRTE routers are not able to deliver. Northbound APIs allow SR-PCE to compute paths in real time. Because of the above, the SR-PCE can construct SLA-aware path computations even across network domains while delivering end-to-end network topology awareness. Again, you should not view SR-PCE as a single all-overseeing device but rather think of a BGP Route-Reflector deployment model where intent is centrally disseminated.

Figure 15-28 shows a screenshot taken from the Crosswork Network Controller's GUI console.

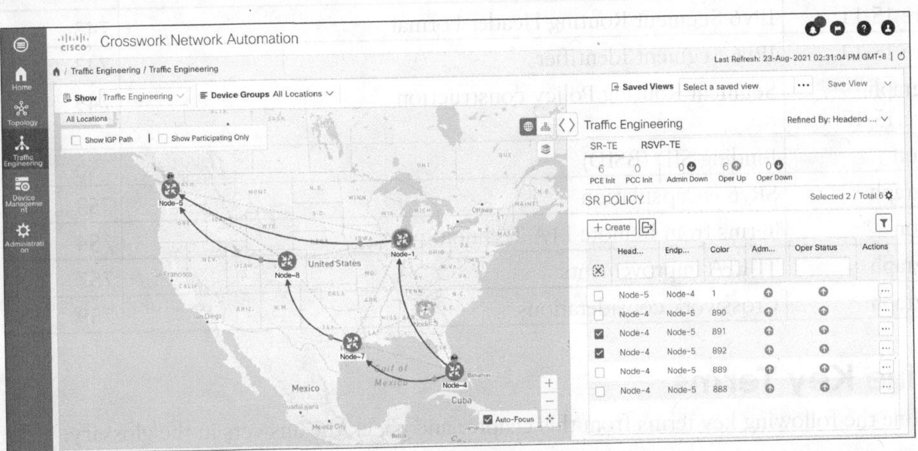

Figure 15-28   *Crosswork Network Controller*

The Cisco Crosswork Optimization Engine stands as a key element within the Crosswork Automation Suite, offering real-time network optimization capabilities. Network operators can enhance network utility and accelerate service deployment through dynamic Traffic Engineering and proactive optimization. Working seamlessly with the Crosswork Optimization Engine, the WAN Automation Engine (WAE) caters to diverse aspects of capacity management. It spans from long-term network engineering to capacity planning and Traffic Engineering, ensuring optimal network operation under various conditions. Furthermore, the WAN Automation Engine serves a valuable role in simulation analysis, aiding in the identification of potential network hotspots during failure scenarios.

Exam Preparation Tasks

As mentioned in the section "How to Use This Book" in the Introduction, you have a few choices for exam preparation: the exercises here, Chapter 23, "Final Preparation," and the exam simulation questions in the Pearson Test Prep Software Online.

Review All Key Topics

Review the most important topics in this chapter, noted with the Key Topic icon in the margin of the page. Table 15-5 lists a reference of these key topics and the page numbers on which each is found.

Table 15-5 Key Topics for Chapter 15

Key Topic Element	Description	Page Number
Table 15-2	LSD Label Ranges	729
Table 15-3	IS-IS TLVs	736
Example 15-3	Commands to Turn on Segment Routing in IS-IS	736
Table 15-4	OSPF Opaque LSAs	738
Figure 15-11	IPv6 Segment Routing Header Format	743
Figure 15-12	IPv6 Segment Identifier	743
Paragraph, Figure 15-17	Segment Routing Policy construction	749
Section	Binding-SID (BSID)	750
Paragraph	SRv6 encapsulation	753
Section	Terms from Remote LFA Technology	754
Paragraph	TI-LFA improvements	757
Paragraph	Crosswork considerations	759

Define Key Terms

Define the following key terms from this chapter and check the answers in the glossary:

BGP control plane, Binding Segment Identifier (BSID), Candidate Paths, Extended P-Space, Flex-Algo, Global Segments, IGP Adjacency Segment, IGP Prefix Segment, IS-IS Control Plane, Label Distribution Protocol (LDP), Label Switching Database (LSD), Local segment, OSPFv2 Control Plane, P-Space, Path Computation Client (PCC), Path Computation Element (PCE), Path Computation Element Protocol (PCEP), PCE-PCC architecture, PQ node, Q-space, Segment Routing, Segment Routing Control Plane, Segment Routing Global Block (SRGB), SR-MPLS (Segment Routing based on MPLS data plane), SRv6 (Segment Routing based on IPv6 data plane), SRv6 control plane, Topology-Independent Loop-free Alternate (TI-LFA)

Command Reference to Check Your Memory

This section includes the most important configuration and EXEC commands covered in this chapter. You might not need to memorize the complete syntax of every command, but you should be able to remember the basic keywords that are needed.

To test your memory of the commands, cover the right side of Table 15-6 with a piece of paper, read the description on the left side, and then see how much of the command you can remember.

The 350-501 exam focuses on practical, hands-on skills that are used by networking professionals. Therefore, you should be able to identify the commands needed to configure and test. Note that not all commands are fully covered in the chapter, but their presence in the table below should lead you to investigate them further to understand this technology.

Table 15-6   CLI Commands to Know

Task	Command Syntax
Define Segment Routing Global Block Range	RP/0/0/CPU0:P3(config)# **segment-routing global-block**
Configure IS-IS advertisements to BGP-LS	RP/0/0/CPU0:P3(config-isis)# **distribute link-state**
Configure IS-IS to generate and accept only new-style type-length-value (TLV) objects	RP/0/0/CPU0:P3(config-isis-af)# **metric-style wide [transition] [level { 1 | 2 }]**
Enable Segment Routing for IPv4 addresses with MPLS data plane	RP/0/0/CPU0:P3(config-isis-af)# **segment-routing mpls**
Enable topology-independent loop-free alternate (TI-LFA) path using the IP fast reroute (FRR) mechanism	RP/0/0/CPU0:P3(config-isis-if)# **fast-reroute per-prefix** RP/0/0/CPU0:P3 (config-isis-if)# **fast-reroute per-prefix ti-lfa**
Configure the Segment Routing Mapping Server (SRMS)	RP/0/0/CPU0:P3(config)# **segment-routing mapping-server prefix-sid-map address-family ipv4 10.1.100.4/32 17000 range 100**
Trace the routes to a destination in a Segment Routing network	RP/0/0/CPU0:P3# **traceroute sr-mpls 10.1.100.2/32**
Set the preference of Segment Routing (SR) labels over Label Distribution Protocol (LDP) labels	RP/0/0/CPU0:P3(config-isis-af)# **segment-routing mpls [sr-prefer]**
Specify or advertise the prefix (node) segment ID (SID) as an index value in IS-IS	RP/0/0/CPU0:P3(config)# **router isis 100** RP/0/0/CPU0:P3(config-isis)# **interface loopback0** RP/0/0/CPU0:P3(config-isis-if)# **address-family ipv4 unicast** RP/0/0/CPU0:P3(config-isis-if-af)# **prefix-sid index 3**
Specify or advertise the prefix (node) segment ID (SID) as an absolute value in OSPF	RP/0/0/CPU0:P3# **configure** RP/0/0/CPU0:P3(config)# **router ospf 1** RP/0/0/CPU0:P3(config-ospf)# **area 0** RP/0/0/CPU0:P3(config-ospf-ar)# **interface loopback0** RP/0/0/CPU0:P3(config-ospf-ar-if)# **prefix-sid absolute 16003**

Task	Command Syntax
Specify the Binding SID (BSID) allocation behavior	RP/0/0/CPU0:P3# **configure** RP/0/0/CPU0:P3(config)# **segment-routing** RP/0/0/CPU0:P3(config-sr)# **traffic-eng** RP/0/0/CPU0:P3(config-sr-te)# **binding-sid explicit fallback-dynamic** RP/0/0/CPU0:P3(config-sr-te)# **policy SAMPLE** RP/0/0/CPU0:P3(config-sr-te-policy)# **binding-sid mpls 1000**
Configure SRv6-TE locator and Binding SID (BSID) behavior	RP/0/0/CPU0:P3# **configure** RP/0/0/CPU0:P3(config)# **segment-routing traffic-eng** RP/0/0/CPU0:P3(config-sr-te)# **srv6 locator loc1 binding-sid dynamic behavior ub6-encaps-reduced**
Globally enable SRv6	RP/0/0/CPU0:P3(config)# **segment-routing srv6**
Configure the SRv6 Locator	RP/0/0/CPU0:P3(config-srv6)# **locators** RP/0/0/CPU0:P3(config-srv6-locators)# **locator myLoc1** RP/0/0/CPU0:P3(config-srv6-locator)# **micro-segment behavior unode psp-usd** RP/0/0/CPU0:P3(config-srv6-locator)# **prefix 2001:0:8::/48**

Review Questions

As a part of the review, we encourage you to provide *a single-sentence answer* (keep your answers as short as possible) to the following questions. If you struggle to complete this answer in a single sentence, this may indicate a lack of clarity or reveal gaps in your understanding. We have constructed these questions to help you consolidate this chapter's information and extract the essence of the covered content.

The answers to these questions appear in Appendix A. For more practice with exam format questions, use the Pearson Test Prep Software Online.

1. How does the implementation of Segment Routing enhance network scalability and simplify Traffic Engineering compared to traditional routing protocols?

2. In what ways can Segment Routing contribute to improved network resiliency and faster convergence times, especially in the face of dynamic changes or failures?

3. How can Segment Routing adapt to support emerging trends such as 5G networks, edge computing, and the increasing demand for network automation?

4. What specific scenarios or network topologies benefit the most from using the TI-LFA loop-free backup path mechanism?

5. Can you name one key benefit of integrating SRv6 to meet the evolving demands of modern applications, services, and emerging technologies?

Bibliography

S. Bryant, C. Filsfils, S. Previdi, M. Shand, and N. So. RFC 7490, *Remote Loop-Free Alternate (LFA) Fast Reroute (FRR)*, https://www.ietf.org/rfc/rfc7490.txt, IETF, April 2015.

P. Camarillo, Ed. RFC 8986, *Segment Routing over IPv6 (SRv6) Network Programming*, https://www.ietf.org/rfc/rfc8986.txt, IETF, February 2021.

D. Dukes, Ed. RFC 8754, *IPv6 Segment Routing Header (SRH)*, https://www.ietf.org/rfc/rfc8754.txt, IETF, March 2020.

A. Farrel, J.-P. Vasseur, and J. Ash. RFC 4655, *A Path Computation Element (PCE)-Based Architecture*, https://www.ietf.org/rfc/rfc4655.txt, IETF, August 2006.

C. Filsfils. *Segment Routing, Part II: Traffic Engineering*, Self-published, 2019 (ISBN: 978-1095963135).

C. Filsfils, K. Talaulikar, Ed., D. Voyer, A. Bogdanov, and P. Mattes. RFC 9256, *Segment Routing Policy Architecture*, https://www.ietf.org/rfc/rfc9256.txt IETF, July 2022.

L. Ginsberg, Ed. RFC 8667, *IS-IS Extensions for Segment Routing*, https://www.ietf.org/rfc/rfc8667.txt, IETF, December 2019.

LabN. RFC 5250, *The OSPF Opaque LSA Option*, https://www.ietf.org/rfc/rfc5250.txt, IETF, July 2008.

J. Liste. *A Guide to a Successful Segment Routing Deployment*, Cisco Live Presentation, 2023.

S. Litkowski, A. Bashandy, C. Filsfils, P. Francois, and B. Decraene. Internet Draft, *Topology Independent Fast Reroute Using Segment Routing*, https://www.ietf.org/archive/id/draft-ietf-rtgwg-segment-routing-ti-lfa-11.html, IETF, June 2023.

P. Pan, G. Swallow, and A. Atlast, Eds. RFC 4090, *Fast Reroute Extensions to RSVP-TE for LSP Tunnels*, https://www.ietf.org/rfc/rfc4090.txt, IETF, May 2005.

S. Previdi, Ed. RFC 8665, *OSPF Extensions for Segment Routing*, https://www.ietf.org/rfc/rfc8665.txt, IETF, December 2019.

S. Previdi. RFC 8670, *BGP Prefix Segment in Large-Scale Data Centers*, https://www.ietf.org/rfc/rfc8670.txt, IETF, December 2019.

S. Previdi and L. Ginsberg, Eds. RFC 8402, *Segment Routing Architecture*, https://www.ietf.org/rfc/rfc8402.txt, IETF, July 2018.

Redback Networks, Inc. RFC 5305, *IS-IS Extensions for Traffic Engineering*, https://www.ietf.org/rfc/rfc5305.txt, IETF, October 2008.

E. Rosen. RFC 8277, *Using BGP to Mind MPLS Labels to Address Prefixes*, https://www.ietf.org/rfc/rfc8277.txt, IETF, October 2017.

A. Roy. Internet Draft, *OSPFv3 LSA Extendibility*, https://datatracker.ietf.org/doc/html/draft-ietf-ospf-ospfv3-lsa-extend-23, IETF, January 2018.

Segment Routing website: https://www.segment-routing.net

## CHAPTER 16

Securing Control Plane

This chapter covers the following exam topics:

1.5 Configure and verify control plane

- 1.5.a Control plane protection techniques (LPTS and CoPP)
- 1.5.b BGP-TTL security and protocol authentication
- 1.5.c BGP prefix suppression
- 1.5.d LDP security (authentication and label allocation filtering)
- 1.5.e BGP sec
- 1.5.f BGP flowspec

Protecting the network from malicious disruptions requires a well-orchestrated approach of implementing robust security measures across various network layers. This and the next two chapters focus on analyzing the latest available defensive techniques, ensuring strict access controls, and regularly monitoring network traffic to detect and respond to potential threats promptly. A comprehensive security strategy—encompassing firewalls, intrusion detection and prevention systems, secure configurations, and timely updates—forms the backbone of secure network operations. By prioritizing these elements, organizations can create a resilient network infrastructure that safeguards against cyber threats and ensures a reliable and secure digital environment.

In response to the rising and constantly evolving intricacy of threats, Cisco has elevated its IOS security features and services for both network devices and infrastructure. These enhancements aim to guarantee the continuous availability of network devices under any circumstances, reinforcing the resilience of the overall network security posture.

"Do I Know This Already?" Quiz

The "Do I Know This Already?" quiz allows you to assess whether you should read this entire chapter thoroughly or jump to the "Exam Preparation Tasks" section. If you are in doubt about your answers to these questions or your own assessment of your knowledge of the topics, read the entire chapter. Table 16-1 lists the major headings in this chapter and their corresponding "Do I Know This Already?" quiz questions. You can find the answers in Appendix A, "Answers to the 'Do I Know This Already?' Quizzes and Review Questions."

Table 16-1 "Do I Know This Already?" Section-to-Question Mapping

Foundation Topics Section	Questions
CoPP	1, 2
LPTS	3
Keeping LDP Safe	4
Keeping BGP Safe	5, 6

1. ARP is an example of a protocol that operates within which network plane?

    a. Control

    b. Data

    c. L2 Ethernet

    d. Management

2. Which of the following best define CoPP functions? (Select all that apply.)

    a. Protects control plane

    b. Safeguards the punt path of the router

    c. Drops non-CEF switched traffic

    d. Applies to all packets directed to the RP

3. Which of the following statements about Local Packet Transport Services (LPTS) policers is correct?

    a. LPTS policers are only applied to control plane traffic destined for the route processor (RP).

    b. LPTS can dynamically adjust the rate limits based on real-time traffic conditions.

    c. LPTS uses static rate limits that must be manually configured for each protocol.

    d. LPTS protects the data plane by filtering inbound and outbound traffic on all interfaces.

4. Which of the following are LDP label filtering techniques? (Select all that apply.)

    a. Label admittance control

    b. Label synchronization control

    c. Label advertisement control

    d. Label allocation filtering

5. RPKI is a function of which of the following?

    a. RTBH

    b. BGP Flowspec

    c. BGPsec

    d. MD5

6. The ROA record contains which of the following fields?

    a. Option 19

    b. max-length

    c. origin prefix

    d. ISP signature

Foundation Topics

Network security has a primary focus in running a network. Network stability and features are equally important, but for businesses to survive, network resources must be protected from someone or something disrupting open access to data, services, and assets. Very early in my network engineering career, I (Brad) saw this play out in front of my eyes. The year was 2003 and (what we did not know at the time) the fastest-spreading Slammer worm hit global networks. At the time, I was managing a moderately sized campus network when calls started coming into our helpdesk department that the network was unusable. I'd had some experiences with networks slowing down, but never unusable in all parts of the campus. Trying to look for clues, I was remotely connected to one of our core routers when my console, an out-of-band connection that did not depend on the network itself, became crawlingly slow. A senior engineer and I left our cubicles and headed to the server room. Our two massive core Cisco 6509 routers with the most robust Supervisor engines were spinning out of control. The CPU utilization bars were at the top of their graphs, jumping from orange to red trying to outdance a *Saturday Night Fever* soundtrack.

Pop-quiz time: What do you do? Remember, you do not know there is a worm raging. The console is unresponsive. We ended up physically pulling out the line cards connecting all the campus floors and buildings until the CPU utilization on the core routers returned to the acceptable green levels. Now, we had the console and knew that the problem was not on the core routers. When we reinserted the line cards, the network tanked again! Why am I telling you this story? For the next four days, the network had to stay down. No one on the campus could do any work. All IT resources (including the networking team and yours truly) were cleaning individual PCs from the Slammer worm. Each day of our company standing idle cost us US$1 million. The annual profit for our division was $50 million (Facebook's 14-hour outage in 2019 reportedly cost $90 million). You can quickly see the pressure of keeping the network up so the business could remain profitable and survive. I have been lucky that my career has survived a few more of these disruptions, and I would encourage you to consider this important element of being a network engineer—quietly building (because you have other pressing daily duties) the security personality of the network domain so, should the unfortunate date come, the network will refuse to get shut down. It is a thankless job until the meltdown is knocking down on your door. Think of this story when reading this chapter.

Consider these important elements of network protection:

1. **Control Plane:** Carries signaling traffic to build domain topology. Think of it as the brain of the network. It runs various routing protocols that communicate with other routers on the network to establish agreed-upon paths for all traffic. These processes are handled by the CPU. If control plane is compromised, many or all operations will stop. Can you think of the protocols that make up the control plane? BGP, IS-IS, OSPF, ARP are some of the examples. On Cisco hardware, you will hear terms the *RP* (route processor) or *RSP* (route switch processor) when control plane is mentioned.

2. **Management Plane:** Carries traffic necessary to operate and monitor the network. SSH, Telnet (stop using it), SNMP, NETCONF, and FTP are some of the examples. Since the router must process these packets for its own use, CPU handles them as well.

3. **Data Plane:** All the traffic the network forwards. Also often referred to as the forwarding plane. The logic is kept simple so that hardware can do fast packet-forwarding. When the data plane encounters packets that require complex processing (for example, packets with IP options), it will punt these to the control plane (RP) to process them.

Some of the best advice I was given early in my career about how to solve networking problems quickly and efficiently was to "be the packet." If you can think like the packet or the router, the solution will become evident. To see what I mean, examine Figure 16-1.

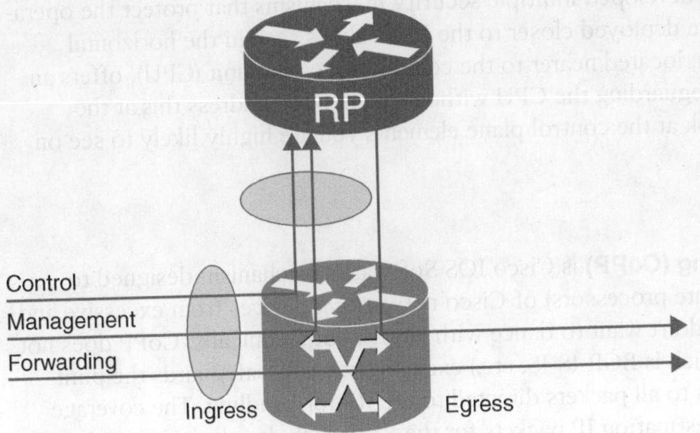

Figure 16-1   *Protecting Router Operations*

Your job is to protect the CPU resources at all costs. Once the CPU gets too many requests, it will slow down because its resources are not infinite. The brain will not be able to support routing protocol updates or topology convergence and will finally stop performing its tasks completely. What options do you, as an operator, have to protect this router's CPU from being overwhelmed? Don't limit yourself to the worm I described earlier. You can be dealing with excessive legitimate updates or software bugs that have the CPU tied up and discarding unnecessary information. What options do you have? Where could you limit or throttle how many requests are coming to the CPU or RP? Well, for starters, you could do this on the ingress interface as the packets are taken off the physical wire and enter the router shown by the vertical oval shape. You certainly could apply an interface ACL to limit what traffic reaches the RP. Would this solution be effective? Be the packet...

Well, the answer is somewhat effective. You can craft an access list that will limit the sources and types of traffic that the RP will receive, but here are some of the limitations that immediately entered my mind.

In Figure 16-1, we have one ingress interface. What if you have a multiline card "refrigerator size" chassis that goes up to 44RUs (rack units) and can have hundreds of physical interfaces (I'm not even talking about virtual subinterfaces)? Applying our ACL can become a laborious task.

1.   Is there traffic that is not easily caught with an ACL? What about exception IP packets? IP options set in the header? What about IP packets with unreachable destinations? These *will* go to the CPU regardless of whether we entered our RP as the destination IP address in the ACL. What about non-IP traffic? What does our ACL look like for this traffic? There are many more of these and other reasons for why the forwarding plane traffic can be punted (sent) to the RP for processing. The forwarding plane doesn't understand what to do with some of the traffic. I would struggle to build an ACL that would even remotely catch all these categories.

2.   Our ACL will also struggle to control the rate at which packets are coming. These can be legitimate updates, but if they keep the CPU overwhelmed, they will have the effect of a denial-of-service (DoS) attack.

For these reasons, Cisco has developed multiple security mechanisms that protect the operation of a router's RP. They are deployed closer to the RP itself, as seen in the horizontal oval in Figure 16-1. This area, located nearer to the central processing unit (CPU), offers an improved chokepoint for safeguarding the CPU without the need to address this at the interface level. Next, let's look at the control plane elements you are highly likely to see on the exam.

CoPP

Cisco **Control Plane Policing (CoPP)** is Cisco IOS Software's mechanism designed to protect the control plane (route processors) of Cisco networking devices from excessive and potentially harmful traffic. I don't want to dance with words, but technically, CoPP does not protect the control plane (which is BGP, IS-IS, etc.) exclusively. CoPP safeguards the punt path of the router and applies to all packets directed to the RP for handling. The coverage is beyond simply receiving destination IP packets for the RP. It includes all the exception IP traffic and non-IP packets we discussed earlier. CoPP uses the **Modular QoS CLI (MQC)** framework for policy construction and offers the flexibility to not only permit or deny specific packets but also to apply rate limiting.

One of the best ways to learn how things work is to reduce them to the most basic elements and see how they work (or do not). In Example 16-1, I applied the following configuration to PE2 (running IOS XE at the moment). This is not a lesson on how to work with MQC, but if you can read, you will follow this logic:

1.   I created a class-map CoPP that matches all traffic in the access-list 100.

2.   Access-list 100 catches any ICMP traffic.

3.   Policy map LIMIT_ICMP takes class CoPP and polices it to the target bit rate (cir) of 8000 bits per second. Any packets below this level will be transmitted to the RP (control plane); anything exceeding this level will be dropped.

4.   I assigned policy map LIMIT_ICMP to the control plane.

Example 16-1   *CoPP Basic Policy*

```
PE2# show running-config
! Output omitted for brevity
!class-map match-all CoPP
 match access-group 100
!
policy-map LIMIT_ICMP
 class CoPP
  police cir 8000
   conform-action transmit
   exceed-action drop
!
control-plane
 service-policy input LIMIT_ICMP
```

```
!
ip access-list extended 100
 10 permit icmp any any
!
```

We get to verify whether I made a mistake or not in Example 16-2. From P3, we ping PE2 100 times, which will exceed the newly assigned bit rate on PE2. Notice that six ping packets received no reply on P3. PE2 shows the same thing: six packets exceeded the rate and were dropped.

Example 16-2 *CoPP Verification*

```
P3#ping 10.1.100.2 repeat 100
Type escape sequence to abort.
Sending 100, 100-byte ICMP Echos to 10.1.100.2, timeout is 2 seconds:
!!!!!!!!!!!!!!!!!!.!!!!!!!!!!!!!!!!!.!!!!!!!!!!!!!!!!!.!!!!!!!!!!!!!!!!!.!!!!!!!!!
!!!!!!!.!!!!!!!!!!!!!!!!!!.!!!!!!!!
Success rate is 94 percent (94/100), round-trip min/avg/max = 1/4/117 ms
P3#

PE2# show policy-map control-plane
 Control Plane

  Service-policy input: LIMIT_ICMP

   Class-map: CoPP (match-all)
    100 packets, 10000 bytes
    5 minute offered rate 2000 bps, drop rate 0000 bps
    Match: access-group 100
    police:
      cir 8000 bps, bc 1500 bytes
    conformed 94 packets, 9400 bytes; actions:
      transmit
    exceeded 6 packets, 600 bytes; actions:
      drop
    conformed 2000 bps, exceeded 0000 bps

   Class-map: class-default (match-any)
    221 packets, 11631 bytes
    5 minute offered rate 0000 bps, drop rate 0000 bps
    Match: any
PE2#
```

The CoPP lesson is over! Well, not quite. Remember that we boiled this down to the basic elements—rate-limiting inbound ICMP traffic to see how the CoPP feature worked. Many options for specifying outbound traffic, different types of traffic, protocols, and actions to take are available. Be the packet and build a QoS policy for traffic to and from the router's control plane. Think about traffic that is not **Cisco Express Forwarding (CEF)** switched. Your goal is to protect the CPU from bombardment with extreme rates of incoming traffic.

Each network has its own peculiar behavior and concerns. It is up to the networking team to come up with a defensive control plane strategy that makes sense and works. In Example 16-3, I share with you a template that I used a long time ago. Do not use it as is (obviously!) because the addressing will be different, rate limits will not be correct for your environment, and it is missing things like SSH. Use this opportunity as an exercise to modernize this template to apply to your lab or network. If you come up with something really good, please share with us, and we'll make the best ones available to the wider community so that we all can learn. From what I recall, there were a few specific aspects I liked when I used it. First, it is modular; plus, it is easy to categorize and observe BGP, management, and other traffic destined for my control plane. Second, it deals with undesirable traffic. See if you can figure this out. Third, it has a "catch-all" class defined to help me see what I have missed and who or what else may be quietly knocking on the control plane's door.

Example 16-3 *A Sample CoPP Template*

```
!-- ACL for CoPP Routing class-map
!
access-list 150 permit tcp any gt 1024 192.168.1.0 0.0.0.255 eq bgp
access-list 150 permit tcp any eq bgp 192.168.1.0 0.0.0.255 gt 1024 established
access-list 150 permit tcp any gt 1024 192.168.1.0 0.0.0.255 eq 639
access-list 150 permit tcp any eq 639 192.168.1.0 0.0.0.255 gt 1024 established
access-list 150 permit tcp any 192.168.1.0 0.0.0.255 eq 646
access-list 150 permit udp any 192.168.1.0 0.0.0.255 eq 646
access-list 150 permit ospf any 192.168.1.0 0.0.0.255
access-list 150 permit ospf any host 224.0.0.5
access-list 150 permit ospf any host 224.0.0.6
access-list 150 permit eigrp any 192.168.1.0 0.0.0.255
access-list 150 permit eigrp any host 224.0.0.10
access-list 150 permit udp any any eq pim-auto-rp
!---etc--- for other routing protocol traffic...
!
!-- ACL for CoPP Management class-map
!
access-list 151 permit tcp 10.100.100.0 0.0.0.255 192.168.1.0 0.0.0.255 eq telnet
access-list 151 permit tcp 10.100.100.0 0.0.0.255 eq telnet 192.168.1.0 0.0.0.255
established
access-list 151 permit tcp 10.100.100.0 0.0.0.255 192.168.1.0 0.0.0.255 eq 22
access-list 151 permit tcp 10.100.100.0 0.0.0.255 eq 22 192.168.1.0 0.0.0.255
established
access-list 151 permit udp 10.100.100.0 0.0.0.255 192.168.1.0 0.0.0.255 eq snmp
access-list 151 permit tcp 10.100.100.0 0.0.0.255 192.168.1.0 0.0.0.255 eq www
access-list 151 permit udp 10.100.100.0 0.0.0.255 192.168.1.0 0.0.0.255 eq 443
access-list 151 permit tcp 10.100.100.0 0.0.0.255 192.168.1.0 0.0.0.255 eq ftp
access-list 151 permit tcp 10.100.100.0 0.0.0.255 192.168.1.0 0.0.0.255 eq ftp-data
access-list 151 permit udp 10.100.100.0 0.0.0.255 192.168.1.0 0.0.0.255 eq syslog
access-list 151 permit udp 10.100.101.0 0.0.0.255 eq domain 192.168.1.0 0.0.0.255
access-list 151 permit udp 10.100.102.0 0.0.0.255 192.168.1.0 0.0.0.255 eq ntp
!---etc--- for known good management traffic...
!
```

```
!-- ACL for CoPP Normal class-map
!
access-list 152 permit icmp any 192.168.1.0 0.0.0.255 echo
access-list 152 permit icmp any 192.168.1.0 0.0.0.255 echo-reply
access-list 152 permit icmp any 192.168.1.0 0.0.0.255 ttl-exceeded
access-list 152 permit icmp any 192.168.1.0 0.0.0.255 packet-too-big
access-list 152 permit icmp any 192.168.1.0 0.0.0.255 port-unreachable
access-list 152 permit icmp any 192.168.1.0 0.0.0.255 unreachable
access-list 152 permit pim any any
access-list 152 permit igmp any any
access-list 152 permit gre any any
!---etc--- for other known good traffic...
!
!-- ACL for CoPP Undesirable class-map
!
access-list 153 permit icmp any any fragments
access-list 153 permit udp any any fragments
access-list 153 permit tcp any any fragments
access-list 153 permit ip any any fragments
access-list 153 permit udp any any eq 1434
access-list 153 permit tcp any any eq 639 rst
access-list 153 permit tcp any any eq bgp rst
!--- etc. all other known bad things here
!
!-- ACL for CoPP Catch-All class-map
!
access-list 154 permit tcp any any
access-list 154 permit udp any any
access-list 154 permit icmp any any
access-list 154 permit ip any any
!
!-- CoPP Routing class-map
!
class-map match-all Routing
 match access-group 150
!
!-- CoPP Management class-map
!
class-map match-all Management
 match access-group 151
!
!-- CoPP Normal class-map
!
class-map match-all Normal
 match access-group 152
!
```

```
!-- CoPP Undesirable class-map
!
class-map match-all Undesirable
 match access-group 153
!
!-- CoPP Catch-All-IP class-map
class-map match-all Catch-All-IP
 match access-group 154
!
policy-map Router_CoPP
 class Undesirable
 police 8000 1500 1500 conform-action drop exceed-action drop
 class Routing
 police 1000000 50000 50000 conform-action transmit exceed-action transmit
 class Management
 police 100000 20000 20000 conform-action transmit exceed-action drop
 class Normal
 police 50000 5000 5000 conform-action transmit exceed-action drop
 class Catch-All-IP
 police 50000 5000 5000 conform-action transmit exceed-action drop
 class class-default

 police 8000 1500 1500 conform-action transmit exceed-action transmit
!
control-plane
 service-policy input Router_CoPP
```

By implementing CoPP, network administrators can improve the overall security and stability of their Cisco devices by selectively allowing or rate-limiting traffic that is destined for the punt path (OK, control plane on the exam). This helps ensure that the device can effectively process legitimate control plane traffic while mitigating the impact of malicious or excessive traffic.

LPTS

There is no CoPP in Cisco IOS XR. Instead, the **Local Packet Transport Services (LPTS)** feature takes the CoPP concept to another level by introducing *automatic* rate limiting for all packets requiring processing by any route processor on the device. LPTS manages tables that outline various packet flows directed to the route processor. It employs a predefined set of policers on which it applies them based on the incoming control traffic's flow type. The automated control provided by LPTS is crucial for maintaining network health, especially in large-scale, high-speed networks where manual configuration of these functions by network engineers and operators becomes increasingly challenging. Remember the template exercise we had you do in IOS XE? You get this for free in XR. Well, not quite, since you've already paid for it. Study Figure 16-2, which is a representation of a distributed chassis system (ASR9K is a good example).

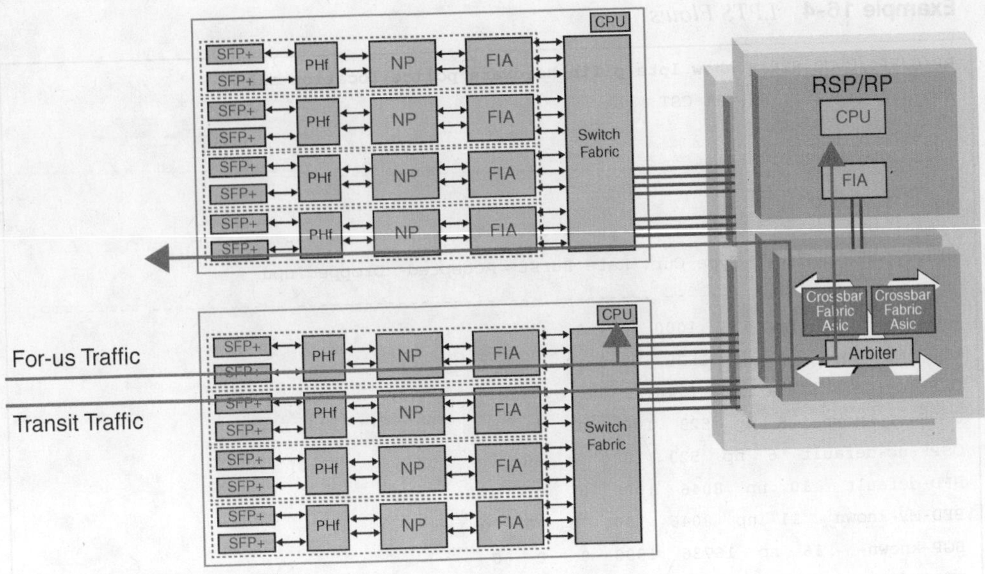

Figure 16-2   *LPTS Architecture*

Figure 16-2 shows two line cards attached to this dual RP/RSP system. Notice that both the RP and line card elements have their own CPUs. For the purposes of this topic, the packet walk is not complicated. Traffic comes into the ingress card on the bottom from the wire, travels through the pluggable optic, hits the PHY element, goes through the network processor (NP), connects to the Fabric Interface ASIC, and hits the chassis' switch fabric.

In the case of the transit traffic, notice how it leaves the switch fabric and immediately finds the egress line card. Of great interest to us is the "For-us" traffic, which is the traffic the system must process in the control plane (CPU/RP/RSP). Follow the top arrow to see that some traffic will be processed by the local line card CPU, whereas other traffic will be sent to the RP. The network processor element has a table called **Internal Forwarding Information Base (iFIB)**, which decides to punt the packets to either the line card CPU or the RSP CPU. Which traffic will go to the line card CPU? Layer 2 traffic, BFD, ARP. Examples of the type of traffic to go to the system RP would be management, Layer 3 control plane traffic, ICMP, and others.

LPTS implementation is platform dependent because various systems (ASR9K, NCS 5500, Cisco 8000) differ in resource abundance. Having said this, IOS XR software classifies the "For-us" traffic into close to 100 flows that are hardware-policed before they arrive at the CPUs. For example, if the LPTS policer is configured to send 1000 packets per second, each NP on the line card can only send (punt) 1000 pps to either the local line card CPU or the RP CPU.

Would you like to see LPTS flows on a router and iFIB? Let's look at Example 16-4.

Example 16-4 *LPTS Flows*

```
RP/0/RP0/CPU0:8201# show lpts pifib hardware police location all
Sun Jan 14 08:21:01.481 CST


-------------------------------------------------------------------
    Node 0/RP0/CPU0:
-------------------------------------------------------------------
FlowType      Policer Type Cur. Rate Burst  Accepted  Dropped npu
-------------------------------------------------------------------
Fragment       2  np  523   1000  0   0   0
OSPF-mc-known  3  np  1528  1000  0   0   0
OSPF-mc-default 4 np  1046  1000  0   0   0
OSPF-uc-known  5  np  523   1000  0   0   0
OSPF-uc-default 6 np  523   1000  0   0   0
BFD-default    10 np  8046  1000  0   0   0
BFD-MP-known   11 np  8046  1000  0   0   0
BGP-known      16 np  16736 1000  0   0   0
BGP-cfg-peer   17 np  1528  1000  0   0   0
BGP-default    18 np  1046  1000  0   0   0
PIM-mcast-default 19 np 523 1000  0   0   0
PIM-mcast-known 20 np 1528 1000   0   0   0
PIM-ucast      21 np  523   1000  0   0   0
IGMP           22 np  1528  1000  0   0   0
ICMP-local     23 np  523   1000  0   0   0
ICMP-control   25 np  2092  1000  0   0   0
ICMP-default   26 np  523   1000  0   0   0
LDP-TCP-known  28 np  2092  1000  39209 0  0
LDP-TCP-cfg-peer 29 np 1046 1000  0   0   0
LDP-TCP-default 30 np  523  1000  0   0   0
LDP-UDP        31 np  523   1000  278618 0 0
All-routers    32 np  523   1000  0   0   0
RSVP-default   38 np  523   1000  0   0   0
RSVP-known     39 np  1528  1000  0   0   0
SNMP           47 np  523   1000  0   0   0
SSH-known      48 np  523   1000  0   0   0
SSH-default    49 np  523   1000  0   0   0
HTTP-known     50 np  523   1000  0   0   0
SHTTP-known    52 np  523   1000  0   0   0
TELNET-known   54 np  523   1000  0   0   0
TELNET-default 55 np  523   1000  0   0   0
UDP-known      60 np  24461 1000  0   0   0
UDP-default    63 np  523   1000  2   0   0
TCP-known      64 np  24461 1000  0   0   0
TCP-default    67 np  523   1000  0   0   0
```

```
Raw-default   71  np  523   1000  0   0   0
ip-sla        72  np  9655  1000  0   0   0
GRE       77  np  523   1000  0   0   0
VRRP      78  np  523   1000  0   0   0
MPLS-oam      80  np  523   1000  0   0   0
DNS       83  np  523   1000  0   0   0
NTP-known     87  np  523   1000  0   0   0
RP/0/RP0/CPU0:8201#
```

Would you like to see what LPTS uses to identify a packet? In that case, let's look at Example 16-5. This router runs MPLS LDP, so let's see what we can find. This Cisco 8000 has two LDP neighbors, and we can decipher these identification tuples in the next command. LPTS can use protocols, source IP, destination IP, ports, VRF, and other fields. In this case, we can see both the TCP and UDP flows for these LDP sessions. We can see that these flows are assigned Critical and High queue priorities.

Example 16-5 *LPTS Identification*

```
RP/0/RP0/CPU0:8201# show mpls ldp neighbor brief
Sun Jan 14 08:22:18.471 CST


Peer    GR NSR Up Time  Discovery Addresses  Labels
          ipv4 ipv6 ipv4 ipv6 ipv4 ipv6
----------------- -- --- ---------- ---------- ---------- ------------
192.168.5.22:0  N N 5d23h  1  0  6  0  12  0
192.168.5.25:0  N N 5d23h  2  0  6  0  12  0
RP/0/RP0/CPU0:8201# show lpts pifib hardware entry location all
Sun Jan 14 08:22:26.822 CST
! Output omitted for brevity
--------------------------------------------------------

L4 Protocol  : 6
L4 remote port : 646
npu id   : 0
Destination IP : 192.168.5.60
Source IP   : 192.168.5.25
Port/Type   : Port:18634
Is Fragment  : 0
vrf   : 0
Listener Tag  : IPv4_STACK
Flow Type   : LDP-TCP-known
DestNode   : Deliver RP0
Type    : Dlvr
Punt Queue Prio : CRITICAL
Interface   : any
Accepted/Dropped : 0/0


--------------------------------------------------------
```

```
L4 Protocol  : 6
L4 remote port : 646
npu id   : 0
Destination IP : 192.168.5.60
Source IP   : 192.168.5.22
Port/Type   : Port:39036
Is Fragment  : 0
vrf    : 0
Listener Tag  : IPv4_STACK
Flow Type   : LDP-TCP-known
DestNode   : Deliver RP0
Type    : Dlvr
Punt Queue Prio : CRITICAL
Interface   : any
Accepted/Dropped : 0/0


------------------------------------------------------
L4 Protocol  : 17
L4 remote port : 0
npu id   : 0
Destination IP : 192.168.5.60
Source IP   : 192.168.5.25
Port/Type   : Port:646
Is Fragment  : 0
vrf    : 0
Listener Tag  : IPv4_LISTENER
Flow Type   : LDP-UDP
DestNode   : Deliver RP0
Type    : Dlvr
Punt Queue Prio : HIGH
Interface   : any
Accepted/Dropped : 0/0


------------------------------------------------------
L4 Protocol  : 17
L4 remote port : 0
npu id   : 0
Destination IP : 224.0.0.2
Source IP   : any
Port/Type   : Port:646
Is Fragment  : 0
vrf    : 0
Listener Tag  : IPv4_LISTENER
Flow Type   : LDP-UDP
DestNode   : Deliver RP0
```

```
Type         : Dlvr
Punt Queue Prio : HIGH
Interface    : any
Accepted/Dropped : 0/0

-----------------------------------------------------------------
```

Do you recall IP exception packets? Let's hop on yet another router, NCS 5500, which also runs IOS XR to see the exception packets along with their assigned default rate of 100 pps (see Example 16-6). Also, observe that the configured rate is 0.

Example 16-6 *LPTS Default Policing*

```
RP/0/RP0/CPU0:55A2# show controllers npu stats traps-all instance all location 0/0/
CPU0
Sun Jan 14 08:55:29.905 CST


Trap Type           NPU Trap TrapStats Policer Packet    Packet

                    ID  ID   ID    Accepted   Dropped
========================================================================================
RxTrapIpv4Ttl0          0 108 0x6c  32010 0        0
RxTrapIpv4Ttl1          0 112 0x70  32010 0        0
RxTrapMplsTtl0          0 141 0x8d  32014 0        0
RxTrapMplsTtl1          0 142 0x8e  32014 0        0
RP/0/RP0/CPU0:55A2# attach location 0/0/CPU0
Sun Jan 14 08:58:34.466 CST
[xr-vm_node0_0_CPU0:~]$ export PS1='#'
# dpa_show puntpolicer | grep -e Def -e 32010
  Def CIR Rate  Conf CIR Rate  CIR Burst    ID
  10 - 0:   100    0  100  32010
#
```

Next, let's change this to the arbitrary higher value of 500 pps. Now, the Configured CIR Rate reflects this change in Example 16-7.

Example 16-7 *LPTS Configuring Policer*

```
RP/0/RP0/CPU0:55A2# configure
Sun Jan 14 09:03:59.329 CST
RP/0/RP0/CPU0:55A2(config)# lpts punt police location 0/0/CPU0
RP/0/RP0/CPU0:55A2(config-lpts-punt-policer-local)# exception ipv4 ttl-error rate ?
  <0-4294967295> Packets Per Second
RP/0/RP0/CPU0:55A2(config-lpts-punt-policer-local)# exception ipv4 ttl-error rate 500
RP/0/RP0/CPU0:55A2(config-lpts-punt-policer-local)# commit
Sun Jan 14 09:05:23.937 CST
```

```
RP/0/RP0/CPU0:55A2(config-lpts-punt-policer-local)# end
RP/0/RP0/CPU0:55A2# attach location 0/0/CPU0
Sun Jan 14 09:05:37.842 CST
Last login: Sun Jan 14 08:58:34 2024 from 172.0.16.1
export PS1='#'
[xr-vm_node0_0_CPU0:~]$ export PS1='#'
# dpa_show puntpolicer | grep -e Def -e 32010
  Def CIR Rate Conf CIR Rate CIR Burst  ID
 10 - 0:   100   500  100  32010
#
```

Just because we can change it, should we? My advice is to leave this alone unless you know what you're doing. Also, realize (why I have shown you examples from different platforms) that different hardware platforms have specific implementations of LPTS. ASR9K has a ton of resources available. Other platforms use different techniques to make up for this limitation. The NCS platform I showed you last uses dynamic flow types to conserve hardware resources. For a more detailed analysis, consult the "Bibliography" section of this chapter. There, you'll find an excellent post that covers this topic by my colleague, Tejas Lad.

Keeping LDP Safe

The LDP control plane needs to be protected. It plays a key role in establishing label-switched paths (LSPs) in MPLS networks, which are essential for efficient data routing. Without proper protection, LDP sessions can be disrupted, leading to potential network outages or degraded performance. Ensuring the integrity and availability of LDP helps maintain the stability and reliability of the entire MPLS network, preventing service interruptions and safeguarding against malicious attacks or configuration errors. I would like to point out the following tools:

- LDP Authentication

- Label Advertisement Control (Outbound Filtering)

- Label Acceptance Control (Inbound Filtering)

- Label Allocation Filtering

The sections that follow delve into these tools in more detail.

LDP Authentication

Recall any of this book's diagrams which show that PE2 (IOS XE) and PE3 (IOS XR) are directly connected to each other and use their respective Loopback0 interfaces as the sources of LDP traffic. Example 16-8 shows an unsecured peering we will modify to support password-protected **Message Digest Algorithm 5 (MD5)** authentication. Note that I switch routers and highlight important details.

Example 16-8 *LDP Authentication*

```
PE2# show mpls ldp neighbors
Peer LDP Ident: 10.1.100.3:0; Local LDP Ident 10.1.100.2:0
        TCP connection: 10.1.100.3.25513 - 10.1.100.2.646
        State: Oper; Msgs sent/rcvd: 1801/1789; Downstream
        Up time: 1d02h
        LDP discovery sources:
          GigabitEthernet2, Src IP addr: 10.1.23.3
    Addresses bound to peer LDP Ident:
      10.1.100.3   10.1.23.3   10.1.34.3
PE2# configure terminal
PE2(config)# access-list 10 permit 10.1.100.3
PE2(config)# mpls ldp password required for 10
PE2(config)# mpls ldp neighbor 10.1.100.3 password ccnp
PE2(config)#
*Jan 14 18:38:06.457: %LDP-5-NBRCHG: LDP Neighbor 10.1.100.3:0 (1) is DOWN
(Session's MD5 password changed)
*Jan 14 18:38:21.812: %TCP-6-BADAUTH: No MD5 digest from 10.1.100.3(48925) to
10.1.100.2(646) tableid - 0s

<!---CHANGING TO PE3---!>
RP/0/0/CPU0:PE3# configure
Sun Jan 14 18:39:23.892 UTC
RP/0/0/CPU0:PE3(config)# mpls ldp
RP/0/0/CPU0:PE3(config-ldp)# neighbor 10.1.100.2:0 password encrypted ccnp
RP/0/0/CPU0:PE3(config)# commit
Sun Jan 14 18:40:00.563 UTC
RP/0/0/CPU0:PE3(config)# end
RP/0/0/CPU0:PE3# show mpls ldp neighbors
Sun Jan 14 18:40:11.673 UTC

Peer LDP Identifier: 10.1.100.2:0
  TCP connection: 10.1.100.2:646 - 10.1.100.3:63080; MD5 on
  Graceful Restart: No
  Session Holdtime: 180 sec
  State: Oper; Msgs sent/rcvd: 8/8; Downstream-Unsolicited
  Up time: 00:00:09
  LDP Discovery Sources:
  IPv4: (1)
   GigabitEthernet0/0/0/2
  IPv6: (0)
  Addresses bound to this peer:
  IPv4: (2)
   10.1.23.2   10.1.100.2
  IPv6: (0)
```

```
<!---CHANGING TO PE2---!>
PE2#
*Jan 14 18:40:02.591: %TCP-6-BADAUTH: No MD5 digest from 10.1.100.3(47847) to
10.1.100.2(646) tableid - 0
*Jan 14 18:40:16.858: %LDP-5-NBRCHG: LDP Neighbor 10.1.100.3:0 (1) is UP
PE2# show mpls ldp neighbor detail
 Peer LDP Ident: 10.1.100.3:0; Local LDP Ident 10.1.100.2:0
        TCP connection: 10.1.100.3.63080 - 10.1.100.2.646; MD5 on
        Password: required, neighbor, in use
        State: Oper; Msgs sent/rcvd: 8/8; Downstream; Last TIB rev sent 10
        Up time: 00:00:34; UID: 2; Peer Id 0
        LDP discovery sources:
         GigabitEthernet2; Src IP addr: 10.1.23.3
          holdtime: 15000 ms, hello interval: 5000 ms
    Addresses bound to peer LDP Ident:
     10.1.100.3   10.1.23.3   10.1.34.3
     Peer holdtime: 180000 ms; KA interval: 60000 ms; Peer state: estab
```

At times, it might be advisable to rotate authentication keys. Example 16-9 shows how to
do this. Make sure that there is some overlap in time to allow for transitions, which last
15 minutes in the shown configuration. We rotate keys every month. Notice that we are
deleting the password we used previously and using the new password **ldp-ccnp**.

Example 16-9 *LDP Authentication*

```
PE2# show running-config
! Output omitted for brevity
mpls ldp password rollover duration 15
access-list 10 permit 10.1.100.3
key chain ldp-ccnp
key 10
key-string ccnp1
send-lifetime 15:00:00 Jan 14 2024 15:30:00 Feb 14 2024
accept-lifetime 15:00:00 Jan 14 2024 15:45:00 Feb 14 2024
key 11
key-string ccnp2
send-lifetime 15:00:00 Feb 14 2024 15:30:00 Mar 14 2024
accept-lifetime 15:00:00 Feb 14 2024 15:45:00 Mar 14 2024
key 12
key-string ccnp3
send-lifetime 15:00:00 Mar 14 2024 15:30:00 Apr 14 2024
accept-lifetime 15:00:00 Mar 14 2024 15:45:00 Apr 14 2024
!
mpls ldp password option 5 for 10 key-chain ldp-ccnp
no mpls ldp neighbor 10.1.100.3 password ccnp
```

Label Advertisement Control (Outbound Filtering)

LDP also has a mechanism to control which labels are advertised to LDP neighbors.

By default, LDP advertises labels for all the prefixes to all its neighbors. When this is not desirable (either for scalability or security reasons), label advertisement control (outbound filtering) can configure LDP to perform outbound filtering for local label advertisement for one or more prefixes to one or more peers (*read this again*). This feature is known as LDP outbound label filtering, or local label advertisement control. In Example 16-10, PE2 (IOS XE) advertises only its Loopback0's label to all neighbors.

Example 16-10   *Outbound Label Filtering*

```
PE2# configure terminal
PE2(config)# no mpls ldp advertise-labels //stop default label advertising
PE2(config)# access-list 11 permit host 10.1.100.2
PE2(config)# access-list 12 permit any
PE2(config)# mpls ldp advertise-labels for 11 ?
  to Access-list specifying controls on LDP peers //advertise only label for L0
  <cr> <cr>
PE2(config)# mpls ldp advertise-labels for 11 to ?
  WORD IP access-list for LDP peers; name or number (1-99)
PE2(config)# mpls ldp advertise-labels for 11 to 12 //advertise to any peer
PE2(config)# end
PE2# show mpls ldp bindings advertisement-acls
Advertisement spec:
    Prefix acl = 11; Peer acl = 12

  lib entry: 10.1.23.0/24, rev 12
  lib entry: 10.1.34.0/24, rev 13
  lib entry: 10.1.100.2/32, rev 14
     Advert acl(s): Prefix acl 11; Peer acl 12
  lib entry: 10.1.100.3/32, rev 15
  lib entry: 10.1.100.4/32, rev 16
PE2#
```

Label Acceptance Control (Inbound Filtering)

What about filtering incoming labels? This feature is available as well. Just like in the case of outbound filtering, by default, LDP accepts labels for all prefixes from all peers. The technical term for this is *liberal label retention mode*, which instructs LDP to keep remote bindings from all peers for a given prefix. To conserve memory, or for security reasons, we can change this behavior by configuring label binding acceptance for a set of prefixes from a given peer. Look at Example 16-11 to see how this is done on PE3 (IOS XR).

Among several LDP labels, PE3 (output snipped) receives an Implicit NULL binding for PE2 prefix 10.1.100.2/32. Why Implicit NULL? Because it is the next hop, so PE3 will pop this label (if you're lost, check out Chapter 10, "MPLS Fundamentals," where this matter is discussed in detail). We will filter this prefix out to remove it from our LFIB database. Notice that once we apply our configuration, the label for the prefix is no longer present in the final output.

Example 16-11 *Outbound Label Filtering*

```
RP/0/0/CPU0:PE3# show mpls ldp bindings
Sun Jan 14 23:02:09.337 UTC
! Output omitted for brevity
10.1.100.2/32, rev 17
  Local binding: label: 16301
  Remote bindings: (2 peers)
  Peer      Label
  ---------------- ---------
  10.1.100.2:0  ImpNull
  10.1.100.4:0  402


RP/0/0/CPU0:PE3# configure
Sun Jan 14 23:02:42.371 UTC
RP/0/0/CPU0:PE3(config)# ipv4 access-list LIMIT_LDP deny host 10.1.100.2
RP/0/0/CPU0:PE3(config)# mpls ldp
RP/0/0/CPU0:PE3(config-ldp)# address-family ipv4
RP/0/0/CPU0:PE3(config-ldp-af)# label remote accept from 10.1.100.2:0 for LIMIT_LDP
RP/0/0/CPU0:PE3(config-ldp-af)# show
Sun Jan 14 23:03:37.950 UTC
Building configuration...
!! IOS XR Configuration 6.6.2.10I
ipv4 access-list LIMIT_LDP
 10 deny ipv4 host 10.1.100.2 any
!
mpls ldp
 address-family ipv4
 label
 remote
 accept
  from 10.1.100.2:0 for LIMIT_LDP
 !
 !
 !
 !
 !
end
RP/0/0/CPU0:PE3(config-ldp-af)# commit
RP/0/0/CPU0:PE3(config-ldp-af)# end
RP/0/0/CPU0:PE3# show mpls ldp bindings
Sun Jan 14 23:04:26.117 UTC
! Output omitted for brevity
10.1.100.2/32, rev 17
  Local binding: label: 16301
```

```
Remote bindings: (1 peers)

  Peer      Label
  ---------------- --------

  10.1.100.4:0   402
```

There are several different approaches you can use to manipulate outbound and inbound prefix distribution to suit your environments. The techniques I have shown you here will serve as the building blocks to control the security aspect of LDP.

Notice that I am trying to show you a wide variety of platforms (ASR9K, Cisco 8000, NCS 5500, ASR1K, and there will be more to come) and software loads (if you have a sharp eye, you noticed that last example was IOS XR version 6.6.2, which is an older version; some of the previous examples were from a software load 7.11.1 from November 2023). The reason for this is that there is no way we can include all possible hardware and software permutations where commands are added or removed. I have no idea what you will see on the exam or in your job role, but it shouldn't matter. Learn to work with the tools you're given. I am coaching you to fix problems, not memorize configurations you found in a book. Study principles, and you will be able to solve any networking problem.

Label Allocation Filtering

The Label Distribution Protocol (LDP) assigns a unique local label to each route it learns from the Interior Gateway Protocol (IGP). If there is no filtering of inbound and outbound labels, these local labels are shared with and acquired by all peers. Sometimes, not all routers on the network need to store all LDP domain labels. Can you think of an example where some routers have no need of certain labels? If you cannot, then look at Figure 16-3.

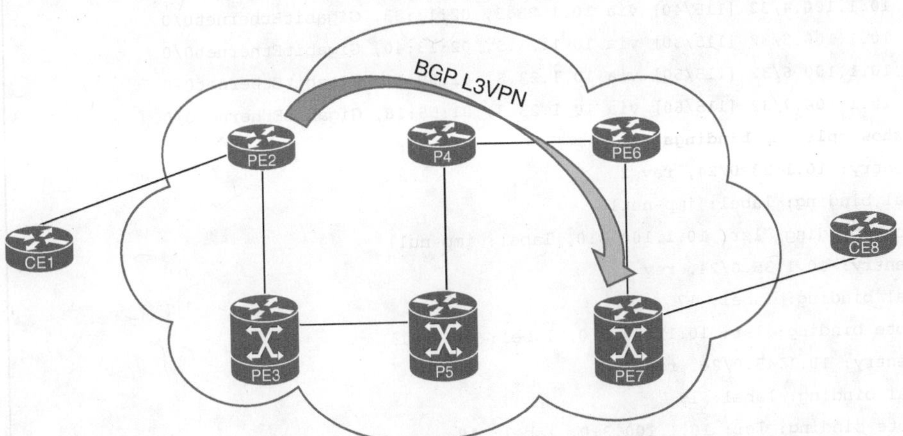

Figure 16-3   *Service and Transport Labels on a Service Provider Network*

We've modified our topology to illustrate routers PE2 and PE7 providing an L3VPN service to a customer. You should be able to visualize the addressing scheme based on the addressing approach we've used in this book. I'm concentrating solely on configuring the LDP portion, because it is our primary focus. However, this setup seamlessly integrates with BGP L3VPN when implemented on top of the presented configuration. PE2 and PE7 run a BGP L3VPN session between them over an MPLS-based network and exchange service VPN labels for this customer. To route the traffic to the customer, they only need to know the

LDP labels for each other's loopbacks; this is how they find the next hop for this VPN. But guess what? Both PE2 and PE7 will learn *all* LDP labels that map /32 loopbacks and interconnecting link prefixes as well. Look for yourself in Example 16-12.

Example 16-12 *LDP Prefixes on PE Routers*

```
PE2# show ip route isis
Codes: L - local, C - connected, S - static, R - RIP, M - mobile, B - BGP
   D - EIGRP, EX - EIGRP external, O - OSPF, IA - OSPF inter area
   N1 - OSPF NSSA external type 1, N2 - OSPF NSSA external type 2
   E1 - OSPF external type 1, E2 - OSPF external type 2
   i - IS-IS, su - IS-IS summary, L1 - IS-IS level-1, L2 - IS-IS level-2
   ia - IS-IS inter area, * - candidate default, U - per-user static route
   o - ODR, P - periodic downloaded static route, H - NHRP, l - LISP
   a - application route
   + - replicated route, % - next hop override, p - overrides from PfR

Gateway of last resort is not set

   10.0.0.0/8 is variably subnetted, 12 subnets, 2 masks
i L2   10.1.35.0/24 [115/20] via 10.1.23.3, 02:13:48, GigabitEthernet0/0
i L2   10.1.45.0/24 [115/30] via 10.1.23.3, 02:13:40, GigabitEthernet0/0
i L2   10.1.46.0/24 [115/40] via 10.1.23.3, 02:13:33, GigabitEthernet0/0
i L2   10.1.67.0/24 [115/50] via 10.1.23.3, 02:08:51, GigabitEthernet0/0
i L2   10.1.100.3/32 [115/20] via 10.1.23.3, 02:26:51, GigabitEthernet0/0
i L2   10.1.100.4/32 [115/40] via 10.1.23.3, 02:13:33, GigabitEthernet0/0
i L2   10.1.100.5/32 [115/30] via 10.1.23.3, 02:13:40, GigabitEthernet0/0
i L2   10.1.100.6/32 [115/50] via 10.1.23.3, 02:09:31, GigabitEthernet0/0
i L2   10.1.100.7/32 [115/60] via 10.1.23.3, 01:58:18, GigabitEthernet0/0
PE2# show mpls ldp bindings
lib entry: 10.1.23.0/24, rev 2
  local binding: label: imp-null
  remote binding: lsr: 10.1.100.3:0, label: imp-null
lib entry: 10.1.35.0/24, rev 8
  local binding: label: 17
  remote binding: lsr: 10.1.100.3:0, label: imp-null
lib entry: 10.1.45.0/24, rev 12
  local binding: label: 19
  remote binding: lsr: 10.1.100.3:0, label: 18
lib entry: 10.1.46.0/24, rev 16
  local binding: label: 21
  remote binding: lsr: 10.1.100.3:0, label: 20
lib entry: 10.1.67.0/24, rev 20
  local binding: label: 23
  remote binding: lsr: 10.1.100.3:0, label: 22
```

```
lib entry: 10.1.100.2/32, rev 4
 local binding: label: imp-null
 remote binding: lsr: 10.1.100.3:0, label: 16
lib entry: 10.1.100.3/32, rev 6
 local binding: label: 16
 remote binding: lsr: 10.1.100.3:0, label: imp-null
lib entry: 10.1.100.4/32, rev 14
 local binding: label: 20
 remote binding: lsr: 10.1.100.3:0, label: 19
lib entry: 10.1.100.5/32, rev 10
 local binding: label: 18
 remote binding: lsr: 10.1.100.3:0, label: 17
lib entry: 10.1.100.6/32, rev 18
 local binding: label: 22
 remote binding: lsr: 10.1.100.3:0, label: 21
lib entry: 10.1.100.7/32, rev 22
 local binding: label: 24
 remote binding: lsr: 10.1.100.3:0, label: 23
PE2#
```

```
RP/0/RP0/CPU0:PE7# show mpls ldp bindings brief
Sat Jan 20 12:59:19.848 UTC


Prefix    Local  Advertised Remote Bindings
    Label (peers) (peers)
----------------- --------- ---------- ---------------
10.1.23.0/24    24008    1    1
10.1.35.0/24    24007    1    1
10.1.45.0/24    24006    1    1
10.1.46.0/24    24001    1    1
10.1.67.0/24    ImpNull    1    1
10.1.100.2/32   24005    1    1
10.1.100.3/32   24004    1    1
10.1.100.4/32   24002    1    1
10.1.100.5/32   24003    1    1
10.1.100.6/32   24000    1    1
10.1.100.7/32   ImpNull    1    1

RP/0/RP0/CPU0:PE7#
```

Just like we said, PE2 and PE7 have allocated a label for each IGP (IS-IS) route, as seen in the **Label Information Base (LIB)** database seen in the output of **show mpls ldp bindings**. The question is: Are all these labels necessary for the operation of this BGP L3VPN on these two PE routers? If you answered No, you are onto something.

Let's remove some of these labels and see what happens, as demonstrated in Example 16-13.

Example 16-13 *Label Allocation Filtering on IOS XR with Host Routes*

```
RP/0/RP0/CPU0:PE7# configure
Sat Jan 20 14:45:57.063 UTC
RP/0/RP0/CPU0:PE7(config)# mpls ldp
RP/0/RP0/CPU0:PE7(config-ldp)# address-family ipv4
RP/0/RP0/CPU0:PE7(config-ldp-af)# label
RP/0/RP0/CPU0:PE7(config-ldp-af-lbl)# local
RP/0/RP0/CPU0:PE7(config-ldp-af-lbl-lcl)# allocate for ?
  WORD       IP access-list
  host-routes Allocate label for host routes only
RP/0/RP0/CPU0:PE7(config-ldp-af-lbl-lcl)# allocate for host-routes
RP/0/RP0/CPU0:PE7(config-ldp-af-lbl-lcl)# commit
Sat Jan 20 14:46:36.589 UTC
RP/0/RP0/CPU0:PE7(config-ldp-af-lbl-lcl)# end
RP/0/RP0/CPU0:PE7# show mpls ldp bindings | brief
Sat Jan 20 14:46:52.640 UTC


Prefix     Local  Advertised Remote Bindings
     Label (peers) (peers)
------------------- --------- ---------- ----------------
10.1.23.0/24   -      0     1
10.1.35.0/24   -      0     1
10.1.45.0/24   -      0     1
10.1.46.0/24   -      0     1
10.1.67.0/24   -      0     1
10.1.100.2/32  24005  1     1
10.1.100.3/32  24004  1     1
10.1.100.4/32  24002  1     1
10.1.100.5/32  24003  1     1
10.1.100.6/32  24000  1     1
10.1.100.7/32  ImpNull 1    1
```

In the output in Example 16-13, notice that we had an option to allocate for only host routes or specify a custom access list. We chose host routes and now all LDP labels associated with transit networks are no longer in the LIB! (Compare this with the output in Example 16-12.)

Now, let's choose the other option and drop all LDP labels but PE2 and PE7 loopbacks, as demonstrated in Example 16-14.

Example 16-14 *Label Allocation Filtering on IOS XR with Access Lists*

```
RP/0/RP0/CPU0:PE7# configure
Sat Jan 20 14:50:44.962 UTC
RP/0/RP0/CPU0:PE7(config)# ipv4 access-list PE2_PE7_LOOPBACKS
RP/0/RP0/CPU0:PE7(config-ipv4-acl)# permit ipv4 host 10.1.100.2 any
RP/0/RP0/CPU0:PE7(config-ipv4-acl)# permit ipv4 host 10.1.100.7 any
RP/0/RP0/CPU0:PE7(config-ipv4-acl)# exit
RP/0/RP0/CPU0:PE7(config)# mpls ldp
```

```
RP/0/RP0/CPU0:PE7(config-ldp)# address-family ipv4
RP/0/RP0/CPU0:PE7(config-ldp-af)# label
RP/0/RP0/CPU0:PE7(config-ldp-af-lbl)# local
RP/0/RP0/CPU0:PE7(config-ldp-af-lbl-lcl)# allocate for PE2_PE7_LOOPBACKS
RP/0/RP0/CPU0:PE7(config-ldp-af-lbl-lcl)# commit
Sat Jan 20 14:55:33.282 UTC
RP/0/RP0/CPU0:PE7(config-ldp-af-lbl-lcl)# end
RP/0/RP0/CPU0:PE7# show mpls ldp bindings brief
Sat Jan 20 14:55:42.769 UTC


Prefix     Local  Advertised Remote Bindings
     Label (peers) (peers)
------------------ --------- -------------------
10.1.23.0/24   -       0      1
10.1.35.0/24   -       0      1
10.1.45.0/24   -       0      1
10.1.46.0/24   -       0      1
10.1.67.0/24   -       0      1
10.1.100.2/32  24005   1      1
10.1.100.3/32  -       0      1
10.1.100.4/32  -       0      1
10.1.100.5/32  -       0      1
10.1.100.6/32  -       0      1
10.1.100.7/32  ImpNull 1      1
```

So, with the access list, we overrode the host routes option and dropped everything but LDP labels for PE2 and PE7's loopbacks—the only PEs we need to make this BGP L3VPN work. Will our connection still work? You bet. Traceroute verifies this (see Example 16-15), and the **Label Forwarding Information Base (LFIB)** knows where to send the packet.

Example 16-15 *Label Allocation Filtering on IOS XR Verified*

```
RP/0/RP0/CPU0:PE7# trace 10.1.100.2
Sat Jan 20 14:56:02.582 UTC


Type escape sequence to abort.
Tracing the route to 10.1.100.2


  1 10.1.67.6 [MPLS: Label 19 Exp 0] 8 msec 8 msec 7 msec
  2 10.1.46.4 [MPLS: Label 20 Exp 0] 10 msec 8 msec 9 msec
  3 10.1.45.5 [MPLS: Label 20 Exp 0] 9 msec 8 msec 8 msec
  4 10.1.35.3 [MPLS: Label 16 Exp 0] 8 msec 8 msec 9 msec
  5 10.1.23.2 9 msec * 9 msec
RP/0/RP0/CPU0:PE7# show mpls forwarding
Sat Jan 20 15:06:33.919 UTC
Local Outgoing Prefix    Outgoing  Next Hop  Bytes
```

```
Label Label  or ID    Interface    Switched
------ ----------- ------------------- ----------- ------------------ ----------
24005 19     10.1.100.2/32  Gi0/0/0/0 10.1.67.6  1760
RP/0/RP0/CPU0:PE7#
```

Is this not something? For optimization and scale purposes, this technique can be useful on larger networks. Operators can choose to minimize the resources that routers allocate and exchange; doing so reduces the pressure on the control plane and speeds up convergence. If certain VPNs are not present on certain PEs, why am I allocating LDP labels for them? Now you know how to do this.

A pop quiz to make sure you understood this topic: Why do we not need these labels for the transit networks and P-Routers' loopbacks in the preceding example? Pause and answer in your head before reading the next sentence. Your answer should be something along the lines of "because we are not sending traffic *to* these networks; we are sending traffic *through* them."

For your homework, can you set this up on PE2, an IOS XE router? Example 16-16 should help you.

Example 16-16 *Label Allocation Filtering on IOS XE*

```
PE2# configure terminal
Enter configuration commands, one per line. End with CNTL/Z.
PE2(config)# mpls ldp ?
 advertise-labels Label advertisements
 backoff    Set LDP session backoff parameters
 discovery   LDP discovery
 entropy-label  Enable Entropy Label for LDP
 explicit-null  Advertise Explicit Null label in place of Implicit Null
 graceful-restart Configure LDP Graceful Restart
 holdtime    LDP session holdtime
 igp     Configure IGP-related LDP parameters
 label     LDP label mode
 logging    Enable LDP logging
 loop-detection Enable LDP Loop Detection
 maxhops    Limit hop count for LDP LSP setup
 neighbor    Configure neighbor parameters
 nsr     Enable Non Stop Routing for LDP
 password    Configure LDP MD5 password
 router-id   Select interface to prefer for LDP identifier address
 session   Configure session parameters
 tcp     Set TCP parameters for LDP
 vrf     Specify a VPN Routing/Forwarding instance
PE2(config)# mpls ldp label
PE2(config-ldp-lbl)# ?
```

```
MPLS LDP label commands:
  allocate Allocate local labels for specified destination prefixes
  default Set a command to its defaults
  exit  Exit from LDP label mode
  no  Negate a command or set its defaults

PE2(config-ldp-lbl)# allocate ?
  global Specify global Routing/Forwarding instance

PE2(config-ldp-lbl)# allocate global ?
  host-routes allocate local label for host routes only
  prefix-list Specify a prefix list for local label filtering
  <cr>    <cr>
PE2(config-ldp-lbl)#
```

Keeping BGP Safe

Border Gateway Protocol (BGP) is a crucial routing protocol that exchanges routing and reachability information between different autonomous systems on the Internet. BGP ensures that data is routed efficiently across the global network. It used to be that few networking engineers got a chance to work with BGP. I remember circa 2005 when my employer finally purchased enough memory for a Cisco 7206VXR for us to accept the entire Internet routing table. Talk about not being able to sleep the night before because of the excitement! Nowadays, things are different. BGP is everywhere. In fact, in my current role with exposure to a massive number of customers who run service provider networks, I encounter far fewer people who feel more comfortable with IS-IS than they do with BGP. BGP scales well. In fact, many IT organizations use it to run their data center environments with VXLAN and use BGP for the control plane, so it is well known.

BGP uses TCP as its transport protocol, and this makes it vulnerable to the same types of attacks that can affect any TCP-based protocol, including denial-of-service (DoS) attacks. Over the years, there have been several ongoing efforts to enhance its security, but incidents do show up. A couple have somehow stayed in my mind. I remember the year was 2008 (the same year I started at Cisco), and Pakistan Telecom unintentionally caused a global BGP incident that disrupted access to YouTube. The company attempted to block access to YouTube within Pakistan but mistakenly announced some of the YouTube IP prefixes into the global BGP routing table. The result was global traffic destined to watch cute puppy videos being redirected through Pakistan instead. This incident made the news and underscored the impact of misconfiguring BGP.

Then, about six years or so ago, Level 3 Communications, a major global Tier 1 ISP, accidentally leaked BGP routes, impacting various networks and causing disruptions. The incident resulted in many IP prefixes being incorrectly propagated. I recall half of my team not being able to use the Cisco Webex video-conferencing platform while our colleagues in the other half of the country were working just fine. Such incidents highlight the importance of BGP security and the need for continuous efforts to address vulnerabilities in the BGP protocol to ensure the stability and security of the global Internet routing infrastructure. Given BGP's impact scale, service providers should exercise utmost caution in implementing robust measures to mitigate the risks associated with potential exploits of the BGP routing protocol.

The sections that follow look at the tools available today, which include the following:

- BGP Authentication

- BGP TTL-Security

- BGP Route Filtering

- BGP Maximum-prefix

- BGP Prefix Suppression

- BGPsec

- BGP Flowspec

BGP Authentication

When it comes to BGP security, put BGP authentication at the top of the list. If another rogue router or attacker can peer up with our BGP speaker, they can feed us undesirable routes that we will amplify. To make this rogue peering harder (it is not impossible; don't kid yourself), MD5-based authentication was introduced and is described in RFC 2385.

BGP neighbor authentication operates symmetrically and, thus, must be activated on both ends of the peering session. MD5-based neighbor authentication involves generating an MD5 hash for each packet transmitted during a BGP session. The recipient BGP neighbor uses the identical algorithm and shared secret to compute its own MD5 hash for comparison. Should the MD5 hash values differ, the receiving BGP neighbor will reject the packet.

RFC 2385 proposed a TCP extension to enhance BGP security. Option 19 was specified to contain the MD5 digest, as seen in Figure 16-4.

Kind=19	Length=18	MD5 Digest...

Figure 16-4 *BGP Extension MD5 Digest Field*

This option allowed BGP to protect itself if an attacker spoofed TCP segments and inserted them into the connection stream. A good attack example would be TCP resets with the goal of dropping existing connections. Thus, "guessing" the TCP sequence numbers just became harder because the attacker would have to acquire the password included in the MD5 digest as well. Since the password itself never appears in the connection stream (only the hash does), the attacker's job becomes far harder.

Let's look at Example 16-17, where we have configured MD5-based authentication. The logic is simple: we enable MD5 authentication on an existing peering and observe the peering session break in the debug output. We can clearly see PE2 complaining that it expects MD5-digest from PE7. When we properly configure PE7, the peering comes back. PE2 runs IOS XE, and PE7 runs IOS XR. Notice that PE2 gets five prefixes from PE7.

Example 16-17 *Turning on MD5-Based Authentication*

```
PE2# show bgp ipv4 unicast summary
BGP router identifier 172.16.3.2, local AS number 65000
BGP table version is 10, main routing table version 10
9 network entries using 1296 bytes of memory
9 path entries using 756 bytes of memory
2/2 BGP path/bestpath attribute entries using 320 bytes of memory
1 BGP AS-PATH entries using 24 bytes of memory
0 BGP route-map cache entries using 0 bytes of memory
0 BGP filter-list cache entries using 0 bytes of memory
BGP using 2396 total bytes of memory
BGP activity 37/28 prefixes, 37/28 paths, scan interval 60 secs


Neighbor  V   AS MsgRcvd MsgSent TblVer InQ OutQ Up/Down State/PfxRcd
10.1.100.7  4  65001  6  7  10 0 0 00:03:16  5
PE2# configure terminal
Enter configuration commands, one per line. End with CNTL/Z.
PE2(config)# router bgp 65000
PE2(config-router)# neighbor 10.1.100.7 password ccnp
PE2(config-router)# end
PE2# debug ip bgp
*Jan 15 20:33:00.837: %SYS-5-LOG_CONFIG_CHANGE: Console logging: level debugging,
xml disabled, filtering disabled
*Jan 15 20:33:02.198: %SYS-5-CONFIG_I: Configured from console by console
PE2#
*Jan 15 20:33:04.143: BGP: 10.1.100.7 open failed: Connection timed out; remote host
not responding
*Jan 15 20:33:04.143: BGP: 10.1.100.7 Active open failed - tcb is not available,
open active delayed 11264ms (35000ms max, 60% jitter)
*Jan 15 20:33:04.143: BGP: ses global 10.1.100.7 (0x111E6870:0) act Reset (Active
open failed).
*Jan 15 20:33:04.146: BGP: 10.1.100.7 active went from Active to Idle
*Jan 15 20:33:04.147: BGP: nbr global 10.1.100.7 Active open failed - open timer
running
*Jan 15 20:33:04.147: BGP: nbr global 10.1.100.7 Active open failed - open timer
running
*Jan 15 20:33:15.100: BGP: 10.1.100.7 active went from Idle to Active
*Jan 15 20:33:15.100: BGP: 10.1.100.7 open active, local address 10.1.100.2
*Jan 15 20:33:22.513: %TCP-6-BADAUTH: No MD5 digest from 10.1.100.7(56433) to
10.1.100.2(179) tableid - 0
*Jan 15 20:33:24.513: %TCP-6-BADAUTH: No MD5 digest from 10.1.100.7(56433) to
10.1.100.2(179) tableid - 0
*Jan 15 20:33:28.514: %TCP-6-BADAUTH: No MD5 digest from 10.1.100.7(56433) to
10.1.100.2(179) tableid - 0

<!---CHANGING TO PE7---!>
RP/0/RP0/CPU0:PE7# configure
Mon Jan 15 20:34:03.447 UTC
```

```
RP/0/RP0/CPU0:PE7(config)# router bgp 65001
RP/0/RP0/CPU0:PE7(config-bgp)# neighbor 10.1.100.2 password 0 ccnp
RP/0/RP0/CPU0:PE7(config-bgp-nbr)# commit
Mon Jan 15 20:37:03.596 UTC

<!---CHANGING TO PE2---!>
*Jan 15 20:37:06.839: BGP: nbr global 10.1.100.7 Active open failed - open timer
running
*Jan 15 20:37:18.814: BGP: 10.1.100.7 active went from Idle to Active
*Jan 15 20:37:18.814: BGP: 10.1.100.7 open active, local address 10.1.100.2
*Jan 15 20:37:18.822: BGP: ses global 10.1.100.7 (0xD97E1A8:0) act Adding topology
IPv4 Unicast:base
*Jan 15 20:37:18.822: BGP: ses global 10.1.100.7 (0xD97E1A8:0) act Send OPEN
*Jan 15 20:37:18.823: BGP: ses global 10.1.100.7 (0xD97E1A8:0) act Building Enhanced
Refresh capability
*Jan 15 20:37:18.823: BGP: 10.1.100.7 active went from Active to OpenSent
*Jan 15 20:37:18.823: BGP: 10.1.100.7 active sending OPEN, version 4, my as: 65000,
holdtime 180 seconds, ID AC100302
*Jan 15 20:37:18.832: BGP: 10.1.100.7 active rcv message type 1, length (excl.
header) 56
*Jan 15 20:37:18.832: BGP: ses global 10.1.100.7 (0xD97E1A8:0) act Receive OPEN
*Jan 15 20:37:18.832: BGP: 10.1.100.7 active rcv OPEN, version 4, holdtime 180
seconds
*Jan 15 20:37:18.832: BGP: 10.1.100.7 active rcv OPEN w/ OPTION parameter len: 46
*Jan 15 20:37:18.833: BGP: 10.1.100.7 active rcvd OPEN w/ optional parameter type 2
(Capability) len 6
*Jan 15 20:37:18.833: BGP: 10.1.100.7 active OPEN has CAPABILITY code: 1, length 4
*Jan 15 20:37:18.833: BGP: 10.1.100.7 active OPEN has MP_EXT CAP for afi/safi: 1/1
*Jan 15 20:37:18.833: BGP: 10.1.100.7 active rcvd OPEN w/ optional parameter type 2
(Capability) len 2
*Jan 15 20:37:18.833: BGP: 10.1.100.7 active OPEN has CAPABILITY code: 128, length 0
*Jan 15 20:37:18.833: BGP: 10.1.100.7 active OPEN has ROUTE-REFRESH capability(old)
for all address-families
*Jan 15 20:37:18.833: BGP: 10.1.100.7 active rcvd OPEN w/ optional parameter type 2
(Capability) len 2
*Jan 15 20:37:18.834: BGP: 10.1.100.7 active OPEN has CAPABILITY code: 2, length 0
*Jan 15 20:37:18.834: BGP: 10.1.100.7 active OPEN has ROUTE-REFRESH capability(new)
for all address-families
*Jan 15 20:37:18.834: BGP: 10.1.100.7 active rcvd OPEN w/ optional parameter type 2
(Capability) len 6
*Jan 15 20:37:18.834: BGP: 10.1.100.7 active OPEN has CAPABILITY code: 65, length 4
*Jan 15 20:37:18.834: BGP: 10.1.100.7 active OPEN has 4-byte ASN CAP for: 65001
*Jan 15 20:37:18.834: BGP: 10.1.100.7 active rcvd OPEN w/ optional parameter type 2
(Capability) len 20
*Jan 15 20:37:18.835: BGP: 10.1.100.7 active OPEN has CAPABILITY code: 5, length 18
*Jan 15 20:37:18.835: BGP: 10.1.100.7 active unrecognized capability code: 5
- ignored
*Jan 15 20:37:18.835: BGP: 10.1.100.7 active rcvd OPEN w/ remote AS 65001, 4-byte
remote AS 65001
```

```
*Jan 15 20:37:18.835: BGP: 10.1.100.7 active went from OpenSent to OpenConfirm
*Jan 15 20:37:18.836: BGP: 10.1.100.7 active went from OpenConfirm to Established
*Jan 15 20:37:18.836: BGP: ses global 10.1.100.7 (0xD97E1A8:1) act Assigned ID
*Jan 15 20:37:18.836: BGP: ses global 10.1.100.7 (0xD97E1A8:1) Up
*Jan 15 20:37:18.837: %BGP-5-ADJCHANGE: neighbor 10.1.100.7 Up
PE2# show bgp ipv4 unicast summary
BGP router identifier 172.16.3.2, local AS number 65000
BGP table version is 1, main routing table version 1
5 network entries using 720 bytes of memory
5 path entries using 420 bytes of memory
2/0 BGP path/bestpath attribute entries using 320 bytes of memory
1 BGP AS-PATH entries using 24 bytes of memory
0 BGP route-map cache entries using 0 bytes of memory
0 BGP filter-list cache entries using 0 bytes of memory
BGP using 1484 total bytes of memory
BGP activity 46/41 prefixes, 46/41 paths, scan interval 60 secs

Neighbor  V   AS MsgRcvd MsgSent TblVer InQ OutQ Up/Down State/PfxRcd
10.1.100.7  4   65001  4  2  1 0 0 00:00:05  5
PE2#
```

Short, memorable, simple. Pop-quiz time: Can you think of what issues you may run into when setting up MD5-based authentication for BGP? Do not read further; challenge yourself to think. Well, I have seen a couple. Remember that we're dealing with TCP-based connections. If you have some form of NAT or PAT present between your two BGP speakers, this connection will give you problems. Additionally, look out for firewalls because some vendors notoriously randomize TCP sequence numbers or strip TCP options altogether. Once our Option 19 is removed from the TCP header, the authentication check will result in failure on the receiving router. Time to call the security team (unless you are them).

BGP TTL-Security

Suppose we got our MD5-based authentication working and feel more secure. There are other scenarios where attackers aim to overwhelm the BGP process itself. They might deploy a barrage of TCP SYN packets directed at our BGP router. The BGP MD5 neighbor authentication method does not provide protection against this type of attack. In fact, it can potentially worsen the situation by prompting the router CPU to allocate resources in computing MD5 hashes for a large volume of attack packets. The BGP **Time-to-Live (TTL)** security check is a mechanism implemented in the Border Gateway Protocol to verify the TTL field in BGP packets. It is designed to stave off DoS attackers.

TTL is a counter in network packets that limits the time or hops a packet can traverse through a network before being discarded. In the context of BGP, the TTL security check involves verifying the TTL value in BGP update messages. BGP routers can be configured to check the TTL field to ensure that it is within an expected range. If the TTL is outside the expected range, the BGP router can discard the BGP update message.

The purpose of this security check is to prevent certain attacks, such as TTL exhaustion attacks, where an attacker manipulates BGP messages with incorrect TTL values to disrupt the normal operation of the BGP routing infrastructure. By enforcing TTL checks, BGP routers can help ensure that BGP messages are legitimate and originate from valid sources. Examine the diagram in Figure 16-5 with all routers running IOS XE.

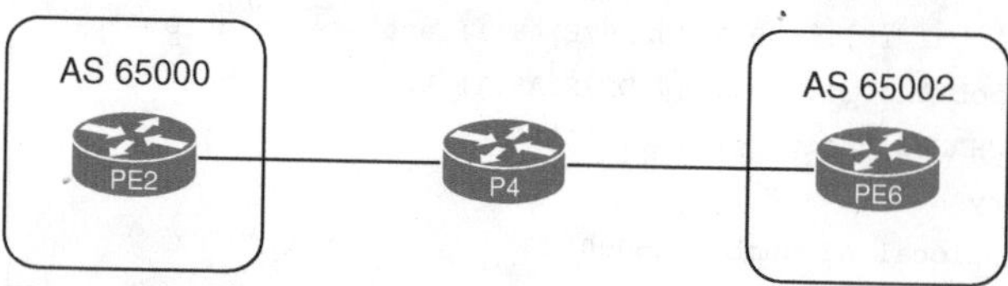

Figure 16-5 *BGP Security Reference Diagram*

Recall that, by default, EBGP connections have a TTL value of 1, since they are assumed to be directly connected. (Notice we have chosen a different, "nondirect" BGP setup to work through this feature in the diagram in Figure 16-5; you will see why soon.) These packets will expire in transit as soon as they go through the first router. This approach works to limit EBGP peers to directly connected networks. It also has the following vulnerability: a remote attacker can easily adjust the TTL value of sent packets. To the target router, it would look as though they came from a directed peer. For this reason, RFC 5082 describes a simple solution that inverts the direction in which TTL is counted.

When the BGP TTL security check is activated, the initial TTL value for an External BGP (EBGP) packet is adjusted to 255 instead of 1 (a big difference!). Additionally, a minimum TTL value is enforced for all BGP packets associated with that specific EBGP session. For instance, if the TTL security check is configured with a value of 1, the BGP router receiving the packets anticipates a TTL of 254 (the initial value of 255 minus one hop).

This is a nontrivial distinction from how EBGP functions out of the box. The IP packet's 8-bit TTL field has a maximum value of 255. Rather than exclusively accepting packets with a TTL set to 1, a more stringent rule is to admit only those packets with a TTL of 255, thereby ensuring that the originator is precisely one hop away. Just by flipping the direction of a TTL count, the task of spoofing a TTL value has become significantly more challenging. Can you think why? Because each router in the path to the target router will decrement the TTL by 1. As a result, when the target router gets the packet, it will be able to tell how many "router hops" away the pretending BGP speaker is. So now, the infrastructure rats out the attacker! As the IP header TTL value decreases with each router hop along the packet's path to its final (target) destination, this security measure restricts the peering diameter to routers in the actual path or only directly connected routers. Now, forging the TTL field has become far more challenging...but not impossible. Can you think of at least one way an attacker can overcome this defense? One way to do this would be to compromise the routers in the path and reset the packet's TTL value on those routers. (Always try to think a step ahead of what can happen.)

Back to Figure 16-5. Because PE2 and PE6 are not directly connected (the intermediate router P4 is present and decrements the packet's TTL by 1), we had to build the EBGP multihop connection between PE2 and PE6. Realize that EBGP multihop and TTL security are mutually exclusive. (What?! Think about what we just discussed again, and it will make sense.) In this case, we will remove EBGP multihop and enable TTL security. Router PE6 will send a packet with a TTL value of 255, which will become 254 as it crosses P4. That means if PE2 is configured for the TTL security value of 1 (the initial TTL value minus the hop count, i.e., 255 − 1), our connection should succeed. Hang on to this theory...

Let's see BGP TTL security in action in Example 16-18.

Example 16-18   *Verifying EBGP Multihop*

```
PE2# show running-config | section bgp
router bgp 65000
 bgp log-neighbor-changes
 no bgp default ipv4-unicast
 neighbor 10.1.100.6 remote-as 65002
 neighbor 10.1.100.6 ebgp-multihop 2
 neighbor 10.1.100.6 update-source Loopback0

PE6# show running-config | section bgp
router bgp 65002
 bgp log-neighbor-changes
 neighbor 10.1.100.2 remote-as 65000
 neighbor 10.1.100.2 ebgp-multihop 2
 neighbor 10.1.100.2 update-source Loopback0

PE2# trace 10.1.100.6
Type escape sequence to abort.
Tracing the route to 10.1.100.6
VRF info: (vrf in name/id, vrf out name/id)
  1 10.1.24.4 2 msec 2 msec 2 msec
  2 10.1.46.6 3 msec 4 msec *
PE2# show ip bgp summary | begin Neighbor
Neighbor  V   AS MsgRcvd MsgSent TblVer InQ OutQ Up/Down State/PfxRcd
10.1.100.6  4   65002   5   8   1321 0 0 00:02:53   4
PE2# show ip bgp neighbors 10.1.100.6 | include TTL
Connection is ECN Disabled, Mininum incoming TTL 0, Outgoing TTL 2
```

Quite ordinary and standard. PE2 and PE6 are EBGP peers two hops away from each other, as confirmed in the traceroute output. Notice how the **ebgp-multihop 2** command leads to the minimum necessary TTL of 0 but the outgoing TTL of 2. We are going to change this behavior with **ttl-security**, as demonstrated in Example 16-19.

Example 16-19   *BGP TTL Security Two Hops*

```
PE6# configure terminal
Enter configuration commands, one per line. End with CNTL/Z.
PE6(config)# router bgp 65002
PE6(config-router)# no neighbor 10.1.100.2 ebgp-multihop 2
PE6(config-router)# neighbor 10.1.100.2 ttl-security hops 2
PE6(config-router)# end
PE6# clear ip bgp *
PE6# show ip bgp summary
BGP router identifier 172.16.63.6, local AS number 65002
BGP table version is 1, main routing table version 1
```

```
Neighbor  V   AS MsgRcvd MsgSent TblVer InQ OutQ Up/Down State/PfxRcd
10.1.100.2  4   65000  0  0  1 0 0 00:00:14 Active
PE6# debug ip bgp

BGP debugging is on for address family: IPv4 Unicast
PE6# configure terminal

Enter configuration commands, one per line. End with CNTL/Z.
PE6(config)# logging console

PE6(config)#

*Jan 18 19:34:33.565: %SYS-5-LOG_CONFIG_CHANGE: Console logging: level debugging,
xml disabled, filtering disabled
PE6(config)#

*Jan 18 19:34:48.099: BGP: topo global:IPv4 Unicast:base Scanning routing tables
*Jan 18 19:34:48.099: BGP: topo global:IPv4 Multicast:base Scanning routing tables
*Jan 18 19:34:48.099: BGP: topo global:L2VPN E-VPN:base Scanning routing tables
*Jan 18 19:34:48.100: BGP: topo global:MVPNv4 Unicast:base Scanning routing tables
*Jan 18 19:34:50.868: BGP: ses global 10.1.100.2 (0x1022DE88:0) act Reset (Active
open failed).
```

So, what did we learn? If one side is EBGP multihop and the other is TTL security, BGP
peering does not get established. Why? Looks as though PE2 does not like it and sends us a
Reset. TTL values are different. So, let's get PE2 to follow the TTL security approach as well,
but instead of doing two hops, let's try one hop and see what happens, as demonstrated in
Example 16-20.

Example 16-20   *BGP TTL Security One Hop*

```
PE2(config)# router bgp 65000
PE2(config-router)# neighbor 10.1.100.6 ttl-security hops 1
PE2(config-router)# end
PE2# clear ip bgp *
PE2# show bgp summary
*Jan 18 19:43:12.176: BGP: 10.1.100.6 Active open failed - no route to peer, open
active delayed 8192ms (35000ms max, 60% jitter)gp summ
BGP router identifier 172.16.23.2, local AS number 65000
BGP table version is 1, main routing table version 1
4 network entries using 576 bytes of memory
4 path entries using 336 bytes of memory
1/0 BGP path/bestpath attribute entries using 160 bytes of memory
0 BGP route-map cache entries using 0 bytes of memory
0 BGP filter-list cache entries using 0 bytes of memory
BGP using 1072 total bytes of memory
BGP activity 16/12 prefixes, 16/12 paths, scan interval 60 secs


Neighbor  V   AS MsgRcvd MsgSent TblVer InQ OutQ Up/Down State/PfxRcd
10.1.100.6  4   65002  0  0  1 0 0 00:00:56 Idle
```

So, we know that hop count 1 is not enough because the connection sits in the Idle state. For that reason, let's change the hop count to 2 and turn the debug on (see Example 16-21).

Example 16-21   *BGP TTL Security Two Hop on PE2*

```
PE2(config-router)# neighbor 10.1.100.6 ttl-security hops 2
PE2(config-router)# do debug ip bgp
BGP debugging is on for address family: IPv4 Unicast
PE2(config-router)#
*Jan 18 19:50:54.060: BGP: 10.1.100.6 active went from Idle to Active
*Jan 18 19:50:54.060: BGP: 10.1.100.6 open active, local address 10.1.100.2
*Jan 18 19:50:54.067: BGP: ses global 10.1.100.6 (0x1071C518:0) act Adding topology
IPv4 Unicast:base
*Jan 18 19:50:54.068: BGP: ses global 10.1.100.6 (0x1071C518:0) act Send OPEN
*Jan 18 19:50:54.068: BGP: ses global 10.1.100.6 (0x1071C518:0) act Building
Enhanced Refresh capability
*Jan 18 19:50:54.068: BGP: 10.1.100.6 active went from Active to OpenSent
*Jan 18 19:50:54.069: BGP: 10.1.100.6 active sending OPEN, version 4, my as:
65000, holdtime 180 seconds, ID AC101702
*Jan 18 19:50:54.076: BGP: 10.1.100.6 active rcv message type 1, length (excl.
header) 38
*Jan 18 19:50:54.076: BGP: ses global 10.1.100.6 (0x1071C518:0) act Receive OPEN
*Jan 18 19:50:54.076: BGP: 10.1.100.6 active rcv OPEN, version 4, holdtime 180 seconds
*Jan 18 19:50:54.077: BGP: 10.1.100.6 active rcv OPEN w/ OPTION parameter len: 28
*Jan 18 19:50:54.077: BGP: 10.1.100.6 active rcvd OPEN w/ optional parameter type 2
(Capability) len 6
*Jan 18 19:50:54.077: BGP: 10.1.100.6 active OPEN has CAPABILITY code: 1, length 4
*Jan 18 19:50:54.077: BGP: 10.1.100.6 active OPEN has MP_EXT CAP for afi/safi: 1/1
*Jan 18 19:50:54.077: BGP: 10.1.100.6 active rcvd OPEN w/ optional parameter type 2
(Capability) len 2
*Jan 18 19:50:54.077: BGP: 10.1.100.6 active OPEN has CAPABILITY code: 128, length 0
*Jan 18 19:50:54.078: BGP: 10.1.100.6 active OPEN has ROUTE-REFRESH capability(old)
for all address-families
*Jan 18 19:50:54.078: BGP: 10.1.100.6 active rcvd OPEN w/ optional parameter type 2
(Capability) len 2
*Jan 18 19:50:54.078: BGP: 10.1.100.6 active OPEN has CAPABILITY code: 2, length 0
*Jan 18 19:50:54.078: BGP: 10.1.100.6 active OPEN has ROUTE-REFRESH capability(new)
for all address-families
*Jan 18 19:50:54.078: BGP: 10.1.100.6 active rcvd OPEN w/ optional parameter type 2
(Capability) len 2
*Jan 18 19:50:54.078: BGP: 10.1.100.6 active OPEN has CAPABILITY code: 70, length 0
*Jan 18 19:50:54.078: BGP: ses global 10.1.100.6 (0x1071C518:0) act Enhanced Refresh
cap received in open message
*Jan 18 19:50:54.079: BGP: 10.1.100.6 active rcvd OPEN w/ optional parameter type 2
(Capability) len 6
*Jan 18 19:50:54.079: BGP: 10.1.100.6 active OPEN has CAPABILITY code: 65, length 4
*Jan 18 19:50:54.079: BGP: 10.1.100.6 active OPEN has 4-byte ASN CAP for: 65002
*Jan 18 19:50:54.079: BGP: 10.1.100.6 active rcvd OPEN w/ remote AS 65002, 4-byte
remote AS 65002
```

```
*Jan 18 19:50:54.079: BGP: 10.1.100.6 active went from OpenSent to OpenConfirm
*Jan 18 19:50:54.082: BGP: 10.1.100.6 active went from OpenConfirm to Established
*Jan 18 19:50:54.082: BGP: ses global 10.1.100.6 (0x1071C518:1) act Assigned ID
*Jan 18 19:50:54.083: BGP: ses global 10.1.100.6 (0x1071C518:1) Up
*Jan 18 19:50:54.083: %BGP-5-ADJCHANGE: neighbor 10.1.100.6 Up
PE2# show ip bgp neighbor | include TTL
Connection is ECN Disabled, Mininum incoming TTL 253, Outgoing TTL 255
```

As soon as we change TTL security hops to 2, the connection comes up. Look, though, how
the minimum requested TTL is 253 now and the outgoing is 255. So, now we know how TTL
security totally flips the TTL value as described in RFC 2385 (recall that these were 0 and 2,
respectively, under the **ebgp-multihop** command).

Pop-quiz time: On PE2, when we change TTL security hops to 3, will the connection come
up? (I'm humming the *Jeopardy* show theme.) The answer should be yes, because the
minimal value is expected.

There's no better way to see how a vendor implements an RFC than to verify it ourselves, as
demonstrated in Example 16-22.

Example 16-22   *BGP TTL Security Three Hops*

```
PE2# configure terminal
Enter configuration commands, one per line. End with CNTL/Z.
PE2(config)# router bgp 65000
PE2(config-router)# neighbor 10.1.100.6 ttl-security hops 3
PE2(config-router)# end
PE2# clear ip bgp *
*Jan 18 19:56:29.817: %SYS-5-CONFIG_I: Configured from console by console
PE2#
*Jan 18 19:56:34.062: BGP: 10.1.100.6 went from Established to Closing
*Jan 18 19:56:34.062: BGP: ses global 10.1.100.6 (0xE8687A8:1) Send NOTIFICATION 6/4
(Administrative Reset) 0 bytes
*Jan 18 19:56:34.063: %BGP-3-NOTIFICATION_MANY: sent to 1 sessions 6/4
(Administrative Reset) for all peers
*Jan 18 19:56:34.063: BGP: system reset due to User reset
*Jan 18 19:56:34.079: BGP: 10.1.100.6 went from Closing to Idle
*Jan 18 19:56:34.080: %BGP-5-ADJCHANGE: neighbor 10.1.100.6 Down User reset
*Jan 18 19:56:34.080: %BGP_SESSION-5-ADJCHANGE: neighbor 10.1.100.6 IPv4 Unicast
topology base removed from session User reset
*Jan 18 19:56:44.273: BGP: 10.1.100.6 active went from Idle to Active
*Jan 18 19:56:44.273: BGP: 10.1.100.6 open active, local address 10.1.100.2
*Jan 18 19:56:44.282: BGP: ses global 10.1.100.6 (0xE8687A8:0) act Adding topology
IPv4 Unicast:base
*Jan 18 19:56:44.282: BGP: ses global 10.1.100.6 (0xE8687A8:0) act Send OPEN
*Jan 18 19:56:44.283: BGP: ses global 10.1.100.6 (0xE8687A8:0) act Building Enhanced
Refresh capability
*Jan 18 19:56:44.283: BGP: 10.1.100.6 active went from Active to OpenSent
*Jan 18 19:56:44.283: BGP: 10.1.100.6 active sending OPEN, version 4, my as: 65000,
holdtime 180 seconds, ID AC101702
```

```
*Jan 18 19:56:44.295: BGP: 10.1.100.6 active rcv message type 1, length
(excl. header) 38
*Jan 18 19:56:44.295: BGP: ses global 10.1.100.6 (0xE8687A8:0) act Receive OPEN
*Jan 18 19:56:44.296: BGP: 10.1.100.6 active rcv OPEN, version 4, holdtime 180
seconds
*Jan 18 19:56:44.296: BGP: 10.1.100.6 active rcv OPEN w/ OPTION parameter len: 28
*Jan 18 19:56:44.296: BGP: 10.1.100.6 active rcvd OPEN w/ optional parameter type 2
(Capability) len 6
*Jan 18 19:56:44.297: BGP: 10.1.100.6 active OPEN has CAPABILITY code: 1, length 4
*Jan 18 19:56:44.297: BGP: 10.1.100.6 active OPEN has MP_EXT CAP for afi/safi: 1/1
*Jan 18 19:56:44.297: BGP: 10.1.100.6 active rcvd OPEN w/ optional parameter type 2
(Capability) len 2
*Jan 18 19:56:44.297: BGP: 10.1.100.6 active OPEN has CAPABILITY code: 128, length 0
*Jan 18 19:56:44.298: BGP: 10.1.100.6 active OPEN has ROUTE-REFRESH capability(old)
for all address-families
*Jan 18 19:56:44.298: BGP: 10.1.100.6 active rcvd OPEN w/ optional parameter type 2
(Capability) len 2
*Jan 18 19:56:44.298: BGP: 10.1.100.6 active OPEN has CAPABILITY code: 2, length 0
*Jan 18 19:56:44.298: BGP: 10.1.100.6 active OPEN has ROUTE-REFRESH capability(new)
for all address-families
*Jan 18 19:56:44.299: BGP: 10.1.100.6 active rcvd OPEN w/ optional parameter type 2
(Capability) len 2
*Jan 18 19:56:44.299: BGP: 10.1.100.6 active OPEN has CAPABILITY code: 70, length 0
*Jan 18 19:56:44.299: BGP: ses global 10.1.100.6 (0xE8687A8:0) act Enhanced Refresh
cap received in open message
*Jan 18 19:56:44.299: BGP: 10.1.100.6 active rcvd OPEN w/ optional parameter type 2
(Capability) len 6
*Jan 18 19:56:44.300: BGP: 10.1.100.6 active OPEN has CAPABILITY code: 65, length 4
*Jan 18 19:56:44.300: BGP: 10.1.100.6 active OPEN has 4-byte ASN CAP for: 65002
*Jan 18 19:56:44.300: BGP: 10.1.100.6 active rcvd OPEN w/ remote AS 65002, 4-byte
remote AS 65002
*Jan 18 19:56:44.300: BGP: 10.1.100.6 active went from OpenSent to OpenConfirm
*Jan 18 19:56:44.303: BGP: ses global 10.1.100.6 (0xE8687A8:0) act read request no-op
*Jan 18 19:56:44.304: BGP: 10.1.100.6 active went from OpenConfirm to Established
*Jan 18 19:56:44.305: BGP: ses global 10.1.100.6 (0xE8687A8:1) act Assigned ID
*Jan 18 19:56:44.305: BGP: ses global 10.1.100.6 (0xE8687A8:1) Up
*Jan 18 19:56:44.307: %BGP-5-ADJCHANGE: neighbor 10.1.100.6 Up
PE2# show ip bgp neighbors | include TTL
Connection is ECN Disabled, Mininum incoming TTL 252, Outgoing TTL 255
```

So, basically, the minimum we expect is 252. We know the TTL will come in at 254, so
the connection works. Hmm, makes sense. But wait…why did this *not* work under the **ttl-
security 1** command? Think about this. At PE6, TTL = 255; at P4, TTL = 254. We were
accepting a value of 254 at PE2 at that time. We know that 255 minus 1 hop count at
P4 = 254, a minimum TTL of 254. Why did PE3 sit "Idle" in Example 16-20? Well, this
illustrates the difficulty of this technology and the Cisco SP CCNP exam in general. Cisco
routers decrement the TTL on the ingress interface. Then, to get it to the control plane,
it is decremented one more time, making TTL 253 acceptable for the BGP connection.
In the case of our topology, the minimum acceptable value is 253. Will you see this on

the exam? Most likely not, but unless you have configured some of these examples before, the exam questions will puzzle you; that is the harsh reality. I've shown you how this works to encourage you to read the book for the theory and to practice these setups on your own. Do you want to be good at your job *and* pass the exam? It's going to take this depth of knowledge to work quickly through the exam questions.

Are you ready to be done with TTL security? Well, I'll leave you with this: If you try to set up TTL security between IOS XE and IOS XR, you will find that the implementations differ, and the results may surprise you. As you have seen, in IOS XE, the hops value indicates how many hops the BGP neighbor can be away. In IOS XR, the only acceptable value is TTL 255. If you would like to see the minimum necessary configuration for TTL security on IOS XR, see Example 16-23 (P5 and PE7 are directly connected).

Example 16-23 *BGP TTL Security*

```
RP/0/RP0/CPU0:P5# show running-config router bgp
Fri Jan 19 02:01:07.489 UTC
router bgp 65005
 bgp router-id 10.1.100.5
 address-family ipv4 unicast
 !
 neighbor 10.1.57.7
 remote-as 65007
 ttl-security
 address-family ipv4 unicast
 route-policy PASS-ALL in
 route-policy PASS-ALL out
 !
 !
!
RP/0/RP0/CPU0:P5#

RP/0/RP0/CPU0:PE7# show running-config router bgp
Fri Jan 19 02:01:53.753 UTC
router bgp 65007
 bgp router-id 10.1.100.7
 address-family ipv4 unicast
 !
 neighbor 10.1.57.5
 remote-as 65005
 ttl-security
 address-family ipv4 unicast
 route-policy PASS-ALL in
 route-policy PASS-ALL out
 !
 !
 !
```

```
RP/0/RP0/CPU0:PE7# show bgp summary
Fri Jan 19 02:03:02.345 UTC
BGP router identifier 10.1.100.7, local AS number 65007
BGP generic scan interval 60 secs
Non-stop routing is enabled
BGP table state: Active
Table ID: 0xe0000000 RD version: 4
BGP main routing table version 4
BGP NSR Initial initsync version 3 (Reached)
BGP NSR/ISSU Sync-Group versions 0/0
BGP scan interval 60 secs


BGP is operating in STANDALONE mode.


Process    RcvTblVer bRIB/RIB LabelVer ImportVer SendTblVer StandbyVer
Speaker       4        4         4        4          4          0


Neighbor   Spk AS MsgRcvd MsgSent TblVer InQ OutQ Up/Down St/PfxRcd
10.1.57.5    0 65005   18      17     4   0   0 00:10:41      0


RP/0/RP0/CPU0:PE7# show bgp neighbor
Fri Jan 19 02:03:43.741 UTC


BGP neighbor is 10.1.57.5
  Remote AS 65005, local AS 65007, external link
  Remote router ID 10.1.100.5
  BGP state = Established, up for 00:11:22
  NSR State: None
  Last read 00:00:17, Last read before reset 00:11:52
  Hold time is 180, keepalive interval is 60 seconds
  Configured hold time: 180, keepalive: 60, min acceptable hold time: 3
  Last write 00:00:17, attempted 19, written 19
  Second last write 00:01:17, attempted 19, written 19
  Last write before reset 00:12:49, attempted 19, written 19
  Second last write before reset 00:13:49, attempted 23, written 23
  Last write pulse rcvd Jan 19 02:03:26.245 last full not set pulse count 35
  Last write pulse rcvd before reset 00:12:49
  Socket not armed for io, armed for read, armed for write
  Last write thread event before reset 00:12:49, second last 00:12:49
  Last KA expiry before reset 00:12:49, second last 00:00:00
  Last KA error before reset 00:00:00, KA not sent 00:00:00
  Last KA start before reset 00:12:49, second last 00:13:49
  Precedence: internet
  Non-stop routing is enabled
```

```
Enforcing first AS is enabled
Multi-protocol capability received
Neighbor capabilities:
Route refresh: advertised (old + new) and received (old + new)
4-byte AS: advertised and received
Address family IPv4 Unicast: advertised and received
Received 19 messages, 1 notifications, 0 in queue
Sent 18 messages, 0 notifications, 0 in queue
Minimum time between advertisement runs is 30 secs
Inbound message logging enabled, 3 messages buffered
Outbound message logging enabled, 3 messages buffered

For Address Family: IPv4 Unicast
BGP neighbor version 4
Update group: 0.2 Filter-group: 0.2 No Refresh request being processed
Extended Nexthop Encoding: advertised and received
Route refresh request: received 0, sent 0
Policy for incoming advertisements is PASS-ALL
Policy for outgoing advertisements is PASS-ALL
0 accepted prefixes, 0 are bestpaths
Exact no. of prefixes denied : 0.
Cumulative no. of prefixes denied: 0.
Prefix advertised 0, suppressed 0, withdrawn 0
An EoR was not received during read-only mode
Last ack version 4, Last synced ack version 0
Outstanding version objects: current 0, max 0, refresh 0
Additional-paths operation: None
Advertise routes with local-label via Unicast SAFI

Connections established 2; dropped 1
Local host: 10.1.57.7, Local port: 179, IF Handle: 0x01000018
Foreign host: 10.1.57.5, Foreign port: 55799
Last reset 00:11:52, due to BGP Notification received: administrative reset
Time since last notification received from neighbor: 00:11:52
Error Code: administrative reset
Notification data received:
None
TTL security is configured
RP/0/RP0/CPU0:PE7#
```

The neighbor is up, and TTL security is configured.

In summary, we must configure TTL security on each router involved. Remember that it protects EBGP peering session only in the incoming direction and has no impact on outgoing IP packets. Implementing BGP TTL security checks is one of the lightweight measures taken to enhance the overall security and robustness of the BGP protocol, which is crucial for the proper functioning of the global Internet routing system.

BGP Route Filtering

There are several reasons and ways that operators can limit the number and which prefixes make it to the BGP process. Route filtering can control which routes are accepted, advertised, or rejected, thereby preventing the propagation of malicious or incorrect routing information that could lead to network attacks or disruptions. BGP filtering and manipulation techniques include route policies, route maps, prefix lists, and AS_PATH access lists. No diagram is necessary here because we're going to use directly connected PE6 and PE7 in different autonomous systems (ASes). You must learn to visualize topologies without looking at pictures. For that reason, Example 16-24 shows route advertisements between BGP speakers.

Example 16-24 *Base BGP Configuration*

```
PE6# show running-config | section bgp
router bgp 65006
 bgp router-id 10.1.100.6
 bgp log-neighbor-changes
 no bgp default ipv4-unicast
 neighbor 10.1.67.7 remote-as 65007
 !
 address-family ipv4
 network 172.16.61.0 mask 255.255.255.0
 network 172.16.62.0 mask 255.255.255.0
 network 172.16.63.0 mask 255.255.255.0
 neighbor 10.1.67.7 activate
 neighbor 10.1.67.7 soft-reconfiguration inbound
 exit-address-family
PE6# show ip bgp neighbors 10.1.67.7 advertised-routes
BGP table version is 7, local router ID is 172.16.63.6
Status codes: s suppressed, d damped, h history, * valid, > best, i - internal,
    r RIB-failure, S Stale, m multipath, b backup-path, f RT-Filter,
    x best-external, a additional-path, c RIB-compressed,
    t secondary path,
Origin codes: i - IGP, e - EGP, ? - incomplete
RPKI validation codes: V valid, I invalid, N Not found

   Network    Next Hop   Metric LocPrf Weight Path
*> 172.16.61.0/24 0.0.0.0      0       32768 i
*> 172.16.62.0/24 0.0.0.0      0       32768 i
*> 172.16.63.0/24 0.0.0.0      0       32768 i


Total number of prefixes 3
PE6# show ip bgp neighbors 10.1.67.7 received-routes
BGP table version is 7, local router ID is 172.16.63.6
Status codes: s suppressed, d damped, h history, * valid, > best, i - internal,
    r RIB-failure, S Stale, m multipath, b backup-path, f RT-Filter,
    x best-external, a additional-path, c RIB-compressed,
    t secondary path,
```

```
   Origin codes: i - IGP, e - EGP, ? - incomplete
   RPKI validation codes: V valid, I invalid, N Not found

   Network    Next Hop    Metric LocPrf Weight Path
 *> 172.16.71.0/24 10.1.67.7      0       0 65007 i
 *> 172.16.72.0/24 10.1.67.7      0       0 65007 i
 *> 172.16.73.0/24 10.1.67.7      0       0 65007 i


Total number of prefixes 3
PE6#
```

```
RP/0/RP0/CPU0:PE7# show running-config router bgp
Sat Jan 20 18:04:41.951 UTC
router bgp 65007
 bgp router-id 10.1.100.7
 address-family ipv4 unicast
 network 172.16.71.0/24
 network 172.16.72.0/24
 network 172.16.73.0/24
 !
 neighbor 10.1.67.6
 remote-as 65006
 address-family ipv4 unicast
 route-policy PASS-ALL in
 route-policy PASS-ALL out
 soft-reconfiguration inbound always
 !
 !
 !
RP/0/RP0/CPU0:PE7# show ip bgp nei 10.1.67.6 advertised-routes
Sat Jan 20 18:04:55.615 UTC
Network    Next Hop    From   AS Path
172.16.71.0/24  10.1.67.7  Local   65007i
172.16.72.0/24  10.1.67.7  Local   65007i
172.16.73.0/24  10.1.67.7  Local   65007i

Processed 3 prefixes, 3 paths
RP/0/RP0/CPU0:PE7# show ip bgp nei 10.1.67.6 received-routes
Sat Jan 20 18:04:58.207 UTC
BGP router identifier 10.1.100.7, local AS number 65007
BGP generic scan interval 60 secs
Non-stop routing is enabled
BGP table state: Active
Table ID: 0xe0000000 RD version: 38
BGP main routing table version 38
BGP NSR Initial initsync version 5 (Reached)
```

```
BGP NSR/ISSU Sync-Group versions 0/0
BGP scan interval 60 secs

Status codes: s suppressed, d damped, h history, * valid, > best
    i - internal, r RIB-failure, S stale, N Nexthop-discard
Origin codes: i - IGP, e - EGP, ? - incomplete
 Network    Next Hop   Metric LocPrf Weight Path
*> 172.16.61.0/24  10.1.67.6     0       0 65006 i
*> 172.16.62.0/24  10.1.67.6     0       0 65006 i
*> 172.16.63.0/24  10.1.67.6     0       0 65006 i

Processed 3 prefixes, 3 paths
RP/0/RP0/CPU0:PE7#
```

What can you tell from a quick scan? (I'm using the highlighting method to help you learn
how to absorb router configurations fast, yet accurately.) PE6 and PE7 are EBGP peers
exchanging three routes each. Let's restrict this on the IOS XE, where BGP implementation
of prefix filtering is done with distribute lists to maintain consistency with other IGPs, as
demonstrated in Example 16-25.

Example 16-25   *BGP Filtering with a Distribute List with IOS XE*

```
PE6# configure terminal
Enter configuration commands, one per line. End with CNTL/Z.
PE6(config-ext-nacl)# router bgp 65006
PE6(config-router)# address-family ipv4 unicast
PE6(config-router-af)# neighbor 10.1.67.7 distribute-list LIMIT-BGP ?
 in Filter incoming updates
 out Filter outgoing updates

PE6(config-router-af)# neighbor 10.1.67.7 distribute-list LIMIT-BGP in
PE6(config-router-af)# exit
PE6(config)# ip access-list extended LIMIT-BGP
PE6(config-ext-nacl)# permit ip 172.16.71.0 0.0.0.255 host 255.255.255.0
PE6(config-ext-nacl)# permit ip 172.16.72.0 0.0.0.255 host 255.255.255.0
PE6(config-ext-nacl)# end
PE6# clear ip bgp *
PE6# show running-config | section bgp
router bgp 65006
 bgp router-id 10.1.100.6
 bgp log-neighbor-changes
 no bgp default ipv4-unicast
 neighbor 10.1.67.7 remote-as 65007
 !
 address-family ipv4
 network 172.16.61.0 mask 255.255.255.0
 network 172.16.62.0 mask 255.255.255.0
```

```
  network 172.16.63.0 mask 255.255.255.0
  neighbor 10.1.67.7 activate
  neighbor 10.1.67.7 soft-reconfiguration inbound
  neighbor 10.1.67.7 distribute-list LIMIT-BGP in
 exit-address-family
PE6#sh access-lists
Extended IP access list LIMIT-BGP
  10 permit ip 172.16.71.0 0.0.0.255 host 255.255.255.0 (2 matches)
  20 permit ip 172.16.72.0 0.0.0.255 host 255.255.255.0 (1 match)
PE6# show bgp summary
BGP router identifier 10.1.100.6, local AS number 65006
BGP table version is 1, main routing table version 1
3 network entries using 432 bytes of memory
3 path entries using 252 bytes of memory
2/0 BGP path/bestpath attribute entries using 320 bytes of memory
1 BGP AS-PATH entries using 24 bytes of memory
0 BGP route-map cache entries using 0 bytes of memory
0 BGP filter-list cache entries using 0 bytes of memory
BGP using 1028 total bytes of memory
1 received paths for inbound soft reconfiguration
BGP activity 36/33 prefixes, 45/42 paths, scan interval 60 secs

Neighbor   V   AS MsgRcvd MsgSent TblVer InQ OutQ Up/Down State/PfxRcd
10.1.67.7  4   65007  4  2  1 0 0 00:00:05  2
PE6# show ip bgp neighbors 10.1.67.7 received-routes
BGP table version is 1, local router ID is 10.1.100.6
Status codes: s suppressed, d damped, h history, * valid, > best, i - internal,
    r RIB-failure, S Stale, m multipath, b backup-path, f RT-Filter,
    x best-external, a additional-path, c RIB-compressed,
    t secondary path,
Origin codes: i - IGP, e - EGP, ? - incomplete
RPKI validation codes: V valid, I invalid, N Not found

  Network      Next Hop   Metric LocPrf Weight Path
* 172.16.71.0/24 10.1.67.7   0       0 65007 i
* 172.16.72.0/24 10.1.67.7   0       0 65007 i
* 172.16.73.0/24 10.1.67.7   0       0 65007 i

Total number of prefixes 3
PE6# show bgp ipv4 unicast
BGP table version is 1, local router ID is 10.1.100.6
Status codes: s suppressed, d damped, h history, * valid, > best, i - internal,
    r RIB-failure, S Stale, m multipath, b backup-path, f RT-Filter,
    x best-external, a additional-path, c RIB-compressed,
    t secondary path,
```

```
Origin codes: i - IGP, e - EGP, ? - incomplete
RPKI validation codes: V valid, I invalid, N Not found


  Network    Next Hop    Metric LocPrf Weight Path
* 172.16.71.0/24 10.1.67.7      0        0 65007 i
* 172.16.72.0/24 10.1.67.7      0        0 65007 i

PE6#
```

Were you able to follow what we did? (Try again if you're not following; you will get faster at this.) We applied a distribute list on PE6 in the inbound direction for 172.16.71.0 and 172.16.72.0 networks with a /24 prefix length coming in via BGP. Even though the Adj-RIB-In contains all routes coming from PE7, the Loc-RIB no longer contains the 172.16.73.0/24 prefix. If you did not understand the preceding sentence, please revisit Chapter 7, "BGP Fundamentals." In addition to the distribute list, you should master using route maps as well. Now, let's replicate the same configuration with the route-map approach, as demonstrated in Example 16-26.

Example 16-26   *BGP Filtering with Route Maps in IOS XE*

```
PE6# configure terminal
Enter configuration commands, one per line. End with CNTL/Z.
PE6(config)# router bgp 65006
PE6(config-router)# address-family ipv4 unicast
PE6(config-router-af)# no neighbor 10.1.67.7 distribute-list LIMIT-BGP in
PE6(config-router-af)# neighbor 10.1.67.7 route-map LIMIT-BGP in
PE6(config-router-af)# exit
PE6(config-router)# exit
PE6(config)# ip prefix-list PREFIX-71 seq 5 permit 172.16.71.0/24
PE6(config)# ip prefix-list PREFIX-72 seq 10 permit 172.16.72.0/24
PE6(config)# route-map LIMIT-BGP permit 5
PE6(config-route-map)# match ip address prefix-list PREFIX-71
PE6(config-route-map)# route-map LIMIT-BGP permit 10
PE6(config-route-map)# match ip address prefix-list PREFIX-72
PE6(config-route-map)# route-map LIMIT-BGP deny 15
PE6(config-route-map)# end
PE6# show running-config | section bgp
router bgp 65006
 bgp router-id 10.1.100.6
 bgp log-neighbor-changes
 no bgp default ipv4-unicast
 neighbor 10.1.67.7 remote-as 65007
 !
 address-family ipv4
 network 172.16.61.0 mask 255.255.255.0
 network 172.16.62.0 mask 255.255.255.0
 network 172.16.63.0 mask 255.255.255.0
 neighbor 10.1.67.7 activate
```

```
  neighbor 10.1.67.7 soft-reconfiguration inbound
  neighbor 10.1.67.7 route-map LIMIT-BGP in
 exit-address-family
PE6# show ip prefix-list
ip prefix-list PE2_PE7_LOOPBACKS: 2 entries
  seq 5 permit 10.1.100.2/32
  seq 10 permit 10.1.100.7/32
ip prefix-list PREFIX-71: 1 entries
  seq 5 permit 172.16.71.0/24
ip prefix-list PREFIX-72: 1 entries
  seq 10 permit 172.16.72.0/24
PE6# show route-map
route-map LIMIT-BGP, permit, sequence 5
 Match clauses:
  ip address prefix-lists: PREFIX-71
 Set clauses:
 Policy routing matches: 0 packets, 0 bytes
route-map LIMIT-BGP, permit, sequence 10
 Match clauses:
  ip address prefix-lists: PREFIX-72
 Set clauses:
 Policy routing matches: 0 packets, 0 bytes
route-map LIMIT-BGP, deny, sequence 15
 Match clauses:
 Set clauses:
 Policy routing matches: 0 packets, 0 bytes
PE6# clear ip bgp *
PE6# show bgp summary
BGP router identifier 10.1.100.6, local AS number 65006
BGP table version is 1, main routing table version 1
3 network entries using 432 bytes of memory
3 path entries using 252 bytes of memory
2/0 BGP path/bestpath attribute entries using 320 bytes of memory
1 BGP AS-PATH entries using 24 bytes of memory
0 BGP route-map cache entries using 0 bytes of memory
0 BGP filter-list cache entries using 0 bytes of memory
BGP using 1028 total bytes of memory
1 received paths for inbound soft reconfiguration
BGP activity 60/57 prefixes, 69/66 paths, scan interval 60 secs

Neighbor  V   AS MsgRcvd MsgSent TblVer InQ OutQ Up/Down State/PfxRcd
10.1.67.7  4  65007  4  2  1 0 0 00:00:06  2
PE6# show ip bgp ipv4 unicast
BGP table version is 1, local router ID is 10.1.100.6
```

```
Status codes: s suppressed, d damped, h history, * valid, > best, i - internal,
    r RIB-failure, S Stale, m multipath, b backup-path, f RT-Filter,
    x best-external, a additional-path, c RIB-compressed,
    t secondary path,
Origin codes: i - IGP, e - EGP, ? - incomplete
RPKI validation codes: V valid, I invalid, N Not found

   Network     Next Hop    Metric LocPrf Weight Path
 * 172.16.71.0/24 10.1.67.7      0         0 65007 i
 * 172.16.72.0/24 10.1.67.7      0         0 65007 i
PE6#
```

Practice these techniques; you will need them. Also, before we move to IOS XR, recall that in IOS XE, this is the order in which BGP processes route filtering techniques:

- Inbound direction:
  - Route map
  - Filter list
  - Prefix or distribute list
- Outbound direction:
  - Prefix or distribute list
  - Filter list
  - Route map

Fine. XR time? IOS XR has a far simpler approach by using route policies only to filter prefixes to and from BGP peers. Let's suppress PE7's outbound advertisement for 172.16.72.0/24, which PE6 still has in its Loc-RIB. Remember the PASS-ALL route policies we need to use? We can modify what we advertise to PE6, as demonstrated in Example 16-27.

Example 16-27 *Route Policy Language for BGP Filtering in IOS XR*

```
RP/0/RP0/CPU0:PE7# show run router bgp
Sat Jan 20 19:57:51.870 UTC
router bgp 65007
 bgp router-id 10.1.100.7
 address-family ipv4 unicast
 network 172.16.71.0/24
 network 172.16.72.0/24
 network 172.16.73.0/24
 !
 neighbor 10.1.67.6
 remote-as 65006
 address-family ipv4 unicast
 route-policy PASS-ALL in
```

```
  route-policy PASS-ALL out
  soft-reconfiguration inbound always
  !
  !
```

```
RP/0/RP0/CPU0:PE7# configure
Sat Jan 20 19:59:38.794 UTC
RP/0/RP0/CPU0:PE7(config)# router bgp 65007
RP/0/RP0/CPU0:PE7(config-bgp)# neighbor 10.1.67.6
RP/0/RP0/CPU0:PE7(config-bgp-nbr)# address-family ipv4 unicast
RP/0/RP0/CPU0:PE7(config-bgp-nbr-af)# no route-policy PASS-ALL out
RP/0/RP0/CPU0:PE7(config-bgp-nbr-af)# route-policy PASS-71-ONLY out
RP/0/RP0/CPU0:PE7(config-bgp-nbr-af)# exit

RP/0/RP0/CPU0:PE7(config-bgp)# exit
RP/0/RP0/CPU0:PE7(config)# route-policy PASS-71-ONLY
RP/0/RP0/CPU0:PE7(config-rpl)# if destination in (172.16.71.0/24) then pass endif
RP/0/RP0/CPU0:PE7(config-rpl)# exit
RP/0/RP0/CPU0:PE7(config)# show
Sat Jan 20 20:02:05.973 UTC
Building configuration...
!! IOS XR Configuration 7.7.1
!
route-policy PASS-71-ONLY
  if destination in (172.16.71.0/24) then
  pass
  endif
end-policy
!
end
!
router bgp 65007
 neighbor 10.1.67.6
 address-family ipv4 unicast
 no route-policy PASS-ALL out
 route-policy PASS-71-ONLY out
 !
 !
!
end
RP/0/RP0/CPU0:PE7(config)# commit
Sat Jan 20 20:03:35.830 UTC
RP/0/RP0/CPU0:PE7(config)# end
RP/0/RP0/CPU0:PE7# clear ip bgp *
Sat Jan 20 20:03:45.844 UTC
```

```
RP/0/RP0/CPU0:PE7# show bgp neighbor 10.1.67.6 advertised-routes
Sat Jan 20 20:04:13.509 UTC
Network     Next Hop   From    AS Path
172.16.71.0/24   10.1.67.7   Local    65007i


Processed 1 prefixes, 1 paths
RP/0/RP0/CPU0:PE7#
```

```
PE6# show ip bgp nei 10.1.67.7 received-routes
BGP table version is 9, local router ID is 10.1.100.6
Status codes: s suppressed, d damped, h history, * valid, > best, i - internal,
     r RIB-failure, S Stale, m multipath, b backup-path, f RT-Filter,
     x best-external, a additional-path, c RIB-compressed,
     t secondary path,
Origin codes: i - IGP, e - EGP, ? - incomplete
RPKI validation codes: V valid, I invalid, N Not found

  Network     Next Hop   Metric LocPrf Weight Path
*> 172.16.71.0/24 10.1.67.7    0    0 65007 i


Total number of prefixes 1
PE6#
```

Did you follow this? You should be able to do so to be quick on the exam. Here, we removed
the outbound PASS-ALL policy from PE6 and replaced it with a route policy that only
advertises the 172.16.71.0/24 network. We verified that it is the only prefix PE7 sends to
PE6 and confirmed the same on PE6 by no longer seeing the 172.16.72.0/24 prefix we were
accepting with PE6's route map.

A few things to think about for sure. Bottom line? There are many permutations of how BGP
routes can be filtered in different IOS flavors, but the concept itself is simple. Be sure to practice these in both directions so you can breeze through such questions and configuration tasks
on the exam.

BGP Maximum-prefix

So now you are getting fast at limiting BGP route updates. Good. Another denial-of-service
technique would be to send an extraordinarily large number of routes to overwhelm the BGP
process and resources on a router. This can be guarded against by specifying the number of
prefixes the router will accept from a neighbor. Before we leave this topology, let's quickly
enable and verify this, as demonstrated in Example 16-28.

Example 16-28 *BGP Maximum Prefixes Accepted from a BGP Neighbor*

```
PE6# configure terminal
Enter configuration commands, one per line. End with CNTL/Z.
PE6(config)# router bgp 65006
PE6(config-router)# address-family ipv4
PE6(config-router-af)# neighbor 10.1.67.7 maximum-prefix ?
 <1-2147483647> maximum no. of prefix limit
```

```
PE6(config-router-af)# neighbor 10.1.67.7 maximum-prefix 1000
PE6(config-router-af)# end
PE6# show bgp nei | i Maximum
 Maximum prefixes allowed 1000
Maximum output segment queue size: 50
PE6#
```

```
RP/0/RP0/CPU0:PE7# configure
Sun Jan 21 13:39:05.123 UTC
RP/0/RP0/CPU0:PE7(config)# router bgp 65007
RP/0/RP0/CPU0:PE7(config-bgp)# neighbor 10.1.67.6
RP/0/RP0/CPU0:PE7(config-bgp-nbr)# address-family ipv4 unicast
RP/0/RP0/CPU0:PE7(config-bgp-nbr-af)# maximum-prefix ?
 <1-4294967295> maximum no. of prefix limit
RP/0/RP0/CPU0:PE7(config-bgp-nbr-af)# maximum-prefix 1000
RP/0/RP0/CPU0:PE7(config-bgp-nbr-af)# commit
Sun Jan 21 13:41:00.192 UTC
RP/0/RP0/CPU0:PE7(config-bgp-nbr-af)# end
RP/0/RP0/CPU0:PE7# show ip bgp neighbors | include Maximum
Sun Jan 21 13:41:34.028 UTC
 Maximum prefixes allowed 1000
RP/0/RP0/CPU0:PE7#
```

BGP Prefix Suppression

BGP prefix suppression does not advertise (suppresses) routes that are in an RIB-failure state. By default, in Cisco IOS, these routes are advertised. Since we have our PE6-PE7 setup handy, let's look at this feature. In Example 16-29, the PE7 route is advertised in BGP, and PE6 uses its routing table as well.

Example 16-29 *Introducing RIB Failure in BGP*

```
PE6# show ip bgp
BGP table version is 5, local router ID is 10.1.100.6
Status codes: s suppressed, d damped, h history, * valid, > best, i - internal,
              r RIB-failure, S Stale, m multipath, b backup-path, f RT-Filter,
              x best-external, a additional-path, c RIB-compressed,
              t secondary path,
Origin codes: i - IGP, e - EGP, ? - incomplete
RPKI validation codes: V valid, I invalid, N Not found


   Network     Next Hop    Metric LocPrf Weight Path
 *> 172.16.61.0/24 0.0.0.0       0       32768 i
 *> 172.16.62.0/24 0.0.0.0       0       32768 i
 *> 172.16.63.0/24 0.0.0.0       0       32768 i
 *> 172.16.71.0/24 10.1.67.7     0        0 65007 i
```

```
PE6# show ip route bgp
Codes: L - local, C - connected, S - static, R - RIP, M - mobile, B - BGP
   D - EIGRP, EX - EIGRP external, O - OSPF, IA - OSPF inter area
   N1 - OSPF NSSA external type 1, N2 - OSPF NSSA external type 2
   E1 - OSPF external type 1, E2 - OSPF external type 2
   i - IS-IS, su - IS-IS summary, L1 - IS-IS level-1, L2 - IS-IS level-2
   ia - IS-IS inter area, * - candidate default, U - per-user static route
   o - ODR, P - periodic downloaded static route, H - NHRP, l - LISP
   a - application route
   + - replicated route, % - next hop override, p - overrides from PfR


Gateway of last resort is not set


      172.16.0.0/16 is variably subnetted, 7 subnets, 2 masks
B     172.16.71.0/24 [20/0] via 10.1.67.7, 00:59:17
PE6#
```

Everything is working the way it's supposed to. But now, let's break this. How would you
introduce an RIB-failure scenario? Well, there are several ways I can think of, but let's create
a route with a lower administrative distance (AD) than 20, which is EBGP's AD, as shown in
Example 16-29. We'll point this route to some ridiculous next hop (PE2, but it doesn't
matter), as demonstrated in Example 16-30.

Example 16-30 *Introducing RIB Failure in BGP, Continued*

```
PE6# configure terminal
Enter configuration commands, one per line. End with CNTL/Z.
PE6(config)# ip route 172.16.71.0 255.255.255.0 10.1.100.2
PE6(config)# end
PE6# show ip route static
Codes: L - local, C - connected, S - static, R - RIP, M - mobile, B - BGP
   D - EIGRP, EX - EIGRP external, O - OSPF, IA - OSPF inter area
   N1 - OSPF NSSA external type 1, N2 - OSPF NSSA external type 2
   E1 - OSPF external type 1, E2 - OSPF external type 2
   i - IS-IS, su - IS-IS summary, L1 - IS-IS level-1, L2 - IS-IS level-2
   ia - IS-IS inter area, * - candidate default, U - per-user static route
   o - ODR, P - periodic downloaded static route, H - NHRP, l - LISP
   a - application route
   + - replicated route, % - next hop override, p - overrides from PfR


Gateway of last resort is not set


      172.16.0.0/16 is variably subnetted, 7 subnets, 2 masks
S     172.16.71.0/24 [1/0] via 10.1.100.2
```

```
PE6# show ip bgp
BGP table version is 6, local router ID is 10.1.100.6
Status codes: s suppressed, d damped, h history, * valid, > best, i - internal,
    r RIB-failure, S Stale, m multipath, b backup-path, f RT-Filter,
    x best-external, a additional-path, c RIB-compressed,
    t secondary path,
Origin codes: i - IGP, e - EGP, ? - incomplete
RPKI validation codes: V valid, I invalid, N Not found


  Network    Next Hop   Metric LocPrf Weight Path
 *> 172.16.61.0/24 0.0.0.0       0    32768 i
 *> 172.16.62.0/24 0.0.0.0       0    32768 i
 *> 172.16.63.0/24 0.0.0.0       0    32768 i
 r> 172.16.71.0/24 10.1.67.7     0     0 65007 i
PE6# show ip bgp rib-failure
 Network    Next Hop       RIB-failure RIB-NH Matches
 172.16.71.0/24  10.1.67.7    Higher admin distance    No
PE6#
```

That did it. As seen in the output of **show ip bgp rib-failure**, we have a route with a next
hop of PE7, which is outranked by another route with a lower (better) AD and a nonmatching
next hop (RIB-NH). We've got ourselves a genuine problem. Why? Because (I quickly set up
another BGP peering with router P4, but it can be any other router for that matter) PE6 still
advertises this route to its neighbors. You don't believe me? Example 16-31 shows this failure
as a legitimate route.

Example 16-31   *RIB Failure Appears as a Legitimate Route on P4*

```
P4# show ip bgp
BGP table version is 5, local router ID is 10.1.100.4
Status codes: s suppressed, d damped, h history, * valid, > best, i - internal,
    r RIB-failure, S Stale, m multipath, b backup-path, f RT-Filter,
    x best-external, a additional-path, c RIB-compressed,
    t secondary path,
Origin codes: i - IGP, e - EGP, ? - incomplete
RPKI validation codes: V valid, I invalid, N Not found


  Network    Next Hop   Metric LocPrf Weight Path
 *>i 172.16.61.0/24 10.1.100.6    0 100  0 i
 *>i 172.16.62.0/24 10.1.100.6    0 100  0 i
 *>i 172.16.63.0/24 10.1.100.6    0 100  0 i
 *>i 172.16.71.0/24 10.1.67.7     0 100  0 65007 i
P4#
```

P4 doesn't know anything about a mischievous network operator tampering with the routing
table on PE6. We cannot allow this to continue, so let's fix this with the **bgp suppress-
inactive** command on PE6, as demonstrated in Example 16-32.

Example 16-32 *Suppressing Inactive Prefixes*

```
PE6(config-router)# bgp suppress-inactive
```

```
P4# show ip bgp
BGP table version is 6, local router ID is 10.1.100.4
Status codes: s suppressed, d damped, h history, * valid, > best, i - internal,
    r RIB-failure, S Stale, m multipath, b backup-path, f RT-Filter,
    x best-external, a additional-path, c RIB-compressed,
    t secondary path,
Origin codes: i - IGP, e - EGP, ? - incomplete
RPKI validation codes: V valid, I invalid, N Not found

  Network     Next Hop   Metric LocPrf Weight Path
 *>i 172.16.61.0/24 10.1.100.6    0 100   0 i
 *>i 172.16.62.0/24 10.1.100.6    0 100   0 i
 *>i 172.16.63.0/24 10.1.100.6    0 100   0 i
P4#
```

As you can see, the prefix is no longer advertised. What is important here? The routes in the RIB-Failure state and with RIB-NH Matches set to No are not advertised when **bgp suppress-inactive** is enabled. Would you like some homework? Instead of pointing this route to PE2, set Null0 as the next hop. You'll get the RIB Failure, but the RIB-NH will still get a match (it will say **Yes** or **n/a**), and the route will continue to be advertised despite the broken prefix. It's well worth your time to set this up. For the restless and exhausted who are crawling to finish the book, I include Example 16-33.

Example 16-33 *RIB-NH Not Working*

```
PE6# show ip bgp rib-failure
  Network     Next Hop      RIB-failure RIB-NH Matches
 172.16.71.0/24 10.1.67.7    Higher admin distance    n/a
```

BGPsec

Do you recall the Pakistan Telecom mistakenly announcing some YouTube IP prefixes into the global BGP routing table from earlier in the chapter? Let this be a memorable lesson about how any autonomous system can announce any prefix. BGP cannot discriminate between correct and incorrect information. It just quickly propagates both to routers around the world.

The Internet Engineering Task Force (IETF) created the **Resource Public Key Infrastructure (RPKI)** security framework to enhance the security and reliability of Internet routing. Using a system of public keys and certificates, it cryptographically signs records to associate the route with originating AS numbers. Now, networks can confirm the legitimacy of where BGP announcements originate. In the future, RPKI may hold a path toward achieving comprehensive path validation.

RPKI has a database repository that stores and makes publicly available signed records that validate that certain autonomous systems are authorized to generate certain prefixes in BGP.

Local Internet Registries (LIRs) use these public certificates to create **Route Origin Authorization (ROA)** records confirming the validity of routing resources. Network operators can download such RPKI records and make routing decisions based on this information.

An ROA record contains the following fields and looks like Table 16-2.

Table 16-2   Route Origin Authorization Record

Prefix	172.16.0.0/16
Max-Length	/20
Origin-AS	AS65002

RFC 6482 has more information on this. Consider these fields:

- An origin AS.

- A prefix.

- Max length. If the max length field is omitted, the ROA will cover only the prefix and nothing more specific. For the most part, this field should be left blank to advertise only the explicitly announced prefixes. Of course, there are exceptions, and RFC 9319 is a good reference for current best practices.

- An ROA name (optional).

How does this work on routers? Cisco's documentation refers to this as *BGP Origin Validation*. You will need an RPKI server that is managed by third-party software. It verifies public key certificates and is configured to allow specific prefixes or ranges of prefixes to originate from specific autonomous systems. If you're interested in observing something fascinating, check out the U.S. Department of Commerce division that tracks Internet prefix validation at https://rpki-monitor.antd.nist.gov/.

Then, the router is configured to establish a TCP connection with the RPKI server using the **bgp rpki server** command. When configured or booted, the router initiates a TCP connection to the specified IP address and port number and downloads a list of prefixes and authorized origin AS numbers from one or more router/RPKI servers using the RPKI-Router protocol (RTR). Typically, more than a single RPKI server is recommended, and the records from all used servers go into what is called an SOVC table. The file bgp_sovc.h mentions that it stands for Secure(d) Origin Validation Cache. I doubt this level of detail is on the exam… but good to know. RFC 6810 and RFC 6811 describe the process of downloading the Validated ROA Payloads (VRPs) from the RPKI server and using the downloaded VRPs to validate the received route.

When you do debugs and show commands, you no longer need to wonder what it does. The router will gather details regarding which autonomous systems are authorized to announce specific routes—clarifying the origin AS for each route. If you create ROAs for your own prefixes on the server, other networks can download them and validate them. Figure 16-6 helps visualize this process.

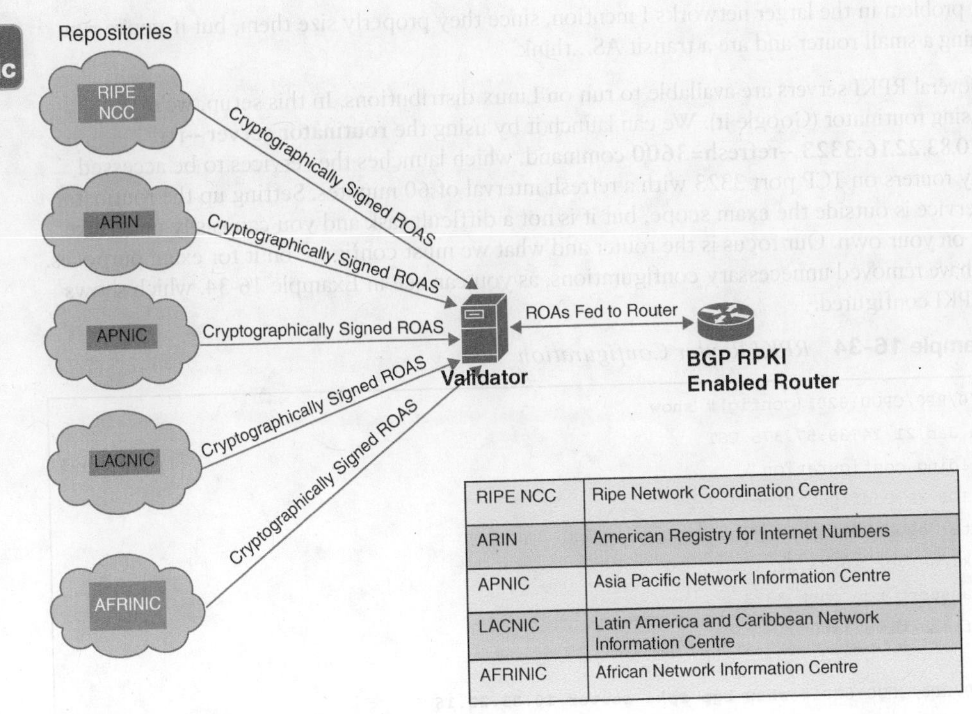

RIPE NCC	Ripe Network Coordination Centre
ARIN	American Registry for Internet Numbers
APNIC	Asia Pacific Network Information Centre
LACNIC	Latin America and Caribbean Network Information Centre
AFRINIC	African Network Information Centre

Figure 16-6 *RPKI Architecture*

Once downloaded, prefixes are classified as:

- **Valid:** Signifies that the prefix has a corresponding AS record.

- **Invalid:** Indicates that the prefix falls into either of these two conditions:

  - It has one or more Route Origin Authorizations (ROAs), but there's no matching ROA where the origin AS matches the origin AS's AS-PATH.

  - It matches one or more ROAs at the minimum length specified, but it exceeds the specified maximum length.

- **Not Found:** Cannot be found in the valid or invalid prefixes.

What do you think happens? In a nutshell, Valid prefixes will be installed into the BGP table. Invalid prefixes will not be advertised to any peers and will be withdrawn from advertising if they are already advertised. Cisco IOS drops them by default. Not Found prefixes will be installed but will not be considered until there are no Valid prefix options. You can modify this behavior, if necessary, but *think* about what you're doing here. Not Founds should not be discarded because most Internet prefixes do not have ROAs, so if you just wanted to run a "clean" Internet routing table, you've just cut off your organization from a large portion of the Internet. What about the Invalids? In the past three years, many of my customers, like Microsoft, T-Mobile, Lumen, Comcast, Orange, AWS, and many others, have started filtering out invalid prefixes. Nevertheless, *think* when using these features, because routers with weaker control planes can struggle looking up all these ROA records. This will not be a problem in the larger networks I mention, since they properly size them, but if you're running a small router and are a transit AS...think.

Several RPKI servers are available to run on Linux distributions. In this setup, we're using routinator (Google it). We can launch it by using the **routinator server --rtr 10.83.22.16:3323 --refresh=3600** command, which launches the services to be accessed by routers on TCP port 3323 with a refresh interval of 60 minutes. Setting up the routinator service is outside the exam scope, but it is not a difficult task and you can easily undertake it on your own. Our focus is the router and what we must configure on it for exam purposes. I have removed unnecessary configurations, as you can see in Example 16-34, which shows RPKI configured.

Example 16-34   *RPKI Router Configuration*

```
RP/0/RP0/CPU0:8201(config)# show
Sun Jan 21 14:39:57.375 CST
Building configuration...
!! IOS XR Configuration 7.7.2
router bgp 65001
 rpki server 10.83.22.16
  transport tcp port 3323
  refresh-time 3600


RP/0/RP0/CPU0:8201# show bgp rpki server 10.83.22.16
Sun Jan 21 14:49:09.931 CST
RPKI Cache-Server 10.83.22.16
 Transport: TCP port 3323
 Bind source: (not configured)
 Connect state: ESTAB
 Conn attempts: 1
 Total byte RX: 3516256
 Total byte TX: 2400
 Last reset
 Timest: Jan 20 09:23:14 (18:25:55 ago)
 Reason: protocol error
RP/0/RP0/CPU0:8201# show bgp rpki server summary
Sun Jan 21 14:51:45.857 CST
Hostname/Address  Transport  State   Time      ROAs (IPv4/IPv6)

10.83.22.16    TCP:3323  ESTAB   18:38:21  202334/22460
RP/0/RP0/CPU0:8201# show bgp rpki table ipv4
Sun Jan 21 14:55:33.830 CST
! Output omitted for brevity
 Network      Maxlen  Origin-AS   Server
 10.16.0.0/24    24     13335     10.83.22.16
 10.16.9.0/22    22     38803     10.83.22.16
 10.16.9.0/24    24     38803     10.83.22.16
```

```
10.16.11.0/24   24    38803   10.83.22.16
10.16.11.0/24   24    38803   10.83.22.16
10.17.4.0/24    24    38803   10.83.22.16
10.17.1.0/24    24    13335   10.83.22.16
10.17.4.0/22    22    4134    10.83.22.16
```

Now, let's look at the results in Example 16-35.

Example 16-35   *RPKI Prefix Download*

```
RP/0/RP0/CPU0:8201# show bgp origin-as validity
Sun Jan 21 16:24:20.585 CST
Building configuration...
!! IOS XR Configuration 7.7.2
! Output omitted for brevity
Status codes: s suppressed, d damped, h history, * valid, > best
    i - internal, r RIB-failure, S stale, N Nexthop-discard
Origin codes: i - IGP, e - EGP, ? - incomplete
Origin-AS validation codes: V valid, I invalid, N not-found, D disabled
  Network    Next Hop   Metric LocPrf Weight Path
D*> 23.73.96.0/19   10.80.17.1     0      0 9500 ?
D*> 27.252.0.0/17  10.80.17.1     0      0 9500 ?
D*> 10.83.22.1/32  10.80.17.1     0      0 9500 ?
```

As you can see from the output in Example 16-35, the router downloads BGP prefixes but does not use them yet—why you see them marked as Disabled. When BGP origin validation is enabled in Example 16-36, the routes are classified with familiar-to-us markings.

Example 16-36   *RPKI Prefix Marking and Usage*

```
RP/0/RP0/CPU0:8201# configure
Sun Jan 21 16:46:01.123 CST
RP/0/RP0/CPU0:8201(config)# router bgp 65001
RP/0/RP0/CPU0:8201(config-bgp)# address-family ipv4 unicast
RP/0/RP0/CPU0:8201(config-router-af)# bgp origin-as validation enable
RP/0/RP0/CPU0:8201(config-router-af)# bgp bestpath origin-as use validity
RP/0/RP0/CPU0:8201(config-router-af)# commit
RP/0/RP0/CPU0:8201(config-router-af)# end
RP/0/RP0/CPU0:8201# show bgp origin-as validity
Sun Jan 21 16:50:33.862 CST
! Output omitted for brevity
Status codes: s suppressed, d damped, h history, * valid, > best
    i - internal, r RIB-failure, S stale, N Nexthop-discard
Origin codes: i - IGP, e - EGP, ? - incomplete
Origin-AS validation codes: V valid, I invalid, N not-found, D disabled
  Network    Next Hop   Metric LocPrf Weight Path
I*> 23.73.96.0/19  10.80.17.1     0      0 9500 ?
V*> 27.252.0.0/17  10.80.17.1     0      0 9500 ?
N*> 10.83.22.1/32  10.80.17.1     0      0 9500 ?
```

The first command makes the router scan the prefixes to properly classify their status, and the following commands enable the router to use marked routes (Invalid, Valid, and Not Found) for pathing decisions. Do you remember what these classifications mean? Time to review if you've forgotten.

What could you do with these routes now? Honestly, anything you want. In Example 16-37, we will construct our logic, but feel free to use your imagination.

Example 16-37 *RPKI Route Map*

```
RP/0/RP0/CPU0:8201# configure
Sun Jan 21 17:41:57.155 CST
RP/0/RP0/CPU0:8201(config-bgp)# neighbor 10.1.100.6
RP/0/RP0/CPU0:8201(config-bgp-nbr)# address-family ipv4 unicast
RP/0/RP0/CPU0:8201(config-bgp-nbr-af)# route-policy RPKI out
RP/0/RP0/CPU0:8201(config-bgp-nbr-af)# bestpath origin-as allow invalid
RP/0/RP0/CPU0:8201(config-bgp-nbr-af)# exit
RP/0/RP0/CPU0:8201(config-bgp-nbr)# exit
RP/0/RP0/CPU0:8201(config-bgp)# exit
RP/0/RP0/CPU0:8201(config)# route-policy RPKI
RP/0/RP0/CPU0:8201(config-rpl)# if validation-state is invalid then
RP/0/RP0/CPU0:8201(config-rpl-if)# set local-preference 50
RP/0/RP0/CPU0:8201(config-rpl-if)# elseif validation-state is not-found then
RP/0/RP0/CPU0:8201(config-rpl-elseif)# set local-preference 100
RP/0/RP0/CPU0:8201(config-rpl-elseif)# elseif validation-state is valid then
RP/0/RP0/CPU0:8201(config-rpl-elseif)# set local-preference 200
RP/0/RP0/CPU0:8201(config-rpl-elseif)# else pass endif
RP/0/RP0/CPU0:8201(config-rpl)# end-policy
RP/0/RP0/CPU0:8201(config)# show
Sun Jan 21 17:50:33.027 CST
Building configuration...
!! IOS XR Configuration 7.7.2
!
route-policy RPKI
  if validation-state is invalid then
  set local-preference 50
  elseif validation-state is not-found then
  set local-preference 100
  elseif validation-state is valid then
  set local-preference 200
  else
  pass
  endif
end-policy
!
router bgp 65001
 neighbor 10.1.100.6
  address-family ipv4 unicast
```

```
   bestpath origin-as allow invalid //Necessary to allow invalids to be used for best
path
   route-policy RPKI out
   !
   !
   !
 end

RP/0/RP0/CPU0:8201(config)#
```

See if you can figure out what my intent was here. This should not be hard.

What is the short and sweet version on all this? RPKI prevents route hijacking for prefixes originated by an AS without authorization and route misorigination when prefixes are mistakenly originated by an AS that does not own them (think YouTube).

So where does **BGP Security (BGPsec)** come in? It is the next evolution of BGP security to verify that a received route advertisement follows the claimed AS-path. RFC 8205 published an extension to BGP that enables routers to generate, propagate, and validate BGP update messages with the BGPsec PATH attribute set (it contains digital signatures). The entire AS_PATH set can be validated to have gone through legitimate autonomous systems. Figure 16-7 shows what that validation looks like.

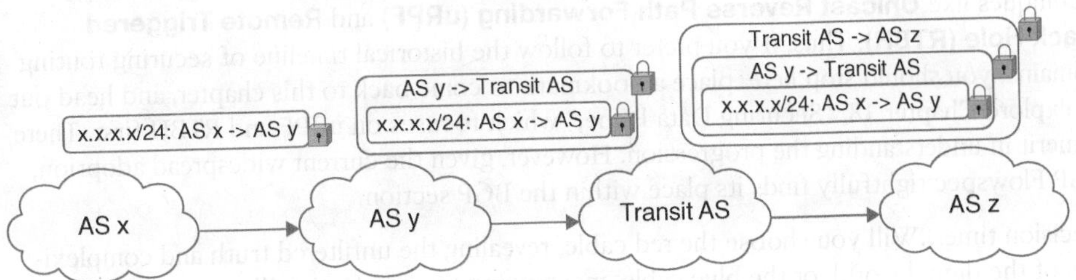

Figure 16-7 *BGP AS-PATH Validation*

Each autonomous system signs a statement: "I received this route with the specified AS-path and am transmitting it to AS such-n-such." The AS includes this statement along with its signature in the route advertisement, subsequently forwarding it to the next AS. This process establishes a certificate chain integrated into every route advertisement. The recipient of a route has the capability to authenticate that the asserted AS-PATH corresponds to the genuine AS-PATH.

Sounds good? Yes, it does. Clean Internet. Kind of like having a spotless commercial kitchen—no crumbs, no clutter, just pure digital hygiene. What is the reality, though? Well, here comes my educated opinion, but opinions do not make you pass exams. First, this would require a central authority to govern which ASNs own which prefixes. Second, everybody in the Internet's ecosystem would have to cooperate with each other at the same time. (I have a hard time getting full cooperation from my direct team peers who like me!) If you ever managed even a medium-sized network, you have seen what "real" export/import/redistribute policy implementations look like. Many are poorly implemented, some cannot be touched, some are not understood due to legacy technical debt. Now think of Internet exchanges. Do you think they all run "clean" and pristine? In the past two years with the war in Ukraine and other regions of the world, have you seen authoritarian governments shut off access? From a business perspective (which drives *everything*), are you going to tell me you will turn down profit from customers who do not want or care about this? Many more reasons exist, but I am desperately trying to keep down the page count for this book. To me, it all boils down to this: I do not know who you are. Even I did, why should I trust *you* and your ASN? Who can validate to me that you are honest and have my best interests in mind?

If you would like to see BGP attacks develop in real time, Cisco has a tool called BGP Stream to observe BGP events on the Internet. A few years ago, Cisco purchased BGPMon and rebranded it into Crosswork Cloud. This tool allows users to track and analyze BGP-related events, providing valuable insights into the security of network routing. Check out www.bgpstream.com. One last thing: do not confuse the Crosswork platform we discussed in Chapter 15, "Segment Routing," with Crosswork Cloud. Crosswork is an on-premises suite of applications to manage service provider products (routing, optical, etc). Crosswork Cloud serves your BGP needs on the Internet.

Also, if you're interested in a broader range of BGP vulnerabilities, you can check out RFC 4272, which is mentioned at the conclusion of this chapter. Flowspec time.

BGP Flowspec

At the time of writing this book, **BGP Flow Specification (BGP Flowspec)** sits at the pinnacle of BGP routing security. Initially, my inclination was to position this section toward the end of the chapter as a chronological and technical evolution beyond long-standing techniques like **Unicast Reverse Path Forwarding (uRPF)** and **Remote Triggered Black Hole (RTBH)**. Thus, if you prefer to follow the historical timeline of securing routing domains, you should stop here, place a bookmark to come back to this chapter, and head out to explore Chapter 18, "Securing Data Plane," which focuses on uRPF and RTBH first. There is merit in understanding the progression. However, given the current widespread adoption, BGP Flowspec rightfully finds its place within the BGP section.

Decision time...Will you choose the red cable, revealing the unfiltered truth and complexities of the digital world, or the blue cable, maintaining the comforting illusion of simplicity and familiarity? The decision is yours, Networking Neo. You will find the blue cable in the RTBH filtering section of Chapter 18.

Aha... You've taken the red cable—the path of revelation and insight. Buckle up, the truth awaits, and this journey will reshape your understanding of BGP's towering capabilities. Without further ado, allow me to present the advancements brought forth by this powerful construct.

BGP Flowspec is short for Border Gateway Protocol Flow Specification and is a mechanism designed to enhance the security and control of BGP routing. It allows network operators to specify rules or filters for the permitted traffic flows based on various criteria, such as source/destination IP addresses, ports, and protocols—a *vast* improvement of what you will see in later sections. By leveraging BGP Flowspec, we can dynamically distribute traffic filtering rules across the network, providing a *flexible, granular, and scalable approach* to mitigate specific security threats or traffic anomalies in real time. This makes BGP Flowspec a valuable tool for improving network security and mitigating distributed denial-of-service (DDoS) attacks.

Last year, Cisco and other vendors (everyone who is anyone in router networking) were thrown into a bucket to build a massive network, and they all ran BGP Flowspec from a non-Cisco controller. The multivendor aspect is massive. RFC 8955 (originally introduced by RFC 5575) is your friend to help you understand the specifics. We are interested in how to configure it, which is the best way to understand it. Go ahead and read the RFC, practice this in the lab, and you will do well on the exam.

If I were to speak of benefits to using BGP Flowspec in layman's terms, avoiding the technical jargon that you will have to master for the exam, I would point out the following. *Flowspec* (I will use this shortened form for the remainder of this section instead of *BGP Flowspec*) allows me to

1. Drop the traffic with a high degree of granularity (see Table 16-4 later) at the edge. A big disadvantage of uRPF and specifically RTBH (that you will learn or have learned already if you followed my earlier advice) is that, essentially, it completes the attacker's intent—making the resource unavailable. Flowspec can pluck out the exact offending flows.

2. Dump this traffic into a VRF, where I can analyze it at my own pace until I decide what I should do. This buys me time.

3. Let the offending traffic in but police it to a far lower rate.

Flowspec information is disseminated throughout the network via BGP Network Layer Reachability Information (NRLI). Note the following BGP address family indicators (AFI) and subsequent address family identifiers (SAFI) to distribute BGP Flowspec rules in Table 16-3.

Table 16-3   BGP AFI/SAFI for Flowspec Dissemination

BGP Address Families	Usage
AFI 1/SAFI 133	Disseminate IPv4 Flowspec rules
AFI 1/SAFI 134	Disseminate VPNv4 Flowspec rules
AFI 2/SAFI 133	Disseminate IPv6 Flowspec rules
AFI 2/SAFI 134	Disseminate VPNv6 Flowspec rules

Where possible and clear, I try to reuse the vendor's own documentation to illustrate their solutions. In Figure 16-8, Cisco shows the Flowspec controller on the left and the client on the right; both are routers in our case. The logic is rather simple in this client/server architecture. The controller on the left matches certain traffic, defines the rules, and creates the Flowspec NRLI entry in the conversation with the client (the BGP speaker on the right). The client receives this information, passes it to its internal Flowspec Manager, and configures the Enhanced Policy-Based Routing (E-PBR) element to program the hardware to follow the controller's instructions.

The configuration on the client is straightforward, but rather than configuring it, let's look at the "before-and-after" output in Example 16-38, which explains it better.

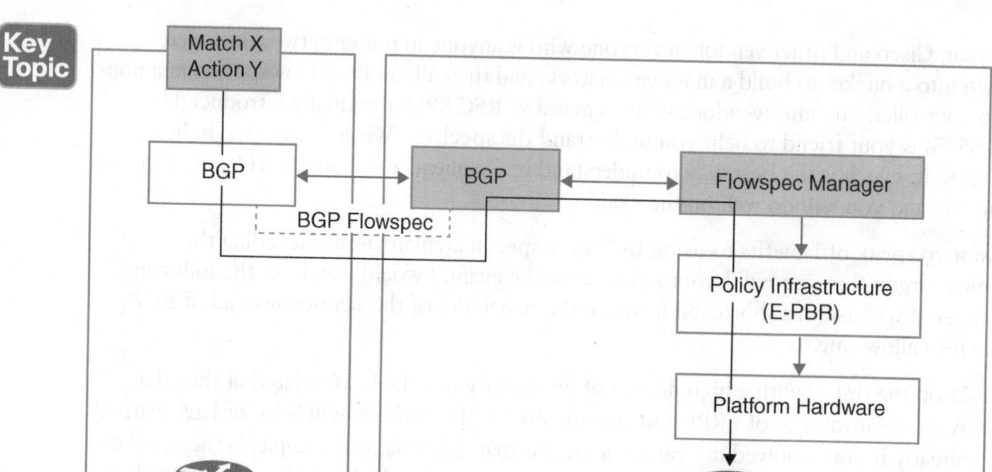

Figure 16-8 *Flowspec Logical Flow Diagram*

Example 16-38 *Flowspec Configuration Before and After on the Client*

```
RP/0/RP0/CPU0:P5# show running-config router bgp
Tue Jan 23 23:18:36.733 UTC
router bgp 65000
 bgp router-id 10.1.100.5
 address-family ipv4 unicast
 !
 neighbor 10.1.100.7
  remote-as 65000
  update-source Loopback0
  address-family ipv4 unicast
   route-policy PASS-ALL in
   route-policy PASS-ALL out
   soft-reconfiguration inbound always
  !
 !
!

RP/0/RP0/CPU0:P5# show running-config
Tue Jan 23 23:42:14.237 UTC
Building configuration...
! Output omitted for brevity
route-policy DROP-ALL
  drop
end-policy
!
route-policy PASS-ALL
  pass
end-policy
!
```

```
router bgp 65000
 bgp router-id 10.1.100.5
 address-family ipv4 unicast
 !
 address-family ipv4 flowspec
 !
 neighbor 10.1.100.7
 remote-as 65000
 update-source Loopback0
 address-family ipv4 unicast
 route-policy PASS-ALL in
 route-policy PASS-ALL out
 soft-reconfiguration inbound always
 !
 address-family ipv4 flowspec
 route-policy PASS-ALL in
 route-policy DROP-ALL out
 !
 !
 !
flowspec
 address-family ipv4
 local-install interface-all
 !
 !
end
RP/0/RP0/CPU0:P5#
```

So, what exactly did I add on the client in Example 16-38? I had a basic BGP configuration;
then I added a drop policy. Then, under the bgp process, I activated the **flowspec address-
family** for IP version 4 for the BGP process. Then again, under the neighbor, which happens
to be the Flowspec server, I added a drop policy for the outbound updates. Then, lastly, I
activated the local Flowspec engine for the IPv4 traffic (for all interfaces). Now comes a bit
more complex *server* configuration in Example 16-39.

Example 16-39 *Flowspec Configuration Before and After on the Server*

```
RP/0/RP0/CPU0:PE7# show running-config router bgp
Mon Jan 23 23:52:29.914 UTC
router bgp 65000
 bgp router-id 10.1.100.7
 address-family ipv4 unicast
 !
 neighbor 10.1.100.5
 remote-as 65000
 update-source Loopback0
 address-family ipv4 unicast
 route-policy PASS-ALL in
```

```
    route-policy PASS-ALL out
    soft-reconfiguration inbound always
   !
  !
  neighbor 10.1.100.6
   remote-as 65000
   update-source Loopback0
   address-family ipv4 unicast
    route-policy PASS-ALL in
    route-policy PASS-ALL out
    soft-reconfiguration inbound always
   !
  !
 !
RP/0/RP0/CPU0:PE7#
RP/0/RP0/CPU0:PE7# show running-config
Wed Jan 24 00:08:37.219 UTC
! Output omitted for brevity
class-map type traffic match-all DROP
 match destination-address ipv4 172.16.52.0 255.255.255.0
 end-class-map
!
class-map type traffic match-all ACCEPT
 match destination-address ipv4 172.16.51.0 255.255.255.0
 end-class-map
!
class-map type traffic match-all POLICE
 match destination-address ipv4 172.16.53.0 255.255.255.0
 end-class-map
!
policy-map type pbr CONTROL-IPV4
 class type traffic DROP
  drop
 !
 class type traffic POLICE
  police rate 10 mbps
 !
 !
 class type traffic ACCEPT
  set dscp ef
 !
 class type traffic class-default
 !
 end-policy-map
!
! Output omitted for brevity
```

```
route-policy DROP-ALL
 drop
end-policy
!
route-policy PASS-ALL
 pass
end-policy
!
router bgp 65000
 bgp router-id 10.1.100.7
 address-family ipv4 unicast
 !
 address-family ipv4 flowspec
 !
 neighbor 10.1.100.5
  remote-as 65000
  update-source Loopback0
  address-family ipv4 unicast
   route-policy PASS-ALL in
   route-policy PASS-ALL out
   soft-reconfiguration inbound always
  !
  address-family ipv4 flowspec
   route-policy PASS-ALL in
   route-policy PASS-ALL out
  !
 neighbor 10.1.100.6
  remote-as 65000
  update-source Loopback0
  address-family ipv4 unicast
   route-policy PASS-ALL in
   route-policy PASS-ALL out
   soft-reconfiguration inbound always
  !
 !
!
flowspec
 address-family ipv4
 service-policy type pbr CONTROL-IPV4
 !
!
end

RP/0/RP0/CPU0:PE7#
```

If you have a keen eye, you will notice that most components we configured on the client apply on the server as well. I am not highlighting them. What is more important is what I highlight, since it represents a policy this server will push to the client. Notice at the very bottom, we define a Policy-Based Routing (BPR) policy CONTROL-IPV4, since this is what we intend to demonstrate. Next, let's move up to the top of Example 16-39 to examine what is in the policy. First, we define the traffic that we want to DROP, ACCEPT, and POLICE, as identified by networks 172.16.52.0/24, 172.16.51.0/24, and 172.16.53.0/24 respectively. Next, via the policy map, we drop traffic, accept and mark with **ef**, and police to 10 Mbps. Obviously, you can choose various actions, but I selected these to illustrate Flowspec. Finally, let's validate whether this configuration has been applied on the client, as in Example 16-40.

Example 16-40 *BGP Flowspec on the Client*

```
RP/0/RP0/CPU0:P5# show flowspec ipv4 detail
Wed Jan 24 00:24:26.148 UTC


AFI: IPv4
  Flow    :Dest:172.16.51.0/24
  Actions  :DSCP: ef (bgp.1)
  Flow    :Dest:172.16.52.0/24
  Actions  :Traffic-rate: 0 bps (bgp.1)
  Flow    :Dest:172.16.53.0/24
  Actions  :Traffic-rate: 10000000 bps (bgp.1)
RP/0/RP0/CPU0:P5#
```

There are many verification commands you can explore and run, but I will leave them up to you. You can clearly see that we have a policy that marks 51 with ef, drops 52, and rate-limits 53 to 10 Mbps. Are you ready to do this on IOS XE? It should be simple after you modify PE7's BGP peering with PE6 (that is a part of your homework). Example 16-41 shows what happens on PE6.

Example 16-41 *BGP Flowspec IOS XE Client*

```
PE6# configure terminal
Enter configuration commands, one per line. End with CNTL/Z.
PE6(config)# flowspec
PE6(config-flowspec)# address-family ipv4
PE6(config-flowspec-afi)# local-install interface-all
PE6(config-flowspec-afi)# router bgp 65000
PE6(config-router)# address-family ipv4 flowspec
PE6(config-router-af)# neighbor 10.1.100.7 activate
PE6(config-router-af)# end
PE6# show flowspec ipv4 detail
AFI: IPv4
  Flow    :Dest:172.16.51.0/24
  Actions  :DSCP: ef (bgp.1)
  Statistics          (packets/bytes)
    Matched    :       0/0
    Dropped    :       0/0
```

```
Flow    :Dest:172.16.52.0/24
Actions :Traffic-rate: 0 bps (bgp.1)
Statistics      (packets/bytes)
 Matched    :      0/0
 Dropped    :      0/0
Flow    :Dest:172.16.53.0/24
Actions :Traffic-rate: 10000000 bps (bgp.1)
Statistics      (packets/bytes)
 Matched    :      0/0
 Dropped    :      0/0
PE6#
```

Far more powerful and granular than the RTBH solution (which we will examine together later). So, the question is: What can we match on? I refer you to RFC 8955. Use Table 16-4 as a starting point, and it is best to consult individual implementations for specific hardware and software. Not what you wanted to hear, but I feel your pain, and this certainly should make you feel better.

Table 16-4   BGP Flowspec NLRI Types

BGP Flowspec NLRI type	QoS Match Fields	Value Input Method
Type 1	IPv4 or IPv6 destination address	Prefix length
Type 2	IPv4 or IPv6 source address	Prefix length
Type 3	IPv4 last next header or IPv6 protocol	Multivalue range
Type 4	IPv4 or IPv6 source or destination port	Multivalue range
Type 5	IPv4 or IPv6 destination port	Multivalue range
Type 6	IPv4 or IPv6 source port	Multivalue range
Type 7	IPv4 or IPv6 ICMP type	Single value
Type 8	IPv4 or IPv6 ICMP code	Single value
Type 9	IPv4 or IPv6 TCP flags (2 bytes include reserved bits)	Bit mask
Type 10	IPv4 or IPv6 packet length	Multivalue range
Type 11	IPv4 or IPv6 DSCP	Multivalue range
Type 12	IPv4 fragmentation bits	Bit mask

Also, Table 16-5 shows possible traffic filtering actions you can deploy based on BGP communities, as taken from RFC 5575.

Table 16-5   BGP Flowspec Traffic Filtering Actions

BGP Community	Action	Description
0x8006	traffic-rate	Rate-limits traffic in bytes per second before dropping
0x8007	traffic-action	Samples traffic to gather attack information
0x8008	redirect	Directs traffic into a VRF
0x8009	traffic-marking	Changes DSCP codes

In my perspective, BGP Flowspec is highly adaptable and constrained only by the creativity of operators, positioning it as one of the most effective and versatile tools currently accessible for securing BGP routing. Other solutions, such as third-party scrubbers and their containerized implementations on routers, are coming to the market, but they are outside of this exam's scope as of the time of writing.

What about homework? I suggest you set up BGP Flowspec for IPv6 and VRF address families. Try to think of steering the traffic differently. Maybe set a different next hop. The reason I encourage you to do this is that the exam is heavy on configurations. If you have never configured BGP Flowspec and rely on recalling screenshots from this book, it will be challenging for you to figure out what is wrong with the configuration or what needs to be added to conserve time so that you can score points. I have boiled Flowspec down to the most basic logic—*common configurations on client and server* and *then policies configured on the server to influence client's behavior.*

Let's move on to lighter topics in Chapter 17, since we have spent much of this chapter configuring things.

Exam Preparation Tasks

As mentioned in the section "How to Use This Book" in the Introduction, you have a few choices for exam preparation: the exercises here, Chapter 23, "Final Preparation," and the exam simulation questions in the Pearson Test Prep Software Online.

Review All Key Topics

Review the most important topics in this chapter, noted with the Key Topic icon in the margin of the page. Table 16-6 lists a reference of these key topics and the page numbers on which each is found.

Table 16-6 Key Topics for Chapter 16

Key Topic Element	Description	Page Number
List	Elements of network protection	766
List	Control Plane Policing (CoPP)	768
Figure 16-2	LPTS Architecture	773
Paragraph	Platforms and software loads	783
Example 16-14	Label Allocation Filtering on IOS XR with Access-Lists	786
Paragraph	BGP TTL security check	794
Paragraph	TTL security on each router	802
List	The order in which BGP processes route filtering techniques	809
Paragraph	Permutations of how BGP routes can be filtered	811
Section	BGP Prefix Suppression	812
Table 16-2	Route Origin Authorization Record	816
Figure 16-6	RPKI Architecture	817
Figure 16-7	BGP AS-PATH Validation	821

Key Topic Element	Description	Page Number
Paragraph	BGP Flowspec	822
Table 16-3	BGP AFI/SAFI for Flowspec Dissemination	823
Figure 16-8	Flowspec Logical Flow Diagram	824
Table 16-4	BGP Flowspec NLRI Types	829
Table 16-5	BGP Flowspec Traffic Filtering Actions	829

Define Key Terms

Define the following key terms from this chapter and check the answers in the glossary:

BGP Flow Specification (BGP Flowspec), BGP Security (BGPsec), Cisco Express Forwarding (CEF), Control Plane Policing (CoPP), Internal Forwarding Information Base (iFIB), Label Forwarding Information Base (LFIB), Label Information Base (LIB), Local Packet Transport Services (LPTS), Message Digest Algorithm 5 (MD5), Modular QoS CLI (MQC), Remote Triggered Black Hole (RTBH), Resource Public Key Infrastructure (RPKI), Route Origin Authorization (ROA), Time-to-Live (TTL), Unicast Reverse Path Forwarding (uRPF)

Command Reference to Check Your Memory

This section includes the most important configuration and EXEC commands covered in this chapter. You might not need to memorize the complete syntax of every command, but you should be able to remember the basic keywords that are needed.

To test your memory of the commands, cover the right side of Table 16-7 with a piece of paper, read the description on the left side, and then see how much of the command you can remember.

The 350-501 exam focuses on practical, hands-on skills that are used by networking professionals. Therefore, you should be able to identify the commands needed to configure and test. Note that not all commands are fully covered in the chapter, but their presence in the following table should lead you to investigate them further to understand this technology.

Table 16-7   CLI Commands to Know

Task	Command Syntax
Enter the control plane configuration mode	Router(config)# **control-plane**
Apply the QoS service policy to the control plane	Router(config-cp)# **service-policy input** *service-policy-name*
Configure the ingress policers and enter pifib policer global configuration mode	RP/0/RSP0/CPU0:router(config)# **lpts pifib hardware police location 0/2/CPU0**
Display the policer configuration value set	RP/0/RSP0/CPU0:router# **show lpts pifib hardware police** [location {all | *node_id*}]
Configure a password key for computing MD5 checksums for the session TCP connection with the specified neighbor	Router(config)# **mpls ldp neighbor** [**vrf** *vrf-name*] *ip-address* **password** [0 | 7] *password-string*

Task	Command Syntax
Specify the access control list (ACL) to be used to filter label bindings for the specified LDP neighbor	RP/0/0/CPU0:P3(config)# **mpls ldp neighbor** [**vrf** *vpn-name*] *nbr-address* **labels accept** *acl*
Verify that the label switch router (LSR) has remote bindings only from a specified peer for prefixes permitted by the access list	Router(config)# **show mpls ldp bindings**
Configure local label allocation filters for learned routes for LDP	Router(config)# **allocate global prefix-list** {*list-name* | *list-number*}
Configure local label allocation filters for learned routes for LDP for host routes only	Router(config)# **allocate global host-routes**
Accept and attempt BGP connections to external peers residing on networks that are not directly connected	Router(config-router)# **neighbor** {*ip-address* | *ipv6-address* | *peer-group-name*} **ebgp-multihop** [*ttl*]
Configure the maximum number of hops that separate two external BGP (eBGP) peers	Router(config-router)# **neighbor** *neighbor-address* **ttl-security hops** *hop-count*
Distribute BGP neighbor information as specified in an access list	Router(config-router)# **neighbor** {*ip-address* | *peer-group-name*}**distribute-list** {*access-list-number* | *expanded-list-number* | *access-list-name*} {**in** | **out**}
Apply a route map to incoming or outgoing routes	Router(config-router)# **neighbor** {*ip-address* | *peer-group-name* | *ipv6-address*}**route-map** *map-name* {**in** | **out**}
Control how many prefixes can be received from a neighbor	Router(config-router)# **neighbor** { *ip-address* | *peer-group-name* } **maximum-prefix** *maximum* [*threshold*] [discard-extra] [restart *restart-interval*] [warning-only]
Suppress the advertisement of routes that are not installed in the routing information base (RIB)	Router(config-router)# **bgp suppress-inactive**
Control how many prefixes can be received from a neighbor	Router(config-router)# **neighbor** { *ip-address* | *peer-group-name* } **maximum-prefix** *maximum* [*threshold*] [discard-extra] [restart *restart-interval*] [warning-only]
Configure the router to connect to the specified RPKI server and download prefix information at intervals specified by the **refresh** *seconds* keyword and argument	RP/0/RSP0/CPU0:router(config-router)#**bgp rpki server tcp** {*ipv4-address* | *ipv6-address*} **port** *port-number* **refresh** *seconds*
Fetch ROAs from the validator	RP/0/RSP0/CPU0:router(config-router-af)#**bgp origin-as validation enable**
Enable the router to use prefix validation state information while making the best path calculation	RP/0/RSP0/CPU0:router(config-router-af)#**bgp bestpath origin-as use validity**

Task	Command Syntax
Specify either the IPv4, IPv6, VPN4, or VPN6 address family and enter address family configuration submode, and initialize the global address family for flowspec policy mapping	RP/0/RSP0/CPU0:router(config-bgp)# **address-family ipv4 flowspec**
Enter the flowspec configuration mode	RP/0/RSP0/CPU0:router(config)# **flowspec**
Install the flowspec policy on all interfaces	RP/0/RSP0/CPU0:router(config-flowspec)# **local-install interface-all**
Attach a policy map to an IPv4 interface to be used as the service policy for that interface	RP/0/RSP0/CPU0:router(config-flowspec-af)# **service-policy type pbr policy1**
Enter control plane configuration mode	RP/0/RP0/CPU0:router(config)# **control-plane**

Review Questions

As a part of the review, we encourage you to provide *a single-sentence answer* (keep your answers as short as possible) to the following questions. If you struggle to complete this answer in a single sentence, this may indicate a lack of clarity or reveal gaps in your understanding. We have constructed these questions to help you consolidate this chapter's information and extract the essence of the covered content.

The answers to these questions appear in Appendix A. For more practice with exam format questions, use the Pearson Test Prep Software Online.

1. Can you explain the key objective of Control Plane Policing (CoPP) in a network security context?

2. How does BGP Flowspec enhance network security and traffic engineering?

3. How does BGPsec contribute to enhancing the security of the Border Gateway Protocol (BGP)? In your answer, provide an overview of the key mechanisms and benefits of BGPsec, and explain how it addresses security vulnerabilities in BGP routing. Try to keep the answer to two sentences.

Bibliography

BGP Configuration Guide for Cisco 8000 Series Routers, IOS XR Release 7.11.x, https://www.cisco.com/c/en/us/td/docs/iosxr/cisco8000/bgp/711x/configuration/guide/b-bgp-cg-8k-711x/implementing-bgp.html. Accessed August 8, 2024.

Y. Gilad, S. Goldberg, K. Sriram, J. Snijders, and B. Maddison. RFC 9319, *The Use of maxLength in the Resource Public Key Infrastructure (RPKI)*, IETF, https://datatracker.ietf.org/doc/html/rfc9319.txt, October 2022.

V. Gill, J. Heasley, D. Meyer, P. Savola, and C. Pignataro. RFC 5082, *The Generalized TTL Security Mechanism (GTSM)*, IETF, https://www.ietf.org/rfc/rfc5082.txt, October 2007.

A. Heffernan. RFC 2385, *Protection of BGP Sessions via the TCP MD5 Signature Option*, IETF, https://www.ietf.org/rfc/rfc2385.txt, August 1998.

T. Lad. *Introduction to NCS55xx and NCS5xx LPTS*, https://xrdocs.io/ncs5500/tutorials/introduction-to-ncs55xx-and-ncs5xx-lpts/. Accessed August 8, 2024.

M. Lepinski and K. Sriram. RFC 8205, *BGPsec Protocol Specification*, IETF, https://www.ietf.org/rfc/rfc8205.txt, September 2017.

M. Lepinski, S. Kent, and D. Kong. RFC 6842, *A Profile for Route Origin Authorizations (ROAs)*, IETF, https://www.ietf.org/rfc/rfc6842.txt, February 2012.

C. Loibl, S. Hares, R. Raszuk, D. McPherson, and M. Bacher. RFC 8955, *Dissemination of Flow Specification Rules*, IETF, https://www.ietf.org/rfc/rfc8955.txt, September 2017.

P. Marques, N. Sheth, R. Raszuk, B. Greene, J. Mauch, and D. McPherson. RFC 5575, *Dissemination of Flow Specification Rules*, IETF, https://www.ietf.org/rfc/rfc5575.txt, August 2009.

S. Murphy. RFC 4272, *BGP Security Vulnerabilities Analysis*, IETF, https://www.ietf.org/rfc/rfc4272.txt, January 2006.

Understand BGP RPKI with XR7 Cisco8000 Whitepaper, https://www.cisco.com/c/en/us/support/docs/ip/border-gateway-protocol-bgp/217020-bgp-rpki-with-xr7-cisco8000-whitepaper.html. Accessed August 8, 2024.

## CHAPTER 17

Securing Management Plane

This chapter covers the following exam topics:

1.6 Describe management plane security

- 1.6.a Traceback
- 1.6.b AAA and TACACS
- 1.6.c RestAPI security
- 1.6.d DDoS

In today's interconnected world, routers serve as the backbone of network infrastructure, managing data traffic and facilitating communication between devices. However, this critical role also makes routers lucrative targets for malicious actors seeking to disrupt network operations or compromise sensitive information. Therefore, establishing robust security measures to protect the management plane of routers is essential. This chapter examines the details of securing router management interfaces, implementing access control mechanisms, and deploying security protocols to defend against potential threats and vulnerabilities.

"Do I Know This Already?" Quiz

The "Do I Know This Already?" quiz allows you to assess whether you should read this entire chapter thoroughly or jump to the "Exam Preparation Tasks" section. If you are in doubt about your answers to these questions or your own assessment of your knowledge of the topics, read the entire chapter. Table 17-1 lists the major headings in this chapter and their corresponding "Do I Know This Already?" quiz questions. You can find the answers in Appendix A, "Answers to the 'Do I Know This Already?' Quizzes and Review Questions."

Table 17-1 "Do I Know This Already?" Section-to-Question Mapping

Foundation Topics Section	Questions
Management Plane Protection Fundamentals	1–2
Tracebacks	3
AAA and TACACS	4
REST APIs	5
DDoS	6

CAUTION   The goal of self-assessment is to gauge your mastery of the topics in this chapter. If you do not know the answer to a question or are only partially sure of the answer, you should mark that question as wrong for purposes of the self-assessment. Giving yourself credit for an answer you correctly guess skews your self-assessment results and might provide you with a false sense of security.

1. MPP can be described as which of the following?

    a. Stateful

    b. MQC-driven

    c. Supports limited protocols

    d. Not supported on IOS XR

2. MPP controls all except which of the following?

    a. IPv6 traffic

    b. Virtual interfaces

    c. Loopback Interfaces

    d. VRF interfaces

3. You are troubleshooting a network issue and need to identify the source of certain packets in a high-security environment. Which of the following techniques would you use to trace the traffic back to its origin?

    a. Implement packet capture on all network segments and analyze the memory stack for errors.

    b. Apply deep packet inspection (DPI) to analyze payloads and determine the source of the traffic.

    c. Configure BGP Flowspec to filter and redirect suspicious traffic to a secure location for analysis.

    d. Use tracebacks to follow the path of the traffic across the network infrastructure.

4. You are configuring AAA on a network device and encounter an issue where users can authenticate, but their command privileges are inconsistent. Which of the following is the most likely cause?

    a. The AAA server is configured with RADIUS instead of TACACS.

    b. The device's AAA authorization configuration is missing the command authorization method.

    c. TACACS is only configured for accounting, not authorization.

    d. The local database is used as a fallback for authentication but not for command authorization.

5. Which package format is predominantly utilized by Cisco IOS XE's REST API service for data exchange?

    a. XML

    b. JSON

    c. YAML

    d. CSV

6. During a DDoS attack mitigation, you notice that legitimate traffic is also being dropped. Which of the following is the most likely cause?

   a. The network's ACLs are incorrectly configured to block specific IP addresses instead of ranges.

   b. The DDoS mitigation system is set to operate only during certain hours, leading to inconsistent protection.

   c. The router's CPU is overwhelmed, causing it to drop packets before reaching the mitigation system.

   d. The DDoS mitigation system is using rate limiting based on the total packet count, affecting all incoming traffic.

Foundation Topics

Management Plane Protection Fundamentals

The management plane concerns all tasks related to achieving network management objectives. This involves interactive management sessions (Telnet, SSH, configuration of any kind—API, orchestration tools, FTP, TFTP, HTTP/S, SCP, SNMP, NTP) and the collection of statistics (through SNMP, NetFlow, Telemetry). Ensuring the security of a network device is of utmost importance, particularly in safeguarding the management plane. Once the management plane is compromised, recovering or stabilizing the network can become a formidable challenge.

The topic is massive. Encrypting passwords; using password levels (0,7) and login password retry lockouts; disabling password recovery; disabling unused services; enabling keepalives for TCP; timing out EXEC sessions; limiting access to the network infrastructure with ACLs; filtering ICMP and IP fragments; controlling access to Console and AUX ports, vty and tty lines, and central authentication; controlling SNMP; logging to a central location; sampling the attack; driving it to the "honeypot" areas—areas that look legitimate to attackers but only serve as a means for attack analysis—there are so many more things to consider. A general recommendation is to consult OS hardening guides from both the vendor and government security organizations that publish practical guides.

For the purposes of the exam, I (Brad) suggest focusing on the management plane features of IOS XE and IOS XR. Cisco IOS software includes a feature called **Management Plane Protection (MPP)**, which allows you to control the interfaces through which network management packets can enter a device. With MPP, you can specify certain router interfaces as designated management interfaces. Once MPP is activated, only these specified interfaces will accept network management traffic for the device, preventing other interfaces from handling such traffic. This helps enhance the security of the device by restricting where management traffic is allowed. Notice how we designate interface g0/0 for management purposes, and are shown protocols we can allow to use it, in Example 17-1.

Example 17-1   *MPP Usage in IOS XE*

```
PE2# configure terminal
Enter configuration commands, one per line. End with CNTL/Z.
PE2(config)# control-plane host
PE2(config-cp-host)# ?
```

```
Control Plane host configuration commands:
  exit      Exit from control-plane host configuration mode
  management-interface Configure interface for receiving network management
           traffic
  no        Negate or set default values of a command
PE2(config-cp-host)# management-interface g0/0 ?
  allow Allowed network management protocols on selected interface


PE2(config-cp-host)# management-interface gigabitEthernet 1 allow ?
  beep Beep Protocol
  ftp  File Transfer Protocol
  http HTTP Protocol
  https HTTPS Protocol
  snmp Simple Network Management Protocol
  ssh  Secure Shell Protocol
  telnet Telnet Protocol
  tftp Trivial File Transfer Protocol
  tl1  Transaction Language Session Protocol
  <cr> <cr>


PE2(config-cp-host)# management-interface interface gigabitEthernet 1 allow
telnet ssh snmp https
PE2(config-cp-host)# do show management-interface
Management interface GigabitEthernet1
        Protocol  Packets processed
          https    26
          ssh     12
          snmp    2
          telnet   45
```

I recommend that you explore these features and become acquainted with them while studying these on command line. Some aspects that caught my attention are as follows:

- This feature (MPP) is not stateful.

- Loopback and virtual interfaces that are not associated with physical ports are not available for configuration. At first, I thought about making Loopback0 my management interface but noticed this option was not available.

- The dedicated management interface configuration is not supported. This would be an out-of-band interface that only processes management traffic, but other platforms allow exactly that.

- There is not a separate option for Secure Copy Protocol (SCP) in the output in Example 17-1. It falls under SSH, which kind of makes sense, but you cannot configure SCP directly.

■ The final observation is that there is currently no option to control IPv6 packets. While the configurations provide control over IPv4 traffic, IPv6 traffic passes through unregulated, because the commands appear to have no impact on it.

There might be others; it's good to explore. The same feature is present in IOS XR, where things get more interesting. Look at Example 17-2, which offers the choice of both in-band and out-of-band interfaces. A quick look down the configuration tree reveals that we now have access to loopback and virtual interfaces as well.

Example 17-2 *MPP Options in IOS XR*

```
RP/0/RP0/CPU0:8201# configure
RP/0/RP0/CPU0:8201(config)# control-plane ?
 local     Locally originated packets
 management-plane Configure management plane protection
 <cr>

RP/0/RP0/CPU0:8201(config)# control-plane management-plane ?
 inband   Configure an inband interface/protocol
 out-of-band Configure an out-of-band interface/protocol
 <cr>

RP/0/RP0/CPU0:8201(config)# control-plane management-plane inband ?
 interface Configure an inband interface
 <cr>

RP/0/RP0/CPU0:8201(config)# control-plane management-plane inband interface ?
 BVI      Bridge-Group Virtual Interface | short name is BV
 Bundle-Ether  Aggregated Ethernet interface(s) | short name is BE
 EightHundredGigE EightHundredGigabitEthernet/IEEE 802.3 interface(s) | short name is EH
 FiftyGigE    FiftyGigabitEthernet/IEEE 802.3 interface(s) | short name is Fi
 FortyGigE    FortyGigabitEthernet/IEEE 802.3 interface(s) | short name is Fo
 FourHundredGigE FourHundredGigabitEthernet/IEEE 802.3 interface(s) | short name is FH
 GCC0     OTN GCC0 interface(s) | short name is G0
 GCC1     OTN GCC1 interface(s) | short name is G1
 GCC2     OTN GCC2 interface(s) | short name is G2
 GigabitEthernet GigabitEthernet/IEEE 802.3 interface(s) | short name is Gi
 HundredGigE  HundredGigabitEthernet/IEEE 802.3 interface(s) | short name is Hu
 Loopback   Loopback interface(s) | short name is Lo
 Null     Null interface | short name is Nu
 PTP     Ethernet/IEEE 802.3 interface(s) | short name is PTP
 TenGigE    TenGigabitEthernet/IEEE 802.3 interface(s) | short name is Te
 TwentyFiveGigE TwentyFiveGigabitEthernet/IEEE 802.3 interface(s) | short name is TF
 TwoHundredGigE TwoHundredGigabitEthernet/IEEE 802.3 interface(s) | short name is TH
 all     configure all the interfaces
 lpts     LPTS Interface(s) | short name is lpts
 nve     Network Virtualization Endpoint Interface(s) | short name is nve
 tunnel-ip   GRE/IPinIP Tunnel Interface(s)
 tunnel-ipsec  IPSec Tunnel interface(s) | short name is tsec
```

```
tunnel-mte  MPLS Traffic Engineering P2MP Tunnel interface(s) | short name is tmte
tunnel-te   MPLS Traffic Engineering Tunnel interface(s) | short name is tt
tunnel-tp   MPLS Transport Protocol Tunnel interface | short name is tp
RP/0/RP0/CPU0:8201(config)# control-plane management-plane inband interface
loopback 0 ?
allow Allow a protocol on this interface
<cr>
RP/0/RP0/CPU0:8201(config)# control-plane management-plane inband interface
loopback 0 allow ?
HTTP  HTTP(S)
NETCONF NETCONF version 1.1 protocol
SNMP  SNMP (all versions)
SSH   Secure Shell (v1 & v2)
TFTP  TFTP
Telnet Telnet
XML   XML
all  All Protocols
RP/0/RP0/CPU0:8201(config)# control-plane management-plane inband interface
loopback 0 allow all ?
peer Configure peer address on this interface
<cr>
RP/0/RP0/CPU0:8201(config)# control-plane management-plane inband interface
loopback 0 allow all peer ?
address Configure peer address on this interface
<cr>
RP/0/RP0/CPU0:8201(config)#$ interface loopback 0 allow all peer address ?
ipv4 Configure peer IPv4 address on this interface
ipv6 Configure peer IPv6 address on this interface
RP/0/RP0/CPU0:8201(config)#$ interface loopback 0 allow all peer address ipv4 ?
A.B.C.D   Enter IPv4 address
A.B.C.D/length Enter IPv4 address with prefix
RP/0/RP0/CPU0:8201(config)#$ interface loopback 0 allow all peer address ipv4
10.1.100.100 ?
<cr>
RP/0/RP0/CPU0:8201(config)# control-plane management-plane out-of-band ?
interface Configure an outband interface
vrf  configure mpp outband vrf
<cr>
RP/0/RP0/CPU0:8201(config)# control-plane management-plane out-of-band interface ?
BVI     Bridge-Group Virtual Interface | short name is BV
Bundle-Ether  Aggregated Ethernet interface(s) | short name is BE
EightHundredGigE EightHundredGigabitEthernet/IEEE 802.3 interface(s) | short name is EH
FiftyGigE    FiftyGigabitEthernet/IEEE 802.3 interface(s) | short name is Fi
FortyGigE    FortyGigabitEthernet/IEEE 802.3 interface(s) | short name is Fo
FourHundredGigE FourHundredGigabitEthernet/IEEE 802.3 interface(s) | short name is FH
GCC0    OTN GCC0 interface(s) | short name is G0
GCC1    OTN GCC1 interface(s) | short name is G1
GCC2    OTN GCC2 interface(s) | short name is G2
```

```
  GigabitEthernet GigabitEthernet/IEEE 802.3 interface(s) | short name is Gi
  HundredGigE  HundredGigabitEthernet/IEEE 802.3 interface(s) | short name is Hu
  Loopback    Loopback interface(s) | short name is Lo
  MgmtEth    Ethernet/IEEE 802.3 interface(s) | short name is Mg
  Null     Null interface | short name is Nu
  PTP      Ethernet/IEEE 802.3 interface(s) | short name is PTP
  TenGigE    TenGigabitEthernet/IEEE 802.3 interface(s) | short name is Te
  TwentyFiveGigE TwentyFiveGigabitEthernet/IEEE 802.3 interface(s) | short name is TF
  TwoHundredGigE TwoHundredGigabitEthernet/IEEE 802.3 interface(s) | short name is TH
  all      configure all the interfaces
  lpts     LPTS Interface(s) | short name is lpts
  nve      Network Virtualization Endpoint Interface(s) | short name is nve
  tunnel-ip   GRE/IPinIP Tunnel Interface(s)
  tunnel-ipsec  IPSec Tunnel interface(s) | short name is tsec
  tunnel-mte  MPLS Traffic Engineering P2MP Tunnel interface(s) | short name is tmte
  tunnel-te   MPLS Traffic Engineering Tunnel interface(s) | short name is tt
  tunnel-tp   MPLS Transport Protocol Tunnel interface | short name is tp
RP/0/RP0/CPU0:8201(config)# control-plane management-plane out-of-band interface
loopback 0 ?
  allow Allow a protocol on this interface
  <cr>

RP/0/RP0/CPU0:8201(config)# control-plane management-plane out-of-band interface
loopback 0 allow ?
  HTTP   HTTP(S)
  NETCONF NETCONF version 1.1 protocol
  SNMP   SNMP (all versions)
  SSH   Secure Shell (v1 & v2)
  TFTP   TFTP
  Telnet Telnet
  XML   XML
  all  All Protocols
RP/0/RP0/CPU0:8201(config)# control-plane management-plane out-of-band interface
loopback 0 allow all ?
  peer Configure peer address on this interface
  <cr>
RP/0/RP0/CPU0:8201(config)#$-band interface loopback 0 allow all peer ?
  address Configure peer address on this interface
  <cr>
RP/0/RP0/CPU0:8201(config)#$-band interface loopback 0 allow all peer address ?
  ipv4 Configure peer IPv4 address on this interface
  ipv6 Configure peer IPv6 address on this interface
RP/0/RP0/CPU0:8201(config)#$-band interface loopback 0 allow all peer address ipv6 ?
  X:X::X    Enter IPv6 address
  X:X::X/length Enter IPv6 address with prefix
RP/0/RP0/CPU0:8201(config)#
```

As we follow the decision tree, notice the peer-filtering option that allows management traffic from specific peers, or a range of peers, to be configured.

Also, notice that MPP allows us to choose specific router interfaces (out-of-band) for managing the device—an option we did not see on IOS XE. Only through these chosen management interfaces can device management traffic enter. Once MPP is on, no interfaces other than the selected management ones will accept network management traffic for the device. I like this limitation to designated interfaces because it gives better control and boosts the security of the device. The forwarded (or customer) traffic cannot interfere with router management, so the possibility of denial-of-service (DoS) attacks is significantly reduced. What is also convenient is that we can run dynamic routing protocols on these interfaces to build an independent management overlay network with access to route policies and routing tools. You can specify a VRF in one of the options, and the rest of the decision tree looks very similar.

So, what are the benefits of this feature on IOS XR? In my opinion:

- Operators can present fewer interfaces to packet flooding and attacks.

- Fewer ACLs are necessary to restrict access to the device.

- Per-interface ACLs to restrict access to the device are not necessary.

Tracebacks

In the context of Cisco networking devices, the term *traceback* has, for many years, referred to debugging messages generated by a router in response to a critical error or an exception. A traceback is a stack trace. It shows the sequence of function calls and their corresponding memory addresses at the time of the error. Tracebacks contain information about the sequence of events leading up to the error, including the functions or processes involved, memory addresses, and the point at which the error occurred. This information is valuable for troubleshooting and diagnosing the root cause of the problem.

What can you find in a Cisco traceback message?

- Timestamp to indicate when the traceback occurred.

- Severity Level to indicate the severity of the error (e.g., critical, major).

- Error message to describe the error or exception.

- Process name to identify the task that encountered the error.

- Location/module to indicate the location in the code where the error occurred.

- Stack trace to show the sequence of function calls and memory addresses leading up to the error.

In Example 17-3, the traceback indicates a memory allocation failure, and the stack trace shows the sequence of function calls that led to the error. Analyzing tracebacks requires expertise in Cisco networking, and network administrators or engineers typically use this information to identify and resolve issues within the network infrastructure when requested by Cisco Technical Assistance Center (TAC).

Example 17-3 *Traceback Messages on a Router Console*

```
%SYS-2-MALLOCFAIL: Memory allocation of 65536 bytes failed from 0x8016F834,
alignment 8
 Pool: Processor Free: 18160 Cause: Not enough free memory
 Alternate Pool: None Free: 0 Cause: No Alternate pool

-Process= "Exec", ipl= 0, pid= 109
-Traceback= 8016F834 80238C68 80238D94 801DA870 801B3FB8 801B44C8 801B61C0 801B6EBC
```

The exam specifically asks for traceback knowledge in the context of management plane security. I have been in networking for over 20 years, and the tracebacks described in this chapter are the ones I have encountered often. While doing extensive research for this book, I came across many references to tracebacks as methods to trace back (retrace) the source of a network attack. I am certain that service providers did this and still do this, but the networks that I have worked on (which are many) did not bother to focus on this specific function. It was too difficult due to the use of spoofed packets. By the time the packet arrived on my network(s), it had gone through so many devices that performed NAT, that for us to trace it back to the real source would be akin to finding a vegetarian at a Texas barbecue—not impossible, but highly improbable!

For these reasons, many providers resorted to techniques like source address validation (look up RFC 2827 and RFC 3704; this is some good stuff if you ask me), denial of RFC 1918 private address at the edge of their networks, denial of their own addresses from external sources, denial of multicast source addresses, and the use of Unicast Reverse Path Forwarding (uRPF)—my favorite tool of the past, which I will describe in detail in the upcoming section, although it is not the most effective tool on dual-home networks, in my opinion.

The idea of pinpointing the attacker sounds romantic, but I have never caught anyone red-handed. Two times in my career I have been to world-class security operations centers (SOCs) that performed this function, although they never called it tracebacks, so go figure. In my experience, these were not networking people, these were security coders, and what they did was nothing short of digital magic. If you search on the Internet, you will find several in-depth academic papers from the early 2000s on the traceback subject detailing mathematical formulas and approaches for packet market, logging, and other methods to seek out the original attacker. My experience has been more of a block-and-tackle—stick to simple working strategies, deliver results, and move on, not chasing attackers. Prior to joining Cisco, I had a few dealings with our ISP when we chased offending IP addresses—turned out to be boring and fruitless efforts, unlike what you see in the movies. It is in the context of denial of service that you may encounter tracebacks on the exam. I have included a couple of links in the "Bibliography" section for you to look at the traceback approaches.

Nevertheless, what can you do to trace such events and address exam questions? The first one I would suggest is "classification" ACLs on the interfaces. They monitor traffic on an interface without changing the network's security rules because they identify specific protocols, source addresses, or destinations. Instead of allowing all traffic, an ACL can be set up to classify traffic by specific protocols or ports; this provides better insight into network traffic because each type has its own counter. Additionally, an administrator can break down the default deny rule at the end of an ACL into detailed rules to identify the types of blocked traffic. Both deny and permit ACL entries can have the **log** option appended to the end.

Example 17-4 shows how to expand the **ipv4 permit any any** ACL to monitor for fragmented and ICMP traffic. I issue 100 pings and 100 traceroutes that are caught by the ACL, which happens to also register unexpected TCP fragments.

Example 17-4   *An Example of a "Classification" Permit ACL*

```
RP/0/RP0/CPU0:P3# show access-lists
ipv4 access-list CLASSIFY-ACL
 10 permit tcp any any fragments log (57 matches)
 15 permit udp any any fragments
 20 permit icmp any any fragments
 25 permit ipv4 any any fragments log
 30 permit icmp any any (200 matches)
 35 permit ipv4 any any
RP/0/RP0/CPU0:P3#
```

Using NetFlow and exporting these entries for either manual or tool-specific analysis can help you find clues to abnormal events. NetFlow tracks network flows to detect unusual and security-related activities. You can view and analyze NetFlow data using the command-line interface or export it to a NetFlow collector, which can be either commercial or free. These collectors analyze network behavior and usage over time by aggregating and trending the data.

Example 17-5 provides a quick example of observing which connections show up in the router's flow cache where we grab two working interfaces and quickly enable NetFlow. We discover that BGP entries are present with this basic example. If the packet flow is excessive for certain applications, we focus on those flows next.

Example 17-5   *Tracking Flows on the Routers with NetFlow*

```
P4# show ip interface brief
Interface      IP-Address  OK? Method Status      Protocol
GigabitEthernet0/0   unassigned  YES NVRAM administratively down down
GigabitEthernet0/1   172.16.48.4 YES manual up       up
GigabitEthernet0/2   10.1.24.4 YES manual up       up
GigabitEthernet0/3   unassigned  YES NVRAM administratively down down
Loopback0      10.1.100.4  YES manual up       up
P4# configure terminal
Enter configuration commands, one per line. End with CNTL/Z.
P4(config)# interface gigabitEthernet 0/2
P4(config-if)# ip flow ingress
P4(config-if)# ip flow egress
P4(config-if)# interface gigabitEthernet 0/1
P4(config-if)# ip flow egress
P4(config-if)# ip flow ingress
P4(config-if)# do show ip cache flow
IP packet size distribution (25 total packets):
   1-32 64 96 128 160 192 224 256 288 320 352 384 416 448 480
   .000 .760 .000 .240 .000 .000 .000 .000 .000 .000 .000 .000 .000 .000 .000
```

```
 512  544  576 1024 1536 2048 2560 3072 3584 4096 4608
.000 .000 .000 .000 .000 .000 .000 .000 .000 .000 .000

IP Flow Switching Cache, 278544 bytes
  3 active, 4093 inactive, 6 added
  173 ager polls, 0 flow alloc failures
  Active flows timeout in 30 minutes
  Inactive flows timeout in 15 seconds
IP Sub Flow Cache, 34056 bytes
  0 active, 1024 inactive, 0 added, 0 added to flow
  0 alloc failures, 0 force free
  1 chunk, 1 chunk added
  last clearing of statistics never
Protocol    Total   Flows Packets Bytes Packets Active(Sec) Idle(Sec)
--------    Flows   /Sec  /Flow /Pkt  /Sec   /Flow   /Flow
TCP-BGP        2   0.0   1 46  0.0    0.4    15.4
TCP-other      1   0.0   2 49  0.0    4.7    15.8
Total:         3   0.0   1 47  0.0    1.8    15.5

SrcIf     SrcIPaddress DstIf    DstIPaddress Pr SrcP DstP Pkts
Gi0/2     10.1.24.2    Null     224.0.0.2    11 0286 0286 13
Gi0/2     10.1.24.2    Null     224.0.0.5    59 0000 0000  6
Gi0/2     10.1.100.2   Local    10.1.100.4   06 0286 A395  1
```

AAA and TACACS

Authentication, authorization, and accounting (AAA) is a framework for admitting users to the network, controlling their access to network resources, and tracking their activities for usage and billing purposes. Simply put:

- **Authentication** is the process of identifying a user or application based on a challenge and response prior to being allowed access to the network and network services.

- **Authorization** is the process of establishing what users or applications can and cannot do based on their network profile.

- **Accounting** is the process of tracking services that users or applications access and the amount of network resources being consumed.

Terminal Access Controller Access Control System (TACACS) is a network security protocol that provides centralized AAA services. TACACS is commonly used in network devices such as routers and switches to control access to network resources and facilitate the AAA services model. Here's a breakdown for how TACACS functions:

1. **Authentication:** TACACS verifies the identity of users attempting to access a network device. When a user tries to log in, TACACS checks the provided credentials (such as username and password) against a centralized TACACS server. This ensures that only authorized individuals can gain access to the network.

2. **Authorization:** Once a user is authenticated, TACACS determines the level of access or permissions that the user has within the network device. Authorization policies are centrally managed and enforced, allowing administrators to specify what commands or operations a user is allowed to perform on the device.

3. **Accounting:** TACACS maintains a detailed record of all actions performed by users on the network device. This includes information about login/logout times, executed commands, and any changes made to the device configuration. Accounting data is useful for auditing, monitoring, and troubleshooting network activities.

It's important to note that there are two main versions of TACACS: TACACS+ and TACACS (often referred to as TACACS Classic). TACACS+ is the newer and more secure version, providing additional features and improvements over the original TACACS protocol.

REST APIs

In modern network and application architectures, developers often use **application programming interfaces (APIs)** to speed up the development process; however, this convenience of deploying software intermediaries can pose risks for the application and network itself. When connecting to external services, hidden vulnerabilities in these applications may expose databases or back-end resources, including network devices, to potential attacks. API security involves protecting the application from these vulnerabilities that could be introduced through **Representational State Transfer (REST)** API calls, OpenAPI, gRPC, GraphQL, and other ad hoc interfaces.

One of the better resources for networking engineers (and developers) to learn about currently available methodologies, documentation, and tools is the Open Worldwide Application Security Project (OWASP), an online community with access to free resources that enhance application security. Feel free to browse this and other resources because this topic is considerably large. What are the general guidelines to be familiar with, specifically for the exam itself? The following best practices come to mind:

- **Authenticate all communication:** API keys serve the dual purpose of identifying objects and authorizing access. This capability becomes valuable for blocking anonymous traffic and managing calls to your API. It is important to note that this is not ideal for securing the traffic to and from your API because the keys can be easily stolen. To prevent misuse of API keys, secret keys along with unique temporary access tokens should be used. It's crucial to maintain strict credential discipline to avoid exposing secrets or passwords.

- **Encrypt all data:** Methods such as Transport Layer Security (TLS) are available to this end, and signatures should be employed when data is modified.

- **Secure all APIs:** This practice applies to both external and internal resources. Before accessing any resources, it is essential to validate all transactions, reducing the potential for harm. To deter hopping attacks, implement a strategy of segmenting access to resources. By dividing and controlling the pathways to various resources, you can enhance security and prevent unauthorized lateral movements within your system.

- **Log all transactions and actively monitor for any signs of unwanted or suspicious behaviors:** Regularly analyzing transaction logs enhances the ability to detect anomalies, providing a robust defense against unauthorized access or malicious activities.

- **Identify API vulnerabilities:** The intricate interactions between various components make it difficult to pinpoint potential weaknesses. Vulnerabilities can arise from issues such as inadequate authentication mechanisms, insufficient data validation, or flawed access controls. Conduct thorough assessments and understand how data flows through the API to recognizing potential points of failure. Vulnerabilities may evolve over time as new threats and attack vectors emerge. Regular and comprehensive security assessments, including penetration testing and code reviews, are essential to stay ahead of risks.

Natively, no APIs exist in IOS XE. REST APIs are delivered as an open virtual application (.OVA) package file to be loaded into the router configuration as a virtual container image. Once the container is enabled, the HTTPS protocol will be used to transport for full Cisco REST API access.

When it comes to REST API security, basic authentication is not the best approach for authentication. Herein, the client transmits the username and password in a Base64-encoded string via an HTTP request. While it boasts simplicity, its security is questionable, given that the credentials are plainly encoded within the code. A paramount concern lies in securing the connection between the client and server, because interception of credentials presents a plausible threat in the absence of robust security measures.

A far better alternative is token-based authentication, which typically requires clients to procure a token as evidence of authorization. This token is commonly acquired through secure access to a web portal or via API calls. Notable token-based authentication methods encompass **JSON Web Tokens (JWTs)**, **OAuth 2.0** access tokens, and API keys. Clients can access Cisco routers by incorporating the token ID into a customized HTTPS header known as an *x-auth-token*. As an example, JWTs are a compact, URL-safe means of representing claims to be transferred between two parties. The claims in a JWT are encoded as a JSON object that is used as the payload of a JSON Web Signature (JWS) structure or as the plaintext of a JSON Web Encryption (JWE) structure, enabling a digital signature or encryption. They are commonly used for authentication and information exchange in web applications and APIs.

As an example, I attempt to program several IOS XR routers with a Layer2 VPN SRTE policy by using Postman (an API tool). I need to obtain a JWT token (also called a *bearer*) to access the Cisco Crosswork Controller API so that the controller can program the routers. In Figure 17-1, I make the first request to obtain the ticket.

Notice the middle arrow, which points to the successful status code 201, indicating that the ticket request has been approved (after I pressed the Send button at the top right) and then the lower arrow, which shows the ticket itself after the last slash (/) in the location string for the Crosswork platform. Figure 17-2 captures me sending the request for the JWT token that needs the ticket (stored in variable) obtained in step 1.

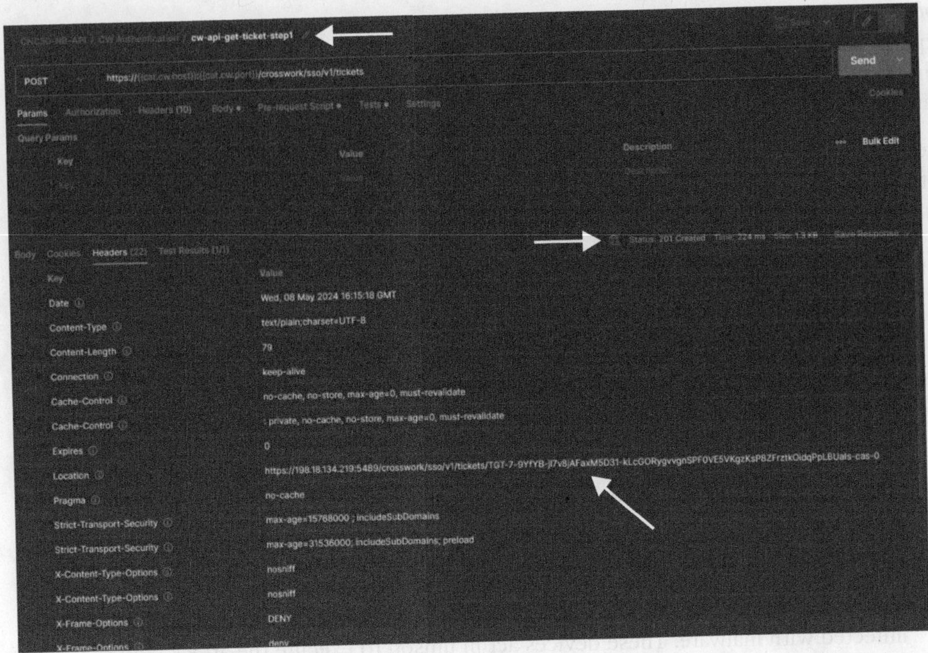

Figure 17-1   *Step 1: Obtaining a Ticket*

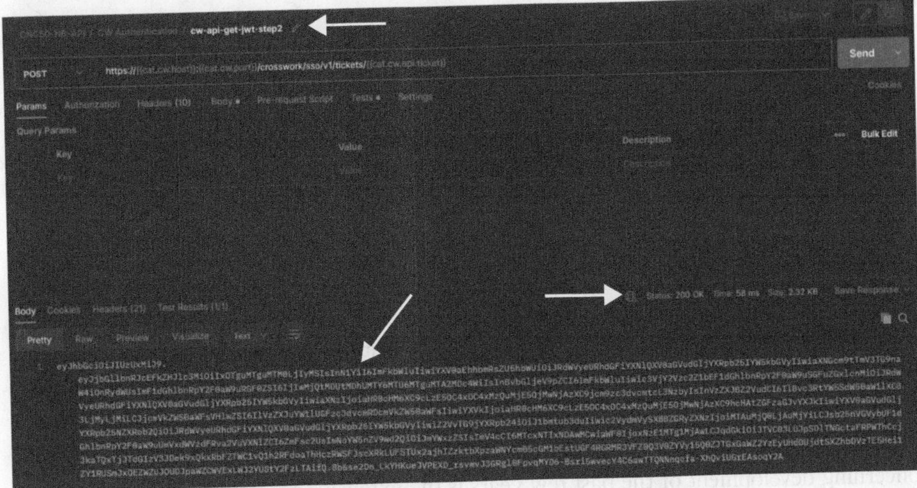

Figure 17-2   *Step 2: Retrieving a Token*

You can see the status of 200 (OK) and the body of the token itself. I am now authorized to deploy the L2VPN SRTE policy, which I do not show here.

DDoS

A network **distributed denial-of-service (DDoS)** attack is a malicious attempt to disrupt the regular functioning of a targeted network by overwhelming it with a flood of traffic. In a typical DDoS attack, multiple compromised computers or devices, often referred to as a *botnet*, are used to send a massive volume of requests to a target network or system. These requests are designed to consume the available bandwidth, exhaust processing capacity, or other critical resources. What is the goal? Rendering the target unable to respond to legitimate user requests.

The following list outlines several perspectives on network DDoS attacks as learned from both lamentable and successful personal experiences, along with observing customers continuously evolve their network to new threats:

- **Distributed DDoS Attacks:** These attacks involve a large number of devices or systems distributed across the Internet. Each device in the botnet contributes to the overall attack, making it difficult to neutralize by simply blocking a single source.

- **Volume-Based DDoS Attacks:** These attacks focus on overwhelming the target network with high traffic volume. The goal is to saturate the network's bandwidth, exhaust its resources, and cause disruptions in service.

- **TCP/IP Protocol Exploitation:** These attacks often exploit vulnerabilities in the TCP/IP protocol stack, taking advantage of weaknesses in how devices handle connection requests, open ports, or process packets.

- **Highly Coordinated Botnets:** This network of compromised computers or devices is infected with malware. These devices act in unison to execute the attack, and the real owners of the compromised devices may be unaware of their involvement.

- **Tools to Fight DDoS:** Organizations use various strategies to mitigate the impact of network DDoS attacks, such as deploying intrusion prevention systems (IPSs), firewalls, content delivery networks (CDNs), DDoS scrubbers (cloud-based, on-prem, and most recently container-based, which run on routers themselves), RTBH, and several tools shown in this chapter. These measures aim to filter out malicious traffic and ensure the availability of network resources.

The primary targets for DDoS attackers today include online gaming and gambling platforms, service providers, cloud services (such as AWS and Azure), governments, financial services, and online retailers. The motivations behind these attacks vary, ranging from gaining a competitive advantage to achieving financial gain, disrupting operations, inflicting reputational damage, committing data theft, and even engaging in espionage. With the constant evolution of attack techniques, organizations must implement strong security measures and response mechanisms to effectively protect online services, websites, and other Internet-facing systems from the significant threat posed by network DDoS attacks.

A concerning development of the past few years is the extensive accessibility of tools helping malicious actors in launching potent DDoS attacks effortlessly, rapidly, and at a low cost. Such tools can be purchased or rented with a preconfigured, ready-to-use botnet. Specific organizations can be targeted with readily available public information for constructing a DDoS attack. Thus, attackers no longer need to acquire in-depth computer knowledge (like you are doing now) to defeat sophisticated network defenses. The most disturbing trend is to use DDoS-as-a-Service, where a contractor is engaged to construct and carry out a DDoS attack. Here, you are trying to pass the exam, and a seasoned security wizard is picking the lock to your network...

As attackers continually develop new techniques, organizations need robust security measures and response mechanisms to defend against these disruptive and potentially damaging attacks.

Exam Preparation Tasks

As mentioned in the section "How to Use This Book" in the Introduction, you have a few choices for exam preparation: the exercises here, Chapter 23, "Final Preparation," and the exam simulation questions in the Pearson Test Prep Software Online.

Review All Key Topics

Review the most important topics in this chapter, noted with the Key Topic icon in the margin of the page. Table 17-2 lists the key topic and the page number on which it is found.

Table 17-2   Key Topics for Chapter 17

Key Topic Element	Description	Page Number
List	Rest API best practices	847

Define Key Terms

Define the following key terms from this chapter and check the answers in the glossary:

application programming interfaces (API); authentication, authorization, and accounting (AAA); distributed denial-of-service (DDoS); JSON Web Tokens (JWTs); Management Plane Protection (MPP); OAuth 2.0; Representational State Transfer (REST); Terminal Access Controller Access Control System (TACACS)

Command Reference to Check Your Memory

This section includes the most important configuration and EXEC commands covered in this chapter. You might not need to memorize the complete syntax of every command, but you should be able to remember the basic keywords that are needed.

To test your memory of the commands, cover the right side of Table 17-3 with a piece of paper, read the description on the left side, and then see how much of the command you can remember.

The 350-501 exam focuses on practical, hands-on skills that are used by networking professionals. Therefore, you should be able to identify the commands needed to configure and test. Note that not all commands are fully covered in the chapter, but their presence in the following table should lead you to investigate them further to understand this technology.

Table 17-3   CLI Commands to Know

Task	Command Syntax
Enter control plane host configuration mode	Router(config)# **control-plane host**
Configure an interface to be a management interface, which will accept management protocols, and specify which management protocols are allowed	Router(config-cp-host)# **management-interface** *interface* **allow** *protocols*

Task	Command Syntax
Display information about the management interface	Router# **show management-interface** [*interface* | **protocol** *protocol-name*]
Configure management plane protection to allow and disallow protocols and enter management plane protection configuration mode	RP/0/RP0/CPU0:router(config-ctrl)# **management-plane**
Configure a specific inband interface	RP/0/RP0/CPU0:router(config-mpp-inband)# **interface HundredGigE 0/2/0/10**
Configure the peer IPv4 address in which management traffic is allowed on the interface	RP/0/RP0/CPU0:router(config-telnet-peer)# **address ipv4 10.1.0.0/16**

Review Questions

As a part of the review, we encourage you to provide *a single-sentence answer* (keep your answers as short as possible) to the following questions. If you struggle to complete this answer in a single sentence, this may indicate a lack of clarity or reveal gaps in your understanding. We have constructed these questions to help you consolidate this chapter's information and extract the essence of the covered content.

The answers to these questions appear in Appendix A. For more practice with exam format questions, use the Pearson Test Prep Software Online.

1. Can you discuss the intricate balance between securing the management plane from unauthorized access and maintaining operational efficiency, highlighting potential challenges and trade-offs faced by network administrators in implementing MPP policies across diverse network environments?

2. In the realm of REST API security, can you describe the methods associated with protecting against common threats such as SQL injection, cross-site scripting (XSS), and unauthorized access to sensitive data?

3. In the context of distributed-denial-of-service (DDoS) attacks, can you discuss the evolving tactics used by cybersecurity professionals to stop network attacks?

Bibliography

F. Baker and P. Savola. RFC 3704, *Ingress Filtering for Multihomed Networks*, IETF, https://www.ietf.org/rfc/rfc3704.txt, March 2004.

P. Ferguson and D. Senie. RFC 2827, *Network Ingress Filtering: Defeating Denial of Service Attacks Which Employ IP Source Address Spoofing*, IETF, https://www.ietf.org/rfc/rfc2827.txt, May 2000.

C. Gong and K. Sarac. *IP Traceback Based on Packet Marking and Logging*. https://personal.utdallas.edu/~ksarac/research/publications/ICC05.pdf

IANA. RFC 3330, *Special-Use IPv4 Addresses*, IETF, https://www.ietf.org/rfc/rfc3330.txt, September 2002.

Open Worldwide Application Security Project (OWASP). https://owasp.org/

S. Savage, D. Wetherall, A. Karlin, and T. Anderson. *Practical Network Support for IP Traceback*. SIGCOMM 2000 Conference Presentation. https://cseweb.ucsd.edu/~savage/papers/Sigcomm00.pdf

CHAPTER 18

Securing Data Plane

This chapter covers the following exam topics:

1.7 Implement data plane security

- 1.7.a uRPF
- 1.7.b ACLs
- 1.7.c RTBH
- 1.7.d MACsec

Securing the data plane of routers is paramount in ensuring the reliable and secure transmission of network traffic. This chapter examines essential strategies and best practices for fortifying the data plane against various threats and vulnerabilities. By implementing robust security measures such as access control lists (ACLs), packet filtering, and encryption protocols, network administrators can effectively safeguard against unauthorized access, data breaches, and malicious attacks. Additionally, the chapter explores advanced techniques for traffic monitoring, anomaly detection, and intrusion prevention to bolster the resilience and integrity of the data plane, ultimately ensuring the uninterrupted flow of data.

"Do I Know This Already?" Quiz

The "Do I Know This Already?" quiz allows you to assess whether you should read this entire chapter thoroughly or jump to the "Exam Preparation Tasks" section. If you are in doubt about your answers to these questions or your own assessment of your knowledge of the topics, read the entire chapter. Table 18-1 lists the major headings in this chapter and their corresponding "Do I Know This Already?" quiz questions. You can find the answers in Appendix A, "Answers to the 'Do I Know This Already?' Quizzes and Review Questions."

Table 18-1 "Do I Know This Already?" Section-to-Question Mapping

Foundation Topics Section	Questions
Unicast Reverse Path Forwarding (uRPF)	1
Access Control Lists (ACLs)	2
Remote Triggered Black Hole (RTBH) Filtering	3–4
Media Access Control Security (MACsec)	5

CAUTION The goal of self-assessment is to gauge your mastery of the topics in this chapter. If you do not know the answer to a question or are only partially sure of the answer, you should mark that question as wrong for purposes of the self-assessment. Giving yourself credit for an answer you correctly guess skews your self-assessment results and might provide you with a false sense of security.

1. Which of the following is a valid uRPF operational mode?

   a. Stringent

   b. Restricted

   c. Loose

   d. Unrestricted

2. Which of the following scenarios is the most likely reason for legitimate traffic being blocked when transit ACLs are implemented on a network?

   a. The transit ACLs are configured to allow only TCP traffic, inadvertently blocking all UDP and ICMP traffic.

   b. The transit ACLs are applied to the outbound interface rather than the inbound, causing the ACL to be ignored.

   c. The transit ACLs include an explicit "permit all" statement at the end, rendering the ACL ineffective.

   d. The transit ACLs are placed on the wrong device in the network, leading to the blockage of local traffic instead of transit traffic.

3. RTBH relies on which of the following?

   a. BGP Flowspec

   b. BGP communities

   c. BGP distribute-lists

   d. BGPsec

4. Which of the following are RTBH flavors? (Select all that apply.)

   a. Source-based

   b. Prefix-based

   c. Destination-based

   d. Trigger-based

5. Which of the following best describes the function of MACsec?

   a. Encrypting Layer 2 frames

   b. Securing traffic at Layer 3

   c. Encrypting data payloads at the application layer

   d. Implementing IPsec for Layer 2 security

Foundation Topics

With the control and management planes out of the way, we can focus on securing the forwarding plane—the one that carries end-user and customer traffic.

Unicast Reverse Path Forwarding (uRPF)

Unicast Reverse Path Forwarding (uRPF) used to be one of my favorite tools to use. The issue is not that it has lost popularity; rather, in larger networks, intricate routing is often in place, and you should strive to avoid any disruptions. It is still a very useful tool, but you will understand my perspective once we go through our example.

uRPF can prevent malicious traffic from entering the network by verifying whether there is a route to the source of the incoming packets. It works exceptionally well by discarding packets with spoofed IP addresses. Attackers construct packets with source addresses that are different from the source of the sender; this hides their identity. The crafted packet looks as though it came from a legitimate network, while the response will arrive somewhere else. If your network is "somewhere else," you have just become the victim of an attack! It looks as though legitimate networks are sending an extraordinary volume of traffic to your network. If the TCP protocol is used, the three-way-handshake can somewhat limit the potential damage because it will prevent sessions from being established. In the case of connectionless UDP, massive volumes of traffic can be sent to unprotected devices.

uRPF reduces the forwarding of IP packets that might be spoofing an address. Based on RFC 2827 and RFC 3704, uRPF can verify that the source IP address of the incoming packet has a resolvable route in the routing table.

How does uRPF make this distinction? The decision is based on entries in the receiving router's Forwarding Information Base (FIB). For uRPF to work, you need to enable Cisco Express Forwarding, or CEF (on by default now), on the router. There are three operational modes, each achieving different objectives:

- **Loose Mode (Loose uRPF):** This mode is more lenient compared to strict mode. In this mode, the router checks whether the source address exists in the routing table, but it doesn't necessarily need to match the interface from which the packet was received. This mode is suitable for multihomed scenarios where asymmetric routing is common.

- **Strict Mode (Strict uRPF):** In this mode, a router checks whether the source address of the incoming packet exists in the routing table and matches the interface from which the packet was received. If the check fails, the packet is discarded. Strict uRPF is effective but may pose challenges in asymmetric routing scenarios (and that is where you have to be careful with it, as I mentioned). I (Brad) frequently see it being used on access-facing ports.

- **VRF Mode (VRF uRPF):** Virtual Routing and Forwarding (VRF) uRPF is used in environments where multiple routing instances or virtual networks (that is, VRFs) coexist. Each VRF operates independently, and uRPF can be applied within each VRF to validate source addresses within their respective routing contexts.

These uRPF modes allow network administrators to choose the level of strictness in verifying source addresses, providing flexibility based on the specific requirements and characteristics of the network.

As stated previously, the best way to understand something is to break it down to its most basic elements, and we plan to do just that. To do so, let's examine Figure 18-1.

In this figure, R2 receives a packet destined to its loopback interface, and the administrator has turned on the uRPF feature in loose mode. R2 looks in its forwarding table (CEF) and asks a single question that I would like you to remember: Is the source IP address in my FIB?

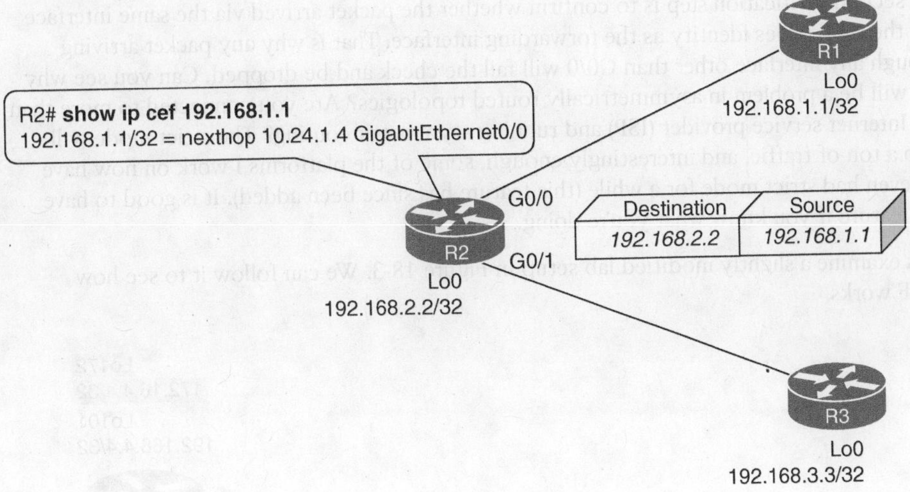

Figure 18-1 *uRPF Loose Mode*

With this feature turned on, if there was no entry in the FIB table (i.e., the route for this network was missing, relying on a default route to return the traffic), R2 would drop this packet. In our scenario, there is a CEF entry to the source of the packet pointing to interface G0/0. R2 only cares if there is an entry. It doesn't matter where this packet came from (R1, R3, R100…). There is a CEF entry, so this traffic is assumed legitimate.

Now let's examine Figure 18-2, where the administrator has turned on uRPF in strict mode.

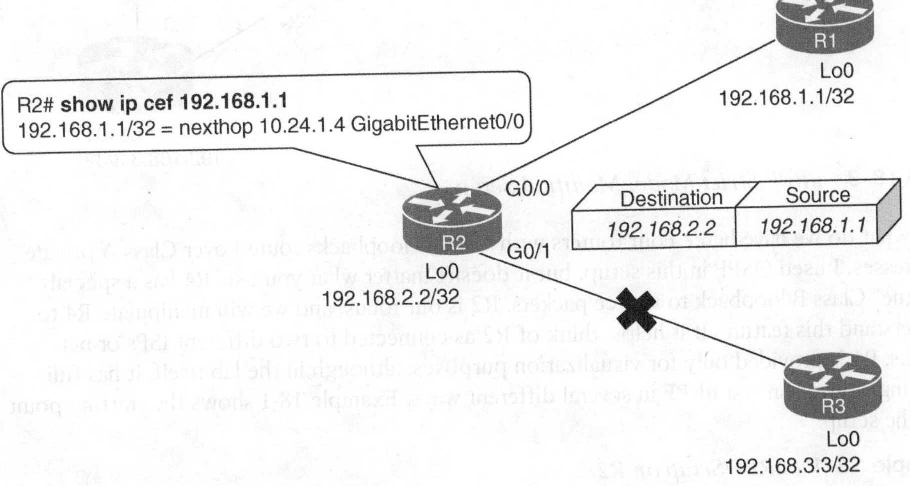

Figure 18-2 *uRPF Strict Mode*

What has changed here from the previous figure? Our router is asking additional questions:

Is the source IP address in my FIB?

Is the source reachable through the interface that the packet arrived through?

The second verification step is to confirm whether the packet arrived via the same interface that the CEF tables identify as the forwarding interface. That is why any packet arriving through any interface other than G0/0 will fail the check and be dropped. Can you see why this will be a problem in asymmetrically routed topologies? Are you connected to more than one Internet service provider (ISP) and running asymmetric routing? The strict mode will drop a ton of traffic, and interestingly enough, some of the platforms I work on now have not even had strict mode for a while (this feature has since been added). It is good to have this feature if you know what you're doing.

Let's examine a slightly modified lab setup in Figure 18-3. We can follow it to see how uRPF works.

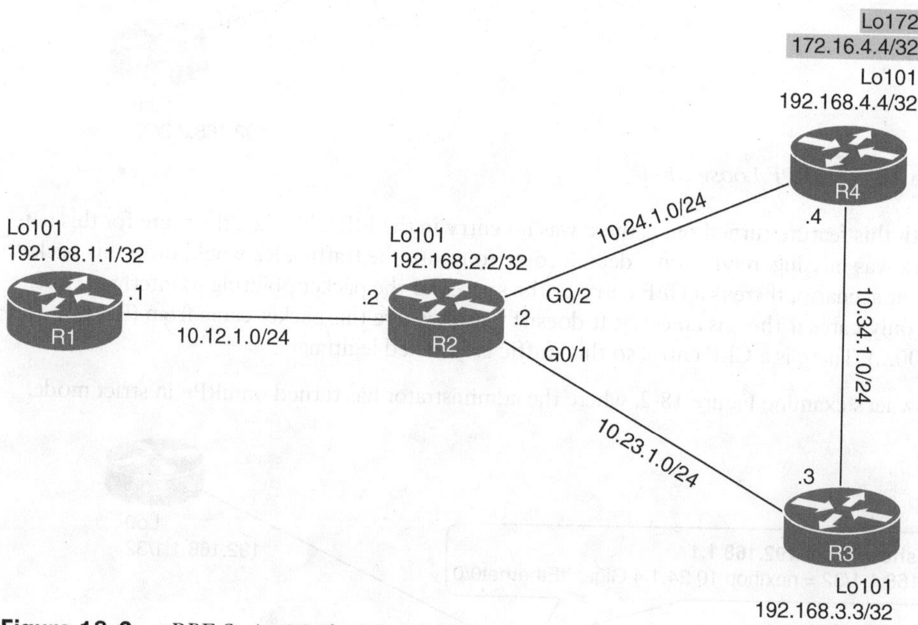

Figure 18-3 *uRPF Strict Mode: Modified Setup*

So, what do we have here? Four routers with Class C loopbacks routed over Class A private addresses. I used OSPF in this setup, but it doesn't matter what you use. R4 has a special "rogue" Class B loopback to source packets. R2 is our focus, and we will manipulate R4 to understand this feature. If it helps, think of R2 as connected to two different ISPs or networks. R1 is provided only for visualization purposes, although in the lab itself, it has full routing, so we can test uRPF in several different ways. Example 18-1 shows the starting point for the setup.

Example 18-1 *uRPF Setup on R2*

```
R2# show ip interface brief | exclude una
Interface           IP-Address      OK? Method Status        Protocol
GigabitEthernet0/0  10.12.1.2       YES TFTP   up            up
GigabitEthernet0/1  10.23.1.2       YES TFTP   up            up
GigabitEthernet0/2  10.24.1.2       YES TFTP   up            up
Loopback101         192.168.2.2     YES TFTP   up            up
```

```
R2# show ip route
Codes: L - local, C - connected, S - static, R - RIP, M - mobile, B - BGP
       D - EIGRP, EX - EIGRP external, O - OSPF, IA - OSPF inter area
       N1 - OSPF NSSA external type 1, N2 - OSPF NSSA external type 2
       E1 - OSPF external type 1, E2 - OSPF external type 2
       i - IS-IS, su - IS-IS summary, L1 - IS-IS level-1, L2 - IS-IS level-2
       ia - IS-IS inter area, * - candidate default, U - per-user static route
       o - ODR, P - periodic downloaded static route, H - NHRP, l - LISP
       a - application route
       + - replicated route, % - next hop override, p - overrides from PfR

Gateway of last resort is 10.24.1.4 to network 0.0.0.0

S*    0.0.0.0/0 [1/0] via 10.24.1.4
      10.0.0.0/8 is variably subnetted, 7 subnets, 2 masks
C        10.12.1.0/24 is directly connected, GigabitEthernet0/0
L        10.12.1.2/32 is directly connected, GigabitEthernet0/0
C        10.23.1.0/24 is directly connected, GigabitEthernet0/1
L        10.23.1.2/32 is directly connected, GigabitEthernet0/1
C        10.24.1.0/24 is directly connected, GigabitEthernet0/2
L        10.24.1.2/32 is directly connected, GigabitEthernet0/2
O        10.34.1.0/24 [110/2] via 10.24.1.4, 02:01:17, GigabitEthernet0/2
                      [110/2] via 10.23.1.3, 00:00:37, GigabitEthernet0/1
      192.168.1.0/32 is subnetted, 1 subnets
O        192.168.1.1 [110/2] via 10.12.1.1, 02:01:37, GigabitEthernet0/0
      192.168.2.0/32 is subnetted, 1 subnets
C        192.168.2.2 is directly connected, Loopback101
      192.168.3.0/32 is subnetted, 1 subnets
O        192.168.3.3 [110/2] via 10.23.1.3, 00:00:37, GigabitEthernet0/1
      192.168.4.0/32 is subnetted, 1 subnets
O        192.168.4.4 [110/2] via 10.24.1.4, 02:01:17, GigabitEthernet0/2
R2# ping 172.16.4.4
Type escape sequence to abort.
Sending 5, 100-byte ICMP Echos to 172.16.4.4, timeout is 2 seconds:
!!!!!
Success rate is 100 percent (5/5), round-trip min/avg/max = 2/2/3 ms
```

Of particular interest to us are interfaces GigabitEthernet0/1 and GigabitEthernet0/2, since they lead to R4 and R3. Note that we have full reachability between Class C loopbacks, but the route to the "rogue" 172.16.4.4/32 is not explicitly present. In this case, the default route takes care of reaching this prefix. Still fully reachable, but not via OSPF. Example 18-2 demonstrates pre-uRPF reachability.

Example 18-2 *uRPF Setup on R3 and R4*

```
R3# show ip interface brief | exclude unassigned
Interface           IP-Address     OK? Method Status     Protocol
GigabitEthernet0/0     10.34.1.3    YES TFTP   up           up
GigabitEthernet0/1     10.23.1.3    YES TFTP   up           up
Loopback101           192.168.3.3   YES TFTP   up           up

R4# show ip interface brief | exclude unassigned
Interface           IP-Address     OK? Method Status     Protocol
GigabitEthernet0/0     10.24.1.4    YES TFTP   up           up
GigabitEthernet0/1     10.34.1.4    YES TFTP   up           up
Loopback101           192.168.4.4   YES TFTP   up         up
Loopback172           172.16.4.4    YES manual up         up
R4# ping 192.168.2.2 source looopback101
Type escape sequence to abort.
Sending 5, 100-byte ICMP Echos to 192.168.2.2, timeout is 2 seconds:
Packet sent with a source address of 192.168.4.4
!!!!!
Success rate is 100 percent (5/5), round-trip min/avg/max = 2/2/3 ms
R4# ping 192.168.2.2 source loopback172
Type escape sequence to abort.
Sending 5, 100-byte ICMP Echos to 192.168.2.2, timeout is 2 seconds:
Packet sent with a source address of 172.16.4.4
!!J!!
Success rate is 100 percent (5/5), round-trip min/avg/max = 1/1/3 ms
R4#
```

On R3 and R4, we see the links completing this triangle-shaped network, with the second
octet representing the connection between routers (10.**34**.1.3 = connection between routers
R3 and R4, etc.). Notice our rogue Loopback172 as well on R4, since we plan to test uRPF
for packets sourced from this interface. Full reachability exists because we can ping R2. Note
that we sourced our pings from different interfaces—Loopback101, which is present in R2's
CEF table due to its OSPF origin, and Loopback172, which is neither in R2's CEF tables
nor explicitly known. Nevertheless, the default static route on R2 takes care of reaching the
172.16.4.4/32 prefix. Now, it's time to set up uRPF, as demonstrated in Example 18-3.

Example 18-3 *uRPF Setup*

```
R2# show running-config interface gigabitEthernet 0/2
Building configuration...
Current configuration : 130 bytes
!
interface GigabitEthernet0/2
 description to
 ip address 10.24.1.2 255.255.255.0
 duplex auto
```

```
 speed auto
 media-type rj45
end
R2# configure terminal
Enter configuration commands, one per line. End with CNTL/Z.
R2(config)# interface gigabitEthernet 0/2
R2(config-if)# ip verify unicast source reachable-via ?
 any Source is reachable via any interface
 rx  Source is reachable via interface on which packet was received
R2(config-if)# ip verify unicast source reachable-via any ?
 <1-199>     IP access list (standard or extended)
 <1300-2699>  IP expanded access list (standard or extended)
 allow-default  Allow default route to match when checking source address
 allow-self-ping Allow router to ping itself (opens vulnerability in
         verification)
 <cr>      <cr>
R2(config-if)# ip verify unicast source reachable-via any
R2(config-if)#
```

Let's look at the interface we are about to configure and rapidly get to the fork in the road—**any** and **rx** options to enable uRPF loose or strict modes, respectively. Here, we pick the first option and check what's behind it. We can see the access list and other options we are not interested in at the moment, since we are after a basic understanding of how uRPF functions. Interface GigabigEthernet0/2 now has uRPF loose mode on the interface leading to R4. What do you believe should happen on R4 now? It's a good idea to think through what will happen before consulting the output in Example 18-4.

Example 18-4   *uRPF R4 Verification*

```
R4# ping 192.168.2.2 source loopback101
Type escape sequence to abort.
Sending 5, 100-byte ICMP Echos to 192.168.2.2, timeout is 2 seconds:
Packet sent with a source address of 192.168.4.4
!!!!!
Success rate is 100 percent (5/5), round-trip min/avg/max = 2/2/4 ms
R4# ping 192.168.2.2 source loopback172
Type escape sequence to abort.
Sending 5, 100-byte ICMP Echos to 192.168.2.2, timeout is 2 seconds:
Packet sent with a source address of 172.16.4.4
.....
Success rate is 0 percent (0/5)
R4#
```

If you followed the explanation, you can see that the rogue network—which is not present in R2's CEF table—fails to receive R2's replies, whereas the network known via OSPF has no issue. Same commands, same "everything" on R4. I just "up-arrowed" on the command line.

Are you curious about what is taking place on R2? I don't know about you, but the mystery surrounding R2's thinking beckons me like an unsolved equation. (#MathHumor. #EyeRoll.) Example 18-5 reveals the reason behind the unsuccessful pings.

Example 18-5 *uRPF R4 Verification*

```
R2(config-if)# end
R2# show ip cef 192.168.4.4
192.168.4.4/32
  nexthop 10.24.1.4 GigabitEthernet0/2
R2# show ip cef 172.16.4.4
0.0.0.0/0
  nexthop 10.24.1.4 GigabitEthernet0/2
R2#
```

The rogue prefix is missing from R2's CEF table, and R2 is not interested in networks that are outside of its forwarding table. uRPF works.

Pop-quiz time: Can you fix this "problem" without configuring anything on R2? (My side goal for this book is to promote "a-few-steps-ahead" thinking, fostering a mindset reminiscent of strategic chess methodology.) Can you think of a way to resolve this by only configuring R4?

I'm not suggesting acting out a hacker mindset, but knowing exactly how the technology works (you're getting a good idea now) gives birth to ideas on how to influence router decisions. Here's my suggestion: R4 advertises the following network over OSPF. Do you think if we were to add the rogue network to this section, we could make R2 return replies to my ICMP requests? I hope you answered yes. Example 18-6 provides the verification.

Example 18-6 *uRPF R4 Changes R2's Mindset*

```
R4# show running-config | section ospf
router ospf 1
 network 10.0.0.0 0.255.255.255 area 0
 network 192.168.0.0 0.0.255.255 area 0
R4# configure terminal
Enter configuration commands, one per line. End with CNTL/Z.
R4(config)# router ospf 1
R4(config-router)# network 172.16.0.0 0.0.255.255 area 0
R4(config-router)# end
R4# ping 192.168.2.2 so loopback172
Type escape sequence to abort.
Sending 5, 100-byte ICMP Echos to 192.168.2.2, timeout is 2 seconds:
Packet sent with a source address of 172.16.4.4
!!!!!
Success rate is 100 percent (5/5), round-trip min/avg/max = 1/2/3 ms
R4#


R2# show ip cef 172.16.4.4
172.16.4.4/32
  nexthop 10.24.1.4 GigabitEthernet0/2
R2#
```

This approach works because R4's OSPF update populated R2's CEF table; the reason is that R2 does not restrict which networks it accepts in our scenario, and the rogue network immediately shows up in the forwarding table.

Are you ready to break this again? I am. Enter uRPF strict mode. Recall that we have the additional criteria of whether the route back lies through the arrival path. At the moment, it does. Even if we were to enable uRPF strict mode on R2 now, the packets would arrive through the same GigabitEthernet0/2 interface. We need to change this, and to this end, we now will enlist router R3's assistance without even touching any of its configurations. I propose adding a static route going to R3. R3 will then forward it to R2, which will, in turn, use the same GigabitEthernet0/2 interface to respond—and voila, we've got ourselves some genuine asymmetric routing!

Example 18-7 verifies this approach from both sides—a double hop through R3 and a direct hop from R2. Because we are still using the loose mode on R2, regardless of the fact that R2 receives the packet on GigabitEthernet0/1 interface, it replies because loose mode only looks for a CEF entry, not the forwarding interface.

Example 18-7   *uRPF R3 Reroutes R4's Traffic*

```
R4# configure terminal
Enter configuration commands, one per line. End with CNTL/Z.
R4(config)# ip route 192.168.2.2 255.255.255.255 10.34.1.3
R4(config)# do trace 192.168.2.2 source 172.16.4.4
Type escape sequence to abort.
Tracing the route to 192.168.2.2
VRF info: (vrf in name/id, vrf out name/id)
  1 10.34.1.3 2 msec 2 msec 2 msec
  2 10.23.1.2 2 msec 3 msec *
R4(config)#

R2# trace 172.16.4.4
Type escape sequence to abort.
Tracing the route to 172.16.4.4
VRF info: (vrf in name/id, vrf out name/id)
  1 10.24.1.4 2 msec * 2 msec
R2#
```

It's time to lock down R2, so let's configure both our "Internet-facing" GigabitEthernet0/1 and GigabitEthernet0/2 for uRPF strict mode, as demonstrated in Example 18-8.

Example 18-8   *uRPF Strict Mode Enabled on R2*

```
R2# configure terminal
Enter configuration commands, one per line. End with CNTL/Z.
R2(config)# interface gigabitEthernet 0/1
R2(config-if)# ip verify unicast source reachable-via ?
  any Source is reachable via any interface
  rx  Source is reachable via interface on which packet was received
```

```
R2(config-if)# ip verify unicast source reachable-via rx
R2(config-if)# interface gigabitEthernet 0/2
R2(config-if)# ip verify unicast source reachable-via rx
R2(config-if)#
```

In Example 18-9, we are at the configuration fork again and decide to take the other road—enabling uRPF strict mode on both interfaces. Do you think R2 stopped this asymmetric routing behavior? Let's see.

Example 18-9 *R4 Traffic Fails*

```
R4(config)# do ping 192.168.2.2 so 172.16.4.4
Type escape sequence to abort.
Sending 5, 100-byte ICMP Echos to 192.168.2.2, timeout is 2 seconds:
Packet sent with a source address of 172.16.4.4
.....
Success rate is 0 percent (0/5)
R4(config)#
```

uRPF blocked this traffic. Can we validate that the feature is working when we remove asymmetric routing? you ask. I like the way you're thinking, since I was going to do this anyway (see Example 18-10).

Example 18-10 *R4 Traffic Succeeds*

```
R4(config)# no ip route 192.168.2.2 255.255.255.255 10.34.1.3
R4(config)# do ping 192.168.2.2 so 172.16.4.4
Type escape sequence to abort.
Sending 5, 100-byte ICMP Echos to 192.168.2.2, timeout is 2 seconds:
Packet sent with a source address of 172.16.4.4
!!!!!
Success rate is 100 percent (5/5), round-trip min/avg/max = 2/2/4 ms
R4(config)#
```

Are we done? Almost. Don't forget to fully verify this on R2, as demonstrated in Example 18-11. Five drops on GigabitEthernet0/1, none on GigabitEthernet0/2.

Example 18-11 *R2 uRPF Interface Verification*

```
R2# show ip interface gigabitEthernet 0/1 | include verif
  IP verify source reachable-via RX
    5 verification drops
    0 suppressed verification drops
    0 verification drop-rate
R2# show ip interface gigabitEthernet 0/2 | include verif
  IP verify source reachable-via RX
    0 verification drops
    0 suppressed verification drops
    0 verification drop-rate
```

```
R2# show ip cef switching statistics feature
IPv4 CEF input features:
    Feature          Drop   Consume    Punt Punt2Host Gave route
    uRPF               5       0          0    0       0
Total                  5       0          0    0       0
IPv4 CEF output features:
    Feature          Drop   Consume    Punt Punt2Host New i/f
Total                  0       0          0    0       0
IPv4 CEF post-encap features:
    Feature          Drop   Consume    Punt Punt2Host New i/f
Total                  0       0          0    0       0
IPv4 CEF for us features:
    Feature          Drop   Consume    Punt Punt2Host New i/f
Total                  0       0          0    0       0
IPv4 CEF punt features:
    Feature          Drop   Consume    Punt Punt2Host New i/f
Total                  0       0          0    0       0
IPv4 CEF local features:
    Feature          Drop   Consume    Punt Punt2Host Gave route
Total                  0       0          0    0       0
R2#
```

IOS XR works the same way.

We have not yet discussed the third uRPF option: the VRF mode. The VRF mode simply verifies that the forwarding considers the virtual forwarding instance from which they arrived.

Homework? I propose two tasks:

1. Configure this scenario in VRF mode in your lab and turn in your work for extra credit.

2. Can you figure out the purpose of the **allow-default** option in Example 18-3?

Access Control Lists (ACLs)

What do access control lists have to do with data plane protection? Well, a lot.

Infrastructure access control lists (iACLs) are what typically we think of when discussing ACLs. They generally focus on filtering traffic destined for the network itself.

The regulation of network traffic can also be achieved through the utilization of transit access control lists (tACLs). tACLs offer filtering capabilities for traffic passing through the network (data plane). Employing tACLs proves advantageous when there is a need to filter specific groups of devices or control transit traffic. While the conventional approach for such filtering involves firewalls, there are scenarios where executing these filtering functions directly on a Cisco IOS XE device within the network becomes advantageous, especially in the absence of a dedicated firewall. Transit ACLs also serve as a suitable platform for implementing static anti-spoofing measures.

Thus, on routers at the edge of your network, you should drop traffic that does not belong on your network. Think of this function as the first line of defense against invalid traffic coming from the Internet. Can you think of the types of traffic that should not enter your network externally? Here is a strategy to consider:

1. **RFC 1918 Networks:** Why should private external addresses enter your network? They are not routable on the Internet, right? (Do not accept this traffic.)

2. **RFC 3330 Addresses:** Class D and Class E addresses, among others (do you remember what these are from your CCNA days? It might be a good time to consult the RFC), address source ranges I do not want to see. (Do not accept this traffic.)

3. **RFC 2827 Anti-Spoofing:** Your own address space must never become the source of packets from outside your BGP autonomous system (AS). (Do not accept this traffic.)

4. Examples of traffic you might need:

   - ICMP from service provider addresses

   - Routing protocols coming from outside of your network

   - **IPsec** for tunnel terminations

   - External permitted traffic to your internal protected resources (DMZ/VPN)

   - External permitted return traffic for your internally sourced traffic

5. Drop everything else.

Here's your homework: Can you think of why you should or should not use this approach on the largest network you have ever worked on? This is a good practice to cultivate critical thinking and consider multiple dimensions of network security. By leveraging tACLs, network administrators can fine-tune traffic regulation based on specific criteria, fostering a proactive approach to security. This not only enhances the network's resilience but also provides a versatile solution, particularly in scenarios where dedicated firewalls might be absent. Embracing such practices encourages a comprehensive understanding of network dynamics, empowering professionals to make informed decisions and bolster the overall security posture.

Remote Triggered Black Hole (RTBH) Filtering

We are at the last stop before we complete the security section of the book. I have put in the time to make it just as exciting as some our previous setups. Wait…Or are you here because you have opted for the blue cable? A wise decision, I must admit, offering a sense of comfort and much needed history. However, before facing the networking exam, you must also grasp the red cable to uncover the truth behind the far more powerful Flowspec. But blue cable it is…

Remote Triggered Black Hole (RTBH) has been around for a long time. I used it when I first started my networking career. It is a decent vendor-agnostic solution for mitigating DDoS attacks. It relies on BGP and BGP policies for its implementation. It provides a way to drop malicious traffic based on a *victim's destination* or *attacker's source*. I suggest you reread the preceding sentence, because it clearly defines the difference between the two available implementations:

- Remote Triggered Black Hole (destination-based)

- Source-Based Remote Triggered Black Hole (source-based)

Let's start with the first approach. Based on RFC 3382, all the way back in 2004, destination-based RTBH works on the principle of advertising a prefix with a BGP community attribute (RTBH) that causes the edge of the network to block traffic destined for this prefix. Figure 18-4 shows the diagram we will use to learn RTBH.

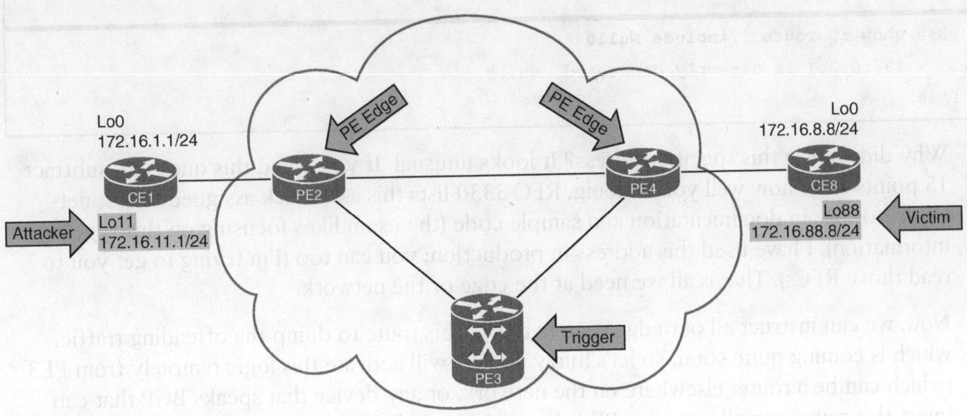

Figure 18-4   *RTBH Reference Diagram*

In Figure 18-4, the service provider network in the middle runs iBGP over an IS-IS underlay. It transports routes between customers CE1 and CE8. There is end-to-end reachability, as validated in Example 18-12. Notice that we're sourcing pings from two networks, one of which will soon have an attacker on it.

Example 18-12   *Network Is Quiet*

```
CE1# ping 172.16.88.8 source loopback0
Type escape sequence to abort.
Sending 5, 100-byte ICMP Echos to 172.16.88.8, timeout is 2 seconds:
Packet sent with a source address of 172.16.1.1
!!!!!
Success rate is 100 percent (5/5), round-trip min/avg/max = 1/2/3 ms
CE1# ping 172.16.88.8 source loopback11
Type escape sequence to abort.
Sending 5, 100-byte ICMP Echos to 172.16.88.8, timeout is 2 seconds:
Packet sent with a source address of 172.16.11.1
!!!!!
Success rate is 100 percent (5/5), round-trip min/avg/max = 1/1/2 ms
CE1#
```

Luckily for us, we are prepared, so let me show you what we've set up. At the edges of the network (Routers PE2 and PE4), we have preconfigured a route that can dump all traffic. Example 18-13 shows them verified two different ways, but this "magic" route is configured identically on both routers.

Example 18-13 *Bit Bucket Routes Configured*

```
PE2# show running-config | include Null0
ip route 192.0.2.1 255.255.255.255 Null0
PE2#
```

```
PE4# show ip route | include Null0
S    192.0.2.1 is directly connected, Null0
PE4#
```

Why did we use this specific address? It looks unusual. If you asked this question, subtract 15 points from how well you're doing. RFC 3330 lists this as a block assigned to test networks for use in documentation and sample code (the exam likes focusing on this type of information). I have used this address in production; you can too (I'm trying to get you to read those RFCs). That is all we need at the edge of the network.

Now, we can instruct all our edge routers to use this route to dump the offending traffic, which is coming quite soon, so let's hurry up. We will activate this logic remotely from PE3 (which can be a router elsewhere on the network, or any device that speaks BGP that can inject this route into all our edge PEs). Example 18-14 kicks off the exciting part of the configuration.

Example 18-14 *Trigger Router Configuration on IOS XR*

```
RP/0/RP0/CPU0:PE3# show running-config
! Output omitted for brevity
route-policy RTBH
 if tag is 666 then
  set next-hop 192.0.2.1
  set local-preference 1000
  set community (no-export)
  set origin igp
 endif
end-policy
router bgp 305
 bgp router-id 10.1.100.3
 address-family ipv4 unicast
  redistribute static route-policy RTBH
 !
 neighbor 10.1.100.2
  remote-as 305
  update-source Loopback0
  address-family ipv4 unicast
  !
 !
 neighbor 10.1.100.4
  remote-as 305
  update-source Loopback0
```

```
address-family ipv4 unicast
 !
 !
!
end
```

We have set up a trigger policy that will signal to our network to drop traffic destined to the future victim. Presently, there is no victim. The policy states, "any route tagged with a community value of 666, set its next hop as the bit bucket magic address, set the highest local preference, do not export this route outside of the BGP domain, and set its origin as IGP." We will import this policy into BGP's address-family IPv4 unicast, and BGP will disseminate this to its neighbors. (IOS XR sends BGP communities, by default, in IBGP sessions, not EBGP. Did you know this? Watch those exam points.) On a production network, please do what makes sense (using route reflectors, etc.). Here, I'm trying to keep things simple so that you can learn fast. We're ready. Fortunately, we are just in time because your phone is ringing. It's the helpdesk.

Back to Figure 18-4, where you figure out that customer CE8, highlighted in gray, is unfortunate to have the attacker who picked out one of CE8's networks from subnet 172.16.88.0/24 as a victim. Customer CE8 notifies you that the volume of traffic to the servers on the subnet is unsustainable, and the link between PE4 and CE8 is peaking in bandwidth. A quick look at your internal network monitoring graphs validates the problem. What are we to do? I don't know about you, but at least two thoughts flash through my mind. First, I must help the customer. Second, I would like to get this volume of traffic off my network; it wastes my bandwidth too!

Now, it's time to use our trigger to signal to the network to drop this traffic, as shown in Example 18-15.

Example 18-15 *Trigger Router in Action*

```
RP/0/RP0/CPU0:PE3# configure
Tue Jan 30 23:28:05.323 UTC
RP/0/RP0/CPU0:PE3(config)# router static
RP/0/RP0/CPU0:PE3(config-static)# address-family ipv4 unicast
RP/0/RP0/CPU0:PE3(config-static-afi)# 172.16.88.0/24 null 0 tag 666
RP/0/RP0/CPU0:PE3(config-static-afi)# root
RP/0/RP0/CPU0:PE3(config)# show
Tue Jan 30 23:28:51.650 UTC
Building configuration...
!! IOS XR Configuration 7.7.1
router static
 address-family ipv4 unicast
  172.16.88.0/24 Null0 tag 666
 !
!
end
RP/0/RP0/CPU0:PE3(config)# commit
Tue Jan 30 23:29:01.111 UTC
RP/0/RP0/CPU0:PE3(config)#
```

That was fast! Let's pause time here. We'll get back to the attack. We simply created a static route to Null0, tagged it with 666, quickly checked what we are about to drop on the network, and committed the configuration.

Next, let's look at the results in Example 18-16.

Example 18-16 *CE1 Verified*

```
CE1# ping 172.16.88.8 source loopback11
Type escape sequence to abort.
Sending 5, 100-byte ICMP Echos to 172.16.88.8, timeout is 2 seconds:
Packet sent with a source address of 172.16.11.1
U.U.U
Success rate is 0 percent (0/5)
CE1# ping 172.16.88.8 source loopback0
Type escape sequence to abort.
Sending 5, 100-byte ICMP Echos to 172.16.88.8, timeout is 2 seconds:
Packet sent with a source address of 172.16.1.1
U.U.U
Success rate is 0 percent (0/5)
CE1#
```

Success! We are dropping traffic closest to the attacker on CE1 from the attacker's subnet. But wait...the other subnet (172.16.1.0/24 with no attackers on it) on CE1 is affected as well! Hang on. What is going on? Example 18-17 examines this further.

Example 18-17 *CE1 Verification Continues*

```
CE1# ping 172.16.8.8 source loopback0
Type escape sequence to abort.
Sending 5, 100-byte ICMP Echos to 172.16.8.8, timeout is 2 seconds:
Packet sent with a source address of 172.16.1.1
!!!!!
Success rate is 100 percent (5/5), round-trip min/avg/max = 1/2/3 ms
CE1# ping 172.16.8.8 source loopback11
Type escape sequence to abort.
Sending 5, 100-byte ICMP Echos to 172.16.8.8, timeout is 2 seconds:
Packet sent with a source address of 172.16.11.1
!!!!!
Success rate is 100 percent (5/5), round-trip min/avg/max = 1/1/2 ms
CE1#
```

Quick changes of destination CE8's network reveals that CE1 can reach 172.16.8.0/24, including the attacker's subnet! Now you're beginning to get the picture of what is going on. Let's jump on any of the edge PEs and get the full picture. PE2 is closest to where I am heading, as shown in Example 18-18.

Example 18-18 *PE2 Verified*

```
PE2# show ip bgp 172.16.88.0
BGP routing table entry for 172.16.88.0/24, version 21
Paths: (1 available, best #1, table default, not advertised to EBGP peer)
 Not advertised to any peer
 Refresh Epoch 1
 Local, (received & used)
  192.0.2.1 from 10.1.100.3 (10.1.100.3)
    Origin IGP, metric 0, localpref 1000, valid, internal, best
    Community: no-export
    rx pathid: 0, tx pathid: 0x0
    Updated on Jan 30 2024 23:29:02 UTC
PE2# show ip route 172.16.88.0
Routing entry for 172.16.88.0/24
 Known via "bgp 305", distance 200, metric 0, type internal
 Last update from 192.0.2.1 00:18:36 ago
 Routing Descriptor Blocks:
 * 192.0.2.1, from 10.1.100.3, 00:18:36 ago
    opaque_ptr 0x7F16EDB8C4F0
    Route metric is 0, traffic share count is 1
    AS Hops 0
    MPLS label: none
PE2#
```

Now the puzzle is complete: edge routers send all traffic destined to 172.16.88.0/24 into a Remote Triggered Black Hole (RTBH). Even PE4 follows this behavior. So, do you call this success? You tell me. CE8's attack has stopped, and the traffic between PE4 and CE8 is back to normal. Yet no one can reach 172.16.88.0/24 network. There may have been other servers on that network the attacker was not touching, but we just took them offline when we configured the /24 prefix. We completed the attack (!), knocking the customer's services offline. A good attorney could pin us as accomplices, since we helped the attacker. I sure hope those were not servers taking credit card transactions, because I am not interested in updating my resume yet.

Jokes aside, destination-based RTBH is not a bad strategy when you wish to stop an attack on a single IP address or prefix. But even at that—we just took down the victim—what does the victim do next? Get a different IP address? This may create more problems than he has now. How do I know? I've done it before myself. Who knows who else we took offline? I hope you understand destination-based RTBH now. Let's fast-forward here: once you remove the route from the signaling router, the routes will disappear from the edge routers.

What about source-based RTBH? The networking community needed something not so heavy-handed as we just experienced. In 2009, RFC 5635 introduced a process whereby a route with an RTBH community matching the attacker's source address could be distributed to all edge devices. The logic is the same. See if you can follow it:

1.   Instead of using the victim's destination address, the attacker's source address is used.

2. Once the edge router receives the route, an import policy would change the route's next hop to Null0 (discard), just like in the previous example.

3. Now that the source is known at the edge, the uRPF strict mode technique (we shared earlier) drops the attacker's traffic. How? The attacker's unicast traffic fails the RFP check because it now points to the network's internal bit bucket. Clever.

What do you think? Well, it's better than dropping all traffic like we did in the destination-based example. What's not to like? you ask. Get a thick pad and long pencil. Many times, the attacker's source address is not known (remember me trying to chase this with an ISP?). Many times, there are too many sources, so how do you block them all? Scale is definitely an issue. What about NAT or Carrier-Grade NAT (CGNAT)—with real source addresses hidden by these widely deployed techniques, and you have just blocked legitimate users from someone's system? Would you like to take this up a notch? The source address you blocked is a legitimate public DNS or NTP or whatever address used for services...

Here's my favorite: at which edge locations do you deploy uRPF? If you answered "all," you just broke many other applications and multihomed networks with asymmetric routing. Minus another 15 points. So, things are not that simple. What would I suggest if this source-based RTBH were the only tool at my disposal? I would enable uRPF at the locations that are more likely to see this attack. What does that mean? Exactly.

Opinion time. What do I dislike about both of these approaches (D-RTBH and S-RTBH)? Aside from the technical limitations I've already discussed, consider the operational complexity of these approaches. Let's say you've discovered your network is under attack. What comes next? Think about your network right now. Are any of these mechanisms in place? Do you have to call your provider's helpdesk number or reach out through a website to report the issue? What is their response time? Are you comfortable that they will not fat-finger another address of yours? Maybe you are a trusted customer and can add a custom community to a route that is recognized by the service provider as an RTBH notification. Maybe *you* are the service provider, and your trusted customer made a configuration mistake and added the wrong route. It's like having a stone axe when you need a surgical scalpel.

For those with blue cables in their hand, it's time to go back to Chapter 16, "Securing Control Plane," and pull the red cable if you have not already done so.

Media Access Control Security (MACsec)

Media Access Control Security (MACsec) is a Layer 2 security protocol that encrypts Ethernet traffic between MACsec-capable routers on a hop-by-hop (a point-to-point Ethernet link) basis. It operates at a line rate and uses the IEEE 802.1AE standard for encryption, ensuring data confidentiality. MACsec protects against various security threats at Layer 2, such as packet sniffing, eavesdropping, and spoofing attacks. It employs AES encryption to secure data on physical media, preventing unauthorized access and tampering. You should know that it operates differently from end-to-end Layer 3 encryption methods. While Layer 3 encryption hides packet contents from network devices they traverse, MACsec encrypts packets at each hop within Layer 2. This approach enables the network to inspect, monitor, and apply policies to traffic as it traverses, ensuring compliance with existing policies.

Frames are encrypted upon leaving the wire, typically after or when passing through the PHY (router physical hardware) following network process unit (NPU, which performs high-speed packet processing and forwarding) operations. They are decrypted before entering the destination router's NPU, providing the NPU with full visibility of the data and enabling it to deliver necessary services to these packets. MACsec offers the ability to secure an Ethernet link, including all control plane protocol packets except EAPoL. It employs the IEEE 802.1X **MACsec Key Agreement (MKA)** protocol to exchange session keys and manage encryption keys.

Familiarize yourself with the following terms because this newly introduced topic is highly likely to be featured on the exam:

- A **MACsec Key Agreement (MKA)**, defined in IEEE 802.1X, serves as a protocol for discovering MACsec peers and managing keys.

- A **secure channel (SC)** establishes a secure relationship to ensure frame security between members of a connectivity association (CA). It is supported by a sequence of secure associations (SAs), allowing the periodic use of fresh keys without terminating the relationship.

- The **secure channel identifier (SCI)** is a globally unique identifier for a secure channel, consisting of a globally unique MAC address and a port identifier unique within the system allocated that address.

- The **Connectivity Association Key (CAK)** serves as a long-lived master key for generating all other keys used in MACsec. It typically appears as a preshared key (PSK) configured through a key chain, represented as a hex string of 16 bytes for AES 128-bit cipher and 32 bytes for 256-bit cipher.

- The **CAK Key Name (CKN)** identifies the CAK and is represented as a hex string of 1 to 32 bytes. Consistency of CKN on both sides is crucial for successful session formation.

- The **Secure Association Key (SAK)**, obtained from the elected key server from the CAK, encrypts and decrypts traffic.

- The **key server (KS)** controls key generation and distribution of SAK to clients (non-KS). The device with the lowest key server priority value is preferred to win key server election. In case of a tie, the lowest value of SCI prevails.

As the data frames get ready to egress the interface, MACsec inserts two tags—the SecTAG and **Integrity Check Value (ICV)**—as shown in Figure 18-5. These are crucial because the receiving interface checks them to ensure that the data was not compromised while traversing the link. If the data integrity check detects anything irregular about the traffic, the traffic is dropped.

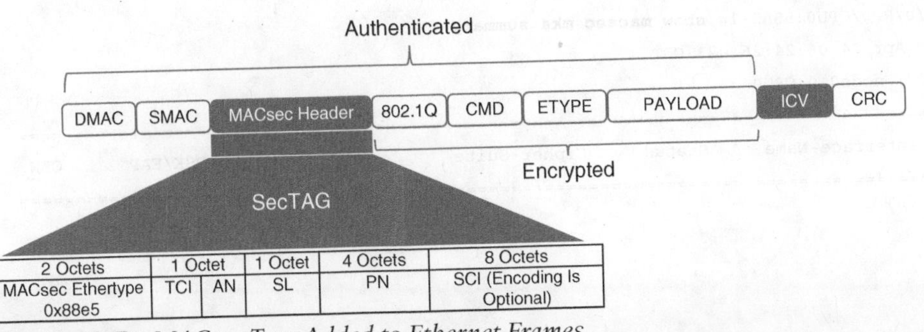

Figure 18-5 *MACsec Tags Added to Ethernet Frames*

The following are key aspects of the MACsec header structure:

- The first two octets are MACsec Ethertype; 0x88e5 designates that the following frame is a MACsec frame.

- The third octet is the TAG Control Information (TCI)/Association Number field. The TCI designates the MACsec version number.

- The fourth SL octet is short length, which is set to the length of the encrypted data.

- Octets 5 through 8 are the packet numbers and are used for replay protection and the construction of the initialization vector (along with the secure channel identifier).

- Octets 9 through 16 are the secure channel identifiers (SCIs). Each connectivity association (CA) is a virtual port, and each virtual port is designated a secure channel identifier that is the concatenation of the MAC address of the physical interface and a 16-bit port ID.

In Cisco's implementation, a 16-byte SecTAG and a 16-byte ICV are consistently employed, resulting in a data plane overhead of 32 bytes.

The MACsec configuration is surprisingly simple, as demonstrated in Example 18-19.

Example 18-19 *Enabling MACsec on the First Peer*

```
RP/0/RP0/CPU0:55A2-1# conf
Wed Apr 24 06:20:20.487 CDT
Current Configuration Session  Line      User     Date                Lock
00001000-0000dd74-00000000     vty1      CISCO15  Wed Apr 24 06:11:22 2024
RP/0/RP0/CPU0:55A2-1(config)# key chain psk1
RP/0/RP0/CPU0:55A2-1(config-psk1)# macsec
RP/0/RP0/CPU0:55A2-1(config-psk1-MacSec)# key 01
RP/0/RP0/CPU0:55A2-1(config-psk1-MacSec-01)# key-string 0123456789abcde-
f0123456789abcdef0123456789abcdef0123456789abcdef cryptographic-algorithm
aes-256-cmac
RP/0/RP0/CPU0:55A2-1(config-psk1-MacSec-01)# lifetime 00:00:00 April 24 2024
infinite
RP/0/RP0/CPU0:55A2-1(config-psk1-MacSec-01)# interface HundredGigE0/0/1/0
RP/0/RP0/CPU0:55A2-1(config-if)# macsec psk-keychain psk1
RP/0/RP0/CPU0:55A2-1(config-if)# commit
Wed Apr 24 06:24:15.359 CDT
RP/0/RP0/CPU0:55A2-1(config-if)# end
RP/0/RP0/CPU0:55A2-1# show macsec mka summary
Wed Apr 24 06:24:26.023 CDT
NODE: node0_0_CPU0

==========================================================================

  Interface-Name     Status     Cipher-Suite      KeyChain      PSK/EAP     CKN

==========================================================================
```

```
    Hu0/0/1/0              Init          NONE            psk1           PRIMARY      01
    Hu0/0/2/0/0            Init          NONE            macsec_skip    PRIMARY      11
Total MACSec Sessions   : 2
    Secured Sessions    : 0
    Pending Sessions    : 2
    Suspended Sessions  : 0
    Active  Sessions    : 0
RP/0/RP0/CPU0:55A2-1#
```

Because only one device has been configured, the session is in the Init phase. After I commit an identical configuration on the point-to-point peer, observe that the link is now encrypted with MACsec, along with self-explanatory verification commands. See if you can locate the term; we covered the MACsec header in the output in Example 18-20. Also, I am deliberately showing the second incomplete peering, so you will learn to recognize those.

Example 18-20   *Complete MACsec Configuration and Verification*

```
RP/0/RP0/CPU0:55A2-1# show macsec mka summary
Wed Apr 24 06:32:39.257 CDT
NODE: node0_0_CPU0

===============================================================================
  Interface-Name      Status      Cipher-Suite        KeyChain        PSK/EAP    CKN
===============================================================================
    Hu0/0/1/0         Secured   GCM-AES-XPN-256        psk1            PRIMARY    01
    Hu0/0/2/0/0       Init          NONE               macsec_skip     PRIMARY    11
Total MACSec Sessions   : 2
    Secured Sessions    : 1
    Pending Sessions    : 1
    Suspended Sessions  : 0
    Active  Sessions    : 0
RP/0/RP0/CPU0:55A2-1# show macsec mka session
Wed Apr 24 06:32:58.061 CDT
NODE: node0_0_CPU0

===============================================================================
  Interface-Name      Local-TxSCI         #Peers    Status    Key-Server PSK/EAP CKN
===============================================================================
    Hu0/0/1/0         0032.1797.5c28/0001    1      Secured     YES       PRIMARY  01
    Hu0/0/2/0/0       0032.1797.5c58/0001    0      Init        YES       PRIMARY  11
RP/0/RP0/CPU0:55A2-1# show macsec mka interface HundredGigE 0/0/1/0
Wed Apr 24 06:33:29.567 CDT

===============================================================================
  Interface-Name      KeyChain-Name    Fallback-KeyChain      Policy Name
===============================================================================
    Hu0/0/1/0            psk1              - NA -            DEFAULT-POLICY
RP/0/RP0/CPU0:55A2-1# show macsec mka session detail
Wed Apr 24 06:33:50.462 CDT
```

```
  NODE: node0_0_CPU0


  MKA Detailed Status for MKA Session

  =====================================
  Status: Secured - Secured MKA Session with MACsec
  Local Tx-SCI                       : 0032.1797.5c28/0001
  Local Tx-SSCI                      : 2
  Interface MAC Address              : 0032.1797.5c28
  MKA Port Identifier                : 1
  Interface Name                     : Hu0/0/1/0
  CAK Name (CKN)                     : 01
  CA Authentication Mode             : PRIMARY-PSK
  Keychain                           : psk1
  Member Identifier (MI)             : C353E1E7E91398602F96ED54
  Message Number (MN)                : 288
  Authenticator                      : NO
  Key Server                         : YES
  MKA Cipher Suite                   : AES-256-CMAC
  Configured MACSec Cipher Suite     : GCM-AES-XPN-256
  Key Distribution Mode              : SAK
  Latest SAK Status                  : Rx & Tx
  Latest SAK AN                      : 0
  Latest SAK KI (KN)                 : C353E1E7E91398602F96ED5400000001 (1)
  Old SAK Status                     : FIRST-SAK
  Old SAK AN                         : 0
  Old SAK KI (KN)                    : FIRST-SAK (0)
  SAK Transmit Wait Time             : 0s (Not waiting for any peers to respond)
  SAK Retire Time                    : 0s (No Old SAK to retire)
  Time to SAK Rekey                  : NA
  Time to exit suspension            : NA
  MKA Policy Name                    : DEFAULT-POLICY
  Key Server Priority                : 16
  Delay Protection                   : FALSE
  Replay Window Size                 : 64
  Include ICV Indicator              : FALSE
  Confidentiality Offset             : 0
  Algorithm Agility                  : 80C201
  SAK Cipher Suite                   : 0080C20001000004 (GCM-AES-XPN-256)
  MACsec Capability                  : 3 (MACsec Integrity, Confidentiality, & Offset)
  MACsec Desired                     : YES
  # of MACsec Capable Live Peers           : 1
  # of MACsec Capable Live Peers Responded : 1
  # of MACSec Suspended Peers              : 0
```

```
Live Peer List:
-------------------------------------------------------------------------------
        MI                          MN          Rx-SCI              SSCI  KS-Priority
-------------------------------------------------------------------------------
4C2223CB5241F2DEA9F60EBF            50      7c31.0e18.6028/0001       1       16

Potential Peer List:
-------------------------------------------------------------------------------
        MI                          MN          Rx-SCI              SSCI  KS-Priority
-------------------------------------------------------------------------------

Suspended Peer List:
-------------------------------------------------------------------------------
     Rx-SCI              SSCI
-------------------------------------------------------------------------------

Peers Status:
  Last Tx MKPDU           : 2024 Apr 24 06:33:50.273
  Peer Count              : 1
  RxSCI                   : 7C310E1860280001
    MI                    : 4C2223CB5241F2DEA9F60EBF
    Peer CAK              : Match
    Latest Rx MKPDU       : 2024 Apr 24 06:33:49.453


MKA Detailed Status for MKA Session

======================================
Status: Init - Searching for Peer (Waiting to receive first Peer MKPDU)
Local Tx-SCI                  : 0032.1797.5c58/0001
Local Tx-SSCI                 : 0
Interface MAC Address         : 0032.1797.5c58
MKA Port Identifier           : 1
Interface Name                : Hu0/0/2/0/0
CAK Name (CKN)                : 11
CA Authentication Mode        : PRIMARY-PSK
Keychain                      : macsec_skip
Member Identifier (MI)        : 5C70E0C1817C1BBFF98DF8F1
Message Number (MN)           : 1
Authenticator                 : NO
Key Server                    : YES
MKA Cipher Suite              : AES-128-CMAC
Configured MACSec Cipher Suite : GCM-AES-XPN-256
Key Distribution Mode         : NONE
Latest SAK Status             : No Rx, No Tx
Latest SAK AN                 : 0
Latest SAK KI (KN)            : FIRST-SAK-INITIALIZING (0)
Old SAK Status                : FIRST-SAK
Old SAK AN                    : 0
Old SAK KI (KN)               : FIRST-SAK (0)
```

```
SAK Transmit Wait Time           : 0s (Not waiting for any peers to respond)
SAK Retire Time                  : 0s (No Old SAK to retire)
Time to SAK Rekey                : NA
Time to exit suspension          : NA
MKA Policy Name                  : pqc-demo
Key Server Priority              : 16
Delay Protection                 : FALSE
Replay Window Size               : 64
Include ICV Indicator            : FALSE
Confidentiality Offset           : 0
Algorithm Agility                : 80C201
SAK Cipher Suite                 : (NONE)
MACsec Capability                : 3 (MACsec Integrity, Confidentiality, & Offset)
MACsec Desired                   : YES
# of MACsec Capable Live Peers            : 0
# of MACsec Capable Live Peers Responded  : 0
# of MACSec Suspended Peers               : 0
Live Peer List:
-------------------------------------------------------------------------------
       MI                MN             Rx-SCI          SSCI KS-Priority
-------------------------------------------------------------------------------
Potential Peer List:
-------------------------------------------------------------------------------
       MI                MN             Rx-SCI          SSCI KS-Priority
-------------------------------------------------------------------------------
Suspended Peer List:
-------------------------------------------------------------------------------
     Rx-SCI          SSCI
-------------------------------------------------------------------------------
Peers Status:
Last Tx MKPDU          : 1969 Dec 31 18:00:00.000
Peer Count             : 0
RP/0/RP0/CPU0:55A2-1#
```

When dealing with numerous MACsec-enabled devices, some operators choose a centralized approach to managing MACsec keys, rather than generating them individually on each device as I have demonstrated here. The centralized management method can be particularly advantageous when dealing with dozens or even hundreds of MACsec peerings, potentially saving significant time and effort. Customers have the option to configure 802.1x EAP profiles with remote RADIUS authentication and CA certificates for centralized MACsec key management. While the implementation of this topic falls outside the scope of the exam, it's important to acknowledge its feasibility and real-world application.

No more homework; this was a hard chapter. I will tell you this: I have thoroughly enjoyed writing it and attempting to make technology come alive.

Exam Preparation Tasks

As mentioned in the section "How to Use This Book" in the Introduction, you have a few choices for exam preparation: the exercises here, Chapter 23, "Final Preparation," and the exam simulation questions in the Pearson Test Prep Software Online.

Review All Key Topics

Review the most important topics in this chapter, noted with the Key Topic icon in the margin of the page. Table 18-2 lists a reference of these key topics and the page numbers on which each is found.

Table 18-2   Key Topics for Chapter 18

Key Topic Element	Description	Page Number
List	uRPF modes	856
Paragraph, list	RTBH implementations	866
Paragraph, list	RTBH mechanics	871
List	MACsec components	873
Figure 18-5	MACsec Tags Added to Ethernet Frames	873

Define Key Terms

Define the following key terms from this chapter and check the answers in the glossary:

Connectivity Association Key (CAK), Integrity Check Value (ICV), IPsec, key server (KS), MACsec Key Agreement (MKA), Media Access Control Security (MACsec), Remote Triggered Black Hole (RTBH), Unicast Reverse Path Forwarding (uRPF)

Command Reference to Check Your Memory

This section includes the most important configuration and EXEC commands covered in this chapter. You might not need to memorize the complete syntax of every command, but you should be able to remember the basic keywords that are needed.

To test your memory of the commands, cover the right side of Table 18-3 with a piece of paper, read the description on the left side, and then see how much of the command you can remember.

The 350-501 exam focuses on practical, hands-on skills that are used by networking professionals. Therefore, you should be able to identify the commands needed to configure and test. Note that not all commands are fully covered in the chapter, but their presence in the following table should lead you to investigate them further to understand this technology.

Table 18-3   CLI Commands to Know

Task	Command Syntax
Configure IPv4 commands for uRPF to work in loose mode	Router(config-if)# **ipv4 verify unicast source reachable-via any**
Configure IPv6 commands for uRPF to work in strict mode	Router(config-if)# **ipv6 verify unicast source reachable-via tx**
Display the summary of MACsec sessions	Router# **show macsec mka summary**

Review Questions

As a part of the review, we encourage you to provide *a single-sentence answer* (keep your answers as short as possible) to the following questions. If you struggle to complete this answer in a single sentence, this may indicate a lack of clarity or reveal gaps in your understanding. We have constructed these questions to help you consolidate this chapter's information and extract the essence of the covered content.

The answers to these questions appear in Appendix A. For more practice with exam format questions, use the Pearson Test Prep Software Online.

1. What implications should network administrators consider when choosing between loose and strict uRPF modes?

2. Can you name one operational challenge associated with fine-tuning RTBH policies?

3. Can you explain the role of the Secure Association Key (SAK) Agreement in MACsec and how it contributes to ensuring the security of Ethernet frames transmitted over a secured link?

Bibliography

B. Brown, "Facebook's Catastrophic Blackout Could Cost $90 Million in Lost Revenue," CCN article, https://www.ccn.com/facebooks-blackout-90-million-lost-revenue/, October 3, 2020.

R. Bush and R. Austein. RFC 6810, *The Resource Public Key Infrastructure (RPKI) to Router Protocol*, IETF, https://www.ietf.org/rfc/rfc6810.txt, January 2013.

P. Ferguson and D. Senie. RFC 2827, *Network Ingress Filtering: Defeating Denial of Service Attacks Which Employ IP Source Address Spoofing*, IETF, https://www.ietf.org/rfc/rfc2827.txt, May 2000.

W. Kumari and D. McPherson. RFC 5635, *Remote Triggered Black Hole Filtering with Unicast Reverse Path Forwarding (uRPF)*, IETF, https://www.ietf.org/rfc/rfc5635.txt, August 2009.

P. Mohapatra, J. Scudder, D. Ward, R. Bush, and R. Austein. RFC 6810, *BGP Prefix Origin Validation*, IETF, https://www.ietf.org/rfc/rfc6811.txt, January 2013.

V. Ng, *MACsec on NCS-5500—Technology and Platform Overview*, Cisco XRDOCS Tutorial, https://xrdocs.io/ncs5500/tutorials/macsec-on-ncs-5500-technology-and-platform-overview/. Last accessed July 16, 2024.

D. Turk. RFC 3832, *Configuring BGP to Block Denial of Service Attacks*, IETF, https://www.ietf.org/rfc/rfc3882.txt, September 2004.

IPv6 Transitions

This chapter covers the following exam topic:

2.7 Describe IPv6 transition (NAT44, NAT64, CGNAT, MAP-T and DS Lite)

As the world exhausts its supply of IPv4 addresses, the transition to IPv6 has become imperative for sustaining the growth of the Internet and accommodating the proliferation of connected devices. This chapter explores the intricate process of transitioning from IPv4 to IPv6, encompassing the challenges, strategies, and best practices involved in migration efforts. From the coexistence of IPv4 and IPv6 to the deployment of dual-stack networks and the implementation of transition mechanisms such as tunneling and translation, this chapter examines the multifaceted landscape of IPv6 transitions. By examining real-world deployment scenarios, you will gain insights into the evolving transition strategies and the critical role of IPv6 in shaping the future of networking infrastructure. This chapter covers the content you are very likely to see on the exam.

"Do I Know This Already?" Quiz

The "Do I Know This Already?" quiz allows you to assess whether you should read this entire chapter thoroughly or jump to the "Exam Preparation Tasks" section. If you are in doubt about your answers to these questions or your own assessment of your knowledge of the topics, read the entire chapter. Table 19-1 lists the major headings in this chapter and their corresponding "Do I Know This Already?" quiz questions. You can find the answers in Appendix A, "Answers to the 'Do I Know This Already?' Quizzes and Review Questions."

Table 19-1 "Do I Know This Already?" Section-to-Question Mapping

Foundation Topics Section	Questions
Introduction	1
NAT44	2
CGNAT	3
NAT64	4
DS-Lite	5
MAP-T	6

CAUTION The goal of self-assessment is to gauge your mastery of the topics in this chapter. If you do not know the answer to a question or are only partially sure of the answer, you should mark that question as wrong for purposes of the self-assessment. Giving yourself credit for an answer you correctly guess skews your self-assessment results and might provide you with a false sense of security.

1. Which of the following is a benefit of Stateless NAT in IPv6 deployments?

   a. It allows for seamless communication between IPv4 and IPv6 networks without the need for address translation.

   b. It reduces network latency by eliminating the need for address resolution during packet forwarding.

   c. It provides enhanced security by hiding internal IPv6 addresses from external networks.

   d. It allows for the coexistence of IPv4 and IPv6 networks without the need for complex address mapping tables.

2. Which of the following accurately describes the purpose of static NAT?

   a. It allows multiple internal hosts to share a single public IP address by dynamically assigning unique port numbers to each outgoing connection.

   b. It assigns a unique public IP address to each internal host, ensuring one-to-one mapping between internal and external addresses.

   c. It translates internal IP addresses to reserved IP ranges before forwarding packets to external networks, ensuring compatibility with public IP addresses.

   d. It allows external hosts to initiate connections to internal hosts by dynamically updating the NAT translation table.

3. Which of the following accurately describes the function of CGNAT?

   a. Multiple internal hosts share a single public IP address by dynamically assigning unique port numbers to each outgoing connection.

   b. A unique public IP address ensures one-to-one mapping between internal and external addresses.

   c. Internal IP addresses are mapped to reserved IP ranges before being forwarded to external networks, ensuring compatibility with public IP addresses.

   d. External hosts initiate connections to internal hosts by dynamically updating the NAT translation table.

4. Which of the following accurately describes NAT64?

   a. IPv6-only hosts communicate with IPv4-only hosts.

   b. A unique public IPv6 address for each internal IPv4 host ensures a one-to-one mapping between internal and external addresses.

   c. IPv4 addresses are mapped to reserved IPv6 ranges for packet forwarding to external IPv6 networks.

   d. IPv4-only hosts initiate connections to IPv6-only hosts by dynamically updating the NAT translation table.

5. Which of the following is correct regarding Dual-Stack Lite (DS-Lite) environments?

   a. They provide a unique public IPv4 address to each internal IPv6 host.

   b. They provide IPv6 addresses to reserved IPv4 ranges.

   c. They encapsulate IPv4 packets within IPv6 headers.

   d. IPv6-only hosts initiate connections to IPv4-only hosts.

6. MAP-T translates which of the following?

   a. IPv6 to IPv4 and vice versa on customer edge (CE) devices and border routers

   b. IPv4 to IPv6 and vice versa on customer edge (CE) devices and border routers

   c. IPv6 to reserved IPv4 ranges and vice versa on CE devices and border routers

   d. IPv4 to reserved IPv6 ranges and vice versa on CE devices and border routers

Foundation Topics

Introduction

A long, long time ago, in the ancient scrolls of networking lore, there lay a whisper of prophecy, foretelling the dawn of IPv6 addressing. As a youthful enthusiast, a seeker of knowledge, I (Brad) eagerly absorbed and believed these tales, convinced that its arrival and domination were imminent. For many moons (in the early 2000s), I wrestled with the enigmatic language of hexadecimals, decoding its cryptic charms. Now, 25 years hence, I still cling to that belief. With each passing year and the gradual depletion of IPv4 addresses, I find myself amused by the irony of it all. IPv6 remains the unicorn of the networking realm, forever just beyond our grasp, calling to us like a captivating siren's melody. Yet, amidst this ever-shifting landscape, if packets journey and addresses are sought, the legend persists—a steadfast beacon illuminating our path. You, too, must become a believer and ready yourself to champion this age-old prophecy. Reflect, for why else would this subject be on the exam?

Every network engineer travels the winding path and comes upon a fork in the road, where the road diverges. To your left is the path of dual-stacking IPv4/IPv6—a safer route favored by many. The network becomes bilingual: it can speak IPv4 or IPv6 languages to its target audience (IP destination). To your right stretches the IPv6-only road—a more perilous journey, given IPv4's enduring persistence. Translations must be performed, and these approaches have a definite learning curve. The "dual-stackers" have kicked the can down the road and lack immediate motivation to abandon IPv4 or hasten IPv6. The "IPv6ers" feel they are making the right decision by stepping into the future. Which path will you choose? For some of us, the right choice was to take the fork. This Cisco exam wants you to know the tools responsible for keeping IPv4 alive.

NAT44

Sharing is caring. And sharing is the reason IPv4 is still around. While there are not enough IPv4 addresses for all devices on the planet, the industry devised multiple approaches to conserve and reuse the finite limited pool of approximately 4.3 billion unique addresses. DHCP was one of them. Since not all devices need to be online at the same time, DHCP temporarily leased addresses and reclaimed them for the use of other occupants at defined intervals. As more and more devices demanded permanent network presence, a far more powerful sharing approach allowed concurrent use of defined IPv4 ranges by introducing the ever-present RFC 1918 private address space. Network Address Translation (NAT) allowed conservation of unique globally routed Internet addresses. Private enterprises could use the same address range on their internal networks and translate them to a limited set of public IPv4 addresses. A NAT device (a router or a firewall) mapped internal addresses to external ones and remembered these connections for future usage. If internal addresses were mapped to a block of addresses, the term *NAT* was used. If a more frugal, many-to-one mapping took place, it was called *PAT* (for Port Address Translation), or *NAPT* (for Network Address and Port Translation), or *address overloading*, and other names. This industry is notorious for calling the same thing multiple names. At the time, no one called it **NAT44**, because it was not necessary. It was simply NAT (I was there that day). There was no necessity to differentiate it from technologies like NAT64, as IPv6 had not yet been introduced, and thus, there was no existing mechanism to translate between IPv4 and IPv6. Call it what you want, but NAT and NAT44 do the same thing—take an IPv4 address and translate it to another IPv4 address. If you are this far into the book, chances are you have seen NAT, participated in it, and perhaps even purchased a souvenir tee-shirt.

If NAT is relatively new to you, the following is my attempt at the world's shortest practical NAT44 tutorial. Master the terms *inside local*, *inside global*, *outside global*, and *outside local*. The terms *inside* and *outside* denote the physical location of the device address, while *local* and *global* describe the viewpoint from which the address is observed in relation to the NAT device. Examine Figure 19-1 (an example of a specific static NAT translation) to understand these terms.

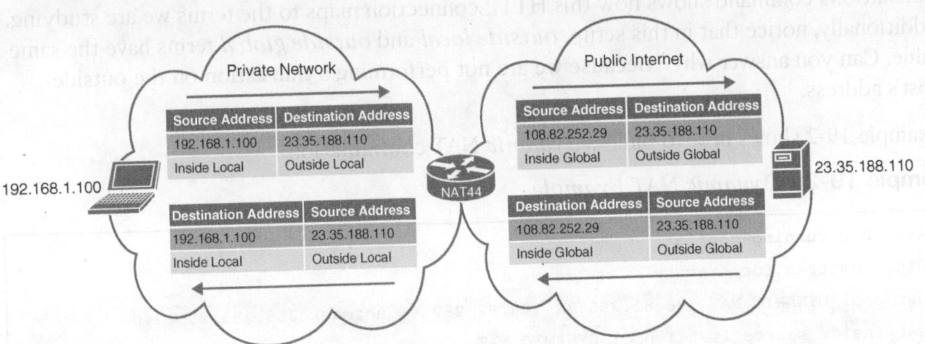

Figure 19-1 *NAT Terms as Defined by Cisco*

My laptop, with a local IP address of 192.168.1.100, is always considered "inside" because it resides on my private network. When I connect to 23.35.188.110 (www.cisco.com), which is physically external to my network and therefore "outside," the terms *local* and *global* describe how these devices are viewed from different perspectives. *Local* refers to how an IP address is seen within its own network—my laptop's IP is 192.168.1.100 locally—while *global* refers to how the address is perceived by the external world. For example, www.cisco.com is globally identified by the IP 23.35.188.110. Thus, *inside local* is my laptop's IP within my private network, *inside global* would be how my laptop's IP appears to the outside world, *outside global* is the global IP of www.cisco.com, and *outside local* is how www.cisco.com's IP is viewed within my private network. Despite the router's position, *inside* and *outside* always refer to the physical location of the devices, while *local* and *global* relate to the perspective from which the IP address is observed.

Observe what you learned in the most basic *static* NAT44 translation in Example 19-1.

Example 19-1 *Static NAT Example*

```
NAT44# show running-config
! Output omitted for brevity
interface GigabitEthernet1
 ip address 192.168.1.1 255.255.255.0
 ip nat inside
!
```

```
interface GigabitEthernet2
 ip address 108.82.252.1 255.255.255.0
 ip nat outside
!
ip nat inside source static 192.168.1.100 108.82.252.29
NAT44# show ip nat translations
Pro  Inside global          Inside local       Outside local        Outside global
---  108.82.252.29          192.168.1.100      ---                  ---
tcp  108.82.252.29:24333    192.168.1.100:24333 23.35.188.110:80    23.35.188.110:80
Total number of translations: 2
```

Observe that the router's interfaces are configured for inside and outside properties along with a *static* one-to-one NAT translation. More importantly, the output of the **show ip nat translations** command shows how this HTTP connection maps to the terms we are studying. Additionally, notice that in this setup, *outside local* and *outside global* terms have the same value. Can you answer why? Because we are not performing a translation on the outside host's address.

Example 19-2 shows how to build a *dynamic* NAT configuration.

Example 19-2 *Dynamic NAT Example*

```
NAT44# show running-config
! Output omitted for brevity
ip nat pool DYNAMIC_NAT 108.82.252.32 108.82.252.46 netmask 255.255.255.240
ip nat inside source list 1 pool DYNAMIC_NAT
!
ip access-list standard 1
 10 permit 192.168.1.0 0.0.0.255
```

We create a pool (range of IP addresses) called DYNAMIC_NAT that we will use to translate our *inside local* addresses in access-list 1 to *inside global* addresses.

Example 19-3 shows how to build *Port Address Translation* (PAT) where many local addresses will use a single global address.

Example 19-3 *PAT Example*

```
NAT44# show running-config
! Output omitted for brevity
ip nat inside source list 1 interface GigabitEthernet2 overload
ip access-list standard 1
 10 permit 192.168.1.0 0.0.0.255
```

PAT allows multiple internal IP addresses to be mapped to a single public IP address, using different ports for each session. This capability is useful for scenarios where you have only one public IP address. In the preceding scenario, we are using the IP address of the router's publicly facing interface for PAT.

Example 19-4 shows another common use of NAT called NAT with Port Forwarding. Can you guess what it does?

Example 19-4 *NAT Port Forwarding Example*

```
NAT44# show running-config
! Output omitted for brevity
ip nat inside source static tcp 192.168.1.100 80 108.82.252.50 80 extendable
```

This configuration is used to forward traffic from a specific port on the public IP to a specific port on an internal IP address. Scenario: you want to forward HTTP traffic (port 80) from the public IP address 108.82.252.50 to an internal web server at 192.168.1.100.

A less common form of NAT is known as *outside* NAT, where the translation occurs on the external, or "outside," addresses rather than the internal, or "inside," addresses. This is often used in scenarios where you need to manipulate the source IP address of incoming traffic before it reaches the internal network. Let's configure an outside NAT rule to translate the external www.cisco.com address to an internal address within our network and see the output in Example 19-5.

Example 19-5 *Outside NAT Example*

```
NAT44# show running-config
! Output omitted for brevity
ip nat outside source static 23.35.188.110 10.10.10.10 add-route
NAT44# show ip nat translations
Pro  Inside global          Inside local         Outside local        Outside global
---  ---                    ---                  10.10.10.10          23.35.188.110
tcp  192.168.1.100:25370    192.168.1.100:25370  10.10.10.10:80       23.35.188.110:80
Total number of translations: 2
```

Observe how we map www.cisco.com to an internal 10.10.10.10 address. The **show ip nat translations** command shows that internally (*outside local*) we connected 10.10.10.10 to the physical (*outside global*) address associated with the website.

There are other uses and types of NAT44, such as bidirectional NAT, which performs both inside NAT and outside NAT simultaneously, allowing translation of both source and destination IP addresses. There is policy NAT, which applies specific NAT rules based on criteria such as source or destination IP addresses, ports, or protocols. Bypass NAT refers to a configuration where specific traffic is exempted from undergoing NAT. In other words, packets that match certain criteria are routed without their source or destination IP addresses being translated; this capability is useful in internal and VPN applications. Somehow, though, I doubt you will see this level of complexity on the exam.

CGNAT

Carrier-Grade NAT (CGNAT) may be new to you. Also referred to as CGN, Large-Scale NAT, LSN, **NAT444**, and double-NAT, there is nothing I know of that is "carrier-grade" in it. It simply refers to the original NAT function being performed twice; a second NAT is done on the already-performed NAT44, as shown in Figure 19-2.

Figure 19-2 *NAT444, aka Carrier-Grade NAT*

A customer runs their own private RFC 1918 addresses. The service provider does not want to route the customer's addresses on their own internal RFC 1918–based network, so the customer will be "NAT44d" to the 10.100.x.x address block, transported across the service provider's network toward the Internet where the second NAT function (NAT444) will take place to give the customer a globally unique Internet routable address.

NOTE Cisco routers that perform Network Address Translation (NAT) functions include various models from Cisco's Integrated Services Routers (ISR) series, such as the ISR 4000 series, ISR 1000 series, and ISR 900 series. Additionally, Cisco's Aggregation Services Routers (ASR) series, including models like the ASR 1000 series, along with the enterprise-grade Catalyst 8000 series, also support NAT functionality. On XR-based platforms, older CRS routers, along with the ASR 9000 series with VSM modules, offered such NAT capabilities. Nowadays, NAT functions have been offloaded from the XR-based platforms (NCS, SiliconOne 8000, newer ASR 9000).

NAT64

Welcome to the road less traveled but getting to be more and more popular. More service providers are choosing to internally deploy IPv6 transport networks and assign IPv6 addresses to their customers. The customers still have to access IPv4 resources on the Internet, and since there is no native IPv6→IPv4 conversion, a **NAT64** device takes IPv6 traffic on one side, IPv4 on the other, and converts between the two, as shown in Figure 19-3.

Figure 19-3 *NAT64*

There are two NAT64 types:

- Stateless NAT64

- Stateful NAT64

The sections that follow cover these in more detail.

Stateless NAT64

In the stateless NAT64 approach, the translation occurs without maintaining any session state information. Each IPv6 packet is independently translated into an IPv4 packet, and vice versa. This is typically used for simple translation scenarios where maintaining session state is unnecessary or impractical. Effective, but due to its one-to-one translation mechanism, it does not "help" to deplete IPv4 addresses.

RFC 6052 describes the use of IPv4-translatable IPv6 addresses. An IPv4/IPv6 translator (which can be a router) can translate between two address types without keeping any per-flow state. What may show up on the exam? The well-known IPv6 prefix (WKP) 64:ff9b::/96 has been assigned to perform this algorithmic mapping. In addition, the following "network-specific" prefixes unique to an organization should be of the following lengths: 32, 40, 48, 56, 64, and 96 (as you can see, WKP is /96). When these are used, a translator can convert between IPv4 and IPv6. What makes it a bit harder is that routers do not speak decimal IPv4 and hexadecimal IPv6, so converting addresses can be tricky for humans at first. I'll show you how this works in a minute.

As of the time of writing, the exam doesn't require you to configure NAT64, so analyzing its implementation might seem excessive to some. Personally, however, I find it more intuitive and memorable to understand the solution by examining the actual configuration rather than relying solely on diagrams or descriptions. Imagine three routers in a row (IPV6, NAT64, and IPV4), with the middle NAT64 performing the translation as illustrated in Figure 19-4.

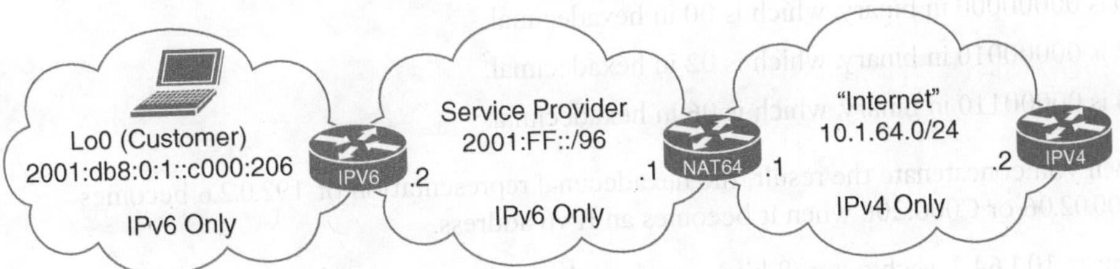

Figure 19-4   *NAT64 Stateless*

Router IPV6 has a Loopback0 interface, which represents a customer that runs only IPv6. There are no IPv4 addresses on this router. The customer tries to reach 10.1.64.2 on router IPV4, which does not speak IPv6. In this case, router NAT64 provides stateless translations. Example 19-6 shows a working configuration.

Example 19-6   *NAT64 Stateless Configuration*

```
NAT64# show running-config
! Output omitted for brevity
ipv6 unicast-routing
!
interface GigabitEthernet1
 ip address 10.1.64.1 255.255.255.0
 nat64 enable
!
interface GigabitEthernet2
 no ip address
```

```
nat64 enable
ipv6 address 2001:FF::1/96
ipv6 enable
!
nat64 prefix stateless 2001:DB8:0:1::/96
nat64 route 192.0.2.0/24 GigabitEthernet2
```

Wrapping your head around this configuration takes a minute. Most important are the two lines at the bottom of the translator's configuration. You see prefix 2001:DB8:0:1::/96 to "allow" the IPv6 side to see IPv6 NATted IPv4 addresses (read slowly) and prefix 192.0.2.0/24 to "allow" the IPv4 side of the diagram to reach IPv6 addresses. Customer 2001:DB8:0:1::C000:206 will ping 2001:DB8:0:1::A01:4002 to reach 10.1.64.2. How is this possible? The translator will take the destination address, strip off the IPv6 network 2001:DB8:0:1::, and convert the remaining A01:4002 from hexadecimal into decimal 10.1.64.2. (OK, it doesn't actually do this. This is easily done in binary, but I am describing this in human-speak.) The return traffic, sourced from 10.1.64.2, will use the other NAT64 range 192.0.2.0/24 to convert 192.0.2.6 to the hexadecimal C000:206 and prepend it with the IPv6 prefix of 2001:DB8:0:1. This sounds like voodoo, but it's not. Let me help.

Convert 192.0.2.6, each octet (8 bits), into hexadecimal:

192 is 11000000 in binary, which is C0 in hexadecimal.

0 is 00000000 in binary, which is 00 in hexadecimal.

2 is 00000010 in binary, which is 02 in hexadecimal.

6 is 00000110 in binary, which is 06 in hexadecimal.

When you concatenate the result, the hexadecimal representation of 192.0.2.6 becomes C0.00.02.06 or C000:206 when it becomes an IPv6 address.

Convert 10.1.64.2, each octet (8 bits), into hexadecimal:

10 is 0x0A in hexadecimal.

1 is 0x01 in hexadecimal.

64 is 0x40 in hexadecimal.

2 is 0x02 in hexadecimal.

Concatenate the hexadecimal representations into 0A.01.40.02. Therefore, the IPv4 address 10.1.64.2 in hexadecimal IPv6 format is 0A01:4002.

You can try this on your own. It doesn't take long to get good at this, but a far more interesting investment of time is to see this work in Example 19-7.

Example 19-7 *NAT64 Stateless Verification*

```
IPV4# ping 192.0.2.6
Type escape sequence to abort.
Sending 5, 100-byte ICMP Echos to 192.0.2.6, timeout is 2 seconds:
!!!!!
Success rate is 100 percent (5/5), round-trip min/avg/max = 23/29/33 ms
IPV4#
```

```
NAT64# show nat64 translations

Proto  Original IPv4        Translated IPv4
       Translated IPv6      Original IPv6
--------------------------------------------------------------------------


Total number of translations: 0

NAT64# show nat64 statistics
NAT64 Statistics

Total active translations: 0 (0 static, 0 dynamic; 0 extended)
Sessions found: 0
Sessions created: 0
Expired translations: 0
Global Stats:
   Packets translated (IPv4 -> IPv6)
      Stateless: 5
      Stateful: 0
      nat46: 0
      MAP-T: 0
      MAP-E: 0
   Packets translated (IPv6 -> IPv4)
      Stateless: 5
      Stateful: 0
      nat46: 0
      MAP-T: 0
      MAP-E: 0
```

```
IPV6# debug ipv6 icmp
  ICMPv6 Packet debugging is on
IPV6#
*Mar 25 22:42:20.412: ICMPv6: Received echo request, Src=2001:DB8:0:1::A01:4002,
Dst=2001:DB8:0:1::C000:206
*Mar 25 22:42:20.413: ICMPv6: Echo request received,  Src: 2001:DB8:0:1::A01:4002
Dst: 2001:DB8:0:1::C000:206 if_input: GigabitEthernet1 if_output: Loopback0
in_tableid: 0x0 out_tableid: 0x0 pak->ip_tableid: 0x0
*Mar 25 22:42:20.414: ICMPv6: Sent echo reply, Src=2001:DB8:0:1::C000:206,
Dst=2001:DB8:0:1::A01:4002
*Mar 25 22:42:20.446: ICMPv6: Received echo request, Src=2001:DB8:0:1::A01:4002,
Dst=2001:DB8:0:1::C000:206
*Mar 25 22:42:20.446: ICMPv6: Echo request received,  Src: 2001:DB8:0:1::A01:4002
Dst: 2001:DB8:0:1::C000:206 if_input: GigabitEthernet1 if_output: Loopback0
in_tableid: 0x0 out_tableid: 0x0 pak->ip_tableid: 0x0
*Mar 25 22:42:20.447: ICMPv6: Sent echo reply, Src=2001:DB8:0:1::C000:206,
Dst=2001:DB8:0:1::A01:4002
```

```
*Mar 25 22:42:20.479: ICMPv6: Received echo request, Src=2001:DB8:0:1::A01:4002,
Dst=2001:DB8:0:1::C000:206
*Mar 25 22:42:20.480: ICMPv6: Echo request received,  Src: 2001:DB8:0:1::A01:4002
Dst: 2001:DB8:0:1::C000:206 if_input: GigabitEthernet1 if_output: Loopback0
in_tableid: 0x0 out_tableid: 0x0 pak->ip_tableid: 0x0
*Mar 25 22:42:20.482: ICMPv6: Sent echo reply, Src=2001:DB8:0:1::C000:206,
Dst=2001:DB8:0:1::A01:4002
*Mar 25 22:42:20.504: ICMPv6: Received echo request, Src=2001:DB8:0:1::A01:4002,
Dst=2001:DB8:0:1::C000:206
*Mar 25 22:42:20.506: ICMPv6: Echo request received,  Src: 2001:DB8:0:1::A01:4002
Dst: 2001:DB8:0:1::C000:206 if_input: GigabitEthernet1 if_output: Loopback0
in_tableid: 0x0 out_tableid: 0x0 pak->ip_tableid: 0x0
*Mar 25 22:42:20.509: ICMPv6: Sent echo reply, Src=2001:DB8:0:1::C000:206,
Dst=2001:DB8:0:1::A01:4002
*Mar 25 22:42:20.541: ICMPv6: Received echo request, Src=2001:DB8:0:1::A01:4002,
Dst=2001:DB8:0:1::C000:206
*Mar 25 22:42:20.543: ICMPv6: Echo request received,  Src: 2001:DB8:0:1::A01:4002
Dst: 2001:DB8:0:1::C000:206 if_input: GigabitEthernet1 if_output: Loopback0
in_tableid: 0x0 out_tableid: 0x0 pak->ip_tableid: 0x0
*Mar 25 22:42:20.544: ICMPv6: Sent echo reply, Src=2001:DB8:0:1::C000:206,
Dst=2001:DB8:0:1::A01:4002
IPV6#ping 2001:DB8:0:1::A01:4002 source loopback0
Type escape sequence to abort.
Sending 5, 100-byte ICMP Echos to 2001:DB8:0:1::A01:4002, timeout is 2 seconds:
Packet sent with a source address of 2001:DB8:0:1::C000:206
!!!!!
Success rate is 100 percent (5/5), round-trip min/avg/max = 1/1/1 ms
```

What did you see? Pings succeed; the NAT64 device shows zero translations. Why? Because we do not keep state; that is, we are stateless. Having said this, these pings show up in the NAT64 statistics, and we see this in action on router IPV6 from the debug output, which accounts for all given pings describing to you where they were sourced from. When we turn around and ping the IPv6 address associated with the IPv4 destination, which was our intent to begin with, pings succeed because the translator converts it in the opposite direction. Not an easy topic to grasp, but it works. Read this description again thoroughly, and it will make sense.

Stateful NAT64

If you were surprised by the complexity of the logarithmic stateless mappings, it is your lucky day, since stateful NAT64 does not use it. In this approach, translation occurs while maintaining session state information. This means that the translation process considers the context of each packet exchange, ensuring that related packets are correctly translated and forwarded. It is far more complex (in its operations, not in your understanding of it) than stateless NAT64 but offers advantages such as better support for applications that require session continuity and improved security through better control over packet flows. This option multiplexes multiple IPv6 devices even into a single IPv4 address, essentially providing the PAT (or overload) function, like IPv4. State is established for each flow within the NAT64 device, ensuring accurate translation and routing for individual packet exchanges.

Example 19-8 shows a working configuration from our earlier diagram where I removed only the stateless NAT64 configurations; everything else is the same. See if you can follow it.

Example 19-8 *NAT64 Stateful Configuration and Verification*

```
NAT64# show running-config | include ^nat|permit|^ipv6 a
ipv6 access-list NAT64
  sequence 10 permit ipv6 2001:DB8:0:1::/64 any
  sequence 20 permit ipv6 2001:FF::/64 any
nat64 prefix stateful 2001:DB8:9999::/96
nat64 v4 pool V4POOL 10.1.64.100 10.1.64.120
nat64 v6v4 list NAT64 pool V4POOL

IPV6# ping 2001:DB8:9999::10.1.64.2
Type escape sequence to abort.
Sending 5, 100-byte ICMP Echos to 2001:DB8:9999::A01:4002, timeout is 2 seconds:
!!!!!
Success rate is 100 percent (5/5), round-trip min/avg/max = 1/1/2 ms
IPV6#ping 2001:DB8:9999::10.1.64.2 source loopback0
Type escape sequence to abort.
Sending 5, 100-byte ICMP Echos to 2001:DB8:9999::A01:4002, timeout is 2 seconds:
Packet sent with a source address of 2001:DB8:0:1::C000:206
!!!!!
Success rate is 100 percent (5/5), round-trip min/avg/max = 1/1/2 ms

NAT64# show nat64 translations

Proto  Original IPv4             Translated IPv4
       Translated IPv6          Original IPv6
-------------------------------------------------------------------

illegal ---                     ---
        10.1.64.101              2001:db8:0:1::c000:206
illegal ---                     ---
        10.1.64.100              2001:ff::2
icmp    10.1.64.2:5081          [2001:db8:9999::a01:4002]:5081
        10.1.64.100:5081        [2001:ff::2]:5081
icmp    10.1.64.2:1245          [2001:db8:9999::a01:4002]:1245
        10.1.64.101:1245        [2001:db8:0:1::c000:206]:1245


Total number of translations: 4


NAT64# show nat64 prefix stateful global


Global Stateful Prefix: is valid, 2001:DB8:9999::/96


IFs Using Global Prefix
```

```
   Gi2

   Gi1


NAT64# show ipv6 cef 2001:db8:9999::10.1.64.2
2001:DB8:9999::/96
   nexthop ::100.0.0.1 NVI0
```

What happened here? I added a crude access list with two entries (one for the "customer loopback0" interface and the other for the interfaces connected to NAT64), which I will use to ping the IPv4 address 10.1.64.2 (router IPV4). Then, I defined an arbitrary prefix 2001:DB8:9999::/96 for my NAT64 range. Then, I defined a v4 pool V4POOL of 20 addresses to work with on the IPv4 side of the diagram. I could have included the additional **overload** keyword at the end; this would make the router do Port Address Translation (PAT), tying my connections to a single IP address if necessary. Finally, I attached the networks I am picking up in the access list to use the V4POOL of IPv4 addresses.

I deliberately pinged from the GigabitEthernet1 and Loopback0 interfaces, and as you can see, they both succeed. On router NAT64, both translations show up, with the first one grabbing the first available 10.1.64.100 address from the pool and the second one using 10.1.64.101. Simple. I could have pinged with the cryptic hexadecimal address, and the results would have been the same (remember, routers do not care about the inferior human-readable formats). Lastly, I included a couple of commands I found useful that show the interfaces involved in NAT64, along with the Cisco Express Forwarding (CEF) table showing that the next hop for the IPv4 destination goes to this 100.0.0.1 NVI0 NAT virtual interface. It's conceivable that an astute test designer could incorporate this scenario into an exam. What is the 100.0.0.1 address? SMH...

Be clear in your mind that the scenario I just described allows only outbound IPv6→IPv4 communication, because we are discussing IPv6-only hosts communication toward IPv4-only hosts. If you need the communication to flow originating from the IPv4-only sides toward IPv6-only hosts, static NAT64 is necessary, as I show in Example 19-9. Be careful, though, because I am switching routers in the process.

Example 19-9 *Static Stateful NAT64*

```
IPV4# ping 10.1.64.100
Type escape sequence to abort.
Sending 5, 100-byte ICMP Echos to 10.1.64.100, timeout is 2 seconds:
.....
Success rate is 0 percent (0/5)
IPV4# ping 10.1.64.121
Type escape sequence to abort.
Sending 5, 100-byte ICMP Echos to 10.1.64.121, timeout is 2 seconds:
.....
Success rate is 0 percent (0/5)

NAT64(config)# nat64 v6v4 static 2001:db8:0:1::c000:206 10.1.64.121
NAT64(config)# do show nat64 translations
```

```
Proto  Original IPv4        Translated IPv4
       Translated IPv6      Original IPv6
- - - - - - - - - - - - - - - - - - - - - - - - - - - - - - - - - - - - - - - -

illegal ---                 ---
        10.1.64.121              2001:db8:0:1::c000:206


Total number of translations: 1
```

```
IPV4# ping 10.1.64.121
Type escape sequence to abort.
Sending 5, 100-byte ICMP Echos to 10.1.64.121, timeout is 2 seconds:
.!!!!
Success rate is 80 percent (4/5), round-trip min/avg/max = 2/2/4 ms
```

Both the visual I provided and the configuration outputs should help you tackle the exam as well as real-life configurations. Both stateless and stateful NAT64 play important roles in facilitating communication between IPv6 and IPv4 networks, but the choice between them depends on the specific requirements of the network deployment and the applications being used. My role is to describe and teach the mechanics of how these approaches function. I will leave the practicality or preference of these approaches to you and industry influencers.

DNS64

DNS64 is a mechanism used in IPv6 networks to assist NAT64 to provide communication with IPv4-only resources. It works alongside NAT64 to enable IPv6-only clients to access IPv4-only resources seamlessly.

When an IPv6-only client requests a resource using a domain name, DNS64 intercepts the DNS query and performs a lookup for the corresponding IPv4 address. If the authoritative DNS server reports that the resource has only an IPv4 address and not an IPv6 address, DNS64 will *synthesize* the AAAA record by combining the IPv4 address with a well-known prefix (WKP) or an ISP-assigned prefix, called a network-specific prefix (NSP). This synthesized IPv6 address allows the IPv6-only client to communicate with the IPv4-only resource through NAT64. The NAT64 device translates packets between IPv6 and IPv4, ensuring end-to-end communication between the IPv6-only client and the IPv4-only resource. You already know what WKP looks like. Can you recognize it on the exam? It is 64:ff9b::/96. What does an NSP record look like? You have been using them all along in our examples. It can be 2001:db8::/32, or it can be 2001:db8:9999::/64. So, let's pretend that our IPv6-only host contacts www.stopipv6.com. Since there is no such record (see Example 19-10 for contrasting with www.cisco.com), DNS64 will use the A record and convert it for use.

Example 19-10 *Checking AAAA DNS records*

```
350-501@SPCOR ~ % dig stopipv6.com aaaa

; <<>> DiG 9.10.6 <<>> stopipv6.com aaaa
;; global options: +cmd
```

```
;; Got answer:
;; ->>HEADER<<- opcode: QUERY, status: NOERROR, id: 56936
;; flags: qr rd ra; QUERY: 1, ANSWER: 0, AUTHORITY: 0, ADDITIONAL: 1

;; OPT PSEUDOSECTION:
; EDNS: version: 0, flags:; udp: 4096
;; QUESTION SECTION:
;stopipv6.com.                    IN      AAAA

;; Query time: 1204 msec
;; SERVER: 2600:1700:5810:22a0::1#53(2600:1700:5810:22a0::1)
;; WHEN: Tue Mar 26 10:33:46 EDT 2024
;; MSG SIZE  rcvd: 41


350-501@SPCOR ~ % dig www.cisco.com aaaa

; <<>> DiG 9.10.6 <<>> www.cisco.com aaaa
;; global options: +cmd
;; Got answer:
;; ->>HEADER<<- opcode: QUERY, status: NOERROR, id: 43688
;; flags: qr rd ra; QUERY: 1, ANSWER: 7, AUTHORITY: 0, ADDITIONAL: 1

;; OPT PSEUDOSECTION:
; EDNS: version: 0, flags:; udp: 4096
;; QUESTION SECTION:
;www.cisco.com.                   IN      AAAA

;; ANSWER SECTION:
www.cisco.com.          822     IN      CNAME   www.cisco.com.akadns.net.
www.cisco.com.akadns.net. 292   IN      CNAME   wwwds.cisco.com.edgekey.net.
wwwds.cisco.com.edgekey.net. 15204 IN   CNAME   wwwds.cisco.com.edgekey.net.
globalredir.akadns.net.
wwwds.cisco.com.edgekey.net.globalredir.akadns.net. 802 IN CNAME e2867.dsca.
akamaiedge.net.
e2867.dsca.akamaiedge.net. 1    IN      CNAME   user-att-108-82-200-0.e2867.
dsca.akamaiedge.net.
user-att-108-82-200-0.e2867.dsca.akamaiedge.net. 20 IN AAAA 2600:1408:ec00:287::b33
user-att-108-82-200-0.e2867.dsca.akamaiedge.net. 20 IN AAAA 2600:1408:ec00:286::b33

;; Query time: 19 msec
;; SERVER: 192.168.1.254#53(192.168.1.254)
;; WHEN: Tue Mar 26 10:33:58 EDT 2024
;; MSG SIZE  rcvd: 300
```

In our case, www.stopipv6.com is nonexistent. For documentation purposes, let's pretend that the record returned is 192.0.2.99. Can you put your algorithmic mapping skills to test and determine which two synthesized records would be passed to our IPv6-only host? Don't look at Figure 19-5 until you have tried because it contains the depiction and the answer.

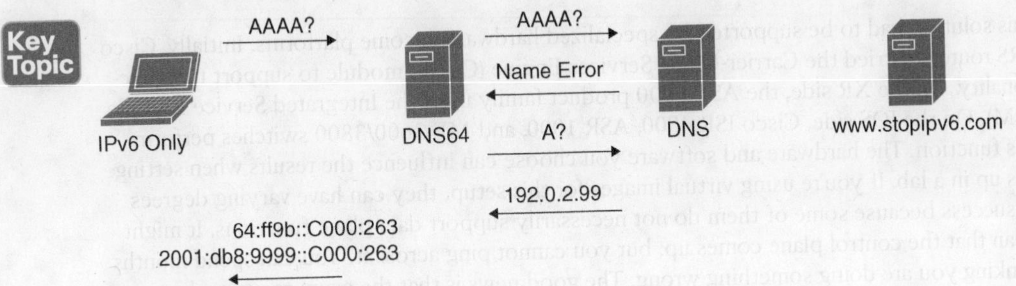

Figure 19-5 *DNS64 Record Returned*

DS-Lite

Many service providers have either fully implemented IPv6 across their networks or have adopted it partially, recognizing its significance in addressing the limitations of IPv4 and accommodating the growing demand for Internet-connected devices. Notice that CPEs in such cases are provisioned natively with IPv6; however, the customer on the top left of Figure 19-6 still runs IPv4 and needs access to IPv4 addresses somewhere beyond the SP network.

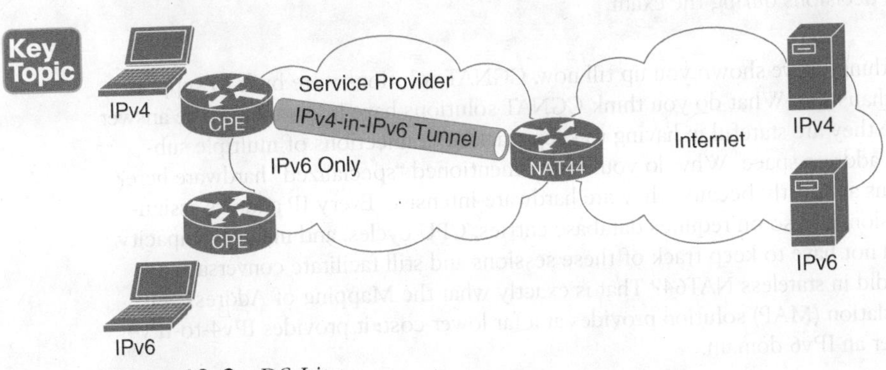

Figure 19-6 *DS-Lite*

Any IPv4 coming from a customer's LAN will be tunneled to a gateway (router NAT44), which will translate the private subscriber IPv4 addressing into a globally routable IPv4 address. Other subscribers that use IPv6 (at the bottom left) will be routed natively over the service provider's infrastructure. For our IPv4 customer, though, it is a *bridging function* from the CPE to a single IPv4 NAT operation; hence, it is NAT44. When a device sends an IPv4 packet, the CPE gateway encapsulates it in IPv6, with the destination address of the IPv6 packet being set to the address of the **DS-Lite**–enabled large-scale NAT (LSN) gateway.

19

What is the best way to remember DS-Lite? It is IPv4-in-IPv6+NAT. Again, there are multiple names to describe this technology, so Carrier-Grade IPv6 (CGv6), LSN, and Carrier-Grade NAT (CGN) have been used in various references. RFCs 6333 and 6908, which are mentioned in the "Bibliography" section of this chapter, will give you a more detailed background.

This solution had to be supported by specialized hardware in some platforms. Initially, Cisco CRS routers carried the Carrier-Grade Services Engine (CGSE) module to support this functionality. On the XR side, the ASR 9000 product family used the Integrated Service Module (ISM). On the IOS side, Cisco ISR 4000, ASR 1000, and ME 3600/3800 switches perform this function. The hardware and software you choose can influence the results when setting this up in a lab. If you're using virtual images for this setup, they can have varying degrees of success because some of them do not necessarily support data plane functions. It might mean that the control plane comes up, but you cannot ping across it. You can spend months thinking you are doing something wrong. The good news is that the exam requests the "describe" level of knowledge, so be sure you understand what I mention here. Take a break at this point before moving on; this knowledge has to settle.

MAP-E

NOTE   I want to clarify that MAP-E is not included in the exam blueprint, and I'm not here to waste your time with unnecessary details. However, I've included this section to help you better understand MAP-T, which *is* on the exam blueprint. While you can choose to skip this part or use it as a reference later, I believe this background information will be crucial in making informed decisions during the exam.

Consider everything I have shown you up till now. CGNAT solutions were built to support IPv4 address exhaustion. What do you think CGNAT solutions have in common? The answer is state, because they are stateful in having to keep track of connections of multiple subscribers sharing address space. Why do you think I mentioned "specialized" hardware here? CGNAT solutions are costly because they are hardware-intensive. Every IP address assignment, lease, session, and so on requires database entries, CPU cycles, and memory capacity. What if you did not have to keep track of these sessions and still facilitate conversations kind of like we did in stateless NAT64? That is exactly what the Mapping of Address and Port using Translation (MAP) solution provides at a far lower cost: it provides IPv4-to-IPv4 connectivity over an IPv6 domain.

Mapping of Address and Port Encapsulated (MAP-E) provides IPv4 as a service over a single-stack IPv6 core. It uses the same stateless algorithm I introduced earlier to embed portions of the customer's allocated IPv4 address into the IPv6 prefix assigned to the client. If you are very observant, you may have spotted references to it in Example 19-7. In MAP-E, IPv4 traffic is encapsulated within an IPv6 header before being transmitted over the IPv6 network. Upon reaching the network operator's boundary router, the IPv6 header is removed, and the encapsulated IPv4 traffic is forwarded to the IPv4 Internet. See Figure 19-7 for a visualization.

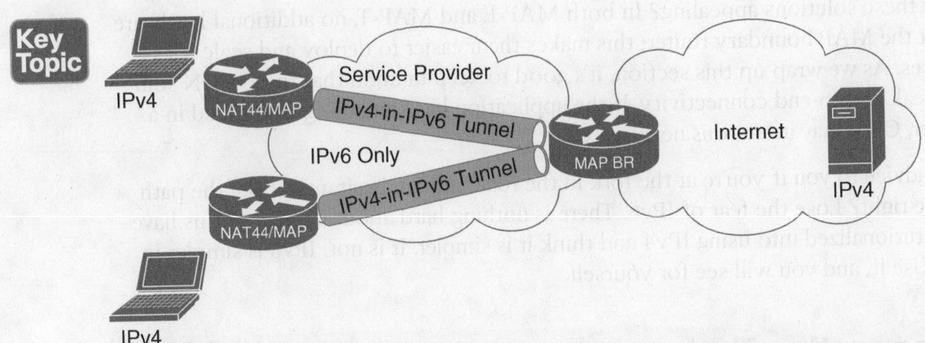

Figure 19-7 *MAP-E*

The CPE router acts as MAP at Customer Edge (MAP-CE). It uses NAT44 to change private IPv4 addresses and ports into a range of addresses and ports set by the MAP rule. This rule is based on the IPv6 prefix it's given. The router then encapsulates the IPv4 packet into an IPv6 packet and sends it to either another device in the MAP network or to a MAP border router if the destination isn't covered by the MAP rule (exit point from the MAP domain).

The MAP border router (BR) has a list of MAP rules for the MAP areas it serves. These rules tell the BR how to handle traffic it received from CPE routers. It checks the source IPv4 address and ports and figures out the destination IPv6 address for incoming IPv4 traffic. MAP-E functions similarly to DS-Lite, but *DS-Lite bridges traffic while MAP-E has a NAT function present at the CPE*. They both tunnel IPv4 traffic over IPv6 though.

MAP-T

In the **Mapping of Address and Port Translated (MAP-T)** method, the IPv4 packet header undergoes mapping to the IPv6 header and vice versa. The mapping algorithm is identical to MAP-E. The distinction between MAP-E and MAP-T lies in their approaches: MAP-E uses IPv6 encapsulation and decapsulation for IPv4 traffic, whereas MAP-T utilizes NAT64 to perform translation between IPv4 and IPv6. *Double stateless translation (NAT46 in the CE and NAT64 in the BR)* is used navigate through the ISP's IPv6 single-stack network. Observe Figure 19-8.

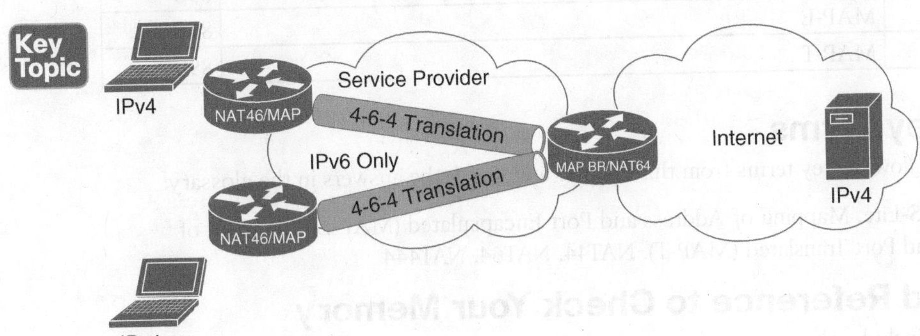

Figure 19-8 *MAP-T*

What makes these solutions appealing? In both MAP-E and MAP-T, no additional hardware is required at the MAP boundary router; this makes them easier to deploy and scale for future services. As we wrap up this section, it's good to keep in mind that these CGN solutions may break end-to-end connectivity. If the application has something embedded in a packet header, CGN may affect this negatively.

What is my advice to you if you're at the fork in the road and are hesitant to take the path leading to the right? Lose the fear of IPv6. There is nothing hard about it. Many of us have become institutionalized into using IPv4 and think it is simpler. It is not. IPv6 is simpler in many ways. Use it, and you will see for yourself.

Exam Preparation Tasks

As mentioned in the section "How to Use This Book" in the Introduction, you have a few choices for exam preparation: the exercises here, Chapter 23, "Final Preparation," and the exam simulation questions in the Pearson Test Prep Software Online.

Review All Key Topics

Review the most important topics in this chapter, noted with the Key Topic icon in the margin of the page. Table 19-2 lists a reference of these key topics and the page numbers on which each is found.

Table 19-2   Key Topics for Chapter 19

Key Topic Element	Description	Page Number
Figure 19-1	NAT Terms as Defined by Cisco	885
Figure 19-2	NAT444, aka Carrier-Grade NAT	888
Figure 19-3	NAT64	888
Figure 19-4	NAT64 Stateless	889
Figure 19-5	DNS64 Record Returned	897
Figure 19-6	DS-Lite	897
Paragraph	Best way to remember DS-Lite	898
Figure 19-7	MAP-E	899
Figure 19-8	MAP-T	899

Define Key Terms

Define the following key terms from this chapter and check the answers in the glossary:

DNS64, DS-Lite, Mapping of Address and Port Encapsulated (MAP-E), Mapping of Address and Port Translated (MAP-T), NAT44, NAT64, NAT444

Command Reference to Check Your Memory

This section includes the most important configuration and EXEC commands covered in this chapter. You might not need to memorize the complete syntax of every command, but you should be able to remember the basic keywords that are needed.

To test your memory of the commands, cover the right side of Table 19-3 with a piece of paper, read the description on the left side, and then see how much of the command you can remember.

The 350-501 exam focuses on practical, hands-on skills that are used by networking professionals. Therefore, you should be able to identify the commands needed to configure and test. Note that not all commands are fully covered in the chapter, but their presence in the following table should lead you to investigate them further to understand this technology.

Table 19-3   CLI Commands to Know

Task	Command Syntax
Display translated IPv4 and IPv6 addresses	**show nat64 translations**
Display the global and interface-specific statistics of the packets that are translated and dropped	**show nat64 statistics**

Review Questions

As a part of the review, we encourage you to provide *a single-sentence answer* (keep your answers as short as possible) to the following questions. If you struggle to complete this answer in a single sentence, this may indicate a lack of clarity or reveal gaps in your understanding. We have constructed these questions to help you consolidate this chapter's information and extract the essence of the covered content.

The answers to these questions appear in Appendix A. For more practice with exam format questions, use the Pearson Test Prep Software Online.

1. What are the complexities and challenges associated with implementing Dual-Stack Lite (DS-Lite) in modern network environments?

2. Can you explain the role and function of the border router in facilitating communication between IPv4 and IPv6 networks?

3. How does the performance and scalability of stateless NAT64 compare to stateful NAT64 in handling large volumes of concurrent translations, particularly in scenarios with diverse application protocols and traffic patterns?

Bibliography

C. Bao, C. Huitema, M. Bagnulo, M. Boudadair, and X. Li. RFC 6052, *IPv6 Addressing of IPv4/IPv6 Translators*, IETF, https://www.ietf.org/rfc/rfc6052.txt, October 2010.

N. Bhaskar, A. Gall, J. Lingard, and S. Venaas. RFC 5059, *Bootstrap Router (BSR) Mechanism for Protocol Independent Multicast (PIM)*, IETF, https://www.ietf.org/rfc/rfc5059.txt, January 2008.

A. Durand, R. Droms, J. Woodyatt, and Y. Lee. RFC 6333, *Dual-Stack Lite Broadband Deployments Following IPv4 Exhaustion*, IETF, https://www.ietf.org/rfc/rfc6333.txt, August 2011.

B. Haberman and D. Thaler. RFC 3306, *Unicast-Prefix-Based IPv6 Multicast Addresses*, IETF, https://www.ietf.org/rfc/rfc3306.txt, August 2002.

H. Holbrook and B. Cain. RFC 4607, *Source-Specific Multicast for IP*, IETF, https://www.ietf.org/rfc/rfc4607.txt, August 2006.

Y. Lee, R. Maglione, C. Williams, C. Jacquenet, and M. Boucadair. RFC 6908, *Deployment Considerations for Dual-Stack Lite*, IETF, https://www.ietf.org/rfc/rfc6908.txt, March 2013.

X. Li, W. Dec, O. Troan, S. Matsushima, and T. Murakami. RFC 7599, *Mapping of Address and Port Using Translation (MAP-T)*, IETF, https://www.ietf.org/rfc/rfc7599.txt, July 2015.

O. Troan, W. Dec, X. Li, C. Bao, S. Matsushima, T. Murakami, and T. Taylor. RFC 7597, *Mapping of Address and Port with Encapsulation (MAP-E)*, IETF, https://www.ietf.org/rfc/rfc7597.txt, July 2015.

## CHAPTER 20

High Availability Designs

This chapter covers the following exam topics:

2.8 Implement high availability

- 2.8.a NSF / graceful restart
- 2.8.b NSR
- 2.8.c BFD
- 2.8.d Link aggregation

In the fast-paced world of modern networking, ensuring high availability is paramount to the success of any organization. Downtime can result in significant financial losses, reputational damage, and diminished customer satisfaction. Therefore, designing resilient and highly available network architectures has become a critical focus for network engineers and architects. This chapter looks at high-availability designs, explores their fundamental principles, best practices, and advanced techniques employed to minimize downtime and maximize network reliability. It is our intent to provide comprehensive insights into building robust network infrastructures capable of withstanding failures and ensuring uninterrupted service delivery.

"Do I Know This Already?" Quiz

The "Do I Know This Already?" quiz allows you to assess whether you should read this entire chapter thoroughly or jump to the "Exam Preparation Tasks" section. If you are in doubt about your answers to these questions or your own assessment of your knowledge of the topics, read the entire chapter. Table 20-1 lists the major headings in this chapter and their corresponding "Do I Know This Already?" quiz questions. You can find the answers in Appendix A, "Answers to the 'Do I Know This Already?' Quizzes and Review Questions."

Table 20-1 "Do I Know This Already?" Section-to-Question Mapping

Foundation Topics Section	Questions
NSF	1
NSR	2
BFD	3
Link Aggregation	4

CAUTION The goal of self-assessment is to gauge your mastery of the topics in this chapter. If you do not know the answer to a question or are only partially sure of the answer, you should mark that question as wrong for purposes of the self-assessment. Giving yourself credit for an answer you correctly guess skews your self-assessment results and might provide you with a false sense of security.

1. What is non-stop forwarding?
   a. NSF allows routers to forward packets without interruption even when the power source is temporarily disconnected.
   b. NSF refers to the capability of routers to continue forwarding packets without interruption, regardless of changes in the network topology or configuration.
   c. NSF ensures that routers continue to forward packets at the same rate, even during maintenance or configuration changes.
   d. NSF ensures uninterrupted packet forwarding during routing protocol convergence or router switchover events.

2. Which of these statements best describes NSR?
   a. NSR allows routers to continue forwarding packets even when the primary routing table is unavailable.
   b. NSR ensures that routing protocols remain operational in the event of a network outage, preventing disruptions in data transmission.
   c. NSR enables routers with redundant route processors to maintain uninterrupted routing functionality during a route processor (RP) failover event.
   d. NSR maintains routing tables across multiple devices, ensuring redundancy and fault tolerance in the network.

3. What are the key parameters used by Bidirectional Forwarding Detection (BFD) to detect link failures? (Select all that apply.)
   a. Interval
   b. Continuous low-overhead signaling
   c. Multiplier
   d. Detection time

4. LACP aggregates links based on
   a. Speed
   b. VLAN tags
   c. IP addresses
   d. MAC addresses

Foundation Topics

High availability in networks refers to the ability of a network infrastructure to remain operational and accessible for users, even in the face of failures or disruptions. It involves designing and implementing redundant components, failover mechanisms, and robust protocols to minimize downtime and ensure continuous service delivery. Most fixed router systems have a signal route processor (RP). In contrast, modular or chassis-based systems can feature redundant route processors to ensure high availability and reliability. The active (primary) RP handles the main control plane functions, including routing protocol operations, management tasks, and overall device control. The standby (backup) RP takes over automatically if the primary RP fails, ensuring minimal downtime and continued operation. This ensures control plane redundancy. In addition, chassis-based routers can feature distributed line cards (or modular interface cards) to handle data plane functions independently and, when necessary, provide data plane redundancy as well.

The key elements of high availability in networks for the SPCOR exam include

- **Redundant Components:** Critical network devices such as routers, switches, and firewalls are deployed in redundant configurations. Redundancy can be achieved through hardware redundancy (e.g., redundant power supplies, network interface cards, and more specifically, route processors) and device redundancy (e.g., active-standby, or active-active configurations).

- **Fault Tolerance:** Networks are designed with fault-tolerant architectures to mitigate the impact of component failures. This may involve implementing redundant network paths, redundant data centers, geographic diversity, and software tools like NSF, SSO, and NSR to minimize disruptions to the network's forwarding plane.

- **Failover and Load-Balancing Mechanisms:** Failover mechanisms automatically redirect network traffic to redundant components in the event of a failure. Load balancing distributes network traffic across multiple redundant paths or devices to prevent overload and ensure optimal resource utilization. This could involve protocols such as Virtual Router Redundancy Protocol (VRRP), Hot Standby Router Protocol (HSRP), or link aggregation techniques like EtherChannel.

- **Rapid Detection and Recovery:** High availability systems employ rapid detection mechanisms to identify failures or anomalies in the network. This is often achieved through **Bidirectional Forwarding Detection (BFD)** which signals rapid recovery mechanisms to initiate failover processes to restore service quickly.

Modern routing platforms have separated control (routing) and forwarding (data) planes. The advantage of this approach is that if one plane's traffic load becomes too heavy, the other plane is not affected. Routing updates should not disrupt data being forwarded at high rates, just like an overwhelming volume of data traffic should not interrupt routing topology construction and maintenance. Use the cheat sheet in Table 20-2 to quickly orient yourself with the terms necessary to understand this topic section.

Table 20-2   High Availability Cheat Sheet

Name	Description
NSF	**Non-Stop Forwarding:** The forwarding plane continues to operate if the control plane stops.
SSO	**Stateful Switchover:** Fast switchover to the backup control plane occurs.
NSR	**Non-Stop Routing:** This technology reduces the impact of disrupted peering sessions.
GR	**Graceful Restart:** Cisco-specific non-stop forwarding (NSF) awareness is applied to the *routing* (not *forwarding*) plane.

NSF

In systems with redundant route processors (RPs), when the routing plane temporarily disappears, the data (forwarding) plane should remain operational without interruption. I'm sure you have heard the term *hitless upgrades* before—no impact. **Non-stop forwarding (NSF)** ensures uninterrupted packet forwarding during software upgrades or hardware failures. Typically, when a device experiences a failure, there is a brief interruption in packet forwarding as the device switches over to a standby RP.

NSF minimizes this interruption, and the router continues to forward packets even during such events. If the switchover process to the standby RP takes too long, this can become a problem for the forwarding plane. Should the control plane topology change, there is no way to signal this change to the forwarding plane, and the forwarding plane can start blackholing (discarding network traffic, preventing it from reaching its destination) the traffic since the Forwarding Information Base (FIB) has become invalid.

Stateful Switchover (SSO) minimizes the time to restore control plane functions. The standby RP retains configurations and preserves the forwarding state during a switchover, reducing the time needed to use the newly activated control plane.

The exam will test your NSF implementation skills. What do you need to know? First, NSF and SSO cannot be separated from each other for the reasons described here. For the device to be configured with NSF, SSO must be enabled. Second, NSF works and is configured with individual routing components (BGP, OSPF, IS-IS, EIGRP, IPv6). Only EIGRP is enabled by default. You must manually configure the others I mention. This also means that NSF implementations are protocol specific: if sham-links or virtual links are not supported, that is the function of OSPF. BGP and EIGRP will have their own considerations. Third, Cisco makes the following distinctions:

- An **NSF-aware device** is one that is running NSF-compatible software. It does not reset neighboring adjacency and supplies router verification information after switchover.

- An **NSF-capable device** is one that is configured to support NSF and can rebuild routing information from either NSF-aware or NSF-capable neighboring devices. It keeps forwarding packets during a switchover.

IS-IS NSF

Let's start with IS-IS. An IS-IS process restarts. This could happen for different reasons. An RP failover occurs, or an administrator reloads the IS-IS process, or an IS-IS software upgrade takes place, or a link flaps. This is a problem, since instability has been introduced into your routing domain. *NSF maintains packet forwarding along known routes while restoring routing protocol information.* During IS-IS process restarts, two tasks need to be performed: relearn available neighbors without resetting relationships and reacquire link-state database contents.

To this end, IS-IS NSF offers two options:

- **IETF NSF:** If neighbors are NSF-aware (they support RFC 5306), they assist in rebuilding routing info after a failover. *This a is stateless solution and requires neighbor assistance.* Stateless means that there is no adjacency check or checks on the content of the LSP database. The "restarting" router simply informs neighbors about a restart event. A new TLV Type 211 is included in IIH PDUs to convey information during a (re)start. The "supporting" router will receive the IIH PDU and respond back to the "restarting" router with its own IIH PDU TLV Type 211, along with a complete set of CNSPs. The "restarting" router receives both and cancels the IS-IS adjacency timer. All is well, the packet forwarding is "hitless."

- **Cisco NSF:** This approach "improves" on the IETF's methodology. It resolves the problem of reacquiring IS-IS neighbor adjacency and LSPs by storing the necessary state on the standby RP for recovery *without needing special cooperation from neighbors.* Therefore, it is stateful, and state is recovered from neighbors using standard IS-IS features. The "restarting" router's newly active RP (which was in standby moments ago) uses "checkpointed" (a concept of taking a snapshot of data and synchronizing or saving it to a particular location) data to immediately restore the routing information and sends IIH PDU with TLV 211 to the IS-IS neighbor. Realize that the neighbor does not have to be NSF-aware (why this is an improvement over the IETF approach). The neighbor router is *unaware that a restart took place* and sends IIH PDU back with TLV Type 211 to the "restarting" router. The restarting router receives the hello packet and cancels the adjacency timer. All is well, the packet forwarding is "hitless."

Cisco's approach is suitable for networks where other routers haven't implemented the IETF standard NSF. When you mix Cisco and IETF NSFs, the IETF will disable Cisco NSFs on other segments, and you will have problems.

I (Brad) highly recommend you slowly reread what I mentioned here several times. I deliberately am not including a picture because it distracts from understanding the difference. You can draw your own diagram from this description, which will be a fine investment of your time. You will forget a picture drawn by someone else before the exam.

Where does **Graceful Restart (GR)** come in? GR is the capability of the control plane to delay advertising the absence of a peer (going through control-plane switchover) for a "grace period," and thus minimizes disruption during that time. RFC 3847, *Restart Signaling for IS-IS,* and RFC 3478, *Graceful Restart Mechanism for Label Distribution Protocol*, are the basis behind Cisco's implementation of IS-IS NSF capabilities.

Example 20-1 shows how to work with IS-IS, so you need to be familiar with these commands.

Example 20-1   *IS-IS NSF Configuration Options*

```
RP/0/RP0/CPU0:NCS-5508-2# configure
Wed Mar 27 15:18:21.195 CDT
RP/0/RP0/CPU0:NCS-5508-2(config)# router isis lab
RP/0/RP0/CPU0:NCS-5508-2(config-isis)# nsf ?
  cisco              Checkpoint NSF restart
  ietf               IETF NSF restart
  interface-expires  # of times T1 can expire waiting for the restart ACK
  interface-timer    Timer used to wait for a restart ACK (seconds)
  lifetime           Maximum route lifetime following restart (seconds)
RP/0/RP0/CPU0:NCS-5508-2(config-isis)# nsf ietf
RP/0/RP0/CPU0:NCS-5508-2(config-isis)# nsf interface-?
interface-expires  interface-timer
RP/0/RP0/CPU0:NCS-5508-2(config-isis)# nsf interface-expires ?
  <1-10>  expiry count
```

```
RP/0/RP0/CPU0:NCS-5508-2(config-isis)# nsf interface-expires 1
RP/0/RP0/CPU0:NCS-5508-2(config-isis)# nsf interface-?
interface-expires  interface-timer
RP/0/RP0/CPU0:NCS-5508-2(config-isis)# nsf interface-timer 15
RP/0/RP0/CPU0:NCS-5508-2(config-isis)# nsf lifetime ?
  <5-300>  seconds
RP/0/RP0/CPU0:NCS-5508-2(config-isis)# nsf lifetime 20
RP/0/RP0/CPU0:NCS-5508-2(config-isis)# commit
Wed Mar 27 15:20:45.564 CDT
RP/0/RP0/CPU0:NCS-5508-2(config-isis)# do show run router isis lab
Wed Mar 27 15:20:54.677 CDT
router isis lab
 is-type level-2-only
 net 49.0001.1921.6800.5022.00
 distribute link-state
 nsf ietf
 nsf lifetime 20
 nsf interface-timer 15
 nsf interface-expires 1
RP/0/RP0/CPU0:NCS-5508-2(config-isis)# end
RP/0/RP0/CPU0:NCS-5508-2# show isis protocol
Wed Mar 27 15:22:22.375 CDT

IS-IS Router: lab
  System Id: 1921.6800.5022
  Job Id: 1013
  Process Id: 7378
  Instance Id: 0
  IS Levels: level-2-only
  Manual area address(es):
    49.0001
  Routing for area address(es):
    49.0001
  LSP MTU: 1492
  LSP Full: level-1: No, level-2: No
  Non-stop forwarding: IETF NSF Restart enabled
  Most recent startup mode: Cold Restart
  TE connection status: Up
  XTC connection status: Up
  Overload Bit: not configured
  Maximum Metric: not configured
  Topologies supported by IS-IS:
    IPv4 Unicast
```

```
RP/0/RP0/CPU0:NCS-5508-2# configure
Wed Mar 27 15:50:54.776 CDT
RP/0/RP0/CPU0:NCS-5508-2(config)# router isis lab
RP/0/RP0/CPU0:NCS-5508-2(config-isis)# nsf cisco
RP/0/RP0/CPU0:NCS-5508-2(config-isis)# commit
Wed Mar 27 15:51:43.787 CDT
RP/0/RP0/CPU0:NCS-5508-2(config-isis)# do show isis protocols | include Non-stop
Wed Mar 27 15:52:24.264 CDT
 Non-stop forwarding: Cisco Proprietary NSF Restart enabled
RP/0/RP0/CPU0:NCS-5508-2(config-isis)# do show isis neighbor detail
Wed Mar 27 15:56:16.056 CDT

IS-IS lab neighbors:
System Id       Interface       SNPA          State Holdtime Type IETF-NSF
MIG-8201-1      FH0/1/0/22      *PtoP*        Up    26       L2   Capable
  Area Address(es): 49.0001
  IPv4 Address(es): 44.44.24.9*
  Topologies: 'IPv4 Unicast'
  Uptime: 6w0d
8808_1          FH0/1/0/18      *PtoP*        Up    26       L2   Capable
  Area Address(es): 49.0001
  IPv4 Address(es): 40.40.12.1*
  Topologies: 'IPv4 Unicast'
  Uptime: 6w0d
Total neighbor count: 2
```

Familiarize yourself with the shown NSF options as well as how to enable and verify NSF state within a specific protocol.

OSPF NSF

OSPF Graceful Restart allows you to reset the OSPF process without interrupting data forwarding. Everything you learned in the previous IS-IS example still applies. It is just done a bit differently because it is a different link-state protocol. OSPF also offers two options: Cisco NSF and IETF NSF. Regardless of the implementation, there are two modes:

- **Restarting Mode:** This is the router performing non-stop forwarding recovery because of an RP switchover, which may have resulted from an RP crash or a software upgrade on the active RP.

- **Helper Mode:** When a neighboring router is restarting, this router is helping in the non-stop forwarding recovery.

Here are the two options:

- **Cisco OSPF NSF:** Pre-RFC 3623. To prevent neighbor adjacency disruptions, Cisco introduced a new bit called *Restart Signal* in the Hello protocol. When this bit is set in a Hello packet, it signals that the router is undergoing a route processor switchover.

Upon receiving such a Hello packet, a neighbor router would disregard the usual two-way connectivity check. The Restart Signal bit would reset when the neighbor adjacency is restored.

■ **IETF OSPF NSF:** Described in RFC 3623; ensures multivendor interoperability. A "restarting" NSF-capable router originates "grace-LSAs" to notify its neighbors that it will perform a Graceful Restart within the specified amount of time or grace period. During this grace period, the neighboring OSPF routers (helper routers) continue to announce the restarting router in their LSAs as if it were fully adjacent, as long as the network topology remains static.

The concept is the same as in IS-IS, and if you carefully read through the output in Example 20-2, you will understand what they do.

Example 20-2 *OSPF NSF Configuration Options*

```
RP/0/RP0/CPU0:8808_1# configure
Wed Mar 27 18:13:26.797 CDT
RP/0/RP0/CPU0:8808_1(config)# router ospf 1
RP/0/RP0/CPU0:8808_1(config-ospf)# nsf ?
  cisco             Enable Cisco Non Stop Forwarding
  flush-delay-time  Maximum time allowed for external route learning (seconds)
  ietf              Enable ietf graceful restart
  interval          Minimum interval between NSF restarts (seconds)
  lifetime          Maximum route lifetime following restart (seconds)
  wait-time         Maximum time allowed for neigbor discovery (seconds)
RP/0/RP0/CPU0:8808_1(config-ospf)# nsf cisco ?
  enforce  Cancel NSF restart when non-NSF-aware neighbors detected
  <cr>
RP/0/RP0/CPU0:8808_1(config-ospf)# nsf interval ?
  <90-3600>  seconds
RP/0/RP0/CPU0:8808_1(config-ospf)# nsf wait-time ?
  <1-120>  seconds
RP/0/RP0/CPU0:8808_1(config-ospf)# nsf lifetime ?
  <90-1800>  seconds
RP/0/RP0/CPU0:8808_1(config-ospf)# nsf ?
  cisco             Enable Cisco Non Stop Forwarding
  flush-delay-time  Maximum time allowed for external route learning (seconds)
  ietf              Enable ietf graceful restart
  interval          Minimum interval between NSF restarts (seconds)
  lifetime          Maximum route lifetime following restart (seconds)
  wait-time         Maximum time allowed for neigbor discovery (seconds)
RP/0/RP0/CPU0:8808_1(config-ospf)# nsf ietf ?
  helper               router's helper support level
  strict-lsa-checking  terminate graceful restart helper mode if lsa changed
  <cr>
```

```
RP/0/RP0/CPU0:8808_1(config-ospf)# nsf ietf helper ?
  disable  router's helper support disabled
RP/0/RP0/CPU0:8808_1(config-ospf)# nsf ietf helper disable ?
  <cr>
RP/0/RP0/CPU0:8808_1(config-ospf)#
```

Peers that support NSF can collaborate using Graceful Restart extensions for BGP. RFC 4724 describes this behavior. You may remember that the Capability Code for Graceful Restart Capability is 64; this is how BGP advertises GR intent either globally or per address family. Example 20-3 shows how to work with BGP NSF Graceful Restart.

Example 20-3 *BGP NSF Graceful Restart*

```
P4(config)# router bgp 65000
P4(config-router)# neighbor 10.100.46.6 remote-as 65001
P4(config-router)# bgp graceful-?
graceful-restart  graceful-shutdown
P4(config-router)# bgp graceful-restart ?
  all            Enable BGP GR for all platforms (even non-NSF capable ones)
  extended       Enable Graceful-Restart Extension
  restart-time   Set the max time needed to restart and come back up
  stalepath-time Set the max time to hold onto restarting peer's stale paths
  <cr>           <cr>
P4(config-router)# bgp graceful-restart restart-time ?
  <1-3600>  Delay value (seconds)
P4(config-router)# bgp graceful-restart
All BGP sessions must be reset to take the new GR config
P4(config-router)# bgp update-delay ?
  <1-3600>  Delay value (seconds)
P4(config-router)# bgp graceful-restart stalepath-time ?
  <1-3600>  Delay value (seconds).
P4(config-router)# bgp graceful-restart stalepath-time 360
P4(config-router)# do show running-config | begin router bgp
router bgp 65000
 bgp log-neighbor-changes
 bgp graceful-restart
 neighbor 10.100.46.6 remote-as 65001
!
```

```
PE6(config-router)# do clear ip bgp *
PE6(config-router)# do show ip bgp summary
BGP router identifier 10.100.100.6, local AS number 65001
BGP table version is 1, main routing table version 1

Neighbor        V     AS MsgRcvd MsgSent  TblVer  InQ OutQ Up/Down   State/PfxRcd
10.100.46.4     4  65000       4       4       1    0    0 00:00:00             0
```

```
PE6(config-router)# do show ip bgp neighbor | include Grace
   Graceful Restart Capability: advertised and received
 Graceful-Restart is enabled, restart-time 120 seconds, stalepath-time 360 seconds
PE6(config-router)#
```

On P4 (grab any router, I quickly stood up a BGP session), you can see a few available parameters for Graceful Restart. I am showing options for **restart-time**, which is the maximum wait time until a peer is declared dead. The **update-delay** specifies the maximum time the router should expect BGP updates from the router that has reconnected after a restart. The **stalepath-time** indicates how long after reconnecting with a router that has restarted a router will continue to use stale routes. I left the values on their default (120, 120, 360 seconds) settings, as can be seen in the output of router R6 after I cleared the BGP session.

Be aware that OSPFv3 is also supported for Graceful Restart.

NSR

What do you think the one common problem is with the control plane switchover processes I have described in the preceding sections? Please do not read ahead. I would like you to *analyze and access* what you have read, even though you may not come up with an answer or the answer I'm looking for.

I am wasting this line in the book to prevent wandering eyes from seeing the key word to focus on. What they have in common are broken protocol adjacencies or peerings. Stateful or not, there is a moment of disruption. What if other events take place on the network at this moment? A neighboring router can advertise a path that has been rerouted because of a failure. When our "restarting" router comes back online, it can readvertise the failed path back into the network, and the network is disrupted again until many routers recompute a solution. There is also the inconvenience of the GR extensions that need to be supported on routers. It seems that no solution is perfect, and there is always room for improvement.

Non-stop routing (NSR) brings *routing awareness to the standby control plane*. This ensures that in the event of failover, the newly active routing plane can seamlessly take control of established sessions. This process is internal to the device, so GR extensions or neighbor dependencies are no longer necessary. It suppresses routing changes for devices with redundant route processors during processor switchover events (RP failover or ISSU) and, thus, reduces network instability and downtime. Switching from the active to standby RP has no impact on the other routers in the network. All information needed to continue the routing protocol peering state is transferred to the standby processor prior to the switchover, so it can continue immediately when a switchover occurs.

Obviously, NSR works *only* on platforms with dual RPs. Example 20-4 shows how to work with NSR.

Example 20-4   *NSR Configurations*

```
RP/0/RP0/CPU0:8808_1# show isis nsr status
Thu Mar 28 05:48:40.255 CDT


IS-IS lab NSR(v1a) is not enabled
IS-IS lab NSR(v1a) STATUS (Not Ready):
```

```
                     V1 Standby     V2 Active    V2 Standby
   SYNC STATUS:        FALSE(0)       FALSE(0)     FALSE(0)
   PEER CHG COUNT:          0              0            0
   UP TIME:             not up         not up       not up
RP/0/RP0/CPU0:8808_1# configure
Thu Mar 28 05:48:46.997 CDT
RP/0/RP0/CPU0:8808_1(config)# router isis lab
RP/0/RP0/CPU0:8808_1(config-isis)# nsr ?
   <cr>
RP/0/RP0/CPU0:8808_1(config-isis)# nsr
RP/0/RP0/CPU0:8808_1(config-isis)# commit
Thu Mar 28 05:49:20.984 CDT
RP/0/RP0/CPU0:8808_1(config-isis)# end
RP/0/RP0/CPU0:8808_1# show isis nsr status
Thu Mar 28 05:56:07.758 CDT


IS-IS lab NSR(v1a) STATUS (HA Ready):
                     V1 Standby     V2 Active    V2 Standby
   SYNC STATUS:        TRUE           FALSE(0)     FALSE(0)
   PEER CHG COUNT:          1              0            0
   UP TIME:             00:04:01       not up       not up
RP/0/RP0/CPU0:8808_1# show isis nsr statistics
Thu Mar 28 05:56:51.371 CDT


IS-IS lab NSR(v1a) MANDATORY STATS :
                     V1 Active   V1 Standby   V2 Active   V2 Standby
   L1 ADJ:                0            0           0           0
   L2 ADJ:                1            1           0           0
   LIVE INTERFACE:        3            3           0           0
   PTP INTERFACE:         2            2           0           0
   LAN INTERFACE:         0            0           0           0
   LOOPBACK INTERFACE:    0            0           0           0
   TE Tunnel:             0            0           0           0
   TE LINK:               1            1           0           0
   NSR OPTIONAL STATS :
   L1 LSP:                0            0           0           0
   L2 LSP:                3            3           0           0
   IPV4 ROUTES:           5            5           0           0
   IPV6 ROUTES:           0            0           0           0
RP/0/RP0/CPU0:8808_1# show isis nsr ?
   adjacency    IS-IS NSR Adjacency(cisco-support)
   interface    IS-IS NSR Interface(cisco-support)
   statistics   IS-IS NSR statistics data
   status       IS-IS NSR Status
```

```
RP/0/RP0/CPU0:8808_1# show isis nsr interface
Thu Mar 28 05:57:49.458 CDT


IS-IS lab Interfaces
Nii0                              Enabled
  Adjacency Formation:            Enabled
  Prefix Advertisement:           Disabled (No cfg topology can participate)
  IPv4 BFD:                       Disabled
  IPv6 BFD:                       Disabled
  BFD Min Interval:               150
  BFD Multiplier:                 3
  Bandwidth:                      0

  Circuit Type:                   level-2-only (Configured: level-1-2)
  Media Type:                     P2P
  Circuit Number:                 0
  Extended Circuit Number:        65537
  Last IIH Received:              05:57:45 (4.31 sec ago), 128 octets
  Last IIH Sent:                  05:57:43 (6.11 sec ago), 137 octets
  Sending next P2P IIH in:        22 s

  Level-2
    Adjacency Count:              1
    LSP Pacing Interval:          33 ms
    PSNP Entry Queue Size:        0
    Hello Interval:               30 s
    Hello Multiplier:             3

  CLNS I/O
    Protocol State:               Up
    MTU:                          9200

  IPv4 Unicast Topology:          Enabled
    Adjacency Formation:          Running
    Prefix Advertisement:         Disabled (Global prefixes are not known)
        Policy (L1/L2):           -/-
    Metric (L1/L2):               10/10
    Metric fallback:
      Bandwidth (L1/L2):          Inactive/Inactive
      Anomaly (L1/L2):            Inactive/Inactive
    Weight (L1/L2):               0/0
    MPLS Max Label Stack:         1/3/7/0 (PRI/BKP/SRTE/SRAT)
    MPLS LDP Sync (L1/L2):        Disabled/Disabled
    FRR (L1/L2):                  L1 Not Enabled      L2 Not Enabled
      FRR Type:                   None                None
```

```
          IPv6 Unicast Topology:    Enabled
            Adjacency Formation:    Running
          Prefix Advertisement:     Disabled (Global prefixes are not known)
                 Policy (L1/L2):    -/-
          Metric (L1/L2):           10/10
          Metric fallback:
            Bandwidth (L1/L2):      Inactive/Inactive
              Anomaly (L1/L2):      Inactive/Inactive
          Weight (L1/L2):           0/0
          MPLS Max Label Stack:     1/3/7/0 (PRI/BKP/SRTE/SRAT)
          MPLS LDP Sync (L1/L2):    Disabled/Disabled
          FRR (L1/L2):              L1 Not Enabled      L2 Not Enabled
              FRR Type:             None                None

      IPv4 Address Family:          Enabled
        Protocol State:             Up
        Global Prefix(es):          None (No global addresses are configured)
      IPv6 Address Family:          Enabled
        Protocol State:             Up
        Forwarding Address(es): ::
RP/0/RP0/CPU0:8808_1# show isis nsr interface brief
Thu Mar 28 05:58:10.764 CDT


IS-IS lab Interfaces

    Interface    All    Adjs    Adj Topos  Adv Topos  CLNS   MTU    Prio
                 OK     L1  L2   Run/Cfg    Run/Cfg                 L1  L2
    ------------ ---    --------- ---------  ---------  ----   ----   ---------
Ni0              Yes    -   1     2/2        0/2        Up     9200   -   -
Ni1              No     -   -     1/2        0/2        Up     9200   -   -
Ni2              No     -   -     1/2        0/2        Up     9200   -   -
RP/0/RP0/CPU0:8808_1# show isis nsr adjacency
Thu Mar 28 06:05:47.222 CDT


IS-IS lab Level-2 adjacencies:
System Id      Interface           SNPA          State Hold Changed  NSF IPv4 IPv6
                                                                         BFD  BFD
8808_1-v1S Nii0                    *PtoP*         Up    82   00:15:57 Yes None None


Total adjacency count: 1


RP/0/RP0/CPU0:8808_1# show redundancy
Thu Mar 28 06:24:24.401 CDT
```

```
Redundancy information for node 0/RP0/CPU0:

===========================================
Node 0/RP0/CPU0 is in ACTIVE role
Partner node (0/RP1/CPU0) is in STANDBY role
Standby node in 0/RP1/CPU0 is ready
Standby node in 0/RP1/CPU0 is NSR-ready
```

This example is self-explanatory; there's not a whole lot to configure. The **show redundancy** command shows that both RPs are present. Non-stop routing is enabled by default for OSPF, OSPFv3, and BGP, while it's not the case for IS-IS (as observed), requiring manual activation. You use the **nsr disable** command to turn off NSR.

What makes this topic challenging for the exam? Different vendors describe different solutions for Graceful Restart, so if you're coming from a non-Cisco world, this can cause confusion. Focus your mind on what I described in this chapter, and you should do well with the exam questions.

BFD

Bidirectional Forwarding Detection (BFD), described in RFC 5880, is a lightweight protocol used to detect connectivity failures between two routers or devices in a timely manner. It operates at the network layer (Layer 3) and provides rapid detection of link failures across various network technologies, including Ethernet, MPLS, and IP.

BFD works by establishing a session between two routers or devices, known as BFD peers, and exchanging periodic control packets, or "heartbeat" messages, at a high frequency. If a router stops receiving these packets within a specified interval, it assumes that the link or neighbor has failed and can quickly trigger failover mechanisms, such as updating routing tables or initiating alternate paths. Key characteristics of BFD include the following:

- **Rapid Detection:** BFD detects link failures quickly, typically within milliseconds or microseconds, allowing for rapid convergence in the event of network disruptions.

- **Low Overhead:** BFD packets are small and lightweight, minimizing the impact on network resources and allowing for efficient operation even on low-bandwidth links.

- **Protocol Independence:** BFD can be used with various network protocols, including OSPF, BGP, and IS-IS, even static routing, enabling consistent and reliable failure detection across different routing domains.

- **Flexible Configuration:** BFD allows for flexible configuration of detection timers and parameters, allowing network administrators to adjust settings based on network requirements and performance considerations.

BFD is UDP-based, and what I always found interesting is that BFD adjacencies (unlike IS-IS, OSFP, RSVP) do not go down on the control plane restarts we have been covering in this chapter. The reason is that BFD deals with the forwarding plane outages. BFD operates in two main modes:

- **Asynchronous Mode:** In this mode, BFD operates independently of any routing protocol. It continuously sends BFD control packets at a predefined interval to detect connectivity failures. Asynchronous mode is commonly used for directly connected links or in scenarios where BFD sessions are established between devices that do not share a common routing protocol.

- **Demand Mode:** In Demand mode, BFD sessions are established dynamically when there is traffic to be forwarded. BFD control packets are sent only when there is data traffic flowing between peers. Interestingly enough, Cisco and other vendors do not support this mode.

An optional feature of BFD is the Echo function, which allows for the verification of bidirectional connectivity between two BFD peers. One BFD peer acts as the initiator and sends periodic Echo packets to the other peer. Upon receiving an Echo packet, the receiving peer responds with a corresponding Echo reply packet. This exchange verifies that both peers are capable of receiving and responding to packets, confirming bidirectional connectivity.

Again, there is no Demand mode support with Cisco, because it supports only the Asynchronous mode. The echo function is enabled by default, but you do not have to use it.

Figure 20-1 shows the difference between these two approaches for how BFD is supposed to function.

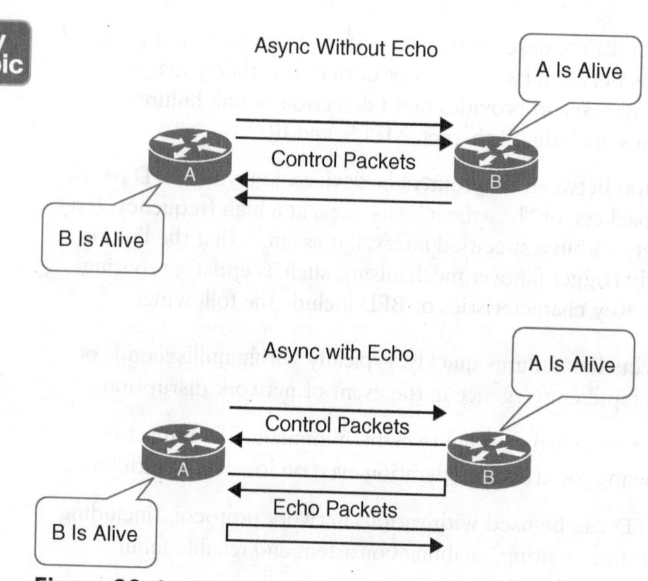

Figure 20-1 *BFD Modes on IOS XR*

Without the Echo function, both routers send independent control packets to each other. If a few packets are missing in a row, the router declares its peer dead.

With the Echo function, a router will send control packets and an echo packet with a source and destination address of the interface itself and a destination UDP port of 3785. The neighbor reflects the Echo back to the originator without processing it (which minimizes its process load of the packet) and increases the possible sensitivity of BFD. Example 20-5 shows how to configure BFD.

Example 20-5 *BFD Configurations*

```
RP/0/RP0/CPU0:8808_1(config)# show
Thu Mar 28 11:39:06.900 CDT
Building configuration...
!! IOS XR Configuration 7.7.1
router static
 address-family ipv4 unicast
  192.0.5.0/24 BVI200 10.1.58.5 bfd fast-detect
  192.0.5.0/24 HundredGigE0/1/0/18 10.1.58.5 bfd fast-detect
  192.0.6.0/24 10.1.99.99 bfd fast-detect multihop 10.1.58.8
 !
!
router isis lab
 interface FourHundredGigE0/0/0/0
  bfd minimum-interval 6500
  bfd multiplier 7
  bfd fast-detect ipv4
  address-family ipv4 unicast
  !
router ospf 1
 area 0
  interface FourHundredGigE0/1/0/18
   bfd minimum-interval 6500
   bfd fast-detect
   bfd multiplier 7
  !
 !
!
router bgp 65000
 neighbor 10.1.58.5
  remote-as 65001
  bfd fast-detect
  bfd multiplier 7
  bfd minimum-interval 6500
 !
!
end
RP/0/RP0/CPU0:8808_1# show bfd session
Thu Mar 28 12:38:00.416 CDT
Interface          Dest Addr             Local det time(int*mult)      State
                                         Echo        Async   H/W  NPU
------------------ ---------------      ----------------- ----------------  ----------
FH0/0/0/0          40.40.12.2           0s(0s*0)          45s(6500ms*7)   UP
                                                                  Yes  0/0/CPU0
```

```
RP/0/RP0/CPU0:8808_1# show bfd session detail
Thu Mar 28 12:38:12.703 CDT
I/f: FourHundredGigE0/0/0/0, Location: 0/0/CPU0
Dest: 40.40.12.2
Src: 40.40.12.1
 State: UP for 0d:0h:1m:22s, number of times UP: 1
 Session type: PR/V4/SH
Received parameters:
 Version: 1, desired tx interval: 6500 ms, required rx interval: 6500 ms
 Required echo rx interval: 0 ms, multiplier: 7, diag: None
 My discr: 2150645764, your discr: 2147549185, state UP, D/F/P/C/A: 0/0/0/1/0
Transmitted parameters:
 Version: 1, desired tx interval: 1 s, required rx interval: 1 s
 Required echo rx interval: 1 ms, multiplier: 7, diag: None
 My discr: 2147549185, your discr: 2150645764, state UP, D/F/P/C/A: 0/0/0/1/0
Timer Values:
 Local negotiated async tx interval: 6500 ms
 Remote negotiated async tx interval: 6500 ms
 Desired echo tx interval: 0 s, local negotiated echo tx interval: 0 ms
 Echo detection time: 0 ms(0 ms*7), async detection time: 45 s(6500 ms*7)
Local Stats:
 Intervals between async packets:
   Tx: Number of intervals=2, min=650 ms, max=4249 ms, avg=2449 ms
       Last packet transmitted 82 s ago
   Rx: Number of intervals=1, min=650 ms, max=650 ms, avg=650 ms
       Last packet received 82 s ago
 Intervals between echo packets:
   Tx: Number of intervals=0, min=0 s, max=0 s, avg=0 s
       Last packet transmitted 0 s ago
   Rx: Number of intervals=0, min=0 s, max=0 s, avg=0 s
       Last packet received 0 s ago
 Latency of echo packets (time between tx and rx):
   Number of packets: 0, min=0 ms, max=0 ms, avg=0 ms
Session owner information:

                        Desired               Adjusted
 Client           Interval   Multiplier  Interval   Multiplier
 ----------------- ---------- ----------- ---------- -----------
 isis-lab          6500 ms      7         6500 ms      7

H/W Offload Info:
 H/W Offload capability : Y, Hosted NPU      : 0/0/CPU0
 Async Offloaded        : Y, Echo Offloaded : N
 Async rx/tx            : 2/3
```

```
Platform Info:
NPU ID: 0
Async RTC ID            : 0          Echo RTC ID            : 0
Async Feature Mask  : 0x0           Echo Feature Mask  : 0x0
Async Session ID    : 0x1           Echo Session ID    : 0x0
Async Tx Key            : 0x80010001  Echo Tx Key           : 0x0
Async Tx Stats addr : 0x0   Echo Tx Stats addr : 0x0
Async Rx Stats addr : 0x0   Echo Rx Stats addr : 0x0
RP/0/RP0/CPU0:8808_1# show bfd interfaces location 0/0/CPU0
Thu Mar 28 12:39:07.722 CDT
FourHundredGigE0/0/0/0
Ifhandle 0x168 Base Caps 30
Threaded IFH 1 IFNAME 1 Echo usage 0 Flags 0x2 Iftype 0xcd
Number of sessions 1 Enabled
Number of invalid IPv4 async:            0,  Number of invalid IPv4 echo:    0
Number of invalid IPv6 async:            0,  Number of invalid IPv6 echo:    0
Number of invalid Label async:           0
RP/0/RP0/CPU0:8808_1#
```

I provided a configuration that enables BFD on three types of static routes: single-hops, directly connected next tops, and multihops. Next, you see BFD configurations for IS-IS, OSPF, and BGP. Notice that I set the BFD minimum interval to 6500 milliseconds with a multiplier of 7 (the default is 3) for all the dynamic protocols. I only commit the IS-IS portion to limit the output of the verification commands. The **show bfd session** command is the most important one, but you also have others to study in the output.

Link Aggregation

Since we're writing this book for a Cisco exam, I would like you to answer **Exam question number 1**:

What does **LACP** do?

   a. Joins multiple physical links together into a single logical path

   b. Divides the traffic across multiple physical links based on packet header hash

   c. None of the above

   d. A and B

What is your answer? Is it C? That is the right answer. If you talk about **Link Aggregation Group (LAG)** IEEE802.3ad standard, then the right answer would have been D. LACP is an option in the LAG standard that provides Dynamic Control Protocol to run on LAG links to prevent you from plugging things into the wrong port. Think of it as a "miscabling" protocol that makes the devices send a system ID so that the correct dynamic LAG can be created. In static LAG, if you plug something into the wrong port, you will blackhole some of the traffic, but LACP will help you avoid this situation. Some of us have been doing this for so long that we have forgotten this and use LACP to describe grouping links together. Technically, LACP does not do this and is not necessary to group links together. It is helpful to group links together correctly. We should use it for the reason I described earlier, but LAG works without it. Let me refresh your memory in Example 20-6.

Example 20-6 *LAG Configuration on IOS XR and IOS*

```
RP/0/RP0/CPU0:PE3# show running-config
Thu Mar 28 21:35:00.978 UTC
! Output omitted for brevity
interface Bundle-Ether1
!
interface GigabitEthernet0/0/0/1
 bundle id 1 mode on
!
interface GigabitEthernet0/0/0/2
 bundle id 1 mode on
RP/0/RP0/CPU0:PE3# show interfaces bundle-ether 1
Thu Mar 28 21:36:21.841 UTC
Bundle-Ether1 is up, line protocol is up
  Interface state transitions: 3
  Hardware is Aggregated Ethernet interface(s), address is 0004.de35.4730
  Internet address is Unknown
  MTU 1514 bytes, BW 2000000 Kbit (Max: 2000000 Kbit)
     reliability 255/255, txload 0/255, rxload 0/255
  Encapsulation ARPA,
  Full-duplex, 2000Mb/s
  loopback not set,
  Last link flapped 00:51:29
    No. of members in this bundle: 2
      GigabitEthernet0/0/0/1        Full-duplex  1000Mb/s        Active
      GigabitEthernet0/0/0/2        Full-duplex  1000Mb/s        Active
  Last input 00:49:27, output never
  Last clearing of "show interface" counters never
  5 minute input rate 0 bits/sec, 0 packets/sec
  5 minute output rate 0 bits/sec, 0 packets/sec
     250 packets input, 31000 bytes, 0 total input drops
     0 drops for unrecognized upper-level protocol
     Received 0 broadcast packets, 0 multicast packets
              0 runts, 0 giants, 0 throttles, 0 parity
     0 input errors, 0 CRC, 0 frame, 0 overrun, 0 ignored, 0 abort
     150 packets output, 18600 bytes, 0 total output drops
     Output 0 broadcast packets, 0 multicast packets
     0 output errors, 0 underruns, 0 applique, 0 resets
     0 output buffer failures, 0 output buffers swapped out
     0 carrier transitions
RP/0/RP0/CPU0:PE3# show bundle
Thu Mar 28 21:55:31.231 UTC
Bundle-Ether1
  Status:                                          Up
  Local links <active/standby/configured>:         2 / 0 / 2
  Local bandwidth <effective/available>:           2000000 (2000000) kbps
```

```
MAC address (source):                        0004.de35.4730 (Chassis pool)
Inter-chassis link:                          No
Minimum active links / bandwidth:            1 / 1 kbps
Maximum active links:                        24
Wait while timer:                            2000 ms
Load balancing:
  Link order signaling:                      Not configured
  Hash type:                                 Default
  Locality threshold:                        None
LACP:                                        Not operational
  Flap suppression timer:                    Off
  Cisco extensions:                          Disabled
  Non-revertive:                             Disabled
mLACP:                                       Not configured
IPv4 BFD:                                    Not configured
IPv6 BFD:                                    Not configured


Port                 Device          State       Port ID           B/W, kbps
-------------------- --------------- ----------- ----------------- ----------
Gi0/0/0/1            Local           Active      0x8000, 0x0000      1000000
    Link is Active
Gi0/0/0/2            Local           Active      0x8000, 0x0000      1000000
    Link is Active
RP/0/RP0/CPU0:PE3#

PE2# show running-config
Building configuration...
! Output omitted for brevity
interface Port-channel1
 no ip address
!
interface GigabitEthernet1
 no ip address
!
interface GigabitEthernet2
 no ip address
 channel-group 1
PE2# show interface port-channel 1
Port-channel1 is up, line protocol is up
  Hardware is GEChannel, address is 001e.bd96.b0c0 (bia 001e.bd96.b0c0)
  MTU 1500 bytes, BW 1000000 Kbit/sec, DLY 10 usec,
     reliability 255/255, txload 1/255, rxload 1/255
  Encapsulation ARPA, loopback not set
  Keepalive set (10 sec)
  ARP type: ARPA, ARP Timeout 04:00:00
```

```
       No. of active members in this channel: 1
          Member 0 : GigabitEthernet2 , Full-duplex, 1000Mb/s
       No. of PF_JUMBO supported members in this channel : 1
    Last input never, output never, output hang never
    Last clearing of "show interface" counters 02:49:52
    Input queue: 0/375/0/0 (size/max/drops/flushes); Total output drops: 0
    Queueing strategy: fifo
    Output queue: 0/40 (size/max)
    5 minute input rate 0 bits/sec, 0 packets/sec
    5 minute output rate 0 bits/sec, 0 packets/sec
       134 packets input, 16616 bytes, 0 no buffer
       Received 0 broadcasts (0 IP multicasts)
       0 runts, 0 giants, 0 throttles
       0 input errors, 0 CRC, 0 frame, 0 overrun, 0 ignored
       0 watchdog, 0 multicast, 0 pause input
PE2#
```

The appropriateness of this topic reveals itself in the fact that I unintentionally made this mistake in Example 20-6, which I leave to your observation without correcting it. As you can see, as I bundled the two links between IOS XR and IOS, I made the mistake of not enabling interface GigabitEthernet1 as a member of the LAG bundle. Despite this, interfaces bundle-ether1 and port-channel1 both showed up in "Up, Up" status, so I copied the output into this book. It is not until I went to highlight the appropriate parts that I noticed that there was only a single member 0 on the IOS side, which made me look in the **show running-config** section. Thus, I did not "need" LACP to take this work, but I needed LACP to make it work correctly. In the current state, I am blackholing some traffic.

So, here is my top-10 list for the exam:

1. LAG groups multiple point-to-point links into one logical link to provide higher bidirectional bandwidth, redundancy, and load balancing between two routers.

2. The router assigns a virtual interface to the bundled link.

3. Component links can be dynamically added or deleted from the virtual interface.

4. The virtual interface is treated as a single interface on which you can configure an IP address (make the bundle L3 instead of L2) and other software features that the link bundle will use.

5. Packets sent to the link bundle are forwarded to one of the bundle's links.

6. There is a maximum of 64 member links in a single bundle.

7. Failure of a single link does not cause a loss of connectivity (you saw that), because traffic can flow on the available links if one of the links within a bundle fails.

8. You can add bandwidth without interrupting the packet flow.

9. Routers support mixed speed bundle members in a bundle.

10. IEEE 802.3ad—Standard technology employs a Link Aggregation Control Protocol (LACP) to ensure that all the member links in a bundle are compatible. The system automatically removes the links from a bundle that are incompatible or have failed.

Let's deal with LACP now. **Exam question number 2:** Previously, in Example 20-6, on PE3, we set the bundle mode to "on" in the beginning of the output. Is LACP running? Go check and then look at Example 20-7.

Example 20-7   *LACP Mode On*

```
RP/0/RP0/CPU0:PE3(config)# interface gigabitEthernet 0/0/0/1
RP/0/RP0/CPU0:PE3(config-if)# bundle id 1 mode ?
  active   Run LACP in active mode over the port.
  inherit  Run LACP as configured in bundle.
  on       Do not run LACP over the port.
  passive  Run LACP in passive mode over the port.
RP/0/RP0/CPU0:PE3(config-if)# do show lacp bundle-ether1
Fri Mar 29 09:55:14.256 UTC
Bundle Bundle-Ether1 is not running LACP
RP/0/RP0/CPU0:PE3(config-if)#
```

The answer is no; LACP is not running. Let's turn it on and see what happens. (Recall that the IOS side PE2 still has the unintended error I have not corrected.) I hope you already know that Active mode initiates connections, Passive mode accepts them. You cannot have both Passive sides connect successfully. Example 20-8 observes our unsuccessful attempt.

Example 20-8   *LACP Mode Active on PE3 Only*

```
RP/0/RP0/CPU0:PE3(config-if)# bundle id 1 mode active
RP/0/RP0/CPU0:PE3(config-if)# interface gigabitEthernet 0/0/0/2
RP/0/RP0/CPU0:PE3(config-if)# bundle id 1 mode active
RP/0/RP0/CPU0:PE3(config-if)# commit
Fri Mar 29 10:01:20.492 UTC
RP/0/RP0/CPU0:PE3(config-if)# do show lacp bundle-ether1
Fri Mar 29 10:01:32.980 UTC
State: a - Port is marked as Aggregatable.
       s - Port is Synchronized with peer.
       c - Port is marked as Collecting.
       d - Port is marked as Distributing.
       A - Device is in Active mode.
       F - Device requests PDUs from the peer at fast rate.
       D - Port is using default values for partner information.
       E - Information about partner has expired.


Bundle-Ether1

  Port            (rate)  State    Port ID        Key     System ID
  ------------------- -------- ------------- ------ ----------------------
Local
  Gi0/0/0/1          1s    a---A-D- 0x8000,0x0001 0x0001 0x8000,00-50-0b-49-a5-2b
  Partner           30s    -----FD- 0x0000,0x0000 0x0000 0x0000,00-00-00-00-00-00
```

```
  Gi0/0/0/2              1s   a---A-D-  0x8000,0x0002 0x0001 0x8000,00-50-0b-49-a5-2b
  Partner               30s   -----FD-  0x0000,0x0000 0x0000 0x0000,00-00-00-00-00-00


  Port              Receive      Period Selection  Mux        A Churn P Churn
  ----------------- ------------ ------ ---------- ---------- ------- -------
Local
  Gi0/0/0/1         Defaulted    Fast   Unselect   Detached   Monitor Monitor
  Gi0/0/0/2         Defaulted    Fast   Unselect   Detached   Monitor Monitor
RP/0/RP0/CPU0:PE3(config-if)# do show bundle
Fri Mar 29 10:03:42.444 UTC
Bundle-Ether1
  Status:                                          Down
  Local links <active/standby/configured>:         0 / 0 / 2
  Local bandwidth <effective/available>:           0 (0) kbps
  MAC address (source):                            0050.0b49.a52a (Chassis pool)
  Inter-chassis link:                              No
  Minimum active links / bandwidth:                1 / 1 kbps
  Maximum active links:                            24
  Wait while timer:                                2000 ms
  Load balancing:
    Link order signaling:                          Not configured
    Hash type:                                     Default
    Locality threshold:                            None
  LACP:                                            Operational
    Flap suppression timer:                        Off
    Cisco extensions:                              Disabled
    Non-revertive:                                 Disabled
  mLACP:                                           Not configured
  IPv4 BFD:                                        Not configured
  IPv6 BFD:                                        Not configured


  Port              Device          State        Port ID          B/W, kbps
  ----------------- --------------- ------------ ---------------- ----------
  Gi0/0/0/1         Local           Configured   0x8000, 0x0001    1000000
    Link is Defaulted; LACPDUs are not being received from the partner
  Gi0/0/0/2         Local           Configured   0x8000, 0x0002    1000000
    Link is Defaulted; LACPDUs are not being received from the partner
RP/0/RP0/CPU0:PE3(config-if)# do sh lacp system-id
Fri Mar 29 10:05:42.828 UTC
Priority  MAC Address
--------  -----------------
  0x8000  00-50-0b-49-a5-2b
RP/0/RP0/CPU0:PE3(config-if)#
```

This is not good. LACP is up, but the bundle is down. The reason is that both links have defaulted because no LACP data units were received from the other side. *Please understand the states I highlighted in the output shown in Example 20-8.* Also, notice the system ID; this is how LACP knows legitimate ports (belonging to the same system ID) from the ports you miscabled that are possibly going to a coffee machine. Let's fix only interface GigabitEthernet2 on PE2 and rerun the commands, as shown in Example 20-9.

Example 20-9 *LACP Mode Passive on One Interface on PE2*

```
PE2(config-if)# interface gigabitEthernet 2
PE2(config-if)# channel-group 1 mode ?
  active   Enable LACP unconditionally
  passive  Enable LACP only if a LACP device is detected
  <cr>     <cr>

PE2(config-if)# channel-group 1 mode passive
Interface already configured in Port-Channel-1.
PE2(config-if)# no channel-group 1
PE2(config-if)# channel-group 1 mode passive
PE2(config-if)#
```

```
RP/0/RP0/CPU0:PE3(config-if)# do show lacp bundle-ether1
Fri Mar 29 10:12:39.551 UTC
State: a - Port is marked as Aggregatable.
       s - Port is Synchronized with peer.
       c - Port is marked as Collecting.
       d - Port is marked as Distributing.
       A - Device is in Active mode.
       F - Device requests PDUs from the peer at fast rate.
       D - Port is using default values for partner information.
       E - Information about partner has expired.


Bundle-Ether1

  Port              (rate)  State     Port ID        Key     System ID
  ----------------- ------- --------- -------------- ------- -----------------------
Local
  Gi0/0/0/1         1s      a---A-D-  0x8000,0x0001  0x0001  0x8000,00-50-0b-49-a5-2b
    Partner         30s     -----FD-  0x0000,0x0000  0x0000  0x0000,00-00-00-00-00-00
  Gi0/0/0/2         30s     ascdA---  0x8000,0x0002  0x0001  0x8000,00-50-0b-49-a5-2b
    Partner         30s     ascd----  0x8000,0x0001  0x0001  0x8000,00-1e-bd-f7-9a-00


  Port              Receive    Period  Selection  Mux       A Churn  P Churn
  ----------------- ---------- ------- ---------- --------- -------- -------
Local
  Gi0/0/0/1         Defaulted  Fast    Unselect   Detached  Churn    Churn
  Gi0/0/0/2         Current    Slow    Selected   Distrib   None     None
RP/0/RP0/CPU0:PE3(config-if)# do show bundle
Fri Mar 29 10:12:51.008 UTC
```

```
Bundle-Ether1
  Status:                                         Up
  Local links <active/standby/configured>:        1 / 0 / 2
  Local bandwidth <effective/available>:          1000000 (1000000) kbps
  MAC address (source):                           0050.0b49.a52a (Chassis pool)
  Inter-chassis link:                             No
  Minimum active links / bandwidth:               1 / 1 kbps
  Maximum active links:                           24
  Wait while timer:                               2000 ms
  Load balancing:
    Link order signaling:                         Not configured
    Hash type:                                    Default
    Locality threshold:                           None
  LACP:                                           Operational
    Flap suppression timer:                       Off
    Cisco extensions:                             Disabled
    Non-revertive:                                Disabled
  mLACP:                                          Not configured
  IPv4 BFD:                                       Not configured
  IPv6 BFD:                                       Not configured

  Port                  Device          State       Port ID          B/W, kbps
  --------------------  --------------  ----------  --------------   ----------
  Gi0/0/0/1             Local           Configured  0x8000, 0x0001     1000000
      Link is Defaulted; LACPDUs are not being received from the partner
  Gi0/0/0/2             Local           Active      0x8000, 0x0002     1000000
      Link is Active
RP/0/RP0/CPU0:PE3(config-if)#
```

As you can see, I had to delete and re-enter the command on PE2. Observe the states that
changed on PE3, and Gi0/0/0/2 shows active. Important: the bundle shows in the "Up" state
(not "Down" as before), but one of the member interfaces is not healthy. This would have
been good to know when I misconfigured PE2 and is the reason why LACP is important:
it would have ratted out my mistake instead of me blackholing some of the traffic.
Example 20-10 shows how to get this to work properly.

Example 20-10 *LACP Mode Passive on Both Interfaces on PE2*

```
PE2(config-if)# interface gigabitEthernet 1
PE2(config-if)# channel-group 1 mode passive
PE2(config-if)#
```

```
RP/0/RP0/CPU0:PE3(config-if)# do show bundle
Fri Mar 29 10:23:40.390 UTC
```

```
Bundle-Ether1
  Status:                                        Up
  Local links <active/standby/configured>:       1 / 0 / 2
  Local bandwidth <effective/available>:         1000000 (1000000) kbps
  MAC address (source):                          0050.0b49.a52a (Chassis pool)
  Inter-chassis link:                            No
  Minimum active links / bandwidth:              1 / 1 kbps
  Maximum active links:                          24
  Wait while timer:                              2000 ms
  Load balancing:
    Link order signaling:                        Not configured
    Hash type:                                   Default
    Locality threshold:                          None
  LACP:                                          Operational
    Flap suppression timer:                      Off
    Cisco extensions:                            Disabled
    Non-revertive:                               Disabled
  mLACP:                                         Not configured
  IPv4 BFD:                                      Not configured
  IPv6 BFD:                                      Not configured

  Port                  Device          State         Port ID          B/W, kbps
  --------------------  --------------  ----------    --------------    ----------
  Gi0/0/0/1             Local           Negotiating   0x8000, 0x0001     1000000
      Wait-while timer is running
  Gi0/0/0/2             Local           Active        0x8000, 0x0002     1000000
      Link is Active
RP/0/RP0/CPU0:PE3(config-if)# do sh bundle
Fri Mar 29 10:23:48.137 UTC

Bundle-Ether1
  Status:                                        Up
  Local links <active/standby/configured>:       2 / 0 / 2
  Local bandwidth <effective/available>:         2000000 (2000000) kbps
  MAC address (source):                          0050.0b49.a52a (Chassis pool)
  Inter-chassis link:                            No
  Minimum active links / bandwidth:              1 / 1 kbps
  Maximum active links:                          24
  Wait while timer:                              2000 ms
  Load balancing:
    Link order signaling:                        Not configured
    Hash type:                                   Default
    Locality threshold:                          None
  LACP:                                          Operational
    Flap suppression timer:                      Off
```

```
    Cisco extensions:                  Disabled
    Non-revertive:                     Disabled
  mLACP:                               Not configured
  IPv4 BFD:                            Not configured
  IPv6 BFD:                            Not configured


  Port              Device         State       Port ID          B/W, kbps
  ----------------  -------------  ----------  ---------------  ----------
  Gi0/0/0/1         Local          Active      0x8000, 0x0001    1000000
      Link is Active
  Gi0/0/0/2         Local          Active      0x8000, 0x0002    1000000
      Link is Active
RP/0/RP0/CPU0:PE3(config-if)# do show lacp bundle-ether1
Fri Mar 29 10:23:54.420 UTC
State: a - Port is marked as Aggregatable.
       s - Port is Synchronized with peer.
       c - Port is marked as Collecting.
       d - Port is marked as Distributing.
       A - Device is in Active mode.
       F - Device requests PDUs from the peer at fast rate.
       D - Port is using default values for partner information.
       E - Information about partner has expired.


Bundle-Ether1


  Port             (rate)  State    Port ID          Key     System ID
  ---------------  ------  -------  ---------------  ------  ----------------------
Local
  Gi0/0/0/1        30s     ascdA--- 0x8000,0x0001  0x0001  0x8000,00-50-0b-49-a5-2b
    Partner        30s     ascd---- 0x8000,0x0001  0x0001  0x8000,00-1e-bd-f7-9a-00
  Gi0/0/0/2        30s     ascdA--- 0x8000,0x0002  0x0001  0x8000,00-50-0b-49-a5-2b
    Partner        30s     ascd---- 0x8000,0x0001  0x0001  0x8000,00-1e-bd-f7-9a-00


  Port                     Receive   Period Selection  Mux       A Churn P Churn
  ---------------          --------  ------ ----------  --------  ------- -------
Local
  Gi0/0/0/1                Current   Slow   Selected    Distrib   None    None
  Gi0/0/0/2                Current   Slow   Selected    Distrib   None    None
RP/0/RP0/CPU0:PE3(config-if)#
```

Notice that I catch it right in the middle of the Negotiating stage, and finally, the bundle is
fully working. We are at Layer 2 right now.

 Here's some homework. Create subinterfaces for the bundle and then, separately, turn the
bundle into a Layer 3 interface. Example 20-11 gives a clue on how to work with Layer 2
subinterfaces.

Example 20-11 *Layer 2 Subinterfaces on a Bundle*

```
RP/0/RP0/CPU0:PE3(config)# interface bundle-ether 1.100 l2transport
RP/0/RP0/CPU0:PE3(config-subif)# encapsulation dot1q 100
RP/0/RP0/CPU0:PE3(config-subif)#
```

The minimum links parameter specifies the minimum number of active physical links required for the LAG to be considered operational. If the number of active links falls below this threshold, the entire LAG is considered down, and traffic is not forwarded. This ensures a certain level of redundancy and bandwidth availability. If the link count drops below this level, the LAG shuts down to prevent suboptimal performance. The maximum links parameter can define the maximum number of physical links that can be active in a LAG at any given time. This controls the number of active links to avoid exceeding the desired bandwidth or hardware capabilities. Extra links that exceed the maximum become backup links, waiting to take over if one of the active links fails. Example 20-12 takes you through these options in IOS XR and IOS. Examine them carefully.

Example 20-12 *Minimum and Maximum LACP Links and Bandwidth Examined*

```
RP/0/RP0/CPU0:PE3# show running-config
RP/0/RP0/CPU0:PE3(config)# interface bundle-ether 1
RP/0/RP0/CPU0:PE3(config-if)# bundle ?
  lacp-delay       Set the lacp-delay timeout for members of this bundle
  lacp-fallback    Set the lacp-fallback for members of this bundle
  load-balancing   Load balancing commands on a bundle
  logging          logging events for the members of this bundle
  maximum-active   Set a limit on the number of links that can be active
  minimum-active   Set the minimum criteria for the bundle to be active
  shutdown         Bring all links in the bundle down to Standby state
  wait-while       Set the wait-while timeout for members of this bundle
RP/0/RP0/CPU0:PE3(config-if)# bundle maximum-active ?
  links  Set the maximum number of active links in this bundle
RP/0/RP0/CPU0:PE3(config-if)# bundle maximum-active links ?
  <1-64>  Maximum number of active links in this bundle
RP/0/RP0/CPU0:PE3(config-if)# bundle maximum-active links 64 ?
  hot-standby  Hot-standby behaviour (non-standard, only effective on links with
  LACP enabled)
  <cr>
RP/0/RP0/CPU0:PE3(config-if)# bundle minimum-active ?
  bandwidth  Set the bandwidth (in kbps) needed to bring up this bundle
  links      Set the number of active links needed to bring up this bundle
RP/0/RP0/CPU0:PE3(config-if)# bundle minimum-active links ?
  <1-64>  Number of active links needed to bring up this bundle
RP/0/RP0/CPU0:PE3(config-if)# bundle minimum-active links 64 ?
  <cr>
```

```
RP/0/RP0/CPU0:PE3(config-if)# bundle minimum-active bandwidth ?
 <1-4294967295>  Bandwidth needed to bring up this bundle (in kbps)
 gbps            Set the bandwidth in gbps
 kbps            Set the bandwidth in kbps
 mbps            Set the bandwidth in mbps
RP/0/RP0/CPU0:PE3(config-if)# bundle minimum-active bandwidth 1000000 ?
 <cr>
RP/0/RP0/CPU0:PE3(config-if)# bundle minimum-active bandwidth gbps 1 ?
 <cr>
RP/0/RP0/CPU0:PE3#
```

```
PE2(config)# interface port-channel 1
PE2(config-if)# lacp ?
 device-id       LACP device id on members of this interface
 failover        Link failover options
 fast-switchover Enable LACP fast switchover on this port channel
 max-bundle      LACP maximum number of ports to bundle in this port channel
 min-bundle      LACP minimum number of ports to bundle in this port channel
PE2(config-if)# lacp max-bundle ?
 <1-4>  Max number of ports to bundle in this Port Channel
PE2(config-if)# lacp max-bundle 4 ?
 <cr>  <cr>
PE2(config-if)# lacp min-bundle ?
 <1-4>  Minimum number of ports to bundle in this Port Channel
```

Notice that you have a choice of how to configure hashing for load-balancing purposes.
This distributes traffic across active links based on a hash of packet header fields, balancing
the load while preserving packet order within a flow. By default, load balancing on Layer 2
link bundles is done based on the MAC source and destination address (SA/DA) fields in the
incoming packet header. The standard hash calculation typically uses a 5-tuple, incorporating
the following parameters:

- Source IP address

- Destination IP address

- Router ID

- Source port (Layer 4)

- Destination port (Layer 4)

Example 20-13 show the options to change the hash that controls link selection.

Example 20-13 *Load Balancing on a Bundled Link*

```
RP/0/RP0/CPU0:PE3(config)# interface bundle-ether 1
RP/0/RP0/CPU0:PE3(config-if)# bundle load-balancing hash ?
  dst-ip  Use the destination IP as the hash function
  src-ip  Use the source IP as the hash function
RP/0/RP0/CPU0:PE3(config-if)# bundle load-balancing hash dst-ip ?
  <cr>
RP/0/RP0/CPU0:PE3(config-if)# bundle load-balancing hash src-ip ?
  <cr>
```

To sum up Link Aggregation Groups: LAG is good, LACP is better, but a fatter pipe is my choice.

Exam Preparation Tasks

As mentioned in the section "How to Use This Book" in the Introduction, you have a few choices for exam preparation: the exercises here, Chapter 23, "Final Preparation," and the exam simulation questions in the Pearson Test Prep Software Online.

Review All Key Topics

Review the most important topics in this chapter, noted with the Key Topic icon in the margin of the page. Table 20-3 lists a reference of these key topics and the page numbers on which each is found.

Table 20-3 Key Topics for Chapter 20

Key Topic Element	Description	Page Number
Table 20-2	High Availability Cheat Sheet	906
List	IS-IS NSF Options	907
Figure 20-1	BFD Modes on IOS XR	918
List	LACP Top Ten	924

Define Key Terms

Define the following key terms from this chapter and check the answers in the glossary:

Bidirectional Forwarding Detection (BFD), Graceful Restart (GR), LACP, Link Aggregation Group (LAG), non-stop forwarding (NSF), non-stop routing (NSR), Stateful Switchover (SSO)

Command Reference to Check Your Memory

This section includes the most important configuration and EXEC commands covered in this chapter. You might not need to memorize the complete syntax of every command, but you should be able to remember the basic keywords that are needed.

To test your memory of the commands, cover the right side of Table 20-4 with a piece of paper, read the description on the left side, and then see how much of the command you can remember.

The 350-501 exam focuses on practical, hands-on skills that are used by networking professionals. Therefore, you should be able to identify the commands needed to configure and test. Note that not all commands are fully covered in the chapter, but their presence in the following table should lead you to investigate them further to understand this technology.

Table 20-4   CLI Commands to Know

Task	Command Syntax
Enable non-stop forwarding (NSF) on the next restart	nsf { cisco | ietf }
Activate Border Gateway Protocol (BGP) non-stop routing (NSR)	nsr
Enable graceful restart support	bgp graceful-restart
Enable Bidirectional Forwarding Detection (BFD) to detect failures in the path between adjacent forwarding engines	bfd fast-detect [disable | ipv4]
Specify the minimum control packet interval for BFD sessions for the corresponding BFD configuration scope	bfd minimum-interval *milliseconds*
Enable the option to use Cisco or IETF mode for BFD	bfd mode { cisco | ietf }
Set the Bidirectional Forwarding Detection (BFD) multiplier	bfd multiplier *multiplier*
Disable echo mode on a router or on an individual interface	echo disable
Add a port to an aggregated interface (or bundle)	bundle id *bundle-id* [mode {active | on | passive}]

Review Questions

As a part of the review, we encourage you to provide *a single-sentence answer* (keep your answers as short as possible) to the following questions. If you struggle to complete this answer in a single sentence, this may indicate a lack of clarity or reveal gaps in your understanding. We have constructed these questions to help you consolidate this chapter's information and extract the essence of the covered content.

The answers to these questions appear in Appendix A. For more practice with exam format questions, use the Pearson Test Prep Software Online.

1. How does non-stop forwarding (NSF) challenge traditional notions of fault tolerance and resilience, and what implications does it have for the design and implementation of high availability solutions in mission-critical environments?

2. How does non-stop routing (NSR) reshape our understanding of network resilience, and what considerations should be considered when implementing NSR in complex network environments to ensure seamless failover and uninterrupted service delivery?

3. In Link Aggregation Control Protocol (LACP), what mechanisms are in place to prevent link flapping and ensure stable link aggregation across diverse network environments, and how do these mechanisms contribute to overall network stability and performance?

Bibliography

D. Katz and D. Ward. RFC 5880, *Bidirectional Forwarding Detection (BFD)*, IETF, https://www.ietf.org/rfc/rfc5880.txt, June 2010.

M. Leelanivas, Y. Rekhter, and R. Aggarwal. RFC 3478, *Graceful Restart Mechanism for Label Distribution Protocol*, IETF, https://www.ietf.org/rfc/rfc3478.txt, February 2003.

J. Moy, P. Pillay-Esnault, and A. Lindem. RFC 3623, *Graceful OSPF Restart*, IETF, https://www.ietf.org/rfc/rfc3623.txt, November 2003.

S. Sangli, E. Chen, R. Fernando, J. Scudder, and Y. Rekhter. RFC 4724, *Graceful Restart Mechanism for BGP*, IETF, https://www.ietf.org/rfc/rfc4724.txt, January 2007.

M. Shand and L. Ginsberg. RFC 3847, *Restart Signaling for Intermediate System to Intermediate System (IS-IS)*, IETF, https://www.ietf.org/rfc/rfc3847.txt, July 2004.

M. Shand and L. Ginsberg. RFC 5306, *Restart Signaling for IS-IS*, IETF, https://www.ietf.org/rfc/rfc5306.txt, October 2008.

CHAPTER 21

Quality of Service

This chapter covers the following exam topics:

1.4 Describe QoS architecture

- 1.4.e IPv6 flow label

4.5 Implement QoS services

- 4.5.a Classification and marking
- 4.5.b Congestion avoidance, traffic policing, and shaping

Quality of Service (QoS) is a critical aspect of modern networking that prioritizes certain types of traffic over others to ensure optimal performance and resource allocation. In today's complex network environments, where diverse applications compete for bandwidth and resources, QoS plays a crucial role in ensuring that critical services receive the necessary level of performance and reliability. By implementing QoS mechanisms, such as traffic classification, congestion management, and traffic shaping, network administrators can effectively manage network congestion, minimize latency, and guarantee bandwidth for mission-critical applications. QoS enables organizations to meet their service-level agreements (SLAs) and deliver a consistent and reliable user experience, making it an indispensable tool for modern network management. This chapter covers the content you are very likely to see on the exam.

"Do I Know This Already?" Quiz

The "Do I Know This Already?" quiz allows you to assess whether you should read this entire chapter thoroughly or jump to the "Exam Preparation Tasks" section. If you are in doubt about your answers to these questions or your own assessment of your knowledge of the topics, read the entire chapter. Table 21-1 lists the major headings in this chapter and their corresponding "Do I Know This Already?" quiz questions. You can find the answers in Appendix A, "Answers to the 'Do I Know This Already?' Quizzes and Review Questions."

Table 21-1   "Do I Know This Already?" Section-to-Question Mapping

Foundation Topics Section	Questions
Traffic Classification	1
Traffic Policing	2
Traffic Shaping	3
Congestion Avoidance	4
Traffic Marking	5
IPv6 Flow Label	6

1. Which of the following statements best describes the process of QoS traffic classification?

    a. Performed solely at the ingress point of the network

    b. Involves assigning traffic to different classes

    c. Used to prioritize high-bandwidth applications

    d. Affects only the scheduling of packets in a router's output queue

2. What is the main advantage of using a Dual-Rate Three-Color Marker?

    a. DRTCM is used for marking traffic in dual-core processors.

    b. DRTCM allows for separate rates for marking packets as either conforming or exceeding the committed information rate (CIR).

    c. In DRTCM, the green color indicates the highest priority traffic, followed by yellow and then red.

    d. DRTCM uses three different markers to classify traffic based on its destination address.

3. What is the purpose of the token bucket algorithm?

    a. Dynamically adjusts the transmission rate based on network congestion

    b. Limits the average transmission rate of a traffic flow over a specified time interval

    c. Prioritizes certain types of traffic over others by assigning different token replenishment rates to each traffic class

    d. Enforces traffic policies by categorizing traffic into different classes and applying shaping rules

4. Which of the following statements best describes the purpose of QoS congestion avoidance?

    a. Immediately drops packets once a queue reaches its maximum capacity

    b. Operates solely on TCP traffic, dynamically adjusting window sizes to control the flow of data and prevent congestion, while UDP traffic remains unaffected by these mechanisms

    c. Prioritizes high-priority traffic during periods of congestion by increasing the probability of dropping lower-priority packets first, ensuring that high-priority traffic always gets through

    d. Proactively manages queue lengths and packet loss probabilities to prevent congestion from occurring

5. Which best describes the functionality of traffic marking?

   a. Tags packets with a unique identifier to trace their path through the network

   b. Prioritizes marked packets over unmarked packets, ensuring that marked packets are transmitted first

   c. Separates different types of multicast traffic to prevent network congestion

   d. Involves setting specific bits in the packet header, such as DSCP or IP precedence, to indicate the level of service a packet should receive

6. What is the purpose of the IPv6 flow label field?

   a. To identify the source and destination IP addresses of packets

   b. To specify ToS for packets traveling through the network

   c. Used for encryption and decryption of packet contents

   d. To label packets belonging to the same flow

Foundation Topics

Quality of Service (QoS) is a method used to prioritize and give special treatment to specific traffic flows, ensuring higher-priority packets are forwarded preferentially. The primary goal of implementing QoS in a network is to improve the service quality for certain types of traffic. A traffic flow can be broadly defined as a packet traveling from its source interface to its destination interface. To achieve end-to-end QoS delivery, it's essential to identify, classify, and prioritize traffic flows on all routers along the data forwarding path within the network. Cisco QoS implementations vary across different software and hardware platforms. However, it's important not to be discouraged by these differences. By understanding the underlying principles of QoS, you can apply them effectively regardless of the platform or software implementation. Additionally, remember that QoS is just one of the topics covered in the exam. The current exam blueprint allocates 25 percent of the 20 percent assigned to this section to QoS. Therefore, you should focus on mastering the main concepts and learn to configure these because you are likely to encounter questions related to these topics.

Cisco QoS largely relies on these techniques to provide for end-to-end QoS delivery across a heterogeneous network:

- **Packet classification and marking methods:** These methods are used to identify traffic flows and enable the division of network traffic into various priority levels or service classes.

- **Congestion management (Policing, Shaping):** These strategies are used to regulate congestion once it arises. One approach used by network devices to manage excessive incoming traffic is to use queuing algorithms to organize the traffic and then decide on a method to prioritize its transmission onto an output link.

- **Congestion avoidance:** Weighted Random Early Detection/Random Early Detection (WRED/RED) techniques vary across hardware platform implementations but can be grouped as monitoring network traffic patterns to predict and prevent congestion at typical bottlenecks before congestion issues arise.

The human mind poorly remembers concrete things long term. Analogies help us recall content because they are visual in nature, but you should be careful with analogies: they all finally break down, so use them to recall things, not to construct something that you have not tested. Multiple analogies exist to help with QoS concepts, but the one that has worked for me has to do with bank tellers. During the lunch rush, customers need to be served quickly to prevent frustration or losing them to another bank. What are the tellers to do? They classify the arriving customers and send the most valuable ones through a priority lane, because the bank cannot risk losing their business. The rest of the customers must be processed simultaneously through multiple queues to quickly reduce the total number of customers in a single line. Lastly, if customers keep coming in, the queues are filling up, and the tellers begin to struggle, they can send a person outside to tell customers to come back another time or use a different branch because the wait time is too long (that is where WRED/RED comes in). Finally, when lunch time is over, everything returns to normal. Refer to this analogy to recall and remember QoS mechanisms you learn in this book or outside.

In Cisco's network software, QoS functionalities are activated using the Modular Quality of Service Command-Line Interface (MQC) feature. One of MQC's primary objectives is to offer a platform-agnostic interface for QoS configuration across various Cisco platforms. MQC is a command-line interface framework that enables the creation of policies and their attachment to interfaces. These policies consist of a traffic class and one or more QoS features. A traffic class serves to classify traffic, while the QoS features within the policy dictate how the classified traffic should be handled. Use Figure 21-1 to solidify your understanding of how to approach working with MQC.

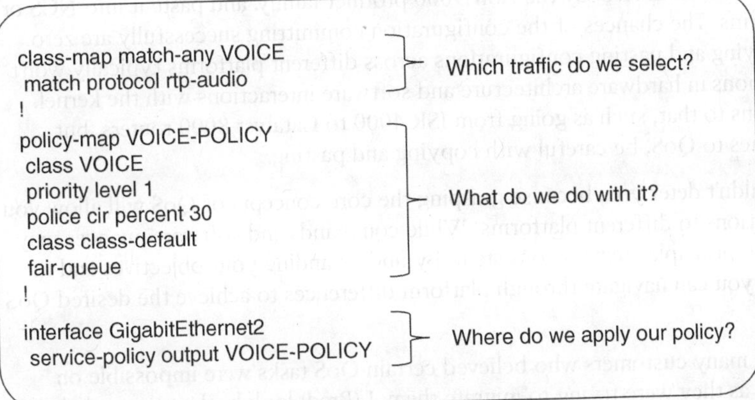

Figure 21-1   *MQC Framework Visualized and Remembered*

Selected traffic (voice in this case) will receive certain treatment on a particular interface. Select, take an action, apply at a certain place. The logic of prioritizing voice traffic is as follows:

Step 1.   Select (class-map): Identify RTP audio packets so they can be treated differently from other traffic classes.

Step 2.   Take an action (policy-map): Define QoS policies for voice traffic. Within this policy-map, there are two classes:

  ■ *class VOICE*: Prioritizes voice traffic by assigning it to priority level 1, which typically maps to expedited forwarding (EF) behavior. Additionally, we apply a traffic policing rate of 30 percent of the interface bandwidth, ensuring that voice traffic does not exceed this rate.

■ *class class-default*: This class handles all other traffic that doesn't match the VOICE class. It's configured with fair-queueing, which provides fair treatment to non-voice traffic.

Step 3.   **Apply it (interface GigabitEthernet2 outbound):** This part applies the VOICE-POLICY policy-map to the GigabitEthernet2 interface's outbound traffic. When the policy-map is applied to the interface, the defined QoS policies will be enforced on the outgoing traffic from this interface.

NOTE   Expedited Forwarding (EF) behavior is a QoS mechanism used to ensure low latency and low jitter for critical network traffic, such as voice or video. It is typically implemented by assigning a high priority to packets marked with the EF codepoint in the Differentiated Services (DiffServ) model, ensuring they are forwarded quickly and consistently through the network. Other types of markings in the DiffServ model include Assured Forwarding (AF) and Best Effort (BE), which provide different levels of service based on the priority and requirements of the traffic. Example 21-3 shows a longer list of these markings.

Use this IOS-based example as the cornerstone of MQC principles and as a guide when you are given a requirement. Also, recognize that MQC configurations are platform-specific. This configuration cannot be pasted directly into IOS XR. Moreover, you cannot take an IOS XR QoS configuration, from let's say the ASR 9000 product family, and paste it into NCS or Cisco 8000 platforms. The chances of the configuration committing successfully are zero. Why? Simply copying and pasting configurations across different platforms typically won't work due to variations in hardware architecture and software interactions with the kernel. There are exceptions to that, such as going from ISR 4000 to Catalyst 8000 routers, but again, when it comes to QoS, be careful with copying and pasting.

However, this shouldn't deter you, because grasping the core concepts of QoS will allow you to adapt configurations to different platforms. While commands and software nuances may vary, the underlying principles remain consistent. By understanding your objectives and the desired outcomes, you can navigate through platform differences to achieve the desired QoS implementation.

I have encountered many customers who believed certain QoS tasks were impossible on different platforms as they were trying to migrate them. I (Brad) look back at these challenges as most memorable and most rewarding. Every time it is an opportunity to showcase creative problem-solving skills and demonstrate that, with the right understanding and approach, virtually any QoS requirement can be addressed effectively.

Traffic Classification

The **class-map** command is used to define traffic classes for the purpose of traffic classification. We would like to categorize different types of traffic flows based on specific criteria, such as packet attributes (e.g., IP addresses, protocols, port numbers) or Quality of Service (QoS) markings. Example 21-1 compares traffic classification options in IOS XR and IOS.

Example 21-1   *QoS Traffic Classification*

```
RP/0/RP0/CPU0:PE3(config)# class-map ?
  match-all  Match all match criteria
  match-any  Match any match criteria (default)
  type       The type of class-map
  WORD       Name of the classmap
RP/0/RP0/CPU0:PE3(config)# class-map GROUP1
RP/0/RP0/CPU0:PE3(config-cmap)# match ?
  access-group         Match access group
  atm                  Match based on ATM specific criteria
  cac                  Match based on CAC fields
  cos                  Match based on IEEE 802.1Q/ISL Class Of Service value
  dei                  Match based on DEI bit (0/1)
  description          Set description for this class-map
  destination-address  Match based on destination address
  destination-port     Match based on destination port
  discard-class        Match based on discard class (upto 8 Ids)
  dscp                 Match based on IP DSCP value (upto 8 values or ranges)
  ethertype            Match based on ethertype (Upto 8 values or ranges)
  flow-key             Match based on flow keys
  fr-de                Match based on FrameRelay DE bit
  fragment-type        Fragment type for a packet
  frame-relay          Match based on frame-relay specific criteria
  ipv4                 Match based on ipv4 icmp
  ipv6                 Match based on IPv6
  mpls                 Match based on MPLS specific values
  not                  Negate match criteria
  packet               Match based on packet length
  precedence           Match based on IP precedence values
  protocol             Match based on L3 protocol (Upto 8 values or ranges)
  qos-group            Match based on QoS Group (upto 8 Ids or ranges)
  source-address       Match based on source address
  source-port          Match based on source port
  tcp-flag             Match based on TCP flags
  vlan                 Match based on Vlan Ids (Upto 8 values or ranges)
  vpls                 Match based on VPLS fields
  <cr>

PE2(config)# class-map GROUP1
PE2(config-cmap)# match ?
  access-group   Access group
  any            Any packets
  application    Application to match
  cac            Call Admission Control
```

```
class-map               Class map
cos                     IEEE 802.1Q/ISL class of service/user priority values
destination-address     Destination address
discard-class           Discard behavior identifier
dscp                    Match DSCP in IPv4 and IPv6 packets
group-object            Match object-group
input-interface         Select an input interface to match
ip                      IP specific values
metadata                Metadata to match
mpls                    Multi Protocol Label Switching specific values
not                     Negate this match result
packet                  Layer 3 Packet length
precedence              Match Precedence in IPv4 and IPv6 packets
protocol                Protocol
qos-group               Qos-group
security-group          Security group
source-address          Source address
traffic-category        Match on traffic-category
vlan                    VLANs to match
```

MQC differences between IOS and IOS XR are apparent even at the top of the configuration tree. You do not have to remember these differences for the exam. Just read and compare the outputs in your mind. For example, you know that a class-map can select one, several, any, or all criteria you specify with **match-any** or **match-all** statements. Observe that IOS and IOS XR syntax is different even here. The list of categories has differences as well, but generally, you can group them into two categories—Layer 2 and Layer 3. Figure 21-2 examines what some of these options mean.

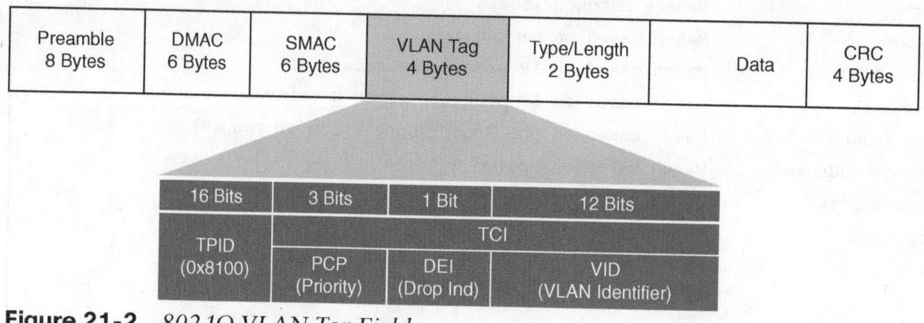

Figure 21-2 *802.1Q VLAN Tag Fields*

Let's look at the Layer 2 Ethernet frame format first. Can you see the PCP (priority) and DEI (drop indicator) fields shown in Figure 21-2 in the class-map output of Example 21-1? They are the **cos** and **dei** options, respectively. You can match Layer 2 frames with a technique broadly known as Class of Service (CoS), which uses a 3-bit field called the Priority Code Point (PCP) within an Ethernet frame header when using VLAN tagged frames as defined by IEEE 802.1Q. It specifies a priority value between 0 and 7 to differentiate traffic. Example 21-2 shows the values that can be selected with the **cos** option.

Example 21-2 *Values for Class of Service*

```
RP/0/RP0/CPU0:PE3(config)# class-map GROUP1
RP/0/RP0/CPU0:PE3(config-cmap)# match cos ?
  <0-7>  COS value
  inner  Match inner cos values (Upto 8 values)
RP/0/RP0/CPU0:PE3(config-cmap)#
```

Can you think of a drawback to using CoS? What if your frames must travel across non-802.1Q or non-802.1p non-Ethernet WAN links? These CoS markings can be lost when frames traverse, and thus, for a more consistent experience, it's advisable to use a more persistent marking method, such as Layer 3 IP DSCP marking. This can be achieved by translating CoS markings into another form of marking or by adopting an alternative marking mechanism altogether.

At the Layer 3 network layer, the classification of IP packets commonly relies on criteria such as the source or destination IP address, or the content of the Type of Service (ToS) byte. Initially, only the first three bits of the ToS byte were used for marking and were referred to as IP precedence. The values ranged from 0 to 7, enabling the segregation of traffic into as many as six practical classes of service (settings 6 and 7 were designated for internal network purposes).

Differentiated Services Code Point (DSCP) represents a modern model that replaces the old approach but is compatible with IP precedence. The model redefines the ToS byte as the DiffServ field, using six prioritization bits to classify up to 64 values (ranging from 0 to 63), with 32 being frequently utilized. Each value in DiffServ is referred to as a DSCP. Figure 21-3 shows the TOS byte format, which consists of three components.

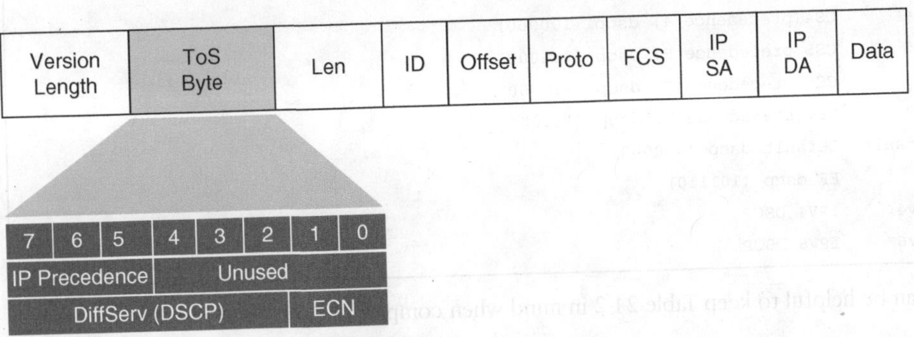

Figure 21-3 *IP Precedence and DSCP*

Observe how packets can be selected on these fields in Example 21-3.

Example 21-3 *IP Precedence and DSCP*

```
RP/0/RP0/CPU0:PE3(config-cmap)# match precedence ?
  <0-7>          Precedence value
  critical       Critical precedence (5)
  flash          Flash precedence (3)
  flash-override Flash override precedence (4)
```

```
    immediate          Immediate precedence (2)
    internet           Internetwork control precedence (6)
    ipv4               IPV4 precedence
    ipv6               IPV6 precedence
    network            Network control precedence (7)
    priority           Priority precedence (1)
    routine            Routine precedence (0)
RP/0/RP0/CPU0:PE3(config-cmap)# match dscp ?
    <0-63>    Differentiated services codepoint value
    <0-63>-   Lower limit of the DSCP range to match.
    af11      AF11 dscp (001010)
    af12      AF12 dscp (001100)
    af13      AF13 dscp (001110)
    af21      AF21 dscp (010010)
    af22      AF22 dscp (010100)
    af23      AF23 dscp (010110)
    af31      AF31 dscp (011010)
    af32      AF32 dscp (011100)
    af33      AF33 dscp (011110)
    af41      AF41 dscp (100010)
    af42      AF42 dscp (100100)
    af43      AF43 dscp (100110)
    cs1       CS1(precedence 1) dscp (001000)
    cs2       CS2(precedence 2) dscp (010000)
    cs3       CS3(precedence 3) dscp (011000)
    cs4       CS4(precedence 4) dscp (100000)
    cs5       CS5(precedence 5) dscp (101000)
    cs6       CS6(precedence 6) dscp (110000)
    cs7       CS7(precedence 7) dscp (111000)
    default   Default dscp (000000)
    ef        EF dscp (101110)
    ipv4      IPV4 DSCP
    ipv6      IPV6 DSCP
```

It can be helpful to keep Table 21-2 in mind when comparing **CoS**, **ToS**, and **DSCP**.

Table 21-2   CoS, ToS, and DSCP Compared

Feature	DSCP (Differentiated Services Code Point)	CoS (Class of Service)	ToS (Type of Service)
Definition	A 6-bit field in the IP header used for packet classification and QoS policies	A 3-bit field in the Ethernet frame header used for prioritizing packets on Layer 2	An 8-bit field in the IP header used for specifying packet priority (deprecated)
Field Location	IP Header (IPv4 ToS/ IPv6 Traffic Class)	Ethernet Frame Header (802.1Q tag)	IP Header (Deprecated in favor of DSCP)

Feature	DSCP (Differentiated Services Code Point)	CoS (Class of Service)	ToS (Type of Service)
Bit Length	6 bits	3 bits	8 bits (3 bits Precedence, 4 bits ToS)
Number of Values	64 values (0–63)	8 values (0–7)	256 values (0–255)
Typical Use	Differentiating traffic types for QoS policies (e.g., EF, AF classes)	Prioritizing traffic on Layer 2 networks (e.g., VLANs)	Initially for QoS, now replaced by DSCP
Common Values	EF (46), AF (10, 12, 14, 18, 20, 22, 26, 28, 30), Default (0)	0 (Best Effort), 5 (Voice), 6 (Video)	0 (Routine), 1 (Priority), 2 (Immediate), 3 (Flash), 4 (Flash Override), 5 (CRITIC/ECP), 6 (Internetwork Control), 7 (Network Control)
Application Layer	Layer 3 (Network Layer)	Layer 2 (Data Link Layer)	Layer 3 (Network Layer)
Purpose	Ensuring end-to-end QoS across IP networks	Providing QoS on Ethernet networks (e.g., VLAN prioritization)	Providing priority handling of IP packets (outdated)

Next, MPLS. When IP packets are transmitted between sites, the IP precedence field (the first three bits of the DSCP field in the IP packet header) determines the CoS. This marking specifies the desired treatment for the packet, such as guaranteed bandwidth or latency. In MPLS networks, if the service provider's network uses MPLS, the IP precedence bits are typically transferred into the MPLS experimental field at the network's edge. However, the service provider may wish to assign a different QoS value to MPLS packets based on their service offerings.

The MPLS experimental field allows the service provider to implement QoS without modifying the value in the customer's IP precedence field. This approach ensures that the IP header remains available for customer use, and the IP packet marking remains unchanged as it traverses the MPLS network, providing a true end-to-end QoS solution. Example 21-4 demonstrates how to configure this.

Example 21-4   *MPLS EXP Field*

```
RP/0/RP0/CPU0:PE3(config)# class-map GROUP1
RP/0/RP0/CPU0:PE3(config-cmap)# match mpls ?
  disposition    Match MPLS Label Disposition
  experimental   Match MPLS experimental values
RP/0/RP0/CPU0:PE3(config-cmap)# match mpls experimental ?
  imposition   Match imposition label (Upto 8 values)
  topmost      Match topmost label (Upto 8 values)
RP/0/RP0/CPU0:PE3(config-cmap)# match mpls experimental topmost ?
  <0-7>   MPLS experimental label
```

```
RP/0/RP0/CPU0:PE3(config-cmap)# match mpls experimental imposition ?
  <0-7>  MPLS experimental label
RP/0/RP0/CPU0:PE3(config-cmap)# match cos ?
  <0-7>  COS value
  inner  Match inner cos values (Upto 8 values)
RP/0/RP0/CPU0:PE3(config-cmap)#
```

Figure 21-4 shows the MPLS header fields.

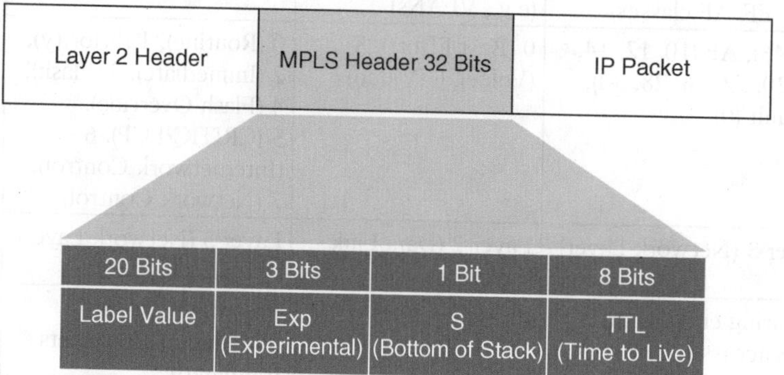

Figure 21-4 *MPLS EXP Field*

While most traffic in service provider networks will be MPLS-based, the focus of our discussion is on working with Modular Quality of Service Command-Line Interface (MQC). It is essential to be proficient with this tool. One of the simplest ways to match traffic is by using an access list, as illustrated in Example 21-5. Realize, though, that you won't be able to match MPLS-based traffic with the access list shown.

Example 21-5 *Matching on Access-lists*

```
RP/0/RP0/CPU0:PE3(config)# class-map GROUP1
RP/0/RP0/CPU0:PE3(config-cmap)# match access-group ?
  ipv4  IPv4 access list
  ipv6  IPv6 access list
RP/0/RP0/CPU0:PE3(config-cmap)# match access-group ipv4 ?
  WORD  Access list name - maximum 64 characters
RP/0/RP0/CPU0:PE3(config-cmap)#
```

Traffic Policing

Traffic policing allows you to control the maximum rate of traffic that is transmitted or received on an interface. Policing will drop excess traffic to control traffic flow within specified rate limits. Alternatively, it can re-mark the excess traffic (possibly with a lower priority) and then send it to the network. Service providers typically sell services at a sub rate access (1 Gbps or 10 Gbps on physical 100 Gbps link), and traffic above that rate needs to be limited.

Traffic policing or rate limiting on Cisco routers uses a token bucket mechanism to regulate traffic flow. Tokens represent a fixed number of bits that the network will accept and are placed into a "bucket" at a specified rate. If you put more bits on the network than there are available tokens in the bucket, the router will drop the exceeding bits. You can find plenty of pictures in other books and on the Internet for this.

For the exam, I challenge you to understand this from a router point of view. To do that, set up three or four IOS routers in a row (one of them can be IOS XR for later use; you will find it annoying to commit and roll back changes, so practice first on IOS). Remove all unnecessary components—no traffic generators, no iperf-like tools (used for throughput testing), maybe even no dynamic routing protocols to minimize the noise. The simpler you make it, the faster you will understand how everything works together and retain it—as additional components tend to distract our minds. I did just that, except that I was too lazy to run static routes and have OSPF turned on. The reason I have four routers is so that you can use these for different scenarios even outside of this book. Figure 21-5 provides a visual for the topology.

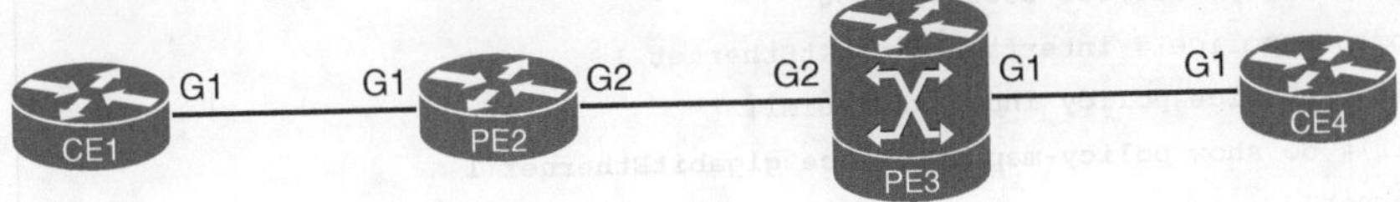

Figure 21-5   *QoS Topology*

Let's look at how to configure traffic policing. Example 21-6 shows how to configure traffic policing on IOS-based devices (some differences might arise between switches and routers).

Example 21-6   *Policing ICMP Traffic*

```
PE2# configure terminal
Enter configuration commands, one per line.  End with CNTL/Z.
PE2(config)# class-map match-all ICMP
PE2(config-cmap)# match protocol icmp
PE2(config-cmap)# policy-map RATE-LIMIT
PE2(config-pmap)# class ICMP
PE2(config-pmap-c)# police ?
  <8000-10000000000>  Target Bit Rate (bIts per second) (postfix k, m, g
                      optional; decimal point allo
  cir                 Committed information rate
  rate                Specify police rate, PCR for hierarchical policies or SCR
                      for single-level ATM 4.0 policer policies

PE2(config-pmap-c)# police cir ?
  <8000-10000000000>  Target Bit Rate (bIts per second) (postfix k, m, g
                      optional; decimal point allo
  percent             % of interface bandwidth for Committed information rate
```

```
PE2(config-pmap-c)# police cir 8000 ?
  <1000-512000000>  Burst bytes
  account           Overhead Accounting
  bc                Conform burst
  conform-action    action when rate is less than conform burst
  pir               Peak Information Rate
  <cr>              <cr>

PE2(config-pmap-c)# police cir 8000 bc ?
  <1000-512000000>  Burst bytes
  account           Overhead Accounting
  conform-action    action when rate is less than conform burst
  pir               Peak Information Rate
  <cr>              <cr>


PE2(config-pmap-c)# police cir 8000 bc 1000
PE2(config-pmap-c-police)# interface gigabitEthernet 1
PE2(config-if)# service-policy input RATE-LIMIT
PE2(config-if)# do show policy-map interface gigabitEthernet 1
 GigabitEthernet2

  Service-policy input: RATE-LIMIT

    Class-map: ICMP (match-all)
      0 packets, 0 bytes
      30 second offered rate 0000 bps, drop rate 0000 bps
      Match: protocol icmp
      police:
          cir 8000 bps, bc 1000 bytes
        conformed 0 packets, 0 bytes; actions:
          transmit
        exceeded 0 packets, 0 bytes; actions:
          drop
        conformed 0000 bps, exceeded 0000 bps

    Class-map: class-default (match-any)
      1 packets, 114 bytes
      30 second offered rate 0000 bps, drop rate 0000 bps
      Match: any
```

What do we have here? On PE2, I defined a class that selects all ICMP traffic (we will be pinging in our tests), created a policy-map RATE-LIMIT that polices the traffic rate to 8000 bits with a burst capacity of another 8000 bits (expressed in bytes; I'm not sure why Cisco does the bit/byte switch), and applied this policy map to the input of interface GigabitEthernet1. Why did I choose those values? It simplifies calculations for us humans. We are going to meter the packet rate for ICMP traffic to 8000 bits per given interval and drop packets that exceed this rate.

NOTE   In QoS policing, the interval refers to the time period over which the amount of data sent is measured and controlled. This interval is determined by the rate at which tokens are added to the bucket. The exam does not cover these details, but the token arrival rate is calculated as follows: (time between packets * policer rate) /8 bits per byte.

Also, if you have forgotten the CIR, Bc, Be, and PIR parameters, refer to Table 21-3 to recall their definitions.

Table 21-3   Traffic Policing and Shaping Parameters

Term	Definition
CIR (Committed Information Rate)	The average data rate guaranteed by the network provider over a specific time period
Bc (Committed Burst)	The maximum amount of data that can be sent during a time interval when the network is not congested, typically measured in bits or bytes
Be (Excess Burst)	The additional data beyond Bc that can be transmitted if the network has available bandwidth, but with no delivery guarantees
PIR (Peak Information Rate)	The maximum data rate allowed at any moment, including both Bc and Be, providing a cap on the highest possible transmission rate

To understand how this works, let's send a single packet through this policy and see what happens in Example 21-7.

Example 21-7   *A Single ICMP Packet*

```
CE1# ping 10.1.100.4 repeat 1 size 100 source loopback0
Type escape sequence to abort.
Sending 1, 100-byte ICMP Echos to 10.1.100.4, timeout is 2 seconds:
Packet sent with a source address of 10.1.100.1
!
Success rate is 100 percent (1/1), round-trip min/avg/max = 4/4/4 ms
CE1#

PE2(config-if)# do show policy-map RATE-LIMIT
  Policy Map RATE-LIMIT
    Class ICMP
     police cir 8000 bc 1000
       conform-action transmit
       exceed-action drop
PE2(config-if)# do show policy-map interface gigabitEthernet 1
  GigabitEthernet1

  Service-policy input: RATE-LIMIT
```

```
    Class-map: ICMP (match-all)
      1 packets, 114 bytes
      30 second offered rate 0000 bps, drop rate 0000 bps
      Match: protocol icmp
      police:
            cir 8000 bps, bc 1000 bytes
          conformed 1 packets, 114 bytes; actions:
            transmit
          exceeded 0 packets, 0 bytes; actions:
            drop
          conformed 0000 bps, exceeded 0000 bps

    Class-map: class-default (match-any)
      428 packets, 48688 bytes
      30 second offered rate 0000 bps, drop rate 0000 bps
      Match: any
```

We send a single ICMP packet size 100 bytes beyond PE2. Of great interest to us is what
happens on PE2. You can see that our bucket is 8000 bits (1000 bytes) and see our packet is
caught by the policy. It is now 114 bytes (912 bits)—the Ethernet frame adds a 6-byte Destination Address + 6 byte Source Address + 2 byte type = 14 bytes. That is about 11 percent
of the available token bucket. Let's clear the counters and generate 10 such packets because
this amount will put more bits on the interfaces than there are tokens in the bucket.
Example 21-8 shows this in action.

Example 21-8 *Ten ICMP Packets*

```
PE2(config-if)# do clear counters
Clear "show interface" counters on all interfaces [confirm]
PE2(config-if)#

CE1# ping 10.1.100.4 repeat 10 size 100 source loopback0
Type escape sequence to abort.
Sending 10, 100-byte ICMP Echos to 10.1.100.4, timeout is 2 seconds:
Packet sent with a source address of 10.1.100.1
!!!!!!!!!.
Success rate is 90 percent (9/10), round-trip min/avg/max = 2/3/4 ms

PE2(config-if)# do show policy-map interface gigabitEthernet 1
GigabitEthernet1

  Service-policy input: RATE-LIMIT

    Class-map: ICMP (match-all)
      10 packets, 1140 bytes
      30 second offered rate 0000 bps, drop rate 0000 bps
      Match: protocol icmp
      police:
```

```
         cir 8000 bps, bc 1000 bytes
       conformed 9 packets, 1026 bytes; actions:
         transmit
       exceeded 1 packets, 114 bytes; actions:
         drop
       conformed 0000 bps, exceeded 0000 bps


   Class-map: class-default (match-any)
     9 packets, 1026 bytes
     30 second offered rate 0000 bps, drop rate 0000 bps
     Match: any
```

In this case, 10 packets multiplied by 114 bytes = 1140 bytes (9120 bits); we do not have that many tokens for this time interval. Also, 9 packets equaled 1026 bytes (8208 bits), just over the top; we must have had some more tokens show up. One packet got rejected and dropped. Let's send 100 packets to observe the bucket being replenished in Example 21-9.

Example 21-9   *One Hundred ICMP Packets*

```
PE2(config-if)# do clear counters
Clear "show interface" counters on all interfaces [confirm]
PE2(config-if)#
```

```
CE1# ping 10.1.100.4 repeat 100 size 100 source loopback0
Type escape sequence to abort.
Sending 100, 100-byte ICMP Echos to 10.1.100.4, timeout is 2 seconds:
Packet sent with a source address of 10.1.100.1
!!!!!!!!!.!!!!!!!!!!.!!!!!!!!!.!!!!!!!!!!.!!!!!!!!!!.!!!!!!!!!!.!!!!!!!!!.!!!!!
!!!.!!!!!!!!!!.!!!!!!!!!!.!!!!!!!!!!
Success rate is 90 percent (90/100), round-trip min/avg/max = 2/2/4 ms
```

```
PE2(config-if)# do show policy-map interface gigabitEthernet 1
 GigabitEthernet1

  Service-policy input: RATE-LIMIT

    Class-map: ICMP (match-all)
      10 packets, 1140 bytes
      30 second offered rate 0000 bps, drop rate 0000 bps
      Match: protocol icmp
      police:
          cir 8000 bps, bc 1000 bytes
        conformed 9 packets, 1026 bytes; actions:
          transmit
        exceeded 1 packets, 114 bytes; actions:
          drop
        conformed 0000 bps, exceeded 0000 bps
```

```
        Class-map: class-default (match-any)
          9 packets, 1026 bytes
          30 second offered rate 0000 bps, drop rate 0000 bps
          Match: any
PE2(config-if)# do show policy-map interface gigabitEthernet 1
  GigabitEthernet1

  Service-policy input: RATE-LIMIT

    Class-map: ICMP (match-all)
      100 packets, 11400 bytes
      30 second offered rate 2000 bps, drop rate 0000 bps
      Match: protocol icmp
      police:
          cir 8000 bps, bc 1000 bytes
        conformed 90 packets, 10260 bytes; actions:
          transmit
        exceeded 10 packets, 1140 bytes; actions:
          drop
        conformed 2000 bps, exceeded 0000 bps

    Class-map: class-default (match-any)
      5 packets, 570 bytes
      30 second offered rate 0000 bps, drop rate 0000 bps
      Match: any
```

Interesting. You can see that every 8 or 9 packets (given our replenishment rate) we had
1 packet timeout. Last one, which will become important later, let's increase the packet size
to 500 bytes (4000 bits). With 14 bytes of overhead, I bet the second packet will put us over
8000 bits and will not succeed. Example 21-10 continues our experiment.

Example 21-10   *Ten ICMP 500-Byte Packets*

```
PE2(config-if)# do clear counters
Clear "show interface" counters on all interfaces [confirm]
PE2(config-if)#

CE1# ping 10.1.100.4 repeat 10 size 500 source loopback0
Type escape sequence to abort.
Sending 10, 500-byte ICMP Echos to 10.1.100.4, timeout is 2 seconds:
Packet sent with a source address of 10.1.100.1
!.!.!.!.!.
Success rate is 50 percent (5/10), round-trip min/avg/max = 3/4/5 ms

PE2(config-if)# do show policy-map interface gigabitEthernet 1
  GigabitEthernet1
```

```
Service-policy input: RATE-LIMIT

  Class-map: ICMP (match-all)
    10 packets, 5140 bytes
    30 second offered rate 0000 bps, drop rate 0000 bps
    Match: protocol icmp
    police:
        cir 8000 bps, bc 1000 bytes
      conformed 5 packets, 2570 bytes; actions:
        transmit
      exceeded 5 packets, 2570 bytes; actions:
        drop
      conformed 0000 bps, exceeded 0000 bps

  Class-map: class-default (match-any)
    13 packets, 1486 bytes
    30 second offered rate 0000 bps, drop rate 0000 bps
    Match: any
```

Every interval, we replenish enough tokens to allow a single 500-byte packet in, with every other packet exceeding our bucket supply. Important…Keep this very example in mind; I will refer to it later.

Is there a name for what you just saw? It is called a Single-Rate Two-Color Marker. Why? We had one bucket, we "colored" (we did not do anything but had an opportunity to), and we had a choice for two actions—conform and drop. Let's call this "1R2C"—a single bucket with two actions. There are other available markers. Would you like to see the "1R3C" (Single-Rate Three-Color) marker? There are two token buckets—a Conformed Burst bucket (Bc) and an exceed burst bucket (Be). Why would we need this? This approach supports bursty traffic, as in data. VoIP traffic typically maintains a consistent and stable flow, whereas data traffic may experience periods of both low activity and sudden spikes. In the 1R2C approach, once the bucket is full, the extra tokens coming every interval are "spilled," or wasted. What if we were to allow for bursting? What if we were to allow for bursting, as in 500-byte ping packets? The second bucket will have enough tokens to help with most of the traffic pattern I chose. Let's see what happens in Example 21-11.

Example 21-11   *Single-Rate Three-Color Marker*

```
PE2(config-pmap-c-police)# do show policy-map

Policy Map RATE-LIMIT
  Class ICMP
    police cir 8000 bc 1000 be 1000
      conform-action set-dscp-transmit af11
      exceed-action set-dscp-transmit af12
      violate-action set-dscp-transmit af13
```

```
CE1# ping 10.1.100.4 repeat 10 size 500 source loopback0
Type escape sequence to abort.
Sending 10, 500-byte ICMP Echos to 10.1.100.4, timeout is 2 seconds:
Packet sent with a source address of 10.1.100.1
!!!!!!!!!!.
Success rate is 90 percent (9/10), round-trip min/avg/max = 2/2/3 ms


PE2(config-pmap-c-police)# do show policy-map interface gigabitEthrnet 1
  GigabitEthernet1

  Service-policy input: RATE-LIMIT

    Class-map: ICMP (match-all)
      10 packets, 5140 bytes
      30 second offered rate 0000 bps, drop rate 0000 bps
      Match: protocol icmp
      police:
          cir 8000 bps, bc 1000 bytes, be 1500 bytes
        conformed 2 packets, 1028 bytes; actions:
          set-dscp-transmit af11
        exceeded 2 packets, 1028 bytes; actions:
          set-dscp-transmit af12
        violated 6 packets, 3084 bytes; actions:
          set-dscp-transmit af13
        conformed 0000 bps, exceeded 0000 bps, violated 0000 bps

    Class-map: class-default (match-any)
      5 packets, 570 bytes
      30 second offered rate 0000 bps, drop rate 0000 bps
      Match: any
```

In the configuration in Example 21-11, I showed "coloring" three ways—marking each category with its own DSCP value. I could have chosen other options such as allow and drop, but we are just learning the mechanics. As you can see, under 1R3C, 9 out of 10 pings succeeded (as the token replenishment rate accounted for almost all the traffic) and got marked (or colored) appropriately. Incidentally, you just learned one of the ways to mark packets transiting your network. In 1R3C, token replenishment of the Conformed Burst (Bc) occurs at the rate of CIR (8000 in our case). Token replenishment of the Excess Burst (Be) occurs at the rate of CIR as well, but only when the Bc bucket is full. When the Bc bucket is full of tokens, the additional tokens spill over into the Be bucket. It is very tempting to look at pictures. Let the picture be in your head. It is far more permanent this way (in my humble opinion).

Are you ready for the 2R3C—Dual-Rate Three-Color Marker? Still the same two Bc and Be buckets, but this method has a Peak Information Rate (PIR) element. PIR provides a separate and independent (not the spillover method) replenishment rate of the Be bucket, as demonstrated in Example 21-12.

Example 21-12 *Dual-Rate Three-Color Marker*

```
PE2(config-pmap-c)# police cir 8000 bc 1000 pir ?
  <8000-10000000000>  Target Bit Rate (bits per second) (postfix k, m, g optional;
decimal point allo

PE2(config-pmap-c)# police cir 8000 bc 1000 pir 8000
PE2(config-pmap-c-police)# do show policy-map


  Policy Map RATE-LIMIT
    Class ICMP
      police cir 8000 bc 1000 pir 8000 be 1500
        conform-action set-dscp-transmit af11
        exceed-action set-dscp-transmit af12
        violate-action set-dscp-transmit af13
```

```
CE1# ping 10.1.100.4 repeat 10 size 500 source loopback0
Type escape sequence to abort.
Sending 10, 500-byte ICMP Echos to 10.1.100.4, timeout is 2 seconds:
Packet sent with a source address of 10.1.100.1
!!!!!!!!!!.
Success rate is 90 percent (9/10), round-trip min/avg/max = 3/3/4 ms
```

```
PE2(config-pmap-c-police)# do show policy-map interface gigabitEthernet 1
  GigabitEthernet1

  Service-policy input: RATE-LIMIT

    Class-map: ICMP (match-all)
      10 packets, 5140 bytes
      30 second offered rate 2000 bps, drop rate 0000 bps
      Match: protocol icmp
      police:
          cir 8000 bps, bc 1000 bytes
          pir 8000 bps, be 1500 bytes
        conformed 1 packets, 514 bytes; actions:
          set-dscp-transmit af11
        exceeded 1 packets, 514 bytes; actions:
          set-dscp-transmit af12
        violated 8 packets, 4112 bytes; actions:
          set-dscp-transmit af13
        conformed 0000 bps, exceeded 0000 bps, violated 1000 bps

    Class-map: class-default (match-any)
      3 packets, 342 bytes
      30 second offered rate 0000 bps, drop rate 0000 bps
      Match: any
```

On the surface (CE1), the results look similar, but PE2 reveals a different story because only one packet conforms, one exceeds, and eight packets are in violation. What would be an example of when to use this approach? Let's imagine a service provider that wants to offer different, decreasing levels of assurances (green, yellow, and red) for their residential and business broadband customers. This service provider is "selling" more bandwidth than they physically offer. By using 2R3C, the provider can discard all red packets, because they exceeded the peak rate, can forward yellow packets as best effort, and forward green packets with a low drop probability.

A word on the hierarchical nature of MQC. Depending on what hardware you run (the knowledge of hardware is not tested on this exam), you can build structured cascading (hierarchical, nested, multilevel) policies. I would like to give you a good example in this section that can apply to other aspects of MQC (shaping, marking, etc.). Refer to Example 21-13 for the related configuration items. Attempt reading it first on your own and see if this makes sense to you. I provide the explanation right after the example.

Example 21-13 *An Example of Hierarchical Policing*

```
RP/0/RP0/CPU0:PE3(config)# show
Building configuration...
!! IOS XR Configuration 7.7.1
ipv4 access-list 100
 10 permit ipv4 host 10.1.100.1 any
!
ipv4 access-list 200
 10 permit ipv4 host 10.1.100.2 any
!
class-map match-all USER1
 match access-group ipv4 100
 end-class-map
!
class-map match-all USER2
 match access-group ipv4 200
 end-class-map
!
policy-map CHILD
 class USER1
  police rate 350 mbps
  !
 !
 class USER2
  police rate 350 mbps
  !
 !
 class class-default
 !
 end-policy-map
!
```

```
policy-map PARENT
 class class-default
  service-policy CHILD
  police rate 500 mbps
  !
 !
 end-policy-map
!
end
RP/0/RP0/CPU0:PE3(config)# interface gigabitEthernet 0/0/0/2
RP/0/RP0/CPU0:PE3(config-if)# service-policy input PARENT
RP/0/RP0/CPU0:PE3(config-if)# commit
RP/0/RP0/CPU0:PE3(config-if)# do show policy-map interface gigabitEthernet 0/0/0/2


GigabitEthernet0/0/0/2 input: PARENT

Class class-default
  Classification statistics          (packets/bytes)     (rate - kbps)
    Matched                 :               0/0                 0
    Transmitted             : N/A
    Total Dropped           :               0/0                 0
  Policing statistics                (packets/bytes)     (rate - kbps)
    Policed(conform)        :               0/0                 0
    Policed(exceed)         :               0/0                 0
    Policed(violate)        :               0/0                 0
    Policed and dropped     :               0/0


  Policy CHILD Class USER1
  Classification statistics          (packets/bytes)     (rate - kbps)
    Matched                 :               0/0                 0
    Transmitted             : N/A
    Total Dropped           :               0/0                 0
  Policing statistics                (packets/bytes)     (rate - kbps)
    Policed(conform)        :               0/0                 0
    Policed(exceed)         :               0/0                 0
    Policed(violate)        :               0/0                 0
    Policed and dropped     :               0/0
    Policed and dropped(parent policer)  : N/A


  Policy CHILD Class USER2
  Classification statistics          (packets/bytes)     (rate - kbps)
    Matched                 :               0/0                 0
    Transmitted             : N/A
    Total Dropped           :               0/0                 0
```

```
    Policing statistics                        (packets/bytes)      (rate - kbps)
       Policed(conform)           :              0/0                    0
       Policed(exceed)            :              0/0                    0
       Policed(violate)           :              0/0                    0
       Policed and dropped :                     0/0
       Policed and dropped(parent policer)   : N/A

    Policy CHILD Class class-default
       Classification statistics                (packets/bytes)      (rate - kbps)
       Matched                    :              0/0                    0
       Transmitted                : N/A
       Total Dropped              :              0/0                    0
GigabitEthernet0/0/0/2 direction output: Service Policy not installed
```

I am showing you the configuration right before I commit it in an IOS XR router. The PARENT policy polices all traffic to 500 Mb, but has a CHILD policy attached to it, which will police CE1 and PE2's loopbacks to 350 Mb each. Use this as a reference model to create MQC configurations that are only limited by your imagination and business requirements.

NOTE   Priority queuing (not covered extensively in this volume due to exam requirements) and traffic policing are complementary QoS mechanisms in network traffic management. Priority queuing ensures that high-priority traffic, such as voice and video, is transmitted before lower-priority traffic, minimizing delay and jitter. Traffic policing regulates the rate of traffic entering the network, comparing it against predefined limits (CIR, Bc, Be, PIR) and marking down or dropping excess traffic to prevent congestion and ensure fair bandwidth distribution. Together, they complement each other because priority queuing ensures critical traffic gets timely delivery, while traffic policing ensures no single traffic flow exceeds its allocated bandwidth, maintaining overall network performance and fairness.

Traffic Shaping

Traffic shaping is a network traffic management technique used to control the rate of data transmission in a network. It regulates the flow of packets by delaying or buffering excess traffic to ensure that it conforms to a predefined traffic profile or rate. This allows network administrators to manage network resources effectively, prevent network congestion, and prioritize critical traffic flows.

Do you recall our example from the policing section where we were only able to get every other 500-byte packet through? I captured the output in Example 21-14 right after setting up that example. I thought, "I bet if I can slow down the sending rate, or shape packets to the policed rate, I can get all 500-byte packets through." Why? Because I am slowing down the packets *below* the policing token refreshment rate.

Example 21-14 *Traffic Shaping 500-Byte Packets Through a Policer*

```
CE1# show running-config
! Output omitted for brevity
class-map match-all ICMP
 match protocol icmp
!
policy-map SHAPE-AVG
 class ICMP
  shape average 8000
!
interface GigabitEthernet1
 ip address 10.1.12.1 255.255.255.0
 service-policy output SHAPE-AVG
!
CE1# ping 10.1.100.4 repeat 10 size 500 source loopback0
Type escape sequence to abort.
Sending 10, 500-byte ICMP Echos to 10.1.100.4, timeout is 2 seconds:
Packet sent with a source address of 10.1.100.1
!!!!!!!!!!
Success rate is 100 percent (10/10), round-trip min/avg/max = 4/455/514 ms

PE2# show policy-map interface gigabitEthernet 1 input
 GigabitEthernet1

  Service-policy input: RATE-LIMIT

    Class-map: ICMP (match-all)
      10 packets, 5140 bytes
      30 second offered rate 0000 bps, drop rate 0000 bps
      Match: protocol icmp
      police:
          cir 8000 bps, bc 1000 bytes
        conformed 10 packets, 5140 bytes; actions:
          transmit
        exceeded 0 packets, 0 bytes; actions:
          drop
        conformed 0000 bps, exceeded 0000 bps

    Class-map: class-default (match-any)
      10 packets, 1140 bytes
      30 second offered rate 0000 bps, drop rate 0000 bps
      Match: any
```

How about that?! The packets were moving visibly slower, as you can see the round-trip time takes a lot longer (look at the latency!). Same number of packets, same number of bytes, but we shaped (slowed down) the traffic until PE2's token bucket got refilled. Sometimes it feels like magic! Traffic shaping allowed me to control the speed of traffic that was leaving an interface. I essentially matched the flow of the traffic to the speed of the interface (a downstream policing router in our case) receiving the packet. Figure 21-6 shows a good picture from www.cisco.com that visualizes traffic shaping (slowing down).

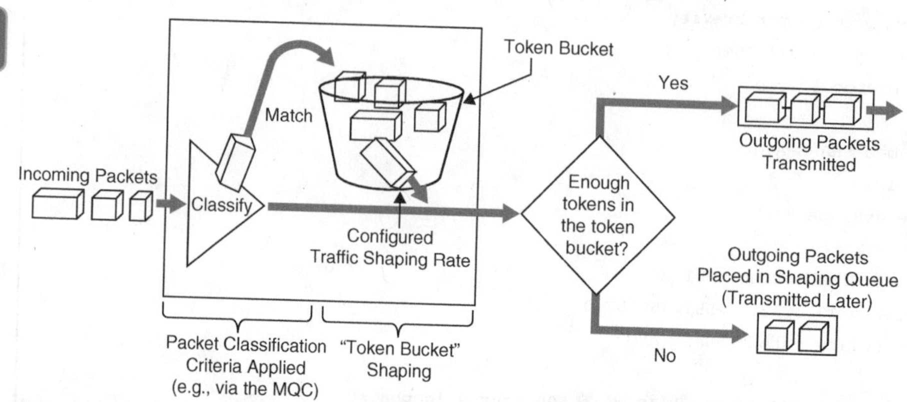

Figure 21-6 *Traffic Shaping*

When does shaping help? When you have a larger central site that has a higher-speed link than a remote site. When you have multiple remote sites, and their cumulative bandwidth is overwhelming a central site.

Both policing and shaping have their places because they limit the bandwidth that traffic can achieve. Can you think of the downsides to these approaches? Do not read further until you've had a chance to answer on your own. Policing drops traffic far more often, which can cause TCP retransmissions. Shaping, on the other hand, will introduce variable delay (remember the wildly different round-trip times for ICMP in Example 21-14), and this can lead to excessive jitter.

Some people may find it helpful to visually compare policing and shaping. Figure 21-7 shows how policing harshly removes the peaks of traffic rates while shaping fills in the valleys by spreading the peaks over time.

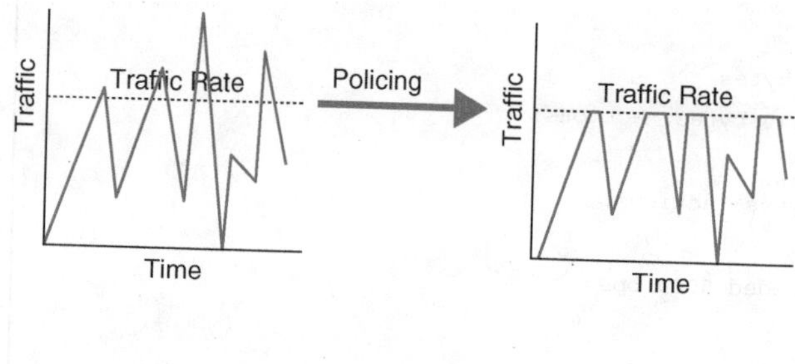

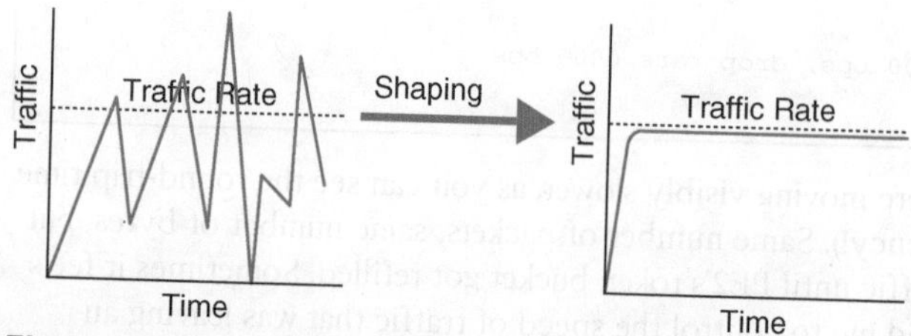

Figure 21-7 *Traffic Policing vs Shaping*

Congestion Avoidance

I am not covering the topic of queuing (which is another congestion management technique in addition to policing and shaping) in this book, since the blueprint does not ask for it and we must focus on topics tested for obvious reasons. Congestion avoidance, though, is on the exam. Remember the "tellers at the bank" analogy? We identify customers, control how many people we let into our bank (policing), direct them into designated prioritized lanes (queuing), and make sure that queues are not packed so tellers are overwhelmed (shaping). But today is an extraordinary day. Too many customers are showing up at lunch, our bank lobby is already full, the tellers are working double-time, and customers keep arriving. If we do not manage what happens outside of the bank doors, customers will get upset, so we would like to avoid this. Congestion avoidance refers to techniques to monitor traffic flows to anticipate and avoid congestion at common bottlenecks. We will send out one of the bank managers to profusely apologize to arriving customers who are determined to visit our branch today. We will politely send them to another nearby branch, ask them to use online services today, come back tomorrow… Avoidance techniques are implemented *before* congestion occurs, as compared with congestion management techniques that control congestion *after* it has occurred.

MQC uses the "tail-drop" technique to deal with queues being full. Tail drop avoids congestion by dropping the incoming packets when the output queue is full until congestion is eliminated. After seeing that tellers are busy and customer lanes will not be processed in time, the bank manager closes the lanes to new walk-ins. Just like the manager, tail drop treats all traffic flows equally and does not care about classes of service (the bank has enough work taking care of existing customers waiting in service lanes). Packets are not classified but are placed into a first-in, first-out (FIFO) queue (first-come-first-served basis) and will be forwarded at a rate determined by the underlying link bandwidth. How does the manager determine when to close the lane? The **queue-limit** command is used to define the maximum threshold for a class. When the maximum threshold is reached, the enqueued packets to the class queue result in tail drop (packet drop). Since we spend so much time policing on IOS, let's continue to work IOS XR on PE3 in Example 21-15.

Example 21-15 *Configuring Tail Drop*

```
RP/0/RP0/CPU0:PE3(config)# show

Building configuration...
!! IOS XR Configuration 7.7.1
ipv4 access-list 100
 10 permit ipv4 host 10.1.100.1 any
!
!
class-map match-any QOS1
 match access-group ipv4 100
 end-class-map
!
!
policy-map TAIL-DROP
 class QOS1
  queue-limit 100 ms
```

```
    priority level 1
   !
   class class-default
   !
   end-policy-map
   !
  interface GigabitEthernet0/0/0/1
   service-policy output TAIL-DROP
  !
 end

 RP/0/RP0/CPU0:PE3(config)# commit
 Tue Apr  2 15:43:35.749 UTC
 RP/0/RP0/CPU0:PE3(config)# do show qos interface gigabitEthernet 0/0/0/1 output
 Tue Apr  2 15:43:50.758 UTC
 Interface: GigabitEthernet0_0_0_1 output
 Bandwidth configured: 1000000 kbps Bandwidth programmed: 1000000 kbps
 ANCP user configured: 0 kbps ANCP programmed in HW: 0 kbps
 Port Shaper programmed in HW: 0 kbps
 Policy: TAIL-DROP Total number of classes: 2
 ----------------------------------------------------------------------
 Level: 0 Policy: TAIL-DROP Class: QOS1
 Bandwidth: 0 kbps, BW sum for Level 0: 0 kbps, Excess Ratio: 0
 QueueID: 24 (Priority 1)
 Queue Limit: 12500 kbytes (100 ms)
 ----------------------------------------------------------------------
 Level: 0 Policy: TAIL-DROP Class: class-default
 Bandwidth: 0 kbps, BW sum for Level 0: 0 kbps, Excess Ratio: 1
 QueueID: 25 (Priority Normal)
 Queue Limit: 625 kbytes
 ----------------------------------------------------------------------
```

I created a new class QOS1 (I could have done this on the class-default, but I'm trying
to show you the difference), and now you can see that QOS1 has a larger output queue.
Implementations differ between Cisco's hardware and software, so learn principles; do not
memorize commands. In this case, you must configure one of the following commands:
priority, shape average, bandwidth, or **bandwidth remaining,** except for the default class.
So, now you know how the manager can regulate the length of each teller lane (length of the
networking queues).

Another congestion avoidance technique is Random Early Detection (RED). It makes use of
TCP's congestion control system by selectively dropping packets before congestion becomes
severe. RED signals TCP sources to reduce their transmission rates and allows the network
to recover from congestion. This approach ensures that TCP adjusts its transmission rate to
match the network's capacity, facilitating smoother data delivery. RED works by spreading
packet losses over time and keeping queue depths relatively low, even during traffic spikes.

When activated on an interface, RED starts dropping packets once congestion surpasses a predefined threshold, as configured by the operator. This proactive approach helps maintain network stability and prevents excessive queuing delays.

NOTE   If too many packets are dropped, TCP connections may enter resynchronization, leading to multiple TCP flows simultaneously retransmitting lost packets. This can exacerbate congestion, causing massive outages as the network becomes overwhelmed with retransmissions, significantly degrading performance and potentially leading to a collapse in network throughput. Mechanisms such as RED help counteract this phenomenon.

How would you say this in English? The manager keeps looking outside the window, monitors the customer walk-in rate before the lobby gets too full, and blasts out an email to the customer base to try later today. The manager anticipates and avoids the problem early. Example 21-16 translates this into CLI commands.

Example 21-16   *Configuring Random Early Detection*

```
RP/0/RP0/CPU0:PE3(config)# show
Tue Apr  2 16:11:10.459 UTC
Building configuration...
!! IOS XR Configuration 7.7.1
!
policy-map RED
 class QOS1
  random-detect default
  priority level 1
 !
 class class-default
 !
 end-policy-map
!
interface GigabitEthernet0/0/0/1
 service-policy output RED
 no service-policy output TAIL-DROP
!
end

RP/0/RP0/CPU0:PE3(config)# commit
RP/0/RP0/CPU0:PE3(config)# do show qos interface gigabitEthernet 0/0/0/1 output
Interface: GigabitEthernet0_0_0_1 output
Bandwidth configured: 1000000 kbps Bandwidth programmed: 1000000 kbps
ANCP user configured: 0 kbps ANCP programmed in HW: 0 kbps
Port Shaper programmed in HW: 0 kbps
Policy: RED Total number of classes: 2
----------------------------------------------------------------------
```

```
Level: 0 Policy: RED Class: QOS1
Bandwidth: 0 kbps, BW sum for Level 0: 0 kbps, Excess Ratio: 0
QueueID: 56 (Priority 1)
Queue Limit: 12500 kbytes
WRED Type: RED Default 6 Curves: 1
Thresholds Min : 6250 (6250) kbytes Max: 12500 (12500) kbytes
-----------------------------------------------------------------
Level: 0 Policy: RED Class: class-default
Bandwidth: 0 kbps, BW sum for Level 0: 0 kbps, Excess Ratio: 1
QueueID: 57 (Priority Normal)
Queue Limit: 625 kbytes
-----------------------------------------------------------------
```

The big difference is that RED *randomly* drops packets without considering individual flows; it lacks per-flow intelligence. The underlying principle is that aggressive flows tend to dominate incoming traffic, increasing the likelihood that RED will drop packets from these aggressive sessions. Consequently, RED essentially penalizes more aggressive sessions by slowing them down with a higher probability of packet drops.

By prompting aggressive sessions to throttle their transmission rates, RED is a more equitable distribution of network resources and prevents any single session from monopolizing bandwidth. Ultimately, it enables smoother and more consistent utilization of available bandwidth, minimizing fluctuations in network traffic.

Some Cisco routing platforms also implement Weighted Random Early Detection (WRED). WRED *selectively drops packets based on specified criteria*, such as discard class, allowing for differentiated treatment of various types of traffic. The configuration of WRED involves using the **random-detect** command along with different discard class values, specifying a range or list of valid values for the field. Additionally, minimum and maximum queue thresholds are set to determine the point at which packets are dropped. It's crucial to ensure that the WRED maximum threshold value closely aligns with the queue limit, as packet drops commence once this threshold is reached.

The virtual IOS XR platform I'm using does not support displaying what I would like to show you, but Example 21-17 illustrates the configuration and the mechanics of WRED on PE2, which runs IOS.

Example 21-17 *Configuring Weighted Random Early Detection*

```
PE2(config-if)# do show running-config
! Output omitted for brevity
class-map match-all QOS1
 match access-group 100
!
policy-map WRED
 class QOS1
  bandwidth remaining percent 30
  random-detect
  random-detect precedence 3 1200 3000 10
!
```

```
interface GigabitEthernet2
 ip address 10.1.23.2 255.255.255.0
 service-policy output WRED
!
PE2(config-if)# do show policy-map interface gigabitEthernet 2
 GigabitEthernet2

  Service-policy output: WRED

    Class-map: QOS1 (match-all)
      0 packets, 0 bytes
      30 second offered rate 0000 bps, drop rate 0000 bps
      Match: access-group 100
      Queueing
      queue limit 416 packets
      (queue depth/total drops/no-buffer drops) 0/0/0
      (pkts output/bytes output) 0/0
      bandwidth remaining 30%
        Exp-weight-constant: 9 (1/512)
        Mean queue depth: 0 packets

        class    Transmitted    Random drop   Tail drop   Minimum   Maximum   Mark
                 pkts/bytes     pkts/bytes    pkts/bytes  thresh    thresh    prob

        0           0/0            0/0           0/0        104       208      1/10
        1           0/0            0/0           0/0        117       208      1/10
        2           0/0            0/0           0/0        130       208      1/10
        3           0/0            0/0           0/0       1200      3000      1/10
        4           0/0            0/0           0/0        156       208      1/10
        5           0/0            0/0           0/0        169       208      1/10
        6           0/0            0/0           0/0        182       208      1/10
        7           0/0            0/0           0/0        195       208      1/10

    Class-map: class-default (match-any)
      13 packets, 1482 bytes
      30 second offered rate 0000 bps, drop rate 0000 bps
      Match: any

      queue limit 416 packets
      (queue depth/total drops/no-buffer drops) 0/0/0
      (pkts output/bytes output) 0/0
```

Notice that for class QOS1, eight classes are defined. A minimum and maximum threshold
are also defined, which is what I changed for class 3. This means that per each class (as we
select traffic for each class), we can define *different* thresholds and the drop probability, and
a router can construct the exponential curve it needs to determine drop probability for any
average queue depth. Figure 21-8 shows drop probability thresholds.

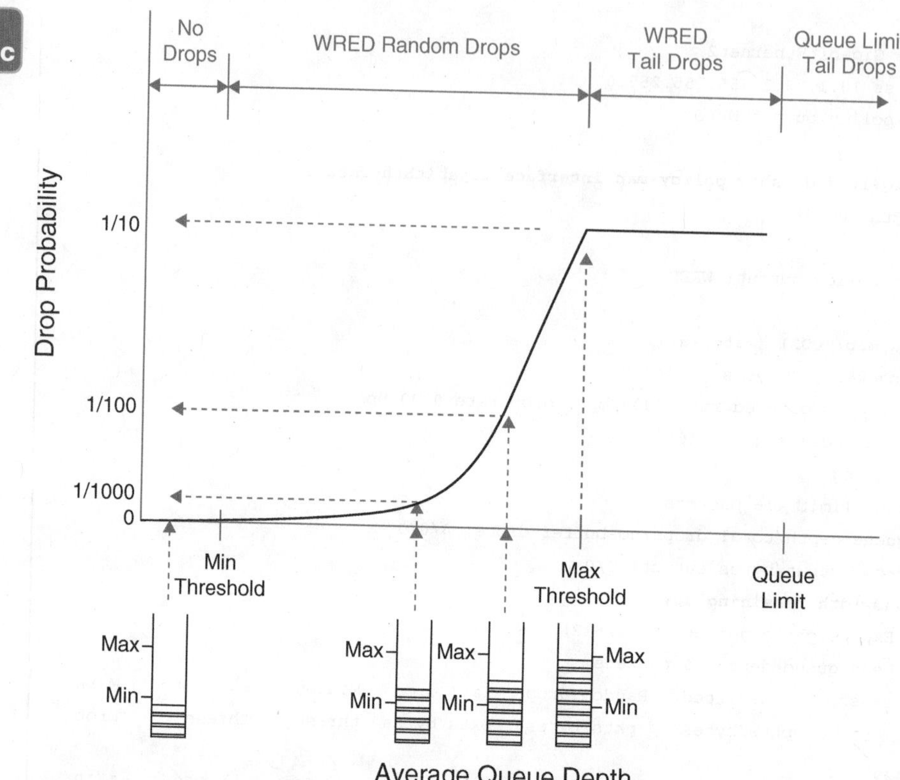

Figure 21-8 *WRED Drop Probabilities*

You can see that, at the minimum specified threshold, the router will drop 1 out of 1000 packets and 1 out of 10 packets at the maximum specified threshold. The router fills in the rest of the graph and will drop 1 out of 100 packets somewhere in between. It sounds scientific, but my experiences are from the practical world and not from the academic side and can tell you that tuning WRED parameters is not typical. Based on interactions with customers, I suggest you do not attempt this unless you have a thorough understanding of how tuning will impact applications in that class. Leave the default values because they will suffice for most use cases. In some of the newer and best routers made, WRED is not even an option, and there is arguable empirical evidence that RED is more efficient than WRED (I happen to be an advocate of this thinking). I will not get into these differences in this book, and they are not a part of the exam. If you want the short answer: WRED can work when most of the traffic is TCP-based, so if you have UDP, there is no way to signal a slow-down, and voice and video (UDP-based) networks do not tolerate dropped packets well.

Traffic Marking

Before reading further, can you answer this question: Why would you want to mark packets? So, we can treat the packet differently when it crosses our network, you may answer. You are right, but also try thinking beyond the obvious. One reason may be to perform a complex classification only once. If we can mark a class, we can use simpler, less CPU-intensive classification methods elsewhere in the network. Another reason may be that, contractually, you receive data from a customer at a specific rate. Instead of discarding packets that surpass that rate, you can mark them with a lower service class. Another reason may be that an encryption function is applied to traffic downstream; therefore, performing a complex classification, such as application recognition, may no longer be possible, so this may be the checkpoint at which to apply markings prior to packets becoming obscured.

You saw me mark packets with the policing tool in MQC in the example of the Single-Rate Three-Color Marker; that is one way to do this. There is also a simpler way, as shown in Example 21-18.

Example 21-18 *Marking Packets Directly in the Policy Map*

```
PE2(config)# policy-map MARK-ICMP
PE2(config-pmap)# class ICMP
PE2(config-pmap-c)# set dscp af41
PE2(config-pmap-c)# interface gigabit Ethernet 1
PE2(config-if)# service-policy input MARK-ICMP
PE2(config-if)#
```

```
CE1# ping 10.1.100.4
Type escape sequence to abort.
Sending 5, 100-byte ICMP Echos to 10.1.100.4, timeout is 2 seconds:
!!!!!
Success rate is 100 percent (5/5), round-trip min/avg/max = 1/1/2 ms
```

```
PE2(config-if)# do show policy-map interface gigabitEthernet 1
 GigabitEthernet1

  Service-policy input: MARK-ICMP

    Class-map: ICMP (match-all)
      5 packets, 570 bytes
      30 second offered rate 0000 bps, drop rate 0000 bps
      Match: protocol icmp
      QoS Set
        dscp af41
          Packets marked 5

    Class-map: class-default (match-any)
      32 packets, 3698 bytes
      30 second offered rate 0000 bps, drop rate 0000 bps
      Match: any
! Notice I had to reload the system before these markings showed up—see output below
! this line
!
PE2(config-if)# do show policy-map interface gigabitEthernet 1
 GigabitEthernet1

  Service-policy input: MARK-ICMP
```

```
   Class-map: ICMP (match-all)
     0 packets, 0 bytes
     30 second offered rate 0000 bps, drop rate 0000 bps
     Match: protocol icmp
     QoS Set
       dscp af41
         Marker statistics: Disabled
PE2(config-if)# no service-policy input MARK-ICMP
PE2(config)# platform qos marker-statistics
Either a) A system RELOAD or
       b) Remove all service-policies, re-apply the change
          to the 'platform qos marker-statistics', re-apply all service-policies
is required before this command will be activated.
PE2(config-if)# service-policy input MARK-ICMP
PE2(config-if)# do write memory
Building configuration...
[OK]
PE2(config-if)# do reload
```

A short policy applied to the interface did the trick. The packets are now marked or re-marked. Observe that I had to issue the **platform qos marker-statistics** command and reload the router before the statistics showed up.

What other techniques should you be familiar with when it comes to marking? Sometimes it is not possible to access and mark every field in a packet. For example, if an IP packet has been encapsulated in MPLS, it is not possible to mark the DSCP value within the IP header because you would have to decapsulate MPLS first. In this case, you can mark the MPLS experimental (EXP) bits. You should also know that you can configure multiple markings at the same time. Let's kill these two birds with one stone in Example 21-19, taken from output for **show running-config.**

Example 21-19 *Multiple Markings Imposed; MPLS EXP Is One*

```
policy-map MARK-ICMP
  class ICMP
    set cos 4
    set mpls exp topmost 4
    set dscp af41
```

This marking policy may seem straightforward, but its simplicity belies its significant impact and carefully considered design. When an MPLS packet crosses an interface with this policy attached, the Layer 2 COS field and EXP bits will get marked. If an IP datagram is encapsulated within the MPLS packet, its DSCP value remains unchanged because we cannot access the inner content of the MPLS packet. However, when a non-MPLS IP packet traverses the same interface, both its Layer 2 COS and Layer 3 DSCP values will be marked accordingly. This approach demonstrates a clever and comprehensive method of handling **traffic markings.**

There is one other marking technique that I believe is important to understand—the internal marking designators. Cisco routers offer the capability to assign and manage two internal values, namely **qos-group** and **discard-class**, which accompany the packet *within* the router without altering the packet's actual contents. Usually, these markings are applied within an ingress policy and are reused for classification into a traffic class or RED drop profile within an egress policy. For instance, if you need to classify traffic based on a user's IP address at egress but find that encryption is enabled, by making the IP address invisible, you can classify the traffic at ingress (before encryption) and assign an appropriate qos-group value. Subsequently, at egress, you can classify based on the qos-group and implement the appropriate action accordingly. In IOS XR, we use this technique for various reasons frequently. Example 21-20 shows how that is done.

Example 21-20   *Using Internal Marking Within the Router*

```
class-map EGRESS-ICMP
  match qos-group 4
!
policy-map MARK-ICMP
  class ICMP
    set qos-group 4
!
policy-map EGRESS-ICMP
  class EGRESS-ICMP
    bandwidth remaining percent 10
!
interface GigabitEthernet1
  service-policy input MARK-ICMP
!
interface GigabitEthernet2
  service-policy output EGRESS-ICMP
```

We mark ICMP traffic on the ingress interface to the internal qos-group 4. We select this internal marking on the egress interface with the match statement and assign it a certain bandwidth. Do you remember when we could not mark the inner IP header because of the MPLS encapsulation? Example 21-21 shows the workaround to work with this traffic.

Example 21-21   *Using Internal Marking to Start Dropping ICMP Traffic During Congestion*

```
class-map EGRESS-ICMP
  match qos-group 4
!
policy-map MARK-ICMP
  class ICMP
    set qos-group 4
    set discard-class 1
!
```

```
policy-map EGRESS-ICMP
  class EGRESS-ICMP
    bandwidth remaining percent 10
    random-detect discard-class-based
    random-detect discard-class 1 25 40
!
interface GigabithEthernet1
  service-policy input MARK-ICMP
!
interface GigabitEthernet2
  service-policy output EGRESS-ICMP
```

```
CE1# ping 10.1.100.4 repeat 10 size 500 source loopback0
Type escape sequence to abort.
Sending 10, 500-byte ICMP Echos to 10.1.100.4, timeout is 2 seconds:
Packet sent with a source address of 10.1.100.1 .
!!!!!!!!!!
Success rate is 100 percent (10/10), round-trip min/avg/max = 30/418/514 ms
```

```
PE2# show policy-map interface gigabitEthernet 2
 GigabitEthernet2

  Service-policy output: EGRESS-ICMP

    Class-map: EGRESS-ICMP (match-all)
      10 packets, 5140 bytes
      30 second offered rate 0000 bps, drop rate 0000 bps
      Match: qos-group 4
      Queueing
      queue limit 416 packets
      (queue depth/total drops/no-buffer drops) 0/0/0
      (pkts output/bytes output) 10/5140
      bandwidth remaining 10%
        Exp-weight-constant: 9 (1/512)
        Mean queue depth: 0 packets
```

discard-class	Transmitted pkts/bytes	Random drop pkts/bytes	Tail drop pkts/bytes	Minimum thresh	Maximum thresh	Mark prob
0	0/0	0/0	0/0	104	208	1/10
1	10/5140	0/0	0/0	25	40	1/10
2	0/0	0/0	0/0	130	208	1/10
3	0/0	0/0	0/0	143	208	1/10
4	0/0	0/0	0/0	156	208	1/10
5	0/0	0/0	0/0	169	208	1/10
6	0/0	0/0	0/0	182	208	1/10
7	0/0	0/0	0/0	195	208	1/10

```
Class-map: class-default (match-any)
   42 packets, 4788 bytes
   30 second offered rate 0000 bps, drop rate 0000 bps
   Match: any

   queue limit 416 packets
   (queue depth/total drops/no-buffer drops) 0/0/0
   (pkts output/bytes output) 0/0
```

As you can see, I apply the policy, ping yet again with our 10 packets, and can account for them making it into the right discard queue. It's satisfying when a strategy falls into place seamlessly.

In summary for the QoS section, the MQC approach stands as the primary methodology for configuring QoS across Cisco IOS and IOS XR Software. As you have seen in the examples, it offers several advantages:

- Provides a highly scalable framework for QoS control.

- Implements a consistent CLI structure for all QoS features (although individual command syntax can differ).

- Segregates the classification engine from the policy configuration; this allows for class and policy reuse.

- Allows for inline real-time modification of policies; this is evident in the last two examples if you configured them. You did not have to modify the entire configuration, just the discard-class sections, and you did not even have to reapply these to the interfaces.

IPv6 Flow Label

We have one remaining task to address, and this section would be the suitable place to handle it. IPv6 offers QoS marking support through a dedicated field in the IPv6 header. Comparable to the Type of Service (ToS) field in the IPv4 header, the Traffic Class field, comprising 8 bits, enables originating nodes and forwarding routers to differentiate and prioritize various classes of IPv6 packets. RFC 3697 describes this in detail, and I have referenced it at the end of the chapter. Look at the IPv6 header structure in Figure 21-9.

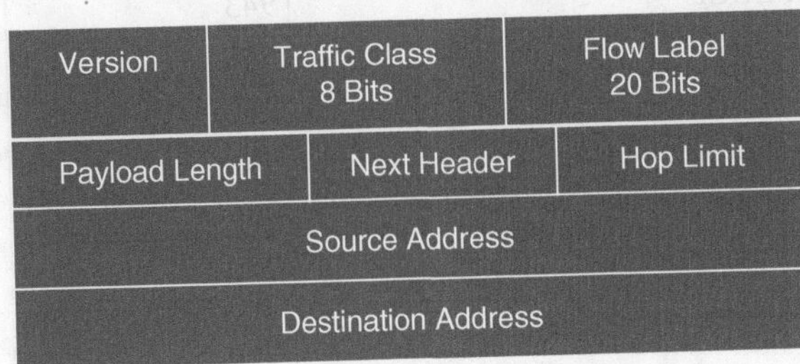

Figure 21-9 *Flow Label in the IPv6 Header*

Do you see that 8-bit Traffic Class field in the top middle? It can be used to set specific precedence or Differentiated Services Code Point (DSCP) values in the exact same way as you do in IPv4. Next to it, top right, is the IPv6 Flow label. At 20-bits long, the Flow Label field enables per-flow processing for differentiation at the IP layer and can be used for special sender requests set by the source node. The source can now tag packets belonging to a specific flow. A Flow Label value of zero signifies packets that are not associated with any flow. Packet classifiers use the combination of Flow Label, Source Address, and Destination Address fields to determine the flow to which a particular packet belongs.

One significant benefit of the Flow Label is that transit routers can identify packet flows without needing to inspect the inner packet contents. This feature proves particularly advantageous in scenarios involving encryption and other similar situations, simplifying flow identification without the need for packet decryption. While it's a commendable concept, I haven't observed its widespread usage. Perhaps I should explore more to encounter it in action.

Considering the wide assortment of scenarios that you may encounter on the exam regarding this topic, prioritizing the study of QoS principles and practical application through hands-on practice becomes indispensable in being able to solve exam questions.

Exam Preparation Tasks

As mentioned in the section "How to Use This Book" in the Introduction, you have a few choices for exam preparation: the exercises here, Chapter 23, "Final Preparation," and the exam simulation questions in the Pearson Test Prep Software Online.

Review All Key Topics

Review the most important topics in this chapter, noted with the Key Topic icon in the margin of the page. Table 21-4 lists a reference of these key topics and the page numbers on which each is found.

Table 21-4　Key Topics for Chapter 21

Key Topic Element	Description	Page Number
List	QoS Techniques	938
Figure 21-1	MQC Framework Visualized and Remembered	939
Figure 21-2	802.1Q VLAN Tag Fields	942
Figure 21-3	IP Precedence and DSCP	943
Figure 21-4	MPLS EXP Field	946
Figure 21-6	Traffic Shaping	960
Paragraph	RED/WRED packet drop behaviors	964
Figure 21-8	WRED Drop Probabilities	966
Paragraph, Example 21-20	Internal marking designators	969
List	MQC Advantages	971
Figure 21-9	Flow Label in the IPv6 Header	971

Define Key Terms

Define the following key terms from this chapter and check the answers in the glossary:

CoS, DSCP, ToS, traffic marking, traffic policing, traffic shaping

Command Reference to Check Your Memory

This section includes the most important configuration and EXEC commands covered in this chapter. You might not need to memorize the complete syntax of every command, but you should be able to remember the basic keywords that are needed.

To test your memory of the commands, cover the right side of Table 21-5 with a piece of paper, read the description on the left side, and then see how much of the command you can remember.

The 350-501 exam focuses on practical, hands-on skills that are used by networking professionals. Therefore, you should be able to identify the commands needed to configure and test. Note that not all commands are fully covered in the chapter, but their presence in the following table should lead you to investigate them further to understand this technology.

Table 21-5   CLI Commands to Know

Task	Command Syntax
Match packets to the specified class	**class-map [match-all	match-any]** *class-map-name*
Create or specify the name of the traffic policy and enter QoS policy-map configuration mode	**policy-map** *policy-map-name*
Attach a policy map to an interface	**service-policy {input	output }** *policy-map-name*
Specify maximum bandwidth usage by a traffic class	**police** *bps burst-normal burst-max* **conform-action** *action* **exceed-action** *action* **violate-action** *action*
Shape traffic according to the keyword and rate specified	**shape [average	peak]** *mean-rate [burst-size]* *[excess-burst-size]*
Enable WRED or distributed WRED (DWRED)	**random-detect**

Review Questions

As a part of the review, we encourage you to provide *a single-sentence answer* (keep your answers as short as possible) to the following questions. If you struggle to complete this answer in a single sentence, this may indicate a lack of clarity or reveal gaps in your understanding. We have constructed these questions to help you consolidate this chapter's information and extract the essence of the covered content.

The answers to these questions appear in Appendix A. For more practice with exam format questions, use the Pearson Test Prep Software Online.

1. How does QoS traffic shaping dynamically adapt to meet SLA requirements and minimize packet loss across heterogeneous traffic flows and network segments?

2. How does Random Early Detection (RED) algorithmically determine appropriate queue limits in a network environment characterized by diverse traffic patterns and varying congestion levels, ensuring effective congestion avoidance without causing excessive packet drops or degradation in overall network performance?

3. In the context of traffic policing, can you discuss the intricate relationship between burst size, committed information rate (CIR), and Excess Burst size (EBS), and how these parameters interact to shape traffic behavior in a network?

Bibliography

J. Rajahalme, A. Conta, B. Carpenter, and S. Deering. RFC 3697, *IVv6 Flow Label Specification*, IETF, https://www.ietf.org/rfc/rfc3697.txt, March 2004.

Automation and Assurance

This chapter covers the following exam topics:

5.0 Automation and Assurance

- 5.1 Describe the programmable APIs used to include Cisco devices in network automation
- 5.2 Interpret an external script to configure a Cisco device using a REST API
- 5.3 Describe the role of Network Services Orchestration (NSO)
- 5.4 Describe the high-level principles and benefits of a data modeling language, such as YANG
- 5.5 Describe configuration management tools, such as Ansible and Terraform
- 5.6 Describe Secure ZTP
- 5.7 Configure dial-in/out, TCP, TLS and mTLS certificates using gRPC and gNMI
- 5.8 Configure and verify NetFlow/IPFIX
- 5.9 Configure and verify NETCONF and RESTCONF
- 5.10 Configure and verify SNMP (v2c/v3)

Network automation is the process of automating the configuration, management, testing, deployment, and operation of physical and virtual devices within a network. With everyday network tasks and functions automated, and repetitive processes controlled and managed automatically, network service availability improves.

Any type of network can use network automation. Hardware- and software-based solutions enable data centers, service providers, and enterprises to implement network automation to improve efficiency, reduce human error, and lower operating expenses.

One of the biggest issues for network managers is the growth of IT costs for network operations. The growth of data and devices is starting to outpace IT capabilities, making manual approaches nearly impossible. Yet up to 95 percent of network changes are performed manually, resulting in operational costs two to three times higher than the cost of the network. Increased IT automation, centrally and remotely managed, is essential for businesses to keep pace in the digital world.

"Do I Know This Already?" Quiz

The "Do I Know This Already?" quiz allows you to assess whether you should read this entire chapter thoroughly or jump to the "Exam Preparation Tasks" section. If you are in doubt about your answers to these questions or your own assessment of your knowledge of the topics, read the entire chapter. Table 22-1 lists the major headings in this chapter and their corresponding "Do I Know This Already?" quiz questions. You can find the answers in Appendix A, "Answers to the 'Do I Know This Already?' Quizzes and Review Questions."

Table 22-1 "Do I Know This Already?" Section-to-Question Mapping

Foundation Topics Section	Questions
REST APIs	1
NETCONF	2
YANG	3
gRPC	4
Network Services Orchestrator (NSO)	5
Secure ZTP	6
NetFlow/IPFIX	7
SNMP	8
Ansible and Terraform	9

CAUTION   The goal of self-assessment is to gauge your mastery of the topics in this chapter. If you do not know the answer to a question or are only partially sure of the answer, you should mark that question as wrong for purposes of the self-assessment. Giving yourself credit for an answer you correctly guess skews your self-assessment results and might provide you with a false sense of security.

1. What would be a factor to consider and account for from a security perspective when dealing with public APIs? (Choose two.)

   a. Data volume exchanged between client and server

   b. Rate limiting user traffic within a period of time

   c. Client and server operating system

   d. Internet provider SLA

2. When you are using NETCONF as a network management tool, what is the device running a server called?

   a. NETCONF agent

   b. NETCONF manager

   c. NETCONF client

   d. NETCONF server

3. Which notation does Cisco IOS XR use for YANG data models?

   a. Cisco-IOS-XR-<suffix><technology><platform>

   b. Cisco-IOS-XR-<platform><technology><suffix>

   c. Cisco-IOS-XR-<technology><platform><suffix>

   d. Cisco-IOS-XR-<technology><suffix><platform>

4. When the **grpc tls-mutual** command is used for gRPC authentication, what are the client requirements?

   a. Username/password/CA/client key

   b. Username/password/CA

   c. Password

   d. Username/password

5. Which component of the NSO architecture is responsible for managing the VNFs?

   a. ESC

   b. CDB

   c. MIB

   d. NSO

6. In the secure ZTP process, which option is associated with the DHCP server for IPv4 support?

   a. 143

   b. 134

   c. 136

   d. 163

7. Which information cannot be collected using NetFlow compared to IPFIX?

   a. TCP flags

   b. Memory usage

   c. Interface status

   d. CPU load

8. In which SNMPv3 mode is Data Encryption Standard (DES) supported?

   a. AuthPriv

   b. AuthnoPriv

   c. NoAuthpriv

   d. NoAuthnoPriv

9. In which feature or aspect do Ansible and Terraform differ?

   a. Infrastructure

   b. Code

   c. Cloud support

   d. Architecture

Foundation Topics

REST APIs

An **application programming interface (API)** is composed of software to communicate in a simplified manner; it is a collection of communication protocols and subroutines used by various programs to communicate between them. Programmers can make use of various API tools to make their programs easier and simpler. Also, an API provides programmers with an efficient way to develop their software programs.

The working of an API can be clearly explained with a few simple steps. Think of a client/ server architecture where the client sends a request via a medium to the server and receives a response through the same medium. An API acts as the communication medium between two programs or systems for functioning. The client is the user or customer who sends the request, the medium is the application interface programming, and the server is the backend, where the request is accepted and a response is provided. The fundamental mechanics of how APIs work are as follows:

Step 1.   The client initiates a request via the API's **Uniform Resource Identifier (URI)**.

Step 2.   The API makes a call to the server after receiving the request.

Step 3.   The server sends the response back to the API with the information.

Step 4.   The API transfers the data to the client.

APIs are considered safe (generally speaking) because they include authorization credentials and an API gateway to limit access to minimize security threats. To provide additional security layers for the data, HTTP headers, query string parameters, or cookies can be considered to add more security and protection.

Because APIs can be public, more security enhancements were added (with the authentication in place) to account for denial-of-service (DoS) attacks. These enhancements include changing the number of requests rate limiting in a timely manner, the number of requests from a specific IP endpoint, and the data volume.

Representational State Transfer, or REST, is most often referred to in the context of Restful APIs. The transport protocol for REST APIs is HTTP.

There are two types of APIs: synchronous and asynchronous. These APIs differ in the way they respond and the time it takes them to handle a request.

When a PC is initiating an API call to the server, for example, it will wait for a response from the server and will reserve all resources in a suspended state waiting for an update from the server. The server might respond in seconds, and after the response is sent to the PC, the resources will be functional again and data processing could start again. We can summarize this process behavior as delay, interruptions, application hang (performance). This is how synchronous mode works.

To resolve the issue of the PC and the application that is running on it waiting and causing delays, the asynchronous mode comes into the picture. The PC will initialize asynchronous API calls to the server but will not hang, and other stuff running will keep running to avoid any delays. Once the server sends a response, the PC will capture it and continue working on it in addition to performing the other functions.

Surely, the enhancement of asynchronous mode over synchronous mode regarding delays and performance involves more complexity from a perspective of building the structure but comes with better user experience.

Another categorization of APIs is northbound and southbound APIs, which are from the most common APIs deployed within the automation world.

To make this discussion clearer, let's look at Figure 22-1. The SDN architecture in this figure relies on a central controller to control all the entities. The data plane is the forwarding plane, which needs to communicate with the controller to reach the applications layer.

Cisco DNA Center is one example of a controller for which we use northbound APIs to reach out to an application from the controller. The APIs use HTTPs and TLS-based communication. Security or application policies could be included in these northbound APIs. This information will be received from the data plane and forwarded to the application layer.

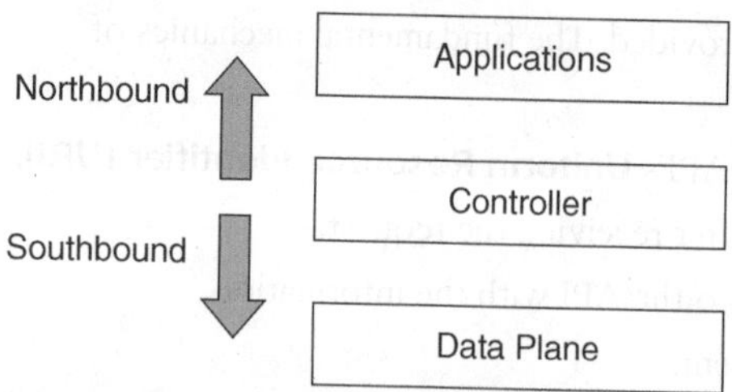

Figure 22-1 *Basic SDN Architecture and API Interaction*

Southbound APIs, which are communicated from the controller down to the data plane, can be something like Simple Network Management Protocol (SNMP), **Representational State Transfer Configuration (RESTCONF)**, and **Network Configuration Protocol (NETCONF)**, which we discuss later in the chapter. Northbound APIs are REST APIs.

Simply, when a client tries to communicate with a server over a REST API and needs to retrieve information from the server, it will send an HTTP GET request. If we want to delete something, we can send a DELETE request. When the client tries to communicate with the server, regardless of the action needed, it will try to use the resources located on the server. The resources from the REST API are called Uniform Resource Identifiers (URIs). What distinguishes a REST API HTTP request is that it targets the resource itself directly.

Also, the reliable part of REST APIs is what we call *status codes*. For each operation that takes place, a status code gives an indication about the operation. For example, the 2xx code indicates the successful receipt of the client request. Table 22-2 shows the high-level status codes and their respective meanings. For more information on the HTTP status codes associated with REST APIs, look at https://restfulapi.net/http-status-codes/.

Table 22-2 HTTP Status Codes

Status Code Category	Description
1xx: Informational	Communicates transfer protocol-level information.
2xx: Success	Indicates that the client's request was accepted successfully.
3xx: Redirection	Indicates that the client must take some additional action to complete their request.
4xx: Client error	This category of error status codes points the finger at clients.
5xx: Server error	The server takes responsibility for these error status codes.

You can visit http://httpbin.org to see the different HTTP codes and operations. For example, Figure 22-2 shows the different HTTP methods that can be used for communication between the client and server using REST APIs.

What Is SOAP?

We have been talking about REST as a method for accessing web services, but technically, REST is effectively an architecture, not a protocol. **Simple Object Access Protocol (SOAP)** is another method you can use to access web services.

HTTP Methods Testing Different HTTP Verbs

DELETE	/delete	The Request's DELETE Parameters
GET	/get	The Request's Query Parameters
PATCH	/patch	The Request's PATCH Parameters
POST	/post	The Request's POST Parameters
PUT	/put	The Request's PUT Parameters

Figure 22-2 *HTTP Methods for Client/Server Communications*

SOAP will use also HTTP as the default transport method although Simple Mail Transfer Protocol (SMTP) is another option you can use. SOAP is more comprehensive compared to REST, especially from a security perspective; however, SOAP is fairly resource-intensive, so you need to consider the cost in resources.

When a client sends an HTTP message to the server, the response is mainly in JSON format and could also hold XML format. For SOAP, it is all XML formats. Although we don't dive deep into the details here, SOAP has a specified message format structure, as shown in Figure 22-3, with a respective function for each block, and it is all XML!

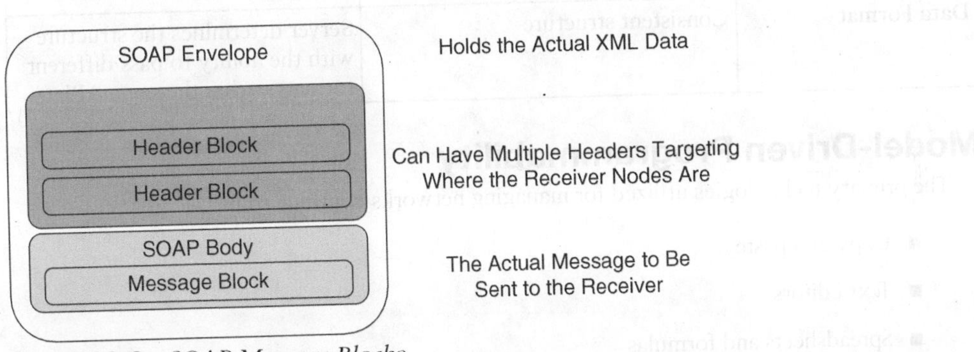

Figure 22-3 *SOAP Message Blocks*

What Is RPC?

A **remote procedure call (RPC)** is a method used to remotely execute code as it is locally performed. The client will send an RPC call (request) to the server to execute a certain function. The server will receive the request and take its time to conduct the request, and the client will wait for the execution to be performed (which is like REST API in synchronous mode). When the server finishes the execution, it will send an RPC call back (response) to the client. This type of communication is vulnerable to brute-force attacks (denial of service) due to the time the client will take during which the call is executed.

In RPC, the client conducts a function (procedure) on the server with data value(s) passed to the server. In contrast, a REST client requests the server to conduct an action targeting a specific resource, and the actions are limited to create, read, update, and delete actions, which are conveyed as HTTP methods. In a nutshell, RPC is designed for actions, whereas REST is designed for resource-centric operations.

Another difference between REST and RPC is from a transport perspective. RPC relies on UDP/TCP to function properly, whereas HTTP is the transport protocol for REST. HTTP usually is considered an application layer protocol, not a transport layer protocol, and therefore, user interactions kick off the activity.

NOTE Create, read, update, and delete operations (actions) are grouped as CRUD.

To clarify, Table 22-3 lists some functional differences between RPC and REST.

Table 22-3 RPC and REST Functional Differences

Aspect	RPC	REST
What is it?	A system that allows remote clients to call a procedure (because it is local)	A structured data exchange between server and client, defined by a set of rules
Usage	Conduct actions remotely to the server	Create, read, update, and delete
Recommendations	Complex calculations or remote process triggering	Uniform data and data structure exposure
State	Stateless/Stateful	Stateless
Data Format	Consistent structure	Server determines the structure with the ability to pass different formats within the same API

Model-Driven Programmability

The primary technologies utilized for managing networks continue to be

- Copy and paste
- Text editors
- Spreadsheets and formulas
- CLI commands

In recent years, there has been a massive increase in the following:

- Number of applications running on network
- Criticality of applications to organizations
- Rate of change in applications

In the past, network configuration and monitoring were the realm of the network engineer and the trusty command-line interface. That is no longer the case.

Development and operations, commonly known as DevOps, have become a successful and dominant approach used in many organizations. Plus, DevOps teams are looking at how to expand their reach into the network.

New web applications are using microservice architectures to build overlay container networks. As the model matures, these applications look to integration with the underlying network for performance and segmentation.

The requirement for an effective, scalable way to configure and manage network devices has been around for quite a while. SNMP was originally proposed in 1988 in RFC 1067. SNMP was designed to provide a standard interface for network management systems to configure and retrieve monitoring information.

SNMP has since been updated with SNMPv2 and SNMPv3. These updates focus on increasing performance and security, as we discuss later in the "SNMP" section of this chapter. However, it is worth mentioning some of the limitations associated with SNMP that moved people to adopt new solutions to ease network management as well as to adapt to application and network requirements:

- **Typical Configuration:** SNMPv2 read-only community strings.

- **Typical Usage:** Interface statistics queries and traps.

- **Empirical Observation:** SNMP is not used for configuration due to

  - Lack of writeable MIBs

  - Security concerns

  - Difficulty to replay and roll back

  - Special applications

What do we need to overcome the limitations of SNMP and adapt to the new digital transformation requirements and applications needed? From a manageability perspective, we seek the following:

- A programmatic interface for device configuration

- Separation of configuration and state data

- The ability to configure "services" and not "devices"

- Integrated error checking and recovery

- Support for transactions and rollback

Many vendors, including Cisco, also saw the need and began offering new APIs using interface models such as

- SOAP

- REST

- JSON-RPC

- XML

Building on RFC 3535, the Internet Engineering Task Force (IETF) developed NETCONF and YANG to offer a standard protocol and data modeling language for programmatic network management.

Before we move on to YANG, NETCONF, and RESTCONF, the sections that follow cover some important programmatic concepts that you need to understand.

Client/Server Model

Client and *server* are terms that can mean different things in different contexts, such as programmatic interfaces or API interactions.

- The *server* is a piece of software or a service running on a device that listens for and responds to incoming communications.

- The *client* is the application that connects to a server to make a request of some type.

NETCONF was originally proposed in RFC 4741 in 2006 and YANG in RFC 6020 in 2010. Both are new technologies that continue to evolve and gain acceptance from customers and vendors.

The NETCONF protocol provides a programmatic interface to tackle many of the challenges of SNMP. As developers have begun using it, there has been interest in providing interface options that align closer with REST APIs and other programmatic standards. RESTCONF and **gRPC** are alternatives to NETCONF that address some of these goals.

Google began the gRPC, an open-source project to provide a modern RPC framework to use in any environment for multiple purposes, not network configuration.

No matter which transport protocol is used (that is, NETCONF, RESTCONF, or gRPC), the YANG data models define the APIs and are the same.

Although many vendors and organizations are rapidly adopting all these technologies, NETCONF and YANG are the most widely available standard interfaces on networking devices today. Having a solid understanding of their use and implementation is the best place to start. Figure 22-4 illustrates a high-level model-driven programmability architecture.

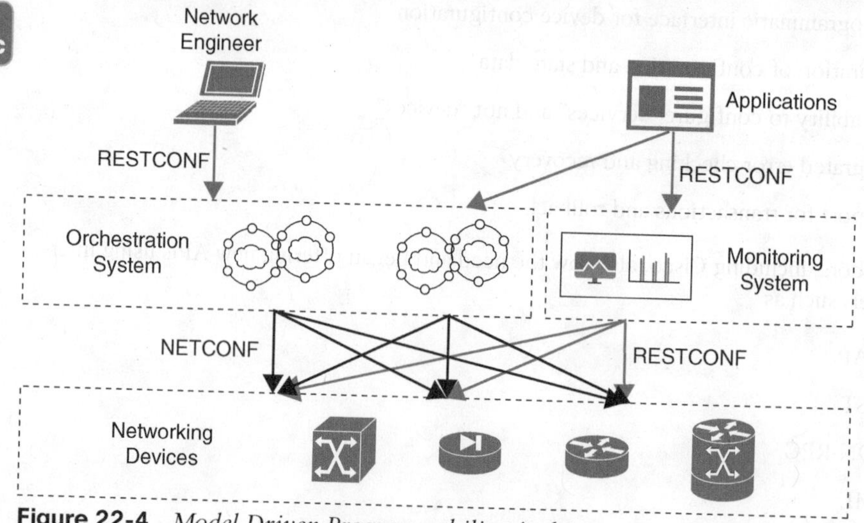

Figure 22-4 *Model-Driven Programmability Architecture*

Network orchestration and monitoring systems also use NETCONF and RESTCONF as their northbound and southbound APIs:

■ The term *northbound APIs* refers to APIs that an application exposes externally.

■ The term *southbound APIs* refers to APIs that an application uses to initiate connections with other systems.

Also, as the network becomes more programmatic, you will find that the network engineer might not be the only source of network configuration changes. Applications are also beginning to use network interfaces to directly query application state from monitoring systems and to drive configuration updates directly.

Typically, the service data models are supported on network orchestration solutions rather than directly by individual network elements. Network operations use the service models to program the orchestrator. The orchestration platform then uses the device data models to perform the actual end configuration.

Clients and Servers with NETCONF

When NETCONF is used as a network management protocol, the device runs a server called a *NETCONF agent*. You or a network management system uses a client called a *NETCONF Manager* to connect to it, as shown in Figure 22-5.

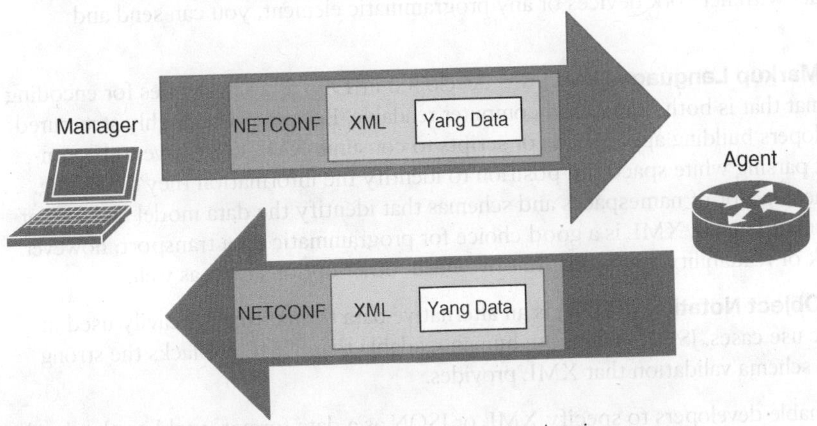

Figure 22-5 *NETCONF Client/Server Communications*

Understanding Transport Protocols and Data Models

Figure 22-6 shows the functional block of a TCP/IP-based network frame from a high-level perspective.

Figure 22-6 *TCP/IP Network Frame Format*

As an application communicates over the network, the relevant data is packaged for transport over the network. This division is shown in Figure 22-6. Often you don't think about these distinctions as you work with applications like HTTP, TELNET, or SMTP, and luckily, you don't need to. With NETCONF and YANG, however, understanding this distinction is important.

NETCONF, RESTCONF, and gRPC describe the protocols and methods for transport of network management data.

YANG describes the data model used by the network elements, both internally and when packaged for transmission.

A data model is a well-understood and agreed-upon method to describe something:

- NETCONF was described and standardized as a transport protocol several years before YANG was defined.

- Before YANG models existed, NETCONF used vendor-specific data models.

- Presently, YANG-based data models are the primary network data model format. However, you might still find devices that offer non-YANG data.

- YANG data models can be used without NETCONF. RESTCONF is a great example of this.

As you interact with network devices or any programmatic element, you can send and receive data.

Extensible Markup Language (XML) was developed in 1996 as a set of rules for encoding data in a format that is both human and computer readable. Because of its highly structured format, developers building applications or scripts to consume XML don't have to be concerned about parsing white space and position to identify the information they're seeking. XML uses the concept of namespaces and schemas that identify the data model and format that the information uses. XML is a good choice for programmatic data transport; however, due to its lack of readability and significant overhead, other options exist as well.

JavaScript Object Notation (JSON) is an alternative data format that is heavily used in programmatic use cases. JSON is far more human readable than XML but lacks the strong structure and schema validation that XML provides.

Many APIs enable developers to specify XML or JSON as a data format, enabling the developers or application to choose which type fits a specific use case best. For your usage here, NETCONF uses XML, while RESTCONF provides either XML or JSON options.

When getting started with YANG, you may find yourself confused because the word *YANG* refers to different things. All are related, but they are different enough to cause confusion if you think there is one YANG.

YANG is a language for describing data models. Although it can describe any data model, it was originally designed for networking data models. YANG also is a structured and strongly typed language, and both are beneficial qualities for a data modeling language. Here are some aspects of the language to note:

- Every data model is a module, a self-contained top-level hierarchy of nodes.

- Data types can be imported from another YANG module or defined within a module.

- It uses containers to group related nodes.

- It uses lists to identify nodes that are stored in sequence.

- A leaf represents each individual attribute of a node.

- Every leaf must have an associated type.

Beginners may feel intimidated by the YANG language. It is a robust language for describing complicated topics. For now, read the examples, and there's no need to write in YANG for some time, if ever.

The model can be displayed and represented in various formats, depending on the requirements at the time. Some options include

- YANG language

- Clear text

- XML

- JSON

- HTML

To familiarize yourself with the structures of the mentioned formats, Example 22-1 shows JSON code and the matching code using XML language.

Example 22-1 *JSON and XML Format Message Examples*

```
! JSON Format message.
{"menu": {
  "id": "file",
  "value": "File",
  "popup": {
    "menuitem": [
      {"value": "New", "onclick": "CreateNewDoc()"},
      {"value": "Open", "onclick": "OpenDoc()"},
      {"value": "Close", "onclick": "CloseDoc()"}
    ]
  }
}}

! XML Format message.
<menu id="file" value="File">
  <popup>
    <menuitem value="New" onclick="CreateNewDoc()" />
    <menuitem value="Open" onclick="OpenDoc()" />
    <menuitem value="Close" onclick="CloseDoc()" />
  </popup>
</menu>
```

NETCONF

The IETF developed Network Configuration (NETCONF) to offer a standard protocol and data modeling language for programmatic network management. NETCONF was originally proposed in RFC 4741.

NETCONF is the primary transport protocol used with YANG data models today. It defines how a manager (client) and agent (server) communicate in a standard fashion. Figure 22-7 shows the main building blocks of NETCONF.

XML			
	Content	Configuration/ Operational Data	<data>
	Operations	Actions to Take	<get>, <get-config>, <edit-config>, etc.
	Messages	Remote Procedure Call (RPC)	<rpc>, <rpc-reply>
	Transport	TCP/IP Method	SSH

Figure 22-7   *NETCONF Building Blocks*

NETCONF uses SSH as the underlying method for communicating over the network. NETCONF authentication options are the same as for any SSH communication. You can use the usernames and passwords or certificates the same way you use SSH for CLI communications.

Directly interacting with NETCONF over an SSH channel is not the best plan. Manually crafting the XML and remote procedure calls (RPCs) is error prone and requires more effort. Rather, you should use code libraries and tools that do all the connection handling for you.

NETCONF Capabilities

As mentioned previously, NETCONF is a transport protocol, but it doesn't provide access to configure or retrieve device information as part of the basic protocol. NETCONF uses YANG and non-YANG data models to detail what capabilities a device provides. The list of these capabilities is exchanged during initial communication between a manager and agent as part of the "hello" phase.

Messages that are sent with NETCONF use RPCs, a standard framework for clients to send a request to a server to perform an action and return the results.

Figure 22-8 shows the basic data stores commonly used with XML.

When the IETF was considering a replacement for SNMP, some of the key requirements were

- An integrated method for configuration validation

- Error checking and handling

- Rollback

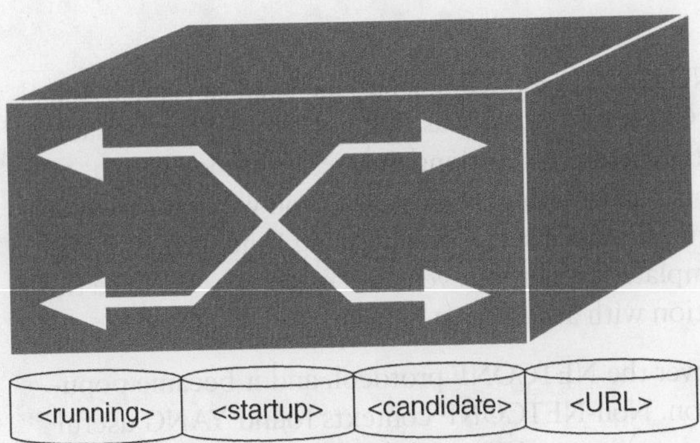

Figure 22-8 *XML Data Stores*

To address this need, NETCONF includes data stores to provide targets of individual operation events. Each container holds a copy of the configuration data that can be prevalidated before committing to active configuration.

Another benefit of data stores is that before committing a set of changes to various network devices, a network management system can look at the configurations for those devices in its data store to verify that they are consistent.

Here are some data store key points:

- A container may hold an entire or partial configuration.

- Not all devices support all data stores (running is the only mandatory data store).

- Not all data stores are writeable.

- IOS supports a URL data store to enable <config-copy>.

- Every NETCONF message must target a data store.

Understanding NETCONF Operations

A NETCONF RPC request uses one of the XML elements shown in Table 22-4 to specify the action it is requesting.

Table 22-4 XML Elements

Operation	Description
<get>	Retrieve running configuration and device state information
<get-config>	Retrieve all or part of specified configuration data store
<edit-config>	Load all or part of a configuration to the specified configuration data store
<copy-config>	Replace an entire configuration data store with another
<delete-config>	Delete a configuration data store
<commit>	Copy the candidate data store to the running data store
<lock> / <unlock>	Lock or unlock the entire configuration data store computer
<close-session>	Close the NETCONF session gracefully
<kill-session>	Force the NETCONF session to end

YANG

As noted elsewhere in the chapter, YANG is a data modeling language used to model your configuration data. We've been using a CLI for decades. Was that not enough and scalable? It is still a handy way of interacting with different networking devices, but imagine that you have a big network with different vendors participating. In that case, you will have to understand the syntax for each vendor configuration tool set to be operating functionally. It will be a difficult task to create a unified template for all those vendors, especially because the network trend is moving into that direction with automation in sight.

YANG was created to define data sent over the NETCONF protocol, and it became popular after NET's success and rapid adoption. Non-NETCONF contexts found YANG useful because it had a good model for defining attributes, APIs, and notifications of a model.

Example 22-2 defines a YANG model for a module that defines the system's hostname and interfaces.

Example 22-2 *YANG Model Example*

```
module acme-system {
        namespace "http://spcor.cisco.com/system";
        prefix "acme";


        organization "SPCOR";
        contact "admin@spcor.cisco.com";
        description
            "The module for entities implementing the ACME system.";


        revision 2024-11-05 {
            description "Initial revision.";
        }


        container system {
            leaf host-name {
                type string;
                description "Hostname for this system";
            }



        list interface {
            key "name";
            description "List of interfaces in the system";
            leaf name {
                type string;
            }
                leaf type {
                    type string;
                }
                leaf mtu {
                    type int32;
```

The system model mentioned earlier can be used to create multiple network or host objects, including routers, switches, and hosts. The data models they support are defined in YANG files that XR devices ship with, using a management protocol (e.g., NETCONF, gRPC, REST-CONF). One option is programmatically querying a device for the list of models it supports and retrieving the model files. In addition, the XR models are publicly available for download on Github. In this chapter, we will use that repository to explore the native XR models.

The names of XR data models use the following notation:

Cisco-IOS-XR-*<platform><technology><suffix>*

Cisco-IOS-XR is the prefix for XR models, followed by a platform substring that can be optional (like ncs5500 or asr9k), followed by a technology substring (e.g., ipv4-bgp), and finally ending with a suffix that indicates whether the model defines configuration data (cfg), operational data (oper), or an action (act).

gRPC

YANG files are included with XR devices to define the data models they can support. A device's list of supported models can be retrieved by programmatically querying it with a management protocol like NETCONF or gRPC. Protocol Buffers (Protobuf) is the base for gRPC, which is an open-source binary serialization protocol.

gRPC provides a flexible, efficient, automated mechanism for serializing structured data, like XML, but is smaller and simpler to use. gRPC employs HTTP/2, which supports multiplexing, a request/response mechanism, and can handle many requests concurrently. gRPC has several advantages. But how do you capitalize on those advantages? One way is to create an RPC and then convert it into a corresponding binary data format and transfer it to/from the server. Does this method seem interesting because creating an RPC is very easy? Another method is to have an interface that creates RPCs and handles their conversion into corresponding data bytes at the client side and server side.

And that's when **gNMI** comes into play. The gNMI, or gRPC Network Management Interface, uses Protocol Buffers to handle data translation (JSON to binary and vice versa) and provides RPCs to control network devices. All of the functionality is provided using gRPC.

A router with minimum version IOS-XR 7 and either of two open-source tools—pygnmi and gnmic—can be used as server and client, respectively.

How will communications between the server and client be secured? gRPC supports all authentication modes listed in Table 22-5. These authentication modes make sure only authorized entities can access gRPC services. Upon receiving a gRPC request, the device will authenticate the user and then perform various authorization checks to validate the user.

Table 22-5   gRPC Authentication Methods

Type	Authentication Method	Authorization Method	Configuration	Client Requirements
Metadata with TLS	Username/password	Username	**grpc**	Username/password/CA
Metadata without TLS	Username/password	Username	**grpc no-tls**	Username/password

Type	Authentication Method	Authorization Method	Configuration	Client Requirements
Metadata with mutual TLS	Username/password	Username	**grpc tls-mutual**	Username/password/CA/client key
Certificate based	Client's certificate (common name field)	Username from client's certificate (common name field)	**grpc tls-mutual** **grpc certificate authentication**	Username/password/CA/client key

Because gNMI uses HTTP/2, TLS can be used to secure the connection. But for now, let's begin without TLS.

To configure a gRPC server on the router (metadata with no TLS), use the commands shown in Example 22-3 (IOS XR–based software).

Example 22-3 *gRPC no-tls Authentication*

```
RP/0/0/CPU0:R2# configure terminal
RP/0/0/CPU0:R2 (config)# grpc
RP/0/0/CPU0:R2 (config-grpc)# port 57777
RP/0/0/CPU0:R2config-grpc)# no-tls
```

NOTE All 64-bit IOS XR platforms support gRPC and TCP protocols. All 32-bit IOS XR platforms support only the TCP protocol and do not support the gRPC protocol.

Cisco gRPC IDL uses the Protocol Buffers interface definition language (IDL) to define service methods and define parameters and return types as protocol buffer message types.

Network Services Orchestrator (NSO)

Relative to the same pain points we have already discussed, networks are becoming increasingly complex, and traditional manual management methods are not sufficient. This requires organizations to have adaptive tools to run daily operations smoothly.

Cisco **Network Services Orchestrator (NSO)** was developed to offer automation and orchestration capabilities to assist organizations to adapt and scale. Automating regular tasks will give businesses more space from operational efficiency, reduce errors, and accelerate services.

The beauty of NSO away from the integrated capabilities of deployment, configuration, and management is that it provides both multivendor and multitechnology support. It acts as a centralized point of orchestration to abstract the underlying network complexity. This will eventually ensure consistency and accuracy by reducing human errors and configurations.

NSO is adopted by several types of organizations:

- **Service Providers:** Provision services seamlessly and oversee complicated infrastructures.

- **Enterprises:** Provide enhanced service delivery by automating network operations.

- **Cloud Providers:** Provide multitenant support and automated service provisioning.

How Does It Work?

NSO adopts a model-focused strategy, establishing and overseeing network services through either a visual interface or programming. This strategy centered on models enables the following:

- **Rapid Service Deployment:** Administrations may be made and conveyed quickly and reliably, dodging human setup issues.

- **Centralized Management:** Network administrators may manage all services from a single point of entry, which increases operational efficiency.

- **Visibility and Control:** NSO provides a comprehensive view of the network and allows for fine-grained control over service behavior.

Benefits

Cisco NSO introduced a digital transition in the ability to manage centrally and added distinguished features to what the market holds. Some key benefits that focus on new digital transformation requirements are as follows:

- It works with different network devices and vendors to provide multivendor support, and ensures interoperability and flexibility in the network environment.

- Automation and efficiency can improve operational efficiency by reducing manual configuration errors and repetitive tasks.

- API-driven architecture allows for custom automation and integration workflows by enabling integration with third-party tools and systems.

- Real-time network visibility allows for proactive troubleshooting and performance optimization because it provides real-time monitoring and visibility into the network.

Cisco NSO can support large and complex network infrastructures in terms of scalability, but it can also be used in terms of flexibility.

The Cisco NSO architecture is like a central hub that helps manage and automate network services. It consists of several key components that work together. Figure 22-9 shows the NSO structure as described in the list that follows.

- **Configuration Database (CDB)** is a storage space that stores all network service configurations. It includes the service manager, which is mainly utilized to create and modify service configurations. CDB possesses a device manager that interacts directly with network devices to apply these configurations, in addition to a service manager. Finally, CDB has a package manager that organizes and manages the different service packages.

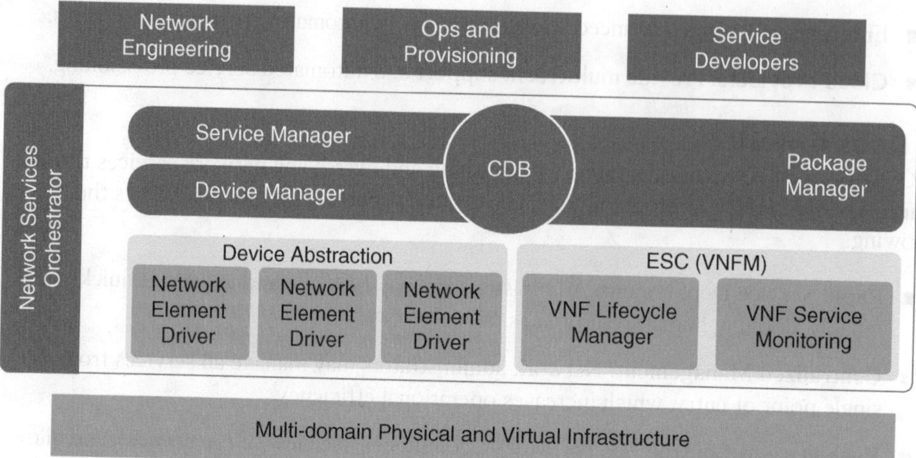

Figure 22-9 *NSO Architecture*

- Device abstraction acts as a translator between the network devices and the NSO system. Furthermore, it assists the NSO in understanding the specifics of each device and communicating with them effectively.

- The **Elastic Services Controller (ESC)** acts as a manager for the virtual network functions (VNFs). In terms of its functioning, it is responsible for managing the lifecycle of VNFs; apart from this, it also monitors the performance of VNFs and ensures they are running smoothly.

NOTE   Cisco NSO architecture is like a smart system that keeps track of network configurations, talks to network devices, and manages virtual functions.

NSO Use Cases

Cisco NSO can be used across many industries and network environments. Examples of common use cases include

- **Service Orchestration:** Automating the process of providing and deploying network services like VPNs, firewalls, and load balancers.

- **Configuration Management:** Maintaining and managing network device configurations in a consistent and scalable manner.

- **Network Automation:** Improving operational efficiency and reducing manual errors by streamlining repetitive tasks and workflows.

- **Multivendor Support:** Using different vendor devices to integrate and orchestrate services across heterogeneous network environments.

- **Self-Service Portals:** Empowering end users to request and provide network services through self-service portals, enhancing agility and responsiveness.

Network Service Orchestration Tools

Network service orchestration tools are a type of software program that helps automate provisioning, configuration, and management of network devices.

These tools assist in streamlining complex network operations and reducing manual errors; they also enhance overall network efficiency.

Further, network service orchestration can be classified into the following three categories:

- Policy-based automation (PBA)

- Software-defined networking (SDN)

- Intent-based networking systems (IBNS)

Secure ZTP

Device management has always been a headache and a management burden, and the associated human errors could dramatically affect network stability.

Secure Zero Touch Provisioning (Secure ZTP) can help seamlessly provision a remarkable number of devices within minutes in a secure fashion.

Security is a major aspect of data centers, and provisioning devices remotely could hold some risks that will require you to provide more secure access to the devices. Secure ZTP combines both automation and secure device onboarding, which eliminates potential security risks or malicious attacks.

The purpose of authentication is to authenticate clients and validate information received from the server.

For the onboarding process of end devices to take place, there are three major steps:

Step 1.   **Router Validation:** The ZTP server authenticates the router before providing bootstrapping data with the assistance of a trust anchor certificate (a SUDI certificate) that will require you to make sure the certificate authority (CA) is preinstalled (this is a prerequisite for Cisco CA on a ZTP server to validate client/server SUDI certificates). The required certificates are as follows:

subject=O = Cisco, CN = ACT2 SUDI CA

subject=O = Cisco Systems, CN = Cisco Root CA 2048

subject=CN = High Assurance SUDI CA, O = Cisco

subject=O = Cisco, CN = Cisco Root CA 2099

Step 2.   **Server Validation:** It is now the device's turn to validate the server to make sure correct network onboarding takes place. Once the process is complete, the server sends the bootstrapping data or artifact to the router.

Step 3.   **Artifact Validation:** At this step, bootstrapping data or the artifact received from the server is validated by configuration.

Secure ZTP Components

Before we dive deep into the operation process of secure ZTP, it is worth examining the constructional components of secure ZTP:

- **Onboarding Device (Router):** You need to configure, provision, or onboard this Cisco device. Secure ZTP requires hardware TAM on the platform (a SUDI certificate embedded in the TAM).

- **DHCP Server:** The server will provide the URL to access the bootstrapping information.

- **ZTP Server:** This can be any server to be used as a source for secure ZTP bootstrapping information (it could be HTTPs or RESTCONF).

The artifacts included in the ZTP server are as follows:

- **Cisco IOS XR Software Images**

- **Bootstrapping Data**

- **ZTP Scripts:** The following libraries are included in the scripts (you can build a script to initiate the ZTP process):

  - **Python Library:** This includes IOS XR CLI (show/configuration commands) as well as YANG-XML.

  - **Bash Library:** This includes IOS XR CLI (show/configuration commands).

  - **Bootstrapping data:** This is a collection of data that a router gets from the ZTP server during the secure ZTP process. You must create and upload the bootstrapping data in the ZTP server. Bootstrapping data has three main artifacts:

  - **Conveyed Information:** This information contains the required bootstrapping data (redirect or onboarding information for device provisioning).

  - **Redirect Information:** This information is used to redirect a device to another server (a list of bootstrap servers with a hostname, optional port, and optional trust anchor certificate for bootstrap server authentication).

  - **Onboarding information:** This is necessary data for device self-bootstrap and secure connection establishment to other systems. Information about boot images, the initial configuration to be committed, and executable scripts are specified in the onboarding information.

- **Report Progress:** The router will report the bootstrapping progress to the ZTP server using API calls after it gets the onboarding information from the ZTP server.

Initial Setup

The following steps are part of the initial setup of the secure ZTP process, which ensures that all components are in place and able to onboard devices properly:

Step 1.   Contact Cisco support to get the voucher. To assure this, you should provide the following information:

- Domain Certificate: This is the trusted digital certificate issued by the certificate authority.

- Order details (which contain serial numbers). Example 22-4 shows a sample.

Example 22-4   *Serial Number Output for Secure ZTP*

```
{
        "expires-on": "2024-10-21T19:31:42Z",
        "assertion": "verified",
        "serial-number": "JADA123456789",
        "idevid-issuer": "base64encodedvalue==",
        "pinned-domain-cert": "base64endvalue==",
        "last-renewal-date": "2029-10-07T19:31:42Z"
}
```

Step 2.   Upload bootstrapping data to the ZTP server.

Step 3.   Set up the DHCP server to provide a URL redirect to the router.

Step 4.   Power on the router.

Step 5.   Enable the Secure ZTP option on the target router.

How Secure ZTP Works

Before we go through the functionality of secure ZTP, please ensure that the network is configured with DHCP and ZTP servers. Now, we can summarize the functionality of secure ZTP with the following steps:

Step 1.   Once the device (IOS XR image) is booted, the secure ZTP process verifies whether the secure ZTP mode is enabled (**secure-ztp-mode**); otherwise, the device will boot normally.

Step 2.   DHCP Discovery:

- A DHCP request is initiated from the router toward the DHCP server.

- The DHCP server responds with DHCPv4 143 address option (IPv4) or DHCPv6 136 address option (IPv6) with the addition of URLs to access bootstrap servers for extra configuration, as shown in Figure 22-10.

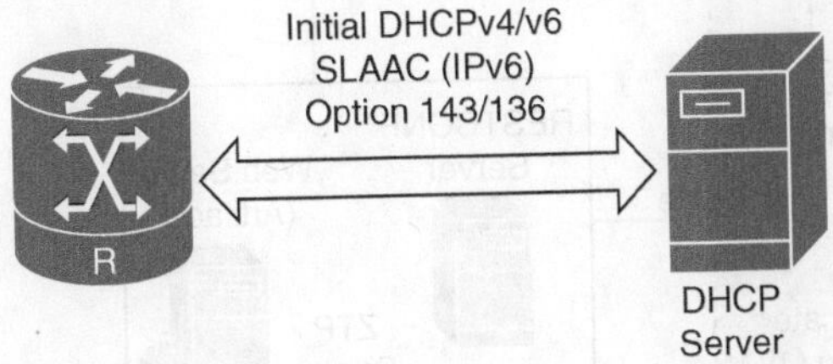

Figure 22-10   *Secure ZTP DHCP Server Communications*

Step 3.   **Router Validation:**

- When the URL is received from the DHCP server, an HTTPs request is sent from the router to either the RESTCONF or HTTPs server using the specified URL. In addition to the HTTPs request, the router sends a client certificate provided by the manufacturer (the SUDI certificate), which authenticates itself to the ZTP server. Figure 22-11 illustrates the router validation process.

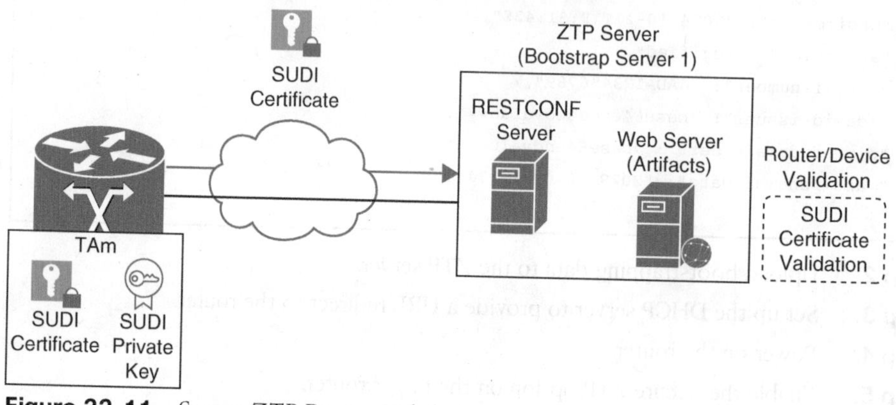

Figure 22-11 *Secure ZTP Router Validation*

- RESTCONF or the HTTPs server validates the received SUDI certificate with the public certificate it has (Cisco issues the public certificate to make sure the onboarded device is a Cisco device).

- After the onboarding device is authenticated, the required artifacts are sent by the web server with the secure ZTP YANG model to the onboarding device.

Step 4.   **Server Validation:** The router receives the YANG model that contains the owner certificate, voucher, and conveyed information. The router to one of the preconfigured trust anchors validates the voucher by verifying its signature. After the router gets the onboarding information, the bootstrap progress is reported to the ZTP server. Figure 22-12 shows the functional process of server validation.

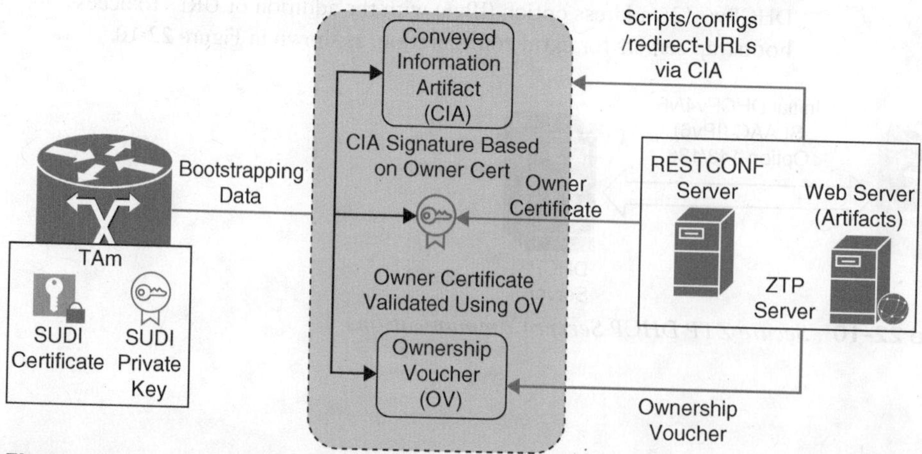

Figure 22-12 *Secure ZTP Server Validation*

NetFlow/IPFIX

Using common network monitoring tools, we can check for information about things such as CPU load, memory usage, and interface status and load. Other tools, like NBAR, allow us to see what kinds of protocols are used.

One thing we can't do with those tools is track all flows in our network. A *flow* is a stream of packets that share the same characteristics as source/destination port, source/destination address, protocol, type, service marking, and so on.

NetFlow allows us to track these flows on our network. We can use this information to solve problems like bottlenecks, identify what applications are used, find how much bandwidth they use, and so on.

For each flow, NetFlow will track the number of packets sent, bytes sent, packet sizes, and more. You can configure your router to keep track of all flows and then export them to a central server where we analyze our traffic. Example 22-5 shows the basic commands to activate NetFlow.

Example 22-5 *NetFlow IOS Configuration Example*

```
R3(config)# ip flow-export destination 10.1.1.1 2055
R3(config)# ip flow-export version 9
R3(config)# interface GigabitEthernet0/1
R3(config-if)# ip route-cache flow

R3# show ip flow export
Flow export v9 is enabled for main cache
  Export source and destination details :
  VRF ID : Default
    Destination(1)   10.1.1.1 (2055)
  Version 9 flow records
  0 flows exported in 0 udp datagrams
  0 flows failed due to lack of export packet
  0 export packets were sent up to process level
  0 export packets were dropped due to no fib
  0 export packets were dropped due to adjacency issues
  0 export packets were dropped due to fragmentation failures
  0 export packets were dropped due to encapsulation fixup failures
```

In 2013, IETF developed the **IP Flow Information Export (IPFIX)** protocol as an evolution to NetFlow. The goal was to extend NetFlow's capabilities by offering a more comprehensive and standardized protocol.

There are some similarities between IPFIX and NetFlow, but the following advantages were introduced:

- Greater flexibility in data types that can be exported

- Extra customization features

- Increased performance and scalability

- Enhancements from an interoperability perspective with other monitoring tools

Like NetFlow, IPFIX collects data from network devices and exports it to a collector for analysis. IPFIX collects not only general information, but a wider range of data types. In addition, information such as TCP flags, packet timestamps, and other fields such as application layer data can be collected, which offers more extensive capabilities.

The extensive capabilities that IPFIX offers are useful for detecting anomalies, identifying traffic patterns, and optimizing performance. For security people, this will help in uncovering threats.

The basic steps involved in configuring IPFIX are as follows:

Step 1.   Configuring an Exporter map with IPFIX as an exporter, as shown in Example 22-6.

Example 22-6   *IPFIX Exporter Map Configuration*

```
RP/0/0/CPU0:R2# show running-config flow exporter-map EXPORT_MAP
flow exporter-map EXPORT_MAP
 destination 10.1.1.1
 source Loopback 0
 transport udp 1025
 exit
version ipfix
 template data timeout 600
 options sampler-table
```

Step 2.   Configuring a Monitor map, as illustrated in Example 22-7.

Example 22-7   *IPFIX Monitor Map Configuration*

```
RP/0/0/CPU0:R2# show running-config monitor-map MONITOR_MAP
flow monitor-map MONITOR_MAP
  record ipv4
   option filtered
  exporter fem_ipfix
  cache entries 10000
  cache timeout active 1800
  cache timeout inactive 15
  exit
```

Step 3.   Configuring a Sampler map, as in Example 22-8.

Example 22-8   *IPFIX Sampler Map Configuration*

```
RP/0/0/CPU0:R2# show running-config sampler-map SAMPLER_MAP
sampler-map SAMPLER_MAP
 random 1 out-of 65535
exit
sampler-map fsm1
 random 1 out-of 65535
exit
```

Step 4.   Applying the Monitor map and Sampler map to an interface, as in Example 22-9.

Example 22-9   *IPFIX Interface Attachment*

```
RP/0/0/CPU0:R2# configure
RP/0/0/CPU0:R2(config)# interface GigabitEthernet0/0/0/0
RP/0/0/CPU0:R2(config-if)# flow ipv4 monitor fmm1 sampler fsm1 ingress
```

We can use the **show flow flow-exporter map** command to verify that the exporter version configured is IPFIX, as shown in Example 22-10.

Example 22-10   *IPFIX Validation*

```
RP/0/0/CPU0:R2# show flow exporter-map EXPORT_MAP
Flow Exporter Map : EXPORT_MAP
-------------------------------------------------------------

Id                    : 3
Packet-Length         : 1468
DestinationIpAddr     : 10.1.1.1
VRFName               : default
SourceIfName          : Loopback0
SourceIpAddr          : 4.4.0.1
DSCP                  : 40
TransportProtocol     : UDP
TransportDestPort     : 9001

Export Version: IPFIX

  Common Template Timeout : 1800 seconds
  Options Template Timeout : 1800 seconds
  Data Template Timeout : 1800 seconds
  Interface-Table Export Timeout : 0 seconds
  Sampler-Table Export Timeout : 0 seconds
  VRF-Table Export Timeout : 0 seconds
```

Streaming Telemetry

Streaming telemetry is a new paradigm for monitoring network health. It provides a mechanism to efficiently stream configuration and operational data of interest from Cisco IOS XR routers. This streamed data is transmitted in a structured format to remote management stations for monitoring and troubleshooting purposes.

With telemetry data, you create a data lake. Analyzing this data, you proactively monitor your network, monitor CPU and memory utilization, identify patterns, troubleshoot your network predictively, and devise strategies to create a resilient network using automation.

Telemetry works on a subscription model, where you subscribe to the data of interest through sensor paths. The sensor paths describe OpenConfig data models or native Cisco data models. You can access the OpenConfig and Native data models for telemetry from Github, a software development platform that provides hosting services for version control. You choose who initiates the subscription by establishing a telemetry session between the router and the receiver. The session is established using either a dial-out mode or a dial-in mode, described in the "Scale-Up Your Network Monitoring Strategy Using Telemetry" article.

The router continually attempts to establish a session with each destination in the subscription and streams data to the receiver. The dial-out mode of subscriptions is persistent. Even when a session terminates, the router continually attempts to re-establish a new session with the receiver at regular intervals.

Figure 22-13 provides a high-level illustration of a dial-out model operation.

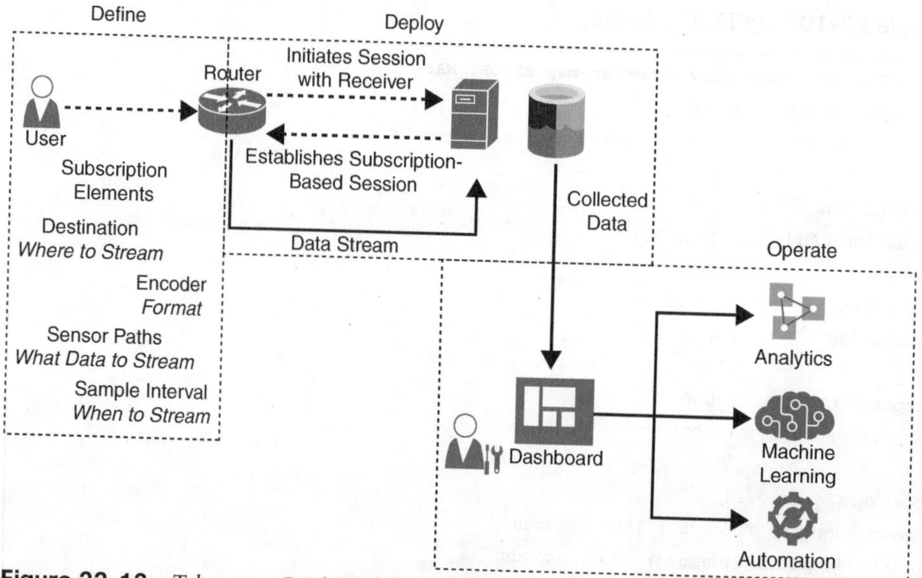

Figure 22-13   *Telemetry Dial-Out Operation*

Telemetry involves the following workflow:

1.   **Define:** You define a subscription to stream data from the router to the receiver. To define a subscription, you create a destination group and a sensor group.

2.   **Deploy:** The router establishes a subscription-based telemetry session and streams data to the receiver. You verify subscription deployment on the router.

3.   **Operate:** You consume and analyze telemetry data using open-source tools, and take necessary actions based on the analysis.

Let's go through a dial-out example for which the router will initiate the session to the destination based on subscriptions.

The process to configure a dial-out mode involves the following:

Step 1.   **Create a destination group using the data model or CLI:** Destination, address, port, encoding, and transport that the router uses to send out the telemetry data, as shown in Example 22-11.

Example 22-11 *Dial-Out Destination Group Using CLI*

```
RP/0/RP0/CPU0:XR1(config)# telemetry model-driven
RP/0/RP0/CPU0:XR1(config-model-driven)# destination-group TELE_GROUP
RP/0/RP0/CPU0:XR1(config-model-driven-dest)# address-family ipv4 10.1.1.100 port
5432
RP/0/RP0/CPU0:XR1(config-model-driven-dest-addr)# encoding ?
  gpb                  GPB encoding
  json                 JSON encoding
  self-describing-gpb  Self describing GPB encoding
RP/0/RP0/CPU0:XR1(config-model-driven-dest-addr)# encoding self-describing-gpb
RP/0/RP0/CPU0:XR1(config-model-driven-dest-addr)# protocol ?
  grpc  gRPC
  tcp   TCP
  udp   UDP
RP/0/RP0/CPU0:XR1(config-model-driven-dest-addr)# protocol tcp
```

Step 2.   **Create a sensor group using the data model or CLI:** List of YANG models to
be streamed, as in Example 22-12.

Example 22-12 *Dial-Out Sensor Group Using CLI*

```
RP/0/RP0/CPU0:XR1(config)# telemetry model-driven
RP/0/RP0/CPU0:XR1(config-model-driven)# sensor-group TELE_SNSR_GROUP
RP/0/RP0/CPU0:XR1(config-model-driven-snsr-grp)# sensor-path Cisco-IOS-XR-infra-
statsd-oper:infra-statistics/interfaces/interface/latest/generic-counters
```

Step 3.   **Create a subscription using the data model or CLI:** Determines the streaming
method and associates the destination group to a sensor group. The source
interface is used to establish the session to stream data to the destination, as
illustrated in Example 22-13.

Example 22-13 *Dial-Out Subscription Definition Using CLI*

```
RP/0/RP0/CPU0:XR1(config)# telemetry model-driven
RP/0/RP0/CPU0:XR1(config-model-driven-subs)# sensor-group-id TELE_SNSR_GROUP
RP/0/RP0/CPU0:XR1(config-model-driven-subs)# destination-id TELE_GROUP
```

Example 22-14 will help validate and verify the three steps we have used to activate the
dial-out.

Example 22-14 *Dial-Out Validation*

```
RP/0/RP0/CPU0:XR1# show telemetry model-driven subscription TELE_SUBSCRIPTION
Subscription:  TELE_SUBSCRIPTION
-------------
  State:         NA
  Sensor groups:
  Id: TELE_SNSR_GROUP
    Sample Interval:        30000 ms
```

```
     Heartbeat Interval:    NA

     Sensor Path:           Cisco-IOS-XR-infra-statsd-oper:infra-statistics/
interfaces/interface/latest/generic-counters
     Sensor Path State:     Resolved


 Destination Groups:
 Group Id: TELE_GROUP
    Destination IP:        10.1.100.1
    Destination Port:      5432
    Encoding:              self-describing-gpb
    Transport:             tcp
    State:                 NA
    TLS :                  False


 Collection Groups:
 ------------------
 No active collection groups
```

SNMP

Simple Network Management Protocol (SNMP) is a standard protocol used for collecting and gathering information about network devices. The main goal is to be able to monitor several aspects about the devices connected over IP networks with the ability to manage them.

Before going through SNMP details and the functional blocks, we should answer a question: Will SNMP disappear? For the time being, no, for a variety of different reasons:

- SNMP and the associated MIB models are still good options for monitoring.

- Management Information Base (MIB) version 2 modules can be translated to YANG modules, as depicted in RFC 6643.

- YANG can be used for configuration and monitoring new features, with SNMP continuing its function in the current state.

The structure of the SNMP environment solely consists of the manager and an agent. The manager is the device that pulls the SNMP agent for information. The agents are responsible for gathering the information about the local devices and storing them in a queried format, which will construct a database called the Management Information Base (MIB).

The following protocol data units (PDUs) describe the exact messaging types that are allowed by the protocol:

- **Get:** A manager sends a Get message to an agent to request the value of a specific OID. This request is answered with a Response message that is sent back to the manager with the data.

- **GetNext:** A GetNext message allows a manager to request the next sequential object in the MIB. This is a way that you can traverse the structure of the MIB without worrying about what OIDs to query.

- **Set:** A manager sends a Set message to an agent to change the value held by a variable on the agent. This can be used to control configuration information or otherwise modify the state of remote hosts. This is the only write operation defined by the protocol.

- **GetBulk:** This manager-to-agent request functions as if multiple GetNext requests were made. The reply back to the manager will contain as much data as possible (within the constraints set by the request) as the packet allows.

- **Response:** This message, sent by an agent, is used to send any requested information back to the manager. It serves as both a transport for the data requested and an acknowledgment of receipt of the request. If the requested data cannot be returned, the response contains error fields that can be set with further information. A response message must be returned for any of the preceding requests, as well as Inform messages.

- **Trap:** A trap message is generally sent by an agent to a manager. Traps are asynchronous notifications in that they are unsolicited by the manager receiving them. They are mainly used by agents to inform managers of events that are happening on their managed devices.

- **Inform:** To confirm the receipt of a trap, a manager sends an Inform message back to the agent. If the agent does not receive this message, it may continue to resend the trap message.

SNMPv2c

The most widely used SNMP is v2c, which relies on a *community*, which is a common phrase that is shared between the manager and the managed host.

To protect our device, we can configure an access list and attach it to the SNMP statement to limit the authorized managers who will pull information. Let's check Example 22-15 for a basic SNMPv2 example.

Example 22-15   *SNMPv2 Basic Configuration Example*

```
R3(config)# access-list 10 permit host 10.1.100.1
R3(config)# snmp-server community secure ro 10
```

SNMPv3

The Simple Network Management Protocol version 3 (SNMPv3) feature provides secure access to devices by authenticating and encrypting data packets over the network. SNMPv3 is an interoperable, standards-based protocol that is defined in RFCs 3413 to 3415. This module discusses the security features provided in SNMPv3 and describes how to configure the security mechanism to handle SNMP packets.

SNMPv3 is a security model in which an authentication strategy is set up for a user and the group in which the user resides. Security level is the permitted level of security within a security model. A combination of a security model and a security level determines which security mechanism is used when handling an SNMP packet.

The security features provided in SNMPv3 are as follows:

- **Message Integrity:** Ensures that a packet has not been tampered with during transit.

- **Authentication:** Determines that the message is from a valid source.

- **Encryption:** Scrambles the content of a packet to prevent it from being learned by an unauthorized source.

Table 22-6 shows the security levels and models supported by SNMPv3.

Table22-6 SNMPv3 Security Levels

Level	Authentication	Encryption	Description
NoAuthNoPriv	Username	No	Uses a username match for authentication
AuthNoPriv	Messages Digest Algorithm 5 (MD5) or Secure Hash Algorithm (SHA)	No	Provides authentication based on the Hashed Message Authentication Code (HMAC)-MD5 or HMAC-SHA algorithms
AuthPriv	Messages Digest Algorithm 5 (MD5) or Secure Hash Algorithm (SHA)	Data Encryption Standard (DES)	Provides authentication based on the HMAC-MD5 or HMAC-SHA algorithms. In addition to authentication, provides DES 56-bit encryption based on the Cipher Block Chaining (CBC)-DES (DES-56) standard.

Example 22-16 demonstrates how to configure SNMPv3.

Example 22-16 *SNMPv3 Configuration Example*

```
R3(config)# access-list 10 permit host 10.1.100.1
R3(config)# snmp-server community secure ro 10
R3(config)# snmp-server group SNMP_GROUP v3 auth access 10
R3(config)# snmp-server user SNMP_USER SNMP_GROUP v3 auth md5 SPCORPASS access 10

%SNMP-6-AUTHPROTOCOLMD5: Authentication protocol md5 support will be deprecated in future

R3# show snmp user
User name: SNMP_USER
Engine ID: 80000009030050999200410O
storage-type: nonvolatile          active access-list: 10
Authentication Protocol: MD5
Privacy Protocol: None
Group-name: SNMP_GROUP
R3#show snmp group
groupname: ILMI                    security model:v1
contextname: <no context specified>    storage-type: permanent
```

```
readview : *ilmi                              writeview: *ilmi
notifyview: <no notifyview specified>
row status: active


groupname: ILMI                               security model:v2c
contextname: <no context specified>           storage-type: permanent
readview : *ilmi                              writeview: *ilmi
notifyview: <no notifyview specified>
row status: active


groupname: secure                             security model:v1
contextname: <no context specified>           storage-type: permanent
readview : v1default                          writeview: <no writeview specified>
notifyview: <no notifyview specified>
row status: active         access-list: 10


groupname: secure                             security model:v2c
contextname: <no context specified>           storage-type: permanent
readview : v1default                          writeview: <no writeview specified>
notifyview: <no notifyview specified>
row status: active         access-list: 10


groupname: SNMP_GROUP                          security model:v3 noauth
contextname: <no context specified>           storage-type: nonvolatile
readview : v1default                          writeview: <no writeview specified>
notifyview: <no notifyview specified>
row status: active


groupname: SNMP_GROUP                          security model:v3 auth
contextname: <no context specified>           storage-type: nonvolatile
readview : v1default                          writeview: <no writeview specified>
notifyview: <no notifyview specified>
row status: active         access-list: 10
AthPriv
```

```
R3(config)# snmp-server group SNMP_GROUP v3 auth md5 SPCORPASS priv aes 256
SPCORPRIV access 10
```

```
%SNMP-6-AUTHPROTOCOLMD5: Authentication protocol md5 support will be deprecated in future
```

```
R3# show snmp user
User name: SNMP_USER
Engine ID: 80000009030050999200410D
storage-type: nonvolatile         active access-list: 10
Authentication Protocol: MD5
Privacy Protocol: AES256
Group-name: SNMP_GROUP
```

```
! IOS XR
RP/0/0/CPU0:R2(config)# snmp-server group SNMP_GROUP v3 auth ipv4 SNMP_ACL
RP/0/0/CPU0:R2(config)# snmp-server user SNMP_USER SNMP_GROUP v3 auth md5 clear
SPCORPASS IPv4 SNMP_ACL
```

Ansible and Terraform

Ansible is used to automate and configure apps. It can work with Docker, Amazon EC2, or Kubernetes. Ansible has been the product of Red Hat Inc. since 2012. It is a configuration management tool, and it is open source. Ansible's architecture is agentless and serverless, and it supports modules for managing Windows and UNIX-like hosts. Ansible depends on SSH/PowerShell sessions.

Ansible executes a DevOps paradigm. It executes all the ad hoc commands. Ansible's imperative nature makes it suitable for traditional configuration management. It is used for various goals like automation and potential migration. Ansible for DevOps has been gaining momentum and embraced in cloud solutions, especially automation.

Terraform is an open-source command-line tool that can be used to provision any kind of infrastructure on many different platforms and services. Terraform can be written in HashiCorp Config Language (HCL). This language is easy to learn and easy to troubleshoot. It's between human-friendly and machine-readable code. Many cloud engineers who use this tool for provisioning assets have asked for Terraform training. In fact, Terraform in Azure and AWS has become quite popular.

Table 22-7 lists the differences between the two platforms from a feature perspective.

Table 22-7   Ansible and Terraform Comparison

Feature	Ansible	Terraform
Code	Open source	Open source
Infrastructure	Ansible provides support for mutable infrastructure.	Terraform provides support for immutable infrastructure.
Architecture	Client only	Client only
Cloud	All CSPs	All CSPs
Lifecycle (State) Management	It does not have lifecycle management.	It is dependent on lifecycle or state management.
Agent Requirement	Ansible does not require any extra agents to be installed on the server to install.	Terraform also does not require any extra agent to install.
Master Server	Ansible is masterless. Some other tools like Chef and Puppet require the master server to store the changes and distribute the updates; however, there are disadvantages, such as extra security and infrastructure maintenance, which incur cost.	Terraform is also masterless. It communicates with the cloud providers using API. They don't require any extra infrastructure authentication mechanism.

Exam Preparation Tasks

As mentioned in the section "How to Use This Book" in the Introduction, you have a few choices for exam preparation: the exercises here, Chapter 23, "Final Preparation," and the exam simulation questions in the Pearson Test Prep Software Online.

Review All Key Topics

Review the most important topics in this chapter, noted with the Key Topic icon in the margin of the page. Table 22-8 lists a reference of these key topics and the page numbers on which each is found.

Table 22-8   Key Topics for Chapter 22

Key Topic Element	Description	Page Number
List	API functionality	979
Table 22-2	HTTP Status Codes	980
Figure 22-4	Model-Driven Programmability Architecture	984
Section	Network Services Orchestrator (NSO)	992
Section	Secure ZTP Components	996
List	IPFIX over NetFlow advantages	999

Define Key Terms

Define the following key terms from this chapter and check the answers in the glossary:

Ansible, Application Programming Interface (API), Configuration Database (CDB), Elastic Services Controller (ESC), Extensible Markup Language (XML), gNMI (Network Management Interface), gRPC (remote procedure call), IP Flow Information Export (IPFIX), JavaScript Object Notation (JSON), Network Configuration Protocol (NETCONF), Network Services Orchestrator (NSO), Remote Procedure Call (RPC), Representational State Transfer (REST), Representational State Transfer Configuration (RESTCONF), Secure Zero Touch Provisioning (Secure ZTP), Simple Network Management Protocol (SNMP), Simple Object Access Protocol (SOAP), Terraform, Uniform Resource Identifier (URI)

Command Reference to Check Your Memory

This section includes the most important commands covered in this chapter. You might not need to memorize the complete syntax of every command, but you should be able to remember the basic keywords that are needed.

To test your memory of the commands, cover the right side of Table 22-9 with a piece of paper, read the description on the left side, and then see how much of the command you can remember.

The SPCOR 350-501 exam focuses on practical, hands-on skills that are used by networking professionals. Therefore, you should be able to identify the commands needed to configure and test. Note that not all commands are fully covered in the chapter, but their presence in the following table should lead you to investigate them further to understand this technology.

Table 22-9   CLI Commands to Know

Task	Command Syntax
Configure GRPC dial-in	**grpc**
Configure TCP dial-out	**telemetry model-driven**
Define the telemetry destination group	**destination-group** *group-name*
Define the telemetry destination sensor	**sensor-group** *group-name*
Configure the NetFlow IP address and port	**ip flow-export destination** *ip-address port-number*
Configure an export map on IOS XR for IPFIX	**flow exporter-map** *map-name*
Configure a monitor map on IOS XR for IPFIX	**flow monitor-map** *map-name*
Configure SNMPv3 (group name, security level, and ACL)	**snmp-server group** *group-name* **v3 auth access** *ACL-number*
Define SNMPv3 user and group association with encryption and ACL	**snmp-server user** *user group-name* **v3 auth md5** *password* **access** *ACL-number*

Review Questions

As a part of the review, we encourage you to provide *a single-sentence answer* (keep your answers as short as possible) to the following questions. If you struggle to complete this answer in a single sentence, this may indicate a lack of clarity or reveal gaps in your understanding. We have constructed these questions to help you consolidate this chapter's information and extract the essence of the covered content.

The answers to these questions appear in Appendix A. For more practice with exam format questions, use the Pearson Test Prep Software Online.

1.   NETCONF will not configure or retrieve device information as part of the basic protocol. What tools are used to accomplish this?

2.   What are advantages of using IPFIX instead of NetFlow?

3.   Will SNMP disappear after the innovation of programmability?

4.   What constructional element of the Telemetry solution do you think is the source of robustness?

Bibliography

M. Bjorklund. RFC 6020, *YANG—A Data Modeling Language for the Network Configuration Protocol (NETCONF)*, IETF, https://www.ietf.org/rfc/rfc6020.txt, October 2010.

J. Case, M. Fedor, M. Shcoffstall, and J. Davin. RFC 1067, *A Simple Network Management Protocol*, IETF, https://www.ietf.org/rfc/rfc1067.txt, August 1988.

J. Case, M. Fedor, M. Shcoffstall, and C. Davin. RFC 1098, *A Simple Network Management Protocol (SNMP)*, IETF, https://www.ietf.org/rfc/rfc1098.txt, April 1989.

Cisco Systems. *Programmability Configuration Guide for Cisco 8000 Series Routers, IOS XR Release 7.9.x*. https://www.cisco.com/c/en/us/td/docs/iosxr/cisco8000/programmability/79x/b-programmability-cg-8000-79x/use-grpc-protocol-to-define-network-operation-with-data-models.html. Accessed August 22, 2024.

Cisco Systems. *Scale-Up Your Network Monitoring Strategy Using Telemetry*. https://www.cisco.com/c/en/us/td/docs/iosxr/ncs5500/telemetry/75x/b-telemetry-cg-ncs5500-75x/scale-up-your-network-monitoring-strategy-using-telemetry.pdf

Cisco Systems. *System Setup and Software Installation Guide for Cisco NCS 540 Series Routers, IOS XR Release 7.11.x*, https://www.cisco.com/c/en/us/td/docs/iosxr/ncs5xx/system-setup/711x/b-system-setup-cg-711x-ncs540/configure-secure-ztp.html. Accessed August 19, 2024.

H. Dahir, J. Davis, S. Clark, and Q. Snyder. *Cisco Certified DevNet Professional DEVCOR 350-901 Official Cert Guide*, Cisco Press, 2022.

R. Enns. RFC 4741, *NETCONF Configuration Protocol*, IETF, https://www.ietf.org/rfc/rfc4741.txt, December 2006.

gRPC. https://grpc.io./. Accessed August 19, 2024.

J. Schoenwaelder. RFC 3535, *Overview of the 2002 IAB Network Management Workshop*, IETF, https://www.ietf.org/rfc/rfc3535.txt, May 2003.

J. Schoenwaelder. RFC 6643, *Translation of Structure of Management Information Version 2 (SMIv2) MIB Modules to YANG Modules*, IETF, https://www.ietf.org/rfc/rfc6643.txt, July 2012.

A. Sharma. *IO-XR7 Innovations*. Cisco Live Presentation, https://www.ciscolive.com/c/dam/r/ciscolive/us/docs/2021/pdf/BRKSPG-2024.pdf. Accessed August 19, 2024.

K. Watsen, I. Farrer, and M. Abrahamsson. RFC 8572, *Secure Zero Touch Provisioning (SZTP)*, IETF, https://www.ietf.org/rfc/rfc8572.txt, April 2019.

## CHAPTER 23

Final Preparation

The first 22 chapters of this book cover the technologies, protocols, design concepts, and considerations required for your preparation in passing the Cisco Implementing and Operating Cisco Service Provider Network Core Technologies (SPCOR 350-501) exam. This is the exam required for the CCNP Service Provider, CCIE Service Provider, and Cisco Certified Specialist–Service Provider Core certifications. If you are pursuing the CCNP Service Provider certification, you still need to select and pass a concentration exam to achieve that certification. If you are preparing for the CCIE certification, you must also pass the hands-on eight-hour lab.

Chapters 1 through 22 cover the information necessary to pass the exam. However, most people need more preparation than simply reading the first 22 chapters of this book. This chapter, along with the Introduction of the book, suggests hands-on activities and a study plan that will help you complete your preparation for the exam.

Hands-on Activities

As mentioned, you should not expect to pass the SPCOR 350-501 exam by just reading this book. The SPCOR 350-501 exam requires hands-on experience with many of the Cisco technologies, tools, and techniques discussed in this book. The most effective way to learn the skills necessary to pass the exam is to build your own lab, break it, and fix it.

Suggested Plan for Final Review and Study

This section provides a suggested study plan from the point at which you finish reading Chapter 22 until you take the Implementing and Operating Cisco Service Provider Network Core Technologies (SPCOR 350-501) exam. You can ignore this plan, use it as is, or modify it to better meet your needs:

Step 1. **Review key topics and DIKTA questions:** You can use the table at the end of each chapter that lists the key topics in each chapter or just flip through the pages looking for key topics. Also, reviewing the "Do I Know This Already?" (DIKTA) questions from the beginning of the chapter can be helpful.

Step 2. **Review the Exam Blueprint:** Cisco maintains a list of testable content known as the Implementing and Operating Cisco Service Provider Network Core Technologies (SPCOR 350-501) Exam Blueprint. Review it and ensure you are familiar with every item that is listed. You can download a copy at https://learningcontent.cisco.com/documents/350_501_SPCOR_v1.0.pdf.

Step 3. **Study "Review Questions" sections:** Go through the review questions at the end of each chapter to identify areas in which you need more study.

Step 4. **Use the Pearson Cert Practice Test engine to practice:** The Pearson Test Prep software provides a bank of unique exam-realistic questions available only with this book.

Summary

The tools and suggestions listed in this chapter have been designed with one goal in mind: to help you develop the skills required to pass the Implementing and Operating Cisco Service Provider Network Core Technologies (SPCOR 350-501) exam to achieve the CCNP Service Provider or CCIE Service Provider certifications.

This book has been developed from the beginning both to present you with a collection of facts and to help you learn how to apply those facts. Regardless of your experience level before reading this book, it is our hope that the broad range of preparation tools, and even the structure of the book, will help you pass the exam with ease.

## CHAPTER 24

CCNP SPCOR (350-501) Exam Updates

The Purpose of This Chapter

For all the other chapters, the content should remain unchanged throughout this edition of the book. However, this chapter will change over time, with an updated online PDF posted so you can see the latest version of the chapter even after you purchase this book.

Why do we need a chapter that updates over time? For two reasons:

1. To add more technical content to the book before it is time to replace the current book edition with the next edition. This chapter will include additional technology content and possibly additional PDFs containing more content.

2. To communicate detail about the next version of the exam, to tell you about our publishing plans for that edition, and to help you understand what that means to you.

After the initial publication of this book, Cisco Press will provide supplemental updates as digital downloads for minor exam updates. If an exam has major changes or accumulates enough minor changes, we will then announce a new edition. We will do our best to provide any updates to you free of charge before we release a new edition. However, if the updates are significant enough in between editions, we may release the updates as a low-priced standalone eBook.

If we do produce a free updated version of this chapter, you can access it on the book's companion website. Simply go to the companion website page and go to the "Exam Updates Chapter" section of the page.

If you have not yet accessed the companion website, follow this process:

Step 1. Browse to www.ciscopress.com/register.

Step 2. Enter the print book ISBN (even if you are using an eBook): 9780135324806.

Step 3. After registering the book, go to your account page and select the Registered Products tab.

Step 4. Click the Access Bonus Content link to access the companion website. Select the **Exam Updates Chapter** link or scroll down to that section to check for updates.

About Possible Exam Updates

Cisco introduced CCNA and CCNP in 1998. For the first 25 years of those certification tracks, Cisco updated the exams on average every 3–4 years. However, Cisco did not pre-announce the exam changes, so exam changes felt very sudden. Usually, a new exam would be announced, with new exam topics, giving you 3–6 months before your only option was to take the new exam. As a result, you could be studying with no idea about Cisco's plans, and the next day, you had a 3–6-month timeline to either pass the old exam or pivot to prepare for the new exam.

Thankfully, Cisco changed its exam release approach in 2023. Called the Cisco Certification Roadmap (https://cisco.com/go/certroadmap), the new plan includes these features:

1. Cisco considers changes to all exam tracks (CCNA, CCNP Enterprise, CCNP Security, and so on) annually.

2. Cisco uses a predefined annual schedule for each track, so even before any announcements, you know the timing of possible changes to the exam you are studying for.

3. The schedule moves in a quarterly sequence:

    a. Privately review the exam to consider what to change.

    b. Publicly announce if an exam is changing, and if so, announce details like exam topics and release date.

    c. Release the new exam.

4. Exam changes might not occur each year. If changes occur, Cisco characterizes them as minor (less than 20 percent change) or major (more than 20 percent change).

Impact on You and Your Study Plan

Cisco's new policy helps you plan, but it also means that the exam might change before you pass the current exam. That impacts you, affecting how we deliver this book to you. This chapter provides a way for Cisco Press to communicate in detail about those changes as they occur. But you should watch other spaces as well.

For those other information sources to watch, bookmark and check these sites for news. In particular:

- **Cisco:** Check their Certification Roadmap page: https://cisco.com/go/certroadmap. Make sure to sign up for automatic notifications from Cisco on that page.

- **Publisher:** Check this page for new certification products, offers, discounts, and free downloads related to the more frequent exam updates: https://www.ciscopress.com/newcert.

- **Cisco Learning Network:** Subscribe to the CCNA Community at https://learningnetwork.cisco.com/s/ccnp-service-provider, where we expect ongoing discussions about exam changes over time. If you have questions, search for "roadmap" in the CCNP community, and if you do not find an answer, ask a new one!

As changes arise, we will update this chapter with more detail about exam and book content. At that point, we will publish an updated version of this chapter, listing our content plans. That detail will likely include the following:

- Content removed, so if you plan to take the new exam version, you can ignore those when studying.

- New content planned per new exam topics, so you know what's coming.

The remainder of the chapter shows the new content that may change over time.

News About the Next Exam Release

This statement was last updated in 2024, before the publication of the *CCNP SPCOR (350-501) Official Cert Guide*.

This version of this chapter has no news to share about the next exam release.

In the most recent version of this chapter, the 350-501 exam version number was Version 1.1.

Updated Technical Content

The current version of this chapter has no additional technical content.

Answers to the "Do I Know This Already?" Quizzes and Review Questions

Chapter 1

"Do I Know This Already?" Quiz

1. b
2. b and c
3. d
4. d
5. c
6. a and b

Review Questions

1. Possible answers include: Distributed intelligence allows for quick and efficient decision-making at each node, while a central controller oversees the networkwide optimization.

2. Possible answers include: It facilitates flexible and efficient wavelength management in DWDM systems by allowing on-the-fly addition, removal, or redirection of wavelengths.

3. Possible answers include: Multiple Input Multiple Output (MIMO) improves data throughput by transmitting multiple streams simultaneously, enhances spectral efficiency, and increases link reliability through the use of multiple antennas.

4. Possible answers include: E-LAN tends to be more cost-effective for providing multipoint connectivity because it allows communication between multiple sites in a LAN-like configuration, whereas E-Tree establishes a hierarchical structure with a root site and multiple leaf sites, which might involve additional configuration and potentially higher costs due to the specific topology.

Chapter 2

"Do I Know This Already?" Quiz

1. b and d
2. a, c, and d
3. d
4. d

Review Questions

1. Possible answers include: Cisco IOS XR provides robust configuration management capabilities tailored for service provider networks with key features such as configuration rollback, commit confirm, and configuration replace, to facilitate safe and efficient handling of configuration changes because these mechanisms help minimize errors and enhance network stability.

2. Possible answers include: Cisco IOS XR facilitates modularity in configuration management through its hierarchical structure, allowing you to organize configurations into separate modules for scalability, manageability, and fault isolation.

3. Possible answers include: **install add source** *<source-location>* **package** *<package-name>*.

Chapter 3

"Do I Know This Already?" Quiz

1. a, b, and d
2. b
3. d
4. b

Review Questions

1. Possible answers include: VNFI encompasses the virtualized resources and management capabilities required for deploying and managing virtualized network functions (VNFs), addressing challenges in resource allocation, performance optimization, and scalability across distributed environments, with considerations for emerging technologies such as edge computing and 5G networks.

2. Possible answers include: The **docker create** command only creates a new container based on an image but does not start it, whereas the **docker start** command starts an existing container that has been previously created but is currently stopped, but it does not create a new container.

3. Possible answers include: The key challenges include resource constraints, security requirements, and network integration, while strategies involve optimizing resource utilization, implementing robust security measures, and leveraging network automation for efficient deployment.

4. Possible answers include: While it's technically possible to run Kubernetes on certain Cisco devices, such as Cisco UCS servers or other x86-based hardware that supports virtualization, it's not a common or recommended use case for Cisco routers.

Chapter 4

"Do I Know This Already?" Quiz

1. c
2. b
3. b
4. a, b, and c
5. c
6. d
7. a
8. a and c
9. d
10. c

Review Questions

1. Possible answers include: Path vector protocols, like BGP, provide flexible policy-based routing and prevent routing loops by explicitly propagating the path information along with each route advertisement.

2. Possible answers include: The primary advantage of using route maps is their capability to selectively filter, modify, or manipulate routes based on defined criteria, enabling precise control over routing behavior and policy enforcement in network configurations.

3. Possible answers include: The primary advantage of using RPL is its ability to create modular and reusable policy components, streamlining network management and enhancing scalability and flexibility.

Chapter 5

"Do I Know This Already?" Quiz

1. a
2. a and d
3. a and d
4. b
5. b

Review Questions

1. Possible answers include: The single key advantage of the IS-IS protocol over OSPF in a service provider network lies in its superior scalability in large networks due to the scope of link-state advertisements (LSAs) and the reduction of the complexity of the network's link-state database.

2. Possible answers include: IS-IS areas are used to regulate the formation of adjacencies; levels control LSP flooding.

Chapter 6

"Do I Know This Already?" Quiz

1. d
2. b and c
3. b
4. a and c
5. c
6. a, b, and d
7. b

Review Questions

1. Possible answers include: OSPF administrators should assess the network's size, traffic patterns, and administrative requirements to determine whether a flat OSPF design's simplicity outweighs the scalability benefits of hierarchical OSPF area structures.

2. Possible answers include: OSPF calculates the cost of a route based on the inverse of the bandwidth of the link, where higher bandwidth corresponds to lower cost, and this cost calculation is influenced by factors such as network delay and interface type in determining the optimal path for routing.

3. Possible answers include: OSPFv3 accommodates IPv6 addressing, enhances address configuration flexibility, and bolsters security features.

Chapter 7

"Do I Know This Already?" Quiz

1. b and d
2. a
3. c
4. c
5. a
6. b
7. d
8. b
9. b and c
10. a

Review Questions

1. Possible answers include: The iBGP relation will become an eBGP relation, which means we have to account for any configuration aspects related to iBGP, such as ebgp-multihop.

2. Possible answers include: Large service providers have a predefined list of communities that assist in controlling their incoming/outgoing traffic; in addition, they propose manipulation of use case path attributes for their customers.

3. Possible answers include: Address Family Identifiers (AFIs), or extensions, have been introduced to account for new services, protocols, and applications.

4. Possible answers include: BGP AIGP will take effect when several autonomous systems are working under the same administration for which we need to ensure an optimal path in both inbound and outbound directions to guarantee symmetrical routing by relying on the IGP metric that will be carried among the autonomous systems. The same holds true for MPLS service providers where there are many provider edge (PE) devices and many routes for which we will segment the IGP and rely on BGP for labeled traffic between the IGP islands.

5. Possible answers include: The loopback interface is a virtual interface, and although it will not be impacted by physical failure, an IGP will be responsible for finding an alternate path to ensure proper loopback-to-loopback connectivity. This will turn the BGP session from a one-hop to a multiple-hop relationship.

Chapter 8

"Do I Know This Already?" Quiz

1. b
2. b
3. a
4. b
5. a

Review Questions

1. Possible answers include: BGP next-hop tracking determines if the next hop is reachable, validates the next hop, and then verifies the reachability of neighbors after the next-hop calculation.

2. Possible answers include: Usually, we build an iBGP session by using loopback interfaces as the source for that iBGP session. Most of the time, we include redundancy internally for the loopbacks to reach each other and therefore maintain the iBGP session.

Chapter 9

"Do I Know This Already?" Quiz

1. a
2. a and d
3. c
4. c
5. d
6. b

Review Questions

1. Possible answers include: PIM Sparse mode minimizes resource consumption and operational complexity through mechanisms such as shared trees and rendezvous points (RPs).

2. Possible answers include: IGMPv3 effectively handles Source-Specific Multicast (SSM) by allowing receivers to specify their desired multicast sources, reducing unnecessary traffic and optimizing resource utilization.

3. Possible answers include: The rendezvous point (RP) serves as a centralized router responsible for receiving multicast traffic from sources and forwarding it to multicast group members upon request, while routers use shared trees and source-specific trees to build and maintain multicast distribution paths, offering efficient multicast traffic delivery in IPv4 networks.

Chapter 10

"Do I Know This Already?" Quiz

1. c
2. a
3. b
4. b
5. c
6. c
7. d
8. b

Review Questions

1. Possible answers include: The OSPF process will advertise the loopback network with a /32 mask, treating it as a host route, which means no label will be assigned for this network because no exact match will be found in the IGP RIB.

2. Possible answers include: PhP will remove the outermost label on the MPLS device residing before the last device in the LSP. This will reserve extra label lookup and speed up packet transport.

3. Possible answers include: The implicit null label is used by default and works well when the network has no QoS requirements, or if the QoS is end-to-end between customer edges.

Chapter 11

"Do I Know This Already?" Quiz

1. b
2. b
3. c

    4. a and c

    5. c

    6. a

Review Questions

1. Possible answers include: EVPN solves all-active per-flow redundancy, MAC flip-flopping over pseudowire, and duplicate frames flooding from the core.

2. Possible answers include: In a traditional VPLS deployment, all provider edge (PE) routers in the service provider's network participate in a single VPLS instance. As the number of customer sites and VPLS subscribers grows, the control plane and data plane overhead associated with maintaining full-mesh connectivity between all PE routers can become significant, leading to scalability challenges.

3. Possible answers include: Two fundamental scale-limiting factors of plain/flat VPLS architecture are signaling overhead and packet replication.

Chapter 12

"Do I Know This Already?" Quiz

    1. b

    2. c

    3. d

    4. b

    5. b

    6. c

    7. a

Review Questions

1. Possible answers include: The purpose of a route distinguisher is to maintain the uniqueness of customer routes as they pass through the service provider core network.

2. Possible answers include: NG-MVPN introduced support for hierarchical multicast trees, multicast flow identification, and optimized multicast traffic delivery.

3. Possible answers include: An important property of the C-multicast Import RT is that it is unique across all VRFs and all PEs. The uniqueness property is accomplished by embedding the PE's IP address and a locally assigned number into the RT (the PE assigns a distinct number for each VRF present on the PE).

Chapter 13

"Do I Know This Already?" Quiz

    1. b

    2. d

    3. a

   4. b

   5. c

   6. a

Review Questions

   1. Possible answers include: You should consider security, scalability, resource utilization, and complexity.

   2. Possible answers include: You will rely on BGP and send-label capabilities between the IGP islands, in addition to LDP functionality within the IGP islands.

Chapter 14

"Do I Know This Already?" Quiz

   1. b

   2. b

   3. b

   4. a

   5. b

Review Questions

   1. Possible answers include: RSVP does not follow the IGP, which allows the headend node to make independent decisions.

   2. Possible answers include: The choice of which bandwidth allocation model to use depends on the way in which bandwidth allocation and preemption will be managed between the tunnels of different classes. If traffic engineering is required for only one of the deployed traffic classes (e.g., for EF traffic only), then DS-TE is not required, and the standard single bandwidth pool TE is sufficient.

   3. Possible answers include: MPLS TE provides a mechanism to route traffic along explicitly defined LSPs according to resource requirements. MPLS TE LSPs are created by the RSVP signaling protocol. Constraint-based routing is used to meet TE requirements.

Chapter 15

"Do I Know This Already?" Quiz

   1. a and b

   2. a and d

   3. a and c

   4. a

   5. b

   6. d

7. c and d

8. d

9. c

10. b and c

Review Questions

1. Possible answers include: Unlike traditional routing, Segment Routing embeds routing information directly into packets, eliminating the need for complex routing tables at each node.

2. Possible answers include: By enabling fast and efficient rerouting in the event of link or node failures, the explicit use of segments allows for predefined alternate paths, reducing convergence times.

3. Possible answers include: Flex-Algo provides programmability and flexibility in defining and steering paths to accommodate diverse services and traffic types.

4. Possible answers include: Networks with stringent requirements for service availability, such as those supporting real-time applications or critical services, can leverage TI-LFA to ensure a reliable response to failures with minimal disruption.

5. Possible answers include: SRv6's ability to encode instructions directly into IPv6 headers enable network operators to dynamically steer traffic, create service chains, and adapt to changing network conditions without the need for complex protocols or overlays.

Chapter 16

"Do I Know This Already?" Quiz

1. a

2. a, b, and d

3. a

4. c and d

5. c

6. b

Review Questions

1. Possible answers include: Control Plane Policing (CoPP) safeguards the control plane from excessive traffic, an example of which is preventing denial-of-service attacks targeting routing protocols.

2. Possible answers include: BGP Flowspec allows the specification and distribution of traffic filtering rules using BGP with DDoS mitigation being the best example.

3. Possible answers include: BGPsec enhances BGP security by validating the authenticity of route announcements. It employs cryptographic signatures to verify the legitimacy of BGP updates, preventing malicious route hijacking.

Chapter 17

"Do I Know This Already?" Quiz

1. c
2. a
3. d
4. b
5. b
6. d

Review Questions

1. Possible answers include: Cisco Management Plane Protection (MPP) involves striking a delicate balance between bolstering security by restricting access to management protocols and ensuring operational efficiency to facilitate legitimate management tasks; such balance requires careful consideration of access control policies, potential impact on network management workflows, and ongoing monitoring and adjustment to mitigate risks effectively.

2. Possible answers include: In REST API security, mitigating threats like SQL injection and XSS requires robust input validation, output encoding, and strict access control measures to prevent unauthorized access to sensitive data and maintain the integrity of API endpoints.

3. Possible answers include: To counter evolving DDoS attack tactics, cybersecurity professionals employ a combination of advanced detection mechanisms, such as anomaly detection and machine learning, along with agile mitigation strategies, including traffic filtering, rate limiting, and DDoS scrubbing services, to swiftly identify and neutralize sophisticated attacks, bolstering network resilience, and enhancing overall security posture.

Chapter 18

"Do I Know This Already?" Quiz

1. c
2. a
3. b
4. a and c
5. a

Review Questions

1. Possible answers include: Strict mode provides stronger security but can pose challenges in asymmetric routing scenarios, while loose mode is more flexible but may be susceptible to IP spoofing.

2. Possible answers include: Challenges may include precise policy definition or coordination with upstream providers for effective traffic diversion.

3. Possible answers include: The Secure Association Key (SAK) in MACsec is a dynamically generated per-session encryption key used to encrypt and decrypt Ethernet frames, ensuring confidentiality and integrity of data transmitted over a secured link.

Chapter 19

"Do I Know This Already?" Quiz

1. d
2. b
3. a
4. a
5. c
6. b

Review Questions

1. Possible answers include: DS-Lite poses challenges due to its dual-stack nature, requiring careful management of IPv4 and IPv6 address spaces, along with the intricacies of NAT traversal and scalability concerns.

2. Possible answers include: The border router is a critical component of MAP-T deployment because it performs the translation between IPv4 and IPv6 addresses, allowing seamless communication between IPv4-only and IPv6-only networks.

3. Possible answers include: Stateless NAT64 typically offers higher scalability but lacks session awareness, while stateful NAT64 provides session tracking capabilities for improved protocol support and security, albeit with potentially lower scalability.

Chapter 20

"Do I Know This Already?" Quiz

1. d
2. c
3. a, c, and d
4. a

Review Questions

1. Possible answers include: Non-stop forwarding (NSF) ensures uninterrupted packet forwarding during control plane disruptions by allowing the forwarding plane to continue operations independently.

2. Possible answers include: Non-stop routing (NSR) enhances network resilience by allowing routers to maintain routing table information during control plane disruptions.

3. Possible answers include: LACP utilizes a variety of mechanisms such as fast timers, periodic transmissions, and neighbor verification to prevent link flapping and maintain stable link aggregation.

Chapter 21

"Do I Know This Already?" Quiz

1. b
2. b
3. b
4. d
5. d
6. d

Review Questions

1. Possible answers include: QoS traffic shaping dynamically adjusts traffic flows through token bucket algorithms.

2. Possible answers include: RED dynamically adjusts queue limits based on congestion indicators such as average queue length and packet drop probability.

3. Possible answers include: In traffic policing, the burst size determines the maximum allowed burst of traffic above the committed information rate (CIR), while the Excess Burst size (EBS) represents the additional burst that can be accommodated before packets are dropped, both crucial for regulating traffic flows without compromising network performance.

Chapter 22

"Do I Know This Already?" Quiz

1. b and c
2. a
3. b
4. a
5. a
6. a
7. a
8. a
9. a

Review Questions

1. Possible answers include: NETCONF is a transport protocol; NETCONF uses YANG and non-YANG data models to detail what "capabilities" a device provides.

2. Possible answers include: Using IPFIX instead of NetFlow provides greater flexibility in data types that can be exported, extra customization features, increased performance and scalability, and enhancements from an interoperability perspective with other monitoring tools.

3. Possible answers include: SNMP can still be used in parallel with new tools such as YANG focusing on the current network and new features to be managed using new tools. People still like the simplicity of SNMP and integrated MIB modules.

4. Possible answers include: Elements of the Telemetry solution that provide robustness include the data lake, for which you will analyze the data, monitor proactively, and identify patterns.

Index

Numerics

4G/5G, 31, 32–33

802.1ad, 535–537

C-bridge component, 539

NNI ports, 539

PBB (provider backbone bridging), 539–541

ports, 537–538

S-bridge component, 538–539

service provider bridges, 538

A

AAA (authentication, authorization, and accounting), 846–847

abort command, 56

ABR (area border router), 11, 12

AC (attachment circuit), 504

ACL (access control list), 865–866, 946

classification, 844–845

troubleshooting, 308–309

address families

BGP, 244–246

troubleshooting, 310–311

address-family command, 115, 246

adjacency/ies. *See also* IS-IS; OSPF (Open Shortest Path First)

authentication

on IOS, 185

on IOS XR, 184–185

debugging, 135

IS-IS, 129–131

multi-area

intra-area routing, 201–202

on IOS, 203–204

on IOS XR, 204

OSPF auto-cost reference, 202

OSPF costs, 202–203

states, 163

AFI (address family identifier), 111, 244

AFRINIC (African Network Information Centre), 233

aggregate-address command, 278–280

AIGP (Accumulated IGP) path attribute, 275–276

algorithm

constraint-based routing, 668

Dijkstra's Shortest Path First, 162

SPF, 110

Ansible, 1008

API (application programming interface), 978–979

asynchronous, 979

northbound, 979, 985

REST (Representational State Transfer), 847–848, 979–980, 980

security, 979

SOAP (Simple Object Access Protocol), 980–981

southbound, 980, 985

synchronous, 979

APNIC (Asia-Pacific Network Information Centre), 233

C

Register your product at **ciscopress.com/register** to unlock additional benefits:

- Save 35%* on your next purchase with an exclusive discount code
- Find companion files, errata, and product updates if available
- Sign up to receive special offers on new editions and related titles

Get more when you shop at **ciscopress.com**:

- Everyday discounts on books, eBooks, video courses, and more
- Free U.S. shipping on all orders
- Multi-format eBooks to read on your preferred device
- Print and eBook Best Value Packs

Discount code valid for 30 days; may not be combined with any other offer and is not redeemable for cash. Offer subject to change.

Cisco Press